International Handbook of Research on Conceptual Change

The International Handbook of Research on Conceptual Change consists of 27 chapters that clarify the nature of conceptual change research, describe its most important findings and demonstrate their importance for education. It is organized into six sections that include detailed discussions of key theoretical and methodological issues, the roots of conceptual change research in the philosophy and history of science, mechanisms of conceptual change, and learner characteristics. It also contains chapters that describe conceptual change research in content areas such as physics, astronomy, biology, medicine and health, and history. A particular focus is given to students' difficulties in learning more advanced and counter-intuitive concepts.

Chapter authors, solicited from all areas of the world, include leading conceptual change researchers from psychology and education, the philosophy and history of science, and from a variety of content areas. Such interdisciplinary and international expertise is missing from previous treatments of conceptual change research. To ensure continuity across the book, authors were instructed to follow a common chapter structure:

- an undeviating focus on conceptual change
- a literature review with highlights of important findings
- a discussion of methodological strengths, weaknesses, and open methodological and theoretical problems
- a state-of-the-art description of their field that includes educational implications (when relevant).

Stella Vosniadou is Professor of Cognitive Psychology in the Department of Philosophy and History of Science at the National and Kapodistrian University of Athens. She is the current chair of the interdisciplinary graduate program in Cognitive Science between the University of Athens and the Economic University of Athens, and director of the Cognitive Science Laboratory at the University of Athens. Professor Vosniadou has served as a president of the European Association for Research on Learning and Instruction (EARLI) and organizer and chair of the 1997 EARLI conference in Athens, Greece.

EDUCATIONAL PSYCHOLOGY HANDBOOK SERIES

Series Editor: Patricia A. Alexander
University of Maryland

International Handbook of Research on Conceptual Change

Edited by

Stella Vosniadou
University of Athens, Greece

Routledge
Taylor & Francis Group

NEW YORK AND LONDON

First published 2008
by Routledge
270 Madison Ave, New York, NY 10016

Simultaneously published in the UK
by Routledge
2 Park Square, Milton Park, Abingdon, Oxon OX14 4RN

Routledge is an imprint of the Taylor & Francis Group, an informa business

© 2008 Taylor & Francis

Typeset in Times and Helvetica by EvS Communication Networx, Inc.
Printed and bound in the United States of America on acid-free paper by Sheridan Books, Inc.

Library of Congress Cataloging in Publication Data

International handbook of research on conceptual change / edited by Stella Vosniadou.
p. cm. — (Educational psychology handbook series)
Includes bibliographical references.
1. Concept learning—Research. 2. Concepts—Research. I. Vosniadou, Stella.
LB1062.I58 2008
370.15'23—dc22
2007041601

ISBN10: 0-8058-6044-4 (hbk)
ISBN10: 0-8058-6045-2 (pbk)

ISBN13: 978-0-8058-6044-3 (hbk)
ISBN13: 978-0-8058-6045-0 (pbk)

This book is dedicated to Giyoo Hatano
whose work in Conceptual Change was an inspiration to all of us

Contents

Contributors

Patricia A. Alexander
University of Maryland

Theodore Arabatzis
University of Athens

William F. Brewer
University of Illinois at Urbana-Champaign

David E. Brown
University of Illinois at Urbana-Champaign

Michelene T. H. Chi
University of Pittsburgh

John Clement
University of Massachusetts at Amherst

Andrea A. diSessa
University of California at Berkeley

Reinders Duit
IPN – Leibniz Institute for Science Education,
University of Kiel

E. Margaret Evans
University of Michigan

Richard F. Gunstone
Monash University

Liza Haglund
Stockholm University

Ola Halldén
Stockholm University

David Hammer
University of Maryland

Giyoo Hatano
Chiba University

Kayoko Inagaki
Chiba University

David Jonassen
University of Missouri

Frank C. Keil
Yale University

David R. Kaufman
Columbia University

Alla Keselman
Columbia University

Vasso Kindi
University of Athens

John T. Leach
The University of Leeds

Gaea Leinhardt
University of Pittsburgh

Marcia C. Linn
University of California at Berkeley

Lee Martin
University of California at Davis

Ference Marton
Göteborg University

Lucia Mason
University of Padova

Naomi Miyake
Chukyo University

P. Karen Murphy
The Pennsylvania State University

Nancy J. Nersessian
Georgia Institute of Technology

George E. Newman
Yale University

Ming Fai Pang
The University of Hong Kong

Vimla L. Patel
Columbia University

Anita K. Ravi
University of Pittsburgh

Max Scheja
Stockholm University

Daniel L. Schwartz
Stanford University

Philip H. Scott
The University of Leeds

Robert S. Siegler
Carnegie Mellon University

Gale M. Sinatra
University of Nevada

Irini Skopeliti
University of Athens

Carol L. Smith
University of Massachusetts at Boston

Matija Svetina
University of Ljubljana

Paul Thagard
University of Waterloo

David F. Treagust
Curtin University of Technology

Xenia Vamvakoussi
University of Athens

Sashank Varma
Stanford University

Stella Vosniadou
University of Athens

Richard T. White
Monash University

Ari Widodo
Indonesian University of Education

Marianne Wiser
Clark University

Conceptual Change Research: An Introduction

Stella Vosniadou

The purpose of editing the *International Handbook of Research on Conceptual Change* is to collect and present in a cohesive manner the results of an impressive body of research conducted approximately in the last 20 years in the area of conceptual change. We hope that the chapters in this volume will help to better define and clarify the nature of research on conceptual change, describe and explain some of the most important findings of this research, and demonstrate their importance for education and the design of instruction.

CONCEPTUAL CHANGE IN THE PHILOSOPHY AND HISTORY OF SCIENCE

The roots of the conceptual change approach to learning can be found in Thomas Kuhn's work on theory change in the philosophy and history of science. Kuhn's classic book *The Structure of Scientific Revolutions* (1962) has been translated in 18 languages and has sold about 20 million copies, making it probably the best-selling book on the philosophy and history of science ever (see Machamer, 2007). It has had a tremendous influence not only on historians and philosophers of science, who have debated endlessly the issues that he and his fellow philosopher Feyerabend have raised, but in many other subject-matter areas including psychology and education.

As discussed also in Vosniadou (2007), Kuhn, together with certain other philosophers of science like Feyerabend, Lakatos, and Toulmin, questioned the attempts by logical positivists and logical empiricists to treat scientific theories as sets of axioms that could be formulated in mathematical logic. According to the 'received view', a theory that enjoys a high degree of confirmation cannot ever be disconfirmed, but can only be expanded to a theory with a wider scope, or absorbed into a more inclusive and comprehensive theory (see Suppe, 1977). Kuhn proposed that normal science operates within sets of shared beliefs, assumptions, commitments and practices that constitute *paradigms*. Discoveries emerge over time that cannot be accommodated within the existing paradigm. When these anomalies accumulate, science enters a period of crisis which is eventually resolved by a revolutionary change in paradigm, a *paradigm shift*. According to Kuhn, different paradigms are incommensurable. Scientific knowledge grows as we move from one to another paradigm, but it is no longer possible to imagine the results of scientific revolutions as a cumulative, linear progression.

Kuhn argued for a contextual view of concepts according to which they are not abstract, rule-based definitions comprising of certain necessary and sufficient characteristics but Wittgenstein-like terms related in a network of interrelated family resemblances. He claimed that concepts are embedded in theoretical frameworks — paradigms — from which they obtain their meaning. When there is a paradigm shift, there is 'conceptual change,' i.e., the meaning of the concepts embedded in the paradigm also change. The scientific concepts in the new paradigm, even when they keep the name they had in the old paradigm, are markedly different from the old ones. The difference lies in that they are embedded in a different theory, have different interconnections to other concepts, and apply to different phenomena. This is the historicist view of scientific concepts as entities that undergo significant changes over time, evolving and developing.[1]

Kuhn's ideas about conceptual change were brought to developmental psychology through the work of Susan Carey (1985) and in science education through the work of Michael Posner and his colleagues (Posner, Strike, Hewson, & Gertzog, 1982). They both stressed the rational aspects of theory change,[2] Carey (1985), in order to describe how children's knowledge structures change with the course of spontaneous cognitive development, and Posner et al. (1982) to explain the difficulties students face when they must learn new science concepts.

THE CONCEPTUAL CHANGE APPROACH IN SCIENCE EDUCATION

In the area of science education, Kuhn's proposals seemed to provide a much needed theoretical framework for explaining students' difficulties in understanding science concepts. As noted by White and Gunstone (chapter 23, this volume), in the 1970s researchers started paying greater attention to students' ideas and explanations of physical phenomena. They started to realize that students held various pre-conceptions, misconceptions, or alternative beliefs, some of which proved to be very persistent and robust (e.g., Viennot, 1979; Driver & Easley, 1978; McCloskey, 1983). In some cases these misconceptions appeared be very similar to earlier theories in the history of science, such as, for example, the impetus theory in mechanics (McCloskey, 1983).

On the basis of the above, Posner et al. (1982) drew an analogy between the kinds of changes needed to be made by students learning science and Kuhn's explanation of theory change in science. They claimed that students need to undergo radical conceptual change when it comes to understanding scientific concepts like 'force' or 'heat' or 'energy'. They need to replace their preconceptions or misconceptions with the new scientific concepts through instruction. Combining Kuhn's ideas with Piaget's notion of accommodation and assimilation, Posner et al. (1982) derived an instructional theory, according to which there are four fundamental conditions that need to be fulfilled before conceptual change can happen in science learning: (1) there must be dissatisfaction with existing conceptions, (2) there must be a new conception that is intelligible, (3) the new conception must appear to be plausible, and (4) the new conception should suggest the possibility of a fruitful program.

This theoretical framework, known as the 'classical approach' to conceptual change, became the leading paradigm that guided research and instructional practices in science education for many years. According to it, the student is like a scientist, the process of (science) learning is a rational process of theory replacement, conceptual change is like a gestalt shift that happens over a short period of time, and cognitive conflict is the major instructional strategy for promoting conceptual change. Practically all of the above-mentioned tenets of the classical approach have undergone serious criticisms, some of which resemble the criticisms voiced against Kuhn's (1962) theory in the history and philosophy of science (see Vosniadou, Baltas, & Vamvakoussi, 2007; Arabatzis & Kindi, chapter 13, this volume).

CONCEPTUAL CHANGE IN LEARNING AND INSTRUCTION

The theoretical and methodological discussions that have taken place in the process of re-framing the 'classical approach' have been some of the most interesting in the field of learning and instruction. Over the years, researchers realized that the issues raised by the classical approach in science education are much larger issues, having to do with the nature of concepts and the processes of conceptual change, and that they can apply to many areas of learning and not only to the learning of science. In this process, it could be argued that conceptual change research itself has undergone a radical conceptual change.

Today, most researchers would agree that research on conceptual change investigates how concepts change with learning and development in specific subject-matter areas or domains of knowledge, focusing more specifically on explaining students' difficulties in learning the more advanced and counter-intuitive concepts in these areas. It is acknowledged that conceptual change research is not restricted to physics but makes a larger claim about learning that transcends many domains (physics, mathematics, biology, psychology, history, political science, medicine, gender studies, cultural studies), and can apply not only to education, but also to the problems investigated by developmental psychology, evolutionary psychology, and cognitive science (Carey, 1985, Hatano & Inagaki, 1994, Wellman, 2002). Recently, the term 'controversial conceptual change' has been used to refer to research in certain areas of learning, such as evolution and environmental changes, or issues related to political and ideological differences and peace education, where the processes of change is influenced by strong emotions.

In the pages that follow, we will outline some of the open questions and issues that are of concern to conceptual change researchers in the area of learning and instruction and which form the backbone of the present volume.

Cohesion Versus Fragmentation

One of the most important questions in conceptual change research concerns the claim that students' knowledge can be described as 'theory-like'. Some use the term 'theory' explicitly, others imply it or use less loaded terms, like the construct of 'schema' (Chi, chapter 3, this volume). The word 'theory' is used by most researchers to denote a structure consisting of a relatively coherent body of domain specific knowledge that is characterized by a distinct ontology and a causality and can give rise to prediction and explanation. This is not assumed to be a socially shared, scientific theory, accompanied by metaconceptual awareness and explicit hypothesis testing. Learning and development is then seen as requiring the re-organization of this structure — i.e., ontological categorical shifts and changes in causality — and not simply its enrichment. For example, Chi (chapter 3, this volume) argues that several ontological category shifts can happen during development and learning, such as categorizing a concept like *force* or *energy* as an 'entity' as opposed to a 'process', or characterizing a process as 'direct' as opposed to 'emergent'. Similarly, Inagaki & Hatano (chapter 9, this volume) argue that there is a change from intentional to vitalistic and then to mechanical causality in children's explanations of biological phenomena.

Some researchers are radically opposed to the idea that initial knowledge structures are theory-like (e.g., diSessa, chapter 2, this volume). This disagreement has given rise to a number of interesting debates in the field, including that between diSessa (chapter 2, this volume) and Vosniadou, Vamvakoussi, and Skopeliti (chapter 1, this volume) on 'coherence versus fragmentation'. The chapters in this volume help to clarify some of the important issue in this debate. In addition, Brown and Hammer (chapter 6, this volume) describe a complex dynamics systems account of knowledge acquisition in physics that they believe can bring together important aspects of both the 'pieces' and the 'theory' perspectives.

The Nature of Concepts and Kinds of Conceptual Change

There is no doubt that we need a better understanding of what concepts are and how they change with development and learning. Researchers usually avoid dealing directly with the question of what concepts are, although many in this volume would adopt the historicist view of concepts as changing and evolving and as embedded in larger theoretical frameworks from which they derive their meaning (see Murphy & Medin, 1985), an approach that is not without its critics (e.g., Fodor, 1996).

On the issue of how concept change, there seems to be some agreement that concepts change in many ways, from the more mundane to the most radical (e.g., Thagard, 1992, chapter 14, this volume). The most radical kinds of conceptual changes are usually described as changes in the hierarchical tree in which a concept belongs. These changes may require that a concept shifts from one ontological category to another (e.g., seeing turberculosis as an infectious disease, Thagard, chapter 14, this volume; or assigning the earth to the category 'atronomical object' rather than 'physical object'—Vosniadou et al. (chapter 1, this volume). Sometimes the creation of new ontological categories is needed, as in the case when the category of 'emergent processes' must be created (Chi, 1992). These are fundamental reorganizations of the knowledge base, because assigning a concept to a category means that all the properties and presuppositions that belong to the category will now also apply to the concept (see Chi, chapter 3, this volume; Vosniadou et al., chapter 1, this volume).

Processes and Mechanisms of Conceptual Change

One of the most controversial claims in Kuhn's (1962) original explanation of theory change in science which was adopted by the classical approach is that the change from one theoretical framework to the other is an abrupt and sudden change that takes place in a short period of time. It appears that Kuhn was influenced by Gestalt psychology and saw this shift in terms of the gestalt ideas of re-structuring produced by insight. Although it is possible that such abrupt restructuring may happen in individuals during the learning process, this does not appear to be the usual road to conceptual change.

The empirical evidence so far has shown that the course of conceptual change is a conservative and slow process. Even when researchers claim that radical conceptual changes are happening in the long run, these are usually the end state of a slow and gradual process and not of a sudden and radical gestalt type of shift (Caravita & Hallden, 1994; Vosniadou, 2003; Hatano & Inagaki, 1994; Wiser & Smith, chapter 8, this volume, Vosniadou et al., chapter 1, this volume). This is an important issue in conceptual change research and has various implications for instruction. If a student holds theory A and needs to change to theory B, which is incommensurable with theory A, how can this be best done? It is clear that the extreme position on 'global incommensurability' can not be true. There is usually some basis from which a student will start to slowly revise his initial views to make them more compatible with the scientific theory presented through instruction.

Vosniadou et al. (chapter 1) claim that learners use mainly additive, enrichment types of mechanisms that are largely unconscious and that these mechanisms can produce conceptual changes in the long run, assuming that they operate on a knowledge base that has a theory-like structure and also that the learner is exposed to new information coming from observation and from culture. They do so, by changing one by one the beliefs and presuppositions of the initial 'theory' that are in conflict with the instructed view. They also claim that enrichment mechanisms can account for the formation of certain misconceptions, which they call 'synthetic models' because they reveal students' attempts to synthesize two incompatible pieces of information — one coming from the scientific concepts presented through information and the other coming from students' prior knowledge. Chi (chapter 3) also argues that many misconceptions can occur when new information is added on to the wrong schema. A great deal of the schema literature in the 1970s which shows the kinds of comprehension and memory errors that can happen when a wrong schema is activated and used is very relevant here.

Following on some of the above ideas, some researchers make a distinction between 'spontaneous' conceptual change that happens in the process of cognitive development and 'instruction-induced' conceptual change produced as a result of instruction (Vosniadou et al., chapter 1; Inagaki & Hatano, chapter 9). In other chapters of the Handbook, Wiser and Smith, Keil and Newman and also Inagaki and Hatano focus on spontaneous conceptual development and describe some of the kinds of conceptual reorganizations that happen in the knowledge base. Vosniadou et al. and Chi focus more on the kinds of conceptual reorganizations that happen as the result of learning and instruction. It appears that 'instruction–induced' conceptual change is more difficult to happen and is likely to lead to the formation of misconceptions and the creations of inert knowledge.

Another critical question concerns the kind of mechanisms that can support and promote radical conceptual change more directly and without producing misconceptions. A number of chapters deal with this issue. Nersserssian explains the importance of mental models and model-based reasoning, while Clement discusses the role of explanatory models and analogy for conceptual change in physics. Miyake elaborates on how collaboration and reflection can promote conceptual change. These are important ideas that need to be studied carefully.

Some chapters include discussions on methodological issues related to the study of conceptual change. Siegler and Svetina show that the same processes of conceptual change are involved in short-term learning and long-term development and describe a methodology to study both. Keil and Newman describe some criteria thereby which we can distinguish radical conceptual change from less radical one.

Conceptual Change in Mathematics

The application of the conceptual change approach in mathematics learning and teaching is a relatively new attempt. Although there has been a great deal of research in the tradition of misconceptions during the 1970s and 1980s, the mathematics education community has been reluctant to adopt the conceptual change approach, which was developed mainly in the context of physical sciences. This is because mathematics has been traditionally regarded as a discipline with particular characteristics that differentiate it even from its nearest neighbors, the physical sciences. Thomas Kuhn himself exempted mathematics from the pattern of scientific development and change presented in *The Structure of Scientific Revolutions* (see Mahoney, 1997). He did this because mathematics is based on deductive proof and not on experiment, is proven to be very tolerant to anomalies and it does not display the radical incommensurability of theory before and after revolution. Unlike science, the formulation of a new theory in mathematics usually carries mathematics to a more general level of analysis and enables a wider perspective that makes possible solutions that have been impossible to formulate before (Corry, 1993; Dauben, 1984).

However, from a learning point of view, it appears that students are confronted with similar situations when they learn mathematics and science. As it is the case that students develop a naïve physics on the basis of everyday experience, they also develop a naïve mathematics which appears to consist of certain core principles or presuppositions (such as the presupposition of discreteness in the number concept) that facilitate some kinds of learning but inhibit others (Dehaene, 1998; Gelman, 2000; Lipton & Spelke, 2003). Such similarities support the argument that the conceptual change approach can be fruitfully applied in the case of mathematics learning.

The Student as a Scientist?

Even the researchers, who support the view that concepts are embedded in theory-like structures from very early on in childhood, agree that there are some very fundamental differences between students and scientists. Some of these differences have to do with students' lack of metaconceptual awareness, difficulties in engaging in systematic hypothesis testing, lack of knowledge about the role of theories and scientific models, and general epistemological understanding (see Wiser & Smith, chapter 8, this volume).

More specifically, it appears that students are not aware of the beliefs and presuppositions that constrain their learning and reasoning and, most important, they are not aware of the hypothetical nature of their beliefs. In other words, they do not understand that their beliefs are hypotheses, as opposed to true facts about the world, and that they can be tested and falsified. They do not understand that other people may have different kinds of beliefs, not to mention being able to seriously entertain and examine different points of view. As it follows from all that, they do not engage in systematic hypothesis testing that would enable them to evaluate the relevance of empirical evidence and engage in intentional theory change (e.g., Kuhn, Amsel, & Loughlin, 1988).

Another important difference between students and scientists centers around the nature of epistemic beliefs. Epistemic beliefs are the beliefs individuals hold about the nature of knowledge and the processes of knowing. Research has shown that unlike scientists, many students can be described to hold absolutistic, objectivist, and non-constructivist personal epistemologies that do not contribute to learning and conceptual change. A number of studies have shown negative correlations between beliefs that knowledge is certain, unstable and given by authority and conceptual change (Mason & Gava, 2007; Stathopoulou & Vosniadou, 2006, 2007).

The development of students' personal epistemology, metaconceptual awareness and intentional learning are important aspects of an instructional approach for the fostering of conceptual change. Indeed, current approaches place a great deal of emphasis on instructional interventions that improve the above-mentioned abilities, mainly through the use of various sociocultural supports, such as classroom discussion and collaborative learning (Miyake, chapter 17, this volume; Sinatra & Mason, chapter 21, this volume; Vosniadou et al., chapter 1, this volume; Wiser & Smith, chapter 8, this volume).

Another criticism of the classical approach to conceptual change is that it represents 'cold' as opposed to 'hot' cognition, i.e., that it does not take into consideration that affective and motivational factors can have an important influence on conceptual change. Effective teaching for conceptual change, should find ways to increase students' motivation to change their beliefs and persuade them that conceptual change is necessary (Pintrich, Marx, & Boyle, 1993; Sinatra & Dole, 1998; Alexander, 2001). In the last years some attention has started to be paid to motivational and affective factors in conceptual change, as discussed in the chapters by Sinatra and Mason, and Murphy and Alexander (chapters 21 and 22).

The Role of Sociocultural Factors

The classical approach emphasized the use of cognitive, internal mechanisms to promote conceptual change and has not paid much attention to sociocultural variables. Most researchers in this area now agree that conceptual change should not be seen as only an individual, internal, cognitive process, but as a social activity that takes place in a complex sociocultural world (see Hatano, 1994; Caravita & Hallden, 1994; Vosniadou, 2007). It is interesting to note that this point is actually very much in line with Kuhn's (1962) own arguments that the notion of 'theory', conceived as a set of propositions, is too narrow to account for the activities of scientists and should be replaced with a 'paradigm'. The introduction of the notion of 'paradigm' by Kuhn shifted the emphasis from individuals' minds to the role that the scientific community and their group commitments, shared examples, and tacit knowledge play in scientific discovery and change and helped philosophers and historians of science think about science as a social activity. Hoddeson (2007) and Machamer (2007) also point out how Kuhn's influence helped historians of science to think about science as a social activity. The influence of sociocultural factors in conceptual change is discussed extensively in the chapters by Vosniadou et al., Inakagi and Hatano, and Miyake (Chapter 1, 9, and 17, respectively).

Instruction for Conceptual Change

Researchers have just started to understand and explore the full implications of the conceptual change approach for the design of curricula and instruction. In addition, there is a vast gap between our theoretical and empirical knowledge and classroom practice. Teachers are not well informed about conceptual change issues and do not use the recommended instructional strategies for promoting conceptual change in the classroom (Duit et al., chapter 24, this volume).

Following on Posner et al. (1982), the traditional approach to promoting conceptual change in science education has used cognitive conflict as a means of creating the necessary dissatisfaction with the learners' 'preconceptions'. The use of cognitive conflict makes sense within the 'classical approach' where conceptual change is seen to involve a sudden and quick re-structuring. However, it has been pointed out that extensive use of cognitive conflict is not a good instructional strategy for producing conceptual change, because it focuses on inappropriate prior knowledge that cannot be used constructively in the learning process (Smith, diSessa, & Roschelle, 1993). As we have come to realize that the process of conceptual change is a slow one, we have also started to see how moderate uses of cognitive conflict can be useful in a long-term, teacher-supported program of instruction. The empirical evidence so far supports the conclusion that moderate uses of cognitive conflict can be helpful in promoting conceptual change, especially if they are combined with constructive strategies, like analogies, in a comprehensive, long-term program of teacher facilitated conceptual change. These issues are extensively discussed by John Clement (chapter 16).

Another approach is to emphasize the use of constructive methods to promote conceptual change (e.g., Linn, chapter 27, this volume, diSessa, chapter 2, this volume). It is also suggested that the problem of conceptual change should be anticipated in the design of curricula as well as in everyday teaching practices so that students are exposed from early on to experiences and examples that help them build some of the prior knowledge required to understand the more advanced scientific or mathematical concepts to which they will exposed later on and construct the necessary bridging devices instead of strengthening initial conceptions that result in inflexible thinking (Greer, 2006; Vosniadou et al., chapter 1, this volume).

Finally, some researchers emphasize the need to develop in students the metaconceptual awareness and intentional learning strategies discussed earlier that will allow them to avoid misconception producing enrichment mechanisms in situations that require conceptual change. These researchers also stress the importance of teaching students the conscious, deliberate, top-down mechanisms that can promote cross-domain mapping, such as the deliberate use of analogies and model-based reasoning, as well as the epistemological sophistication and uses of hypothesis testing that make children different from scientists (e.g., Wiser & Smith, chapter 8, this volume; Clement, chapter 16, this volume).

A ROADMAP TO THE BOOK

The *International Handbook of Research on Conceptual Change* is divided into six sections. The first section is entitled *Theoretical Issues in Conceptual Change Research.* It consists of five chapters that focus on fundamental theoretical issues in conceptual change research, such as the definition of concepts and of conceptual change, the specification of the different kinds of conceptual changes that can take place, the coherence versus fragmentation debate, as well as some methodological issues. In the first chapter, Vosniadou, Vamvakoussi and Skopeliti describe the kinds of conceptual changes that take place in the learning of science and mathematics. They argue that science and mathematics concepts are difficult to learn because they are embedded in naïve, framework theories of physics and mathematics, which are different explanatory frameworks from those that are now scientifically accepted. These naïve framework theories are not fragmented observations but form a relatively coherent explanatory system which is based and continuously re-confirmed by everyday experience. Students are not aware of these differences and employ the usual enrichment mechanisms to add scientific and mathematical information to existing knowledge structure, destroying their coherence and creating internal inconsistency and misconceptions. In order to foster conceptual change, students must (1) become aware of the inconsistencies between their naïve theories and the scientific ones, and (2) use the top-down, conscious and deliberate mechanisms for intentional learning mentioned earlier. In other words, instruction-induced conceptual change requires not only the restructuring of students' naïve theories but also the restructuring of their modes of learning and reasoning, the creation of metaconceptual awareness and intentionality and the development of epistemological sophistication. In order to accomplish these changes substantial cognitive effort and sociocultural support are necessary.

In the second chapter, diSessa explains and advocates a "knowledge in pieces" approach to conceptual change. He enriches and redefines the debate between 'coherence' and 'fragmentation' views, discussing three main issues: (a) the grain-size of elements necessary to understand conceptual change, (b) the very meaning of coherence, and (c) the problem of accounting for empirically evident sensitivity to context. The chapter also answers a set of questions that display misconceptions about, and prejudices toward, positions that hold for substantial fragmentation in naïve conceptions. Questions include whether "pieces" advocates are fretting about peripheral complexities and ignoring the big picture, and how instructional realities and possibilities play out from opposing points of view. Finally, the chapter identifies the basic differences in the research programs represented by the two sides of the debate. diSessa argues that two of the characteristic strengths of the knowledge in pieces approach are in dealing with the long road to competence, and in treating evident diversity across students, across domains, and across contexts within a domain.

In the third chapter, Chi argues that learning failures and misunderstandings typically occur either when the cues in the new materials activate no relevant prior schema, or when the cues activate incomplete and under-developed prior schema. She goes on to propose that misconceptions are a special type of learning failures, i.e., a unique case in which an inappropriate schema is activated for assimilation and generation. In her chapter she provides a theoretical account for this particular type of learning failures, using natural selection as an example.

Keil and Newman argue that one of the great challenges in the study of conceptual change involves disentangling what changes from what remains the same. They examine this challenge by discussing in detail two different cases of conceptual change. The first case involves intuitions about causality and order. The second case involves intuitions about biological processes. In the first case, they argue, an apparently unchanging pattern of judgments over a large age range masks what is in reality a dramatic conceptual change at an underlying level. On the contrary, in the second case, apparently dramatic changes in judgments, suggesting marked conceptual change, are in fact quite misleading. More broadly they explore the different kinds of conceptual change that can occur as well as other kinds of developmental change that can masquerade as conceptual change.

In the last chapter, Siegler and Svetina describe a method, the microgenetic/cross sectional design, that can yield data that can resolve the theoretical disputes regarding the nature of the processes of change that take place during learning and development. The basic logic that underlies this design is that combining cross-sectional and microgenetic components within the same experiment can yield maximally comparable data. The cross-sectional component of the design involves presenting the same tasks and measures to children of different ages. The microgenetic component involves randomly selecting a subset of children from the youngest group of the same population, presenting them an experience that is designed to promote improvement on the task of primary interest, and then comparing their performance on a posttest to that of peers who did not receive the experience. Experiments using this method and the findings that they have yielded basically support Vygotsky's and Werner's position that short-term and long-term change share many similarities, including progress through similar sequences of qualitatively distinct knowledge states.

The second part of the book is entitled *The Conceptual Change Approach in the Content Areas*. It consists of seven chapters that describe the processes of knowledge acquisition and conceptual change in different subject matter areas such as physics, astronomy, matter, biology, medicine, and history. In the first chapter Brown and Hammer present a comprehensive discussion of the different perspectives in the area of physics education and describe how they attempt to explain students' difficulties in physics despite ample instruction. They then present their own theoretical perspective, which is a complex dynamics systems account that considers discourse dynamics as theoretically continuous with conceptual dynamics.

In the second chapter, Brewer provides an extensive review and analysis of the empirical studies in the area of conceptual development in observational astronomy. He also discusses in detail some of the methodological questions and problems that have emerged from research on children's naïve models of observational astronomy and defends the structured interview technique as the method of choice for scientific research in this area. He goes on to argue that children's ideas and explanations of phenomena in observational astronomy have all the essential characteristics of naïve theories or models, i.e., contain theoretical entities and provide explanations and predictions.

The chapter by Wiser and Smith provides a detailed description of the long progression involved in the learning of the concepts of matter and materials. They argue that students not only have considerable difficulties understanding the atomic-molecular theory of matter which is taught at school but that they also have considerable difficulties understanding the macroscopic concept of matter and its relationships to certain other key concepts in this area, such as the concepts of weight, density, volume, solid, liquid and gas. They go on to provide a very interesting account of the conceptual changes that are needed in this area and to show how they interrelate with changes in mathematical and epistemological understanding.

The next two chapters deal with conceptual change in biology. The chapter by Inagaki and Hatano is a reprint of the seventh chapter of their book *Young Children's Naïve Thinking about the Biological World*. In this chapter, they discuss the nature of conceptual change as a fundamental restructuring of (conceptual) knowledge in general. They then describe the conceptual changes that take place in the course of development of biological knowledge, paying particular attention to outlining some of the mechanisms of conceptual change. The second chapter on biology is written by Margaret Evans who reviews the empirical research on the Darwinian theory of evolution, particularly the one conducted in diverse religious and cultural contexts. She argues that although the Darwinian theory of evolution has revolutionized scientists' understanding of the biological world, almost half of the U.S. public endorses creationist ('God made it') explanations for the origin of humans, and most of the rest endorse pre-Darwinian evolutionary concepts. This evidence motivates the hypothesis that evolution is counterintuitive because of initial constraints on cognition. These constraints give rise to cognitive biases or intuitive theories that appear to limit humans' view of nature: Species are separated by fixed boundaries in an unchanging world (essentialism) and animate behavior is directed towards a goal that satisfies both an organism's goals (teleology) and its intentions (theory of mind). The human species, in particular, occupies a privileged position. Such intuitions appear early in childhood and persist into adulthood. The scientific and religious communities provide information that serve to reinforce or radically modify such basic intuitions. The core question is the extent to which the human mind is capable of conceptual change when confronted with scientific evidence that appears to flatly contradict such a self-serving view of the world.

The domains of medicine and healthcare are discussed in the next chapter by Kaufman, Keselman, and Patel. This chapter reviews two bodies of conceptual understanding research pertaining to: (1) health professionals and medical students in biomedical domains and (2) lay individuals in the domain of health. In the first, the authors discuss studies pertaining to the understanding of core biomedical concepts, the nature and development of expertise, and the use of basic science knowledge in clinical reasoning. In the second, they examine cross-cultural research pertaining to lay understanding and reasoning about nutritional disorders and HIV-related issues and interventions designed to promote conceptual change in understanding about HIV and diabetes. Conceptual understanding of health issues gives individuals the power to derive predictions and explanations of health-related phenomena, and may mediate health decisions and behavior. At the end of the chapter, the authors present a study elucidating the terminological and conceptual gaps that can impede the public's comprehension of consumer health resources.

The last chapter in Part II is written by Leinhardt and Ravi. The authors trace the ways in which history as a domain has undergone a conceptual shift. They start with the ideas expressed by Herodotus that suggest components of history might include author identity and position, purpose, and evidential rules. They show that current ideas of what history is include those fundamentals but also add layered positioning with respect to other accounts, such as periodicity, interpretive argument, and rationale for remembrance. They use the Boston Massacre as an example to show how accounts that observe the same set of evidential rules can differ dramatically with respect to issues such as periodicity and argument. Finally, they examine some of the literature that exists to see if and how students manage these shifts in considering what history is. The accounts of student knowledge show that students can and do attend to ideas such as authorship albeit awkwardly and do move from an accuracy driven definition to a criterion driven understanding of historical phenomena.

The third part of the book is entitled *Conceptual Change in the Philosophy and History of Science* and consists of two chapters. The first one, by Arabatzis and Kindi, provides information about the roots of the conceptual change approach in the philosophy and history of science, including a critical analysis of Thomas Kuhn's more recent work in which he attempted to address some of the difficulties faced by his original account of conceptual change and to articulate further his key philosophical notion of incommensurability. They conclude by discussing a post-Kuhnian approach to conceptual change, which aims at a reapprochement of history and philosophy of science, on the one hand, and cognitive science, on the other. In the second chapter, Paul Thagard examines three central concepts in biology, psychology, and medicine: the concepts of life, mind, and disease, respectively. He argues that all three concepts have undergone a progression that involved shifts in theoretical understanding from the theological to the qualitative to the mechanistic. He attempts to show how concepts with a mechanistic underpinning differ from theological and qualitative ones, and discusses some of the psychological impediments to students' acquisition of a mechanistic understanding of life, disease, and mind. He concludes with three generalizations about the nature of conceptual change in the history of science: there has been a shift from conceptualizations in terms of simple properties to ones in terms of complex relations; conceptual change is theory change; and conceptual change is often emotional as well as cognitive.

Part IV includes four chapters that focus on *Mechanisms of Conceptual Change,* and more specifically on the role of transfer, collaboration, mental models and analogies. In the first chapter of this section, Nerserssian argues that although the notion of 'mental model' underlies much research in conceptual change, the notion of what a mental model is, and how mental modeling can lead to conceptual change have not been clarified. Drawing on literature across the 'mental models framework', Nerserssian develops an analysis that creates a synthesis of research from the areas of situation and discourse models, mental spatial simulation, mental animation, and embodied and distributed cognition. It is argued that research findings and interpretations in these literatures support a notion of mental modeling that is close to Craik's original conception, which in current terms would be called a 'perceptual mental model' and that this notion supports the idea that internal and external representations are 'coupled' in reasoning processes. Finally, the notion of 'model-based reasoning' in conceptual change is discussed specifically with respect to research on conceptual change in science. Analogical, imagistic, and simulative modeling are argued to be productive means of conceptual change in that they involve abstractive reasoning processes by means of which truly novel combinations of here-to-fore unrepresented structures and behaviors can emerge.

In the next chapter, John Clement discusses two traditional approaches to promote conceptual change through instruction: the use of dissonance producing strategies like cognitive conflict, and the use of constructive strategies, involving for example analogies. He then goes on to argue that these seemingly disparate approaches can be combined successfully in a model evolution approach that includes many cycles of model evaluation and revision. Each revision can also utilize other contributing strategies besides dissonance promoters and analogies, expanding the image of conceptual change teaching to one that includes multiple strategies. Because it breaks learning down into small pieces, a model evolution approach holds out the possibility of enabling students to do a significant share of the reasoning in a process of co-construction with the teacher.

Naomi Miyake examines the role of collaboration and reflection as social mechanisms that promote conceptual change and reviews some of the instructional applications of these mechanisms. In the first section of the chapter she introduces descriptive research to document cases where simple conversation led to relatively substantial conceptual change. In the second section, she introduces two research projects that tried to reveal underlying mechanisms of how the collaborative reflection contributes to conceptual change, relying on some detailed protocol analyses, from two different perspectives. One perspective focuses more on the process of convergence; the other emphasizes the divergent, individualistic concept formation through social interaction. In the third section, she reviews some instructional applications of the above approaches, including the Hypothesis-Experiment-Instruction and some Computer Supported Collaborative Learning (CSCL) studies. She concludes with a call for a longer-term perspective to support life-long learning, to make it possible for every citizen to develop sustainable abilities to keep changing their own concepts whenever necessary.

In the last chapter of Part IV, Schwartz, Varma, and Martin write about Dynamic Transfer and Innovation. They argue that transfer occurs when people use learning from one situation in another, for example, when they use their knowledge of water flow to understand electrical current. Transfer is relevant to conceptual change, because new concepts build on a foundation of prior learning. The contribution of the transfer literature to conceptual change comes from its explanations of why people retrieve and change their ideas in some contexts, but not others. Because transfer can precipitate changes to the environment as well as concepts, they use the broader term innovation of which conceptual change is a subset. Transfer addresses two critical issues for innovation: the knowledge problem and the inertia problem. The knowledge problem asks how prior knowledge of one sort can contribute to creating new knowledge of another sort. The inertia problem asks why people often fail to innovate, even though they have the relevant prior knowledge. People often transfer for repetition rather than innovation. The chapter proposes two types of transfer to address these problems. Similarity transfer occurs when people are able to recognize that they have well-formed prior ideas that can be profitably used to describe another situation in a new way. Dynamic transfer occurs when component competencies are coordinated through interaction with the environment to yield novel concepts or material structures. The two types of transfer can work together so that people transfer the idea of being innovative when it is appropriate to do so.

The fifth part, *The Context and the Learner,* includes two chapters that describe contextual approaches to conceptual change and two chapters that focus on the characteristics of the learner and particularly on how achievement goals, epistemic motives and beliefs, interest, self-efficacy, and affect and emotions might affect conceptual change. In their chapter, Halden, Scheja, and Haglund propose a theoretical methodological approach to analyzing personal meaning making based on intentional analysis. This approach focuses on learners' interaction with the learning material and with their surroundings, emphasizing the potentialities of learning. Adopting this approach to conceptual change, the authors argue, not only reveals students' ways of contextualising concepts and learning tasks, but also enables teachers to link the students' personal conceptions to ways of thinking endorsed within the discipline.

In the second chapter, Marton and Fai Pang discuss conceptual change from the point of view of phenomenography. Phenomenography attempts to capture the learner's changing experiences of understanding and utilize them to produce new understandings through teaching. It represents a distinct ontological and epistemological position from other approaches to conceptual change, insofar as it considers the different understandings as capabilities for making sense of certain things in certain ways, rather than stored internal representations. As discernment is a function of experienced variation and invariance, changes in understandings are primarily seen in terms of the patterns of variation and invariance in how the phenomenon that is understood appears to the learner. The authors present in their chapter a detailed example of differing ways of making sense of price and pricing in order to illustrate how phenomenology describes students' different understandings and to demonstrate how new understandings are brought about in teaching.

Sinatra and Mason try to capture the "warming trend" in conceptual change research (Sinatra,

2005). This trend is evident in recent models of conceptual change that seek to characterize the role of hot constructs that affect conceptual change beyond effects attributable to background knowledge (Murphy & Mason, 2006). In their chapter, they argue that learner characteristics that act at the intentional level can play a determining role in fostering conceptual change (Sinatra & Pintrich, 2003). They also review current theory and research on how key hot constructs such as, achievement goals, epistemic motives and beliefs, interest, self-efficacy, and affect and emotions might affect the change process.

Murphy and Alexander attempt to ascertain, through meta-analytic and best evidence synthesis techniques, the quantifiable effects of approaches to conceptual change on learners' knowledge, beliefs, and interest. They concentrate on empirical research published in the last decade focusing on learning within K–12 classroom settings, and describe particular design features of this empirical literature, such as the domains or topics studied or the ethnicity, ages, or abilities of participants. Drawing on those design features and the major findings of the identified works, they then turn their attention to three significant trends that arose from the synthesis of the identified literature. Those trends shed light on the researchers' conceptualizations and operationalizations of concepts and conceptual change, as well as the conditions under which transformations in learners' knowledge, beliefs, and interest were documented.

Instruction to Promote Conceptual Change is the title of Part VI. In the first chapter of this part, White and Gunstone show how research into alternative conceptions spread rapidly in the 1970s and became very prominent in science education affecting science teaching. In the second chapter, Duit, Treagust, and Widodo also provide an overview of the development of conceptual change perspectives since the 1970s. They argue that the theoretical frameworks and research methods that have been developed within the conceptual change approach allow fine-grained analyses of teaching and learning processes to better understand the consequence of practice in the science classroom. On the other hand, they also provide research findings from various studies on the practice of science instruction showing that there is a large gap between what is known in research and what may be set in practice in normal science classes. Teachers usually are not well informed about actual views of efficient teaching and learning available in the research community. Most teachers hold views about teaching and learning that are limited when seen from recent inclusive conceptual change perspectives. Consequently, their instructional repertoires are far from teaching based on these conceptual change perspectives. It is argued that teachers must become familiar with the recent state of conceptual change research so that they can change their instructional repertoires. They also think that the recent conceptual change perspectives may also provide powerful pedagogical frameworks for understanding the conceptual change processes required in the case of teacher professional development.

John Leach and Philip Scott describe an approach that draws on individual and sociocultural perspectives to promote conceptual change through teaching. They argue that the acquisition and participation metaphors for learning have been the subject of much debate in the academic community since the early 1990s. Learning is portrayed either as a process of *participation* in social activity, or as the *acquisition* of something by a cognizing individual. Significant attention has been given in the literature to the relative merits of each metaphor for describing learning in various settings. However, much less attention has been given to the implications of each metaphor for planning and executing teaching. In their chapter they present the key aspects of individual and sociocultural perspectives that have been used to theorize science learning, considering in detail the advantages and limitations of these perspectives in informing the planning of teaching for conceptual understanding in science. They then present their own approach to planning and conducting science teaching that is informed by both individual and sociocultural perspectives.

In the next chapter, David Jonassen focuses on the advantages of model-based reasoning for conceptual change. He argues that model-based reasoning is fostered by learner construction of qualitative and quantitative models using technology-based modeling tools. Model building is a powerful strategy for engaging, supporting, and assessing conceptual change in learners because these models scaffold and externalize internal, mental models by providing multiple formalisms for representing conceptual understanding and change. Building models of domain content, problems, systems, experiences, or thinking processes using different representational formalisms represent different kinds of conceptual understanding that foster different kinds of conceptual change.

In the last chapter, Marcia Linn argues that research on conceptual change takes a variety of positions around the question: Should we encourage learners to extinguish the ideas that experts dispute or should we help students distinguish among normative and personally-constructed views? The chapter introduces the knowledge integration framework as a promising way to respond to these issues. Conceptual change is identified as the individuals' lifelong trajectory of understanding of a given topic or discipline. Five issues that a comprehensive perspective on conceptual change needs to explain are identified and discussed: (1) the role of memory and forgetting, (2) the role of development from childhood to adulthood, (3) the impact of the disciplinary context of the topic, (4) the form of explanation (causal, atomic level, descriptive, colloquial), and (5) the design and impact of instruction.

ACKNOWLEDGMENTS

This book is dedicated to Giyoo Hatano whose work in conceptual change was an inspiration to all of us. Giyoo was one of the original editors of this volume and instrumental for its conception. His untimely death did not allow him to complete this project. We have reprinted in this volume chapter 7 from his book with Kayoko Inagaki entitled *Young Children's Naïve Thinking about the Biological World.* I am indebted to Kayoko Inagaki for her permission to reprint this chapter and to Naomi Miyake for her extensive discussion of Giyoo's work in her chapter.

I would like to thank Pat Alexander who suggested to me the idea of editing a handbook in this area and who supported it all along as the series editor for Educational Psychology. I would also like to express my thanks to the editorial director of the series, Lane Akers who has been extremely helpful and supportive all along the many months it took to complete this project. All the authors who contributed chapters for the volume were extremely cooperative. I would like to thank them for that.

This volume would not have been possible without the help of a special group of the graduate students who helped directly or indirectly to make this Handbook a reality. More specifically I would like to thank Irini Skopeliti, Xenia Vamvakoussi, Konstantinos P. Christou and Svetlana Gerakakis. Last but not least, I thank my secretary Spyridoula Efthimiou who has spent hours formatting and correcting manuscripts and references for this book.

NOTES

1. A detailed presentation of Kuhn's views and the criticism they received from philosophers of science can be found in the chapter by Arabatzis and Kindi (chapter 13, this volume).
2. A very interesting phenomenon since Kuhn's theory directly challenged the rationality of theory-choice in science.

REFERENCES

Alexander, P. A. (2001). Persuasion: Rethinking the nature of change in students' knowledge and beliefs: Introduction to special issue on persuasion. *International Journal of Educational Research, 35*, 629–631.

Caravita, S., & Hallden, O. (1994) Re-framing the problem of conceptual change. *Learning and Instruction, 4*, 89–111.

Carey, S. (1985). *Conceptual change in childhood*. Cambridge, MA: MIT Press.

Chi, M. T. H. (1992). Conceptual change within and across ontological categories: Examples from learning and discovery in science. In R. Giere (Ed.), *Cognitive models of science: Minnesota Studies in the Philosophy of Science* (pp. 129–186). University of Minnesota Press: Minneapolis, MN.

Corry, L. (1993). Kuhnian issues, scientific revolutions and the history of mathematics. *Studies in History and Philosophy of Science, 24*, 95–117.

Dauben, J., (1984). Conceptual revolutions and the history of mathematics: Two studies in the growth of knowledge. Originally appeared in E. Mendelsohn (Ed.), *Transformation and tradition in the sciences, Essays in Honor of I. Bernard Cohen* (pp. 81–103). Cambridge University Press. Reprinted in D. Gilies (Ed.) *Revolutions in mathematics* (pp. 15–20). Oxford University Press, 1992.

Dehaene, S. (1998). *The number sense: How the mind creates mathematics*. Harmondsworth, Middlesex, England: The Penguin Press (First published by Oxford University Press, 1997).

Driver, R., & Easley, J. (1978). Pupils and paradigms: A review of literature related to concept development in adolescent science students. *Studies in Science Education, 5*, 61–84.

Fodor, J. (1996). Deconstructing Dennett's Darwin. *Mind and Langage, 11*, 246–262.

Gelman, R. (2000). The epigenesis of mathematical thinking. *Journal of Applied Developmental Psychology, 21*, 27–37.

Greer, B. (2006). Designing for conceptual change. In J. Novotná, H. Moraová, M. Krátká, & N. Stehlíková (Eds), *Proceedings of the 30th conference of the international group for the psychology of mathematics education* (Vol. 1, pp. 175–178). Prague: PME.

Hatano, G. (Guest Editor). (1994). Introduction: Conceptual Change — Japanese Perspectives. *Special Issue of Human Development, 37*(4), 189–197.

Hatano, G., & Inagaki, K. (1994). Young children's naive theory of biology. *Cognition, 50*, 171–188.

Hatano, G., & Inagaki, K. (2003). When is conceptual change intended? A cognitive-sociocultural view. In G. M. Sinatra & P. R. Pintrich (Eds.), *Intentional conceptual change* (pp. 407–427). Mahwah, NJ: Erlbaum.

Hoddeson, L. (2007). In the wake of Tomas Kuhn's theory of scientific revolutions: The perspective of an historian of science. In S. Vosniadou, A., Baltas, & X., Vamvakoussi, (Eds.). *Reframing the conceptual change approach in learning and instruction* (pp. 25–34). Oxford: Elsevier.

Kuhn, D., Amsel, E., & O'Loughlin, M. (1988). *The development of scientific thinking skills*. San Diego, CA: Academic Press.

Kuhn, T. (1962). *The structure of scientific revolutions*. Chicago: Chicago Press.

Lipton, J. S., & Spelke, E. S. (2003). Origins of number sense: large numbers discrimination in human infants. *Psychological Science, 4*, 396–401.

Machamer, P. (2007). Kuhn's philosophical successes? In S. Vosniadou, A., Baltas, & X., Vamvakoussi, (Eds.), *Reframing the conceptual change approach in learning and instruction* (pp. 35–46). Oxford: Elsevier.

Mahoney, M. S. (1997). Revolution in mathematics. Unpublished manuscript.

Mason, L., & Gava, M. (2007). Effects of epistemological beliefs and learning text structure on conceptual change. In S. Vosniadou, A., Baltas, & X., Vamvakoussi (Eds.), *Reframing the conceptual change approach in learning and instruction*. (pp. 165–196). Oxford: Elsevier.

McCloskey, M. (1983). Intuitive physics. *Scientific American, 248*(4), 122–130.

Murphy, P., & Mason, L. (2006). Changing knowledge and beliefs. In P. A. Alexander & P. H. Winne (Eds.), *Handbook of educational psychology* (pp. 305–324). Mahwah, NJ: Erlbaum.

Murphy, G. L., & Medin, D. L. (1985). The role of theories in conceptual coherence. *Psychological Review, 92*(3), 289–316.

Pintrich, P. R., Marx, R. W., & Boyle, R. A. (1993). Beyond cold conceptual change: The role of motivational beliefs and classroom contextual factors in the process of conceptual change. *Review of Educational Research, 63*, 167–199.

Posner, G. J., Strike, K. A., Hewson, P. W., & Gertzog, W. A. (1982). Accommodation of a scientific conception: towards a theory of conceptual change. *Science Education, 66*, 211–227.

Sinatra, G. (2005). The 'warming trend' in conceptual change research: The legacy of Paul R. Pintrich. *Educational Psychologist, 40*(2), 107–115.

Sinatra, G. M., & Dole, J. A. (1998). Case studies in conceptual change: A social psychological perspective. In B. Guzzetti & C. Hynd (Eds.), *Perspectives on conceptual change: Multiple ways to understand knowing and learning in a complex world* (pp. 39–53). Mahwah, NJ: Erlbaum.

Sinatra, G. M., & Pintrich, P. R. (Eds.). (2003). *Intentional conceptual change*. Mahwah, NJ: Erlbaum.

Smith, J. P., diSessa, A. A., & Roschelle, J. (1993). Misconceptions reconceived: A constructivist analysis of knowledge in transition. *The Journal of the Learning Sciences, 3*, 115–163.

Stathopoulou, C., & Vosniadou, S. (2006). Exploring the relationship between physics-related epistemological beliefs and physics understanding. *Contemporary Educational Psychology 32*, 255–281.

Stathopoulou, C., & Vosniadou, S. (2007). Conceptual change in physics and physics-related epistemological Beliefs: A relationship under scrutiny. In S. Vosniadou, A. Baltas, & X. Vamvakoussi (Eds.), *Reframing the conceptual change approach in learning and instruction* (pp. 145–164). Oxford: Elsevier.

Suppe, F. (1977). The search for philosophic understanding if scientific theories. In F. Suppe (Ed.). *The structure of scientific theories* (pp. 3–241). Urbana & Chicago: University of Illinois Press.

Thagard, P. (1992). *Conceptual revolutions*. Princeton, NJ: Princeton University Press.

Viennot L. (1979). Spontaneous reasoning in elementary dynamics. *European Journal of Science Education, 1*(2), 205–221.

Vosniadou, S. (2003). Exploring the relationships between conceptual change and intentional learning. In G. M. Sinatra & P. R. Pintrich (Eds.), *Intentional conceptual change* (pp. 377–406). Mahwah, NJ: Erlbaum.

Vosniadou, S. (2007). The cognitive—situative divide and the problem of conceptual change. *Educational Psychologist, 42*(1), 55–66.

Vosniadou, S., Baltas, A., & Vamvakoussi, X. (Eds.). (2007). *Reframing the conceptual change approach in learning and instruction*. Oxford: Elsevier.

Wellman, H. M. (2002). Understanding the psychological world: Developing a theory of mind. In U. Goswami (Ed.), *Handbook of childhood cognitive development* (pp. 167–187). Oxford: Blackwell.

I

THEORETICAL ISSUES IN CONCEPTUAL CHANGE RESEARCH

1

The Framework Theory Approach to the Problem of Conceptual Change

Stella Vosniadou, Xenia Vamvakoussi, and Irini Skopeliti
National and Kapodistrian University of Athens

INTRODUCTION

The term *conceptual change* was introduced by Thomas Kuhn (1962) to indicate that the concepts embedded in a scientific theory change their meaning when the theory (paradigm) changes.[1] Kuhn promoted a contextual view of concepts as having an internal structure embedded in theoretical frameworks from which they obtain their meaning. When a theoretical framework changes, the meanings of the concepts subsumed in it also changes, making them 'incommensurable' to the same concepts subsumed under the previous theoretical framework.[2] The notion of incommensurability received considerable criticism from philosophers and historians of science, forcing Kuhn to eventually change his position from that of 'global incommensurability' to 'local incommensurability'. Local incommensurability refers to only a partial change in the meaning of concepts.

Susan Carey (see, Carey, 1985, 1991, in press; Carey & Spelke, 1994) has been instrumental in clarifying how conceptual change can be seen in the context of cognitive development. Carey (1991) supported the notion of 'local incommensurability' attempting to divorce conceptual change from issues of reference (Kitcher, 1983).[3] She identified several kinds of conceptual changes that could be considered as radical conceptual change and provided the empirical evidence to support the claim that they occur in the course of spontaneous cognitive development. Conceptual change according to Carey (1991) requires the re-assignment of a concept to a different ontological category or the creation of new ontological categories — as when the concept of the 'earth' becomes subsumed under the category of astronomical objects as opposed to physical objects (Vosniadou & Skopeliti, 2005). It can also involve the differentiation or coalescence of concepts — such as the differentiation between heat and temperature or weight and density (Carey, 1991; Carey & Spelke, 1994; Wiser & Carey, 1983; Wiser & Smith, chapter 8, this volume).

Other researchers have interpreted the term *conceptual change* more broadly to indicate all the different kinds of conceptual changes that happen in the process of learning and development as well as in the history of science and not only the ones that accompany theory change

(Thagard, 1992; chapter 14, this volume). Thagard (chapter 14, this volume) provides such a list of conceptual changes, starting with some of the simpler kinds, i.e., those that involve adding a new instance or a new rule to an existing concept, and ending with some of the more radical, i.e., those involved in theory change. The latter are the ones requiring changes in the ontological category tree in which a concept belongs, with corresponding changes in causality, for example, when concepts like 'life', 'disease' and 'mind' change from being embedded within theological explanations to qualitative and then to mechanistic frameworks. Chi (chapter 3, this volume) also distinguishes between three kinds of conceptual changes that happen in the process of learning: belief revision, mental model transformation, and categorical shift. Similar distinctions are also made by Keil and Newman (chapter 4, this volume), Wiser and Smith (chapter 8, this volume), Inagaki and Hatano (2003; chapter 9, this volume), to characterize the process of cognitive development.

The focus of the present chapter is to describe and explain the kinds of conceptual changes that take place when students are exposed to counter-intuitive concepts in science and mathematics (Vosniadou, 2006; Vosniadou & Verschaffel, 2004). We are interested in what Inagaki and Hatano (chapter 9, this volume) call 'instruction induced conceptual change', as compared to the kinds of conceptual changes that happen spontaneously in development. We argue that many science concepts are difficult to learn because they are embedded within scientific theories that violate fundamental principles of the naïve, framework theory of physics within which everyday physics concepts are subsumed. In other words, the learning of many science concepts requires the more radical kind of conceptual changes that involve ontological category shifts.

At the heart of our theoretical approach is the idea that initial explanations of the physical world in naive physics are not fragmented observations but form a coherent whole, a *framework theory*. The change of the framework theory is difficult because it forms a coherent explanatory system, it is based on everyday experience, and it is constantly re-confirmed by our everyday experiences in the context of lay culture. After all, the currently accepted scientific explanations are the product of a long historical development of science characterized by radical theory changes that have restructured our representations of the physical world. More recently we have started to work in the area of mathematics. Although the domain of mathematics is very different from that of science, we believe that the same analysis can roughly apply in the case of learning mathematics (see Vosniadou & Verschaffel, 2004; Verschaffel & Vosniadou, 2004)

The first section of this chapter presents two examples of conceptual change, one coming from the area of physics (observational astronomy) and the other from the area of mathematics (rational number). The second section provides a more detailed analysis of the theoretical position which also explains its similarities and differences with other approaches dealing with the problem of conceptual change in learning and development. The chapter concludes with a discussion of some of the implications of the framework theory approach for the design of instruction in science and mathematics.

It is our contention that the problem of conceptual change commonly posed in instruction is one of the major reasons behind students' widespread failure to understand concepts in science and mathematics. An overwhelming body of educational research has documented the considerable difficulties students encounter in these areas. These difficulties are not present only in the case of the weaker or younger students. They are present even in the brighter college students, attending the most prestigious universities. Absence of critical thinking, knowledge fragmentation, lack of transfer, and misconceptions characterize the reasoning and problem solving of many students, particularly in those cases where the new, to-be-acquired information conflicts with the structure of existing, experience-based, lay knowledge. Finally, it is also our contention that, to a large extent, the general ineffectiveness of instructional interventions in this area could be attributed to the inadequate attention that has been given so far to the problem of conceptual change.

TWO EXAMPLES OF INSTRUCTION-INDUCED CONCEPTUAL CHANGE

The Concept of the Earth[4]

Children's Initial Concept

A substantial body of cross-cultural research supports the conclusion that during the pre-school years children construct an initial concept of the earth based on interpretations of everyday experience in the context of lay culture. According to this initial concept, the earth is a flat, stable, stationary, and supported physical object. Objects located on the earth obey the laws of an up/down gravity, and space is organised in terms of the dimensions of up and down. The sky and solar objects are located above the top of this flat earth which is thought to occupy a geocentric universe (see Brewer, chapter 7, this volume; Vosniadou & Brewer, 1992, 1994; Nussbaum, 1979, 1985).

Scientific Concept

As shown in Table 1.1, the scientific concept of the earth, to which children are exposed at least as soon as they enter elementary school, violates practically all of the presuppositions that apply to children's initial earth concept. According to the scientific concept, the earth is a planet — an unsupported, spherical, astronomical object — which rotates around its axis and revolves around the sun in a heliocentric solar system. People live all around the spherical earth and gravity operates towards the center of the earth. Understanding the scientific concept of the earth requires that children re-categorize the earth to a new ontological category — from a physical object to an astronomical object. We consider this re-categorization to be a form of radical conceptual change.

Conceptual Change

The hypothesis that the acquisition of the scientific concept of the earth requires conceptual change was tested directly in an empirical study by Vosniadou and Skopeliti (2005). In this study, 62 first- and fifth-grade children were shown 10 cards with the words 'sun, moon, star, earth, planet, house, cat, rock, tree, and car' and were asked three categorization questions. The results, which are described in detail in Table 1.2, showed that great majority of the children were able to distinguish physical from solar objects and that there was a developmental shift in their categorizations of the earth.

TABLE 1.1
Concept of the Earth

Initial	*Scientific*
Earth as a physical object	*Earth as an astronomical object (planet)*
Flat	Spherical
Stationary	Rotating around its axis Revolving around Sun
Supported	Unsupported
Up/down Gravity	Gravity towards the center of earth
Geocentric system	Heliocentric system

TABLE 1.2
Frequencies/Percentages of Children's Response Types to the Categorization Test

Questions	Response Types	1st grade	5th grade
1. I want you to put together the things that you think should go together, i.e., belong to the same group.	1. Distinguishes solar from physical objects and groups Earth with solar. (Two categories.)	21%	47%
	2. Distinguishes solar from physical objects and groups Earth with solar. (Many categories.)	13%	32%
	3. Distinguishes solar from physical objects and groups Earth with physical. (Many categories.)	20%	5%
	4. Does not distinguish physical from solar objects.	44%	16%
	5. Don't know.	2%	
2. Could you make only two groups from these things?	1. Distinguishes solar from physical objects and groups Earth with solar.	27%	79%
	2. Distinguishes solar from physical objects and groups Earth with physical.	11%	5%
	3. Does not distinguish physical from solar objects.	36%	16%
	4. Don't know / Cannot do it	16%	
3. Could you put in one group the things that go with the Earth and in another the things that do not?	1. Distinguishes solar from physical objects and groups Earth with solar.	42%	90%
	2. Distinguishes solar from physical objects and groups Earth with physical.	35%	10%
	3. Does not distinguish physical from solar objects.	23%	—

Children's responses, particularly to the third question, which asked them explicitly to put together the things that go with the earth in one group and the things that do not go with the earth in a different group, were very revealing. At grade one, 35% of the children categorized the earth as a physical object and 42% as a solar object, while at grade five only one child categorized the earth as a physical object and 90% categorized it as a solar object. Further, children's responses to an earth shape questionnaire similar to the one used by Vosniadou and Brewer (1992) showed significant correlations between children's categorizations and their earth shape models.

We concluded that the results support the hypothesis that there is a change in the categorization of the earth from a physical to a solar object, and that the re-categorization of the earth as a solar object may precede children's full understanding of the earth as a spherical planet, rotating around its axis and revolving around the sun.

Internal Inconsistency and Synthetic Models

The re-categorization of the earth as a solar object does not take place overnight. A series of cross-sectional developmental studies (e.g., Blown & Bryce, 2006; Diakidoy, Vosniadou & Hawks, 1997; Nussbaum, 1979; Nussbaum & Novak, 1976; Vosniadou & Brewer, 1992, 1994) as well as some longitudinal studies (Kikas, 1998; Maria, 1993, 1997a, 1997b), support the hypothesis that the process of acquiring the scientific concept of the earth is a slow and gradual process which gives rise to the construction of alternative conceptions of the earth as well as to internally inconsistent responses. A list of the alternative representations constructed by elementary school children in the Vosniadou and Brewer (1992) study appears in Figure 1.1. These accounted for about 90% of the overall responses of the third- and fifth-grade children and 65% of the overall responses of the first-grade children. The overall responses of the remaining children were categorized as mixed.[5]

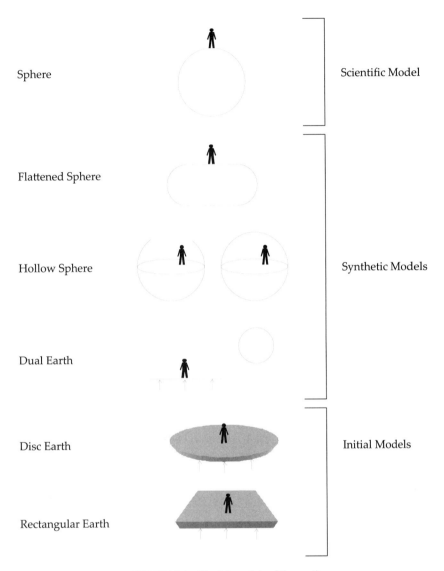

FIGURE 1.1   Mental models of the earth.

The internally consistent responses formed a range of alternative models of the earth, starting from the initial representation of a flat earth to the scientific representation of a sphere. The younger children tended to represent the earth as a square, rectangle, or disc-like flat, physical object, supported by ground below and the sky and solar objects above its top. Some children formed the interesting model of a dual earth, according to which there are two earths: a flat one on which people live and a spherical one which is up in the sky and which is a planet. Another common mis-representation of the earth was that of a hollow sphere. According to that model, the earth is spherical but hollow inside. People live on flat ground inside the bottom part of the hollow sphere. Alternatively, the earth was conceptualized like a flattened sphere or truncated sphere with people living on its flat top, covered by the dome of the sky above its top.

These alternative representations of the earth were not rare. In fact, only 23 of the 60 children in the Vosniadou and Brewer (1992) study had constructed the culturally accepted representation of the earth as a sphere. These findings have been confirmed by many cross-cultural studies conducted both in our lab (e.g., Diakidoy, Vosniadou & Hawks, 1997; Samarapungavan, Vosniadou, & Brewer, 1996; Vosniadou, Skopeliti, & Ikospentaki, 2004, 2005), as well as by a number of independent investigators (Blown & Bryce, 2006; Hayes, Goodhew, Heit, & Gillan, 2003; Mali & Howe, 1979).[6]

The Process of Conceptual Change

Given that the spherical representation of the earth is so ubiquitous in our culture, one wonders why children have such great difficulty understanding it and why they form the alternative representations noted above. The explanation we have given is that the change from a flat earth to a spherical earth concept is not a change in a simple belief (Chi, chapter 3, this volume), but a radical conceptual change. This is because the initial concept of the earth is embedded within a larger, framework theory of physics, forming a complex construction which is supported by a whole system of observations, beliefs and presuppositions constituting a relative coherent and systematic explanatory structure (Vosniadou & Brewer, 1992, 1994; Vosniadou, 2007b). Figure 1.2 shows some of the observations, beliefs and presuppositions of the assumed conceptual structure that underlies the initial concept of the earth.

Two assumptions are made here which will be discussed in greater detail in the next section. One is that the concept of the earth is embedded within a domain-specific, framework theory of physics, i.e., a naïve physics. The second is that categorization is a powerful process that plays an important role as a mechanism in learning (Bransford, Brown, & Cocking, 1999; Chi, chapter 3, this volume; Chi & Koeske, 1983; Medin & Rips, 2005). Knowing that an object belongs to a given category allows us to infer certain characteristics of the object which can either support learning or hinder it, if the category to which it is assigned is inappropriate. In the case of the earth, its categorization as a physical object allows young children to make a host of inferences about the way they interpret observational evidence received from experience and draw conclusions regarding certain inaccessible, unobservable properties of the earth (e.g., that it is supported

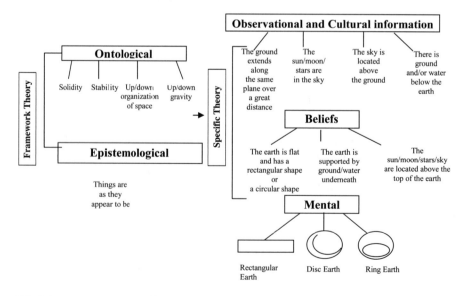

FIGURE 1.2   Hypothetical conceptual structure underlying children's mental models of the earth.

or that it has an end). These inferences are not subject to conscious awareness and can stand as powerful presuppositions constraining the process of learning science.

An examination of children's alternative models of the earth, as well as their internally inconsistent responses, suggests that children use enrichment type of learning mechanisms to add the new (scientific) information to their initial concept of the earth. While the use of such mechanisms can be very appropriate in most situations where the new, to-be-acquired, information is consistent with what is already known, they are not very productive when the new information belongs to a scientific concept embedded within a theoretical framework incompatible — incommensurate we might say — with children's initial concept of the earth.

As we have argued so far, the scientific concept of the earth is embedded within a different explanatory framework — that of an astronomical object — a framework that differs in many of its presuppositions from the presuppositions of the initial concept of the earth, which is categorized as a physical object embedded within a naïve physics. In cases such as these, where the new information comes in conflict with what is already known, the use of additive, bottom-up enrichment mechanisms can only lead the learner into small changes which may either fragment what is already known creating internally inconsistent pieces of knowledge, or at best lead into the creation of alternative models or misconceptions.

We have interpreted the alternative models of the earth to be 'synthetic models' because they seem to result from children's attempts to synthesize the information that comes from the scientific concept, and particularly the information that the earth is a sphere, with aspects of the initial concept of the earth, i.e., that it is a solid, stable, supported physical object, with an up/down organization of space and gravity. If we look carefully at all the alternative models of the earth in Figure 1.1, we can see that in all cases they represent attempts on the part of the children to solve the problem of how it is possible for the earth to be spherical and flat at the same time and how it is possible for people to live on this spherical earth without falling down.

Furthermore, the process of conceptual change appears to involve a gradual lifting of the presuppositions of the framework theory allowing the formation of more sophisticated models of the earth, until conceptual change has been achieved. Although most of the empirical support for synthetic models comes from cross-sectional studies, the developmental pattern is clear (see also Brewer, chapter 7, this volume). The less sophisticated and more fragmented responses occur at the younger ages while the more sophisticated synthetic models, and of course the scientific model, are found in the older children. Thus, children start with the model of a square or rectangular, supported, stable, and flat earth that meet all the presuppositions of the earth as a physical object. The model of the disc earth shows some possible influence from the culture reflected in the change in the assumed shape of the earth from rectangular to round (but flat). This model could be an initial model or it could result from some exposure to scientific information about the shape of the earth. The dual model of the earth is an interesting construction that shows how scientific information can be incorporated into the knowledge base in a way that does not affect existing knowledge structures that contradict it. In this model the children believe that the spherical earth is different from the flat earth on which we live — it is a planet up in the sky.

The models of the hollow sphere and the truncated sphere are more sophisticated and are usually formed by older children. The model of the hollow sphere presupposes an understanding that the earth is spherical and not supported, but it is constrained by an up/down gravity presupposition. The children who construct this model believe that people live on flat ground inside the earth because they would fall 'down' if they lived on the surface of the spherical earth. Similarly, the up/down gravity presupposition constrains the understanding of the spherical earth in children who have constructed a flattened or truncated sphere, who also believe that people live on flat ground above the top of the earth. These children can see the earth as a spherical, suspended and sometimes rotating object but they still organise space and gravity in terms of the directions of up/down. These are some of the most fundamental presuppositions of a naïve, framework theory of physics.

It should be mentioned here that the children placed in the category 'mixed' also use enrichment types of learning mechanisms to add the new information to their initial concept. The difference from the 'synthetic' models category is that the children placed in the mixed category were either not aware of the internal contradiction in their responses or could not find a way to solve this contradiction through the creation of a 'synthetic model'. Synthetic models are actually quite creative constructions as they provide unique solutions to the problem of incommensurability and have explanatory power. As we will argue later on, we believe that in order to avoid internal inconsistency, or the creation of synthetic models, the learner must first of all become aware of the incongruity that exists between the incoming information and his/her prior knowledge. Metaconceptual awareness and intentional learning are required for conceptual change to be achieved. Learners must also avoid the use of simple, additive mechanisms. Conscious, intentional and top-down learning mechanisms, such as the deliberate use of analogy and cross-domain mappings, are much better mechanisms than additive, enrichment-type mechanisms for producing radical conceptual change. These issues will be discussed in greater detail in the last section of the chapter.

The Concept of Number

Children's Initial Concept

It appears that children form an initial concept of number which allows them to deal with number-related tasks long before they are exposed to formal instruction in mathematics. Summarizing the relevant empirical findings, Gelman (1994) concludes that by four or five years of age children are able to 'count in principled ways, invent solutions to novel counting problems, detect errors in counting trails generated by others and make up counting algorithms to solve simple addition and subtraction problems, at least for a limited range of the numbers' (p. 68). These abilities reflect a concept of number close to the mathematical concept of natural numbers.

The first years of instruction are dedicated to natural number arithmetic. Thus, the initial understandings of number are compatible with school instruction. As a result, the natural number concept is further confirmed and strengthened. By the middle of the elementary school years most children have built a rich and productive number concept, which is based on counting, and which carries all the basic presuppositions of natural numbers described in Table 1.3.

A basic characteristic of this initial understanding of numbers is that numbers are discrete i.e., that every number has a unique successor. In fact, there seems to be some evidence that the property of discreteness of numbers may be neurobiologically based, in the sense that humans are predisposed to learn and reason with natural numbers (Dehaene, 1998; Gelman, 2000). Another characteristic is that numbers can be ordered by means of their position on the count list, with numerals with more digits corresponding to bigger numbers (see also Smith, Solomon, & Carey, 2005). Numbers are involved in the operations of addition and subtraction which can be supported by counting-based strategies (e.g., Resnick, 1986). The operation of multiplication is interpreted as repeated addition while division is interpreted as partitioning, where the divisor is smaller than the dividend (Fischbein et al., 1985). All four operations are seen as having predictable outcomes, in the sense that addition and multiplication 'make bigger', whereas subtraction and division 'make smaller' (Fischbein et al., 1985; Moskal & Magone, 2000). Finally, it is also assumed that every number has only one symbolic representation, that there is a unique numeral that corresponds to each number.

TABLE 1.3
Concept of the Number

Children's number concept (before they are exposed to rational number instruction)	*The mathematical concept of rational number*
▪ Numbers are *counting numbers*	▪ Not based on counting
▪ Numbers are discrete: There is no other number between a number and its next ▪ There is a smallest number (0 or 1)	▪ Dense: Between any two, non equal numbers there are infinitely many numbers ▪ There is no smallest numbers
▪ Numbers can be ordered by means of their position in the count list ▪ "Longer" numbers (i.e. with more digits) are bigger	▪ Ordering is not counting-based ▪ "Longer" numbers are not necessarily bigger, e.g., 3.2 > 3.197

▪ Addition and multiplication "make bigger"
▪ Subtraction and division "make smaller"
	▪ The magnitude of the outcome depends on the numbers involved, e.g.,
	  • Adding a negative number "makes smaller"
	  • Multiplying by a number smaller than one "makes smaller"

▪ Every number has only one symbolic representation	▪ Any number can be represented either as a fraction, or as a decimal. In addition, any number can be represented in various ways as a fraction or decimal.

The Mathematical Concept of Rational Number

All of the above-mentioned assumptions underlying students' number concept are in contrast with the mathematical concept of rational number introduced through instruction: Rational numbers are not based on counting and they are dense and not discrete. In other words, no rational number has a successor within the rational number set, and there are infinitely many numbers between any two, non equal, rational numbers. Counting-based strategies cannot support the ordering of rational numbers (for example, 1/4 is bigger than 1/5). In addition, 'longer' rational numbers are not necessarily 'bigger' (for instance, 3.2 is bigger than 3.197). Operations with rational numbers do not have predictable results – in the sense that addition and multiplication may result either in bigger, or in smaller outcomes, as in the case of 4+ (–2), or 3 × 1/2. Multiplication cannot always be conceptualized as repeated addition, (consider the case 0.3 × 1/2) and it is difficult to understand division as partitioning when the divisor is bigger than the dividend (e.g., 2:8), or when the divisor is smaller than one (e.g., 2:0.5).

Finally, rational numbers do not have only one symbolic representation. Rather, they can be represented symbolically either as decimals, or as fractions. For example, the number one half can be represented as 0.5 and also as 1/2. To make things more complicated, the one half can be represented also as 0.50, 0.500, 2/4, 4/8, etc. This presents the learner with yet another difficulty: one must realise that fractions and decimals[7] are alternative representations of rational numbers (and not different kinds of numbers), despite their differences in notation, ordering, operations and contexts of use.

Conceptual Change

There is a great deal of empirical evidence showing that rational number reasoning is very difficult for students at all levels of instruction and in particular when new information about rational numbers comes in contrast with prior natural number knowledge (Moss, 2005; Ni &

Zhou, 2005). For instance, many students believe that 'longer decimals are bigger' (e.g., Moskal and Magone, 2000), that 'multiplication makes bigger' and 'division makes smaller' (Fischbein et al., 1985), or that 'the bigger the terms of a fraction, the bigger the fraction' (e.g., Stafylidou & Vosniadou, 2004). Students at elementary, secondary and even university levels do not realize that rational and real numbers are dense (e.g., Malara, 2001; Merenluoto & Lehtinen, 2002, 2004; Neumann, 1998; Tirosh, Fischbein, Graeber, & Wilson, 1999; Vamvakoussi & Vosniadou 2004, 2007, in preparation). They have many difficulties interpreting and dealing with rational number notation, in particular when it comes to fractions (Gelman, 1991; Moss, 2005; Stafylidou & Vosniadou, 2004). They do not realize that it is possible for different symbols (e.g., decimals and fractions) to represent the same number and thus they treat different symbolic representations as if they were different numbers (Khoury & Zazkis, 1994; O'Connor, 2001; Vamvakoussi & Vosniadou, 2007).

Internal Inconsistency and Synthetic Models

Some of the difficulties secondary school students have in understanding rational numbers were investigated in a series of studies in our lab, focusing mostly on the discreteness/density divide and its interaction with students' interpretation of rational number notation (Vamvakoussi & Vosniadou 2004, 2007, in preparation). It was hypothesized that the presupposition of discreteness which is a characteristic of the initial concept of number, would constrain students' understanding of rational numbers causing fragmentation, internal inconsistency and misconceptions which could be interpreted as 'synthetic models'. This hypothesis is consistent with the existing empirical evidence for students (e.g., Malara, 2001; Merenluoto & Lehtinen, 2002, 2004; Neumann, 1998), as well as for prospective teachers (e.g., Tirosh, Fischbein, Graeber, & Wilson, 1999). This is because the initial concept of number forms a coherent explanatory system that produces correct predictions and explanations in most everyday situations where number reasoning is required.

It was also predicted that students would have difficulty understanding that decimals and fractions are interchangeable representations of rational numbers, and not different kinds of numbers. This could be for various reasons. First, decimals and fractions take their meaning from the situations in which they are used and these situations are usually qualitatively different (Resnick, 1986). In addition, there are considerable differences both between the operations and between the ordering of decimals and fractions. Finally, students may categorize rational numbers on the basis of their notation, which may be considered a superficial characteristic by the mathematically versed person, but not by the novices in the domain (see Markovitz & Sowder, 1991; Chi, Feltovich, & Glaser, 1981).

The results confirmed that the presupposition of discreteness is strong for the younger students (seventh graders) and remains robust even for older students (ninth and eleventh graders), despite noticeable developmental differences. Students from all age groups answer frequently that there is a finite number of numbers in a given interval, regardless of whether they are asked in an interview (Vamvakoussi & Vosniadou, 2004), in an open-ended questionnaire (Vamvakoussi & Vosniadou, 2007), or a forced choice questionnaire (Vamvakoussi & Vosniadou, 2007, in preparation). Figure 1.3 presents the distribution of the 549 participants in our third study (Vamvakoussi & Vosniadou, in preparation), based on the number of finite versus infinite responses they gave to the question 'How many numbers are there between X and Y', where the pair X and Y could be integers, decimals or fractions (in a total of ten items, consisting of two integer, four decimal, and four fraction questions). FIN students gave at least seven finite responses while INF students gave at least seven infinite responses. FIN/INF included all the remaining students. As

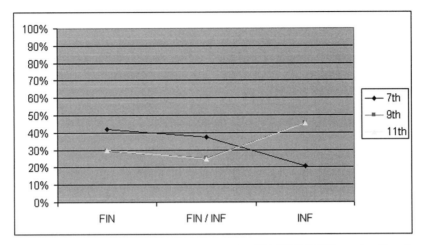

FIGURE 1.3   Percent of participants placed in categories FIN, FIN/INF, INF as a function of grade.

can be seen, the seventh-grade students gave mostly finite responses, while the older students were placed mostly in the FIN/INF and INF categories. Nevertheless, 30% of the ninth- and eleventh-grade students were still categorised in the most naïve, FIN category.

Second, the results showed that the presupposition of discreteness is not 'lifted' overnight. In other words, it is not the case that students become aware of the infinity of numbers at some point and then consistently apply it to all the given intervals. Rather, there seems to be a pattern of development during which information regarding the dense structure of numbers is slowly added on to existing conceptual structures: This developmental pattern seems to be roughly the following: The presupposition of discreteness is lifted first for integers and then for decimals and fractions. Then, there is some indication that students apply the notion of infinity first to decimals and then to fractions. Finally, when infinity is initially applied to decimals and fractions, it seems to be restricted to numbers of the same symbolic representation within an interval, i.e., only decimals between decimals and integers, and only fractions between fractions.

To illustrate these points, a more refined sub-categorization of the participants within the categories FIN, FIN/INF, and INF in the Vamvakoussi and Vosniadou (in preparation) study is presented in Table 4. As can be seen, we can identify an *initial, all finite model* in the category FIN, as well a kind of an *integers only* synthetic model consisting of students who seem to apply the notion of infinity in integers but not in decimals and fractions. In the category FIN/INF we see the emergence of the *decimal – fraction distinction*. Students in this sub-category answer differently when the interval ends are fractions, as compared to when they are decimals. More specifically, these students may a) give an INF answer for decimals, but a FIN answer for fractions, or b) give an FIN answer for decimals, but an INF answer for fractions. Usually, this distinction is in favour of decimals. Finally in the INF category the most interesting distinction is between the *same kind of numbers model* and the *sophisticated model*. In both of these models the students give only INF responses, however, in the *same kind of numbers model* they prefer to place decimals between decimals and fractions between fractions, while in the *sophisticated model* they are willing to accept that the numbers in any given interval may have different symbolic representations.

To sum up, it appears that students form an initial understanding of number roughly as natural number. This initial concept then stands in the way of understanding the concept of rational number presented to students through instruction. Understanding the mathematical concept of rational number requires a re-structuring of the initial concept of number. This is not easy.

TABLE 1.4
Synthetic Models of Rational Numbers Intervals

Category type	Models	7th grade (N = 181)	9th grade (N = 166)	11th grade (N = 202)	Total
FIN (N = 185)	All Finite — Initial Model	19 (25.0%)	21 (42.9%)	15 (25.0%)	55 (29.7%)
	All or mostly Finite for decimals and fractions	20 (26.3%)	10 (20.4%)	11 (18.3%)	41 (22.2%)
	Infinite for integers, mostly Finite for decimals and fractions	16 (21.1%)	5 (10.2%)	15 (25.0%)	36 (19.5%)
	Mixed 1	21 (27.6%)	13 (26.5%)	19 (31.7%)	53 (28.6%)
	Total by FIN	76	49	60	185
FIN / INF (N = 160)	Infinite for Integers, mostly Finite for decimals & fractions	2 (2.9%)	2 (4.8%)	5 (10.0%)	9 (5.6%)
	Mostly infinite for decimals, mostly finite for fractions	23 (33.8%)	6 (14.3%)	10 (20%)	39 (24.4%)
	Mostly finite for decimals, mostly infinite for fractions	8 (11.8%)	3 (7.1%)	10 (20%)	21 (13.1%)
	Mixed 2	35 (51.5%)	31 (73.8%)	25 (50.0%)	91 (56.9%)
	Total by FIN / INF	68	42	50	160
INF (N = 204)	Mostly infinite for decimals, mostly finite for fractions	1 (2.7%)	3 (4%)	4 (4.3%)	8 (3.9%)
	Mostly finite for decimals, mostly infinite for fractions	0 (0%)	0 (0%)	2 (2.2%)	2 (1%)
	All Infinite — Advanced Model	3 (8.1%)	5 (6.7%)	12 (13.0%)	20 (9.8%)
	All Infinite — Sophisticated Model	5 (13.5%)	33 (44.0%)	38 (41.3%)	76 (37.3%)
	Mixed 3	28 (75.7%)	34 (45.3%)	36 (39.1%)	98 (48%)
	Total by INF	37	75	92	204

Students need to realize that certain presuppositions, like the discreteness of numbers, are valid only in specific contexts. Also, learning about rational numbers requires from students to construct meanings for new symbolic notations — fractions and decimals — not encountered before (Gelman, 1991; Stafylidou & Vosniadou, 2004). In addition to the difficulty of interpreting decimal and fractional notation in its own right, students have to realize that different symbolic notations refer to the same object, i.e., that decimals and fractions are interchangeable representations of rational numbers, and not different kinds of numbers.

The empirical evidence suggests that students are using conservative, additive, enrichment types of mechanisms to add new information to existing but incompatible conceptual structures. These mechanisms create internal inconsistency and 'misconceptions' of the rational number concept which can be explained as 'synthetic models'. One of these synthetic models is to conceptualize the rational numbers set as consisting of three different and unrelated 'sets' of numbers: whole numbers, decimals, and fractions. As they come to understand the principle of density through instruction, students then apply this principle additively to the different 'sets' of numbers. As a result, students come to think differently for integers, decimals, and fractions in terms of their structure (discrete vs. dense). They also become reluctant to accept that there might be fractions between two decimals, or vice versa (see also Neumann, 1998).

Summary

Despite the enormous differences in the two concepts we analyzed, which are embedded in very different domains of thought, we can observe certain important similarities. In both cases we have a situation where the new concept, regardless of whether it is of a scientific or a mathematical nature, comes in conflict in practically all its major ontological presuppositions with the expected prior knowledge of the student. In both cases there is adequate empirical evidence to support the conclusion that an initial concept of the earth and an initial concept of number is constructed early on, in the process of spontaneous knowledge acquisition on the basis of everyday experience in the context of lay culture. This concept is embedded within a naïve theory of physics or of number that forms a narrow but relatively coherent explanatory structure. The new information presented through instruction comes in conflict with the presuppositions of the existing framework theory. Being largely unaware of this conflict, students assimilate the new information into the existing but incompatible knowledge base using enrichment type mechanisms which result in internally inconsistent responses or in the formation of synthetic models. Enrichment type mechanisms can be very successful in many cases of knowledge acquisition but fail in situations that require conceptual change, because of the incompatibility between the way knowledge is structured in the students' knowledge base and the structure of the scientific or mathematical concept presented through instruction.

THE FRAMEWORK THEORY APPROACH

The framework theory approach is based on cognitive/developmental research and attempts to provide a broad theoretical basis for understanding how conceptual change is achieved in the process of learning science. There are certain fundamental assumptions which characterize this approach which are discussed below. In short, it is claimed that there is enough empirical evidence coming from research in cognitive development to support they view that concepts are embedded in domain specific 'framework theories' which represent different explanatory frameworks from currently accepted science and mathematics (see Carey, 1991; Carey & Spelke, 1994; Hatano, 1994; Keil, 1994). These framework theories are constructed early on and are based on children's interpretations of their common everyday experiences in the context of lay culture. Because learners use additive, enrichment types of learning mechanisms to assimilate the new incompatible information to existent knowledge structures, the process of learning science and mathematics is slow and gradual and characterized by fragmentation, internal inconsistency and misconceptions, some of which can be interpreted as 'synthetic models' (Vosniadou & Brewer, 1992, 1994; Vosniadou, Baltas, & Vamvakoussi, 2007).

Domain Specificity

Most theories of learning and development, such as Piagetian and Vygotskian approaches, information processing or sociocultural theories are *domain general*. They focus on principles, stages, mechanisms, strategies, etc., that are meant to characterize all aspects of development and learning. In contrast, domain specific approaches focus on the description and explanation of the changes that take place in the content and structure of knowledge with learning and development as well as on mechanisms and strategies that are specific to these changes.

The idea that human cognition includes domain-specific mechanisms for learning is based on a number of independent research traditions and sets of empirical findings, some coming from animal studies (Gallistel, 1990), others based on Chomsky's work in linguistics (Chomsky, 1988). Some cognitive developmental psychologists see domain specificity through the notion of domain specific *constraints* on learning (Keil, 1981, 1990). It is argued that such constraints are needed in order to restrict the indeterminacy of experience (Goodman, 1972) and guide, amongst others, the development of language (Markman, 1989), numeric understanding (Gelman, 1990), or physical and psychological knowledge (Wellman & Gelman, 1998).

There is some debate in the literature as to whether domain specific constraints should be seen as hardwired and innate as opposed to acquired, and as having representational content or not (see Elman et al., 1996). Hatano and Inagaki (2000) suggested that constraints are innate domain specific biases or preferences that mitigate the interaction between a learning system and the environment. They also introduced the notion of 'sociocultural constraints'. They argue that sociocultural factors can also guide learning and development by restricting the possible range of alternative actions thus leading the learner to select the most appropriate behaviour (see also Hatano & Miyake, 1991; Keil, 1994).

Finally, some domain specific approaches focus on the description of the development of expertise in different subject-matter areas, such as physics (Chi, Feltovich, & Glaser, 1981), mathematics (VanLehn, 1990; Mayer, 1985) or chess (Chase & Simon, 1973), without necessarily appealing to innate modules or constraints.

Our position is that it is more profitable to study learning from a domain specific point of view that allows us to make hypothesis about the way a specific content is structured (and re-structured), without necessarily committing ourselves to innate constraints or modules. We also believe that domain-specific approaches should be seen as complimentary rather than contradictory to domain general approaches. It is very likely that both domain general and domain specific mechanisms apply in development and learning (Keil, 1994).

FRAMEWORK THEORIES, SPECIFIC THEORIES AND MENTAL MODELS

The human child is a complex organism capable of engaging in quick and efficient learning immediately after birth. Cognitive developmental research has provided substantial empirical evidence to support the view that children organize the multiplicity of their sensory experiences under the influence of everyday culture and language into narrow but relatively coherent, domains of thought from very early on (Baillargeon, 1995; Carey & Spelke, 1994; Gelman, 1990). It appears that at least four well-defined domains of thought can be distinguished and considered roughly as 'framework theories' — physics, psychology, mathematics, and language.

Each one of these domains has its unique ontology — applies to a distinct set of entities. For example, physics applies to physical entities, psychology applies to physical but only animate entities, mathematics to numbers and their operations, and language to lexical items and their operations. Each domain is also governed by a distinct system of principles and rules of operation. Physical entities obey the laws of mechanical causality as opposed to psychological entities that are governed under intentional causality. Language and mathematics have their own unique rules and principles of organisation. We are not going to delve further into these differences here.[8] The important point to make is that in all these cases we are not dealing with a collection of unrelated pieces of knowledge but with coherent and principle-based systems.

Each one of these domains of thought has certain procedures for identifying the entities that belong to the domain. For example, it appears that the criterion of self-initiated vs. non-self-initiated movement is used by infants to distinguish physical from psychological entities. Once categorized as a physical or psychological object, an entity inherits all the characteristics and properties of the entities that belong to the domain. As mentioned earlier, categorization is a very important learning mechanism in this respect. We assume that concepts are embedded in framework theories (such as a naïve physics, psychology, mathematics, etc.) and that they inherit all the properties of the framework theory to which they belong. In addition, they may contain additional information which belongs specifically to the concept — has the form of a 'specific theory'. The hypothesized internal structure of the initial concept of the 'earth' is described in Figure 1.2. This structure includes specific information about the earth, coming from observation and from the culture (i.e., that the earth is flat, the sky is above the earth, etc.), but interpreted within the constraints of the framework theory. The concept of the earth is not stable (although reference is), but evolves and develops with knowledge acquisition, with changes happening both at the level of the specific theory and at the level of the framework theory.

Finally, we assume that human beings have a cognitive system that allows them to create analog mental representations of physical objects that embody the internal structure of the concept and can be run in the mind's eye to generate predictions and explanations of phenomena (see Nersserssian, chapter15, this volume, for a discussion of some of these issues). For example, we can create a mental model of the earth and we can use this model to answer questions like 'What will happen if you were to walk for many days on the earth? Is there an end/edge to the earth? Can you fall from this earth?' Depending on our mental model of the earth we can answer this question in different ways. In our previous work (Vosniadou & Brewer, 1992, 1994 — see also Brewer, chapter 7, this volume) we provided numerous examples that demonstrate beyond any possible doubt that even very young children are capable of using the earth, the moon, and the sun as theoretical entities in models that can be run in the mind to make predictions and provide explanations of phenomena.

Conceptual Change

There is substantial evidence that cognitive development is characterized by conceptual change. For example, in the domain of biology, cross sectional developmental studies show that the biological knowledge of the 10-year-old is qualitatively different from that of the 4- to 6-year-old child (Carey, 1985; Carey, 1991; Keil, 1994; Hatano and Inagaki, 1997; Inagaki & Hatano, 2003, chapter 9, this volume), although there is considerable disagreement as to how exactly this development proceeds. Theory changes in the domain of biology have been described in terms of three fundamental components: the ontological distinctions between living/non-living and mind/body, the modes of inference that children employ to produce predictions regarding the behaviour of biological kinds, and third, the causal-explanatory framework children employ — e.g., intentional as opposed to vitalistic or mechanistic causality (Inagaki & Hatano, 2003).

Similar re-organizations of conceptual knowledge across early childhood years can be found amongst others, in children's concept of mind (Wellman, 1990), concept of matter (Smith, Carey, & Wiser, 1985; Wiser & Smith, chapter 8, this volume), concept of force (Chi, 1992; Ioannides & Vosniadou, 2002), concept of number (Smith, Solomon, & Carey, 2005), and concept of the earth (Vosniadou & Brewer, 1992, 1994). As described earlier, the empirical evidence in the area of observational astronomy has shown that considerable qualitative changes take place in children's concept of the earth between the ages of 4 and 12. Pre-school children think about the earth as a stable, stationary and flat physical object located in the centre of the universe. On the contrary, most children at the end of the elementary school years think of the earth as a spherical astronomical object, rotating around it and revolving around the sun in a heliocentric solar system. In this process, a significant ontological shift takes place in the concept of the earth which is categorized as a *physical object* by the majority of first graders but as a *solar, astronomical object* by the majority of sixth graders (Vosniadou & Skopeliti, 2005). Similar ontological shifts have been pointed out in the case of the concept of force and of heat amongst others (Chi, 1992; Ioannides & Vosniadou, 2002; Wiser & Carey, 1983).

Mechanisms of Conceptual Change and the Problem of Incommensurability

Conceptual change can happen either through the use of bottom-up, implicit and additive mechanisms, or through the use of top-down, deliberate and intentional learning mechanisms, assuming of course, a continuous interaction between an individual and a larger, surrounding cultural context. Examples of the former can be mechanisms like the Piagetian assimilation and accommodation, the use of similarity-based analogical reasoning (Vosniadou, 1989), internalization (Vygotsky, 1978), or even the appropriation of cultural practices of the situated theorists (Rogoff, 1990). Examples of the latter are the deliberate use of analogy and models that allow mappings across domains, the construction of thought experiments and limited case analyses, and translations from physical language to the language of mathematics (see Carey & Spelke, 1994; Nersessian, 1992; Vosniadou, 2007c). It is also very important to mention several social kinds of mechanisms that can facilitate conceptual change, like collaboration (Miyake, chapter17, this volume) and class discussion (Hatano & Inagaki, 2003).

According to Carey (1991), ordinary, intuitive, cognitive development involves radical conceptual changes of the nature described earlier which cannot be explained if we assume that children only use enrichment types of mechanisms. She agrees with Spelke (1991) that enrichment types of mechanisms cannot produce radical conceptual change but can only form new beliefs over concepts already available. In Carey and Spelke (1994), the evidence supporting the claim for spontaneous conceptual change is again reviewed and certain possible mechanisms are discussed that are mainly based in mappings across different domains of thought. For example, changing conceptions of number (from natural number to rational number) is thought to depend on the construction of mappings between number and physical objects as the child learns measurement (see also Gelman, 1991). Similarly, the development of mechanistic biology and mechanistic psychology require mappings from the domain of psychology to physics.

We also believe that cross domain mappings and the use of thought experiments and limited case analyses are powerful mechanisms for conceptual change and that they should be encouraged in instruction. However, the results of many empirical studies can be interpreted to suggest that most of the conceptual changes that happen spontaneously in cognitive development are the product of additive, enrichment types of mechanisms. These types of mechanisms are capable of producing radical conceptual change if we assume that a) the knowledge base has a theory-like internal structure, and b) new information is coming in through observation and from the culture. In other words, these mechanisms presuppose that children will grow in a culture with a developed science and that they will be exposed to the re-structured concepts either through participation in the adult lay culture and language or through systematic science and math instruction.

For example, young children usually categorize plants as non-living things. However, everyday experiences with plants, such as watering plants, seeing them become bigger, or noticing that they can die, in the context of an adult culture and language, can slowly lead the children to understand that plants are similar to animals in certain properties, such as feeding, growing, and dying. These similarities can eventually make children re-categorize plants as living things, rather than as inanimate objects, despite the fact that they lack self-initiated movement (Inagaki & Hatano, 2003). This category change can be described as branch jumping (Thagard, 1988), or as an ontological category shift (Chi, 1992), and represents a considerable re-organization of the concept of living thing (Carey, 1985), that can be characterized as requiring conceptual change. Similar ontological category changes can be produced when children are given direct feedback on plants' capacity for goal-directed movement (see Opfer & Siegler, 2004). In fact, it appears that learning about teleology is more effective than learning about the need for water and food on the categorization of plants, possibly because the former criterion (goal directed movement) is more critical for categorizing an entity as a living thing than the latter (need for food and water).

Although the use of bottom-up, implicit, additive mechanisms can be useful in producing even radical kinds of conceptual changes under conditions of spontaneous cognitive development, they can also be the source of producing internal inconsistency and synthetic models in many instances where 'instruction-induced conceptual change' is needed. This is the case because the teaching of science usually takes place in a school context where students are required to understand in a short period of time counter-intuitive concepts that took scientific revolutions to be constructed. Furthermore, it is often the case that inappropriate curricula are used by teachers who are not always knowledgeable about the problem of conceptual change and who may not fully understand the magnitude of the difficulties experienced by students (see Duit et al., chapter 24, this volume). In these situations, instruction-induced conceptual change becomes a slow process during which the new, counter-intuitive, scientific, information is assimilated into students' initial concepts, creating internal inconsistency and misconceptions. Many of these misconceptions are *synthetic models*, formed as learners assimilate the scientific information to an existing but incompatible knowledge base without metaconceptual awareness (Vosniadou, 2003, 2007b).

A number of experimental studies in our lab have confirmed that the above mentioned processes are taking place in the learning of science. For example, Figure 1.4 shows the synthetic models of the layers and composition of the earth's interior revealed in the drawings and verbal explanations of students in the first, sixth, and eleventh grades (Ioannidou & Vosniadou, 2001). Most first graders believe that the earth contains only solid materials (i.e., ground and rocks) arranged in flat layers. Notice that the flat layering representation of the assumed earth's interior is used in children's drawings even in those cases where the earth is seen as round. When the students are instructed about the existence of magma inside the earth, they seem to think that the magma is placed at the bottom, rather than in the center, of the spherical earth. It is only later on that the circular layering appears in their drawings, with the magma placed in the center of the spherical earth. Even the eleventh-grade students (as well as most undergraduate perspective teachers) believe that magma is located very deep in the center of the earth, rather than relatively close to its surface, and have difficulties understanding the scientific explanations of volcanoes and earthquakes.

In another study, Kyrkos and Vosniadou (1997) investigated students' understanding of plant development and the concept of photosynthesis, which has shown to be difficult for students to understand (Barker & Carr, 1989; Haslam & Treagust, 1987; Wandersee, 1983). From the perspective of the framework theory approach, students' difficulties arise from the incommensurability between the scientific and naïve explanatory frameworks of plant development. As it is shown in Table 1.5, most first graders consider plants in the context of a psychological framework theory, explaining plant development through an analogy to animals. More specifically, they think that plants take their food (i.e., water and other nutrients) from the ground through their roots and that they grow as food accumulates in small pieces inside them. As instruction about photosynthesis comes in, this initial explanation becomes fragmented, and a number of different synthetic models can be formed. Some of them are shown in Table 1.6. One synthetic model is analogous to the 'dual earth' model of the earth. In other words, students retain their initial

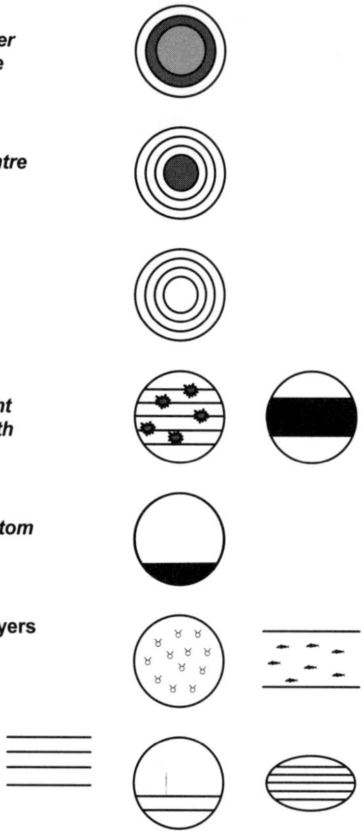

		1st Grade	6th Grade	11th Grade
Spherical Layers *Magma in the layer below the surface*		0	1	1
Spherical Layers *Magma in the centre of the earth*		2	15	12
Spherical Layers *Solid Materials*		2	3	6
Flat Layers *Magma in different places inside earth*		0	0	0
Flat Layers *Magma in the bottom of the earth*		2	0	2
Undetermined Layers *Solid Materials*		4	0	0
Flat Layers *Solid Materials*		14	14	3
	Total	24	24	24

FIGURE 1.4   Frequency of models of the layers and composition of the earth by grade.

explanation of how plants grow through feeding, and add to it some information about photo-synthesis as referring to a different plant function, that of 'breathing': Plants take in dirty air, they clean it, and give out clean air. Another synthetic model is to add to the initial explanation of feeding, a naïve interpretation of photosynthesis. According to this model, plants take food and water from the ground through their roots, but also take food from the air and light through their leaves. A more advanced synthetic model of photosynthesis develops in older children who understand that plants make food by themselves but still think of it in terms of mixing elements and not as a chemical process.

SIMILARITIES AND DIFFERENCES WITH OTHER APPROACHES

Piaget's 'Global Restructuring'

Most approaches to learning, including behaviorist, Piagetian, and Vygotskian sociocultural ap-proaches are domain general approaches based on enrichment type of learning mechanisms.

TABLE 1.5
Explanations of Plant Development

Plant Development (Photosynthesis)	
Initial Explanation	*Scientific Explanation*
Plants take their food from the ground (water or other nutrients) through their roots	Plants create their own food through the process of photosynthesis
Plants grow as food accumulates in small pieces inside them	Photosynthesis is a chemical process during which solar energy is used to transform water + CO2 into organic materials like glucose. Oxygen is also formed and stored in the plant or released in the atmosphere
Plants do not breathe.	Plants take in CO2 from the atmosphere and use it in the process of photosynthesis. To this extent "breathing" in plants is related to growth and development.

Piaget (1970) has described cognitive development as proceeding through a series of stages, each of which is characterized by a different logical-psychological structure. In infancy, intellectual structures take the form of concrete action schemas. During the preschool years, these structures acquire representational status and later develop into concrete operations — described in terms of groupings based on the mathematical notion of sets and their combinations. The last stage of intellectual development, formal operational thought, is characterized by the ability to engage in propositional reasoning, to entertain and systematically evaluate hypotheses, etc. This type of restructuring applies to all domains of thought and has been characterized as 'global restructuring'.

Cognitive development according to Piaget is the product of the natural, spontaneous process of constructive intellectual development and not of explicit learning. Nevertheless, experience will be interpreted differently at different stages depending on the logic of the underlying conceptual structures. The understanding of science concepts is usually thought to require formal operational thinking.

Piaget was instrumental in introducing individual, psychological constructivism (as opposed to social constructivism) to learning research. The importance of prior knowledge and the mechanisms of assimilation, accommodation and equilibration in the context of constructivism are important contributions of Piagetian theory to learning and instruction. Although we agree with the above-mentioned aspects of Piagetian theory, the conceptual change approach described in this chapter differs in important ways from Piaget's views. The differences have mainly to do

TABLE 1.6
Synthetic Models in Photosynthesis (Kyrkos & Vosniadou, 1997)

1. Initial Explanation	Plants take food from the ground, through their roots. Food accumulates inside the plant and makes it grow. They do not breathe.
2. Photosynthesis as breathing, separate from feeding	Photosynthesis is about breathing and it does not affect the initial explanation of feeding. Plants take in dirty air, clean it, and they give out clean air.
3. Photosynthesis as a feeding process	Plants take food from the ground and from water through their roots. They also take food from the air and light through their leaves (O, CO2).
4. Photosynthesis as a revised process of feeding	Plants take food from the ground and from atmosphere and also use water and O or CO2 to make the food in their leaves through the process of photosynthesis (mixture/not a chemical process).

with the emphasis on knowledge acquisition in specific subject-matter areas and the notion of 'domain-specific' as opposed to 'global restructuring'. The present approach focuses on knowledge acquisition in specific subject-matter areas and describes the learning of science concepts as a process that requires the significant re-organization of existing domain-specific knowledge structures. Emphasis is placed, on the one hand, on the influence of initial framework theories on the learning process, and, on the other, on the importance of social, cultural and educational environments in the restructuring process.

The 'Classical Approach' to Conceptual Change

The first attempts to interpret Kuhnian theory in science education resulted in the 'classical approach' which claimed that the learning of science involves the replacement of persistent, theory-like misconceptions (McCloskey, 1983a, 1983b; Posner et al., 1982). Misconceptions were defined as student conceptions that produced systematic patterns of error. Misconceptions were seen as being either the result of instruction or as 'preconceptions' originating prior to instruction. Posner and colleagues (1982) drew an analogy between Piaget's concepts of assimilation and accommodation and the concepts of normal science and scientific revolution offered by philosophers of science such as Kuhn (1962) and derived from this analogy an instructional theory to promote accommodation in students' learning of science. The work of Posner et al. (1982) became the leading paradigm that guided research and practice in science education for many years.

Smith, diSessa, and Rochelle (1993) criticized the misconceptions position on the grounds that it presents a narrow view of learning that focuses only on the mistaken qualities of students' prior knowledge and ignores their productive ideas that can become the basis for achieving a more sophisticated mathematical or scientific understanding. Smith et al. (1993) argued that misconceptions should be reconceived as faulty extensions of productive knowledge, that misconceptions are not always resistant to change, and that instruction that 'confronts misconceptions with a view to replacing them is misguided and unlikely to succeed' (p. 153).

We agree with the attempts by diSessa (1993) and Smith et al. (1993) to provide an account of the knowledge acquisition process that captures the continuity one expects with development and has the possibility of locating knowledge elements in novices' prior knowledge that can be used to build more complex knowledge systems. We also agree with their proposal to move from single units of knowledge to systems of knowledge that consist of complex substructures that may change gradually in different ways. Finally, we agree with Smith et al.'s (1993) urge to researchers to 'move beyond the identification of misconceptions' towards research that focuses on the evolution of expert understandings and particularly on 'detailed descriptions of the evolution of knowledge systems over much longer durations than has been typical of recent detailed studies' (p. 154).

It could be argued that the 'framework theory' approach we propose is really not very different from the traditional misconceptions position criticised by Smith and colleagues (1993). But this is not the case. Our position meets all the criticisms of Smith et al. (1993). First, we are not describing unitary, faulty conceptions but a complex knowledge system consisting of presuppositions, beliefs, and mental models organised in theory-like structures that provide explanation and prediction. This system is not static but constantly developing and evolving and influenced by students' experience and the information they receive from the culture. Second, we make a distinction between initial concepts, based on initial framework theories, prior to instruction, and those that result after instruction. We argue that information presented through instruction can cause students to become internally inconsistent or to form misconceptions and synthetic models. This is the case because the new information is simply added on to prior but incompatible knowledge through constructive, enrichment type mechanisms. Synthetic models are one form of knowledge organisation that can result from this process. Synthetic models are not stable, but dynamic and constantly changing as children's developing knowledge constantly evolves. Finally, it should be clear from the above that our theoretical position is a constructivist one, as it explains misconceptions to result from students constructive attempts to add new information onto existing but incompatible knowledge structures. Last, our approach provides a comprehensive framework within which meaningful and detailed predictions can be made about the knowledge acquisition process.

The 'Knowledge in Pieces' View

diSessa (1988, 1993, chapter 2, this volume) has put forward a different proposal for conceptualizing the development of physical knowledge. He argues that the knowledge system of novices consists of an unstructured collection of many simple elements known as phenomenological primitives (p-prims) that originate from superficial interpretations of physical reality. P-prims are supposed to be organized in a conceptual network and to be activated through a mechanism of recognition that depends on the connections that p-prims have to the other elements of the system. According to this position, the process of learning science is one of collecting and systematizing the pieces of knowledge into larger wholes. This happens as p-prims change their function from relatively isolated, self-explanatory entities to become pieces of a larger system of complex knowledge structures such as physics laws. In the knowledge system of the expert, p-prims 'can no longer be self-explanatory, but must refer to much more complex knowledge structures, physics laws, etc. for justification' (diSessa, 1993, p. 114).

Our position is not inconsistent with the view that something like diSessa's p-prims constitute an element of the knowledge system of novices and experts. We believe that p-prims can be interpreted to refer to the multiplicity of perceptual and sensory experiences obtained through observations of physical objects and interactions with them. In the conceptual system we propose, diSessa's p-prims could take the place of observation-based beliefs. Our proposal that the conceptual system consists of different kinds of knowledge elements (such as beliefs, presuppositions and mental models) is also consistent with diSessa's proposal that we need to focus not on single conceptions but on rich knowledge systems composed of many constituent elements.

diSessa argues that p-prims are basically unstructured or loosely organized in the conceptual system of the novice. It is through instruction and exposure to the scientific theory that p-prims lose their self-explanatory status and become organized in larger theoretical structures such as physical laws. According to diSessa, this change in the function of p-prims is a major change from intuitive to expert physics.

In our view (and to the extent that knowledge elements such as p-prims could be postulated to operate in our conceptual system), p-prims should become organized in knowledge structures much earlier than diSessa believes. If this is so, the process of learning science is not one of simply organizing the unstructured p-prims into physics laws but rather one during which they need to be re-organised into a scientific theory. This is a slow, gradual process, precisely because we are dealing with many knowledge elements.

Sociocultural Approaches

Criticisms from sociocultural theorists point out that conceptual change is not an individual, internal, cognitive process, as it is often seen from a purely cognitive perspective. Rather, they think it should be considered as a social activity that takes place in complex sociocultural settings that also involve the use of symbolic languages, tools, and artefacts. We also believe that it is important to consider the role of sociocultural practices, tools, and contexts in problem solving and reasoning. However, this should not be done without consideration of the crucial role individual minds play in intellectual functioning. As Hatano (1994) aptly expresses, 'although understanding is a social process, it also involves much processing by an active individual mind. It is unlikely that conceptual change is induced only by social consensus. The post-change conceptual systems must have not only coherence but also subjective necessity. Such a system can be built only through an individual minds' active attempts to achieve integration and plausibility' (p. 195).

A second criticism coming from the more radical expression of sociocultural theory raises questions about the very nature of concepts and the ontological status of knowledge itself. From the point of view of sociocultural theory, knowledge is not something that can be acquired, develop, or change but 'a process, an activity that takes place among individuals, the tools and artifacts that they use, and the communities and practices in which they participate' (Greeno et al., 1996, p. 20).

This position emerged in an effort by sociocultural theorists to explain the results of a set of empirical findings showing that learning is highly influenced by contextual and situational factors and that there is often a lack of knowledge transfer, usually in cases where information learned in school needs to transfer to everyday, out of school situations (see Vosniadou, 2006 for a discussion of these issues). For example, studies of math problem solving in practical situations have shown that the procedures used for problem solving at school do not transfer to math problem solving in everyday contexts (Carraher, Carraher, & Schliemann, 1985; Lave, 1988; Scribner, 1984). These findings have led some researchers to propose a highly contextualized view of knowledge as a process of participation in sociocultural activities (see also Sfard, 1998).

While it is important to recognize the problems that cognitive theory has with transfer as identified by sociocultural theorists, the move to deny any objectification of knowledge — and thus of the possibility of any transfer, does not provide a viable solution. There is an enormous body of empirical evidence demonstrating beyond any possible doubt the transfer of prior knowledge and its effects, positive or negative, on reasoning, text comprehension, language communication, problem solving, memory and the acquisition of new knowledge (see Bransford, 1979; Bransford, Brown, & Cocking, 1999, for relevant reviews).

We believe that there is a different interpretation of the results of the practical math studies, which is very much related to the problem of conceptual change. More specifically, we claim that researchers have overlooked the fact that there is an important asymmetry in knowledge transfer; i.e., that it is difficult when scientific or mathematical knowledge acquired in school settings needs to be transfered to everyday situations, but not the other way around. Knowledge acquired in everyday settings is ubiquitous and transfers spontaneously and without any difficulty. The construction of misconceptions and synthetic models is additional evidence for the existence of such knowledge transfer (Vosniadou, 2007a).

As it was earlier discussed, many science and mathematics concepts are difficult to learn because they are embedded in different explanatory frameworks from the initial, framework theories constructed by children early on in development. In these situations, it is very common for knowledge acquired in school settings either to remain unrelated to prior knowledge, or to be added to what is already known through the use of additive, enrichment mechanisms. As mentioned earlier, many misconceptions can be interpreted as synthetic models, resulting from the implicit use of bottom-up, additive learning mechanisms in situations where the new information, belongs to a different explanatory framework from that of prior knowledge. These implicit but constructive attempts are nothing more than the instances of negative transfer where prior knowledge stands in the way of understanding science and math concepts.

Such findings are not easy to explain from a sociocultural perspective, that denies any objectification of knowledge. This is the reason why some sociocultural researchers dismiss the effects of prior knowledge and the evidence for negative knowledge transfer and synthetic models altogether (e.g., Schoultz, Säljö, and Wyndhamn, 2001; Nobes et al., 2005). These researchers consider the empirical findings that demonstrate the presence of misconceptions to be methodological artifacts, caused by flaws in studies conducted from a cognitive perspective that focus on unobservable, inside-the-head, mental structures. They claim that these difficulties disappear when thinking and reasoning is analyzed from a discursive point of view, as a tool dependent activity. However, the strategy to deny the empirical findings regarding misconceptions or the effects of prior knowledge in general, is totally inadequate and does not solve any problems. It is true that children produce fewer misconceptions when forced-choice questionnaires are used and cultural artefacts like a globe are present, but they still have considerable difficulty understanding science and math concepts (see Brewer, chapter 7, this volume; Vosniadou et al., 2004, 2005). Students' difficulties in learning the concepts of current science and mathematics have been documented in hundreds of studies and represent one of the most pressing problems of schooling. They are not going to disappear because they are not consistent with the radical sociocultural perspective. Rather, it is the sociocultural perspective that needs to be modified to allow for the possibility to objectify knowledge.

To sum up, in order to explain the basic empirical findings in learning research and particularly around the problem of transfer, we need to take seriously into consideration the problem of conceptual change. We need to understand the asymmetry that exists in transfer situations and the causes of this asymmetry. This necessitates an approach on concepts that neither denies their existence, like the radical sociocultural perspective, nor considers them as stable and unchanging structures. Rather, concepts should be seen as flexible and malleable structures, influenced by the surrounding context, but also developing and evolving as the larger frameworks within which they are embedded also change.

Finally, a third criticism coming from radical sociocultural theory is the denial of mental representations and mental models. From our point of view, humans' ability to form mental representations of the environment is important because it helps in the de-situation of cognitive activity (Greeno, 1988). Not only can we form mental models of the physical environment, we can also objectify these representations further in the creation of tools and artifacts that can then be used as external, prosthetic devices in thinking. The sociocultural perspective emphasizes the importance of cultural artifacts and the role they play as facilitators of thinking. But it does not explain how human culture created these artifacts in the first place. Model-based reasoning is the key to understanding how humans created the rich cultural environments that mediate our social and intellectual life. Cultural mediating structures can range from symbolic systems like language, mathematics, reading, writing, to artifacts like pencil and paper, calculators and computers. But even traffic lights, supermarket layouts, or categorization systems can be considered as symbolic structures that mediate our activities.

Individuals can form mental models not only of their everyday, physical experiences, but also of the cultural artifacts they use. Cultural artifacts like maps and globes can be internalized and used in instrumental ways in revising representations based on everyday experience. As mentioned earlier, our studies of children's reasoning in astronomy provide important although preliminary information about how individuals can construct mental representations that are neither copies of external reality nor copies of external artifacts, but creative synthetic combinations of both. This suggests that the cognitive system is flexible and capable of utilizing a variety of external and internal representations to adapt to the needs of the situation (Vosniadou, Skopeliti, & Ikospentaki, 2004, 2005).

Some Implications for Instruction

A large body of empirical evidence has been accumulated in the last 20 or so years pointing to the problem of conceptual change, particularly in the areas of science and mathematics. Nevertheless, the relevant findings and results have not yet found their way in everyday classroom practices. This is true both for science teaching (Duit, 2007; Duit et al., chapter 24, this volume) and mathematics (see also Greer, 2004, 2006; Resnick, 2006). Science and mathematics educators often believe that there is little or no prior knowledge that students bring to the learning task. Or, they believe that new concepts can always be built upon prior knowledge. They do not understand that prior knowledge can sometimes hinder the acquisition of new information.

Teaching for conceptual change requires that teachers pay attention to the prior knowledge that students bring to the learning task and find ways not only to enrich this prior knowledge but also to change it, leading eventually to the formation of new structures. This requires the design of appropriate curricula and of instruction that aim towards the creation of motivated, life-long learners who have the necessary metaconceptual awareness and intentional learning strategies to engage in prolonged and meaningful learning (Vosniadou, 2003).

In the context of physics education, instruction for conceptual change has often been associated with the 'classical approach' earlier described, based on the use of cognitive conflict (Posner et al., 1982). An important limitation of this type of instruction is the assumption that conceptual change is something that can happen in a short period of time and involves a rational process of concept replacement, similar to a Gestalt-type of restructuring experience. On the contrary, as we have discussed in this chapter, the process of conceptual change is a gradual and continuous process that involves many interrelated pieces of knowledge and requires a long time to be achieved. In this long process of conceptual change, limited uses of cognitive conflict can be useful as an instructional strategy but only in the context of a larger program of carefully planned curricula and interventions.

There are at least two kinds of directions that can be taken in the development of instructional approaches to promote conceptual change. One direction is to try to narrow the gap between students' framework theories, and the new, to-be-acquired information, thus making the problem of conceptual change less acute. This can be done by taking a long-term perspective in curricula design as well as in everyday teaching practices, carefully planning the sequence of concepts to be taught by identifying the points at which conceptual change is necessary and by looking for bridging devices from early on. For example, we have developed curricula in observational astronomy paying particular attention to the sequence of concepts to be introduced taking into consideration the relevant research findings (Vosniadou, Ioannides, Dimitrakopoulou, & Papademetriou, 2001). More specifically, instructional activities are introduced to facilitate children's understanding of how it is possible for the earth to be spherical when it appears to our senses to be flat, and of how it is possible for people and objects to stand on the surface of this spherical earth without falling down. Explanations of the day/night cycle are given only after children have been introduced to the concept of a spherical earth in a heliocentric solar system, and so on.

It is also important in designing curricula and instruction for young children to anticipate later expansions of meaning of a concept, in order to bridge the conceptual change gap. For example, as Greer (2006) points out, there is a wide body of evidence showing that children face difficulties with the interpretation of the equals sign in the context of algebra, where the meaning of equivalence is essential. This is because their only experience of the use of this sign is formed in the context of arithmetic, where the equals sign is typically interpreted as 'makes'. However, later expansions of meaning could be anticipated if children were exposed to expressions such as 5+5 = 6+4 from an early age.

This recommendation comes in contrast to current practices where insufficient attention is given to the issue of conceptual change and where the implicit belief that learning progresses 'along a simple/complex dimension' (Greer, 2006, p. 178), results in the design of curricula that introduce 'simple' concepts first and more 'complex' concepts later. As Vosniadou & Vamvakoussi (2006) note, the concepts that are considered to be 'simpler' are usually the ones closer to children's intuitive understandings. Thus, children's initial theories are confirmed and strengthened through instruction, resulting in cognitive inflexibility that widens the gap between children's current knowledge and the to-be-acquired information, hindering further understanding.

A more radical proposal has been offered by some mathematics education researchers who suggest that curricula should support the introduction of certain difficult concepts at an earlier stage. For instance, it has been proposed that instead of teaching arithmetic first and algebra second the two strands should be intertwined from an early age (see Carraher, Schliemann, & Brizuela, 2001). There are also interesting proposals about how to teach rational number in ways that can be understood by very young children (Nunes, 2007). We consider these to be interesting proposals that need to be further investigated first at the experimental level.

Regardless of how far one can go in knowledge acquisition relying on social-constructivist types of approaches that build on prior knowledge, the problems of conceptual change requires that teachers also teach to students' mechanisms for knowledge restructuring, such as model-based reasoning, the deliberate uses of bridging analogies, and cross domain mappings. Instructional interventions should also pay attention to the development of students' metaconceptual awareness, epistemological sophistication and intentional learning skills that will allow them to the engage in meaningful, long-term learning (Sinatra & Pintrich, 2003; Wiser & Smith, chapter 8, this volume; Vosniadou, 2003).

We agree with Hatano and Inagaki (2003) that considerable social support is required for this type of instruction. One way teachers can provide the sociocultural environment to encourage metaconceptual awareness is to ask students to participate in dialogical interaction, which is usually whole-class discussion. Whole-classroom dialogue can be effective because it ensures, on the one hand, that students understand the need to revise their beliefs deeply instead of engaging in local repairs (Chinn & Brewer, 1993), and, on the other, that they spend the considerable time and effort needed to engage in the conscious and deliberate belief revision required for conceptual change.

Hatano and Inagaki have conducted a number of educational studies in order to show how individual cognitive mechanisms can combine with sociocultural constraints to promote instruction-induced conceptual change. Most of these studies are conducted using the Japanese science education method known as Hypothesis-Experiment-Instruction (HEI) originally devised by Itakura (Itakura, 1962). This method was utilized extensively by Hatano and his colleagues and it is a promising method for achieving the kind of metaconceptual awareness and intentional learning skills required by students for the deliberate and intentional belief revision needed for instruction based conceptual change (see also Miyake, 1986, chapter 17, this volume).

It is probably clear by now that teaching and learning for conceptual change requires substantial amounts of effort on the part of the teacher, as well as on the part of the learner. For this effort to be invested, there should be an environment within which this is both necessary and appreciated. That is, for teachers to design relevant and meaningful activities (Vosniadou et al., 2001), and for students to be actively engaged, there should be a broader educational community that recognizes and is capable of assessing this kind of effort.

CONCLUSIONS

We argued that science and mathematics concepts are difficult to learn because they are embedded in initial, framework theories of physics and mathematics, which are different explanatory frameworks from those that are now scientifically accepted. These naïve framework theories are not fragmented observations but form a relatively coherent explanatory system which is based and continuously re-confirmed by everyday experience. Students are not aware of these differences and employ the usual enrichment mechanisms to add scientific and mathematical information to existing knowledge structures, destroying their coherence and creating internal inconsistency and misconceptions which are 'synthetic models'.

In order to foster conceptual change through instruction, we can consider the design of curricula and instruction that reduce the gap between students' expected initial knowledge and the to-be-acquired information, so that learners can use their usual constructive, enrichment types of learning mechanisms successfully. It is also important to develop in students the necessary metaconceptual awareness, epistemological sophistication, hypothesis testing skills, and the top-down, conscious and deliberate mechanisms for intentional learning that will prepare them for meaningful, life-long learning. Instruction for conceptual change thus requires not only the restructuring of students' naïve theories but also the restructuring of their modes of learning and reasoning. The above cannot be accomplished without substantial sociocultural support.

NOTES

1. For criticisms of Kunh's views in the philosophy and history of science, see Arabatzis and Kindi (chapter 13, this volume) and Machamer (2007). A more detailed description of our views on conceptual change and incommensurability will be provided later in this chapter.
2. Similar views were simultaneously and independently expressed by the philosopher Paul Feyerabend (1962).
3. Global incommensurability can easily lead to an anti-realist position. If concepts change then it is not clear how they can continue to refer to the same entities or processes. Adopting a realist stance requires an account of concepts that keeps reference constant as the meaning of the concepts changes (see also Putnam, 1992).
4. The term *concept* is used here to denote both individuals' concepts and the socially shared and culturally accepted scientific concepts.
5. The children placed in the 'mixed' category usually gave a mixture of 'scientific' and 'naïve' responses, just like the children grouped under the 'alternative models' category, but their responses were non-systematic and often self-contradictory.
6. There are a number of studies by Siegal, Nobes, and their colleagues (e.g., Nobes, Martin, & Panagiotaki, 2005; Siegal, Butterworth, Newcombe, 2004) criticizing the above-mentioned findings. For extensive and detailed discussions of the theoretical and methodological issues around these studies see Vosniadou, Skopeliti, and Ikospentaki (2004, 2005) as well as Brewer (chapter 7, this volume).
7. The term *decimal* is used here to refer only to the decimal numbers that belong to the rational numbers set.
8. Language development does not seem to be characterised by theory-changes, but some of the difficulties students experience in learning a foreign (or second) language may be of a similar nature.

REFERENCES

Baillargeon, R. (1995). A model of physical reasoning in infancy. In C. Rovee-Collier & L. Lipsitt (Eds.), Advances in infancy research, Vol. 9 (pp. 305–371). Norwood, NJ: Ablex.

Barker, M., & Carr, M. (1989). Teaching and learning about photosynthesis. *International Journal of Science Education, 11*(1), 48–56.

Blown, E. J., & Bryce, T. G. K. (2006). Knowledge restructuring in the development of children's cosmologies. *International Journal of Science Education, 28*(12), 1411–1462.

Bransford, J. (1979). *Human cognition: Learning, understanding, and remembering.* Belmont, CA: Wadsworth.

Bransford, J. D., Brown, A., & Cocking, R. (Eds.). (1999). *How people learn: Mind, brain, experience and school.* Washington, DC: National Academy Press

Carraher, T. N., Carraher, D. W., & Schliemann, A. D. (1985). Mathematics in the streets and in schools. *British Journal of Developmental Psychology, 3*, 21–29.

Carraher, D., Schliemann, A., & Brizuela, B. (2001). Can young students operate on unknowns? In M. van den Heuvel-Panhuizen (Ed.), *Proceedings of the 25th Conference of the International Group for the Psychology of Mathematics Education* (vol.1, pp. 130–140). Utrecht: Utrecht University.

Carey, S. (1985). *Conceptual change in childhood.* Cambridge, MA: MIT Press.

Carey, S. (1991). Knowledge acquisition: Enrichment or conceptual change? In S. Carey & R. Gelman (Eds.), *The epigenisis of mind: Essays on biology and cognition.* Hillsdale, NJ: Erlbaum.

Carey, S. (in press). *The origin of concepts.* Oxford: Oxford University Press.

Carey, S. & Spelke, E. (1994). Domain-specific knowledge and conceptual change. In L. A. Hirschfeld & S. A. Gelman (Eds.), *Mapping the mind: Domain specificity in cognition and culture*, (pp. 169–200). Cambridge, MA: Cambridge University Press.

Chase, W. G. & Simon, H. A. (1973). The mind's eye in chess. In W. G. Chase (Ed.), V*isual information processing* (pp. 215–281). New York: Academic Press.

Chi, M. T. H., Feltovich, P. J., & Glaser, R. (1981). Categorization and representation in physics problems by experts and novices. *Cognitive Science, 5*, 121–152.

Chi, M. T. H., & Koeske, R. D. (1983). Network representation of a child's dinosaur knowledge. *Developmental Psychology 19*(1), 29–39.

Chi, M. T. H. (1992). Conceptual change within and across ontological categories: Examples from learning and discovery in science. In R. Giere (Ed.), *Cognitive models of science: Minnesota Studies in the Philosophy of Science* (pp. 129–186). Minneapolis: University of Minnesota Press.

Chinn, C. A., & Brewer, W. F. (1993). The role of anomalous data in knowledge acquisition: A theoretical framework and implications for science instruction. *Review of Educational Research, 63*, 1–49.

Chomsky, N. (1988). *Language and problems of knowledge.* Cambridge, MA: MIT Press.

Dehaene, S. (1998). *The number sense: How the mind creates mathematics.* Harmondsworth, Middlesex, England: The Penguin Press.

Diakidoy, I. A., Vosniadou, S., & Hawks J. (1997). Conceptual change in Astronomy: Models of the earth and of the day/night cycle in American-Indian children. *European Journal of Psychology of Education, XII*, 159–184.

diSessa, A. A. (1988). Knowledge in pieces. In G. Forman and P. B. Pufall (Eds.), *Constructivism in the computer age* (pp. 49–7). Hillsdale, NJ: Erlbaum.

diSessa, A. (1993). Toward an epistemology of physics. *Cognition and Instruction, 10*(2/3), 105–225.

Duit, R. (2007). Science education research internationally: Conceptions, research methods, domains of research. *Eurasia Journal of Mathematics, Science & Technology Education, 3*(1), 3–15.

Elman, J., Bates, L., Johnson, M., Karmiloff-Smith, A., Parisi, D., & Plunkett K. (1996). *Rethinking innateness. A connectionist perspective on development.* Cambridge, MA: MIT Press.

Feyerabend, P. K. (1962). Explanation, reduction, and empiricism. In H. Feigl & G. Maxwell (Eds.), *Minnesota studies in the philosophy of science* (pp. 28–97*)*.Minneapolis: University of Minnesota Press.

Fischbein, E., Deri, M., Nello, M., & Marino, M. (1985). The role of implicit models in solving problems in multiplication and division. *Journal for Research in Mathematics Education, 16*, 3–17.

Gallistel, R. (1990). *The organization of learning.* Cambridge, MA: MIT Press.

Gelman, R. (1990). First principles organize attention to and learning about relevant data: Number and animate-inanimate distinction as examples. *Cognitive Science, 14*, 79–106.

Gelman, R. (1991). Epigenetic foundations of knowledge structures: Initial and transcendent constructions. In S. Carey and R. Gelman (Eds.), *The epigenesis of mind: Essays on biology and cognition* (pp.293–322). Hilldale, NJ: Erlbaum.

Gelman, R. (1994). Constructivism and supporting environments. In D. Tirosh (Ed.), *Implicit and explicit knowledge: An educational approach* (pp. 55–82). New York: Ablex.

Gelman, R. (2000). The epigenesis of mathematical thinking. *Journal of Applied Developmental Psychology, 21*, 27–37.

Goodman, N. (1972). Seven structures on similarity. In N. Goodman (Ed.), *Problems and projects* (pp. 341–352). New York: Bobbs-Merrill.

Greeno, J. G. (1988). Situations, mental models, and generative knowledge. In D. Klahr & K. Kotovsky (Eds.), *Complex information processing* (pp. 285–318). Hillsdale, NJ: Erlbaum.

Greeno, J. G., Collins, A. M., & Resnick, L. B. (1996). Cognition and learning. In D.C. Berliner & R.C. Calfee (Eds.), *Handbook of educational psychology* (pp. 15–46). New York: McMillan.

Greer, B. (2004). The growth of mathematics through conceptual restructuring. *Learning and Instruction, 14*, 541–548.

Greer, B. (2006). Designing for conceptual change. In J. Novotná, H. Moraová, M. Krátká, & N. Stehlíková (Eds.), *Proceedings of the 30th conference of the international group for the psychology of mathematics education* (Vol. 1, pp. 175–178). Prague: PME.

Haslam, F., & Treagust, D.F. (1987). Diagnosing secondary students' misconceptions of photosynthesis and respiration in plants using a two-tier multiple choice instrument. *Journal of Biological Education, 21*(3), 203–211.

Hatano, G. (Guest Ed.). (1994). Introduction: Conceptual change – Japanese perspectives. *Special Issue of Human Development, 37*(4), 189–197.

Hatano, G., & Inagaki, K. (1997). Qualitative changes in intuitive biology. *European Journal of Psychology of Education, 13*, 111–130.

Hatano, G., & Inagaki, K. (2000). Domain-specific constraints on conceptual development. *International Journal of Behavioural Development, 24*(3), 267–275.

Hatano, G., & Inagaki, K. (2003). When is conceptual change intended? A cognitive-sociocultural view. In G. M. Sinatra & P. R. Pintrich (Eds.), *Intentional conceptual change* (pp. 407–427). Mahwah, NJ: Erlbaum.

Hatano, G., & Miyake, N. (1991). What does a cultural approach offer to research on learning? *Learning and Instruction, 1*, 273–281.

Hayes, B. K., Goodhew, A., Heit, E., & Gillan, J. (2003). The role of diverse instruction in conceptual change. *Journal of Experimental Child Psychology, 86*, 253–276.

Inagaki, K., & Hatano, G. (2003). Conceptual and linguistic factors in inductive projection: How do young children recognize commonalities between animals and plants? In D. Gentner & S. Goldin-Meadow (Eds.), *Language in mind* (pp. 313–333). Cambridge, MA: MIT Press.

Ioannides, C., & Vosniadou, S. (2002). The changing meanings of force. *Cognitive Science Quarterly, 2*(1), 5–62.

Ioannidou, I., & Vosniadou, S. (2001). The development of knowledge about the composition and layering of the earth's interior. *Nea Paedia, 31*, 107–150 (in Greek).

Itakura, K. (1962). Instruction and learning of concept force in static based on Kasetsu-Jikken-Jugyo (Hypothesis – Experiment – Instruction): A new method of science teaching. *Bulletin of National Institute for Educational Research, 52* (in Japanese).

Keil, F. C. (1981). Constraints on knowledge and cognitive development. *Psychological Review 88*, 197–227.

Keil, F. C. (1990). Constraints on constraints: Surveying the epigenetic landscape. *Cognitive Science, 14*, 135–168.

Keil, F. C. (1994). *Concepts, kinds, and cognitive development.* Cambridge, MA: MIT Press.

Khoury, H. A., & Zazkis, R. (1994). On fractions and non-standard representations: Preservice teachers' concepts. *Educational Studies in Mathematics, 27*, 191–204.

Kikas, E. (1998). The impact of teaching on students' definitions and explanations of astronomical phenomena. *Learning and Instruction, 8*(5), 439–454.

Kitcher, P. (1983). *The nature of mathematical knowledge.* Oxford: Oxford University Press.

Kuhn, T. (1962). *The structure of scientific revolutions.* Chicago: Chicago Press.

Kyrkos, Ch., & Vosniadou, S. (1997). *Mental models of plant nutrition: A study of conceptual change in childhood.* Poster presented at the Seventh European Conference for Research on Learning and Instruction, Athens, Greece.

Lave, J. (1988). *Cognition in practice: Mind, mathematics and culture in everyday life.* Cambridge: Cambridge University Press.

Machamer, P. (2007). Kuhn's philosophical successes? In S. Vosniadou, A. Baltas, & X. Vamvakoussi (Eds.), *Reframing the conceptual change approach in learning and instruction* (pp. 35–46). Oxford: Elsevier.

Malara, N. (2001). From fractions to rational numbers in their structure: Outlines for an innovative didactical strategy and the question of density. In: J. Novotná (Ed.), *Proceedings of the 2nd Conference of the European Society for Research Mathematics Education II* (pp. 35–46). Praga: Univerzita Karlova v Praze, Pedagogická Faculta.

Mali, G. B., & Howe, A. (1979). Development of earth and gravity concepts among Nepali children. *Science Education, 63*(5), 685–691.

Maria, K. (1993). *The development of earth concepts.* Paper presented at the Third International Seminar on Misconceptions and Educational Strategies in Science and Mathematics, Ithaca, NY.

Maria, K. (1997a). A case study of conceptual change in a young child. *Elementary School Journal, 98*, 67–88.

Maria, K. (1997b). *Conceptual change in a young girl: A longitudinal case study.* Paper presented at the annual meeting of the National Reading Conference, Scottsdale, AZ.

Markman, E. M. (1989). *Categorization and naming in children: Problems of induction.* MIT Press.

Markovitz, Z., & Sowder, J. (1991). Students' understanding of the relationship between fractions and decimals. *Focus on Learning Problems in Mathematics, 13*(1), 3–11.

Mayer, R. E. (1985). Implications of cognitive psychology for instruction in mathematical problem solving. In E. A. Silver (Ed.), *Teaching and learning mathematical problem solving: Multiple research perspectives* (pp. 123–138). Hillsdale, NJ: Erlbaum.

McCloskey, M. (1983a). Naive theories of motion. In D. Gentner & A. Stevens (Eds.), *Mental models* (pp. 299–324). Hillsdale, NJ: Erlbaum.

McCloskey, M. (1983b). Intuitive physics. *Scientific American, 248*(4), 122–130.

Medin, D. L., & Rips, L. J. (2005) Concepts and categories: Memory, meaning, and metaphysics. In Holyoak, K. J. & Morrison, R. G. (Eds.), *Cambridge handbook of thinking and reasoning* (pp. 37–72). Cambridge: Cambridge University Press.

Merenluoto, K., & Lehtinen, E. (2002). Conceptual change in mathematics: Understanding the real numbers. In M. Limon, & L. Mason (Eds.), *Reconsidering conceptual change: Issues in theory and practice* (pp. 233–258). Dordrecht, The Netherlands: Kluwer.

Merenluoto, K., & Lehtinen, E. (2004). Number concept and conceptual change: Outlines for new teaching strategies. *Learning and Instruction, 14*, 519–534.

Miyake, N. (1986). Constructive interaction and the iterative process of understanding. *Cognitive Science, 10*, 151–177.

Moskal, B. M., & Magone, M. E. (2000). Making sense of what students know: Examining the referents, relationships and modes students displayed in response to a decimal task. *Educational Studies in Mathematics, 43*, 313–335.

Moss, J. (2005). How students learn mathematics in the classroom. Retrieved January 25, 2005, from http://darwin.nap.edu/books/0309089492/html/157.html.

Nersessian, N. (1992). How do scientists think? Capturing the dynamics of conceptual change in science. In R. N. Giere (Ed.), *Minnesota studies in philosophy of science: Vol. 15. Cognitive models of science* (pp. 5–22). Minneapolis: University of Minnesota Press.

Ni, Y., & Zhou, Y-D. (2005). Teaching and learning fraction and rational numbers: The origins and implications of whole number bias. *Educational Psychologist, 40*(1), 27–52.

Neumann, R. (1998). Students' ideas on the density of fractions. In H. G. Weigand, A. Peter-Koop, N. Neil, K. Reiss, G. Torner, & B. Wollring (Eds.), *Proceedings of the Annual Meeting of the Gesellschaft fur Didaktik der Mathematik* (pp. 97–104). Retrieved March 21, 200, from http://webdoc.sub.gwdg.de/ebook/e/gdm/1998/

Nobes, G., Martin, A. E., & Panagiotaki, G. (2005). The development of scientific knowledge of the Earth. *British Journal of Developmental Psychology, 23*, 47–66.

Nunes, T. (2007). *Understanding rational numbers.* Invited Talk at the 12th European Conference for Research on Learning and Instruction, Budapest, Hungary.

Nussbaum, J. (1979). Children's conception of the earth as a cosmic body: A cross-age study. *Scientific Education, 63*, pp. 83–93

Nussbaum, J. (1985). The earth as a cosmic body. In R. Driver, E. Guesne, & A. Tiberghien (Eds.), *Children's ideas in science* (170–192). Milton Keynes: Open University Press.

Nussbaum, J., & Novak, J. D. (1976). An assessment of children's concepts of the earth utilizing structured interviews. *Science Education, 60*, 535–550.

O'Connor, M. C. (2001). "Can any fraction be turned into a decimal?" A case study of a mathematical group discussion. *Educational Studies in Mathematics, 46*, 143–185.

Opfer, J. E., & Siegler, R. S. (2004). Revisiting preschoolers' *living things* concept: A microgenetic analysis of conceptual change in basic biology. *Cognitive Psychology, 49*, 301–332.

Piaget, J. (1970). *Structuralism.* New York: Basic Books.

Posner, G. J., Strike, K. A., Hewson, P. W., & Gertzog, W. A. (1982). Accommodation of a scientific conception: towards a theory of conceptual change. *Science Education, 66*, 211–227.

Putnam, H. (1992). Truth, activation vectors and posession conditions for concepts. *Philosophy and Phenomenological Research, 52*, 431–447.

Resnick, L. B. (1986). The development of mathematicsl intuition. In M. Perimutter (Ed.), *Perspectives on intellectual development: The Minnesota Symposia on Child Psychology* (Vol. 19, pp.159–194). Hillsdale, NJ: Erlbaum.

Resnick, L. B. (2006). The dilemma of mathematical intuition in learning. In J. Novotná, H. Moraová, M. Krátká, & N. Stehlíková (Eds), *Proceedings of the 30th conference of the international group for the psychology of mathematics education* (Vol. 1, pp. 173–175). Prague: PME.

Rogoff, B. (1990). *Apprenticeship in thinking: Cognitive development in social context.* New York: Oxford University Press.

Samarapungavan, A., Vosniadou, S., & Brewer, W. F. (1996). Mental models of the earth, sun, and moon: Indian children's cosmologies. *Cognitive Development, 11*, 491–521.

Schoultz, J., Säljö, R., & Wyndhamn, J. (2001). Heavenly talk: discourse, artifacts, and children's understanding of elementary astronomy. *Human Development, 44*, 103–118.

Scribner, S. (1984). Studying working intelligence. In B. Rogoff & J. Lave (Eds.), *Everyday cognition: Its development in social context* (pp. 9–40). Cambridge, MA: Harvard University Press.

Sfard, A. (1998). On two metaphors for learning and on the dangers of choosing just one. *Educational Researcher, 27*(2), 4–13.

Siegal, M., Butterworth, G., & Newcombe, P.A. (2004). Culture and children's cosmology. *Developmental Science, 7*(3), 308–324.

Sinatra, G. M., & Pintrich, P. R. (Eds.). (2003) *Intentional conceptual change.* Mahwah, NJ: Erlbaum.

Smith, C., Carey, S., & Wiser, M. (1985). On differentiation: A case study of the development of the concepts of size, weight, and density. *Cognition, 21*, 177–237.

Smith, J. P., diSessa, A. A., & Roschelle, J. (1993). Misconceptions reconceived: A constructivist analysis of knowledge in transition. *The Journal of the Learning Sciences, 3*, 115–163.

Smith, C. L., Solomon, G. E. A., & Carey, S. (2005). Never getting to zero: Elementary school students'understanding of the infinite divisibility of number and matter. *Cognitive Psychology, 51*, 101–140.

Spelke, E.S. (1991). Physical knowledge in infancy: Reflections on Piaget's theory. In S. Carey & R. Gelman (Eds.), *The epigenesis of mind: Essays on biology and cognition.* Mahwah, NJ: Erlbaum.

Stafylidou, S., & Vosniadou, S. (2004). Students' understanding of the numerical value of fractions: A conceptual change approach. *Learning and Instruction, 14*, 503–518.

Thagard, P. (1988). *Computational philosophies of science.* A Bradford Book. Cambridge, MA: MIT Press,

Thagard, P. (1992). *Conceptual revolutions.* Princeton, NJ: Princeton University Press.

Tirosh, D., Fischbein, E., Graeber, A. O., & Wilson, J. W. (1999). *Prospective elementary teachers' conceptions of rational numbers.* Retrieved May 5, 2005, from http://jwilson.coe.uga.edu/Texts.Folder/Tirosh/Pros. El.Tchrs.html

Vamvakoussi, X., & Vosniadou, S. (2004). Understanding the structure of the set of rational numbers: A conceptual change approach. *Learning and Instruction, 14,* 453–467.

Vamvakoussi, X., & Vosniadou, S. (2007). How many numbers are there in a rational numbers interval? Constraints, synthetic models and the effect of the number line. In S. Vosniadou, A. Baltas, & X. Vamvakoussi (Eds.), *Reframing the conceptual change approach in learning and instruction* (pp.265–282). Oxford: Elsevier

VanLehn, K. (1990). *Mind bugs: The origins of procedural misconceptions.* Cambridge, MA: MIT Press.

Verschaffel, L., & Vosniadou, S. (Eds.). (2004). The conceptual change approach to mathematics learning and teaching. *Learning and Instruction, 14,* 445–548.

Vosniadou, S. (1989). Analogical reasoning and knowledge acquisition: A developmental perspective. In S. Vosniadou & A. Ortony (Eds.), *Similarity and analogical reasoning* (pp. 413–422). New York: Cambridge University Press.

Vosniadou, S. (2003). Exploring the relationships between conceptual change and intentional learning. In G. M. Sinatra & P. R. Pintrich (Eds.), *Intentional conceptual change* (pp. 377–406). Mahwah, NJ: Erlbaum.

Vosniadou, S. (2006). The conceptual change approach in the learning and teaching of mathematics: An introduction. In Novotná, J., Moraová, H., Krátká, M., & Stehlíková, N. (Eds.), *Proceedings, 30th Conference of the International Group for the Psychology of Mathematics Education* (*Vol. 1*, pp. 155–159). Prague: PME.

Vosniadou, S. (2007a). The cognitive-situative divide and the problem of conceptual change *Educational Psychologist, 42*(1), 55–66.

Vosniadou, S. (2007b). The conceptual change approach and its re-framing. In S. Vosniadou, A. Baltas, & X. Vamvakoussi, (Eds.), *Reframing the conceptual change approach in learning and instruction* (pp. 1–15). Oxford: Elsevier.

Vosniadou, S. (2007 c). Conceptual change and education. *Human Development, 50*(1), 47–54

Vosniadou, S., Baltas, A., & Vamvakoussi, X. (Eds.). (2007). *Reframing the conceptual change approach in learning and instruction.* Oxford: Elsevier.

Vosniadou, S., & Brewer, W. F. (1992). Mental models of the earth: A study of conceptual change in childhood. *Cognitive Psychology, 24,* 535–585.

Vosniadou, S., & Brewer, W. F. (1994). Mental models of the day/night cycle. *Cognitive Science, 18,* 123–183.

Vosniadou, S., Ioannides, C., Dimitrakopoulou, A., & Papademetriou, E. (2001). Designing learning environments to promote conceptual change in science. *Learning and Instruction, 11,* 381–419.

Vosniadou, S., & Skopeliti, I. (2005). Developmental shifts in children's categorization of the earth. In B. G. Bara, L. Barsalou, & M. Bucciarelli (Eds.), *Proceedings of the XXVII Annual Conference of the Cognitive Science Society* (pp. 2325–2330).

Vosniadou, S., Skopeliti, I., & Ikospentaki, K. (2004). Modes of knowing and ways of reasoning in elementary astronomy. *Cognitive Development, 19,* 203–222.

Vosniadou, S., Skopeliti, I., & Ikospentaki, K. (2005). Reconsidering the role of artifacts in reasoning: Children's understanding of the globe as a model of the earth. *Learning and Instruction, 15,* 333–351.

Vosniadou, S., & Vamvakoussi, X. (2006). Examining mathematics learning from a conceptual change point of view: Implications for the design of learning environments. In L. Verschaffel, F. Dochy, M. Boekaerts, & S. Vosniadou (Eds.), *Instructional psychology: Past, present and future trends – Fifteen essays in honour of Erik De Corte* (pp. 55–72). Oxford: Elsevier.

Vosniadou, S. & Verschaffel, L. (2004). Extending the conceptual change approach to mathematics learning and teaching. *Learning and Instruction, 140,* 445–451.

Vygotsky, L. S. (1978). *Mind and society: The development of higher mental processes.* Cambridge, MA: Harvard University Press.

Wandersee, J. H. (1983). Students' misconceptions about photosynthesis: A cross-age study. In H. Helm &

J.D. Novak (Eds.), *Proceedings of the International Seminar: Misconceptions in Science and Mathematics*, (pp. 441–446). Ithaca, NY: Cornell University,.

Wellman, H. M. (1990). *The child's theory of mind.* Cambridge, MA: MIT Press.

Wellman, H. M., & Gelman, S. A. (1998). Knowledge acquisition in foundational domains. In D. Kuhn & R. Siegler (Eds.), *Cognition, perception and language. Volume 2 of the Handbook of child psychology* (5th ed., pp. 523–573). New York: Wiley.

Wiser, M., & Carey, S. (1983). When heat and temperature were one. In D. Gentner & A. Stevens (Eds.), *Mental models* (pp. 267–297). Hillsdale, NJ: Erlbaum.

2

A Bird's-Eye View of the "Pieces" vs. "Coherence" Controversy (From the "Pieces" Side of the Fence)

Andrea A. diSessa
University of California at Berkeley

INTRODUCTION

The central principle of conceptual change research is the constructivist idea that "old" ideas (or mental structures) are influential in supporting or constraining learning (or development). In classroom-relevant study, conceptual change research has laid blame for difficulties in learning at the feet of "entrenched naïve ideas," or, at least, prior ideas that are for various reasons radically different from normative understanding in domains like physics and biology. In physics, naïve ideas said to be like the medieval "impetus theory" of motion must give way to counter-intuitive Newtonian ideas (McCloskey, 1983). Similarly, developmental studies seek to find the great intellectual accomplishments of childhood in dramatic revisions in the way domains are construed. Carey (1985) talked about a shift from a psychological view of the world of biology to a true "mechanistic" biology. Hatano (Inagaki & Hatano, 2002) argued that there is an earlier phase of distinctly biological thinking, called "vitalistic," whose characteristics are, while not psychological, still far from adult biological conceptualization.

Roughly two and one-half decades after the beginnings of modern conceptual change research, one would think that the basic nature of naïve or "old" ideas should be settled. Old ideas, of course, are different in content from new ones. But what in their nature, or in their relation to new ideas, makes them "entrenched," difficult to change, requiring extended experience or exceptional instruction? It is puzzling and ironic, given its centrality, that no consensus exists on this issue.

This chapter looks at a critical fault line concerning the nature of naïve ideas as they relate to learning normative scientific ideas. On the one hand, naïve ideas have been described as coherent, systematic, or even theory-like[1] — similar enough to scientists' carefully laid out and systematic *theories* to deserve the same descriptive term. On the other hand, naïve ideas have also been described as many, diverse, "fragmented," and displaying limited integration or coherence. There are many issues concerning the nature of naïve conceptions. However, I believe that a strong case can be made for the importance of moving toward settling this particular issue, at this particular time. The mere fact that the debate about coherence persists — and in fact has seemed to involve more sharply divided opinions through the years — provides strong motivation. In addition, I believe that the fragmented vs. coherent issue is manifestly epistemologically and empirically fundamental. Our very sense of the nature of knowledge and how it changes is at stake. If we cannot settle on a broad characterization of naïve knowledge, how can we expect to settle other more subtle issues, such as tracking conceptual change in detail? I believe that the state of the art in theoretical sophistication and empirical methodology has advanced far since the early days of conceptual change research. This is a time when we might come at least to a rough consensus on the nature of naïve ideas.

A Thumbnail History

This is not the place for an extended review of the historical development of this debate. However, a few basic points may contextualize current consideration. As hinted above, the issue of fragmentation vs. coherence is hardly new. In diSessa (2006) I trace the debate back into the prehistory of modern studies of conceptual change, to the early 1970s. Then, it was a dispute in the history and philosophy of science. On the coherence side, Kuhn (1970) advocated the view that conceptual systems are integrated enough that bit-by-bit change is sometimes impossible. In such cases, science changes in a revolutionary manner, which Kuhn likened to a gestalt switch. Many early participants in conceptual change research were strongly influenced by Kuhn.

On the fragmentation side, Stephen Toulmin (1972) explicitly contested what he saw as a "cult of systematicity" (Toulmin's words) in Kuhn and other philosophers' positions. Unlike Kuhn, Toulmin had few followers in early conceptual change research, although his line of thinking continued as a minority view. In fact, with few exceptions, the coherence side of the argument has strongly dominated frameworks and assumptions in conceptual change work.

I have been a long-time partisan in this debate, taking the fragmented side of it at least since the early 1980s (diSessa, 1983, 1988). My personal judgment is, also, that the tide has gradually been turning in favor of "fragmentation" assumptions. In recent years, more and more work has appeared favoring the hypothesis of fragmentation, especially in educational studies. See, for example, Izsák (2005), Wagner (2006), and consult the systematic orientation of Linn's "knowledge integration" principles for instructional effectiveness (Linn, 2006).

The Chapter's Intent

This chapter is part of my larger agenda to promote a consideration of this issue as central, and to help foster a sensible resolution. However, I aim here to avoid technical theoretical considerations and detailed empirical argument, although some of that will be referenced for illustration. Instead, I want to take seriously the possibility that, in addition to technical issues and data, basic feelings of sensibility drive researchers' decisions in terms of directions for research. I intend to work here at the level of researchers' own persistent intuitions, motivations, and perspectives. In a sense, this strategy reflects the epistemological orientation of my basic claims about naïve, intuitive knowledge. In particular, the strategy assumes that conviction is at least somewhat distributed in nature, and thus I assume that multiple arguments that can be quickly reached and relatively briefly treated may have surprising effects, alongside in-depth and more "rigorous" arguments.[2]

Many of the issues treated here, especially those in the section on Questions, arise informally and are somewhat disconnected from focused scientific give-and-take. In particular, many of the questions I list are near-transcriptions of comments that have come to me after talks, for example, or in "final words" of reviewers of journal articles after the main work of review has been done. Questioners or reviewers often acknowledge force in the presented arguments, but voice residual feelings concerning implausibilities or problems with the pieces position.

Despite the less-than-usually formal nature of the questions and responses in this chapter, I do want to exert due diligence concerning a few issues close to the core of the debate. In particular, up front, I want to acknowledge that my main concern has been conceptual change in physics. I believe that conceptual change in physics, mechanics in particular, has some special characteristics that may not be true in all domains of conceptual change. In particular, physical intuition is built from a huge and critically important phenomenology — living every day in the physical world and having to negotiate it effectively in order to survive and flourish. To take a historically relevant contrast case, children's cosmologies certainly make interesting study from a conceptual change point of view (for example, Vosniadou & Brewer, 1992). But it is unclear that uninstructed ideas in this domain are nearly as rich and experientially founded as intuitive physics. Biology probably constitutes an intermediate domain — not so salient and instrumentally important in young children's lives as physics, but still grounded in everyday observations that children can make of phenomena of living things. I believe that insights from the "fragmented" position apply to most, if not all domains, more so to the extent that the domains are rich and experientially founded. But assuming physics is a prototype for my arguments avoids unnecessary complexity and qualifications.

So, the first of a few issues that require a little care is with respect to domains of conceptual change; all domains may not work in the same way. The most important set of "due diligence" issues, central to this chapter, are treated in the next section.

What Is at Issue?

In the introduction, I characterized the debate as concerning whether naïve ideas consist of relatively independent fragments, or whether they are coherent wholes. In my own work, I have used the phrase "knowledge in pieces" to describe the general position of "fragmentation" advocates, and also my own particular version of that position. On the "coherence" side, I take those who advocate the "theory theory" (e.g., McCloskey, 1983; Gopnik & Wellman, 1994) — that students' "old" ideas are systematic enough to be called a theory — to be staking out a somewhat extreme version of the coherence position. Some of the more prominent, if less extreme coherence advocates are Susan Carey (e.g., Carey, 1999) and Stella Vosniadou (e.g., Vosniadou, 2002). "Less extreme" refers to explicit acknowledgment of aspects of intuitive "theories" that are different from professional science, such as being less articulately espoused (scientists can describe their theories in language), absence of a well-developed meta-conceptual awareness (scientists know that they have theories), and an acknowledgment of lesser degrees of coherence, smaller breadth of coverage, and so on, compared to professional science.

Slogans like "theory theory" or "knowledge in pieces" are good for drawing attention to positions in a debate, but they are not sufficient even for the rough and ready treatment that I give here. For me, the real debate begins in the issue of grain size: At what grain size and level of detail[3] must we describe intuitive ideas so as to have characterized them adequately enough to understand conceptual change?

While grain size is seldom treated and argued explicitly, one can get a good gestalt simply by looking at researchers' descriptions of naïve ideas. How much and what kind of things are said to characterize the naïve state? Coherence advocates appear to think that (very roughly speaking) a paragraph of natural language text, or a few compact principles (each a sentence or two in length), suffices. Of course, researchers say much more in terms of motivation, implications, and certainly in terms of empirical validation. But descriptions of naïve ideas are seldom elaborate. Early descriptions of "intuitive theories" of mechanics were often in terms of a single phrase or sentence, and seldom more than a paragraph. In recent work, for example, Vosniadou (2002) describes a sufficient number of meanings of force to cover about 90% of subjects, across a wide developmental span (from kindergarten to ninth grade) in a one-page chart, using a sentence or two to describe each meaning. In contrast, in one paper (diSessa, 1993), I describe more than three dozen "elements of intuitive knowledge" in mechanics, using about a paragraph each, while making clear that the descriptions are partial, and that the listing is representative, not by any means complete.

Grain size entails two subsidiary considerations that are equally important in defining what is at issue in the debate between "pieces" and "coherence." The first consideration is *structure*. If one has dozens or hundreds of knowledge elements, the question of how they are organized or relate to each other naturally arises. What is the structure of naïve physics?

Anticipating later argument, I think the "coherence" position has a salient theoretical problem right here. While coherence is a vague word, one important core meaning has inherently to do with relations; that is, the meaning of coherence requires an articulation of structure. What are the relations among parts of, for example, intuitive theories, and how can we even make an overall judgment of "coherent" without the articulation of structure? Definitions of coherence and specifications of relations are too often missing or minimal in descriptions of naïve knowledge by coherence advocates.

My early work on intuitive ideas was aimed mainly to establish a sensible grain size at which to think about such knowledge as a precursor to describing structure (including "systematics" or coherence).[4] To cut a long story very short, I believe it is important and possible to track intuitive ideas at a sub-conceptual grain size ("smaller" and more numerous than scientific concepts). Some of my more recent research has been aimed to establish the "architecture" (specific relational structure) of normative scientific concepts at a grain size consistent with what we see in naïve knowledge. (See, for example, the review of "coordination classes" in diSessa & Wagner, 2005.)So, the *fact* of relational structure is not an issue. How to describe it, and whether and how one can make a judgment of "coherent," is at issue.

The second subsidiary consideration that follows on considering grain size is *contextuality*. When do children or students use what particular ideas? With more elements, it is strongly likely there is a much greater contextuality.

Structure is theoretically intensive (you need a specification of elements and relations), but, in contrast, contextuality provides a sometimes fairly easy empirical window. Do children always say things that are aligned with descriptions of their intuitive ideas, or, in contrast, is it easy to ask questions about slightly different situations that elicit different responses? A fair amount of my empirical work demonstrates circumstances and questions that elicit answers that cannot be covered by the kind of sparse descriptions of naïve ideas offered by coherence advocates. Theoretically, contextuality depends not only on coverage — in our descriptions, have we covered the range of ideas students actually have? — but it depends also on whether descriptions of student knowledge are precise enough that we know when that knowledge should actually be used.

To summarize, I claim that the debate about coherence should be construed, more precisely, as concerning the grain size of mental entities we track. From a knowledge in pieces point of view, "intuitive theories," if they exist, are highly aggregated; I project that we will not be able to describe conceptual change at all perspicuously from such a high level of aggregation. Only with a more appropriate, sub-conceptual grain size can we describe the structure (and, in consequence, define and evaluate coherence) of naïve ideas, and only at that level can we track the re-constitution of naïve elements into normative concepts.

Having refined what is at stake — from "pieces vs. coherence" to "grain size" (and related issues, such as structure and contextuality) — I begin my exposition in earnest by responding to a set of common questions that I take to reveal prejudices against, or misunderstanding of, the pieces perspective.

QUESTIONS ABOUT KNOWLEDGE IN PIECES

More or Less

What is all the fuss about? Isn't the dispute just a matter of degree?

Certainly, no one can believe that people are 100% coherent and consistent, and no one can believe people have nothing more than a completely incoherent jumble of ad hoc ideas. Might this even be an issue of "half full" vs. "half empty," and might it not depend on delicacies, for example, on the nature of the empirical probe?

As a preliminary, I note that the relevant question of coherence, as I construe it here, is distinct from the issue of whether people can track a coherent line of reasoning. Instead, it is about the relational structure of the totality of domain-relevant knowledge. For example, it is conceivable that people could, in every instance, track coherent lines of reasoning, and yet, in terms of the totality of ways of thinking, they might track different and incommensurable lines on different occasions.

The implicit model I see lying behind the topic question here is that there is some number that defines the coherence of a set of ideas (say, an intuitive theory), and the dispute is about estimates of that number. On a 10-point scale, we can safely rule out 1 (complete incoherence) and 10 (complete coherence). However, after that, what is a good estimate? Given still fairly sketchy empirical results, why should anyone make such a fuss about whether one's predilection puts an estimate in the upper or lower half of the coherence scale, especially since the answer might depend on empirical technique, topic, operationalization of "coherent," and so on?

The flaw in this temporizing question is that there is a prior, unaddressed issue, before we can even get to disputes about quantitative measures. We must ask what is the legitimate grain size at which we should begin to formulate a measure — or even a conception — of coherence? Here, the positions of "pieces" and "coherence" are asymmetrical. On the "pieces" side, I fully agree that concepts and theories define legitimate grain sizes to consider. However, I also believe that there exists an entire other universe of sub-conceptual elements that must be tracked in order to see the construction of concepts and theories — that is, in order to understand conceptual change. Later in the chapter I describe how I decompose a so-called "naïve theory" into multiple intuitive elements, which are independently validated empirically.

Assessing coherence requires yet another step beyond agreeing, even roughly, on grain size. That is, we need to describe the relations among elements that we examine in order to determine coherence. We must consider *structure*. For example, mathematicians might insist that coherence means deductive coherence. Pursuing this line, we could characterize deductive coherence as follows:

> Elements are either propositions or terms; terms may be undefined, or defined; propositions are either axioms or they must be proven; and the relation "proven" is highly restrictive in the usual way.

No one that I know supports the axiomatic version of coherence for naïve ideas, which is very nearly categorical (either you have it, or you don't; there is no 10-point scale). However, neither do they deny it,[5] nor are there forthcoming specific proposals as to what relations coherence does entail.[6]

Contrast a different sort of relation by which one might assess coherence. Let us say that two ideas are coherent if one vaguely seems to imply the other, or even if they merely seem related in some unspecified sense. That is a very different kind of coherence, and probably has very different consequences for conceptual change. The bottom line is that I do not believe coherence can be assessed *at all*, hence coherence advocates have no ground to stand on, until we have a better agreement on what grain size, what kind of elements are at issue (their ontology, e.g., "propositions," "axioms," or "p-prims"), and what sort of relations we are attending to (e.g., "provable," or "vaguely related"). In my own work, I have talked about several different kinds of relations one might investigate in naïve or expert knowledge systems, such as mutual plausibility, mutual use, common abstractions, and so on (see the Systematicity section of diSessa, 1993).[7] Each would support a different judgment about the level of coherence in a knowledge system. More recent work (e.g., diSessa & Wagner, 2005) I propose a categorical criterion of coherence, called "alignment," which I believe to be important in assessing fully developed scientific concepts.

To be honest, even without agreements on elements and relations, I think empirical and theoretical work from the pieces community provides suggestive constraints on levels of coherence. For example, in listing dozens of elements that seem to have, at best, sketchy relations of any sort with one another, future more definitive assessments of coherence seem bounded. The mere fact of a large number of elements makes a very high level of coherence implausible, whatever the relational measure. Furthermore, my own theory of the development of intuitive elements (diSessa, 1993) suggests largely independent developmental trajectories, which would make a high degree of coherence improbable.

To sum up, the underlying important issues are primarily grain size and, then, structure (e.g., relational coherence). Until we make progress in settling these, discussion about the level of coherence is, at best, heuristic and uncertain. In these terms, the dispute between pieces and coherence advocates is more categorical. I believe that there is a large family of sub-conceptual elements — multiple elements that play a role in the construction of scientific concepts — and the structure of that family of elements and their contributions to instructed concepts must be charted in order to understand conceptual change. Coherence advocates, to the extent they do not recognize or articulate any sub-conceptual structure, are simply playing a different game.

Partisanship

Aren't partisans driving toward extremes in the debate between pieces vs. coherence? Isn't the resolution — and more sensible researchers — likely somewhere in the middle?

My rhetorical strategy has been to pick "pieces vs. coherence" as banner in the deeper disputes about grain size and such. There is no easy "middle" to retreat to. The conceptual change research community, in my view, must get down to brass tacks, define and defend its choices of grain size, ontology, and relational structure. I assume that my own takes on this are wrong or incomplete in at least some measure. But, I am standing for the need to articulate sub-conceptual architectures.

Forests and Trees

Isn't the "pieces" point of view wallowing in a "fine and esoteric level of detail,"[8] while the big picture of conceptual change is missed?

Coherence is (should be) a content-independent measure of a system of knowledge. That is, very different ways of thinking about the universe might still each be internally coherent. The "forests and trees" question seems to admit that the details of cognition are complex (who could deny that?), but it focuses on something like a schematic or structural core that explains important aspects of conceptual structure and change. Coherence advocates presumably would want to maintain that the core is coherent, even if the noisy fringe is not.

In responding to this important and interesting question, I want to sketch a set of issues that need to be treated. Secondarily, I sketch the kind of the data that supports the "pieces" position on these issues. The full set of issues constitutes a critical framework that, I argue, should be systematically applied to claims concerning the existence of deep-structural conceptual frameworks.

The first issue is whether the core schematizations exist at all. As social scientists, we should be well aware that easy generalizations, stereotypes, can be asserted, but they often turn out to be hard to validate as reliable.

As a field, I think conceptual change research has spent a huge amount of time finding problems and questions that evoke "interesting" and somewhat uniform responses. The reverse enterprise of evaluating the actual contextual range of such schematization is thinly populated with studies, and, in my view, offers easy opportunities to critique proposed "core schematizations."

In recent work (diSessa, Gillespie, & Esterly, 2004), we took a characterization of children's meanings of force by Ioannides and Vosniadou (2002) and used a simple strategy. We identified features of situations that we had good reason to believe would affect student responses, and then we validated that changes in these aspects made substantial differences in student responses. The differences in responses constituted a contextuality that Ioannides and Vosniadou's conceptions of force could not account for, since their models simply did not mention the features that we manipulated. The main judgment Ioannides and Vosniadou looked at in subjects was whether or not a force existed in a situation. We found that the existence and magnitude of forces that subjects saw depended on things such as whether a block is seen as leaning on another block, or, being leaned on. It also depended on whether a ball moving in a circle was doing so because it was tied by a string to a center, or, in contrast, being guided by a circular tube. In another case, we found a significant number of students who saw that a struck bell emits a force (disconnected from the bell, itself), which violated the stated contexts in which students were supposed to see forces, and also, more subtly, the basic ontology of force, according to Ioannides and Vosniadou.

The basic design of our study was straightforward. Almost all of the critical attributes that we used to test judgments of force were previously documented (e.g., diSessa, 1993), although not in large N studies. My personal feeling is that data on complexities and contextualities are easy to come by, so that there is a reservoir of resources within easy reach for advocates of "pieces." Sociologically, forgoing easy tests of generality seems an example of the fact that coherence advocates are generally not focused on possible contextual refutation of the generalities they propose, even when relevant potential contextualities are documented in the literature.

That same work (diSessa, Gillespie, & Esterly, 2004) actually found a more direct problem with the generalities discovered by Ioannides and Vosniadou. As part of preliminary work for our study, we performed a near replication of their experiment, with dramatically different results ($p < .00001$). We found little or no trace of systematic answers that display coherent and consistently applied meanings of force. The methodological issues here are complex, so I do not want to explain or rely heavily on them. Nonetheless, the general point is that assertions of generality are rarely tested in "far replications" (e.g., by different groups of researchers, or even slightly varying methodologies) or by deliberate attempts to test that generality across a wide range of contexts.

Even if a proposed "core conceptual structure" can be robustly validated, I think a second criterion is important and often neglected. "Core" should mean "important." Yet many studies of conceptual change name features of naïve knowledge without demonstrating their importance at the same time that they ignore what I take to be important aspects. (Examples appear in the following two paragraphs.) Thus, the dismissive reference to "esoteric detail" by coherence advocates is pre-judgmental, and also ironic (if my judgments about omitted important considerations are valid). Establishing importance, of course, is a difficult challenge. However, it is a little-recognized consideration that, I believe, dogs claims about so-called core conceptual structures.

Using this same pair of recent studies (Ioannides & Vosniadou, 2002; diSessa et al., 2004), I can illustrate the issue of importance. Ioannides and Vosniadou focused nearly exclusively on children's takes on the sheer existence of a force. However, we argued that conceptual competence involves many issues other than mere existence. Students may give completely normative answers concerning when a force exists, and even its magnitude, but they may still draw critically flawed inferences. One of the oldest and most robust findings in conceptual change in physics is that students infer speed from the existence of a force (Viennot, 1979; Clement, 1983); they do not infer, as $F = ma$ would have, acceleration. I do not claim that it is evident that inferences are much more important than existence (although I believe it to be true), but only make the point that importance of "core conceptual structure" needs documenting and discussion before we can accept claims that "pieces" overlooks important core structure.

The Ioannides and Vosniadou case illustrates potentially missing important aspects of concepts. Uncalibrated importance for documented aspects is equally easy to illustrate. For example, the influential work of Clement and Brown (e.g., Brown, 1994) documented the widespread misconception that a table does not exert an upward force on a book lying on it. Yet that substantial body of work provided no demonstration that effective instruction that "fixed" the misconception had any significant effect in bringing students, generally, toward a Newtonian concept of force.

"Trust that generalities might appear, despite the 'noise of details'," is an orientation of coherence advocates with not a great deal of empirical validation. Mere assertions (1) that a "core structure" organizes a lot of data (from a database selected to demonstrate "the core"), (2) that claimed structure is core to the whole family of ideas that children display, and (3) that such structure poses the central problem of conceptual change will not suffice.

A third element of critique exists, even if we give away "existence" and "importance" of a simple, coherent core. That is, might a "pieces" explanation of "core structures" be more perspicuous than a "coherence" explanation? In this case, what I have in mind is explaining "high-level" regularities from a sub-conceptual point of view.

One of the best known of intuitive conceptualizations is the idea that, in throwing an object up in the air, we impart an internal force to it. The force gradually dies out, allowing other forces, such as gravity to "take over." McCloskey (1983) first popularized this "naïve theory," and Ioannides & Vosniadou's (2002) "acquired force" meaning is essentially the same idea.

In diSessa (1988), I conjectured the possibility that this so-called theory is actually a compound construction involving roughly six sub-conceptual elements that happen to apply to situations like tossing a ball into the air. The core of this conjecture is that a conflict — an object going up while being pulled down by gravity — is intuitively evident in a toss. A conceptually critical part of the toss, the peak, shows a typical intuitive pattern, called "overcoming" (diSessa, 1993), where a weakening influence is overcome by another (or a constant influence is overcome by a strengthening one). The upward "impetus" force may be invented to provide a weakening influence that is overcome by gravity at the peak of the toss.

The potential advantages of such a decomposition are these: (1) The assembly of a core conceptualization out of independently validated elements provides a good sketch of how such a "theory" could have come about. (2) The core conceptualization's properties are a consequence of the properties of independently validated elements. (The "theory" follows from joint use of a number of "principles," in the way that physicists sometimes use several basic principles in composition to solve a problem.) (3) Contextuality may be better handled by the "pieces" decomposition. That is, on many occasions students use the pieces, whereas they do not invoke the "full theory." In particular, high school and college students seldom (never, in my interviewing experience) use impetus to explain the fall from rest of a dropped object, where there is no conflict between motion and a known force, gravity. If a push from a hand imparts a force in a toss, should not gravity in a drop also impart one? But subjects never assert that gravity imparts such a force to the dropped object.[9]

Several years after conjecturing the decomposition of McCloskey's impetus theory, I was lucky enough to catch on video the apparent construction of the impetus theory on the fly (diSessa, 1996). The student exhibited the following behaviors: (1) She began to construct the theory only after showing apparently competent use of the corresponding Newtonian analysis. (2) The initiating event was the interviewer's pointing out the peak of the toss for analysis, where, I conjectured, overcoming is salient and begins the search for a conflicting "opponent" to gravity. (3) The subject initially tried a different "opponent" to gravity, air resistance, to fill the needed niche for overcoming; she came up with impetus only as a second try. This last shows the quasi-independence of elements (impetus does not always go together with overcoming, even in a toss), and also that construction of the impetus theory may be piecemeal. While catching construction events like this is undoubtedly extremely rare, these data show, in a case, the possibility of construction as conjectured, consistent with a multiple pieces interpretation.

I am not providing sufficient detail here in explaining this particular analysis and its empirical basis to make a convincing case to skeptics. But, in the spirit of this chapter, the point is that *even if* "important, core generalizations" can be validated, a pieces approach to them can have a number of important advantages.

To sum up this section, my belief is that coherence advocates trust that they will find core, coherent structures far beyond what is empirically warranted. (1) They ignore "noise," seldom test the contextual breadth of the constructions, and almost never deliberately challenge the existence of their proposed core structures. (2) They trust the importance of core structure, without explicit argument or validation. (3) And finally, they seldom or never consider that the decomposition of "core structure" might be exceptionally illuminating of its conceptual and contextual properties, and of the way in which it might have come to exist.

Parsimony

> Scientific theories should be parsimonious. Isn't the pieces view just like the epicycles that were proposed arbitrarily to explain details of planetary motion before Kepler and Newton created a simplifying explanation? You can always explain anything if you allow any number of parameters.

Despite the fact that there are many "parameters" in the pool of sub-conceptual pieces of knowledge that I conjecture to explain a principle part of naïve physics knowledge, each of these pieces is motivated by data and subject to empirical validation. They are not arbitrary.

The larger issue is when are we forced to accept complexity as part of science? Plenty of historical precedents exist for the ultimate scientific story being much more complicated than older scientific or non-scientific explanations. The four elements of the Greeks turned into over a hundred. A more closely related case is biology and evolution. Explaining the nature of present biological organisms simply requires a lot of time and a lot of detail. Part of the reason for the complexity is that present-day organisms developed over a long period of time, and their current forms express much historical detail, including "accidents" of history (the "choice" of a way to solve a biological problem, like energy storage) that are simply not given by simple, rational rules, or necessity.[10] The conceptual ecology of humans is, in my view, similarly dependent on a complex history, some of it biological, but much of it experiential and dependent on early ideas and how they seeded later ones. In a nutshell, the complexities of a long historical development seldom or never admit of a simple, "rational" reconstruction.

Passions run high among coherence advocates concerning basic expectations about the complexity of human thought. For example a reviewer of a paper of mine who was, on the whole positive, said that, "The subjective impact of the study is disturbingly 'anarchistic'." Why should complexity be disturbing? Another, published characterization of "knowledge in pieces" portrays it, obviously negatively, as holding that naïve knowledge is a "fragmented, inconsistent jumble" (Samarapungavan & Weirs, 1997, p. 179).

In the end, dispositions that "estimate" the complexity with which we must deal in order to understand a field need to acquiesce to growing empirical and theoretical arguments. Arguments based on a priori dispositions either in favor or in opposition to a complex, sub-conceptual knowledge system in humans are weak.

Robustness

> How can a large collection of "fragile," random pieces account for the obvious robustness of intuitive ideas?

"Fragile" and "random" are prejudiced descriptors that do not capture much of my view of knowledge in pieces. Elements of intuitive knowledge are contextual in that there are many of them, and they each have quite specific contextual boundaries. The region of applicability of an element might, however, be quite broad. For example, the idea that "increased effort" begets "greater results" applies across the physics/psychology boundary, which professional physical ideas like "force" do not cross.

None of the more important elements are "random" in any reasonable sense. They are important to human's understanding the world, and are often if not always productive in everyday thinking. They are reliably activated by situations within their span of applicability; reliable activation, in fact, is critical to their empirical tractability. The former feature, productivity, in fact, explains a "resistance" to change that the conventional idea of "misconceptions" misses. If ideas are just wrong, why would people hold tightly to them? Even more, conceptual change is more difficult because, used in the proper context, many intuitive ideas will be productive *in normative physics* as well; they are constituents of correct science.

The need for shifting contextuality in the course of learning is much more characteristic of difficulty than the fact of contextuality, per se. Even when intuitive elements are used in normative physics, they are used in new contexts and in new ways. Creating that contextuality in students' use of those ideas is not easy. And, the ultimate problem is that multiple changes in the contextuality of multiple elements must all be coordinated to create a plausible successor to old ways of thinking.

Let me illustrate the nature, importance, and difficulty in shifting contextuality. Consider my analysis of the "impetus theory" in a toss. The intuitive elements, such as balancing, and so on, are not wrong. Students will be doing a lot of "balancing" of forces and balancing equations when they come to solve physics problems correctly. Furthermore, I have conjectured that balancing will become an important part of "conservation of energy" (diSessa, 1993). So, in net, learning that "balance is wrong" is simply not appropriate. It is just that balancing is not a productive way of thinking about *this* situation.

The composite entities — scientific concepts, for example — that go into a proper physics analysis are complicated and take extended construction. Knowledge in pieces explains — actually in many ways — why change is difficult. Elements need to be re-contextualized, not erased, and many coordinated changes are necessary to create normative scientific concepts. These explanations are not tautological, as an unanalyzed appeal to "entrenchment," for example, may be. The systems view of knowledge in pieces can also explain why change is easy in some instances (say, a single, weak intuitive element applies, and alternative intuitive analyses exist that are in line with normative physics). In general, knowledge in pieces emphasizes how change is possible (due to the existence of relevant, productive pieces), and even sometimes easy. (See the discussion of "narratives" in diSessa, 1996.) In contrast, I believe it is fair to say strong coherence theories are much less interested in the details of success cases.

The complex construction of scientific concepts explains why change is also difficult in other cases that are rarely, if ever, highlighted from a coherence point of view. What happens when students do not show strong attachment to an intuitive view? Surely learning physics means coming to understand some situations that are completely baffling before instruction. That is another kind of conceptual change that is often ignored.

Complexity in Instruction

> Isn't the pieces point of view too complicated to be useful in instruction? How is a teacher supposed to make sense of "hundreds or thousands" of intuitive knowledge elements?

The issue of instructional implications of knowledge in pieces is huge, and it deserves a chapter on its own. However, I make a few general points.

First, facts about the world are not beholden to us to make our lives easier. If, in fact, naïve conceptual architectures involve thousands of elements, we need to learn to deal with it. In responding to the previous question, I noted that simplicity is attractive, but it must be accountable to the facts of the matter. In similar manner, claims that have easy practical implications are also attractive. But, again, that attractiveness has little or nothing to do with validity. Educationally oriented researchers would love to have conceptual change turn out such that we can easily teach better. But that is no basis for evaluating theories or data.

A second issue is explaining complex and maybe unsettling scientific results to teachers and other professionals. This issue is important and challenging to deal with. Again, however, judging science by how easy it is to explain to non-scientists is not a valid strategy.[11]

Preliminaries aside, what are the implications of knowledge in pieces for instruction? What can teachers do in view of those facts of the matter, if they are valid?

1. *Deep learning just takes time.* There are several ways to motivate the idea that, if we are to achieve deep results from instruction, we need to take adequate time to do it. However, I believe knowledge in pieces is both fundamentally correct and has the implication that, to draw out useful intuitive ideas and to assemble a good, normative concept, we cannot instructionally escape time and effort. Clark (2006) takes the issue of the amount of time it takes to create an integrated understanding head-on.
2. *Deep learning requires learning in many contexts.* Complex contextuality is a fact of the matter in a knowledge in pieces perspective. Scientific understanding unifies contexts that are "plainly" (in naïve eyes) different. That takes specific attention, it takes many contexts of use, and it takes time.[12]
3. *Students have a richness of conceptual resources to draw on. Attend to their ideas and help them build on the best of them.* I am not at all sure teachers have the same negative reaction to the idea that students have a lot of ideas that some researchers do. In fact, I believe that attending to students carefully in a classroom lends more experiential cogency to knowledge in pieces claims, compared to claims for the existence of a few core and coherent structures. I think it is a powerful and useful lesson for teachers to attend to nuances in student ideas, and to try to figure out how to use them productively.

   Given the fact of many ideas in intuitive knowledge ecologies, I believe it is both suggested and correct that it is a losing strategy to focus a lot of energy on teaching students that some particular ideas they have are just wrong. In the early days of conceptual change research, "elicit and confront" (prove to students that their intuitive theories are inadequate) was probably the most widely drawn instructional implication. I believe the strategy of confrontation has diminished visibility mainly because it does not work reliably. Knowledge in pieces provides a principled explanation of why it must fail: Pieces, one at a time are not true or false; assemblies are the relevant scale; normative assemblies often re-use naïve knowledge, although with different contextualities, so "dismissing" knowledge elements is a poor strategy.

4. *Coaching students meta-conceptually is very different from a knowledge in pieces perspective.* In recent years, the influence of students' ideas about knowledge and learning has come, more and more, to be considered significant. For example, students who think learning is unproblematic and fact-by-fact appear to be at a significant disadvantage. (See Hofer & Pintrich, 2002, for representative state-of-the-art work.) Naturally, our theoretical and empirical views of the nature of knowledge, both naïve and expert, and how expert knowledge is produced will strongly influence what we can and should cultivate in our students' views of knowledge. Hammer and Elby (2002) represent the knowledge in pieces perspective concerning students' meta-conceptual knowledge.

5. *Conceptual change in science is different for different students.* "One theory fits all," does not work. In general, learning researchers need to attend to diversity more adequately than they have in the past. Coherence views — especially those that emphasize only core and supposedly influential structure — do not provide us good leverage for dealing with diversity. Only with a more complex view of knowledge can we understand students' diversities and produce instruction that is well-adapted to individuals or classes of students. Diversity is important enough to deserve more discussion later in this chapter.

6. *Assessment is a completely different matter from a knowledge in pieces perspective.* Strongly coherent, monolithic prior ideas can easily be monitored by any of a wide range of indicators; there is only one thing to test for. In contrast, assessing the presence, relative strength, and contextuality of a diverse collection of elements is more difficult, but (I claim) more valid and more informative. If normative ideas are as strongly held together as naïve ones (consult later discussion), then success at conceptual change is similarly much easier to assess, compared to a more distributed view of expertise. Along the road to competence, a knowledge in pieces perspective allows textured formative assessment of individuals who might take different tracks to competence. Prototypically complex and instructionally informative assessments of different elements of student knowledge on the way to competence are exploited by Minstrell's "facet" methodology of assessment (e.g., Hunt & Minstrell, 1994).

This list emphasizes advice to teachers, including thoughts concerning assessment. However, there are other avenues of help that theories of conceptual change can provide concerning instruction. For example, they can provide a finer grain size at which one can look at events of learning and failure to learn. (We can worry about how to explain and convey the import of such investigations to teachers once we have carried them out.) Design of instructional materials, especially, can make use of such studies. Exemplary studies of learning at a fine grain scale include Clark (2006), Izsák (2005), Wagner (2006), and Parnafes (2005).

Validation in Instruction

Hasn't research validated the power of teaching against "misconceptions" or "naïve theories"?

To be sure, there are instructional methods developed by people who believe in coherence and naïve theories. But the modest success of those instructional interventions does not provide definitive validation of their authors' theories. To begin, there is an increasing literature from knowledge in pieces advocates that shows significant effectiveness in instruction that they develop. I mentioned Linn and Minstrell, and there are others. Second, I think that the very simple idea of engaging students' ideas is surprisingly powerful, independent of particular theoretical direction. So, many of the good properties of conceptual change inspired instruction come independent of specific theories of students' ideas. Third, many instructional methods are sensible within both theoretical perspectives, if for different reasons. Most contemporary researchers of whatever theoretical persuasion believe that classroom discussion and visual, manipulable models can be powerful. Finally, detailed tracking of conceptual change in students through an instructional process, such as what would be necessary to validate one or another view of conceptual change, are almost nonexistent. Standard "before and after" tests may show *the fact* of conceptual change, but not how it happened. (See diSessa & Wagner (2005) for a discussion of why performance tests are very weak in determining conceptual development.)

Demeaning of Children

> Isn't the pieces point of view dismissive of children as incoherent thinkers?

I believe that it is proper to criticize many researchers for undervaluing students' naïve knowledge. Worse, it is too temptingly easy to "explain" students' problems (without really explaining) by saying that they have poor quality knowledge. I have attended too many talks where researchers deride or even ridicule students' knowledge, using deprecating terms such as "pseudo-concepts" and comparing "misconceptions" to familiar phenomena such as intransigent ignorance or backwardness.

Although attitudes toward students do not follow strictly from theoretical orientations, I take knowledge in pieces to be a highly positive view of students' naïve knowledge. The most central part of this positive view is that many naïve pieces, although not all, actually become part of high quality technical competence. The rich naïve cognitive ecology constitutes a generative pool of resources. Just as sub-conceptual elements can combine to create "the impetus theory," better combinations of those or different elements are possible. In contrast, for most coherence advocates, especially theory theorists, new "good" knowledge must be generated *ab initio* by general processes such as analogy or abstraction, if any explanation of the generation of good knowledge is given at all. Most theory theorists, I believe, are only constructivist in the negative sense; naïve knowledge provides problems with which we need to deal. They have no account of content resources in naïve knowledge that become involved in normative understanding.

Knowledge in pieces also provides a different view of expertise. Expert understanding is not monolithic, homogeneous, and logically consistent, either (as Toulmin counseled us, over 30 years ago). Instead, it is sometimes fragmented, often heuristic, and surprisingly more amenable to error that most expect. I do not take this as a denigrating view of the best knowledge that human beings can produce; it is just a realistic and analytical view. As a side effect of this recalibration of professional knowledge, students' knowledge looks much more like scientists' knowledge, even if a shift in systematicity is necessary to transition from naïve to expert.

Western people *prefer* to think of themselves as rational, "logical," and consistent. It is an assumed standard for "good" knowledge. But this is a bias based on terms that are not scientifically defined or empirically validated. Improved theory and sound empirical work will prepare for valid judgments of this sort, if any are forthcoming. These are not reliable assumptions going in.

KEY RESEARCH QUESTIONS AND MOTIVATING PHENOMENA

Research programs are often thought to be defined by theories and empirical results. However, especially in early stages, it is important to look at the central questions that researchers ask and the phenomena that motivate their inquiry.

Charting the Long Path to Competence

In terms of central research questions, almost all conceptual change researchers are concerned with the difficulty of acquiring particular concepts. Almost all researchers also agree that the path to conceptual change is long and difficult. However, explicitly charting that long path is particularly characteristic of knowledge in pieces researchers. The idea of knowledge in pieces, itself, provides a first approximation model of what happens in the extended development of a new concept. A great number of elements must be collected and joined in appropriate ways to produce working, normative concepts or theories. Theory theorists, to my mind, seem particularly unconcerned with empirically charting details in this long and gradual process.

Charting the long path to competence is a non-negotiable focus of attention for conceptual change research. Implausible, bordering on impossible, alternatives include that, during the long period of "learning," nothing happens for a long time. Then, for some reason, conceptual change happens. I also believe that the long path of change is not a question that we can or should put off for future research. I am not so concerned about how one charts gradual change of state so much as that we must begin to hypothesize and validate paths.

Here is an illuminating possibility for "how the long and difficult path to conceptual change" may be conceptualized. I can imagine a gradual change in parameters of a system that keep it in a stable working mode. (For example, a tower of blocks might be stable as one gradually slides the upper blocks to the side.) But eventually, at a tipping point, a fairly rapid shift occurs to a new working mode. (The blocks, eventually, fall.) Physical scientists might call this a phase shift (e.g., after a long process of cooling, water becomes ice at a particular temperature). If conceptual change worked like this, it would validate a more coherence-oriented theory than I prefer. Still, with such a model, there is a locus of change (e.g., internal parameters of some sort) that is theoretically focused and (one should require) empirically tractable. Creating *any models at all* of the progress that is happening on "the long road to conceptual change" is the proximal goal that I am advocating here, more important than judgments of pieces or coherence. Of course, once we get started seriously on the modeling enterprise, criteria for adequacy of models will become much more important.

Focus on the long path to change is undermined by the absence of process studies of conceptual change in the field. "Before and after" snapshot validations are too prominent as evaluations of conceptual change, as attractive as they might be to test educational outcomes. In addition, I believe there is a real paucity of models of incremental change offered by the "coherence community."

The Meaning of Coherence

A second key question that is characteristic of the knowledge in pieces perspective has already been discussed at some length: What is the meaning of "coherent," and how should it be empirically determined? As discussed, coherence advocates tend not to ask this question, as if "coherence" were self-evident, or they provide what I regard as unhelpful answers.[13]

Micro-Development; Complex Contextuality; Multiple Strands of Conceptual Change

Turning from basic questions to phenomenological focus, there is a longer list of distinctive considerations. I start with three related foci, *micro-development*, *contextuality*, and *multiple strands* of development. First — this is no surprise — knowledge in pieces advocates attend to micro-developmental phenomena. Of the relatively few micro-genetic studies of conceptual change, aiming to track moment-by-moment changes in knowledge, essentially all of them are by knowledge in pieces advocates. An exemplary case is the work of Wagner (2006), which looks at an extended corpus of interviews to track students' learning the so-called law of large numbers. From the bird's eye view, the important point is simply that there is a lot of fine-structure to attend to and make sense of. Note that I am focusing here on phenomena, not on how one accounts for them. If one could account for the sort of phenomena I am pointing to here with a coherence-based framework, excellent! But the first step is to attend to those phenomena.

Wagner's work also highlights the importance of tracking the related phenomenology of the complex, delicate contextual dependencies of ideas, showing that a wide breadth of application of "the same idea" comes slowly, almost one context at a time, and is hard won. His work also tracks the influence of ideas as components of concepts, which is theory-characteristic of knowledge in pieces. For example, the idea of "representativeness" (to paraphrase, "bigger samples are more representative of reality") occurs to one subject only late in her learning of the law of large numbers, and it makes a difference in terms of the range of contexts in which that subject could confidently apply the law.

I mentioned before that in my own work I have used the phenomenon of unexpected contextuality to challenge coherence inspired work (diSessa et. al., 2004). One of my prior extended case studies showed that one subject maintained two contradictory (to expert eyes) models of a toss — the impetus model and the correct model — through an extended interview and instructional process (diSessa, 1996; diSessa, Elby, & Hammer, 2002). The mere fact of students' use of multiple models is downplayed in most coherence research, and it is not the focus of systematic empirical study.

In general, careful study of micro-developmental phenomena leads to a focus on *multiple strands* of a "single" conceptual change. The case study above showed development in the student's normative model of a toss with instruction, but this did not affect her use of and confidence in her naïve model! One of the critiques we offered of coherence accounts of conceptual change concerning "force" is that aspects of it seem quite separable. For example, in diSessa et al. (2006), we charted a dramatic developmental shift *from correct to incorrect*, of children's expectation of the effect of a force in cases of circular motion. The details are not relevant, but see Table 2.1 for the numbers. Our contention is that this shift is important and that no simple "coherent" account

TABLE 2.1
Responses to an Item Asking for the Effect of an Off-Center Force on a Circular Object. Does the Object Move in the Direction of the Force or Opposite It?

	Aligned (correct)	Opposite (incorrect)
High School	0%	100%
Middle School	17%	83%
Elementary School	50%	38%
Pre-School	62%	38%

of conceptual change can include both the general advance in sophistication of meanings of force that is conjectured, and, at the same time, this "backward" trajectory with respect to the important issue of the motion implications of the existence of a force.

"Out of the Shadows Learning"

Although it has not received a lot of empirical attention, a phenomenon I call *out of the shadows learning* is critically important and theoretically diagnostic. "Out of the shadows" refers to a situation where a minor intuitive idea, or one simply not connected by novices to the phenomenology of an expert domain, becomes importantly involved in developing an expert conception. This is, of course, a completely expectable phenomenon from a knowledge in pieces perspective. It is central to the assumption of generativity in intuitive knowledge, which I discussed in defending knowledge in pieces against claims that it demeaned children's or students' knowledge. Wagner's "representativeness" might constitute an example of out of the shadows learning. A much more dramatic possibility, which I have written about in several places, is that a "small" contextually bound idea that force can flow (diSessa et. al., 2006), could become a central organizing concept in learning mechanics (diSessa, 1980).

Other Things Students Say

A focus of attention related to the "out of the shadows" phenomenon is making sense of the huge range of things students and children say that do not relate to the theories or coherent conceptions attributed to them. Even the most die-hard theory theorist must admit that children have a wide variety of things to say about domains (physics, biology, psychology) that are not easily assimilable to their core "theories." This is often treated as "noise" in coherence advocates' studies. Noise is often eliminated by tuning the instruments of investigation. But, conceptual noise is often signal for pieces advocates. Even if it is unimportant (which I contest), it is a legitimate focus of study, and coherence advocates, in general, have nothing whatsoever, theoretically or empirically, to say about it. Of course, I expect that the "noise" will yield to analysis in the same terms that "theories" and "concepts" will — that is, in terms of pieces that form part of new concepts and theories. Before we have a definitive resolution to such issues, it is still illuminating that coherence advocates minimize and ignore "other things students say," while pieces advocates seek to understand them and bring them under the umbrella of a more powerful, general, theory of concepts and conceptual change.

I propose a simple pseudo experiment. Walk around the house with a student, pushing, prodding, tossing, dropping, bouncing, and watching things. Definitely include splashing and floating in water (since studies of intuitive physics have essentially ignored liquids)! How much can be brought under the umbrella of any existing coherence model of physics knowledge? Or, talk with a child for an hour about her friends and family. How much of that can be brought under the umbrella of a naïve theory of mind? Of course, no one can yet do a complete knowledge in pieces account of all this diversity, either. But the perspective recognizes that someday we should be able to account for all that noise.

Diversity

In my view, coherence approaches to conceptual change inevitably simplify complexities in learning and conceptual performance in the search of single, easy-to-say conceptions. In contrast, a knowledge in pieces perspective focuses on exposing and understanding *diversity* of several kinds in conceptualization. In the first instance, as I mentioned already, I do not think one should presume that all conceptual change works in the same way. Different domains, or even different concepts in the same domain, might be quite different. While mapping out the dimensions of this diversity and validating implications has not proceeded far, it is a possibility that deserves continuing attention.

Diversity in the way people handle concepts across different contexts has already been extensively discussed here, as *contextuality*. *Individual diversity*, how different students approach conceptual change differently (and, presumably, need different kinds of help in instruction), has essentially no representation in coherence approaches to conceptual change. Case studies, almost unique to the knowledge in pieces perspective, are one way to get at diversity across individuals. The case of J, which I have used in several ways here, revealed remarkable, if not unique, individual characteristics (diSessa, Elby, & Hammer, 2002). In particular, although J developed a fine normative model of a toss, she retained and continued to use her initial model on occasion, despite direct challenge and direct contrast to the normative model. In contrast, another case study (unpublished) showed a student with the same initial model, who spontaneously changed her model to the normative one — explicitly renouncing her old model — during one protocol segment of less than 10 minutes duration.

Of these forms of diversity, contextual diversity has had the most empirical attention. However, the whole package of forms of diversity (individual, contextual, domain-relative) is important and expected from a knowledge in pieces perspective. None of them are typically mentioned within the coherence community. I underscore that in this section, particularly, I am not arguing that results in this area are the least bit definitive, but only that certain phenomenological foci are very salient from the pieces side, and hardly discernable from the coherence side. Of course, the salience of the phenomenon leads to a set of key question. In the case of diversity: What are the dimensions of diversity in its various forms; how do we account for them in terms of our theories of concepts and conceptual change?

INTELLECTUAL TRADITIONS

Intellectual traditions are powerful resources in science. They provide:

- toolkits of specific empirical and theoretical strategies;
- (sometimes) formalisms for expressing results and for reasoning about implications;
- implicit and explicit standards for what counts as an explanation.

More generally, traditions provide:

- a pre-selection of classes of phenomenology that can go together for scientific analysis;
- "eye-glasses" for seeing what is important and general in those phenomena;
- productive assumptions and simplifications that keep us from wandering aimlessly among a myriad of possibilities;
- work-a-day practices that keep us from inventing anew each day what we should be doing.

But, of course, intellectual traditions constrain, as well as enable.

- Particular empirical strategies are always better for investigating some phenomena compared to others.

- Any theoretical repertoire, similarly, restricts "what we can say and naturally attend to."
- Predispositions toward what constitutes noise and what constitutes signal can obscure new and powerful connections, and also hide limitations.
- Particular modes of analysis always favor certain categories and assumptions over others.
- Established practices are resistant to enlargement of, or merely changing, the empirical or theoretical landscape.

This section briefly discusses three intellectual traditions that are relevant to conceptual change research. I believe that these traditions, even at a bird's eye level, help explain the fault line between coherence and pieces.

Cognitive Modeling

One of the main lines of influence that created cognitive science was the idea that thinking could be modeled in detail as a complex process. While the most visible part of this line involved explicit symbolic or connectionist modeling on computers, there is a significant "softer and broader" movement in the same spirit. Minsky's "society of mind" (Minsky, 1988) is a good exemplar. In my own work I usually acknowledge the influence of that line of thinking by evoking the idea of "complex knowledge systems" (e.g., diSessa & Wagner, 2005). In this view, the idea that thinking — or even just "a concept" — might consist of many elements of different sorts, interconnected in complex ways, is just common sense. Literally no one espousing any form of this perspective, no cognitive modeler, would believe that a paragraph of natural language text could remotely describe the operation of a concept, much less a theory. While one might believe this to be merely a distinction between what it takes to *describe* a concept and what it takes to *implement* one, I believe the distinction is both epistemological and profound.

Two examples of ways of thinking, inside and outside the cognitive modeling perspective, may advance my argument. Both involve the idea of emergence.

Same system, different performances: Within the complex knowledge system perspective, thinking or "concept use" is the phenomenological presentation of a complex system in operation. The system, itself, much less its pieces, looks nothing like its appearance. A familiar example is that birds flock in such a way as to give the appearance of having a leader. However, there is nothing like the concept of "leader" in the simple rules that each bird follows. The fact of a leader might emerge from a rule like (anthropomorphism aside) "all things equal, it's convivial to fly slightly behind and to the side of a colleague."

If there are many rules, or, more generally speaking, elements, the gap between a system and its appearances gets even starker. A single system, even if it is distinctly identifiable, might behave differently on different occasions, or different parts of it might be used to provide the same behavior (function) on different occasions. In my own work, the latter property — different parts of a system provide "the same function" on different occasions — has been particularly important. I describe the particular subset of a concept-system that performs the function of "the concept" in particular circumstances as a *concept projection* (diSessa & Wagner, 2005).

To some, this discussion might sound like it introduces a technical and esoteric set of distinctions. But I think it is completely intuitive, even obvious, to anyone adhering to a complex knowledge systems perspective. Anecdotally, in my own work I found myself using the idea of concept projection implicitly, without naming it. However, feedback from readers of my papers and audiences of my talks convinced me that the idea was counter-intuitive to many, and needed naming and specific attention. The contrasting intuition, I believe, is that there is a much more direct and holistic ontological connection between the use of a concept and "the concept," itself. One may tend to assume that a concept is "the same" in each use.

Different systems, common elements: The second way of thinking connected with emergence has to do with the degree of connection between a system or its behavior and any element in it. From a complex knowledge system perspective, because of the gap between the system itself and its performance, no particular connection between the system and an element in it can be assumed. For example, two very different systems may use exactly the same element, and yet behave completely differently. To take a technical example, two programs that use the same command cannot be assumed to have anything of much consequence to do with one another.[14]

The contrary intuition is that different systems must have different elements. Let me recount an experience. Several years ago, I made an empirical case that intuitive psychological and sociological ways of thinking might have something in common with intuitive physics (diSessa, 2000). For example, the idea that more effort begets greater effect is common to psychological effort in accomplishing intellectual tasks, and physical effort in accomplishing physical tasks. I found myself in extended arguments with developmental psychologist colleagues about my claims. The discussion had nothing to do with the data that I presented in that paper. Instead, my colleagues insisted that children demonstrably learn to distinguish the physical from psychological (or biological) early on, a fact that I can grant. However, from my point of view, even granting two different systems of thought are used in different situations (physical and psychological, for example), and even granting that children always know which system to use, it does not follow that there is nothing whatsoever in common between those systems. I felt that I was hearing, quite directly, the argument that different systems must have no elements in common.

My developmental colleagues and I were not debating the plausibility of my claims, but their very possibility. Is it possible that two different knowledge systems that are even perceived by children as applying in distinct contexts could have anything (any element) in common? My common sense is that there is no way one can rule that out a priori, even if it is false. Of course, my colleagues were probably not thinking in systems terms, and that is precisely the point. Complex systems thinking is not a part of the common sense of all scientists.[15]

To summarize, the intellectual traditions behind the complex knowledge system perspective make particular ways of thinking about conceptual change possible. Sometimes those traditions can make certain possibilities seem, more than possible, but also plausible, and even necessary. This fact obtains even when specific, technical results are not at issue. Other communities may not find those ways of thinking at all congenial.

Developmental Psychology

The "hard core" of coherence points of view, I believe, is in the community of developmental psychologists who are contributing to conceptual change research. I make sense of this for myself by thinking about Piaget, and successor perspectives on development. Piaget, of course, wanted to have a unified theory of intelligence. In the most reductionist version of his program, one global structure of intelligence succeeded another, and the two were quite distinct from one another.

There are few clear examples of complex systems thinking in Piaget's theorizing. Core structures were described without a great deal of concern about the nature of elements in them, or their specific relations. When he articulated models of "structures," the high end of complexity is represented by what I would call "simple" logical schemes like the 4 element group articulated in his theory of "groupments."

One of the most significant changes in post-Piagetian developmental psychology was to move from assumptions of a unified intelligence to recognizing the particularities of specific domains (Hirschfeld & Gelman, 1994). However, as an adherent of a complex systems point of view, my perception is that one step away from Piaget was taken, whereas two are needed. Shifting the assumption that few, relatively simple and compact descriptions can suffice from "intelligence in general" to "knowledge domains" just does not go far enough. This is essentially a restatement of my conviction that we must deal with the phenomenology of complex systems in dealing with conceptual change, and that my sense for the size and complexity of such descriptions is quite different from that displayed, as a generality, in developmental psychology.

This brief "intellectual line" story about why coherence ideas seem particularly entrenched in developmental psychology is even more speculative than my account of important, general ideas available in complex systems thinking. Among other things, it seems ironic that Piaget, a biologist by training and at heart (although not an ecologist) would not display sensitivity to complex systems and how to think about them. Perhaps he did not have sufficient models for complex systems in cognition, as opposed to the evident "many parts" of biological systems. But, in the bigger picture, this story is also less important than the one about cognitive modeling. My main goal is to point out ways of thinking that I think are important in understanding conceptual change, and what communities might have an inside track on some of them. The fact that certain simple, if unfamiliar, ideas do not have much play in the coherence community is much more important and salient than the reasons for that discrepancy.

Education

Education is a complicated case because it enfolds many disparate intellectual traditions. However, I have already made a few comments about how and why I believe education, as a perspective, tends toward knowledge in pieces.

I believe that educators, particularly teachers, come naturally into contact with the complexity of students' ideas. Classrooms — at least open classrooms that rely on student discussion — are full of a rich phenomenology of thinking, unconstrained by carefully developed instruments and protocols designed to filter out "noise." I also believe that a central diversity in ways of thinking is manifest and commonsensical in teaching situations. My experience in speaking with teachers is that they find knowledge in pieces interesting and not counter intuitive, even if it is difficult to understand. If they do not have relevant complex systems intuitions, at least they do not have the opposite intuitions.

Another point about the educational context is that the instinct to find and use "out of the shadows" knowledge that students have for productive purposes is widespread. In addition, education has, in principle, a strong accountability for "having a concept." Students must display a robust understanding of force, across many contexts (problems). My theory-based view of this is that, educationally, the full and complex system that constitutes a concept is at issue, not presumed-to-be reliable indicators, tested in a small range of contexts. More generally, the long road to competence is not only experientially rich for teachers and materials designers, it is vital to understand for instrumental purposes. While developmental psychologists generally have avoided tracking moment-by-moment process data concerning the changes they study,[16] educators feel responsible for causing relevant change during a conversation or in a worked problem. While it may be difficult, there is a strong feeling among educators that we can and should be able to track and understand such changes.

I think that judgments of importance are more natural in education than in developmental or experimental psychology. For example, I remarked, above, that the Ioannides/Vosniadou concept of force omitted consideration of potentially critical inferential aspects of the concept: what may one infer from the existence of a force? Importance is, in part, an educational judgment. If we want to do conceptual change research relevant to real-world educational problems, we should not ignore, as if it were a "minor" issue, aspects of a concept that are educationally critical. Individual studies, of course, must be limited in their goals. However, omitting important considerations from whole lines of study is the serious problem.

Education seems to me, thus, to be a natural generator of foci of attention that are also natural in the knowledge in pieces perspective. Certain ways of thinking that are salient in instructional contexts — holding to strong tests of competence, building on weak but relevant student knowledge, attending to incremental change on the long road to competence — are synergistic with a complex knowledge system analysis. In view of these observations, it is natural that educationally-oriented researchers are those who are pushing the current trend toward knowledge in pieces analyses.

SUMMARY

The purpose of this chapter is to deliberately take an unusual approach to an important controversy in conceptual change research — the nature of intuitive or naïve ideas: Are they coherent, systematic enough, perhaps, to describe as a theory? Or are they fragmented and piecemeal, large in number and displaying only limited systematicity? The standard mode of approaching such a debate would be to marshal careful argument about theory, and comparative critique of empirical results in the service of competitive argumentation. Instead, this chapter reviews the debate assuming that researchers' reasons for taking sides are as much or more in a distributed set of heuristics, dispositions, intuitions, or lack of intuitions, compared to logic and compelling data. I have attempted to bring the "fringe" of the dispute to center stage. In this mode, I try to counter dispositions and intuitions lined up against knowledge in pieces, and highlight those that support it. I also hope to shed some light why some intellectual traditions line up on one side or on the other.

Reformulating the Debate: Grain Size, Relational Structure, and Contextuality

The first important move in thinking about "pieces vs. coherence" was to penetrate the rhetorical veneer to what I take to be the deeper and more consequential issues. While the "pieces vs. coherence" debate is ostensibly about degree of coherence, I made the case that the primary and prior issue is grain size in describing conceptual structure. In short, I believe a good tracking of concepts and conceptual change necessarily entails an extensive accounting at a sub-conceptual grain size. We must necessarily say a lot about intuitive mental ecologies to account for their properties and to account for the emergence of new concepts. Coherence, in fact, is not defined or sensibly operationalized unless we say more precisely than is usually done not only something about the size and kind of pieces, but also what kind of *relational structure* exists among them. Furthermore, a smaller grain size and a greater number of elements means that *contextuality* — exactly when elements are used and how such context/knowledge links change in learning — becomes much more important theoretically and empirically.

Questions

I used several strategies to approach my goals. To begin, I treated a number of questions about the pieces perspective that I have often heard. These seem disconnected from technical debates, but genuinely part of people's reactions to knowledge in pieces.

First, some people think that the debate is overdone and polarized, particularly in view of the fact that the empirical resolution on conceptual structure is still quite weak. Through a fuzzy lens, what is the point of arguing fine points about degree of coherence? My response is that, given my reformulation of the core issues as concerning grain size, the debate is much more categorical. Do we need careful models of conceptual knowledge, including significant numbers of sub-conceptual elements, or can we get away with naming concepts and describing them in a sentence or two of natural language? The pieces side advocates refined models and extensive description, not only of content, but also of form. Without such models, establishing degree of coherence is not only empirically difficult, it is theoretically beyond reach.

A harder question concerns whether knowledge in pieces is putting forward esoteric details, while coherence folks are getting at the central parts of conceptual structure. My first response is to affirm that a sea of complexities is easy to see and draw out. Developing a theory powerful enough to treat those complexities, instead of just ignoring them, seems to be within reach for the knowledge in pieces perspective, but essentially written out of the realm of possibility by coherence advocates. The reverse is not true. Knowledge in pieces can treat large-scale conceptual structure as configurations of pieces, and that is in fact an important part of the knowledge in pieces program. Empirical work of exactly this sort has been done. I claim it provides a more powerful theory of "big chunks" by understanding their properties as stemming from their constituents, and also by providing hints as to how the chunks might have been constructed.

Whether coherence advocates have even got the big chunks roughly right is another question. I note that empirical work is ambiguous. In particular, claimed chunks seem easy to break by attending to attributes that knowledge in pieces shows are relevant, but that coherence stories ignore. We find that subjects only sometimes show anything like the chunks claimed. Coherence advocates do very little, if any, boundary setting on the contextuality of their "core structure." Furthermore, they seldom test or even explicitly argue that "core" also means "important." For example, even if a structure is there, is it consequential in learning school physics? I showed examples of aspects of the concept of force that research has shown are important (e.g., what follows from the existence of a force?), which are not treated by what I take to be among the best coherence stories. Although knowledge in pieces advocates attend to detail, ironically, coherence advocates sometimes ignore validated-as-important aspects of concepts because they do not fit their supposed "core" naïve "theories" or "concepts."

Many people feel that knowledge in pieces is just too complicated. It violates scientific parsimony. I believe this point is easily dispatched. Science is sometimes complicated, even if we prefer otherwise. We have to look at the complexity of the phenomena and then see how complex our theories must be. Besides, the idea of many elements, per se, is simply not conceptually complicated. Long lists are hardly intractable.

Some biased characterizations of knowledge in pieces (pieces and their use are random, insubstantial) make it seem unlikely that such a view can account for apparent robustness of some intuitive ideas. But, pieces can be substantial, even if their boundaries of application do not mesh with those of scientific concepts. Furthermore, the fundamental fact that new concepts require complex composition and coordination of old pieces can explain difficulty in creating new concepts without question-begging attribution of "entrenchment" or other such characteristics.

Complaints that knowledge in pieces makes instruction difficult, in the first instance, have no bearing on scientific cogency. Furthermore, I believe coherence types just have not thought much about instructional applications of pieces; I provided suggestive examples of help it can provide in instruction. Finally, I think the feeling that instruction based on coherence ideas has been effective ignores the fact that instruction based on knowledge in pieces also has been shown effective. Indeed, instruction based on these two perspectives often uses similar strategies (computer models, classroom discussion, etc.). So, instructional effectiveness may not be very diagnostic of the validity of the theories of designers.

Does knowledge in pieces demean children? I think this is hardly the case. In the first instance, knowledge in pieces validates much of the knowledge that they have, not only in its own terms (everyday use), but also in supplying rich resources that become part of normative competence. In addition, knowledge in pieces applies to scientists, not just children. The main problem may be that it is not the way we prefer, for non-scientific reasons, to think about ourselves.

Motivating Phenomena and Key Research Questions

After responding to informal questions, I approached the debate in another way, in terms of central research questions and motivating phenomenology (again, in contrast to specific theories or empirical results). The biggest issue for me here is treating the long, presumably complex road to conceptual change that everyone agrees exists. But, then, how do theories that specify concepts in sparse and categorical (as opposed to contextual) terms parameterize and describe that change? Knowledge in pieces has many ways to deal with slow, difficult change. The prototypical phenomenon is that many elements need to be accumulated, and their contextual places gradually established. Empirical work has shown provocative instances of "one little contextual piece at a time makes a correspondingly small difference in competence."

Once we chose a smaller grain size, a whole range of possible developmental phenomena become theoretically approachable, and thus more empirically tractable and interesting. There is no reason conceptual competence cannot contain several nearly distinct strands, and I alluded to an example that showed that, over a long ranges of age (but before instruction), students get *worse*, conceptually, concerning at least one aspect of competence with the idea of force. There is even provocative data that early students of physics get systematically worse in some ways (Thaden-Koch, Mestre, Dufresne, Gerace, & Leonard, 2004). How can "coherence" explain that, in the face of claimed steady increase in sophistication?

One of my favorite foci of attention is "out of the shadows learning," when peripheral student knowledge (which coherence advocates generally treat as noise), becomes central to normative competence. While empirical work in this area is still weak, the phenomenon is strongly diagnostic of the differences between pieces and coherence, and hence worthy of attention.

Finally, I pointed out a substantial list of kinds of diversity: individual diversity, diversity in how domain affects conceptual change, and that central bugaboo (for coherence advocates), contextual diversity. I maintain that these diversities are phenomenologically rich, important, but comparatively intractable from a coherence point of view. They are certainly not prominent in research by that community.

Intellectual Traditions

My last strategy for addressing the goals of this chapter was speculative. What can we learn about the pieces vs. coherence controversy by looking at intellectual traditions? I considered developmental psychology — a bastion of coherence advocates. In developmental psychology, the small grain size and complexity of knowledge in pieces has, almost forever, been out of fashion. In contrast, I looked at some simple intuitions from cognitive modeling and related traditions that make knowledge in pieces commonsensical. For example, pieces are just not diagnostic of the system that contains them. In contrast, coherence advocates seem to assume that pieces, if they exist, are uniquely characteristic of systems that contain them. The logic seems to be, "Since children think differently about psychological issues than about physical issues, there are no pieces in common between those systems." Slightly more subtly, outside of certain traditions one tends to assume that each instance of a phenomenon implicates the same underlying structures. Each instance of use of a concept uses "the same knowledge." But, any programmer knows that implementing a function often requires different code for different cases.

CODA

From focal phenomenology, to driving intuitions and assumptions, to theoretical repertoire, to empirical technique (e.g., case studies vs. closed coding confirmation of use of a "theory"), knowledge in pieces and coherence approaches are more like different paradigms[17] than they are merely different claims about conceptual change. They are certainly more than a difference of opinion concerning the degree of coherence in naïve thought. Kuhn thought that we could not speak across certain such differences. But that, and even understanding some of the more intractable aspects of difference (because they are marginal to direct scientific debate), are precisely the goals of this chapter.

ACKNOWLEDGMENTS

I wish to thank members of the Boxer Research Group, UC Berkeley, for ideas and early critique of the content of this chapter. David Brown provided helpful commentary and a new "question from critics" to address. Comments and corrections by Stella Vosniadou are gratefully acknowledged. Joseph Wagner and Karen Chang provided helpful editorial suggestions. The Spencer Foundation's support of my current (grant number MG-200500036) and past conceptual change work is also gratefully acknowledged.

NOTES

1. "Theory-like" probably entails other attributes besides coherence, which under other circumstances might deserve discussion. I believe naïve ideas are "abstract and explanatory," given sufficient qualifications on the meanings of these terms. Many take "domain characteristic" also as part of "theory-like." This is more problematic as a characterization of naïve ideas. See later discussion about whether any naïve ideas cross the physics/psychology boundary.
2. It would be illuminating to put the assumptions behind my strategy here to the test. One could empirically study the profile of intuitions, the salience of certain phenomena, and the familiarity with certain kinds of arguments and correlate them with researchers' basic commitments in terms of "pieces vs. coherence."
3. There are three related, but distinguishable issues here, which I treat in this chapter mostly as "the same issue." Grain size relative to, for example, concepts, is one. A second is how much theoretical precision and explicit consideration is required even to specify the *kind* of knowledge at issue. My view of intuitive knowledge requires an extended treatment (see diSessa, 1993). Third, how much empirical detail is involved in describing any relevant theoretical object, say, a particular concept?
4. However, I feel my work has often been misrepresented in this regard, as denying that any structure exists. See later quotations in this chapter.
5. Given that naïve ideas and theories are so often presented in a sentence or two, I suspect the implicit model for coherence is that of a system of propositions. Even this leaves open the possibility of many measures of coherence. For inspiration, see Thagard (2000). If Thagard is an advocate of coherence, then he constitutes a notable counter-example to the claim that advocates of coherence never define coherence.
6. I will have to resort on several occasions to denials that "coherence" advocates provide answers to certain questions. Documenting the absence of something is difficult to do, even if my expositional strategy included enough detail to support attempts at validation. I am, of course, open to correction on facts of the matter in terms of published work.
7. My default model for "relational structure" involves mapping specific relations among specific elements, similar to Thagard (2000). Although this is restrictive, I do not believe we are far enough along to need more general relational models, such as resonances in a complex, continuous-parameter dynamical system.
8. This is essentially a quote from the reviewer of a journal article I submitted.
9. A second issue of contextuality is the noted fact (McCloskey, 1983) that students seldom use the impetus theory when objects are carried. My explanation of this fact is that another of the many intuitive

schemata NOT involved in the "impetus theory" better fits situations of carrying. So, an empirically noted exception to the "theory" (or an unmotivated "branch" of it) is also explained in a pieces perspective, by the contextuality of independent elements.

10. Another provocative analogy is the structure of a society, which is also complex and dependent on many contingencies of history.

11. I am more sympathetic with researchers who claim, themselves, not to understand the complexity of knowledge in pieces. However, the essential complexity, the fact of many elements, doesn't seem at all complex. If there are, indeed, other "complexities," we need to work them out in terms of, for example, claims by coherence advocates of specific confusions and unclarities in the knowledge in pieces perspective.

12. This issue has become a central theoretical and empirical project in some recent work (e.g., diSessa & Wagner, 2005).

13. One of my "favorite" unhelpful answers to "what is coherence," is that coherence is the state of having no contradictions. This implies, however, that any system of pieces that *have no relation whatsoever with one another* is coherent. Another unhelpful specification is that coherence describes a system that is well-connected or integrated, begging the fundamental *structure* question of *what sort of relations* one is talking about.

14. It is slightly dangerous to use an example that suggests that these ideas are particular to symbolic information processing models of thought. I believe the basic phenomena are common to a wide range of complex systems, including neural or connectionist models, and even more general dynamical systems.

15. I feel the need to rehearse again, at least in a footnote, the purpose and strategy of this chapter. I am not claiming I am right about any of the particular issues in this section. I aim to be evoking ways of thinking that "belong" to different communities, which may account for systematic difference in point of view. That there is little research on the cognitive characteristics of different scientific communities is a bit of a deterrent to making a good case like this. However, that does not mean the possibility will not be helpful to both communities in understanding their differences. That is precisely the point.

16. Micro-genetic analyses (see Siegler and Svetina, chapter 5, this volume) constitute an important class of exceptions.

17. Kuhn's later phrase, "disciplinary matrix" is certainly more descriptive and apt than "paradigm," although it is less recognizable.

REFERENCES

Brown, D. E. (1994). Facilitating conceptual change using analogies and explanatory models. *International Journal of Science Education, 16*(2) 201–214.

Carey, S. (1985). *Conceptual change in childhood.* Cambridge, MA: MIT Press/Bradford Books.

Carey, S. (1999). Sources of conceptual change. In E. Scholnick, K. Nelson, S. Gelman, & P. Miller (Eds.), *Conceptual development: Piaget's legacy* (pp. 293–326). Mahwah, NJ: Erlbaum .

Clark, D. B. (2006). Longitudinal conceptual change in students' understanding of thermal equilibrium: An examination of the process of conceptual restructuring. *Cognition and Instruction, 24*(4), 467–563.

diSessa, A. A. (1980). Momentum flow as an alternative perspective in elementary mechanics. *American Journal of Physics, 48,* 365–369.

diSessa, A. A. (1983). Phenomenology and the evolution of intuition. In D. Gentner & A. Stevens (Eds.), *Mental models* (pp. 15–33). Hillsdale, NJ: Erlbaum.

diSessa, A. A. (1988). Knowledge in pieces. In G. Forman & P. Pufall (Eds.), *Constructivism in the computer age* (pp. 49–70). Hillsdale, NJ: Erlbaum.

diSessa, A. A. (1993). Toward an epistemology of physics. *Cognition and Instruction, 10*(2-3), 105–225.

diSessa, A. A. (1996). What do "just plain folk" know about physics? In D. R. Olson & N. Torrance (Eds.), *Handbook of education and human development: New models of learning, teaching, and schooling* (pp. 709–730). Oxford, UK: Blackwell.

diSessa, A. A. (2000). Does the mind know the difference between the physical and social worlds? In L.

Nucci, G. Saxe, & E. Turiel (Eds.), *Culture, development and knowledge* (pp. 141–166). Mahwah, NJ: Erlbaum.

diSessa, A. A. (2006). A history of conceptual change research: Threads and fault lines. In R. K. Sawyer (Ed.), *The Cambridge handbook of the learning sciences* (pp. 265–281). Cambridge, UK: Cambridge University Press.

diSessa, A. A., Elby, A., & Hammer, D. (2002). J's epistemological stance and strategies. In G. Sinatra and P. Pintrich (Eds.), *Intentional conceptual change* (pp. 237–290). Mahwah, NJ: Erlbaum.

diSessa, A. A., Gillespie, N., & Esterly, J. (2004). Coherence vs. fragmentation in the development of the concept of force. *Cognitive Science, 28*, 843–900.

diSessa, A. A., & Wagner, J. F. (2005). What coordination has to say about transfer. In J. Mestre (Ed.), *Transfer of learning from a modern multi-disciplinary perspective* (pp. 121–154). Greenwich, CT: Information Age.

Gopnik, A., & Wellman, H. M. (1994). The theory theory. In L. A. Hirschfeld & S. A. Gelman (Eds.), *Mapping the mind: Domain specificity in cognition and culture* (pp. 257–293). New York: Cambridge University Press.

Hammer, D., & Elby, A. (2002). On the form of a personal epistemology. In B. K. Hofer & P. R. Pintrich (Eds.), *Personal epistemology: The psychology of beliefs about knowledge and knowing* (pp. 169–190). Mahwah, NJ: Erlbaum.

Hirschfeld, L., & Gelman, S. (1994). *Mapping the mind: Domain specificity in cognition and culture.* New York: Cambridge University Press.

Hofer, B., & Pintrich, P. (2002). *Personal epistemology: The psychology of beliefs about knowledge and knowing.* Mahwah, NJ Erlbaum.

Hunt, E., & Minstrell, J. (1994). A cognitive approach to the teaching of physics. In K. McGilly (Ed.), *Classroom lessons: Integrating cognitive theory and classroom practice* (pp. 51–74). Cambridge, MA: MIT Press.

Inagaki, K., & Hatano, G. (2002). *Young children's naive thinking about the biological world.* New York: Psychology Press.

Ioannides, C., &Vosniadou, S. (2002). The changing meanings of force. *Cognitive Science Quarterly, 2*, 5–61.

Izsák, A. (2005). "You have to count the squares": Applying knowledge in pieces to learning rectangular area. *Journal of the Learning Sciences, 14*(3), 361–403.

Kuhn, T. S. (1970). *The structure of scientific revolutions.* Second Edition. Chicago: University of Chicago Press.

Linn, M. C. (2006). The knowledge integration perspective on learning and instruction. In R. K. Sawyer (Ed.), *The Cambridge handbook of the learning sciences* (pp. 242–264). Cambridge, UK: Cambridge University Press.

McCloskey, M. (1983). Naïve theories of motion. In D. Gentner & A. Stevens (Eds.), *Mental models* (pp. 299–324). Hillsdale, NJ: Erlbaum.

Minsky, M. (1988). *Society of mind.* New York: Simon & Schuster.

Parnafes, O. (2005). The development of conceptual understanding through the use of computer-based representations. Unpublished doctoral dissertation, University of California at Berkeley.

Samarapungavan, A., & Wiers, R. (1997). Children's thoughts on the origin of species: A study of explanatory coherence. *Cognitive Science, 21*(2), 147–177.

Thaden-Koch, T., Mestre, J., Dufresne, R., Gerace, W., & Leonard, W. (2004). When transfer fails: Effect of knowledge, expectations and observations on transfer in physics. In J. Mestre (Ed.), *Transfer of learning: Research and perspectives.* Greenwich, CT: Information Age Publishing.

Thagard, P. (2000). *Coherence in thought and action.* Cambridge, MA: MIT Press.

Toulmin, S. (1972). *Human understanding.* Vol. 1. Oxford, UK: Clarendon Press.

Vosniadou, S. (2002). On the nature of naïve physics. In M. Limón & L. Mason (Eds.), *Reconsidering conceptual change: Issues in theory and practice* (pp. 61–76). Dordrecht: Kluwer.

Vosniadou, S., & Brewer, W. (1992). Mental models of the earth: A study of conceptual change in childhood. *Cognitive Psychology, 24*, 535–585.

Wagner, J. F. (2006). Transfer in pieces. *Cognition and Instruction, 24*(1), 1–71.

3

Three Types of Conceptual Change: Belief Revision, Mental Model Transformation, and Categorical Shift

Michelene T. H. Chi
University of Pittsburgh

CONCEPTUAL CHANGE KIND OF LEARNING

Learning of complex material, such as concepts encountered in science classrooms, can occur under at least three different conditions of prior knowledge. First, a student may have no prior knowledge of the to-be-learned concepts, although they may have some related knowledge. In this case, prior knowledge is *missing*, and learning consists of *adding* new knowledge. Second, a student may have some correct prior knowledge about the to-be-learned concepts, but that knowledge is *incomplete*. In this incomplete knowledge case, learning can be conceived of as *gap filling*. In both *missing* and *incomplete* knowledge conditions, knowledge acquisition is of the *enriching* kind (Carey, 1991). In a third condition, a student may have acquired ideas, either in school or from everyday experience, that are "in conflict with" the to-be-learned concepts (Vosniadou, 2004). Knowledge acquisition under this third case is of the *conceptual change* kind. It is customary to assume in this case that the prior "in conflict with" knowledge is incorrect or misconceived, and the to-be-learned information is correct, by some normative standard. Thus, learning in this third condition is not *adding* new knowledge or *gap filling* incomplete knowledge; rather, learning is *changing* prior misconceived knowledge to correct knowledge. This chapter focuses on this conceptual change kind of learning.

Although this definition of conceptual change appears straightforward, conceptual change kind of learning entails several complex, non-transparent, and interleaved issues. Some of the key non-transparent ideas are: (a) In what ways is knowledge misconceived? (b) Why is such misconceived knowledge often resistant to change? (c) What constitutes a *change* in prior knowledge? and (d) How should instruction be designed to promote conceptual change? The existence of decades of research on conceptual change speaks to the complexity of these issues. This chapter hopes to add clarity to some of these issues by laying out three different grain sizes in which knowledge can be "in conflict with" the to-be-learned materials, postulating for each grain size the processes by which such "in conflict with knowledge" can be changed, and speculating on the kind of instruction that might achieve such change. We start by providing some definitions and assumptions about concepts and categories in conceptual change.

"CONCEPTS" AND "CATEGORIES" IN CONCEPTUAL CHANGE

In this section, we elaborate on (1) the scope of the term "concepts" in conceptual change research, (2) the assumptions about the role of categorization in learning and conceptual change, and (3) the relationships among different levels and kinds of "categories."

Scope of Concepts

Several decades of psychological literature (see Medin & Rips, 2005, for a recent review; and see Jackendoff along with the Forum published in *Mind & Language*, 1989, for a broader view) have dealt with determining how concepts can be identified and defined. That classic literature has typically been devoted to defining isolated and static concepts and categories such as *robins* and *birds*. From that literature, we adopt the common assumptions that a concept has several perceptual features and conceptual attributes, and a concept can be viewed as belonging to some category. For example, a *robin* has a red breast (a perceptual feature), lives in a temperate climate (more of a conceptual attribute), and belongs to the category of *birds*. (Throughout this chapter, we will use the term features to refer to perceptual properties, "attributes" to refer to conceptual properties, and italicize category terms and scientific concepts.)

Although prior conflicting ideas are often referred to as mis*conceptions* and learning that involves altering such incorrect ideas is referred to as *conceptual* change, the grain size of that prior knowledge does not have to be at the level of a concept, in the traditional sense of static concepts typically studied by psychologists, such as *chairs* and *furniture*. Even though psychologists have begun to expand the notion of a category beyond concrete static types to include explanation-based categories such as *food items for a diet* (e.g., popcorn, diet soda, lean turkey, Barsalou, 1983) or principle-based categories (such as physics problems that share the same principle, Chi, Feltovich, & Glaser, 1981), the kind of misconceived knowledge in subject matter domains taught in schools (especially science domains) are at a much larger grain size, more complex and inter-related. For example, students are expected to learn about systems (such as the *circulatory system*) consisting of many inter-related components (such as *blood, organs*, etc). Students are also expected to learn not only about static concepts, but also about dynamic concepts, such as the processes of *heat transfer* and *natural selection*. In short, the term "concepts" in conceptual change research often refers to a broader scope than isolated and static concepts.

ROLE OF HIERARCHICAL CATEGORIZATION IN LEARNING

Categorizing is the process of identifying or assigning a concept to a category to which it belongs. One of the most important assumptions about categorizing that we also adopt is its role in learning (Bransford, Brown, & Cocking, 1999). Categorization is an important learning mechanism because a concept, once categorized, can "inherit" features and attributes from its category membership. For example, we can infer that *robins lay eggs* even if we were never told that fact, as long as we know that *robins are birds* and *birds lay eggs*. By knowing that *robins are a kind of bird* allows us to infer that *robins* inherit the properties of *birds*. Thus, categorizing, or assigning a concept to a correct category, is powerful because a learner can use knowledge of the category to make many inferences and attributions about a novel concept/phenomenon (Medin & Rips, 2005). Even young children can do this. For example, 4- to 7-year-old dinosaur aficionados can generate many appropriate inferences about an unfamiliar dinosaur once they have categorized it on the basis of surface features (Chi & Koeske, 1983; Gobbo & Chi, 1986).

Besides the common assumption that categorization allows new concepts to inherit categorical properties, we propose two additional assumptions about the role of categorization in learning. The first new assumption is that when learners have *no* obvious basic category to assign a new concept or phenomenon — they will assign it to the next higher level of category that is appropriate. For example, suppose an observer in a museum sees a strange large creature (a *gavial*) with four short legs, scaly skin and a flat bill-like snout. Not knowing that it's a kind of *reptile*, like a crocodile, the observer would categorize it at the next level up, as a kind of *animal*, since it appears to have the properties of *animals,* can move on its own, eat, and so forth. (The second new assumption will be described in the next section.)

As illustrated above, the type of relationships cognitive psychologists have explored about inheritance of properties are hierarchical ones. Hierarchical relationships among categories are primarily inclusive in nature. For example, *living beings* include *animals*, and *animals* include *reptiles* and *birds*, and *birds* include *robins*. (See Figure 3.1, left-most hierarchical tree.) *Living beings,* in turn, can be subsumed under an even higher category, such as *objects*; and *conobjects* can be subsumed under yet an even higher category such as *Entities*. The classic psychological research that dealt mostly with hierarchical relationships among categories asked questions such as: What level within this hierarchy is the most "basic" and useful? How does correct categorization support reasoning and inferencing? Can priming the correct super-ordinate category enhance recognition?

Little research has focused on incorrect hierarchical categorization, perhaps because it is not wrong but merely too specific or overly general. As in the preceding *gavial* example, the overly general hierarchical categorization of *gavial* as an *animal* is not that damaging, since the observer can still benefit from correct inferences and attributions inherited from the *animal* category. For example, the observer can understand new instruction about *gavials,* such as that *they breathe air through their snouts*. The observer can assimilate this new piece of information because it is compatible with what s/he knows about *animals* in general. Therefore, categorizing a concept at a higher categorical level is not damaging to learning.

Lateral and Ontological Categories

Research in cognitive psychology has paid much less attention to the role of "lateral" (rather than hierarchical) categories. For example, *artifacts* can be considered a lateral category more-or-less "parallel" to *living beings* (see Figure 3.1). *Artifacts* does not include the subcategories of *living beings*, such as *animals, reptiles, birds,* or *robins*. Instead, *artifacts* includes a different set of subcategories, such as *furniture* and *toys,* and *furniture* includes subcategories such as *tables* and *chairs* (see Figure 3.1) In short, *artifacts* and *living beings* can be thought of as occupying different branches of the same hierarchical tree (Thagard, 1990), in this case the *Entities* tree. We will refer to categories on different branches as "lateral" (vs. hierarchical) categories and, when lateral categories occur at about the same level within a tree, we will refer to them as "parallel."

Although *artifacts* and *living beings* can both be subsumed under the higher-level category of *objects* and therefore share higher-level properties of *objects* such as "has shape" and "can be thrown," the properties of *artifacts* and *living beings* tend to be distinct and mutually exclusive. For example, *living beings* "can move" on their own volition, whereas *artifacts* cannot; *living beings* "can reproduce" whereas *artifacts* cannot. (Examples of properties of each category are shown in quotes in Figure 3.1.). Gelman (1988) and Schwartz (1977) might have referred to these categories as different in "*kind.*"

Having mutually exclusive properties means that it does not make sense to talk about a concept of one category as having a property from a lateral category. Conversely, a concept can be

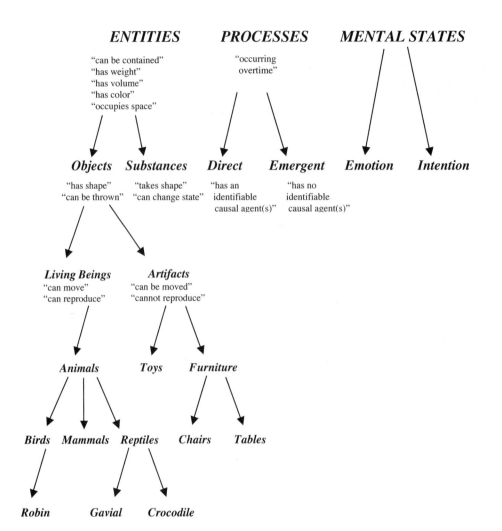

FIGURE 3.1   Distinct ontological trees: hierarchical and lateral categories within a tree and between trees.

described as having a property of its own category whether or not it is true. For example, *living beings* can reproduce whereas *artifacts* cannot. This means that Fido (a dog), being a *living being*, has the potential to reproduce even though Fido (a specific dog), having been neutered, cannot. On the other hand, a *toy dog* (an instance of an *artifact*) does not have this potential. Thus, it makes sense to say that Fido will have grey puppies even though Fido cannot have puppies, but it does not make sense to say that the mechanical toy dog will have puppies. Thus, a property of a category can be applied to members of that category or its subcategories, whether or not it is true, whereas it cannot be applied to a member of a lateral category. Thus, having mutually exclusive properties means that it does not make sense to talk about a concept as having a property of a lateral category, whereas it does make sense to talk about a concept as having a property of its own category even if it is false.

To take another example, an *object* such as a piece of clear glass, being an *Entity*, can have the property of "color," even though a specific piece of glass is colorless. That is, it is acceptable and sensible to say "the glass is green" even though it is not, whereas it makes no sense to say "the baseball game is green." This is because a baseball game, being a *direct* process, which is a category on an alternative tree, cannot take on the property of "color," so that it does not make sense to say that "the baseball game is green." Thus, one way to determine that two categories are laterally distinct (either within the same tree or between trees) is to use such a sensibility judgment task (Keil, 1979). Although in the past, we and others have called such lateral categories *ontological* (Chi, 1997; Keil, 1981), we reserve the term *ontologies* to refer to categories between different trees (as shown in Figure 3.1), since categories on different trees never share any properties, given that they do not share any super-ordinate level categories. For example, *Entities* have properties such as "can be contained" and "has volume," whereas *Processes* have properties such as "occurring over time." Thus, no process, whether it's an event such as a baseball game, a procedure such as baking a cake, or a state change such as melting, can have the property of "has volume," "has color," or "can be contained," whereas no entity, such as a cake or a ball, can have the property of "lasting two hours." Thus, each tree might be considered an "ontology" (and its name will be capitalized) (Chi, 1997, 2005), in that the trees refer to a system of taxonomic categories for certain existences in the world, as defined by philosophers (Sommers, 1971). Thus, in this chapter, we will refer to categories that occupy different trees as different "ontologically", and categories that occupy parallel branches within a tree as different laterally or in "kind."

The goal of our research is not to lay out the exact ordering and structure of hierarchical and lateral categories and trees, nor to decide which categories deserve the name ontology, or how many kinds or ontologies there are. The nature of categorical structure is an epistemological issue. Our goal instead is to focus on the role of lateral and ontological categories in conceptual change kind of learning. Thus, Figure 3.1 is offered merely as an example of a crude and intuitive rendition of categorical structures. It is by no means the absolute or the correct one.

Our second additional assumption about categorization and learning is that, when an observer or learner cannot classify a concept or phenomenon, instead of assigning it more generally to a higher-level category (as mentioned in the first additional assumption above), the observer may instead assign it to a lateral category. Using the gavial example again, the observer might categorize it as a *mammal* rather than an *animal*.

The central question to pose about lateral and ontological categories is the cost of category mistakes. We define a category mistake as the case when a concept has been assigned inappropriately to a lateral or alternative ontological category. In contrast to incorrect hierarchical categorization, category mistakes are damaging in that categorical inferences and attributions will be erroneous, creating a barrier to correct learning with deep understanding. The central thesis of our explanation is that such category mistakes account for the existence of robust misconceptions and their resistance to change. This explanation will be addressed in detail later in this chapter.

KNOWLEDGE MISCONCEIVED AT THREE GRAIN SIZES

Superficially, the notion of misconceived knowledge seems easy to define objectively, in that it is incorrect and to-be-learned material is correct. However, this contrast between correct and incorrect knowledge is too simplistic because it cannot address the issue of why such incorrect knowledge is often resistant to change. In order to understand the difference between incorrect knowledge and misconceived/conflicting knowledge, we need to consider the representation of knowledge at three different grain sizes: individual beliefs, mental models, and categories. Although our framework does not necessarily commit to any notions of hierarchy in these grain sizes, one could presume that they occur at different "levels," with individual beliefs at the lowest level and categories at the highest. What is critical, however, is our proposal that the grain size at which one considers misconceived knowledge determines the level at which instruction should target conceptual change. More specifically, how conflict is defined (between misconceived knowledge and to-be-learned material) determines how instruction should be designed.

In this section, we will focus on each of the three grain sizes of conflicting knowledge. In particular, we will examine how students' ideas conflict with to-be-learned information, the kind of conceptual change that occurs, and the type of instruction or confrontation that might trigger conceptual change. In the discussion below, our examples will be drawn primarily from science domains for three reasons. First, it is relatively easy to agree on what is considered correct or normative scientific information and thus to contrast it with misconceived knowledge, which, by definition, implies prior knowledge that is incorrect as compared to some normative or scientifically-based information. Second, misconceptions historically were recognized largely in science domains. Third, we draw our examples from science domains for which we have some data, primarily taken from concepts such as the *human circulatory system* and *heat transfer*. For the headings of the three subsections below, the first segment serves as a label for how knowledge is misconceived, the second segment describes the kind of conceptual change that can occur, and the third segment refers to the kind of confrontation and/or instruction that may produce conceptual change.

FALSE BELIEFS: BELIEF REVISION FROM REFUTATION

Students' prior knowledge can be represented at the grain size of a single idea, corresponding more-or-less to information specified in a single sentence or statement. We will refer to single ideas as "beliefs." As described earlier, students' prior beliefs can be *missing* or *incomplete*, but learning under these two conditions of prior knowledge would not constitute conceptual change, since missing beliefs can simply be added and gaps in incomplete beliefs can be filled. For example, a student might not know that *a human heart has four chambers*, and telling the student this piece of information would be *adding* to her prior beliefs. Similarly, a student might know that the upper chambers are called *atria,* but not that the lower chambers are called *ventricles.* Telling the student the name of the lower chambers can be thought of as *filling* a gap in her knowledge about the names of the chambers. We had a priori considered processes of adding and gap-filling as an enrichment kind of learning.

For conceptual change to occur, prior knowledge must conflict with new information. When prior knowledge conflicts with new information at the grain size of a single idea, we can refer to that idea as a *false belief*, as in incorrectly thinking that "the *heart* is responsible for reoxygenating blood" or that "*all* blood vessels have valves." Such false beliefs conflict with correct text sentences that describe the *lungs* as being responsible for oxygenating blood or only *veins* but not arteries as having valves (Chi, de Leeuw, Chiu, & LaVancher, 1994; Chi & Roscoe, 2002). Thus, false beliefs and correct information are in conflict in the sense that they *contradict* each other. For example, it is the *lungs* and not the *heart* that oxygenate blood.

If false beliefs and correct information conflict in the contradictory sense, then one would expect that designing instruction that is targeted at refuting false beliefs might succeed at correcting them, resulting in *belief revision*. It appears that this is true (Broughton, Sinatra, & Reynolds, 2007; Guzetti, Snyder, Glass, & Gamas, 1993). That is, false beliefs for some subject matter domains can be corrected when learners are explicitly confronted with the correct information by contradiction and refutation. In Chi and Roscoe (2002), we reported results by de Leeuw (1993) that focused on eighth-grade students' understanding of the circulatory system. In a pretest assessment, 12 students exhibited a total of 31 "stable" and unique false beliefs of the type exemplified above. As suggested by many others (Engel, Clough, & Driver, 1986; Licht & Thijs, 1990), by "stable," we mean false beliefs that were manifested consistently in students' explanations and answers on more than one occasion, so that they were not simply generated on-the-fly in the context of answering questions. We found that 71% of the 31 prior false beliefs were correctly revised if the text students subsequently read included sentences that directly refuted the false beliefs, such as mentioning that "only veins but not arteries have valves."

Moreover, the false beliefs exemplified above could be revised even when the text sentences did not refute them explicitly, as in directly denying the false beliefs. For example, the text did not explicitly say that "the heart does not oxygenate blood, only lungs do." Instead, the text merely provided the correct information that "the lungs oxygenate blood." Thus, even with such indirect implicit refutation, false beliefs about the circulatory system could be revised, even though they were "in conflict with" the correct information. Thus, we might conclude that conceptual change can sometimes be readily achieved, and it might be described as belief revision through explicit or implicit refutation of prior false beliefs. But such belief revision can be achieved only when misconceived knowledge conflicts in the *contradictory* sense.

There are many false beliefs in other domains that are not so readily revised by refutation at the grain size of a single idea. Consider, for example, false beliefs such as "a thrown object acquires or contains some internal force" or "coldness from the ice flows into the water, making the water colder." Although students can readily learn by *adding* new beliefs about "internal force," such as the equation for its relation to mass and acceleration, the definition of acceleration, and so on, these newly added beliefs cannot correct a student's false belief that "a thrown object acquires or contains some internal force." Moreover, such false beliefs cannot be easily denied or corrected by contradiction. For example, saying that "a thrown object does not acquire or contain internal forces" will not succeed in achieving correct understanding. This is because, as we will propose later, misconceptions about force and temperature/heat do not conflict with normative correct ideas in a *contradictory* sense. Before addressing how these misconceptions about force and heat are misconceived, we should consider misconceived knowledge at the next grain size.

Flawed Mental Models: Mental Model Transformation from Accumulation of Belief Revisions

An organized collection of individual beliefs can be viewed as forming a mental model. A mental model is an internal representation of a concept (such as the *earth*), or an inter-related system of concepts (such as the *circulatory system*) that corresponds in some way to the external structure that it represents (Gentner & Stevens, 1983). For example, mental models can be "run" mentally, much like an animated simulation, to depict changes and generate predictions and outcomes, such as the direction of blood flow. As with beliefs, a mental model can be "in conflict with" the correct scientific model to varying degrees, such as a *missing* or non-existing mental model, or an *incomplete* mental model. For example, some students' prior conceptions of the human circulatory system may be so sparse and disconnected that it is difficult to capture what, if any, structure their mental models have (Chi et al., 1994), so that we could not say whether or not their mental models are "in conflict with" the correct scientific model. In these cases of spare and incomplete mental models, learning would begin by *adding* and *filling* in missing components. Adding and gap-filling a mental model would not constitute conceptual change, by our definition.

In what other ways can mental models be "misconceived," so that learning is the conceptual change kind and not merely the enriching kind? Many of us have proposed that a learner's mental model conflicts with the correct scientific model when it is *flawed*. By flawed, we mean that it is coherent but incorrect (Chi, 2000; Chi et al., 1994; Vosniadou & Brewer, 1994), in the sense that the student can use the mental model to offer similar and consistently incorrect explanations and predictions in response to a variety of questions. The pattern and consistency of the generated explanations allow us to capture the structure of the flawed mental model (Chi et al., 1994; Vosniadou & Brewer, 1992, 1994). We can then validate the accuracy of the flawed mental model by predicting and testing how the student will respond to additional questions. For example, about half of the participants in our studies had an initial 'single-loop' model of the human circulatory system. According to this flawed model, blood goes to the heart to be oxygenated, then it is pumped to the rest of the body, then back to the heart. (In contrast, the correct "double-loop" model has two paths. One path leads from the heart to the lungs, where blood is oxygenated before returning to the heart. The second path leads from the heart to the rest of the body and back to the heart.) In order to confirm that our assessment of the flawed "single-loop" model is accurate, we can design additional questions to see if students will respond as expected, on the basis of the "single-loop" model.

In what way does a flawed "single-loop" model conflict with the correct "double-loop" model? The flawed "single-loop" model conflicts with the correct "double-loop" model in that it results in *different predictions* about where blood goes after it leaves the heart, *different explanations* with respect to where blood is oxygenated, and *different elements* in terms of whether or not lungs play an important role in oxygenation. Thus, we could say that two models are "in conflict with" each other if they make different predictions, generate different explanations, include different elements, and so forth. (Notice that these criteria of conflict — different predictions, different explanations, and different elements — are similar to the ones mentioned by Carey (1985) as compatible with the notion of "incommensurate" from the philosophy of science. In our framework here, we propose that these two conflicting models are not incommensurate and we would reserve the term "incommensurate" for knowledge that is "in conflict" either laterally or ontologically, to be discussed in the next grain size.)

Likewise, Vosniadou and Brewer (1992) have shown that young children have flawed mental models of the earth, including a flattened disk and a hollow sphere. Students with a flattened-disk model consistently say that the shape of the earth is round, that one should look down to see the earth, and that there is an edge from which people can potentially fall off. In short, flawed mental models are coherent in that students retrieve and use them consistently to answer questions and make predictions, allowing researchers to capture the structure of their mental models by analyzing the systematicity in the pattern of their responses (see also McCloskey, 1983; Samarapungavan & Wiers, 1997; Vosniadou & Brewer, 1992; Wiser, 1987). Thus, a flawed mental model "is in conflict" with the correct model in the sense that the two models generate different predictions and explanations and may contain different elements.

In the previous section, we concluded that refuting false beliefs with correct statements that contradicted those beliefs can lead to belief revision. In this section, we refer to successful modification of a flawed mental model as mental model *transformation*. But how should we design instruction to induce mental model transformation, given that we have defined conflicting models in terms of different predictions, explanations, and elements? Since mental models and correct models conflict at the mental model level (flat earth vs. spherical earth; single-loop vs. double-loop), a holistic confrontation may induce successful model transformation. One way to design a holistic confrontation might be to have students examine a visual depiction (e.g., a diagram) of the flawed mental model, then contrast it with a diagram of the correct model, in terms of the predictions, explanations and elements of each model. We are not aware of any instruction offering this kind of holistic confrontation, and we are conducting a study to address its feasibility.

Although we have described conflicting mental models at the mental-model level (such as a flat earth vs. a spherical earth and a single-loop vs. a double-loop), instruction to confront a flawed mental model typically occurs at the belief level. Typically, when a student reads a text, instruction consists of a description of the correct model, one sentence at a time. When a learner's flawed mental model is confronted with a description of the correct model presented one sentence at a time, each sentence can either refute (explicitly or implicitly) an existing belief or not, as discussed in the preceding section on *Belief Revision*.

From the perspective of a mental model, there are two possible outcomes when instruction is presented sentence-by-sentence. In the first case, information presented in a given sentence or sentences may not refute (explicitly or implicitly) any of the learner's prior beliefs. Instead, the information might be new or more elaborated than what the learner knows. In such a case, the learner can assimilate by embedding or *adding* the new information from the sentences into her existing flawed model, so that her mental model is enriched, but continues to be flawed. For example, in the case of a "single-loop" flawed model, learners assume that *blood from the heart goes to the rest of the body to deliver oxygen.* Such models lack the idea that blood also goes to the *lungs,* not to deliver oxygen but to receive oxygen. Upon reading a sentence such as "The right side [of the heart] pumps blood to the lungs and the left side pumps blood to other parts of the body," students with a "single-loop" model may not find it to contradict any beliefs in their flawed single-loop model, since they interpret the sentence to mean that the right side pumps blood to the lungs *to deliver oxygen* (rather than *to receive oxygen*), just as it does to the rest of the body. Therefore, even though at the mental model level, the sentence conflicts with the learner's flawed model, at the belief level, the sentence does not directly contradict the learner's prior beliefs. Thus the learner does not perceive a conflict, and the new information is assimilated into the flawed model (Chi, 2000). In short, assimilation of new information occurs when a learner does not perceive a conflict at the belief level, even though from the researcher's perspective, the new information is in conflict with the learner's flawed mental model.

The second possible outcome of sentence-by-sentence instruction is that new information presented does refute a learner's false beliefs and the learner recognizes the contradiction. Under such circumstances, as described in the preceding section, false beliefs that are explicitly or implicitly refuted do predominantly get revised. The relevant question with respect to mental models is: Does the accumulation of numerous belief revisions eventually result in the transformation of a student's flawed mental model to the correct model? The answer is *yes*, by-and-large.

According to our data, by reading and self-explaining a text passage about the human circulatory system, five of eight students (62.5%) with prior flawed "single-loop" model, transformed their flawed models to the correct model. Similarly, in Vosniadou and Brewer's (1992) data, 12 of 20 children (60%) developmentally acquired the correct spherical model of the earth by the fifth grade, suggesting that their flawed mental models had undergone transformation. In short, again, for domains such as the circulatory system and the earth, coherently flawed mental models can be successfully corrected and transformed into the correct model, in over 60% of the population, with either relatively brief instruction from text (in the case of the circulatory system) or from general development and learning in school (in the case of the earth). Thus, conceptual change can be achieved in that "in conflict" flawed mental models can be transformed into the correct model when false beliefs within a flawed model are refuted by instruction and recognized by students as contradictions, so that the students can self-repair their flawed mental models (Chi, 2000).

Whether or not flawed mental models are successfully transformed into the correct model also depends on whether some critical false beliefs are revised. That is, a flawed mental model is composed of many correct and many false beliefs. The incorrectness of the flawed mental model does not depend on the number of incorrect beliefs, but on the number of critical false beliefs. For example, across the various studies for which we have assessed students' initial mental models of the circulatory system, we found 22 students (about 50%) to have the flawed "single-loop" model prior to instruction. The number of correct beliefs held by these 22 students varied widely, ranging from 5 to 35. Five students held 10–15 correct beliefs, and 4 students held 25–35 correct beliefs, all embedded within the flawed "single-loop" model (see Figure 2 in Chi & Roscoe, 2002). This variability suggests that knowing and learning many correct beliefs does not guarantee successful transformation of a flawed mental model to the correct model. Some critical or important beliefs serve to discriminate a flawed model from a correct model (in terms of generating correct explanations and predictions), and these critical beliefs need to be revised.

To recap, students' knowledge consists of an interrelated system of false beliefs and correct beliefs, forming a coherent but sometimes flawed mental model. A flawed mental model can be said to conflict with a scientific model if it is incorrect but coherent, in the sense that it consistently leads to different predictions and explanations and contains different elements. During instruction, when a specific sentence contradicts a false belief through explicit or implicit refutation, such refutation can cause students to revise their false beliefs when they are aware of the contradictions. Without such awareness, students may assimilate instruction, especially for implicit contradictions. The accumulation of multiple belief revisions can lead eventually to a transformation of a flawed mental model to the correct model for over 60% of the students, either through direct instruction (in the case of the *circulatory system)* or from exposure to everyday experiences (as perhaps in the case of the *earth)*. For students whose flawed mental models were not correctly transformed, this may be due to a lack of awareness of contradictions, especially for critical false beliefs. There may be other ways to design instruction, such as holistic confrontation, that may encourage revision and reduce the likelihood of assimilation or *adding* to a flawed model, so that successful transformation can be achieved by all students.

Category Mistakes: Categorical Shift from Awareness and Building a New Category

The preceding sections described two grain sizes at which conceptual change is often achieved successfully. At the level of false beliefs, we found that refuting them can lead to belief revision. At the level of flawed mental models, multiple refutations can cause multiple belief revisions, the accumulation of which can result in transformation from a flawed mental model to the correct model for a majority of the students. However, we have also mentioned that there are numerous concepts (such as force and heat/temperature) across a variety of domains for which conceptual change cannot be achieved at the belief level. This section begins with an example of failure to transform a flawed mental model successfully, illustrating succinctly what robust misconceptions mean, in that they are *persistent and resistant* to conceptual change.

Robust Misconceptions: An Example

Law and Ogborne (1988) carried out a study in which students were asked to use Prolog to design and build a computational model of their own understanding of motion. The Prolog programming required students to express their ideas in propositional rule-based statements, which we can consider to be analogous to beliefs. Building and running such a model forced students to externalize and formalize their ideas, making them explicit, explorable and capable of offering explanations. Students assessed their models by running their programs, then made modifications based on program results or feedback from their instructor. Since programs could be run, allowing students to make predictions and observe outcomes, we can consider such a program to be analogous to an externalized mental model.

As with our circulatory system data, only some students had clear structural frameworks based on a core set of hypotheses about various aspects of motion that the researchers could identify. We can consider these students as having flawed but coherent mental models. Other students had no clear conceptualization, and these students can be deemed to have missing or incomplete models. For students with coherent but flawed mental models, the question is, can they change their flawed mental model? One way to determine whether they change their mental model is to see whether they change their *implicit* core hypotheses or misconceptions, which include the following set of false beliefs:

a. Force is the deciding factor in determining all aspects of motion;
b. Force is *an entity* which can be possessed, transferred, and dissipated (rather than an interaction);
c. All motions need causes;
d. Agents cause and control motion by acting as *sources* that supply force;
e. Sources that supply force can be internal or external, and the supplied force is referred to as an internal or external force;
f. Weight is an intrinsic property of an object (even though gravity is conceptualized as an external factor that pulls harder on heavier objects).

This set of core hypotheses about force and motion are compatible with various other analyses of students' misconceptions about force and motion in the literature.

The advantage of the Prolog programming environment is that it allowed students to explore the consequences of their externalized beliefs or rules. For example, one student who held the core hypothesis d, that there is a *source* that supplies the force for every motion, wrote the following Prolog rules for determining the cause of motion:

1. _object motion-caused-by itself if _object force-supplied-by _object
2. _object motion-caused-by machine if _object force-supplied-by machine
3. _object1 motion-caused-by _object2 if _object1 force-supplied-by _object2
4. _object motion-caused-by gravity if not (_object under-the-influence-of other-external-force).

She then tested her program for the cause of a falling apple, expecting the computer to say that the motion was caused by gravity (her fourth rule). The reason was that in one of her earlier sessions, she included weight as an external supply of force, along with other forces such as friction and air current. The program's outcome can be thought of as providing explicit refutation of her fourth rule.

When she did not get the result she expected, she modified her fourth rule by excluding gravity as an external force. After this patching, the computer still did not give her the expected answer of gravity as a cause of the apple's fall, since anything placed in air would be affected by air-current, since air current is an external force. She then revised her fourth rule again to read: _object motion-caused by gravity if not (_object motion-caused-by _something). Her problems continued even after various patchings of her other rules.

This example illustrates the point that, despite numerous revisions in response to refutations at the rule or belief level, the revisions and the accumulation of multiple patches did not transform her flawed mental model into a correct model, in that the *implicit* underlying core hypotheses of her program (or misconceptions) were not changed. That is, she still assumed that all motions need causes (hypothesis c), that agents cause and control motion by acting as sources that supply force (hypothesis d), and so forth. As this example illustrates, the student was not resistant to change per se, since she readily revised her rules, but the multiple belief revisions she did undertake did not add up to a correct model transformation since the revisions did not change her underlying core hypotheses.

In short, there are many domains and concepts for which one's initial flawed mental model is not transformed to the correct model, despite repeated corrections or patchings at the individual belief level. This example shows that, even though the student willingly modified individual rules or beliefs as a result of external feedback (or explicit refutation from the program's outcomes), the revised beliefs, cumulatively, did not transform the mental model into the correct model, in that the implicit underlying core hypotheses were still incorrect. Thus, the flawed model was resistant to change. (There are occasions, of course, when students themselves resist making changes by dismissing the feedback or explaining it away. The point here is that, even with the best of intentions and willingness to change, this student could not transform her misconceived view.)

What should we conclude? This suggests that, for robust misconceptions, refutation at the belief or mental-model level is not the right grain size to achieve conceptual change. In such cases, we propose that instruction be designed to target conceptual change at a different grain size, at the categorical level.

CONFLICT BETWEEN LATERAL CATEGORIES

Findings similar to the Law and Ogborne's (1988) study have been documented for several decades, and we can refer to it as the *robust misconception* problem. That is, many misconceptions are not only "in conflict" with the correct scientific conceptions, but moreover, they are robust in that the misconceptions are difficult to revise, so conceptual change is not achieved. The robustness of misconceptions has been demonstrated in literally thousands of studies, about all kinds of science concepts and phenomena, beginning with a book by Novak (1977) and a review by Driver and Easley (1978), both published almost three decades ago. By 2004, there were over 6,000 publications describing students' ideas and instructional attempts to change them (Confrey, 1990; Driver, Squires, Rushworth, & Wood-Robinson, 1994; Duit, 2004; Ram, Nersessian, & Keil, 1997), indicating that conceptual understanding in the presence of misconceptions remains a challenging problem. The daunting task of building conceptual understanding in the presence of robust misconceptions is sometimes referred to as *radical* conceptual change (Carey, 1985). We propose the operational definition that certain misconceptions are robust because they have been mistakenly assigned to an inappropriate lateral category.

Our claim, then, is that some false beliefs and flawed mental models are robustly resistant to change because they have been laterally or ontologically miscategorized. That is, if a misconception belongs to one category and the correct conception belongs to another lateral or ontological category, then they conflict by definition of *kind* and/or *ontology*. This means that conceptual change requires a shift across lateral or ontological categories. In order to support this claim, we have to characterize the nature of misconceptions and the nature of correct information to see whether they in fact belong to two categories that differ either in *kind* or in *ontology*, thereby being "in conflict."

The Lateral Categories to which Misconceptions and Correct Conceptions are Assigned

In order to characterize the nature of misconceptions in terms of the category to which they have been mistakenly assigned, and also to characterize the nature of scientific conceptions in terms of the category to which they have been assigned, we analyzed students' causal explanations of a variety of science concepts, consolidated researchers' findings on misconceptions, and examined the history and philosophy of science literature. In particular, we examined the extent to which robust misconceptions reflect common implicit core hypotheses, as exemplified by the ideas about force and motion listed earlier. From such core hypotheses, we induced the properties of the mistaken category that they characterized. We then determined the lateral category into which correct scientific conceptions fall. We illustrate below two sets of conflicting lateral categories that we have identified: the conflict between two ontological trees — *Entities* (the misconceived view) and *Processes* (*the correct* view), and the conflict between two branches within the *Process* tree, *direct* processes (the misconceived view) and *emergent* processes (the correct view).

Entities Versus Processes

Entities are *objects* or *substances* that have various attributes and behave in various ways (see Figure 3.1, the *Entities* tree). For example, a ball is a physical object with attributes such as mass and volume, and behaviors such as bouncing and rolling. In reviewing students' explanations for four science concepts — force, heat, electricity, and light — we arrived at the commonality that students mistakenly categorize these concepts as *Entities*. On the basis of our analyses across these four concepts, we proposed that misconceptions for some concepts are *Entity*-based (Reiner, Slotta, Chi, & Resnick, 2000). For example, Law and Ogborne's (1988) hypothesis b, described above, indicates that many students view force as a *substance*-kind of *Entity* that can be possessed, transferred and dissipated. Students often explain that a moving object slows down because it has "used up all its force" (McCloskey, 1983), as if force were like a fuel that is consumed. Similarly, students think of heat as physical *objects* such as "hot molecules" or a *material substance* such as "hot stuff" or "hotness" (Wiser & Amin, 2001), as indicated by phrases such as "molecules of heat" or expressions such as "Close the door, you're letting all the heat out." The misconception is that heat can be "contained," as if it were *objects* like marbles or *substances* such as sand or water. In either case, heat is misconceived as a kind of *Entity*.

Not only do such *Entity*-based misconceptions occur for a variety of concepts across a variety of disciplines, but they are held across grade levels, from elementary to college students (Chi, Slotta, & de Leeuw, 1994), as well as across historical periods (Chi, 1992). They may even account for barriers that were only overcome by scientific discoveries (Chi & Hausmann, 2003). In short, robust misconceptions are extremely resistant to change, so that everyday experiences encountered during developmental maturation and formal schooling seem powerless to change them (in contrast to the success with which a majority of flawed mental models can be transformed from everyday experiences or formal schooling, as described earlier).

How are *Entity*-based misconceptions in conflict with scientific conceptions? Our initial conjecture was that scientists view many of these concepts not as *Entities*, but as *Processes*, an ontological tree distinct from *Entities*, verifiable by the predicate test (see Figure 3.1). For example, heat or the sensation of "hotness," is the speed at which molecules jostle: the faster the speed, the "hotter" the molecules feel. Thus, heat is not "hot molecules" or "hot stuff" (an *Entity*), but more accurately, the *speed* of molecules (a *Process*).

The naïve conception of the term "heat" is that it's like "hotness." "Hotness," as we illustrated above, refers to molecular motion, and motion is a *Process*. But the technical term *heat*, although a noun, actually refers not just to the motion of the molecules, but to the transfer of "hotness." That is, *heat* is defined as "the transfer of energy" or *energy in transit from one object or substance to another*, and is therefore a *Process*. The use of a noun to represent a transfer process, and defining heat as the transfer of *energy*, which is also a noun, is unfortunate, because such terminology encourages students to maintain their misconceptions since they can continue to conceive of the term "energy" as a kind of *substance*. In other words, robust misconceptions cannot be easily refuted by merely presenting scientific information in technical terms.

Direct Versus Emergent

Although we were able to explain a good deal of robust misconceptions as category errors involving the ontological trees *Entities* and *Processes* (Chi, 1997), our explanation for the robustness of many misconceptions was incomplete. Whether or not students conceive of heat as an *Entity*, most students nevertheless do recognize that heat transfer is a *Process* because they have experienced the apparent movement of "hotness" from one location to another, for example, from a warm cup to cold hands. Thus, characterizing heat misconceptions as *Entity*-based does not adequately explain why students have difficulty understanding heat transfer. To explain the latter kind of misconceptions, we had to propose conflicts between two additional kinds of lateral categories within the *Process* tree, which we have called *direct* and *emergent* (Chi, 2005). Our claim is that *students* misconceive of some processes as *direct* kinds when in fact they are *emergent* kinds. Table 3.1a and Table 3.1b list two sets of mutually exclusive properties for *emergent* and *direct* processes.

Briefly, a *direct* process is one that usually has an identifiable agent that causes some outcome in a sequential and dependent sort of way. We will describe an everyday example, a less familiar example, and a scientific example, highlighting with each example properties of *emergent* and *direct* processes, as listed in Table 3.1a and Table 3.1b.

Direct Example 1.   In the familiar process of a baseball game, the final outcome might be explained as being due to the excellent work of the pitcher, thus attributing the outcome to a single agent (*Direct* property #1) that has special status (*Direct* property #2). Moreover, the behavior of local events within the game corresponds to or aligns with the global outcome. For example, a team with many home runs in a game is more likely to win. Thus, home runs are positive local events and they align with the positive global outcome of winning the game (*Direct* property #3).

TABLE 3.1A
Five Inter-level Properties Characterizing the Relationship Between the Agent (micro) Level and the Pattern (macro) Level

Emergent Causal Explanations	*Direct Causal Explanations*
1. The entire collection or **all** the agents together "cause" the observable global pattern	1. A **single** agent or a **subgroup** of agents can "cause" the global observable pattern
2. All agents have **equal status** with respect to the pattern	2. One or more agents have **special status** with respect to the pattern
3. Local events and the global pattern can behave in **disjoint** non-matching ways	3. Local events and the global pattern behave in a **corresponding** matched way
4. Agents interact to intentionally achieve **local goals**; ignorant of the global pattern	4. Some agents interact to intentionally achieve the **global goal** and direct their interactions at producing the global pattern
5. Mechanism producing the global pattern: **proportional change** (collective summing across time)	5. Mechanism producing the global pattern: **incremental change** (additive summing across time)

TABLE 3.1B
Five Micro-level Properties Characterizing the Relationship Among Agents' Interaction
in an Emergent and a Direct Process

Interactions among Agents in an Emergent Process	Interactions among Agents in a Direct Process
6. All agents behave in more-or-less the same **uniform** way	6. Agents behave in **distinct** ways
7. All agents interact **randomly** with other agents	7. Agents can interact with predetermined or **restricted** others
8. All agents interact **simultaneously**	8. Agents interact **sequentially**
9. All agents interact **independently** of one another	9. Agents' interactions **depend** on other agents' interactions
10. Interactions among agents are **continuous**	10. Agents' interactions **terminate** when the pattern-level behavior stops

Direct Example 2.   A slightly less familiar example is seeing multiple airplanes flying in a V-formation. This V-pattern is intentional, created by the lead pilot telling the other pilots where to fly in order to achieve the global goal (*Direct* property #4).

Direct Example 3.   A direct process from biology is cell division, which proceeds through a sequence of three stages. The first, interphase, is a period of cell growth. This is followed by mitosis, the division of the cell nucleus, and then cytokinesis, the division of the cytoplasm of a parent cell into two daughter cells. In each phase, the cells behave in distinct ways, either growing or dividing (*Direct* property #6). Such a process has a definite sequence, in which some events cannot occur until others are completed (*Direct* properties #8 and #9).

In contrast, *emergent* processes have neither an identifiable causal agent or agents nor an identifiable sequence of stages. Rather, the outcome results from the collective and simultaneous interactions of all agents. Let's consider three examples here as well.

Emergent Example 1.   The process of a crowd forming a bottleneck, as when the school bell rings and students hurry to get through the narrow classroom door, is an everyday example of an *emergent* process. Although there is an external trigger (the school bell), the global outcome of forming the bottleneck cannot be attributed to any single agent or group of agents, and the process is not sequential. Instead, all the students (*Emergent* property #1) simultaneously (*Emergent* property #8) rush toward the door at about the same speed (*Emergent* property #6), shoving and bumping randomly into whichever student happens to be in the way (*Emergent* property #7).

Emergent Example 2.   A slightly less familiar example is migrating geese flying in a V-formation. In contrast to the airplane example, the V-pattern is not caused by the leader goose telling other geese where to fly. Instead, all the geese are doing the same thing, flying slightly behind another goose because instinctually they seek the area of least resistance. Thus, they are pursuing the local goal of flying with minimal effort (*Emergent* property #4), ignorant of the pattern they form. When all the geese do the same thing at the same time, collectively, a V-pattern emerges (*Emergent* properties #1, #2, #6, and #8).

Emergent Example 3.   An emergent process from biology is the diffusion of oxygen from the lungs to the blood vessels. This process is caused by all the oxygen and carbon dioxide molecules moving and colliding randomly with and independently of each other (*Emergent* properties #6, #7, #8, and #9). From such random collisions, a greater number of oxygen molecules are likely to move from the lungs to the blood than from the blood to the lungs, simply because there are a greater number of them in the lungs than in the blood. The reverse is true for carbon dioxide molecules. Since all molecules move and collide randomly, both kinds of molecules move in both directions, so that some oxygen molecules do move from the blood to the lungs, and some carbon dioxide molecules do move from the lungs to the blood. Thus, the local movements of individual molecules may not match the direction of the movement of the majority of the molecules, thus causing the observed pattern (*Emergent* property #3). Nevertheless, despite local variations, the majority of oxygen molecules move from the lungs to the blood, and the majority of carbon dioxide molecules move in the opposite direction, without any specific intention to move in that global direction (*Emergent* property #4).

To return to our heat example, the technical term "heat" actually refers to the "transfer of hotness." The sensation of hotness moving from one area to another area is understood correctly by students as a *Process*. However, this process is not a *direct* process in that the sensation of hotness moving is not caused by hot molecules moving from one location to another. Rather, the transfer is caused by the collisions of faster jostling "hotter" molecules into slower-moving molecules. That is, when faster-moving molecules bombard slower-moving molecules, it causes the faster-moving molecules to slow down (thus decreasing their hotness) and the slower-moving molecules to move faster (thus increasing their hotness). This is how hotness is transferred. Thus, heat transfer is an *emergent* process. These two sets of examples illustrate general differences between *direct* and *emergent* processes. A more detailed description is provided in Chi (2005).

BEYOND REFUTATION

If misconceptions occur as the result of category mistakes, then instruction needs to focus at the categorical level. When students' misconceived ideas conflict with correct ideas at the lateral category level, then refutation at the belief level will not promote conceptual change, as was shown in the Law and Ogborne study. This is because refutation at the belief level can only cause local revisions at the belief level and not categorical shift. Consider the false belief that "coldness from the ice flows into the water, making the water colder." Essentially, this misconception assumes that ice contains some "cold substance" like tiny cold molecules (the reverse of hot objects, which are often misconceived as containing "hot molecules"), and that this "cold substance" can flow into the surrounding water, which then makes the water colder. To refute this misconception at the belief level, we might point out that ice does not contain a cold substance, that coldness does not flow, and that water does not get colder because it gains coldness. Refutation at the belief level only works when a false belief and the correct conception contradict each other. Moreover, belief level refutation tends to be partial in that many elements of the false beliefs are maintained. For example, it was straightforward to entertain the alternative belief that *lungs* are the source of oxygenation and not the *heart,* because only one element of the false belief had to be changed while many other elements (the concept of oxygenation, etc.) were maintained. But how can a false belief like "ice contains cold substances" be changed? Should a student expect ice to contain an alternative kind of substance if not a "cold" substance? The revision that a student must make has to do with the property "contain," not the feature "coldness" or any other kind of substance. To confront the property "contain" means to confront students at the ontological/categorical level, since "contain" is a property of *Entities* and not *Processes*.

What about at the mental model level? Suppose we think of the ice and water as a system. The misconception is that coldness flows into the water as a *direct* process. Again, where do we begin in terms of either multiple belief-level refutations or holistic confrontation? We will likely achieve only local patchings, as in the Prolog example, because the core hypotheses underlying the mental model are not addressed. The model transformations that were obtained in connection with the circulatory system and the shape of the earth were transformations that occurred within the same ontology. We propose that, in order to achieve radical conceptual change, we need students to make a category shift by reassigning a concept to another lateral category. To do so, we need to confront students at the categorical level.

How Can We Achieve Shifts Across Lateral or Ontological Categories?

Shifting across lateral categories, in the sense of reassigning a concept from one lateral/ontological category to another, can in principle be straightforward and easily achieved for certain misconceptions. Let's take an everyday example to illustrate the ease of such a shift. Suppose a young child sees a *whale* in the ocean and believes it to be a kind of *fish,* since *whales* possess many perceptual features of a *fish*, such as look like sharks and swim in water. Based on that mistaken categorization, the child will likely assume that *whales*, like other *fish*, breathe through gills through osmosis (a conceptual attribute). To promote conceptual change, we might provide belief-level refutation, pointing out that *whales do not breathe through gills, but through a blowhole*. The child may accept this instruction and revise her false belief about gills, but still continue to implicitly assume that whales are *fish* (rather than *mammals*). Assuming that *fish* and *mammals* are lateral categories that differ in *kind*, maintaining that whales are *fish* will cause the child to have difficulty understanding subsequent instruction or answering questions such as: "Why do sharks suffocate when you take them out of the water, but whales do not?" This example illustrates that, when a category mistake is refuted at the belief level, the belief revision results in superficial or shallow understanding only, since the conception is still fundamentally wrong at the categorical level. Any deep explanations offered in response to more complicated questions will continue to be wrong.

However, confronting misconceptions at the categorical level seems straightforward enough for simple concepts such as *whales*. If a child is simply told explicitly that whales are *mammals* rather than *fish,* she might then be able to explain (or at least understand) why whales do not suffocate on land. The fact that most children eventually learn that *whales* are *mammals* (thereby "*whales are fish*" is not a robust misconception) suggests that lateral categorical shifts can occur readily for certain concepts, perhaps even without explicit refutation. But why is categorical shift not easily achieved for robust misconceptions of the *heat* kind?

Although, to our knowledge, no research has investigated confrontation at the categorical level, a closer examination of the relative ease of categorical shift for the *whale* example, suggests that two instructional steps are needed in order to overcome barriers to conceptual change for robust misconceptions. First, students have to be aware that they have made a category mistake, which amounts to confronting their ideas at the categorical level; and second, students must be knowledgeable about the category to which a concept actually belongs. We briefly discuss these two steps below.

Awareness

Shifting across lateral categories per se is not a difficult learning mechanism from a computational perspective or from everyday evidence as illustrated by the *whale* example and by the ease with which people can understand metaphors. For example, metaphors often invoke a predicate from one category and a concept from a lateral category, often from different ontological trees. For instance, *anger* (a *Mental State*) is often treated as a *substance* (an *Entity*) that can be contained, as in "He let out his anger" or "I can barely contain my rage" (Lakoff, 1987). We propose that part of the difficulty of shifting categories for many science concepts has to do with lack of awareness, in that students do not realize that they have to shift their assignment of a concept to a different category. This is because reassigning a phenomenon or concept from one kind to another kind is a low frequency occurrence in everyday life. That is, students do not routinely need to re-categorize, such as shifting a whale from *fish* to *mammal*. This is because, in our everyday environment, our initial categorizations are mostly correct, since they are based on outward perceptual features. For example, when we identify a furry object with a wagging tail that responds to our commands as a real live dog (thus an *animal*), we are almost never wrong, in the sense that it is actually a stuffed dog (thus an *artifact*). The fact that these category mistakes rarely occur in real life makes it difficult for learners to recognize that their understanding or lack of understanding of new concepts may originate from a category error at the lateral level. As with metaphors, the rarity of category mistakes is a ploy that is sometimes used in stories and films to produce interest, drama and suspense, such as in the children's novel *Velveteen Rabbit*. Moreover, if people do make category mistakes, especially across ontological trees, such as confusing reality (either *Entities* or *Processes*) with imagination *(Mental States)*, it is considered bizarre and perhaps a sign of psychological illness.

The rarity of category mistakes in real life also reinforces the strength of commitment to the original category to which a concept is assigned, as well as to the boundary between lateral categories. For example, even four-year-olds treat *living beings* as fundamentally different from *artifacts*, in that they rarely associate *artifacts* with *animal* or human properties (Carey, 1985; Chi, 1988). The commitment to a particular category occurs even as early as age five. Once a concept is categorized, young children are extremely reluctant to change the category to which it is assigned. Keil's work (1989) has shown that, no matter what physical alterations are made to an object (such as a real dog), such as shaving off its fur, replacing its tail, and so on, five-year-olds will not accept such changes as capable of transforming a real dog to a toy dog (thus crossing the boundary between lateral categories *animals* and *artifacts*). However, they will agree that, with appropriate alterations such as replacing black fur with brown fur, one can transform a skunk into a raccoon. This is because skunks and raccoons belong to the same *mammal* category. Thus, once assigned, even five-year-olds honor the boundary between *kinds* and remain committed to the category to which they have assigned a concept.

Even though miscategorization is rare in everyday life, our proposal is that it is the fundamental source of robust misconceptions in science. That is, many phenomena in science look and act like they belong to one category rather than another. For example, geese flying in a V-formation (*Emergent* Example 2) looks like airplanes flying in a V-formation (*Direct* Example 2), heat flowing into a cool room feels like water flowing down a stream. However, the causal explanations for the similar patterns are distinctly different. Thus, learners can be misled by perceptual similarities and treat such pairs of phenomena as having the same causal explanations, resulting in miscategorization of one but not the other. Therefore, students must be made aware of their miscategorization and must learn to discriminate between the two kinds of phenomena. In short, the lack of awareness of the need to shift categories laterally is due to the low frequency of such shifts in the real world and to superficial similarities among many phenomena. Instruction aimed at promoting such shifts must begin by making students aware that they have committed category mistakes.

Building a New Lateral Category

In our hypothetical *whale* example, it seemed relatively easy for children to shift categories simply by being told that whales are *mammals*. Why is this category shift so easy to implement?

Would science students find it easy to shift categories if we simply told them that heat transfer is an *emergent* rather than a *direct* process? The answer is no, obviously, because students are ignorant of the *emergent* category. That is, we assume that an *emergent process* category is not familiar and available to students and therefore they cannot assimilate novel concepts into it. This missing category situation is tractable and suggests an instructional approach of building such a category. Thus, instruction to promote categorical shift must also include instruction about *emergence*. Our prediction is that, to achieve successful conceptual change for robustly misconceived concepts, we need to first teach students the properties of such a category, which is uniquely distinct from the lateral category with which they are familiar and to which they have mistakenly assigned concepts, such as *direct* processes. Once students have successfully built such a lateral category with its distinct set of properties (as shown in Table 3.1a & Table 3.1b), they can begin to assimilate new instruction (for example, about heat transfer) into the category. Preliminary successes using this method have been shown in Slotta, Chi and Joram (1995), and Slotta and Chi (2006). Descriptions of our current successful attempt is forthcoming (Chi, Roscoe, Slotta, Roy, & Chase, submitted).

CAVEATS ABOUT THE ROLE OF REFUTATION IN HIERARCHICAL AND LATERAL CATEGORIES

This chapter addresses the problem of learning for which prior knowledge conflicts with to-be-learned information. This kind of learning is considered the conceptual change kind rather than the enrichment kind. We propose that prior knowledge can be in conflict with to-be-learned information in three ways. First, at a belief level, prior knowledge can be incorrect or false and conflict with correct information in the contradictory sense. In such cases, conceptual change can be achieved by refuting (implicitly or explicitly) the false beliefs, and this can lead to belief revision in some domains of science. Second, at a mental-model level, prior knowledge can be incorrect and conflict with correct information in the coherent-but-flawed sense. In such cases, conceptual change can be achieved by refuting multiple false beliefs within a flawed mental model, especially the critical ones. The cumulative effect of many such belief revisions will transform a flawed mental model into the correct model.

However, three caveats need to be noted about the success of these types of refutations for belief revisions and mental model transformations. First and foremost, the success of these two types of conceptual change hinges on the assumption that the misconception and the correct conception are assigned into the same category or hierarchical categories, as shown in the left branch of Figure 3.2. An example might be mistaking the heart as the source of oxygenation rather than the lungs. Moreover, this kind of refutation can be effective whether presented implicitly or explicitly. Finally, the refutation maintains many of the elements of the misconceptions, whether false beliefs or flawed mental models. For example, in contradicting that the *heart* is the source of oxygenation, we maintained many elements of the false belief and the flawed mental model, such as that *blood is the medium of transporting oxygen and carbon dioxide*, that *oxygen needs to be replenished in the blood,* and so on. In short, the success of belief revision and mental model transformation is domain- and concept-specific. Thus, for concepts such as *heart* versus *lungs* as sources of oxygenation with systems such as *blood circulation*, misconceptions are *within the same hierarchical branch of an ontological tree* as the correct conceptions.

For misconceptions that are categorically misassigned between lateral branches or ontological trees (as shown in the right branch of Figure 3.2), we assume that this happens because learners cannot tell what category the to-be-assigned concept belongs or because they do not have the category to which the new concept should be assigned. Either way, conceptual change requires a

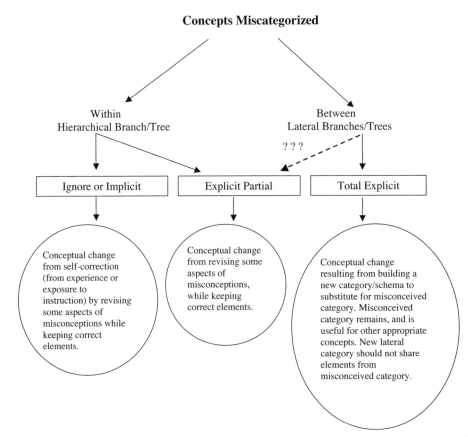

FIGURE 3.2   The type of instruction needed (rectangles) and the processes and types of conceptual change achieved (ovals) depend on how misconceptions are miscategorized.

categorical shift. Such a shift necessitates that the learner is aware that the shift is needed and that the correct category is available. For many robust misconceptions in science, the lateral category to which misconceptions have to be reassigned, *emergent processes,* does not exist in students' knowledge base, so instruction has to build a new category. Because *emergent* and *direct* processes are different in *kind*, with mutually exclusive properties, confrontation needs to reject the misassigned category and build the alternative *emergence* category, perhaps through direct instruction using contrasting cases (see Chi, Roscoe, Slotta, Roy, & Chase, submitted). Of course, the original *direct process* category can remain, as it is important for understanding other *direct processes*. In short, it is difficult to imagine how robust misconceptions can be corrected at a deep level if one maintains many elements of the misconceptions, as in approaches that call for integrating ideas or elements of misconceptions with correct science conceptions. This integrating approach is somewhat analogous to our "explicit partial refutation" approach, shown in Figure 3.2. We denote our skepticism by using a dotted line and question marks to link robust misconceptions with this type of instructional approach to achieve conceptual change, as shown in Figure 3.2.

ACKNOWLEDGMENTS

The author is grateful for funding and support provided by the Spencer Foundation (Grant 200100305). The author will be a professor at Arizona State Universitiy, effective August, 2008.

REFERENCES

Barsalou, L. W. (1983). Ad-hoc categories. *Memory and Cognition, 11*, 211–227.

Bransford, J., Brown, A., & Cocking, R. (Eds.). (1999). *How people learn: Brain, mind, experience, and school.* Washington, DC: National Academy Press.

Broughton, S. H., Sinatra, G. M., & Reynolds, R. E. (2007). The refutation text effect: Influence on learning and attention. Paper presented at the Annual Meeting of the Americal Educational Researchers Association, Chicago, Illinois.

Carey, S. (1985). *Conceptual change in childhood.* Cambridge, MA: MIT Press.

Carey, S. (1991). Knowledge acquisition: Enrichment or conceptual change? In S.Carey & R. Gelman (Eds.), *The epigenesis of mind* (pp. 257–291). Hillsdale: NJ: Erlbaum.

Chi, M. T. H. (1988). Children's lack of access and knowledge reorganization: An example from the concept of animism. In F. Weinert & M. Perlmutter (Eds.), *Memory Development: Universal Changes and Individual Differences* (pp. 169–194). Hillsdale, NJ: Erlbaum.

Chi, M. T. H. (1992). Conceptual change within and across ontological categories: Examples from learning and discovery in science. In R. Giere (Ed.), *Cognitive Models of Science: Minnesota Studies in the Philosophy of Science* (pp. 129–186). Minneapolis: University of Minnesota Press:

Chi, M. T. H. (1997). Creativity: Shifting across ontological categories flexibly. In T. B. Ward, S. M. Smith, & J. Vaid (Eds.), *Conceptual Structures and Processes: Emergence, Discovery and Change.* (pp. 209–234) Washington, DC: American Psychological Association.

Chi, M. T. H. (2000). Cognitive understanding levels. In A.E . Kazdin (Ed.), *Encyclopedia of psychology* (Vol. 2, pp. 146–151. Washington, DC: American Psychological Association.

Chi, M. T. H. (2005). Common sense conceptions of emergent processes: Why some misconceptions are robust. *Journal of the Learning Sciences, 14*, 161–199.

Chi, M. T. H., de Leeuw, N., Chiu, M. H., & LaVancher, C. (1994). Eliciting self-explanations improves understanding. *Cognitive Science, 18,* 439–477.

Chi, M. T. H., Feltovich, P., & Glaser, R. (1981). Categorization and representation of physics problems by experts and novices**.** *Cognitive Science, 5,* 121–152**.**

Chi, M. T. H., & Hausmann, R. G. M. (2003). Do radical discoveries require ontological shifts? In L. V. Shavinina (Ed.) *International Handbook on Innovation* (pp. 430–444). Oxford: Pergamon.

Chi, M. T. H., & Koeske, R. (1983). Network representation of a child's dinosaur knowledge. *Developmental Psychology, 19,* 29–39.

Chi, M. T. H., & Roscoe, R. (2002). The processes and challenges of conceptual change. In M. Limon & L. Mason (Eds.), *Reframing the process of conceptual change: Integrating theory and practice* (pp. 3–27). Dordrecht, The Netherlands: Kluwer.

Chi, M. T. H., Roscoe, R., Slotta, J. D., Roy, M., & Chase, C. (submitted). Domain-general qualitative understanding of emergence transfers to learing of specific science concepts. Submitted to *The Journal of the Learning Sciences.*

Chi, M. T. H., Slotta, J. D., & de Leeuw, N. (1994). From things to processes: A theory of conceptual change for learning science concepts. *Learning and Instruction, 4,* 27–43.

Confrey, J. (1990). A review of the research on student conceptions in mathematics, science and programming. In C. B. Cazden (Ed.), *Review of research in education.* Washington, DC: American Educational Research Association.

de Leeuw, N. (1993). Students' beliefs about the circulatory system: Are misconceptions universal? In *Proceedings of the Fifteenth Annual Conference of the Cognitive Science Society* (pp. 389–393). Hillsdale, NJ: Erlbaum.

Driver, R., & Easley, J. (1978). Pupils and paradigms: A review of literature related to concept development in adolescent science students. *Studies in Science Education, 5,* 61–84.

Driver, R., Squires, A., Rushworth, P., & Wood-Robinson, V. (1994). *Making sense of secondary science.* London: Routledge.

Duit, R. (2004). *Bibliography: Students' and teachers' conceptions and science education database.* Kiel, Germany: University of Kiel.

Engel Clough, E., & Driver, R. (1986). A study of consistency in the use of students' conceptual framework across different task contexts. *Science Eduction, 70,* 473–493.

Gelman, S. (1988). The development of induction within natural kind and artifact categories. *Cognitive Psychology, 20,* 65–95.

Gentner, D., & Stevens, A. L. (Eds.). (1983). *Mental models.* Hillsdale, NJ: Erlbaum.

Gobbo, C., & Chi, M. T. H. (1986). How knowledge is structured and used by expert and novice children. *Cognitive Development, 1,* 221–237.

Guzetti, B. J., Snyder, T. E., Glass, G. V., & Gamas, W. S. (1993). Meta-analysis of instructional interventions from reading education and science education to promote conceptual change in science. *Reading Research Quarterly, 28,* 116–161.

Jackendoff, R. (1989). What is a concept, that a person may grasp it? *Mind and Language, 4,* 68–102.

Keil, F. (1979). *Semantic and conceptual development: An ontological perspective.* Cambridge, MA: Harvard University Press.

Keil, F. (1981). Constraints on knowledge and cognitive development. *Psychological Review, 88,* 197–227.

Keil, F. (1989). *Concepts, kinds, and cognitive development.* Cambridge, MA: MIT Press.

Lakoff, G. (1987). *Women, Fire, and Dangerous Things: What categories reveal about the mind.* Chicago: University of Chicago Press.

Law, N., & Ogborne, J. (1988). Students as expert system developers: A means of eliciting and understanding commonsense reasoning. *Journal of Research on Computing in Education, 26,* 497–514.

Licht, P., & Thijs, G. D. (1990). Method to trace coherence and consistency of preconceptions. *International Journal of Science Education, 12,* 403–416.

McCloskey, M. (1983). Naïve theories of motion. In D. Gentner & A. L. Stevens (Eds.), *Mental models,* (pp. 299–324). Hillsdale, NJ: Erlbaum.

Medin, D. L., & Rips, L. J. (2005) Concepts and categories: Memory, meaning, and metaphysics. In K. J. Holyoak & R. G. Morrison (Eds.), *The Cambridge handbook of thinking and reasoning* (pp. 37–72). New York: Cambridge University Press.

Novak, J. (1977). *A theory of education.* Ithaca, NY: Cornell University Press.

Ram, A., Nersessian, N. J., & Keil, F. C. (1997). Special issue: Conceptual change. *The Journal of the Learning Sciences, 6,* 1–91.

Reiner, M., Slotta, J. D., Chi, M. T. H., & Resnick, L. B. (2000). Naive physics reasoning: A Commitment to substance-based conceptions. *Cognition and Instruction, 18,* 1–34.

Samarapungavan, A., & Wiers, R. W. (1997). Children's thoughts on the origin of species: A study of explanatory coherence. *Cognitive Science, 21,* 147–177.

Schwartz, S. P. (1977). *Naming, necessity, and natural kinds.* Ithaca, NY: Cornell University Press.

Slotta, J. D., & Chi, M.T.H. (2006). The impact of ontology training on conceptual change: Helping students understand the challenging topics in science. *Cognition and Instruction, 24,* 261–289.

Slotta, J. D., Chi, M.T.H., & Joram, E. (1995). Assessing students' misclassifications of physics concepts: An ontological basis for conceptual change. *Cognition and Instruction, 13,* 373–400.

Sommers, F. (1971). Structural ontology. *Philosophia, 1,* 21–42.

Thagard, P. (1990). Concepts and conceptual change. *Syntheses, 82,* 255–274.

Vosniadou, S. (2004). Extending the conceptual change approach to mathematics learning and teaching. *Learning and Instruction, 14,* 445–451.

Vosniadou, S., & Brewer, W. (1992). Mental models of the earth: A study of conceptual change in childhood. *Cognitive Psychology, 24,* 535–585.

Vosniadou, S., & Brewer, W. (1994). Mental models of the day/night cycle. *Cognitive Science, 18,* 123–183.

Wiser, M. (1987). The differentiation of heat and temperature: History of science and novice-expert shift. In S. Strauss (Ed.), *Ontogeny, phylogeny, and historical development* (p. 28–48). Norwood, NJ: Ablex.

Wiser, M., & Amin, T. (2001). "Is heat hot?" inducing conceptual change by integrating everyday and scientific perspectives on thermal phenomena. *Learning and Instruction, 11,* 331–353.

4

Two Tales of Conceptual Change: What Changes and What Remains the Same

Frank C. Keil and George E. Newman
Yale University

Conceptual change is not always synonymous with cognitive development. For example, children can undergo changes in their thought process that would not normally be considered instances of conceptual change. Moreover, these changes may influence concept use in a dramatic manner. In many cases, that dramatic influence can easily appear to be true conceptual change, when in fact it is not. Although it can be relatively easy to delineate in principle a large number of different forms of conceptual change, in practice, it often can be difficult to know which form is actually occurring. Scholars can disagree quite dramatically on whether they are witnessing a true conceptual revolution or a more pedestrian case of conceptual elaboration, or no real conceptual change at all. Thus, it is important to be clear about patterns of cognitive development so as to better distinguish real instances of conceptual change from developmental changes that merely appear to be conceptual.

Here, we suggest that true conceptual change occurs under one of two conditions: either a concept's internal structure changes, or its relations to other concepts changes in ways that are central to its meaning. However, the coherence of such accounts obviously depends on the models one proposes for how concepts are represented. For example, if one favors a minimalist view of concept structure in which concepts such as "dog," "car," and "tiger" are represented in essentially the same way as "red," conceptual change may indeed be a rare event only found in relatively exotic compound concepts (Fodor, 1998). In this essay we'll assume that everyday concepts like "dog" or "car" do have more structure than such minimalist views, either by having an internal structure consisting of sets of features, properties and their interrelations (e.g., Smith & Medin, 1981) or by having an "external" structure consisting of their relation to other concepts that give them their meaning (e.g., Quine & Ullian, 1978). We will not dwell here on these alternatives or on possible hybrid combinations (e.g., Murphy, 2002; Keil, 1989; Keil, Smith, Simons, & Levin, 1998). Our approach is to assume that some kind of structural characterization is needed to explain how concepts are represented, used and acquired and that conceptual change consists of cases where that structure changes.

There are, however, some modest additional assumptions about concept structure that are relevant to almost all commonly described cases of conceptual change. One such assumption is the idea that the structural configuration associated with a concept is domain-specific. Thus, when a child's concept of living things undergoes some type of change, we assume that the change is bounded to the domain of biology. The effect of that change can be quite dramatic for many related concepts within that domain, but relatively minor or non-existent for concepts that are outside of the domain. This assumption might seem to clash with meaning holism, the idea that concepts are inferentially linked together to almost all other concepts in the web of belief. It need not be incompatible, however, as the density of linkages might be quite variable: changes within a domain, where links are dense, may cause far more changes than for concepts in other domains, where the links are sparse.

There is also an assumption that concepts are, to some degree, parts of theory-like structures that provide explanatory insight into why their features co-occur. Thus, the concept of bird includes not only the fact that wings and flight are correlated, but also some causal story of how wings enable flight. Such stories can be incomplete, or even outright wrong, but it is commonly assumed that some set of explanatory beliefs is essential to understanding how we acquire and use concepts and, moreover, how they change. For example, if a series of explanatory gaps grows, it may precipitate a conceptual change to structures and relations that have fewer gaps or inconsistencies (Kuhn, 1962; Carey, 1985). The concepts-in-theories idea does encounter challenges, as people's lay theories are often highly fragmentary (diSessa & Sherin, 1998), or surprisingly incomplete (Rozenblit & Keil, 2002). For our purposes, however, we will assume that some notion of explanatory insight is part of most accounts of what concepts are and how they change, while acknowledging that the explanatory component may not be in the form of detailed, well-developed theories or mechanistic mental models (Keil, 2003, 2006).

There have been several discussions attempting to delineate various kinds of conceptual change (Carey, 1985, 1991, 1999; Chi, 1992; Inagaki & Hatano, 2002; Keil, 1999; Nersessian, 1989; Thagard, 1992; Vosniadou & Brewer, 1987). There may be cases of gradual elaboration of a structure by adding new more fine-grained information that doesn't change the kind of structure involved. There may be dramatic restructuring of a concept similar to historical "revolutions" in thought (Kuhn, 1962). These revolutions could consist either of cases of new concepts "differentiating" out of old ones (Carey, 1999); or a restructuring of how features and properties define concepts (Keil, 1989). Conceptual changes can also sometimes result in a reassignment of ontological categories (Chi, 1992), such as thinking of flames as a process instead of as "stuff."

In addition, we will argue that some kinds of conceptual change may be missed altogether if considered at the wrong level of analysis. For example, one level of analysis may reveal the same judgments at different ages, while another may reveal that the same judgments are in reality occurring for dramatically different reasons. In this chapter, we considers two extremes to illustrate how easy it is to be misled about what is changing and why. We consider first a pattern of judgments over the course of development that seems to be essentially the same. When looked at through the lens of one method and set of stimuli, no significant conceptual change appears to be occurring. We will show, however, that when considered in more detail with other stimuli and questions, a dramatic change may be occurring — one that is masked by certain anchoring phenomena in the real world. In other words, sometimes a causal pattern in the world may be so salient and reliable that children in all ages (even infants) will be able to predict it in the same way, but the basis for the predictions may undergo dramatic conceptual change.

Our second example considers a case of apparently dramatic conceptual change that seems to reflect a genuine revolution in conceptual structure and shifts of ontological categories. We will illustrate, however, that the same patterns of change in judgments could occur without any true conceptual change occurring in the traditional sense. We will consider two alternatives to conceptual change that are often overlooked but which can mimic dramatic changes in conceptual structure. We will then examine how one might tease these cases apart.

CONCEPTUAL REVOLUTIONS UNDERNEATH A SEA OF CALM

The world around us consists of two fundamentally forms of patterns: those that appear random and those that appear to radically depart from randomness by having some sort of order. Order may be perceived in any number of modalities and in many different forms, whether it be via axes of symmetry, spatial or temporal sorting, or complex structural arrangements. Moreover, the way in which we differentiate the causal origins of these patterns (randomness vs. order) may be as distinct as the structural arrangements themselves: whereas any number of underlying causal processes may give rise to apparent randomness, departures from randomness tend only to result from the intentional actions of goal-directed actors (or agents) — e.g., a parent cleans up a child's room by stacking items of like kind in different piles, or a diamond miner sorts rough diamonds by size, color, and quality. As adults, we clearly recognize that agents have the capacity to manipulate, organize, and structure the world around them such that they create patterns that deviate from random or chance occurrences.

We do not, however, see simple bounded objects as capable of having such effects. Throw a stone, roll a ball, or slide a block at a disordered system and it is highly unlikely that any of those events will make a more orderly arrangement. We would be surprised to see such an effect because we normally assume that order arises from the intentional actions of agents, not inanimate objects. Thus, one major division in the world of causal entities is between those that are capable of creating order and those that are not.

Previous work suggests that even infants appear sensitive to this fundamental distinction. By 12 months of age, infants appear to understand that whereas agents are capable of creating order (or reversing entropy on a local scale), inanimate objects are not (Newman, Keil, Kuhlmeier, & Wynn, 2005; under review). Using a standard violation-of-expectation procedure, Newman et al. (2005) presented infants with two types of short, computer-animated movies. In one type of movie (the "Ordering" movie), infants first saw a disordered array of blocks. An opaque screen appeared and moved in front of the blocks, hiding them from view. Then an "entity" moved behind the screen. For half the infants the entity was an inanimate object, a polka-dotted ball that rolled behind the screen. For the other half of the infants, the entity was an animate agent (a ball-like character with a face). In test trials, the screen dropped to reveal the blocks in an ordered arrangement. Thus, it appeared as if the entity (ball or agent) changed the disordered pile of blocks into an ordered pile.

In the other type movie (the "Disordering" movie), infants saw an identical sequence of events, however, the beginning and end-states of the block-arrays were reversed: infants first saw an ordered array of blocks, the entity moved behind the screen, then the screen dropped to reveal the blocks in disarray. Now it appeared as if the entity changed the ordered arrangement of blocks into a disordered pile. The Ordering and Disordering movies were identical, except for the sequence in which the ordered and disordered arrays appeared.

Whereas it is perfectly consistent for a ball to disorganize a group of blocks (e.g., by colliding with them), it is impossible for a ball to organize a group of blocks. Therefore, we predicted that infants in the "Ball" condition should look longer at the movie of a ball creating order than at the movie of a ball creating disorder. In contrast, infants in the "Agent" condition should look equally long at the movies of an agent creating order and an agent creating disorder, because both outcomes are consistent with actions that agents are capable of completing. Consistent with these predictions, infants looked reliably longer when the ball apparently caused a disordered array to become ordered, than when it caused an ordered array to become disordered. In contrast, when infants saw identical events involving an agent, they did not differentiate between ordered and disordered outcomes, suggesting that infants did not apply the same sorts of expectations to the agent as they did the ball.

It was unclear, however, from this initial study exactly why infants in the Agent condition failed to distinguish between the Ordering and Disordering events. It may be that infants, like adults, appreciate that agents can cause either order or disorder; thus, they found neither event unexpected. Alternatively, it may be that infants were simply unable to generate predictions about the agent's actions. Perhaps infants selectively apply the principle of entropy to inanimate objects without making firm predictions about the capacities of agents.

To distinguish between these two possibilities, a second study explored whether infants can in fact form positive expectations about an agent's ability to create order. Borrowing from a series of studies in which infants attribute consistent, object-specific goals to human hands but not to inanimate sticks (Leslie, 1984; Woodward, 1998), we asked whether infants appreciate that an agent may have the "goal" to cause order, and whether they recognize that goal as different from a goal to cause disorder.

Infants were familiarized to short movie sequences involving real objects (instead of computer-animated cartoons), in which a hand or a claw appeared to create order. Infants in the Hand condition first saw a disordered pile of blocks, and an opaque barrier was raised to cover the blocks. Then, an experimenter's hand traveled behind the barrier, appeared to manipulate the objects and then exited the display. The barrier was dropped to reveal the blocks in an ordered arrangement. After infants saw this event three times, they were shown two different types of test events involving new blocks (i.e., different shapes and colors). In the Ordering event, the hand continued to create order by changing a disordered pile of blocks into an ordered array (similar to the familiarization trials). In the Disordering event, the sequence of events was reversed: the hand appeared to cause disorder, changing an ordered arrangement of blocks into a disordered array.

A second group of infants in a Claw condition saw exactly the same series of events, however, instead of a hand, infants saw events in which a claw-like stick appeared to either organize or disorganize arrays of objects: Infants were first familiarized to the claw creating order and then saw the claw either continuing to create order, or creating disorder.

When infants were familiarized to the hand creating order, they expected the hand to continue to create order: thus, they looked reliably longer when the hand changed its goal and appeared to cause disorder than when it continued to create order. Thus, infants appeared to recognize that the goal to create order was distinct from the goal to create disorder, and they expected such a goal to remain consistent across subsequent test events involving novel arrays of objects. In contrast, when infants saw the identical sequence of events involving the claw, they did not look longer when the claw changed to cause disorder. In fact, infants in the Claw condition continued to look longer at the claw creating order, presumably because they continued to find that sequence of events unexpected.

Together, these studies suggest that by 12 months of age, infants appreciate that intentional agents are capable of creating order in ways that inanimate objects are not. Moreover, on the surface it would seem as though infants have, roughly, the same appreciation as adults: infants expect that causal interactions involving only inanimate objects should result in more disorderly arrangements. They know, for instance, that an inanimate ball can cause an ordered array to become disordered, but not a disordered array to become ordered (also see Friedman, 2002). Infants, however, also appear capable of making predictions about the actions of agents. They expect an agent who creates order to remain an "orderer" and thus find it "unexpected" when the agent changes its goal to become a "disorderer." Without previous exposure to the agent's goals, however, infants do not appear to distinguish between an agent creating order and an agent creating disorder. Thus, infants appear sensitive whether or not an agent has the apparent goal to create order.

For adults, it is this second understanding of order as the product of intentional goal-directed action that seems particularly important to how we interpret and explain the existence of order in the world. The capacity to create more ordered structures from less ordered ones represents one of the most salient aspects of human agency. Evidence that humans are capable of creating order is present in virtually every aspect of our daily lives, from buildings, to artifacts, to visual art. In fact, we often associate ordered arrangements with the mental plans that produce them, rather than the physical or mechanical causes that may have brought them into existence. For example, even in situations where order is physically caused by inanimate objects, such as robots on an assembly line, we often associate the change from relative disorder to order with the *mental* plan to create order (e.g., a blueprint, or the robot's designer), rather than the mechanical causes that may have produced such a change (e.g., the robot itself).

Although the work discussed above suggests that, at some level, infants like adults may think of order in terms of intentional goal-directed action rather than pure mechanical causes, the nature of looking-time measures prevents drawing any strong conclusions about how infants may be representing such events. The present case is one where robust patterns in the world may support an early-emerging conceptual distinction that is relatively continuous across development. However, it may also be that infants and adults represent such a distinction in fundamentally different ways, while producing a pattern of responses that only *appears* to be the same.

A potential method for exploring this issue is to investigate how young children may represent similar conceptual distinctions. For example, do we see evidence of similar patterns of reasoning in young children (e.g., preschoolers), who might be better able to articulate a basis for their response? In contrast to the infant studies, previous work indicates that in certain circumstances, children may actually have a great deal of difficulty reasoning about the effects of random forces (e.g., Piaget & Inhelder, 1975; Shultz & Cottington, 1981). However, more recent studies that reduce task demands have found that children as young as four-years-old appreciate that random forces are only likely to produce disordered arrangements (Friedman, 2001). Thus, it is unclear from previous work whether an understanding of causality and order undergoes any sort of conceptual change between infancy and adulthood.

THE CAUSE REMAINS THE SAME

Here, we briefly describe two experiments that attempted to address this issue directly. In our first study we simply wanted to replicate the pattern of responses observed with infants. Using a paradigm similar to the first infant study, we contrasted agents versus inanimate causes. We tested whether preschoolers (3- to 6-year-olds) appreciate that inanimate forces (e.g., the wind blowing) are only capable of producing disorder, while agents (e.g., a person) can produce either order or disorder.

Children were first presented with a cartoon drawing of a room. The drawing depicted six different piles of blocks distributed around the room. For each child, the experimenter said, "This is a picture of Billy's room, and these are some of the things that are in his room. One day, Billy went outside to play, and this is how things looked before he went outside." Children in the Person condition were then presented with a cartoon drawing of a teenage girl. The experimenter said, "This is a picture of Billy's older sister, Julie. While Billy was outside playing, Julie went into his room and changed some of his things." The experimenter then presented two different test cards. One test card depicted an ordered array of blocks. The other test card depicted a disordered array of blocks. The ordered and disordered arrays were both different than the arrays presented in the initial drawing, but were composed of the same blocks. Children were then asked, "Which one of these piles looks most like if Julie changed it?" Children were presented with six different pairs of ordered and disordered arrangements. Each ordered arrangement was organized along a different perceptual dimension, such as color, shape, or spatial arrangement.

The other half of the children were assigned to the Wind condition. Children in this condition were presented with exactly the same series of pictures. However, instead of a drawing of teenage girl, children were shown a cartoon drawing of an open window. The experimenter said, "This is a picture of the window in Billy's room. The window was open, and the wind was blowing really strong. While Billy was outside playing, the wind blew in his room and changed some of his things." Analogous to the Person condition, the experimenter then presented two different test cards. One card depicted an ordered array of blocks, while the other card depicted a disordered array of blocks. Children were then asked, "Which one of these piles looks most like if the wind changed it?"

We predicted that children in the Person condition should be likely to say that the person could make either the ordered or disordered arrangements, because both outcomes are consistent with actions that agents are capable of completing. Thus, children's pattern of response should mirror the looking time pattern of infants. In contrast, whereas a strong gust of wind can disorganize a group of blocks, it is highly unlikely that the wind blowing could organize a group of blocks. Therefore, we predicted that children in the Wind condition should be significantly more likely to say that the wind made the disordered arrangement than to say that the wind made the ordered arrangement.

The results from this study were consistent with these predictions. Children in the Person condition reported that the person could make either the ordered or disordered arrangement. In contrast, children in the Wind condition were significantly more likely to say that the wind blowing could only create the disordered arrangement. Splitting the sample into two age groups (5- to 6-year-olds and 3- to 4-year-olds) revealed no differences in the pattern of responding across the two age ranges.

For each item in this study, children were also asked to explain *why* they thought the particular causal agent (person or wind) would produce the arrangement they selected. Interestingly, children were often unable to articulate the basis for their response. In fact, children's most common justification was simply to describe the visual array, such as merely redescribing that the wind had knocked over the blocks. Thus, children rarely described the nature of the causal agent when describing the ordered and disordered arrays.

Results from this study suggested that children as young as three- to four-years-old appreciate that, whereas agents can cause either order or disorder, inanimate forces such as the wind are only likely to cause disorder. This pattern of judgments is consistent with infants' looking time preferences: 12-month-olds look longer when an inanimate ball creates order than when it creates disorder, yet, they look equally long at an agent creating either order or disorder. Furthermore, we did not observe any differences in judgments between three-year-olds and six-year-olds. Thus, beliefs about the unique connection between order and agency appear to be relatively unchanging throughout early development. However, though preschoolers clearly appreciate that agents are unique in their ability to create order, it is still uncertain from their justifications (or lack thereof) how they might be representing such an understanding. Although the overall pattern of judgments may be the same, perhaps young children and adults represent an identical causal pattern in fundamentally different ways. Here we briefly consider three possibilities for how children may initially be representing such an understanding.

EARLY CONCEPTUAL MODELS FOR AN ABILITY TO CREATE ORDER

One possibility may be that children's expectations about the ability to create order emerge from the psychological domain. Perhaps children start with the appreciation that only agents are responsible for order. Such an expectation would be plausible given early exposure to many instances in which people create ordered arrangements. From an association between agents and order, children may then come to expect that inanimate causes rarely bring about order. In contrast, expectations about the causes of *disorder* may receive little systematic feedback. Hence, children may accept that either agents or inanimate causes are capable of causing disorder. This view predicts that, initially, children may be likely to describe both animate and inanimate causes in terms of psychological characteristics. For instance, "people create order because they want to, while the wind doesn't know how."

A second possibility is that children's expectations about order emerge from an understanding of physical causality. Children may first appreciate that inanimate causes lack the capacity to physically bring about ordered arrangements, whereas agents (e.g., human hands) are capable of causing many different types of change. Such an appreciation may not include a detailed understanding of mechanism, but rather may consist of only a very general notion that agents are not necessarily subject to the same physical laws that govern simple inanimate objects. In other words, young children and infants may have a relatively abstract, intuitive appreciation that agents and inanimate objects differ in their capacities to bring about certain types of physical change. This view predicts that young children may represent the difference between inanimate causes and agents in terms of physical characteristics. For instance, "the wind can't create order because it can't pick stuff up, while people can move things around in many ways."

A third possibility is that young children represent the connection between causality and order as two distinct understandings: a) that animate entities tend to produce order, and b) that inanimate forces are only capable of bringing about disorder. This view predicts that whereas children may be likely to discuss inanimate causes in terms of mechanical characteristics, they may be more likely to describe agents and order in terms of psychological characteristics. For instance, "a ball causes disorder because it can only knock things over, while an agent causes order because they want to." Intuitively, this third possibility seems the most similar to the adult appreciation.

ANTHROPOMORPHIZING ORDER

One way to experimentally distinguish between the interpretations outlined above may be to explore what types of entities young children view as capable of creating order. Given that preschoolers are often likely to anthropomorphize and over-attribute human-like mental states to many different types of entities (e.g., Lutz, 2003), the first and third views predict that younger children may be more liberal than older children in the types of entities that they view as capable of creating order. In other words, if children do explain agents and order via psychological characteristics then beliefs about the ability to create order may follow beliefs about an organism's mental capacities. Thus, younger children may say that a wider-range of entities can create order than older children, because they believe a wider-range of entities to have more human-like mental capacities.

Our second study specifically probed children's judgments about the kinds of agents capable of creating ordered arrangements. We wanted to explore how narrowly or broadly children might construe an "ability to create order". Using a similar design as the first study we presented children with changes from disorder to order and asked about different entities that may be capable of causing such a change. We also explored whether children make any conceptual distinctions between different *types* of order and the type of entity involved.

Young elementary school children (ranging from Kindergarteners to second graders) were presented with photographs of real objects. Children were first shown a photograph of a dis-ordered arrangement (e.g., a scrambled pile of red and black beans). Then, they were shown a photograph of the same objects in an ordered array (e.g., two neat piles of beans, organized by color). The experimenter said, "Here are some objects. The objects used to look like this (dis-ordered photo), but a little while later they looked like this (ordered photo)." The experimenter would ask, "What do you notice about these pictures? What has changed?" For children who were unable to articulate the difference between the two pictures, the experimenter helped ex-plain the differences. For instance, he said, "Look, in this picture they are all messed up. But, in this picture they are put into neat piles. All of the black ones are over here while all of the red ones are over there."

After the child acknowledged the difference between the disordered and ordered photo-graphs, the experimenter asked (pointing to the ordered photo), "How do you think it got to be this way?" The experimenter then presented four cartoon drawings of different "agents." The four agents were drawings of a teenage girl, a baby, a cat, and an open window. The experimenter then pointed to each the agents saying, "Which one of these do you think changed the objects? Was it the big girl, the baby, the kitty cat, or the wind blowing really strong?" After the child selected a particular agent the experimenter asked (pointing to the remaining agents), "Do you think that any of the other ones could have changed the objects?" This process was repeated until either the child said that none of the other agents were capable of causing the ordered array, or the child said that all of the agents were capable of causing the ordered array. This same procedure was repeated for ten different sets of items. The ten items were designed to represent five different types of order, with two exemplars of each, i.e., grouping by color, grouping by shape, grouping by spatial arrangement, grouping by category, and grouping by "complimentarity" (e.g., small objects that were always placed *inside* of rings, though the exact spatial arrangement was not ordered). Additionally, children were asked to justify the basis for their response for three of the items. For instance, the experiment asked, "Why do you think that the girl made the objects look like that?" or "Why couldn't the baby make the blocks look like that?"

For each child, we tallied the total number of times that they chose a particular agent (e.g., person, baby, cat, or wind). Unsurprisingly, both Kindergartners and second graders were sig-nificantly more likely to say a person could make order than any of the other agents; and overall, children did not distinguish between different kinds of order and the type of agent responsible — suggesting that their appreciation of an ability to create order might be fairly abstract. How-ever, there was a rather curious result: second graders were significantly more likely to say that the baby could create different types of order than were kindergarteners (no other differences between the age groups were observed). This finding that *older* children were more likely to say that the baby could create order than were younger children was quite surprising. In fact, this result was directly opposite the prediction that younger children should judge a wider-range of entities to be capable of creating order than older children. Instead, we found that *younger* chil-dren appeared more restrictive in their judgments than older children. To explore what might be responsible for this counterintuitive pattern, we more closely examined children's justifications.

Children's justifications were coded into one of three categories. For this analysis we com-bined across "positive" justifications (e.g., explanations for why a particular entity could cause order) and "negative" justifications (e.g., explanations for why a particular entity could not cause order). The justifications were coded as either "Physical" (e.g., "the (agent) couldn't do it be-cause it doesn't have hands", "it can't pick it up", "it is too little", "the blocks are too heavy", or "the (agent) has hands", "the (agent) is big"), "Mental" (e.g., "doesn't know how", "not smart enough", "can't do it on purpose", or "because they want to"), or "Other" (e.g., "b/c only the per-son could do it", "can only make it messy", "can only mess around with it"). Using this coding scheme, we found a significant difference between younger and older children's justifications: Younger children were reliably more likely to provide "Physical" justifications, while older children were reliably more likely to provide "Mental" justifications. Thus, despite a similar response pattern, Kindergarteners and second-graders seem to causally account for order in very different ways.

Such a pattern potentially explains the counterintuitive finding that older children are *more* likely report that a baby can create order than are younger children. Perhaps because older children are coding order more in terms of psychological characteristics, they are more likely to think that a baby can create order than are younger children (note that this explanation assumes that children are over-attributing adult-like mental capacities to infants). In contrast, younger children may be coding the identical pattern in terms of physical characteristics. As such, they may correctly recognize that an infant lacks the physical dexterity to create ordered structures; thus they are less likely to report that an infant can create order.

A SHIFT IN STRUCTURE?

The studies discussed here with children suggest that despite an apparently consistent pattern of responding across multiple age ranges, there may actually be quite a dramatic shift in how children account for ordered arrangements: Five- to six-year-olds appear to represent the capacity to create order more in terms of the physical characteristics that may produce ordered structures (e.g., hands, adult dexterity). In contrast, seven- and eight-year-olds seem to account for the identical causal patterns more in terms of psychological characteristics (e.g., the plan to create order). Such a shift is potentially indicative of a conceptual reassignment in ontological categories, of the sort discussed above. Initially, young children and perhaps infants may situate the capacity to create order more in the physical domain (along with other types of physical changes, such as causal contact). Under this view, early appreciations of order may consist of only of the very general notion that agents are not subject to the same physical laws that govern simple inanimate objects. This understanding, however, may still include notions of intentionality despite emerging from the physical domain: the intentional actions of agents (and their causal powers) might be viewed as a sort of break from the deterministic affects of physical causes.

Seven- and eight-year-olds, on the other hand, appear to appreciate that the mental plan to produce order is a necessary prerequisite for bringing about ordered arrangements. In this sense, their understanding of an ability to create order may be more heavily tied to the psychological domain. Again, such a reassignment does not preclude an understanding of physical process; rather, it merely suggests that an understanding of the capacity to create order in older children may have stronger ties to other types of psychological concepts (mental representations, design, etc.) than in younger children. Thus, in terms of the potential representations outlined earlier, children seem to be shifting from a predominately physical account of order to a more nuanced view that incorporates an understanding of the mental capacities necessary to bring about ordered structures.

It could be argued that in fact there is less conceptual change going on here than meets the eye. Perhaps the younger children are interpreting the "why" question as one about how the action was actually performed while older children are interpreting the same question as about underlying causes. If this alternative were correct, then different kinds of questions might prompt more similar responses across ages. We don't, however, think that this alternative can fully explain these results as the younger children did sometimes refer to underlying causes (e.g., that the infant was physically too weak to cause order) — but only an extensive series of studies can determine for sure whether this rather dramatic change in justifications is more than simply a shift in the understanding of a question, rather than a deeper sort of conceptual change. Our point here is only to note that a pattern of judgments, which at one level might suggest no conceptual change at all, might reveal dramatic change when examined at a different level of analysis.

If this difference in understanding is borne out, then we have a case where developmental constancy in judgments about which agent is responsible for creating order masks an underlying conceptual change concerning the kinds of causal reasons behind that change. One empirical prediction here is that if children really are shifting from physical to psychological understandings of order, then at some point in development we should observe a fairly dramatic shift in children's understanding of the requisite mental capacities necessary to produce order. For example, younger children may be more likely to endorse the plausibility of ordering devices that lack true mental underpinnings (such as purely mechanical robots). Similarly, as children shift from physical to psychological explanations they may begin to more accurately match varying complexities of order with appropriately complex mental capacities. For example, younger children may simply think that any human is capable of causing any type of order, while older children may more accurately report that more complicated structures require sufficiently greater mental abilities. If, however, task demands are part of the story and younger children are simply interpreting "why" questions in a different manner, follow-up studies should reveal that when the question is clarified, they can fully grasp the relatively intricate ways in which mental states are related to order. We think that this is unlikely, but recognize the need for further studies in this area.

In short, even infants understand quite well that agents are the likely causes of ordered events, and judgments linking order to agents remain highly consistent from infancy on into adulthood. The correlation is simply too strong and salient in the world to ignore. As a result, there is great deal of developmental continuity in judgments concerning what cause (agent vs. inanimate cause) goes with what outcome. Yet, the basis for such judgments (when viewed from a different level of analysis) may change dramatically as children come to understand a different causal basis for ordering events.

False Revolutions — Surface Change without Deep Conceptual Change

In marked contrast to cases of consistent judgment patterns over time, there are many examples in cognitive development where children's judgments seem to change dramatically. In some instances, such changes may appear to be direct reflections of changes in conceptual structure, when in fact other kinds of developmental change may be at work. One classic case along these lines concerns the development of transitive reasoning. It was long believed, following Piaget, that younger children simply didn't have the ability to engage in transitive reasoning because they were missing some kind of logical operator that enabled them to know that inequalities such as $A > B$ and $B > C$, logically entailed $A > C$. Yet, in a now classic study, Bryant and Trabasso (1971) illustrated how the main developmental change might be caused by general memory limitations instead of profound conceptual change. When young children were extensively trained on sets of inequalities and could easily remember each of them, the transitive inferences seemed to naturally fall out. Thus, there may not be any change in the concept of transitivity, but rather, merely a change in the ability to hold enough inequalities in mind so as to use them as the foundation for transitive inferences. This kind of change is therefore a domain-general one of changing abilities to memorize arbitrary relations, not a result of a specific problem with a transitive operator. Developmental changes in domain-general capacities may have effects on performance in specific tasks, but should not be confused with conceptual changes of mental representations or operations that are much more focused, such as transitive reasoning.

More broadly, developmental psychology over the past few decades has witnessed several cases where changes in memory capacity or attention, rather than changes in knowledge structures or conceptual systems, seem to be the basis for developmental change. In cases of conservation (Gelman, 1969; McGarrigle & Donaldson, 1974), egocentrism (Shatz & Gelman, 1973), or classification (Mandler, 2004), memory and attention limitations have often provided compelling alternative explanations. In most cases, however, the arguments have been against domain-general conceptual changes of the sort proposed by global stage theorists such as Piaget. Changes in memory and attention capacity can also be domain-general, but they are not normally considered instances of conceptual change (given the characterization that we developed at the beginning of the chapter). We don't, for example, normally think of changes in memory and attention as involving changes in causal beliefs in an explanatory structure. Nor do we think of memory and attention capacity changes as causing changes in ontological status, such as shifting from seeing a flame as a substance to seeing it as an event, or from seeing ordered arrangements as a predominately physical, rather than a mental creation.

Presently, we consider conceptual change in folk-biological thought, a case where qualitative conceptual change seems to be quite compelling, namely that a child may shift from thinking of living things as members of one domain with one kind of relations to being members of a different domain with very different kinds of relations. Biological thought has often been considered a paradigmatic instance of conceptual change. We consider the case of biology here because the kind of conceptual change that has been proposed (a revolutionary restructuring of an entire domain) is among the most dramatic and interesting forms in that literature. Thus, if we can show that a case of an apparent shift in ontological types and networks of causal relations is in fact something far less dramatic, we have illustrated the challenges of inferring conceptual change from only one level of evidence.

Conceptual Change in Folk-Biology

One of the most fascinating and influential claims of conceptual change is the idea that young children (e.g., preschoolers) have no real sense of the biological world per se, but instead understand the living world in terms of two earlier emerging systems: a naïve physics and a naïve psychology (Carey, 1985). There is now abundant evidence that even infants can have dramatically different expectations about agents who they consider psychological, as opposed objects that they view as merely mechanical (Carey & Spelke, 1994; Leslie, 1994). For example, there is ample evidence that infants see goal-directed actors as different from inanimate objects (Kuhlmeier, Bloom, & Wynn 2004; Meltzoff, 1995; Poulin-Dubois, Lepage, & Ferland, 1996; Woodward, 1998), and they expect these two kinds of objects to interact differently with the environment (Gergely, Nadasdy, Csibra, & Biro, 1995; Rakison & Poulin-Dubois, 2001; Saxe, Tenenbaum, & Carey, 2005; Spelke, Phillips, & Woodward, 1995). Indeed, the case of order and agents, just considered, relies on the ability of infants to distinguish intentional psychological agents from unintentional mechanical causes. Infants may not yet be able to figure out how intentional agents create order (in terms of specific mental capacities), but they may well code that the category of things that comprises intentional agents has particular causal powers that the other category (inanimate objects) does not.

It has been argued that unlike the early-emerging systems of psychology and physics, the grand revolution for biology is one where living kinds are first interpreted in a Procrustean manner as being part of either psychology or mechanics (Carey, 1985). In essence, psychology and mechanics are alleged to be the only early explanatory frameworks of any generality. Thus, by necessity, other causal patterns must be absorbed into one of these two domains until a new theory can emerge that is more specific to biology. A young child might view a plant as fundamentally the same sort of thing as a rock or an icicle, and see a dog as fundamentally the same sort of thing as an intentional human agent. However, somewhere around seven or eight years of age, a new domain of biological thought emerges along with the dramatic insight that dogs, plants, people, and bugs are all in the same domain of living things. Thus, the child no longer needs the crutches of psychology and physics to interpret biological properties and processes. A newly emergent understanding of reproduction, nutrition, and basic physiology makes it possible to see the ontological commonality to all living things (Carey, 1985).

Evidence of this dramatic shift in conceptual structure is argued to be apparent in patterns of reasoning, such as property induction. For example, a child might be taught that a particular biological entity has a novel property, such as "an omentum." The child is then asked what other types of entities might also have that property (Carey, 1985). In other cases a more familiar property known to be true of humans, such as having babies, might be asked of other living and nonliving things (Carey, 1985). These induction tasks often reveal dramatic developmental changes in judgments. Younger children's inductions appear to be based on the extent to which an entity is psychologically similar to humans. Thus, dogs can have babies because the predicate "have babies" is understood in terms of its associated *psychological* roles such as being nurturing, protective and caring. By contrast, a supposed ignorance of the biological aspects of having babies, such as the need for a species to reproduce, causes young children to argue that other animals, such as worms, cannot have babies.

Older children, however, show a dramatic shift in their induction patterns, judging that appropriate biological properties apply to all living things. For example, older children will appropriately attribute biological properties, such as reproduction to all animals and often plants, but not to nonliving kinds. Such patterns are thought to reflect the emergence of theories unique to biological process. Later studies with different groups of children do not always find such developmental shifts (e.g., Ross, Medin, Coley, & Atran, 2003). For example, young children in rural Native American (Menominee) culture show adult-like patterns of induction (Ross et al., 2003), and in a somewhat different version of the task, Japanese children are also considerably more precocious (Hatano & Inagaki, 1994). In both cases, however, it could be argued that children in other cultures simply undergo the revolution to developing true biological thought much earlier. In other words, deep and profound conceptual change is occurring on a culture-wide basis. But, the special practices of a particular culture may alter the timetable for which such change happens.

There are, however, alternative accounts of how children's inductions might be changing; accounts in which changes in the pattern of judgment may occur without the mechanism of underlying conceptual change. In the following sections we more deeply consider two such alternatives. Our purpose is not to unilaterally decide whether or not profound conceptual change is *really* occurring. Instead, it is to more simply consider how other forms of change, besides conceptual change, might be responsible for dramatic shifts in judgment.

SHIFTING RELEVANCE: ONE FORM OF NON-CONCEPTUAL CHANGE

How might a child's patterns of judgment dramatically shift without underlying conceptual change? One way is through the notion of shifting relevance. Shifting relevance is a different mechanism for producing dramatic changes in judgments without necessarily implying underlying conceptual change. With respect to biology, there is strong evidence that developmental changes in patterns of induction may be explained by shifting relevance (Gurthiel, Vera, & Keil,

1998; Keil, 2003, 2006). A key feature of the notion of shifting relevance is that one often has to decide which conceptual domain is relevant before engaging in reasoning about an entity. For example, when predicting the motion path of a person we normally draw upon inferences from the psychological domain. We assume that a person's goals, beliefs and desires may best predict their movements. But, we could also treat the person as a brute physical object and reason about their motion path accordingly. We might very well do so, for example, if we knew that the person was in a coma, or in free-fall. Thus, our domain of mechanical physics is completely developed; it just doesn't spring to mind first when evaluating the motions of humans.

For induction tasks, similar influences may be at work. There are indeed multiple ways of construing predicates like "sleeps" and "has babies." Although it may be true that younger children interpret such phrases in psychological terms, they may do so not because they lack a conceptual domain of biology, but rather because they don't understand that biology is the preferred domain for the task at hand. In other words, younger children's confusion might occur in deciphering which conceptual domain (psychology, biology, or physics) is the most relevant way to construe a given property. For example, consider the question, "Does a worm think?" One might respond yes if "thinks" is understood in the biological sense as the raw, neural computation to process information so as to guide behavior. But, more likely, one will respond "no" because one interprets "thinks" in terms of mental states. Thus, the way in which "thinks" is understood may dramatically shift the types of entities to which "thinks" is thought to apply.

Many tasks contain terms that could be understood in one conceptual domain or another, an ambiguity that often is clarified by context, but which may be clarified in different ways at different ages. If both domains can be readily used once their relevance is made clear, then a shifting relevance account of developmental change in induction is supported. To test the shifting relevance possibility, Gutheil, Vera, and Keil (1998, p. 37) provided contextual cues to young children. The first kind of cue elaborated on the meaning of a term in a biological or psychological manner, such as:

> This person eats because he needs food to eat and grow. The food gives him energy to move. If he doesn't eat he will die (biological context for 'eat').

and,

> This person eats because he loves to be at meals with his family and friends. Meals bring the family together to eat and have fun. If he didn't eat, he would never see his family all together (psychological context for "eat").

This cue was provided only in talking about humans. Children were then presented with the standard induction task used by Carey (1985). As seen in Figure 4.1 (from Gutheil et al., 1998), the two contexts either made four-year-olds look just like Carey's four-year-olds, with a gradual drop off in induction suggestive of judgments relying upon a psychological system of interpretation or, with the biological context, made the four-year-olds look just like the seven-year-olds in the Carey studies who had presumably undergone a major conceptual revolution and understood the domain of biology proper. The four-year-olds in this study were not taught anything about the applicability of these terms to entities other than people, but once the biological sense of the terms was made clear, they immediately saw the relevance of biological similarities and judged accordingly. The presence of such induction patterns in four-year-olds suggests that the seven-year-olds might not differ because they have a new domain of biological thought, but more because they realize the greater relevance of a long existing conceptual realm of biology to the task at hand.

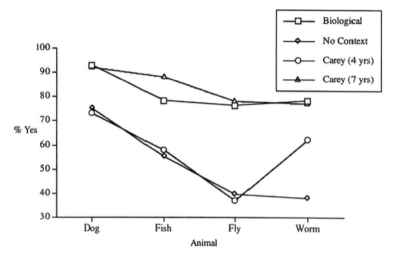

FIGURE 4.1   Children's patterns of induction can be shifted radically depending on whether they think that the biological or psychological sense of terms are implied (from Gutheil et al., 1998).

However, it might be argued that elaborating on the terms in ways done in the first study somehow allowed children to see the specific relevance of those terms without really engaging the broader domain of biological thought. To explore this issue, Gutheil et al. (1998) conducted a second study in which they didn't elaborate at all about the terms and instead merely provided a very general context for thinking in biological terms, a kind of conceptual system "priming." To cause such priming, they used the following passage:

Let's talk about people, okay? You know how machines have inside parts that let them do things, like motors that make trucks move or batteries that make flashlights light up? Well, people have inside parts that let them do things in all sorts of interesting ways as well. We all can breathe by ourselves and we can all move around by ourselves and we all have the same kinds of stuff inside that lets us do this. People aren't the only things in the world that can do things like move around and breathe, right? We're going to look at the pictures of people and other things and talk about them. While we look at the pictures, try to think about all the different kinds of things in the world that can do things like move around by themselves, and breathe by themselves, and have the same kinds of stuff inside. Okay, here we go. (Gutheil et al., 1998, p. 43)

This simple thirty-second passage caused the same sort of shift as the more specific elaborations used in the first study. Simply putting four-year-old children into a biological frame of mind was enough to induce a pattern of judgments much like seven-year-olds. No specific biological terms were ever discussed, just the general idea of people functioning like complex machines.

It is clear how such patterns could, at least in principle, explain how shifts in judgments could occur without appealing to conceptual change: The four-year-olds could have exactly the same sense of biology as seven-year-olds, but just not appreciate all of the contexts to which biology (vs. psychology) applies. In practice, the story is probably not that simple. Indeed, increasing elaboration of knowledge, one of the most conservative forms of conceptual change may indeed be the mechanism that shifts relevance (Gutheil et al., 1998). Thus, as conceptual knowledge in an area becomes more articulated and richer, the child starts to appreciate more and more of its explanatory power for a wider range of phenomena. This same effect can be found in adults as they immerse themselves in a particular discipline. For example, consider undergraduates who become entranced with Marxist theory and use it to explain an enormous range of social, economic, and political phenomena. Similarly, those who become immersed in Freudian theory may start to see its relevance everywhere, such as in literary and artistic analysis. In such cases, it would probably be appropriate to describe these changes as conceptual change.

Moreover, shifting relevance may also engender conceptual change through different means. We have argued that changes in judgment patterns can occur simply as a reordering of default biases — i.e., which domain (or, mode of construal) first comes to mind in a task. But it may also be that other mental processes, such as analogies, similarly attract a certain mode of construal as relevant, while reflecting conceptual change at a deeper level. For example, a person might realize that some techniques in computer programming, such as recursion, can be used in writing down cooking recipes. This is an example of realizing the relevance of one domain to another. That realization, however, may additionally require conceptual elaborations of the understandings of recipes, which suddenly makes the computer programming routines more relevant. Thus, certain shifts in relevance via analogical insight may have relations to deeper sorts of conceptual change and elaboration.

We don't, however, think that the biological induction case described above can be explained in this way because the shift is so easily malleable. Even briefly priming the domain of biology can cause a dramatic flip in judgment patterns. In other words, this type of shift doesn't seem to require the corresponding shifts in conceptual elaboration. Indeed, one way to delineate these two notions of shifting relevance is by the nature of their affects: Shifts in relevance that occur in brief contexts (perhaps with specific types of conceptual primes) and with minimal elaboration may reflect minimal conceptual change, while those that occur more spontaneously and with greater elaboration (often through analogical insight) may have more complex change occurring.

In short, patterns of judgments that suggest dramatic conceptual change may actually reflect developmental changes that are not conceptual, such as shifting relevance. On the other hand, conceptual change may also, in turn, drive changes in children's ability to determine relevance via elaboration. Again, such analyses are not intended to unilaterally decide whether or not profound conceptual change is *really* occurring. Instead, we briefly considered how other forms of change, besides conceptual change, might be responsible for dramatic shifts in judgments. It is critical for researchers to be aware of this interplay between factors such as shifting relevance, depth of elaboration, etc. when making claims about conceptual change, and to consider that in some cases, the appearance of conceptual change may actually mask developmental changes of a different sort.

Increasing Access: A Second Form of Non-conceptual Change

A more general sort of change thought to underlie many types of developmental change, and possibly forms of conceptual change, is the notion of increasing access. The idea of increasing access has been in the literature for many years. Some of the most eloquent and compelling proposals for its role in cognitive development are present in seminal papers by Rozin (1976) and Fodor (1972). In both cases, the authors argued against global stages of cognitive development, such as those proposed by Vygotksy, Bruner, and Piaget, and instead suggested that a child may possess necessary logical operators or representational capacities but may have a much more limited use of them. The possible reasons for the limitations are many, but often revolve around memory and attention limitations, and the automaticity of related skills. Thus, a child might fail to recognize that liquid quantities are conserved (as in Piaget's classic task) because the end states are so compelling that they interfere with reflection about the earlier states and processes that produced them. Piaget certainly thought that the end states contributed to the failure to conserve. However, he linked a focus on end states to missing quasi-logical operators. Instead, the "increasing access" alternative posits fully intact operators that simply can't be accessed due to a sort of attentional override.

For Rozin, the "access" concerned access of the conscious mind to prior unconscious cognitive abilities, such as phonological principles used in speech that needed to be accessed for reading. Some tasks require an ability to retrieve information that one is already using very fluently and use it in new ways. But not all patterns of increasing access need to bring implicit knowledge into the explicit arena. Increasing access to a cognitive capacity may also occur because other cognitive structures and processes now enable a child to use an already present capacity in new tasks. For example, we can think of increasing memory skills as allowing a child to access transitive reasoning skills in a wider and wider range of situations that require more memory. Or increasing executive skills at shifting and controlling focus might allow conservation based reasoning to apply to a wider range of tasks. In all these cases, underlying conceptual change does not have to be occurring.

Can such an increasing access story also work for induction about biological properties? There have not been systematic studies exploring this option, but it is one way of explaining the cross-cultural differences in biological knowledge that have been found. For example, differences in when biological thought comes online in varying cultures (e.g., Ross et al., 2003) have been explained via the influence and practices of a particular culture. But, at the cognitive level, the influence of culture (in this context) may be to rehearse and emphasize necessary premises for reasoning about the biological domain. Just as in Bryant and Trabasso (1971), a particular culture may extensively train a certain set of inferences about biological process, such that an already existing domain of biological thought can be accessed more readily. Thus, without true conceptual change, judgments may shift depending on how access to certain biological concepts is reinforced, or perhaps inhibited in a given culture.

Briefly consider a culture that emphasizes the continuous reproductive cycle present in all living things versus a culture that emphasizes the animistic, anthropomorphic aspects of living kinds. Clearly, these two different sorts of influences may have profound consequences in establishing access to biological versus psychological concepts. Thus, a child raised in the biologically-heavy conceptual environment may more easily access concepts such as heredity and reproduction, than the child raised in the psychologically-heavy environment. As we saw in the previous section, such types of reinforcement may have dramatic influence for shifting relevance, and in turn, the resulting patterns of judgment.

Indeed, there is some empirical support for this idea. For example, Waxman, Medin, and Ross (in press) gave children from several different cultures versions of the adoption paradigm: children were told about a baby pig that was adopted and raised solely by other cows. They were then asked about many of the pig's properties, for example, what things would be pig-like and what would be cow-like. Across all cultures, they found evidence for a strong biological component to children's understanding of property inheritance. However, Native American children seemed to have more firm commitments about the biological mechanism underlying the transmission of properties from parent to offspring. Under the "increasing access" view, such patterns may result not from the presence or absence of theories about biological mechanism, but rather, the ease with which children are capable of retrieving them (as determined by their prevalence in a particular culture). Indeed, this interpretation does not seem to be all that different from the one made by Waxman et al. (in press): "In sum, the results (of Experiments 1 and 2) suggest that children may be more likely to consider biological (blood) than non-biological (nurturance) processes as candidate essences, and that in identifying candidate biological processes, they are sensitive to community-wide discourse."

Of course, conceptual change proper may also play an important role in either culture-wide or culture-specific change. The purpose of this section is simply to illustrate how increasing access might work (perhaps in tandem with shifting relevance) to give the illusion of deep conceptual change, when in fact, there is none. When considering whether or not one is witnessing true conceptual change, it is important to consider the many ways that task-specific or culture-specific factors may shape a pattern of judgments, perhaps in even dramatic ways.

CONCLUSIONS

Our general purpose in this chapter has been to argue that the study of conceptual change encompasses a rich and diverse set of mental phenomena: sometimes dramatic conceptual change may underlie a sea of apparent conceptual calm while, at other times, a surface of marked conceptual change may derive from other sorts changes in processing. It is important whenever examining patterns of development to realize the many distinct ways in which underlying cognitive processes could cause changes in judgments. All too often, researchers come to a task with a particular theoretical model that can indeed explain the developmental pattern but that causes them to neglect several other models that can also explain the same pattern. This is not to say that there is no way to tell theories apart; rather, when one explicitly considers the full range of possible accounts, it is then possible to design follow-up studies that can distinguish between different theoretical interpretations. However, the pluralism of patterns of change, both conceptual and not, does need to be acknowledged to motivate the right sorts of experimental designs.

Similarly, there are cases where a powerful pattern in the real world, such as that holding between agents and order, may result in common judgments across a wide range of ages (as discussed in the first section). A closer look, however, can reveal how at a different level of analysis dramatic conceptual change may still be occurring. In such cases as well, one needs to consider the full range of alternative models and what sorts of experimental results might distinguish among them. The only way to know what is really going on is to consider the many additional factors that may influence judgments (some of which we outlined here) and engage in close analyses of task performance — often from several different perspectives to see how they converge on the phenomena of interest. Thus, one key component of conceptual change (as a psychological construct) may be to engage lively and challenging theoretical discussion about what is *really* changing and why.

ACKNOWLEDGMENT

Preparation of this paper and some of the research described therein was supported by NIH grant # R37HD023922 to F. Keil.

REFERENCES

Bryant, P. E., & Trabasso, T. (1971). Transitive inferences and memory in young children. *Nature, 232*, 456–458.

Carey, S. (1985). *Conceptual change in childhood*. Cambridge, MA: MIT Press.

Carey, S. (1991). Knowledge acquisition: Enrichment or conceptual change? In S. Carey & R. Gelman (Eds.), *The epigenesis of mind: Essays on biology and cognition* (pp. 257–291). Hillsdale, NJ: Erlbaum.

Carey, S. (1999). Sources of conceptual change. In E. Scholnick, K. Nelson, S. Gelman, & P. Miller (Eds.), *Conceptual development: Piaget's legacy* (pp. 293–326). Mahwah, NJ: Erlbaum.

Carey, S., & Spelke, E. S. (1994). Domain specific knowledge and conceptual change. In L. Hirschfeld, & S. Gelman (Eds.), *Mapping the mind: Domain specificity in cognition and culture* (pp. 169–200). Cambridge: Cambridge University Press.

Chi, M. (1992). Conceptual change within and across ontological categories: Examples from learning and discovery in science. *Minnesota Studies in the Philosophy of Science, 15*, 129–186.

diSessa, A. A., & Sherin, B. L. (1998). What Changes in Conceptual Change? *International Journal of Science Education, 20*, 1155.

Fodor, J. A. (1972). Some reflections on L.S. Vygotsky's Thought And Language, *Cognition, 1*, 83–95.

Fodor, J. A. (1998). *Concepts: Where cognitive science went wrong.* New York: Oxford University Press.

Friedman, W., (2001). The development of an intuitive understanding of entropy. *Child Development, 72*, 460–473.

Friedman, W., (2002). Arrows of time in infancy: The representation of temporal-causal invariances. *Cognitive Psychology, 44*, 252–296.

Gelman, R. (1969). Conservation acquisition: A problem of learning to attend to relevant attributes. *Journal of Experimental Child Psychology, 7*, 167–187.

Gergely, G., Nadasdy, Z., Csibra, G., & Biro, S. (1995). Taking the intentional stance at 12 months of age. *Cognition, 56*, 165–193.

Gutheil, G., Vera, A., & Keil, F. C. (1998). Do houseflies think?: Patterns of induction and biological beliefs in development, *Cognition, 66*, 33–49.

Hatano, G., & Inagaki, K. (1994). Young children's naive theory of biology. *Cognition, 50*, 171–188.

Inagaki, K., & Hatano, G. (2002). *Young children's naïve thinking about the biological world.* New York: Psychology Press.

Keil, F. C. (1989). *Concepts, kinds, and cognitive development.* Cambridge: MIT Press.

Keil, F. C. (1999) Cognition, content and development. In M. Bennett (Ed.), *Developmental psychology: Prospects & achievements* (pp. 165–184). London: Psychology Press.

Keil, F. C. (2003). That's life: Coming to understand biology. *Human Development, 46*, 369–377.

Keil, F. C. (2006). Cognitive science and cognitive development. In W. Damon & R. Lerner (Series Eds.) & D. Kuhn & R. S. Siegler (Vol. Eds.), *Handbook of child psychology: Vol 2: Cognition, perception, and language* (6th ed., pp. 609-635). New York: Wiley.

Keil, F. C., Smith, C. S., Simons, D., & Levin, D. (1998). Two dogmas of conceptual empiricism, *Cognition, 65*, 103–135.

Kuhlmeier, V., Bloom, P., & Wynn, K., (2004). Do 5-month-old infants see humans as material objects? *Cognition, 94*, 95.

Kuhn, T. (1962). *The structure of scientific revolutions.* Chicago, IL: University of Chicago Press.

Leslie, A. (1984). Infant perception of a manual pick-up event. *British Journal of Developmental Psychology, 2*, 19–32.

Leslie, A. M. (1994). ToMM, ToBy, and Agency: Core architecture and domain specificity. In L. Hirschfeld & S. Gelman (Eds.), *Mapping the mind: Domain specificity in cognition and culture* (pp. 119–148). New York: Cambridge University Press.

Lutz, D. J. (2003). Young children's understanding of the biological and behavioral processes underlying life and death. Unpublished Doctoral Dissertation

Mandler, J. M. (2004). *The foundations of mind: The origins of the conceptual system.* New York: Oxford University Press.

McGarrigle, J., & Donaldson, M. (1974). Conservation accidents. *Cognition, 3*, 341–350.

Meltzoff, A. (1995). Understanding the intentions of others: Re-enactment of intended acts by 18-month-old children, *Developmental Psychology, 31*, 838–850.

Murphy, G. L. (2002). *The big book of concepts.* Cambridge, MA: MIT Press.

Nersessian, N. (1989). Conceptual change in science and in science education. *Synthese*, 163–183.

Newman, G. E., Keil, F. C., Kuhlmeier, V., & Wynn, K. (2005, April). 12 Month-olds Know That Agents Defy Entropy: Exploring the Relationship Between Order and Intentionality. Society for Research in Child Development, Atlanta, GA.

Newman, G. E., Keil, F. C., Kuhlmeier, V., & Wynn, K. (under review). One-year-olds appreciate that only intentional agents can create order.

Piaget, J., & Inhelder, B. (1975). *The origin of the idea of chance in children*. New York: Norton.

Poulin-Dubois, D., Lepage, A., & Ferland, D. (1996). Infants' concept of animacy. *Cognitive Development, 11*, 19.

Quine, W. V., & Ullian, J.S. (1978). *The web of belief*. New York: Random House.

Rakison, D., & Poulin-Dubois, D. (2001). Developmental origin of the animate–inanimate distinction. *Psychological Bulletin, 127*, 209.

Ross, N., Medin, D. L., Coley, J. D., & Atran, S. (2003). Cultural and Experiential Differences in the Development of Folkbiological Induction. *Cognitive Development, 18*, 25–47.

Rozin, P. (1976). The evolution of intelligence and access to the cognitive unconscious. In J. M. Sprague & A. N. Epstein (Eds.), *Progress in psychobiology and physiological psychology, Vol. 6* (pp. 245–280). New York: Academic Press.

Saxe, R., Tenenbaum, J. B., & Carey, S. (2005). Secret agents: Inferences about hidden causes by 10- and 12-month-old infants. *Psychological Science, 16,* 995–1001.

Shatz, M., & Gelman, R. (1973). The development of communication skills: Modifications in the speech of young children as a function of listener. *Monographs of the Society for Research in Child Development, 38*, 1–38.

Shultz, T. R., & Cottington, M. (1981). Development of the concept of energy conservation and entropy. *Journal of Experimental Child Psychology, 31*, 131–152.

Smith, E. E., & Medin, D. L. (1981). *Categories and concepts*. Cambridge, MA: Harvard University Press.

Spelke, E., Phillips, A., & Woodward, A. (1995). Infants' knowledge of object motion and human action. In D. Sperber, D. Premack, & A. J. Premack (Ed.), *Causal cognition: A multidisciplinary debate* (chapter 3). Oxford: Oxford University Press.

Thagard, P. (1992). *Conceptual revolutions*. Princeton, NJ: Princeton University Press.

Vosniadou, S., & Brewer, W. F. (1987). Theories of knowledge restructuring in development. *Review of Educational Research, 57,* 51–67.

Waxman, S. R., Medin, D. L., & Ross, N. (in press). Folkbiological reasoning from a cross-cultural developmental perspective: Early essentialist notions are shaped by cultural beliefs. *Developmental Psychology*.

Woodward, A. (1998). Infants selectively encode the goal object of an actor's reach. *Cognition, 69*, 1–34.

5

Relations Between Short- and Long-Term Changes in Children's Thinking

Robert S. Siegler
Carnegie Mellon University

Matija Svetina
University of Ljubljana

The relation between short-term and long-term change (a.k.a. learning and development, microgenetic and macrogenetic change) is among the enduring issues in developmental psychology. Classic theories of cognitive development have taken strong stances on this issue; indeed, part of the reason that these theories are considered classic is that they include clear and well-argued positions about the relation of short-term and long-term change. The stances that have been taken by the classic theorists, however, vary considerably.

Werner (1948, 1957) and Vygotsky (1934/1962) viewed short-term change as a speeded-up version of long-term change. That is, they believed that the two involved the same qualitatively distinct understandings, that the understandings emerged in the same order, and that they emerged through the same underlying processes. Learning theorists (e.g., Bijou & Baer, 1961) also viewed short- and long-term change as fundamentally similar but, unlike Werner and Vygotsky, they viewed both as occurring through gradual incremental processes and not including qualitatively distinct stages. Piaget (e.g., 1964, 1970) expressed a third perspective; he viewed the two types of change, which he referred to as learning and development, as fundamentally dissimilar. In his view, development created new cognitive structures; learning merely filled-in the details of specific content. The contrast among these positions is evident in the following quotations from Vygotsky, Piaget, and Bijou:

> This (microgenetic) analysis permits us to uncover the very essence of the genetic (developmental) process of concept formation in a schematic form, and thus gives us the key to the understanding of the process as it unfolds in real life. (Vygotsky, 1962, p. 69)

> By contrast (with development), learning under external reinforcement (e.g., permitting the subject to observe the results of the deduction he should have made or informing him verbally)

produces either very little change in logical thinking or a striking momentary change with no real comprehension. (Piaget, 1970, p. 714)

...development reflects the convergence of the basic principles of behavior analysis. (Bijou & Ribes, 1996, p. 10)

The relation of short-term to long-term change continues to be of major interest within contemporary theories: dynamic systems (Fischer & Bidell, 2006; Thelen & Smith, 2006; van Geert, 1998), neo-Piagetian (Case, 1998; Karmiloff-Smith, 1992; Liben, 1987), sociocultural (Cole, 2006; Gauvain, 2001), and information processing (Rogers & McClelland, 2004; Munakata, 2006; Siegler, 2006). However, a lack of empirical data directly relevant to comparing the two types of changes has prevented understanding from proceeding very far.

In this chapter, we describe an experimental design that can help advance understanding of the relation between short- and long-term change: *the microgenetic/cross-sectional design*. The purpose of this experimental design is to provide maximally parallel information about change at varying time scales. To convey the main characteristics and uses of the approach, we first describe the microgenetic method for obtaining data about short-term change, then describe how it can be combined with standard cross-sectional designs, and then describe findings from two studies in which we have used microgenetic/cross-sectional designs. The two studies document surprisingly close parallels between short-term changes, elicited by directly relevant experiences, and long-term changes, elicited by the combination of maturation and the myriad tangentially relevant experiences that occur in the course of children's everyday lives.

Both of these main examples involve strategic change, because these are the contexts in which the microgenetic/cross-sectional design has been applied within a single study. However, the argument applies as strongly to conceptual change as it does to strategic change, as indicated by situations in which separate studies have applied microgenetic and cross-sectional methods to the same task and age range. Consider John Opfer's studies of acquisition of the concept of living things. Opfer and Gelman's (2001) cross-sectional study showed that 5- and 10-year-olds differ in parallel ways in their judgments of which objects are alive and which objects tend to move toward desirable goals. Five-year-olds judged animals to be the only living things and to be the only type of thing that would move differentially toward goals, such as food and water, which would promote their functioning. In contrast, 10-year-olds believed that both plants and animals were alive and that both would move toward goals that promoted their functioning. Opfer and Siegler's (2004) microgenetic study of acquisition of the same concept demonstrated that presenting 5-year-olds with information that plants as well as animals would move toward goals that promoted their functioning led the large majority of children to infer that plants as well as animals were alive. Presenting peers with information that plants as well as animals grow and need water did not promote this inference nearly as often.

Opfer's cross-sectional and microgenetic studies provided stronger evidence than either could alone that movement toward functional goals was crucial in acquisition of understanding of living things. They also strongly suggest that although the two examples below concern strategic change, the microgenetic/cross-sectional approach is equally applicable to examining conceptual change. Perhaps most important, they support the central conclusion of the present chapter: short-term changes, produced by specific experiences designed to stimulate formation of a strategy or concept, are surprisingly similar to long-term changes, produced by maturation and general experience. Evidence for this conclusion is described below, followed by a hypothesis regarding why the parallel patterns of change arise.

THE MICROGENETIC METHOD

Over the past 25 years, microgenetic designs have been used increasingly often to study cognitive development (for a recent review of research using the approach, see Siegler, 2006). The main reason for the increasing use of such designs is the precise descriptions of changing competence that they often yield. The microgenetic method is defined by three main characteristics.

1. Observations span the period of rapidly changing competence.
2. The density of observations within this period is high, relative to the rate of change of the knowledge or skills of interest.
3. The observations of changing performance are analyzed intensively, with the goal of inferring the representations and processes that gave rise to them.

The second characteristic is especially important. Intensively examining performance while it is changing provides the high temporal resolution needed to describe the process of change. The detailed data about changes yielded by such studies also allow us to discriminate between alternative underlying mechanisms. Many mechanisms could potentially produce changes of a general sort (e.g., moving from not understanding X at 5 years of age to understanding X at 7 years of age). However, far fewer mechanisms could give rise to the highly specific data about changes in strategy use, particular errors, solution times, and breadth and rate of generalization that can emerge from microgenetic studies. In other words, the detailed data generated by microgenetic studies constrain the range of mechanisms that could produce the changes.

Microgenetic methods have proven useful for testing predictions of a wide variety of theoretical approaches and for studying a wide variety of topics and age groups. They have been used to test predictions from diverse theoretical approaches: information processing (Alibali, 1999; Chen & Siegler, 2000), dynamic systems (Spencer, Vereijken, Diedrich, & Thelen, 2000; van Geert, 2002), neo-Piagetian (Pine & Messer, 2000; Thornton, 1999), and sociocultural (Duncan & Pratt, 1997; Foreman & MacPhail, 1993). They also have been used to study development in a wide range of content areas: language (Gershkoff-Stowe & Smith, 1997), memory (Schlagmüller & Schneider, 2002), attention (Miller & Aloise-Young, 1995), locomotion (Thelen & Ulrich, 1991), mathematics (Goldin-Meadow & Alibali, 2002), theory of mind (Amsterlaw & Wellman, 2006), biology (Opfer & Siegler, 2004), and physics reasoning (Perry & Lewis, 1999), among them. Moreover, they have proved applicable to a wide range of populations: infants (Adolph, 1997), toddlers (Chen & Siegler, 2000), preschoolers (Johnson & Mervis, 1994), school-age children (Schauble, 1996), adolescents (Kuhn et al., 1995), and adults (Granott, 1998).

In addition to this broad applicability, microgenetic studies have suggested a conceptual framework for thinking about cognitive growth (Siegler, 1996). This framework distinguishes among five dimensions of growth: its path, rate, breadth, sources, and variability. The *path of change* concerns distinct knowledge states through which children progress while gaining competence. The *rate of change* involves the amount of time and experience needed to produce initial use of an approach and the amount of time and experience separating initial use of an approach from consistent use of it. The *breadth of change* involves how widely the new approach is generalized to other problems, contexts, and related capabilities. The *sources of change* are the causes that set the change in motion. The *variability of change* involves differences among children on the other dimensions of change.

An especially encouraging characteristic of microgenetic studies is that despite the diversity of theoretical approaches, content areas, and populations associated with their use, they have yielded rather consistent findings regarding these dimensions of change (Chinn, 2006; Kuhn,

1995; Miller & Coyle, 1999; Siegler, 2006). A common finding regarding the path of change is that just before discovery of a new approach, children shift from relatively consistent use of a single incorrect approach to more variable incorrect behavior (Alibali, 1999; Goldin-Meadow, 2001; Graham & Perry, 1993; Siegler, 1995). The rate of change tends to be gradual, with less sophisticated, earlier emerging approaches continuing to be used well after more sophisticated approaches also are used (Amsterlaw & Wellman, 2006; Bjorklund, Miller, Coyle, & Slawinski, 1997; Kuhn et al., 1995). The breadth of change often is fairly narrow, though some generalization to conceptually related tasks also is common (Kuhn et al., 1995; Schauble, 1990, 1996; Siegler, 2002). Variability of learning tends to be high; children learn via different paths, at different rates, and with differing degrees of generalization. Finally, certain sources of cognitive growth, such as encouragement to explain observations of physical phenomena or other people's reasoning, operate over a wide age range and in diverse content domains (Calin-Jageman & Ratner, 2005; Pine & Messer, 2000; Siegler, 2002).

The inherent importance of understanding how change occurs, together with the information that microgenetic studies have yielded about change, have led to widespread agreement that such studies are useful for understanding children's learning. There also is widespread agreement that at a general level, the short-term changes that are seen in microgenetic studies resemble the longer term changes that are seen in cross-sectional and longitudinal studies (e.g., Fischer & Bidell, 1998; Granott, 1998; Miller & Coyle, 1999). There is much less agreement, however, as to the level of specificity of the parallels. Miller and Coyle (1999), Pressley (1992), and Kuhn and Franklin (2006) all have noted that the degree of similarity between microgenetic and age-related change is uncertain, both at the level of the descriptive course of change and at the level of underlying mechanisms. They also have noted that the conditions used to elicit change in microgenetic studies often differ from those that elicit it in the everyday environment. Even when the eliciting events are basically similar, the higher density of relevant experiences and the more consistent feedback in the laboratory setting could result in the changes being quite different in their specifics. These issues led Miller and Coyle (1999, p. 212) to conclude: "Although the microgenetic method reveals how behavior *can* change, it is less clear whether behavior typically *does* change in this way in the natural environment" (italics in original). The goal of the microgenetic/cross-sectional approach is to provide maximally comparable circumstances in which to address this issue.

THE MICROGENETIC/CROSS-SECTIONAL DESIGN

The basic logic that underlies this design is that combining cross-sectional and microgenetic components within the same experiment should yield maximally comparable data. The cross-sectional component of the design involves presenting the same tasks and measures to children of different ages. The microgenetic component involves randomly selecting a subset of children from the youngest group of the same population, presenting them an experience that is designed to promote improvement on the task of primary interest, and then comparing their performance on a posttest to that of peers who did not receive the experience.

Assuming that the experimental condition produces significant improvement on the task of greatest interest, the next step is to identify an age range within the cross-sectional part of the design over which comparable amounts of growth occur on the task. This step involves selecting a global measure of performance on the task of interest, such as percent correct answers, and then locating within the cross-sectional sample two comparison groups, one for performance at pretest and one for performance at posttest. Age peers who were not assigned to the experimental condition ordinarily provide the pretest comparison group. The posttest comparison group is the age group within the cross-sectional sample whose performance on the global measure was most similar to the posttest performance of children in the experimental condition. Identification of cross-sectional and microgenetic samples that showed comparable global change (e.g., from 25% to 75% correct) allows analysis of the degree of similarity of the pattern of changes on the finer grain measures and thus of the degree of similarity of the patterns of short-term and long-term change. Choosing a comparison age range over which comparable overall change occurred is essential, because the crucial issue is the degree of similarity of the *pattern* of microgenetic and age-related change when the overall amount of change is equated. The pattern of change can involve whether the same qualitatively distinct knowledge states occur, whether these knowledge states emerge in the same order, whether the same types of errors are most common, and whether the same quantitative measures reveal change or absence of change. All of these aspects of the pattern of change were examined in the present studies.

A MICROGENETIC/CROSS-SECTIONAL STUDY OF MATRIX COMPLETION

In an initial microgenetic/cross-sectional study, Siegler and Svetina (2002) examined the development of matrix completion. The matrix completion task that we presented was modeled after one used by Inhelder and Piaget (1964). As illustrated in Figure 5.1, each problem involved a 2×2 matrix. Objects were present in the top row and the left column; the bottom right square was empty. Six alternative responses that could complete the matrix were presented alongside it. The task was to choose the response alternative that, if inserted into the empty square, would result in the two objects at the bottom being related in the same way as the top objects at the top, and the two objects on the right being related in the same way as the two objects on the left. All objects in the problems varied along four dimensions: form, size, color, and orientation (facing left or right). Thus, one way of thinking about the item in Figure 5.1 is: "A large, gray mouse facing right is to a large gray bird facing right, as a small gray mouse facing left is to a ___." The child could then search for a small, gray bird facing left and select the response alternative that matched that description.

This task was of interest for several reasons. It assesses in a particularly direct way children's ability to focus on multiple dimensions; consistently correct performance requires considering all four dimensions. The task, and the hypothesized underlying ability of multiple classification, play a central role within Piaget's theory. The task also assesses analogical reasoning ability,

FIGURE 5.1 Example of a matrix completion problem.

TABLE 5.1
Tasks Presented to Children of Different Ages and in Different Conditions in Each Session

	Session						
	1	*2*	*3*	*4*	*5*	*6*	*7*
6-year-olds							
Experimental	MC, C, R	MC*	MC*	MC*	MC*	MC	MC & C
Control	MC, C, R						MC & C
7-year-olds	MC, C, R						
8-year-olds	MC, C, R						

MC = Matrix Completion. C = Conservation. R = Ravens Progressive Matrices Test.
*Feedback and self-explanation questions given.

which plays a central role in information processing theories (e.g., Gentner, 1989; Halford, 1993; Tomasello, 2006). Moreover, performance on matrix completion problems is predictive of school achievement, which has led to such problems being included on many intelligence tests.

Another reason for our interest in this matrix completion task was that it allowed assessment of the detailed patterning of change. The six possible answers on each problem included only one that was correct on all dimensions, but it included four others that were correct on three of the four dimensions (the remaining answer was incorrect on all dimensions). Thus, children could improve on one or more of the dimensions (e.g., size) by more consistently choosing alternatives on which those dimensions were correct, even if the children did not consistently choose the correct answer. Similarly, by asking why children believed that the answer they had chosen was correct, we could examine their explicit understanding of the importance of each dimension for making the correct choice.

Siegler and Svetina's (2002) study of matrix completion included seven sessions. Sessions 1–6 were presented at weekly intervals; Session 7 was presented two months after Session 6. The tasks presented in each session are described in Table 5.1.

In Session 1, 6-, 7-, and 8-year-olds were presented the matrix completion task, as well as tests of intelligence, short-term memory, and conservation knowledge. This session provided all of the data for the cross-sectional component of the study; it also provided the pretest measures for the microgenetic component.

The 6-year-olds were randomly assigned to the experimental or control group. In each of the four sessions after the pretest (Sessions 2–5), children in the experimental condition were presented 22 matrix completion problems with feedback and requests to explain why the correct answer was correct on each problem. The combination of feedback and requests to explain correct answers had been found in previous studies to promote learning on a number of tasks, including biological reasoning, geometry, number conservation, mathematical equality, and computer programming problems (Bielaczyc, Pirolli, & Brown, 1995; Chi, de Leeuw, Chiu, & LaVancher, 1994; Siegler, 1995, 2002). The combination was expected to be effective in promoting understanding of matrix completion as well. In Session 6, children in the experimental condition were presented another 22 problems but without feedback; the goal was to assess their knowledge at the end of the instructional experience.

In Session 7, matrix completion and conservation problems were presented to 6-year-olds in the experimental group and to a control group that included 6-year-olds who had participated in Session 1 but not in Sessions 2–6. Comparing changes in matrix completion performance between Sessions 1 and 7 allowed us to test whether the experimental condition produced changes greater than would have occurred without participation in Sessions 2–6. Comparing performance in Sessions 6 and 7 provided a measure of the stability of learning among children in the experimental group (because the two sessions were separated by two months). Examining differences between the experimental and control groups in conservation performance in Sessions 1 and 7 provided a measure of the breadth of learning (because no direct experience with conservation was provided in Sessions 2–6). Differences in conservation performance between children in the experimental and control groups in Session 7 but not Session 1 would indicate that the matrix completion experience generalized beyond the immediate task.

The combination of microgenetic and cross-sectional components within this design enabled us to compare the short-term learning within the microgenetic condition to the long-term learning within the cross-sectional comparison on 10 measures of matrix completion performance: percentage of correct answers; percentage of answers that were correct on the dimensions of form, size, orientation, and color; percentage of explanations that cited each of these four dimensions; and predominant type of errors. The data also allowed two other, less direct comparisons, one of stability of learning over time and the other of generalization of learning to novel tasks. The reason why these comparisons were less direct was that the cross-sectional data did not provide information regarding stability over time or generalization across tasks, because the same children were not measured at different ages. However, because Piaget (e.g., 1964) identified stability and generalization as among the key properties that differentiate development from learning, and because individual differences in intellectual achievement tend to be positively correlated across tasks and stable over time (Brody, 1992), it seemed worthwhile to determine whether stability and generalization also are present within short-term microgenetic change.

Findings Regarding Microgenetic Changes

Changes over sessions were analyzed along five dimensions: the source, path, rate, breadth, and variability of change.

Source of Change

As shown in Figure 5.2, the combination of problem solving practice, feedback, and self-explanations resulted in increased learning over the seven sessions. In Session 1, the experimental

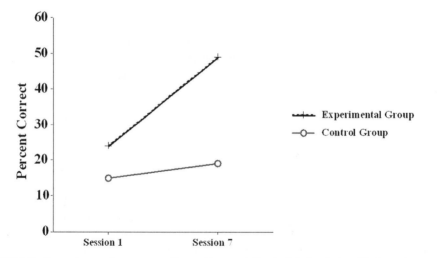

FIGURE 5.2   Percent correct answers on the matrix completion task in the first and last sessions among 6-year-olds in the control and experimental groups.

and control group children produced similar numbers of correct answers; in Session 7, children in the experimental group produced more correct answers. Viewed from a different perspective, number of correct answers increased between Sessions 1 and 7 among children in the experimental group but not among peers in the control group.

Variability of Change

Individual children's performance fit one of three patterns: precocious, nonlearner, or learner. Some children (17%) fit the precocious pattern, which required generation of at least 80% correct answers in the first session and a mean of at least 80% correct over the last three sessions. Other children (53%) fit the nonlearner pattern, defined as fewer than 33% correct answers in the first session and a mean of fewer than 33% correct in the last three sessions. The remaining children (30%) fit the learner pattern, defined as fewer than 33% correct in the first session and a mean of more than 80% correct over the last three sessions. Note that these patterns were far from inherently exhaustive; if a child answered between 33% and 80% correct in either the first session or the last three sessions, the child would not have fit into any of the categories. Lending external validation to these individual difference patterns, children who fit the precocious pattern on the matrix completion task scored significantly higher on the Ravens IQ test than did those who fit the nonlearner pattern, with children who fit the learner pattern in-between and not differing significantly from either of the other two groups.

Path of Change

A backward trials graph (Figure 5.3) illustrated the path that led to the learners discovering how to solve matrix completion problems. In this type of graph, the 0 trial block is the point at which each child meets the criterion of discovery, in this case three consecutive correct answers on the six-choice task. Percent correct in this 0 trial block is by definition 100%. The –1 trial block refers to the 3 trials just before the 0 trial block, the –2 trial block refers to the 3 trials before that, and so on. Thus, the graph illustrates what was occurring just before the discovery and just after it.

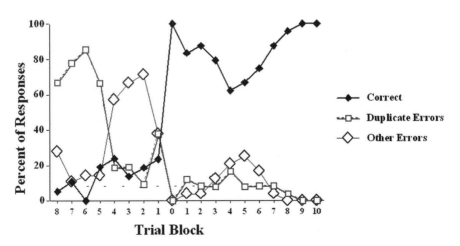

FIGURE 5.3 Percentage of answers that were correct, that were duplicates of an object already in the matrix, or that followed other incorrect forms on the trial blocks leading up to and following each child's discovery of the correct solution strategy.

As shown in Figure 5.3, most of children's early errors were duplicates, that is, answers that were identical to the object directly above or alongside the empty square in the 2×2 matrix (e.g., the small gray mouse facing left). However, about 12 trials (4 trial blocks) before the discovery, the frequency of duplicate errors greatly decreased and the frequency of other errors considerably increased. Thus, children rejected the predominant incorrect approach well before they discovered the correct approach.

In the trial blocks immediately after the discovery, accuracy decreased somewhat from the 100% level during the trial block of discovery; it took about a dozen trials on average before the learners were again consistently correct (Figure 5.3). However, in all trial blocks after the discovery, percent correct was much higher than in any trial block before the discovery.

Rate of Change

Viewed from the perspective of the overall group, learning occurred gradually over the first four sessions (25%, 36%, 43%, and 50% correct in Sessions 1–4). It remained steady at around 50% in Sessions 4–7. In contrast, at the level of individual learners, change was quite abrupt. Returning to the data from the backward trials graph (Figure 5.3), percent correct increased from 20% correct on the 12 trials before each child's discovery to 78% correct on the 12 trials of that child after it (the 3 trials in the 0 trial block were not included in this comparison, because they were correct by definition).

Breadth of Change

Children in the experimental condition generalized their experience with the matrix completion problems to improve their conservation performance. As shown in Figure 5.4, precocious children did well on the conservation problems from the beginning, nonlearners did poorly both before and after experience with the matrix completion problems, and learners answered inaccurately before experience with the matrix completion problems but accurately after the experience. The transfer shown by the learners was evident even after IQ was partialed out. Learning to consider multiple relevant dimensions on the matrix completion task may have led children also to consider multiple relevant dimensions on the conservation problems.

Findings Regarding Changes with Age

Consistent with Inhelder and Piaget's (1964) findings, and those of a variety of researchers since then, children's matrix completion performance improved considerably between 6- and 8-years. Percentage of correct answers increased from 20% for 6-year-olds to 48% for 7-year-olds to 78% for 8-year-olds. Percent correct answers on each of the four dimensions also increased over this age span, though the only dimension that was cited more often by children was orientation. At all ages, the same type of error, duplicate errors, predominated. Percent correct conservation answers improved from 24% correct at age 6 years to 62% at 7 years and 74% correct at 8 years.

RELATIONS BETWEEN SHORT-TERM AND LONG-TERM CHANGE

The change in percent correct answers between Sessions 1 and 7 of children in the experimental condition of the microgenetic part of the study was almost identical to that shown between 6 and 7 years by children in the cross-sectional part. In both cases, children progressed from about 20%

TABLE 5.2
Microgenetic and Age-Related Changes

Variable	Observed Changes		Match
	Over Sessions *(1 to 7)*	*Over Age* *(6 to 7 years)*	
Total % correct	Increase	Increase	+
% Form correct	No change	No change	+
% Orientation correct	Increase	Increase	+
% Size correct	Increase	Increase	+
% Color correct	No change	No change	+
% Form cited	No change	No change	+
% Orientation cited	No change	Increase	-
% Size cited	No change	No change	+
% Color cited	No change	No change	+
Predominant Error	Duplicates	Duplicates	+
Stability Over Time	Yes	Predicted	+
Transfer to Conservation	Yes	Predicted	+

to 50% correct. This allowed us to compare the patterning of changes over the seven sessions with changes from 6 years to 7 years.

Table 5.2 is a comparison of the presence or absence of microgenetic and age-related changes on 12 variables. On all but one measure, changes either were present in both microgenetic and cross-sectional comparisons or were present under neither condition. In addition, duplicate errors predominated under both conditions, and the absolute percentage of duplicate errors was nearly identical: 57% duplicate errors among 6- and 7-year-olds versus 59% over the seven sessions (chance was 31%). The changes within the experimental condition of the microgenetic study also met criteria that Piaget (1964) claimed were basic characteristics of development but not of learning: transfer to related problems and stability over time. The data showing transfer to conservation were discussed earlier and are shown in Figure 5.4. The data on stability over time are best summarized by the correlation of $r = .98$ between percent correct matrix completion answers in Sessions 6 and 7, which were separated by two months. Such transfer and stability over time could not be assessed within this (or other) cross-sectional designs, but the data from the present study did indicate parallels between the observed microgenetic changes and the theoretically predicted developmental change.

Discussion of Matrix Completion Findings

The results of Siegler and Svetina (2002) revealed striking similarities between short- and long-term changes. On five measures, changes were present in both the microgenetic and cross-sectional comparisons; on five measures, changes were absent on both measures; and the main type of error was the same on both. On only one measure were the outcomes different for cross-sectional and microgenetic comparisons. This indicates that parallels between short- and long-term changes are not just present at a general level; the parallels, at least with regard to acquisition of matrix completion, are quite specific.

In most ways, the results of the microgenetic component of this study were representative

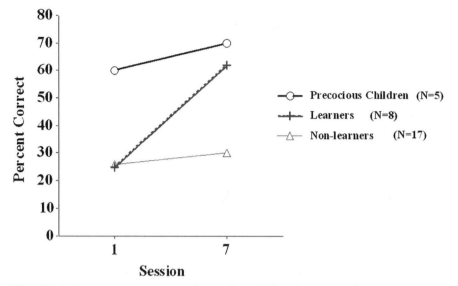

FIGURE 5.4   Percent correct answers of precocious children, learners, and non-learners on the conservation task in Sessions 1 and 7.

of microgenetic findings in general. One exception, however, involved the rate of uptake of the newly discovered strategy, which was considerably faster in this study than in most others.

Once children met the discovery criterion for the matrix completion task, they showed relatively few regressions to previous approaches, both within- and between-sessions. One likely reason was the large difference in accuracy yielded by the correct strategy and the two other approaches that children used to solve matrix completion problems. Duplicate responses were always wrong, and choosing randomly among the response alternatives yielded only 17% correct answers. Large differences in accuracy between old and new strategies have been found to be related to rate of uptake of newly discovered strategies in general (Siegler, 2006).

Siegler and Svetina (2002) suggested that another factor also might have been influential — the logic underlying the new strategy. The tasks on which uptake of new strategies have been fastest — number conservation, mathematical equality, 20 Questions, and matrix completion, among them — have tended to be ones on which the new strategy was logically as well as empirically superior (Goldin-Meadow & Alibali, 2002; Siegler, 1995; Siegler & Svetina, 2002; Thornton, 1999). The role of the logic underlying strategies in this variable — whether new strategies are logically, as well as empirically, superior — was directly examined in Siegler and Svetina's (2006) study of class inclusion.

A MICROGENETIC/CROSS-SECTIONAL STUDY OF CLASS INCLUSION

On standard class inclusion problems, children are presented with drawings of two types of objects, with both types being subsets of the same set: dogs, cats, and animals; bananas, strawberries, and fruit; trucks, buses, and vehicles; and so on. The experimenter asks children to indicate whether the larger subset or the set has a greater number of objects. For example, children might be presented pictures of five dogs and three cats and asked, "Here we have dogs, cats, and animals: Do we have more dogs or more animals?"

This task was of particular interest because it allowed us to examine whether young children learn more effectively from logical or empirical explanations of the utility of new strategies.

Correct answers to class inclusion problems can be justified deductively, for example by saying, "Dogs are a kind of animal, there are also other animals, so there must be more animals than dogs." The same conclusion can be justified inductively, for example by saying, "Counting indicated that there are five dogs and that there are eight animals, so there are more animals." The existence of both logical and empirical justifications for the same conclusion allowed us to examine whether 5-year-olds would learn more from explanations of correct answers that cited the logical relation or whether they would learn more from explanations of correct answers that cited the empirical relation.

Each possibility was plausible. Supporting the possibility that 5-year-olds prefer empirical explanations were findings that 5-year-olds rely on empirical strategies in many situations in which older individuals rely on logical strategies. Most 5-year-olds solve class inclusion problems via the empirical procedure of comparing the number of objects in the two subsets (e.g., five dogs vs. three cats) (Piaget, 1964). Children of this age also rely on empirical relations on other problems that older individuals would solve deductively. For example, when presented tautologies (e.g., "I either am holding a green chip in my hand or I'm not") or contradictions ("I am holding and not holding a green chip in my hand"), and asked whether they needed the experimenter to open her hands to tell if the statement was true or false, most 5-year-olds chose the empirical strategy; they said they needed the experimenter to open her hands to tell (Osherson & Markman, 1975). Most 5-year-olds also confuse logically determinate and logically indeterminate problems and attempt empirical solutions to scientific reasoning problems that have logical solutions (Fay & Klahr, 1996; Klahr & Chen, 2003).

Also favoring the prediction that children should learn more from empirical explanations, 5-year-olds seem to have a particular fondness for the type of empirical strategy relevant to class inclusion, counting. They use counting even when it is inappropriate to do so. For example, K. Miller (1984) found that 5-year-olds created "fair" divisions of food between two birds by counting out equal numbers of pieces of food, even though the sizes of the "food" differed. Similarly, Levin (1989) found that 5-year-olds often counted the passage of two temporal durations and judged the higher number to indicate the longer time, regardless of whether the counting had proceeded at the same speed. This reliance on counting strategies, and on empirical rather than logical strategies in general, suggested that 5-year-olds would learn empirical strategies more readily than logical ones.

Other arguments, however, suggested that the rate and completeness of uptake of logical strategies might be as great or greater than that of empirical approaches. The above-cited findings of young children using empirical strategies in situations where older children and adults use logical ones may reflect the young children not understanding the logical strategies. If the logic was made clear to them, they might prefer the logical strategies or have no preference between the two. In addition, as noted earlier, several of the microgenetic studies in which newly discovered strategies have been adopted most rapidly have involved acquisition of logical reasoning strategies. Thus, the fact that young children use empirical strategies to solve problems that adults and older children solve via logical strategies does not imply that children would choose empirical strategies if they understood that logical strategies would solve the problems.

Moreover, there were reasons to think that young children might prefer logical reasoning strategies if they understood how to execute and apply them to particular problems. Logical strategies often have large advantages in speed and accuracy. In the context of class inclusion, solving the problem logically both avoids the possibility of errors in counting and numerical comparison and takes less time. Foreseeing these benefits, or learning about them through experience with the strategies, might lead children to consistently adopt new logical strategies more rapidly than new empirical ones. In addition, to the extent that children are searching for basic logical understanding of domains, as theorists such as Gelman and Williams (1998) and Keil (2006) have proposed, logical strategies might be adopted faster and more completely than empirical strategies precisely because they are logically compelling. Therefore, we expected that the logical explanations would increase learning at least as much as the empirical explanations would.

Siegler and Svetina (2006) used a microgenetic/cross-sectional design to address this issue in the context of class inclusion. In the cross-sectional component of the study, 5-, 6-, 7-, 8-, 9-, and 10-year-olds were presented 10 class inclusion problems in a single session. The problems differed only in the exact types and numbers of objects that they included.

In the microgenetic part of the study, 5-year-olds were presented with 10 class inclusion problems in each of three sessions. These children were randomly assigned to four groups. Children in all four groups received feedback on whether each of their answers was correct, but the groups varied in the explanations that the experimenter provided to children regarding why the correct answer was correct. Consider the explanation that children in each group received following incorrect answers to a problem that involved six dogs and three cats. (In all groups, the explanations were attributed to a teacher who was not present but had given these explanations to the experimenter.) Children in the *empirical explanations group* were told that the teacher had said there were more animals than dogs because there were nine animals but only six dogs. To illustrate the counting procedure that yielded this outcome, the experimenter pointed to each animal in turn before saying there were nine, and to each dog in turn before saying there were six. Children in the *logical explanations group* were told that the teacher had said there were more animals than dogs because dogs are just a type of animal, so if there were dogs and some other animals, there must be more animals than dogs. Children in the *logical and empirical explanations group* were provided both explanations. Children in the *no explanations group* were given feedback on the correctness of their answer (as were children in the other three groups) but were not provided any explanation.

On trials on which children answered incorrectly, they were asked to judge how smart the teacher's explanation of the correct answer was. This was intended to provide a measure of conceptual understanding of the logical and empirical explanations. Previous studies have shown that conceptual understanding, as indexed by ability to answer questions about the intelligence of strategies, often diverges from procedural knowledge, as indexed by use of correct strategies. Sometimes conceptual understanding precedes use of correct strategies (Siegler & Crowley, 1994), sometimes the reverse is true (Briars & Siegler, 1984), and sometimes the two types of knowledge are highly similar (Cauley, 1998). Regarding class inclusion, it seemed very likely that adults would view the logical explanations as more conceptually advanced than the empirical ones; results of the study would reveal whether children have similar understanding and whether the understanding precedes or follows success in solving class inclusion problems.

Findings Regarding Microgenetic Change

The same dimensions of change that were used to analyze changes in matrix completion knowledge were used to analyze changes in knowledge of class inclusion.

Source of Change

In keeping with the experimental prediction, exposure to logical explanations led to children learning more than they did without the logical explanations (with feedback alone). Contrary to expectation, exposure to empirical explanations did not enhance learning beyond that produced by feedback alone, though there was some tendency in this direction. The differences in the effectiveness of the logical and empirical explanations increased over the three sessions. In Session 1, there was no difference between the groups that received logical explanations alone and empirical explanations alone, but differences were present in Sessions 2 and 3.

Path of Change

Previous cross-sectional studies of the development of class inclusion suggested that children proceed through three levels of understanding: systematically incorrect performance, chance-level performance, and correct performance (Chapman & McBride, 1992; Hodkin, 1987; McCabe, Siegel, Spence, & Wilkinson, 1982). The main basis for this conclusion was that percentage of correct answers at different ages improved from around 25% at 5 years of age to around 50% at 6 or 7 years of age to around 90% by 9 or 10 years of age. Within the microgenetic component of Siegler and Svetina (2006), some children progressed through these three phases, although others progressed directly from systematically incorrect to consistently correct performance. The exact numbers in each group varied with the exact criterion of discovery, but by all criteria, there were substantial numbers of children showing each pattern.

Rate of Change

The trial of discovery was operationally defined as the first trial within the first set of five consecutive correct answers that the child generated. Thus, if a child answered incorrectly on trials 1 and 4 and correctly on trials 5–9, the child would be said to have made the discovery on trial 5. The results did not vary substantially with the particular criterion of discovery; for example, 70% of children made the discovery at some time during the three sessions by the five consecutive correct answers criterion, and 74% would have made it if a three consecutive correct answers criterion had been used.

Most children who ever met the criterion for discovering a correct approach met it quite early in the experiment. Among the children who met the criterion in any of the three sessions, 82% met it in Session 1.

To examine the rate of discovery more precisely, we graphed the cumulative percentage of discoveries that had occurred by each of the 30 trials within the microgenetic experiment (Figure 5.5). In addition to illustrating that more children in the two groups that received logical explanations made the discovery, Figure 5.5 also illustrates that the difference between those who did and did not receive logical explanations arose through the logical explanations condition stimulating discoveries over a longer period. The difference is particularly clear in comparing the rate of discovery of children who only received the logical explanations with that of children who only received the empirical ones. Through the first five trials, more children who only received empirical explanations than who only received logical ones made the discovery (35% vs. 20% of the children in the two groups). In contrast, many more children who received logical explanations made the discovery after the fifth trial (45% vs. 15%). Viewed from a different perspective, 69% of children who received logical explanations who had not yet made the discovery by trial 5 made it afterward, whereas only 30% of children who received empirical explanations did. This pattern suggests that the logical explanations may have been difficult for the 5-year-olds to understand, but with repeated exposure, the children understood and learned from them, with the amount of learning eventually exceeding that from the empirical explanations.

Once children met the criterion of discovery, they answered correctly and, surprisingly, consistently, even more consistently than the children in Siegler and Svetina (2002) study. Children in previous multi-session microgenetic studies have often shown a great deal of regression to previous strategies from one session to the next (e.g., Miller & Aloise-Young, 1995; Siegler & Stern,

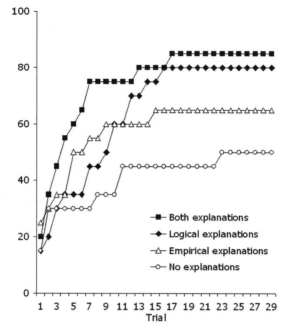

FIGURE 5.5   Cumulative percentage of children in each experimental condition reaching the discovery criterion.

1998), but this was not the case in the class inclusion study. Children who discovered the correct strategy in Session N answered correctly on 97% of the first five questions in Session N+1. The findings did not depend on the original discovery criteria requiring a relatively long string of consecutive correct answers. When a looser discovery criterion of three consecutive correct answers was used, children who met the criterion in one session answered 91% of problems correctly on the first three trials of the following session. This occurred under all four conditions; in none of them did children average even 10% errors after having met the discovery criterion.

Breadth of Learning

To examine the relation between conceptual and procedural knowledge of class inclusion, we first checked whether adults shared our intuition that the logical explanation was more conceptually advanced than the empirical one. We presented college students, who presumably understood class inclusion, each type of strategy and asked them to rate how smart they were. Almost all (59 of 60) of the college students rated the logical explanation as smarter than the empirical one.

The question then became whether 5-year-olds who did not initially solve class inclusion problems also would evaluate logical explanations as smarter. To find out, we compared the evaluations of logical and empirical explanations of children who received both types of explanations. Before the discovery, children in this group judged logical explanations to be smarter than empirical explanations (means of 2.8 vs. 2.2 on a 3-point scale with "3" being "very smart"). There were too few incorrect answers (the only problems on which children's evaluations were sought) to do a comparable evaluation of their views after the discovery. However, the difference in evaluations before the discovery, together with the greater learning from hearing logical explanations than empirical ones, indicated that even before children consistently solved class inclusion problems, they, like college students, found logical explanations more persuasive.

Variability of Change

Striking individual differences were present in both the rate and the path of change. With regard to the rate of change, children could be divided into fast learners, medium-rate learners, slow-learners, and non-learners. The fast-learner pattern (28% of children) was operationally defined as 90% or more correct answers in each of the three sessions. These children learned extremely quickly — the criterion of at least 90% correct in all three sessions meant that a child in this group could only advance one incorrect answer in the first session. Another 29% of 5-year-olds fit the medium-rate learner pattern, which was defined as fewer than 90% correct answers in Session 1 and 90% or more correct answers in Sessions 2 and 3. An additional 6% of children fit the slow-learner pattern, which was defined as fewer than 90% correct answers in Sessions 1 and 2, and at least 90% correct in Session 3. Finally, 28% of children fit the non-learner pattern, which was defined as 30% or fewer correct in all three sessions. Note that all four patterns, which together fit the response patterns of 91% of the children, departed strongly from a chance distribution, which would have yielded 50% correct in each session.

Analyses of variations in children's paths of change involved setting criteria for each hypothesized level of performance — consistently incorrect, chance, and consistently correct — and examining the fit of the criteria to individual children's performance. The period of below chance performance was defined as the trials before children generated two consecutive correct answers; the period of chance performance was defined as the trials in which children had responded correctly on two consecutive trials but not on five consecutive trials; and the period of consistently correct performance was defined as the trials following children having met the discovery criterion of five consecutive correct answers.

All children followed one of five paths. About half the children showed stability rather than change. The stability took two forms. One form of stability, shown by 19% of children, involved consistently correct responding. These children met the discovery criterion on the first five trials of the first session and answered 95% of subsequent problems correctly. The other form of stability, shown by 30% of children, involved consistently incorrect responding. These children answered only 6% of problems correctly, and none ever met the discovery criterion.

The other half of children showed one of three patterns of change. Some children (14% of the sample) progressed through all three hypothesized periods. In the first period, their accuracy was below chance (12% correct); in the second period, it was at chance (52% correct); and in the third period, it was far above chance (89% correct). Other children (30% of the sample) progressed directly from below chance to consistently correct performance. Their first two consecutive correct answers were immediately followed by three more consecutive correct answers. Before the discovery, they answered correctly on 16% of trials; after it, they answered correctly on 94% of trials. The relative sizes of this group and the group that progressed through all three approaches depended on the exact criteria for chance responding: If the criterion for a period of chance responding had been at least one correct response but not five consecutive correct responses, the numbers of children in the two groups would have been reversed. Finally, a few children (8% of the sample) answered the first two questions correctly, then generated chance level performance for an average of five trials (47% correct), and then, after the discovery, answered consistently correctly (97% correct). These children may have begun with the correct approach, regressed to chance level responding, and then answered consistently correctly, or they may have started at a chance level and proceeded to consistently correct responding.

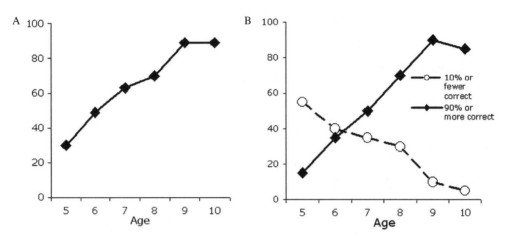

FIGURE 5.6   (A) Percent correct answers among 5- to 10-year-olds in cross-sectional experiment. (B) Percentage of 5- to 10-year-olds advancing 10% or fewer correct answers or 90% or more correct answers.

Findings Regarding Changes with Age

In the cross-sectional part of the study, groups of 20 children of each age between 5 and 10 years were presented a single session of 10 trials without feedback or explanations. As shown in Figure 5.6A, mean percent correct increased gradually with age—from well below chance (30% correct) among 5-year-olds, to chance (56% correct) for 6- and 7-year-olds, to well above chance (89% correct) among 9- and 10-year-olds. Thus, as in previous cross-sectional studies of class inclusion, percent correct improved from below chance to chance to consistently correct in this age range.

The data on individual performance, however, told quite a different story (Figure 5.6B). Simply put, at no age did many children perform at chance level. At all six ages, at least 70% of children answered either no more than 10% or at least 90% of problems correctly. Summed across the six age groups, this was true of 88% of children. Thus, at the level that could be revealed by cross-sectional sampling, the period between stable below chance performance and stable correct performance appeared to be very brief or nonexistent.

Relations Between Short-Term and Long-Term Change

The design used to study class inclusion included fewer measures that could be used to compare short- and long-term changes than did the design used to study matrix completion. The study of class inclusion did identify some marked similarities in the path and rate of such changes, though. When examined at a high level of aggregation — mean percent correct at different ages and in different sessions — the rate of change looked gradual in both cases. At this aggregated level, both microgenetic and cross-sectional data were consistent with previous suggestions that children first use a strategy that produces below-chance performance (because children compare the two subsets), then a strategy that produces chance performance (guessing or oscillating between correct and incorrect responding), and then a strategy that produces consistently correct performance (counting or logical deduction).

When examined at a more refined level — individual children's trial-by-trial performance — the data told quite a different story. The large majority of children of all ages in the cross-sectional sample were consistently correct or consistently incorrect. What changed with age was the percentage of children in each group. The large majority of children in the microgenetic sample also fit this pattern. Many children shifted from consistently incorrect to consistently correct performance without any transitional strategy. Even among those children who showed an intermediate state of chance-level performance, the state was very short-lived, usually only a few trials. Thus, as in Siegler and Svetina's (2002) study of matrix completion, short- and long-term changes in acquisition of knowledge about class inclusion showed clear parallels.

CONCLUSIONS

The present findings present evidence that short-term and long-term change show many highly specific parallels, as well as other, more general ones. This was especially evident in the findings of Siegler and Svetina (2002). In almost all instances, a given measure either showed change over both short and long time periods or showed an absence of change over both. Stability of change, a feature said by Piaget to characterize true developmental change but not learning, could hardly have been higher than the $r = .98$ correlation observed over the two-month period within the microgenetic sample. Not only did the same type of error predominate in both microgenetic and cross-sectional data sets; the percentage of such duplicate errors was virtually identical at the end of the microgenetic sessions as among the older children.

The parallels were especially striking, because the sources of change surely differed. We do not know what aspects of maturation and what experiences lead to improvements between 5 and 9 years in class inclusion and matrix completion performance, but we can be reasonably sure that the relevant experiences do not ordinarily resemble the experimental procedures of presenting these unusual tasks, telling children the correct answer, and then asking them to explain why that answer is correct. Indeed, it seems unlikely that most children ever encounter class inclusion problems outside the laboratory, much less encounter the present instructional procedure for helping children learn to solve them. Matrix completion problems are somewhat more common in the everyday environment, but it still seems likely that most children become able to solve them without prior, directly relevant, instructional experience with them. These observations raise the issue: Why would cognitive change at short and long time intervals show so many parallels, even when the sources that set the changes in motion clearly differ?

One possibility is that cognitive change is analogous to physical change in the locations of inanimate objects. Consider a stone perched near the top of a mountain. Any of a variety of events may set the stone in motion — erosion of objects around it, another stone or inanimate object colliding with it, an animal kicking or stepping on it, a thunderstorm with heavy winds and rain lashing it, and so on. Once set in motion, however, the stone's motion would be similar, as long as the amount and direction of forces impacting it were similar.

Cognitive change may be similar. Any number of particular experiences and maturational changes seem likely to be sufficient to set specific cognitive changes in motion. Once they are in motion, the changes may show many similarities. This can be seen by comparing the changes produced by different short-term experiences. Regardless of the particular source of change that produced improvements in class inclusion in Siegler and Svetina (2006), children moved from below chance to consistently correct performance with little or no transitional period. Regardless of the particular source of change, once children initially showed consistently correct performance, they almost never regressed to chance or below chance performance. Regardless of the particular source of change, most children either showed substantial change in the first session or they never did.

None of this is to say that different sources of change consistently promote equal amounts of learning. This is clearly not the case. However, the different effectiveness of various sources of change may reflect the likelihood that they will be sufficiently strong to set the change in motion, rather than how the change will proceed once it is set in motion. Again, the analogy to the stone on the mountain may illustrate the point. The forces accompanying different sources of motion vary, and therefore the likelihood that they will set the stone in motion also will vary. However, for forces of equal strength and direction, once the stone begins to move, its subsequent motion is determined by the characteristics of the object and the landscape, rather than by the source of the motion. Analogously, given a constant task and highly similar initial knowledge states, cognitive change may show surprising similarity regardless of the source that sets the change in motion.

REFERENCES

Adolph, K. E. (1997). Learning in the development of infant locomotion. *Monographs of the Society for Research in Child Development, 62* 3(Serial No. 251).

Alibali, M. W. (1999). How children change their minds: Strategy change can be gradual or abrupt. *Developmental Psychology, 35,* 127–145.

Amsterlaw, J., & Wellman, H. (2006). Theories of mind in transition: A microgenetic study of the development of false belief understanding. *Journal of Cognition and Development, 7,* 139–172.

Bielaczyc, K., Pirolli, P. L., & Brown, A. L. (1995). Training in self-explanation and self-regulation strategies: Investigating the effects of knowledge acquisition activities on problem solving. *Cognition and Instruction, 13,* 221–252.

Bijou, S., & Baer, D. M. (1961). *Child development: Vol. 1: A systematic and empirical theory.* New York: Appleton-Century-Crofts.

Bijou, S. W., & Ribes, E. (1996). Introduction. In S. W. Bijou & E. Ribes (Eds.), *New directions in behavior development* (pp. 9–13). Reno, NV: Context Press.

Bjorklund, D. F., Miller, P. H., Coyle, T. R., & Slawinski, J. L. (1997). Instructing children to use memory strategies: Evidence of utilization deficiencies in memory training studies. *Developmental Review, 17,* 411–441.

Briars, D. J., & Siegler, R. S. (1984). A featural analysis of preschoolers' counting knowledge. *Developmental Psychology, 20,* 607–618.

Brody, N. (1992). *Intelligence* (2nd ed.). San Diego: Academic Press.

Calin-Jageman, R. J., & Ratner, H. H. (2005). The role of encoding in the self-explanation effect. *Cognition and Instruction, 23,* 523–543.

Case, R. (1998). The development of conceptual structures. In W. Damon (Series Ed.), D. Kuhn & R. S. Siegler (Vol. Eds.), *Handbook of child psychology: Vol. 2: Cognition, perception & language* (5th ed., pp. 745–800). New York: Wiley.

Cauley, K. M. (1998). Construction of logical knowledge: Study of borrowing in subtraction. *Journal of Educational Psychology, 80,* 202–205.

Chapman, M., & McBride, M. L. (1992). Beyond competence and performance: Children's class inclusion strategies, superordinate class cues, and verbal justifications. *Developmental Psychology, 28,* 319–327.

Chen, Z., & Siegler, R. S. (2000). Across the great divide: Bridging the gap between understanding of toddlers' and older children's thinking. *Monographs of the Society for Research in Child Development, 65*(2, Serial No. 261).

Chi, M. T. H., de Leeuw, N., Chiu, M.-H., & LaVancher, C. (1994). Eliciting self-explanations improves understanding. *Cognitive Science, 18,* 439–477.

Chinn, C. A. (2006, in press). The microgenetic method: Current work and extensions to classroom research. To appear in J. L. Green, G. Camilli, & P. B. Elmore (Eds.), *Handbook of complementary methods in education research* (3rd ed.). Mahwah, NJ: Erlbaum.

Cole, M. (2006). Culture and cognitive development in phylogenetic, historical, and ontogenetic perspective. In W. Damon & R. M. Lerner (Series Eds.), D. Kuhn & R. S. Siegler (Vol. Eds.), *Handbook of child psychology: Volume 2: Cognition, perception, and language* (6th ed., pp. 636–683). Hoboken, NJ: Wiley.

Duncan, R. M., & Pratt, M. W. (1997). Microgenetic change in the quantity and quality of preschoolers' private speech. *International Journal of Behavioral Development, 20*, 367–383.

Fay, A. L., & Klahr, D. (1996). Knowing about guessing and guessing about knowing: Preschoolers' understanding of indeterminacy. *Child Development, 67*, 689–719.

Fischer, K. W., & Bidell, T. R. (1998). Dynamic development of psychological structures in action and thought. In W. Damon (Series Ed.), R. M. Lerner (Vol. Ed.), *Handbook of child psychology: Vol. 1: Theoretical models of human development* (5th ed., pp. 467–562). New York: Wiley.

Fischer, K. W., & Bidell, T. R. (2006). Dynamic development of action and thought. In W. Damon & R. M. Lerner (Series Eds.), R. M. Lerner (Vol. Ed.), *Handbook of child psychology: Volume 1: Theoretical models of human development* (6th ed., pp. 313–399). Hoboken, NJ: Wiley.

Foreman, E. A., & MacPhail, J. (1993). Vygotskian perspective in children's collaborative problem solving activity. In E. A. Forman, N. Minick, & C. A. Stone (Eds.), *Contexts for learning: Sociocultural dynamics in children's development* (pp. 213–229). Oxford: Oxford University Press.

Gauvain, M. (2001). *The social context of cognitive development*. New York: Guilford.

Gelman, R., & Williams, E. (1998). Enabling constraints for cognitive development and learning: Domain specificity and epigenesis. In W. Damon (Series Ed.), D. Kuhn & R. S. Siegler (Vol. Eds.), *Handbook of child psychology: Vol. 2: Cognition, perception & language* (5th ed., pp. 575–630). New York: Wiley.

Gentner, D. (1989). The mechanisms of analogical learning. In S. Vosniadou & A. Ortony (Eds.), *Similarity and anlogical reasoning* (pp. 199–241). New York: Cambridge University Press.

Gershkoff-Stowe, L., & Smith, L. B. (1997). A curvilinear trend in naming errors as a function of early vocabulary growth. *Cognitive Psychology, 34*, 37–71.

Goldin-Meadow, S. (2001). Giving the mind a hand: The role of gesture in cognitive change. In J. L. McClelland & R. S. Siegler (Eds.), *Mechanisms of cognitive development: Behavioral and neural perspectives* (pp. 5–31). Mahwah, NJ: Erlbaum.

Goldin-Meadow, S., & Alibali, M. W. (2002). Looking at the hands through time: A microgenetic perspective on learning and instruction. In N. Granott & J. Parziale (Eds.), *Microdevelopment: Transition processes in development and learning* (pp 80–105). Cambridge, UK: Cambridge University Press.

Graham, T., & Perry, M. (1993). Indexing transitional knowledge. *Developmental Psychology, 29*, 779–788

Granott, N. (1998). A paradigm shift in the study of development: Essay review of *Emerging Minds* by R. S. Siegler. *Human Development, 41*, 360–365.

Halford, G. S. (1993). *Children's understanding: The development of mental models*. Hillsdale, NJ: Erlbaum.

Hodkin, B. (1987). Performance model analysis in class inclusion: An illustration with two language conditions. *Developmental Psychology, 23*, 683–689.

Inhelder, B., & Piaget, J. (1964). *The early growth of logic in the child: Classification and seriation*. London: Routledge.

Johnson, K. E., & Mervis, C. B. (1994). Microgenetic analysis of first steps in children's acquisition of expertise on shorebirds. *Developmental Psychology, 30*, 418–435.

Karmiloff-Smith, A. (1992). *Beyond modularity: A developmental perspective on cognitive science*. Cambridge, MA: MIT Press.

Keil, F. C. (2006). Cognitive science and cognitive development. In W. Damon & R. M. Lerner (Series Eds.), D. Kuhn & R. S. Siegler (Vol. Eds.), *Handbook of child psychology: Volume 2: Cognition, perception, and language* (6th ed., pp. 609–635). Hoboken, NJ: Wiley.

Klahr, D., & Chen, Z. (2003). Overcoming the positive-capture strategy in young children: Learning about indeterminacy. *Child Development, 74*, 1275–1296.

Kuhn, D. (1995). Microgenetic study of change: What has it told us? *Psychological Science, 6*, 133–139

Kuhn, D., & Franklin, S. (2006). The second decade: What develops (and how). In W. Damon & R. M.

Lerner (Series Eds.), D. Kuhn & R. S. Siegler (Vol. Eds.), *Handbook of child psychology: Volume 2: Cognition, perception, and language* (6th ed., pp. 953–993). Hoboken, NJ: Wiley.

Kuhn, D., Garcia-Mila, M., Zohar, A., & Anderson, C. (1995). Strategies of knowledge acquisition. *Monographs of the Society for Research in Child Development, 60*(4, Serial No. 245).

Levin, I. (1989). Principles underlying time measurement: The development of children's constraints on counting time. In I. Levin & D. Zakay (Eds.), *Time and human cognition: A life-span perspective* (pp. 145–183). Amsterdam: North-Holland.

Liben, L. S. (Ed.). (1987). *Development and learning: Conflict or congruence*. Hillsdale, NJ: Erlbaum.

McCabe, A. E., Siegel, L. S., Spence, I., & Wilkinson, A. (1982). Class-inclusion reasoning: Patterns of performance from three to eight years. *Child Development, 53*, 780–785.

Miller, K. (1984). Child as the measurer of all things: Measurement of procedures and the development of quantitative concepts. In C. Sophian (Ed.), *Origins of cognitive skills: The eighteenth annual Carnegie symposium on cognition* (pp. 193–228). Hillsdale, NJ: Erlbaum.

Miller, P. H., & Aloise-Young, P. A. (1995). Preschoolers' strategic behavior and performance on a same-different task. *Journal of Experimental Child Psychology, 60*, 284–303.

Miller, P. H., & Coyle, T. R. (1999). Developmental change: Lessons from microgenesis. In E. K. Scholnick, K. Nelson, S. A. Gelman, & P. H. Miller (Eds.), *Conceptual development: Piaget's legacy* (pp. 209–239). Mahwah, NJ: Erlbaum.

Munakata, Y. (2006). Information processing approaches to development. In W. Damon & R. M. Lerner (Series Eds.), D. Kuhn & R. S. Siegler (Vol. Eds.), *Handbook of child psychology: Volume 2: Cognition, perception, and language* (6th ed., pp. 426–463). Hoboken, NJ: Wiley.

Opfer, J. E., & Gelman, S. A. (2001). Children's and adults' models for predicting teleological action: The development of a biology-based model. *Child Development, 72*, 1367–1381.

Opfer, J. E., & Siegler, R. S. (2004). Revisiting preschoolers' *living things* concept: A microgenetic analysis of conceptual change in basic biology. *Cognitive Psychology, 49*, 301–332.

Osherson, D. N., & Markman, E. (1975). Language and the ability to evaluate contradictions and tautologies. *Cognition, 3*, 213–226.

Perry, M., & Lewis, J. L. (1999). Verbal imprecision as an index of knowledge in transition. *Developmental Psychology, 35*, 749–759.

Piaget, J. (1964). Development and learning. In T. Ripple & V. Rockcastle (Eds.), *Piaget rediscovered* (pp. 7–19). Ithaca, NY: Cornell University Press.

Piaget, J. (1970). *Psychology and epistemology*. New York: W. W. Norton.

Pine, K. J., & Messer, D. J. (2000). The effect of explaining another's actions on children's implicit theories of balance. *Cognition and Instruction, 18*, 35–51.

Pressley, M. (1992). How *not* to study strategy discovery. *American Psychologist, 47*, 1240–1241.

Rogers, T. T., & McClelland, J. L. (2004). *Semantic cognition: A parallel distributed processing approach*. Cambridge, MA: Bradford Books/MIT Press.

Schauble, L. (1990). Belief revision in children: The role of prior knowledge and strategies for generating evidence. *Journal of Experimental Child Psychology, 49*, 31–57.

Schauble, L. (1996). The development of scientific reasoning in knowledge-rich contexts. *Developmental Psychology, 32*, 102–119.

Schlagmüller, M., & Schneider, W. (2002). The development of organizational strategies in children: Evidence from a microgenetic longitudinal study. *Journal of Experimental Child Psychology, 81*, 298–319.

Siegler, R. S. (1995). How does change occur: A microgenetic study of number conservation. *Cognitive Psychology, 25*, 225–273.

Siegler, R. S. (1996). Unidimensional thinking, multidimensional thinking, and characteristic tendencies of thought. In A. J. Sameroff & M. M. Haith (Eds.), *The five to seven year shift: The age of reason and responsibility* (pp. 63–84). Chicago: University of Chicago Press.

Siegler, R. S. (2002). Microgenetic studies of self-explanations. In N. Granott & J. Parziale (Eds.), *Microdevelopment: Transition processes in development and learning* (pp. 31–58). New York: Cambridge University.

Siegler, R. S. (2006). Microgenetic analyses of learning. In W. Damon & R. M. Lerner (Series Eds.), D. Kuhn & R. S. Siegler (Vol. Eds.), *Handbook of child psychology: Volume 2: Cognition, perception, and language* (6th ed., pp. 464–510). Hoboken, NJ: Wiley.

Siegler, R. S., & Crowley, K. (1994). Constraints on learning in non-privileged domains. *Cognitive Psychology, 27*, 194–227.

Siegler, R. S., & Stern, E. (1998). A microgenetic analysis of conscious and unconscious strategy discoveries. *Journal of Experimental Psychology: General, 127*, 377–397.

Siegler, R. S., & Svetina, M. (2002). A microgenetic/cross-sectional study of matrix completion: Comparing short-term and long-term change. *Child Development, 73*, 793–809.

Siegler, R. S., & Svetina, M. (2006). What leads children to adopt new strategies? A microgenetic/cross sectional study of class inclusion. *Child Development, 77*, 996–1015.

Spencer, J. P., Vereijken, B., Diedrich, F. J., & Thelen, E. (2000). Posture and the emergence of manual skills. *Developmental Science, 3*, 216–233.

Thelen, E., & Smith, L. B. (2006). Dynamic systems theories. In W. Damon & R. M. Lerner (Series Eds.), R. M. Lerner (Vol. Ed.), *Handbook of child psychology: Volume 1: Theoretical models of human development* (6th ed., pp. 258–312). Hoboken, NJ: Wiley.

Thelen, E., & Ulrich, B. D. (1991). Hidden skills. *Monographs of the Society for Research in Child Development, 56*(1Serial No. 223).

Thornton, S. (1999). Creating the conditions for cognitive change: The interaction between task structures and specific strategies. *Child Development, 70*, 588–603.

Tomasello, M. (2006). Acquiring linguistic constructions. In W. Damon & R. M. Lerner (Series Eds.), D. Kuhn & R. S. Siegler (Vol. Eds.), *Handbook of child psychology: Volume 2: Cognition, perception, and language* (6th ed., pp. 255–298). Hoboken, NJ: Wiley.

van Geert, P. (1998). A dynamic systems model of basic developmental mechanisms: Piaget, Vygotsky, and beyond. *Psychological Review, 105*, 634–677.

van Geert, P. (2002). Developmental dynamics, intentional action, and fuzzy sets. In N. Granott & J. Parziale (Eds.), *Microdevelopment: Transition processes in development and learning* (pp. 319–343). Cambridge, UK: Cambridge University Press.

Vygotsky, L. (1934/1962). *Thought and language*. New York: Wiley.

Werner, H. (1948). *Comparative psychology of mental development*. New York: International Universities Press.

Werner, H. (1957). The concept of development from a comparative and organismic point of view. In D. B. Harris (Ed.), *The concept of development: An issue in the study of human behavior* (pp. 125–148). Minneapolis: University of Minnesota Press.

II
CONCEPTUAL CHANGE IN THE CONTENT AREAS

6

Conceptual Change in Physics[1]

David E. Brown
University of Illinois at Urbana-Champaign

David Hammer
University of Maryland

INTRODUCTION

In the late 1980s, a video was released which took on something of a cult status in the science education community. This video, *A Private Universe* (Sadler, Schneps, & Woll, 1989), began by showing interviews of Harvard University students at graduation dressed in their graduation robes. They were asked two questions, "what causes the seasons?" and "what causes the phases of the moon?" Of the 25 or so who were interviewed, over 20 had substantial problems answering the questions. Many confidently and eloquently expounded ideas at odds with the most elementary treatments of these questions.

One graduate after another explained that the earth is closer to the sun in the summer, in answer to the first question. It is a reasonable first guess, if one has had no instruction, but it cannot account for the commonly known fact that the southern hemisphere experiences summer when the northern hemisphere experiences winter. Further, virtually all students have been taught some form of explanation for this phenomenon in their early schooling. Further still, one of the students who gave this explanation mentioned later that he had had a course in the physics of planetary motion. In a few minutes of riveting footage, *A Private Universe* illustrated pointedly what had been demonstrated in numerous research papers on science learning: even the "best and brightest" students are not learning what educators may think they are learning from their science education.

It was a public display of what research in science education had been documenting in the literature for most of the decade, mostly in mechanics, that even after substantial instruction in physics, students have conceptual difficulties with the most basic ideas (Champagne, Klopfer, & Anderson, 1980; Clement, 1982; Halloun & Hestenes, 1985a; McCloskey, 1983; Peters, 1981; Trowbridge & McDermott, 1980; Whitaker, 1983). Ask college students how the forces compare between a bowling ball and pin when they collide, and a substantial majority of students answer that the bowling ball exerts a greater force, even after a full year of physics (Brown, 1989), when it is a straightforward application of Newton's Third Law to see that the forces are equal. Ask students to identify the forces on a moving object and, again after physics instruction, students will often indicate a force in the direction of motion, when simple applications of Newton's First or Second Laws say otherwise (Clement, 1982, McCloskey, 1983). The Force Concept Inventory (Halloun & Hestenes, 1985b) had provided a simple means for physics professors to replicate these findings with their own students. *A Private Universe* gave a final boost to a movement to transform science education to promote conceptual change.

Some of the findings and assumptions at the core of this movement have been the subject of controversy, as we discuss below, but there is widespread agreement about some of the basic phenomena:

- Many questions, phrased in a qualitative or "conceptual" way, remain difficult for students despite ample related instruction, including students who can solve standard, quantitative textbook questions about the same topics.
- Incorrect answers to these questions tend to cluster into a small number of alternatives.
- Students often show confidence in their incorrect answers.

These difficulties are clearly of serious concern to physics educators. For many, it is a surprise to find that students can solve quantitative problems without having even a basic understanding of the ideas behind the solution methods. For example, a student may be able to apply F = ma accurately to find a if given F and m, but if asked to explain what the equation means might say something like: "It means that the force of an object depends on how heavy it is and how fast it's moving." This involves alternative ways of thinking about all three variables — force as a property of an object, mass as weight, and acceleration as speed.

The research of the 1980s thus showed that students could come away from instruction having memorized some facts and solution algorithms but with their conceptual understanding essentially unchanged. And so educators became interested in teaching for "conceptual change." But what does "conceptual change" mean? What are students' "conceptions" initially, and how do they change?

Most of the literature on conceptual change has understood conceptions, such as that the earth is closer to the sun in the summer, as units of knowledge; some have taken the unit at a larger grain-size in the form of a naïve theory. While this was an early view of conceptual change, and continues to be widely held in the physics education community, current research has largely come to reject unitary views of conceptions and conceptual change. In the following section, we review several perspectives on intuitive physics and on how it changes as students develop expertise. From there we will discuss our own views and some possible new directions for research.

PERSPECTIVES ON STUDENTS' CONCEPTIONS AND CONCEPTUAL CHANGE

In this section we discuss four perspectives on conceptions and conceptual change. To help present and distinguish the different views, we will describe them all with respect to a common example. For convenience, we use a simple, idealized example, which we construct based on familiar experiences in interviews and instruction.

Consider the following question: A puck slides on a frictionless surface at a constant velocity. Show any forces acting on the puck, and describe the motion of the puck.

Before instruction, a student may say and draw the following (see Figure 6.1):

There's a downward force of gravity, and there's a force of motion in the direction it's traveling. This force of motion will gradually die away and the puck will eventually come to a stop, but not for a while since the surface is slippery.

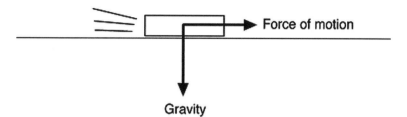

Force of motion

Gravity

FIGURE 6.1   Student's initial drawing showing evidence of conceptual difficulties.

After instruction the student gives a different (and correct) answer, and when asked she explains (see Figure 6. 2):

> I was thinking the force would make it move, but we've learned that forces make things *change* how they move, so I don't think there's a force moving it anymore. And I know the force up by the table has to cancel the force downward by gravity, so they have to be equal and opposite. Before I didn't think we call it a force, what the table does, but we did that thing with the spring, and now I can see that the table's pushing up. Since there's no friction, that's all the forces.

We take it as well established and uncontroversial that most students would give an answer similar to the first response, prior to instruction and in many cases after instruction, and that a change to the second way of understanding the moving puck is difficult to achieve. But there are a number of different views of the nature of that change and why it is so difficult. Taking this simple before-and-after as an instance for reference, we review four theoretical perspectives. These perspectives move from a view of students' conceptions as unitary, coherent, and consistent naïve theories to a view of students' ways of talking about phenomena as highly contextual and fluid.

Students' Ideas a s Like Theories in the History of Science

Discussion in the late 1970s and early 1980s tended to focus on student conceptions as similar to earlier theories in the history of science (Driver & Easley, 1978; Posner, Strike, Hewson, & Gertzog, 1982; Hewson & Hewson, 1984; McCloskey, 1983). For example, McCloskey (1983) compared students' ideas of force and motion to medieval impetus theory, which posited "impetus" as the causal agent of motion, "injected" into a moving object and then fading or draining

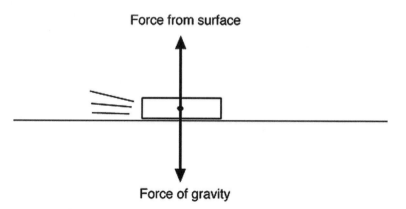

Force from surface

Force of gravity

FIGURE 6.2   Student's final drawing showing evidence of conceptual change.

away. (Impetus theorists differed over whether impetus would simply fade away on its own or be drained away by impediments to the object's motion.)

From this perspective, the student's original answer to the sliding puck question reflected a naïve theory of motion, similar to the medieval impetus theories, by which motion is caused by "force" as an externally applied or internally stored influence. Thus she understood a "force of motion" as "injected" into the puck, and the motion as dying away as the force weakens. By her original theory, if there is motion, there is force. Similarly, her later answer reflected a more sophisticated theoretical framework, in which forces cause changes in motion. By her new theory, if the sum of all the forces on an object is zero, then it moves with a constant velocity, and force is not something an object can "store" or exert on itself. The change in her understanding was not simply a change in the relationship between force and motion, but a change in her understanding of what constitutes force. Her conceptual change, in this way, involves a "strong restructuring" (Carey, 1985) from one framework to another, analogous to theoretical "revolutions" (Kuhn, 1970) in the history of science (McCloskey & Kargon, 1988).

Understanding student conceptions and conceptual change in this way, as analogous to historical theories and progress, researchers outlined the requirements for such a conceptual shift to take place (Posner et. al., 1982; Strike & Posner, 1985; Hewson & Hewson, 1984). First, there needs to be dissatisfaction with the existing theory. Just as scientists would not be convinced of a new theoretical framework without compelling evidence that their existing theory is inadequate, students need to experience problems with prior conceptions in order for them to change. Then, the new theory needs to be seen as intelligible (able to be understood), plausible (believable as a potentially true theory), and fruitful (opening up new avenues of thought or investigation not possible with the old theory).

This view of students' conceptual change, then, provided an organizing scheme for education research and development. First, it shifted educators' understanding of student errors. Whereas previously students were seen as just making mistakes, now they were seen as scientists applying alternative theories to interpretations of phenomena. This helped to make sense of why students seemed "resistant" to new ideas, and it drew attention to the need to understand their existing theories: The field needed research to lay out these alternative theoretical frameworks. Second, it guided educators to understand the need for instruction not merely to present new ideas but to elicit and address students' existing ideas.

While this view got the ball rolling on considering students' content specific conceptual views as an educationally interesting area for research, the hardcore view of students' pre-instructional ideas as similar in essence to historical theories is not widely held by current researchers. First, although there is clearly overlap in how students think about motion (e.g., a continuing force is needed to keep things moving), impetus theories were developed by a community of scholars over many years and were expressed carefully in writing. Strike and Posner (1992), revisiting and revising their views on conceptual change, critiqued their own perspective as having depicted the student as too rational. They argued that rationality in theory development and selection "may be taken for granted in scientific communities" (p. 152) but not in students: "The major modifications required are to take into account the immaturity and novice standing of the learner and to deemphasize those aspects of the sociology of scientific communities that have figured in the philosophical theories of conceptual change" (p. 152).

Second, impetus theorists were deliberate and systematic in applying their principles to explaining motion in all circumstances. The theory of misconceptions did not claim students are deliberate in adhering to a set of principles; rather, they treated the apparent coherence of student reasoning as a property of the conceptual framework. Strike and Posner's critique of assuming rationality applies not only to the development of theory but to its application as well. The original theory of misconceptions asks us to believe that students tacitly adhere to essentially the same principles that impetus theorists followed with care. That does not seem plausible, and in fact there is abundant evidence that students are not typically systematic (Huffman & Heller, 1995; Maloney & Siegler, 1993; Smith, diSessa, & Roschelle, 1993/1994; Steinberg & Sabella, 1997; Tytler, 1998; Taber, 2000).

There are also reasons for concern regarding the instructional implications of the perspective of misconceptions as unitary ideas, some of which derive not from the original formulation of the perspective but from how it has been appropriated by the larger science education community. In general use, the perspective often degenerates into a general view of students as *worse* than blank slates: they are slates that have bad ideas written on them in hard-to-erase chalk. With students' prior knowledge understood as systematically misconceived, educational thinking about curriculum design and instruction focuses on systematically eliciting and confronting the ideas in that prior knowledge, the confrontation coming in the form of conflicting experience, evidence, or arguments (Nussbaum & Novick, 1982; Dawson & Rowell, 1984; Closset 1985; Thorley & Treagust, 1987). Without question, in particular circumstances this approach is effective, but it is also clear that in other circumstances it is inappropriate. Strike and Posner (1992), reflecting on their early work and what had become of it in the literature, expressed concern that the misconceptions perspective "may easily lead teachers or researchers to believe that learners enter instruction with articulated misconceptions. In fact, the actual misconception may be generated on the spot" (p. 158).

Moreover, applied systematically as the principal approach to science instruction, the strategy of elicitation and confrontation may have negative effects. Students could learn or have reinforced the notion that ideas in physics are "counter-intuitive," detached from common sense and everyday experience, with the corollary that their prior knowledge and experience is a liability. There is evidence (Halloun, 1998; Hammer, 1994; May & Etkina, 2002; Redish, Steinberg, & Saul, 1998) that by the time they are in college, many students do not expect physics to make sense, and the problem gets worse as a result of college physics courses (Redish et al., 1998).

Students' Ideas as Generated from Deeper Implicit Conceptions

We now turn to a cognitive view that is often compared to the first view of students' ideas as theories. However, while these researchers view students' ideas as theory-like in some ways, the view of theory in this context is that of coherent, underlying, and organizing presuppositions rather than specific theories as in the previous section. This work draws on numerous psychological studies exploring the naïve theories of children, adolescents, and adults. In this use, the term "theory" denotes some level of psychological coherence, which may be at an unconscious or implicit level, not the coherence of a scientific theory that is conscious and open to scrutiny.

For example, Spelke (1991) and Baillargeon (1992) have spearheaded work focusing on the "naïve theories" of infants, well before they are able to articulate their ideas using language. Through clever experiments they determine what surprises babies, based, for example, on how long they stare at a new event. From these results they have found that babies have surprisingly adult expectations: that solid objects can't move through each other, that objects that move together are likely connected, and that inanimate objects don't move on their own. This last expectation could be called a baby's "theory of inertia" (Spelke, Katz, Purcell, Ehrlich, & Breinlinger, 1994). Such a theory is clearly not the carefully articulated theory of a community of scientists, but it provides an underlying, organizing basis for perception and reasoning.

From this perspective, the student answering the puck question would not be viewed as having a coherent impetus theory, but rather as having an implicit "framework theory" (Vosniadou,

1994) consisting of presuppositions including "that 'rest is the natural state of physical objects' and 'motion needs to be explained' and that 'abstract entities such as force, heat, weight, etc. are properties of objects'" (Ioannides & Vosniadou, 2002, p. 8). These would constrain the construction of a specific model of the situation to include force as a property of the moving puck. The change to an expert understanding would be difficult because it would involve a change to the framework presuppositions.

The framework theory serves as something of a nucleus around which observations and other knowledge are organized into models in specific situations, which, as Strike and Posner (1992) argued, may be constructed on the spot. Such student models are not unitary in the sense earlier misconceptions research posited. However, once a model is constructed, it may take on generative characteristics of its own, as Vosniadou and Brewer (1992) showed may happen with student-constructed models of the earth. For example, some children think of a fishbowl with people living inside, constructed to bring together the idea of a ball-shaped earth with the framework theoretical presupposition of a universal up-and-down, and then use that model in further reasoning.

Such a perspective helps to make sense of the observations about students' answers to conceptual questions while avoiding some of the difficulties of the hardcore "theory-theory" perspective discussed earlier. This perspective also treats students' conceptions as composed of elements, such as implicit presuppositions of the framework theory, observations, metaconceptual aspects, etc. However, one prediction of this theory is that children's responses to classes of situations will be consistent, since they would access the same framework theory for a variety of instances. While Vosniadou has found such consistency in her work (Ioannides & Vosniadou, 2002; Vosniadou & Brewer, 1992), these results have been challenged (diSessa, Gillespie, & Esterly, 2004) with data showing substantially less consistency. The next perspective moves yet further away from the view of students' ideas as theories, proposing a conceptual system of many small pieces that activate, sometimes in groups, to give rise to what we see as students' ideas.

Students' Knowledge as a Collection of Primitives

The most prominent voice in this camp is Andrea diSessa and colleagues. DiSessa's framework, most thoroughly presented in his 1993 monograph, "Towards an Epistemology of Physics," directly challenges accounts of novices as holding "alternative frameworks" or "naïve theories." In this view, the intuitive physics of a novice "does not come close to the expert's in depth and systematicity" but the elements of that intuitive physics are the raw material for constructing expert understanding: "the development of scientific knowledge about the physical world is possible only through reorganized intuitive knowledge" (p. 108).

Rather than understanding intuitive physics as comprised of intuitive theories, to be confronted, overcome, and replaced, diSessa understands it in terms of cognitive building blocks he calls "phenomenological primitives" or "p-prims." They are "phenomenological" in the sense that they are minimal abstractions from experience; they are closely tied to familiar phenomena. And they are "primitive" both in how people use them, as the obviously true ideas at the bottom level of explanation, and in their role in diSessa's model of cognitive structure as "nearly minimal memory elements, evoked as a whole…perhaps as atomic and isolated a mental structure as one can find" (p. 112).

P-prims work by being "cued" or "activated," and a key difference between this account and views of naïve theories is that any p-prim may or may not be activated. In this account, the student's "misconception" that motion causes force comes about as a result of a high cuing-priority for the p-prims "force as mover" and "continuous force." The former is a primitive sense of an initial force acting on an object causing it to move, such as a shove or a toss; the latter is similar but of a force continuously applied, such as a car engine. Taking this perspective, the student's initial reasoning about the puck reflected her activation of *continuous force*, in understanding the force in the direction of the puck's motion, and the p-prim *supporting* (which does not entail a force), in understanding what the ice does to the puck to keep it from falling. Thus many circumstances cue these primitives, leading to the observations that support impetus theory interpretations of student understanding.

One would expect, however, that other questions would activate different p-prims. For example, if there were a pebble on top of the puck, a student reasoning about the forces acting on the pebble might not see any in the direction of motion, activating only *supporting* or *guiding* to understand what the puck does to the pebble. The empirical support for diSessa's view over theory-oriented views is that it is not difficult to identify circumstances that do not cue these primitives. It is common knowledge and experience for example that, sitting in a vehicle, one cannot tell how quickly it is moving without looking outside; people do not wonder why they cannot tell how quickly they are moving by the sensation of the force that is moving them. In fact, they know there is no such force, and they do not find it problematic (unless an interviewer calls it to their attention). For intuitive physics, the situation of riding in a steadily moving car is simply static, not dynamic, and the motion it involves needs no explanation. The *car's* motion needs explanation, not the passengers'.

This perspective nicely captures the contextuality observed in students' answers to questions asked in slightly different ways. It does not, however, reject robust patterns of reasoning, such as the phenomena of misconceptions, although this account is often misread to depict intuitive physics as randomly incoherent. In fact, diSessa discusses "systematicity" at length in his monograph (1993; see also diSessa & Sherin, 1998; diSessa, et al., 2004). Rather, it rejects attributing coherence as structurally encoded in the knowledge system; on this account, "systematicity" arises in a complex dynamic, to which we return below. Thus diSessa's account differs from the early views of intuitive physics much as does Vosniadou's (1994) and Strike and Posner's (1992) revisionist version: while the dynamics of novices' reasoning may produce similar results to articulate, intentional theories, the structure of intuitive knowledge is not well-compared to the structure of those theories.

The differences between diSessa's account and Vosniadou's are more subtle. Where Vosniadou posits framework presuppositions that act as "constraints" on reasoning and intuitive modeling, diSessa posits elements that are more central in the knowledge system, and so may be cued with high priority in a wide variety of circumstances. For Vosniadou, presuppositions that differ from expert reasoning must be revised; in this sense they are structural misconceptions, albeit at an implicit rather than conscious level. For diSessa, development to expertise may require the addition of new primitives, but existing primitives change only in activation priorities, not in their semantics.

Students' Ideas as Modes of Discourse

While the previous perspective treats well differences in student answers based on problem situation, there are other aspects of contextuality not explicitly dealt with in this perspective. It is the latter that we explore in this final section, a perspective that is in many ways diametrically opposed to the first perspective and that takes most seriously the contextuality and fluidity of students' ways of talking about phenomena. While earlier perspectives consider a student's "talking about" phenomena as something to be explained with some kind of model of what goes on in the student's mind, discourse perspectives tend to shy away from such mentalism. To a discourse theorist, explanations of students "talking about" phenomena are to be found in the dynamics of social interchange (Lemke, 1990; Edwards, 1993; Saljo, 1999; Hallden, 1999; Givry & Roth, 2006). Such a perspective focuses on phenomenology rather than on modeling cognition. Many discourse theorists would maintain that students' explanations, predictions, discussions, etc., are not best thought of as arising from the cognition of individual students. Rather, the appropriate focus is the discourse itself and the social and sociocultural dynamics that contribute to the discourse.

From a discourse perspective, concepts are not viewed as mental entities. Rather they are viewed as tools for social interchange. Consider the concept "banana." Saljo (1999) discusses this interesting case, showing how the concept can be different in different social contexts. When querying a botanist, the "banana" is quite easy to define, and the botanist has very little trouble classifying various fruits as a banana or not a banana. However, politically, the botanist's definition of banana causes problems. European countries that eat a lot of bananas do not want to use the botanists' definition of banana for tariff reasons — they want to exclude a kind of banana grown in the European Union that is not the typical yellow, tasty fruit one puts on breakfast cereal. "Politicians, even prime ministers, bureaucrats, businessmen, consumer organizations, ship owners and freight companies, and experts of different kinds have been involved in trying to establish what counts as a banana and what does not" (p. 82).

From a discourse perspective, the exchanges about the sliding puck are viewed not as indications of what is in the student's mind, but rather as indicative of the nature of the social exchange. Consider that the exchange likely takes place in a physics classroom, or at the very least the student knows that these are questions about physics. As such, modes of discourse pertinent to physics class are needed for this interchange. By this view, the change that took place reflects the student's having been enculturated into physics discourse, having learned to talk about Newton's first law, about free body diagrams, about frictionless surfaces, etc. By contrast, if she were talking to one of her friends about hockey, she might well say: "I wouldn't want to be hit with a slap shot — the puck has a lot of force and could really hurt." The modes of discourse in this context are different, and as such different ways of talking about moving pucks are needed. Just as banana means something different in scientific versus political interchange, what counts as a force in one social context is different than what counts as a force in another social context.

This perspective focuses attention on important social and discursive dynamics. It also recognizes the discursive contextuality of conceptions. In an everyday context, the geocentric view of the solar system is expected, and to employ a different view would be confusing. However, when discussing the solar system, a heliocentric view is needed. But even astronomers make use of a geocentric perspective when giving coordinates of astronomical bodies using altitude and azimuth. In this case the geocentric perspective is useful for discourse about particular problems.

So we see value in this discursive perspective, value in focusing on dynamics that can be undervalued in a perspective focused solely on cognitive aspects. However, the danger in such a perspective is to reify social dynamics at the expense of cognitive dynamics. In this we agree with Vosniadou, Ioannides, Dimitrakopoulou, and Papademetriou (2001, p. 395):

> Moving in the direction of taking into consideration situational and cultural variables does not necessarily mean the abandonment of the level of mental representations and its replacement with discourse analysis as suggested by some radical situationists (e.g., Saljo, 1999). A theory of conceptual change needs to provide a description of the internal representations and processes that go on during cognitive activity but should also try to relate these internal representations to external, situational variables that influence them.

Roth and Duit (2003) discuss "the structural coupling between collective conversation and individual contributions" (p. 870). While they privilege discourse in their treatment (with even the "individual contributions" considered as individual discourse), we agree that there is an interdependence, in our view between conceptual dynamics and discourse dynamics. We see the field moving toward such a consideration of dynamics at various levels as interdependent. We discuss this dynamic perspective in the next section as an integrative perspective that helps to make sense of findings from each of the previous four perspectives.

A COMPLEX SYSTEMS PERSPECTIVE ON STUDENTS' CONCEPTIONS

To review, the original perspective of misconceptions identified and called attention to the phenomena that all of this research has addressed: despite having had instruction, and often despite evident abilities at textbook problem solving, physics students continue to show sensible but naïve misunderstandings when responding to simple conceptual questions. There is wide consensus now as well that at least some of these misunderstandings vary with context (Strike & Posner, 1992; diSessa, 1993; Vosniadou 1994), as there is consensus that some naïve views students express are consistent with expert understanding (Clement, Brown, & Zietsman, 1989; Minstrell, 1992, 2000). The points of debate over conceptual phenomenology concern the extent to which students' reasoning is consistent with a core set of tacitly held ideas, and the extent to which it varies with question or context.

In our view, there is strong evidence at both ends of this phenomenological spectrum. There are clearly "systematicities" in student reasoning, to use diSessa's term, that appear across a wide range of circumstances, as research since the first papers on misconceptions has documented. It is also clear "that students may change their local, situational models, move from one misconception to another, or even be internally inconsistent" (Vosniadou, 1994, p. 65), as research has amply documented as well. An adequate model of intuitive knowledge must account for the full range of established phenomena.

The field has been making progress in constructing such a model, reflected particularly in diSessa's and Vosniadou's work, and we see this progress as toward a complex systems account of knowledge and learning. Our purpose in this section is to promote that progress. We will review the concept of a complex system, and then we will argue that a complex systems perspective can integrate findings from previous work. In particular, we will argue that, couched within a complex systems approach, the differences in diSessa's and Vosniadou's models mostly disappear, and discourse dynamics can be seen as theoretically continuous with conceptual dynamics.

Complex Systems

Complex systems theory concerns dynamical systems in which there are interactions among components that include feedback, such that what happens to one part of the system can affect another part, which can then affect the first part. This feedback makes the system *non-linear*, such that a small change can lead to a disproportional effect. A complex system need not have many components — a double pendulum is a simple non-linear dynamical system — but a great deal of complex systems research involves systems with many components. In recent years there has been growing interest in modeling cognition and development as a complex, dynamical system (Thelen, 1992; Thelen & Smith, 1994; Bogartz, 1994; van Geert, 1994, 1998).

One of the central ideas in a complex systems perspective is that robust order and structure can emerge from the interaction of a large number of random interactions, without the overall direction of an intelligent agent, much as tossing a coin billions of times reliably results in very close to 50% heads and 50% tails. Structure and coherence can emerge out of a dynamic system of interacting simpler agents.

To help get a sense of this, consider a cocktail party to which a number of people are invited. If you look into the cocktail party, in which people are free to move about, you would likely see them organize into a collection of small groups. No one has told the partygoers to get into groups; it arises from individuals making independent choices of where to place themselves. If you look later, it still looks this way, although if you look closely the groups have changed — some no longer exist, others have grown larger, etc. If you look at another party, the actual groups that form and the places in which they form after the same amount of time will vary from the first party, although one can predict with near certainty what the general look of the party will be. Of course, environmental factors can influence these results. If tables or bars are present at the cocktail party, it is a sure bet that groups of people will tend to gather around these (although not all tables will have groups, and for any given table it may be impossible to predict in advance whether it will have a group or not, how many will be in the group, who will be in the group, etc.). If the tables are rearranged, this will have an effect on the arrangement of the groups.

The cocktail party can be taken as a metaphor for many complex systems. In general, after a certain amount of time, complex dynamic systems may "settle" into stable patterns, or "attractors." The patterns may be robust, but they are not fixed features; larger scale patterns arise from the independent actions and interactions of individual elements at a smaller scale. In one respect, however, this example may be misleading. One might understand it as a property of individuals that they prefer to be in groups of a certain size, and so there would be a direct correspondence between small scale features and large scale patterns. In most dynamic systems, properties of elements do not correspond so directly with large-scale patterns. For example, it is not a feature of people in cars that they hope to be in traffic jams, but that is another reliable result of many individual choices under appropriate conditions, with robust, predictable patterns (e.g., that the location of traffic delay moves backwards along a highway).

Many phenomena are well-modeled with a complex systems approach, from disease propagation to cellular function, and chemical reactions to stock market pricing. Dynamic systems occur over a wide range in size and stability—sound, smoke rings, hurricanes, and trade winds are all dynamic processes that arise from a common set of fundamental mechanisms at the level of air molecules. Research on how people think about these systems has shown a tendency toward reasoning in terms of unitary, centralized structures (Resnick, 1996; Wilensky & Resnick, 1999; Wilensky & Reisman, 2006). That is, people often think that stable patterns come about because of inherent, fixed properties of the system.

Such reasoning is evident also in considering student "misconceptions" as unitary entities. As discussed below, considering students' conceptual thought as a complex dynamic system does not in any way deny the existence of stabilities in student reasoning (and the need to understand these stabilities). But considering students' conceptual thought as a complex dynamic system accounts for observations that a unitary account finds problematic (e.g., students answering one way in one context and a different way in a different context); it positions conceptual dynamics as theoretically continuous with discursive and sociocultural dynamics; and it brings to the fore new and potentially fruitful research directions.

Complex Systems Theory and Conceptual Change

While there has been a great deal of interest in complex systems within cognitive science, there has been little discussion of its application to theories of conceptual change. It is in this light that we view the promise of diSessa's and Vosniadou's frameworks as the beginnings of complex systems accounts.

Complex systems theory describes the full spectrum of phenomena in the literature on conceptual change, from the robust, lasting patterns of reasoning to fleeting, context-sensitive variability. Each may be described in terms of dynamic cognitive structures, arising from the interactions of smaller conceptual elements or resources (which themselves develop from even smaller elements). The nature of complex systems is such that these dynamic stabilities would generally develop. However, it may be the case that these stabilities or structures dynamically dissipate and reform rather quickly in different contexts. Or it may be the case that these structures remain largely the same across a wide variety of contexts. The complex systems perspective argues that such emergent stabilities generally develop, but the nature and extent of such structuring is a matter for empirical investigation. Our goals for the remainder of this chapter are to sketch possible connections between dynamic systems theory and students' conceptions and learning. We suggest that dynamic systems can make sense of established ideas and, more important, that it points in particular directions that might advance research on conceptual change.

Core Features of Complex Systems

Some widely applicable ideas of complex systems include the following: intrinsic dynamism, non-linearity, emergent structures, and embeddedness (Wiener, 1961; von Bertalanffy, 1973; von Foerster, 1996; Powers, 1973; Thelen & Smith, 1994; van Geert, 1994).

Intrinsic Dynamism

Elements of the system are in constant and dynamic interaction. One type of this remaining the same but changing is "dynamic equilibrium." Systems in dynamic equilibrium are "thing-like" in that in many respects they remain the same, but they are not "thing-like" in that the mechanisms that produce them are dynamic. It is much easier to think of a person as an enduring individual than it is to think of the processes that are in dynamic flux, producing the perceptually stable person. In many cases it is appropriate to ignore the dynamics and treat the dynamic system as having an enduring identity. However, when the orientation is toward changing the system, as in conceptual change, treating the system as unitary is inappropriate.

Non-linearity

Some dynamic systems are *linear* such that perturbations lead to proportional results: double the tension on a cord in a system of pulleys, for example, and the tension is doubled throughout. Non-linear systems are characterized by feedback such that a change in one part of the system causes change in another part which then causes changes in the original part. This generally leads to non-proportional results much larger or much smaller than the original perturbation.

For example, consider a simple ecosystem of rabbits and grass (see Figure 6.3). If the rabbits get enough grass to eat they will have the energy to live and to reproduce. However, if the rabbits do not have enough to eat, they will start to die of starvation. If the population of rabbits gets too high, they will eat too much grass. This will decrease the population of grass to the point where the rabbits will not have enough to eat. Many rabbits will die of starvation. Enough rabbits may die that the grass can grow almost without check, greatly increasing the population of grass. In this environment of plenty, the remaining rabbits (if there are any!) will flourish, increasing the rabbit population, returning us to another surplus of rabbits that will eat too much grass.

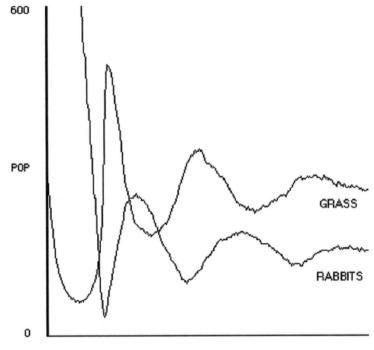

FIGURE 6.3   The populations of rabbits and grass swing through extreme highs and lows before, in this case, tending toward dynamic equilibrium values (an "attractor state"). From a NetLogo simulation (see Wilensky, 2001).

Changing the number of rabbits leads to a change in the amount of grass which then affects the number of rabbits, and so the system is non-linear. Still, it can produce predictable results and a dynamic stability. In simulations of this simple ecosystem, depending on the starting conditions the rabbit population may die out in one of the early oscillations, or the system may settle into an "attractor state" with a dynamic equilibrium of rabbits and grass, as shown in Figure 6.3. Whether the system reaches that equilibrium can be sensitive to the starting conditions, and may do so in ways that may be counter-intuitive: Start with a little more grass for the rabbits to eat, and the rabbits may die out. Otherwise, however, the equilibrium is stable with changes of rabbits or grass: The addition of a group of rabbits, for example, will upset this equilibrium, but after some time the system will return to the same state. And, of course, the dynamic would be entirely different if the change is to introduce a single pair of foxes. Similarly, the conceptual system seems to be non-linear — under many circumstances, even a great deal of instruction can lead to little change, while in other situations small influences can lead to major insights.

Emergence

Because elements of the system are in constant and dynamic interaction, structures and patterns emerge as a result of these dynamics. Such structures are typically not predictable based on the individual elements of the system, and so the structures need to be studied at an appropriate grain size. In the cocktail party system, small groups emerge naturally as a result of the social dynamics of the party. Similarly, students' conceptions may be understood to emerge from the dynamics of smaller conceptual pieces.

Embeddedness

Complex systems often have the feature that they are embedded within complex systems at a larger scale and have complex systems at a smaller scale embedded within them. Consider the human body, for example, with its circulatory, nervous, digestive, immune and other systems. Each can be modeled as a complex system in itself, but each of course is composed of cells, which are also complex systems, and they are all part of the larger system of the body as a whole. On a still larger scale, the nervous system of a modern day human is a result of the dynamic processes of evolution; at still lower scales are the systems of chemical interactions. Depending on the clinical or scholarly matter at hand, it may be essential to consider more than one level of organization in understanding bodily phenomena.

In a similar way, research on cognition could expect multiple levels of organization, from neurons to simple conceptual components (such as p-prims) to more elaborate conceptions to minds as complex systems. On still larger scales, this approach could be continuous with models of social and cultural dynamics, again as complex systems but at a larger scale of organization. In terms of conceptual change, dynamics at various levels are embedded in each other and interact — evolutionary, neural, protoconceptual, conceptual, metaconceptual, social, sociocultural, etc. In investigations of students' conceptions, often the conceptual level is predominantly (and often appropriately) the focus. However, in instructional planning, typically there is explicit or implicit recognition that other levels must be considered as well.

Connections and Refinements to Existing Research

It is not difficult to find alignments between ideas from complex dynamic systems and existing research on conceptual change. As we have discussed, complex dynamic systems show stabilities, and the stabilities can be robust, which provides an account of the observation that brought conceptual change ideas to the fore in physics education — that patterns in students' reasoning can be difficult to change. This account is clearly similar to both diSessa's and Vosniadou's, with conceptions understood as resulting from knowledge elements at a lower level of organization; it is closer to diSessa's in that the lower level is itself dynamic, in contrast to Vosniadou's view of constrained presuppositions.[1] In its non-linearity, the account matches the familiar experience that amount of instruction is not proportional to amount of conceptual learning. Moreover, a complex systems account leads easily to views of situational and social dynamics at larger levels of organization.

While we argue that the field has been moving toward a complex systems perspective on conceptions and conceptual change, none of the perspectives reviewed previously takes a full-blown dynamic perspective. The misconceptions and discourse perspectives tend to privilege one level of organization in their accounts, of conceptions or of discourse practices, often to the implicit or explicit exclusion of consideration of dynamics at other levels. For example, radical discourse theorists often say explicitly that consideration of conceptual dynamics is misguided (Edwards, 1993; Saljo, 1999; Roth & Duit, 2003). In our view, adopting a complex systems perspective can incorporate existing ideas into an integrative framework. The phenomena of misconceptions and of discourse can be understood as emergent from complex dynamics at different levels of organization.

Vosniadou's and diSessa's accounts both describe complex knowledge systems, taking student ideas in particular situations as emergent phenomena arising from the activity of lower-level knowledge elements. Each, however, posits a bottom level to the cognitive structure. In Vosniadou's theory, the bottom level is comprised of the framework presuppositions, such as that "space is organized in terms of the directions of up and down" (1994, p. 49), or that "hotness is a transferable property of physical objects" (p. 48), which act as constraints on further reasoning. Conceptual change requires revising the presuppositions. In diSessa's view, the bottom level is comprised of phenomenological primitives, such as "force as mover" or "Ohm's p-prim," which may or may not be activated in any particular moment. They are not constraints on reasoning, because they may or may not be cued at any particular moment. But as primitive elements — "atomic and isolated" mental structures (1993, p. 112), once formed they are not themselves subject to revision. For diSessa, conceptual change requires revising, not the primitives, but how and when they are activated.

DiSessa's model is of a complex system, taking p-prims as the fundamental elements. Adopting a complex systems perspective more broadly, p-prims could be seen as stable dynamic structures, as might Vosniadou's presuppositions. In this way, the two theories could be understood as different possible dynamics of a system. P-prims describe structures that are more stable than presuppositions, which in Vosniadou's account can ultimately change; presuppositions act like p-prims in the limit of universally high cuing and reliability priorities — think of Ohm's p-prim, which diSessa describes as more "central" than others, as essentially always cued in contexts that invite thinking about effort or resistance. The system could admit other possible dynamics as well, such as structures with both properties — essentially always cued and too stable to disrupt — so as to act as 'permanent' properties of the system.[2] The important point here is that, framed as emergent structures in a dynamic system, there is no principled reason to suppose the system must act only one way or the other. One possible outcome of the debate, then, is that one or the other version of the dynamic may apply within different regions, and the question for research becomes one of delineating those regions.

In this way, too, a complex systems approach helps answer questions that arise within each of these accounts. In Vosniadou's account, the framework presuppositions act as fixed constraints to the dynamics of the system. What happens to change that? There are several possibilities within a complex systems account, of presuppositions having some kind of accessible internal structure, some kind of activation priority like diSessa's p-prims, or as we noted having their output suppressed.

In diSessa's framework, p-prims are varied to the point that they can seem like different kinds of cognitive objects. Ohm's p-prim, for example, has a very general schematisation of a causal agent acting through a resistance to produce a result (p. 217), which may apply to a wide range of phenomenology — from pushing a box across the floor to giving students continuous encouragement to work hard. Some other p-prims could be seen as general in this way; *continuous push* could be understood to schematise any causal agent maintaining an effect. But other p-prims, such as *Force as spinner*, can apply only to a much more narrow set of circumstances (Brown, 1993; Redish, 2004). Moreover, Ohm's p-prim involves schematisations of resistance and effort, ideas that are repeated in other primitives in diSessa's account. A number of primitives involve similarities in meaning, suggesting that it might be fruitful to look further into the substructure of p-prims rather than treating them as atomic and isolated, as diSessa has mostly done so far.

Thus we see a complex systems perspective as allowing a synthesis of prior research in conceptual change. In the following section we further discuss how this perspective can make sense of a number of well-established findings in the literature on conceptual change in physics. We then explore what it would suggest as promising directions for future research and instructional practice.

A COMPLEX SYSTEMS PERSPECTIVE ON EXISTING AND FUTURE RESEARCH AND INSTRUCTIONAL PRACTICE

For the past 25 years, research in conceptual change has been organized primarily by the ways of thinking introduced in the early research on misconceptions and alternative frameworks: Students have ideas, sensible but incompatible with scientific expertise, and these ideas pose difficulties for constructive conceptual change. The first task for research, then, is to identify those ideas, and that has been a powerful organizing scheme.

A researcher looking for a new, do-able and publishable project needs only to identify a domain of science in which there has not been sufficient charting of students' misconceptions and difficulties. Existing research offers a range of methodological models for how to proceed, such as by posing problems within that domain in clinical interviews, observing students' work in classroom interactions, and designing instruments to assess conceptual understanding. The best work employs a range of these methods, such as starting with observations to find likely candidates of misunderstanding, designing clinical interviews to explore those candidates, and gathering qualitative data of the range of possible lines of reasoning. Thus the incorrect ideas discovered in observations and interviews provide ideas for item construction in the instrument, in how to pose questions and what possibilities to include in the choices for answers. (For a bibliography of several thousand articles identifying misconceptions and difficulties, see Duit, 2006.).

In these respects, then, the question "What are students' misconceptions" (or, many studies in physics ask, "What are students' difficulties") has been extremely generative; we might describe it as paradigmatic. As thinking moves on from the misconceptions paradigm, however, the need opens up for lines of inquiry that have the same fertility and generativity for research.

Our purpose in this section is to lay out a research agenda from within a complex systems paradigm, illustrating its generativity. We begin by revisiting established empirical findings, to reconsider them from within a dynamic systems perspective. We then turn to promising new areas for research.

Established Findings and Implications from a Complex Systems Perspective

The core findings and implications from conceptual change research may all be re-expressed in terms of complex dynamic systems. We discuss several of these established findings below.

Students' Conceptual Dynamics Exhibit Conceptual Attractors

One characteristic of students' conceptual dynamics that became salient early on is that often inappropriate ideas are comparatively undisturbed by instruction (Champagne et al., 1980; Clement, 1982; Halloun & Hestenes, 1985a; McCloskey, 1983; Peters, 1981; Trowbridge & McDermott, 1980; Whitaker, 1983). For example, Brown (1989) discusses students' conceptions of force, presenting evidence that a conception of force as a property of objects explains much evidence from diagnostic tests focusing on the interactions of objects (e.g., a bowling ball striking a bowling pin), both before and after physics instruction. Objects that have more force then exert more force. In many cases these conceptions of physical phenomena are similar even across cultures (Driver, Squires, Rushworth, & Wood-Robinson, 1994).

From a complex systems perspective, these are strong conceptual attractors, dynamically emergent stabilities. We would expect to find a range in the phenomena of stability, from momentary thoughts to long-lasting patterns of reasoning; we would expect to find patterns that tend to emerge under specific conditions and others that emerge in a wide variety of situations.

This enables a dynamic perspective to embrace both the stability of students' ideas as well as the fluidity and contextuality of their ideas.

Instruction Must Pay Attention to Conceptual Attractors

Since the earliest articles on conceptual change, researchers have argued that instruction must pay attention to student conceptions. A complex systems perspective provides a new lens on earlier work and its implications. It predicts that learning will not be a linear accretion of knowledge, whether through instruction or through induction from experiment. Even after extensive instruction, students' reasoning may remain unchanged, as so many studies have shown. On the other hand, however, in some situations brief interventions can have dramatic effects (Duckworth, 1987; Mayer 1995; Clement 1989; Rosenberg, Hammer, & Phelan, 2006).

As we have noted, there is an extensive literature on instruction taking student conceptions into account (Duit, 2006), especially within physics. Reviewing this work from a complex systems perspective gives new insight into the effectiveness of this perspective.

For example, Hewson and Hewson (1983) critiqued traditional instruction as simply introducing new information without paying attention to students' existing ways of making sense of ideas related to the concept of density. They found significant improvement from encouraging students to consider their existing ideas. Minstrell (1984) found that even when he took substantial extra time to carefully outline the logical arguments for Newton's first law in a high school physics class, most students reverted to naïve ideas later. When he involved students in activities that had them consider their naïve ideas, most correctly answered conceptual questions on Newton's first law toward the end of the year. McDermott and Shaffer (1992; Shaffer & McDermott, 1992) had similar results from helping students consider their own reasoning about electricity and electrical circuits.

In each of these cases, large interventions of one kind had little effect, and improvement resulted from changes in the kinds of interventions rather than simply the extent. From a complex systems perspective, these early studies all illustrate a familiar occurrence in non-linear dynamics — the results in student learning were not proportional to the instructional "perturbation."

In each of these cases, a central aspect of the new instructional dynamic was that it engaged students in reflection about different perspectives; students became aware of different possibilities for making sense of the phenomena they were studying. White and Frederiksen (1998) focused explicitly on this aspect of their instructional design, of the role of metacognition in student learning and conceptual change, in the context of their *ThinkerTools* computational environment for middle school students to explore forces and motion. In other words, the system involves not only conceptual knowledge but metacognitive knowledge as well, and we may frame White and Frederiksen's findings in terms of interdependence is among embedded conceptual and metacognitive stabilities.

Students' Conceptual Dynamics Exhibit Fluidity and Contextuality

While there is clear evidence of conceptual attractors, there is also clear evidence of contextual sensitivities (diSessa, 1993; Maloney & Siegler, 1993; Smith, diSessa & Roschelle, 1993/1994; Mestre, Thaden-Koch, Dufresne, & Gerace, 2004; Tytler, 1998; Hammer, 2004). For example, Maloney and Siegler (1993) studied students' reasoning on a variety of kinetic energy and momentum problems to show evidence that they held multiple, conflicting conceptions, and the particular conception they applied depended on the problem they were shown. Elby (2000) showed that students were more likely to reason about graphs as though they are pictures, such as to misinterpret a velocity graph as depicting position, when the graphs contain "compelling visual attributes" such as a pointed maximum or an intersection. Parnafes (under review) recently observed students describing a motion as "fast" in the sense of frequency when observing a high frequency, low amplitude oscillation, but shifting to describing another motion as "fast" in the sense of linear velocity.

These studies illustrate a phenomenology of variation among different local stabilities: Ask students one question, and they show one, often robust pattern of reasoning; ask them a different question or change the context, and the same students show a different pattern. This mix of stabilities and variability is quintessential to complex systems. As we have emphasized, however, the variability in complex systems is not without structure, and knowledge-in-pieces accounts do not present reasoning as incoherent.

Instruction Can Draw on Fluidity and Contextuality

A complex systems perspective entails a view of knowledge and reasoning in terms of manifold resources that can activate in various ways at various times, rather than of unitary, systematic (mis)conceptions (Hammer, 1996, 2000). For teachers, it means thinking of student reasoning in any particular moment as possibly only a local stability, and it implies the possibility of other stabilities, of different sets of resources becoming active in other contexts. This suggests instructional strategies to help students find other possibilities in their existing knowledge, to focus attention on building from productive resources, rather than to focus primarily on eliciting and confronting wrong ideas. As well, it suggests caution in interpreting students' correct reasoning as evidence that they "got it."

The same students that have strong non-Newtonian intuitions in some contexts have strong Newtonian intuitions in other contexts (Clement, Brown, & Zietsman, 1989). Students do not only have wrong ideas or misconceptions, and a constructivist understanding of learning holds that sophisticated understandings must develop from the same conceptual system that produces misconceived responses. The underlying basis of the use of analogies and models (Gutwill, Frederiksen, & White, 1999; Dagher, 1998; Gilbert & Boulter, 2000; Clement & Steinberg, 2002; Clement, chapter 16, this volume) is that students will have conceptual resources in one context that they can use in a different context. In other words, analogies and models may be understood in terms of drawing connections among different parts of the cognitive system, and these connections may give rise to new stabilities.

For example, students tend to think of a spring as exerting a force back on a hand that compresses it. That intuition can serve as a conceptual "anchor" for students to recognize the upward force by a table on a book, and an instructor can facilitate this connection by presenting bridging analogies, such as a book on a bendy table (Minstrell, 1982). Brown and Clement (1989) and Brown (1993) show that this is not an abstract transfer (upward force in one context means upward force in another context), but rather that the construction of a conscious explanatory model in the table context (the table as microscopically springy) allows the attachment of appropriate intuitions to that context. When such bridging analogies and explanatory models are used in classroom instruction, students show significant gains on conceptual questions (Clement, 1993).

That analogies and models can be helpful in instruction is another strong result of the literature (for reviews see Duit, 1991; Dagher, 1998). However, the traditional view of analogy is rather static. In a "structure-mapping" account (Gentner 1983, 1989), the analogical base is construed to have a well-defined structure from the outset that is mapped to the target domain. For example, an analogy may map the structure of the solar system (the base) to an atom (the target), with a large central body and orbiting smaller bodies, with superficial features including the size and luminescence of the sun irrelevant.

From a complex systems perspective, the process can be much more dynamic, a fluid recruiting of conceptual resources from different parts of the system that then interact and settle into new patterns. The structure of the base need not be so stable as to remain constant in the process; the "base" may not exist prior to the analogy. Atkins (2004) presented a dynamic view of analogical reasoning in her analyses of several case studies. She connected the study of analogical reasoning to research on categorization, arguing that the generation of an analogy is essentially the nomination of a category, and that it is often misleading to expect a mapping from an intact, stable base to a target. As categories can be ad hoc, such as things to take from your house in a fire (Barsalou, 1987), analogies including analogical bases can be as well. Recent work on ongoing model construction, critique, and revision is consonant with this view as well (Clement, 1989; Wong, 1993a, 1993b; Dagher, 1998; Frederiksen, White, & Gutwill, 1999; Gilbert & Boulter, 2000; Clement & Steinberg, 2002; see also Clement, chapter 16, this volume, for a much more extended discussion of this area of research).

While some segments of the community have focused attention on conceptual change, other segments have focused attention on students learning science as inquiry. Research on analogies in physics classes, for example, has focused almost exclusively on instructional analogies, in the interest of promoting conceptual change, but a small number of studies have focused on understanding and promoting student abilities to generate and work with their own analogies (Wong, 1993a, 1993b; Atkins, 2004; May, Hammer, & Roy, 2006). Conceptual change and inquiry are often treated as distinct objectives (National Research Council, 1996), but a complex systems perspective would suggest they are interdependent, much as White and Frederiksen (1998) treated them in developing and analyzing the results of their *ThinkerTools* curriculum. In this way, a complex systems perspective supports views of the importance of meta-level aspects of student reasoning (Hennessey, 2002; Gunstone, 1992; Andre & Windschitl, 2002; Hewson, 1985).

Research on student epistemologies has begun to consider them as dynamic systems as well, comprised of manifold epistemological resources that are again context sensitive in their activation with multiple stabilities (Hammer & Elby, 2003; Redish, 2004; Rosenberg et al., 2006), such that students who approach learning as memorization in one moment may approach it as a personal construction of meaning in another. These epistemological resources may be seen in dynamic interaction with conceptual resources. For example, a stable Newtonian concept of *force* may involve a stable commitment to principled consistency in reasoning, because there are many apparent inconsistencies with that concept in unrefined intuition (Hammer, Elby, Scherr, & Redish, 2005). Without a commitment to consistency, a student would experience no need to reconcile those inconsistencies (diSessa, Elby, & Hammer, 2002).

New Emphases for Research

We have discussed existing work as seen from a complex systems perspective. A fully dynamic perspective, which we argue the field is moving toward, also has a number of implications for what may be generative areas for further research.

Identifying Productive Resources

With the extensive body of literature on student difficulties and misconceptions in place, the field would also benefit from complementary research to identify possible conceptual progenitors of expert understanding in students' intuitions. In a sense, this work is already underway, as research in curriculum development to address identified student difficulties invariably involves instructional strategies of guiding students toward helpful prior knowledge (Heron, 2004a, 2004b). But relatively few studies have made it an explicit agenda to identify helpful "facets" (Minstrell, 1992; Minstrell, 2000) of students' prior knowledge, the "preconceptions that are not misconceptions" (Clement, et al., 1989), such as how thinking about compressing springs provides useful conceptual resources for reasoning about the upward force by a table on a book. The possibilities are as rich as they have been for identifying misconceptions and difficulties.

Studying Transitions Among Multiple Stabilities

Naïve reasoning about springs and tables illustrates the phenomenon of multiple stabilities: Thinking about an object sitting on a visibly compressed spring, people think of the spring as pushing up; thinking about an object on a table, people think differently. The strategy of a bridging analogy is about facilitating a transition in student thinking from one stability to the other. We see a promising emphasis for new research in describing the dynamics of transitions from one to another, both as it happens spontaneously and as it may be facilitated by instruction.

To use Parnafes' (under review) work as an example, recall that students who look at a small amplitude, high frequency oscillation are likely to speak of the motion as "fast" in the sense of frequency, and those who look at high amplitude, low frequency oscillations are likely to speak of "fast" in the sense of translational velocity. What might be the dynamics of their transition from one meaning of "fast" to the other? Perhaps there are interesting phenomena in their reasoning about middle frequencies and amplitudes; is it possible for small, subtle cues to tip students into one meaning or the other? Similarly, Elby's work (2000) showed different patterns in students' interpretations of graphs depending on the presence or absence of eye-catching features. How subtle can the difference be and still show the correlation?

Studies of conceptual dynamics are more challenging, methodologically, than identifying misconceptions, but work of this kind has already been underway. Research in cognitive psychology began to emphasize microgenetic studies in the 1990s, trying to identify particular developmental changes as they occur, with a high density of observations "from the beginning of the change to the time at which it reaches a relatively stable state" (Siegler & Crowley, 1991, p. 606; see also Siegler, 1996; Siegler & Svetina, chapter 5, this volume). That "stable state" need not be developmental, in the sense of a new, fixed part of the learner's reasoning; it might be one of multiple possible stabilities, and the research could focus on understanding the extent of those stabilities and the nature of the transitions from one stability to another.

Developing Multi-dimensional Accounts of Learning Dynamics

Leander and Brown (1999) discuss six dimensions of embedded dynamics they identified in a microanalysis of a 20-minute discussion in a high school physics class. These dynamics included focal, conceptual, discursive/symbolic, institutional, social, and affective. The focal dynamics were generally unstable, with the focus of the discussion moving between a pendulum, an object on a spring, a tossed pencil, a baby on a rubber band, etc. The conceptual dynamics exhibited substantial stability within individuals, but substantial variability between individuals, leading to much talking past each other. Discursive/symbolic modes or forms of communication varied widely between the teacher and students. Students tended to animate stories about particular situations while the teacher tended to focus on abstractions, bringing in individual situations as examples of these abstractions. Institutional stabilities and instabilities were imposed by institutional structures and policies such as grades, syllabi, standardized tests, etc. This discussion came during a test review, and this institutional stability had noticeable effects on the discussion. Social stabilities and instabilities were exhibited in interpersonal alignments and misalignments, and affective stabilities and instabilities were exhibited in various expressions of emotion such as frustration, laughter, withdrawal, etc.

Research on learning generally identifies a specific target of investigation, be it conceptual understanding, epistemologies, affect, or social dynamics. Educators widely recognize these various aspects are interdependent. For example, research from an explicitly cognitive orientation often has students working in groups in order to take advantage of the social dynamics, while work from a social or sociocultural perspective will often involve students in consideration of discrepant events. In most cases it is difficult to discern the underlying theoretical orientation simply by observing the instruction. Still, there has been relatively little explicit discussion (Cobb, 1994; Roth & Duit, 2003; Vosniadou et al., 2001), largely because it is difficult to conceptualize and articulate the nature of these interdependencies. A complex systems perspective may help provide a theoretical framework.

Investigating Non-linear Conceptual Growth

The almost unquestioned assumption in most instruction is that if we want students to learn more, we need to teach more *at a faster uniform pace*. If we need to build a brick wall faster, we need to put the bricks on top of each other at a faster uniform pace. However, if students' conceptions form a complex dynamic system, we might expect progress in the system to be non-linear; we might think of an analogy to population growth or to phase change rather than to adding bricks in the wall. Instructionally, this would mean expecting a period of slow growth at the outset with more rapid progress later, as ideas connect to and build on the initial conceptual understandings. This is not to say that students are not learning much at the beginning (we would argue that a great deal of learning is occurring as students begin to form initial conceptual understandings), but rather that the number of topics covered in a typical textbook is likely to be less. It would also suggest that to impose a linear rate (in terms of topics per unit of time) may not provide sufficient time for meaningful learning at the outset. This would have implications for what happens later, except for those few students who for whatever reason were already at a place in their exponential learning where their rate of learning matched the pace of instruction, and thus they were able to keep up meaningfully.

We do not know of published studies explicitly taking such an exponential learning perspective, but there are some indications that such an approach could be beneficial. Anecdotal accounts include Max Beberman, one of the leaders of the "New Math" movement and a skilled mathematics teacher who focused closely on students' ideas in his own instruction. He took this approach with some middle school students and found that after one semester he was woefully behind other classes. After a year he was slightly ahead, and after two years he was far ahead of the other classes (Easley, 1993, personal communication). Don DeCoste, a former high school chemistry teacher and current chemistry professor at the University of Illinois, obtained similar results in his own teaching. After one semester teaching high school chemistry (and not moving on until students had a good conceptual grasp), he was well behind the other classes, but after one year he was slightly ahead (DeCoste, 2003, personal communication). Gautreau and Novemsky (1997) discuss the use of non-mathematical, conceptual physics to begin their physics instruction (van Heuvelen's 1991 OCS physics). Even though the experimental classes did not get to practice quantitative problem solving until substantially later in the semester than comparison classes, on tests of quantitative problem solving later in the semester the experimental classes performed substantially better. Benezet (1935) delayed instruction of computational algorithms until sixth grade, focusing in the early grades instead on more conceptual aspects of mathematics such as estimation of quantities. He found the experimental students caught up to traditional students in computation after one year, but they vastly outstripped comparison students in ability to think mathematically. This lesson has gone largely unheeded in the United States. Hiebert, Stigler, Jacobs, Givvin, Garnier, Smith, Hollingsworth, Manaster, Wearne, and Gallimore (2005) critique mathematics instruction in the United States, based on the *Third International Mathematics and Science Study*. In the United States, which did poorly in this comparison, they found that 53% of the time in mathematics classes was spent on review of rather rote procedures, while in other countries, which performed better, much less time was spent on review and much more time on introducing new conceptual material.

Exploring Phenomena and Models at Multiple Scales of Structure

Complex systems are often characterized by a range in dynamical and structural scales. Recent research has focused on a number of interesting properties shared by many self-organizing networks such as the World Wide Web, social networks, or chemical reactions in organisms.

One common property is "self-similarity" (Song, Havlin & Makse, 2005). Like snowflakes, coastlines, trees, and other fractals, many networks have similar structure across a wide range of scales. Look at a branch of a tree coming off the trunk, and it has branches of its own, which have branches, a fractal structure such that a portion of the tree is similar to the tree as a whole. For networks, self-similarity would entail elements clustering in patterns such that at larger scales the clusters are similar to the elements at the smaller scales.

Many of these networks are also "scale free" in another sense: There is a pattern in the connectedness of elements in the network such that a small number of elements have many connections, and a large number of elements have few connections. Specifically, the probability that a particular node in the network has k links to other nodes is proportional to λ/k^λ, where λ is a constant that is typically between 2 and 3 for naturally occurring networks (Barabási, 2002). The few nodes with many links act as hubs, and these networks also tend to have "small-world" connectivity in that it does not take many connections to get from one node to another in the network (Strogatz, 2001). (Six degrees of separation claims small-world structure in society in that nearly all people are connected to each other by no more than six social connections.)

Ideas from network theory are beginning to influence cognitive science. Steyvers and Tennenbaum (2005), for instance, examined the structure of three types of semantic networks: word associations from a database collected from 6,000 subjects (Nelson, McKinney, Gee, & Janczura, 1998), *Roget's Thesaurus* (Roget, 1911), and WordNet (Miller, 1995). In each case they found a nearly scale-free pattern of connections as well as small-world connectivity.

Perhaps these ideas could be generative for research on conceptual change, with its range in scales of phenomena and the range in structural scales of cognitive entities posited to account for those phenomena. Of course, the members and links in the network relevant for research on conceptual change are not easy to identify, but research has already nominated structures at various scales, including diSessa's p-prims and Vosniadou's presuppositions. Brown (1993, 1995) described a hierarchy of structures ranging from core intuitions to conscious models to verbal-symbolic knowledge. A network theory perspective suggests looking for invariances up and down these scales.

Supposing self-similarity, the difference between p-prims and "conceptions" might be fundamentally one of scale. Could Ohm's p-prim, for example, be understood as a network of resources for understanding agency, effect, and resistance — more effort or less resistance leads to more results? Even the understanding of "more" can be seen to have substructure, as Minksy

(1985) famously illustrated in his account of a "society of more." In this way, Ohm's p-prim could be a cognitive object in the sense of a stable, recurring pattern of activations, the same sense in which a framework theory could be seen as an object at a larger scale.

Wittmann (in press) has proposed "resource graphs" to represent and analyze conceptual change based on a network structure. One challenge in this program is that there are too many degrees of freedom in constructing these graphs. Perhaps it will be useful to experiment with supposing a scale-free pattern — Ohm's p-prim as a highly connected "hub," *force as spinner* as a resource with few connections — as a constraint in the construction of resource graphs. Supposing the network has small-world connectivity might suggest, for example, that hub resources play particular roles in metaphors between physical mechanism and anthropomorphic reasoning (e.g., the system is seeking equilibrium, the puck wants to keep moving).

Of course these are speculations; none of this is to suggest that network theory is the answer. It is to suggest only that it may be a source of ideas, much as computer science has been a source of ideas (including ideas central to diSessa's framework), although it is clear there are limitations in what a computational model can accomplish.

CONCLUSION

It has been almost 30 years since seminal work on students' content area conceptions and conceptual change in physics helped define this as a central focus in physics education research (e.g., Driver & Easley, 1978; Viennot, 1979; Posner et al., 1982). Research in the area has since grown to many thousands of articles and books. As the previous discussion documents, the focus in this research has moved from early metaphors of theory change in science toward a view of students' ideas as emergent, dynamic, and embedded. Such a view helps to integrate a wide variety of findings from apparently conflicting orientations and points toward potentially fruitful future research directions in physics education. We propose the complex systems perspective not as a totally new and original approach, but rather as a perspective that we believe the field has been moving toward and that will prove generative for further development of research, theory, and practice.

ACKNOWLEDGMENT

This work was supported in part by the National Science Foundation under Grant Number REC-0440113. The views expressed are those of the authors and not necessarily shared by the Foundation.

NOTES

1. While this is a fair representation of Vosniadou's published work, recently she has expressed a view that is similar to that expounded here — that presuppositions are themselves entities arising out of the dynamic interactions of smaller components (Vosniadou, 2007, personal communication).
2. We might imagine Ohm's p-prim and up-down organization acting in this way, as effectively permanent features of the system. If they were, one would expect that any reasoning in violation of Ohm's p-prim, for example, such that more effort begets less results, would involve the activation of some other knowledge elements that act to mark the reasoning as exceptional — perhaps to suppress the output of Ohm' p-prim.

REFERENCES

Andre, T., & Windschitl, M. (2002). Interest, epistemological belief, and intentional conceptual change. In G. M. Sinatra & P. R. Pintrich (Eds.), *Intentional conceptual change* (pp. 173–197). Mahwah, NJ: Erlbaum.

Atkins, L. J. (2004). *Analogies as categorization phenomena: Studies from scientific discourse.* Unpublished Doctoral dissertation, University of Maryland, College Park.

Baillargeon, R. (1992). The object concept revisited: New directions. In C. E. Granrud (Ed.), *Visual perception and cognition in infancy* (pp. 265–315). (Carnegie Mellon Symposia on Cognition, Vol. 23). Hillsdale, NJ: Erlbaum.

Barabási, A. L. (2002). *Linked: the new science of networks.* Cambridge, MA: Perseus Pub.

Barsalou, L. W. (1987). The instability of graded structure: Implications for the nature of concepts. In U. Neisser (Ed.), *Concepts and conceptual development: Ecological and intellectual factors in categorization* (pp. 101–140). Cambridge: Cambridge University Press.

Benezet, L. P. (1935). The teaching of arithmetic I, II, III: The story of an experiment. *Journal of the National Education Association, 24*(8), 241–244, *24*(9), 301–303, *25*(1), 7–8.

Bogartz, R. S. (1994). The future of dynamic systems models in developmental psychology in the light of the past. *Journal of Experimental Child Psychology, 58*(2), 289–319.

Brown, D. E. (1989). Students' concept of force: The importance of understanding Newton's third law. *Physics Education, 24*, 353–358.

Brown, D. E. (1993). Refocusing core intuitions: A concretizing role for analogy in conceptual change. *Journal of Research in Science Teaching, 30*(10), 1273–1290.

Brown, D. E. (1995, April). Theories in pieces? The nature of students' conceptions and current issues in science education. Paper presented at the annual meeting of the National Association for Research in Science Teaching, San Francisco, CA.

Brown, D. E., & Clement, J. (1989). Overcoming misconceptions via analogical reasoning: Abstract transfer versus explanatory model construction. *Instructional Science, 18*(4), 237–261.

Carey, S. (1985). *Conceptual change in childhood.* Cambridge, MA: The MIT Press.

Champagne, A. B., Klopfer, L. E., & Anderson, J. H. (1980). Factors influencing the learning of classical mechanics. *American Journal of Physics, 48*, 1074–1079.

Clement, J. (1982). Student preconceptions in introductory mechanics. *American Journal of Physics, 50*, 66.

Clement, J. (1989). Learning via model construction and criticism: Protocol evidence on sources of creativity in science. In Glover, J., Ronning, R., & Reynolds, C. (Eds.), *Handbook of creativity: Assessment, theory and research* (pp. 341–381). New York: Plenum,.

Clement, J. (1993). Using bridging analogies and anchoring intuitions to deal with students' preconceptions in physics. *Journal of Research in Science Teaching, 30*, 1241–1257.

Clement, J. J., & Steinberg, M. S. (2002). Step-wise evolution of mental models of electric circuits: A "learning-aloud" case study. *The Journal of the Learning Sciences, 11*(4), 389–452.

Clement, J., Brown, D., & Zeitsman, A. (1989). Not all preconceptions are misconceptions: Finding 'anchoring conceptions' for grounding instruction on students' intuitions. *International Journal of Science Education, 11*, 554–565.

Closset, J. L. (1985). Using cognitive conflict to teach electricity. In R. Duit, Jung, W., Rhoeneck, & C. von (Eds.), *Aspects of understanding electricity* (pp. 267–273). Kiel, Germany: Schmidt & Klaunig.

Cobb, P. (1994). Where is the mind? Constructivist and sociocultural perspectives on mathematical development. *Educational Researcher, 23*(7), 13–20.

Dagher, Z. (1998). The case for analogies in teaching science for understanding. In J. Mintzes, Wandersee, J., & Novak, J. (Eds.), *Teaching science for understanding* (pp. 195–211). San Diego: Academic Press.

Dawson, C. L., & Rowell, J. A. (1984). Displacement of water: Weight or volume? An examination of two conflict based teaching strategies. *Research in Science Education, 14*, 67–77.

DeCoste, D. (May, 2003). Personal communication with David Brown.

diSessa, A. A. (1993). Toward an epistemology of physics. *Cognition and Instruction, 10,* 105–225.

diSessa, A. A., & Sherin, B. L. (1998). What changes in conceptual change? *International Journal of Science Education, 20,* 1155–1191.

diSessa, A. A., Elby, A., & Hammer, D. (2002). J's epistemological stance and strategies. In G. M. Sinatra & P. R. Pintrich (Eds.), *Intentional conceptual change* (pp. 237–290). Mahwah, NJ: Erlbaum.

diSessa, A. A., Gillespie, N. M., & Esterly, J. B. (2004). Coherence versus fragmentation in the development of the concept of force. *Cognitive Science, 28,* 843–900.

Driver, R., & Easley, J. (1978). Pupils and paradigms: a review of literature related to concept development in adolescent science students. *Studies in Science Education, 5,* 61–84.

Driver, R., Squires, A., Rushworth, P., & Wood-Robinson, V. (1994). Making sense of secondary science: Research into children's ideas. New York: Routledge.

Duckworth, E. (1987). *"The having of wonderful ideas" and other essays on teaching and learning.* New York: Teachers College Press.

Duit, R. (1991). On the role of analogies and metaphors in learning science. *Science Education, 30,* 1241–1257.

Duit, R. (2006). *Bibliography: Students' and teachers' conceptions and science education.* Kiel, Germany: IPN. Available at http://www.ipn.uni-kiel.de/aktuell/stcse/stcse.html

Easley, J. (April, 1993). Personal communication with David Brown.

Edwards, D. (1993). But what do children really think?: Discourse analysis and conceptual content in children's talk. *Cognition and Instruction, 11,* 207–225.

Elby, A. (2000). What students' learning of representations tells us about constructivism. *Journal of Mathematical Behavior, 19,* 481–502.

Frederiksen, J. R., White, B. Y., & Gutwill, J. (1999). Dynamic mental models in learning science: The importance of constructing derivational linkages among models. *Journal of Research in Science Teaching, 36*(7), 806–836.

Gautreau, R., & Novemsky, L. (1997). Concepts first: A small group approach to physics learning. *American Journal of Physics, 65,* 418–428.

Gentner, D. (1983). Structure-mapping: A theoretical framework for analogy. *Cognitive Science, 7,* 155–170.

Gentner, D. (1989). The mechanisms of analogical learning. In S. Vosniadou & A. Ortony (Eds.), *Similarity and analogical reasoning* (pp. 199–241). New York: Cambridge University Press.

Gilbert, J. K., & Boulter, C. J. (2000). *Developing models in science education.* Boston: Kluwer Academic.

Givry, D., & Roth, W.-M. (2006). Toward a new conception of conceptions: Interplay of talk, gestures, and structures in the setting. *Journal of Research in Science Teaching, 43*(10), 1086–1109.

Gunstone, R. F. (1992). Constructivism and metacognition: Theoretical issues and classroom studies. In R. Duit, F. Goldberg & H. Niedderer (Eds.), *Research in physics learning: Theoretical issues and empirical studies* (pp. 129–140). Kiel, Germany: IPN.

Gutwill, J. P., Frederiksen, J. R., & White, B. Y. (1999). Making their own connections: Students' understanding of multiple models in basic electricity. *Cognition and Instruction, 17*(3), 249–282.

Hallden, O. (1999). Conceptual change and contextualization. In W. Schnotz, S. Vosniadou, & M. Carretero (Eds.), *New perspectives on conceptual change* (pp. 53–65). Oxford: Pergamon.

Halloun, I. (1998). Views about science and physics achievement. The VASS Story. In E. F. Redish & J. S. Rigden (Eds.), *Proceedings of the International Conference on Undergraduate Physics Education (1996)* (pp. 605–613). Washington, DC: American Institute of Physics.

Halloun, I. A., & Hestenes, D. (1985a). Common sense concepts about motion. *American Journal of Physics, 53*(11), 1056.

Halloun, I. A., & Hestenes, D. (1985b). The initial knowledge state of college physics students. *American Journal of Physics, 53*(11), 1043–1056.

Hammer, D. (1994). Epistemological beliefs in introductory physics. *Cognition and Instruction, 12*(2), 151–183.

Hammer, D. (1996). Misconceptions or p-prims: How may alternative perspectives of cognitive structure influence instructional perceptions and intentions? *Journal of the Learning Sciences, 5,* 97–127.

Hammer, D. (2000). Student resources for learning introductory physics. *American Journal of Physics, Physics Education Research Supplement, 68*(S1), S52–59.

Hammer, D. (2004). The variability of student reasoning, lectures 1–3. In E. Redish & M. Vicentini (Eds.), *Proceedings of the Enrico Fermi Summer School, Course CLVI* (pp. 279–340). Bologna, Italy: Italian Physical Society.

Hammer, D., & Elby, A. (2003). Tapping epistemological resources for learning physics. *Journal of the Learning Sciences, 12*(1), 53–91.

Hammer, D., Elby, A., Scherr, R. E., & Redish, E. F. (2005). Resources, framing, and transfer. In J. Mestre (Ed.), *Transfer of Learning from a Modern Multidisciplinary Perspective* (pp. 89–119). Greenwich, CT: Information Age Publishing.

Hammer, D. & van Zee, E. H. (2006). *Seeing the science in children's thinking: Case studies of student inquiry in physical science.* Portsmouth, NH: Heinemann.

Hennessey, M. G. (2002). Metacognitive aspects of students' reflective discourse: Implications for intentional conceptual change teaching and learning. In G. M. Sinatra & P. R. Pintrich (Eds.), *Intentional conceptual change* (pp. 103–132). Mahwah, NJ: Erlbaum.

Heron, P. R. L. (2004a). Empirical investigations of learning and teaching, part I: Examining and interpreting student thinking. In E. Redish & M. Vicentini (Eds.), *Proceedings of the Enrico Fermi Summer School, Course CLVI* (pp. 341–350). Bologna, Itlay: Italian Physical Society.

Heron, P. R. L. (2004b). Empirical investigations of learning and teaching, part II: Developing research based instructional materials. In E. Redish & M. Vicentini (Eds.), *Proceedings of the Enrico Fermi Summer School, Course CLVI* (pp. 351–366). Bologna, Itlay: Italian Physical Society.

Hewson, M. G., & Hewson, P. W. (1983). Effect of instruction using students' prior knowledge and conceptual change strategies on science learning. *Journal of Research in Science Teaching. 20,* 731–743.

Hewson, P. W. (1985). Epistemological commitments in the learning of science: Examples from dynamics. *European Journal of Science Education, 7*(2), 163–172.

Hewson, P. W., & Hewson, M. G. (1984). The role of conceptual conflict in conceptual change and the design of science instruction. *Instructional Science, 13,* 1–13.

Hiebert, J., Stigler, J. W., Jacobs, J. K., Givvin, K. B., Garnier, H., Smith, M., Hollingsworth, H., Manaster, A., Wearne, D., & Gallimore, R. (2005). Mathematics teaching in the United States today (and tomorrow): Results from the TIMSS 1999 Video Study. *Educational Evaluation and Policy Analysis, 27*(2), 111–132.

Huffman, D., & Heller, P. (1995). What does the Force Concept Inventory actually measure? *The Physics Teacher, 33*(3), 138–143.

Ioannides, C., & Vosniadou, S. (2002). The changing meanings of force. *Cognitive Science Quarterly, 2,* 5–61.

Kuhn, T. (1970). *The structure of scientific revolutions* (2nd ed.). Chicago: University of Chicago Press.

Leander, K., & Brown, D. E. (1999). "You understand, but you don't believe it": Tracing the stabilities and instabilities of interaction in a physics classroom through a multidimensional framework. *Cognition and Instruction, 17*(1), 93–135.

Lemke, J. L. (1990). *Talking science: Language, learning, and values.* Norwood, NJ: Ablex.

Maloney, D. P., & Siegler, R. S. (1993). Conceptual competition in physics learning. *International Journal of Science Education, 15*(3), 283–296.

May, D. B., & Etkina, E. (2002). College physics students' epistemological self-reflection and its relationship to conceptual learning. *American Journal of Physics, 70*(12), 1249–1258.

May, D. B., Hammer, D., & Roy, P. (2006). Children's analogical reasoning in a third-grade science discussion. *Science Education, 90*(2), 316–330.

Mayer, R. E. (1995). The search for insight: Grappling with Gestalt Psychology's unanswered questions. In R. J. Sternberg & J. E. Davidson (Eds.), *The nature of insight* (pp. 3–32). Cambridge, MA: The MIT Press.

McCloskey, M. (1983). Naive theories of motion. In D. Gentner & A. Stevens (Eds.), *Mental models* (pp. 299–324). Hillsdale, NJ: Erlbaum.

McCloskey, M., & Kargon, R. (1988). The meaning and use of historical models in the study of intuitive physics. In S. Strauss (Ed.), *Ontogeny, phylogeny, and historical development* (pp. 49–67). Norwood, NJ: Ablex.

McDermott, L. C., & Shaffer, P. S. (1992). Research as a guide for curriculum development: An example from introductory electricity. Part I. Investigation of student understanding. *American Journal of Physics, 60*, 994–1003.

Mestre, J., Thaden-Koch, T., Dufresne, R., & Gerace, W. (2004). The dependence of knowledge deployment on context among physics novices. In E. Redish & M. Vicentini (Eds.), *Proceedings of the Enrico Fermi Summer School, Course CLVI*. Bologna, Italy: Italian Physical Society.

Miller, G.A. (1995). WordNet: An on-line lexical database [Special issue]. *International Journal of Lexicography, 3*(4).

Minsky, M. L. (1985). *Society of mind*. New York: Simon and Schuster.

Minstrell, J. (1982). Explaining the 'at rest' condition of an object. *The Physics Teacher, 20*, 10–20.

Minstrell, J. (1984). Teaching for the development of understanding of ideas: Forces on moving objects. In C. W. Anderson (Ed.) *Observing classrooms: Perspectives from research and practice,* A.E.T.S. Yearbook vol. 11. Columbus, OH: ERIC Center for Science, Mathematics and Environmental Education.

Minstrell, J. (1992). Facets of students' knowledge and relevant instruction. In R. Duit, F. Goldberg, & H. Niedderer (Eds.), *Research in physics learning: Theoretical issues and empirical studies* (pp. 110–128). Kiel, Germany: IPN.

Minstrell, J. (2000). Student thinking and related assessment: Creating a facet-based learning environment. In N. S. Raju, J. W. Pellegrino, M. W. Bertenthal, K. J. Mitchell, & L. R. Jones (Eds.), *Grading the nation's report card: Research from the evaluation NAEP* (pp. 44–73). Washington, DC: National Academy Press.

National Research Council. (1996). *National science education standards*. Washington, DC: National Academy Press.

Nelson, D. L., McKinney, V. M., Gee, N. R., & Janczura, G. A. (1998). Interpreting the influence of implicitly activated memories on recall and recognition. *Psychological Review, 105,* 299–324.

Nussbaum, J., Novick, S. (1982). Alternative frameworks, conceptual conflict and accommodation: Toward a principled teaching strategy. *Instructional Science, 11*, 183–200.

Parnafes, O. (under review). These are at the same skinniness level, but they're not as high: Understanding the physical world through computational representations.

Peters, P. C. (1981). Even honors students have conceptual difficulties with physics. *American Journal of Physics, 50*(6), 501.

Posner, G. J., Strike, K. A., Hewson, P. W., & Gertzog, W. A. (1982). Accommodation of a scientific conception: Toward a theory of conceptual change. *Science Education, 66,* 211–227.

Powers, W. T. (1973). *Behavior, the control of perception*. Chicago: Aldine.

Redish, E. F. (2002). *Teaching physics*. New York: Wiley.

Redish, E. F. (2004). A theoretical framework for physics education research: Modeling student thinking. In E. Redish & M. Vicentini (Eds.), *Proceedings of the Enrico Fermi Summer School, Course CLVI* (pp. 1–63). Bologna, Italy: Italian Physical Society.

Redish, E. F., Steinberg, R. N., & Saul, J. M. (1998). Student expectations in introductory physics. *American Journal of Physics, 66*(3), 212–224.

Resnick, M. (1996). Beyond the centralized mindset. *Journal of the Learning Sciences, 5*(1), 1–22.

Roget, P. M. (1911). *Roget's Thesaurus of English words and phrases*. New York: Random House.

Rosenberg, S. A., Hammer, D., & Phelan, J. (2006). Multiple epistemological coherences in an eighth-grade discussion of the rock cycle. *Journal of the Learning Sciences, 15*(2), 261–292.

Roth, W-M., & Duit, R. (2003). Emergence, flexibility, and stabilization of language in a physics classroom. *Journal of Research in Science Teaching, 40*, 869–897.

Saljo, R. (1999). Concepts, cognition and discourse: From mental structures to discursive tools. In W. Schnotz, S. Vosniadou, & M. Carretero (Eds.), *New perspectives on conceptual change* (pp. 81–90). Oxford: Pergamon.

Sadler, P. M., Schneps, M. H., & Woll, S. (1989). *A private universe*. Santa Monica, CA: Pyramid Film and Video.

Shaffer, P. S., & McDermott, L. C. (1992). Research as a guide for curriculum development — An example from introductory electricity. Part II: Design of instructional strategies. *American Journal of Physics, 60*, 1003–1013.

Siegler, R. S. (1996). *Emerging minds: The process of change in children's thinking.* New York: Oxford University Press.

Siegler, R. S., & Crowley, K. (1991). The microgenetic method. A direct means for studying cognitive development. *American Psychologist, 46*(6), 606–620.

Song, C., Havlin, S., & Makse, H. A. (2005). Self-similarity of complex networks. *Nature, 433*, 392–395.

Smith, J., diSessa, A., & Roschelle, J. (1993/1994). Misconceptions reconceived: A constructivist analysis of knowledge in transition. *The Journal of the Learning Sciences, 3*(2), 115–163.

Spelke, E .S. (1991). Physical knowledge in infancy: Reflections on Piaget's theory. In S. Carey & R. Gelman (Eds.), *The epigenesis of mind: Essays on biology and cognition* (pp. 133–169). Hillsdale, NJ: Erlbaum.

Spelke, E. S., Katz, G., Purcell, S. E., Ehrlich, S. M., & Breinlinger, K. (1994). Early knowledge of object motion: continuity and inertia. *Cognition, 51*, 131–76.

Steinberg, R. N., & Sabella, M. S. (1997). Performance on multiple-choice diagnostics and complementary exam problems. *The Physics Teacher, 35*(3), 150–155.

Steyvers, M., & Tennenbaum, J. B. (2005). The large-scale structure of semantic networks: Statistical analyses and a model of semantic growth. *Cognitive Science, 29*(1), 41–78.

Strike, K. A., & Posner, G. J. (1985). A conceptual change view of learning and understanding. In L. H. T. West & A. L. Pines (Eds.), *Cognitive structure and conceptual change* (pp. 211–231). New York: Academic Press.

Strike, K. A., & Posner, G. J. (1992). A revisionist theory of conceptual change. In R. A. Duschl & R. J. Hamilton (Eds.), *Philosophy of science, cognitive psychology, and educational theory and practice.* Albany: State University of New York Press.

Strogatz, S. H. (2001). Exploring complex networks. *Nature, 410*(6825), 268–276.

Taber, K. S. (2000). Multiple frameworks?: Evidence of manifold conceptions in individual cognitive structure. *International Journal of Science Education, 22*(4), 399–417.

Thelen, E. (1992). Development as a dynamic system. *Current Directions in Psychological Science, 1*(6), 189–193.

Thelen, E., & Smith, L. (1994). *A dynamic systems approach to the development of cognition and action.* Cambridge, Mass.: MIT Press.

Thorley, N. R., & Treagust, D. F. (1987). Conflict within dyadic interactions as a stimulant for conceptual change in physics. *International Journal of Science Education, 9*(2), 203–216.

Trowbridge, D. E., & McDermott, L. C. (1980). Investigation of student understanding of the concept of velocity in one dimension. *American Journal of Physics, 48*(3), 1020–1028.

Tytler, R. (1998). The nature of students' informal science conceptions. *International Journal of Science Education, 20*(8), 901–927.

van Geert, P. (1994). *Dynamic systems of development: Change between complexity and chaos.* New York: Harvester Wheatsheaf.

van Geert, P. (1998). A dynamic systems model of basic developmental mechanisms: Piaget, Vygotsky, and beyond. *Psychological Review, 105*, 634–677.

Van Heuvelen, A. (1991). Overview, case study physics. *American Journal of Physics, 59*, 898–907.

Viennot, L. (1979). Spontaneous reasoning in elementary dynamics. *European Journal of Science Education, 1*(2), 205–221.

von Bertalanffy, L. (1973). *General systems theory* (rev. ed.). New York: George Braziller.

von Foerster, H. (1996). *Cybernetics of cybernetics* (2nd ed.). Minneapolis, MN: Future Systems.

Vosniadou, S. (1994). Capturing and modeling the process of conceptual change. *Learning & Instruction, 4*, 45–69.

Vosniadou, S. (April, 2007). Personal communication with David Brown.

Vosniadou, S., & Brewer, W. F. (1992). Mental models of the earth: A study of conceptual change in childhood. *Cognitive Psychology, 24*(4), 535–585.

Vosniadou, S., Ioannides, C., Dimitrakopoulou, A., & Papademetriou, E. (2001). Designing learning environments to promote conceptual change in science. *Learning & Instruction, 11*(4-5), 381–419.

Whitaker, R. J. (1983). Aristotle is not dead: student understanding of trajectory motion. *American Journal of Physics, 51*(4), 352.

White, B. (1993). ThinkerTools: Causal models, conceptual change, and science education. *Cognition and Instruction, 10*, 1–100.

White, B. Y., & Frederiksen, J. R. (1998). Inquiry, modeling, and metacognition: Making science accessible to all students. *Cognition and Instruction, 16*(1), 3–118.

Wiener N. (1961). *Cybernetics: or Control and communication in the animal and machine.* Cambridge, MA: M.I.T. Press.

Wilensky, U. (2001). NetLogo Rabbits Grass Weeds model. http://ccl.northwestern.edu/netlogo/models/ RabbitsGrassWeeds. Center for Connected Learning and Computer-Based Modeling, Northwestern University, Evanston, IL.

Wilensky, U., & Reisman, K. (2006). Thinking like a wolf, a sheep or a firefly: Learning biology through constructing and testing computational theories — an embedded modeling approach. *Cognition and Instruction, 24*(2), 171–209.

Wilensky, U., & Resnick, M. (1999). Thinking in levels: A dynamic systems perspective to making sense of the world. *Journal of Science Education and Technology, 8*(1), 3–19.

Wittmann, M. C. (in press). Using resource graphs to represent conceptual change. *Physical Review Special Topics – Physics Education Research.*

Wong, E. D. (1993a). Self-generated analogies as a tool for constructing and evaluating explanations of scientific phenomena. *Journal of Research in Science Teaching, 30*(4), 367–380.

Wong, E. D. (1993b). Understanding the generative capacity of analogies as a tool for explanation. *Journal of Research in Science Teaching, 30*(10), 1259–1272.

7

Naïve Theories of Observational Astronomy: Review, Analysis, and Theoretical Implications

William F. Brewer
University of Illinois at Urbana-Champaign

One of the major discoveries in cognitive psychology, cognitive development, and science education in the last half century has been the understanding that children before instruction and adults after instruction hold a wide variety of theory-like beliefs about the natural world that are not the same as the current scientific theories in those domains (see Carey, 1985; Driver, Guesne, & Tiberghien, 1985; Gopnik & Wellman, 1994; Wandersee, Mintzes, & Novak, 1994). In this chapter I analyze the extensive research that has been carried out on children and adults in the domain of observational astronomy and draw out some of the theoretical implications of this research. I focus on those aspects of observational astronomy where the phenomena have the potential to give rise to naïve theories (e.g., the shape of the earth, the day/night cycle, the seasons, and the phases of the moon).

Before beginning the content of the chapter, I will introduce some terminology: *Naïve theories* and *naïve models* are theory-like and model-like beliefs held by children and (nonscientist) adults. There are a variety of subclasses of naïve theories and naïve models. *Naïve scientific theories* and *naïve scientific models* are the naïve theories and naïve models held by children and (nonscientist) adults that are consistent with the corresponding scientific theories or models held by scientists. *Alternative theories* and *alternative models* are naïve theories and naïve models that are not consistent with the current scientific theory or scientific model. *Synthetic theories* and *synthetic models* are naïve theories and naïve models that include both scientific and alternative components. *Initial theories* and *initial models* are naïve theories and naïve models that give mechanistic accounts of phenomena using objects and constructs from the everyday world (though sometimes supernatural and anthropomorphic accounts are included as initial models). The rationale and conceptual underpinnings for this terminology will be given in detail later in this chapter.

METHODOLOGICAL ISSUES IN THE STUDY OF NAÏVE MODELS

In the last few years there has been a concerted attack on the structured interview procedures that have been used to uncover most of the theoretically important data in the area of the mental representation of the phenomena of observational astronomy. Therefore it is necessary to open this chapter with a detailed discussion of these methodological issues before turning to the actual findings. A structured interview is an open-ended technique in which the individual is asked a predetermined series of open-ended questions selected before the interview to be of interest on theoretical or empirical grounds. The critics of the structured interview have made some very extreme claims based on their methodological attacks. For example, on the basis of the methodological critiques, Panagiotaki, Nobes, and Banerjee (2006a) have stated that "naïve mental models of the earth are largely artifactual" (p. 353). These methodological criticisms of the structured interview procedure must be treated very seriously indeed, since, if taken at face value, they would undercut most of the current scientific findings on naïve theories and naïve models which are heavily based on data from structured interviews. Therefore in the first section of this chapter I will evaluate the force of these methodological attacks.

Methodological Problems with Closed-End Procedures

A number of investigators have argued that structured interviews are subjective and open to bias and should be replaced with objective, unbiased, closed-end multiple-choice procedures. Some representative examples of the arguments against the use of structured interviews and for the use of the forced-choice procedure are: (a) "forced-choice questions are less ambiguous than open questions (because the presentation of possible answers, and the lack of repeated questions, clarifies their meaning)" (Panagiotaki, Nobes, & Banerjee, 2006a, p. 364); (b) "These [forced choice] methods were considered more appropriate than those of the mental model theorists because they rely on recognition rather than recall and so are less memory demanding; they increase participant's awareness of the purpose of questions by providing only relevant answers; and they avoid misinterpretation of responses" (Panagiotaki, Nobes, & Banerjee, 2006b, p. 127).

Question Format in Eyewitness Interviews

In the area of naïve theories of astronomy, it is difficult to resolve the issue of which form of questioning procedure (open-ended or close-end) provides the most accurate account of the underlying form of mental representation. The problem is that the investigators in this domain have no direct way to know what form of mental representation a given individual possesses. However, there is a completely independent area of investigation, the area of eyewitness testimony, where the issues of how to ask questions have enormous consequences for society and so have been widely studied. The investigators in this area have the advantage that in their experiments they can provide the information to the respondent (e.g., by showing a movie or acting out an event) and thus they know what information the individual has been exposed to and can study the validity of various methods of questioning. A typical finding (see Dent, 1991) is that children are much more likely to make errors on closed questions (e.g., true/false, multiple choice) than they are when open-ended questions are used.

Children Choosing an Arbitrary Response

The investigators in the area of eyewitness testimony argue that one of the major problems with closed questions is that children often provide an answer (e.g., "true") regardless of whether they actually have the information being tested. This hypothesis about the reasons for the higher error rate for closed questions is well supported. For example, Waterman, Blades, and Spencer (2001) carried out a study in which half of the questions tested information that had been presented to the child, but the other half of the questions tested information unknown to the child. The children were tested with open-ended (wh-questions) and with closed-end (true/false) questions. The children were essentially at ceiling for both kinds of answerable questions; however, the results were very different for the unanswerable questions. The children had been instructed that if they did not know the answer to the question they should tell the experimenter that they did not know ("If you don't know the answer to a question, that's OK and you can tell me that you don't know"). Yet, on the closed-end questions 76% of children ages 5 to 9 years made an (incorrect) response, compared to only 15% responses on the open-ended questions. The authors concluded "children may provide an inappropriate response to a question which they do not understand or to which they do not know the answer, if the question only requires a yes/no response" (Waterman, Blades, & Spencer, 2001, p. 523).

In a major review of the literature of children's reports, Poole and Lindsay (1998) give the following overall summary of the literature on the form of questioning and response accuracy: "A robust finding is that children's accuracy declines as questioning moves from free-recall questions (e.g., 'Tell me what happened?'), to open-ended but more focused questions (e.g., 'Can you tell me what the man looked like?') to specific questions that inquire about a single detail (e.g., 'What color was his hair?') or that ask children to select from a limited set of options (such as multiple choice or yes-no questions). This finding has been replicated across studies with very different procedures, age groups, subject populations (i.e., normal versus cognitively impaired children)" (Poole & Lindsay, 1998, p. 16).

Thus, the data in an area where it is possible to examine the accuracy of open-ended versus closed-end questioning shows that closed-end multiple choice items used with young children have major methodological difficulties. Now, I will shift to an examination of a number of additional issues that arise with the use of closed-end questions in the area of observational astronomy.

Restricted Response Options

For a closed-end test to correctly identify the alternative models for a given natural science phenomenon, each possible model must appear in the response alternatives. Here, of course, the open-ended procedure has an enormous advantage since it is capable of identifying as wide a range of models as occur and can even identify models never before encountered. In the literature on observational astronomy there are many examples of invalid results due to this methodological difficulty with closed-end procedures. A classic example is a multiple choice item used to test knowledge of observational astronomy on the 1969 National Assessment of Educational Progress. The question was: "One reason that there is day and night on Earth is that the: (a) Sun turns; (b) Moon turns; (c) Earth turns; (d) Sun gets dark at night; (e) I don't know" (Schoon, 1988, p. 82). With open-ended procedures Vosniadou and Brewer (1994) identified 12 different models of the day-night (e.g., the sun and moon revolve around the earth every day; the earth rotates around its axis while the sun and moon are fixed in space on opposite sides of the earth). Clearly, the choice of foils on the NAEP item essentially eliminated the ability of that item to identify such alternative models of the day/night cycle. A number of researchers using multiple choice items in the area of naïve astronomy have understood this point and have first carried out an open-ended investigation to attempt to uncover the possible alternative conceptions and then tried to include one or more of the alternative models on their closed-end tests (e.g., Baxter, 1989; Mant & Summers, 1993; Sadler, 1992; Summers & Mant, 1995).

However, even those investigators who include empirically derived alternatives in their test items often write items that dramatically bias the data. For example in order to study the day/

night cycle Siegal, Butterworth, and Newcombe (2004) used the following item: "Some children say that day happens because the sun goes down in front of one part of the world and comes up underneath to shine in front of the other part. Some other children say that day happens because the world turns around so that the sun only shines on part of the world at one time. What do you think?" (p. 312). This question restricts the child to only two options. Comparison with the open-ended response data reported in Vosniadou and Brewer (1994) shows that the two options provided by Siegal, Butterworth, and Newcombe account for only 7% of the total responses identified by Vosniadou and Brewer. It would appear that Siegal, Butterworth, and Newcombe (2004) did not understand the serious methodological problem that restricted response options pose when using multiple choice procedures in the area of naïve theories of astronomy, since their conclusion in this paper about the methodological issue was: "children appeared more likely to give correct responses when provided with two clear alternatives rather than open-ended 'generative' questions that may carry an ambiguous interpretation" (Siegal, Butterworth, & Newcombe, 2004, p. 322).

Small Item Set

Some of the proponents of the multiple choice technique have deliberately chosen to use the smallest subset of items possible to test the child's understanding of a given construct. For example Nobes et al. (2003) used just four items to study the child's beliefs about the shape of the earth. This methodological decision has severe consequences. With the small number of items each hypothesized type of naïve theory of earth typically corresponds to just one unique pattern of responses. If a child produces a single incorrect response for *any reason*, then that child is likely to be classified as inconsistent or be misclassified in terms of which naïve theory they actually hold. It is thus not surprising that Nobes et al. (2003) find few, if any, naïve models in their study.

Contrast the minimalist multiple choice approach with the open-ended approach of Vosniadou and colleagues (Vosniadou & Brewer, 1992; 1994; Samarapungavan, Vosniadou, & Brewer, 1996). In these studies we used the technique of *converging operations* (Garner, Hake, & Eriksen, 1956), in which we attempted to find different test procedures that would help us converge on the hypothesized underlying mental model. Thus, for example, in Vosniadou and Brewer (1994), in attempting to understand children's models of the day/night cycle, we asked 13 questions such as: "Where is the sun at night?" "How does this happen?" "Where are the stars at night?" and in addition we also asked for a drawing. The data from the larger set of questions provide a much richer and detailed account of what the child believes (though it also brings along with it some difficult issues of how to combine the total set of responses into a global account of the child's beliefs).

Providing Model Information

Most proponents of the multiple choice procedure in the area of naïve models of astronomy (appropriately) attempt to include the scientific view and one or more alternative conceptions among the response alternatives. This opens up the possibility that an individual who has no coherent model will read one of the options (e.g., the distance model for the seasons) find that model attractive, and select it, giving a false indication of their state of knowledge. This difficulty seems an intrinsic problem with the closed-end technique.

Question Content

There is an interesting practical problem for testing more complex theories with multiple choice items. The scientific theory for some phenomena (e.g., the moon's phases) require a full paragraph to write out, so it is difficult to use the full correct scientific theory as a practical multiple choice response option. Thus, those wishing to use closed-end procedures to test naïve theories of the phases have faced real problems. Sadler (1987) constructed an item that asked for an explanation of the phases and used the response: "The moon moves around the Earth" (p. 423) to test for the presence of the scientific model. Clearly this response option dramatically underspecified the scientific model. Bisard, Aron, Francek, and Nelson (1994) tested the scientific model with: "The different shapes of the Moon (or phases) are caused by...viewing reflected sunlight off the Moon during the month" (p. 39). Once again this closed-end item underspecified the scientific model. In Sadler's (1992) dissertation he was reduced to a desperation ploy. For the item investigating knowledge of the phases, he constructed four foils each testing an alternative model of the phases and then used "none of the above" as the response option testing the scientific model. This analysis suggests that closed-end questions focused on complex concepts such as the phases of the moon are likely to give artificially high percentages for understanding of the full scientific model since the test items underspecify the full complex model.

Surface Responses

There is clear evidence that individuals sometimes respond to the surface characteristics of response alternatives in closed-end tests. Depending on how the investigator writes the items, this can result in artificially high responses for the scientific response or lead the students to make a response that clearly is not reflective of their underlying beliefs. On a test of the seasons, Bisard, Aron, Francek, and Nelson (1994) constructed an item to test knowledge of the seasons in which the response testing the scientific model was: "The Earth's northern hemisphere is tilted more directly toward the Sun in June" (p. 39). Bisard and his colleagues used this item with a sample of preservice teachers and found that 89% chose the correct (scientific) alternative. Schoon (1995) also tested knowledge of the seasons with a sample of preservice teachers. The scientific model was tested with a response alternative that did not include the word "tilt": "Summer is warmer because the sun is higher in the sky T/F" (p. 32). Only 15% of his sample chose this response option, and in discussions with these preservice teachers about the test, they argued that the test item was unfair because it did not include the crucial surface item "tilt."

Another example can be found in studies of the day/night cycle. Baxter (1989, 1998) used a closed-end test with pictures to study children's alternative models of the day/night cycle. He found that 69% of his sample of 9 and 10 year old English school children chose the picture of the earth going around the sun. This seems much too high. While open-ended interview studies do occasionally find this model given as an answer for questions about the day/night cycle, the percentages found are much lower (e.g., 2% in Vosniadou & Brewer, 1994). This suggests that many of the children selecting this picture as the answer for the day/night question are simply making a surface response to the picture of the earth going around the sun — a picture they have seen many times in their textbooks in discussions of the earth's annual revolution around the sun.

Response Follow-Up

One of the difficulties with the closed-end techniques, as traditionally used, is that the answers to the questions are taken at face value without a deeper probing of the knowledge that led to the response selection. Vosniadou and Brewer's (1994) study of the day/night cycle provides some empirical evidence that shows the power of using an open-ended follow-up for a closed-end question. In that study we asked children the closed-end question "Does the moon move?" We were thus at risk of obtaining a yes/no answer that was ambiguous with respect to the underlying models. However, the yes/no question was asked in the course of a structured interview and, luckily for us, many of the children chose to elaborate their simple yes/no answers so that we were frequently able to understand why they gave the particular response to the question. The younger (geocentric) children were more likely to say *yes* the moon did move and that it moved up and down relative to the ground. The intermediate age children were more likely to say *no* that the moon did not move, which we interpreted as due to a number of children holding the synthetic model that the earth spins while the sun and moon remain fixed on either side. The oldest children (and adults) were more likely to say *yes* and to indicate that the moon moved around the earth. Note that use of a closed-end question here could have left us with inconsistent and uninterpretable responses, but that many of our children were trying to be good conversational partners and went on to explain their closed-end responses. In retrospect we should not have relied so much on the good will of our children, but, after asking the closed-end question, should have systematically followed up their response (e.g., asking those who said it moved to explain, or show us, how it moved). Clearly, taking the responses to closed-end questions at face value and not being able to follow up responses with additional open-ended questions limits the ability of closed-end questions to reveal the underlying beliefs that actually led to the closed-end response.

Question Presupposition

A difficult problem for investigators writing multiple choice items is that they often mistakenly generate items from their adult (heliocentric) point of view (this is also a problem for open-ended questions — see the discussions later in the chapter). Siegal, Butterworth, and Newcombe (2004) provide a classic case of experimenter presupposition and insensitivity to the child's beliefs. These experimenters were attempting to explore the issue of where on the earth children think people live. For one of their test items, the child was given a small doll and "told with reference to the sphere model 'This little girl has sticky stuff on her. You can put her here (top), here (side), or here (bottom). Show me using the little girl where people in Australia...live on the model" (p. 312). The experimenters' question presupposes the children believe the earth to be a sphere and is insensitive to the beliefs of children who believe the earth is flat.

Empirical Comparisons of Closed Versus Open Procedures

In this section I predict how the difficulties with closed-end procedures outlined above can be expected to distort the data when applied to the study of naïve theories in the area of observational astronomy. The problem of arbitrary responding with closed-end procedures should lead to an inflation in the number of inconsistent responses. The problem of using a restricted response set should lead to an undercount in the number of alternative models. The problem of using a small item set should lead to more inconsistent responses. The problem of surface responding should lead to both an inflation in the number of scientific responses (surface responses to words learned from instruction) and an increase in inconsistent responses (unthinking responses). The inability to follow up responses when using the standard closed-end procedure should lead to fewer alternative models. The use of closed-end items with heliocentric presuppositions should lead to more inconsistent responses and fewer alternative (non-heliocentric) models. Thus, overall, the prediction is that the flaws with closed-end procedures should lead those procedures to produce: (a) more scientific models, (b) fewer alternative models, and (c) more inconsistent responses.

There have been two experimental studies that have compared closed-end and open-ended procedures in the area of earth shape. One study (Panagiotaki, Nobes, & Banerjee, 2006a) was carried out by advocates of the closed-end methodology and one study (Vosniadou, Skopeliti, & Ikospentaki, 2004) was carried out by proponents of the open-ended structured interview techniques. Often studies carried out by individuals with very different theoretical beliefs give different results, but in this case the two studies give very similar findings. Just as predicted above, the closed-end techniques (compared to the findings from structured interviews) lead to (a) more scientific models, (b) fewer alternative models, and (c) more inconsistent responses. This, of course, provides strong support for the analysis presented earlier of the problems with closed-end techniques when used to uncover the naïve models held by young children.

Exemplar of the Failure of the Closed-End Method

The study by Nobes et al. (2003) is an exemplar of the problems associated with the use of the closed-end technique in the area of naïve theories. These authors (Nobes, Moore, Martin, Clifford, Butterworth, Panagiotaki and Siegal) used four multiple choice items to study the shape of the earth. They then used a reasonable procedure (based on Vosniadou and Brewer's model identification methodology) to examine the pattern of data they obtained. They found that the predicted patterns of occurrence of alternative naïve models of the earth (previously uncovered with open-ended techniques) were not above chance. In other publications some of these authors have used their findings to make extreme claims. For example, Panagiotaki, Nobes, and Banerjee (2006a) wrote, "We have suggested that naïve mental models of the earth are methodological artefacts, and that this is at least partly because Vosniadou and Brewer's task is ambiguous and requires recall rather than recognition" (p. 365). However, there is an aspect of their data that Nobes et al. (2003) do not mention in the discussion section of their paper. Not only does their procedure of using a small sample of multiple choice items not find any evidence for alternative models of the earth, it also does not find any evidence for the *scientific model* of the earth (see the data and statistical analysis presented on p. 82). To the best of my knowledge, all previous studies of children's knowledge of the shape of the earth with children in the age range they used have identified some children with the scientific model. Thus, the Nobes et al. (2003) study provides striking evidence that the use of closed-end methodology can lead to a failure to uncover the very phenomena that it was designed to study.

Use of Closed-End Questions — Conclusions

Given the severe methodological problems with the use of closed-end techniques with young children that were described above, there is currently little justification for using these techniques in studies attempting to provide a scientific understanding of the phenomena of naïve theories in young children. This is particularly true given that there is a very well studied and understood methodology (the structured interview) which has proved very successful in answering scientific questions about naïve theories in both young children and adults across a variety of disciplines and across different aspects of the natural world (cf. Wandersee, Mintzes, & Novak, 1994).

However, the structured interview is both time consuming and requires some skill in interpretation, so the cost may be prohibitive for many applied needs. Therefore, it seems to me that if one is sensitive to the methodological issues discussed above, as a practical matter, one may be able to use the less time consuming and expensive closed-end tests to gain a rough distribution of the naïve models in a particular population of individuals. Yet, given the multiple problems outlined above, it still seems risky to use them for the identification of the naïve models of the individual members of a classroom of students.

Methodological Problems with Open-Ended Procedures

Most of the methodological problems discussed above are restricted to closed-end procedures; however open-ended procedures such as structured interviews also have some methodological problems.

Interviewer Bias

It is clear that investigators using open-ended procedures could easily bias the child's responses. There is a good published example in the work of Ivarsson, Schoultz, and Säljö (2002). In this protocol the interviewer is trying to establish what the child believes about the shape of the earth and has presented the child with a flat map of the world: [Interviewer] "Does the earth look like this?" [Child] "Yes, perhaps" [Interviewer] "Perhaps, it does. What does the earth look like in reality?" [Child] "Round" [Interviewer] "Round like a ball." [Child] "Mm" [Interviewer] "But if you're going to make it like a map you have to do it like this right?" [Child] "Mm" [Interviewer] "And then you have to make some bends like this. Why does it look flattened? Why does one draw it like an egg do you think?" The investigators in this study realize that other investigators may have difficulty with the obvious bias introduced by interviewer (cf. p. 91), but they assert that from their "dialogical perspective" there is no problem with this type of intervention by the interviewer. It seems to me that if one is trying to discover what the child believes about the shape of the earth then this kind of investigator intrusion into the open-ended interview process is not acceptable. And, in fact, I find it rather ironic that these investigators use the data gathered in this fashion to conclude: "The claim that children hold such mental models (or framework theories) seems questionable and appears primarily as a product of the methods used" (pp. 95–96).

Question Presupposition

It is obvious that most experimenters using the structured interview procedure do not allow the interviewers to show the dramatic kinds of bias the interviewers showed in the Ivarsson, Schoultz, and Säljö (2002) study. One of the great advantages of the open-ended procedures is that the child can be asked open-ended questions with minimal presuppositions, e.g., "What is the shape of the earth?" "Explain to me why it is hotter in the summer than in the winter."

However, occasionally the researchers using structured interview procedures have failed to construct neutral questions and have asked questions with some form of presupposition. In fact, Piaget (1929/1979), who was one of the early advocates for the use of the structured interview, provides some clear examples. He asked children questions such as "Why does night come?" (p. 291) and "Why is it dark at night?" (p. 293) and obtained answers such as "it is time to go to bed" (p. 293). He interpreted these responses as evidence that children showed "artificialism" (the belief that natural objects exist for human purposes). Oakes (1947, p. 47) also used Piaget's question "Why does night come?" and pointed out the problem of the presupposition with that form of the question. Notice that if one asked more neutral questions such as "Explain to me how day and night happen" or "What happens to the sun at night?" it is quite obvious one would obtain many fewer responses showing artificialism.

One can also find several examples of experimenter presuppositions in Nussbaum's important work on earth shape using open-ended procedures. Nussbaum was not expecting to find children with flat earth models (cf. Nussbaum, 1972, p. 131); thus, the first question of his structured interview was: "How do you know that Earth is round?" (Nussbaum, 1972, p. 72), a question that clearly presupposes a spherical earth. After the initial questions Nussbaum introduced a globe and asked another series of questions with respect to the globe (Nussbaum & Novak, 1976, p. 537). Once again this presumes the child believes the earth is the shape of a globe, a problem Nussbaum, himself, pointed out in a later paper (Nussbaum, 1985, pp. 180–181).

Vosniadou and Brewer were aware of the problem of item presuppositions and tried hard to avoid them. For example in Vosniadou and Brewer (1992) the structured interview questions about where people live on the earth were asked with respect to the child's own drawings (cf. p. 544), not with something provided by the experimenter that presupposed some particular model. However, in Vosniadou and Brewer's study of the day/night cycle (1994) we did make a few question presupposition errors. For example, we asked "Where is the sun at night?" which has a subtle presupposition that the sun physically moves. In retrospect the question might have been better if it was worded: "What happens to the sun at night?" In another part of the interview, in attempting to elicit the children's explanations of the day/night cycle, the structured interview protocol required the interviewer to draw a circular earth, then draw a stick figure on the earth, and finally ask the child to "To make it so it is day for that person" (cf. p. 137). In the published article we point out that this procedure contained presuppositions about the shape of the earth (p. 145). In retrospect we probably should have just asked the child to explain the day/night cycle in an open-ended fashion with no experimenter provided props (e.g., "Explain to me how night and day happen" or "What happens to the sun at night?"). Ironically, our presupposition error produced some very helpful data, since a number of the children with strong flat earth models of the earth overrode the bias in our drawing and drew their own stick figure on a flat place on the paper more consistent with their models. Note that Nussbaum and Novak (1976, p. 544) made a similar presupposition error in their questions and also found children with flat earth naïve models who ignored the investigators' round earth bias and placed people on flat ground below the round earth.

Question Repetition

A second general class of criticism directed at open-ended procedures has been an argument, based on an analysis of the pragmatics of adult-child conversations, that investigators using structured interviews (particularly Vosniadou & Brewer, 1992, 1994) have repeated questions and that this has biased the data. Some representative examples of this form of criticism: (a) "Under repeated questioning in the generative style, the child may vary his or her answers simply in an attempt to provide what the experimenter believes is the right answer" (Siegal, Butterworth, & Newcombe, 2004, p. 310); (b) "This use of repeated questioning can lead children to change their answers because they assume that their first answers must have been incorrect" (Nobes, Martin, & Panagiotaki, 2005, p. 50); (c) "Vosniadou and her colleagues have used repeated and similar questions in their interviews...If a question is asked more than once there is a danger that children will assume that their first answer must have been incorrect. Children will then strive to provide alternative answers in the hope that they will hit upon the 'right one'" (Nobes et al., 2003, p. 76).

The specific attack on Vosniadou and Brewer's work is a nonstarter — examination of the questions used in Vosniadou and Brewer (1992, 1994) shows that there are no repeated questions. What Vosniadou and Brewer's questions show is an attempt to use the method of converging operations. The questions try in a variety of ways to assess the underlying knowledge of the child.

However, even if the specific attack on Vosniadou and Brewer fails, there are more general issues here that need to be discussed. Those using the repeated question criticism often cite the work of Siegal, Waters, and Dinwiddy (1988) as evidence that repeated questions can cause young children to shift their answers. Examination of that paper shows that Siegal, Waters, and

Dinwiddy used a closed-end procedure and *literal* repetition of the closed-end questions. We are once again able to gain some perspective on these issues by use of the research in the area of eyewitness interviewing, where, as discussed earlier, it is possible to carry out experiments with knowledge of the information that the child has been exposed to. Poole and White (1991) carried out a study of question repetition in interviews with young children about an event they had witnessed. The children were asked some open-ended questions ("Tell me what happened when he came into the room") and some closed-end questions ("Did the man hurt Melanie?"). These experimenters manipulated question repetition and found that for closed-end questions the youngest children did show some response shifting as in the Siegal, Waters, & Dinwiddy (1988) study. However, there was no effect of repetition for the open-ended questions.

The critics of repetition in the structured interview procedure have grounded their attack on an analysis of the pragmatics of conversations. Poole and White (1995) provide an insightful analysis into these issues. They point out that "Open-ended questions are often repeated in daily interaction (e.g., 'What was that you said you did in school today?'), and children as well as adults generally respond to such requests by repeating their original story with surprisingly little variation. Repeating open-ended questions appears to be an innocuous procedure, and one that may lead witnesses to recall a useful piece of additional information. The conversational 'implicature' (Grice, 1975) of repeating a specific question is quite different, however (e.g., "Are you sure you don't want something to eat?"), and children are more prone than adults to change answers to yes-no questions" (p. 40).

Overall, it appears that the specific attack on the work of Vosniadou and Brewer (1992, 1994) was based on an inadequate examination of the actual questions used in that work. On the more general issues of question repetition in the study of naïve models, the research in the area of eyewitness interviewing, showing that question repetition is not a problem for open-ended techniques, has uncovered another reason why open-ended techniques are to be preferred to closed-end techniques.

Conversational Pragmatics

Another line of attack on the use of structured interviews has been to argue that investigators using the structured interview procedure have not been sensitive to the conversational pragmatics of the interchange between the investigator and the participant. Some examples of this type of critique are: (a) "many of the answers produced by children in Vosniadou's study can be understood as children fulfilling their communicative obligations by answering something when asked" (Schoultz, Säljö, & Wyndhamn, 2001, p. 115); (b) "the main problem with Vosniadou and her colleagues' methods is not that they use open-ended generative tasks *per se*, but that their instructions and questions are ambiguous and challenging even for educated adults" (Panagiotaki, Nobes, & Banerjee, 2006b, p. 137); (c) "Children's drawing, and their answers to open questions, should be interpreted only as their attempts to solve the puzzle of what the question means, rather than as accurate representations of their views about the earth" (Panagiotaki, Nobes, & Banerjee, 2006a, p. 365); (d) "the 3-D model selection and forced-choice question approach is 'designed to align the child's perception of the purpose and relevance of the questions with that of the experimenter' (Siegal et al., 2004)" (Panagiotaki, Nobes, & Banerjee, 2006a, p. 355); (e) [we used] "forms of questioning in which children were mainly asked to identify — rather than generate — the correct response in a manner designed to align the child's perception of the purpose and relevance of the questions with that of the experiment" (Siegal, Butterworth, & Newcombe, 2004, p. 311).

I agree with the essential point of these methodological comments. It is clear that in attempting to uncover the child's naïve models one wants to use questions that are comprehensible and unambiguous to the child and to make sure that the experimenter and the child are in agreement about the purpose of the questions and procedures used in the experiment. However, these issues of conversational pragmatics are not specific to open-ended procedures, but are relevant to *any* study involving children (or adults). In fact, the open-ended procedures are probably less likely to lead to these types of errors, since the child's open-ended responses can make clear to the interviewer that there has been a miscommunication, whereas with closed-end procedures the investigators simply have the fixed responses to their closed-end questions.

The study by Siegal, Butterworth, and Newcombe (2004) provides some prime examples of how researchers using closed-end materials have failed to be sensitive to the pragmatics of the experimental situation. This study shows how researchers attempting to write closed-end questions for difficult concepts have managed to construct multiple choice items that are "challenging even for educated adults." In that study 4- and 5-year-old children were shown two spheres and asked the following question: "Pretend you are standing just where this little girl is standing at the bottom of the moon. She's looking at her friend who lives down here on the world. Does her friend look the right way up or upside down to her" (p. 312). I leave it to the reader to decide what the right answer is to this multiple choice item used with preschool children.

The same study also provides a good example of another type of problem in the area of conversational pragmatics. In order to study models of the shape of the earth with closed-end procedures Siegal, Butterworth, and Newcombe (2004) presented children with three different physical models (sphere, hemisphere, and disc) of the shape of the earth. In the paper the authors stated that "combining a response to the sphere with one to the disc would allow the child to represent a 'dual earth'" (p. 312). However examination of the exact question asked of the child reveals that in Experiment 1 the children were asked "What is the shape of the earth? Show me *the* best model" (p. 312) [italics not in original] and in Experiment 2 the children were asked "Can you point to *the* model that shows how the world really is?" [italics not in original]. Clearly in this conversation between the experimenter and the child the conversational pragmatics strongly imply that the child should select only one model and thus make it unlikely that a child with a dual earth naïve model would use two physical models to demonstrate their beliefs. The results section of this study show that across 175 children no child selected two objects, and thus no children were classified as having a dual earth model (contrasting with the data from open-ended procedures which typically find this model). Given this flaw in their methodology, which strongly biases the children against giving dual earth responses, it is interesting to note that in the discussion section of their paper Siegal, Butterworth, and Newcombe (2004) state that their data on flat earth models would be similar to the work of Vosniadou and Brewer "if one discounts the dual earth and hollow earth models proposed by V&B as a possible methodological artifact" (p. 321). Overall this study provides a clear example of what can happen if the experimenter does not "align the child's perception of the purpose and relevance of the questions with that of the experiment" (Siegal, Butterworth, & Newcombe, 2004, p. 311).

Situated Cognition and Cultural Artifacts

A fourth line of criticism of the work using structured interviews is the assertion that investigators should use cultural artifacts such as globes during the questioning process. Some representative examples of this argument are: (a) "The claim that children hold such mental model (or framework theories) seems questionable and appears primarily as a product of the methods used. When children are interviewed without any support in the form of a meaningful artefact, they obviously express views that disappear completely when there is a map present" (Ivarsson,

Schoultz, & Säljö, 2002, pp. 95–96); (b) "Schoultz, Säljö, and Wyndhamn (2001) found that, by providing children with a globe, even first grade Swedish children demonstrated sophisticated knowledge of the shape and properties of the earth" (Nobes et al., 2003, p. 73); (c) "Schoultz et al. (2001) asked children about a globe. All these studies found little or no evidence of initial or synthetic mental models. Instead, scientific knowledge was shown to be present from an early age" (Nobes, Martin, & Panagiotaki, 2005, p. 50).

Situated cognition and object affordances.   It is clear from the quotes presented above that these critics of the structured interview think that if a cultural artifact such as a globe is used when interviewing the child, that it will allow the child's "real" models to be expressed. In this section I will show that when viewed in the larger context of situated cognition and object affordances this line of argument is ill-formed.

Situated cognition is the name for a complex intellectual movement within the cognitive sciences. Norman (1993) described a radical version of the position as a view which focuses "entirely upon the structures of the world and how they constrain and guide human behavior. Human knowledge and interaction cannot be divorced from the world. To do so is to study a disembodied intelligence, one that is artificial, unreal, and uncharacteristic of actual behavior. What really matters is the situation and the parts that people play" (p. 4). A more moderate version of the view is that it focuses attention on the role that the environment (particularly cultural artifacts) play in human behavior. Consider the graphic user interface of the computer I am using to write this chapter. The computer off-loads some of my cognitive tasks and so, in some sense, one can think of my cognitive activity as being distributed between my mind and a cultural artifact (the computer).

To help clarify the confusions reflected in the quotes given above, I will introduce the notion of "affordances." The concept of affordance was introduced into psychology by James J. Gibson. He stated that "the *affordances* of the environment are what it *offers* the animal, what it *provides* or *furnishes*, either for good or ill. The verb *to afford* is found in the dictionary, but the noun *affordance* is not. I have made it up. I mean by it something that refers to both the environment and the animal in a way that no existing term does. It implies the complementarity of the animal and the environment" (1986, p. 127). Don Norman modified the notion, applied it to cultural artifacts, and made it more cognitive. He stated "the term *affordance* refers to the perceived and actual properties of the thing, primarily those fundamental properties that determine just how the thing could possibly be used...A chair affords ('is for') support and, therefore, affords sitting" (1988, p. 9).

Situated cognition, affordance, and naïve models.   I want to extend the term *affordance* even farther, make it more cognitive, and argue that a given cultural artifact can afford certain mental representations (e.g., the presence of a globe during an interview may afford spherical mental models). Note, that as applied to naïve models, affordances can be positive or negative. A given cultural artifact might show positive affordances (facilitate) one naïve model while, at the same time, show negative affordances (inhibit) another naïve model.

In keeping with the perspective of situated cognition, it seems to me that reasoning with one particular cultural artifact is not somehow "special" (cf. Vosniadou, Skopeliti, & Ikospentaki, 2005, p. 336 for a similar argument). Different cultural artifacts simply afford different mental representations. Instead of arguing (as in the quotes given above) that cognition involving one cultural artifact is special, I would prefer to analyze the use of the cultural artifacts in terms of their *ecological validity* — how they are likely to be used in everyday life.

There are two conceptually different ways in which cultural artifacts can be used. In the literature on situated cognition the case usually discussed is the use of cultural artifacts (e.g., abacus, pocket calculator) to provide cognitive support for a difficult cognitive phenomenon. However, in instruction, cultural artifacts can play a different role. Often in the area of teaching observational astronomy (e.g., phases, day/night cycle) an attempt is made to use a set of cultural artifacts (e.g., spheres and a light source) to help the student develop a better (internal) naïve model of the phenomenon. If this instruction with cultural artifacts succeeds, it provides a powerful internal mental representation that the student can use without the need for the external cultural artifacts. So, the role of the cultural artifact differs depending on the ecological situation. It seems conceptually efficient to have an internalized model of the day/night cycle if one is trying to decide whether when it is noon in North America it is reasonable to phone someone in Brazil or in Australia. However, for very difficult constructs this may not be possible. Most individuals are unable to manipulate their mental models of the earth — sun — moon to generate the specific directions the crescent moon will be facing early in the lunar cycle versus later in the cycle. So, in this case, it seems that to answer the question one might want to look it up in a book or use a set of physical models and a point source of light to work out the answer.

However, we do need a baseline from which to make comparisons. I propose that we adopt a *Cartesian* baseline (i.e., an individual sitting alone thinking about the world without external cultural artifacts). We should establish the naïve models in an open-ended interview without external cultural artifacts and then see how the data change with the introduction of a particular cultural artifact. It turns out that in making this proposal I am following in the footsteps of the first systematic study in observational astronomy to use structured interviews. In their classic paper, Nussbaum and Novak (1976) state that "in the process of developing the interview, it was observed that visual props were apt to provide the child with some cues that would interfere with the spontaneity and authenticity of his natural thinking (thereby risking the validity of the interview interpretation). It was decided, therefore, to start the interview with a set of questions in the absence of any visual Earth model" (p. 537).

Globes.   There have been a number of studies using the globe in the process of identifying naïve models of the shape of the earth. Vosniadou, Skopeliti, and Ikospentaki (2005) and Skopeliti and Vosniadou (in press) compared young children's naïve models of the earth with and without a globe. The globe showed positive affordance for spherical models, negative affordance for alternative (flat and synthetic) models and increased the number of mixed models. Schoultz, Säljö, and Wyndhamn (2001) also carried out a study of earth shape with the use of a globe. They asserted that 100% of their sample of young school children believed the earth to be spherical. However, given the intrusive interview procedures used in the study by Ivarsson, Schoultz, and Säljö (2002) (see the discussion in the section on interview bias with open-ended procedures), it does not seem wise to compare this data with the other data in this section. Vosniadou, Skopeliti, and Ikospentaki (2005, p. 342) make an interesting point about the information available on a political/geographical globe. When asked if people could live on the bottom of the globe, many of the children in their study looked on the bottom of the globe to see if there were any countries on the bottom before they gave their response. This suggests that some of the children might be letting their beliefs about gravity be overridden by other forms of knowledge about where people live on the earth. This leads me to make a prediction. It seems to me that while a *feature-less* globe may well afford spherical earth models, the presence of a featureless globe might also afford beliefs that one can fall off the bottom of the earth. Ironically it turns out that I am about 250 years late to get credit for this prediction. In 1756 Ferguson made the same prediction! He stated, "When we see a globe hung up in a room we cannot help imagining it to have an upper and an under side, and immediately form a like idea of the Earth; from whence we conclude, that it is as impossible for persons to stand on the under side of the Earth as for pebbles to lie on the under side of the globe, which instantly fall away from it down to the ground" (see Cohen & Lucas, 2002, p. 2).

Physical models. There have been a number of studies that compare individuals' performance in explaining various astronomical phenomena with and without the use of physical models. Osborne, Wadsworth, Black, and Meadows (1994) examined school children's naïve models of the day/night cycle first with an open-ended question, then asked a second time having the children demonstrate their answer with models. They found that the physical models afforded the scientific mental model of the day/night cycle (e.g., for the 8- and 9-year-old children, the number who were scored as saying the earth moved jumped from 0% with the verbal interview to 41% with the use of models). Atwood and Atwood (1995) studied preservice teachers' naïve models of the day/night cycle and found that the use of physical models strongly afforded scientific mental models (70%) compared to a group who explained the day/night cycle without a physical model (32%). Atwood and Atwood (1996) compared preservice teachers on an open-ended written question with a condition involving the use of physical models (a sphere tilted as the earth's axis is tilted) in an interview about the causes of the seasons. They predicted that the physical model would afford the scientific mental model of the seasons, but found little difference between the two groups. In fact, if anything, the tilted physical model afforded various alternative models involving distance. Trundle, Atwood, and Christopher (2002) found that physical models did not afford scientific mental models compared to drawing when preservice teachers were asked to provide explanations of the phases of the moon.

Drawing. Most investigators have not looked at the use of pencil and paper as a cultural artifact, but clearly it is. Vosniadou and Brewer (1992) asked children to draw the earth. Those children who drew a round earth were given a drawing of a house on a flat earth and asked to explain the difference. This confrontation question was extremely valuable in allowing children who believed there were two earths (a flat one we live on and a round one up in space) to express their model. However, in light of the above analysis of the role of cultural artifacts, it seems to me likely that this experimental situation affords flat earth models to some unknown degree. Panagiotaki, Nobes, and Banerjee (2006a) compared earth shape models of young school children with a drawing procedure and with a physical model selection procedure. They found that the drawing procedure appeared to afford synthetic models, but did not afford flat earth models. This suggests that the affordance offered by drawing may only be modest.

Constructing models with play-dough. Several studies of the shape of the earth have asked children to construct models of the earth from play-dough (e.g., Vosniadou, Skopeliti, & Ikospentaki, 2005). There have been no explicit comparisons of this procedure with the same questions asked without this form of cultural artifact, so it is not clear what forms of naïve models it might afford. However, it seems possible that previous experience with modeling balls and ropes with play-dough might positively afford spheres and rings, but perhaps negatively afford hollow spheres.

Use of hands. While not exactly a *cultural* artifact, it appears that human hands can also provide affordances. Rudmann (2005) carried out a study of college students answering open-ended questions about topics such as the day/night cycle, the seasons, and the moon's phases. He observed that 72% of his participants attempted to use their hands as models in trying to answer the questions.

Roald and Mikalsen (2000) carried out a study of children's models of the shape of the earth. This work is relevant to the issue of affordances because they were studying deaf children who use sign language. They argue that there was a tendency for the children to pick a shape for the moon or sun that had an iconic relationship with the sign used by the child (e.g., a child using a sign for moon that involved making a crescent with the fingers was more likely to say the moon was crescent shaped). The sign for earth/world in Norwegian Sign Language involves making a ball with the hands (cf. p. 343), and the data on earth shape show a relatively high level of children (88%) who held a spherical model of the shape of the earth. These findings are certainly suggestive that iconic signs used by the deaf afford the iconically related model.

Three-dimensional earth models with closed-end procedures.   In several of our studies of earth shape, we tested children's beliefs about the shape of the earth with three-dimensional models using closed-end procedures (e.g., Vosniadou & Brewer, 1990; Samarapungavan, Vosniadou, & Brewer, 1996). We used the models because we thought they would allow us to resolve the sometimes imprecise verbal information we obtained from structured interviews. In light of the methodological analysis just presented, the method now seems more problematic. Some of the studies that adopted our procedure (Nobes et al., 2003; Siegal, Butterworth, & Newcombe, 2004) used a very limited set of earth shape models (only 3 models) and thus are examples of the methodological flaw of using a restricted set of response options. However, other studies (Panagiotaki, Nobes, Banerjee, 2006a, 2006b) have used a wider set of empirically derived models. Nevertheless, this procedure probably suffers from several other of the methodological problems common to closed-end procedures. One would expect that this procedure would have problems due to the fact that young children feel the need to make some type of response with closed-end procedures. In addition it seems to me it is quite likely that children with vague naïve models (as revealed in structured interviews) might, by choosing a particular physical model, give the appearance of having a more precise naïve model than they actually do. Note that this argument is supported by the fact that we found very few mixed/unclassified children in Samarapungavan, Vosniadou, and Brewer (1996). (Of course, it is also possible that the reduction in mixed/unclassified children occurred because the physical earth models allowed a more precise measure of the child's actual naïve model.) Identifying dual earth naïve models is particularly problematic with this procedure. The pragmatics of the object selection task make it unlikely that a child will pick two physical models and explain that both of them are "earth." Consistent with this analysis, examination of the results from studies using a closed-end earth model selection task (Panagiotaki, Nobes, Banerjee, 2006a, 2006b; Samarapungavan, Vosniadou, & Brewer, 1996; Vosniadou, Skopeliti, & Ikospentaki, 2004) show essentially no dual earth models. Finally, the use of three-dimensional models raises additional issues of situated cognition. The different shapes and the particular instantiation of those shapes within a given experiment might have very different affordances. In summary, the use of three-dimensional objects in closed-end procedures might have the ability to reveal naïve models that the child finds difficult to express verbally; however the methodological difficulties just outlined suggest it be used with great caution.

Situated cognition — conclusions.   The quotes at the beginning of this section show that a number of critics of open-ended procedures believe that the use of a particular cultural artifact (the globe) reveals the "true" nature of the child's mental representation, and that open-ended interviews, without such artifacts, are methodologically flawed. Analysis of these arguments in terms of the larger issues of situated cognition and the affordances of cultural artifacts shows that this narrow view needs to be reconceptualized in terms of the affordances provided by a particular cultural artifact for particular naïve models. In this larger framework no one cultural artifact has special status.

The data presented above suggest that some cultural artifacts do, in fact, afford particular mental models. But given the differences across studies, this is clearly a topic that needs additional research. The data already available do raise an interesting theoretical question. If a cultural artifact has afforded a particular mental model in a child, does the cultural artifact only temporarily act as a thinking tool or does it modify the child's mental representation when the cultural artifact is no longer available?

Vosniadou and Brewer Model Identification Procedure

Criticisms of the Vosniadou and Brewer model identification procedure.   A fifth line of criticism of the open-ended procedures has been directed at the specific proposals of Vosniadou and Brewer for identifying children's underlying naïve models. Vosniadou and Brewer (1992, 1994) argued that experimenters should develop hypotheses about particular models, develop a series of relevant questions, work out the expected pattern of data for each model, and then test the hypothesized models against data. Representative criticisms of this approach are: (a) "Vosniadou and her colleagues' approach involves searching for mental models derived from their participants' responses, and then classifying the same responses according to these mental models. With this post-hoc, circular process there is a danger of 'finding' consistency — and therefore evidence of mental models — when in reality there is none" (Nobes et al., 2003, p. 83); (b) "it therefore seems likely that synthetic earths are artifacts of the classification system developed by Vosniadou and colleagues. They have defined and categorized the commonest sets of responses given by children to their drawing and model-making tasks in terms of these putative mental models, and these set of responses have been labeled 'consistent' or 'coherent'" (Panagiotaki, Nobes, & Banerjee, 2006a, p. 365); (c) "mental models are *post hoc* inferences that are made to fit the data, as opposed to *a priori* predictions that are tested deductively" (Panagiotaki, Nobes, & Banerjee, 2006a, p. 356).

Logic of Vosniadou and Brewer's Model Identification Methodology   Probably the major contribution of the Vosniadou and Brewer papers on earth shape (Vosniadou & Brewer, 1992) and the day night cycle (Vosniadou & Brewer, 1994) was the methodological proposal about how models should be derived from structured interview data. Previous research in the area of naïve models of observational astronomy (e.g., Nussbaum & Novak, 1976) had used investigator intuitions about the global pattern of responses to discover naïve models. Vosniadou and Brewer proposed that researchers should develop hypotheses about the characteristics of the various naïve models in the domain of interest. Then, we proposed that the investigator should develop a series of theoretically relevant questions and for each hypothesized model generate the pattern of answers to the questions that would be predicted by the hypothesized model. Finally, we argued that the investigator should relate the hypothesized pattern to the actual data obtained, set some criteria, and then report the data on naïve models that are generated by this procedure. This approach provides a transparent path from the item level data to the identified models.

What the critics fail to understand is that in a domain that supports explanatory models, there are strong constraints on the postulated naïve models. The postulated naïve models are not arbitrary constructs. The postulated models have an analogical relation with the phenomena in the world (see the discussion below in the section on the nature of naïve theories). Thus, there are severe constraints (from the characteristics of the physical world) on the characteristics of the naïve models. The experimenter develops hypotheses about a particular naïve model (e.g., the scientific naïve model of the day/night cycle). Given the constraints on this model, the protocols of children with this naïve model must say that the earth spins so that the light from the sun hits different parts of the earth. If the investigator finds a child who also says that the people on the other side of the earth have daytime while we have daytime, then with the Vosniadou and Brewer methodology one does not inductively add that pattern to the criteria for the scientific mental model of the day/night cycle. A child who says that it is daytime on both sides of the earth should not be classified as having a scientific naïve model, since saying that it is daytime on both sides of the earth is inconsistent with the internal constraints of the postulated naïve model.

The critics of the Vosniadou and Brewer model discovery procedure have not understood the logic just described and have claimed it is a purely inductive procedure (see the quotes above). For example, Nobes et al. (2003, p. 83) suggest that by taking the six most frequent patterns of data in their data set they could classify 77% of the children in their sample as having naïve models. A real problem for the critics is that, because of the model-based constraints, Vosniadou and Brewer have always found that there were a substantial number of children that could not be classified as having a naïve model (18% in Vosniadou & Brewer, 1992; 37% in Vosniadou & Brewer, 1994). A "circular process" that used the "commonest sets of responses" in an inductive way would not lead to a large percentage of children failing to fit the postulated models, whereas a model-based approach can lead to this type of finding.

Difficulties with the model identification procedure. While the critics of the Vosniadou and Brewer methodology have simply failed to understand the underlying logic of the approach, there are, in fact, some important issues with respect to the methodology that need to be discussed. First, where do the postulated naïve models come from? The investigator using the Vosniadou and Brewer methodology operates just as any scientist does — the investigator examines the protocols and tries to develop hypotheses that would explain the pattern of responses. The postulated models are not so much inductive as *abductive* (Peirce, 1901–1903/1957). Typically, the problem is not that the investigator is generating too many ad hoc models, but that the investigator is not creative enough to come up with what turn out to be the appropriate naïve models in the domain.

Probably the most troubling issue with the Vosniadou and Brewer methodology is determining how stringent or loose the criteria should be for the pattern of data that will be considered to fit a postulated naïve model. In the real world of data from children, they omit to say some things they believe and they make mistakes in responding. Thus, if one requires that every aspect of the model be included and requires that there be no inconsistencies, then even if many of the children do actually hold naïve mental models, one is likely to identify relatively few of them. Different investigators are likely to come to different decisions about where to set the criteria. But one of the great advantages of the Vosniadou and Brewer approach over the use of global intuitions is that the criteria being used are made public and the readers can decide for themselves if the model fitting criteria are too stringent or too loose.

For readers who are familiar with the work of Chinn and Brewer on scientists' responses to anomalous data (Chinn & Brewer, 1993; Brewer & Chinn, 1994), the section of this chapter just completed, analyzing the recent criticisms of the structured interview technique, is a very thorough and detailed example of the responses we labeled as "Rejection" and "Reinterpretation."

NATURE OF NAÏVE THEORIES AND NAÏVE MODELS

Preliminary Issues

Criticism of Naïve Theories in Observational Astronomy

A number of authors have recently argued that children do not have naïve theories. For example: (a) "young children's concepts lack theoretical structure or coherence, and are not constrained by presuppositions or intuitions. Instead, until children have acquired a scientific model, they are 'theory neutral'" (Nobes et al., 2003, p. 73); (b) "The shift from inconsistent to consistently scientific earth notions does not appear to be influenced by intuitive constraints, nor does it involve the construction of naïve mental models" (Panagiotaki, Nobes, & Banerjee, 2006b, p. 138); (c) "knowledge remains fragmented until the coherent cultural view is acquired. Its fragmented, incoherent content and structure mean that children do not have anything like a naïve theory or 'mental model' of the Earth. The only theory that children acquire is the scientific theory that culture communicates" (Nobes, Martin, & Panagiotaki, 2005, p. 61).

Nature of Theories and Models in Science

To discuss the nature of naïve theories and naïve models, we first need to discuss the nature of theories and models in science. This is a very complex and controversial issue (Suppe, 1977) and cannot be described in detail here. However, a brief overview of the essential core of the accounts of the nature of theories and models should be enough for the purposes of this chapter. I think many current philosophers of science and many working scientists would agree that scientific theories contain theoretical entities (usually nonobservable), provide organized relations among the theoretical entities in the theory, and use the theoretical entities to explain some phenomena. The theory goes beyond the original phenomena, often integrates a range of phenomena, and provides a theoretical or conceptual framework for the phenomena.

There has been much debate about the relationship of models to theories in science (Black, 1962; Campbell, 1920/1957). This is also a very complex topic and cannot be described in detail. For the purposes of this paper I am going to take a strong position on the role of models in science. The physicist Boltzmann (1902) has provided a very nice description of those scientists who emphasize the role of models in science and described them as scientists who believe "physical theory is merely a mental construction of mechanical models, the working of which we make plain to ourselves by the analogy of mechanisms we hold in our hands, and which have so much in common with natural phenomena as to help our comprehension of the latter" (p. 790). In several recent papers (Brewer, 1999, 2001), I have argued that models are a *subclass* of theories that use mechanical/causal and physical/spatial mechanisms, and I am going to take that position in this chapter.

Exemplars of Naïve Theories and Models

In debates about the existence or nonexistence of naïve theories and naïve models in nonscientists, the discussions often involve quantitative data derived through the use of complex methodologies. I think theorists on each side of this debate have undervalued the power of qualitative protocols to resolve this theoretical issue. Therefore, in this section of the chapter I am going to present protocols of individuals that display their beliefs about a number of standard astronomical phenomena: the day/night cycle, the seasons, the phases of the moon, and the shape of the earth:

Sun Around Earth Day/Night Model: Native American Child, Age 6 Years

[Interviewer] "Where is the sun during the day?" [Child] "In the sky." [Interviewer] "Where is the sun at night?" [Child] "It moves to the other side of the earth."...[Interviewer] "Where is the moon during the day?" [Child] "It moves to the other side of the earth." [Interviewer] "So tell me, how does it change from day to night?" [Child] "The sun and the moon move around" (Diakidoy, Vosniadou, & Hawks, 1997, p. 174).

Sun Around Earth Day/Night Model: American Child, Age 9 Years

[Interviewer] "Where is the sun at night?" [Child] "Well, it goes under the earth to China. See, while we have day China has night and while China has night, we have day." [Interviewer] "How does this happen?" [Child] "Well, the moon and sun trade places" (Vosniadou & Brewer, 1994, p. 143).

Distance Model of Seasons: English Child, Age 10 Years

[Child drew a picture with the earth in an elliptical orbit around the sun] [Child] "The Earth is closest to the Sun in summer" (Sharp, Bowker, & Merrick, 1997, p. 75).

Distance Model of Seasons: American Child, Age 7 or 8 Years

[Child] "The earth goes around the sun in sort of an oval path. In winter we are far away from the sun" (Kuse, 1963, p. 215).

Eclipse Model of Phases: American College Student

[Student is asked to explain the phases of the moon] "The Moon goes around the Earth as the Earth goes around the Sun. As the Moon revolves, the Sun cast's [sic] light onto the Earth and the Earth shadow goes onto the Moon. Depending on where the Moon is, it will look like the Moon is in different shapes" (Fanetti, 2001, p. 34).

Eclipse Model of Phases: American Preservice Teacher

[Interviewer] "What do you think explains why we only see a portion of the lit part?" [Student] "Because the Earth is in the way of the sunlight." [Interviewer] "And so the Earth does what?" [Student] "Blocks the rays" (Callison, 1993, p. 248).

Dual Earth Model of Shape of Earth: American Child, Age 4 Years

[Interviewer] "Here's a house and this house is on the earth, right?" [Child] "Un-huh." [Interviewer] "So why does the earth look flat but you said it is a circle?" [Child] "Well, because...well, this world is our world (points to house drawing) and we have grass an stuff and our world isn't this world (points to his own drawing of a circle)." [Interviewer] "Oh okay can you explain that a little more?" [Child] "Because, we have grass and wood chips and stuff and this is the world up in space and we're not up in space" (Jipson, 2000, p. 83).

Dual Earth Model of Shape of Earth: Chinese Child, Age 5 Years

[Interviewer] "Are we on the Earth?" [Child] "No." [Interviewer] "Where are we then?" [Child] "We are not on the Earth because the Earth is in space...we can't fly so we can't go to the Earth." [Interviewer] "Where are we now?" [Child] "On the ground" (Blown & Bryce, 2006, p. 1430).

Hollow Earth Model of Shape of Earth: American Child, Age 9 Years

[Interviewer] "Can people fall off the edge of the earth?" [Child] "No." [Interviewer] "Why wouldn't they fall off?" [Child] "Because they are inside the earth." [Interviewer] "What do you mean inside?" [Child] "They don't fall, they have sidewalks, things down like on the bottom." [Interviewer] "Is the earth round like a ball or round like a thick pancake?" [Child] "Round like a ball." [Interviewer] "When you say that they live inside the earth, do you mean they live inside the ball?" [Child] "Inside the ball. In the middle of it" (Vosniadou & Brewer, 1992, p. 564).

Hollow Earth Model of Shape of Earth: Native American Child, Age 6 or 7 Years

[Interviewer] "Here is a picture of a house. How come the earth is flat here, but you said that it is a circle?" [Child] "Inside is flat and circle is around it."...[Interviewer] "Does the earth have an end or edge? [Child] "No, its too far." ...[Interviewer] "Where do people live on the earth?" [Child] "They live inside." (Diakidoy, Vosniadou, & Hawks, 1997, p. 171).

It seems to me that these qualitative protocols provide powerful and convincing evidence that children and nonscientist adults hold naïve models.

Characteristics of Naïve Theories and Naïve Models

Causal/Mechanical Models

The protocols of the two children who hold a geocentric view and account for the day/night cycle in terms of the *sun and moon orbiting around the earth* are clear examples of naïve models. These children have never seen the sun on the other side of the earth so this must be a theoretical entity postulated to account for the phenomena. They can run the model and derive its predictions (e.g., when we have day it will be night in China). Overall, this theory provides a powerful explanation of the phenomena (the day/night cycle).

The *distance model of the seasons* is another good example of a naïve model. The phenomena evident to the child are that it is cold in winter and hot in summer. These children's protocols show they use the earth and the sun as theoretical entities (i.e., the earth they stand on is totally different in appearance to the earth used as a theoretical construct in their model). Their theory incorporates an unexpressed naïve law — that if you are closer to a hot object it will make you warmer. They know how to manipulate the theoretical entities (e.g., move the solar objects in orbits). With this theoretical machinery they give a very coherent explanation of the seasons.

The *eclipse model of the phases* of the moon is another common naïve model in the area of observational astronomy. Individuals who hold this model use a number of theoretical entities (earth, moon, sun, and shadow), the motions of the three astronomical objects (earth, moon, sun), and a prior theory about light and shadow to explain the phases of the moon. They hypothesize that the moon orbits the earth each month, and when the moon is on the far side, away from the sun, the earth's shadow will move across the moon causing the phases. One can see that the shadow is acting as a theoretical entity in this model; the actual observable phenomenon is that the moon appears to change shape and a shadow is just one possible theoretical mechanism (e.g., there are other naïve theories in which it is assumed that the moon's physical substance actually changes). Once again, the theory appears to explain what is a very puzzling phenomenon.

Earth Shape Models

The earth shape theories do not have the causal mechanical component that is central to the other theories described in the protocols above. However, it seems to me that they are also theories. Thus, the two protocols from children with a *dual earth model* need a theory-based interpretation. These children have resolved the conflict between the fact that the earth seems flat with the information from adults that the earth is round by postulating two theoretical entities (a large flat earth we live on and a small, round earth up in space) where the scientific account only has one entity. This type of disagreement about the number of theoretical entities needed to account for a phenomenon is similar to historical debates in science, such as the status of oxygen in phlogiston theory. Children holding the dual earth view understand the theoretical implications of their model. Most of them state that people can only live on the flat earth — they often reason that people cannot live on the round earth up in space because it is small and round and people would slide off.

The protocols from the two children who hold hollow earth models make the same point. These children have resolved the flat/round conflict by hypothesizing that while the earth is spherical we live on flat parts inside the sphere. In this model the earth is a single entity, but of a rather unexpected shape. Clearly, the hollow earth is a theoretical entity; they have certainly never seen the postulated hollow earth. Overall, it does seem to me that these earth shape models have somewhat weaker explanatory force than do the causal/mechanical naïve models. Nevertheless, the earth shape models do support theory-derived implications. For example, when asked a question such as: "If you were to walk for many days would you ever reach the end/edge of the earth?" children holding these hollow earth models give responses such as "No, you would have to be in a spaceship if you are going to the end of the earth" or "Yes, but you have to go up to get off the earth...You can't walk off the earth because you can't walk up" (unpublished protocols from Vosniadou and Brewer, 1992). Thus, it seems to me that while beliefs about the shape of the earth are not quite as clear cases of naïve theories as are those naïve theories with causal/mechanical components, they still should be considered to be naïve theories — theories that move from the world of everyday objects to the world of astronomically large objects.

The Active Nature of Naïve Models

In a discussion of the nature of naïve models of the phases of the moon, Callison (1993) gave an insightful account of the role of naïve models as a form of mental representation in scientific reasoning. She stated, "In an attempt to comprehend the abstract, 'invisible,' or partially visible scientific phenomena, humans can mentally construct models of that which cannot be observed directly. The constructed mental models become mental visualizations or pictures of the phenomena within the time and space they occupy as well as the space surrounding the phenomena. Once constructed, models can be mentally manipulated through rotation, altering the viewpoint, or frame of reference" (p. 284). In a discussion of mental models in cognitive psychology Collins (1985) made a similar point. He stated, "Mental models are meant to imply a conceptual representation that is qualitative, and that you can run in your mind's eye and see what happens" (p. 80).

Scientific Models are Analogues of the World

In the earlier discussion of the nature of theories in science, I provided a quote from Boltzmann showing that proponents of model-based theories in science have felt that a crucial aspect of models in science is that they have an analogical relationship with the phenomena they describe. More recently, Suppe (1977) has made a similar argument and stated that scientific theories "must include a model — the model being the theory — which, if the theory is true, stands in an iconic relation to its phenomena" (p. 101).

Naïve Models are Analogues of the World

Johnson-Laird has made essentially the same point for mental representations in cognitive psychology. He proposed a new form of cognitive representation, *mental models*, in order to deal with a variety of issues in language comprehension and logical reasoning. In characterizing that form of mental representation, he stated that "A model *represents* a state of affairs and accordingly its structure is not arbitrary like that of a propositional representation, but plays a direct representational or analogical role. Its structure mirrors the relevant aspects of the corresponding state of affairs in the world" (Johnson-Laird, 1980, p. 98). I have argued (Brewer, 1999, 2001, 2003) that it is this structural relationship between the mental representation and the physical world that gives naïve models their enormous power to make successful predictions about phenomena in the natural world.

What are Naïve Theories and Naïve Models?

I propose that *naïve theories* are a form of mental representation that involves theoretical entities (abstract or concrete) and the cognitive interaction of these entities to provide explanations for phenomena in the natural world. *Naïve models* are the subclass of naïve theories in which the mental representations involve physical/spatial and causal/mechanical information. The mental representations in naïve models have an analogical relationship with the physical world, and the mental manipulation of the physical/spatial and causal/mechanical conceptual entities provides predictions about the relevant states of the world (i.e., they can often be run in the mind's eye). The overall conceptual framework of naïve models provide satisfying explanations of the relevant phenomena in the natural world.

Theory Change and Conceptual Change

In *The Structure of Scientific Revolutions* (1962), Thomas Kuhn argued that after a paradigm shift scientists view the world in a different way. One of the characteristics that sometimes occur with major theoretical change is that there is ontological change (e.g., objects of one type are now considered to be objects of another type, cf. Thagard, 1992). Carey (1985) and Chi (1992) have proposed that theory change from one naïve theory to another can also involve ontological change. In a very elegant study, Vosniadou and Skopeliti (2005) have shown that model change in the domain of observational astronomy also leads to ontological change. This study compared 10-year-old children with 6-year-old children. The majority of the 10-year-olds had scientific models, whereas the majority of the 6-year-olds had alternative naïve models (initial or synthetic). The children were given cards with the names of objects on them. Some of the cards had words for ordinary terrestrial objects (e.g., house, rock, and tree) and other cards had words for solar objects (sun, moon, and earth). The children were asked to make two groups out of the total set of cards. The results showed that 79% of the 10-year-old children classified the earth with the other solar objects, whereas only 27% of the 6-year-old-children did this. This strongly suggests that the children's naïve models determined which ontological category the earth belonged in. It tended to be classified as an ordinary terrestrial object by the young children with alternative naïve models of the earth, but tended to be classified as a solar object by those children with scientific naïve models of the earth. Thus, just as is the case with scientific models, it appears that theory change involving naïve models can lead to ontological change. This provides an additional independent source of support for the view that naïve theories and naïve models behave like theories and models in science.

The Theory-Ladenness of Data

In the philosophy and history of science, one of the major insights in the last half century has been the understanding that theories held by scientists interact with their observation and interpretation of data (Hanson, 1958; Kuhn, 1962). Brewer and Lambert (2001) and Brewer and Loschky (2005) have provided an analysis showing that the psychological claims by the philosophers and historians of science are, in fact, supported by current research in cognitive psychology. This allows an independent test of arguments for the similarity of scientific theories and naïve theories. If naïve theories behave like theories in science, then they too should have an impact on the naïve theorist's data.

Callison's (1993) dissertation provides a sample of protocols and drawings by college students explaining the phases of the moon. A number of these students hold the eclipse model of the phases (where the shadow of the earth on the moon produces the phases). This theory has a problem in that the shadow mechanism is only plausible for the configuration where the moon is on the side of the earth away from the sun. Examination of the drawings of the students with eclipse models of the phases shows that most of them only show the moon (with its phases) for the region on the side away from the earth (where their model can generate phase-like data). This is a clear case of theory-driven distortion of the data. Targan (1988, pp. 122–123) presents a protocol that also shows the impact of the eclipse model. One of the participants ignored the sun the investigator had provided on a sheet of paper (which would not have provided an appropriate shadow) and drew in her own sun in the location required by her model. Trundle, Atwood, and Christopher (2006) asked preservice teachers to draw the phases of the moon as they would observe them in the night sky. They found that 48% of the preservice teachers drew the phases as they would be generated from an eclipse model of the moon, not as they actually appear. This is a strong case of a naïve model overriding observational data. Thus, it appears that naïve models impact data in ways similar to those described in the philosophy and history of science, and this provides a second set of findings that support the view that naïve models behave in the same way as scientific models.

The Existence of Naïve Theories and Naïve Models — Conclusions

At the beginning of this section of the chapter, I provided a number of quotes from researchers in the area of observational astronomy who essentially deny the existence of naïve theories in children. Panagiotaki, Nobes, and Banerjee (2006a) provide an additional example of this very strong claim. They state, "Before children acquire scientific knowledge of the earth, they are 'theory free': they simply do not know and have no strongly held views about the earth" (p. 355).

I take the protocols and the analysis of these protocols given above to be a demonstration proof that the claims of these researchers are simply false. The protocols do not allow us to know what percentages of children have naïve models; they do not tell us if the naïve models are constructed on the spot or are in long term memory; but they do allow us to know that some individuals have mental representations that are best described as naïve models. Note that this is not an extreme view. The one professional philosopher of science who has examined this issue also concluded that children's naïve theories have the essential characteristics of scientific theories (Thagard, 1992, p. 257).

An opponent of naïve models might want to argue that the mental representations described as naïve models in this chapter are somehow fundamentally different from models in science and thus should not be characterized as models. However, this is going to be very hard going. Note that in a slightly different physical world some of these naïve models would, in fact, *be* the scientific model. For example, if the earth's axis of rotation was not tilted and if the earth was in a very elliptical orbit around the sun then the distance naïve model of the seasons would be the scientific model. And we know that in the history of Western culture the sun-around-the-earth day/night naïve model was the scientific model for more than a thousand years!

However, I do not want to argue that naïve theories are in all respects the same as scientific theories. Brewer, Samarapungavan, and Chinn (Brewer, 2008; Brewer & Samarapungavan, 1991; Brewer, Chinn, & Samarapungavan, 1998, 2000) have argued that the social institutions of science produce theories that are more internally consistent and more precise fits to the data than are naïve theories. For example, note that while the sun-around-the-earth naïve model provides a very elegant account of most of the data available to the child, it does not account for the behavior of the Foucault pendulum (information not known by the child). The distance naïve model of the seasons does not account for the fact that the seasons in the Northern hemisphere are the opposite of those in the Southern hemisphere. The eclipse naïve model of the phases has severe trouble accounting for the full moon. These issues of empirical adequacy are not unexpected. If the naïve models did not have some problems then they would not be called *alternative models*; they would, in fact, be the scientific models. One additional difference between naïve models and scientific models is that naïve models do not typically incorporate mathematical information and contain only qualitative and very loose quantitative information. Note that the (naïve) scientific theories held by children and nonscientist adults have essentially the same characteristics as alternative naïve theories and are also different from the scientific theories held by scientists in all of the ways just outlined.

Naïve Theories and Naïve Models in other Domains?

I am going to take an agnostic position on the degree of generality of the occurrence of naïve theories and naïve models in other domains. I think the arguments and evidence presented in this chapter have clearly established that naïve theories and naïve models are forms of psychological representation that occur in the domain of observational astronomy. It seems to me that it is up to the experts in other domains to use arguments similar to those used in this chapter and apply them to likely phenomena in their domains to see if it makes sense to talk about naïve theories or naïve models in each domain.

However, it does seem to me that the analyses presented in this chapter do provide some hints as to where one is likely to find naïve theories and naïve models. I think that naïve theories and naïve models are more likely to occur when: (a) the domain supports scientific explanatory theories (thus it is less likely for naïve theories to occur in the domain of traditional botany); (b) the domain involves causal mechanical mechanisms; (c) the domain supports cognitive mechanisms that are already available to the child (e.g., mechanical causation, occlusion, object motion); (d) the phenomena are available to the child (thus initial models for the photoelectric effect or for pulsars are unlikely); and (e) models for the domain occurred early in the history of the culture. Note that observational astronomy meets all these criteria and thus, it is probably not coincidental that we find such strong evidence for naïve theories and naïve models in this domain.

Naïve Models: The Nature of Representation versus the Memory Status

Form of Representation Distinguished from Status in Memory

A number of researchers have attacked the construct of naïve theories or naïve models by arguing that the evidence they are constructed on the fly is evidence against these models as a form of mental representation. These arguments conflate two quite different issues — the nature of the mental representation and its status in memory. If something is to be called a naïve theory or naïve model, then it must meet those criteria outlined earlier in this section of the chapter.

The memory status of a representation is a separate issue, and, in fact, the critics of naïve models have it exactly backwards. If an individual can construct a naïve model on the fly, that is a much more impressive cognitive performance than retrieving it from long term memory. To be able to create an explanation on the spot is an extraordinary intellectual achievement. A model stored in long term memory might have been constructed over many formal or informal instructional episodes, and so the ability to deploy such a model does not seem to be quite as impressive as someone generating the same model for the first time on the spot.

Evidence for Naïve Models Constructed on the Spot versus Models Stored in Long Term Memory

Vosniadou and Brewer (1992, pp. 575–576; 1994, p. 125) have argued that mental models of the shape of the earth are often constructed on the spot for problem solving based on presuppositions stored in long term memory; however, we also argued that some models are probably stored in long term memory. It is difficult to bring empirical evidence to bear on this issue. However, earlier in the chapter I argued that qualitative protocols often have much theoretical power in trying to understand the form of mental representation. I also think they can provide some evidence on the issue of the memory status of naïve models. The following protocol seems to me strong evidence that *some* naïve models are constructed on the spot at the time of questioning:

[College student asked to explain the phases] [Student] "I can only make a guess that there's something blocking the moon from our sight. I can only make that assumption...just an obstruction of our view I don't know like something comes in between." {over 20 exchanges later} [Student] "And so maybe like we're in front of the moon here that must be it. We must be like in front of the moon somehow...if you cover it up and you can only see a little portion of it and it's like it just moves a little over and so you can see a little more...I don't know if that was a very correct explanation, but I'm trying to figure this out as I go" (Lindell, 2001, pp. 163–167).

However, the argument that *all* naïve models are constructed on the spot seems to imply an inability to learn on the part of the child (or adult). Brewer (2003) has argued that with repeated use a model is likely to be stored as a whole in long term memory. Thus, it seems highly likely that if a child has been asked to explain a particular phenomenon (or reflects on some phenomenon on their own), they will come to have the full explanatory theory in long term memory. Consider your own mental model of the day/night cycle. It seems to me that most adults have the ability to retrieve the full model from long term memory and do not have to construct it on the spot. In fact, the protocol given above, suggesting construction on the spot, may have been the first time this student ever had to explain the phenomena at hand, and therefore, by necessity, it had to be generated on the spot.

EMPIRICAL FINDINGS ABOUT NAÏVE MODELS IN OBSERVATIONAL ASTRONOMY

Naïve Models of the Shape of the Earth

Identified Naïve Models of the Shape of the Earth

A framework for classifying models of the shape of the earth. Before beginning the presentation of the data, I want to provide a framework for thinking about naïve models of the shape of the earth. First, one needs to learn to put aside one's adult Copernican world view and look at things from the child's point of view. The adult view that we live on a giant sphere rotating in space really is quite implausible. It goes against a set of very entrenched beliefs derived from long experience with the everyday world. The child faces a formidable problem. Examination of the models that have been reported suggests that there are three major presuppositions that the child has to reconceptualize in order to achieve the naïve scientific model: (a) things that look flat are flat, (b) things fall down to the ground, (c) the earth is supported. Table 7.1 displays the commonly occurring earth shapes crossed with the psychological constructs gravity down vs. gravity to center and earth supported vs. earth not supported. The resulting matrix predicts essentially all of the empirically obtained models of shapes of the earth. All of the cells in this table correspond to logically possible models; however only a subset seem to me to correspond to psychologically plausible models. The table indicates which of the possible models I consider to be psychologically implausible. Take for example the disc model. Many children have been found to believe that the earth is shaped like a disc, that there is dirt "all the way down," and that things fall down to the flat ground. Clearly, this is a psychologically plausible model since many children hold it. It is totally consistent with the three presuppositions listed above — the earth is flat, things fall down to the earth, and the earth is supported by dirt and rocks. However, consider a disc model in which the earth is supported by rocks and dirt, but gravity pulls things to the center of the earth. I consider this model to be psychologically implausible, since one of the points of believing in gravity to the center of the earth is to allow one to account for the evidence that people live on

TABLE 7.1
Set of Possible Earth Shape and Gravity Models

Earth shapes	Earth supported		Earth not supported	
	Gravity down	*Gravity to center*	*Gravity down*	*Gravity to center*
Square/rectangle	D	X	P	X
Disc	D	X	D	X
Infinite plane	P?	X	X	X
Dual earth (one flat; one sphere)	D*	X	D*	X
Hollow sphere & truncated sphere	D	X	D	X
Flattened sphere	X	X	D	D
Sphere	D	X	D	D

Note. D = discovered; D* = model has two entities; P = possible; X = psychologically implausible the other side of the earth. This belief does not make much sense if one has a model of the earth supported by dirt and rocks, and so I have indicated that this is a psychologically implausible model.

The reasoning is similar for the other cells classified as psychologically implausible. For example, many children have been found to believe that we live on a flat area within a sphere in space. These children have accepted the information from the adult culture that the earth is a sphere, have given up the belief that the earth must be supported, but still retain the beliefs that things that look flat are flat and that things fall down to the flat ground. Consider a hollow earth model in which things fall toward the center of the earth. This seems psychologically implausible since if people can live on all sides of a sphere then there is no need for a model in which we live inside the sphere to keep from falling. With the framework displayed in Table 7.1, it should be somewhat easier to understand the data on naïve models of the shape of the earth.

A brief historical note.   Modern work on alternative models of the shape of the earth was initiated by Nussbaum in his thesis (1972) and two subsequent publications (Nussbaum & Novak, 1976; Nussbaum, 1979). However, the alternative models for the shape of the earth are fairly obvious if the investigator is able to put aside their adult preconceptions. G. Stanley Hall's work on "The contents of children's minds on entering school" (initially published in the *Princeton Review* in 1883, and then as a book in 1893) is often taken to be the first empirical study in American developmental psychology. In that work Hall used open-ended questions on a large variety of topics and found that for many young children "The world is square, straight, or flat...If we go to the edge of the world we come to water or may fall off" (1883/1893, pp. 34–35). He states that in his sample of preschool children "About three fourths of all questioned thought the world a plain, and many described it as round like a dollar, while the sky is like a flattened bowl turned over it" (1883/1893, pp. 36–37). Unfortunately, Hall's early work was largely forgotten, and it took almost a century before these issues were taken up in a systematic way by Nussbaum.

Identified naïve models of the shape of the earth.   The major models of the shape of the earth that have been identified are given in Table 7.2. The initial models in this area are that the earth is *flat* (shape unspecified, square, disc, ring, or shape unspecified). All of these models assume that the earth is supported by dirt and rocks all the way down. (Note that the figure we give in Vosniadou and Brewer, 1992, p. 549 for the disc model is inconsistent with this support assumption — it looks more like a disc in space.) These models are consistent with the child's three core presuppositions, and the disc model even has the added advantage of being consistent with the adults saying that the earth is "round." Even though these are initial models held by very young children, the roundness of the disc model is likely influenced by the culture and the square and rectangular models could possibly show some influence from the shape of maps. The next model, the earth as an *indefinite* plane, was suggested by Nussbaum and his colleagues (Nussbaum, 1979; Nussbaum & Sharoni-Dagan, 1983). This is an intriguing idea and came to mind when Stella Vosniadou and I were initially working on children's naïve model's of the earth. However, our data suggested that most of the children with initial models believed the earth had edges and so we argued that they were reasoning by analogy with every day objects, which typically have edges, that the earth also had edges (Vosniadou & Brewer, 1992, p. 578). However, I think Nussbaum's hypothesis deserves more research. The trick is going to be in finding a way to ask the very young child appropriate questions.

The *dual earth* model is a wonderful model that has fooled generations of parents, teachers, and earth shape researchers. Protocols from children with this model were given earlier in the section on the nature of naïve models. The child's solution is an ontological one — their model

TABLE 7. 2
Earth shape: Naïve Models Identified in Interview Studies

Earth shape	Interview studies
Earth supported and Gravity down	
Flat (shape unspecified)	H, 1883; M & H, 1979; V, S & I, 2005; Bl & B, 2006; S & V, i.p.
Rectangle/Square (dirt all the way down; so actually a rectangular or square column)	H, 1883; M & H, 1979; V & B, 1992; S, V& B, 1996; V, A, K & I, 1996; D, V & H, 1997; J, 2000; H, G, H & G, 2003; V, S & I, 2004
Disc (dirt all the way down; so actually a round column)	H, 1883; N, 1979; M & H, 1979; V & B, 1992; S, V & B, 1996; V, A, K & I, 1996; J, 2000; H, G, H & G, 2003; V, S & I, 2004; V, S & I, 2005; Bl & B, 2006; S & V, i.p.
Ring	B, H & V, 1987; V, S & I, 2004
Infinite plane	N, 1979; N & S-D, 1983
Dual earth (the flat one)	N & N, 1976; N, 1979; V & B, 1992; D, V & H, 1997; J, 2000; H, G, H & G, 2003; V, S & I, 2005
Hollow sphere & truncated sphere	M & H, 1979; S, V & B, 1996
Sphere	S, V & B, 1996
Earth Not Supported and Gravity Down	
Disc in space	M & H, 1979; S, V & B, 1996; S, A, K & I, 1996; D, V & H, 1997
Dual earth (the spherical one)	N & N, 1976; N, 1979; V & B, 1992; D, V & H, 1997; J, 2000; H, G, H & G, 2003; V, S & I, 2005
Hollow sphere & truncated sphere in space	N & N, 1976; N, 1979; M & H, 1979; N & S-D, 1983; Sh, 1995; S, V & B, 1996; V, A, K & I, 1996; D, V & H, 1997; S & O, 1998; J, 2000; H, G, H & G, 2003; V, S & I, 2004; V, S & I, 2005; Bl & B, 2006; S & V, i.p.
Flattened sphere (people live on top)	D. V & H, 1997
Sphere (people live on top)	N & N, 1976; N, 1979; M & H, 1979; N & S-D, 1983; Sh, 1995; S, V & B, 1996; S & O, 1998; S, 1999; V, S & I, 2004; V, S & I, 2005; Bl & B, 2006; S & V, i.p.
Earth Not Supported and Gravity to Center	
Flattened sphere (people can live on bottom)	V & B, 1992; Sh, 1995; V, A, K & I, 1996; S, 1999; J, 2000; H, G, H & G, 2003; V, S & I, 2005; S & V, i.p.
Sphere (people can live on bottom) [the naïve scientific model]	N & N, 1976; N, 1979; M & H, 1979; V & B, 1992; Sh, 1995; S, V & B, 1996; V, A, K & I, 1996; D, V & H, 1997; S & O, 1998; S, 1999; J, 2000, H, G, H & G, 2003; V, S & I, 2004; V, S & I, 2005; Bl & B, 2006; S & V, i.p.

has two entities where the scientific model has only one. The child is exposed to pictures of the earth taken from space and is told that this is a picture of the "earth." Since the earth in the picture bears no resemblance to the one we live on, many children come to believe that the "earth" is that spherical object up in space. This leads to a severe problem concerning the child's usage of the term "earth." Some children apparently assume that the word "earth" for adults is a homonym. These children thus use the term "earth" both for the spherical object in space *and* for the flat place we live on (e.g., adults say, "We live on the earth"). Other children apparently use "ground" or "dirt" for the place we live on. For other children, it is not clear that they have a lexical item for the flat place we live on when treated as an object.

All of this ontological and lexical complexity makes it hard to find ways to identify children with a dual earth model. If the researcher shows a child with the homonym solution a picture of the spherical earth from space and asks what it is, the child says, "earth." If the researcher asks the child where we live, the child also says, "earth." Thus, to the researcher, it looks as if the child has the scientific model of the earth. However, there are several additional types of questions that often will uncover the dual earth model. Nussbaum and Novak (1976) noted that when they asked children to point to the earth a subset of the children made what might at first seem a bizarre response — they pointed up to the sky. Nussbaum and Novak argued that these responses made perfect sense if the child held the dual earth model. In Vosniadou and Brewer (1992), we made *pointing up* one of the required responses for a child to be classified as holding a dual earth model; however, we noted (p. 555) that some children holding other models also point up in answer to this question (Nussbaum, 1972, p. 73 also found this). Another way to uncover the dual earth model is to show the child a picture of the earth from space and ask if people live there or if we live there; a child holding the dual earth model will often will say, "no" (typically, quite a surprise to the naïve researcher). If asked "why," the dual earth child will often say that the earth is too small for people to live on or that people would slide off. Another approach that helps to uncover dual earth models is the *confrontation question* introduced by Klein (1982). With this technique the child is asked to draw the earth. Almost all children will draw a circle. Then the child is shown a picture of the earth as we see it — flat with houses and trees on it. Finally, the child is asked to resolve the conflict. This will often give qualitative evidence for the dual earth model (e.g., the child will say we live on *this* one, pointing to the flat picture, not *that* one, pointing to the round drawing). Note that studies that use the confrontation question with young children often uncover substantial numbers of children with this model (e.g., Jipson, 2000; Vosniadou & Brewer, 1992), whereas studies that do not use this question (e.g., Vosniadou & Brewer, 1990; Vosniadou, Skopeliti, & Ikospentaki, 2004) often find no children with dual earth models. Overall, the dual earth naïve model is a creative solution to the problem facing the child who is exposed to the adult culture. By postulating that there are two entities, the child does not have to give up any of the three core presuppositions and yet can give the "correct" answer to most obvious questions from adults (parents, teachers, or researchers).

Now, I shift to the naïve models in which the earth is not supported. Children with a *disc in space* model have given up the presupposition that the earth must be supported but have retained the presuppositions that things that look flat are flat and that things fall down to the flat ground. The *hollow sphere* and *truncated sphere* are perhaps the most counter intuitive earth shape for most adult (It took Stella Vosniadou and me over 2 years to recognize these models in our initial data about the shape of the earth.) Protocols from children with this model were given earlier in the section on the nature of naïve models. In the hollow sphere model the child assumes that the spherical earth is like a round fishbowl or hollowed out pumpkin and that we live on the flat part at the bottom. In some of our initial protocols, there are amusing interchanges between the naïve investigator and the sophisticated child. The child says that the earth is a sphere and that people cannot fall off the earth. The investigator knows that the child has *down gravity* and so points out the "inconsistency" and the exasperated child says, "but you can't fall because you are inside the earth," at which point the investigator assumes the child is just inconsistent and goes on to the next question. In this model the child has given up the belief that the earth must be supported, has found a creative solution to the issue of what looks flat must be flat, but has retained the belief that things fall down to the ground. A similar model is one in which the earth is considered to be a truncated sphere with a sky dome covering the top half to make an overall spherical shape. Both of the models provide a clear solution to the problem of the adults asserting that the earth is a giant sphere in space. However, these models do cause some complexity for the child in where to place the solar objects (cf. Vosniadou and Brewer, 1992).

The *sphere in space* model, in which people live only on the top, solves the problem about the earth being a sphere, requires the child to give up the belief that the earth must be supported and that everything that looks flat is flat. However, it does not require the child to give up the strongly entrenched belief that things fall down.

The *flattened sphere* model, where people can live on the bottom, requires the child to give up the presuppositions that the earth is supported and that things fall down, but retains the presupposition that things that look flat are flat. The *scientific naïve model* is the sphere in space model with gravity acting to the center of the sphere. This model requires the child to give up all three of the core presuppositions.

Issues of Model Classification

Many secondary sources cite the studies by Nussbaum and Novak (1976), Nussbaum (1979), and Vosniadou and Brewer (1992) as essentially identifying the same set of earth shape models. Careful examination of these three papers will show that these researchers have quite different classification schemes. Before I start this analysis, I want to make clear that I think the Nussbaum and Novak (1976) and Nussbaum (1979) studies are the two most important studies ever carried out on children's naïve models of the shape of the earth. In Nussbaum and Novak (1976), the authors define Notion 1 as flat earth models. Examination of the protocols shows that under Notion 1 they included several dual earth models (a major discovery on their part) and at least one (unrecognized) hollow sphere (cf. p. 542). There are no clear examples of disc earth models in this category. To make things more complex, when Nussbaum (1979) described the earlier Nussbaum and Novak (1976) models, he *added* that in Notion 1 "the earth is flat and continues infinitely sideways and downwards" (p. 83). Notion 2 in Nussbaum and Novak (1976) is hard to summarize but is a model of a spherical earth that people live on. They say the children holding Notion 2 "state that the Earth we live on is round like a ball" (Nussbaum & Novak, 1976, p. 543). Yet as an example of this category they give a drawing of a dual earth child who explicitly put the people on the flat ground below the spherical earth. It seems to me that Notion 1 and Notion 2 as expressed in Nussbaum and Novak (1976) are not "natural kinds" (cf. Schwartz, 1977). Notion 3 in Nussbaum and Novak (1976) is the discovery of the spheres in space model in which people live only on the top. In his 1979 paper Nussbaum revised the earlier classification scheme. He said he wanted to collapse the old Notions 1 and 2 into a new Notion 1. He also asserted that the new Notion 1 involves an infinite earth. His protocols show that he now had examples of disc earth models and put them in Notion 1 along with dual earth models (note that two of the three illustrations given in Figure 3, p. 88 are disc models and thus inconsistent with an infinite model). So, once again, it seems to me the revised Notion 1 is not a natural kind. The new Notion 2 now describes hollow earth models — a third major discovery by Nussbaum. In Vosniadou and Brewer (1992), we make disc earth models and dual earth models separate categories and, consistent with Nussbaum, also make hollow sphere models a separate category. However, in that study we failed to identify the spheres in space model in which people live only on the top. (In later studies Stella Vosniadou has, in fact, found this model, e.g., Vosniadou, Skopeliti, & Ikospentaki, 2004, 2005.) It seems to me that this analysis shows that the early investigators had trouble finding a consistent set of categories that captured the natural kinds of naïve models of the shape of the earth, but that now with many years of work and discussion, the classification of the models has become much clearer and more nearly "cuts nature at her joints."

Change of Naïve Models of the Shape of the Earth with Age

The models above are presented in an order that reflects the arguments originally presented in Vosniadou and Brewer (1992) that acquisition of naïve models of the shape of the earth could be conceptualized as the successive giving up of presuppositions. It would be interesting to see if this theory-based order can be found in the empirical results from the studies of naïve models. In order to examine this issue, I propose using a *Model Change Index*. If a model is one that tends to be held by younger children, then in cross-sectional studies that investigate children at different ages ("cross-age studies"), it ought to be the case that fewer older children in the sample should hold those models. In order to turn this reasoning into quantitative form, I propose to examine the data from cross-sectional interview studies that have studied children at two or more ages. If the data for a given model shows a decrease in percent occurrence from a younger age to an older age, then that model is given a minus, and if the data for a given model shows an increase, that model is given a plus (ties are ignored). So, if a study found that 12% of the children in the younger age group gave supernatural responses while 2% of the children from the older age group in that cross-age study gave these responses, then the supernatural category would gain a minus. The overall Model Change Index is the percentage of plus scores across the data for a particular model. This number can range from 0% to 100%, with low percents indicating those models that were decreasing with age and high percents indicating those models that were increasing with age. The Model Change Index thus provides a rough measure of the age-based sophistication of naïve models.

I identified 11 cross-sectional interview studies of the shape of the earth that provided data for at least two naïve models across two or more ages (Blown & Bryce, 2006; Diakidoy, Vosniadou, & Hawks, 1997; Jipson, 2000; Mali & Howe, 1979; Nussbaum, 1979; Nussbaum & Sharoni-Dagan, 1983; Skopeliti & Vosniadou, in press; Sneider & Ohadi, 1998; Vosniadou & Brewer, 1992; Vosniadou, Skopeliti, & Ikospentaki, 2004, 2005). The rank order by the Model Change Index of the earth shape models with sufficient data is: Flat 0%; Rectangular 0%; Disc 27%; Dual earth 33%; Flattened sphere 50%; Hollow earth 56%; Sphere (gravity down) 62%; Sphere (gravity to center) 87%. Even though the Model Change Index is a relatively crude index of knowledge change with age, the empirical findings about model change with age are almost in complete agreement with the theory-based analysis given earlier. The pre-models and initial models decline dramatically with age (there were essentially no samples in which these models showed an increase from a younger age to an older age). Thus, the child appears to start with the initial models which are consistent with all of the core presuppositions and then shift to other models as the adult culture forces the child to give up one or more of the presuppositions. The intermediate and synthetic models tend to increase with age as the child gives up more and more presuppositions. These models then decline, giving intermediate numbers, and as the child gives up all the presuppositions the scientific model increases strongly with age. Note that since the Model Change Index is derived from cross sectional data we do not know if individual children follow this entire trajectory or if this pattern only occurs when one looks across groups of children.

Frequency of Earth Shape Models

The data for interview studies of the shape of the earth is relatively limited, makes use of different categorizations of the data, and is spread over a wide range of different ages. Thus, it is difficult to find an appropriate way to extract the information in the data. The frequencies of the models are changing rapidly across ages; thus, for an early model, the frequencies for older children will be very low or nonexistence, and for more sophisticated models the reverse will happen. Therefore, if one attempts to use medians, the score for many models would be zero, and the means (averaging across many low frequencies) would be low and not reflect the fact that some models actually occur at high frequency over a limited age range. Nevertheless, one would like to try and uncover some of the valuable information about the frequencies of models at different ages that occurs in the studies of naïve models of earth shape; I propose an index called the *Peak-1 Index* ("peak minus one"). To calculate the Peak-1 Index one ranks the frequencies of occurrence for a particular model across all samples (broken down by age) for all relevant studies (in this case, interview studies that present data on the percentages of children who hold a particular model of the shape of the earth). The Peak-1 Index is the percentage frequency of occurrence of the model in the sample with the *next to highest* percentage of occurrence across all the relevant studies. It gives a rough measure of the peak (i.e., highest) frequency of occurrence of a particular model across ages and studies. I chose the next to highest frequency because it seems to me that the highest frequency may often be an outlier and therefore moving down the frequency distribution should provide a more stable index.

The Peak-1 Indexes for naïve models of the shape of the earth where there was enough data to calculate the index are presented in Table 7.3. These percentages reflect the peak occurrence of a particular model and thus the percentages of the Peak-1 Index across models do not add to 100%. The table also includes the age of the children in the particular sample selected by the Peak-1 procedure. These ages are probably a bit less stable than the rank order generated by the Model Change Index, but have the advantage of giving actual ages. The data show that there are a number of initial models (disc models and dual earth models) and a number of synthetic models (hollow earth models and spheres with gravity down) that occur with relatively high frequency. The ages at which the models make their peak occurrence are relatively similar to the rank order given by the Model Change Index and thus also support the argument that the order of the models is determined by the number of presuppositions that must be given up to hold the model. The more presuppositions that must be reconceptualized, the later the model occurs.

TABLE 7.3
Earth Shape: Frequencies of Occurrence of Naïve Models

Models	Peak-1 Index	Age of sample
Flat—gravity down	23%	5 & 6 yrs.
Square—gravity down	5%	7 yrs.
Disc—gravity down	25%	6 yrs.
Dual earth	53%	7 & 8 yrs.
Hollow earth in space—gravity down	30%	11 yrs.
Sphere in space—gravity down	37%	11 yrs.
Flattened sphere in space—gravity to center	9%	6 yrs.
Sphere in space—gravity to center	60%	11 yrs.

Peak-1 Index is the percent occurrence of the model with the next to highest frequency of occurrence across studies (see text for more detail).

Table is based on data from: Blown & Bryce, 2006; Diakidoy, Vosniadou, & Hawks, 1997; Hayes, Goodhew, Heit, & Gillan, 2003; Jipson, 2000; Mali & Howe, 1979; Nussbaum, 1979; Nussbaum & Novak, 1976; Nussbaum & Sharoni-Dagan, 1983; Samarapungavan, Vosniadou, & Brewer, 1996; Skopeliti & Vosniadou, in press; Sneider & Ohadi, 1998; Vosniadou & Brewer, 1992; Vosniadou, Skopeliti & Ikospentaki, 2004, 2005.

Naïve Models of the Day/Night Cycle

Identified Naïve Models of the Day/Night Cycle

The major models of the day/night cycle are presented in Table 7.4. The first three categories are types of responses that were emphasized in Piaget's (1929/1979) early work. These response types are typically found in very young children and are, in some sense, pre-model. *Animistic* responses are responses in which the child treats an inanimate object as animate, e.g., "the sun goes to sleep." *Artificialistic* responses are responses in which the child assumes natural phenomena are designed to serve the purposes of human beings (e.g., [Interviewer] "Why is it dark at night?" [Child] "so we can go to sleep"). Most of the responses that show arificialism are

TABLE 7.4
Day/Night: Naïve Models Identified in Interview Studies

Naïve Models	*Interview Studies*
Animistic	H, 1883; P, 1929; L & P, 1962; Kuse, 1963; V & B, 1990; F, 1997; Sh, 1995; D, V & H, 1997
Artificialism	P, 1929; L & P, 1962; V & B, 1990; O, W, B & M, 1994; F, 1997
Supernatural	H, 1883; P, 1929; O, 1947; L & P, 1962; Kuse, 1963; V & B, 1990; F, 1997
Sun down to ground	H, 1883; L & P, 1962; O, 1947; Kuse, 1963; K, 1982; V & B, 1990, V & B, 1994; O, W, B & M, 1994; F, 1997; D, V, & H, 1997; P & H, 1998; R & M, 2001
Sun behind hills	O, 1947; L & P, 1962; Kuse, 1963; B, 1989; V & B, 1990; F, 1997; Sh, 1995; V, S & I, 2004
Sun behind clouds	P, 1929; O, 1947; L & P, 1962; Y, 1962; Kuse, 1963; B, 1989; V & B, 1990; V & B, 1994; O, W, B & M, 1994; Sh, 1995; S, V & B, 1996; S, 1996; F, 1997; V, S & I, 2004; L, 2005
Sun goes to other countries	L & P, 1962; Y, 1962; Kuse, 1963; Sh, 1995; S, 1996
Sun out into space	J, L & R, 1987; V & B, 1994; O, W, B & M, 1994; S, V, & B, 1996; F, 1997
Sun turns off	H, 1883; Y, 1962; S, 1987; V & B, 1990; R & M, 2001
Night a dark substance	P, 1929; L & P, 1962; Kuse, 1963
Sun has dark & light sides	P, 1929; O, 1947; H, 1950; Kuse, 1963
Sun behind moon	H, 1883; Kuse, 1963; S, 1987; B, 1989; O, W, B & M, 1994; S, 1996; P & H, 1998; R, 2005
Sun down to other side	O, 1947; K, 1982; V & B, 1994; Sh, 1995; S, V & B, 1996; S, 1996
Sun revolves around earth	O, 1947; L & P, 1962; Y, 1962; Kuse, 1963; K, 1982; J, L & R, 1987; S, 1987; B, 1989; V & B, 1994; O, W, B & M, 1994; Sh, 1995; A & A, 1995; S, V & B, 1996; S, 1996; D, V & H, 1997; P & H, 1998; K, 1998a; R & M, 2001, V, S, & I, 2004; L, 2005; R, 2005
Earth revolves around sun	B, 1989; J, L & R, 1987; V & B, 1990; M & S, 1993; V & B, 1994; A & A, 1995; S, 1996; K, 1998a; V, S & I, 2004; R, 2005
Earth rotates into dark space & light space	V & B, 1994; R & M, 2001
Earth rotates: sun & moon fixed	J, L & R, 1987; V & B, 1994; S, V & B, 1996; S, 1996; D, V & H, 1997; P & H, 1998
Earth rotates: sun fixed, moon revolves around earth	O, 1947; L & P, 1962; Kuse, 1963; K, 1982; S, 1987; B, 1989; V & B, 1990; M & S, 1993; V & B, 1994; O, W, B & M, 1994; Sh, 1995; A & A, 1995; S, 1996, S, V & B, 1996; D, V & H, 1997; P & H, 1998; K, 1998a; R & M, 2001; V, S & I, 2004; L, 2005; R, 2005

given in response to questions of the form just quoted. This question form is clearly ambiguous and thus facilitates artificialistic responses. *Supernatural* responses are responses that invoke a supernatural agent, e.g., "God makes it get dark." The category *sun goes down to the ground* is often heterogeneous. In Vosniadou and Brewer (1994, p. 142) we argued that it was important to distinguish responses such as "the sun goes down" which are more description than explanation from "the sun goes down *to the other side* of the earth" which show some growing sophistication about the day/night cycle.

The next set of naïve models tend to make use of causal/mechanistic reasoning and beliefs about occlusion and to apply them to observed solar objects. Understanding mechanical causality (e.g., Leslie & Keeble, 1987) and that objects occlude other objects when they are in front of them (e.g., Aguiar & Baillargeon, 1999) are constructs that occur very early in child development. Thus, as would be expected, naïve models making use of these also occur early in the child's development. The sun goes *behind the hills* or the sun goes *behind the clouds* are classic examples of models that use occlusion to solve the problem of what happens to the sun at night. The sun goes *to other countries* is another ambiguous category; unless it is followed up, it does not distinguish between flat earth and spherical earth models. Placing the sun far *out into space* makes use of the prior belief that light fades with distance. The sun *turns off* is another interesting mechanism. In Vosniadou and Brewer (1994, p. 130, 132), we predicted this model based on our assumption that the child's models are often based on analogy with previous knowledge and we thought turning off a light with a light switch might lead to sun turns off responses. However, we found no examples in our data set. It is comforting to know that our reasoning was solid and that others have found this type of model. The idea that *night is a dark substance* and perhaps covers the sun at night is an intriguing concept that needs greater study (along with the child's understanding of light and shadow). The belief that the sun has *dark and light sides* and rotates to cause day and night is an elegant (though rare) solution to the problem faced by the child. Note that it is more parsimonious than the scientific model! Another ingenious naïve model is to have the *sun behind the moon* during the night and the *moon behind the sun* during the day.

All the remaining daylight models require that the child has adopted the belief that the earth is a large finite object in space. The *sun goes around the earth* (the classic Ptolemaic model) allows the child to retain a geocentric point of view and yet provides a powerful explanation for the day/night cycle. Protocols from children with this model were given earlier in the section on the nature of naïve models.

The *earth goes around the sun* naïve model has always puzzled me. It, unlike all the rest of the naïve mechanical models of the day/night cycle, does not seem to be explanatory. More work on this model is needed to discover if it is explanatory for the child in a way that is not obvious to this researcher or if it is simply a surface confusion of the daily rotation of the earth around its axis with the annual revolution of the earth around the sun (cf. Vosniadou & Brewer, 1994, p. 154, 174).

The remaining naïve models require that the child accept that the earth rotates in some fashion. This requires that the child give up the presumably well entrenched belief that the earth is stable and does not spin. The belief that the earth rotates while the space around the earth is divided into a light half and a dark half is another naïve model that needs additional research (e.g., how does this model relate to the child's understanding of light and shadow?).

The naïve scientific model requires that the child accept that the earth is a sphere in space and that the sphere is rotating on its axis. In Vosniadou and Brewer (1994), we distinguished two basic forms of earth rotation models: *earth rotates — sun and moon fixed* versus *earth rotates — sun fixed, moon revolves around earth*. We found that most of the children in our sample who used the earth's rotation to explain the day/night cycle actually held a subtle synthetic model — that the earth rotated while the sun and moon were fixed in space on opposite sides of the earth. This is an elegant model — simpler than the scientific model. (It does have a problem dealing with the fact that the moon can be visible during the day, but since most of the children do not know this fact, the model has, for them, strong empirical validity.) It is probably the case that many of the responses that have been categorized as showing the full naïve scientific model in the studies listed in the table actually include substantial numbers of cases of the synthetic model in which the sun and moon are fixed. However, the data on adults' models of the day/night cycle (Atwood & Atwood, 1995; Mant & Summers, 1993; Parker & Heywood, 1998) suggest that many adults do have the full naïve scientific model in which the earth spins on its axis, the sun is fixed, but the moon revolves around the earth. Thus, overall, the progression appears to be from early non-mechanistic models, to initial mechanical models in which the solar objects are taken to be the size and shape that they appear to be and to obey the laws of the everyday world (e.g., object occlusion, distance fading). The next set of models requires the child to treat the earth as a large object in space. The adult culture typically imposes the belief that the large object is a sphere, thus leading to the various alternative models of earth shape. The final set of models requires the child to give up the belief that the earth is motionless and accept that the earth rotates.

Change of Naïve Models of the Day/Night Cycle with Age

The models above are presented in an order that reflects a variety of theory-based assumptions. It would again seem to be interesting to see if this theory-based order can be found in the empirical results from the studies of naïve models of the day/night cycle. I identified seven cross-sectional interview studies of the day/night cycle that provided data for at least three naïve models across two or more ages (Diakidoy, Vosniadou, & Hawks, 1997; Kuse, 1963; Osborne, Wadsworth, Black, & Meadows, 1994; Samarapungavan, Vosniadou, & Brewer, 1996; Vosniadou & Brewer, 1990, 1994; Vosniadou, Skopeliti, & Ikospentaki, 2004). The rank order by the Model Change Index (see the detailed description above) of the most common models from these studies is: Animistic 0%; Artificalism 0%; Supernatural 0%; Sun down to ground 0%; Sun behind hills 0%; Sun out into space 0%; Sun behind clouds 25%; Sun goes around earth 54%; Earth around the sun 67%; Earth rotates, sun and moon fixed 80%; Earth rotates, sun fixed, moon revolves 100%. The empirical findings about model change with age are almost in complete agreement with the theory-based analysis given earlier. The pre-models and initial models decline dramatically with age (there were essentially no samples in which these models showed an increase from a younger age to an older age). The intermediate and synthetic models tend to increase with age, up to a point, then decline, giving intermediate numbers; and the scientific model increases strongly with age.

Frequency of Day/Night Models

In order to provide a rough measure of the frequencies of occurrence of the day/night models I calculated the Peak-1 Indexes for those models where there was enough data, and those percentages are presented in Table 7. 5. The data in this table show that there are a range of naïve models occurring with relatively low frequency. To the degree that one can compare, there is fair agreement between the Conceptual Change Index and the age associated with the Peak-1 Indexes. They both show the early occurrence of mechanistic naïve models, the later occurrence of synthetic naïve models, and finally the even later occurrence of models approximating the naïve scientific model.

TABLE 7.5
Day/Night: Frequencies of Occurrence of Naïve Models

Models	Peak-1 Index	Age of sample
Sun behind clouds	10%	6 & 7 yrs
Supernatural	3%	7 yrs.
Sun out into space	5%	8 yrs.
Sun down to other side	11%	8 yrs.
Sun revolves around earth	16%	8 yrs.
Sun behind moon	4%	Adult
Earth rotates: sun & moon fixed	16%	Adult
Earth rotates: sun fixed, moon revolves around earth	68%	Adult

Peak-1 Index is the percent occurrence of the model with the next to highest frequency of occurrence across studies (see text for more detail).
Table is based on data from: Kuse (1963); Mant & Summers (1993); Parker & Heywood (1998); Rudmann (2005); Samarapungavan, Vosniadou & Brewer (1996); Sharp (1995, 1996); Vosniadou & Brewer (1990, 1994).

Reasoning from Ordinary World to the Day/Night Cycle

If the children's naïve models are actually generated by reasoning by analogy with previous knowledge, then it ought to be possible to predict the occurrence of many of these naïve models. In this section I attempt to develop an *a priori* list of plausible factors involved in explaining the day/night cycle. I assume the child is likely to reason from the world of everyday objects and phenomena to the world of astronomy. Thus, imagine you are in a room with an overhead light source — how can you cause it to not be visible? (a) Place some object in front of the light source (object occlusion); (b) Move the light source behind some object (source occlusion); (c) Move the light source so far away that it would not be visible (distance fading); (d) Turn the light source off (change output); (e) Turn away from the light source (occlusion by turning) (see Vosniadou & Brewer, 1994, p. 130 for a similar analysis). Note that all of these a priori mechanisms are, in fact, used in the set of naïve models of the day/night cycle that have been found empirically. This lends considerable support to the argument that children reason from the world of everyday objects to the world of observational astronomy.

Naïve Models of the Seasons

Identified Naïve Models of the Seasons

The major models of the seasonal changes that have been identified are given in Table 7. 6. Only a few pre-model accounts (*animistic, artificialism*) of the seasons have been identified. This is probably an artifact of the samples used to study the seasons. Most investigators have thought the concept of seasons was too hard for very young children to grasp and have not included them in their studies.

There were four mechanistic initial models in which the solar objects are treated as they appear to the child in the ordinary world (*sun out more in summer; sun turns hotter in summer; snow makes winter colder; clouds make winter colder*). At first glance these do not appear to be very powerful models, but notice that most of these could be true in a slightly different solar system (e.g., if the axis of the earth was not tilted and the fusion reactions in the sun varied cyclically over time then the model that the sun turns hotter in summer could be the scientific model).

TABLE 7.6
Seasons: Naïve Models Identified in Interview Studies

Naïve Models	Interview Studies
Animistic	Kuse, 1963
Artificialism	Sh, 1995
Sun out more in summer	Kuse, 1963; F & C, 1989; K, 1998a
Sun turns hotter in summer	F & C, 1989; Sh, 1995, 1996
Snow makes winter colder	Kuse, 1963; F & C, 1989; S, 1996
Clouds make winter colder	Kuse, 1963; B, 1989; S, 1996; R & M, 2001
Distance from sun--unspecified	Kuse, 1963; S, 1987; O, W, B & M, 1994; K, 1998b; D, S, S & B, 1998; R & M, 2001
Sun revolves around earth (geocentric)	B, 1989; S, 1996; A & A, 1996; K, 1998a; D, S, S & B, 1998; R, 2005
Earth revolves around sun	K, 1998a; D, S, S & B 1998; R, 2005
Earth rotation (spin)	F & C, 1989; S, 1996; A & A, 1996; D, S, S & B, 1998
Earth in elliptical orbit around sun	Kuse, 1963; F & C, 1989; M & S, 1993; Sh, 1995, 1996; A & A, 1996; D, S, S & B, 1998; P & H, 1998; R, 2005
Wobbly tilt	S, 1987; F & C, 1989; M & S, 1993; P & H, 1998; R & M, 2001; R, 2005
Tethered tilt	R, 2005
Tilt plus distance (or no mechanism)	Kuse, 1963; B, 1989; M & S, 1993; A & A, 1996; K, 1998b; D, S, S & B, 1998; P & H, 1998; R & M, 2001, R, 2005
Full tilt (fixed axis and spread of heat)	M & S, 1993; A & A, 1996; D, S, S & B, 1998

The core component of most of the more sophisticated alternative models is the belief that coming closer to a source of heat will make you hotter. A response from a child that the seasons are caused by the distance from the sun is too underspecified to allow placement in a particular naïve model since the distance belief is used in a variety of quite different models.

The geocentric naïve model of the seasons (*sun revolves around earth*) postulates that the sun goes around the earth and comes down closer or spends longer in the sky during the summer. This model requires that the child believe the heat/distance relationship and accept that the earth is a large object in space. The equivalent heliocentric naïve model (*earth revolves around the sun*) could simply be an underspecified version of the other heliocentric naïve models, but occasionally a protocol suggests that this is an identifiable model in which one side of the earth faces the sun more during the summer.

The naïve model, *with the earth in an elliptical orbit around the sun*, is a very attractive alternative model and widely found. Protocols from individuals with this model were given earlier in the section on the nature of naïve models. In this model summer occurs when the earth's path along the elliptical orbit is closer to the sun (distance assumption) and winter occurs when its path along the elliptical orbit takes it farther from the sun. This is a classic synthetic model in that it includes the heliocentric component of the scientific model, but retains the entrenched heat/distance belief.

The scientific model of the seasons includes a number of core components: (a) the heliocentric view, (b) the tilt of the earth's axis, (c) the direction of tilt remains fixed as the earth rotates and revolves (i.e., like a gyroscope), and (d) heat from the sun has a lower energy density when it hits at an angle and spreads out. Taken together, these components generate the alternation of the seasons as the earth makes its annual revolution around the sun. The *wobbly tilt* model is an alternative model in which the earth's axis tilt flips toward and away from the sun to produce the seasons. The concept that the earth's axis remains fixed as the earth rotates and revolves is relatively difficult and the wobbly tilt model is a way to generate the seasons without the fixed tilt construct. The *tethered tilt* is an alternative naïve model in which the axis is considered to continue to point at the sun as the earth revolves around the sun (i.e., it is as if the north pole was tethered to the sun as it moved around). This naïve model is unlike most alternative models in that it cannot generate the phenomenon it is supposed to explain (there would be no change in seasons across the year).

Several researchers (Atwood & Atwood, 1996; Mant & Summers, 1993) have noted that many apparent scientific tilt models actually still contain the heat/distance construct. In this type of *tilt plus distance model* the basic spatial arrangement is as in the scientific model, but the mechanism that leads to the temperature differences is that the tilted hemisphere is physically closer to the sun. Finally, the *full tilt* model is the naïve scientific model (including the fixed axis and the spreading of heat mechanism). Note that many of the open-ended and closed-end studies in the literature are underspecified and have not required the individual to show all the core components to be classified as having the naïve scientific model. Thus, in many of these studies the percentages of individuals who are said to hold the scientific model are large overestimates.

Frequency of Models of the Seasons

The frequencies of occurrence of naïve models of the seasons as revealed by the Peak-1 index are given in Table 7.7. There are a wide range of models. The very young children show pre-model beliefs. Then initial models occur which are mechanistic and which assume the solar objects are (in size and shape) as they appear. A number of the models involve a strongly entrenched heat/distance belief. This belief, along with the culturally acquired heliocentric framework, leads to a strong alternative model — the elliptical naïve model of the seasons. Acquiring the naïve scientific model is quite difficult and requires giving up the use of the heat/distance belief as the heat change mechanism and understanding that the tilt of the earth's axis is fixed. The full scientific model is apparently not attained by most college educated adults.

TABLE 7.7
Seasons: Frequencies of Occurrence of Naïve Models

Models	Peak-1 Index	Age of sample
Sun out more in summer	39%	8 yrs.
Sun turns hotter in summer	18%	7 yrs.
Snow makes winter colder	16%	7 yrs.
Clouds make winter colder	4%	7 yrs.
Earth rotation (spin)	11%	Adult
Earth in elliptical orbit around sun	22%	Adult
Tilt plus distance (or no mechanism)	11%	Adult
Full tilt (fixed axis and spread of heat)	6%	Adult

Peak-1 Index is the percent occurrence of the model with the next to highest frequency of occurrence across studies (see text for more detail).
Table is based on data from: Atwood & Atwood (1996); DeLaughter, Stein, Stein, & Bain, (1998); Kuse (1963); Mant & Summers (1993); Parker & Heywood (1998); Rudmann, (2005); Sharp (1995, 1996).

Reasoning from Ordinary World to the Seasons

As with the day/night cycle, there seems to be a good argument that the child's (and adult's) models of the seasons are derived by reasoning by analogy with previous knowledge. Again, I assume the child is likely to reason from the world of everyday objects and phenomena to the world of astronomy. Thus, imagine you are in a cold room with a very weak source of heat. How might you heat yourself? One could: (a) Turn up the heat source (change output); (b) Move the heat source closer (the heat/distance belief); (c) Turn your body as in front of a fireplace; (d) Orient your body perpendicular with the rays from the heat source (reduce heat spreading). And note that if you were in a hot room and wanted to cool down you could: (e) Put something between you and the source of heat (object occlusion); (f) Move the heat source behind something (source occlusion); (g) Use some external source of cooling such as water or ice (external cooling).

As with the day/night cycle, this thought experiment involving reasoning from the ordinary world to the astronomical world predicts essentially all of the explanatory models of the seasons as they have been discovered empirically and thus adds additional support to the argument that children generating naïve models are applying reasoning from the world of everyday objects to the world of astronomical phenomena.

Naïve Models of the Phases of the Moon

Identified Naïve Models of the Phases

The major models of the phases of the moon that have been identified are given in Table 7.8. Several investigators have noted that some children think that there are actual changes in the physical shape of the moon during the phases. This is an issue that needs more investigation. Trying to account for the changing appearance of the moon poses a real problem and, as with the

TABLE 7.8
Phases: Naïve Models Identified in Interview Studies

Naïve Models	Interview Studies
Supernatural	P, 1929; Kuse, 1963
Physical change in shape	H, 1883; Z, 1976; R & M, 2001
Clouds block moon	P, 1929; H, 1950; Kuse, 1963; C, 1982; S, 1987; B, 1989; Sh, 1995; S, 1996; S, K & S, 1999; R & M, 2001; R, 2005
Night blocks moon	H, 1950; Kuse, 1963
Something blocks moon	M & S, 1993; R, 2005
Planets block moon	C, 1982; S, 1987; B, 1989; R, 2005
Moon dark side/light side	C, 1982; S, 1987; C, 1993; R & M, 2001; R, 2005
Earth rotates (spins)	T, 1988; S, 1996; S, K & S, 1999
Moon goes behind sun	T, 1988; B, 1989; C, 1993; M & S, 1993; R, 2005
Reflected sunlight	H, 1950; Kuse, 1963; S, 1987; R & M, 2001
Eclipse	Kuet, 1963; C, 1982; S, 1987; T, 1988; M & S, 1993; C, 1993; S, 1996; P & H, 1998; L, 2001; R & M, 2001; T, A & C, 2002; R, 2005
Scientific model	C, 1982; T, 1988; C, 1993; M & S, 1993; P & H, 1998; L, 2001; T, A & C, 2002; R, 2005

day/night and seasons naïve models, occlusion is brought to bear on the problem, producing a set of occlusion models: *clouds block moon; night blocks moon; planets block moon,* and, for the really desperate, *something blocks moon.* The final initial model to be considered is the belief that the moon has a dark colored side and light colored side and that it rotates to produce the phases; this involves very similar reasoning to the day/night model in which the sun and the moon are the opposite sides of the same solar object.

The remaining models require that the individual have accepted the basic premise of astronomical mental modeling — that the solar objects of appearance are actually large objects in space and that manipulating mental models of these objects can explain the world of appearance. The model that the *earth rotates* makes use of aspects of the scientific naïve model, but it is not clear to me how it can explain the data. The model that the *moon goes behind the sun* could occur in a geocentric form, but, in all the examples identified, it appears to occur in heliocentric versions in which the moon is on an independent orbit around the sun and sometimes the moon goes behind the sun and is occluded. Given that this would require the moon to be occluded by the bright sun, it certainly does not score high on consistency with the observational data of the phases. The response that the phases are due to *reflected sunlight* seems like another desperation ploy invoking scientific terminology

The obvious problem of trying to account for the phases gives rise to an extremely attractive and widespread alternative model — the *eclipse model.* Protocols from individuals with this model were given earlier in the section on the nature of naïve models. This is a model derived from instruction in which the individual imports the entire machinery of a lunar eclipse and applies it to the phases. The shadow of the earth is said, over days, to move across the moon causing the parts of the moon in the shadow to appear dark. The orbital geometry (moon on one side of earth, sun on the other) which is used in the scientific account of a total lunar eclipse is used to explain the occurrence of a new moon.

The full naïve *scientific model* of the phases is very difficult to explain. But, very roughly, it states that the moon revolves around the earth and that the half of the moon facing the sun is always illuminated by the sun. On earth we see portions of the illuminated half and the portions we see are determined by the relative positions of the earth, moon, and sun. The arrangement moon — earth — sun produces a full moon while the arrangement earth — moon — sun produces a new moon. This naïve scientific model requires the complex manipulation of three mental objects along with an understanding of shadows on spheres and is rarely mastered even by educated adults.

Frequency of Models of the Phases

The frequencies of occurrence of naïve models of the phases as revealed by the Peak-1 Index are given in Table 7.9. The results suggest that the initial models in this area show a strong reliance on occlusion. By far the most frequent of the sophisticated alternative models is the eclipse model. There are enough studies of the phases that it is possible to make a strong comparison of the occurrence of the eclipse model and the scientific model. Across eight studies, the median frequency of occurrence of the eclipse naïve model is 40%, whereas for the same eight studies the median frequency of occurrence of the naïve scientific model is 8%.

Overall, the developmental progression of the phase model appears to start with many alternative occlusion models. Then the data are overwhelmed by the widespread occurrence of the eclipse model, with relatively few college educated adults ever coming to hold the naïve scientific model.

TABLE 7.9
Phases: Frequencies of Occurrence of Naïve Models

Models	Peak-1 Index	Age of sample
Clouds block moon	14%	6 yrs.
Night blocks moon	4%	6 yrs.
Something blocks moon	6%	Adult
Planets block moon	2%	Adult
Moon dark side/light side	4%	Adult
Earth rotates (spins)	7%	10 yrs
Moon goes behind sun	4%	Adult
Eclipse	50%	Adult
Scientific model	12%	Adult

Peak-1 Index is the percent occurrence of the model with the next to highest frequency of occurrence across studies (see text for more detail).

Table is based on data from: Callison, 1993; Cohen, 1982; Haupt, 1950; Lindell, 2001; Mant & Summers, 1993; Parker & Heywood, 1998; Rudmann, 2005; Sharp, 1996; Targan, 1988; Trundle, Atwood, & Christopher, 2002.

THEORETICAL IMPLICATIONS OF THE DATA ON NAÏVE MODELS IN OBSERVATIONAL ASTRONOMY

Synthetic Models Should Increase with Instruction

Vosniadou and Brewer's (1992, 1994) claim that in some domains the knowledge acquisition path is one from initial models, to synthetic models, to naïve scientific models, has an interesting if somewhat counter-intuitive implication. We argued that synthetic models result when students attempt to reconcile deeply entrenched beliefs with information about the scientific models in the domain. Thus, for synthetic models to occur, the individual must be exposed to instruction in the scientific models of observational astronomy. Therefore, in some circumstances, instruction may (against the obvious desires of the teachers) produce scientifically incorrect synthetic models. To get this effect one has to examine the distribution of models before instruction has moved a large percentage of the students to the (correct) naïve scientific model.

Schoon (1988) included the eclipse model of the phases in a nicely designed closed-end questionnaire and used it across a wide range of ages. The percentage of students choosing the eclipse model was as follows: 30%, fifth grade; 39%, eighth grade; 54%, eleventh grade; and 70%, college. This pattern of data certainly suggests that increasing education increases the eclipse alternative naïve model of the phases of the moon. In addition to this indirect evidence that instruction leads to alternative models, there is more direct data from a number of instructional studies. After instruction in astronomy, Osborne, Wadsworth, Black, and Meadows (1994, p. 86) found that the number of students who held the distance model of the seasons moved from 55% to 68% for a group of 8- and 9-year-olds and from 44% to 56% in a group of 10- and 11-year-olds. Jipson (2000) developed an instruction program on the shape of the earth for mothers to carry out with their children ages 4 to 8 years. She found that after instruction the number of children holding the hollow sphere naïve model moved from 2 to 8. Sharp, Bowker, & Merrick (1997) carried out a study of the naïve models of three children (ages 10 and 11 years) before and after a several-month-long instructional unit on astronomy. In general, the children moved from initial models to synthetic models. Targan (1988) had college students observe the moon over time and then form groups to discuss what was causing the effect. On a careful open-ended test, Targan found that the number holding the eclipse model of the phases moved from 13% to 43%. However all was not lost; after an intensive and focused program of instruction the number holding the eclipse model dropped to 9%. Overall, these studies provide striking evidence that standard school instruction on observational astronomy can lead to the formation of synthetic alternative naïve models as predicted by Vosniadou and Brewer's account of synthetic models in observational astronomy.

Longitudinal Studies of Naïve Models

Longitudinal studies are difficult to carry out, but provide evidence about the process of model acquisition, and actually allow one to observe the shift of models within the development of a single individual. Kikas (1998a) carried out a study of the long-term impact of instruction about the day/night cycle and the seasons. She found a striking regression to alternative naïve models over four years. For the day/night cycle the percentage of students holding the naïve scientific model dropped from 65% to 20%; while the alternative models increased from 20% to 55%. Tsai and Chang (2005) found similar results with models of the seasons eight months after instruction. With standard instruction the percentage of students holding the naïve scientific model dropped from 68% to 23%, while the alternative models increased from 28% to 59%.

Maria (1993, 1997a, 1997b) carried out an extraordinary microgenetic study of instruction in the shape of the earth, gravity, and the day/night cycle in two (grand) children. With Charlie (age 5:4) there were about 22 sessions of 1 hour and with Jennifer (age 6:6) about 19 sessions of 1 hour occurring over almost a full 2-year period. The data is very rich, and so I can only give a hint of it here. Charlie starts off with a spherical earth model with down gravity. He continues holding the down gravity view through the 5th session despite Maria's hard efforts. He gives a gravity to the center answer during the 6th session, but regresses back to down gravity during the 7th session. He later shifts back to gravity to the center, but, even in the 12th session, we find the following interchange when Maria asks him what would happen if you dug a hole through the earth and dropped a ball in the hole [C] "It would go voo to space" [M] "It would fall right down to space?" [C] "Yup, 'cause it's gravity. No, it would go to the middle" (Maria, 1997a, p. 78).

Looking at these studies the impression one gets is that instruction in observational astronomy is like climbing an ice covered hill. There is forward progress with instruction toward more scientific naïve models and then over time the child slips back to attractive initial and synthetic models. It is obvious that if we are going to deeply understand the process of model change that more researchers are going to have to bite the bullet and carry out longitudinal and microgenetic studies of the change in naïve models over time.

Universals in Naïve Models of Observational Astronomy

Vosniadou and Brewer (1992, 1994) on universals view that young children are generating naïve models in opposition to the scientific model that dominates the adult culture has strong implications. It predicts that there should be some universal aspects to the formation of naïve models. Vosniadou (1994) formulated the claim in terms of two hypotheses: "the hypothesis that entrenched presuppositions are universal predicts that the class of possible initial models of the earth constructed by children in different cultures would be constrained by the same entrenched presuppositions. The cultural mediation hypothesis predicts that children in different cultures will construct different alternative models of the earth from the class of possible models, reflecting their cultural experiences" (p. 422). In essence the claim is that the *presuppositions* (e.g., things that look flat are flat; things fall straight down to the ground) are universal and that the *models* show more impact of culture.

Flat earth models.   The data presented earlier on naïve models for the shape of the earth show that almost all of the alternative earth shape models show constraints imposed by the presuppositions of flatness and gravity down. However, the data show that only a modest percentage of the youngest children have 'pure' flat earth models (i.e., those models showing minimal influence from the cultural spherical model). This suggests that only a relatively small percentage of the youngest children form coherent flat earth models (e.g., flat, disc or rectangular models) before the impact of the cultural model begins to shift them to various forms of synthetic models (e.g., dual earth models, hollow earth models). However, most of this reasoning is based on cross-sectional data, and so the conclusions should be treated with caution until there are careful longitudinal studies.

Cross-cultural data.   There have been a large number of studies on the shape of the earth and on the day/night cycle that can be used to examine the universal/cultural issue (see Bryce & Blown, 2006, for a good review of this literature). First, there have been studies on the shape of the earth and the day/night cycle from a broad sampling of the developed nations — for example: the United States (Vosniadou & Brewer, 1992, 1994); England (Sharp, 1999), Australia (Hayes, Goodhew, Heit, & Gillan, 2003); New Zealand (Blown & Bryce, 2006); Israel (Nussbaum, 1979); and Greece (Vosniadou & Brewer, 1990; Vosniadou, Skopeliti, & Ikospentaki, 2004, 2005). These studies all show the operation of the initial presuppositions and also tend to show a common set of naïve models.

There have also been a number of studies from developing nations, where one might expect an impact of the indigenous cultural models on the child's naïve models. Mali and Howe (1979) studied children from Nepal and found all of the models previously identified in the work of Nussbaum and Novak (1976). They also provide the first report of a hollow sphere model showing support by either dirt or water. Samarapungavan, Vosniadou, and Brewer (1996) studied children from India. They found a distribution of models roughly similar to that of Vosniadou and Brewer (1992, 1994). However, there are in the data some possible influences of the indigenous culture (cultural models which often includes models of the earth floating on water). The data show that 38% of the Indian children held models (disc, hollow sphere) in which the earth was floating on water. Interestingly the only reports in the literature of hollow spheres floating on water are from India and Nepal. Klein (1982) reported data on a sample of Mexican-American children and noted that half of the Mexican-American children gave animistic responses on the day/night question whereas none of the Euro-American children did. Diakidoy, Vosniadou, and Hawks (1997) reported data on Native-American children. The earth shape models were remarkably similar to those found by Vosniadou and Brewer (1992) for Euro-American children, but they found that 23% of the Native-American children gave animistic accounts of the day/night cycle, while they found none of these types of responses in the Euro-American sample. Brewer, Herdrich, and Vosniadou (1987) reported earth shape data on children from Samoa. They found more initial (flat earth) models among the Samoan children than among Euro-American children. There was also one interesting new model among these children — the *ring earth*. There is much evidence for rings as a dominate cultural theme in Samoan culture, so this finding is very suggestive of the influence of the indigenous culture on earth shape models. Fleer's (1997) research is probably the most impressive attempt to date to find a large impact of indigenous culture. This was a study of Australian Aboriginal children and to prime the indigenous beliefs the interview took place in the context of story telling in a campfire scene. The results were a disappointment to the investigator, but of great interest for science. The Aboriginal children showed most of the initial models of the day/night found in Euro-American children with more supernatural and animistic responses.

Limited set of naïve models.   One of the interesting findings in this data is that the particular models uncovered seem to be drawn from a small set of possible models. Why is this? In the philosophy of science it has been argued that theories are underdetermined by data and that for any set of data there are an indefinitely large number of possible theories (cf. Newton-Smith, 2000). It seems to me that, in actual practice, it is hard to come up with many theories that are plausible and account for the data in the domain of interest. I argued earlier that children developing a naïve model reason from the world of every day objects and processes. In the sections of this chapter dealing with the day/night cycle, and the seasons, I tried to develop the set of plausible mechanisms in each of those domains and that set turned out to be small and highly predictive of the empirically obtained models in the area. So, I take the limited set of plausible mechanisms to be the underlying reason that for each sub-domain there is a small set of recurring models.

Universality — conclusions.   Overall, the results of the cross-cultural studies lend strong support to the view that the presuppositions are universal and that as children get older culture has a strong impact on their naïve models. However, the results are not quite as Vosniadou and colleagues had originally envisioned. The initial models and the synthetic models show a relatively limited set of models across cultures. The impact of culture turns out to be the overwhelmingly powerful influence of the scientific model for the diverse set of cultures that have been examined so far. The impact of indigenous cultural models seems limited. Perhaps the best case is the suggestion that in Nepal and India there is some influence of a cultural model with water supporting the earth. There are several other findings suggested by the data. In several of the studies (e.g., Mali & Howe, 1979; Brewer, Herdrich, & Vosniadou, 1987) the data suggests that the impact of the scientific culture occurs later in cultures from developing nations than it does in developed nations. There is also some suggestion that more animistic and supernatural responses occur in cultures from developing nations; however, it is not clear how much of this is due to the indigenous culture and how much is due to the delayed impact of the scientific culture on these children. In general these studies suggest strong universality of the model presuppositions and a surprising degree of universality at the level of the models themselves.

Recapitulation

The Vosniadou and Brewer view also has implications for the history of astronomy. The constraints that lead the children to a limited set of theories may also have been operating in the adults who produced the very earliest cosmologies in different cultures, and therefore we might expect very early cosmological models to show strong similarities to those we have uncovered in young children. I have recently carried out an examination of accounts of the shape of earth and the day/night cycle found in the earliest Greek cosmologies, early Egyptian cosmology, early Hebrew cosmology, and early Chinese cosmology, and have found that they show strong similarities to the child data and thus provide additional support for the finding of a limited set of models with some cultural variation (Brewer. 2004a, 2004b).

Cognitive Generativity

When I was a graduate student and a postdoc, I read Noam Chomsky's work on language. I was bowled over by his insight that language is generative — that human beings understand and produce utterances that they have never encountered before. For me, the work on naïve models of astronomy has the same kind of intellectual power in the nonlinguistic cognitive domain. The data discussed in this chapter show that each year vast numbers of students generate explanatory models such as the hollow earth model of the earth's shape, the elliptical orbit theory of the seasons, the eclipse theory of the phases. That ordinary children can and do construct such models, something often thought restricted to adult scientists, is one of the extraordinary characteristics of human cognition.

ACKNOWLEDGMENT

I would like to thanks Ellen Brewer, Clark Chinn, and Brian Miller for comments on an earlier draft of this chapter.

REFERENCES

Aguiar, A., & Baillargeon, R. (1999). 2.5-month-old infants' reasoning about when objects should and should not be occluded. *Cognitive Psychology, 39*, 116–157.

Atwood, V. A., & Atwood, R. K. (1995). Preservice elementary teachers' conceptions of what causes night and day. *School Science and Mathematics, 95*, 290–294.

Atwood, R. K., & Atwood, V. A. (1996). Preservice elementary teacher's conceptions of the causes of seasons. *Journal of Research in Science Teaching, 33*, 553–563.

Baxter, J. (1989). Children's understanding of familiar astronomical events. *International Journal of Science Education, 11*, 502–513.

Baxter, J. H. (1998). The influences of the national curriculum on children's misconceptions about astronomy and the use of these misconceptions in the development of interactive teaching materials. In L. Gouguenheim, D. McNally & J. R. Percy (Eds.), *New trends in astronomy teaching* (pp. 139–146; IAU Colloquium 162). Cambridge: Cambridge University Press.

Bisard, W. J., Aron, R. H., Francek, M. A., & Nelson, B. D. (1994). Assessing selected physical science and earth science misconceptions of middle school through university preservice teachers. *Journal of College Science Teaching, 24*, 38–42.

Black, M. (1962). Models and archetypes. In M. Black (Ed.), *Models and metaphors* (pp. 219–243). Ithaca, NY: Cornell University Press.

Blown, E. J., & Bryce, T. G. K. (2006). Knowledge restructuring in the development of children's cosmologies. *International Journal of Science Education, 28*, 1411–1462.

Boltzmann, L. (1902). Models. In *The New Volumes of the Encyclopaedia Britannica* (10th ed., Vol. 30, pp. 788–791). London: Adam and Charles Black.

Brewer, W. F. (1999). Scientific theories and naïve theories as forms of mental representation: Psychologism revived. *Science & Education, 8*, 489–505.

Brewer, W. F. (2001). Models in Science and Mental Models in Scientists and Nonscientists. *Mind & Society, 2*, 33–48.

Brewer, W. F. (2003). Mental models. In L. Nadel (Ed.), *Encyclopedia of cognitive science* (Vol. 3, pp. 1–6). London: Nature Publishing Group.

Brewer, W. F. (2004a, May). *Constraints on knowledge acquisition.* Paper presented at the European Association for Research on Learning and Instruction. Fourth European Symposium: Conceptual Change: Philosophical, Historical, Psychological, and Educational Approaches, Delphi, Greece.

Brewer, W. F. (2004b, June). Constraints on knowledge acquisition in the history of astronomy. Paper present-ed at the Second International Conference of Philosophy and Cognitive Science, Guangzhou, China.

Brewer, W. F. (2008). In what sense can the child be considered to be a "little scientist"? In R. A. Duschl & R. E. Grandy (Eds.), *Teaching scientific inquiry* (pp. 38–49). Rotterdam: Sense Publishers.

Brewer, W. F., & Chinn, C. A. (1994). Scientists' responses to anomalous data: Evidence from psychology, history, and philosophy of science. *Philosophy of Science Association, Volume 1*, 304–313.

Brewer, W. F., Chinn, C. A., & Samarapungavan, A. (1998). Explanation in scientists and children. *Minds and machines, 8*, 119–136.

Brewer, W. F., Chinn, C. A., & Samarapungavan, A. (2000). Explanation in scientists and children. In F. C. Keil & R. A. Wilson (Eds.), *Explanation and cognition* (pp. 279–298). Cambridge, MA: MIT Press.

Brewer, W. F., Herdrich, D. J., & Vosniadou, S. (1987 January). Universal and culture-specific aspects of children's cosmological models: Samoan and American data. Third International Conference on Thinking. Honolulu, Hawaii.

Brewer, W. F., & Lambert, B. L. (2001). The theory-ladenness of observation and the theory-ladenness of the rest of the scientific process. *Philosophy of Science, 68*, S176–S186.

Brewer, W. F., & Loschky, L. (2005). Top-down and bottom-up influences on observation: Evidence from cognitive psychology and the history of science. In A. Raftopoulos (Ed.), *Cognitive penetrability of perception: Attention, action, strategies, and bottom-up constraints* (pp. 31–47). Hauppauge, NY: Nova Science Publishers.

Brewer, W. F., & Samarapungavan, A. (1991). Children's theories vs. scientific theories: Differences in reasoning or differences in knowledge? In R. R. Hoffman & D. S. Palermo (Eds.), *Cognition and the symbolic processes: Applied and ecological perspectives* (pp. 209–232). Hillsdale, NJ: Erlbaum.

Bryce, T. G. K., & Blown, E. J. (2006). Cultural mediation of children's cosmologies: A longitudinal study of the astronomy concepts of Chinese and New Zealand children. *International Journal of Science Education, 28*, 1113–1160.

Callison, P. L. (1993). *The effect of teaching strategies using models on preservice elementary teachers' conceptions about earth-sun-moon relationships.* (Doctoral dissertation, Kansas State University, 1993). Dissertation Abstracts International-A, 54/08, 2885.

Campbell, N. R. (1957). *Foundations of science.* New York: Dover. (Originally published as *Physics: The elements*, Cambridge: Cambridge University Press, 1920).

Carey, S. (1985). *Conceptual change in childhood.* Cambridge, MA: MIT Press.

Chi, M. T. H. (1992). Conceptual change within and across ontological categories: Examples from learning and discovery in science. In R. N. Giere (Ed.), *Minnesota studies in the philosophy of science: Vol. 15. Cognitive models of science* (pp. 129–186). Minneapolis: University of Minnesota Press.

Chinn, C. A., & Brewer, W. F. (1993). The role of anomalous data in knowledge acquisition: A theoretical framework and implications for science instruction. *Review of Educational Research, 63*, 1–49.

Cohen, M. R. (1982, February). How can sunlight hit the moon if we are in the dark?: Teacher's concepts of phases of the moon. Paper presented at the Seventh Annual Henry Lester Smith Conference on Educa-tional Research, Bloomington, IN.

Cohen, M. R., & Lucas, K. (2002, August). Toward a model for evolving science standards: Learning from the past, present, and future about the shape of the earth. Paper presented at the meeting of Interna-tional Organization for Science and Technology Education, Foz do Iguaçu, Brazil.

Collins, A. (1985). Component models of physical systems. In *Proceedings of the Seventh Annual Confer-ence of the Cognitive Science Society* (pp. 80–89). Irvine, CA: Cognitive Science Society.

DeLaughter, J. E., Stein, S., Stein, C. A., & Bain, K. R. (1998). Preconceptions abound among students in an introductory earth science course. *Eos, 79*(36), 429–432. Retrieved from http://www.earth.northwest-ern.edu/people/seth/Test/index.html)

Dent, H. R. (1991). Experimental studies of interviewing child witnesses. In J. Doris (Ed.), *The suggestibil-ity of children's recollections* (pp. 138–146). Washington, DC: American Psychological Association.

Diakidoy, I.-A., Vosniadou, S., & Hawks, J. D. (1997). Conceptual change in astronomy: Models of the earth and of the day/night cycle in American-Indian children. *European Journal of Psychology of Education, 12*, 159–184.

Driver, R., Guesne, E., & Tiberghien, A. (Eds.). (1985). *Children's ideas in science*. Milton Keynes, UK: Open University Press.

Fanetti, T. M. (2001). *The relationships of scale concepts on college age students' misconceptions about the cause of the lunar phases*. Unpublished master's thesis. Iowa State University, Ames, Iowa.

Fleer, M. (1997). A cross-cultural study of rural Australian Aboriginal children's understandings of night and day. *Research in Science Education, 27*, 101–116.

Furuness, L. B., & Cohen, M. R. (1989). Children's conceptions of the seasons: A comparison of three interview techniques. Paper presented at the National Association for Research in Science Teaching, San Francisco, CA.

Garner, W. R., Hake, H. W., & Eriksen, C. W. (1956). Operationism and the concept of perception. *Psychological Review, 63*, 149–159.

Gibson, J. J. (1986). *The ecological approach to visual perception*. Hillsdale, NJ: Lawrence Erlbaum.

Gopnik, A., & Wellman, H. M. (1994). The theory theory. In L. A. Hirschfeld & S. A. Gelman (Eds.), *Mapping the mind: Domain specificity in cognition and culture* (pp. 257–293). Cambridge: Cambridge University Press.

Hall, G. S. (1883/1893). The contents of children's minds on entering school. *Princeton Review*, Series 4, *11*, 249–272 (reprinted as: *The contents of children's minds on entering school*. New York: E. L. Kellogg, 1893).

Hanson, N. R. (1958). *Patterns of discovery*. Cambridge: Cambridge University Press.

Haupt, G. W. (1950). First grade concepts of the moon: Part II. By interview. *Science Education, 34*, 224–234.

Hayes, B. K., Goodhew, A., Heit, E., & Gillan, J. (2003). The role of diverse instruction in conceptual change. *Journal of Experimental Child Psychology, 86*, 253–276.

Ivarsson, J., Schoultz, J., & Säljö, R. (2002). Map reading versus mind reading. In M. Limón & L. Mason (Eds.), *Reconsidering conceptual change: Issues in theory and practice* (pp. 77–99). Dordrecht, The Netherlands: Kluwer.

Johnson-Laird, P. N. (1980). Mental models in cognitive science. *Cognitive Science, 4*, 71–115.

Jipson, J. L. (2000). *"It's like a big, blue, ball:" Parent-child conversation and children's understanding of the shape of the earth*. (Doctoral dissertation, University of California, Santa Cruz, 2000). Dissertation Abstracts International-B, 62/02, 1115.

Jones, B. L., Lynch, P. P., & Reesink, C. (1987). Children's conceptions of the earth, sun and moon. *International Journal of Science Education, 9*, 43–53.

Kikas, E. (1998a). The impact of teaching on students' definitions and explanations of astronomical phenomena. *Learning and Instruction, 8*, 439–454.

Kikas, E. (1998b). Pupils' explanations of seasonal changes: Age differences and the influence of teaching. *British Journal of Educational Psychology, 68*, 505–516.

Klein, C. A. (1982). Children's concepts of the earth and sun: A cross cultural study. *Science Education, 65*, 95–107.

Kuethe, J. L. (1963). Science concepts: A study of "sophisticated" errors. *Science Education, 47*, 361–364.

Kuhn, T. S. (1962). *The structure of scientific revolutions*. Chicago: University of Chicago Press.

Kuse, H. R. (1963). *A survey of the sources and extent of primary grade children's concepts of elementary astronomy*. (Doctoral dissertation, University of Colorado, 1963). Dissertation Abstracts International 26/03, 1513.

Laurendeau, M., & Pinard, A. (1962). *Causal thinking in the child*. New York: International Universities Press.

Leslie, A. M., & Keeble, S. (1987). Do six-month-old infants perceive causality? *Cognition, 25*, 265–288.

Lindell, R. S. (2001). *Enhancing college students' understanding of lunar phases*. (Doctoral dissertation, University of Nebraska, 2001). Dissertation Abstracts International-B 62/08, 3655.

Liu, S.-C. (2005). Models of "the heavens and the earth": An investigation of German and Taiwanese students' alternative conceptions of the universe. *International Journal of Science and Mathematics Education, 3*, 295–325.

Mali, G. B., & Howe, A. (1979). Development of earth and gravity concepts among Nepali children. *Science Education, 63*, 685–691.

Mant, J., & Summers, M. (1993). Some primary-school teachers' understanding of the Earth's place in the universe. *Research Papers in Education, 8,* 101–129.

Maria, K. (1993). The development of earth concepts. In *Proceedings of the Third International Seminar on Misconceptions and Educational Strategies in Science and Mathematics* (pp. 1–24). Ithaca, NY: Misconceptions Trust.

Maria, K. (1997a). A case study of conceptual change in a young child. *Elementary School Journal, 98,* 67–88.

Maria, K. (1997b). Conceptual change in a young girl: A longitudinal case study. Paper presented at the National Reading Conference, Scottsdale, AZ.

Newton-Smith, W. H. (2000). Underdetermination of theory by data. In W. H. Newton-Smith (Ed.), *A companion to the philosophy of science* (pp. 532–536). Oxford: Blackwell.

Nobes, G., Martin, A. E., & Panagiotaki, G. (2005). The development of scientific knowledge of the Earth. *British Journal of Developmental Psychology, 23,* 47–64.

Nobes, G., Moore, D. G., Martin, A. E., Clifford, B. R., Butterworth, G., Panagiotaki, G., & Siegal, M. (2003). Children's understanding of the earth in a multicultural community: mental models or fragments of knowledge? *Developmental Science, 6,* 72–85.

Norman, D. A. (1988). *The psychology of everyday things.* New York: Basic Books.

Norman, D. A. (1993). Cognition in the head and in the world: An introduction to the special issue on situated action. *Cognitive Science, 17,* 1–6.

Nussbaum, J. (1972). *An approach to teaching and assessment: The earth concept at the second grade level.* (Doctoral dissertation, Cornell University, 1972). Dissertation Abstracts International-A, 33/07, 3427.

Nussbaum, J. (1979). Children's conceptions of the earth as a cosmic body: A cross age study. *Science Education, 63,* 83–93.

Nussbaum, J. (1985). The earth as a cosmic body. In R. Driver, E. Guesne, & A. Tiberghien (Eds.), *Children's ideas in science* (pp. 170–192). Milton Keynes, UK: Open University Press.

Nussbaum, J., & Novak, J. D. (1976). An assessment of children's concepts of the earth utilizing structured interviews. *Science Education, 60,* 535–550.

Nussbaum, J., & Sharoni-Dagan, N. (1983). Changes in second grade children's preconceptions about the earth as a cosmic body resulting from a short series of audio-tutorial lessons. *Science Education, 67,* 99–114.

Oakes, M. E. (1947). *Children's explanations of natural phenomena.* (Teachers College, Columbia University, Contributions to Education, No. 926). New York: Bureau of Publications, Teachers College, Columbia University.

Osborne, J., Wadsworth, P., Black, P., & Meadows, J. (1994). *The earth in space (Primary Space Project: Science Processes and Concept Exploration Research Report).* Liverpool, UK: Liverpool University Press.

Panagiotaki, G., Nobes, G., & Banerjee, R. (2006a). Children's representations of the earth: A methodological comparison. *British Journal of Developmental Psychology, 24,* 353–372.

Panagiotaki, G., Nobes, G., & Banerjee, R. (2006b). Is the world round or flat? Children's understanding of the earth. *European Journal of Developmental Psychology, 3,* 124–141.

Parker, J., & Heywood, D. (1998). The earth and beyond: Developing primary teachers' understanding of basic astronomical events. *International Journal of Science Education, 20,* 503–520.

Piaget, J. (1929/1979). *The child's conception of the world.* London: Routledge and Kegan Paul (republished: Totowa, NJ: Littlefield, Adams, 1979).

Peirce, C. S. (1901–1903/1957). The logic of abduction. In V. Thomas (Ed.), *Essays in the philosophy of science* (pp. 235–255). New York: Bobbs–Merrill, 1957.

Poole, D. A., & Lindsay, D. S. (1998). Assessing the accuracy of young children's reports: Lessons from the investigation of child sexual abuse. *Applied & Preventive Psychology, 7,* 1–26.

Poole, D. A., & White, L. T. (1991). Effects of question repetition on the eyewitness testimony of children and adults. *Developmental Psychology, 27,* 975–986.

Poole, D. A., & White, L. T. (1995). Tell me again and again: Stability and change in the repeated testimonies of children and adults. In M. S. Zaragoza, J. R. Graham, G. C. N. Hall, R. Hirschman, & Y. S. Ben-Porath (Eds.), *Memory and testimony in the child witness* (pp. 24–43). Thousand Oaks, CA: Sage.

Roald, I., & Mikalsen, Ø. (2000). What are the Earth and the heavenly bodies like? A study of objectual conceptions among Norwegian deaf and hearing pupils. *International Journal of Science Education, 22*, 337–355.

Roald, I., & Mikalsen, Ø. (2001). Configuration and dynamics of the Earth-Sun-Moon system: An investigation into conceptions of deaf and hearing pupils. *International Journal of Science Education, 23*, 423–440.

Rudmann, D. (2005). *Empirical accuracy and consistency in college students' knowledge of classical astronomy.* (Doctoral dissertation, University of Illinois at Urbana-Champaign, 2005). Dissertation Abstracts International-A 67/01, 95.

Sadler, P. M. (1987). Misconceptions in astronomy. In J. D. Novak (Ed.), *Proceedings of the Second International Seminar: Misconceptions and Educational Strategies in Science and Mathematics* (Vol. 3, 422–425). Ithaca, NY: Cornell University.

Sadler, P. M. (1992). *The initial knowledge state of high school astronomy students.* (Doctoral dissertation, Harvard University, 1992). Dissertation Abstracts International-A 53/05, 1470

Samarapungavan, A., Vosniadou, S., & Brewer, W. F. (1996). Mental models of the earth, sun, and moon: Indian children's cosmologies. *Cognitive Development, 11*, 491–521.

Schoon, K. J. (1988). *Misconceptions in the earth and space sciences.* (Doctoral dissertation, Loyola University of Chicago 1988). Dissertation Abstracts International-A 50/04, 915.

Schoon, K. J. (1995). The origin and extent of alternative conceptions in the earth and space sciences: A survey of pre-service elementary teachers. *Journal of Elementary Science Education, 7*, 27–46.

Schoultz, J., Säljö, R., & Wyndhamn, J. (2001). Heavenly talk: Discourse, artifacts, and children's understanding of elementary astronomy. *Human Development, 44*, 103–118.

Schwartz, S. P. (Ed.). (1977). *Naming, necessity, and natural kinds.* Ithaca, NY: Cornell University Press.

Sharp, J. G. (1995). Children's astronomy: Implications for curriculum developments at Key Stage 1 and the future of infant science in England and Wales. *International Journal of Early Years Education, 3*, 17–49.

Sharp, J. G. (1996). Children's astronomical beliefs: A preliminary study of Year 6 children in south-west England. *International Journal of Science Education, 18*, 685–712.

Sharp, J. G. (1999). Young children's ideas about the earth in space. *International Journal of Early Years Education, 7*, 159–172.

Sharp, J. G., Bowker, R., & Merrick, J. (1997). Primary astronomy: Conceptual change and learning in three 10–11 year olds. *Research in Education, 57*, 67–83.

Siegal, M., Butterworth, G., & Newcombe, P. A. (2004). Culture and children's cosmology. *Developmental Science, 7*, 308–324.

Siegal, M., Waters, L. J., & Dinwiddy, L. S. (1988). Misleading children: Causal attributions for inconsistency under repeated questioning. *Journal of Experimental Child Psychology, 45*, 438–456.

Skopeliti, I., & Vosniadou, S. (in press). Reasoning with external representations in elementary astronomy. In S. Vosniadou, D. Kayser & A. Protopapas (Eds.), *Proceedings of the 2nd European Cognitive Science Conference.* Delphi, Greece.

Sneider, C. I., & Ohadi, M. M. (1998). Unraveling students' misconceptions about the earth's shape and gravity. *Science Education, 82*, 265–284.

Stahly, L. L., Krockover, G. H., & Shepardson, D. P. (1999). Third grade students' ideas about the lunar phases. *Journal of Research in Science Teaching, 36*, 159–177.

Summers, M., & Mant, J. (1995). A survey of British primary school teachers' understanding of the Earth's place in the universe. *Educational Research, 1995*, 3–19.

Suppe, F. (Ed.). (1977). *The structure of scientific theories* (2nd ed.). Urbana: University of Illinois Press.

Targan, D. M. (1988). *The assimilation and accommodation of concepts in astronomy.* (Doctoral dissertation, University of Minnesota). Dissertation Abstracts International-A, 49/07, 1755.

Thagard, P. (1992). *Conceptual revolutions.* Princeton, NJ: Princeton University Press.

Trundle, K. C., Atwood, R. K., & Christopher, J. E. (2002). Preservice elementary teachers' conceptions of moon phases before and after instruction. *Journal of Research in Science Teaching, 39*, 633–658.

Trundle, K. C., Atwood, R. K., & Christopher, J. E. (2006). Preservice elementary teachers' knowledge of observable moon phases and pattern of change in phases. *Journal of Science Teacher Education, 17,* 87–101.

Tsai, C.-C., & Chang, C.-Y. (2005). Lasting effects of instruction guided by the conflict map: Experimental study of learning about the causes of the seasons. *Journal of Research in Science Teaching, 42,* 1089–1111.

Vosniadou, S. (1994). Universal and cultural-specific properties of children's mental models of the earth. In L. A. Hirschfeld & S. A. Gelman (Eds.), *Mapping the mind: Domain specificity in cognition and culture* (pp. 412–430). Cambridge: Cambridge University Press.

Vosniadou, S., Archontidou, A., Kalogiannidou, A., & Ioannides, C. (1996). How Greek children understand the shape of the earth: A study of conceptual change in childhood. *Psychological Issues, 7,* 30–51 (in Greek).

Vosniadou, S., & Brewer, W. F. (1990). A cross-cultural investigation of children's conceptions about the earth, the sun, and the moon: Greek and American data. In H. Mandl, E. De Corte, N. Bennett & H. F. Friedrich (Eds.), *Learning and Instruction: European research in an international context: Vol. 2.2. Analysis of complex skills and complex knowledge domains* (pp. 605–629). Oxford: Pergamon Press.

Vosniadou, S., & Brewer, W. F. (1992). Mental models of the earth: A study of conceptual change in childhood. *Cognitive Psychology, 24,* 535–585.

Vosniadou, S., & Brewer, W. F. (1994). Mental models of the day/night cycle. *Cognitive Science, 18,* 123–183.

Vosniadou, S., & Skopeliti, I. (2005). Developmental shifts in children's categorizations of the earth. In *Proceedings of the Twenty Seventh Annual Conference of the Cognitive Science Society* (pp. 2325–2330). Mahwah, NJ: Erlbaum.

Vosniadou, S., Skopeliti, I., & Ikospentaki, K. (2004). Modes of knowing and ways of reasoning in elementary astronomy. *Cognitive Development, 19,* 203–222.

Vosniadou, S., Skopeliti, I., & Ikospentaki, K. (2005). Reconsidering the role of artifacts in reasoning: Children's understanding of the globe as a model of the earth. *Learning and Instruction, 15,* 333–351.

Wandersee, J. H., Mintzes, J. J., & Novak, J. D. (1994). Research on alternative conceptions in science. In D. L. Gabel (Ed.), *Handbook of research on science teaching and learning* (pp. 177–210). New York: Macmillan.

Waterman, A. H., Blades, M., & Spencer, C. (2001). Interviewing children and adults: The effect of question format on the tendency to speculate. *Applied Cognitive Psychology, 15,* 521–531.

Yuckenberg, L. M. (1962). Children's understanding of certain concepts of astronomy in the first grade. *Science Education, 46,* 148–150.

Za'rour, G. I. (1976). Interpretation of natural phenomena by Lebanese school children. *Science Education, 60,* 277–287.

8

Learning and Teaching about Matter in Grades K–8: When Should the Atomic-Molecular Theory be Introduced?

Marianne Wiser
Clark University

Carol L. Smith
University of Massachusetts at Boston

The atomic-molecular theory is one of the most important scientific theories, on par with Darwin's theory of evolution. It is important that it be familiar to students graduating from high school but, like evolution theory, it is highly counterintuitive for most students, and current K–12 science teaching is typically not effective in helping them understand and accept it. Rather, the majority of high school and even college students (including chemistry majors) have many fundamental misconceptions about atoms and molecules, and many fail to understand the central tenets of the theory, as well as its explanatory power.

Recently, researchers have begun investigating the deeper *reasons* for such failure. Significantly, their work suggests that difficulties with the atomic-molecular theory are only the tip of the iceberg. Lurking underneath are fundamental difficulties with conceptualizing matter and materials on a macroscopic scale as well as basic limitations in students' epistemological understanding of what science, and scientific models in particular, are all about. Thus, developing an understanding of the atomic-molecular theory will call for *more* conceptual changes (and also *more types* of conceptual changes) than has often been acknowledged. However, this does not mean that atoms and molecules should not been introduced relatively early in the curriculum, as those concepts interact with understanding matter at the macroscopic level. This raises obvious questions: Which conceptual changes should one work on with students during the elementary and early middle school years? Is there some set of macroscopic concepts and epistemological understandings that should be in place before introducing the idea of atoms? Are there other macroscopic concepts and epistemological understandings that are best developed in combination with learning about atoms and molecules or after those concepts are introduced? In other words, when is learning about atoms part of the problem, and when is it part of the solution?

We will start by sketching out a learning progression for the concepts of matter, weight, density, volume, and material kind from early childhood to middle school, assuming traditional science and math instruction,[1] in order to identify students' state of content and epistemological knowledge at the time the atomic model is introduced (typically in eighth grade, in U.S. schools). We will argue that how far students progress along this trajectory is more variable than commonly realized. For example, there is great variation in the modal patterns of thinking for different populations of students. Further, students in the same grade and in the same school system are often conceptually in quite different places. The reasons for these differences are not yet well understood. At a minimum, this variation shows that developing certain macroscopic conceptions of matter is not "developmentally inevitable" (as is commonly assumed) but critically depends on the instructional and other cultural experiences available to students and their degree of involvement in sense-making about these experiences.

We will then present the major misinterpretations students develop about atoms and molecules during the middle and high school years and discuss the diverse reasons for those misconceptions. These include the important role played by their (inadequate) macroscopic concepts and epistemological knowledge and the interactions among beliefs about atoms, macroscopic concepts, and epistemology. We will argue that a curriculum focused on helping students develop a core set of macroscopic and epistemological understandings during elementary school (e.g., understanding that all matter has weight,[2] model building in science, and so on) would provide students with important resources for making the atomic-molecular theory meaningful. At the same time, we will argue that learning about atoms and molecules early (by late elementary or early middle school) is important both because it helps consolidate macroscopic understandings about matter (e.g., the material nature of gases) and provides a necessary foundation for developing other important macroscopic understandings (e.g., evaporation; chemical reactions). Whether there are benefits to integrating modeling matter at a nanoscopic level even earlier in the curriculum remains an open question.

ASSUMPTIONS GUIDING OUR CONCEPTUAL ANALYSES AND REVIEW

The concept of matter does not develop in isolation but rather in close interaction with the concepts of weight, density, mass, and material kind and, later on, with the concepts of atoms and molecules. We find both individual concepts and the broader network in which they are embedded useful units of analysis. Others (diSessa & Sherin, 1998) argue that it is more useful to focus on levels of description at the subconceptual level, in part because this level has greater "reality" and invariance; they interpret students in clinical interviews as constructing "on the fly" context-specific models of each situation presented to them by using subconceptual elements. They further argue that the structure of concepts is much more complex than has been acknowledged, that concepts have no simple core, and that conceptual change consists of gradual change in the tuning of cueing priorities for different subconceptual elements, rather than radical restructuring.

We do not deny that multiple levels of analysis are important; in fact, we embrace this view. As we will see, the literature on students' beliefs about conservation of weight and matter, and about molecules and atoms, gives plenty of evidence for the context dependency of students' assertions and for explanations being constructed on the spot during interviews. However, students' thinking is not unconstrained. They bring to their interactions with the researcher interrelated epistemologies (the senses are good indicators of physical entities), ontologies (atoms are gas-like), intuitive theories (matter is what can be felt and seen) and models (atoms are embedded in matter), within which they then invent more specific explanations.

Conceptual change undoubtedly involves reorganization of subconceptual elements and progressive shifts in cueing priorities, which curricula should support (e.g., from "if I can see the iodine gas, iodine is still there" to "even if I cannot see water vapor, it is still there because matter does not disappear"; or from "this grain of rice weighs nothing because it feels like nothing" to "it has to weigh something because it is matter; a very sensitive balance scale would show it"). However, these shifts are not simple belief revisions, they are part of conceptual and supraconceptual reorganizations and cannot be stabilized without large-scale restructuring. The scope and depth of the restructuring is what makes conceptual change difficult and therefore it is of great pedagogical relevance. What could be interpreted as a shift in cueing priority (e.g., from heft to balance scale) involves *concurrent and inter-related* changes in concepts (e.g., felt weight moves from core to periphery; weight becomes an extensive property), conceptual relations (any piece of matter weighs something; weight is differentiated from density), ontology and epistemology, as it would in scientific theory change.

Concepts do indeed have a complex structure (Keil & Lockhart, 1999), and their different aspects can be foregrounded in different contexts. We believe, however, they also have a core as well as less essential components; conceptual restructuring often involves movement from core to periphery and vice versa (Carey, 1991). But again, this movement is part of a change in ontology and epistemology: for example, felt weight becomes peripheral *because* students have come to appreciate that objective measures are more precise and reliable, and they support lawful generalizations (e.g., about the relation of weight and volume). This complex shift is also one in which a concept changes status from *explanans* to *explanandum*, a hallmark of theory change in science: Felt weight is primitive in students' early view of matter, whereas later it is accounted for by the scientific concepts of weight, pressure, volume, and density (as well as physiology). We consider that, in the domain of matter at the macroscopic level, the conceptual changes that bring students to a view of matter, weight, volume and density compatible with the scientific theory involve many characteristics of theory change in science.

The case of the atomic-molecular theory is different because few students have a concept of atom or molecule prior to instruction. Thus, learning the atomic-molecular theory is not a matter of revising one's pre-existing concepts and beliefs about atoms and molecules but about developing them in the first place. However, analyzing the beliefs that students develop about matter at the atomic level as a result of instruction also benefits from a multi-level approach because their interpretations are constrained by their macroscopic view of matter and their epistemology. Moreover, this approach allows us to distinguish between kinds of misconceptions. Not all misconceptions are born equal nor are they equally resistant to change. We will argue that some (e.g., that atoms are embedded in "stuff" or that they have all the properties of materials at the macroscopic level) are both prevalent and entrenched because they involve multiple reasons—conceptual, perceptual, metaphysical, or epistemological. They also seem to be ideas that students have developed as they were trying to make sense of information presented in the classroom prior to being interviewed. Others are more fleeting and appear created "on the fly" in an effort to answer the interviewers' probes, without deep commitment on the part of the students. This distinction is important for obvious pedagogical reasons and speaks to the concept/subconcept debate, as an analysis exclusively at the level of subconcepts might not allow for important distinctions between misconceptions.

The goal of this chapter is neither to document nor to try to resolve the intuitive theory versus knowledge-in-pieces debate. The paragraphs above were intended to clarify the framework within which we are writing this chapter. As for the debate, we suspect that consensus will develop around some integrated version (as with Piagetian and Vygotskian approaches, or the trichromatic and opponent-process theories of color vision). As with all theoretical differences, this one will be resolved by making detailed proposals about the role of the different levels — perceptual, subconceptual, conceptual, ontological, epistemological — in constraining knowledge acquisition. Another component will be examining which framework best captures students' patterns of answers to the *same* problems in a variety of contexts, as well as which framework informs more effective teaching studies, and ultimately, curricula. We suspect that scientific domain may be important— students may have a richer network of concepts in some domains than others, which may place more constraints, and therefore produce more coherence, in their reasoning.

A LEARNING PROGRESSION FOR THE CONCEPT OF MATTER AT THE MACROSCOPIC LEVEL

The Early Development of the Concepts of Matter and Material Kind

Infants and young preschool children undoubtedly don't have any explicit explanatory concepts of matter or material kind. In order to have such concepts, children need to not only distinguish multiple levels of description (object, material kind, and matter), but also to inter-relate those levels into representations expressed by "Wood is a kind of material" or "This car is made of wood." Further, for these concepts to be explanatory, children need to use knowledge of properties at one level to explain properties at another. For example, "This cup breaks *because* it is made of glass," or "I can see, feel, and touch this doll *because* it is made of some stuff."

Although explicit concepts of matter and material kind are not present in infancy, their precursors do exist in the form of a concept of object, a concept of "non-solid" (encompassing liquids, aggregates, gels, and other nonrigid materials that in children's experience allow dividing, molding, or pouring), and a sense of substantiality. There is abundant evidence that infants have a robust concept of physical object as a bounded entity that is solid, permanent and enduring, and that has characteristic properties and functions (Baillargeon, 2002; Spelke, 1991). In addition, there is some evidence that, by 8 months, infants make a distinction between discrete objects (that are countable) and continuous entities such as liquids and aggregates (that are not) (Huntley-Fenner, Carey, & Solimando, 2002). This distinction plays an important role in early word learning. For example, even 2-year-old children generalize novel names of nonsolid aggregates to other portions of the same material shaped differently, whereas they generalize novel names of solid objects to other objects of the same shape even if they are made of a different material (Soja, Carey, & Spelke, 1991). Embedded in the notion of both solid objects and nonsolids is a notion of substantiality. Infants perceive properties such as shape, size, texture, and pliability intermodally; they expect things they see to lend themselves to be touched and handled and to interact causally with each other in ways that are constrained by their properties, spatial arrangements, and physical contact. We take this network of expectations to form the precursor of a concept of matter while the distinction between (solid) objects and nonsolids will lead to the distinction between objects and material kinds.

These precursors guide, and are enriched by, children's explorations of the physical world and their interpretations of linguistic input. For example, sensory and motor experience with objects versus nonsolids entrenches the notion that the shape of (inanimate) objects is both invariant and relevant to one's actions on them, whereas it is texture (and other intensive properties) that are both invariant and relevant to one's handling of nonsolids. Language acquisition builds on this distinction — in languages such as English, object names are count nouns whereas names for material kinds are mass nouns — as well as helps them go beyond it as they learn that there are material kind names that label portions of both solid and nonsolid stuff.

Significantly, the first material kind names infants learn are for liquids (water, milk); children are somewhat slower to acquire material kind names for solid materials, although they usually have at least some names by ages 3 or 4 (Bloom, 2000). In Western children's experience, solid materials (cotton, wood, plastic) are more variable in color and texture than nonsolids (milk, water, sand). More crucially, nonsolid materials tend to be associated with unique patterns of sensory-motor experiences (e.g., Playdough has a specific texture and gets molded; milk is white, fluid, and for drinking) whereas it is the kind of object rather than the material it is made of that has the strongest association with sensory-motor activity. Thus, learning the names of solid materials not only requires overcoming the salient object-level description but also constructing the notion of "made of" and articulating the two — this is a spoon and it is made of plastic (Bloom, 2000). This, we propose, is a major and long-drawn conceptual change, drawing on multiple sources.

Linguistic input draws attention to the materials solids are made of, not just with the names of materials (plastic, glass), but also with statements like "This is a plastic spoon" or "This spoon is *made of* plastic." Using "plastic" as an adjective guides generalizations across different kinds of plastic objects and thus encourages linking "plastic" to shininess, lightness, and flexibility. We hypothesize that the combinations of such statements with nonverbal patterns of experiences in which objects made of the same materials have similar appearances and show similar behaviors (rubber objects bounce, glass objects break) help create initial concepts of material kinds for solid objects.

Children would then be in a position to establish similarities between solid and nonsolid materials. They are both characterized by surface appearance and texture, independent of shape and size of the object/sample, and correlated with how the object/sample interacts with other objects (e.g., when dropped, sand makes a pile, water makes a puddle, and rubber objects bounce). Linguistic input is also a factor in this process: the names of materials, whether solid or not, are embedded in the same grammatical construction ("This is sand," "This is plastic"). The role of similarity in fostering inference of additional common properties and thus in conceptual development is well-documented in Gentner's (2003) work. We hypothesize that, once children are aware of similarities between solid and nonsolid materials, the rich sense of what nonsolid materials *are* — that they have the same perceptual and motor affordances all the way through, gained from squeezing and running their hands through them as opposed to being limited to exploring the surface of solid materials — gets mentally applied to solid materials as well, giving "made of" a deeper meaning. (It is also possible that children have enough familiarity with cutting and breaking solid objects to make this inference.) Thereby a new ontological category is formed — material kind — encompassing the materials of objects and nonsolids. When this new material kind level of description is coordinated with the object level of description, children can think of a plastic spoon both as a spoon (an object whose shape is designed for eating) and as made of plastic. It is likely that an essentialist bias makes material kind an explanatory concept — this breaks *because* it is made of glass, this bounces *because* it is made of rubber (Gelman & Markman, 1987). At the same time, infants' sense of substantiality is enriched and becomes the core of young children's concept of matter: things that are seen, touched, and hefted, are now conceived of as made of stuff, in the sense described above.

Evidence for Understanding Material Kind

There are several lines of evidence that children between 3 to 7 years of age are developing concepts of specific material kinds as well as more general concepts of matter and material kind. Those developments are complementary and mutually supportive. First, preschool children not only are learning the names for many kinds of objects, but also for particular kinds of materials.

We take the onset of learning material kind names for solid materials and children's ability to answer questions about what kind of stuff objects are made of as good evidence that they are formulating explicit concepts of material kinds at this time (Bloom, 2000; Dickinson, 1987, 1988).

In addition, young children are beginning to distinguish explicitly between properties that may characterize particular materials (e.g., sweetness, color, texture) from properties that characterize particular objects (e.g., shape, size, function). In an unpublished study, Wiser gave 3- and 4-year-olds pairs of unfamiliar objects (A and B) to hold. The objects were made of different (unfamiliar) materials of significantly different densities and were given unfamiliar labels ("This is a dax and that is a tiv"). Children were asked which one was heavier. Then another pair was placed before the child, the same two shapes but made of the opposite material, and the child was asked, "Which one is a dax?" and "Which is heavier?" The children performed significantly differently on the two questions, showing a stronger association between shape and name and between material kind and heaviness, respectively. In other studies, preschool children made distinctions between properties that varied with the amount or size of the sample (e.g., is big, can be blown away) from properties that characterized the specific material (e.g., is sweet, burns, is white) (Au, 1994). Although children were not as good as adults, the fact that most were above chance in patterns of responding is consistent with their making some distinction between these two levels of description.

In addition, 4- to 6-year-old children know that when a paper cup or a wooden airplane is chopped into pieces, the pieces are still paper or wood but no longer a cup or airplane (Smith, Carey, & Wiser, 1985). This gives further evidence that they distinguish object and material levels of description and have contrasting ways of tracking the identity of objects and materials. This is likely to be because the pieces still have the characteristic (perceptual) properties they associate with the material rather than because they have a deep belief that breaking or grinding does not change material kind or think of material kind as an *underlying* constituent. Evidence for this interpretation comes from the fact that younger children are more likely to justify their judgments by saying that it still *looks like* wood, rather than arguing that it is still wood because that was what it was made of (Smith et al., 1985).

Evidence for Understanding of Matter

The prior studies suggest young children are developing some concept of material kind that is distinct from their concept of object kind. But what evidence is there that they might also be developing some general concept of matter and recognize that there are important commonalities across different materials? And what might those commonalities be?

One of the most basic ontological distinctions, made explicitly even by preschoolers, is a distinction between physical and mental entities. In a series of elegant studies, Estes and Wellman found that 3-, 4-, and 5-year-olds were able to judge that physical objects have a rich variety of "sensory-behavioral" affordances that thoughts of those objects do not (Wellman, 1990). For example, you can see, touch, and feel a cookie but not the thought of a cookie. Physical objects have a public and consistent existence that thoughts of those objects, which are private and fleeting, do not. Of course, making an ontological distinction between physical objects and thoughts does not require that children have an explicit concept of matter: They could be contrasting mental entities and entities with public existence, without representing solids, liquids, and aggregates as alike in that they are *made of some kind of stuff.*

Some direct evidence that they do have a more general concept of matter comes from a small-scale study by Carey (1991) in which 4-, 6-, 10-, and 12-year-old children were explicitly asked to sort entities into different piles: one pile for things that were made of some kind of physical stuff, one pile for things that were not made of some kind of stuff. Children were given a wide range of entities: solids (both inanimate physical objects and biological kinds), liquids (water, coca-cola), powders (sugar), gases (air, steam), nonmaterial physical entities (heat, electricity, shadows, echo) and mental entities (wish, idea). Carey found that about half of the 4-year-olds, three quarters of the 6-year-olds, and all the older children grouped some solids, liquids, and powders as alike in being made of some kind of stuff. Of course, none of these children had the scientists' concept that neatly picked out all solids, liquids, powders, and gases while excluding other nonmaterial physical entities. Indeed, they all made some under- and overextension errors (which we will return to discuss shortly). Nonetheless, the fact that they were making some sensible groupings at a level broader than solid physical object is evidence that preschoolers are developing a broader concept of matter. They not only recognize that these entities are things that can be seen, touched, or produce some physical effect, but they use these properties as evidence that they are all "made of some kind of stuff."

A final piece of evidence that children are developing a more general concept of matter during this time is their increasing success with the classic Piagetian conservation of matter tasks (Piaget & Inhelder, 1974). In these tasks, children are given samples of different materials (a ball of clay, a beaker of water, a certain length of wire) and then watch while the sample is reshaped or divided into smaller samples (e.g., the clay ball is rolled into a sausage or divided into four pieces). Whereas younger children typically think the amount of clay, liquid, or wire has changed because of perceptual appearances, the majority of 7- and 8-year-olds make correct judgments. "Conservation of matter" is somewhat misleading, however, because it connotes the scientific principle that matter is conserved under all physical transformations. What children this age achieve is much more modest and might be better described as a concept of amount of material, which stays invariant if no material is added or removed during the transformation; that is how they generally justify their correct judgments.

Piaget and Inhelder originally explained this development in terms of the development of concrete operations, an account that has been heavily critiqued on both theoretical and empirical grounds. We prefer to view it as a domain-specific achievement, arising from an emerging naïve theory of matter, although our view shares with Piaget and Inhelder's account the hypothesis that an early notion of composition and decomposition is part of this deeper understanding. To think of solids and nonsolids as constituted of homogeneous pieces of stuff is tantamount to having a sense of amount of stuff; adding or removing pieces change this amount, and if nothing is added or removed, the amount stays the same. We suspect it is no coincidence that children are distinguishing this theoretical quantity, which is conserved, from perceptual appearances (it looks different), during the same time that they are learning more about specific materials. They recognize that solid objects are made of something and come to see commonalities among solids, liquids, and powders in that they are all made of some kind of stuff. Further research is needed to establish the links among these developments in the same group of children across a variety of materials.

Summary of the Development of Matter and Material Kind in Early Childhood

We have proposed that the concepts of matter and material kind children bring to elementary school have their roots in infancy—in infants' concepts of solid objects and of nonsolids (aggregates and liquids) and in their sense of substantiality expressed in intermodal expectations that objects can be seen, touched, and handled. Generalizations based on experiences with a variety of objects, liquids, and aggregates, combined with lexical and syntactic input as well as analogical reasoning, foster the development of an intuitive theory of matter and material kind during the preschool and elementary school years. The domain of this theory is solids, liquids, and aggregates. Its core tenets are that matter can be touched, seen, and hefted; that it exists as different material kinds, which have perceptual and inherent properties that explain their behaviors when acted upon; and that its amount (a qualitative notion) does not change under visible mechanical transformations (change of shape, macroscopic division).

The emergence of this theory involves several related conceptual changes. Children coalesce physical objects and nonsolids into a new ontological category — made of "stuff" — that now accounts for the substantiality that was part of infants' perception of objects and nonsolid entities. Conceiving of solid objects as made of specific kinds of stuff allows the differentiation of object level properties and material kind level properties.

Unlike its scientific counterpart, the core of the concepts in children's intuitive theory of matter is perceptually based: An entity is material (made of some stuff) if it can be touched and seen. It can be thought of as composed of homogeneous parts that are touchable and visible; if they were not they could not compose matter. The understanding of conservation young children evince in Piagetian tasks is based on this notion, evoked in the context of witnessed transformations. Other transformations, however, make "matter" disappear, most saliently boiling, dissolution, and burning. According to the intuitive theory, gases are not material. Material kinds are also identified perceptually, according to appearance and behavior (e.g., glass is transparent and breakable) so that, if melting and freezing significantly change the appearance and behavior of a material, they are taken to transform one material kind into another.

The kinds of conceptual restructuring needed to understand the macroscopic scientific theory of matter will be deeper and more complex than those involved in achieving the intuitive theory of matter. We will show in the next section that this conceptual restructuring involves a rich network of concepts (not only matter and material kind but also weight, volume, and density), deeper ontological changes, and radical changes in epistemology. Not surprisingly, the majority of students reach the end of middle school without a good grasp of the scientific concepts and epistemology.

Later Developments in Children's Concepts of Matter and Material Kind: Enrichment, Fragmentation, and (More Rarely) Restructuring

Given that young children's initial concepts of matter and material kind are quite different from the concepts of matter and chemical substance that are the target of elementary and middle school science curricula, what happens when children are exposed to these curricula? How do their ideas (typically) develop and change? In this section, we propose that it is useful to distinguish changes that involve piecemeal elaboration of children's initial concepts from those involving fundamental restructuring. Although some children make fundamental changes in their understanding of matter and material kind during this time, many others do not. Thus, exposure to new facts and information does not necessarily lead to deep (and productive) conceptual changes. Instead, the new information often produces only limited progress toward the scientific view, which, for reasons we explore below, falls severely short of the conceptual revisions necessary to master a macroscopic understanding of matter and material kind consistent with the scientific view. It can also lead to greater fragmentation, confusion, and conceptual incoherence in ways that are not widely recognized in the science education community, in part because this community has not been attentive to describing how students' concepts are articulated.

*Knowledge of Different Kinds of Materials and Range of Entities
Considered to be Matter*

During the elementary school years, the notion of material kind becomes more salient to children, as evidenced by a steady increase in using material kind in spontaneous classifications (Knerl, Watson, & Glazar, 1998). There is also an increase in the number of material kind names that children spontaneously generate when asked to give examples of what things are made of (Smith et al., 1985).

Two studies have investigated changes in children's judgments of what is and is not matter during the elementary school years (Carey, 1991; Stavy, 1991). Carey found that even first graders were significantly above chance in judging solids, aggregates, and some liquids to be matter, in keeping with our proposal that they think of matter as something they can see, feel, and touch. Further support for this assumption comes from their commonly referring to these properties when asked to explain how they could tell something is matter or what properties all matter might have. Stavy's first graders performed less well, possibly because, unlike Carey, she did not offer anchoring for the word "matter" by providing examples of prototypical material and nonmaterial entities (solids vs. mental entities). By seventh grade, the vast majority of children in both studies were correct in making judgments about solids, liquids, and aggregates, but there was less change in the frequency of children's overextensions to nonmaterial entities such as electricity, which remained substantial, and they were only at or slightly above chance in judging that air was matter. Even by eighth grade, many students still believe that air is not matter (Smith, Maclin, Grosslight, & Davis, 1997).

Given that children have explicitly been told that air is matter on numerous occasions, this underextension suggests that what they are told simply doesn't make sense, because it violates their concept of matter as something that can be seen, felt, and touched. Revising the ontology of gases requires a theory that provides uniting common properties for solids, liquids, and gases (e.g., having weight and taking up space); this theory cannot be achieved without extensive and radical conceptual restructuring, not only of matter but of weight and volume (as well as experimental evidence about the weight of gases). Quite strikingly, none of the younger children and only a few of the older children in the previous studies, used having weight as criterial for being matter (Carey, 1991; Stavy, 1991). In the absence of this restructuring, students can either reject that gases are matter, fragment their understanding of matter by introducing unexplained exceptions, give matter the unconstrained meaning of "everything that exists," or accept that "solids, liquids, and gases are matter" without understanding what "matter" really is, relying on similarity to prototypes of solids, liquids, and gases to judge whether something is matter or not.

Conceptualizing Materials as Underlying Constituents

Young children's initial understanding of matter and materials is very much based on perception and action — objects (broadly defined) are "seeable" and tangible (matter), and they exist in a variety of kinds of stuff with certain clusters of perceptually accessible properties (material kinds). This understanding allows them to infer that both smaller and larger samples of a material have some common characteristics, but usually only when reasoning about sizeable chunks that share perceptual properties. Presented with a chunk of iron and the powder that they are told resulted from grinding it, 4-year-olds believe the powder is not iron because it does not look like the chunk (Dickinson, 1987).

A more advanced understanding of objects *being made of* a material is based on the notion of *underlying constituent,* that is, on conceptualizing and visualizing the object as being composed of very small pieces of the material all the way through. This early mental modeling may have its source in sensory-motor experience with aggregates (grains of sand, specks of dirt) and clay-like substances that can be broken into tiny pieces, extended by limiting case thinking. It allows older children to override perceptual dissimilarities and know that iron powder is still iron, because it is made of the same tiny pieces that constituted the chunk. Dickinson (1987) found that it is not until age 12 that most children *consistently* group powders with chunks for all the materials presented while Au (1994) found that even 4-year-olds occasionally maintain material identity after being ground into powder. One can hypothesize that this variability among younger children is due to individual differences in having achieved the notion of underlying constituent. It may also be due to other strategies, such as using similarity between large chunks and powders for some materials or relying on an essentialist bias. Both may allow some children witnessing the transformation and focusing on its history to reason that "it was iron before, you just ground it up, so it is still iron."

There is also evidence that children improve in their understandings that there can be pieces of matter too small to see with the naked eye, that is, that matter can exist even though one cannot see it or touch it. Piaget and Inhelder (1974) originally investigated young children's understanding that dissolved sugar continues to exist. Prior to ages 7 or 8, children frequently denied that the sugar was still there whereas older children were more aware that there were still little pieces of sugar in the water. Several studies have also found that children's understanding of contamination awareness begins to appear at this time (Fallon, Rozin, & Pliner, 1984; Rozin, 1990). In addition, Smith, Solomon, and Carey (2005) directly asked children whether there could be pieces of matter too small to see. The majority of 8-year-olds thought so, typically bringing up the case of germs or other tiny things that can only be seen with a microscope. Nonetheless, when pressed about whether or not one could repeatedly divide matter forever, the majority concluded that one could not because the pieces would eventually disappear.

This constituent view represents progress in conceptualizing matter and material kind but by itself is limited: It is only an extension of children's initial idea that matter is detectable by the (unaided) senses and therefore is still anchored in perception. Thus it does not support conservation of matter without at least some actual or potential perceptual evidence (e.g., taste of sugar; visible with a microscope). Even older students often fail stricter tests for conservation—they believe that if one repeatedly cuts Styrofoam into smaller and smaller pieces, the pieces would disappear (e.g., Smith, 2007; Smith et al., 1997) or fail to maintain conservation of matter across certain phase changes such as boiling, in which matter seems to disappear (Johnson, 1998b; Lee, Eichinger, Anderson, Berkheimer, & Blakeslee, 1993). For similar reasons, this view supports only a limited commitment to conservation of material kind across physical transformations. Transformations that preserve many perceptual properties (e.g., melting chocolate) may be more easily understood correctly than those that do not (e.g., melting wax). Finally, this view by itself does not support conceptualizing gases as material because, being based on perception and imagined mental division, it is "unidirectional": Starting with a chunk, one mentally divides it into little pieces, first really and then potentially visible. But, in children's experience, gases don't start as perceptible chunks; the decomposition schema is constrained by children's ontology and applies to what is conceived of as material to start with.

The Relations of Weight to Matter and Material Kind

The Piagetian conservation literature suggests that during the elementary school years children markedly improve their understanding that weight and volume are conserved when objects get divided into smaller chunks or reshaped. The fact that conservation of matter (in the limited sense discussed previously) emerges prior to conservation of weight and volume (7–8 vs. 9–10 and 12–13, respectively) argues that the former does not depend on the latter, consistent with our findings that very few children use having weight as a criterion for being material.

Conservation of weight in Piaget's tasks, like conservation of amount of matter, is probably reached by reasoning that more stuff is heavier and less stuff is less heavy so weight stays the same if nothing is added or removed, and should not be interpreted in the scientific sense. There may be several reasons that conservation of weight lags behind conservation of matter. For many elementary school children, the core of the concept of weight is still felt weight, so that direct experience with adding and subtracting stuff may not provide (strong) support for their effect on weight; moreover, shape transformations do affect felt weight. It is likely that experience with measuring weight with balance scales is building up an objective aspect to the concept of weight (which may become central for some children and remain peripheral for others). This experience could be enough to link weight to amount of stuff and establish conservation of weight in the restricted sense — adding stuff on one side of the balance scale makes it tip, removing some makes it go up, not doing anything leaves it level. These experiences, as well as many in everyday life based on felt weight, also lead them to formulate a crude empirical generalizations — bigger things tend to be heavier; steel tends to be heavy, plastic tends to be light (Smith et al., 1985).

But this does not mean children have formulated the general principle that weight is a property of all matter nor that they have differentiated weight from density. Many children this age and even much older (eighth grade) still think that a small *visible* piece of Styrofoam and small enough pieces of any material weigh nothing at all (Carey, 1991; Smith et al., 2005, Smith, 2007). Moreover, children's justifications fail to indicate that they have formed a general belief that all matter has weight, either in weight conservation tasks or in matter sorting tasks discussed previously. And, for the majority of those children, the relation between weight and material kind is based on an undifferentiated weight concept conflating heavy and heavy for size These limitations are directly related to the enduring perceptual bases for the concepts of matter and weight: Felt weight does not support the differentiation of weight and density nor does it support the belief that tiny pieces have weight (a microscope may make invisible pieces visible but does not magnify weight).

Why Are Some Conceptual Changes Harder than Others?

There is considerable evidence of enrichment of children's initial understanding of matter and material kinds during the elementary school years. As they get older, children certainly: acquire more knowledge about specific material kinds; are clearer that solids, liquids, and aggregates are matter; develop some generalizations about size, weight, matter, and material kinds; think more clearly of matter as an underlying constituent; and develop conservation of amount of matter and material kind across some physical transformations. These changes are achieved by the majority of students, the ease of their acquisition being consistent with the assumption that they involve elaborating on the (perceptually based) concepts students bring to elementary school, rather than restructuring them.

There is also evidence that new information that is not consistent with children's intuitive ideas creates incoherence and fragmentation. In the starting intuitive theory, matter being something that one can see and feel, that disappears when cut into very tiny pieces, and that does not include gases, as well as material kinds changing identity when they melt, form a (somewhat) coherent set of perceptually-based beliefs. But being told that gases and tiny pieces of a solid chunk are matter and its properties loses its systematicity. As perceptual criteria lose their force, children are left without a notion of what makes material kins what they are, and of what enduring properties matter has. Crude empirical generalizations also can lead to confusion when put to experimental test: How can one account for small steel objects being sometimes heavier and sometimes lighter than bigger plastic objects? This unsatisfactory state of knowledge shows that traditional teaching does not provide the tools for students to create an alternative to their perceptually-based interpretive framework in which to make sense of received information and exploit generalizations they make on their own.

However, Smith and Carey find that some late elementary and middle school children do come to think that all matter must have some weight and that this belief is part of a new framework for thinking about matter and materials. This is often first evident in children's correct responses to questions about the weight of tiny (and/or invisible) pieces of stuff. They support these notions with general principles and modal statements — all matter weighs something, if it is there it must weigh something (Smith, 2007) — that are much stronger kinds of justifications that those reported in the Piagetian weight conservation tasks (Elkind, 1961). Significantly, students who have made these changes have also made other changes in their understanding of matter. For example, they now refrain from talking about matter as something that one can see, feel, or touch and they espouse, in thought experiments, general beliefs that matter *must* continue to exist with repeated division; it can't just disappear. They also differentiate between the weight of objects and the density of materials and have made progress in reconceptualizing weight and size as objective measurable properties (Smith, 2007; Smith et al., 1997). Thus, the fact that these children have made coordinated changes in a variety of concepts (changing what is at the core vs. periphery, making conceptual differentiations and coalescences) argues that they have fundamentally changed their understandings of matter and materials and developed a productive new framework for thinking about them.

The proportion of students who give evidence of achieving this restructuring varies considerably among different student populations. For example, one study with middle-class children in a Montessori school found that the majority of 8- to 9-year-olds understood that small pieces of matter must weigh something when questioned about a small piece of Styrofoam or a grain of rice and clearly differentiated between weight and density in a simple paired comparisons task (Smith et al., 1985). However, this was not the case for 8- to 9- year-olds from another private school, where only a minority showed both understandings (Smith, 2003). Nor is it typically the case for even much older students. In one study of urban seventh graders, only 10% thought that small pieces of matter must weigh something and clearly differentiated weight and density (Smith, Grosslight, Davis, Unger, & Snir, 1994). Among eighth graders in a suburban school, less than one-third of those in the main science track showed these understandings (Smith, 1993) prior to a teaching intervention, compared to two-thirds of students in the higher-math ability science track (Smith et al., 1997).

Why so much variability across populations and among students within the same population? Certainly this variability argues against viewing these achievements as "developmentally" inevitable. Broad factors are undoubtedly one source of variability — amount of content science knowledge being taught, quality of mathematical education, and individual students' academic level among them. We suspect, however, that more specific factors are involved. In keeping with our view that restructuring is not simply the result of a gradual (bottom-up) process that depends upon making enough piecemeal changes to one's initial ideas but also involves top-down processes (e.g., thought experiments, comparison, modeling) and a new epistemology, and therefore metacognitively guided learning, we believe that opportunities for metacognitive engagement, explicit model building, and discourse around these issues should be critical to promoting restructuring. Higher ability students may be more likely to create/seek these opportunities (as well as have more relevant prior knowledge), but classrooms may also vary enormously in the extent to which they provide these opportunities for all their students. (We will return to these issues in the later section that discusses the findings of explicit teaching studies.)

Take, for example, the concept of weight, which is central to a scientific understanding of matter. In order to construct an objective and extensive concept of weight, students need to make the ontological distinction between felt weight and weight as measured by a balance scale, to privilege the latter over the former, and to understand the properties of good measurement. Constructing measures of weight also involves cross-domain mapping between weight and number and reconceptualizing number as rational rather than counting number, another difficult conceptual change. Not surprisingly, there is evidence that these two conceptual changes occur at about the same time and appear to be mutually supportive (Smith et al., 2005).

Relating this additive (extensive) concept of weight to matter requires a mental model of matter with similar formal properties — that is, having the cognitive resources to divide mentally a chunk of matter into arbitrarily small pieces, focusing at the same time on each piece and on the whole, knowing that, even if cut infinitely small, the pieces cannot vanish or the whole would vanish. Bringing weight into this model results in understanding that, since the chunk has weight, each tiny piece of it has a tiny weight — all matter has weight, whether visible directly, or through a microscope, or too small to even imagine. This requires trusting the logic of a mental construct over perceptual evidence, a major epistemological leap of faith. It is likely that appreciating that the model provides a more stable and coherent view of the physical world helps one take the leap. For example, conservation of matter can be established by measuring weight and thus extended to melting, freezing, and dissolving transformations. And if one can imagine infinitely small pieces of a material, it is easier to believe that material kind is preserved even if radical perceptual changes take place.

Thus, as part of this conceptual restructuring, one sees an interesting shift in the relationships between ideas about matter and weight. Whereas early on children developed qualitative insights about matter that "pulled" deeper insights about weight (conservation of matter leads to conservation of weight when samples are cut or reshaped), further insights about matter may depend on their ability to measure weight and volume, which in turn depend upon using mathematical knowledge to inform physical understandings (Lehrer, Schauble, Strom, & Pligge, 2001).

The compositional model described above may contribute to the differentiation of density (which has its origin in "heavy-for-size" in the intuitive theory) from weight, as it makes it possible to contrast amount of matter and weight in a small portion of an object to the amount of matter and weight of the whole object. Constructing the concept of density also relies on new symbolic representations — graphs and (external) models (e.g., Lehrer et al., 2001; Smith et al., 1997). Graphing weight as a function of volume for different material kinds strengthens the additive nature of weight and supports the conceptualization of density, its differentiation from weight, and the mathematical relation between density, weight, and volume. By becoming an inherent characteristic of material kind,[3] density makes material kind a more abstract concept, integrates it more closely with matter (different materials have different densities because the matter of which they are constituted is distributed more or less sparsely), and strengthens the belief that all matter has weight (the reason that Styrofoam feels like nothing is not that it has no weight but that its density is very low). But this concept-building requires understanding that visual representations are tools for investigating and explaining phenomena, a form of hypothetico-deductive thinking that is not part of many students' epistemology.

The material nature of gases is still a challenge even for students who have the mathematical, cognitive, and metacognitive resources to restructure their concept of matter, although they now have a means for investigating the issue. Experiments showing that gases have weight are relevant to students who believe that matter has weight; a mental model of solids and liquids as constituted of tiny pieces might lend itself to a crude gas model, in which those tiny pieces are far apart. However, the atomic-molecular theory will make boiling, evaporation (as well as melting and freezing), and the nature of gases much more meaningful, giving solids, liquids, and gases a common ontology (they are all made of particles separated in space). It is also needed to account for melting and freezing, to understand the nature of chemical reactions and how they differ from physical transformations, and to grasp the difference between element, compound and mixture, all achievements that are beyond the scope of the macroscopic theory.

THE ATOMIC-MOLECULAR MODEL

The atomic-molecular theory is one of the most important contemporary scientific theories; as such it should be familiar to students graduating from high school. It offers parsimonious and elegant explanations of what makes materials different from each other, why and how they change phase, and why and how chemical reactions happen. Its basic tenets are few and simple. All matter is made up of atoms, which are far too small to see through an optical microscope. There is empty space (vacuum) between atoms. Each atom takes up space, has mass, and is in constant motion. All matter that we encounter on earth is made of less than 100 kinds of atoms. Each kind has distinctive properties, including its mass and the way it combines with other atoms or molecules. Atoms can be joined (in different proportions) to form molecules or networks — a process that involves forming chemical bonds between atoms. Some substances (elements) are composed of just one kind of atom. Other substances (compounds) are composed of clusters of atoms bound together. Materials are mixtures of two or more (often many more) substances. Some materials are predominantly a single substance. Changes in matter include physical changes, in which molecules change arrangement and/or motion but remain intact, and chemical changes, in which atoms are rearranged (disconnected and reconnected) into new molecules but the atoms remain intact.

Irrespective of when the atomic-molecular theory is introduced into the curriculum, most 12th-grade students display major misconceptions about the nature, behavior, and structural arrangements of atoms. They also have misconceptions about how the atomic-molecular model accounts for macroscopic properties and phenomena — for example, kinds of materials, weight, volume and density, latent and specific heat, phase changes, and chemical reactions. We will argue that this lack of understanding is not inevitable and is no reason to delay teaching the atomic-molecular theory.

Students working within traditional curricula face three major sources of difficulty in understanding and accepting the atomic-molecular theory. First, they do not have the epistemological knowledge necessary to reconcile everyday perceptual experience of material objects (solids and liquids appear continuous, the ground is solid, materials differ in color and hardness) with some of the basic tenets of the atomic-molecular theory (matter is discontinuous, atoms exist in a vacuum, atoms are neither hard nor soft and they are not colored). In particular, students know little about the nature of scientific models and of their relation to observed characteristics of objects and events. Another source of difficulty is not as widely recognized; it is that few students have the macroscopic conceptions of matter, weight, volume, and density necessary to support a sound understanding of the atomic-molecular theory. A third reason has to do with the way the atomic-molecular theory itself is taught: The information presented to students is not rich enough for them to make sense of the atomic-molecular model and the language and illustrations in textbooks are widely, if unwittingly, misleading.

In this section, we review some of the misconceptions students develop about atoms and molecules (when taught traditionally) and analyze the reasons those misconceptions develop. In later sections, we will consider the implications of these analyses for characterizing the epistemological, ontological, and macroscopic knowledge necessary to achieve a sound understanding of the basic atomic-molecular theory and for devising more effective instruction.

There is often more than one reason for a given misconception, and those reasons are often interlinked, both within levels of analysis (e.g., different beliefs about atoms support each other) and between levels of analysis (e.g., lack of epistemological understanding of models can cause misinterpretations of information about atoms). Some misconceptions are deep and well-entrenched; they tend to be those with interlinked reasons. Others seem more fleeting, probably created on the fly as students are interviewed rather than entrenched beliefs. We will note that not all misconceptions are undesirable, as some are an inherent part of the knowledge construction process. How desirable or undesirable a misconception is cannot be judged by how similar or distant it is from the scientists' conceptions but more on how it functions in supporting further growth and learning. Thus, it is important to distinguish among misconceptions that serve as valuable "stepping stones" for future learning (and might be inherent in the learning process) and those that do not and therefore should be prevented from developing.

Misconceptions about Atoms and Molecules and Some Hypotheses about Their Causes

Synthetic Models of Matter

Many students do not conceive of atoms as the basic constituents of matter but rather as something *in* matter. They view atoms as embedded in a material substrate (Andersson, 1990; Lee et al., 1993; Novick & Nussbaum, 1981), as if, by themselves, they were not sufficient to be the stuff from which things are made. This is an extremely powerful misconception that survives even through college chemistry instruction (Pozo & Crespo, 2005). Many reasons conspire to cause its entrenchment. One comes from students' epistemological commitment to naïve realism and their lack of sophistication in model-based reasoning. As a default position, they assume things are the way they appear. Matter looks continuous thus matter *is* inherently continuous (Harrison & Treagust, 2002; Nakhleh, Samarapungavan, & Saglam, 2005). Another comes from their macroscopic concepts of matter and materials. The Matter-in-Molecules model is a synthetic model (Vosniadou & Brewer, 1992); that is, it is a model resulting from the integration of school information into students' pre-existing intuitive theory (Ben-Zvi, Eylon, & Silberstein, 1986). A third is that textbook illustrations suggest and/or reinforce this model — a piece of substance is represented as a colored cube or sphere (with black boundaries), with small black spheres in it. So does language such as "Atoms *in* solids vibrate, while atoms *in* liquids…," "Molecules are less free to move *in* ice than *in* (liquid) water," "Bonds are the *glue* between atoms," and "Molecules *escape from the water* into the air when water boils." Direct observations may then be interpreted in light of such statements. For example, ice contains air pockets, as does water about to boil; some children think those are atoms (Ault, Novak, & Gowin, 1984).

Even students who are able to "suspend disbelief" to give the atomic-molecular model serious consideration find it impossible to do so on the basis of the information that is typically provided to them. Words used to describe atoms generate a wrong sense of scale about atoms and the gaps between them. For example, "microscopic" suggests that atoms can be seen with a light microscope; "particulate" suggests particles (e.g., of dust), and "nucleus" may lead to the "molecell" concept (Griffiths & Preston, 1992). Metaphysics is another obstacle — the existence of vacuum between atoms violates a deeply held metaphysical principle that vacuum does not exist in nature. The need to "fill the gaps" with stuff is all the more acute because most middle school students have no notion of the bonding forces holding molecules and atoms together, let alone of their magnitude compared to familiar forces (Johnson, 2000). This leaves students without recourse for understanding what holds matter together and prevents us from falling through the floor.

Another synthetic model, adopted by some students, illustrates similar reasons. Atoms are often introduced by asking students to imagine cutting a chunk of substance into smaller and smaller pieces. This generates a mental model of atoms as stacked cubes without space between them (Pfundt, 1981), an interpretation that fits the statement "matter is *made of* atoms" more closely than the Molecules-in-Matter model. It has the advantage of violating neither perceptual evidence nor students' epistemology and metaphysics, but it fails to represent the central idea that atoms are pre-existing constituents of matter, with specific size and mass.

These models of atoms are not scientific models of materials, not because they are wrong per se, but because they do not serve the *function* of scientific models. That is, they do not propose another level of description in order to explain the properties of materials. In the case of the Stacked-Cubes model, this is because atoms are not pre-existing units; they are simply the material itself. In the case of the Molecules-in-Matter models, it is because atoms are embedded in "stuff," thus begging the question of what the "stuff" is made of. Their use is largely unconstrained (e.g., Why can one not cut the stacked cubes into even smaller pieces? Why do atoms escape during boiling but not during melting?), and thus they are not revisable in a systematic way. They also do not contribute to further learning because they do not capture any (or even precursors) of the tenets of the atomic-molecular model upon which one could build. Thus, one of the goals of an effective curriculum should be to prevent their development, a point to which we will return later..

Misconceptions About the Ontology of Atoms and Molecules

Underlying the alternative models students develop about atoms and molecules are fundamental misconceptions about what atoms and molecules are and what things are made of atoms and molecules (their ontology). Learning about atoms and molecules is difficult not only because it involves adding a new ontological level (atoms and molecules share few properties with macroscopic objects), but also because it involves making a fundamental distinction between atoms and molecules within this level (atoms are conserved across chemical transformations, whereas molecules can come in to existence and go out of existence). Creating new ontological levels will require serious theory-building, and in general students lack the epistemological sophistication to realize that is what they are doing. Instructional approaches compound the problem when they present the tenets of the atomic molecular theory as a set of facts rather than as an explanatory model.

Not surprisingly, students typically start by trying to map atoms and molecules onto existing ontological categories rather than creating new ones. Thus, students develop their own ideas of what atoms are and where they are found. Although some of those ideas are highly resistant to change, they do not form an alternative framework—they are context dependent, piecemeal, and not always coherent. Also, they exist in different combinations in different students. Nevertheless, several things unify them: They are developed within the ontological constraints of students' own macroscopic concepts; they are not developed to be explanatory, but out of a need to make sense of information that cannot be meaningful; and they are not useful stepping stones for further learning.

For many students, solid and liquids, which are visible and tangible, form the ontological category *matter,* while gases are something else, usually more closely related to heat and electricity than to matter. This ontological commitment at the macroscopic level, in interaction with students' selective attention to information presented to them about atoms, leads to misconceptions about the nature of atoms. If students formulate the belief "everything has atoms — solids, liquids, and gases," they are likely to think of atoms as nonmaterial, gas-like "specks" embedded in solids and liquids and floating in gases, for example. On the other hand, if they focus on "iron is made of atoms of iron, mercury is made of atoms of mercury, and air is made of atoms," they are likely to construct the (correct) belief that there are different kinds of atoms but to conclude (incorrectly) that some atoms are little pieces of matter (e.g., iron) while others are not (e.g., oxygen). Or, if they focus on "matter is made of atoms," they might conclude that atoms are found only in solids and liquids, which form the domain of their matter concept.

Students' macroscopic concepts of weight and volume also affect their beliefs about what atoms are and where they are found. For many middle school students, weight and volume are still, essentially, properties of objects that can be felt or hefted, or seen, respectively, so that very little pieces of matter don't weigh anything or occupy space. If atoms don't weigh anything, don't "feel like anything," and don't occupy space because they are too small, they cannot be constitutive of matter, which one can touch and see. This would reinforce the need to embed atoms in "stuff." On the other hand, given that gases are not matter, it might make sense that only gases, but not solids and liquids, are made of atoms.

Correlational studies support the link between holding alternative conceptions at the macroscopic level and having difficulties with understanding the atomic-molecular theory as an explanatory model and internalizing its core tenets. Snir, Smith, and Raz (2003) showed that students who were successful in understanding how atoms/molecules explained certain macroscopic phenomena also had sound macroscopic understandings of matter, weight, volume, and density. Lee et al. (1993) showed that macroscopic and atomic-molecular misconceptions coexist at equivalent levels in sixth graders regarding many issues (the material nature of gases, what happens in phase change, dissolving, etc.). Teaching that addresses both levels is much more successful than teaching that addresses just the atomic-molecular level.

Many students make some progress in high school toward viewing atoms as little pieces of matter that weigh something and have something to do with the properties of materials, mostly upon the introduction of the periodic table in their first chemistry course (Wiser, O'Connor, & Higgins, 1995). However, they do not understand that macroscopic properties and events are *emergent.* For example, fluidity has to do with atomic structure and molecular bonds, not with atoms being fluid; substances may differ while being made up of the same atoms (in different arrangements); and liquids taking the shape of their containers does not imply that atoms do. They think of atoms/molecules as little homogeneous parts of macroscopic objects to which they overextend macroscopic properties (i.e., hotness, squishiness, hardness, being solid or liquid, being static, etc.). This is one of the most robust misconceptions about atoms in the literature (Andersson, 1990; Ben-Zvi et al., 1986; Johnson, 1998a, 2000).

Failing to differentiate the properties of atoms and macroscopic properties of materials deeply affects students' understanding of physical transformations. If atoms and molecules have all the properties of macroscopic matter, then they themselves change during phase changes. For example, many students say that molecules change size and weight upon heating and during phase change, liquefy during melting and dissolution, and disappear when liquids boil (Griffiths & Preston, 1992; Lee et al., 1993).

Undoubtedly, a naïve realist epistemology and a lack of knowledge about models are at the root of the overextension of macroscopic properties to atoms and molecules: If at a macroscopic level materials have certain properties, then atoms themselves are that way, too. However, this is not the only cause of overextension. As in the case of the structure of matter, students are not given content information about atomic and molecular bonds that would help them understand how, for example, materials can be flexible without being made of flexible atoms or melt without individual atoms becoming liquid.

The relation between heat and atoms presents the same problems, with an added ontological challenge. In physics, heat is the energy exchanged by objects at different temperatures. For students, it is a (usually immaterial) entity, existing *in* matter, with the intrinsic property of hotness. This concept offers no explanation for why substances melt and boil when heat is added to them. Moreover, after being taught that "everything in the world" is made of atoms, many students infer that there are heat atoms and cold atoms, or that atoms are hot and cold (Wiser, 1986). For students to understand and accept the scientific account of heating and phase change at the atomic-molecular level, they need to be given an account for object-sense interaction so that they understand how hotness can arise from atomic motion. Wiser and Amin (2001) have found that a simple explanation of how atoms interact with thermal skin detectors to cause brain signals interpreted as hotness helped students to make an ontological distinction between heat (as objective molecular energy) and hotness (as a perceptual property in the perceiver's mind).

Color presents still greater pedagogical challenges because it is a purely perceptual property. Atoms are neither flexible nor blue, but groups of atoms are flexible, whereas groups of atoms are not blue. Properties such as fluidity, hardness, and flexibility are perceptual properties but they are also inherent physical properties of materials, which have objective manifestations in the interactions between objects. Moreover, students can use their macroscopic intuitions to grasp that less tightly bound atoms or molecules imply a more flexible material and underlie melting. The conceptual change involved in understanding that those properties are properties of groups of atoms, not of individual atoms, is not as radical as for hotness and color. Color is particularly difficult because the physical phenomenon of light reflection and absorption by groups of atoms and the perceptual mechanism involved in color perception are both complex.

Understanding what a chemical transformation is and how it differs from a physical transformation is difficult to achieve for the reasons just reviewed. At the core of understanding the nature of chemical reactions and accounting for the changes in appearance they create is grasping their emergent nature, differentiating and relating perceptual properties and physical ones, and having a concept of bonds. Atoms are conserved, but they are rearranged into different molecules, and it is the new spatial arrangement that underlie changes in color, density, texture, and so on. Without that knowledge, students infer that what is happening at the macroscopic level is happening to the atoms and molecules themselves — for example, when iron rusts, atoms of iron get covered with rust.

Moreover, understanding the difference between physical and chemical transformations requires the distinction between atom and molecule and between intra- and intermolecular forces. In phase change, molecules are conserved and heat affects the strength of the intermolecular forces, while in chemical reactions, molecules are not conserved but atoms are. Most students do not make these distinctions and will often believe, for example, that water molecules break down into hydrogen and oxygen when water boils (Osborne & Freyberg, 1985). A perhaps subtler consequence of students' epistemological shortcomings and lack of information about atomic and molecular forces is their difficulty in understanding chemical reactions as dynamic interactions between molecules. In keeping with a "mixing" view of chemical reactions at the macroscopic level, some students describe molecules produced in chemical reaction as concatenating without affecting each other (Pozo, 2001).

Summary of the Epistemological, Ontological, and Macrosocopic Knowledge that (would) Make the Atomic-molecular Theory Meaningful

Mastering the atomic-molecular theory requires epistemological, ontological, and macroscopic knowledge that, for many students, is not in place by the time the theory is presented to them — nor is it acquired as they are studying it. Epistemologically, students need to understand the nature and function of scientific models — that their elements are different from the entities they account for, their value is in their explanatory power, they represent hypotheses and are revisable. Students also need to realize the ontological distinction between perceptual and physical properties and to understand how they are linked, rather than treat the perceptual properties of matter from a naïve realist point of view. This more advanced epistemology and new ontological distinction are the basis on which an understanding of emergent properties can be built: Atoms invisible to the naked eye can form visible matter with physical and perceptual properties they themselves do not have.

The relation between the macroscopic theory of matter and the atomic-molecular model is bidirectional—for the latter to account for the former, they have to be understood each in their own right and in compatible ways. This does not mean that the atomic-molecular theory cannot be taught before students have a complete scientific theory of matter at the macroscopic level; in fact, we will argue it should. Obviously, some macroscopic understanding of matter must be in place for the atomic model to be a model of matter. But some aspects of the macroscopic theory (e.g., the idea of chemical reaction, substance, compound and mixtures, as well as a full appreciation of the material nature of gases) take their meanings from the atomic-molecular model and thus are better taught after students have had some exposure to it. (This claim is not uncontroversial and will be developed below.) How to orchestrate macroscopic and nanoscopic teachings to create a learning progression between those two points is a crucial issue that has received little attention. Should students have a rich and solid macroscopic understanding of matter, measurement, and models before atoms are introduced? Or would an early curriculum about atoms contribute to this macroscopic and epistemological understanding, and perhaps avoid (some) prevalent misconceptions about atoms and molecules? These issues can only be explored and settled on the basis of long-term teaching studies. We suspect that multiple learning trajectories are possible but surmise that they will share several important features: The elementary curriculum will have a strong emphasis on developing the macroscopic concepts of matter, weight, volume and density as they pertain to solids and liquids; on a progressively finer grained compositional view of matter; and on measurement, model building, and the distinction between perceptual and objective properties. The idea that matter has structure might be introduced early or late in the curriculum but in a manner consistent with students' macroscopic concepts at the time. It will lead to (if introduced early) or consist of (if introduced later) a particulate[4] model that will include the concepts of unchangeable particles, existing in the vacuum and held by bonds of varying strength. This model will be the basis for the atomic-molecular theory, which itself will be the basis on which to study chemical reactions, substances, compounds and mixtures. Students will be actively involved in developing and/or assessing compositional and particulate models in explanatory contexts (e.g., differences between material kinds and phase changes).

In the last two sections of this paper, we review some teaching interventions that support our view and propose a learning progression that incorporates the features just discussed.

WHAT CONCEPTUAL CHANGES SHOULD BE WORKED
ON IN ELEMENTARY SCHOOL?

In the previous sections we have shown that the scientific theory of matter, both at the macroscopic and atomic level, is far removed from everyday experience and challenges everyday epistemological and ontological assumptions and we have highlighted the many kinds of conceptual changes needed to develop it. In this section, we review both conceptual and empirical arguments for the importance of developing *a robust and mutually supportive set* of macroscopic, ontological, and epistemological understandings in elementary school to provide an appropriate foundation for learning about the atomic-molecular theory in later years.

Overview of Conceptual Changes in Restructuring Macroscopic Concepts and Why They are Important

Table 8.1 provides an overview of some of the important understandings for students to develop during the elementary school years and the kinds of conceptual changes they involve. These changes include: (a) extending and restructuring their macroscopic concepts of weight, size, material kind, and matter so that they are now inter-related and based on objective (measurable) properties and support an understanding of conservation of matter, weight, and material kind across a range of transformations; (b) developing their epistemological understanding of the role of measurement, models, and argument in theory building; and (c) changing their ontological commitments through coalescing solids, liquids, and gases as forms of matter and distinguishing objective from sensory-based properties.

Perception-based concepts do not provide a framework that allows developing either macroscopic or atomic understanding of matter. If matter is something that can be seen, felt, and touched, and if felt weight is central to the concept of weight, then gases are immaterial and weightless and belong to a different ontological kind from solids and liquids. Moreover, the notion that atoms, which are too small to see and feel, are the constituents of matter, is ultimately incoherent. Similarly, such perception-based concepts of weight and matter do not permit students to differentiate weight and density or to understand the conservation of weight across decomposition and phase change. Further, if models are judged by their match with surface appearance rather than explanatory force or ability to represent key relations, then neither the decompositional models of measurement (in which one subdivides continuous magnitudes into unseen identical units) and of matter (in which one subdivides a sample into unseen identical, arbitrarily small pieces) nor the atomic-molecular model of matter are prima facie good models of objects and materials.

In contrast, if students' understanding of measurement and models allow them to conceive of weight and volume as objective, extensive properties and to visualize decomposing matter into tiny pieces that continue to exist even if they are not directly detectable by the senses, then their models of weight and volume can be linked to a compositional model of matter, producing the understanding that any piece of matter, however small, has weight and occupies space. These students also have the basis for coordinating weight and volume in a concept of density, for determining that gases are material and for investigating conservation of matter across a variety of transformations. If they know that matter takes up space and has weight, they can be puzzled by phenomena where weight is conserved but volume changes (e.g., thermal expansion, phase changes). This helps motivate the idea that matter is composed of discrete particles separated by empty space, paving the way for the atomic model. With sound macroscopic understandings of matter, weight, and material kind, they have firm enough expectations to be

TABLE 8.1
Overview of Key Conceptual Changes in Elementary School Years

Key Change	General Description
Changes in concept of material kind	Developing understanding of material kind as a dense causal nexus used to explain some properties of objects; moving from perception-based understanding of material kinds (and their properties) to having an understanding of material kinds as fundamental constituents that maintain their identity across decomposition and phase change and that have objective and measurable characteristic properties (such as density, boiling points); beginning to sort out reliability of properties in identifying materials (e.g., melting and boiling points are more reliable than surface perceptual properties); using multiple criteria, including objective properties and transformation history to trace continuity and discontinuity of material kinds across various transformations.
Changes in concepts of physical quantities	Moving from perception-based understanding of physical quantities to more objective (and differentiated) set of concepts, grounded in measurement and inter-related in a theory of matter (e.g., all matter has weight and takes up space; the weight of an object is the sum of the weight of its parts and a function of its volume and the density of the material it is made of); differentiating weight and density, and length, area, surface area, and volume; developing a sound epistemological understanding of the importance of measurable quantities in science, instead of relying on sense impressions; developing an explicit theory of measure (e.g., understanding attribute-unit relations, need for identical units, use of fractional units and zero point), ability to measure weight, volume; understanding measurement error and what makes a good measurement.
Changes in concept of matter	Developing general concept of matter as causal nexus; moving from perception-based understanding of matter as something you can see, feel, and touch (that can include solids and liquids, but excludes small objects and gases) to understanding matter as fundamental constituent that has weight and volume (that can now include solids, liquids, and gases as forms of matter, and hence all of the same ontological kind); developing understanding that matter and weight are conserved across a wide variety of transformations, although volume and density can change.
Changes in concept of models	Moving from resemblance-based understanding of models as little pictures, replicas, or scale models to more abstract understanding of explanatory models that can be used as reasoning tools and that capture important relationships. Change involves making a distinction between explanation and thing explained; acknowledging emergent properties; explanatory force replaces looks like as criterion for evaluating models.

puzzled by phenomena that can motivate distinguishing chemical from physical change. For example, why under some conditions can materials be combined in any proportion and produce a material with physical properties that are the averages of the properties of its components, while in other conditions materials combine in fixed proportions and produce materials with novel properties?

Evidence that Elementary School Students Can Develop Relevant Macroscopic and Epistemological Understandings

For a long time it had been assumed that developing these macroscopic and epistemological understandings was out of reach of elementary school students because they required abstract "formal operational thought." Elementary school children were assumed to be concrete thinkers, so that their instruction should be primarily piecemeal and factual, laying the observation base for later theorizing in the upper grades. Hence, measurement was taught as a set of procedures to be learned and mastered, not tied to theory development or the solving of important intellectual puzzles. Similarly, students were simply *told* that solids, liquids, and gases were types of matter and that all matter was composed of atoms rather than engaged in active theorizing about the nature of matter and materials that would allow these statements to make sense.

There is now, however, overwhelming evidence that traditional elementary and middle school science instruction (with its emphasis either on cookbook activities, unguided discovery, or didactic instruction) is a resounding failure in building a base for later learning. For example, few middle school students think matter has weight and volume (Smith, 2007; Stavy, 1991), know how to measure weight and volume (Smith, 2007), and differentiate weight and density (Hewson, 1986; Smith et al., 1997). In addition, exposed to science curricula that treat knowledge as unproblematic facts, few students have any appreciation of the coherent nature of scientific theories or of the role of ideas, models, symbolization, and cycles of hypothesis testing in their creation (Carey, Evans, Honda, Jay, & Unger, 1989; Driver, Leach, Millar, & Scott, 1996; Grosslight, Unger, Jay, & Smith, 1991). The fact that students often make little or no progress in developing these understandings with increasing age demonstrates that these understandings do not simply magically appear with unaided "development." Hence, the "let's wait until they are developmentally ready" strategy of science teaching is fundamentally flawed.

We now know these approaches fail because they both over- and underestimate the capacities of elementary school students. They *overestimate* the extent to which students' initial concepts and model-building efforts match those of scientists, and thus the extent to which students can internalize the statements and procedures being taught without being given experiences that enable them to develop a framework in which they make sense. Developing this framework is based on the capacity to engage in symbolization, model-based reasoning, and argumentation (in socially supported instructional contexts) right from the start, a capacity that is severely *underestimated* and therefore ignored in elementary school curricula.

Acher and Arca's work suggests that very young students are capable of developing initial models of the structure of matter when such models are scaffolded by their teacher (Acher & Arca, in press; Acher, Arca, & Sanmarti, 2007). In their studies, 4- to 9-year-olds model materials and their physical transformations via drawing but also via role playing, verbal descriptions, and gestures. The guiding themes of those activities are structure, (large quantity of) discrete parts, bonds between the parts, and the idea that the strength of a structure depends on its bonds. Children start by representing the visible structure of different materials, then are asked to imagine and represent smaller grain structures, and end up modeling phase changes as changes in the strength of bonds. This learning progression allows the construction of progressively more complex models of materials, drawing on children's ability to impose an imaginary discrete structure on a visible continuum as well as their ability to think of structures systematically by thinking of parts and relations among parts. Although Arca and Acher provide evidence of young children's abilities to model and reflect on unseen entities, the curriculum as a whole has not been implemented with a single cohort, nor has it been submitted to systematic assessment. It also raises a large number of questions about its long-term consequences that have not yet been explored: for example, how it interacts with the development of other concepts (e.g., weight and density), what epistemological lessons it teaches, and whether it prevents the development of misconceptions about atoms later on (when concepts of atoms and molecules are explicitly taught).

A number of researchers have taken on the challenge of trying to improve elementary or middle school students' macroscopic understandings of matter, weight, volume, or density by designing innovative curriculum units (Lehrer et al., 2001; Raghavan & Glaser, 1995; Smith, Snir, & Grosslight, 1992; Smith et al., 1997). Although the focus and methods of these curriculum units vary, none relies on simple didactic instruction or unguided inquiry. Rather, a common feature is the curriculum developers' awareness of students' initial views and their sustained attempts to engage students in constructing new representations or models that help them investigate and account for key phenomena. The fact that students make much more progress with these innovative curriculum materials than traditional ones is an important piece of evidence that students' conceptual difficulties can be addressed with more appropriate science instruction.

For example, Smith and her colleagues have designed curriculum units that engage students with thinking about the properties of matter and with building macroscopic models that visually depict the inter-relation among volume, mass, and density of materials (Smith et al., 1997). These units work simultaneously on several fronts: (a) raising explicit questions about the nature and purpose of model-building (especially trying to highlight the importance of a model showing relationships among variables rather than just depicting how something looks); (b) engaging students in reasoning about properties that all matter shares and with thought experiments that challenge them to consider what happens in extreme cases (such as when something is divided into smaller and smaller pieces that get vanishingly small) to foster a coherent and consistent way of reasoning about matter across a wide range of situations; (c) developing students' ability to quantify and measure weight and volume so as to clarify the extensive nature of both physical quantities; and (d) having students construct visual models with distinct yet integrated representations of volume, weight, and density that allow them not only to differentiate among these quantities but also to realize that density is a characteristic property of materials.

This model-based conceptual change approach has been consistently effective in helping seventh- and eighth-grade students from a variety of backgrounds (suburban, inner city) develop more abstract conceptions of matter (matter has mass and takes up space, gases are material); reconceptualize weight as an objective, quantifiable property of matter; and make progress in differentiating weight and density as fundamentally different kinds of magnitudes (Smith, 2007; Smith et al., 1994, 1997). It has been found to be much more effective in bringing about conceptual change than the standard Introductory Physical Science curriculum that addresses these topics (Smith et al., 1997).

An alternative, more mathematically-based approach to helping students construct a concept of density was reported by Lehrer, Schauble, Strom, and Pligge (2001).[5] Their intervention with fifth graders in modeling material kind was part of a much larger sustained multi-year collaboration with participating teachers in which they worked to "reorient mathematics and science instruction around the construction, evaluation, and revision of models" (p. 39). In earlier grades, they had worked on a variety of "big ideas," including developing a theory of measure, as first applied to measuring length and then later area (Lehrer, Jaslow, & Curtis, 2003). In this earlier work students were encouraged to create their own nonstandard units and work through features of a "good" measurement before moving on to more standard units. In the process, they learned important ideas about units (e.g., the idea of iteration, identical unit, covering the measurement space, partitioning units to form fractional units) and about scale (e.g., the importance of a zero-point, the need for appropriate precision, and inherent limitations of measurement in accuracy). In their semester-long work in fifth grade, students first learned to extend these ideas of measure to tackle the problem of developing measures of volume. They next worked with families of magnified rectangles to develop a mathematical expression for "same, but bigger": straight line graphs through the origin showing the ratios of the two sides. Finally, students explored a variety of objects of different volume and material, ultimately testing their conjecture that there might be "families of materials." As part of these investigations, students built on their previous understandings of the measure of volume and the mathematics of similarity. They also constructed a measure of weight, made weight and volume measurements of different size samples of different materials, and wrestled with problems of the reliability and accuracy of measurements (especially when they had to use water displacement methods to estimate the volumes of irregular solids). Finally, they plotted their data about the weight and volume of different objects on a coordinate graph. Their prior work with graphing families of similar rectangles led them to expect that each family of materials might be represented with a line of different slope; when their data points for objects made of the same material did not fall exactly on one line, they discussed the epistemological issue of why this might be and even considered which line would be best to draw through the obtained data points.

Significantly, these sustained investigations using graphical, algebraic, and tabular representations led these fifth-grade students to the conclusion that materials varied in their weight/size ratios, that is, density. Further, they were able to use these insights to make and test novel predictions. This is particularly noteworthy since Rowell and Dawson (1983) had earlier shown that the ability to use straight-line graphical relations to infer the constancy of density eluded most ninth-grade students. Clearly, elementary school children have a greater capacity for mathematical abstraction than is typically acknowledged or encouraged with standard math and science instruction. Further, using mathematical models is an important abstraction tool that aids in the development of science concepts like density.

These cases nicely illustrate some general principles of how conceptual change occurs. Conceptual change occurs in the context of multiple (iterative) cycles of model construction, testing, and revision, which involves both processes of conceptual elaboration and more major restructuring. Although model construction and testing are always constrained by students' initial conceptual and epistemological understandings, students can be led to use conceptual resources and symbolic tools from inside and outside a given domain to represent new organizing relationships if scaffolding is provided by instructional contexts. More specifically, the development of young children's *mathematical* insights and reasoning may play a much more powerful role in enabling the conceptual restructuring of children's physical concepts of matter, weight, volume, and density than many conceptual change researchers have realized.

Evidence that Developing these Understandings Leverages Later Change

Within each of these curricula, there are iterative cycles of model-building, with new insights building off prior ones and leveraging later change. But what is the evidence that this macroscopic and epistemological teaching leverages better understanding of the particulate theory of matter itself? Although there is not yet as much direct empirical evidence on this point, two findings are provocative and indicate that this issue merits further investigation.

First, there is direct evidence that developing a macroscopic understanding of matter (as having weight and taking up space) along with understanding weight and volume as objective measurable properties enables students to come to see gases as material (Smith, 2007; Smith et al., 1997). Given that exploring the behavior of gases is commonly used in developing a particulate theory (see next section, and the work of Nussbaum, 1997), it is critical that students first conceptualize gases as material.

Second, developing an explicit belief that matter has weight and takes up space and differentiating weight and density sets the stage for students to be deeply puzzled by a variety of phenomena in which weight is conserved but volume changes. For example, how can heating a brass ball change its volume but not its weight? How is it possible that when water and alcohol are mixed, the volume of the mixture is less than the sum of the volumes of water and alcohol, although weight is conserved? These phenomena challenge students' belief that matter is fundamentally continuous and thus can be used to introduce the idea that matter is particulate. Significantly, research indicates that fifth- and sixth-grade students who have developed a sound macroscopic understanding of matter, weight, volume, and density were more likely to find these phenomena puzzling than those who have not. They were also more likely to evaluate models based on their capacity to explain phenomena rather than resemble them and hence were more likely to find particulate explanations of these phenomena compelling (Snir et al., 2003).

Further, in a teaching study with seventh graders in which these phenomena were used to introduce the idea that matter is particulate, a strong relationship was found between students' long-term internalization of the assumptions of the particulate model, their macroscopic understanding of matter and physical quantities, and their epistemological understanding of the particulate theory as an explanatory model. Students who remembered and used the basic tenets of the atomic-molecular theory six months later to provide explanations of both taught and novel phenomena were those who had a sound macroscopic understanding of matter and regarded it as a good explanatory model (Snir et al., 2003).

WHEN AND HOW SHOULD THE ATOMIC-MOLECULAR THEORY BE TAUGHT?

Overview of Conceptual Changes Involved in Learning about Atoms, Molecules, and Chemical Reactions: Ontological and Epistemological Challenges

Mastering the atomic-molecular theory involves developing a large network of related concepts and beliefs that pose closely intertwined ontological and epistemological challenges. It rests on a sound macroscopic foundation, which it deepens with its new nanoscopic level. At the same time, it is motivated by macroscopic phenomena that can only be understood superficially, if at all, without it. Thus, new concepts are being constructed simultaneously at the nanoscopic and macroscopic levels, requiring a solid understanding of model-building.

Atoms are strange "objects": They are the sole constituents of matter without having most of its macroscopic properties, and those they have may be the most counterintuitive, given their size — volume, weight, and mass. Moreover, they have properties uniquely their own: They are held together by electro-magnetic forces, move at very high speed, and exist in the vacuum; there are only about 100 different ones, whereas the number of materials surrounding us is practically infinite; and they are never created or destroyed (in physical and chemical reactions).

To make sense of these ontologically counterintuitive entities, students need objective (rather than perceptually-based) concepts of matter, weight, and volume in order for atoms to be understood as the constituents of matter. Believing experimental evidence for the existence of atoms and molecules requires modeling abilities in addition to objective macroscopic concepts, since such evidence is indirect and derived from measurement of macroscopic events.[6] For example, taking the decrease in volume when alcohol and water are mixed as supporting a discontinuous model of matter requires a scientific understanding of weight and volume and the ability to evaluate competing models of matter in terms of how well they can account for these observations.

On the other hand, as we argue in the next section, some concepts such as substance, compound, mixture, and chemical reaction cannot be solely understood at the macroscopic level and thus require some prior understanding of atoms and molecules. But if students are to learn new concepts via modeling, that is, by relating atomic models to experimental observations, they need categories of macroscopic phenomena (e.g., phase change vs. chemical reaction) that will support their model-building. In other words, they have to construct atomic-molecular explanations for phenomena that initially have at best only shallow meaning at the macroscopic level. Thus, the epistemological knowledge required at this stage, although not fundamentally different from that involved in developing a scientific understanding of matter at the macroscopic level, is more crucial and more sophisticated. The disparity between observed phenomena and theoretical models is much greater and the interplay between macroscopic and nanoscopic accounts, more complex. Moreover, the thinking involved in understanding the relation between the properties of atoms and molecules and the macroscopic properties of material kinds and of physical and chemical transformations requires a major shift from the "process" type of causal reasoning students are familiar with to one that acknowledges emergent properties and constraint-based interactions (Chi & Roscoe, 2002).

The Value of Intermediate Models

It is premature to propose a detailed learning progression for these conceptual and epistemological changes for lack of enough (comparative) experimental evidence of how understanding unfolds under different conditions of instruction over long periods of time. Johnson (1998c) notes that students' conceptual development is usually assessed in the context of teaching studies, so that it is hard to disentangle "inevitable" conceptual evolution from the effects of specific teaching.[7] Our position is slightly different. Any conceptual change is the result of teaching, formal or informal, so that the issue is not to disentangle "inevitable" from curriculum-specific change but rather to compare the effects of different curricula. The goal is to determine effective orders in which to present different concepts, experiments, models, and epistemological teachings, so that, at each stage, new information can be assimilated into students' existing framework to further their knowledge in a way suitable for tackling the next part of the curriculum. In the rest of this section, we apply those considerations to one specific issue — the merits, or lack thereof, of "intermediate" models of the structure of matter: Are students' models scientific models? Are they useful stepping stones? Should some of them be taught explicitly?

Based on his extensive three-year longitudinal study of seventh- to ninth-grade students, in which students were introduced to ideas of substance versus mixture and chemical reaction versus phase change at the macroscopic level, and particulate explanations of these phenomena, Johnson (1998a) identified a series of models of matter held by students. We will consider the major ones here: Model X in which matter is continuous and particles are not mentioned; Model A (Particles-in-Matter model; particles do not constitute matter); Model B (a particulate model in which matter is made of spaced particles, and only of those particles, and in which the particles have all the macroscopic properties of a substance, including its state); and Model C (the particulate model taught to the students: a substance is made of particles, specific to the substances they constitute and are held together by different strength attraction forces that account for the three states of matter). None of the students initially conceptualized matter as particulate and none progressed to the taught model directly. A little more than half progressed directly to Model B (in which particles are either solid, liquid, or gas), and the majority of those then progressed to Model C (in which particles are the same in the three states). In contrast, of those who first developed a Particles-in-Matter model (Model A), less than half achieved a particulate model (B or C, in which particles constitute matter) by the end of the study. Only two of those learned the target model (Model C).

These results support our earlier claim that the Particles-in-Matter model (Model A) is not inevitable. There is also no evidence that it is a useful stepping stone, since students who did *not* develop it were far more likely to end up mastering the model being taught (Model C) and to do so more quickly. Johnson does not fully explore the reasons that some students develop Model A while others go directly to a particulate model (Model B). We conjecture that students with more limited (perception-based) understandings of matter and epistemologies that privilege everyday observation over measurement and modeling may be the ones most vulnerable to develop these misconceptions when exposed to teaching about atoms. Consistent with the importance of epistemological understandings, Johnson mentions that Model A students did not refer to their model when explaining phenomena, nor did they integrate information received (e.g., forces) into it. The results also support our claim that forces between particles can (and should) be introduced early in instruction in order to make particulate explanations more coherent and understandable to students. Johnson notes that his students made widespread (and cogent) use of interparticular forces in their explanations of state and phase change. Whether Johnson's curriculum was more effective than a traditional one is likely but cannot be decided without quantitative comparisons with a control group of students taught in a more traditional way.

As to Model B (in which particles are either solid, liquid, or gas-like), some researchers (Chomat, Larcher, & Meheut, 1988; Pozo & Gomez Crespo, 2005) argue that it has none of the epistemological characteristics of a scientific model. Most fundamentally, it is not hypothetico-deductive (and therefore not revisable) because it is the macroscopic appearance of objects that accounts for its particulate description (this is liquid therefore it is made of liquid particles), not the other way around (it is liquid because, at this temperature, its particles have weak bonds). We find it useful to distinguish between two questions — whether students' models have characteristics of scientific models and whether those models are useful stepping stones for the atomic-molecular model. Model B appears to be a stepping stone: In Johnson's study, the majority of the students who reached the target Model C did so via Model B. Moreover, the interview protocols suggest that envisioning phase-specific particles separated in space allowed students to adopt the idea of interparticular forces and different motions and to use those notions in their account of states of matter, while hanging on to the idea that particles are, literally, little pieces of macroscopic matter. At some point, some of them must have understood that different forces were enough to account for the different states and that state-specific particles were redundant, although finer-grained interviews would be needed to ascertain the process by which students move from Model B to Model C. Thus, Model B might not be scientific, but it is revisable "cognitively" in the sense that it scaffolds learning the (more scientific) particulate model.

With unchangeable, discretely spaced particles that characterize a specific material and that are held together by forces (strong in solids, less strong in liquids, very weak in gases), Model C represents an important part of the content of the atomic model and gives a parsimonious account of differences between materials, phase changes, and dissolving. Most importantly, it allows students to understand that (and why) gases are material and unifies the ontology of solids, liquids, and gases. Epistemologically, it embodies the distinction between elements of a model and the observable phenomena to be explained, and, more specifically, that the macroscopic properties of substances are explained by the structure of collections of particles, not by the properties of an individual one. It is revisable: In the context of chemical reactions, the notion of particle can be differentiated between molecule and atom and the notion of interparticular forces between intra-and intermolecular forces that are part of a full-fledged atomic-molecular model. It is likely that while Model C students already know that particles are not modified in phase changes, and therefore differentiate to some extent the ontology of macroscopic matter and of particles, they still think of them as tiny solid pieces. Introducing the notion that molecules are composed of atoms and are created and destroyed in chemical reactions should make the idea of atoms as little pieces of macroscopic matter less plausible. Similarly, students who, while adopting Model B or C, believed there was "air" between the particles, might find it easier to reject this notion when heavy emphasis is placed on chemical bonds, which might make the idea of vacuum less "unbelievable." We therefore agree with Johnson that Model C may be viewed as an intermediate model, scaffolding the transition to a more elaborate version of the atomic-molecular theory.

In a study with ninth graders, Chomat, Larcher, and Meheut (1988) taught a particulate model very similar to Model C, but their emphasis was on explicit modeling and model revision. Their students were asked to build and evaluate progressively more sophisticated models to account for progressively more complicated phenomena. At the end of the intervention, the majority of students showed a solid understanding of the epistemological enterprise and significant gains in their application of the basic model to the different phenomena and macroscopic understanding (e.g., the conservation of mass during thermal dilation and phase change). (Between 75% and 95% of students answered different types of questions correctly.) These findings show that teaching Model C can help students develop nanoscopic, macroscopic, and epistemological knowledge consistent with the scientific view. It also supports Johnson's claim that introducing different aspects of the atomic-molecular model progressively, giving students experience with phenomena supported by each intermediate model, makes good pedagogical sense.

Other studies show that younger students can use discretely spaced particle models (similar to Model C) explanatorily, with appropriate instructional scaffolding and support. For example, Lee et al. (1993) found that over half of their sixth-grade students could use a particulate model to explain conservation of mass and material kind across phase change, thermal expansion, and dissolving. Snir et al. (2003) found fifth- through seventh-grade students (with sound macroscopic understanding of matter) could use such models to explain the loss of volume without loss of mass, when alcohol is mixed with water, the expansion of a metal ball on heating, and why materials combine in fixed proportions in chemical reactions. Nussbaum (1997) has shown that seventh-grade students can use these models to explain many aspects of the behavior of gases, including its compressibility.

In summary, we believe that teaching a particulate model like Johnson's Model C in the context of physical transformations and the nature of gases is a productive way to lead to the atomic-molecular model, especially if such teaching includes explicit epistemological instruction. It is a way to divide and conquer ontological and epistemological challenges: Those involved in learning Model C are less daunting than if the atomic-molecular model had to be learned "from scratch" (especially if Model B is developed spontaneously and acts as scaffold). Those involved in moving from Model C to the atomic-molecular model itself are difficult, but build on, rather than undo, those already mastered. However, comparative studies involving other sequences need to be conducted to validate this hypothesis empirically.

When to Teach the Atomic-Molecular Model

Two main reasons have been advanced for delaying teaching the atomic-molecular theory until (late) high school. One is the complexity of conceptual changes needed to understand it; the other is that it should be motivated by extensive experience with macroscopic phenomena, most notably chemical reactions (Fensham, 1994). We believe this position is misguided for several reasons. First, with the proper elementary school curriculum, students entering middle school could have the macroscopic and epistemological knowledge necessary to develop an intermediate particulate model, which captures some of the tenets of the atomic-molecular theory and can serve as a stepping stone for further learning in high school. Moreover, many topics that are seen as central in elementary and middle school instruction (e.g., phase change and water cycle, the nature of gases, and what makes material kinds different from each other) remain superficially understood without the atomic-molecular theory and motivate learning it. Third, chemical reactions make little sense without the atomic-molecular theory and thus cannot motivate it; on the other hand, they can motivate revising an intermediate particulate model. We now consider those reasons in more detail.

Some proponents of the "delay teaching the atomic-molecular theory" view may be influenced by the Piagetian tradition and believe that the atomic-molecular model is beyond the reach of middle school students because it requires hypothetico-deductive thinking and the coordination of three levels of description — macroscopic, atomic-molecular, and symbolic. This mistakenly assumes that "developmental readiness" is independent from "instructional history" and underestimates young students' capacity for abstract thinking. We have offered experimental evidence in the previous sections that, with proper instruction, elementary school students can undergo conceptual changes and achieve a macroscopic understanding of matter consistent with the scientific view. Middle school students can achieve a productive understanding of a particulate model, which embodies some of the basic tenets of the atomic-molecular model. Moreover, there is ample evidence that even elementary school students can develop a sound epistemological understanding of modeling, measurement, and aspects of hypothetico-deductive reasoning (see, for example, Lehrer & Schauble, 2000).

Many educators worry about the meaningfulness of the atomic-molecular theory when it is first introduced (e.g., Millar, 1990; Stocklmayer & Gilbert, 2002) and argue that it should be presented as answering questions (e.g., why is glass transparent) and explaining events relevant to students' everyday lives (e.g., cooking, medications), rather than more decontextualized laboratory experiments. As Hallden (1990) points out, scientific theories do not (easily) answer the questions students have in mind; everyday phenomena are often much harder to account for than carefully selected laboratory experiments. We agree that this is an important issue but do not see that teaching macroscopic chemistry first bears on it, for several reasons. Chemical reactions themselves are disconnected from everyday life; if students find them interesting, it is usually for their "magical" side, rather than because they raise important theoretical questions (DeVos & Verdonk, 1987; Harrison & Treagust, 2002). More importantly, we doubt that much can be understood about chemical reactions exclusively at the macroscopic level.

For example, the idea that the concepts of substance and element can emerge from patterns of chemical reactions at the macroscopic level, and later be used to give meaning to atoms and molecules (Johnstone, 1982) has little theoretical or experimental support. Although students initially make a distinction between "pure substances" and mixtures, the macroscopic criteria by which they make these distinctions are completely different from those used by chemists, as they rest more on perceptual appearance (pure substances look homogeneous, mixtures do not) and transformational history (pure substances are those found in nature, mixtures are a product of "mixing" things or artificial processes) rather than the macroscopic tests used by chemists (e.g., does it have a fixed boiling or melting point?). Johnson (2002) notes that the idea of pure substance made little sense to his students prior to being taught the atomic model, and, more importantly, that students who were told about "melting point test" did not think of using it to determine whether a chemical reaction has produced a new substance. They had no way of understanding *how* new substances would be produced in the first place. On the other hand, he found that learning about atoms and molecules greatly facilitated developing a concept of chemical substance as something whose identity is maintained across phase change, determined by its properties such as the temperature at which it melts and the manner in which it does so, and being part of chemical combinations and decompositions. In other words, it is not that atoms and molecules account for the concepts of substance, compound, mixture, and chemical change already in place, but rather that they allow students to construct those concepts. Moreover, chemical reactions cannot be understood without the knowledge that gases are material and therefore can react with solids and liquids; and, as we detail below, a particulate model is really needed to consolidate understanding that gases are material. Hence, this is an important case where learning about atoms and molecules is part of the solution, rather than part of the problem, and an important reason that it is important to develop some atomic-molecular understandings early.

A related pedagogical debate is about the context in which to introduce the atomic (or particulate) model — solids and liquids, or gases. Nussbaum (1985, 1997) and Fensham (1994) believe that the atomic model should be introduced in the context of gases because it is easier to believe that gases are made of tiny particles undetectable by the senses, in constant motion, and separated by a vacuum, than to believe the same thing about solids and liquids. However, Pozo and Gomez Crespo (2005) argue that students who adopt the atomic view for gases do so for the wrong epistemological and ontological reasons: They are actually overextending, by analogy, the perceptual properties of gases (which appear to move on their own and be "insubstantial") to atoms and then inferring that solids and liquids, which are substantial and don't move on their own, are not made of atoms (see also Knerl et al., 1998). Johnson (1998b) makes a similar point: it is not that students start with the notion that gases are matter (in the sense that solids are), accept that they are made of atoms, and then extend the atomic model to solids and liquids; rather, it is the atomic model itself that helps make sense of the idea that gases are material. Our own position is that it makes sense to start with a particulate model developed in the context of solids and liquids so that the model is clearly a model of *matter* (in both the student's and the scientist's sense) and then use the model in the context of evaporation and boiling to develop the material nature of gases. In support of this position, Snir et al. (2003) identified a variety of phenomena involving solids and liquids—for example, the loss of volume in the mixture of two (seemingly continuous) liquids, water and alcohol, or the expansion of a metal ball with heating—for which students found particulate explanations (and the idea of space between particles) especially compelling.

CONCLUSIONS

We have used research to establish students' conceptual states when they start learning about matter at the macroscopic level and when they start learning about the atomic-molecular model. We have also analyzed the conceptual difficulties posed by the atomic-molecular theory as it is traditionally taught. A variety of conceptual and epistemological changes are needed to bridge young children's initial understanding of matter and the atomic theory, most of them not facilitated by existing curricula. On the basis of those analyses, and a review of some innovative, successful teaching interventions, we have made the case for a learning progression in which knowledge about matter becomes progressively more scientific while remaining coherent. We assume that this learning progression will involve a number of intermediate constructions that will act as stepping stones but that many dead-ended misconceptions will be avoided.

In this learning progression, some tenets of the atomic-molecular model are in place relatively early (end of elementary school or beginning of middle school), in the rich but not full-fledged form of a particulate model and as part of a science curriculum which, from kindergarten on, imparts epistemological knowledge about measurement and models. The particulate model also allows students to develop a macroscopic understanding of matter consistent with the scientific view. Children working with this kind of curriculum would learn about matter in the context of solids and liquids first. Matter has weight and volume; it exists as different material kinds that differ in various ways, including density and melting point, and are conserved during melting and freezing. They would acquire a progressively finer-grained compositional model of matter, allowing them to think of (homogeneous) objects being constituted of a material kind all the way through, and supporting conservation of amount of matter and weight under certain transformations. They would then start exploring gases — for example, air, water vapor, sublimated iodine, and oxygen involved in rusting — using perception and weight measurements as evidence for their material nature. Existing research does not allow us to specify when or in what form to first introduce a particulate model (e.g., more or less didactically; early or late in elementary school; directly in a "Model C-like" form or as a progression of models about the visible, then microscopic, then nanoscopic structure of matter and its transformations). Also left unspecified, although of crucial importance, are the timetable for and links between specific macroscopic, epistemological, and particulate teaching that will ensure that students have the macroscopic understanding and epistemological resources that make models of matter meaningful and explanatory. In any case, by the beginning of middle school, students would be familiar with the scale and the invariance of particles[8] across phase change, the effects of heating and cooling on the bonds between them, and giving particulate accounts of differences between materials (density, hardness, melting point), thermal expansion, dissolving, melting and freezing, and the mixing of specific materials. The model could then be extended to account for evaporation and boiling and to strengthen students' understanding of the material nature of gases. The ontological differences between macroscopic samples, molecules, and atoms as well as the difference between elements, compounds and mixtures, between physical and chemical reactions (atoms are rearranged in chemical reactions, inter- and intramolecular forces are different), would be explored later in high school, in the context of chemical reactions.

One of the themes running through this proposed learning progression would be understanding the compositional nature of matter both at the macroscopic and nanoscopic level, as it is central to developing an understanding of its conservation and transformations. Envisioning an object as made of macroscopic "chunks" allows a first sense of conservation of amount of matter and weight in Piagetian tasks. Constructing a model of a sample as divisible into arbitrary small pieces supports conservation of amount of matter and weight and of material kind when a solid is ground, melted, or dissolved, giving it a broader scope and a deeper sense. Particulate models do the same thing for boiling and evaporation, and they give meaning to gases being matter. Finally, the atomic-molecular model explains the conservation of amount of matter and weight across chemical transformations while accounting for why substances are not always conserved. Thus, modeling is at the heart of learning about matter throughout the curriculum making epistemological teaching part and parcel of it.

Clearly, much research is needed to understand the ingredients of successful pedagogical approaches, including comparing the effectiveness of curricula targeting different learning trajectories. On the basis of the successful interventions we have reviewed, we predict that all successful curricula will integrate macroscopic, epistemological, and particulate teaching. They will also engage students in explaining phenomena and/or developing and assessing models to account for those phenomena. We also predict that, however successful the curriculum, it will involve students for multiple years, supporting Stavy's (1991) and Johnson's (1998c) plea to dispense with the "quick tell."

NOTES

1. "Traditional instruction" is in contrast to the kind of innovative curricula that we review later in this chapter. These curricula often differ in approach, scope, and epistemological focus rather than content goals per se.
2. This is true only in a gravitational field. However, the more general statement — all matter has mass — would be far less meaningful to students, given that the concept of mass is a difficult and late achievement.
3. This is a case of stepping stone — density will need to be revised as depending on temperature and state.
4. "Particulate" refers to a model that does not make the distinction between atom and molecule. However, as mentioned earlier, we believe that the term "particulate" should not be used pedagogically, as it suggests wrong scale and ontology to students.

5. This approach was also successfully used with 3rd graders (Lehrer, Strom, & Confrey, 2002).
6. Advanced technology (Scanning Tunneling Microscope or STM; Scanning Electron Microscopy or SEM; Atomic Force Microscopy or AFM) allows scientists and students to construct visualizations of matter at the atomic scale and provides powerful evidence for the existence of atoms. Some researchers are beginning to explore its usefulness in the teaching of middle school students (Margel, Eylon, & Schertz, 2004). However, whether one can rightfully claim that the images provided by this technology show "atoms" rather than being evidence for them is a complicated epistemological issue. Moreover, they do not provide evidence for other tenets of the theory, such as there being space between them not filled with matter, nor for the distinction between atomic and macroscopic properties.
7. "Inevitable" does not mean innately determined but rather the only way a concept can evolve given existing cognitive constraints and the kind of information typically received by students.
8. The meaning of "particle" should be explicitly distinguished from its everyday meaning, or particles should be called something else. See footnote 4.

REFERENCES

Acher, A., & Arca, M. (in press). Children's representations in modeling scientific knowledge construction. In C. Andersen, M. N. Scheuer, M. P. Perez Echeveerria, & E. Teubal (Eds.), *Representational systems and practices as learning tools in different fields of knowledge*. Rotterdam, The Netherlands: Sense Publishers.

Acher, A., Arca, M., & Sanmarti, N. (2007). Modeling as a teaching learning process for understanding materials: A case study in primary education. *Science Education, 91*, 398–418.

Andersson, B. (1990). Pupils' conceptions of matter and its transformations (age 12–16). *Studies in Science Education, 18*, 53–85.

Au, T. K-F. (1994). Developing an intuitive understanding of substance kinds. *Cognitive Psychology, 27*, 71–111.

Ault, C. R. Jr., Novak, J. D., & Gowin, D. B. (1984). Constructing Vee maps for clinical interviews on molecule concepts. *Science Education, 68*, 441–442.

Baillargeon, R. (2002). The acquisition of physical knowledge in infancy: A summary in eight lessons. In U. Goswami (Ed.), *Blackwell handbook of childhood cognitive development* (pp. 47–83). London: Blackwell.

Ben-Zvi, R., Eylon, R., & Silberstein, J. (1986). Is an atom of copper malleable? *Journal of Chemical Education, 63*, 64–66.

Bloom, P. (2000). *How children learn the meaning of words*. Cambridge, MA: The MIT Press.

Carey, S. (1991). Knowledge acquisition: Enrichment or conceptual change? In. S. Carey & R. Gelman (Eds.), *The epigenesis of mind* (pp. 257–291). Hillsdale, NJ: Erlbaum.

Carey, S., Evans, R., Honda, M., Jay, E., & Unger, C. (1989). "An experiment is when you try it and see if it works": A study of grade 7 students' understanding of the construction of scientific knowledge. *International Journal of Science Education, 11*, 514–529.

Chi, M. T., & Roscoe, D. (2002). The processes and challenges of conceptual change. In M. Limon & L. Mason (Eds.), *Reconsidering conceptual change: Issues in theory and practice* (pp. 3–27). Dordrecht/London: Kluwer.

Chomat, A., Larcher, C., & Meheut, M. (1988). Modele particulaire et activates de modelisation en class de quatrieme [Particulate models and modeling activities in a 9th grade classroom]. *Aster, 7*, 143–184.

DeVos, W., & Verdonk, A. H. (1987). A new road to reactions, Part 3: A substance and its molecules. *Journal of Chemical Education, 64*, 692–694.

Dickinson, D. K. (1987). The development of material kind. *Science Education, 71*, 615–628.

Dickinson, D. K. (1988). Learning names for materials: Factors constraining and limiting hypotheses about word meaning. *Cognitive Development, 3*, 15–35.

diSessa, A., & Sherin, B. (1998). What changes in conceptual change? *International Journal of Science Education, 20*, 1155–1191.

Driver, R., Leach, J., Millar, R., & Scott, P. (1996). *Young people's images of science*. Buckingham, UK: Open University Press.

Elkind, D. (1961). Children's discovery of conservation of mass, weight, and volume: Piaget replication study 2. *The Journal of Genetic Psychology*, *98*, 219–227.

Fallon, A. E., Rozin, P., & Pliner, P. (1984). The child's conception of food: The development of food rejections with special reference to disgust and contamination sensitivity. *Child Development*, *55*, 566–585.

Fensham, P. J. (1994). Beginning to teach chemistry. In P. Fensham, R. Gunstone, & R. White (Eds.), *The content of science: A constructivist approach to its teaching and learning* (pp. 14–28). London: Falmer Press.

Gelman, S., & Markman, E. (1987). Young children's inductions from natural kinds: The role of categories and appearances. *Child Development*, *58*, 1532–1541.

Gentner, D. (2003). Why we're so smart. In D. Gentner & S. Goldin-Meadow (Eds.), *Language in Mind: Advances in the study of language and thought* (pp. 195–235). Cambridge, MA: MIT Press.

Griffiths, A., & Preston, K. (1992). Grade 12 students' misconceptions relating to fundamental characteristics of atoms and molecules. *Journal of Research in Science Teaching, 29*, 611–628.

Grosslight, L., Unger, C., Jay, E., & Smith, C. (1991). Understanding models and their use in science: Conceptions of middle and high school students and experts. *Journal of Research in Science Teaching, 28*, 799–822.

Hallden, O. (1990). Questions asked in common sense contexts and in scientific contexts. In P. L. Lijnse, P. Licht, W. deVos, & A. J. Warloo (Eds.), *Relating macroscopic phenomena to microscopic particles* (pp. 119–130). Utrecht: The Netherlands University of Utrecht.

Harrison, A., & Treagust, D. (2002). The particulate nature of matter: Challenges in understanding the submicroscopic world. In J. Gilbert, O. de Jong, R. Justi, D. Treagust, & J. van Driel (Eds.), *Chemical education: Towards research-based practice* (Vol. 17, pp. 189–212). Dordrecht: Kluwer.

Hewson, M. G. (1986). The acquisition of scientific knowledge: analysis and representation of student conceptions concerning density. *Science Education*, *70*(2), 159–170.

Huntley-Fenner, G., Carey, S., & Solimando, A. (2002). Objects are individuals but stuff doesn't count: Perceptual rigidity and cohesiveness influences infants' representations of small numbers of discrete entities. *Cognition*, *85*, 203–221.

Johnson, P. (1998a). Progression in children's understanding of a "basic" particle theory: A longitudinal study. *International Journal of Science Education*, *20*, 393–412.

Johnson, P. (1998b). Children's understanding of changes of state involving the gas state, Part 1: Boiling water and the particle theory. *International Journal of Science Education*, *20*, 567–583.

Johnson, P. (1998c). Children's understanding of changes of state involving the gas state, Part 2: Evaporation and condensation below boiling point. *International Journal of Science Education*, *20*, 695–709.

Johnson, P. (2000). Children's understanding of substances, Part 1: Recognizing chemical change. *International Journal of Science Education*, *22*(7), 719–737.

Johnson, P. (2002). Children's understanding of substances, Part 2: Explaining chemical change. *International Journal of Science Education*, *24*(10), 1037–1054.

Johnstone, A. H. (1982). Macro- and microchemistry. *School Science Review*, *64*, 377–379.

Keil, F., & Lockhart, K. (1999). Explanatory understanding in conceptual development. In E. Scholnick, K. Nelson, S. Gelman, & P. Miller (Eds.), *Conceptual development: Piaget's legacy* (pp. 103–130). Mahwah, NJ: Erlbaum.

Knerl, D., Watson, R., & Glazar, S.A. (1998). Survey of research related to the development of the concept of "matter." *International Journal of Science Education*, *20*(3), 257–289.

Lee, O., Eichinger, D. C., Anderson, C. W., Berkheimer, G. D., & Blakeslee, T. D. (1993). Changing middle school students' conceptions of matter and molecules. *Journal of Research in Science Teaching*, *30*(3), 249–270.

Lehrer, R., Jaslow, L., & Curtis, C. (2003). Developing understanding of measurement in elementary grades. In D. Clements & G. Bright (Eds.), *The national council of teachers of mathematics: Yearbook on learning and teaching measurement* (pp. 100–121). Reston, VA: The National Council of Teachers of Mathematics.

Lehrer, R., & Schauble, L. (2000). Developing model-based reasoning in mathematics and science. *Journal of Applied Developmental Psychology*, *21*(1), 39–48.

Lehrer, R., Schauble, L., Strom, D., & Pligge, M. (2001). Similarity of form and substance: Modeling material kind. In S. Carver & D. Klahr (Eds.), *Cognition and instruction: Twenty-five years of progress* (pp. 39–74). Mahwah, NJ: Erlbaum.

Lehrer, R., Strom, D., & Confrey, J. (2002). Grounding metaphors and inscriptional resonance: Children's emerging understanding of mathematical similarity. *Cognition and Instruction*, *20*(3), 359–98.

Margel, H., Eylon, B.-S., & Schertz, Z. (2004). "We actually saw atoms with our own eyes": Conceptions and convictions in using the Scanning Tunneling Microscope in junior high school. *Journal of Chemical Education*, *81*, 558–566.

Millar, R. (1990). What use are particle ideas to children? In P. L. Lijnse, P. Licht, W. deVos, & A. J. Warloo (Eds.), *Relating macroscopic phenomena to microscopic particles* (pp. 283–293). Utrecht: The Netherlands University of Utrecht.

Nakhleh, M. B., Samarapungavan, A., & Saglam, Y. (2005). Middle school children's beliefs about matter. *Journal of Research in Science Teaching*, *42*, 581–612.

National Research Council. (1996). *National science education standards*. Washington, D.C.: National Academy Press.

Novick S., & Nussbaum, J. (1981). Pupils' understanding of the particulate theory of matter: A cross-age study. *Science Education*, *65*, 187–196.

Nussbaum, J. (1985). The particulate nature of matter in the gaseous phase. In R. Driver, E. Guesne, & A. Tiberghien (Eds.), *Children's ideas in science*. Philadelphia: Open University Press.

Nussbaum, J. (1997). History and philosophy of science and the preparation for constructivist teaching: The case of particle theory. In J. Mintzes, J. H. Wandersee, & J. D. Novak (Eds.), *Teaching science for understanding* (pp. 165–194). Boston, MA: Academic Press.

Osborne, R., & Freyberg, P. (1985). *Learning in science: The implications of children's science*. New Zealand: Heinemann.

Pfundt, H. (1981). The atom—The final link in the division process or the first building block? *Chimica Didactica*, *7*, 75–94.

Piaget, J., & Inhelder, B. (1974). *The child's construction of physical quantities*. London: Routledge and Kegan Paul.

Pozo, R. M. del (2001). Prospective teachers' ideas about the relationships between concepts describing the composition of matter. *International Journal of Science Education*, *23*, 353–371.

Pozo, J., & Gomez Crespo, M. (2005). The embodied nature of implicit theories: The consistency of ideas about the nature of matter. *Cognition and Instruction*, *23*(3), 351–387.

Raghavan, K., & Glaser, R. (1995). Model-based analysis and reasoning in science: The MARS curriculum. *Science Education*, *79*(1), 37–61.

Rowell, J. A., & Dawson, C. J. (1983). Laboratory counterexamples and the growth of understanding in science. *European Journal of Science Education*, *5*(2), 203–215.

Rozin, P. (1990). Development in the food domain. *Developmental Psychology*, *26*, 555–562.

Smith, C. (1993). [Weight/density interview data: 8th grade Earth Science sample]. Unpublished raw data.

Smith, C. (2003). [Weight/density interview data: Elementary school sample]. Unpublished raw data.

Smith, C. (2007). Bootstrapping processes in the development of students' commonsense matter theories: Using analogical mappings, thought experiments, and learning to measure to promote conceptual restructuring. *Cognition and Instruction,* *25*(4), 337–338.

Smith, C., Carey, S., & Wiser, M. (1985). On differentiation: A case study of the development of the concepts of size, weight, and density. *Cognition*, *21*(3), 177–237.

Smith, C., Grosslight, L., Davis, H., Unger, C., & Snir, J. (1994). *Using conceptual models to teach inner city students about density: The promise and the prerequisites*. Final report to the McDonnell Foundation.

Smith, C., Maclin, D., Grosslight, L., & Davis, H. (1997). Teaching for understanding: A comparison of two approaches to teaching students about matter and density. *Cognition and Instruction*, *15*(3), 317–393.

Smith, C., Snir, J., & Grosslight, L. (1992). Using conceptual models to facilitate conceptual change: The case of weight/density differentiation. *Cognition and Instruction*, *9*(3), 221–83.

Smith, C., Solomon, G., & Carey, S. (2005). Never getting to zero: Elementary school students' understanding of the infinite divisibility of matter and number. *Cognitive Psychology*, *51*, 101–140.

Snir, J., Smith, C., & Raz, G. (2003). Linking phenomena with competing underlying models: A software tool for introducing students to the particulate model of matter. *Science Education*, *87*, 794–830.

Soja, N., Carey, S., & Spelke, E. (1991). Ontological categories guide young children's inductions of word meaning: Object terms and substance terms. *Cognition*, *38*, 179–211.

Spelke, E. (1991). Physical knowledge in infancy: Reflections on Piaget's theory. In. S. Carey & R. Gelman (Eds.), *The epigenesis of mind* (pp. 257–291). Hillsdale, NJ: Erlbaum.

Stavy, R. (1991). Children's ideas about matter. *School Science and Curriculum*, *91*, 240–244.

Stocklmayer, S., & Gilbert, J. (2002). Informal chemical education. In J. K. Gilbert, O. De Jong, R. Justi, D. F. Treagust, & J. H. Van Driel (Eds.), *Chemical education: Towards research-based practice* (pp.143–164). Dordrecht, The Netherlands: Kluwer.

Vosniadou, S., & Brewer, W. F. (1992). Mental models of the earth: A study of conceptual change in childhood. *Cognitive Psychology*, *24*, 535–585.

Wellman, H. (1990). *The child's theory of mind.* Cambridge: MIT Press.

Wiser, M. (1986). *The differentiation of heat and temperature: An evaluation of the effect of micro-computer teaching on students' misconceptions.* Cambridge, MA: Educational Technology Center, Harvard Graduate School of Education.

Wiser, M., & Amin, T. G. (2001). "Is heat hot?" Inducing conceptual change by integrating everyday and scientific perspectives on thermal phenomena. In L. Mason (Ed.), *Instructional practices for conceptual change in science domains* [Special Issue]. *Learning & Instruction*, *11*, 331–355.

Wiser, M., O'Connor, K., & Higgins, T. (1995, April). *Mutual constraints in the development of the concepts of matter and molecule.* Paper presented at American Educational Research Association (AERA), April 19–21, 1995, San Francisco, CA.

9

Conceptual Change in Naïve Biology

Kayoko Inagaki and Giyoo Hatano[1]
Chiba University

The preceding chapters have revealed that young children, at least older preschoolers, possess a naive theory of biology. Psychologists dealing with other core domains of thought also claim that preschool children have naive theories about the important aspects of the world; for example, they assert that preschool children have naive psychology or a theory of mind (e.g., Perner, 1991; Wellman, 1990). However, that children have naive theories does not mean that their theories are the same as intuitive theories lay adults possess. Because the construction of the initial theory is based on a limited database, it has to be restructured as more and more facts are incorporated into it with increasing age, unless the initial set of observed facts constitutes a representative sample of all relevant facts. Some of the innate or very early tendencies and biases that are helpful at the initial phase may be weakened or given up, as accumulated pieces of prior knowledge come to serve as constraints. This also makes conceptual change or theory change during childhood inevitable.

In this chapter, we discuss conceptual change that spontaneously occurs during childhood, and its mechanisms. More specifically, first, we discuss the nature of conceptual change as a fundamental restructuring of (conceptual) knowledge in general, and we then sketch conceptual change in the course of development of biological knowledge, primarily relying on our experimental evidence. Finally, we return to the general discussion of how conceptual change occurs.

CONCEPTUAL CHANGE AS FUNDAMENTAL RESTRUCTURING

What is Conceptual Change?

The notion of conceptual change in cognitive development has been proposed as an alternative to "enrichment views" (Carey, 1985, 1991). It denotes that conceptual development involves not just enrichment or elaboration of the existing knowledge systems but their considerable re-organization or restructuring. Conceptual change involves change in core concepts, conceptions, or conceptualizations (including rules, models, and theories). To put it differently, it concerns a large-scale restructuring of the existing knowledge system (especially conceptual knowledge in it). The knowledge systems before and after the conceptual change may sometimes be locally in-commensurable (Carey, 1988); that is, some pieces of knowledge in one system cannot properly be translated into the other, as exemplified by the shift from children's undifferentiated concept of heat/temperature to adults' separate concepts of heat and temperature (Wiser & Carey, 1983).

It should be noted that conceptual change seldom occurs suddenly, just as it has taken years for concepts, conceptions, or conceptualizations to change in the history of science. The process of conceptual change tends to be slow and gradual, even if its end result is drastically different from its initial state.

Conceptual change often takes the form of theory change, because concepts and conceptions are embedded in theories; changing one core concept in a theory generates changes in related concepts and eventually leads to a change in the whole set of concepts. Theory change involves changes in causal devices or explanations and/or a large scale change in the range of phenomena or entities that are included. See Keil (1998, 1999) for distinct senses or conceptual change other than theory change.

Types of Conceptual Change

Four types of conceptual change can be distinguished with regard to the relationship between the old, pre-change knowledge system and the new, post-change system. Let us take theory change as an example. First, a new theory emerges from an old theory in the same domain, with the latter being subsumed in, or replaced by, the former. It can be described as A → A', where A and A' denote the old and new theory, respectively.

For example, between the ages 2 and 4 to 5 years, the early theory of mind, which is based solely on desires and perceptions, is transformed into the "representational theory of mind," which includes beliefs as well (Gopnik & Wellman, 1994).

Second, a new theory emerges and develops from an old one within the same domain, and the latter continues to exist with its salience decreased: A → A' & A. Sometimes the old theory is even extended by the new theory. For example, Perner (1991) claims that, although at about 4 years of age, children's understanding of the mind changes from a "situation theory" (where mental states are construed in relation to situations) to a "representational theory" (where mental states are understood as serving representational functions), the latter does not replace the former but merely extends it; even adults may be situation theorists when possible, but they, unlike young children, can take a representational view when necessary. Subbotsky (1997) also proposed a "coexistence model of the development of fundamental structures of mind" by demonstrating that phenomenalistic forms of causal reasoning retain their power in the mind of an educated adult.

Third, a new theory emerges from an old one through differentiation, and new and old theories, representing knowledge systems in different domains, develop separately afterwards: A → A & B. One example is the emergence of a theory of matter from a theory of physics in which objects and materials from which they are made are not fully distinguished (Smith, Carey, & Wiser, 1985). Carey (1985, 1995) argued that naive biology emerges from an intuitive psychology.

Fourth, a new theory emerges through the integration of old subtheories: A & B → C. For example, young Israeli children consider plants as neither living things nor nonliving things, but "growers" (Stavy & Wax, 1989). In contrast, they easily recognize animals as living by attending to their self-initiated movement. In other words, these young children seem to possess different theories for animals and plants. As they grow older, they acquire a theory of living things by integrating these different subtheories of animals and plants.

We consider, in the domain of biology, the second type of theory change as most tenable; the fourth type is also possible at the level of its specific theory. As we will describe in detail later, conceptual change in naive biology takes place approximately between ages 5 and 10 years within the domain. Young children tend to understand biological phenomena by relying on vitalistic causality and personifying inference, whereas older children and adults use mechanical causality and inference based on higher order biological categories. However, vitalistic causality and personifying inference continue to function as a basis of understanding and to be used as a fallback in situations where people do not think they are required to make precise and detailed predictions or explanations based on so-called scientific biology (Hatano & Inagaki, 1997).

Spontaneous Versus Instruction-Based Conceptual Change

Forms of conceptual change can also be distinguished in terms of whether the change occurs spontaneously or is induced by instruction (Hatano & Inagaki, 1997; Vosniadou & Ioannides, 1998). Spontaneous conceptual change is the change that results from children's increasing experience in their physical and sociocultural environment. In other words, it occurs without systematic instruction, though schooling certainly has some general facilitative effects on it. Most of the examples referred to in the preceding section are of this form. This form of change seems to occur readily, because it is commonly found among most children growing up in highly technological societies. An additional example is the change that occurs within young children's belief-desire psychology between ages 3 and 6, i.e., from a copy-container theory of mind representing a static mind that 3-year-old children are supposed to possess to an interpretive homuncular theory representing an active and constructive mind (Wellman, 1990). Cognitive developmentalists have been primarily concerned with this spontaneous conceptual change.

In contrast, researchers who are interested in science education have dealt with instruction-based conceptual change, which occurs by incorporating conceptual devices of science and thereby correcting "misconceptions" (e.g., Vosniadou & Brewer, 1992). This instruction-based conceptual change requires laborious and effortful processes of systematic teaching to be achieved, and even with good teaching, only a limited portion of older children and adults may achieve it (e.g., Clement, 1982).

However, it should be noted that the difference between spontaneous conceptual change and instruction-based conceptual change is not in actuality so large because conceptual development during the middle elementary school years and after is directly or indirectly influenced by systematic science instruction. Even when such science education does not function well, some scientific concepts that students learned in incomplete ways may work for them as something like a placeholder on the students' knowledge system and contribute to restructuring it eventually. Thus conceptual change during and after the elementary school years may often be a mixture of spontaneous and instruction-based conceptual changes.

CONCEPTUAL CHANGE IN THE DOMAIN OF NAIVE BIOLOGY

Returning to the domain of biology, we discuss conceptual change in naive biology. Compared with lay adults' intuitive biology, young children's naive biology has five weaknesses: (a) limited factual knowledge, (b) limited applicability of biological reasoning to classes of biological phenomena (focusing on eating, being vigorous and lively, and growing, almost neglecting, say, reproduction and etiological aspects), (c) a lack of inferences based on complex, hierarchically-organized biological categories, (d) a lack of mechanical causality, and (e) a lack of some conceptual devices, such as "evolution" or "photosynthesis." During the early elementary school years, children gradually overcome weaknesses through enrichment and through spontaneous conceptual change. Specifically, the use of inferences based on complex, hierarchically organized biological categories and of mechanical causality requires fundamental restructuring of biological knowledge, whereas the accumulation of more and more factual knowledge and more coherent application of biological reasoning can be achieved by enrichment only.

In contrast, the acquisition of basic conceptual devices of scientific biology, such as photosynthesis or the Darwinian idea of evolution, requires instruction-based conceptual change, because children almost never acquire them without instruction, and incorporating them meaningfully into the existing body of knowledge can usually be achieved only with its restructuring. For example, one who does not know the phenomenon of photosynthesis cannot understand the basic difference between animals and plants (i.e., plants can produce nutriments themselves) and thus may construct a wrong integrative theory for both animals and plants, accepting the false mapping of water for plants to food for animals. The Darwinian idea of evolution must also be difficult for children to grasp. Because naive biology assumes living things, but not nonliving things, to be able to adjust themselves to their ecological niche or ways of life, children are ready to accept any biological entity's gradual adaptive changes over generations (Evans, 2001) and thus to form a version of the Lamarckian idea of evolution (Marton, 1989). The Darwinian idea of evolution has been fully accepted, even among biologists, since the 19th century. We assume that, unlike spontaneous conceptual change in naive theories, conceptual change through the understanding of conceptual devices is very hard to bring about, even with educational intervention, and thus occurs only among a limited portion of older children or adolescents, as described above in the case of the Darwinian idea of evolution.

In what follows, we primarily consider spontaneous conceptual change. We first sketch qualitative changes in the salient mode of inference and those in preferred causality with increasing age; that is, changes from similarity-based to category-based inference on the one hand, and those from vitalistic to mechanical causality on the other. Next, we show that the pre- and post-change modes of inference and causalities coexist even in adults, although the pre-change mode of inference and causality is no longer salient in adults' biology. It can sometimes be used as a fallback in everyday lives.

Developmental Shift from Similarity-Based to Category-Based Inference

In chapter 3 we characterized young children's biology as human-centered or personifying in nature. Our experimental demonstrations used prediction/explanation questions requiring children to construct their answers. However, we cannot use this method to examine developmental changes in modes of inference from preschoolers to adults, because in this method the change in ways of inference would be confounded with children's increased general verbal abilities with age. Thus, instead of the person analogy task, we, like in Carey (1985), have adopted the task of inductive projection from humans, or the attribution of human properties. This method relies less on children's verbal ability. We considered it as admissible because personification involves both the so-called person analogy and inductive projection from humans to other nonhuman entities, and the latter can be regarded as a special case of the person analogy (Inagaki & Hatano, 2003).

Suppose children are asked the following attribution question, "Does X have a property Y?", where Y is a property that they know people have and that they do not know whether X has. If children have personifying biology, they will make the following inference: First, they will judge whether X is similar to humans, as for the target property. If they judge it as dissimilar, they will answer "No" to the above question. If they perceive some similarity between humans and the target entity X, they will tend to answer "Yes" in proportion to its judged similarity, unless they have additional knowledge that it is impossible for X to have the property Y. We call such a mode of inference "similarity-based attribution," which is the same as Carey's (1985) "comparison-to-people model." The attributional profile of this mode of inference is a gradually decreasing pattern, as shown by the solid line in Figure 9.1, when varied objects are arranged on a continuum

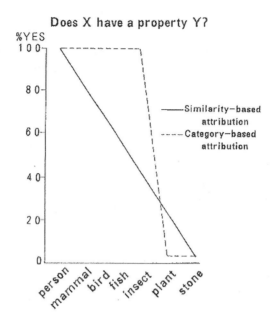

FIGURE 9.1   Hypothetical patterns of attribution (from Inagaki and Sugiyama, 1988).

according to their phylogenetic affinity to a person. Thus similarity-based attribution inevitably generates both under- and overattribution errors, for the objects. By underattribution errors we mean that children fail to attribute a specific (human) property to those objects, and by overattribution errors, we mean erroneous attribution of the property to those not having it.

Another apparently contrasting type of inference is a deductive attribution arrived at by relying on such higher order biological categories as mammals, vertebrates, and so on (e.g., "The grasshopper is an invertebrate and the invertebrates have no bones, so the grasshopper must have no bones"). We call it category-based attribution. This attribution generates correct responses as long as the target object is allocated to the proper category and the attributional boundary is correct. Its attributional profile is a flat pattern with a sharp break as shown in the dotted line in Figure 9.1, although the location of the sharp break on the continuum may vary from uniquely human to restricted-animal to all-living-thing properties.

Carey (1985) claimed that 4-year-olds attribute animal properties based on the "comparison-to-people model," whereas 10-year-olds rely little on it. To put it another way, we can expect that younger children use similarity-based inference, while older children rely on category-based attribution. How does this shift from the similarity-based to the category-based take place? More specifically, is the shift abrupt or gradual? We assume that pure similarity-based attribution progresses toward pure category-based attribution by being more and more strongly constrained by categorical knowledge, as children come to realize its usefulness through various experiences, including formal schooling. Even young children check the plausibility of similarity-based inference with factual knowledge (Inagaki & Hatano, 1987) and, though not often, with inference based on biological functions. Therefore, we can identify an "intermediate" way of attribution, which might be called a constrained similarity-based attribution, that is, inferences primarily based on similarity but constrained by categorical knowledge. The attributional profile of this intermediate way can be a variety of mixed patterns between a flat pattern with a sharp break and a gradually decreasing pattern.

However, we assume that a pattern with a decreasing part on the person/animal side and a flat part of the plant/nonliving thing side would occur most often, because children use object-specific knowledge (Inagaki & Hatano, 1987) or categorical knowledge to reject the "Yes" response obtained by projecting human properties to nonhuman entities. It is not likely that children possess object-specific knowledge that enables them to answer "Yes" when they do not project human properties to the object according to its similarity to people. This likely intermediate pattern would thus reduce overattribution errors to plants and nonliving things more than underattribution errors to those animals that are apparently dissimilar to humans.

We examined whether the above developmental shift from similarity-based to category-based attribution would occur through an analysis of both group data (Inagaki & Sugiyama, 1988, Experiment 1) and of individual data (Experiment 2). For the attribution of unobservable anatomical/physiological properties, we predicted, as Carey (1985) found, that there would be developmental changes from similarity-based to category-based attribution between ages 4 and 10.

In contrast, for mental properties, which were not taught explicitly in school biology, we predicted that there would be a delayed shift, and thus even adults might sometimes make similarity-based attributions. This is because the attribution of mental properties requires more inference than does the attribution of anatomical/physiological properties. For example, when a child is asked, "Does a grasshopper have bones?", he or she can find an answer by making an inference based on knowledge about higher order category membership and category-attribute associations. The child can reason "It is an insect, so it can't possibly have bones." However, for the question of "Does a grasshopper feel happy?" she must further consider that a brain is required to feel happy, along with whether a grasshopper has a brain. As C. Johnson and Wellman (1982) reported, it is fairly difficult for children to grasp associations between a brain and mental properties, especially mental properties such as having feelings and sensations.

We also predicted that intermediate patterns of attribution, that is, the constrained similarity-based attribution, would be found in between the two contrasting patterns of attribution, between younger children and adults for anatomical/physiological properties, and among older children and adults for mental properties. This prediction implies that adults would be able to reduce overattribution errors. For example, they would exclude the possibility that trees feel pain, even when they perceive them to be somewhat similar to people, because they know that plants do not have a central nervous system enabling them to have feelings.

In the first experiment, 20 participants each from five age groups were involved: 4-year-olds (M = 4;9), 5-year-olds (M = 5;9); second graders (M = 8;1), fourth graders (M = 10;2), and college students. Eight phylogenetically different objects were used as targets: a person, a rabbit, a pigeon, a fish, a grasshopper, a tulip, a tree, and a stone. The objects are listed here in the order of perceived similarity to people, as established in another sample, but were presented in a random fashion in the experiment.

The participants were individually asked 10 property questions for each of the eight objects in the format, "Does X have a property Y?" The 10 properties were grouped into three types: (a) unobservable anatomical/physiological properties: having a heart, having bones, breathing, and growth; (b) unobservable mental properties: the abilities to think, feel happy, and feel pain; (c) observable properties: having eyes, the ability to move, and speaking to a person. Questions about the observable properties were included to confirm that there were no developmental differences in attribution accuracy about these properties. In fact, it turned that the participants in all age groups had almost equally high percentages of correct knowledge about these observable properties of the target objects. All the property questions were asked about an object before the inquiry proceeded to another object.

For each of the seven unobservable property questions, we computed proportions of "Yes" response to the eight target objects, phylogenetically ordered from a person to a stone, in each

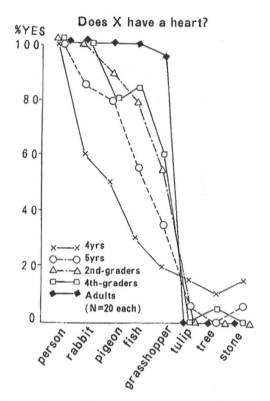

FIGURE 9.2   An example of developmental patterns obtained in attribution of the anatomical physiological properties (from Inagaki and Sugiyama, 1988).

age group. As shown in Figure 9.1, the category-based attribution should be a pattern consisting of a big gap (decline) and two flat parts before and after it, and the similarity-based attribution, a pattern showing gradual decrease from a person to a stone. Thus we examined whether there existed a big gap (an arbitrary criterion of a difference of 40% or more between two consecutive objects) somewhere on the continuum, and whether the two parts before and after the gap were flat (i.e., all the successive differences were less than 10%). Then, we classified the attributional patterns, for each property by each age group, into three types, category-based, similarity-based, and intermediate (e.g., the pattern having a big gap but only one flat part).

Results supported all three of our predictions. For the anatomical/physiological properties, there was a progression from 4-year-olds' predominant reliance of similarity-based attribution to adults' predominant reliance on category-based attribution. The intermediate pattern of attribution was found between similarity-based and category-based attribution, mostly among 5-year-olds, second, and fourth graders. One example is shown in Figure 9.2. Thus, the shift seemed to occur primarily during the elementary school years. For mental properties, participants in all age groups mostly made similarity-based attribution. An illustrative example is shown in Figure 9.3.

For the above findings from the analyses of group data, there exists an alternative interpretation, which is that this apparent similarity-based pattern for a group of participants may have been generated by their disagreement in attributional boundaries. More specifically, the above shift in patterns for anatomical/physiological properties may have been due to greater variability among younger children in the category extensions or in category-attribute associations than among adults, and adults' "similarity-based" patterns for mental properties may have only represented category-based attribution with different category-attribute associations.

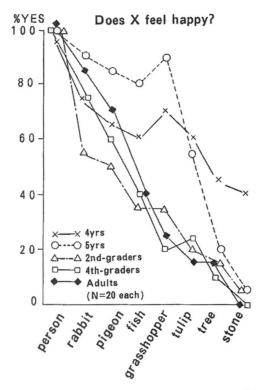

FIGURE 9.3   An example of developmental patterns obtained in attribution of the mental properties. From Inagaki and Sugiyama (1988).

To exclude this alternative interpretation, we conducted Experiment 2, which examined whether the similarity-based pattern would be found within individuals as well.

Another group made up of 5-year-olds and of college students participated in this experiment. Target objects were five members each belonging to the same higher order categories (i.e., mammals, birds, fish, insects, and plants) but differing in appearance (e.g., size), as well as a person and a stone.

Each participant was individually asked to attribute two anatomical/physiological properties (having bones and the heart) and two mental properties (feeling pain and feeling happy) to each of the above 27 objects. The question formats were the same as those of Experiment 1 described above: "Does X have a property Y?" In other words, property questions referred to the name of the target object, but did not refer to the name of the category. All the property questions were asked about an object before the inquiry proceeded to another object.

After all the property questions, the participant was required to classify into five categories all 25 of the above-described objects, excluding the person and the stone. This classification task was added in order to confirm that participants had relied on similarity-based attribution for judgment of these properties even though they were able to classify most of the objects correctly. Thus twenty 5-year-olds and twenty college students who classified most of the objects correctly were used in the analyses.

We classified the responses of each participant for each property into one of three patterns, that is, category-based, similarity-based, and others (classified as neither similarity-based nor category-based). If a participant makes category-based attributions, he or she should always answer "Yes" or always answer "No" to the question of whether each of the five objects belonging to the same category has a target property. Thus, the data pattern will consist of two flat parts

TABLE 9.1
Percentages of Each Attributional Pattern in Each Age Group

Age group	Anatomical/physiological properties			Mental properties		
	S-based	C-based	Others	S-based	C-based	Others
5-year-olds	73	18	10	48	13	40
Adults	10	90	0	53	43	5

Note: S-based means similarlity-based attribution; C-based means category-based attribution. $N = 20 \times 2$ in each age group.

with a sharp break. On the other hand, if the participant makes similarity-based attributions, he or she should give "Yes" responses to some members and "No" responses to others belonging to the same category when the category is located near the boundary of "Yes" responses and "No" responses; as a result, the ratio of "Yes" responses of each category should decrease as the categories become phylogenetically farther from people.

Results of Experiment 2 confirmed our interpretation of the result obtained by analyses of group data in Experiment 1 as shown in Table 9.1. For anatomical/physiological properties, 73% of the preschoolers' patterns fit the definition of similarity-based attribution. In contrast, 90% of the adults' patterns were category-based attributions. The developmental difference in frequency of the two patterns was highly significant.

For mental properties, about half of the young children's patterns reflected similarity-based attributions, versus only 13% reflecting category-based attributions. More than 50% of the adults' patterns were also similarity-based attributions; about 40% were category-based. The difference between young children and adults in ratio of similarity-based to category-based patterns was marginally significant.

The results described above clearly indicate that there exist qualitative changes in the salient mode of inference, that is, from preschoolers' use of inference based on similarity to people to older children's and adults' reliance on higher order category-based inference, and that these changes proceed gradually from preschool years to middle childhood to adult ages.

We hastily add that we are not claiming that young children can never make inferences based on higher order biological categories. They can do so if they are urged to with some help, at least when they possess the pieces of knowledge about the higher order category membership of the target and relevant category-property relationships. However, they seldom possess such pieces of knowledge and are unlikely to rely on category-based inference spontaneously.

To paraphrase this shift, preschool children have a graded concept of living things organized in terms of their similarity to humans, but as they grow older, they come to possess a concept of living things that is divided into hierarchically organized categories, where humans are probably seen just as animals. K. Johnson, Mervis, and Boster (1992) obtained relevant findings for 7-year-olds, and even 10-year-olds, in their experiment, using a triad task, which required the participants to find two similar things from among, say, human/nonhuman primate/nonprimate triads. Whereas the 7- and 10-year-olds tended to treat humans as isolates by showing reluctance to acknowledge similarities between humans and nonhumans, the adults did not show such a tendency; the adults responded by basing their judgments on membership within or outside the primate category.

Interestingly, this change in the salient mode of inference is accompanied with, if not induced by, change in metacognitive beliefs and values about particular modes of inference. Hatano and Inagaki (1991) examined whether the shift from similarity-based to category-based inferences would be induced, at least in part, by a metacognitive belief about the usefulness of higher order categories, namely, the belief that category-based inference is more dependable than similarity-based inference. Children of second, fourth, and sixth grade were required to evaluate, in a questionnaire format, a given set of reasons that were allegedly offered by same-age children in a dialogue with a teacher. That is, they were asked to judge the plausibility of three different types of reasons, each of which was preceded by a "Yes/No" judgment to such a question as, "Does an eel have bones?" or "Does a tiger have a kidney(s)?" Two of the three reasons represented similarity-based inference and category-based inference, respectively. The former referred to the target's surface similarity to people, such as, "I think a tiger has a kidney, because it is generally like a human," and the latter referred to higher order categories like "mammals," such as, "I think a tiger has a kidney, because both a human and a tiger are mammals." The other reason, clearly not category-based nor similarity-based, was a distractor, for example, "I think a tiger does not have a kidney, because it is not as intelligent as a human." The same children were also given a similar attribution task as the one used in Inagaki and Sugiyama (1988).

It was found that as children grew older, the number of respondents who judged the category-based reason to be plausible and the similarity-based one to be implausible significantly increased, whereas the number of respondents who evaluated the similarity-based reason as plausible and the category-based one as implausible decreased, suggesting that children came to acquire a metacognitive belief about the usefulness of higher order categories. Moreover, even among the second-graders, those children who consistently favored category-based reasons tended to show an attributional pattern closer to the pure category-based attribution than was shown by those who favored similarity-based reasons.

Hatano and Inagaki further examined, by using indirect, "projective"-type questions, whether older students differentiated more clearly a fictitious child who gave a category-based reason from a child who gave a similarity-based reason in the rating of his or her academic talent. Another group of second, fourth, and sixth graders were given a questionnaire. It described two hypothetical pairs of children of the same grade as the students, who, in dialogue with their teacher, gave a judgment of whether rabbits and ants had a pancreas (or tigers and grasshoppers had bones) and the reason for it. The reason given by one of each pair was in fact similarity-based, and the other, category-based (these labels were not given). The participating students were asked to rate how good academically the fictitious child who had given the reason would be, and how likable the child would be as a friend, in a four-point scale.

Results were as follows: The fictitious child who had allegedly given a category-based reason was rated significantly higher in academic talent than the allegedly similarity-based child in all grades. However, the older the participant, the greater the magnitude of the difference. That is, the older students were much more negative than the younger ones in the rating of the fictitious child who had given the similarity-based reasons. Since the likeability rating for this fictitious child did not differ significantly, it is not likely that these participants always gave favorable ratings for the category-based child. These results strongly suggest that children become reluctant to use similarity to people as an inferential cue for biological attributions as they grow older. It is likely that conceptual change in modes of biological inference is enhanced by social sanctions; for instance, children may stop relying on similarity to people in order to avoid being regarded as less talented.

PROGRESSION FROM VITALISTIC TO MECHANICAL CAUSALITY

Here, we examine how another essential element of young children's naive biology, namely vitalistic causality, changes as they grow older. In chapter 5 of Inagaki and Hatano (2002), we have seen that young children's naive biology is vitalistic in nature; they tend to apply vitalistic causality to internal bodily phenomena. They consider that internal bodily phenomena are caused by activity of an internal organ having agency, and the organ's activity often involves transmission or exchange of "vital force." Since the vital force is an unspecified substance as illustrated in children's words, "vital power," "source of energy," "something good for health," and so on, vitalistic causality presumes unspecified mechanisms. Vital power seems to be a global conceptual entity that serves as a causal device in children's initial biology. It is expected that, as children learn more and more about biological phenomena including scientific words and their implications, through learning school biology, watching TV programs, or reading books, they come to acquire knowledge that enables them to specify mechanisms. In other words, the global conceptual entity of vital power is specified into a set of particular mechanisms. With this learning of specific mechanisms, children come to recognize mechanical causality (presupposing a specified mechanism) to be more reliable than vitalistic causality, and this induces the shift to mechanical causality.

To confirm this expectation, Inagaki and Hatano (1993, Experiment 2) examined whether young children's reliance on vitalistic causality would progress to the use of mechanical causality as they grow older. Not only 6-year-olds but also 8-year-olds and college students participated in this study. They were asked to choose one from among three possible causal explanations for each of six bodily phenomena, such as blood circulation and respiration. The three explanations represented intentional, vitalistic, and mechanical causality, respectively. Although several of the example questions and three alternative explanations were already shown in chapter 5 of this volume, we present here another example, blood circulation: "Why does the blood flow to different parts of our bodies? (a) Because we move our body, hoping the blood will flow in it [intentional causality]; (b) Because our heart works hard it sends out life and energy with blood [vitalistic]; (c) Because the heart sends the blood by working as a pump [mechanical]."

As shown in Figure 9.4, the 6-year-old children chose vitalistic explanations as most plausible most often (54%) and chose intentional explanations second most often (25%). In contrast, the 8-year-olds chose mechanical causal explanations most often (62%) and opted for some vitalistic ones (34%) as well, but seldom chose intentional explanations. The adults predominantly preferred mechanical explanations to explanations of the other two types.

Results of individual data analyses also confirmed this developmental change in preferred causality. Out of the twenty 6-year-olds, only one chose four or more intentional explanations for the six items (we call them intentional responders), whereas nine chose four or more vitalistic explanations (vitalistic responders). Among 8-year-olds, there was only one vitalistic responder;

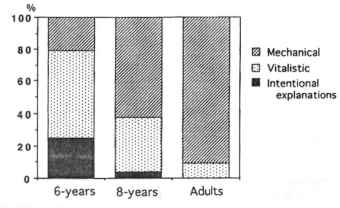

FIGURE 9.4   Percentages of choices for different types of casual explanations.

there were 10 mechanical responders who made four or more mechanical choices; six out of nine "Others" respondents were children who chose vitalistic and mechanical explanations equally (three each), and two were children who made three vitalistic choices and two mechanical choices. Among adults, there were 19 mechanical responders and one vitalistic responder. This pattern of findings also suggests that there exists change in preferred causality from vitalistic to mechanical, with increasing age.

Developmental change in preferred causality for biological phenomena is not confined to Japanese children and adults. Morris, Taplin, and Gelman (2000), carrying out a careful replication of Inagaki and Hatano's (1993) Experiment 2, confirmed this tendency among English-speaking children and adults in Australia. When asked to choose one from among three causal explanations for each of the six bodily phenomena, Australian 5-year-old kindergartners showed a clear preference for vitalistic explanations over mechanical ones, whereas college students and, to a lesser extent, 10-year-old children chose the mechanical explanation most often. Results from the individual data analyses confirmed the results of the group analysis, indicating that 30% of the 5-year-olds were vitalistic responders, while 48% of the 10-year-olds and 80% of the adults were mechanical responders.

Again, we would like to emphasize that the observed shift is for preferred causality, and it is premature to conclude that young children can not rely on mechanical causality in explaining bodily processes. However, they are unlikely to be attracted by mechanical explanations because they do not have well-understood examples of specific mechanisms for bodily processes.

When the above findings on the shift in preferred causalities are combined with those on the shift in the salient mode of inference, we can conclude convincingly that there occurs conceptual change in children's naive biology, from 5 years of age or so through middle childhood and adulthood; from young children's personifying and vitalistic biology to older children's and adults' biology based on category-based inference and mechanical causality.

PRE-CHANGE SYSTEM STILL EXISTS IN ADULTS' INTUITIVE BIOLOGY

Is older children's and adults' intuitive biology no longer personifying at all? Is the similarity-based inference completely replaced by the category-based inference in older children and adults? Does their intuitive biology no longer rely on vitalistic causality? Answers to these questions are not affirmative. The fact that there exists a shift from similarity-based to category-based inferences does not mean that older children and adults never rely on similarity to people in their inferences. Likewise, as discussed in chapter 5, the fact that there is a developmental shift from reliance on vitalistic causality to that on mechanical causality does not denote that adults never take vitalistic views for biological understanding. We first describe the similarity-based inference in adults.

Adults' Reliance on Similarity-Based Inference

Remember that a substantial number of adults as well as older children still relied on similarity to people in attributing mental properties to various animals. As impressively indicated in Table 9.1, even adults showed the similarity-based pattern at a substantial rate (more than 50% of the time) in attributing mental properties to animate entities. This suggests that even adults sometimes rely on similarity-based inference.

This tendency is not limited to attribution of mental or psychological properties. In another experiment using reaction times (Morita, Inagaki, & Hatano, 1988), we found that college students relied on similarity-based attribution to some extent not only for mental properties but also for anatomical/physiological ones in a situation where quick responding was required. In this experiment, four pairs of animals belonging to the same category but differing in judged similarity to humans (e.g., a tiger vs. a fur seal; a tortoise vs. a snake; a penguin vs. a swallow; a mantis vs. a grasshopper) were used as targets, and four additional objects (e.g., a rose, a stone, etc.) as fillers. These four pairs were selected from 16 animals by another group of students who were required to rate them on a 9-point scale in terms of similarity to people. The former of each pair was perceived by these raters as more similar to people than the latter. First, 31 college students were told the correct higher order category that each object belongs to, and then they were required to give Yes/No responses as quickly as possible to 7 property questions for each of the 12 objects (i.e., the four pairs of animals and four fillers). The property questions consisted of two unobservable anatomical/physiological properties (i.e., has bones and breathes), two mental properties (i.e., feels pain and feels sad), two observable animal properties (i.e., has a mouth and has eyes), and one human property (i.e., speaks language). Answers to these questions were to be all "Yes" for humans. There were 84 property questions in all.

It was found that these students made more "Yes" responses to the more human-like members of the animals (e.g., a tortoise in the above example) in attributing unobservable properties. In addition, when their responses were identical within pairs, "Yes" responses were quicker for the more similar members than for the less similar ones, whereas "No" responses were slower for the more similar members than for the less similar ones (see Figure 9.5). The interaction effect was significant. This suggests that even college students use the similarity-to-humans as a cue when relying on category-based inference is nearly impossible because of the time pressure.

It is not feasible to explain the above results in terms of prototypicality, for example, that the more typical member of the pair was more readily assigned target properties shared by most members of the category. This is because the member of the pair that is more similar to humans is not always more prototypical within the category; for example, a penguin is more similar to humans, but less prototypical within the category of birds than a swallow. Moreover, some of the target properties (e.g., feeling sad) are typical of humans, and are in fact not attributed to other animals frequently.

Thus, we can summarize that the college students relied on similarity to people in attributing mental as well as unobservable biological properties under time pressure. This means that

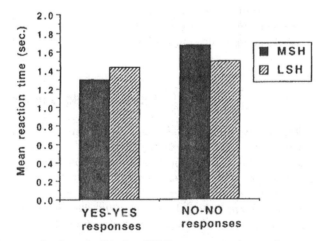

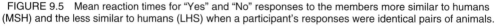

FIGURE 9.5   Mean reaction times for "Yes" and "No" responses to the members more similar to humans (MSH) and the less similar to humans (LHS) when a participant's responses were identical pairs of animals.

the developmental shift from similarity-based to category-based inference is only a part of the whole story; the similarity-based mode of inference is retained and may be used even by adults as a fallback strategy.

Adults' Use of Vitalistic Causality

Inagaki and Hatano (1993) and Morris et al. (2000) revealed that older children and college students preferred more strongly mechanical causality to the vitalistic one. However, this does not necessarily mean that adults never rely on vitalistic causality in any situation. Instead, we claim, vitalistic causality is never completely superseded by mechanical causality with increasing age; rather, it may continue to work as a basis of understanding some biological phenomena and to be used in situations where people are not required to give precise and detailed answers based on scientific biology (Hatano & Inagaki, 1996, 1997). In fact, a few college students in Experiment 2 of Inagaki and Hatano (1993) seemed to use vitalistic causality as an informal or fallback mode of explanation. One student who consistently chose vitalistic explanations answered at the interview after the experiment, "We usually choose those including 'oxygen' or 'the heart works like a pump' because we have learned in school to do so. However, I chose others because they were most convincing and comprehensible to me."

Miller and Bartsch (1997), conducting a modified replication of Inagaki and Hatano's (1993) Experiment 2, found that American college students were vitalists, contrary to Inagaki and Hatano (1993); that is, these students preferred to apply vitalistic explanations for bodily phenomena as often as the 6- and 8-year-olds did. Although we cannot reject a possibility that this result was an artifact produced by methodological problems in their study, as Morris et al. (2000) pointed out (instead of requiring participants to choose one from among three alternatives, they asked the participants to make a choice between intentional and vitalistic explanations, and between vitalistic and mechanical explanations), it is possible that these adults indeed preferred vitalistic explanations for bodily phenomena, because the students may have been interviewed in a situation in which answers based on scientific biology were not highly valued. It is plausible that even adults still consider vitalistic explanations reasonable for bodily phenomena and offer such explanations when they are not obliged to give an answer based on scientific biology.

We should note the fact that not only young children but also a substantial ratio of lay adults hold the idea of resistance to illness as one case of vitalism in everyday life; they believe in folk preventive medicine that advocates the importance of one's resistance to illness and that offers various specific recommendations for improving resistance. When asked what factor was considered the most important as a cause for getting a cold, about 70% of Japanese college students offered physical factors as contributing to illness susceptibility, that is, irregular daily routines or the lack of self-control of health, fatigue, deterioration of physical strength, sudden change of temperature, and so on. For example, "Bodily resistance to illness is lost due to shortage of sleep and/or fatigue," "Insufficient sleep or staying out in cold weather increases bodily susceptibility to illness," or "The body cannot adjust to sudden changes of temperature" (see Inagaki & Hatano, 1999).

We can generalize the above results as follows: Although the pre- and post-change knowledge systems are qualitatively different, there are some continuities between them (Hatano, 1994). The occurrence of conceptual change does not mean that components of the pre-change system are replaced by the post-change system and disappear completely. We claim that old components retain as less salient fallback models or strategies in the new system. This is consistent with recent research findings indicating that multiple models (Yates et al., 1988) or multiple strategies (e.g., Siegler & Jenkins, 1989) coexist within the same individual. This is also in line with the claim offered by Perner (1991) as to the development of theories of mind or the claim by Subbotsky (1997) as to phenomenalistic causal reasoning. An important implication of these claims is that the post-change knowledge system of educated adults may not be as drastically different from young children's pre-change knowledge system as it appears.

Another Conceptual Change?

The qualitative changes that we have discussed so far occur in later childhood, that is, after 5 years of age. Considering that a great majority of investigators now believe that even preschool children possess a form of naive biology, only those changes before 5 years of age can be relevant to the issue of conceptual change that has been the target of debate, namely, whether naive biology emerges from intuitive psychology through conceptual change. Does another conceptual change take place earlier? Since in chapter 8 of Inagaki and Hatano (2002) we discuss in detail the issue of whether young children interpret biological phenomena within the framework of intuitive psychology, we concentrate here on the issue of whether naive biology emerges from naive psychology through conceptual change.

It is true that there are some qualitative changes in children's predictions and explanations for biological phenomena approximately between ages 3 and 5. As we reviewed in the preceding chapters, many studies have shown that 5-year-old children can clearly differentiate human biological properties and phenomena from psychological ones in terms of modifiability and controllability. They also understand illness causality biologically. Around age 5, children understand illness causality biologically. Around age 5, children can distinguish living entities including animals and plants from nonliving things and begin to recognize commonalities between—animals and plants. Some studies have shown that 5-year-olds can choose biological explanations presented from a number of alternative causal explanations for biological phenomena, and at times even offer biological explanations themselves.

In contrast, (a) 3- and 4-year-olds' predictions for biological phenomena are not highly consistent and are easily influenced by contexts or by types of questions. (b) They sometimes rely on psychological causal devices as often as on biological ones for biological phenomena, whereas they seldom apply biological causality to social-psychological phenomena. However, (c) when biological and psychological causal devices are explicitly contrasted, they tend to choose the biological ones for biological phenomena.

We propose two possible interpretations for the observed change during these years. It may be that, although children as young as 3 years of age possess naive biology as well as psychology, psychological knowledge is more readily retrieved generally and thus sometimes interferes with the retrieval of its biological counterpart (as suggested above b). It probably takes a few years before young children clearly recognize that it is not naive psychology but biology that can explain those bodily processes and phenomena that are needed for us to be active and lively but are beyond our intentional control. It could thus be called a kind of conceptual change, somewhat similar to a relevance shift (Keil, 1999). This interpretation is harmonious with Carey's (1985) original position, though it differs from hers in attributing a form of naive biology to young children (based on (c) above). An alternative interpretation is that the observed change is just trivial, because it is a product of the fact that 3-year-olds naive biology is still being established. For many theories, there is some delay between acquisition and firm establishment, and such theories are unlikely to be used promptly until they are well established. Naive psychology as an established neighbor theory may sometimes penetrate into biological reasoning, but only until the establishment of naive biology.

Although more studies are needed, we prefer the second interpretation, because even 3-year-olds respond differently to biological and psychological phenomena unless they respond in a random fashion. In addition, they tend to choose biological causal devices for biological phenomena when these devices are given explicitly. In other words, we assume that the observed change in biological reasoning between ages 3 and 5 is not a matter of conceptual change but of a gradual construction of naive biology.

HOW DOES CONCEPTUAL CHANGE OCCUR?

In this final section, we discuss the issue of how conceptual change occurs in general, using primarily the case of naive biology as an example, because conceptual changes in core domains of thought are considered to be similar to each other in their mechanisms and conditions, though different in content. Although the issue of how conceptual change occurs and the specification of its mechanisms is "one of the fundamental problems of cognitive psychology today" (Vosniadou, 1994, p. 3), the available data are limited. This is partly because recent developmentalists have focused on the specification of the initial form of a naive theory and, to a much lesser extent, on the description of the state after conceptual change, without analyzing the process of change itself (Carey, 1985; Wellman, 1990). Relying on not only findings obtained in conceptual development but also some evidence from the history of science and science education, we thus propose possible mechanisms of conceptual change and conditions for its occurrence. To put it another way, we consider primarily mechanisms and conditions of spontaneous conceptual change, but take into account findings from studies on instruction-based conceptual change or scientists' activities, when they are relevant.

The critical difference between spontaneous and instruction-based conceptual changes seems to be the extent to which a cognizer consciously recognizes incongruity in his or her existing knowledge system and to which he or she intentionally attempts to solve them. Whereas spontaneous conceptual change seems to proceed slowly but steadily without the cognizer's explicit recognition of incongruity, the instruction-based conceptual change usually takes place only when students explicitly recognize the inadequacy of their conceptual knowledge by a teacher's instructional attempts to induce such recognition in them.

It is clear that in every case increased knowledge is required for conceptual change, and that the pre-change system serves as a cognitive constraint on conceptual change. In other words, conceptual change is a cognitive attempt to resume coherence of the knowledge system that has been disturbed by new pieces of information, through complex interactions of constituent elements of the current knowledge system.

Let us propose two contrasting mechanisms, one local and bottom-up, the other goal directed and top-down. If the system includes all candidate concepts, conceptions, and conceptualizations, each of which has its own subjective truth value (i.e., how strongly it is believed to be true), conceptual change can be described as radical changes in the truth-value of a range of connected pieces of knowledge (or beliefs, these two expressions being used interchangeably). We can thus assume that one type of mechanism for conceptual change is the spreading of truth-value alteration. When new inputs change the truth value of some pieces of knowledge, the changes bring about changes in the truth-value of other connected pieces, which may induce further changes in their neighbors. In the long run, there can be a drastic change in almost all pieces through continued spreading and recurring effects as well as further inputs to facilitate the truth-value alteration. This type of conceptual change is a bottom-up process and does not require the cognizer's conscious grasp of incongruity among beliefs and intentional attempt to reduce it. The relationships among beliefs are divided into dyadic relations with one another, each of which is characterized only in terms of whether two beliefs are roughly consonant, dissonant, or neither (one belief's being true implies the other belief's being true, false, or nothing). Here the change is gradual, takes time, and is based on a large amount of input.

The other type of conceptual change, which might be called deliberate belief revision, sometimes occurs. A representative subtype of this is similar to the process of comprehension monitoring (Markman, 1981) or repair (e.g., Ackerman, 1984; Glenberg & Epstein, 1985) in the sense that existing beliefs are consciously and deliberately rewritten (and new beliefs are introduced) in the process, in order to remove recognized inconsistencies (e.g., disconfirmed predictions based on the current set of beliefs) and make the knowledge system coherent again. In another subtype, deliberate belief revision is induced by what we call "discoordination" (Hatano, 1998), that is, the recognition that the current set of beliefs is not well connected or not powerful enough to be the basis for understanding the world. In both cases, removal of incongruity is not achieved as the accumulation of small local changes, as in the case of spreading of the truth-value alteration. It is a top-down, goal-directed process.

Instruction-based conceptual change usually takes the form of deliberate belief revision. In contrast, spontaneous conceptual change usually proceeds less consciously and less deliberately, although it is not always bottom-up. It is often initiated when a new piece of information induces unexpected incongruity. Suppose that children have a conception of birds consisting of a set of beliefs, such as "birds are flying animals," "birds are bigger than bugs," "birds lay eggs," "birds have wings," and so on. If they learn that a penguin is a bird but does not fly, it is dissonant with the first belief; or when they learn that a bat flies but isn't a bird, the target belief may become less trustworthy. As a result of these local, minor truth-value alterations and their recurring effects, children's conception of birds may change, as the flying-animals belief, being dissociated from other beliefs about birds, becomes less and less trustworthy. Alternatively, however, such incongruous pieces of information may induce a deliberate attempt to revise the conception. Of course, we human beings can ignore or tolerate incongruity to some extent, but let us suppose children are sensitive and open to the incongruous information. They may thus be tempted to modify their conception of birds, for instance, into something like, "birds are animals that have a basic body structure convenient for flying, but cannot necessarily fly."

Similarly, children who have found that similarity to people does not always lead to valid attributions, or that their peers often use and highly evaluate category-based inference, may weaken a little their belief in similarity-based inference. Alternatively, they may decide to compare similarity-based and category-based inferences systematically. Those who are afraid that vitalistic explanations are not welcome by adults (including the science teacher) and those who know some mechanical concepts and terms may shift to offering mechanical explanations either via the spreading of truth-value alteration or via deliberate belief revision. We believe that spontaneous conceptual change involves a combination of the two mechanisms.

Conditions for Inducing Conceptual Change

What conditions are likely to induce conceptual change? It should be pointed out that, although accumulated knowledge is a necessary condition for conceptual change (e.g., Carey, 1985), it is not a sufficient condition. We propose three additional conditions, two cognitive requisites that seem necessary and the sociocultural context that is facilitative. Since spontaneous conceptual change occurs without systematic intervention, these conditions are usually met, but theoretically it is significant to conceptualize them explicitly.

First, some metacognitive abilities that enable one to assess and monitor incongruity within the existing knowledge system are needed for conceptual change (especially deliberate belief revision) to occur, because it is an incongruity-reducing process. In most cases, as children grow older, their knowledge accumulates, and, at the same time, their metacognitive knowledge and skills also develop. In other words, the increase of knowledge and the development of metacognitive knowledge and skills proceed hand-in-hand in normal cognitive development. Thus, the necessity of metacognitive knowledge and skills for conceptual change is often overlooked.

However, we can offer solid evidence for the importance of metacognitive ability for conceptual change by examining knowledge that individuals with Williams syndrome have acquired. Individuals with Williams syndrome tend to talk in great detail with only superficial understanding, on the one hand, and lack analytic and metacognitive knowledge and skills, on the other. S. Johnson and Carey (1998) compared individuals with Williams syndrome, whose average verbal mental age was 11 years, with two groups of normally developing children whose average mental ages were 10 years and 6 years, respectively, in terms of the acquisition of general knowledge of animals (e.g., the size of their animal lexicon) and folk-biological concepts that were supposed to be normally acquired through conceptual change between ages 6 and 12 years (e.g., concepts of being alive or dead). They found that, although the participants with Williams syndrome performed at the level of the normal children of age 10 on the tasks concerning general knowledge of animals, their performance on the folk-biological knowledge tasks was at the level of normal 6-year-olds.

Although a number of alternative interpretations could be offered, we consider this finding as strongly suggesting the role of metacognitive skills in the acquisition of knowledge through conceptual change. In the course of normal development, we assume, children use metacognitive skills more or less unconsciously, and as a result, the process of belief revision may proceed slowly and gradually because a piece of new information induces local incongruity. This may be one of the reasons why conceptual change occurring in development takes place gradually over years, as is well illustrated in the developmental shifts in a domain of biology in the previous section.

Some conceptual change observed among scientists may occur more quickly than conceptual change occurring in the course of childhood conceptual development. Scientists can carefully monitor coherence among pieces of knowledge constituting a theory and be sensitive to and respond to a small amount of disconfirmation or discoordination in their knowledge system, thanks to their advanced metacognitive abilities. A good example is the "thought experiment" including limiting case analyses, as represented by Galileo's famous thought experiment showing that heavier objects do not fall faster than lighter ones (Nersessian, 1992). Some science instruction aims at bringing about conceptual change in less time by making students aware of the incongruity in their knowledge through the presentation of contradictory evidence.

The second condition for conceptual change is that an alternative concept, conception, or conceptualization (or the set of its constituent pieces) is available at least potentially in the existing knowledge structure. As indicated above, conceptual change via a spreading of the truth-value alteration is possible only when the candidate pieces of conceptual knowledge are included in the system. The deliberate belief revision is possible only when a cognizer can think of an alternative belief. If people do not think of any alternative theory, model, or interpretation, they may stick to the old conceptual device even when predictions from it are not supported.

An alternative concept, conception, or conceptualization may be prepared gradually and slowly in development of the target naive theory; alternatively, it can be brought in from outside the target theory by using some "borrowing" heuristics. Examples of the former case include the following.

1. Pieces of information needed to construct an alternative idea are accumulated slowly because they are not attended initially (e.g., on a balance beam, young children pay attention to the number of weights but ignore their distance from the center).

2. An idea stays implicit, in other words, it is "implemented" but not represented (e.g., being able to solve a concrete problem but unable to describe how to solve it).
3. An idea is available only in a particular context and has yet to be generalized (e.g., from biological understanding of illness as caused by germs only when there are obvious routes of contagion, such as coughing, to a generalized illness causality in terms of the germ theory).

Analogies and conceptual placeholders are two major "borrowing" heuristics. Conceptual change may often be triggered by an analogy that suggests an alternative view. Using analogies, people map their knowledge about the *source* to the present new case (target) so that they can make a coherent interpretation of the set of observations for the target, or even build a tentative theory.

Analogies are sometimes applied spontaneously, and other times presented by teachers and other adults. Photosynthesis is one of the difficult notions in understanding biology, because it is against the intuitive grasp of the commonality among all living things that naive biology indicates. That plants can produce their own nutriment is usually beyond children's imagination. However, Yuzawa (1988) reported that a "production factory" analogy—processing materials with proper means like baking bread from flour using heat—helped junior high students understand photosynthesis. Dunbar (1995) also reported that scientists in real-world laboratories often rely on analogy to generate new ideas when faced with inconsistent experimental findings.

Another possibility for deriving an alternative concept, conceptions, and conceptualizations is to assume a conceptual placeholder that does not include much substantive information initially. Solomon and Johnson (2000) reported findings suggesting that conceptual change occurs when children are exposed to a scientific concept that can serve as a conceptual peg in a sociocultural context. Here, children of 5 to 6 years of age were first made aware of the inadequacy of their understanding of biological inheritance by a conversation with a teacher, and then they were given a rudimentary notion of genes and opportunities to use this notion. This intervention, though lasting only about 20 minutes, led the children to make adult-like judgments on inheritance to some extent. This strategy is often adopted in science education. However, considering that young children in highly technological societies are often presented with a scientific concept that would serve as a conceptual peg through conversation with adults, watching TV programs, reading a book with adults, and so on in everyday life, spontaneous conceptual change also could occur in a similar way in everyday life, though it would take a longer time than the instruction based one.

Third, sociocultural contexts in which children are exposed to various, sometimes incongruous, pieces of information may make conceptual change more likely to occur. As already mentioned, children's learning that others possess different beliefs from their own may reduce the truth value of relevant beliefs and also induce attempts to revise the beliefs. This is because, though human beings have not only confirmation biases but also tendencies to ignore incongruous information (Festinger, 1957), they cannot do so when they engage in interaction with others for an extended period of time. One of such contexts enhancing conceptual change is social interactions including group discussion. Social interactions can be sources for generating recognized inconsistencies or discoordinations in individuals' existing knowledge systems, because different perspectives are presented in the interactions, and they can also be sources for providing possible solutions. In this sense, discussion can contribute to the occurrence of conceptual change. Indeed, it has been reported that social interaction can be a powerful mechanism for inducing conceptual change among scientists (Dunbar, 1995).

However, a number of studies have revealed that even among less sophisticated thinkers, discursive interactions may induce conceptual change. For example, Hatano and Inagaki (1997) provided data to support this claim; many school-aged children (10 years of age) changed their ways of reasoning about a monkey's physical characteristics through whole-class discussion from reasoning based on the animal's similarity to humans to reasoning based on a more sophisticated (Lamarckian) conception of evolution and specific biological taxonomy. Willams and Tolmie (2000) also reported that socially generated cognitive conflict (or inconsistencies) is effective for acquiring a more advanced conception of inheritance in their intervention study using children aged 8–12. Their dialogue analyses indicated that the effects of group discussion could be attributed to resolution of conceptual conflict within the groups holding different conceptions.

Toward an Integrative and Moderate Model of Conceptual Change

Let us make a brief comparison with other notions of conceptual change proposed so far. At what point does our notion of conceptual change differ from others? We take the position that conceptual change, as a profound change in a child's underlying conceptual structures, can take place during childhood, and, at the same time, we assert that the pre- and post-change knowledge systems have some continuity. In naive biology, for example, the pre- and post-change modes of inference or causalities coexist even among adults, though the former system becomes less salient and is used as a fallback.

How is our notion related to a newly proposed idea that children and adults differ only in shifting the relevance of already present explanatory systems (Keil, 1998, 1997)? This relevance shift notion of "conceptual change" denotes that children and adults differ not in underlying conceptual structures but in the relevance of these structures; children often possess several theories available to them early on, but they differ remarkably from adults in realizing where these theories are most relevant. It should be noted that according to this conceptualization, conceptual change is no longer clearly distinguished from enrichment. We agree with this notion of continuities in conceptual structures among young children, older children, and adults. Even preschool children possess naive theories of core domains, such as biology and psychology, and if they are urged to do so, they may be able to reason using biological categories and relying on mechanical causality in primitive ways. However, this does not mean that all developmental differences are just quantitative, a matter of how salient a variety of competing ideas are and how adaptively they can be applied to problem situations.

In addition, we cannot ignore possibilities that instruction-based conceptual change or instructionally influenced spontaneous conceptual change can take place, especially in later cognitive development. It can produce new conceptual tools through which older children and lay adults can see the world differently than young children do. We should pay more attention to the bridge or interaction between conceptual development and instruction, as claimed and researched by Vosniadou and Ioannides (1998).

Finally, our notion of conceptual change has emphasized the sociocultural factors involved. We fully agree that an increased amount of knowledge is a necessary condition for conceptual change (e.g., Carey, 1985; Smith et al., 1985; Wiser, 1988) and that the pre-change system provides cognitive or internal constraints in conceptual change. However, the roles of other people and tools as sociocultural or interactive constraints are also very important in conceptual change. We believe that most leading investigators studying conceptual change have been too cognitive and too individualistic. The issue of motivation inducing conceptual change has also been neglected, with a few notable exceptions (e.g., Pintrich, Marx, & Boyle, 1993).

NOTE

This chapter is a reprint of chapter 7 from Inagaki and Hatano (2002) "Young Children's Naïve Thinking about the Biological World." Reprinted with permission from Kayoko Inagaki and the Taylor and Francis Group.

REFERENCES

Ackerman, B. P. (1984). The effects of storage and processing complexity on comprehension repair in children and adults. *Journal of Experimental Child Psychology, 37*, 303–334.

Carey, S. (1985). *Conceptual change in childhood*. Cambridge, MA: MIT Press.

Carey, S. (1988). Conceptual differences between children and adults. *Mind and Language, 3*, 167–181.

Carey, S. (1991). Knowledge acquisition: Enrichment or conceptual change? In S. Carey & R. Gelman (Eds.), *The epigenesis of mind: Essays on biology and cognition* (pp. 257–291). Hillsdale, NJ: Erlbaum.

Carey, S. (1995). On the origin of causal understanding. In D. Sperber, D. Premack, & A. J. Premack (Eds.), *Causal cognition: A multidisciplinary debate* (pp. 268–302). Oxford: Clarendon Press.

Clement, J. (1982). Students' preconceptions in introductory mechanics. *American Journal of Physics, 50*, 66–71.

Dunbar, K. (1995). How scientists really reason: Scientific reasoning in real-world laboratories. In R. J. Sternberg & J. E. Davidson (Eds.), *The nature of insight* (pp. 365–395). Cambridge, MA: MIT Press.

Evans, E. M. (2001). Cognitive and contextual factors in the emergence of diverse belief systems: Creation versus evolution. *Cognitive Psychology, 42*, 217–266.

Festinger, L. (1957). *A theory of cognitive dissonance*. Evanston, IL: Row, Peterson.

Glenberg, A. M., & Epstein, W. (1985). Calibration of comprehension. *Journal of Experimental Psychology: Learning, Memory, and Cognition, 11*, 702–718.

Gopnick, A., & Wellman, H. M. (1994). The theory theory. In L. A. Hirschfeld & S. A. Gelman (Eds.), *Mapping the mind: Domain specificity in cognition and culture* (pp. 257–293). New York: Cambridge University Press.

Hatano, G. (1994). Introduction. *Human Development, 37*, 189–197.

Hatano, G. (1998). Comprehension activity in individuals and groups. In M. Sabourin, F. Craik, & M. Robert (Eds.), *Advances in psychological sciences. Vol. 2: Biological and cognitive aspects* (pp. 399–418). Hove, UK: Psychology Press.

Hatano, G., & Inagaki, K. (1991). Learning to trust higher-order categories in biology instruction. Paper presented at the meeting of the American Educational Research Association, Chicago.

Hatano, G., & Inagaki, K. (1996). Cognitive and cultural factors in the acquisition of intuitive biology. In D. R. Olson & N. Torrance (Eds.), *Handbook of education and human development: New models of learning, teaching and schooling* (pp. 683–708). Oxford: Blackwell.

Hatano, G., & Inagaki, K. (1997). Qualitative changes in intuitive biology. *European Journal of Psychology of Education, 12,* 111–130.

Inagaki, K, & Hatano, G. (1987). Young children's spontaneous personification as analogy. *Child Development, 58*, 1013–1020.

Inagaki, K., & Hatano, G. (1993). Young children's understanding of the mind-body distinction. *Child Development, 64*, 1534–1549.

Inagaki, K., & Hatano, G. (1999). Children's understanding of mind-body relationships. In M. Siegal & C. C. Peterson (Eds.), *Children's understanding of biology and health* (pp. 23–44). Cambridge: Cambridge University Press.

Inagaki, K., & Hatano, G. (2003). Conceptual and linguistic factors in inductive projection: How do young children recognize commonalities between animals and plants? In D. Genter & S. Goldin-Meadow

(Eds.), *Language and thought in mind: Advances in the study of language and thought* (pp. 313–333). Cambridge, MA: MIT Press.

Inagaki, K., & Sugiyama, K. (1988). Attributing human characteristics: Developmental changes in over- and underattribution. *Cognitive Development, 3*, 55–70.

Johnson, C. N., & Wellman, H. M. (1982). Children's developing conceptions of the mind and brain. *Child Development, 53*, 222–234.

Johnson, K. E., Mervis, C. B., & Boster, J. S. (1992). Developmental changes within the structure of the mammal domain. *Developmental Psychology, 28*, 74–83.

Johnson, S. C., & Carey, S. (1998). Knowledge enrichment and conceptual change: Knowledge acquisition in people with Williams syndrome. *Cognitive Psychology, 37*, 156–200.

Keil, F. C. (1998). Cognitive science and the origins of thought and knowledge. In W. Damon (Ed.), *Handbook of child psychology*, 5th ed., Vol. 1: R. M. Lerner (Ed.), *Theoretical models of human development* (pp. 341–413). New York: Wiley.

Keil, F. C. (1999). Conceptual change. In R. A. Wilson & F. C. Keil (Eds.), *The MIT encyclopedia of the cognitive sciences* (pp. 179–182). Cambridge, MA: MIT Press.

Markman, E. M. (1981). Comprehension monitoring. In W. P. Dickson (Ed.), *Children's oral communication skills* (pp. 61–84). New York: Academic Press.

Marton, F. (1989). Towards a pedagogy of content. *Educational Psychologist, 24*, 1–23.

Miller, J. L., & Bartsch, K. (1997). Development of biological explanation: Are children vitalists? *Developmental Psychology, 33*, 156–164.

Morita, E., Inagaki, K., & Hatano, G. (1988). The development of biological inferences: Analyses of RTs in children's attribution of human properties. Paper presented at the 30th annual convention of the Japanese Association of Educational Psychology, Naruto. [in Japanese]

Morris, S. C., Taplin, J. E., & Gelman, S. A. (2000). Vitalism in naive biological thinking. *Developmental Psychology, 36*, 582–613.

Nersessian, N. (1992). How do scientists think? Capturing the dynamics of conceptual change in science. In R. N. Giere (Ed.), *Minnesota studies in philosophy of science: Vol. 15. Cognitive models of science* (pp. 3–44). Minneapolis: University of Minnesota Press.

Perner, J. (1991). *Understanding the representational mind.* Cambridge, MA: MITPress.

Pintrich, P. R., Marx, R. W., & Boyle, R. A. (1993). Beyond cold conceptual change: The role of motivational beliefs and classroom contextual factors in the process of conceptual change. *Review of Educational Research, 63*, 167–199.

Siegler, R. S., & Jenkins, E. (1989). *How children discover new strategies.* Hillsdale, NJ: Erlbaum.

Smith, C., Carey, S., & Wiser, M. (1985). On differentiation: A case study of the development of the concepts of size, weight, and density. *Cognition, 21*, 177–237.

Solomon, G. E. A., & Johnson, S. C. (2000). Conceptual change in the classroom: Teaching young children to understand biological inheritance. *British Journal of Developmental Psychology, 18*, 81–96.

Stavy, R., & Wax, N. (1989). Children's conceptions of plants as living things. *Human Development, 32*, 88–94.

Subbotsky, E. (1997). Explanations of unusual events: Phenomenalistic causal judgments in children and adults. *British Journal of Developmental Psychology, 15*, 13–36.

Vosniadou, S. (1994). Introduction. *Learning and Instruction, 4*, 3–6.

Vosniadou, S., & Brewer, W. F. (1992). Mental models of the earth: A study of conceptual change in childhood. *Cognitive Psychology, 24*, 535–585.

Vosniadou, S., & Ioannides, C. (1998). From conceptual development to science education: A psychological point of view. *International Journal of Science Education, 20,* 1213–1230.

Wellman, H. M. (1990). *The child's theory of mind.* Cambridge, MA: MIT Press.

Williams, J. M., & Tolmie, A. (2000). Conceptual change in biology: Group interaction and the understanding of inheritance. *British Journal of Developmental Psychology, 18*, 625–649.

Wiser, M. (1988). The differentiation of heat and temperature: History of science and novice-expert shift. In S. Strauss (Ed.), *Ontogeny, phylogeny, and historical development* (pp. 28–48). Norwood, NJ: Ablex.

Wiser, M., & Carey, S. (1983). When heat and temperature were one. In D. Gentner & A. L. Stevens (Eds.), *Mental models* (pp. 267–297). Hillsdale, NJ: Erlbaum.

Yates, J., Bassman, M., Dunne, M., Jertson, D., Sly, K., & Wendelboe, B. (1988). Are conceptions of motion based on a naive theory or on prototypes? *Cognition, 29,* 251–275.

Yuzawa, M. (1988). Understanding the meaning of the situation of a problem and a reasoning schema. *Japanese Journal of Educational Psychology, 36,* 297–306. [in Japanese with an English summary]

10

Conceptual Change and Evolutionary Biology: A Developmental Analysis

E. Margaret Evans
University of Michigan

Evolution, in a way, contradicts common sense. (Mayr, 1982, p. 309)

Given the reputation of the United States as a world leader in science, it is ironic that its scientific establishment is experiencing a public backlash. The most acrimonious manifestation of this backlash has been the U.S. public's reaction to the Darwinian theory of evolution. With only 40% of the U.S. public accepting evolutionary explanations for human origins, the United States ranks second to last in acceptance rate among 34 industrialized nations. The rate in most of Europe, in contrast, ranges from 70% to 80%, whereas Japan's is 78% (Miller, Scott, & Okamoto, 2006). Explanations for this phenomenon abound, ranging from religious belief to poor scientific training to politicization. According to Mazur's (2005) analysis of several national U.S. samples, *Christian religiosity*, especially fundamentalism, significantly outweighs other contributing factors, including educational level and political orientation. Further, after controlling for these factors, including religiosity, Mazur (2005) found that acceptance of evolution was *not* independently related to other measures of science knowledge, dogmatism (closed-mindedness), geographical locale, or ethnicity.

In this chapter, these overt largely *creationist* rejections of evolutionary origins will be linked to a parallel phenomenon, well known to science teachers and science education researchers, which is students' misunderstanding of natural selection (e.g., Bishop & Anderson, 1990). A developmental framework will be used to help explain the emergence of both sets of ideas in communities with different religious orientations and differing degrees of scientific expertise. By invoking a developmental perspective, cognitive scientists and science educators who are interested in the emergence of early scientific ideas can pinpoint the critical junctures at which commonsense, scientific, and religious reasoning meet, and trace the ensuing conceptual changes (e.g., Duschl, Schweingruber, & Shouse, 2006; Vosniadou, 1994; Vosniadou & Ioannides, 1998).

A recent developmental approach that aligns well with formal science instruction is a description of human reasoning as a series of naïve or folk theories, which map onto fundamental domains of human knowledge, from biology to psychology to physics (Gopnik & Wellman, 1994; Hirschfeld & Gelman, 1994; Wellman & Gelman, 1998). Naïve theories provide the *commonsense* intuitions that first come to mind when humans seek everyday explanations for natural phenomena, from the workings of the human psyche to the movements of celestial objects. Conceptual change, from this perspective, may consist of the elaboration of intuitive concepts embedded in a particular explanatory framework or a more radical shift from one intuitive theory to another, to explain a particular phenomenon, such as from a naïve psychology to a naïve biology (e.g., Carey, 1985). Intuitive theories are not so much discarded as reworked.

In this chapter a synopsis of creationist thought will be followed by a developmental analysis of creationist and evolutionary ideas, utilizing the intuitive theory approach. The ways in which this approach could be integrated with that of domain-general theories will also be described. The premise of this chapter, however, is that a domain-specific explanatory framework is necessary (if not sufficient) to clarify why evolutionary ideas are counterintuitive, and creationist ones contagious (Sperber, 1996). Without it, the public resistance to evolution can only be understood in a piecemeal fashion. Such a framework, informed by a detailed developmental analysis, should also explain why conceptual change in evolutionary biology arouses existential fears. In brief, the basic claim, elaborated in the concluding section, is that an understanding of Darwinian evolution requires a radical shift from an intuitive psychological framework to a naturalistic biological one.

SCIENCE, CREATION SCIENCE, AND INTELLIGENT DESIGN

Creationists exploit the public's uneasiness about questions of origins and their misunderstanding of science to saddle evolution with the problems of a materialistic culture and to claim the imminent demise of evolutionary theory. From a creationist perspective, the failures of evolutionary theory stem from evolutionary biologists' naturalistic explanations for questions of origins, in particular, their acceptance of the mutability of species. Creationists argue that this materialistic world view excludes the supernatural, exposing the public to the misery of a Godless and immoral world (Scott, 2004). These criticisms have been addressed in detail in the media and in several books (e.g., Miller, 1999; Pennock, 2001; Ruse, 2005; Scott, 2004). In this chapter I shall provide enough background material to speak to a few of the core issues: the nature of creationist thought, the public reaction to the creation-evolution debate, and related *nature of science* questions.

Creationism and Science: A Cultural Clash?

Most cultures have a creation myth (see Campbell, 1972). Creationism is the most well known in the West because it draws its support from the King James Bible. Biblical literalists believe that God created each kind of animal with a unique essence, about 6000 to 10,000 years ago (Numbers, 1992, 2003). A cornerstone of this approach is the immutability of living kinds: Each kind has a fixed boundary and only God can create new kinds (Evans, 2001; Kehoe, 1983, 1995). Although the inerrancy of the Bible is a notable feature of Christian fundamentalist thought, it is also found among other religious groups, with about 30% of the U.S. population accepting the Bible as the actual word of God (Doyle, 2003). Fundamentalists from other monotheistic religions also reject evolution, for similar reasons, but the focus of this chapter is on the more explicit challenges posed by Christian Fundamentalism. Clearly, their viewpoint is at odds with that of contemporary evolutionary biologists, many of whom regard *species* boundaries as entirely mutable, with ancestor and descendent species linked in one entangled web, in a common ancestry of naturalistic origin (e.g., Doolittle, 2000).

The media coverage of the evolution-creationist controversy obscures what is actually a broad range of opinions on this topic (Miller, 1999; Ruse, 2005; Scott, 2004). The Gallup polls tend to focus fairly narrowly on the question of human origins and their questions rarely address this kind of complexity. Nevertheless, they do show a fairly consistent pattern over the past twenty years, with approximately 46% of their national sample endorsing the Biblical version of human origins. Only 13% accept the notion of common ancestry, with no reference to God. Importantly, though, 36% appeared to be theistic evolutionist, in that they accept evolution, but under God's guiding hand (Gallup, 2007).[1] The latter is in keeping with the beliefs of theologians from most non-fundamentalist Western religions who happily accept the theory of evolution as the embodiment of God's powers (Ruse, 2005). Indeed, many contemporary scientists reconcile science and religion as "nonoverlapping magisteria" (Gould, 1997) or consider that "God ... exists outside of space and time" (Francis Collins, interviewed by Biema, 2006). This kind of analysis indicates that the two worldviews part company at their extremes, with Biblical literalists in one camp, and scientists, such as Dawkins, who extol the benefits of atheism (Biema, 2006), in the other. Towards the center, however, there appear to be several ways of reconciling these apparently incommensurable positions.

Creation science preceded the more recent intelligent design movement, though both are manifestations of earlier creationist ideas (Evans, 1991, 1994/1995; Mayr, 1982; Scott, 2004). For this reason, the term *creationism* will be used in this chapter in a generic sense to refer to all groups who accept a *direct* role for God in the creation of species. Creation science was a 20th century movement. It emerged along with the publication of several prominent books by creation scientists John C. Whitcomb and Henry M. Morris, which reestablished the importance of the Noachim flood, so-called flood geology, and a literalist view of the Bible (Evans, 2001; Morris & Parker, 1982; Numbers, 1992; Whitcomb, 1972, 1988). Contemporary ideas about intelligent design, in contrast, secede from this literalist viewpoint to accept the geologist's view of the age of the earth. What both creation science and intelligent design have in common, though, is a rejection of a materialist view of the world, including a denial of naturalistic explanations for the origins of species (Scott, 2004). Moreover, both claim that a materialist Western science endorses a purposeless, Godless world. Scott (2004) points out that with methodological naturalism Western science cannot make any kind of statement about the existence, or not, of the supernatural, but this nuanced view is lost on creationists (and even some contemporary scientists).

In contrast to this contemporary angst, a brief glimpse of the history of Western science often shows science and religion working hand in hand, with scientists revealing God's guiding hand as they investigate the mysteries of the natural world (Evans 2000b; Shapin, 1996). The methods they used, however, were naturalistic, including experimentation; only naturalistic methods could be used to investigate natural phenomena. One of the reasons why creation science is often declared an oxymoron is because science cannot be used to investigate the supernatural (Numbers, 1992; Scott, 2004). That is the realm of religion.

All the major scientific and research organizations in the United States have issued policy statements defending the teaching of evolution in the nation's science classrooms and rejecting the idea that creation science or intelligent design should be taught alongside evolution (NSTA, 2003). Moreover, the law is on the science teacher's side. Despite many attempts, neither creation scientists nor leaders of the intelligent design (ID) movement have yet convinced the nation's lawmakers that creationism can be taught in the *science* classroom (Scott, 2004). The trump card, according to Judge Jones in the 2005 Dover trial, is that "ID violates the centuries-old ground rules of science by invoking and permitting supernatural causation" (p. 34, Mervis, 2006). This does not prevent creationists from attempting to impose their beliefs on local or state school boards, who are less susceptible to the legal or scientific arguments.

Is Evolution Immoral?

Leaving aside the question of the authenticity of the scientific account of evolution and of its legal status, many members of the public still feel uneasy about evolutionary theory (Brem, Ranney, & Schindel, 2003). Is it immoral? "If we are merely animals then how should we behave to one another" was one parent's question, and another said, "I don't know what to believe, I just want my kids to go to heaven." (Evans, 1994/1995, 2001). Evolutionary theory is, of course, mute on this point; this is the realm of religion, not science. Yet, some members of the public, including science teachers, associate evolution with a variety of negative ideas and effects, which contributes to their rejection of evolutionary theory (Griffith & Brem, 2004; Hahn, Brem, & Semken, 2005).

One factor in this rejection is the discredited attempt to associate Darwinism with the social inequality of the 19th century, the implication being that such inequality was genetically determined (Scott, 2004). Another is a successful attempt, mostly by creationists, to brand evolutionary theory with outcomes that harm society. A major political figure blamed the Columbine disaster on the teaching of evolution (Krugman, 2003). Others noted that the increased teaching of evolution in the schools *caused* a rise in teenage pregnancy and venereal disease (Chick, 2000). Teenage pregnancy rates are now declining, yet the teaching of evolution continues unabated. It would be just as misleading to state that the teaching of evolution caused the recent decline. This illusory correlation is one of the many ways that creationists use science to mislead the public and associate evolution with a host of contemporary evils.

Creationism and the Nature of Science

In addition to its supposed immorality, an oft-repeated criticism of evolution is that evolution is *only a theory* (Bybee, 2004; NAS, 1998, 1999; Scott, 2004). This criticism again relies on a misuse of science to bolster the case against evolution, but it does raise some interesting nature of science issues. In this case, creationists are using the term *theory* in its everyday sense, as an idea that can easily be discarded.

What does having a theory mean to a scientist? As do many areas of specialization, science incorporates terms commonly used in general discourse and proceeds to give them highly specialized meanings. In everyday language, theory means an idea, or a hunch about something. For scientists, however, a theory is an organized body of knowledge, which explains a set of interrelated facts. It has a great deal of support. In the face of evidence that does not quite fit into the theory, the theory is more likely to be amended than overturned. It takes a lot of counter evidence to overturn a theory. On the other hand, the term *hypothesis*, as used by scientists, is probably closer in meaning to the everyday use of theory. When scientists conduct experiments, it is usually to test whether or not a specific hypothesis can be supported, not an entire theory.

Creationists' belittling of evolution is also tied to ongoing disputes within the scientific community. Richard Dawkins and the late Steven Jay Gould are two leading evolutionary biologists who have had long battles over specific evolutionary hypotheses, though both are staunch anti-creationists. Dawkins argues, for example, that natural selection occurs at the level of the gene, whereas Gould considered it to operate at the level of the species, as well. Creationists have long publicized such arguments as evidence that evolutionary theory is in crisis and will soon be overturned. But, from a scientific point of view, it is just a sign that evolutionary theory is alive and well. New data will be collected to resolve such disputes over these specific hypotheses, which will end up strengthening the predictive power of the theory.

One more *nature of science* issue often raised by creation scientists is that evolutionary theory is not science because it is based on undocumented inference, rather than observation. Classically, creationists point out that the fossil record is incomplete, therefore, it cannot be used as evidence that species have evolved. There are countless examples in science of inferences based on data that could not be directly observed. We now know that there is a space between nerve cells across which chemicals are released for cell communication. This space could not be observed until the advent of the electron microscope in the 1940s. Yet, prior to that date, in order to explain otherwise inexplicable findings about the transmission of information in the nervous system, scientists had determined that there must be a space (see Mazzarello, 2000 for an historical account). How did they know? They could not directly observe the space, but based on available data they made the inference that it must exist. It was the only reasonable explanation for their findings. Crucially, even though scientists can only indirectly observe these phenomena, they are using *naturalistic* methods to obtain data to test their hypotheses. They did not resort to supernatural explanation.

Finally, it turns out that evolution can be observed. Organisms that undergo rapid reproduction from viruses to fruit flies provide opportunities for the direct observation of natural selection in action (Futuyma, 1998). The fossil record, while not complete, does provide evidence of transitional forms between species, some of the most notable examples being those of the ancestors of whales, which, unlike modern whales, had the capacity to walk on land (Gingerich, Raza, Arif, Anwar, & Shou, 1994; Zimmer, 2005).

These criticisms of evolution have proven useful to the scientific community because they highlight some widespread misconceptions about the scientific method, which need to be addressed both in the educational system and in communication with the general public (e.g., NAS, 1998).

Creationism and the Mutability of Species

Beyond nature of science wars, creationist misunderstandings of evolution reveal some intriguing cognitive barriers to evolutionary thought. These biases are core to the intuitive theory approach to be developed in rest of this chapter. Darwinian evolution is not all of one kind. Essentially, it can be divided into two sorts of processes, which are interdependent: microevolution or small-scale evolution and macroevolution or large-scale evolution. *Microevolutionary* processes explain change in gene frequencies within a particular population or species. Given particular environmental pressures and sufficient numbers of generations, these microevolutionary processes eventually yield large phenotypic changes, such as the reptiles and mammals, which are derived from a common ancestor. This is known as *macroevolution* (Futuyma, 1998).

Creationists explicitly reject macroevolution and common descent. Such processes directly contradict the creationist belief that each living kind was present during the Noachim Flood and has a God-given essence, meaning that it cannot change into a different living kind (Whitcomb, 1988). In contrast, by claiming that God built some diversity into the DNA of each living kind, creationists can accept microevolutionary processes such as variation and changes in gene frequency within a living kind (Greenspan, 2002; Morris & Parker, 1982). In a criticism of various evolution exhibits, a creationist claims:

> The evolution of HIV is not disputed by creationists. The only complaint that creationists have with this is the confusing use of the term "evolution" to describe both variation within a species and the origin of new kinds of life. ... The fact that one can mix existing genes to get some variation in species doesn't prove that genes can arise naturally to create new kinds of creatures. (Jones, 2005)

The following example, given by an adult museum visitor, illustrates this type of creationist reasoning in the museum-going lay public (Evans et al., 2006):

Ok, I believe um, God created a pair, a male and female of everything with the ability to diversify. So I guess what I meant at the time of the flood, I believe that's when the continents broke apart and so even though only a few of each things were saved in the flood, they had the genetic background to be able to diversify into all of the, like for instance, dogs, and all the different kinds that we have. And so um, does that help? Just a creationistic view.

Thus, when creationists reject evolution, by and large they are rejecting phylogenetic changes or macroevolution (Poling & Evans, 2004b). In the following example, a museum visitor was asked to explain why there were changes in the average size of beaks in populations of *Galapagos Finches* over several seasons. Although *evolution* is rejected, the visitor describes the microevolutionary process of differential survival with some accuracy (Evans, et al., 2006):

That's a good question. I probably can't explain that. But like I said, because of my biblical world view, I don't believe in evolution. So I don't believe that they evolved because it takes too long. There are too many failures before they evolve into something that finally works, so I just reject that view. *Um, my guess would be that there probably were larger beaked finches but there weren't as many of them and the small beaked ones would have died out because they couldn't get the food.* [italics added]

The practical outcome of this distinction is that in the classroom the teacher could discuss microevolutionary processes without running into difficulties with creationist reasoners (Evans et al., 2007). Further, there is some evidence that the lay public similarly considers evolution to be common descent, without understanding that it also refers to changes in gene frequency in a population (Poling & Evans, 2004b).

One final issue raised by notions of the immutability, or not, of species is the definition of the term *species*, which is problematic for both the scientist and the layperson. For the creationist museum visitors described above, diversity within a specific *living kind*, such as birds or dogs, would not be considered evidence of speciation because the diverse dogs or birds continue to be *same* living kind. When a college-educated population was asked to define species, the majority thought of species as a group of animals that looked alike "'like mice or humans'; only 7% referenced reproductive isolation or common ancestry" (Poling & Evans, 2004b, p. 513). In that same study, even undergraduates who were creationist as well as those who were evolutionist were more likely to agree that highly similar animals (e.g., gorillas, monkeys) share a common ancestor than do dissimilar animals (e.g., rats, whales) (Poling & Evans, 2004b). (For an evolutionary biologist, all living things share a common ancestor.)

Such definitions are similar to the *generic-species* concepts found historically in the folk beliefs of traditional societies across the world (Atran, 1990, 1999). This concept references an everyday understanding of species as living kinds that look alike and which are adapted to a specific environment; usually they are the only representative of a particular genus in that locale (e.g., zebras, lions). The field naturalist, in contrast, is likely to use reproductive isolation as a working definition of species (Futuyma, 1998; Mayr, 1991, 1997), whereas other biologists and philosophers often argue that there is no satisfactory definition that covers all phyla (Doolittle, 2000; Mishler, 1999).

CONCEPTUAL BARRIERS TO EVOLUTIONARY THINKING: A FRAMEWORK

Intuitive theories provide a conceptual framework that makes it possible for individuals to make sense of the everyday world, without any formal training (Atran, 1995, 1998; Wellman & Gelman, 1998). Intuitive reasoning works wonderfully on a day-to-day basis. It only causes difficulty when we try to understand ideas that are outside the realm of everyday experience, such as the theory of evolution. Two cognitive biases stemming from an everyday or intuitive biology (Medin & Atran, 2004; Gelman, 2003) and psychology (Wellman & Gelman, 1998) are particularly problematic: That living things are separate, stable, and unchanging (*essentialism*) and that animate behavior is goal directed (*teleology*) and intentional. Evolutionary concepts, it is claimed, are counterintuitive precisely because they challenge this everyday understanding (Evans, 1991, 1994/1995, 2000a, 2001; Mayr, 1982), which tends to resonate better with a creationist ideology. These biases appear very early in human ontogeny (Wellman & Gelman, 1998).

Evolutionary theory provides us with a dynamic world in which all living kinds are related, through a common ancestry. If we could speed up time, we would "see" species as dynamic and biological change as contingent and non-directional; in effect, species would morph from one to another as environments change, or disappear entirely. Yet, everyday cognition, mired as it is in a particular time and place, appears to obstruct this view of a dynamic world. What is needed is the equivalent of a microscope or telescope, such as a time-machine that transcends human cognitive and perceptual limitations. Although the fossil record and molecular biology provide some of these tools, they lack the sense of immediacy and authenticity of the other instruments. The most potent constraint, though, is derived from an everyday psychology, our expertise at reading minds and understanding human goals and intentions. The powerful analogy provided by the creative abilities of the human appears to underlie the concept of intelligent design, especially when reinforced by a cultural model of God as central planner of the natural world (Evans 2000a, 2001).

Next, I shall focus on the basic claim in this chapter, which is that this network of intuitive beliefs constrains human cognition such that creationist ideas are attractive and easier to spread, whereas evolutionary ideas are less contagious.

Essentialism

A group of well-educated adults bursts into laughter as a leading creation scientist describes the apparently absurd idea entertained by evolutionary biologists that whales originally walked on land (Evans, 1994/1995). On the face of it this does appear to be an odd idea: a land mammal the ancestor of an ocean dweller? Similarly, if children are asked if such a transformation is possible, they are likely to reply "you've got to be kidding" (Evans et al., 2005). What underlies this strong intuition that animal kinds are unique and cannot be transformed into different kinds? Such ideas are widespread. Historians have documented them in early Western philosophers (Mayr, 1982), and they are also found in children (Gelman, 2003). This psychological essentialism (Medin & Ortony, 1989) gives rise to essentialist beliefs in the unique identity of each living kind. Humans act as if each living kind has an underlying essence that makes it what it is. A tiger, for example, is always a tiger, even if you paint out its stripes and remove its legs; it is a deformed tiger, but a tiger, nonetheless. These essentialist beliefs may well have several functions. They appear to help us view the world as stable and unchanging. This is a very useful aspect of everyday reasoning in that we ignore the dynamic aspects of the world around us and focus on the stability. It is much easier for young children, for example, to work out what is happening in a world that is perceived as essentially the same from day to day. Essentialist thinking may also underlie our ability to categorize and make inferences based on those categories (Gelman, 2003; Shipley, 1993). Once a child is told that the three-legged white animal is really a tiger, he or she can easily infer a lot of tiger properties: Its offspring will be tigers, it eats meat, it lives in forests and is dangerous. This categorization ability reduces the amount of information we have to process every time we learn new things. Everyday essentialist reasoning is, however, a significant barrier to evolutionary thinking, in which living kinds are ever changing.

Teleology

A glance at the behavior of an ant colony or a beehive will convince most people that ant and bee activities are purposeful. These insects systematically search for food and bring it back to their home base to fuel the next generation. The human tendency to view behavior as directed towards a goal is very powerful and seen in infancy (Tomasello, Carpenter, Call, Behne, & Moll, 2005). Yet, insects, even ants, cannot reason about goals, because they cannot *think*. They aren't wondering where the next meal is coming from or how to satisfy the voracious appetites of their young. Their behavior only appears to be goal-directed; in reality, insects are responding to environmental cues and internal signals, acquired over their evolutionary history. It is very difficult, however, to describe animal behavior without referring to its purpose or function (Kelemen, 1999, 2004; Keil, 1994, 1995). Why might such teleological (or purposive) thinking be useful?

A reasonable hypothesis is that it helps people tell the difference between living and nonliving things (e.g., Medin & Atran, 2004). If we see a rock plummeting down a mountain-side, we will look for something that might have pushed it. That is part of an everyday naïve physics. Conversely, if we see a cat bounding down the same terrain, one might wonder about its goal — pursuit of a rabbit, fleeing a predator? Even infants can distinguish between these two kinds of movement, one resulting from a physical cause and the other apparently satisfying a function or goal (Tomasello et al., 2005). It could well be that the ability to detect purposeful activity is important to human survival, as it is a signal that an object is a living thing and it might be a source of food or of danger. Researchers hypothesize that along with essentialist reasoning, teleological reasoning forms the basis of our everyday naive biology (Medin & Atran, 2004), and appears early in childhood (Inagaki & Hatano, 2002, 2006). This again raises a barrier to evolutionist reasoning. Evolution is adaptive in the sense that it is contingent on particular environmental conditions, but it is not directed towards the goal of adapting to those conditions.

Intentionality

Humans are a social species exquisitely attuned to shades of meaning. We read human minds and behaviors more easily and earlier than we read books. Unfortunately, it also leads us to assume intentions where none are meant. One child kicks another. Did he or she mean to do it? Was it intentional or accidental? Here's where we get to creationist versus evolutionist reasoning. A watchmaker creates a perfect instrument exquisitely attuned to the measurement of time (Dawkins, 1987). This artifact has been built to satisfy human goals and intentions. Creationists, it would appear, transfer their intuitive understanding of the human as a manufacturer of tools, such as watches, and apply it to objects that have arisen naturally, such as the human eye. They use the artifact analogy to reason that anything as perfect as the human eye must have had a designer, a supernatural creator in this case; this is the crux of the intelligent design argument. The eye could not have arisen naturally. Some researchers argue that creationism and intelligent design are so appealing because they elicit the well honed human capacity for intentional and purposive or goal-directed reasoning — a naïve theory of mind (Evans, 1994/1995, 2000, 2001; Kelemen, 2004).

Conceptual Change

Evolutionary theory is probably one of the most counterintuitive ideas the human mind has encountered, so far. Some historians believe that is why it took such a long time before anyone could discern a natural solution to the problem of "Where did we come from?" (Mayr, 1982).

That is, a solution that did not involve the direct intervention of a supernatural designer. Even when Darwin had solved the problem, it took him many years to assemble a watertight argument, one that would convince every critic (Mayr, 1991). To appreciate evolutionary arguments requires a radical conceptual change. We have to set aside or reconfigure our intuition that species were designed for a purpose, just like artifacts, and that they have unique essences. Specifically, we have to switch from a naïve psychological explanation to a naturalistic explanation that eschews purpose and endorses the idea that living things undergo radical change.

On the surface, it would seem that evolution may be too difficult for children to grasp. But we cannot assume this to be the case. In some ways children are more flexible than adults. An understanding of evolution does not require complex ideas that take years to acquire, such as mathematical reasoning or an understanding of genetics. Darwin and his contemporaries had no knowledge of Mendel's work on genes (Mayr, 1991). It was not until the 20th century that Darwinian evolution and Mendelian genetics were united. In the next section, I shall outline what we know about the development of evolutionary concepts in children and describe the most typical ideas of youth of different ages.

So far the focus has been on conceptual barriers to an understanding of evolution rather than on difficulties understanding the *nature of science*. Although both are important, I shall argue later that the latter are secondary rather than primary. The public misunderstanding of science and its uneasiness about questions of origins are exploited by creationists. The intuition that animals are immutable and that animate behavior is purposive increases susceptibility to a creationist worldview. For such ideas to spread with ease the cognitive contingencies must already be in place (Sperber, 1996). Darwinian evolution, on the other hand, is unsettling and more difficult to reconcile with these basic intuitions. Although it is clearly the case that the public misunderstands the nature of science, that does not explain why antipathy towards the theory of evolution is stronger than to other scientific theories, such as the theory of gravity.

CONCEPTUAL CHANGE AND EVOLUTIONARY BIOLOGY: A DEVELOPMENTAL ANALYSIS

The Emergence of Evolutionist and Creationist Ideas in Different Communities

If human cognition is subject to constraints in the form of intuitions that increase resistance to evolutionary thinking, then the developmental evidence should provide the most powerful support for such a hypothesis (Evans, 2000a, 2001). Such constraints should appear early on, change systematically over development, and persist into adulthood, even when modified by cultural input.

In sum, we should expect to see developmental change in children's understanding of evolutionary ideas, which parallel children's emerging understanding of human minds and of nature. Young children should be highly resistant to the idea that animals can change and quite accepting of the idea that animate motion is purposeful (Evans, 2000a, 2001). Further, the extensive work on children's theory of mind should provide evidence of changes in their everyday psychology that relate to children's understanding of intelligent design. In a series of studies that examined the early emergence of ideas about the origins of species in diverse communities, such relationships were found, though there were some surprises (Evans, 1991, 1994/1995, 2000a, 2000b, 2001).

In the following summary of these studies, the term *Christian fundamentalist* refers to families from communities who attend churches *and* schools that endorse Biblical literalism. *Nonfundamentalist* refers to families from communities in the same locale, but who went to churches that did not endorse a literal reading of the Bible and who attended public schools. Importantly, parents from the two communities had similar educational levels and similar expectations of their children's educational attainment. Further, families from the two communities did not differ in the extent to which they endorsed musical activities and typical childhood hobbies, from stamp collecting onwards. Consistent with their respective ideologies, fundamentalist families were more likely to endorse religious activities, whereas non-fundamentalist families were more likely to include fossils and nature in their preferred activities (Evans, 2001).

Overview

Children and adults from both fundamentalist and non-fundamentalist communities were asked a series of open- and closed-ended questions about the origins of the *very first* of different kinds of animals. Given the ages of the child participants, the term *evolution* was never used. In the coding systems, the term *evolutionist* was applied to responses that endorsed the basic macroevolutionary concept rejected by the Biblical literalists described earlier: that one kind of animal could be the predecessor or successor of a very different kind of animal. This is a transformationist idea. Children's responses were termed *spontaneous generationist* (see Mayr, 1982) if they expressed a naturalistic non-transformationist idea, implying that the very first of a kind just appeared or emerged from the ground ("it came out of the ground"). Such ideas were expressed by the early Greeks (Mayr, 1982). Moreover, they are consistent with the observation that living things apparently emerge out of the ground after the snow thaws or a rainstorm (Evans, 2000a). *Creationist* ideas were those in which a supernatural power was invoked (God made it). In the results shown in Figure 10.1 (Evans, 2001), any of these ideas could be endorsed from zero to three times over three open-ended questions about the origins of humans, sun bears, and tuataras. As can be seen in Figure 10.1, children and adults from the two communities clearly differed in the extent to which they endorsed creationist and evolutionist ideas, with creationism overwhelmingly endorsed in the fundamentalist community, by all age-groups.

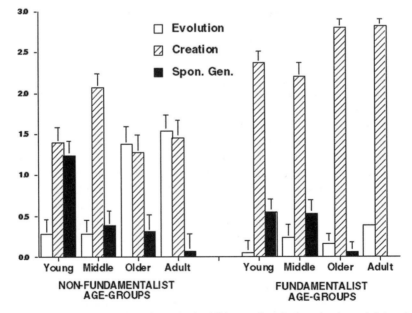

FIGURE 10.1   Beliefs about the origin of species in children and adults from fundamentalist and non-fundamentalist school communities, by age group (Frequency Range 0-3 + SEM).

Overall, the results imply that 5- to 7-year-olds (Young Age-Group) endorse a mixture of spontaneous generationist and creationist ideas, depending on the community of origin. In contrast, 8- to 10-year-olds (Middle Age-Group) endorse creationist ideas, *regardless* of community of origin; in fact, there was no significant difference between the communities for this age-group. By early adolescence (Older Age-Group), however, children's ideas were not significantly different from those of the adult members of their respective communities: evolutionist, creationist, or some mixture of the two (Evans, 2000a, 2001). The pattern of endorsement in the non-fundamentalist community was very similar to that found in national samples (e.g., Gallup, 2007).

Furthermore, consistent with their robust essentialism (Gelman, 2003), 5- to 7-year-olds responded "No" when asked the closed-ended question: Could one species have been the descendent of a completely different kind of animal (see also Samarapungavan & Weirs, 1997). These young children did, however, endorse creationism at higher rates when they were explicitly presented with such ideas: Did God make them? Such results suggest that young children are susceptible to notions of intelligent design, even while they resist notions of species change (Evans, 2001). These findings were interpreted as supporting a constructive interactionist position (e.g., Wozniak & Fischer, 1993). Consistent with their cognitive biases, children spontaneously generate intuitive beliefs about origins, both natural and intentional. Community input reinforces and refines the culturally sanctioned intuitions while purging others, resulting in the distinctive and complex *reflective* belief systems (Sperber, 1996) of the communities at large (Evans, 2000a, 2000b, 2001).

What was most striking about these results were the two age-related shifts: from the mixture of spontaneous generationist and creationist ideas found in the 5- to 7-year-olds to the consistent creationism of the 8- to 9-year olds; and the second shift to the endorsement of evolutionary ideas among early adolescents, at least in the non-fundamentalist communities. A series of follow-up studies examined these shifts in more detail.

Consistent Creationism in 8- to 9-year-olds

Further investigation of the pattern of reasoning of the 8- to 9-year-olds in non-fundamentalist communities, revealed an interesting relationship. It appeared that children in this age-group were beginning to confront existential questions, of eternity and of death, and it was this capacity that helped to motivate the shift to a consistent creationism (Evans, Mull, & Poling, 2001).

One of the reasons the youngest children appeared to endorse spontaneous generationist ideas was that they had failed to grasp the basic premise of the origins question, that, at one time, a particular kind of animal did not exist (Evans, 2000a, 2000b, 2001). In effect, some 5- to -7-year-olds seemed to believe that the animals were always on earth, but someplace else where they could not be seen, such as underground. The origins questions about the *very first* of a particular kind would make little sense to a child who thought they were eternal. To test this hypothesis, in a different study 99 preschool and early school age children, who attended public schools, were asked "Have there always been 'Xs' here on this world" (*impermanence*), where X was one of three randomly presented pictures of North American mammals and three simple artifacts (Evans, Mull, & Poling, 2001). Children responded with simple yes-no answers. As can be seen in Figure 10.2, not until children were 8- to 9-years of age did they consistently accept the idea of the impermanence of animals and of artifacts.

Children in the same study were also asked artificialist (Did a person make it?) and creationist (Did God make it?) questions about each of the same animals and artifacts. Replicating a pattern found among *non-fundamentalist* children in an earlier study (Evans, 2001), but using different measures, it was not until 8- to 9- years of age that children consistently distinguished

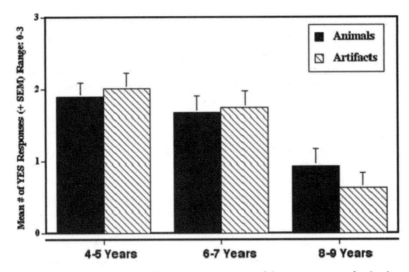

FIGURE 10.2   Were they always here? Children's acceptance of the permanence of animals and artifacts, by age group.

between the creative capabilities of humans and of God (see Figure 10.3). In particular, younger non-fundamentalist children were as likely to state that God made artifacts as humans made artifacts (Evans, Mull, & Poling, 2001). In contrast, *fundamentalist* children from the same age-group seem precocious in that they were significantly more likely to make these distinctions (Evans, 2001). As it seems unlikely that fundamentalist adults explicitly focus on the distinctions between God and human capacities, the conclusion is that children make this inference unaided, perhaps based on repeated exposure to a creationist model.

Children's emerging grasp of core existential concepts should also include death: Entities once created will not continue to exist. Although there is much variation in the age of acquisi-

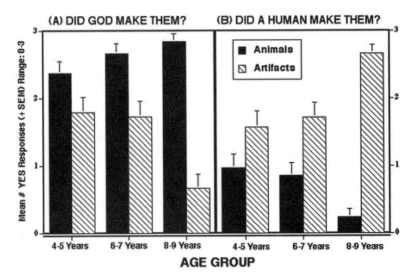

FIGURE 10.3   Children's responses to creationist (A) and artificialist (B) explanations for the origins of animals and artifacts, by age group.

tion, which depends on the measures used, a full understanding of death is often not achieved until children are 7 to 9 years of age (Poling & Evans, 2004b; Slaughter & Lyons, 2003; Speece & Brent, 1984, 1996). Three measures of the death concept, irreversibility, nonfunctionality, and universality (inevitability) were also included in this study, and combined into a composite measure of children's understanding of death (Evans, Mull, & Poling, 2001).

To assess whether the creationism of the children in the study was related to their understanding of existential issues and their capacity to reason about human artificialism, a multiple regression analysis was performed on a composite measure of *coherent* creationism, in which two measures were combined (God made animals, God did not make artifacts): 54% of the variance was explained. Predictor variables included a coherent artificialism (humans make artifacts, not animals), children's understanding of death, children's understanding of the impermanence of objects, and children's age (as a continuous variable). Standardized regression coefficients indicated that age did not add any additional variance beyond the effects of the other variables, all of which contributed variance independently of each other (Evans, Mull, & Poling, 2001).

This study suggests that children's capacity to reason about an intelligent designer is strongly related to their understanding of artifact origins as well as their grasp of existential concepts, rather than other age-related factors. This capability increases children's susceptibility to cultural input, which is why older children are more likely than younger children to evoke God as the designer. What else is needed?

Final and Ultimate-Causal Reasoning in 8- to 9-year-olds

The *final* or teleological cause reasoning of the creationist world view is eschewed by modern science, because the typical scientist should be concerned with proximate cause mechanisms, the immediate cause of the event in question (Root-Bernstein, 1984; Shapin, 1996). Ernst Mayr, the preeminent evolutionary biologist, disagrees with this viewpoint, however. Mayr argued that evolutionary biology differs from the physical sciences because it consider the *ultimate* causes, more specifically the evolutionary reasons, for the existence of a particular biological structure or behavior, as well as the proximate causes (1985, 1988). Thus the evolutionary biologist asks both how and why questions: How does a particular organ work? Why does that organ have that particular structure and function? (Evans 2000a, 2001; Southerland, Abrams, Cummins, & Anzelmo, 2001).

This integration of causal levels is one of the reasons that evolutionary biology appears to challenge the creationist world view. The causal status of proximate *causes* and that of the more distal *reasons* (or purpose) for a behavior or event has been the subject of much philosophical and psychological debate (e.g., Malle, 2004; Sehon 2005). A *reason* explanation is also called teleological reasoning, but if it is conceptualized as a more distal causal level, the evolutionary cause, some of the angst surrounding the creation/evolution debate should melt away. In effect, many of those scientists and theologians described earlier have managed to accommodate those causal levels by considering God as the first cause (Baker, 2006), the reason why life exists, and evolutionary causes as critical links in a naturalistic causal chain set into motion by God. The problems really arise when God is thought of as the more immediate or proximate cause of the origin of species, a central planner, as in the Biblical literalist account.

The focus here is on children and when they begin to make sense of these crucial distinctions. The short answer is that, as yet, not very much is known about this issue. To understand origins questions children have to integrate proximate and more distal causes into a complex causal structure. Only then can they consider *how* and *why* something came into existence (see also Abrams, Southerland, & Cummins, 2001; Southerland et al., 2001). There is plenty of evidence that young children use proximate cause reasoning (e.g., Wellman & Gelman, 1998). In the spontaneous generationist reasoning of the 5- to 7-year-olds, for example, they easily explain how the animal became visible (it came out of the ground), but they do not explain how it got there in the first place. Yet, the ease with which 5- to 7-year-olds agreed that "God did it," when offered the opportunity to do so in closed-ended questions (Evans, 2001), not only suggests a role for "testimony" (Harris & Koenig, 2006) in children's endorsement, but also suggests that they can incorporate distal cause reasoning.

The evidence presented earlier, however, demonstrated that for younger children, at least, this information is not yet integrated into a knowledge structure, in that "God did it" is just a loosely associated piece of information, no different from "a person did it" (Evans 2000a, 2001). Furthermore, younger children appeared to consider God as the proximate cause of the event in the sense that he directly makes objects/species in the way that people make artifacts, rather than considering the final cause, the reason why he made the object. Further evidence to support this argument is found in a recent study in which children were asked open-ended questions about the origins of the very first artifacts: Younger children gave single cause answers, whereas older children were more likely to integrate different causal levels (Evans, Mull, Poling, & Szymanowski, 2005). The following responses to the question: How do you think the very first chair got here on earth? illustrate this age-related shift:

From the store (6 years); God made it (6.8 years) Humans build it (6.8 years).

God makes trees, so we can cut the trees down, and make chairs out of wood (8.3 years).

God gave people the idea to make a chair (11. 8 years).

Moreover, in some recent work investigating the development of a folk theory of intentionality (Malle & Knobe, 1997), it was not until 8- to 9-years of age that children appeared to be converging on the adult theory (Mull & Evans, 2007). The *intentionality* inherent in an action such as that of a child knocking over a glass, for example, is interpreted differently by different age-groups. One-year-olds both recognize and respond appropriately to goal-directed actions such as the hand movements or visual gaze that are the immediate precursors to an action (Tomasello et al., 2005). Preschoolers often report that an action occurred because of the protagonist's desires: "he wanted to knock over the glass" (Mull & Evans, 2007). Five- to seven-year olds report the immediate or behavioral concomitants of the action, such as looking and pushing. Older children are more likely to report the more distal causes underlying the action, such as the knowledge, skills, and beliefs of the perpetrator: "he knew what he was doing when he looked and pushed the glass" (Mull & Evans, 2007).

This research indicates that it is not until they about 8- to 9-years of age that children fully describe the reasons, in particular the prior intentions, that make up a folk theory of intentionality (Mull & Evans, 2007). At this point they integrate an understanding of proximate cause goal-directed actions, apparent at all ages, with more distal mental state explanations. Researchers investigating school-age children's understanding of the mental processes that underlie more complex actions report a similar age-related trajectory (Amsterlaw, 1999; Flavell et al., 1995, 2000). These findings could well explain why it is often not until 8- to 9-years of age that children begin to fully conceptualize God as intelligent designer; younger children are less likely to integrate the immediate causes of an action (he made it) with the final causes (the reasons why he made it). If the same capacity underlies the ability to reason about ultimate or evolutionary causes, then it is not too surprising that it is not until the end of the grade school years that children typically begin to reason in evolutionary terms.

Evolutionary Ideas (macro- and micro-) in Older Schoolchildren

In sum, the work described so far indicates that to reason about the origins of novel entities, artifacts or animals, children should have confronted core existential questions and be able to integrate proximate and ultimate causes into a complex causal chain. This emerging cognitive capacity is necessary, but not sufficient. It is related to final cause creationist reasoning as well as ultimate cause evolutionary reasoning. What else might predict acceptance of evolutionary ideas? In this section both micro- and macro-evolutionary concepts are considered.

Clearly, exposure to a particular cultural environment is critical, but which aspects of that environment have predictive value? As described earlier, by early adolescence, children raised in more religious contexts, such as Christian fundamentalist homes and schools, were more likely to maintain and extend their creationist ideas, whereas their non-fundamentalist counterparts were more likely to endorse evolutionist views (Evans, 2001). Importantly, that research also revealed that the latter endorsement was related to several factors other than community of origin.

Independent of the consistency of parent evolutionist beliefs, an understanding of the fossil evidence and a willingness to accept the (incorrect) idea that animals change in response to environmental factors (e.g., giraffes' long necks result from their habit of stretching their necks to reach into tall trees to obtain food) predicted preadolescents' macroevolutionary ideas. Even though the mechanism they endorse is incorrect, they acknowledged the critical role of environmental pressure in species changes (Evans 2000a, 2000b). Children from fundamentalist families believed that animals would not change, because "God made it that way so it can't change" (11-year-old; Evans, 2001). Altogether, on open-ended questions, these factors explained 76% of the variance in the frequency of preadolescents' evolutionary ideas. Predictors of the frequency of preadolescents' creationist ideas included the consistency of parent creationist ideas, attendance at a Christian fundamentalist school, and a lack of knowledge of the fossil evidence, altogether accounting for 67% of the variance (Evans, 2001).

One of the surprising findings in Evans' (2001) study was that many of the participants had mixed beliefs, endorsing both evolutionist and creationist ideas. Moreover, many in the non-fundamentalist community, while accepting that non-human species evolved, believed that humans were created by God. A more recent in-depth investigation of this finding revealed a much more nuanced acceptance or rejection of evolution than national or international surveys would allow. In this study, we hypothesized that an acceptance of radical within-species change, such as the metamorphosis of caterpillars into butterflies (Rosengren, Gelman, Kalish, & McCormick, 1991), would predict acceptance of evolutionary origins, because in both cases such an acceptance requires a modification of core essentialist constraints on species concepts (Evans, Rosengren, Szymanowksi, Smith, & Johnson, 2005). The relation between an acceptance of macroevolutionary change and the nature of the living kind was examined in 115 6- to 12-year-olds and their parents from both Biblical literalist and theistic evolutionist families (defined by parental belief system). Participants of all ages were more likely to accept evolutionary ideas for animals that undergo metamorphosis and were taxonomically distant from the human, in the following order: Butterflies > frogs > non-human mammals > humans (Figure 10.4).

Moreover, among theistic evolutionist families, metamorphosis understanding was related to evolutionary concepts, independently of the child's age. This was not the case in Biblical literalist families however, where older children understood metamorphosis but still retained their explicit belief that each "kind" has a unique and God-given essence that cannot change. Although, one clear implication of these studies is that teaching children about metamorphosis may provide them with the basis for modifying an early cognitive constraint, namely an essentialist bias, there is an important caveat. Metamorphosis as a model for species change introduces an inaccurate if

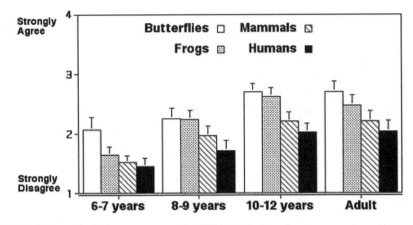

FIGURE 10.4   Did it evolve? Mean agreement (+SEM) for butterflies, frogs, mammals and humans, by age group.

prevalent analogy: Evolutionary change is like developmental change.

One further, critical factor related to evolutionist and creationist ideas in a population is the acceptance of the human as an animal (Carey, 1985). In the same study, children were also asked whether humans, other mammals, butterflies, frogs, and artifacts were animals (Evans et al., 2005). Apart from the human, children of all ages were quite clear which were animals and which were not. For the human there was both a developmental and a community influence, with older children from theistic evolutionist families most likely to agree that the human was an animal (see Figure 10.5). Moreover, independently of other relevant factors, such as parental promotion of religious interest in the child, and the child's age, acceptance of the human as an animal was positively related to children's macroevolutionary ideas ($\beta = .29$; $p < .01$).

Early adolescents have the capacity to reason about original cause. They may also accept that populations of animals undergo macroevolutionary change. The latter acceptance is most likely to occur if the essentialist bias that species are unchanging has been modified by exposure to evidence of species change, from fossils, to metamorphosis, to adaptive variation. Moreover, many of the children who endorsed macroevolutionary ideas also spontaneously invoked some

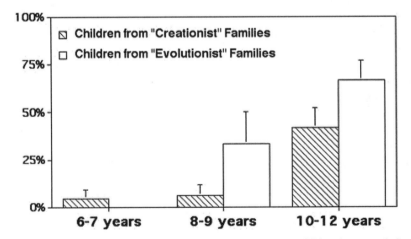

FIGURE 10.5   Is the human an animal? Percentage agreement among children from mostly "creationist" and mostly "evolutionist" families, by age group.

kind of evolutionary cause that would explain these changes. In most cases this was a teleological cause, such as a need-based or developmental change in response to environmental factors, seen also in other studies with these age-groups (e.g., Abrams et al., 2001; Brumby, 1979; Deadman & Kelly, 1978; Southerland et al., 2001); presumably no-one taught them this, it is one that they inferred with minimal input. But there were occasional instances of something approaching a Darwinian mechanism.

Here is the response of a 10-year-old girl with no formal exposure to evolutionary theory, who had been asked about the adaptation of a novel animal called a spiggle (it looked like a mixture of a pig and a squirrel) to its newly aquatic environment — a previously dry island that had been flooded. Note the sequence of causal chains in her response (Evans, 2000a):

> If there are spiggles that weren't streamlined, they wouldn't be well equipped for the life they lived so the streamlined webbed spiggles would live and — slowly the stronger webbed ones would survive and eventually all would be like this. (p. 248)

A typical response from a younger child was:

> [they] watched the fishes, copied them, one spiggle got to swim and taught the others. (p. 230)

Both of these responses were original. The younger child was using his understanding of human activities as goal-directed and intentional to model how spiggles could change. The 10-year-old, in contrast, thought that the spiggle population can vary (some are streamlined, some are not), and that the aquatic environment acts as a selection force, with the streamlined, webbed spiggles surviving. There is no reference to intentional or goal-directed actions. She has almost described the mechanism of natural selection.

High School and College Students' Understanding of Evolution

The focus of this chapter, thus far, has been on concepts of species origins rather on mechanisms of change within a population. What has been demonstrated is that by early adolescence those children who accept the idea of common ancestry, that one kind of animal could have been the descendent of a completely different kind, are also likely to endorse pre-Darwinian teleological ideas of evolutionary change. The main focus of the extensive research on high-school and college students' misunderstanding of evolution has been on mechanisms of microevolutionary change, in particular students' understanding of natural selection (Catley, 2006; Poling & Evans, 2004b). This research has also addressed the issue of what kinds of teaching methods are required for students to shift from a pre-Darwinian mechanism of individual change to the Darwinian mechanisms of natural selection in a population. This work has been detailed elsewhere (e.g., Anderson, Fisher, & Norman, 2002; Catley, 2006; Poling & Evans, 2004b; Shtulman, 2006). In this section, some of the most relevant conclusions will be summarized and related to the developmental studies and more recent research on museum visitors' understanding.

What is striking about this research is the extensive documentation of the overlap between students' intuitive notions of evolutionary change and pre-Darwinian evolutionary concepts (e.g., Chambers, 1994; Mayr, 1982; Shtulman, 2006), though they are certainly not identical (Evans, 2001; Kampourakis & Zogza, 2007). Students' ideas focus on individual change rather than population change and utilize commonsense concepts, similar to those found in younger children: (1) that evolutionary change is need-based and adaptive, in a teleological sense, (2) that it is developmental and progressive: an emergence from an underdeveloped form, and (3) that it is not so much a dynamic process as a series of discrete events (e.g., Banet & Ayuso, 2003; Bizzo, 1994; Clough & Wood-Robinson, 1985a, 1985b; Dagher & BouJaoude, 1997; Deadman & Kelly, 1978; Ferrari & Chi, 1998).

Such ideas are found at all grade levels, including science undergraduates and medical students, and are remarkably resistant to instruction (Bishop & Anderson, 1990; Brumby, 1982, 1984; Lawson & Worsnop, 1992). More recent studies of the effects of classroom instruction that include students' understanding of the nature of science and the nature of knowledge have yielded more promising results (Bell, Lederman, & Abd-El-Khalick, 2000; Passmore & Stewart, 2002; Sandoval & Morrison, 2003; Sandoval & Reiser, 2004; Scharmann, 2005; Sinatra et al., 2003). Even so, the effects are not large. One possible explanation for such results is that these studies include students who are uninterested in the topic and who are merely learning enough material to pass the course, not to acquire the deep understanding necessary for understanding evolutionary concepts.

Natural History Museum Visitors' Understanding of Evolution

What about a population that would be expected to have a good grasp of evolutionary theory and who have a demonstrated interest in natural history, such as natural history museum visitors? On average, such visitors are more highly educated than the general population; 60% or more have a college education (Korn, 1995). Additionally, of course, they are interested enough in natural history to voluntarily visit such a museum, where they are likely to encounter exhibits on evolution (Diamond & Scotchmoor, 2006). As such, they would be expected to be more knowledgeable about natural history and more accepting of evolution than the general population.

It is indeed the case that museum visitors are less likely to be creationist and more likely to accept evolutionary origins than the general population (Spiegel et al., 2006). But, just like the rest of the population, it depends on the target species. When asked about *human* origins, 28% of a sample attending three Midwest museums were creationist (Evans et al., 2006), compared with 46% in the general population (Gallup, 2007). However, only 6% of the same sample held consistently creationist views, regardless of the species, which included HIV, diatom, fruit-fly, ant, finch, and whale, as well as the human. What is more surprising is that only 34% of the same sample could be described as knowledgeable about evolution, and, even then, none of the visitors consistently invoked Darwinian reasoning across all seven species. Just like participants in earlier studies, most visitors used mixed reasoning, for some species they were informed Darwinian reasoners, for others they invoked novice naturalistic reasoning, and, occasionally, but most often for the human, they were creationist (Diamond & Evans, 2007; Evans, Spiegel, Gram, Frazier, Cover, Tare, & Diamond, 2006).

These kinds of findings are not only replicated in other museum settings across the United States (Spiegel et al., 2006), but are also found among visitors from international communities, where the acceptance rate of evolutionary origins, common descent, is much higher. Silver and Kisiel (2006) compared U.S., Canadian, English, and Australian natural history museum visitors and found that only about 30% had a reasonable grasp of natural selection. In the United States and in other English-speaking countries, museum visitors exhibit the same kinds of misunderstandings of evolution found in young children and in school-age and college students, with a preponderance of teleological, intentional, and essentialist explanations. The universality of these ideas is quite striking.

Two examples will suffice. When asked to explain why there were now 800 species of fruit flies on the Hawaiian Islands, when several million years ago there were only a few such flies, 50% of a natural history museum sample used the kind of essentialist, proximate cause explanations described earlier in young children:

Obviously people have brought the fruit flies in. And Dole probably, Dole pineapple people probably brought them in. (Diamond & Evans, 2007, p. 1503)

In response to a question about changes in beak size in the Galapagos finches over seasons, this museum visitor invoked the classic teleological story of the giraffe's neck, to describe biological change:

Evolution for survival. …Well, in order to survive, their body parts had to adjust to certain things, similar to the way giraffes' necks probably grew long as they reached for the plants at the top of the trees, so the beak grew longer in order to deal with the tougher seeds. (Diamond & Evans, 2007, 1504)

MISUNDERSTANDING EVOLUTIONARY BIOLOGY: IMPLICATIONS FOR THEORIES OF CONCEPTUAL CHANGE

In the final section, a summary of the developmental research is followed by a discussion of the strengths and weaknesses of the intuitive theory approach and a consideration of a potential research agenda based on this theoretical framework.

Summary

Cognitive biases that are intrinsic components of an intuitive psychology and biology (e.g., Astuti, Solomon, & Carey, 2004; Carey, 1985, 1995; Hatano & Inagaki, 1999; Inagaki & Hatano, 2002; Keil, 1994, 1995; Medin & Atran, 2004; Wellman & Gelman, 1998), intention, essentialism, and teleology, make it difficult for children and adults to accept and explain the core tenets of evolutionary theory: That naturalistic, non-teleological, and non-intentional processes result in population change, speciation, common descent, and the interrelationship of all living things. These final steps, especially common descent, are explicitly rejected by Biblical literalists, even when they endorse changes in gene frequency in a population. Speciation and phylogenetic change challenge the Biblically-based tenet that each living kind has an unchanging God-given essence (Evans, 2001, 2005; Morris & Parker, 1982).

The developmental evidence demonstrates that in comparison with older children, 5- to 7-year-olds are more likely to believe that animals and artifacts are eternal and unchanging and use simple proximate cause reasoning to explain the origins of animals and artifacts ("it was in the store," "it came from someplace else"). Thus, for the younger children in these studies, the whole question of "origins" is often moot. From their perspective, the animals were always here on earth, perhaps hidden somewhere, and unlikely to change. Therefore, it makes little sense to ask how "the very first" of a species got here on earth. This kind of intuitive reasoning is hypothesized to give rise to a view of species as unvarying and stable. For example, 5- to 7-year-olds are unlikely to accept that animals undergo radical changes over their lifetime. If asked to pick the adult of a tadpole, younger children typically pick a bigger tadpole, not a frog (Rosengren et al., 1991).

Children aged 8- to 9-years are in an interesting transitional phase (Evans, 2005). They are more likely than their younger siblings to endorse life-cycle and within-species variation and change, but less likely than 10- to 12-year-olds to accept common descent. The majority endorse some form of creationist or intelligent design ideas, regardless of home background. One of the reasons for these age-related differences is that children of this age group are beginning to confront existential questions. Unlike 5- to 7-year-olds, they know more about death, and they realize that animals are not eternal, in that they were not always here on earth. So the question now arises:

How did they get there in the first place? These children appeal to their intuitions about human intentions and design and apply it to species: If tools can be designed, so can animals. Simultaneously, they are integrating levels of cause, proximate and more distal, into the kind of complex causal structure that is necessary for the ultimate cause reasoning of the evolutionary biologist.

Depending on their family belief system, creationist or not, and their exposure to fossil and natural history knowledge regarding animal change, 10- to 12 year-olds are more willing than younger children to accept that one kind of animal could have descended from a completely different kind. Regardless of age, children who accepted that the human was an animal and who understood metamorphosis were more likely to accept common descent (Evans, Rosengren, Szymanowski, Smith, & Johnson, 2005). The latter finding implies that these children endorse a common misconception, that species change is analogous to developmental change in individuals. There was an important caveat, however. Children from Biblical literalist families (God created each kind) accepted metamorphosis but did not accept common descent for humans or other mammals. Yet, irrespective of background, all age groups were more likely to accept common descent for butterflies and frogs than for mammals or humans.

Such results are in keeping with earlier findings that about 30% of older children and adults entertain mixed beliefs, accepting evolutionary origins for non-human species and creationism for humans, for example (Evans, 2001; Sinatra et al., 2003). Further, a recent study of museum visitors' explanations of biological change in diverse organisms revealed a similar inconsistency: their endorsement of evolutionary or creationist origins depended (1) on the organism under discussion, as well as (2) whether the question was about microevolutionary or macroevolutionary change (Evans et al., 2006).

In sum, intentional, teleological, and essentialist views of species origins are found historically in children and in students and adults from different cultural backgrounds. Microevolutionary questions elicit naïve biological explanations in museum visitors and students of all ages from the United States (e.g., Bishop & Anderson, 1990, Brumby, 1982, 1984; Clough & Wood-Robinson, 1985a, 1985b; Spiegel et al., 2006), Japan (Inagaki & Hatano, 2006), Netherlands (Samarapungavan & Wiers, 1997), and other cultural settings where they have been tested (e.g., Dagher & BouJaoude, 1997; Silver & Kisiel, 2006). Typically, they take the form of the erroneous pre-Darwinian microevolutionary concept, that individuals in a population change over the life-span in response to the demands of a novel environment and that subsequent generations inherit these changes (Chambers, 1994; Mayr, 1982). This goal-directed or teleological concept of species change, in response to an individual organism's needs, can persist in the face of focused instruction (e.g., Anderson et al., 2002; Bishop & Anderson, 1990). On the other hand, macroevolutionary or *origins* questions are more likely to elicit *intentional* creationist or intelligent design explanations, especially in the United States.

The Explanatory Potential of Intuitive Theories

The intuitive theory or developmental constraint approach described in this chapter offers a robust theoretical framework for integrating a large body of data on the misunderstanding of evolution. It provides a developmental framework for understanding the persistence of essentialist, teleological, and intentional concepts of evolution in the lay public and in students, before and after instruction (Evans, 1994/1995, 2000a, 2000b, 2001). It links these misunderstandings to broader cultural and developmental factors, such as the rejection by Biblical literalists of macroevolutionary change and young children's resistance to between-species transformations, both of which, it is argued, are tied to essentialist reasoning patterns. It can be related to discussions of emergent knowledge in other conceptual domains, such as diSessa's phenomenological primitives in a naïve physics (diSessa, 1993; diSessa et al., 2004; Southerland et al., 2001). Moreover, the focus on evolutionary biology, in this chapter, provides data to amply support a more recent consensus in the science education community that "Children's rich but naïve understandings of the natural world can be built on to develop their understanding of scientific concepts" (Duschl, Schweingruber, & Shouse, 2006, pp. 11–14).

It can also predict contextual effects: To the extent that a naïve psychological framework is elicited then evolution will be rejected. Naturalistic, non-teleological, evolutionary concepts of species change run counter to the folk concepts of intentionality (Malle, 2004; Malle & Knobe, 1997) that are the foundation of a naïve psychology (e.g., Wellman, 2002). The human, of course, is the quintessential intentional entity. In support of the prediction, the human, and species closely related to the human, is more likely to elicit intentional explanations such as intelligent design and creationism (Evans, 2001; Evans et al., 2005; Sinatra et al., 2003). As well, species that are taxonomically distant from the human are more likely to elicit naïve biological explanations, including naturalistic proximate cause explanations and non-intentional, teleological evolutionary explanations. Further, unlike evolutionists, creationists do not consider the human to be an animal (Evans et al., 2005). In cultures that do not share Western monotheistic beliefs in the privileged human, the relationship between the human and other primates is much more likely to be acknowledged (Inagaki & Hatano, 2006).

Creationists are particularly resistant to the idea of evolutionary origins, macroevolution, but, for the most part, they will accept microevolutionary processes governing within-species change (Evans, Hazel, Nesse, Weder, Murdock, Gervasi, & Witt, 2007). Why might that be? The obvious explanation is that evolutionary origins directly contradict the received word of God that each kind was specially created with an unique immutable essence: one kind cannot become another — a reified essentialist notion (Evans, 2001). Change over the lifespan of an organism is endorsed, however (Morris & Parker, 1982). More subtly, though, if the mutability of kinds is accepted, then this might well arouse existential angst, particularly concerning the extinction of the human. In contrast to a sample of evolutionary biologists, for example, midwestern parents and children were more likely to reject the possibility of human extinction than the extinction of non-human species (Poling & Evans, 2004a).

In addition to intentions and goals, a naïve psychological framework also encompasses emotions, beliefs, and desires (Wellman, 2002). This licenses another prediction that the extent to which a naïve psychology is elicited, then evolution will be associated with negative feelings and emotions. As described earlier, the apparent purposeless of evolutionary explanations elicits deep-seated concerns, even when evolution is accepted (Brem et al., 2003; Jackson, Doster, Meadows, & Wood, 1995). Parents respond to these concerns by worrying whether they can raise moral children: "if children are nothing more than apes evolved then we cannot expect them to act more than that to one another…" (Evans, 1994/1995, p. 124; 2000b). Even teachers respond to these concerns with heightened levels of stress (Griffith & Brem, 2004; Hahn et al., 2005).

Causal Flexibility and Explanatory Coherence

Although the exact nature of the cognitive biases associated with the intuitive theory approach has been the source of a lively and often contentious debate (e.g., Astuti, Solomon, & Carey, 2004; Carey, 1985, 1995; Hatano & Inagaki, 1999; Keil, 1994, 1995; Medin & Atran, 2004), this has only strengthened the subsequent research. Teleological explanation is considered of key importance (Evans, 1994/1995; Inagaki & Hatano, 2002; Keil, 1994; Kelemen, 1999; Opfer, 2002). One contentious issue is whether this explanatory mode is necessarily linked to the mental state explanations of a naïve psychology, especially in young children (Kelemen, 2004).

The research described in this chapter suggests that this is not the case. More specifically, it would appear that when linked to intentional mental state explanations, teleology motivates a naïve psychology, but when linked to functional explanations that serve the organism itself, it motivates a naïve biology (Poling & Evans, 2002, 2004b; Keil, 1994). Children discriminate between these explanatory modes (Schult & Wellman, 1997) and use them flexibly (Gutheil, Vera, & Keil, 1998). Even though 6- to 7-year-olds often favor psychological explanations for biological phenomena (Carey, 1985), they agree that animals breathe because they *need* to (a functional explanation that serves the organism) and not because they *want* to (a mental state explanation) (Poling & Evans, 2002). This kind of evidence suggests that although mental state explanations may be a default, they are not the only ones available to young children (Gutheil, Vera, & Keil, 1998). This capacity to shift explanations depending on the context is called *causal flexibility* (Poling & Evans, 2002), and it is demonstrated in children and adults when they shift explanatory modes depending on the species. It should be a fundamental component in any explanation of conceptual change.

The evidence presented in this chapter suggests that as children learn more about change and diversity in the biological world (and provided they are not reared in a fundamentalist environment) they shift from a naïve psychological framework to a naïve biological one, to explain species change. Initially, the latter yields a non-Darwinian teleo-functional explanation (see Inagaki & Hatano, 2006) for evolutionary change. With more experience of the natural world, essentialist and teleological biases guide the burgeoning biologist as he/she investigates the patterns of similarity and differences in species and links them to adaptive functions.

It should be noted that the claim is *not* that the evolutionary biologist is freed of a teleo-essentialist bias, but that it is reconfigured in the process of re-representing the realities of the biological world. For the evolutionary biologist, genes reflect essences and adaptation reflects ancestral environments, encoded genetically. These changes indicate the emergence of a richer and more coherent knowledge structure; an age-related but not an age-dependent shift.

While their beliefs appear to be locally coherent, this set of findings suggests that explanatory coherence writ large (Thagard, 1989), is not necessarily found in a lay population (Evans, 2001). In many cases, participants in these studies shifted between explanations, such as creationist and evolutionist, depending on the target organism and on their interpretation of the question (see also Gutheil, Vera, & Keil, 1998; Poling & Evans, 2002; and in the physical domain, diSessa, 1993; diSessa et al., 2004). Further, these findings suggest that conceptual change is not necessarily achieved by radically reconfiguring a preexisting conceptual structure, but by sidelining one particular conceptual framework in favor of another, as circumstances change (Keil 1994; Keil & Newman, chapter 4, this volume). Meanwhile, with development, both biological and intentional frameworks are undergoing conceptual enrichment and change fueled by the acquisition of culturally and experientially provided information.

As in the history of science (Thagard, chapter 14, this volume), these studies demonstrate shifts from intentional to mechanistic-biological explanations of origins. Yet, at least ontogenetically, this is not a progressive tendency. It is not that young children are unable to conceive of a naturalistic explanation for species origins, but that the explanations they do utilize, such as spontaneous generation, are, as yet, inadequate to the task. For children, this is a proximate cause mechanism that explains how species became visible, but not how they originated *ex nihilo*. Plausibly, such naturalistic explanations could eventually yield a pre-Darwinian evolutionary explanation in children who are not exposed to the attractive creationist alternative (Evans, 1994/1995, 2000, 2001; Samarapungavan & Weirs, 1997). Mayr (1982) makes a similar argument historically: Were it not for the impact of Christianity, the spontaneous generationist ideas of early Greek philosophers could have yielded evolutionary explanations, in that both were non-teleological and naturalistic.

In children who are exposed to creationism, to a greater or lesser degree, the shift to an intentional mode, in which species are treated as artifacts of God, is accompanied by the capacity to integrate both proximate and final causes into an explanatory framework. Intriguingly, this pattern of complex causal reasoning also underlies the ability to appreciate ultimate cause evolutionary explanations for the origins of species.

Integrating Domain-specific and Domain-general Approaches

The preceding sections have detailed the emergence of domain-specific intuitive reasoning processes utilizing a developmental framework, which yield testable hypotheses regarding an everyday understanding of evolutionary biology. The data provided so far offer support for this framework theory. A weakness of this approach, however, is that it does not directly address "the interplay between domain-specific and domain-general knowledge over the course of development" (Duschl et al., 2006, pp. 11–15).

Clearly, students' personal epistemology (e.g., Hofer & Pintrich, 1997; Muis, Bendixen, & Haerle, 2006; Sinatra et al., 2003; Sinatra & Mason, chapter 21, this volume), in particular their understanding of the nature of science (e.g., Abd-El-Khalick & Akerson, 2004; Bell et al., 2000) and their ability to distinguish between belief and knowledge (Southerland, Sinatra, & Matthews, 2001; Sinatra, 2005), as well as more general reasoning processes (Kuhn, 1999; Lawson, & Worsnop, 1992), all play a role in their understanding of evolutionary biology. From a domain-general perspective alone, though, it would be difficult to explain why the term evolution arouses such misgivings (Brem et al., 2003) or explain the existence of contextual effects, such as the consistent finding that creationist concepts are more likely to be evoked for human origins and for macroevolutionary processes (Evans, 2000b, 2001; Evans et al., 2005, 2007).

On the other hand, the developmental data presented here have domain-general implications, in particular the integration of proximate and more distal causal levels to explain evolutionary concepts. The ability to link causal levels must underlie a range of domains that consider existential issues, from philosophy and religion to evolutionary biology. Researchers, in particular Lawson and his colleagues, have related students' domain-general reasoning processes, using a Piagetian framework, to their misunderstanding of science (e.g., Lawson, Alkhoury, Benford, Clark, & Falconer, 2000), and of evolution (Lawson & Worsnop, 1992). They suggest a hierarchy of descriptive, hypothetical and theoretical concepts that range from more to less observable (Lawson et al., 2000), which could potentially be tied to an intuitive theory framework.

There are several possible ways of integrating these perspectives (Duschl et al., 2006). One possibility, relevant to the current topic, is to consider how domain-specific processes may become available to other domains as intuitive theories are extended and developed. Mathematics, for example, is essential to a theoretical physics, even though it probably plays no role in an intuitive physics. Children's theory of mind or intuitive psychology, likewise, may be extended to inform a personal epistemology, which, in turn, can be utilized in a number of academic domains. As described earlier, although preschoolers and young school-age children may reference unobservable mental states, such as know, think, and believe, the complexities of the thinking process, such as being in two minds or having conflicting ideas, are not grasped until they are 8- to 9-years of age or older (Carpendale & Chandler, 1996; Flavell, Green, & Flavell, 1995; Mull & Evans, 2007). This emerging ability to reflect upon their own knowledge (Wellman & Johnson, in press) allows children to integrate diverse views of knowledge, and to actively consider the distinction between knowledge and belief (Southerland et al., 2001).

Thus, even though very young children can distinguish between domains at an intuitive level, in the sense that they can tell the difference between an apple and a thought about an apple (Wellman, 2002), their ability to reflect upon the nature of their own and others' knowledge requires a different level of analysis (Wellman & Johnson, in press). There is a recursive quality to this ability, the capacity to re-represent representations, which may be tied to other processes such as the emergence of executive function (Wellman, 2002) and the integration of causal levels (Mull & Evans, 2007). It is quite plausible, therefore, that this reflective capacity is a function of an elaborated intuitive psychology, focusing on the nature of knowledge, which then becomes more broadly accessible to other domains, including academic domains (Muis et al., 2006).

A Research Agenda?

This analysis would not be complete without suggesting a research agenda, one that integrates disparate disciplines. No longer can it be said that students' understanding of evolution is under-researched (Cummins et al., 1994), but what is lacking is a coherent theoretical framework, particularly one that integrates the developmental origins of adult resistance to evolution (Bloom & Weisberg, 2007).

Clearly, a multifaceted approach is needed. At the level of basic research, we need to know much more about the development of intuitive cognitive biases, essentialism, teleology, and intention, and their relationship to intuitive and folk theories of biology and psychology (e.g., Coley, Solomon, & Shafto, 2002; Kelemen & DiYanni, 2005). This requires a philosophical as well as a psychological analysis (e.g., Sehon, 2005). A key task, which builds on this research, is to establish how these initial constraints are reconfigured to support Darwinian evolutionary explanations, in formal (e.g., Rudolph & Stewart, 1998; Shtulman, 2006) and informal (Diamond & Scotchmoor, 2006; Weiss, 2006) educational settings. New techniques, particularly modeling techniques, for teaching evolutionary biology and science (e.g., Alters, 2005; Jensen & Finley, 1996; Lehrer & Schauble, 2006; Southerland & Sinatra, 2003; Wilensky & Resnick, 1999) should be informed by a developmental constraints framework. As well, it is important to make evolution more engaging for students, especially those who are not science majors, by focusing on topics that might intrigue them, such as Darwinian medicine (e.g., Nesse & Wilson, 1996) or forensics (Mindell, 2006).

One of the contextual factors emphasized in this analysis is the resistance to macroevolutionary concepts, even when microevolutionary concepts are deemed acceptable. Several investigators are focusing their efforts on students' understanding of common descent and of cladograms that introduce *tree thinking*, a modeling technique used by evolutionary biologists to represent evolutionary relationships between organisms. Students can also be exposed to these concepts via an understanding of geological or deep time (Dodick & Orion, 2003). As it turns out, though, tree thinking is not that easy, in that students have difficulty both with the spatial relationships as well as the underlying evolutionary concepts (Baum, DeWitt-Smith, & Donovan, 2005; Novick & Catley, 2007). Although the introduction of modeling as an abstract concept is often problematic (e.g., Windschitl & Thompson, 2006), simplified tree-diagrams could be made sufficiently concrete so that they convey evolutionary relationships over time in a way that transcends cognitive or perceptual biases.

Besides the tools of evolutionary biology, such as tree-diagrams, which are often opaque, the language of evolution is also a potential barrier to understanding. Darwin struggled with this language (Beer, 2000). Evolutionary biologists use everyday terms such as adaptation and design in a highly specialized manner, but the language provides traps for the unwary. In fact, biologists have long been criticized for their teleological terminology (e.g., Jungwirth, 1975; Sprinkle, 2006). In a recent article on evolution and cancer in *Scientific American*, science writer Carl Zimmer describes cancer cells that "trick the body into supplying them with energy to grow even larger" (2007, p. 69). Even the title is problematic: *Evolved for Cancer*. This evocative but teleological/intentional language powerfully conveys the basic idea, but amazingly no-one has studied what effect this may have on the naïve reader. Does the reader immediately grasp the metaphor? If, as in this case, the language of biology mirrors students' intuitive cognitive biases, does it reinforce these biases or could it scaffold an understanding of Darwinian evolution?

No intervention focusing on evolutionary concepts is likely to work, at least in the United States, without extracting an emotional cost. Entrenched creationist beliefs (Chinn & Brewer, 2000) that are strongly rooted in a literal reading of the Bible are unlikely to change, but most of this research indicates that about two-thirds of the U.S. public are confused rather than resistant. Even so, unlike the physical sciences, evolutionary biology arouses existential anxieties. Addressing these issues raises many problems (Pennock, 2002). Furthermore, there are important epistemological issues, which have not yet been satisfactorily resolved at the philosophical or the psychological level but which need to be addressed. How is the relationship between religion and science to be disambiguated? Judge Jones of the Dover trial (Mervis, 2006) focused on the distinction between supernatural and natural causation, rather than differences in standards of evidence. Can such ideas even be raised in the science classroom? If so, how can this be achieved?

To solve these problems requires an approach that integrates the multiple factors and multiple disciplines referenced in this chapter. Evolutionary theory is the foundational theory for a broad range of endeavors from the biological, health, and social sciences to the computational sciences. In addition to its intrinsic importance, evolution should be part of the knowledge base of any informed citizen of the 21st century, who should grasp the evolutionary issues that underlie the impact of human activities on the natural world. Besides these important applied outcomes, investigations of the reasons why evolution is so easily misunderstood should provide insights into the way the human mind processes information about natural and supernatural causation, potentially impacting many disciplines.

CONCLUSION

The evidence presented in this chapter supports the position that the human mind seems almost incapable of conceptual change when confronted with scientific data that contradict a self-serving view of the world. About one-half of the U.S. public embraces creationist ideas about the origins of species. Even among those members of the public who accept evolutionary origins, including common ancestry, most invoke intuitive non-Darwinian teleological concepts to explain species change. Moreover, only about one-third of those with a demonstrated interest in natural history, such as museum visitors, grasp Darwinian evolutionary concepts. The latter patterns are replicated in other industrial societies.

As this chapter demonstrates, though, there are glimmers of hope, exemplified in the following conversation between a 12-year-old boy and his mother, as they sat next to the mythologist, Joseph Campbell, at a lunch counter (1972):

Boy: "Jimmy wrote a paper today on the evolution of man, and Teacher said he was wrong, that Adam and Eve were our first parents."
Mother: "Well, Teacher was right. Our first parents *were* Adam and Eve."
Boy: "Yes, I know, but this was a *scientific* paper."
Mother: "Oh those scientists!" she said angrily. "These are only theories."
Boy   "Yes I know," was his cool and calm reply; "but they have been factualized: they found the bones." (pp. 1–2)

Campbell goes on to argue that it would behoove scientists to understand the "life-supporting nature of myths" before they are overthrown by "young truth-seekers of this kind" (p. 2) (Evans, 1994/1995).

ACKNOWLEDGMENT

This material is based upon work supported by the Spencer Foundation and the National Science Foundation (#0540152 [#0411406 & #0540152]). Thanks to Sarah Brem, Karl Rosengren and Gale Sinatra for helpful discussions.

NOTE

1. The reported percentages of the population that endorse evolution or creation vary minimally depending on the type of question (Miller et al., 2006)

REFERENCES

Abd-El-Khalick, F., & Akerson, V. L. (2004). Learning as conceptual change: Factors mediating the development of preservice elementary teachers' views of nature of science. *Science Education, 88*, 785–810.

Abrams, E., Southerland, S., & Cummins, C. L. (2001). The how's and why's of biological change: how learners neglect physical mechanisms in their search for meaning. *International Journal of Science Education, 23*, 1271–1281.

Alters, B. (2005). *Teaching biological evolution in higher education.* Sudbury, MA: Jones & Bartlett Publishers.

Amsterlaw, J. (1999). Children's beliefs about everyday reasoning. *Child Development, 77*, 443–464.

Anderson, D. L., Fisher, K. M., & Norman, G. J. (2002). Development and evaluation of the conceptual inventory of the natural selection. *Journal of Research of Science Teaching, 39*, 952–978.

Astuti, R., Solomon, G. E. A., & Carey, S. (2004). *Constraints on conceptual development* (Vol. 69). Boston, MA: Blackwell Publishing.

Atran, S. (1990). *Cognitive foundations of natural history: Towards an anthropology of science.* Cambridge: Cambridge University Press.

Atran, S. (1995). Causal constraints on categories and categorical constraints on biological reasoning across cultures. In D. Sperber, D. Premack, & A. J. Premack (Eds.), *Causal cognition: A multidisciplinary debate* (pp. 205–233). Oxford: Clarendon Press.

Atran, S. (1998). Folk Biology and the anthropology of science: Cognitive universals and cultural particulars. *Behavioral and Brain Sciences, 21*, 547–609.

Atran, S. (1999). The universal primacy of generic species in folkbiological taxonomy: Implications for human biological, cultural and scientific evolution. In R. A. Wilson (Ed.), *Species: New interdisciplinary essays* (pp. 231–262). Cambridge, MA: MIT Press.

Baker, C. (2006). *The evolution dialogues: Science, christianity, and the quest for understanding.* Washington, DC: American Association for the Advancement of Science.

Banet, E., & Ayuso, G. E. (2003). Teaching of biological inheritance and evolution of living beings in secondary school. *International Journal of Science Education, 25*, 373–407.

Baum, D. A., DeWitt-Smith, S., & Donovan, S. (2005). The tree-thinking challenge. *Science, 310*, 979–980.

Beer, G. (2000). *Darwin's plots: Evolutionary narrative in Darwin, George Eliot and Nineteenth-Century Fiction.* Cambridge, UK: Cambridge University Press.

Bell, R. L., Lederman, N. G., & Abd-El-Khalick, F. (2000). Developing and acting upon one's conception of the nature of science: A follow-up study. *Journal of Research in Science Teaching, 37*, 563–581.

Biema, D. V. (November 13, 2006). God vs. science. *Time, 168*, 48–55.

Bishop, B. A., & Anderson, C. W. (1990). Student conceptions of natural selection and its role in evolution. *Journal of Research in Science Teaching, 27*, 415–427.

Bizzo, N. M. V. (1994). From down house landlord to Brazilian high school students: What has happened to evolutionary knowledge on the way. *Journal of Research in Science Teaching, 31*, 537–556.

Bloom, P., & Weisberg, D. S. (2007). Childhood origins of adult resistance to science. *Science, 316*, 996–997.

Brem, S. K., Ranney, M., & Schindel, J. (2003). Perceived consequences of evolution: College students perceive negative personal and social impact in evolutionary theory. *Science Education, 87*, 181–206.

Brumby, M. (1979). Problems in learning the concept of natural selection. *Journal of Biological Education, 13*, 119–122.

Brumby, M. (1982). Students' perceptions of the concept of life. *Science Education, 66*, 613–622.

Brumby, M. N. (1984). Misconceptions about the concept of natural selection by medical biology students. *Science Education, 684*, 493–503.

Bybee, R. W. (2004). *Evolution in Perspective: The Science Teacher's Compendium*: National Science Teachers Association Press.

Campbell, J. (1972). *Myths to live by*. New York: Viking Penguin, Inc.

Carey, S. (1985). *Conceptual change in childhood*. Cambridge. MA: MIT Press.

Carey, S. (1995). On the origins of causal understanding. In D. Sperber, D. Premack, & A. Premack (Eds.), *Causal Cognition: A Multidisciplinary Debate* (pp. 268–302). Oxford: Clarendon Press.

Carpendale, J. I., & Chandler, M. J. (1996). On the distinction between false belief understanding and subscribing to an interpretive theory of mind. *Child Development, 67*, 1686–1706.

Catley, K. M. (2006). Darwin's missing link—A novel paradigm for evolution education. *Science Education, 90*, 767–783.

Chambers, R. (1994). *Vestiges of the natural history of creation and other evolutionary writings originally published in 1844 and 1845*. Chicago and London: The University of Chicago Press.

Chick, J. T. (2000). *English-big daddy*. http://www.chick.com/reading/tracts/0055/0055_01.asp

Chinn, C. A., & Brewer, W. F. (2000). Knowledge change in science, religion, and magic. In K. Rosengren, C. Johnson & P. Harris (Eds.), *Imagining the impossible: The development of magical, scientific, and religious thinking in contemporary society* (pp. 334–371). Cambridge: Cambridge University Press.

Clough, E. E., & Wood-Robinson, C. (1985a). How secondary students interpret instances of biological adaptation. *Journal of Biological Education, 19*, 125–130.

Clough, E. E., & Wood-Robinson, C. (1985b). Children's understanding of inheritance. *Journal of Biological Education, 19*, 304–310.

Coley, J. D., Solomon, G. E. A., & Shafto, P. (2002). The development of folkbiology: A cognitive science perspective on children's understanding of the biological world. In P. H. Kahn & S. R. Kellert (Eds.), *Children and nature: Psychological, sociocultural and evolutionary investigations*. Cambridge, MA: The MIT Press.

Cummins, C. L., Demastes, S. S., & Hafner, M. S. (1994). Evolution: Biological education's under-researched unifying theme. *Journal of Research in Science Teaching, 31*, 445–448.

Dagher, Z. R., & BouJaoude, S. (1997). Scientific views and religious beliefs of college students: The case of biological evolution. *Journal of Research in Science Teaching, 34*, 429–445.

Dawkins, R. (1987). *The blind watchmaker*. New York: Norton.

Deadman, J. A., & Kelly, P. J. (1978). What do secondary school boys understand about evolution and heredity before they are taught about the topics. *Journal of Biological Education, 12*, 7–15.

Diamond, J., & Evans, E. M. (2007). Museums teach evolution. *Evolution, 61*, 1500–1506.

Diamond, J., & Scotchmoor, J. (2006). Exhibiting Evolution. *Museums and Social Issues, 1*, 21–48.

diSessa, A. A. (1993). Toward an epistemology of physics. *Cognition and Instruction, 10*, 105–225.

diSessa, A. A., Gillespie, N. M., & Esterly, J. B. (2004). Coherence versus fragmentation in the development of the concept of force. *Cognitive Science, 28*, 843–900.

Dodick, J., & Orion, N. (2003). Measuring student understanding of geological time. *Science Education, 87*, 708–731.

Doolittle, W. (2000). Uprooting the tree of life. *Scientific American, 282*(2), 90–95.

Doyle, R. (2003, March). Sizing up evangelicals: Fundamentalism persists but shows signs of moderation. *Scientific American, 228*, 37.

Duschl, R. A., Schweingruber, H. A., & Shouse, A. W. (Eds.). (2006). *Taking Science to School: Learning and Teaching Science in Grades K-8*. Washington, DC.: The National Academies Press.

Evans, E. M. (1991). Understanding fossils, dinosaurs, and the origins of species: Ontogenetic and historic comparisons. *Abstracts Society for Research in Child Development, 8,* 246.

Evans, E. M. (1994/1995). *God or Darwin? The development of beliefs about the origin of species.* Dissertation Abstracts International Section A: Humanities & Social Sciences; Vol 558-A Feb 1995; 2335 AAM9500920: University of Michigan.

Evans, E. M. (2000a). The emergence of beliefs about the origins of species in school-age children. *Merrill-Palmer Quarterly: A Journal of Developmental Psychology, 46,* 221–254.

Evans, E. M. (2000b). Beyond Scopes: Why creationism is here to stay. In K. Rosengren, C. Johnson, & P. Harris (Eds.), *Imagining the impossible: Magical, scientific and religious thinking in children.* (pp. 305–331) Cambridge: Cambridge University Press.

Evans, E. M. (2001). Cognitive and contextual factors in the emergence of diverse belief systems: Creation versus evolution. *Cognitive Psychology, 42,* 217–266.

Evans, E. M. (2005) Teaching and learning about evolution. In J. Diamond (Ed.) *The virus and the whale: Explore evolution in creatures small and large.* NSTA Press: Arlington, VA.

Evans, E. M., Mull, M., & Poling, D. (2001, April). Confronting the existential questions: Children's understanding of death and origins. Biennial Meeting of the Society for Research In Child Development, Minneapolis, MN.

Evans, E. M., Mull, M. S., Poling, D. A., & Szymanowksi, K. (2005, April). God as master planner: A late emerging aspect of a theory of mind? Biennial meeting of the Society for Research in Child Development, Atlanta, GA.

Evans, E. M., Rosengren, K. S., Szymanowksi, K., Smith P. H. & Johnson, K. (2005, October). Culture, cognition, and creationism. Biennial meeting of the Cognitive Development Society, San Diego, CA.

Evans, E. M., Spiegel, A., Gram, W., Frazier, B. F., Cover, S., Tare, M. & Diamond, J. (2006, April). A conceptual guide to museum visitors' understanding of evolution. Annual Meeting of the American Education Research Association, San Francisco.

Evans, E. M., Hazel, A., Nesse, R., Weder, A. B., Murdock, C., Gervasi, S. & Witt, A. (2007, May). Learning Darwinian medicine: Cognitive and cultural constraints. Annual Meeting of the American Institute of Biological Sciences, Washington, D.C.

Ferrari, M., & Chi, M. T. H. (1998). The nature of naive explanations of natural selection. *International Journal of Science Education, 20*(10), 1231–1256.

Flavell, J. H., Green, F. L., & Flavell, E. R., (1995). *Young children's knowledge about thinking, 60* (1, Serial No. 243).

Flavell, J. H., Green, F. L., & Flavell, E. R. (2000). Development of children's awareness of their own thoughts. *Journal of Cognition and Development,* 97–112.

Futuyma, D. J. (1998). *Evolutionary biology* (3rd ed.). Sunderland, MA: Sinauer Associates

Gallup (2007). *Evolution, Creationism, Intelligent Design.* Retrieved February 2, 2008, from the Gallup Poll Web site: http://www.gallup.com/poll/21814/Evolution-Creationism-Intelligent-Design.aspx

Gelman, S. A. (2003). *The essential child: Origins of essentialism in everyday thought.* Oxford: Oxford University Press.

Gingerich, P. D., Raza, S. M., Arif, M., Anwar, M., & Shou, X. (1994). New whale from the Eocene of Pakistan and the origin of cetacean swimming. *Nature, 368,* 844–847.

Gopnik, A., & Wellman, H. M. (1994). The Theory Theory. In L. A. Hirschfeld & S. A. Gelman (Eds.), *Mapping the mind: Domain specificity in cognition and culture* (pp. 257–293). New York: Cambridge University Press.

Gould, S. J. (March, 1997). Nonoverlapping magisteria. *Natural History, 106,* 16–22 & 60–62.

Greenspan, N. S. (2002). Not-so-intelligent design. *The Scientist, 165,* 12.

Griffith, J. A., & Brem, S. K. (2004). Teaching evolutionary biology: Pressures, stress, and coping. *Journal of Research in Science Teaching, 41*(8), 791–809.

Gutheil, G., Vera, A., & Keil, F. C. (1998). Do houseflies think? Patterns of induction and biological beliefs in development. *Cognition, 66,* 33–49.

Hahn, D., Brem, S. K., & Semken, S. (2005). Exploring the social, moral, and temporal qualities of preservice teachers' narratives of evolution. *Journal of Geosciences Education,* 456–461.

Harris, P. L., & Koenig, M. A. (2006). Trust in testimony: How children learn about science and religion. *Child Development, 77*, 505–524.

Hatano, G., & Inagaki, K. (1999). A developmental perspective on informal biology. In D. L. Medin & S. Atran (Eds.), *Folkbiology* (pp. 321–354). Cambridge, MA: MIT Press.

Hirschfeld, L. A., & Gelman, S. A. (1994). Towards a topography of mind: An introduction to domain specificity. In L. A. Hirschfeld & S. A. Gelman (Eds.), *Mapping the mind: Domain specificity in cognition and culture* (pp. 3–36). Cambridge: CUP.

Hofer, B. K., & Pintrich, P. R. (1997). The development of epistemological theories: Beliefs about knowledge and knowing and their relation to learning. *Review of Educational Research, 67*, 88–140.

Inagaki, K., & Hatano, G. (2002). *Young children's naive thinking about the biological world*. New York: Psychology Press.

Inagaki, K., & Hatano, G. (2006). Young children's conception of the biological world. *Current Directions in Psychological Science, 15*, 177–181.

Jackson, D. F., Doster, E. C., Meadows, L., & Wood, T. (1995). Hearts and minds in the science classroom: The education of a confirmed evolutionist. *Journal of Research in Science Teaching, 32*, 585–611.

Jensen, M. S., & Finley, F. N. (1996). Changes in students' understanding of evolution resulting from different curricular and instructional strategies. *Journal of Research in Science Teaching, 33*(8), 870–900.

Jones, D.-W. (December, 2005). *Smart Sponsors*, from http://www.scienceagainstevolution.org/v10i3f.htm

Jungwirth, E. (1975). Preconceived adaptation and inverted evolution: A case of distorted concept formation in high school biology. *Australian Science Teacher's Journal, 21*, 95–100.

Kampourakis, K., & Zogza, V. (2007). Students' preconceptions about evolution: How accurate is the characterization as "Lamarckian" when considering the history of evolutionary thought? *Science & Education, 16*, 393–422.

Kargbo, D. B., Hobbs, E. D., & Gaalen, L. (1980). Children's beliefs about inherited characteristics. *Journal of Biological Education, 14*, 137–146.

Kehoe, A. B. (1983). The word of God. In L. R. Godfrey (Ed.), *Scientists confront creationism* (pp. 1–12). New York: Norton.

Kehoe, A. B. (1995). Scientific creationism: World view, not science. In F. B. Harrold & R. A. Eve (Eds.), *Cult archeology and creationism: Understanding pseudoscientific beliefs about the past* (pp. 11–20). Iowa City: University of Iowa Press.

Keil, F. (1995). The growth of causal understandings of natural kinds. In D. Sperber, D. Premack, & A. J. Premack (Eds.), *Causal cognition: A multidisciplinary debate* (pp. 235–267). New York: Oxford University Press.

Keil, F. C. (1994). The birth and nurturance of concepts by domains: The origins of concepts of living things. In L. A. Hirschfeld & S. A. Gelman (Eds.), *Mapping the mind: Domain specificity in cognition and culture* (pp. 234–254). Cambridge: CUP.

Kelemen, D. (1999). Why are rocks pointy? Children's preference for teleological explanations of the natural world. *Developmental Psychology, 35*, 1440–1452.

Kelemen, D. (2004). Are children intuitive theists? Reasoning about purpose and design in nature. *Psychological Science, 15*, 295–301.

Kelemen, D., & DiYanni, C. (2005). Intuitions about origins: Purpose and intelligent design in children's reasoning about nature. *Journal of Cognition and Development, 6*, 3–31.

Korn, R. (1995). An analysis of difference between visitors at natural history museums and science centers. *Curator: The Museum Journal, 38*, 150–160.

Krugman, P. (2003). *The great unraveling: Losing our way in the new century*. New York: Norton.

Kuhn, D. (1999). A developmental model of critical thinking. *Educational Researcher, 28*, 16–25.

Lawson, A. E., & Worsnop, W. A. (1992). Learning about evolution and rejecting a belief in special creation: Effects of reflective reasoning skill, prior knowledge, prior belief and religious commitment. *Journal of Research in Science Teaching, 29*, 143–166.

Lawson, A. E., Alkhoury, S., Benford, R., Clark, B. R., & Falconer, K. A. (2000). What kinds of scientific concepts exist? Concept construction and intellectual development in college biology. *Journal of Research in Science Teaching, 9*, 996–1018.

Lehrer, R., & Schauble, L. (2006). Scientific thinking and science literacy. In W. Damon, R. Lerner, K. A. Renninger, & I. E. Sigel (Eds.), *Handbook of child psychology, Sixth Edition, Volume Four: Child psychology in practice* (pp. 153–196). Hoboken, NJ: Wiley.

Malle, B. F. (2004). *How the mind explains behavior: Folk explanations, meaning, and social interaction.* Cambridge, MA: The MIT Press.

Malle, B. F., & Knobe, J. (1997). The folk concept of intentionality. *Journal of Experimental Social Psychology, 33,* 101–121.

Mayr, E. (1982). *The growth of biological thought: Diversity, evolution and inheritance.* Cambridge, MA: Harvard University Press.

Mayr, E. (1985). How biology differs from the physical sciences. In D. J. Depew & B. H. Weber (Eds.), *Evolution at a crossroads: The new biology and the new philosophy of science* (pp. 43–63). Cambridge. MA: The MIT Press.

Mayr, E. (1988). *Towards a new philosophy of biology.* Cambridge, MA: Harvard University Press.

Mayr, E. (1991). *One long argument: Charles Darwin and the genesis of modern evolutionary thought.* Cambridge, MA: Harvard University Press.

Mayr, E. (1997). *This is biology: The science of the living world.* Cambridge, MA: Belknap/Harvard.

Mazur, A. (2005). Believers and disbelievers in evolution. *Politics and the Life Sciences, 8*(November), 55–61.

Mazzarello, P. (2000). *Hidden structure: The scientific life of Camillo Golgi* (Translated & Edited by H. A. Buchtel & A. Badiani). Oxford: University of Oxford Press.

Medin, D. L., & Atran, S. (2004). The native mind: Biological categorization and reasoning in development and across cultures. *Psychological Review, 111,* 960–983.

Medin, D., & Ortony, A. (1989). Comments on Part 1: Psychological essentialism. In S. Vosniadou & A. Ortony (Eds.), *Similarity and analogical reasoning* (pp. 179–193). New York: Cambridge University Press.

Mervis, J. (6 January, 2006). Judge Jones defines science-and why intelligent design isn't. *Science, 311,* 34.

Miller, J. D., Scott, E. C., & Okamoto, S. (2006). Public acceptance of evolution. *Science, 313,* 765–766.

Miller, K. R. (1999). *Finding Darwin's God.* New York: Harper Collins.

Mindell, D. P. (2006). *The evolving world: Evolution in everyday life.* Cambridge, MA: Harvard University Press.

Mishler, B. D. (1999). Getting rid of species? In R. A. Wilson (Ed.), *Species: New Interdisciplinary essays* (pp. 307–315). Cambridge, MA: MIT Press.

Morris, H. M., & Parker, G. E. (1982). *What is creation science.* El Cajon, CA: Master Books.

Muis, K. R., Bendixen, L. D., & Haerle, F. C. (2006). Domain generality and domain specificity in personal epistemology research: Philosophical and empirical reflections in the development of a theoretical framework. *Educational Psychology Review, 18,* 3–54.

Mull, M. S., & Evans, E. M. (2007). *Did she mean to do it? Acquiring a folk theory of intention.* Manuscript submitted for publication.

National Academy of Sciences. (1998). *Teaching about Evolution and the Nature of Science.* Washington, DC: National Academy Press.

National Academy of Sciences. (1999). *Science and creationism: A view from the National Academy of Sciences* (2nd ed.). Washington, DC: National Academy Press.

National Science Teachers Association. (2003). *NSTA Position Statement: The Teaching of Evolution.* Retrieved February, 2, 2008, from the NSTA Web site: http://www.nsta.org/about/positions/evolution.aspx

Nesse, R. M., & Williams, G. C. (1996). *Why we get sick: The new science of Darwinian medicine.* New York: Vintage Books.

Novick, L. R., & Catley, K. M. (2007). Understanding phylogenies in biology: The influence of a Gestalt perceptual principle. *Journal of Experimental Psychology: Applied, 13,* 197–223.

Numbers, R. L. (1992). *The creationists: The evolution of scientific creationism.* New York: Knopf.

Numbers, R. L. (2003). Science without God: Natural laws and Christian beliefs. In D. C. Lindberg & R. L.

Numbers (Eds.), *When science and Christianity meet* (pp. 265–285). Chicago: University of Chicago Press.

Opfer, J. E. (2002). Identifying living and sentient kinds from dynamic information: the case of goal-directed versus aimless autonomous movement in conceptual change. *Cognition, 86*, 97–122.

Passmore, C., & Stewart, J. (2002). A modeling approach to teaching evolutionary biology in high schools. *Journal of Research in Science Teaching, 39*, 185–204.

Pennock, R. T. (2002). Should creationism be taught in the public schools? *Science and Education, 11*, 111–133.

Pennock, R. T. (Ed.). (2001). *Intelligent design, creationism and its critics: Philosophical, theological, and scientific perspectives.* Cambridge, MA: The MIT Press.

Poling, D. A., & Evans, E. M. (2002). Why do birds of a feather flock together? Developmental change in the use of multiple explanations: Intention, teleology, essentialism. *British Journal of Developmental Psychology, 20,* 89–112.

Poling, D. A., & Evans, E. M. (2004a). Are dinosaurs the rule or the exception? Developing concepts of death and extinction. *Cognitive Development, 19,* 363–383.

Poling, D. A., & Evans, E. M. (2004b). Religious belief, scientific expertise, and folk ecology. *Journal of Cognition and Culture: Studies in the Cognitive Anthropology of Science, 4,* 485–524.

Root-Bernstein, R. (1984). On defining a scientific theory: Creationism considered. In A. Montagu (Ed.), *Science and creationism* (pp. 64–93). New York: Oxford University Press.

Rosengren, K. S., Gelman, S. A., Kalish, C. W., & McCormick, M. (1991). As time goes by: Children's early understanding of growth in animals. *Child Development, 62*, 1302–1320.

Rudolph, J. L., & Stewart, J. (1998). Evolution and the nature of science: On the historical discord and its implications for education. *Journal of Research in Science Teaching, 35*, 1069–1089.

Ruse, M. (2005). *The Evolution-Creation Struggle.* Cambridge, MA: Harvard University Press.

Samarapungavan, A., & Wiers, R. W. (1997). Children's thoughts on the origin of species: A study of explanatory coherence. *Cognitive Science, 21*, 147–177.

Sandoval, W. A., & Morrison, K. (2003). High School students' ideas about theories and theory change after a biological inquiry unit. *Journal of Research in Science Teaching, 40*, 369–392.

Sandoval, W. A., & Reiser, B. J. (2004). Explanation-driven inquiry: Integrating conceptual and epistemic scaffolds for scientific inquiry. *Science Education, 88*, 345–371.

Scharmann, L. C. (2005). A proactive strategy for teaching evolution. *The American Biology Teacher, 67,* 12–16.

Schult, C. A., & Wellman, H. M. (1997). Explaining human movements and actions: Children's understanding of the limits of psychological explanation. *Cognition, 62*, 291–324.

Scott, E. C. (2004). *Evolution vs. creationism.* Westport, CT: Greenwood Press.

Sehon, S. (2005). *Teleological realism: Mind, agency, and explanation.* Cambridge, MA: MIT Press.

Shapin, S. (1996). *The scientific revolution.* Chicago: University of Chicago Press.

Shipley, E. F. (1993). Categories, hierarchies, and induction. In D. L. Medin (Ed.), *The psychology of learning and motivation* (pp. 265–301). San Diego, CA: Academic Press.

Shtulman, A. (2006). Qualitative differences between naive and scientific theories of evolution. *Cognitive Psychology, 52*, 170–194.

Silver, L. A., & Kisiel, J. (2006, July). *A comparative study of American, Australian, and Canadian museum visitors' understanding of the nature of evolutionary theory.* Paper presented at the Visitor Studies Association, Grand Rapids, MI.

Sinatra, G. M. (2001). Knowledge, beliefs, and learning. *Educational Psychology Review, 13*, 321–323.

Sinatra, G. M. (2005). The warming trend in conceptual change research: The legacy of Paul R. Pintrich. *Educational Psychologist, 40,* 107–115.

Sinatra, G. M., Southerland, S. A., McConaughy, F., & Demastes, J. W. (2003). Intentions and beliefs in students' understanding and acceptance of biological evolution. *Journal of Research in Science Teaching, 40*5, 510–528.

Slaughter, V., & Lyons, M. (2003). Learning about life and death in early childhood. *Cognitive Psychology, 46*, 1–30.

Southerland, S. A., & Sinatra, G. M. (2003). Learning about biological evolution: A special case of intentional conceptual change. In G. M. Sinatra & P. R. Pintrich (Eds.), *Intentional Conceptual Change* (pp. 317–345). Mahwah, NJ: Erlbaum.

Southerland, S. A., Abrams, E., Cummins, C. L., & Anzelmo, J. (2001). Understanding students' explanations of biological phenomena: Conceptual frameworks or P-Prims. *Science Education, 85,* 328–348.

Southerland, S. A., Sinatra, G. M., & Matthews, M. R. (2001). Belief, knowledge, and science education. *Educational Psychology Review, 13,* 325–351.

Speece, M. W., & Brent, S. B. (1984). Children's understanding of death: a review of three components of the death concept. *Child Development, 55,* 1671–1686.

Speece, M. W., & Brent, S. B. (1996). The development of children's understanding of death. In C. A. Corr & D. M. Corr (Eds.), *Handbook of childhood death and bereavement* (pp. 29–50). New York: Springer.

Sperber, D. (1996). *Explaining culture: A naturalistic approach.* Oxford: Blackwell.

Spiegel, A. N., Evans, E. M., Gram, W., & Diamond, J. (2006). Museum visitors' understanding of evolution. *Museums & Social Issues, 1,* 67–84.

Sprinkle, R. H. (2006, February). Unremembered intimacies. Review of "Beasts of the Earth: Animals, Humans, and Disease" by E. F. Torrey & R. H. Yolken. *BioScience, 56,* 166–167.

Thagard, P. (1989). Explanatory coherence. *Behavioral and Brain Science, 12,* 435–502.

Tomasello, M., Carpenter, M., Call, J., Behne, T., & Moll, H. (2005). Understanding and sharing intentions: The origins of cultural cognition. *Behavioral and Brain Sciences, 28,* 675–735.

Vosniadou, S. (1994). Universal and culture-specific properties of children's mental models of the earth. In L. A. Hirschfeld & S. A. Gelman (Eds.), *Mapping the mind: Domain specificity in cognition and culture* (pp. 412–431). Cambridge: Cambridge University Press.

Vosniadou, S., & Ioannides, C. (1998). From conceptual development to science education: a psychological point of view. *International Journal of Science Education, 20,* 1213–1231.

Weiss, M. (2006, March/April). Beyond the evolution battle: Addressing public misunderstanding. *ASTC Dimensions: Bimonthly News Journal of the Association of Science-Technology Centers,* 3–5.

Wellman, H. M. (2002). Understanding the psychological world: Developing a theory of mind. In U. Goswami (Ed.), *Blackwell handbook of childhood cognitive development* (pp. 167–187). Boston, MA: Blackwell Publishing.

Wellman, H. M., & Gelman, S. A. (1998). Knowledge acquisition in foundational domains. In W. Damon, D. Kuhn & R. Siegler (Eds.), *Handbook of child psychology: Vol. 2. Cognition, perception and language* (5th ed., pp. 523–574). New York: Wiley.

Wellman, H. M., & Johnson, C. N. (in press, 2007). Developing Dualism: From intuitive understanding to transcendental ideas. To appear in A. Antonettti, A. Corradini & E. J. Lowe (Eds.), *Psycho-physical Dualism today: An interdisciplinary approach.*

Whitcomb, J. C. (1972). *The early earth: An introduction to biblical creationism.* Grand Rapids, MI: Baker Book House.

Whitcomb, J. C. (1988). *The world that perished: An introduction to biblical catastrophism.* Grand Rapids, MI: Baker Book House.

Wilensky, U., & Resnick, M. (1999). Thinking in levels: A dynamic systems approach to making sense of the world. *Journal of Science Education and Technology, 8*(1), 3–18.

Windschitl, M., & Thompson, J. (2006). Transcending simple forms of school science investigation: The impact of preservice instruction on teachers' understanding of model based inquiry. *American Educational Research Journal, 43,* 783–835.

Wozniak, R. H., & Fischer, K. W. (1993). Development in context: An introduction. In R. H. Wozniak & K. W. Fischer (Eds.), *Development in context: Acting and thinking in specific environments* (pp. xi–xvi). Hillsdale, NJ: Erlbaum.

Zimmer, C. (2005). Evolution in seven organisms. In J. Diamond (Ed.), *The virus and the whale: Explore evolution in creatures large and small* (pp. 13–24). Arlington, VA: NSTA Press.

Zimmer, C. (2007, January). Evolved for cancer. *Scientific American, 296,* 68–75.

11

Changing Conceptions in Medicine and Health

David R. Kaufman, Alla Keselman, and Vimla L. Patel
Columbia University

This chapter concerns the nature of conceptual knowledge and the process of conceptual change in the domains of medicine and health. Biomedicine is a complex and diverse knowledge-rich domain. We are particularly interested in scientific knowledge as it pertains to clinical practice and as it relates to lay individual's reasoning about matters of health and illness. The chapter raises a number of questions. Physicians receive extensive training in the biomedical sciences. How do they use this complex scientific knowledge when they make diagnostic and treatment decisions? How does this knowledge support decision heuristics that are the products of experience? What are the implications for medical education? The issues are somewhat different in the field of health cognition. The term *lay people* refers to individuals who have no formal training in the health sciences. What kind of health-related knowledge do lay people need to have to take good care of their health? How will this change in response to the shifting demands of the health-care system? How does knowledge affect reasoning and how does it change with learning? And finally, how can health professionals and lay people effectively communicate with each other despite many conceptual differences in their understanding of health and disease? These are some of the framing issues that guide the discussion in this chapter.

The role of basic science knowledge[1] in the practice of medicine has been the subject of debate for almost a century. Since the Flexner Report (1910) recommended the partitioning of the medical curriculum into a basic science component and an applied component, medical educators have argued over how to best promote clinical skills as well as foster robust conceptual change (Barzansky, 1992). Researchers in the field of medical cognition have similarly put forth competing visions concerning the nature of medical expertise and the acquisition of conceptual biomedical knowledge for the past 25 years (Elstein, Shulman, & Sprafka, 1978; Patel & Groen, 1986; Boshuizen & Schmidt, 1992; Clough, Shea, & Hamilton, 2004). Investigators in the area of health cognition have focused on how the beliefs held by lay people inform their health-related decisions and practices. Similarly, health educators and public health communicators are interested in how best to inform and educate people so that they are more responsive to health-related messages.

The domains of medicine and health care are currently undergoing significant transformation. These changes have been partially spurred by new developments in biological science and advances in the treatment of clinical diseases. Medical schools are confronted with the challenges of introducing new core knowledge into an increasingly crowded curriculum. The Internet and other health information technologies are increasingly having a significant impact on clinical practice. Clinical practitioners are continuously under pressure to maintain (or extend) their standard of competency. This requires that practitioners keep up with the latest scientific developments as they relate to their practices. Keeping up entails finding, reading, evaluating, comprehending, and incorporating the new information into one's patient care regimens. Although the availability of electronic resources can greatly facilitate this process, they also introduce new challenges related to how to productively use these technologies to address information needs and foster conceptual understanding.

The lay public has also been affected by changes in the healthcare system. The system has been impacted by societal changes such as population demographics, prevalence of certain diseases, and availability of financial resources. More than 100 million individuals suffer from chronic illness in the United States (National Academy on an Aging Society Report, 1999), and it has been reported that health care for people with chronic disease consumes approximately 78% of all health care spending in this country (Information Technology Association of America E-Health Committee, 2004). Infectious diseases are the leading causes of death worldwide and the third leading cause of death in the United States. There is a great deal of interest in both reducing the spread of infection and preparing the general public for outbreaks of infectious disease (Centers for Disease Control, 2005; Slaughter, Keselman, Kushniruk, & Patel, 2005). Most proposed solutions presuppose a greatly increased role for technology used by patients and health consumers. In keeping with these solutions, the application of information and communication technologies to health care has grown exponentially in recent years. Our concern is the ways in which these technologies can facilitate meaningful or conceptual learning and, in particular, the ways in which they fall short. Meaningful learning is the product of mindful engagement with materials and leads to genuine conceptual understanding. It is to be distinguished with procedural learning which focuses on the mastery of a particular procedure (e.g., following a therapeutic regimen). We are also concerned with tools and interventions that aim to facilitate communication and understanding.

The term *e-health* refers to the interaction of an individual with an electronic device or communication technology to access or receive health information, direction, and support on matters pertaining to health (Robinson, Patrick, Eng, & Gustafson, 1998). The emergence of e-health technologies has opened up new horizons for promoting increased self-reliance in patients who are chronically ill and encouraging greater involvement in health-related decisions. It also provides an avenue for tailoring public health messages to the lay public in the event of an outbreak. This necessitates the development of new skills and knowledge on the part of the individuals. Although there is enthusiasm for these applications, there is also recognition that the evidence for the efficacy of e-health applications is not yet indisputable. The field is still in its formative stages, and developments in technology exceed a sound scientific knowledge base (McCray, 2005). There is also recognition that those who are most in need are often those who benefit the least. The Digital Divide refers to the gap between those groups who have access to computers and the Internet and those who do not (National Telecommunications and Information Administration, 1999). Lower income households, people of color, individuals with less than high school education, and adults older than 65 years of age are significantly less likely to have such access. Although health information technologies for patients and consumers are arguably in their formative phase, it is not clear that they are oriented to produce meaningful conceptual learning.

The chapter will review research related to the process of understanding biomedical concepts and how acquisition of biomedical knowledge can support reasoning and decision making in medicine and health care domains by medical students, trained clinicians, patients, and health consumers. The chapter is divided into the following two superordinate sections: (1) conceptual understanding in biomedical domains and (2) conceptual understanding in the domain of health. In the first, we focus predominantly on research concerned with the role of biomedical knowledge in clinical reasoning. The second section is concerned with the ways in which health consumers and patients understand concepts and employ knowledge in a range of health-related contexts. The areas differ in important respects. Clinical medicine is a professional domain necessitating advanced knowledge acquisition, learning that takes place once one has mastered the basics. Lay health cognition, on the other hand, typically focuses on individuals who may lack the prerequisite literacies for productively engaging the healthcare system. The use of informal and experiential knowledge is more central to matters of lay health.

Both lay health and medical cognition draw on a core foundation of biological knowledge. There are numerous competencies involved in the practice of medicine and health, some of which are fostered in the context of actual practice and others of which are best acquired through a formal learning process. As mentioned previously, over the last 30 years, much work has gone into understanding how to enhance the medical student experience and produce skilled practitioners. Patients and health consumers are increasingly required to assume a more central role in matters pertaining to their own or their families' health. This necessitates new sets of skills and knowledge. Lay health is a comparatively new area of research, and most of the efforts are concerned with understanding the barriers to productive participation in the healthcare system. It should be noted that the research disciplines of lay health cognition and medical cognition have historically been framed by different issues and employ different methodologies to study cognitive processes. However, it is our contention that unifying these seemingly disparate strands can provide insights into the promotion of conceptual change and effective medical and healthcare practices. These insights may also contribute to our understanding of conceptual change in the biological sciences.

CONCEPTUAL UNDERSTANDING IN BIOMEDICAL DOMAIN

The Acquisition of Biomedical Knowledge and Clinical Reasoning

It is convenient to partition medical knowledge into two types of knowledge: clinical knowledge, including knowledge of disease entities and associated findings as well as investigative procedures and therapeutic management; and basic science knowledge, incorporating subject matter such as biochemistry, anatomy, and physiology. The relationship between biomedical knowledge and clinical reasoning has been the source of considerable controversy in different disciplines including medical education, medical artificial intelligence and research in medical cognition (Patel, Kaufman, & Arocha, 2000; Patel, Arocha, & Kaufman, 1994). It is generally agreed that basic science or biomedical knowledge provides a foundation for clinical knowledge. However, the precise role of basic science knowledge in clinical performance is the subject of some debate. In this section, we consider some of the epistemological issues and the consequences for cognitive research and implications for training. These issues are addressed in greater detail elsewhere (Patel et al., 2000, 1994; Kaufman & Patel, 1998). The core issues regarding conceptual change in biomedicine that are addressed are how to (1) characterize the complex nature of biomedicine, (2) understand differences in the organization of knowledge between experts and novices, and (3) identify different ways in which to promote learning of basic science concepts so that they may be useful in the practice of clinical medicine.

Unlike most other domains that are the subject of conceptual change research, medicine is a domain of advanced knowledge acquisition (Feltovich, Spiro, & Coulson, 1993). Such a domain necessitates learning that takes place beyond the initial or introductory stages. For example, medical students are expected to have substantial backgrounds in the biological sciences. Much of the basic science subject matter in medical schools is predicated on the fact that students have a basic mastery of the introductory materials, so that instructors can focus on more advanced topics. According to Feltovich, Spiro, and Coulson (1989), advanced and introductory learning have very different goals and necessitate different instructional methods. For example, a basic goal of introductory learning is exposure to large areas of content without much emphasis on conceptual mastery of knowledge. Advanced knowledge acquisition carries the expectation of students attaining a deeper understanding of the content material and the ability to use it flexibly and productively in diverse contexts.

In the traditional approach to medical education, medical students are taught basic science courses for the first two years of their studies followed by two years that primarily emphasize the acquisition of clinical skills and knowledge. This model predominated for most of the last century. However, the growth of biomedical and clinical knowledge placed increasing pressures on medical schools to accommodate more classes. As a consequence, science training became increasingly detached from clinical practice. This in part led to the growing popularity of problem-based learning (PBL) which offers clinically integrated curricula. In PBL programs, instruction involves the introduction of clinically meaningful problems at the beginning of the curriculum, based on the assumption that scientific knowledge taught abstractly does not help students to integrate this knowledge with clinical practice (Norman & Schmidt, 2000). PBL also stresses self-directed learning, problem-solving skills and effective collaboration skills. In general, research evaluating the performance of PBL and conventional curricula programs has found negligible differences in terms of clinical skills (Albanese & Mitchell, 1993; Colliver, 2004; Jolly, 2006). Nevertheless, the different curricula make rather different assumptions about how best to foster conceptual change. PBL programs are predicated on the necessity of connecting scientific concepts to the conditions of application, whereas conventional curricula (CC) emphasize the importance of fostering a foundation of general scientific knowledge that is broadly applicable. The CC runs the risk of imparting inert knowledge, much of which is not retained beyond medical school. For example, students may learn models of cardiovascular physiology that are not readily applicable to clinical contexts. On the other hand, PBL curricula may promote knowledge that is so tightly coupled to context (e.g., a featured clinical case of hypothyroidism) as to have minimum generality beyond the immediate set of problems.

In general, cognitive research contrasting the two curricula supports these assertions regarding the strength and limitations of the two models (Norman & Schmidt, 2000). The findings are briefly summarized here, but presented in detail in Patel et al. (2000). Patel, Groen, & Norman (1993) conducted a series of studies that contrasted the performance of PBL versus CC students in their abilities to integrate basic science knowledge (BSK) in a diagnostic reasoning task. To prime the students' use of this knowledge, relevant basic science texts (roughly a page in length) were presented either before or prior to the presentation of a clinical case. There was a third condition in which the students were not exposed to the basic science texts. When basic science information was provided prior to the clinical problem, the students showed a lack of integration of basic science into the clinical context in both schools. When the basic science texts were presented after the clinical problem, there was integration of basic science into students' clinical explanations in both schools. This suggests that the clinical cases establish a context that enables biomedical knowledge to be readily integrated, but biomedical knowledge when given before provides a causal model within which clinical knowledge cannot be integrated.

There were a number of differences in the ways the students from the two schools employed basic science information in the context of clinical reasoning. PBL students used BSK spontaneously (without prompting) and more readily integrated it into their explanations, but included much information that was not relevant to the problem. CC students did not spontaneously integrate BSK into their explanations and used it only when they experienced difficulty with the patient problems. Although they used it more sparingly than the PBL students, it served to integrate disparate parts of the diagnostic problem and rendered a diagnostic solution as more sensible. Students from the PBL School integrated the biomedical knowledge within the clinical structure very tightly, making the transfer of the biomedical knowledge to another context difficult. Patel and colleagues proposed that the differences in the utilization of biomedical concepts in clinical problem solving between PBL and CC students could conceivably be due to the emphasis on premature integration of causal models with clinical problems, as stressed in the PBL curriculum. Interestingly, similar differences in reasoning were evident in residents trained in either PBL or CC curricula (Patel, Arocha, & Leccisi, 2001). This shows the long-term impact of instruction and training in the two curricular formats. It is important to characterize the ways in which learning activities (e.g., small group sessions) employed in the different systems contribute to the differences in clinical performance of trainees from the two schools, (Patel, Arocha, Chaudhari, Karlin, & Briedis, 2005; Schmidt, Vermeulen, & Van Der Molen, 2006).

This is coextensive with an ongoing debate in educational and cognitive research related to the optimal balance between abstract and situation-specific learning (Anderson, Reder, & Simon, 1995). Abstract learning can serve to improve the generality and extensibility of a concept to a range of situations, but it increases the risk of inert knowledge. Contextualized or situated learning can increase the applicability of concepts to particular clinical problems, but they may serve to limit the scope of its application to other problems. Although medical educational approaches are not the focal point of this chapter, it serves as a subtext for much of the conceptual issues in cognitive research that is discussed.

Epistemological Issues and Diagnostic Reasoning

It had been widely believed that biomedical and clinical knowledge could be seamlessly integrated into a coherent knowledge structure that supported all facets of medical practice and patient management. This was evident in the writings of Feinstein (1973), who proposed an elaborate theory of diagnostic reasoning as a logical process. The objective was to develop explanatory models of decision making that incorporated physiological causality, and thereby went beyond probabilistic models that only considered the correlations of symptoms to clinical disorders. Diagnostic reasoning is described as a process of passing through a series of explanatory stations during which the input data of a patient's manifestations are converted to the output — a particular disease. The process involves not merely coordinating systems with disease categories, but identifying the structural or functional source of the manifestation. The model suggests that medical diagnosis is akin to diagnostic troubleshooting in electronics, with a primary goal of finding the structural fault or systemic perturbation (Kaufman & Patel, 1998). From this perspective, clinical and biomedical knowledge become intricately intertwined, providing medical practice with a sound scientific basis.

Blois (1988) had the insight that medical reasoning could be construed as a vertical reasoning process across disparate knowledge sources that draw on different domains including biochemistry, anatomy and physiology. In addition, the multi-level knowledge can be arranged as a hierarchical schema of scientific sources. This is illustrated in the context of Wilson's Disease (Table 11.1), a central nervous system disorder caused by a metabolic defect in which the body

TABLE 11.1
Attributes of Wilson's Disease at Different Levels in the Hierarchy (adapted from Blois, 1988)

Level	Disease Attribute	Field
Patient as a whole	Malaise, bizarre behavior, labile effect	Clinical Medicine
Physiologic Systems	Intention tremor, dysarthia, chorea	Physiology
Organs	Kayser-Fleischer ring, ascites	Physiology
Cells	Alzheimer type II cells, abnormal glycogen deposits, necrosis of neurons	Physiology, Pathology
Biopolymers	Decreased serum ceruplasmin, increased alkaline phospotase	Biochemistry
Molecules	Aminoaciduria	Chemistry
Atoms	Decreased serum copper, increased urinary copper	Physics

cannot properly eliminate copper from the blood. The lower-level abnormalities such as urinary copper are revealed by laboratory tests and the higher-level findings come from patient history (e.g., malaise) and physical examinations. Every level has relatively distinct set of concepts and unique language for describing causal processes. Each level also references specialized bodies of knowledge, and it's not likely that an individual will be equally expert at all levels. The ascending levels introduce a greater degree of uncertainty in ascribing causality. For example, it's more difficult to explain the cause of the patient's bizarre behavior than it is to account for his or her tremor or ascites (excess fluid in the abdomen caused by liver dysfunction). It should be noted that relatively few diseases can be traced across levels in this manner. It is also not proposed as a model of how clinicians do or should reason. The example serves to highlight the challenge of integrating information from qualitatively different sources of information drawn from different domains of biomedicine.

Medical AI introduces some important distinctions for thinking about conceptual knowledge and diagnostic reasoning. A complete discussion of these issues is beyond the scope of this chapter. In our view these distinctions are useful in illuminating dimensions of human reasoning and conceptual knowledge. Feinstein's analysis is consistent with a *fault model* that emphasizes deep system knowledge and finding the root cause of the problem. A *shallow system* reasons by relating observations to intermediate hypotheses, which partition the problem space, and further associating intermediate hypotheses with diagnostic hypotheses. The knowledge-base would include only entities related to taxonomic classification: diagnostic hypotheses and clinical findings. A *deep system* has explicit representations of structural components (e.g., arteries and valves) and their relations (e.g., pressure flow), the functions of these components, and their relationship to behavioral states (Chandrasakeran, Smith, & Sticklen, 1989; Kuipers, 1987). The causal and diagnostic knowledge can be generated by *running* or simulating the system and qualitatively deriving behavioral sequences that can identify and explain the malfunction.

Alternatively, diagnostic reasoning can be viewed as a process of heuristic classification involving the instantiation of specific slots in a disease schema, which is consistent with a shallow system (Clancey, 1988). In this perspective, the primary goal of diagnostic reasoning is to discriminate between and classify a cluster of patient findings as belonging to a specific disease category. Diagnostic reasoning is viewed as a process of coordinating theory and evidence rather than one of finding fault in the system. As expertise develops, the disease knowledge of a clinician becomes more dependent on clinical experience; clinical problem-solving is increasingly guided by the use of clinical case exemplars drawn from prior exposure, and less dependent on a robust understanding of the system in question. This is not to suggest that basic science does not play an important role in medicine; rather the process of diagnosis, particularly in dealing with routine problems, is largely one of classification. Basic science knowledge is important in dealing with more complex problems and resolving anomalies. In addition, it is unlikely that clinicians could acquire a basic understanding of the categorical structure of disease without a sound foundation in the biomedical sciences.

In summary, there are different ways of construing the role of basic science knowledge in diagnostic reasoning. Feinstein articulates the received approach in which clinical reasoning is rooted in a deep understanding of biomedical knowledge. Although Blois does not speak directly to the controversy, he proposes an ontological approach in which to understand how disparate sources of biomedical knowledge, drawing on varying scientific sources, can play a role in reasoning about a single case. The work in medical AI serves to sharpen our understanding between a heuristic or associative method which emphasizes categorization and a deep knowledge method which implies causal reasoning and more extensive conceptual knowledge.

Conceptual Change and the Development of Medical Expertise

The term *medical cognition* refers to a body of research pertaining to cognitive processes, such as perception, text comprehension, conceptual understanding, problem solving and decision making in medical practice or in experimental tasks representative of medical practice. A focal point of this research has been in understanding the nature of expertise. A well organized knowledge base is one of the hallmarks of expertise (Chase & Simon, 1973; Chi, Feltovich, & Glaser, 1981). It is generally agreed that an expert's problem solving ability is a result of years of domain related experience in which he or she develops a richly interconnected network of knowledge. This knowledge is specifically tuned to the tasks that the experts routinely perform. In general, experts are able to organize information into meaningfully interrelated chunks, selectively attend to relevant information and employ highly efficient knowledge-based problem solving strategies (Ericsson & Smith, 1991; Feltovich, Spiro, & Coulson, 1997).

There are several methods common to the study of medical cognition including an online think aloud protocol generated while the subject is reasoning about a medical case, free recall of which provides a measure of memory for domain-related stimuli and pathophysiological explanation. The latter is a post-hoc task that asks the clinician, student or scientist to provide an explanation of the underlying pathophysiology of the case. The protocols from this task can be used to examine the use of basic science concepts in clinical explanations. Most of the studies discussed in this section employ one or more of these tasks. The free recall and pathophysiological explanation tasks are often used in tandem to provide a more in-depth characterization of the participants' clinical case representations. Free recall is generally used as a measure of case comprehension. Pathophysiological explanation provides a more explicit measure of clinical reasoning as evidenced by both the kinds of knowledge used (e.g., basic science and clinical) and the patterns of inferences.

In the early 1980s, researchers and educators commonly believed that biomedical knowledge played an integrative role in diagnostic reasoning (van de Wiel, 1997; Johnson, Duran, Hassebrock, Moller, Prietula, Feltovich, & Swanson, 1981; Lesgold, Rubinson, Feltovich, Glaser, Klopfer, & Wang, 1988; Feltovich, Johnson, Moller, & Swanson, 1984). As discussed previously, diagnostic reasoning expertise was partially predicated on having a deep understanding of the pathophysiology of disease. Feltovich studied expert-novice differences in the diagnosis of pediatric cardiology cases. This is a domain in which diagnosis can be differentiated by subtle differences in anatomical abnormalities and related perturbations. For example in one case, subjects needed to distinguish whether an obstruction impeding blood flow was in the aorta, immediately upstream (subvalvular) or immediately downstream (supravalvular) from the aortic valve. Each of these problems produces a somewhat different symptom profile. The results indicate a developmental pattern in terms of both diagnostic accuracy and clinical reasoning with a marked improvement as a function of expertise. Feltovich et al. concluded that experts' knowledge of disease is extensively cross-referenced with a rich network of connections among diseases that can present similar symptoms. This knowledge base is characterized by a deep understanding of the pathophysiology of congenital heart disease. Novices, on the other hand, have comparatively sparse knowledge and less precise understanding of the relation between the pathophysiology of disease and clinical symptoms.

Lesgold et al. studied the abilities of expert radiologists and trainees at different levels to interpret chest x-ray photographs. Lesgold et al. (1988) found that expert radiologists were able to rapidly detect a general pattern of disease, which resulted in a general localization of the anatomical defect and served to constrain the possible diagnostic interpretations. Novices, on the on other hand, had greater difficulty focusing in on important structures and were less able to differentiate noise (e.g., shadows) from substance (e.g., a tumor). The authors concluded that the knowledge that underlies expertise in radiology includes the mental representation of anatomy, a theory of anatomical perturbation and the ability to transform the visual image into a three dimensional representation.

Crowley, Naus, Stewart, and Friedman (2003) studied differences in expertise in breast pathology. The results suggest systematic differences between subjects at varying levels of expertise corresponding to accuracy of diagnosis, and all aspects of task performance including feature detection, identification and data interpretation. The authors propose a model of visual diagnostic competence that involves development of effective search strategies, fast and accurate recognition of anatomic location, acquisition of visual data interpretation skills and explicit feature identification strategies that result from a well-organized knowledge base.

On the basis of this early research in medical cognition, one may presuppose that basic science knowledge is the primary engine of clinical reasoning. Patel and colleagues (Patel & Groen, 1986; Patel, Evans, & Kaufman, 1989) conducted a series of studies that endeavored to elucidate differences in reasoning strategies and use of basic science knowledge by subjects at varying levels of expertise. It is useful to introduce a distinction that has been shown to discriminate between novice and expert reasoning in a range of domains (Larkin, McDermott, Simon, & Simon, 1980). Forward or data-driven reasoning is a strategy in which hypotheses are generated from data, for example, weight loss may indicate a hypermetabolic state. Backward or hypothesis-driven reasoning is a strategy in which one reasons backward, drawing implication from a hypothesis and attempting to find data that elucidate it. Hypothyroidism may cause the observed weight gain is an example of a backward reasoning inference. Forward reasoning is rapid and based on domain knowledge and can be error-prone in the absence of adequate domain knowledge. Backward reasoning is slower and may make heavy demands on working memory (because one has to keep track of goals and hypotheses). It is more likely to be used when domain knowledge is inadequate. In general, much of clinical reasoning employs a mixture of backward and forward reasoning (Patel & Kaufman, 1995). Clinical reasoning can be characterized as a two-stage process: diagnostic reasoning is marked by a pattern of (forward) inference from observation to hypothesis; and predictive reasoning is marked by (backward) inference from hypothesis to observations.

In several related experiments, experts made minimal use of biomedical knowledge when solving clinical problems and when providing pathophysiological explanations (Patel & Groen, 1986; Patel, Evans, & Groen, 1989). The studies are summarized in detail elsewhere (Patel, Evans, & Groen, 1989; Patel & Kaufman, 1995) and will be presented in brief. Patel and Groen (1986) showed that when diagnosis was accurate, all expert cardiologists explained routine problems by means of forward reasoning. With inaccurate diagnoses, however, a mixture of forward and backward reasoning was used. In either case, the inferences employed almost exclusively clinical knowledge. In another study (Patel, Groen, & Arocha, 1990), cardiologists and endocrinologists were asked to read endocrinology and cardiology cases (provided as written text), recall case information, and explain the underlying pathophysiology of the problems. The clinicians were asked to work on problems both within and outside their domains of expertise. Surprisingly, the clinicians did not employ principles from basic biomedical science, even when they were working outside their own domain of expertise; rather, they relied on clinical associations and classifications to formulate solutions. The results suggest that basic science did not contribute directly to reasoning in clinical problem solving for experienced clinicians. When clinicians were presented with unusually difficult cases, they tended to employ biomedical information in a backward-directed causal reasoning manner, in order to provide coherence to the explanation of clinical cues that could not be easily accounted for by the primary diagnostic hypothesis that was being considered (Joseph & Patel, 1990; Patel et al., 1990).

Experiments with medical students reveal an interesting developmental pattern. In one study, medical students were presented with basic science material immediately prior to being given a clinical case (Patel, Groen, & Scott, 1988). Such a procedure was designed to increase the likelihood that subjects would use related information from separate knowledge sources. The subjects were asked to read four texts, recall in writing what they had read, and then explain the clinical problem in terms of the basic science texts. The subjects included students in their first year of medical school, second-year medical students who had completed all basic medical sciences but had not begun any clinical work; and final-year medical students just prior to their graduation. In general, subjects' recall of the basic science texts was very limited, indicating a lack of well-developed knowledge structures in which to organize this information. In their clinical explanations, the first year students had limited prior knowledge of pathophysiology and tended to employ concepts from normal physiology (e.g., thermal regulation of body temperature rather than infection leading to fever). The second-year students made extensive use of basic science knowledge. However, their explanations made equal use of case relevant and case irrelevant concepts. Fourth-year students provided explanations and also made use of basic science information, but were more selective and systematic in applying it to the clinical problems. It is interesting to note that the fourth-year students' greater use of basic science actually resulted in more consistent inferences. Our results can be interpreted as indicating that basic science knowledge is used differently by the three groups of subjects.

In a related study with subjects at the same levels of training, the order of materials was reversed. The clinical problem was presented and this was followed by three basic science texts. The fourth-year students were able to use the basic science information effectively for both diagnostic and predictive reasoning. The second-year students were also able to use in the predictive reasoning phase, but not for diagnostic reasoning. The first-year students were not able to use the basic science information any more effectively when it was given after the clinical problem than when it was given before the clinical problem. These results suggest that reasoning toward a diagnosis from the facts of a case is frustrated by attempting to employ basic science knowledge unless the student has already developed a diagnostic hypothesis. Interestingly, the addition of basic science knowledge seems to improve the accuracy of diagnoses offered by final-year medical students, but does not improve the accuracy of diagnoses by first- and second-year students. Patel, Evans, and Groen (1989) concluded that final-year students, who have had some clinical experience, rely on clinically relevant features in a case to classify the diagnosis and make selective predictions of findings partially based on basic science concepts from the texts (Patel et al., 1989). In other words, as evidenced in more experienced clinicians, the diagnostic process was largely contingent on reasoning about clinical findings and basic science knowledge did not contribute to the organization of information, but provided a mechanism for adding coherence or checking plausibility.

There have been numerous other studies that suggest the integration of basic and clinical knowledge is not seamless (e.g., Woods, Brooks, & Norman, 2005; Arocha, Patel, & Patel, 1993; Patel, Groen, & Norman, 1993). Pathophysiological information is used by physicians and senior medical students either when the problem solving process breaks down (i.e., no obvious solution) or to explain loose ends (i.e., leftover findings) that cannot be accounted for by the diagnostic hypothesis or hypotheses. In general, there is evidence to suggest that unprompted use of biomedical concepts in clinical reasoning decreases as a function of expertise (Patel & Kaufman, 1995). In addition, there is evidence to suggest that students have difficulty in applying basic science concepts in contexts that differ from the initial conditions of learning (Patel et al., 1993). This problem of transfer is of course common to many different domains of learning.

In summary, the use of basic science differs in the various subdomains of medicine and appears to play a more central role in perceptual domains such as radiology and dermatology. Basic science is used sparingly by experts in familiar or routine problems, but is used more extensively in complex cases. The relative use of BSK is associated with particular patterns of inference. Backward reasoning involves causal inferences that more liberally draw on biomedical concepts whereas forward reasoning is more of a heuristically driven reasoning that makes minimal use of these concepts. Experts reasoning about routine problems within their domain typically engage in forward reasoning; novices and experts dealing with non-routine problems are more likely to resort to backward reasoning. There are also developmental patterns that reflect medical students' conceptual organization of knowledge and experience with clinical problems. Not surprisingly, senior students can more readily attend to selective features of a problem and systematically use BSK in pathophysiological explanations. Basic science knowledge can be used to facilitate diagnostic reasoning but may actually frustrate it when a student has not developed a diagnostic hypothesis.

Mental Models and Conceptual Complexity

Although there is a substantial body of research examining the use of biomedical knowledge in clinical contexts, there have been comparatively few in-depth studies examining students' and practitioners' conceptual understanding of basic science phenomena. In this type of research, as is more common in other domains such as physics (diSessa, 1993; Vosniadou, 1994), participants' understanding of concepts is closely scrutinized through in-depth interviews and tasks that require the use of the same concepts in different problem contexts. The focus in these studies is not on clinical reasoning per se, but on students and practitioners' mental models of biological systems.

As mentioned previously, medicine is an advanced domain of knowledge acquisition in which the goals of learning are oriented towards a greater depth of understanding at least in theory if not always in practice. The acquisition of the prerequisite clinical and biomedical domain knowledge to practice medicine typically occurs over a 10-year period. Conceptual knowledge is not only characterized by growth, but reorganization necessitated by the nature of the task demands. For example, the biological knowledge acquired by an undergraduate premedical student is at least partially oriented towards attaining a satisfactory grade. It would stand to reason that her knowledge is tuned towards answering questions on a test. In medical school, the basic science assessments are oriented towards the pathophysiology of disease and increasingly towards a certain level of integration with clinical knowledge as required by licensing examinations as well as the demands of clinical practice. Conceptual knowledge undergoes multiple conceptual reorganizations over the course of those years. The development of expert conceptual knowledge involves a shift from the novice's flat and disconnected knowledge to the expert's systematic multi-layered structures (diSessa, 1993).

As in other domains of science, students exhibit misconceptions. These misconceptions are rooted in prior knowledge that may have been adequate or even productive at an earlier point in the students' learning. The patterns of misunderstanding are not the result of a single erroneous piece of knowledge, but reflect networks of knowledge elements, which in themselves may be correct, partially correct or faulty (Spiro, Feltovich, Coulson, & Anderson, 1989; Patel et al., 2000). It is useful to conceptualize subjects' understandings in terms of progressions of mental models (Kaufman et al., 1998). Mental Models are dynamic knowledge structures that enable one to understand how a system works. One can "run" a mental model to predict future states of a system or to explain the cause of a change in state of a system. As a consequence, mental models can be characterized in terms of their predictive and explanatory power.

Patel, Kaufman, and Magder (1991) examined medical students' understanding of concepts related to ventilation-perfusion matching, an important concept in pulmonary and circulatory physiology. They found that students at the end of first year of the medical school exhibited significant misconceptions in reasoning about ventilation-perfusion matching in the context of a clinical problem. Specifically, students had considerable difficulty in conceptualizing the cardio-pulmonary system as a closed mechanistic system. Students' explanations revealed that they reasoned about each lung as if it were semi-autonomous and did not impose constraints on the other lung's functioning. It was also observed that students were not able to map clinical findings onto pathophysiological manifestations. In general, the novices' mental models were too brittle to be able to predict the pathophysiological consequences of anatomical abnormalities. The students were also not capable of formulating adequate explanations to account for clinical manifestations.

Feltovich and colleagues (1989) have explored students understanding of concepts pertaining to cardiovascular physiology. In one study, they documented significant misconceptions in students' understanding of the structure and function of the cardiovascular system. Congestive heart failure is a syndrome in which the heart's effectiveness as a pump can diminish greatly, and as a result the rate of blood flow slows dramatically. The misconception that was expressed by over 60% of first and second year medical students in a study, and by some medical practitioners, was that heart failure is caused by the heart getting too big, which in turn stretches the cardiac muscle fibres. This explanation places too strong an emphasis on mechanical factors rather than biochemical factors. The primary cause of congestive heart failure is activational, meaning that it is resulting from a failure to meet the heart's metabolic and energy requirements. The authors characterized multiple component beliefs that contributed to the misconception, some of which can be traced to formal learning experiences. For example, textbooks frequently present a graphic depiction of single cardiac muscle fiber to discuss length-tension relationships (the force a muscle is capable of generating at different lengths). As a consequence, participants assume that sum of the parts of the system to account for the function of an intact system — failing to consider the emergent properties.

Kaufman and colleagues (Kaufman, Patel, & Magder, 1996; Kaufman & Patel, 1998) investigated students, residents, cardiologists and physiologists' mental models of biomedical concepts in the domain of cardiovascular physiology. The findings are described in detail in Patel et al. (2000). In the experiment, subjects were presented with questions and problems pertaining to the concepts of cardiac output, venous return, and the mechanical properties of the cardiovascular and circulatory system. *Cardiac output* is the total amount of blood pumped from the heart per unit time. *Venous return* refers to the amount of blood returning to the heart per unit time. The circulatory system is a closed system, and therefore the blood pumped out by the heart must inevitably return to the heart. The stimulus material included several areas of questions and problems including basic physiology (e.g., explain the effects of an increase in preload on stroke volume); applied physiology (e.g., extreme exercise); pathophysiology (e.g., the hemodynamic effects of haemorrhage); medical disorders (e.g., congestive heart failure) and brief patient problems. Most of the questions involved predictions pertaining to the effects of changes (an increase or decrease) in variables such as preload (tension in the heart prior to contraction) on changes in circulation. This afforded us an opportunity to investigate subjects' reasoning within and across levels in the hierarchical chain of biomedicine as described by Blois (1988).

In general, we observed a progression of mental models as a function of expertise. This was evidenced in predictive accuracy which increased with expertise, from 42% in a premedical student to 91% in the most experienced cardiologist (Kaufman & Patel, 1998). It was also noted in the quality of explanations in response to individual questions and problems and in terms of overall coherence of the subjects' representations of cardiovascular and circulatory system (see Patel et al., 2000). However, we also found a wide range of conceptual errors in subjects at different levels of expertise. First year medical students began their learning with preconceptions that evidenced a lack of basic understanding of prerequisite concepts. For example, one subject was lacking in basic physical science knowledge and had difficulties reasoning about pressure gradients. These misconceptions would appear to result from formal learning. For example, a misconception was manifested in the responses of six subjects, including two fourth year students and two cardiology residents. It was related to a confounding of venous resistance and venous compliance. Venous return is determined primarily by vascular compliance and by venous resistance. Vascular compliance describes the properties of a vessel to distend to accommodate more blood volume per unit pressure. Vascular resistance is the forces opposing blood flow determined by the frictional loss of energy due to the radius of the vessels and the viscosity of blood. In other words, increasing resistance has the effect of diminishing blood flow, all things being equal.

The notion is that since an increase in venous resistance is associated with a decrease in compliance, then the net effect of resistance would be to increase venous return. This is quite counterintuitive given both commonsense and biomedical meaning of resistance, which all of these subjects clearly understood as impeding blood flow. This may suggest that this misconception is a function of formal learning rather than acquired through experience. It also necessitates that subjects integrate the forces affecting cardiac output and venous return, which proved to be a significant challenge for many subjects. The more expert subjects, including the final year medical students and physicians, experienced more difficulty in responding to the basic physiology than they did applying the same concepts in more clinically-oriented problems. On several occasions, the physicians would use clinical analogies to explain physiological processes, often leading to faulty explanations (Kaufman et al., 1996). One of the problems is that reasoning about a patient's condition typically invokes a simpler inference scheme with fewer steps and less temporal precision. In other words, rigorous reasoning about physiological states often necessitates more fine-grained analysis of cause-effect relations and a more precise time line. However, when provided with pathophysiological conditions or medical disorders requiring pathophysiological explanations (e.g., congestive heart failure), the physicians drew on their clinical knowledge to great effect. The closer the distance in the analogical mapping (e.g., from clinical science to pathophysiology), the more likely there was to be a successful transfer of knowledge.

This section serves to highlight the conceptual complexity of basic science knowledge in medicine. As in other domains, novices as well as more experienced subjects exhibit misconceptions that lead to faulty patterns of reasoning. Mental models, even in expert subjects, tend to be imperfect and, at times, imprecise. Experienced physicians who are less than experts show evidence of significant faults in their understanding of biomedical knowledge. However, these faults do not necessarily impair their ability to engage in clinical reasoning except under circumstances where such knowledge is necessary (e.g., a complex case). In these situations, they would most likely consult with or refer the patient to an expert cardiologist. The studies in the above section were concentrated in the domain of cardiovascular physiology, which constitutes an extensive and diverse body of knowledge. It's not tenable that a medical student would acquire a deep and expansive understanding of the domain based on such a limited exposure to these set of related ideas. Their experiences are insufficient to generate feedback to correct faulty assumptions. It's possible that mental models are too brittle to be used effectively in clinical contexts and this could explain some of the findings in the earlier section related to the non-productive use of basic science knowledge. It is reasonable to expect students who go on to study cardiology would acquire deeper and more robust understanding as a consequence of both formal learning (e.g. studying for board examinations) and experience in seeing a diversity of patients with heart problems.

Reconciling Basic Science and Clinical Knowledge: Is One World Enough?

In the prior sections we reviewed empirical and epistemological literature concerning the role of biomedical knowledge in clinical reasoning. Two competing cognitive theories have emerged to explain the conceptual organization of knowledge and its development: the "two-world hypothesis" theory and "knowledge encapsulation." Patel and Groen (1991) expressed the idea that these two knowledge bases constituted "two worlds" connected at discrete points. Schmidt and Boshuizen propose a learning mechanism, *knowledge encapsulation*, for explaining how biomedical knowledge becomes subsumed under clinical knowledge in the development of expertise (Schmidt & Boshuizen, 1993; Boshuizen & Schmidt, 1992). The process of knowledge encapsulation involves the subsumption of biomedical propositions and associative relations under a small number of higher level clinical propositions with the same explanatory power. They argue that through repeated application of knowledge in medical training and practice, networks of causal biomedical knowledge becomes incorporated into a comprehensive clinical concept (van de Wiel, 1997). Basic science knowledge can be "unpacked" as needed and relatively easily, but is not typically used as a first line of explanation by medical experts. The knowledge encapsulation thesis has spawned an impressive body of research. In this section, we consider both hypotheses, starting with the two world hypothesis.

The crux of the two-world hypothesis is that these two bodies of knowledge differ in important respects, including in terms of the nature of constituent knowledge elements (kinds of core concepts) and in the nature of reasoning they support. For example, clinical reasoning involves the coordination of diagnostic hypotheses with clinical evidence, and incorporates an elaborate taxonomy that relates clinical symptoms to disorders. Biomedical reasoning involves the use of causal models at varying levels of abstraction (e.g., organ and cellular levels). The evidence from medical problem solving studies suggests that routine diagnostic reasoning is largely a heuristic classification process in which clusters of associated findings become attached to hypotheses. Basic science knowledge is not typically evident in expert think aloud protocols in these circumstances. Perhaps the central role played by basic science may not be in facilitating clinical reasoning per se, but in facilitating explanation and coherent communication (Patel et al., 1989; Patel & Kaufman, 1995: Patel et al., 2005).

Under conditions of uncertainty, physicians resort to scientific explanations which are coherent, even when they are not completely accurate. The role of basic science, aside from providing the concepts and vocabulary required to formulate clinical problems, is to create a basis for establishing and assessing coherence in the explanation of biomedical phenomena. Basic science does not provide the axioms, the analogies, or the abstractions required to support clinical problem solving. Rather, it provides the principles that make it possible to organize observations that defy ready clinical classification and analysis. Biomedical knowledge also provides a means for explaining, justifying and communicating medical decisions. Woods and colleagues (2005) conducted an experiment in which undergraduates were taught four disorders by either using basic science mechanisms or through the use of probabilistic associations (symptoms × disease). There was no difference in accuracy between the groups in an immediate test. But after a week-long delay, the mechanism group performed better. The authors concluded that the real benefit of basic science is that it facilitates retention and retrieval. In the absence of basic science, the relationships between symptoms and diagnoses may seem to be largely arbitrary and not very memorable. Basic science knowledge is associated with genuine understanding.

The two-world hypothesis is consistent with a model of conceptual change in which clinical knowledge and basic science knowledge undergo both a joint and separate process of reorganization. This is partly a function of the kinds of learning experiences that students undergo. As the students increase their clinical work, the prioritization of knowledge also shifts to concepts that support the process of clinical reasoning. Schmidt and Boshuizen (1993) offer a different explanation for this phenomenon. They propose that the development of expertise in medicine can be characterized by a developmental process marked by phases in which the learner employs qualitatively different knowledge bases when diagnosing a case. In the early part of their training, students acquire "rich elaborated causal networks explaining the causes and consequences of disease" in terms of biomedical knowledge (p. 207). Through repeated exposure to patient problems, the basic science knowledge becomes encapsulated into high-level simplified causal models explaining signs and symptoms. These models are indexed by diagnostic labels. The knowledge structures acquired through different developmental phases do not fade into oblivion, rather they sedimentate into multiple layers which are accessed when the more recently acquired structures are inadequate to explain a clinical problem.

There is ample evidence in the expertise literature to suggest that novices and intermediates require additional processing time and effort to accomplish a task as compared to experts. For example, in pathophysiological explanations, intermediates generate lengthy lines of reasoning that employ numerous biomedical concepts. On the other hand, expert physicians use shortcuts in their line of reasoning, skipping intervening steps (Kuipers & Kassirer, 1984; Schmidt & Boshuizen, 1993; van de Wiel, 1997). An example drawn from a study by van de Wiel, Boshuizen and Schmidt (2000) illustrates the difference in reasoning. They asked fourth year medical students and practicing physicians to explain a clinical case of heart failure. When asked to explain the patient's shortness of breath, a physician stated that "Mitral valve insufficiency causes pulmonary congestion and hence shortness of breath" (p. 331). A fourth year student provided a much lengthier explanation that invoked the dysfunction of valves, left ventricle leakage, and disruption of blood flow effecting pulmonary circulation causing lung congestion leading to shortness of breath. The line of reasoning between the two participants is rather similar, but the clinician expressed it in a compact fashion.

The intermediate effect is a phenomenon in which performance is characterized by a u-shaped (or inverted u-shaped) curve. This is similar to the well documented developmental phenomenon in which a child regresses to an earlier stage in learning to perform a new behavior because it is not yet fully assimilated (Strauss & Stavy, 1982). The intermediate effect has been found in a variety of medical cognition tasks and with a great number of performance indicators. Intermediates typically generate more irrelevant information in clinical case recall (Patel, Groen & Frederiksen, 1986; Schmidt & Boshuizen, 1993; van de Wiel et al., 2000), make more interpretation errors when identifying dermatology disorders (Norman, Brooks, & Allen, 1989), make more diagnostic errors of radiological images (Lesgold et al., 1988), and generate a higher number of inaccurate diagnostic hypotheses in case explanations (Arocha et al., 1993). A common finding is that intermediates (typically senior medical students) recall more information than either novices or experts when asked to recall information from a clinical case. Novices lack the knowledge to integrate the information and experts selectively attend to and recall only the relevant information. Similarly in pathophysiological explanation tasks, intermediates tend to use more biomedical knowledge and more elaborations than either novices or experts. The extra processing is due to the fact that these subjects have accumulated a great deal of conceptual knowledge, but it has not been fully assimilated or organized in such a way that it is tuned to clinical performance task.

Schmidt and colleagues (Schmidt & Boshuizen, 1993; van de Wiel et al., 2000) have conducted several studies in which they have manipulated the processing time in free recall and explanation tasks by varying the case exposures varied the time of case exposure (3'30", 1'15" and 30"). They have demonstrated that intermediates are adversely affected by having less time to process the stimulus material whereas experts were largely unaffected by a reduction in time. The argument is that the immediate activation of a small number of highly relevant encapsulating concepts enables experts to rapidly formulate an adequate representation of a patient problem. On the other hand, students have yet to develop knowledge in an encapsulated form, rely more on biomedical knowledge and require more time to construct a coherent case representation (van de Wiel, 1997). In other studies, they demonstrated that expert clinicians could unfold their abbreviated lines of reasoning into longer chains of inferences that evoked more elaborate causal models when the situation warranted it (Schmidt & Boshuizen, 1993; Rikers et al., 2002). This was seen as further evidence to support the knowledge encapsulation theory.

Is one world enough to accommodate the diverse kinds of biomedical and clinical knowledge? The knowledge encapsulation theory suggests that the acquisition of biomedical knowledge can best be characterized in terms of increasing differentiation of a single knowledge base. The two-world hypothesis argues that clinical and biomedical knowledge are qualitatively different and are likely fostered by different kinds of learning experiences. It is best to conceptualize them as two or more distinct kinds of knowledge structures. However, the competing theories agree on a number of important points. Both recognize the importance of biomedical knowledge in making sense of complex diagnostic problems. Although expert clinicians do not employ such knowledge in routine situations, it continues to fulfill an important role in clinical practice. In addition, both theories differ from the classical view, for example as espoused by Feinstein, that diagnostic reasoning is fundamentally a process of identifying the structural or functional source of the manifestation.

In our view, knowledge encapsulation represents a relatively idealized perspective on the integration of basic science into clinical knowledge. However, encapsulation may very well play a role in fostering conceptual change. In an earlier paper (Patel et al., 2000), we argued that it is not tenable to develop such neatly packaged knowledge structures, given the fact that biomedical knowledge consists of complex multi-leveled hierarchical structures and given the relatively short exposure in medical schools to a vast range of biomedical concepts (usually less than 2 years). In addition, basic science knowledge plays a very different role in different clinical domains. It is more central to domains such as radiology, anesthesiology and nephrology whereby a robust knowledge of anatomical structures, physiology and biology are critical to the development of expertise (Norman, 2000). On the other hand, the use of biomedical knowledge is less pervasive in routine medical problem solving in other domains of medicine such as cardiology and endocrinology.

The knowledge encapsulation theory, on the one hand, may overstate the capabilities of experts to rapidly activate elaborated biomedical models when circumstances warrant it. On the other hand, by focusing on lines of reasoning, the theory may undermine the generative nature of expert mental models. The nature of possible mental models is determined by the elements that comprise a domain or its ontology, the goals of the agent, and the inferential character of the task environment (Williams, Hollan, & Stevens, 1983). Lines of reasoning would suggest that experts have access to limited patterns of inference resulting from repeated exposure to similar cases. There is evidence to suggest that they do have access to a repertoire of such patterns and use it as circumstances warrant it (van de Wiel et al., 2000). It is apparent that people learn to circumvent long chains of reasoning and chunk or compile knowledge across intermediate states of inference (Newell, 1990; Chandrasakeran et al., 1989). This results in shorter more direct inferences which are stored in long term memory and are directly available to be retrieved in the appropriate contexts. Chandrasakeran and colleagues (1989) refer to this sort of knowledge as *compiled causal knowledge*. This refers to knowledge of causal expectations that people compile directly from experience and partly by chunking results from previous problem-solving endeavors (Kaufman & Patel, 1998).

However, experts are also capable of solving novel and complex problems which necessitate the generation of new causal models. Experts and skilled students can dynamically formulate models on the fly on the basis of a representation of structure-function relations of a device (Frederiksen, White, & Gutwill, 1999). In the context of clinical medicine, this ability enables them to work out the consequences of a pathophysiological process that is anomalous or one not previously encountered (Kaufman & Patel, 1998). This is necessary when encapsulated knowledge is not available. As mentioned in an earlier section, mastery of a biomedical knowledge may be characterized as a progression of mental models which reflect increasingly sophisticated and robust understandings of pathophysiological processes. Given the vast quantities of knowledge that need to be assimilated in a four year medical curricula, it is not likely that one can develop robust understanding of the pathophysiology of disease. Clinical practice offers selective exposure to certain kinds of clinical cases. Even experts' mental models can be somewhat brittle when stretched to the limits of their understanding (Kaufman & Patel, 1998).

Knowledge encapsulation may partially account for the process of conceptual change in biomedicine. Clearly, the diversity of biomedical knowledge and clinical reasoning tasks necessitates multiple mechanisms of learning. The two theories have stimulated much research in the area of medical cognition and contributed to debates regarding how to teach basic science in medical school.

Summary and Discussion

This section of the chapter is concerned with the role of biomedical knowledge in clinical reasoning. The paradox of basic science knowledge is that although it is central to the practice of medicine, it is used somewhat sparingly and often ineffectually by medical students as well as physicians. This can be partially explained by both the conceptual complexity of the domain which spans great depth and breadth of knowledge and their in situ clinical learning experiences which orient them towards the acquisition of skills and the use of a heuristic classification process. Routine diagnostic reasoning may not require the use of deeper models, but problems of greater complexity clearly do. Research on conceptual understanding reveals relatively systemic misconceptions that appear to impact the reasoning of both students and physicians. Although there is no evidence that such deficits in knowledge adversely effect patient care, acquisitions of more robust mental models could yield insights into more difficult medical problems.

As in other domains of advanced knowledge acquisition, students undergo a process of continuous knowledge reorganization that is the product of both formal learning and clinical practice. In addition to its theoretical significance, understanding this developmental process has practical importance for developing medical curricula. Systematic differences in conceptual knowledge are evidenced among students at different levels as well as between students in problem-based learning and conventional curricula. For example, PBL students demonstrated more elaborate and better integrated schema when employing basic science information in the context of clinical reasoning. On the other hand, they were less able to transfer this knowledge to related problems and were less selective in their use of relevant concepts in comparison to the CC students.

In general, studies comparing graduates of PBL and conventional curricula programs have not found significant differences in terms of the development of clinical skills (Colliver, 2004; Jolly, 2006). Small group teaching (SGT) is one of the characteristics of PBL, though many conventional curricula have begun incorporate it as well. Patel, Arocha, Branch, and Karlin (2004) investigated the relationship between SGT and lecture teaching and how biomedical and clinical knowledge is integrated across these teaching formats. Whereas the lecture served as a means to broadly cover core biomedical material, the small groups allowed for further discussion and integration of the biomedical and clinical knowledge in an interactive and intimate environment. Thus, the use of both lecture based and small group teaching formats in the medical curriculum support the objective of providing students with a strong foundation in biomedical knowledge, which can be integrated and used in clinical practice.

The section also considered two competing theoretical perspectives that explain the development and use of biomedical knowledge in clinical contexts: knowledge encapsulation and the two-world hypothesis. The two theoretical approaches have led to a substantial body of research that in our view has advanced our understanding of medical cognition. Despite the numerous studies, the dispute cannot be resolved solely on the basis of empirical evidence. The knowledge encapsulation theory, in some sense, captures the way clinicians *ought* to use biomedical knowledge. In this respect, we should encourage learning activities that move students towards the development of encapsulated knowledge. On our part, we favor the two-world hypothesis as an explanation that is more consistent with the ways in which clinicians and medical students *actually* employ biomedical knowledge in the context of clinical reasoning.

Something about that the role of biological knowledge in clinical practice may change in the future, given genomics, personalized medicine, etc… So, the two worlds may be sort of coming together in the future. The volume of biomedical knowledge continues to accelerate, especially in the areas of cellular and molecular biology (Shaywitz, Martin, & Ausiello, 2000). A recent report by the Association of American Medical Colleges (2001) proposes that "Medical practice should be based on a sound understanding of the scientific basis of contemporary approaches to the diagnosis and management of disease. Therefore, knowledge and understanding of the scientific principles that govern human biology provide doctors not only with a rationale for the contemporary practice of medicine, but also with a framework for incorporating new knowledge into their practices in the future."

Medical curricular reform is faced with competing pressures. For example, recent reports also commissioned by the Association of American Medical Colleges (2006) advocate reforming medical education in view to promote a more patient-centered approach and a more rigorous approach for ensuring that students and residents are acquiring the knowledge, skills, attitudes and values deemed necessary to provide high-quality patient care. Although these are laudable goals, the focus on clinical skills and competencies introduces additional demands on an already crowded curriculum. On the other hand, a more patient-centered approach may contribute to bridging gaps in understanding between health professionals and lay people. This is the subject of the next section.

CONCEPTUAL UNDERSTANDING IN THE DOMAIN OF HEALTH

Of all scientific disciplines, knowledge related to health sciences arguably has the greatest bearing on the daily lives of individuals. In sickness and in health, we are health consumers, regardless of our occupation, demographics characteristics and social status. As we make routine decisions about nutrition, exercise, immunization, as well as non-routine decisions about medical treatment options, we implicitly and explicitly draw upon our health knowledge. The active role of health consumers is becoming widely recognized by health care organizations and policy makers. The objective of many consumer health initiatives is to empower health consumers and enable them to act as partners in their health care (Hack, Degner, Parker, & The SCRN Communication Team, 2005). Unfortunately, lack of knowledge and non-normative understanding of health concepts present a barrier to achieving this goal. The emphasis on educated health consumerism creates new obligations and opportunities for science and health education, and requires good understanding of lay health knowledge and its relationship to reasoning and decision making.

Research in medical cognition has been ongoing for more than 30 years, and there are relatively stable paradigms for experimental research. Health cognition is a comparatively new discipline and we are just beginning to define the central issues. Most works on lay understanding of health concepts are conducted in applied domains of public health and consumer health education. There have been comparatively few cognitive studies of conceptual change in the domain of health, especially with adults. However, general conceptual change theory has much to offer to the applied, intervention-focused consumer health research. Basic tenets of conceptual change theory suggest that: (1) individuals' prior knowledge exercises strong influence over their emergent beliefs and theories, and (2) conceptual change requires some genuine understanding, and mere knowledge accretion as a mode of learning is less likely to result in usable knowledge. Integrating these tenets into consumer health works has the potential to enrich consumer health research and interventions. At the same time, due to its complex, "ill-structured," knowledge-rich nature, health domain presents a fertile area for a study of science learning and conceptual change.

Medical professionals train for many years before they become certified to practice. The vast majority of lay individuals receives minimal or no formal training in matters of health, and cannot be expected to have the extensive biomedical knowledge of health professionals. They may lack the knowledge of biomedical concepts, necessary for understanding disease etiology and mechanism. For example, McGregor (2003) interviewed patients with localized prostate cancer (ten Scotland residents between the ages of 53 and 75, representing diverse educational and professional backgrounds) about their understanding of their disease. Most men had little understanding of the function of the prostate gland. They also had limited understanding of the side-effects of the possible treatments. However, while lay people may have limited biomedical knowledge, they possess many other kinds of knowledge — cultural, social, and experiential — that they draw upon in reasoning about health and diseases (Patel et al., 2000). Knowledge derived from these sources may be non-normative and differ significantly from the medical view. However, we will argue that this knowledge is often organized into complex causal networks, with evidence of causality grounded in narratives, memorable instances and superficially plausible links. To the extent that these knowledge networks make logical sense given beliefs of their holders, they are consistent and have a coherent structure. Lay individuals often possess both cultural/experiential/personal knowledge and some formal "school" knowledge of health concepts (Sivaramakrishnan & Patel, 1993). The two systems are often in conflict, and reasoning, while drawing on the knowledge from different sources, presents a challenge. In the rest of this section, we will review research pertaining to lay understanding of health issues in indigenous and Western cultures. We will then explore the role that biomedical knowledge plays in health reasoning and the effect of conceptual change interventions on reasoning.

Studies presented in this chapter are not meant to provide an exhaustive review of the literature on lay understanding of health concepts, but rather to present studies that draw on our own research and illustrate basic trends in this literature. In doing so, we adapt a life-span approach to conceptual change in health understanding, focusing on adults to a greater extent and on children to a lesser extent than is customary in conceptual change literature. Finally, one of our basic premises is that lay understanding of health concepts has bearing on consumer health decisions and behavior. Conceptual understanding of health issues gives individuals the power to derive predictions and explanations of a wide range of health-related phenomena, which can then be applied in decision making. Such conceptual competence does not guarantee correct performance (which is affected by a broad range of other cognitive and non-cognitive factors) but provides the necessary knowledge base.

Lay Health Knowledge across Cultures

Studies of lay health theories in non-Western cultures reveal causal beliefs that are non-biological in nature. Sivaramakrishnan and Patel (1993) conducted studies of reasoning about childhood nutritional diseases by mothers in rural India. Many unschooled mothers explained symptoms of malnutrition by referring to the concept of *therai,* a toad that falls on a pregnant mother and sucks the nutrients from the fetus. Treatment for the condition involves tying a live toad in a leather pouch to the child's neck or waist. The study also demonstrated co-existence of supernatural and biological explanations. For example, after explaining the concept of *therai* and its causal role in *Marasmus* disease (malnutrition), one of the participants added that *Marasmus* may also be caused by worms and should then be treated by worm medicine. Similar blends of supernatural and biological causality can be observed in other studies. In her interviews with mothers of malnourished children in Pakistan, Mull (1991) showed that the majority of mothers correctly viewed diarrhea as predisposing to malnutrition. However, few mothers viewed diarrhea or the lack of food as the cause of the disease. Most explained that the condition was caused by the shadow of an unclean woman, thrown on the child or the mother. Although these explanations are obviously non-normative from the point of view of Western biomedical theories, their narrative structure is coherent, with all propositions (clauses) of the narrative tied into one causal system. They are also less dissonant with indigenous medical frameworks. For example, East Indian Ayurvedic medicine is based on the concept of "humors" that constitute the human body. Illness and health are the result of the balance or imbalance of these humors.

Combinations of normative and non-normative health concepts and reliance on cultural and experiential knowledge in lay heath reasoning are not limited to non-Western cultures. Keselman and colleagues conducted a study of New York City adolescents' understanding of HIV and reasoning about HIV-related issues (Keselman, Kaufman, & Patel, 2004). Middle and high school students of urban schools were interviewed about their conceptual understanding of HIV. They were also asked to evaluate scenarios with myths about HIV. On the basis of their responses to the interview, students' understanding of HIV biology was classified into three models, naïve, intermediate, and advanced. Students were assigned to models on the basis of their understanding of three factors: (1) core concept of HIV, (2) mechanism of HIV infection, and (3) disease progression. Factual knowledge that HIV is an incurable sexually transmitted disease did not affect model assignment. Of the 21 participants in the study, 11 (nine middle school students and two high school students) were classified at the naïve level of HIV understanding. Seven (one middle school and six high school students) students were classified at the intermediate level, and three (high school) students were classified at the advanced level. Students at the naïve level showed no understanding of biological concepts of a virus, infection, and immune system. Lack of awareness of hidden biological processes often led to explanations in which cause and effect had to be deduced from the "tangible" events. These included young adolescents' beliefs that HIV was caused by dirt (poor hygiene after sex), or by the sexual act itself. Adolescents' perception of causality in terms of input-output relationships may be rooted in intuitive biology that has originated during childhood attempts to make sense of the world, and survived into adulthood. In a study of adolescents' understanding of food spoilage and infectious diseases, Au and Romo (1999) recorded causal explanations that were similarly grounded in tangible relationships. Like explanations by mothers in Sivaramakrishnan and Patel's (1993) study, explanations often had narrative structure. The following quote from a seventh-grader illustrates an incorrect, but conceptually complex explanation of HIV infection mechanism, "See, most people, like, they don't actually wash after having sex. See, if the person is dirty, … you know, like the dirt, it goes into skin, like, it stays there for a long time, then it starts to go further in, then it starts mixing with your blood, and that's how AIDS could probably form."

In addition to personal experiences and culturally-based medical practices, individuals' understanding of health issues may also be influenced by social group norms and discourse practices. For example, Bogart and Thornburn (2005) conducted a survey of African American's beliefs about the origin of HIV. They found that 20% of men and 12% of women somewhat agreed to strongly agreed that "HIV/AIDS is a man-made virus that the federal government made to kill and wipe out black people." Ross, Essien, and Torres (2006) found that genocidal conspiracy theories were also relatively widespread in other racial/ethnic groups. For some groups, beliefs affected health behavior: conspiracy beliefs were associated with reduction of condom use among African American men.

The Role of Causality in Lay Conceptual Knowledge of Health

Narrative structure of lay explanations of disease causality in Sivaramakrishnan and Patel (1993) and Keselman, Kaufman, and Patel (2004) studies provides some evidence about the important role that perceived causality plays in lay disease concept. More direct evidence comes from studies that involved experimental methodology. For example, Kim and Ahn (2002) conducted experiments that related lay participants' causal theories about psychiatric disorders to their categorization decisions. Participants in the studies were asked about their understanding of causal relationships among various symptoms of real and artificial mental disorders. Symptoms in participants' models were then categorized in terms of depth of cause (X, where X causes Y, which causes Z), intermediate causes (Y) and terminal effects (Z). Participants were also presented with lists of symptoms, characterizing the disorders, and asked them to classify conditions as either belonging or not belonging to the disorder, when one of the symptoms was absent. For example, they asked participants if the diagnosis of anorexia nervosa would hold true if the symptom "refusal to maintain minimum body weight" was absent. The findings suggest that symptoms perceived as "deeper" causes are viewed as more central to the disorders than those that are perceived as "intermediate" causes or effects. Intermediate causes are perceived as more important than effects. Finally, symptoms that were not part of the coherent causal system (causally unrelated) were seen as less central than causally connected factors.

Although Kim and Ahn's study does not mirror the real life conditions of patients (participants are given descriptions of diseases and their prior understanding of mental health issues is not considered), it has implications for health education. The study points to the flaws of intervention that provide facts without supplying well-connected causal explanations, as these accurate facts are likely to be ignored in favor of non-normative but rich concepts. Indeed, the following section will illustrate many instances where participants in interview studies reason and make decisions on the basis of incorrect but causally complex cultural/experiential theories, rather than accurate but superficial knowledge of biomedical facts.

Formal Learning and Lay Health Knowledge

In explaining diseases and reasoning about health issues, lay individuals typically draw both on their cultural/experiential knowledge and on their "school" knowledge. Attempts to resolve discrepancies between "informal" and "formal" knowledge are not easy, and often violate coherence of explanations and lead to inconsistencies in reasoning (Driver, Asoko, Leach, Mortimer, & Scott, 1994). Studies also suggest that "formal" knowledge is more likely to be used (and to be helpful) when it has a certain depth and involves genuine understanding rather than mere knowledge of facts.

To study the effect of education on explanations disease causality, Sivaramakrishnan and Patel (1993) interviewed 22 mothers of East Indian origins living in Canada. Five of the participants had no formal education, five completed 10 years of secondary school, and 12 were educated in Indian universities. University educated mothers were assumed to be familiar with Western biomedical concepts, because these studies would have been part of their university curricula. The study showed that educated mothers were more likely than their less educated counterparts to identify dietary deficiency as a cause of malnutrition. Participants with no formal education often explained the symptoms of *Marasmus* by referring to indigestion. Their explanations were typically coherent and consistent with an Ayurvedic framework, in which the concept of proper digestion of food is central to good health. Mothers with university education were more likely to refer to Western biomedical concepts (e.g., enzyme production) in their explanations. However, their reasoning was still largely grounded in Ayurvedic interpretation, in which all digestive problems are traced to the liver. Drawing on two medical systems also lead to opportunistic and inconsistent use of concepts and contributed to the fragmentation of reasoning.

Similar to many Indian mothers in Sivaramakrishnan and Patel studies (1993), participants in Keselman, Kaufman, and Patel's (2004) study whose HIV understanding was classified at the naïve level relied on their cultural and experiential knowledge while reasoning about HIV myths. They also used their knowledge opportunistically: if their informal/experiential knowledge did not correspond to their factual biomedical knowledge, they drew upon the experience. This is illustrated by the reasoning of a ninth grader. This student had little understanding of HIV biology, yet was able to state in the interview that he knew that there was no cure for HIV, and that he had learned this at school, in HIV education activities. Later, he was presented with a myth suggesting that HIV could be expelled from the body by urine and sweat, and recommended exercise in order to increase sweating. The student replied, "Yeah, this is true, this is true. Cause people can stop by like that. By exercising, like they said. Like that lady, like I told you, she exercised her way out of cancer, so I think this is true, you can exercise your way out of HIV probably." In the absence of robust biological knowledge, experiential analogy outweighed accurate, but conflicting factual knowledge.

Students at the intermediate level had greater understanding of HIV biology: they knew that HIV was a biological entity that entered the body with bodily fluids and compromised the immune system. However, because their knowledge lacked depth and was somewhat fragmented, students often could not connect these concepts into logical chains, and switched to relying on their experiential knowledge and memories of media stories, which sometimes led them to accept myths as true. In contrast, students at the advanced level had robust understanding of HIV biology. They knew that HIV was a virus that entered the body through bodily fluids and then penetrated T-cells of the immune system and eventually destroyed them by taking over their reproductive mechanism. These students consistently relied on biological reasoning to point to the flaws in the logic of the myths. Findings from both studies reviewed in this sub-section illustrate that the basic tenet of conceptual change theory — that to be applicable to reasoning across a range of situations, knowledge needs to be sufficiently robust and coherent.

Promoting Conceptual Change

Many public health initiatives are concerned with the challenge of facilitating behavioral change, by influencing many cognitive and non-cognitive factors that affect health behaviors (e.g., motivation, self-efficacy, perceived difficulty of the change). While we view this task as extremely important, an extensive review of behavioral change interventions is beyond the scope of this paper. We also understand that knowledge is necessary but not sufficient component of behavioral change. Our goal is to show that helping individuals develop moderately deep understanding of health issues is possible, and provides them with a knowledge base for reasoning about real or realistic situations. We then provide examples of situations in which health knowledge has been shown to positively impact health behaviors.

In a follow-up to the study of adolescents' understanding of HIV, Keselman, Kaufman, Kramer, and Patel (2007) conducted a middle school science intervention in HIV biology, which combined scientific reasoning and science writing activities. Part of the intervention involved teacher-led lectures. Students also reviewed media articles about viral diseases and developed explanations of occurrences described in the articles. Finally, students in one of the two conditions assumed the role of HIV counselors and responded to letters from fictional characters to an HIV counseling clinic. The emphasis of the intervention was on building a deeper, more meaningful, well-integrated knowledge network that could support reasoning about authentic tasks.

In the course of the intervention, many students developed reasonably robust understanding of the concepts of virus, viral transmission and the immune system, advancing from the naïve to the intermediate model of HIV understanding. They also showed improved ability to apply their understanding to reasoning about realistic problem scenarios about HIV. Pre- and post-test assessments required students to read a letter from a fictional young woman, whose friend had been diagnosed with HIV. The friendship was crumbling because the author of the letter became afraid of all types of contact with her friend and feared sharing the friend's clean utensils and towels at her house. At the pretest, a half of the students in both groups (incorrectly) acknowledged that the fear was justified. Most of them gave advice about ways to save the friendship while taking necessary precautions (e.g., using disposable utensils). At the time of the post-test, most students in the writing group pointed out that HIV could not be contracted via casual household contact, such as sharing utensils or towels. Most of them also supported their statements by providing biological explanations of reasonable conceptual depth (e.g., "You'll never get it with spit because not a lot of virus live on the spit and viruses die outside of your body."). The study suggests that positive relationship between conceptual understanding and critical reasoning about health issues can be fostered in a classroom environment.

Although knowledge is not a sufficient condition for behavioral change, there is evidence that understanding of health concepts leads to improved health practices. Recently, much of consumer health research has focused on the study of health literacy, or "the degree to which individuals have the capacity to obtain, process, and understand basic information and services needed to make appropriate decisions regarding their health" (Nielsen-Bohlman, Panzer, & Kindig, 2004). While health literacy is a concept that is distinct from conceptual knowledge, studies suggest that health literacy is independently related to disease knowledge among patients (Gazmararian, Williams, Peel, & Baker, 2003). Studies in domains ranging from diabetes to HIV show that inadequate health literacy is related to suboptimal health practices and lower health outcome (Baker, Gazmararian, Williams, Scott, Parker, Green, Ren, & Peel, 2002; Schillinger, Grumbach, Piette, Wang, Osmond, Daher, Palacios, Sullivan, & Bindman, 2002; Kalichman et al., 2000).

Donovan and Ward (2001) developed an intervention that aimed to facilitate patients' coping with cancer pain (RIDPAIN). The intervention is based on the recognition that the beliefs that form an individuals' cognitive representation of an illness create the basis for reacting to new information and making decisions. Traditional interventions typically teach new coping skills without first addressing misconceptions in existing beliefs. Donovan and Ward argue that such interventions provide knowledge inconsistent with existing beliefs, and thus less likely to be translated into behavior.

Donovan and Ward propose a "representational approach" to patient education. Steps of their intervention are based on Leventhal's common sense model (CSM), which proposes that people's representation of illness has five core components: identity, cause, timeline, consequences and cure or control (Leventhal & Diefenbach, 1991). The first step of the intervention is representational assessment, during which patients describe their beliefs about their illness along the five dimensions of the CSM. In the second step, a nurse helps patients explore their misconceptions. In the third step, the nurse and the patients describe the problems associated with the misconceptions, thus setting the ground for conceptual change. The forth step involves correcting misconceptions and filling knowledge gaps with accurate information. The final step involves summarizing new information and discussing its benefits. Assessment of RIDPAIN showed that participants held a wide range of misconceptions about cancer pain management. Of the 77% of participants who participated in a follow-up 2 months after the intervention, 83% said the intervention changed their understanding of pain medication, 85% said they felt more confident using pain medication, and 57% reported changes in their pain management as a result of the intervention.

At present, only a few works examine the effect of conceptual change in the domain of health on heath behavior. The work in this area is distributed across a range of disciplines. Studies in science education and cognitive psychology focus on conceptual understanding and learning, but do not necessarily relate them to behavioral change. Studies in public health focus on health behavior, but treat health knowledge as a collection of facts that can be adequately assessed via survey methodology. Relating conceptual knowledge to health behavior is a challenging task, because barriers to translating knowledge into action range from non-cognitive (e.g., social support) to cognitive (e.g., deficiencies in lay reasoning). However, requirements of educated health consumerism call for a dialogue and an integration of knowledge amassed by the communities of science education and psychology on the one hand, and health education and public health on the other.

Patients' Understanding and Management of Chronic Illness

More than 100 million individuals suffer from chronic illness in the United States (National Academy on an Aging Society Report, 1999), and it has been reported that healthcare for people with chronic disease consumes approximately 78% of all healthcare spending in this country (Information Technology Association of America E-Health Committee, 2004). In particular, the prevalence of type 2 diabetes has increased rapidly in the past two decades and is projected to continue to grow at this rapid pace (Schulze & Hu, 2005). Patient self-management is increasingly seen as a necessary adjunct to the currently strained healthcare system (Wagner & Groves, 2002).

Recent advances in health information technologies promise to improve the quality of care and quality of life for chronically ill individuals. However, substantial challenges remain in targeting digital divide populations who are likely to be older, less educated and novice computer users. There are a number of barriers that preclude chronically ill patients from employing health technologies productively (Kaufman, Patel, Hilliman, Morin, Pevzner, Weinstock, Goland, Shea, & Starren, 2003). Low health literacy and the lack of adequate domain knowledge represent an impediment for adapting and maintaining a self-management program. For example, diabetes patients with inadequate health literacy were more likely to have poor control of their blood sugar and associated complications (Schillinger et al., 2002). Low health literacy can limit patient understanding of information about treatments and outcomes and is a barrier to participation in the decision making process. Diabetes self-management necessitates a basic understanding of blood glucose regulation and metabolism. In addition to measuring their blood glucose, patients with diabetes must carefully regulate their diet, exercise, and stress levels.

Lippa and Altman Klein (2006) studied the different ways in which people understood diabetes. They focused on three particular areas of knowledge: (1) problem detection which involved perceiving, through experienced symptoms or through measuring blood glucose, abnormally high or low glucose values; (2) functional relationships which involve recognizing the cause or potential cause of an abnormal value (e.g., diet, exercise, medication); and (3) problem solving which involves taking effective action (e.g., half a glass of orange juice to ameliorate low blood glucose) to restore a glucose imbalance. The authors characterized a progression of mental models beginning with rudimentary models of self management in which the patient was lacking a basic understanding on how to gain control. The majority of subjects possessed a "recipe model" which involves following procedures ritualistically and a basic understanding of their consequences (e.g., too much bread will raise blood sugar levels). These patients have relatively little insight into their illness and reported leaving the decision making to healthcare professionals. Such a model works fine under routine circumstances, but not under conditions of unexpected events. The "control model" involved a more sophisticated understanding of glucose regulation. These patients understood that the problem involved several interacting factors and were able to use this knowledge to guide their behavior, provide an explanatory mechanism and facilitate prediction of future events (e.g., effects of food intake on tomorrow's blood glucose levels).

It is likely that patients with different mental models of their illness will respond differently to diabetes education and e-health initiatives. Kaufman and colleagues (2003, 2006) conducted a cognitive evaluation of older adults with diabetes use of a comprehensive telemedicine system. They documented a range of problems, many of which can be subsumed under the following three categories: (1) perceptual-motor skills, especially in relation to the use of the mouse, (2) mental models which refer to a basic understanding of the system, and (3) health literacy, including literacy and numeracy. One of the most striking findings corresponded to problems with numeracy and representational fluency (e.g., ability to read a table or understand a chart). Kaufman et al. (2003) observed patients who had varying levels of difficulty in reading a table of their glucose and blood pressure values. Interestingly, some participants who could readily read their blood pressure values off the meter were not able to recognize a representation of the same values in a tabular form. In addition, individuals who had maintained blood glucose logs for many years were not able to understand the tabular representations in which the values are embodied in rows and cells. This limitation precluded them from effectively using the Web-based record system to monitor changes in blood pressure and blood glucose.

In order to promote health among seniors and reduce healthcare disparities, it is essential that we enable older adults and other "digital divide individuals" to use health information tools effectively. The Internet is emerging as a vital resource for consumers for health information and is increasingly serving as a mediator of health education, health-related decision making and healthcare management. However, the substantial digital divide among the elderly, especially those who are from lower SES strata, less educated and ethnic and racial minorities, often leaves those who are most in need with less access to health information. In response to this problem, various educational initiatives have targeted low SES seniors in view to train them to use online health information more productively and to become agents of change in managing their own health (Kaufman & Rockoff, 2006).

Consumer Health Vocabulary

The non-normative nature of lay health knowledge points to the problem of the gap between lay and professional understanding of health concepts. When lay people and health professionals use language to communicate with each other, the gulf of understanding translates into a language gap. Studies show that both gaps contribute to misunderstandings and the loss of crucial information on both sides, and may reduce compliance with medical recommendations (Patel, Arocha, & Kushniruk, 2002; Ong, de Haes, Hoos, & Lammes, 1995; Quirt et al., 1997; Chapman, Abraham, Jenkins, & Fallowfield, 2003). This problem becomes even more prominent in the area of e-health (e.g., health oriented Internet sites and decision support tools), which does not allow the negotiation of meaning through clarifications. Conceptual change research may guide consumer health informatics work on bridging the gap between lay and professional health terms and concepts.

In order to communicate with the lay public effectively, health professionals and designers of e-health tools need to (1) understand lay cognitive representations of health concepts and (2) know the terms that lay individuals use to refer to those concepts. One of the challenges lies in understanding the relationship between lay health terms and concepts. Depending on the nature of this relationship, the gap may be primarily terminological or primarily conceptual. In the case of a primarily terminological gap, an individual's understanding of a health concept is relatively normative, but the term used to refer to the concept is not part of any standard medical vocabulary. Examples of such non-standard terms include "high blood" for hypertension and "locked bowels" for constipation (Sugarman & Butter, 1985). Conceptual gaps occur when lay individuals use standard biomedical terms, but their understanding of the underlying concepts is different from that of health professionals. For example, the patient may use the term *hypertension*, understanding it as "nervous" or "easily upset" (Gibbs, Gibbs, & Henrich, 1987). We can propose two hypotheses: primarily conceptual gaps are more difficult to detect and correct and that most misunderstanding between lay individuals and health professionals are probably attributable to both conceptual and terminological gaps.

With respect to e-health communication, the crux of the problem lies in mapping lay and professional health terms and concepts in a consistent, comprehensive manner that could be converted into a computational algorithm. Compared to concept mapping, the problem of terminological matching is more manageable, and initiatives in the field of consumer health informatics undertook the challenge. One such project is Consumer Health Vocabulary Initiative, conducted jointly by Decision Systems Group at Harvard Medical School and the National Library of Medicine (http://www.consumerhealthvocab.org/). The project combines computational and human review approaches in order to extract consumer health terms from the body of search queries submitted to MedLinePlus (an online health information resource of the US National Library of Medicine) and relate these terms to entries in formal biomedical vocabularies (Zeng & Tse, 2006).

The rationale for relating consumer health terms to biomedical terms is developing software tools that help lay individuals seek health information online. Search engines with access to consumer health vocabularies will connect searchers to relevant documents, even when searchers formulate their queries in non-standard terms (e.g., "clot buster" for "thrombolytic agents"). Making use of consumer health terms in consumer health materials is also likely to improve their comprehension. However, in order to meet lay individuals' health information needs and provide them with clear, comprehensible information, we need to reach beyond surface-level term familiarity, relating it to the domain of conceptual understanding.

Keselman, Kaufman, Kramer, and Patel (2007) conducted a pilot study, presenting 52 health consumers with a survey instrument, assessing surface-level and conceptual familiarity with 15 health terms. Surface-level familiarity test items assessed participants' ability to associate health terms with relevant terms at a super-category level (e.g., sphincter → muscle). Concept familiarity test items assessed the ability to associate written terms with brief phrases describing the meaning or "gists" (e.g., sphincter → a ring of muscles that opens and closes). Each multiple choice question included four answer options: one correct answer, two plausible "distractors" and the "don't know" option. The terms varied in frequency with which they could be found across a range of consumer health information resources. A regression model converted these frequencies into predicted "term familiarity likelihood" scores. Results showed that while familiarity likelihood scores predicted both surface-level/terminological and conceptual familiarity, conceptual familiarity scores continuously lagged behind surface level familiarity scores. The gap between surface-level and conceptual familiarity scores was greater for "easy" terms, predicted as "likely" to be familiar. While the findings of this pilot study should not be viewed as conclusive evidence, they caution developers of consumer health vocabularies against equating knowledge of terms with a genuine understanding of the underlying concept. Moreover, the nature and degree of the gap between terminological and conceptual knowledge is likely to be affected by a number of factors. Understanding these factors may be essential for developing software tools to support consumer health information seeking. The field of cognitive psychology and science education can provide consumer health information specialists with the language and the methods for an in-depth analysis of these issues.

Summary and Discussion

The current health system encourages lay individuals to be active participants in their care. Not surprisingly, many individuals are ill-prepared to take on such a role. Research presented in this chapter has been oriented towards documenting the barriers to participation. On the one hand, individuals have a lifetime of experience grappling with health concepts, and lay health beliefs have a certain measure of causal coherence. On the other hand, lay knowledge lacks the depth and breadth of professional understanding. An even more significant characteristic of lay knowledge is the discrepancy between formal and cultural/experiential knowledge — apparent across cultures. Causality is not always biomedical causality, and stability of experiential and cultural beliefs may supersede accurate formal knowledge. This was in evidence in the study of middle school students' understanding of HIV and Indian mothers' understanding of childhood nutritional disorders. Culturally and socially grounded beliefs about health were shown to exert a powerful role in subjects' reasoning.

As in other domains of science (e.g., Vosniadou, 1994), health concepts can be characterized in terms of progressions of models of understanding, with more advanced models of understanding providing a better basis for critical thinking. Keselman and colleagues (2004) demonstrated that students' understanding of concepts related to HIV affected their ability to reason about myths pertaining to the cause and spread of the virus. A follow-up study demonstrated that an educational intervention targeting understanding could result in genuine conceptual change and facilitate critical reasoning and problem solving. Strengthening the ties between biology and health sciences education could potentially achieve greater understanding in ways that public health could not possibly achieve.

An individual's conceptual models of disease and treatment can impact a patients' quality of health and their ability to effectively adhere to certain regimens. It is also associated with their ability to participate effectively in various e-health initiatives.

In this context, depth of conceptual understanding has real consequences and is very likely to influence health outcomes. Efforts to educate lay people in both school and medical settings are promising. Technology also provides an additional resource, but many are prevented from benefiting because of digital divide. When it comes to doctor-patient communication, a vocabulary gap may also contribute to the lack of mutual understanding. Health cognition is an emerging research discipline and at present lacks the stable mature paradigms that are characteristic of medical cognition research. More theory-based research and interventions are needed.

CONCLUSIONS

This chapter has reviewed two bodies of literature in relation to medicine and health. Both domains are grounded in the world of biology, and they intersect in professional contexts (i.e., physicians treat patients). There is, of course, a great asymmetry in terms of knowledge that favors the physician. Physicians receive years of extensive training, whereas most health consumers and patients have very little formal experience to draw on. On the other hand, clinicians frequently do not make "optimal" use of biomedical knowledge. Lay people, in many cases, may lack the prior knowledge necessary to comprehend and synthesize personally relevant health information. From the educational perspective, professional learning requires knowledge consolidation and integration. Conceptual change is an explicit goal of health professions education, but not necessarily health education.

At present, research in medical and health cognition are largely separate enterprises. There is a need for research that can bridge the two disciplines. The two health knowledge systems, lay and professional, intersect when they attempt to communicate about disease or prevention. A number of consumer health initiatives aim to create and support partnership between clinician and patient in view to share decision making and for the patient to assume a greater role in managing their own health. Partnership requires shared model and common language, which represents a substantial challenge. In addition, physicians need to be able to gauge patients' level of understanding. Unfortunately, a patient's comprehension is not something that can be easily assessed in the context of a brief clinical encounter.

The Internet and related computing technologies have broadened the access to health information and are increasingly serving as mediators of health education, decision making, and management. Although research in e-health is still in its formative stages, there is growing evidence to suggest that it can improve health and behavioral outcomes (Neuhauser & Kreps, 2003). E-health interventions such as the Comprehensive Health Enhancement Support System have demonstrated a positive impact on health behaviors (Gustafson, McTavish, Hawkins, Shaw, McDowell, Chen, Volrathongchai, & Landucci, 2005). Bass (2003) examined the relationship of Internet health information use with patient behavior among newly diagnosed cancer patients. The authors of the study concluded that patients who are newly diagnosed with cancer perceive the Internet as a powerful tool, both for acquiring information and for enhancing confidence to make informed decisions. However, as discussed previously, the digital divide may serve to increase healthcare disparities if individuals are unable to secure access to and productively use online health information. Although there are several barriers (e.g., access to the Internet), low health literacy has been recognized as a primary factor in increasing the divide. Lack of domain conceptual knowledge is a primary obstacle to these patients for making sense of health information. E-health initiatives are primarily oriented towards the promotion of information access rather than meaningful learning. These initiatives target adults who are unlikely to undergo the in-depth learning experiences necessary to master substantial body of biomedical knowledge. Strengthening links between science and health education in secondary school may go some way toward producing future generations of literate health consumers. Consumer health informatics can gain insight from conceptual change research into how to better foster conceptual understanding and empower those on the other side of the divide.

NOTE

1. The terms *basic science knowledge* and *biomedical knowledge* both reference subject matter such as anatomy, physiology and biochemistry that is foundational to medicine. The terms are used interchangeably. Pathophysiology refers to abnormal physiological or biochemical function and may also reference perturbations in anatomical structure.

REFERENCES

Albanese, M., & Mitchell, S. (1993). Problem-based learning: A review of literature on its outcomes and implementation issues. *Academic Medicine, 68*(1), 52–81.

Anderson, J. R., Reder, L. M., & Simon, H. A. (1995). Situated learning and education. *Educational Researcher, 25*(4) 5–11.

Arocha, J. F., Patel, V. L., & Patel, Y. C. (1993). Hypothesis generation and the coordination of theory and evidence in novice diagnostic reasoning. *Medical Decision Making, 13*(8), 198–211.

Association of American Medical Colleges. (2001). *Report IV: Contemporary issues in medicine: Basic science and clinical research.* Medical school objectives project. Washington, DC.

Association of American Medical Colleges. (2006). *Implementing the vision: Group on educational affairs responds to the IIME Dean's Committee report.* Washington, DC.

Au, T. K. F., & Romo, L. F. (1999). Mechanical causality in children's "folkbiology." In D. L. Medin & S. Atran (Eds.), *Folkbiology* (pp. 355–401). Cambridge, MA: MIT Press.

Baker, D. W., Gazmararian, J. A., Williams M. V., Scott, T., Parker, R. M., Green, D., Ren, J., & Peel J. (2002). Functional health literacy and the risk of hospital admission among Medicare managed care enrollees. *American Journal of Public Health, 92*(8), 1278–1283.

Barzansky, B. (1992). The growth and divergence of the basic sciences. In B. Barzansky & N. Gevitz (Eds.), *Beyond Flexner: Medical education in the twentieth century* (pp. 1–18). New York: Greenwood Press.

Bass, S. B. (2003). How will internet use affect the patient? A review of computer network and closed internet-based system studies and the implication in understanding how the use of the Internet affects patient populations. *Journal of Health Psychology, 8*(1), 25–38.

Blois, M. S. (1988). Medicine and the nature of vertical reasoning. *New England Journal of Medicine, 319*(14), 847–851.

Bogart, L. M., & Thornburn, S. (2005). Are HIV/AIDS conspiracy beliefs a barrier to HIV prevention among African Americans? *Journal of Acquired Immune Deficiency Syndromes, 38*(2), 213–218.

Boshuizen, H. P. A., & Schmidt, H. G. (1992). On the role of biomedical knowledge in clinical reasoning by experts, intermediates, and novices. *Cognitive Science, 16*(2), 153–184.

Chandrasekaran, B., Smith, J. W., & Sticklen, J. (1989). Deep models and their relation to diagnosis. *Artificial Intelligence in Medicine, 1*(1), 29–40.

Chapman, K., Abraham, C., Jenkins, V., & Fallowfield, L. (2003). Lay understanding of terms used in cancer consultations. *Psycho-Oncology, 12*(6), 557–566.

Chase, W. G., & Simon, H. A. (1973). Perception in chess. *Cognitive Psychology, 4*(1), 55–81.

Chi, M. T. H., Feltovich, P. J., & Glaser, R. (1981). Categorization and representation of physics problems by experts and novices. *Cognitive Science, 5*(1), 121–52.

Clancey, W. J. (1988). Acquiring, representing and evaluating a competence model of diagnostic strategy. In M. T. H. Chi, R. Glaser, & M. J. Farr (Eds.), *The nature of expertise* (pp. 343–418). Hillsdale, NJ: Erlbaum.

Center for Disease Control. (2005). Health protection goals. http://www.cdc.gov/osi/goals/goals.html

Clough, R. W., Shea, S. L, & Hamilton, W. R. (2004). Weaving basic science and social sciences into a case-based, clinically oriented medical curriculum: One school's approach. *Academic Medicine 79*(11),1073–1083.

Colliver, J. A. (2004). Full-curriculum interventions and small-scale studies of transfer: implications for psychology-type theory. *Medical Education, 38*(12), 1212–1214.

Crowley, R. S., Naus, G. J., Stewart, J., & Friedman, C. P. (2003). Development of visual diagnostic expertise in pathology — an information-processing study. *Journal of the American Medical Informatics Association, 10*(1), 39–51.

diSessa, A. A. (1993). Towards an epistemology of physics. *Cognition and Instruction, 10*(2 & 3), 105–225.

Donovan, H., & Ward, S. (2001). A representational approach to patient education. *Journal of Nursing Scholarship, 33*(3), 211–216.

Driver, R., Asoko, H., Leach, J., Mortimer, E., & Scott, P. (1994). Constructing scientific knowledge in the classroom. *Educational Researcher , 23*(7), 5–12.

Elstein, A., Shulman, L., & Sprafka, S. (1978). *Medical problem solving: An analysis of clinical reasoning.* Cambridge, MA: Harvard University Press.

Ericsson, A., & Smith, J. (1991). Prospects and limits of the empirical study of expertise: An introduction. In A. Ericsson & J. Smith (Eds.), *Toward a general theory of expertise: Prospects and limits* (pp. 1–38). New York: Cambridge University Press.

Feinstein, A. R. (1973). An analysis of diagnostic reasoning: The domain and disorders of clinical macrobiology. *Yale Journal of Biological Medicine, 46*(4), 264–283.

Feltovich, P. J., Johnson, P. E., Moller, J. H., & Swanson, D. B. (1984). LCS: The role and development of medical knowledge in diagnostic expertise. In W. J. Clancey & E. H. Shortliffe (Eds.), *Readings in medical artificial intelligence: The first decade* (pp. 275–319). Reading, MA: Addison-Wesley.

Feltovich, P. J., Spiro, R., & Coulson, R. (1989). The nature of conceptual understanding in biomedicine: The deep structure of complex ideas and the development of misconceptions. In D. Evans & V. Patel (Eds.), *Cognitive science in medicine: Biomedical modeling.* Cambridge, MA: MIT Press.

Feltovich, P. J., Spiro, R. J., & Coulson, R. L. (1993). Learning, teaching, and testing for complex conceptual understanding. In N. Frederiksen & I. Bejar (Eds.), *Test theory for a new generation of tests* (pp. 181–217). Hillsdale, NJ: Erlbaum.

Feltovich, P., Spiro, R., & Coulson, R. (1997). Issues of expert flexibility in contexts characterized by complexity and change. In P. J. Feltovich, K. M. Ford, & R. R. Hoffman (Eds.), *Expertise in context: Human and machine* (pp. 125–146). Menlo Park, CA: AAAI/MIT Press.

Flexner, A. (1910). *Medical education in the United States and Canada. A report to the Carnegie Foundation for the Advancement of Teaching.* Boston, MA: Updyke.

Frederiksen, J. R., White, B. Y., & Gutwill, J. (1999). Dynamic mental models in learning science: The importance of constructing derivational linkages among models. *Journal of Research in Science Teaching, 36*(7), 806–836.

Gazmararian, J. A., Williams, M. V., Peel, J., & Baker, D. W. (2003). Health literacy and knowledge of chronic disease. *Patient Education and Counseling, 51*(3), 267–275.

Gibbs, R., Gibbs, P., & Heinrich, J. (1987). Patient understanding of commonly used medical vocabulary. *Journal of Family Practice, 25*(2), 176–178.

Gustafson, D. H., McTavish, F. M., Hawkins, R., Shaw, B., McDowell, H., Chen, W. C., Volrathongchai, K., & Landucci, G. (2005). Use and impact of eHealth System by low-income women with breast cancer. *Journal of Health Communication, 10*(s1), 195–218.

Hack, T. F., Degner, L. F., Parker, P. A., & The SCRN Communication Team. (2005). The communication goals and needs of cancer patients: A review. *Psycho-oncology, 14*(10), 831–845.

Information Technology Association of America E-Health Committee (2004, May). *Chronic care improvement: How Medicare transformation can save lives, save money and stimulate an emerging technology industry.* Information Technology Association of America, 2004.

Jolly B. (2006). Problem-based Learning. *Medical Education, 40*,494–495.

Johnson, P. E., Duran, A. S., Hassebrock, F., Moller, J., Prietula, M., Feltovich, P., & Swanson, D. B. (1981). Expertise and error in diagnostic reasoning. *Cognitive Science, 5*(2), 235–283.

Joseph, G. M. & Patel, V.L. (1990). Domain knowledge and hypothesis generation in diagnostic reasoning. *Medical Decision Making, 10*(1), 31–46.

Kalichman, S. C., Benotsch, E., Suarez, T., Catz, S., Miller, J., & Rompa, D. (2000). Health literacy and health-related knowledge among persons living with HIV/AIDS. *American Journal of Preventive Medicine, 18*, 325–231.

Kaufman, D. R. Patel, V. L., & Magder, S (1996). The explanatory role of spontaneously generated analogies in a reasoning about physiological concepts. *International Journal of Science Education, 18*(4), 369–386.

Kaufman, D. R., & Patel, V. L. (1998) Progressions of mental models in understanding circulatory physiology. In I. Singh & R. Parasuraman (Eds.), *Human cognition: A multidisciplinary perspective* (pp. 300–326). New Delhi, India: Sage.

Kaufman, D. R., Patel, V. L., Hilliman, C., Morin, P. C., Pevzner, J., Weinstock, J., Goland, R., Shea, S., & Starren, J. (2003). Usability in the real world: Assessing medical information technologies in patients' homes. *Journal of Biomedical Informatics, 36*(1& 2), 45–60.

Kaufman, D. R., Pevzner, J, Hilliman, C., Weinstock, R. S., Teresi, J., Shea, S., & Starren, J. (2006). Redesigning a telehealth diabetes management program for a digital divide seniors population. *Home, Healthcare, Management & Practice. 18*(3), 223–234.

Kaufman, D. R., & Rockoff, M. L. (2006). Promoting online health information-seeking in seniors: a community-based organizations approach. *Generations, 30*(2), 55–57.

Keselman A., Kaufman, D. R., Kramer, S., & Patel, V. L. (2007). Fostering conceptual change and critical reasoning about HIV and AIDS. *Journal of Research in Science Teaching, 44*(6), 844–863.

Keselman, A., Kaufman, D.R., & Patel, V.L. (2004). "You can exercise your way out of HIV" and other stories: The role of biological knowledge in adolescents' evaluation of myths. *Journal of Science Education, 88*(4) 548–573.

Keselman, A., Tse, T., Crowell, J., Browne, A., Ngo, L., & Zeng, Q. (2007). Assessing consumer health vocabulary familiarity: An exploratory study. *Journal of Medical Internet Research, 9*(1), e5.

Kim, N. S., & Ahn, W. (2002). The influence of naive causal theories on lay concepts of mental illness. *American Journal of Psychology, 115*(1), 33–65.

Kuipers, B. (1987). Qualitative simulation as causal explanation. IEEE Transactions. *Systems, Man, and Cybernetics, 17*(3), 432–444.

Kuipers, B. J., & Kassirer, J. P. (1984). Causal reasoning in medicine: Analysis of a protocol. *Cognitive Science, 8*(4), 363–385.

Larkin, J. H., McDermott, J., Simon, H. A., & Simon, D. P. (1980). Expert and novice performances in solving physics problems. *Science, 208*, 1335–1342.

Lesgold, A. M., Rubinson, H., Feltovich, P. J., Glaser, R., Klopfer, D., & Wang, Y. (1988). Expertise in a complex skill: Diagnosing x-ray pictures. In M. T. H. Chi, R. Glaser, & M. Farr (Eds.), *The Nature of expertise* (pp. 311–342). Hillsdale, NJ: Erlbaum.

Leventhal, H., & Diefenbach, M. (1991). The active side of illness cognition. In J.A. Skelton & R. T. Croyle (Eds.), *Mental representations in health and illness.* (pp. 247–272). New York: Springer-Verlag.

Lippa, K. D. & Klein, H. A. (2006). How patients understand diabetes self care. Proceedings of the 50th Annual Meeting of the Human Factors and Ergonomic Society.

McGregor, S. (2003). What information patients with localised prostate cancer hear and understand. *Patient Education and Counseling, 49*(3), 273–278.

McCray, A. T. (2005). Promoting health literacy. *Journal of the American Medical Informatics Association, 11*(6),439–447.

Mull, D. S. (1991). Traditional perceptions of marasmus in Pakistan. *Social Science and Medicine, 32*(2), 175–191.

National Academy on Aging Society Report. (1999). *Chronic conditions: A challenge for the 21st century.* The Gerontological Society of America. Washington, D.C.

National Telecommunications and Information Administration. (1999). *Falling through the net: Defining the digital divide.* U.S Department of Commerce. Washington, D.C.

Newell, A. (1990). *Unified theories of cognition.* Cambridge, MA: Harvard University Press.

Neuhauser, L., & Kreps, G. L. (2003). Rethinking communication in the E-health era. *Journal of Health Psychology, 8*(1), 7–23.

Nielsen-Bohlman, L., Panzer, A. M., & Kindig, D. A. (2004). *Health literacy: A prescription to end confusion.* Washington, DC: Institute of Medicine, The National Academies Press.

Norman G. (2000). The essential role of basic science in medical education: the perspective from psychology. *Clinical Investigative Medicine, 23*(1), 47–51

Norman, G. R., Brooks, L. R., & Allen, S. W. (1989). Recall by expert medical practitioners and novices as a record of processing attention. *Journal of Experimental Psychology: Learning, Memory, & Cognition, 15*(6), 1166–1174.

Norman G. R., & Schmidt, H. G. (2000). Effectiveness of problem-based learning curricula: theory, practice and paper darts. *Medical Education, 34*(11), 721–728.

Ong, L. M., de Haes, J. C. J. M., Hoos, A. M., & Lammes, F. B. (1995). Doctor–patient communication: A review of the literature. *Social Science and Medicine, 40*(10), 903–918.

Patel, V. L., Arocha, J., Branch, T., & Karlin, D. R. (2004). Relationships between small group problem-solving activity and lectures in health science curricula. *Journal of Dental Education, 68*(10),1058–1080.

Patel, V. L., Arocha, J. F., Chaudhari, S., Karlin, D. R., & Briedis, D. J. (2005). Knowledge integration and reasoning as a function of instruction in a hybrid medical curriculum. *Journal of Dental Education, 69*(11), 186–211.

Patel, V. L., Arocha, J. F., & Kaufman, D. R. (1994). Diagnostic reasoning and expertise. *The Psychology of Learning and Motivation: Advances in Research and Theory, 31*, 137–252.

Patel, V. L., Arocha, J., & Kushniruk, A. W. (2002). Patients' and physicians' understanding of health and biomedical concepts: Relationship to the design of EMR systems. *Journal of Biomedical Informatics, 35*(1), 8–16.

Patel, V. L., Arocha, J., & Leccisi, M. (2001). Impact of undergraduate medical training on housestaff problem solving performance: Implications for health education in problem-based curricula." *Journal of Dental Education, 65*(11), 1199–1218.

Patel, V. L., Evans, D. A., & Groen, G. J. (1989). Biomedical knowledge and clinical reasoning. In D. A. Evans & V. L. Patel (Eds.), *Cognitive science in medicine: Biomedical modeling* (pp. 49–108). Cambridge, MA: MIT Press.

Patel, V. L., Evans, D.A., & Kaufman, D. R. (1989). Cognitive framework for doctor-patient interaction. In D. A. Evans & V. L. Patel (Eds.), *Cognitive science in medicine: Biomedical modeling* (pp. 253–308). Cambridge, MA: The MIT Press.

Patel, V. L., & Groen, G. J. (1986). Knowledge-based solution strategies in medical reasoning. *Cognitive Science, 10*(1), 91–116.

Patel, V. L., & Groen, G. J. (1991). The general and specific nature of medical expertise: A critical look. In A. Ericsson & J. Smith (Eds.), *Toward a general theory of expertise: Prospects and limits* (pp. 93–125). New York: Cambridge University Press.

Patel, V. L., Groen, G. J., & Arocha, J. F. (1990). Medical expertise as a function of task difficulty. *Memory & Cognition, 18*(4), 394–406.

Patel, V. L., Groen, G. J., & Frederiksen, C. H. (1986). Differences between students and physicians in memory for clinical cases. *Medical Education, 20*(1), 3–9.

Patel, V. L., Groen, G. J., & Norman, G. R. (1993). Reasoning and instruction in medical curricula. *Cognition & Instruction, 10*(4), 335–378.

Patel, V. L., Groen, G. J., & Scott, H. S. (1988). Biomedical knowledge in explanations of clinical problems by medical students. *Medical Education, 22*(5), 398–406.

Patel, V. L., & Kaufman, D. R. (1995). Clinical reasoning and biomedical knowledge: Implications for teaching. In J. Higgs & M. Jones (Eds.), *Clinical reasoning in the health professions* (pp. 117–128). Oxford: Butterworth Heinemenn.

Patel, V.L., Kaufman, D. R., & Arocha, J. F. (2000). Conceptual change in the biomedical and health sciences domain. In R. Glaser (Ed.), *Advances in Instructional Psychology* (pp. 329–392). Hillsdale, NJ: Erlbaum.

Patel, V. L., Kaufman, D. R., & Magder, S. (1991). Causal reasoning about complex physiological concepts in cardiovascular physiology by medical students. *International Journal of Science Education, 13*(2), 171–185.

Quirt C. F., Mackillop, W. J., Ginsburg, A. D., Sheldon, L., Brundage, M., Dixon, P., & Ginsburg, L. (1997). *Lung Cancer, 18*(1), 1–20.

Rikers, R. M. J. P., Schmidt, H. G., Boshuizen, H. P. A., Linssen, G. C., Wesseling, G., & Paas, F. G. (2002). The robustness of medical expertise: Clinical case processing by medical experts and subexperts. *American Journal of Psychology, 114*(4), 609–629.

Robinson, T. N., Patrick, K., Eng, T. R., & Gustafson, D. (1998). An evidence-based approach to interactive health communication: a challenge to medicine in the Information Age. *Journal of the American Medical Association, 280*(14), 1264–1269.

Ross, M. W., Essien, E. J., & Torres, I. (2006). Conspiracy beliefs about the origin of HIV/AIDS in four racial/ethnic groups. *Journal of Acquired Immune Deficiency Syndromes, 41*(3), 342–344.

Schillinger, D., Grumbach, K., Piette, J., Wang, F., Osmond, D., Daher, C., Palacios, J., Sullivan, G. D., & Bindman, A. B. (2002). Association of health literacy with diabetes outcomes. *Journal of the American Medical Association, 288*(4), 475–482.

Schmidt, H. G., & Boshuizen, H. P. A. (1993). On acquiring expertise in medicine. *Educational Psychology Review, 5*(1), 1–17.

Schmidt, H. G., Vermeulen, L., & Van der Molen, H. T. (2006). Long-term effects of problem-based learning: a comparison of competencies acquired by graduates of a problem-based and a conventional medical school. *Medical Education, 40*(6), 562–567.

Shaywitz, D. A., Martin, J B., & Ausiello, D. A. (2000). Patient-oriented research: principles and new approaches to training. *American Journal of Medicine, 109*(2), 136–140.

Schulze, M. B., & Hu, F. B. (2005). Primary prevention of diabetes: What can be done and how much can be prevented? *Annual Review of Public Health, 26,* 445–467.

Sivaramakrishnan, M., & Patel, V. L. (1993). Reasoning about childhood nutritional deficiencies by mothers in rural India: A cognitive analysis. *Social Science & Medicine, 37*(7), 937–952.

Slaughter, L., Keselman, A., Kushniruk, A., & Patel, V. L. (2005). A framework for capturing the interactions between laypersons' understanding of disease, information gathering behaviors, and actions taken during an epidemic. *Journal of Biomedical Informatics, 38*(4), 298–313.

Spiro, R. J., Feltovich, P. J., Coulson, R. L., & Anderson, D. K. (1989). Multiple analogies for complex concepts: Antidotes for analogy-induced misconceptions in advanced knowledge acquisition. In S. Vosniadou & R. Ortony (Eds.), *Similarity and analogical reasoning* (pp. 498–531). Cambridge, MA: Cambridge University Press.

Strauss, S., & Stavy, R. (1982). *U-shaped behavioral growth*. New York: Academic Press.

Sugarman J., & Butter, R. R. (1985). Understanding the patient: Medical words the doctor may not know. *North Carolina Medical Journal, 46*(7), 415–417.

Wagner, E., & Groves, T. (2002). Care for chronic diseases. *British Medical Journal, 325*(7370), 913–914.

Williams, D., Hollan, J. D., & Stevens, A. L. (1983). Human reasoning about a simple physical system. In D. Gentner & A. L. Stevens (Eds.), *Mental models* (pp. 131–153) Hillsdale, NJ: Erlbaum.

Woods, N. N., Brooks, L. R., & Norman, G. R. (2005). The value of basic science in clinical diagnosis: Creating coherence among signs and symptoms. *Medical Education, 39*(1), 107–112.

van de Wiel, M. (1997). *Knowledge encapsulation. Studies on the development of medical expertise*. Dissertation. Ponsen and Looijen.

van de Wiel, M. W. J., Boshuizen, H. P. A., & Schmidt. H. G. (2000). Knowledge restructuring in expertise development: Evidence from pathophysiological representations of clinical cases by students and physicians. *European Journal of Cognitive Psychology, 12*(3), 323–355.

Vosniadou, S. (1994). Conceptual Change in the Physical Sciences. *Learning and Instruction, 4*(1), 121.

Zeng, Q. T., & Tse, T. (2006). Exploring and developing consumer health vocabularies. *Journal of American Medical Informatics Association, 13*(1), 24–29.

12

Changing Historical Conceptions of History

Gaea Leinhardt and Anita K. Ravi
University of Pittsburgh

The issue of conceptual change is not normally the framing idea for discussions about historical knowledge, reasoning, learning, or disciplinary progress. The lone exception to this is the work of Torney-Purta (1994) in which she uses the ideas of ontological shift suggested by Chi (1992) to examine the reasoning of adolescents as they include a more varied array of political and historical causes in their reasoning tasks. Unfortunately, however, the careful psychological work that she conducted is somewhat sparse from the historical point of view. If we coordinate the idea of changing ideas about what history is, that is engage in some historical analysis, with the examination of a simple case of historical reasoning we might make some interesting progress in the direction of considering conceptual change in history more deeply. In this chapter we start by considering a range of differing definitions of the scope and purposes of history, drawing on authors from Herodotus to Schama. These definitions range from history as a singular heroic, accurate, causal account (of, say, the Persian Wars and their causes) to history as an interpretation of conditions and perspectives that surround a particular circumstance (of, say, the role of landscape in historical memory) and back to a characterization of national identity through historical accounts. Within any of these definitions, assumptions are made such as honesty, completeness, and accuracy of the account as well as public identification of the author. We use these alternative purposes and definitions of history as the bases for an exploration of one easily understood example of an historical event, the Boston Massacre, and consider what challenges these issues might pose for the learner.

The Boston Massacre is often considered a defining moment for the start of the American Revolution. Yet it is a curious event and it is unclear why this event is selected from an array of similar and often far more powerful moments of conflict as a major focus in the events leading up to the American Revolution. Thus, we use this event as a lens to show how the "history" has moved from heroic narrative to contentious argument surrounding ideas of law and order. We then conclude with hints at an answer to the questions of why this event and not some other one is particularly anointed. We use these discussions as a way to consider some fragments of empirical work on the ways in which students come to understand history as a constructed, contested, and authored account. We discuss Peter Lee and Roslyn Ashby's developmental account of students' beliefs about history and we consider the trace of one student's learning over time in one class-

328

room to examine the ways in which conceptual change might support the developing understandings and competencies of the student.

SOME IMPORTANT DISTINCTIONS

Consider how Herodotus (writing in the mid-5th century B.C.E.), often assumed to be the father of history, opens his famous accounts of the Persian Wars:

> Herodotus of Helicarnassus hereby publishes the results of his inquiries, hoping to do two things: to preserve the memory of the past by putting on record the astonishing achievements of both the Greek and the non-Greek peoples; and more particularly, to show how the two races came into conflict. (Goold, 1920; Herodotus, 1987, 2006)[1]

There are several important elements in these sentences. First, Herodotus identifies himself in the text; he is not an anonymous committee of authors. Second, he tells us where he is from so we can infer his position with regard to the people and activities he describes; he does not just give a publisher's address. Third, he tells us why he is writing the account, namely to preserve the memory of astonishing achievements and to show how the conflict arose. Thus, Herodotus chose to cover both the events and the surrounding culture of the main actors. In contrast to both what had gone before and what was to come later, Herodotus, the narrator, tells us that he is responsible for his words and that he knows these things because they were told to him or he saw them. What is challenging for the student is not the history in and of itself but the presence of the historian who must also be understood. The layered and evolving nature of history is one of the hallmarks of historical thinking, as Collingwood (1946) and von Wright (1971) both pointed out so clearly.

By 400 B.C.E. the central elements of the discipline of history were in place: identifiable authorship, stated sources, commitment to accuracy, and stated purpose for the particular account. The form of historical account was also set as distinctly narrative. None of the major branches of science can make the same claims about structure and form. Only the arts and mathematics might present such a suggestion. This means that the idea of conceptual change either of person or of field has a slightly different cast in history than it might have in other fields. To review, history is told by a specific historian with a known position vis-à-vis the account given, it has a purpose that is stated in any given account, and it has a commitment to accuracy. From the very earliest times, then, readers or hearers of historical accounts were aware that who was telling the tale had something to do with what was being said and why.

Simon Schama (1991) adds to this set of issues. In a piece for the *New York Times Magazine*, "Clio Has a Problem," he wrote:

> History isn't a how-to manual full of analogies to explain whatever this week's crisis happens to be — Saddam as Hitler, Kuwait as Munich — and certainly not some carefully prepared tonic for self-esteem. As an irreproachable historian, R.G. Collingwood, once put it, we study what man has done to discover what man is. History is an indispensable form of self-knowledge...To know our past is to grow up. History's mission then is to illuminate the human condition from the witness of memory...History has always been "a debatable land" as Macaulay noted. "It lies on the confines of two distinct territories. It is under the jurisdiction of two hostile powers...Instead of being equally shared between its two rulers, the Reason and the Imagination, it falls alternately under the sole and absolute domination of each" (p. 32)

In this short essay, Schama argues for a particular kind of constrained purpose in doing history and the need for narrative in historical accounts. This nuance adds to the task of the student still again: She must learn the content, the author, and the style and must recognize the way each influences the other.

WHAT COUNTS AS HISTORY?

The non-historian often makes several naïve assumptions about history. First, everything that happened in the past counts as history. Thus, the task of history is to build a complete and neutral account of the sequence of events. The second naïve assumption is that the major "problem" for history is getting the smallest of detail correct in some archeological sense. These two assumptions have some truth since history is a domain constrained by chronology and it strives to be accurate with respect to the details of actions and actors. However, history as a domain is concerned primarily with the selection and interpretation of events and situations from the past, not simply a complete recording of all that has ever happened. Because some things are selected and other things are left unmentioned, there is an inherent interpretation. And, because there is a purposiveness, there is also a sense of argumentation within any good historical narrative. Historians have an obligation to keep repositioning themselves with respect to new understandings and appreciation of different "voices" that might be salient for any given account.

Important things that happened in the past count as history. But what is or is not important? According to Homer, Herodotus, and Thucydides, the epic struggles of men and the personal (or god-derived) flaws that make them win or lose are important. The naïve learner may assume that whatever is presented is by definition important and what is not presented is not important. Modern historians have noted other things that might be important, should not be forgotten, but are at risk of being forgotten; these phenomena are more likely to be related to large amorphous social movements, such as the struggle for women's right to vote, or for labor groups to organize, or the personal and social limitations of warring factions that emerge from familial practices (see Mallon, 1983). The accounts of Herodotus and Thucydides focus on the ways men come into conflict and the accuracy of those accounts; there are other struggles that they chose not to discuss. Picking and choosing the events, social systems, and historical actors is also a part of historical activity.

The preservation of memory is also a function of history, and, in turn, what is preserved in memory becomes the fodder for history. In this sense, history can be taken to be a remembrance of the purely local because for that community it is "important." Such local memorabilia may be associated with cultural heroes from a community. For example, there is very small museum in Puerto Rico devoted to Pablo Casals. The National Library of Wales (www.llgc.org.uk/drych) has chosen to catalogue, in its virtual museum, the existence of a unique web site dealing with issues of substance abuse world wide, which was developed and maintained by Jim Young, alongside reproductions of the oldest Welsh Bible and the earliest book printed in Welsh (*Yny lhyvyr hwnn*). On the volcanic Western Islands of Vestmannaeyjar in Iceland one can find a small building containing various war memorabilia, swords, medals, and orders, from Icelandic soldiers of the First World War. Pablo Casals is memorialized historically as the son of a Puerto Rican mother; Jim Young is honored as a creative Welsh member of the Internet generation working for social good; the Bible (and book) written in Welsh are symbols of the preservation of the national language and its connection to both the religious and modern world; and finally the swords and medals residing in a small corner of Iceland connect a local population with a sweep of larger world events. Each example illustrates local efforts to preserve memory and commemorate local citizens' roles in the larger historical context. As Sam Wineburg (Wineburg, Mosborg, Porat, & Duncan, 2007) and his colleagues have pointed out these memories, whether formally preserved or not, are often ignored or denigrated by the formal historical account — yet it is the intergenerational memories that tend to survive over time.

We have *multiple meanings* of history, then. One is the pure complete account, an account that permits accurate reenactment and commemoration; a second is an epic heroic tale of national identity and virtue; and a third is a contentious, argued, analytic, and interpretive account. The assertion being made in this chapter is that conceptual change in history means moving from a singular account of either of the first two to a challenged account of the third. What is challenged in the latter approach is not so much the facts of a given case but the meaning of it — when it began and ended, how it was perceived by others at the time, how it is authored, and what portions of the record remain for use and interpretation. The conceptual change we seek to describe for both the discipline and the learner is the movement from notions of history as story to history as the conditions and considerations that produce the "story."

WORKING THROUGH AN EXAMPLE: THE BOSTON MASSACRE

On the night of March 5th, 1770, a small conflict took place between a group of civilians in Boston and a group of British soldiers stationed there. The result was that five men were shot and killed by the British soldiers. During the 1770s, there were numerous events that were similar to this one, including an event 6 weeks earlier in which a young boy had been killed by British troops (Zobel, 1970). Why then is this particular skirmish so important in the national consciousness that it is present in virtually every U. S. history textbook? To begin to explore that question more carefully we need to consider some paradigmatic accounts that fit with the issues of history discussed above: the accurate reenactment account and the epic tale account.

As recently as 2005, the History Channel on U. S. television presented a special on the Boston Massacre in which the entire focus was on whether or not Crispus Attucks was the first man to fall in the lead-up to the Revolution. Historians, doctors, and an armament specialist were all consulted and gave grave statements on camera. Careful reconstructions of the scene based on testimony from the second trial that emerged from the incident (the first trial notes having been lost), from refiring of rifles of the day, and from medical testimony about Attucks' wounds claimed to have solved this historical "mystery." Why is that important? Crispus Attucks was of African descent, and as writers of the day and later poet laureates proclaimed he was the first fallen son and that has a certain historical irony to it. In this example the tools of scientific analysis are marshaled to "prove" the accuracy of a particular historical claim. But the account overall is rather ahistorical.[2]

Two competing and conflicting national identity accounts also exist. These two accounts weave their way through U.S. history textbooks depending on the political mood of the country over the course of the 20th century. In the first account, brave unarmed patriots confront surly occupying British troops and throw snowballs at them. The cruel British troops fire into the unarmed crowd and kill the patriots. The citizens of Boston and the surrounding communities arrange a somber and very large funeral for the fallen men, the occupying forces retreat to an island in Boston harbor, and the community ultimately honors the patriots with a monument on the Boston Commons and a brass plaque in the street where the event took place. What is noble and to be remembered is the *sacrifice for freedom*. In the second account, an unruly mob pesters, badmouths, and assaults frightened, cold, young conscripts unwillingly stationed in Boston. Although not armed with guns, the mob is armed with ice balls laced with shellfish shells and small rocks, and large wooden staves. They taunt the troops, daring them to fire, and they hit them with their staves. Accidentally the troops start to fire, church bells are rung, the mob increases in size, and the troops retreat. Both the acting governor, Hutchinson, and the military leader in charge promptly arrest the British men involved. Fearful of further mob action the American patriot and future president, John Adams, cousin of the firebrand leader of the Sons of Liberty, Sam Adams, agrees to defend the soldiers in a court of law. Adams' sense of fairness and justice saves the day and the men are acquitted and sent home. What is to be remembered here is the value of *law* over mob rule, *and* the importance of *justice* even when it does not support personal political aims.

Both of these versions serve the purpose of history as a national identity account. Both versions are routinely presented in U. S. history textbooks. But the historical significance of this small event and the work of historical account construction is seriously masked by all three accounts, the TV and the textbook ones. These three kinds of accounts also change as conceptions of what history is change.

What does an altered account look like? Let's consider four features that would produce a more nuanced account. First, when did this episode begin and when did it end? This issue is referred to as *periodicity*; the ambiguity surrounding the beginning and ending of a particular historical phenomenon is one location where differences in meaning may be worked out. Second, what happened (most probably) and what were the reactions to it? Interpretive actions in history require fidelity to the record not just any old story; pieces are selected in order to form the *argument* being made (Voss, 1998; Voss & Wiley, 2006). Third, who wrote the account and for what purposes? The *source* of an account, as several have noted (Wineburg, 1991, 1994; Britt, Rouet, Georgi, & Perfetti, 1994), becomes quite invisible to the student reader who tends to read through the account like a window and does not see the purposive moves of the author. Fourth, how have we chosen to remember this event and why and who benefits from keeping the *memory* alive.

At first pass, the event (as contrasted to a social system or process) is perhaps the cleanest, most concrete way of describing the past: It is located in a specific time and place; particular individuals are involved; there is a narrative structure to it that gives a beginning, middle, and end; and one can speak of the impact, or significance, of the event. So, one could say that the Boston Massacre took place on March 5, 1770, for example, and explicate the event from there. However, the concept of causality challenges the simple narrative details. Although the event did happen on March 5, 1770, the particular causes of this event call into question both the beginning point and the end of this conflict as well as it is or ramifications, of this conflict. Some might argue that the roots of the Boston Massacre lie in the Stamp Act riots of 1763 when, in response to British-imposed taxes on everyday paper items such as newsprint or marriage licenses, farmers and townspeople in central Massachusetts dragged a British tax collector out of his office and tarred and feathered him, initiating a series of riots in which similar behavior was repeated elsewhere in the colonies. This "mob" action in response to British policy was the first overtly violent series of events in which people lost their lives. Others might argue that the roots or beginnings of the Boston Massacre lie in the arrival of thousands of British troops in Boston in 1768. By order of the British government via the Quartering Act of 1765, Bostonians were compelled to provide housing for these soldiers. Needless to say, most refused to house these soldiers who were seen as a hostile imposition by a distant government, and as a result, these soldiers were left to camp outdoors during some very cold Boston winters. The mere presence of 4,000 soldiers in a city of 15,000 residents led to countless conflicts and skirmishes between colonists and soldiers in the 2 years leading up to March 5, 1770. Still others (Beard & Beard, 1943; Zinn, 2003) might argue that this was at heart a labor dispute between the poor dockworkers and the unpaid and cold soldiers who scavenged for work and had been in a serious scuffle early on the day of March 5th. Choosing one of the three "beginnings" mentioned above (or others) is essential to the construction of a historical narrative of the event. Each choice implies that relevant evidence be brought to bear in defense of that choice. The task is not to create an "accurate" account of the event per se, although accuracy is a primary tenant of the discipline. The task is to create a plausible argument about the causes of the Boston Massacre that takes into account historical evidence and also requires the historian to impose an order on the past by selecting relevant material to make the argument.

Making the argument about the beginning of an event also requires selecting and defending an ending point. The process of making a case for the end-point requires that the historian consider why the event has been called up in the first place — its historical purpose and standing in a particular account. If one were making the case that the Boston Massacre event was really an instance in which the rule of law was summoned to put an end to the perceived lawlessness of the "mob," then the ending to this story lies with the trial and release of the seven British soldiers. Defended by none other than John Adams, future third president of the United States, these British soldiers were found not guilty of murder. In defending the troops, Adams knew he was taking an unpopular position. But Adams was a complicated figure. He feared and hated mob violence. He believed in and respected the law. He also understood politically that if increased governance within the colony was a goal, then it had to be shown that real law was supported and followed.

If one were making the case that the Boston Massacre was one in a series of many events in which the "common man" took matters into his own hands to protest the policies of a faraway and unresponsive government, then one could argue that the end of this type of conflict comes years after the end of the Revolution: with Shays' Rebellion in 1787. In this case, the primary conflict was between the newly formed state government of Massachusetts and a group of farmers in Western Massachusetts who were about to lose their farms due to their inability to pay taxes. These citizens felt there was an undue burden being placed on them financially by a faraway state government in Boston run primarily by merchants. Each year, their pleas to the government to help revive the local economy fell on deaf ears. In 1786 these farmers, led by Daniel Shays, protested yet another tax placed on whiskey. In 1787, on the eve of many foreclosures, Shays and several thousand followers raided the local armory in Springfield (the largest store of guns and ammunition in New England) and proceeded to do battle with soldiers representing their own state government. Although they lost the battle, their efforts were enough to initiate a constitutional convention and the creation of a new government, thus provoking the government to be responsive to those it represented (Richards, 2002).

Finally, if one were making the case that the Boston Massacre represented yet another instance in which the colonists, writ large, forced the British to reverse their policies once again (as they had done with the Stamp Act), then one could argue that the ending lies with the removal of the British soldiers to Castle Rock, an island off the coast of Massachusetts, immediately following the event. The initial arrival of 4,000 troops into the city of Boston was meant to assert a huge presence in a city that was thought to be unruly and mobbish to begin with. When the British government agreed to the removal of the troops, at the urging of Massachusetts colonial governor Hutchinson, it was prior to the trial and marked a retreat from this original intent.

Although the beginnings and endings of a particular historical account may shift, this does not mean that the account is up for grabs. Rather, what the historian selects as the beginning and end point have particular purposes in the construction of the account *and where it sits* in the broader stream of history — in this case, where the Boston Massacre sits in the stream of events leading up to, or perhaps immediately following, the American Revolution. As the historian brings relevant accurate information to bear, it is brought with a purposeful argument in mind.

We have considered the periodicity, or beginnings and endings, of historical accounts as one feature that defines the practice and construction of history. Next we will consider describing "what happened" and how historical actors reacted at the time of the event. As in the recounting of the first sentence of Herodotus' *The Peloponnesian Wars*, one of his goals was "to show how the two races came into conflict." In other words, he intended to tell the story of a particular conflict, recounting "what happened." In seeking to describe accurately "what happened" before, during, and after a specific event, modern historians turn to primary accounts produced by those who witnessed or experienced the event.

Almost as soon as the Boston Massacre "ended," there was a flurry of activity on the part of many individuals to get their version of the story down on paper. As a result, multiple conflicting accounts of the event appeared almost immediately. Captain Preston, the leader of the British soldiers and participant in the event, immediately wrote a letter to his superior officers in Britain. Several newspaper accounts were generated in local newspapers throughout the colonies. Paul Revere created an engraving of the event, which depicted the British soldiers firing on a defenseless, unarmed crowd of colonists; Sam Adams dubbed the event the "Boston Massacre," even though five people died. The Revere engraving was reproduced in newspapers across the colonies as a piece of propaganda meant to incite sympathy toward the colonists and anger toward the British soldiers. Such a flurry of written activity indicates that those who participated in the event understood its importance, especially in the context of 1770 colonial America. There had been conflicts and skirmishes between British officials and colonists since the Stamp Act Riots. Yet the significance of this event is in the particulars: The conflict took place in front of the Boston customs house, symbol of British economic control; it involved British soldiers firing on fellow citizens; and unlike the aftermath of the Stamp Act riots, the colonial leadership stepped in to take control of how the event was played out and was perceived. The trial itself produced its own set of newspaper reports, both in the colonies and in Great Britain, along with three sets of court transcripts of the trial. So, in seeking to describe "what happened," the historian has a myriad of sources at his/her disposal.

The historian must be conscious of the fact that many of those sources were authored by individuals who themselves sought to put their own spin on events: to tell their own story. In constructing a narrative of this event, then, one must be aware of how the various historical actors position themselves in relation to the event as they are telling the story from their particular perspective. Maintaining fidelity to the historical record involves taking all of these features into account: what was put down on paper, the intentions of historical actors, and how the event fit into their own schema of a path toward independence.

Just as the primary sources that comprise the raw materials of history are authored, so, too, are the accounts produced by historians. While historians may not introduce and position themselves outright, as Herodotus did, they are very much a part of the narratives they construct. The common reference for history in the classroom is almost always the textbook: a lengthy and weighty tome whose text appears authorless, colorless, and yet authoritative (Schama, 1991). Under such weight, and stymied by the textbook committee list at the front of the book listing 10, 15, or 20 contributors, it is easy to lose sight of how even the textbook narrative was produced by specific people in a specific time and place; that it, too, is positioned. In the work of the historian, notions of periodicity and telling "what happened" are reflective of the individual telling the story. Who we are and the times in which we live play into the structure of the historical narratives we produce. The story of the Boston Massacre as recounted by Morrison and Commager in the 1930s and 1940s or by Schlesinger in the 1960s is quite different from that of Zinn in the 1980s.[3]

So, the conceptual change we seek to consider in history involves notions of periodicity, selections of materials to tell what happened, and authorship. Finally, the construction of history rests on how we have chosen to remember a particular piece of history and why. This notion of historical memory is integral to the construction of historical accounts. In the aftermath of the Boston Massacre, once the engraving made by Revere had served the purpose of inciting ire against the British, once the trial was over, there was a concerted effort on the part of the leadership of the revolution to, as Young (1999) argues, "erase the mob side of the Revolution." The Sons of Liberty were comprised of the leaders in the colonial communities — merchants, lawyers, skilled craftsmen. Not represented in this group were the "common man" — the laborers, dockworkers, shoemakers, farmers — those who participated in the events surrounding the Boston Massacre and the Stamp Act riots. The Boston Tea party, an event that followed the Boston Massacre, was orchestrated by the Sons of Liberty, taking their cue from the types of protest initiated by the "common man" in these earlier events. The leadership was interested in controlling the method, type, and timing of protests against the British, and were not as interested in involving all members of society in the process. And since the colonial leadership eventually won — both the Revolution and the fight for stable government via the Constitution — they also won the ability to control the memory of the Revolution. Those who founded the United States sought to paint their independence as one anchored in the rational and scholarly traditions of Western thought and ideas: the rule of law above all else, the ability of man to make rational decisions.

In the tradition of heroic tales of national identity, the birth of one's nation is the cornerstone of such efforts. The History Channel documentary mentioned earlier is one example of why it matters who participated in key events leading to independence. The appearance or non-appearance of Crispus Attucks in accounts of the Boston Massacre is reflective of trends in historical memory throughout our brief history. We know that Attucks was there at the Boston customs house and that he died that day. But why focus on him? What about the other colonists who died? Because he was of African decent is one answer. He represented a class of free blacks living in the North in colonial times. There is also a question as to how involved he was with the Sons of Liberty — did this group include blacks in its membership? Attucks drops out of the story for quite awhile until he is resurrected as a significant historical figure in an 1888 commemoration which memorialized his participation in the Boston Massacre conflict. Yet he is absent from accounts of the event both before and after 1888. His resurgence in high school textbooks coincided with a movement in the late 1970s and 1980s to produce a more inclusive account of U. S. history that looked at the contributions of many different racial and ethnic groups to the historical record. Yet, reviving him in this way via textbook accounts contributed to an understanding of him as a token participant. If we are to look across all the accounts produced about this one individual, then we may begin to paint a picture of his actions and contributions to the Revolutionary effort and why he is worth remembering and studying. In looking across these varied accounts we are also in dialogue with the historical memory of him as a historical figure in the mythic event that was the birth of the nation.

We have engaged in the activity of telling and retelling, stating and challenging the story of the Boston Massacre to document how the field of history itself has shifted in significant ways. The structures of the discipline as stated by Herodotus have remained as anchors but the emphasis and the meaning has changed profoundly.[4] Peter Seixas (2000) asks whether or not we should include or exclude students from this shift — some suggest that we should start with the simple single line of story and then only later add the layers of complexity. However, the historian Florencia Mallon and others have no doubt of the requirement that students be brought into the truth of the matter from the beginning (as cited in Leinhardt, Stainton, & Virgi, 1994). We turn now to considering what this might imply for the learner.

WHAT MIGHT THIS EVOLUTION IN HISTORY MEAN
FOR THE STUDENT LEARNER?

What are the challenges that these different aspects of history pose to the learner? We think that there are three challenges that are complex enough that they require fairly fundamental shifts of thought on the part of the student (and teacher). First, history is authored both through the selective surviving record (some things survive and others do not and this is not a random process) and by the deliverer of a current account. Second, history is argued, interpreted, and narrated by an author while maintaining a quest for truth. Third, history is selected both in terms of beginnings and endings and in terms of inclusion and omission. The first of these challenges is to keep an eye on both the history and the historian. This duality requires a somewhat continuous juggling of perspective.

In discussing the way in which ideas of learning and conceptual change might be considered from a linked perspective between the cognitive and situative, Greeno and van de Sande (2007) introduce the idea following MacWhinney (2005), of "perspectival understanding." They define perspectival understanding as "a cognitive arrangement of entities and some of their properties, organized in relation to each other, with a point of view. The viewer may be enmeshed in the perspective (enactive/projective) or the viewer may be viewing from the outside, representing and operating on the entities in the perspective (depictive/descriptive). Construction of a perspectival understanding is a process of constraint satisfaction." (Greeno & van de Sande, 2007, p. 14). What this would mean for the student of history is that he or she would need to include in their account of the Boston Massacre the specifics of the event itself (enactive/projective) but at the same time recognize that they had learned about these specifics from an author with a viewpoint and a position. Do teachers teach this? If they do, do students "get it?"

Our first example of efforts to embed this changed definition of history in instruction and curriculum comes from the United Kingdom's national project. Lee and Ashby (2000) were part of the national effort carried out in the United Kingdom to alter history instruction so that it included not only the substantive historical content (events and people in time) but also what the authors referred to as second-order or procedural ideas. The goal of the redesign of instruction was to trace the ways that ideas about the nature of history and potential historical participation changed over time and development. In the terms of Greeno and van de Sande, this means that students were being queried as to their competence and awareness of perspectival shift between the contents of an account and the purposes and authoring of the account. They must bring two different cognitive aspects into focus: the account itself, and the purpose and contestation of the account.

Lee and Ashby (2000) examined the thinking and responses of a cross-section of students ranging in age from 8 to 14 in four separate panels of data. Students were given a variety of tasks in which they read two short accounts of the same historical event, such as the Roman presence in the British Isles, the collapse of the Roman Empire, or the Saxon settlement of Britain. Students were then asked questions at the end of each pair of accounts, such as the following: If two historians follow the same practices and look at the same evidence, can they disagree? If there are differing accounts of when the Roman Empire ended, how could one decide when it actually ended or would there be additional dates? Is it the case that in real history there is only one true account of what happened? (All questions have been paraphrased.) These questions all relate to what Lee and Ashby refer to as secondary historical understandings and to issues of what Greeno and van de Sande (2007) following Pickering (1995) refer to as conceptual agency. What we want to describe here is how the answers to these questions help us to understand how students do or do not address the ideas of authorship, periodicity, and argument as accounts develop or change over time.

In considering the differences in selecting the date for the end of the Roman Empire, children started with one of two positions: It was a factual problem that required getting the right history, or it was a fundamentally unknowable problem since we cannot interview or talk to people who were present at the scene, so to speak (Lee & Ashby, 2000, pp. 205–207). Some children (ages 12–13) thought perhaps one might find the scrap of paper where someone might have written it down. (The mental picture is of someone scribbling next to the grocery list, "and today Rome fell.") Still others imagined that this was an issue of error but one that could be resolved either by splitting the difference numerically (476 and 1453) or by imagining that it was a long process. A few students (some of the older ones) believed it was an issue of criteria. One would have to decide on the criteria for what should count as a collapse of the Roman Empire and then systematically apply them.

As a follow up to this question, Lee and Ashby asked the students how one could decide. One 14-year-old came up with several criteria: Determine when Rome stopped having an influence on the rest of the world or when the "Eastern half stopped being like the old Roman Empire" (Lee & Ashby, 2000, p. 108). What is especially intriguing about this level of understanding is that it suggests that the Roman Empire itself is an historical construct not a place or a government. That is, even if the Eastern Empire stayed intact but lost the Roman ideals of citizenship and law, it could be considered to have "fallen." Lee and Ashby note a developmental trend, under the influence of instruction, in student responses that moves from seeing the history as a simple matter of greater factual detail to considering the possibilities of multiple endings (a sort of tolerance for inconsistency) to working toward a criterion-based approach. The notion of layering of the historical account is most definitely included as an instructional goal from the very beginning. Further, in including the idea of authoring Lee and Ashby rightly connect it to the other rhetorical aspects of history construction that we identified through the discussion of the Boston Massacre.

In considering ideas of why authors might come to different conclusions or write different accounts, younger students assumed differences lay with errors while older students saw authors as both positioned and in some cases as interpreting information. The Lee and Ashby work is unique in its depth, but it echoes the earlier work of Ola Halldén (1994), in which young people's ideas about the substance and procedures of history emerge over time. In Halldén's work, the idea of a meta-awareness of what history is emerges from classroom discourses and is explored in a manner quite consistent with the suggestions of Greeno and van de Sande. However, the goals of instruction at the time in Sweden did not include a layered understanding of both the contents of history and position of the historian presenting the content.

Studies of history learning in the United States take place in a very different context from the European one. Absent recognized, agreed-upon national standards in history; absent the ability to purchase a rich curriculum that embodies notions of history as construction; teachers, schools, and school districts in the United States are left to develop their own curricula. As such, the research we have in the United States is not of the same scope and scale as the Lee and Ashby work in Great Britain. However, there are important glimmerings that emerge from studies of U.S. classroom instruction. In one study of student history learning at the high school level in the United States, we can see through lesson transcripts that the teacher continuously prompted students to understand that their depictive accounts shared a positional feature with respect to other historians (Leinhardt, 1993). With respect to the historian the students' ideas were enmeshed, so that the historian's voice was inherently unrecognized. Consider the following excerpt from a U. S. history class (students were approximately 15 years old) (Leinhardt, 1993, p. 57):

T[eacher]:...That takes me to the point of Beard [an historian] saying, that these were just
self-centered men who went to Philadelphia so that they would be paid, uh, for their

bonds that they had taken out during the Revolutionary War…Was that true?…Or, would you modify to some extent?…

S[tudent]1:   Yes.

T: We have a Beardian philosopher here. They are interested in themselves period….

S2:   I would say that by, making, their own personal economy better, and stronger they would strengthen that of the whole country. And by giving themselves the opportunity they would also give the opportunity to others.

T: …What kind of historian's view does that coincide with?…

Ss: Hofstader.

T: Hofstader and also?

Ss: Commager.

In this exchange, we see that the teacher is asking students to link the position of their own accounts about the planners of the Constitution with that of historians. But historians as such are not a natural part of the accounts that students provided either early in the school term or later. They may be able to state that Beard had an economic self-interest, interpretive stance, or that Commager had a more glorifying one; but historians' positions were not present within the students' depictive accounts either in speech or in writing. Even 2 months later in the term when a student, Paul, gave a lengthy description of the beginning of the Civil War, one that rested heavily on a Beardian-style interpretation of economic conditions, he told the tale as if it were unfiltered fact (Leinhardt, 1993, p. 71):

Paul:…And after this basically the South, the South, the South had lost all its aces. Ah, it was not going to get the ships that it needed in time to fight the war with the North to break the blockade. It had lost its card of King Cotton to begin with and as far as mediation there was now no hope of that due to the fact that the North had gained support among the English people in general.

In this exchange, we hear an account that sounds uncontested; it is a simple summary of the position of the South near the beginning of the Civil War. Given that all of the students had been prompted steadily to recognize the positioned and layered feature of all of the accounts they were reading, and given the fact that Paul turned out to be one of the best of the students, it seems evident that students do not easily pick up on the idea of authoring as a notion of contested accounting.

We see more evidence of this in the work of Sam Wineburg (1991), in which he compared responses by students and historians to historical texts. The notable finding from this study and others in the same vein was that students did not use sourcing information in interpreting the texts themselves. The source information — who wrote it and from what perspective — was not seen as integral to the interpretation. He argues, however, that students cannot discuss or understand the validity of source information if they are unaware that it exists. In textbook-driven instruction, students are not taught to understand how the history they read was produced. As in the example of Paul, the responsibility for making authorship visible falls on the teacher. Likewise, in the work of Perfetti and his colleagues (Britt et al., 1994), students were shown to need a great deal of support to gradually include this kind of information in their understandings of historical accounts. It is important to recognize that historical instruction does not always include this layer of authorship. If Halldén (1994) was accurate in his description of the purposes of upper-level Swedish instruction in history, then the purpose was simply to learn the national identity tale not to question how the tale was constructed or why certain elements were included or not. In the United States, the decision to include or exclude the contested aspects of national identity is a matter left to the discretion of the teacher. However, upper level exams such as the Advanced Placement do hold students accountable for at least some sense of both positioned authorship and an awareness of purposiveness in account construction.

CONCLUSIONS

We can see in these episodes of student learning both in the U. S. and in Europe some of the ways in which history as a discipline has undergone a conceptual shift such that ideas of beginnings and ending, ideas of interpretation and argument, and ideas of significance and who gets to decide what is and is not are now recognized as a legitimate part of the disciplinary practice. These secondary or procedural ideas of Lee and Ashby (2000) relate in some interesting ways to the ideas of conceptual and disciplinary agency discussed by Greeno and van de Sande (2007). These two ideas of agency refer to following the disciplinary practices and to seeing the discipline as the authoritative source in contrast to following practices that relate to the judgment, utility, and importance of actions and considering the authority to be the group engaged in the particular and local practice. Agency and perspective help to make "room" for a recognition that the work of students should include the ideas of historical practice. These concepts also suggest a need for refocusing the object of understanding to include both the content of history, the historian, and the argument. Peter Lee and Rosalyn Ashby's design experiment in history instruction and learning certainly included reference to the consideration of the historian as having a position and as building an account that supports that position, but it does not point to nor make the distinction between the differing types of agency. The data do not yet demonstrate a strong case for conceptual change taking place in history learning per se, although we certainly see developmental growth; data do indicate a press toward instruction and research that reflects the shifts within the discipline itself.[5]

We have suggested in this chapter that student conceptual growth or change in history is somewhat different than in other domains because it is the field itself that has undergone a conceptual shift. New elements have been considered worthy of inclusion in the field — for example, phenomena whose record is pictorial or folkloric in nature. There are new ways of organizing the field with a shift from taking extant political social orders as given and seeing events set down upon them, to using communication regions (the Atlantic or Pacific rim), navigational growth, or natural occurrences as the backdrop for investigation. But these may not be shifts in kind in the way that Chi (1992) might describe, even though they have enormous impact on the field. They are shifts in focus and emphasis. Such shifts also impact the particular combination of narrative and expository presentation — as suggested by our early quote from Schama (1991) about imagination and reason — but not the rhetoric of argument or causality. Likewise, while the idea of authorship and its tight connection to purpose or intent has come to the foreground in recent disciplinary scholarship, it was always a vital part of the account from Herodotus (550 B.C.E.) to Macaulay (1855/1897) to Schama (1991).

The task for the history learner is, first, to come to see their world as having histories, whether that is a social-political event, such as a war or election, or an economic and social one, such as the distribution and selection of food, or the arrangement of buildings and factories in towns and cities; and, secondly, the task is to see the presentation of those histories as purposeful and authored; and, we would add, even when such histories are local and familial. The historical example of the Boston Massacre illustrates the nuances of how one would come to understand an historical event within this extended framework. Incorporating these practices and perspectives into classroom instruction is indeed the goal of our own work with schools and many school districts around the United States.

NOTES

1. These multiple references refer to the many varieties of translations that appear for Herodotus; all contain the ideas discussed.
2. In critiquing the television history, we do not mean to criticize history on television or the idea that history could expand its medium from text to video. For example, the documentary history of Ken Burns, whether it is about the Civil War, jazz, or baseball, meets the strictest criteria of textual history and is to be applauded for its general interest, provocativeness, and educational value.
3. In addition, historians are in constant dialogue with their contemporary colleagues and with historians who have gone before them. For example, it would be ridiculous to put forth an argument in 2006 that the Revolution was, in fact, not so revolutionary without referencing the work of Alfred Young, who argued in 1999 that the American Revolution was not so radical, especially placed in the context of other European revolutions of the same period (the French Revolution, for example) (Young, 1999). The historian making such an argument today would need to demonstrate a command of this earlier argument and then place his/her own account/argument in this historical trajectory. In other words, the historian is attuned to the historiography of his or her particular period, mindful of how that period has been studied by other historians.
4. We can compare this shift in history to that of, say, physics, where there has been much discussion of the shift from an Aristotelian account of motion to a Newtonian one. The historical shift is one of perspective and focus which may indeed be challenging; but it is not as complex or difficult for the learner as the one in physics.
5. We have chosen not to emphasize the observed differences in history learning that surround different classes of historical topics. The different topics include event like narratives such as the Boston Massacre in contrast to the social structural elements such as constitutional arrangements or economic systems that require a more expository development with far less agency. Events are easier to learn and teach than systems (Young & Leinhardt, 1998) this is consistent with Chi's (2005) assertion that emergent systems are harder to learn than more causal ones.

REFERENCES

Beard, C., & Beard, M. (1943). *The American spirit.* New York: Macmillan.
Britt, M. A., Rouet, J. F., Georgi, M. C., & Perfetti, C. A. (1994). Learning from historical texts: From causal analysis to argument models. In G. Leinhardt, I. Beck, & C. Stainton (Eds.), *Teaching and learning in history* (pp. 47–84). Hillsdale, NJ: Erlbaum.
Chi, M. T. H. (1992). Conceptual change within and across ontological categories: Examples from learning and discovery in science. In R. Giere (Ed.), *Cognitive models of science: Minnesota studies in the philosophy of science* (pp 129-186). Minneapolis: University of Minnesota Press.
Chi, M. T. H. (2005). Commonsense conceptions of emergent processes: Why some misconceptions are robust. *The Journal of the Learning Sciences, 14*(2), 161-199.
Collingwood, R. G. (1946). *The idea of history.* London: Oxford University Press.
Goold, G. P. (Ed.) (1920). *Herodotus* (Vol. 1; A. D. Godley, Trans.) Cambridge, MA: Harvard University Press.
Greeno, J. G., & van de Sande, C. (2007). Perspectival understanding of conceptions and conceptual growth in interaction. *Educational Psychologist, 42*(1), 9–23.
Halldén, O. (1994). On the paradox of understanding history in an educational setting. In G. Leinhardt, I. Beck, & C. Stainton (Eds.), *Teaching and learning in history* (pp. 27–46). Hillsdale, NJ: Erlbaum.
Herodotus (1987). *The history* (D. Grene, Trans.). Chicago: University of Chicago Press.
Herodotus (2006). Available at: http://www.livius.org/he-hg/herodotus/herodotus01.htm. Downloaded 06/09/2006/02:22pm.
Lee, P., & Ashby, R. (2000). Progression in historical understanding among students ages 7–14. In P. N. Stearns, P. Seixas, & S. Wineburg (Eds.), *Knowing, teaching, and learning history* (pp. 199–222). New York: New York University Press.

Leinhardt, G. (1993). Weaving instructional explanations in history. *British Journal of Educational Psychology*, *63*, 46–74.

Leinhardt, G., Stainton, C., & Virjii, S. M. (1994). A Sense of history. *Educational Psychologist*, *29*(2), 79–88.

Macaulay, T. B. (1897). *England in 1685: Being chapter III of the history of England.* Boston: Ginn & Co.

MacWhinney, B. (2005). The emergence of grammar from perspective. In D. Pecher & R. A. Zwann (Eds.), *The grounding of cognition: The role of perception and action in memory, language and thinking* (pp. 198–223). Cambridge: Cambridge University Press.

Mallon, F. A. (1983). *The defense of community in Peru's central highlands.* Princeton, NJ: Princeton University Press.

Pickering, A. (1995). *The mangle of practice.* Chicago: University of Chicago Press.

Richards, L. L. (2002). *Shays's Rebellion: The American Revolution's final battle.* Philadelphia: University of Pennsylvania Press.

Schama, S. (1991, September 8). Clio has problem. *New York Times Magazine*, pp. 30–33.

Seixas, P. (2000). Schweigen! Die Kinder! or Does postmodern history have a place in schools? In P. N. Stearns, P. Seixas, & S. Wineburg (Eds.), *Knowing, teaching, and learning history* (pp. 19–37). New York: New York University Press.

Torney-Purta, J. (1994). Dimensions of adolescents' reasoning about political and historical issues: Ontological switches, developmental processes, and situated learning. In M. Carretero & J. Voss (Eds.), *Cognitive and instructional processes in history and the social sciences* (pp. 103–122). Hillsdale, NJ: Erlbaum.

von Wright, G. H. (1971). *Explanation and understanding.* Ithaca, NY: Cornell University Press.

Voss, J. F. (1998). Issues in the learning of history. *Issues in Education, 4*(2), 163–209.

Voss, J. F., & Wiley, J. (2006). Expertise in history. In K. A. Ericsson, N. Charness, P. J. Feltovich & R. R. Hoffman (Eds.), *The Cambridge handbook of expertise and expert performance* (pp. 159–184). Cambridge, UK: Cambridge University Press.

Wineburg, S. (1991). On the reading of historical texts: Notes on the breach between school and academy. *American Educational Research Journal*, *28*, 495–519.

Wineburg, S. (1994). The cognitive representation of historical texts. In G. Leinhardt, I. Beck, & C. Stainton (Eds.), *Teaching and learning in history* (pp. 85–135). Hillsdale, NJ: Erlbaum.

Wineburg, S., Mosborg, S., Porat, D., & Duncan, A. (2007). Common belief and the Cultural Curriculum: An intergenerational study of historical consciousness. *American Educational Research Journal, 44* (1), 40–76.

Young, A. F. (1993). *Beyond the American Revolution: Exploration and in the history of American radicalism.* DeKalb, IL: Northern Illinois University Press.

Young, A. F. (1999). *The shoemaker and the Tea Party: Memory and the American Revolution.* Boston: Beacon Press.

Young, K. M. & Leinhardt, G. (1998a). Wildflowers, sheep, and democracy: The role of analogy in the teaching and learning of history. In J. F. Voss, & M. Carretero (vol. Eds.), *International review of history education (vol. 2). Learning and reasoning in history* (pp. 154–199). London: Woburn Press.

Young, K. M., & Leinhardt, G (1998b). Writing from primary documents: A way of knowing in history. *Written Communication, 15*(1), 25–86.

Zinn, H. (2003). *A people's history of the United States.* New York: HarperCollins.

Zobel, H. B. (1970). *The Boston Massacre.* New York: Norton.

III

CONCEPTUAL CHANGE IN THE PHILOSOPHY AND HISTORY OF SCIENCE

13

The Problem of Conceptual Change in the Philosophy and History of Science

Theodore Arabatzis and Vasso Kindi
University of Athens

INTRODUCTION

The problem of conceptual change has been widely discussed in the philosophy of science since the early 1960s, when Thomas Kuhn and Paul Feyerabend, among others, launched a powerful critique against logical positivism, a critique based on a close reading of the history of the physical sciences. One of their most far-reaching theses was that scientific concepts are historical entities that evolve over time and are replaced by altogether different ones. In their view, the older concepts and their descendants refer to completely different entities. The very subject matter of scientific investigation shifts along with conceptual change. Furthermore, because of such ontological shifts, the possibility of giving an account of theory change as a rational process is undermined. In post-Kuhnian philosophy of science, there has been considerable effort to come to terms with those ontological and epistemological implications of conceptual change.

In this chapter, we give an overview of the problem of conceptual change in 20th century philosophy of science. We start with the logical positivist analysis of scientific concepts. Then, we discuss the "historicist" view of concepts and conceptual change, as expounded in the early writings of Kuhn and Feyerabend. The following sections examine the reception of historicist views by the philosophical community, focusing on the writings of D. Shapere, I. Scheffler, D. Davidson, and H. Putnam. Then, we analyze Kuhn's more recent work, in which he attempted to address some of the difficulties faced by his original account of conceptual change, by articulating further his key philosophical notion of incommensurability. We conclude by discussing a post-Kuhnian approach to conceptual change, which aims at a rapprochement of history and philosophy of science, on the one hand, and cognitive science, on the other.

THE LOGICAL POSITIVIST ANALYSIS OF CONCEPTS

The logical positivists in their manifesto entitled "Wissenschaftliche Weltauffassung: Die Wiener Kreis" ("The Scientific Conception of the World: The Vienna Circle"; Hahn, Carnap, & Neurath, 1996), published for the first time in 1929, specify the goal of their scientific outlook: "unified science".

The endeavor is to link and harmonize the achievements of individual investigators in their various fields of science. From this aim follows the emphasis on *collective efforts*, and also the emphasis on what can be grasped intersubjectively; from this springs the search for a neutral system of formulae, for a symbolism freed from the slag of historical languages; and also the search for a total system of concepts. (Hahn et al., 1996, p. 328)

What is interesting in this passage for our purposes is the reference to "a neutral system of formulae" and "a total system of concepts". Logical positivists aimed at reaching the goal of unified science[1], by ordering all concepts into a reductive system, what they called a 'constitutive system'.[2] The idea was that any concept, from any branch of science, had to be "statable by step-wise reduction to other concepts, down to the concepts of the lowest level which refer directly to the given" (ibid., p. 331). On this lowest level there were supposed to lie concepts of "the experience and qualities of the individual psyche", on the next, physical objects, then, other minds and, lastly, the objects of social science (ibid.). The philosophers belonging to the movement of logical positivism never succeeded in executing this very ambitious project; they knew it was difficult but they were optimistic that the advance of science would offer the means to carry it out. The method logical positivists used to move in and deal with this hierarchical system of concepts was logical analysis, undertaken with the help of the, then modern, symbolic logic, i.e., the formal logic developed by Frege and Russell at the turn of the 20th century. This tool allowed logical positivists to formulate statements in a first-order formal language, that of propositional or predicate logic, which gave them the rigor, clarity and precision they required. The aim was to move from statement to statement by tautological transformations representing, thus, thought and inference as a mechanical, automatically controlled process (ibid., pp. 330, 331). The reason behind all this was the determination to keep metaphysics out of the scientific world-conception (ibid., p. 329). They wanted to cancel out the "metaphysical aberration" (ibid.), to remove "the metaphysical and theological debris of millennia" (ibid., p. 339), to free concepts from "metaphysical admixtures which had clung to them from ancient time" (ibid., p. 334). They were suspicious of metaphysics in general but they were mostly concerned with the metaphysical philosophy of their day as it was expressed in the work of Heidegger, Bergson, Fichte, Hegel, and Schelling (Carnap, 1959, p. 80). So, the project, which had an ultimate political objective of liberation and enlightenment, consisted in manipulating an ordered system of concepts, arranged in statements, by means of a language that contained only structural formulae (Hahn et al., 1996, pp. 331–332). The emphasis on mere structure, mere form, and not content was thought to guarantee intersubjectivity and unity.[3] Let us see in more detail how they understood concepts and how they dealt with them.

Carnap in his essay "Logical Foundations of the Unity of Science" (1981), first published in the *International Encyclopedia of Unified Science* (1938), assigns to the theory of science the study, in the abstract,[4] of the linguistic expressions of science (p. 113). These expressions form statements, which form, in turn, ordered systems, the theories. The task of the philosopher is to study the relations between statements. For instance, when philosophers discuss the problem of confirmation — how scientific theories are confirmed by evidence — they consider the relations between observation statements and statements which express scientific hypotheses. When they discuss explanation — how scientists explain, for example, individual phenomena — they consider the relations between the *explanans* and the *explanandum*, that is, the relations between statements which express general laws and initial conditions on the one hand (the explanans), and a statement expressing the particular event to be explained on the other.

Each statement has as components terms which may express concepts. Carnap says that he prefers 'terms' to 'concepts' because he fears that 'concepts' may be understood psychologically:

Instead of the word 'term' the word 'concept' could be taken, which is more frequently used by logicians. But the word 'term' is more clear, since it shows that we mean signs, e.g., words, expressions consisting of words, artificial symbols, etc., of course with the meaning they have in the language in question. We do not mean 'concept' in its psychological sense, i.e., images or thoughts somehow connected with a word; that would not belong to logic. (ibid., p. 118)

We see again in this passage the emphasis on the structural formulae of syntax (words, signs, and artificial symbols) and the rejection of any psychological accompaniments of language as not belonging to logic.

Frege, whose lectures Carnap had attended at Jena, was himself concerned that concepts may be understood psychologically[5] and urged the distinction between the psychological and the logical.[6] In his introduction to *The Foundations of Arithmetic* (1980b, p. x), he states it as the first of his fundamental principles: "always to separate sharply the psychological from the logical, the subjective from the objective". He developed a notation to capture what is logical in concepts — their conceptual content — that is, what is relevant to logical inference. This notation is Frege's *Begriffsschrift* (concept-script),[7] a "formula language of pure thought", modeled upon that of arithmetic, in which signs stand for concepts with sharp boundaries.[8] The psychological trappings, the clothing of thought, which may differ from language to language, were left out (Frege, 1979d, p. 142)[9] and the vagueness and ambiguity of natural languages were avoided.[10] With this tool, Frege undertook to provide a detailed analysis of the concepts of arithmetic and a foundation for its theorems (1980a, p. 8), aiming ultimately to show that mathematics can be reduced to logic. Frege hoped to extend the domain of this formal language to the fields of geometry and physics, both of which were considered to place value on the validity of proofs. He saw his notation as realizing Leibniz's "gigantic idea" of a *lingua characterica* (Frege, 1979a, pp. 9, 10, 13; also 1980a, p. 6),[11] and hoped that it would expand to comprise not only all existing symbolic languages (such as those of arithmetic, geometry and chemistry) but also new ones to be developed.

According to Frege, the meaning of terms cannot be sought in the ideas or images (*Vorstellungen*) that may be formed in the speakers' minds. These are private and subjective whereas meanings are objective in the sense of being independent and common to the speakers of language. A painter, a horseman, and a zoologist may connect different ideas with the term '*Bucephalus*'; yet, so far as they communicate, they all share the sign's sense which belongs to mankind's "common store of thoughts which is transmitted from one generation to another" (Frege, 1997a, p. 154). Frege, in his "Über Sinn und Bedeutung" (1997a), first published in 1892, distinguished between sense (*Sinn*) and meaning[12] (*Bedeutung*) and placed sense in a Platonic realm of abstract, timeless, unvarying entities, a third realm, which is different from the realm of physical things in the external world and the realm of mental objects of consciousness in the inner world (Frege, 1997c, pp. 336–337; 1979d, p. 148). Meaning or reference was sought in the world of objects. In general, one might say that the sense of a linguistic expression is a description of conditions that have to be met in order for the expression's meaning or reference to be determined. Sense, that is, helps to pick out objects in the world by describing them in a certain way. For example, the sense of the name 'Bucephalus' is "The horse of Alexander the Great" while its meaning or referent is the actual horse that belonged to Alexander.

Carnap compared the Fregean distinction between sense and meaning (sense and nominatum in his translation) to his distinction between the intension and extension of concepts (Carnap, 1988, pp. 118–133). Following Church's reading of Frege,[13] he thought that the two pairs coincide.[14] The sense or intension of a concept-word or predicate is a concept described by a conjunction of properties, while the meaning or extension of the concept-word is the class of objects that fall under it. For example, the intension of the concept-word 'horse' is "a four legged, solid-hoofed animal with a flowing mane and tail" and its referent is the concept's extension, i.e., the set of horses in the world.[15] Carnap claimed that the determination of intensions (as well as of extensions) is an empirical matter carried out by science, which achieves increasing precision and clarity in the description of properties some of which are selected as essential (Carnap, 1988, p. 241). Carnap's ultimate aim, as described at least in the *Aufbau* (1969, pp. v–viii), and here again it can be said that he follows Frege, was to achieve a rational reconstruction of the concepts of all fields of knowledge with the help of the formalism and logic that had been developed by Frege, but also Russell and Whitehead.[16] This task, which was shared, as we have seen, by other members of the Vienna Circle, involved the explication of concepts, i.e., their clarification in the direction of greater exactness through their reduction, originally to basic concepts of sensory experience (for instance, sense data of the form "a red of a certain type at a certain visual field place at a certain time"), and later, in order to ensure a greater inter-subjective agreement, through reduction to a physical basis, which contained as basic concepts observable properties and relations of physical things. It should be noted, however, that Carnap's logical reconstruction was not at all concerned with the actual concepts and the empirical work of the sciences. Carnap, just like the rest of the logical positivists, concentrated on logical form and structure to ensure inter-subjective objectivity (Friedman, 1999, pp. 95–101). His concepts are mere knots in a system of structural relations and have only formal, structural properties.

The different executions of this project formed the so-called received (Putnam 1975a), orthodox (Feigl, 1970) or standard view (Hempel, 1970) of scientific theories conceived as an axiomatic, hypothetico-deductive, empirically uninterpreted calculus, which was then interpreted observationally by means of bridge principles or correspondence rules[17]. The idea was that there is a "theoretical scenario" involving laws, theoretical concepts and entities, which is brought to apply, by bridge principles, to the empirical phenomena it is supposed to explain. For example, the kinetic theory of gases with its assumptions about gas molecules and the laws that govern them serves as the theoretical scenario to explain phenomena such as temperature and pressure using bridge principles which state, for instance, that the temperature of a gas (empirical concept) is proportional to the mean kinetic energy of its molecules (theoretical concept) (Hempel, 1970). Feigl (1970, p. 6) graphically illustrates this model (see Figure 13.1).

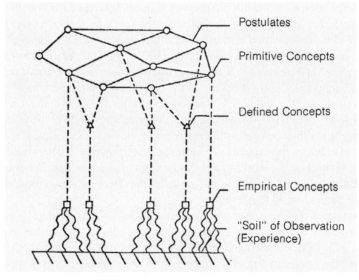

FIGURE 13.1   Feigl's diagram of theories.

In Figure 13.1, the uninterpreted theoretical scenario is a system of abstract postulates, which, while hovering over empirical facts, is linked to experience by means of correspondence rules. The primitive concepts in the theoretical scenario are implicitly defined[18] by the set of postulates that contain them and are used to explicitly define other concepts. As Feigl pointedly observes (1970, p. 5), "[c]oncepts thus defined are devoid of empirical content. One may well hesitate to speak of 'concepts' here, since strictly speaking, even 'logical' meaning as understood by Frege and Russell is absent. Any postulate system if taken (as erstwhile) *empirically uninterpreted* merely establishes a network of symbols. The symbols are to be manipulated according to preassigned formation and transformation rules and their 'meanings' are, if one can speak of meanings here at all, purely formal." The idea is that the validity of inferences could be checked automatically, by electronic computers (Feigl, 1970, p. 4).

We see, then, that in the context of logical positivism, whose reign lasted for more than 30 years and shaped what is still known as philosophy of science, there is no substantive account of concepts. Carnap even goes as far as stating that 'object' understood in its widest sense and 'concept' are one and the same in the metaphysically[19] neutral language that he employs (Carnap, 1969, p. 10). What mattered to Carnap and the logical positivists was to be able to manipulate mechanically signs in the effort to bring to the study of science, and, thus, to philosophy, the rigor and clarity of mathematics and logic. Their concerns were purely logical (i.e., the logical relations among statements and terms); the actual theories and concepts of science were only the occasion to exercise their logical insights. They had no ambition to influence the practice of scientists. "It should be stressed and not merely bashfully admitted", says Feigl, "that the rational reconstruction of theories is a highly artificial hindsight operation which has little to do with the work of the creative scientist" (Feigl, 1970, p. 13). And Carl Hempel (1970, p. 148) notes that "the standard construal was never claimed to provide a descriptive account of the actual formulation and use of theories by scientists in the on going process of scientific inquiry".

Conceptual change was far from their priorities, if non-existent as a matter of concern. The standard account of theories "could at best represent a theory quick frozen, as it were, at one momentary stage of what is in fact a continually developing system of ideas" (ibid., p. 148). Responding to the criticism by Feyerabend and Kuhn, which we will consider later on in this chapter, Hempel (1970, pp. 153–155), as late as the 1970s, considers the question of change in the meaning of terms. He challenges the operationist idea that different methods of measurement indicate different concepts and inquires whether in theory change what we have is change in the meaning of terms or just a revision of the laws in which the terms appear.[20] Do we have new concepts in the new theory or are the concepts of the old used to express new laws which prove the previously held laws false? "[A] satisfactory resolution of the issue would require a more adequate theory of the notion of sameness of meaning than seems yet to be at hand" (ibid., pp. 155–156).

THE "HISTORICIST" VIEW OF CONCEPTS AND CONCEPTUAL CHANGE

The issue of conceptual change, which was understood as change in the meaning of theoretical terms in the sciences, became the focus of attention in the early 1960s with the work most notably of Paul Feyerabend and Thomas Kuhn. The novel idea which these two philosophers introduced was that theory change in the sciences may involve change in the meaning of terms, in which case there is radical discontinuity in the development of scientific knowledge. The logical positivists, and those who were working in the tradition of their philosophy, did not deny that in the course of scientific development theories evolve, are modified or abandoned. They did not deny that new theoretical terms and new concepts are introduced with the advent of a new theory. But they did deny, at least implicitly, that these developments effect radical discontinuity and interfere with the meanings of the terms that are retained. Carnap, for instance, in his important paper "Testability and Meaning" (1936–37, pp. 441–453) explains what is to be done if a new term is to be introduced in the language of science[21]: it has either to be defined in terms of antecedently available vocabulary, if we want to fix its meaning once and for all, or, if we want to fix its meaning now for certain cases and wait for fuller determination in the future, its meaning has to be determined by pairs of reduction sentences, i.e., sentences which describe experimental conditions that have to be fulfilled in order for the new term to apply. Nowhere in both alternatives does Carnap ever consider the possibility of discontinuity which would have implied that it may not be possible to determine the meaning of the new term by reducing it to concepts already available. The reason this possibility was not even imaginable may be sought in the confidence that logical positivists had that the observational and physicalist language which they had placed at the bottom of their formulation of theories could guarantee continuity and intersubjective validity.[22] They had an entity idea of meaning and thought that there is a steady influx of neutral empirical content from the observation level to the abstract level of theory and into the empty syntactical shells of the theoretical terms of science. For instance, the abstract, theoretical predicate Q acquires meaning by being connected to certain observation predicates, which belong to sentences that are easily decided as to their truth or falsity with the help of some observations.[23] Some of these sentences, which may be added to or modified, constitute the necessary and sufficient conditions that have to obtain in order for the predicate to apply and the corresponding concept to be circumscribed.[24]

Both Kuhn and Feyerabend had a different idea of meaning drawing upon Wittgenstein's later philosophy. Feyerabend, in his seminal paper "Explanation, Reduction and Empiricism" (1981a, p. 24), which was first published in 1962, explicitly invoked Wittgenstein when he spoke of his contextual theory of meaning while Kuhn in his landmark book *The Structure of Scientific Revolutions* (1970, p. 45), which was also published for the first time in 1962, referred to Wittgenstein in connection with the notion of family resemblance.

Wittgenstein spoke of meaning as use rejecting an entity idea of meaning (the entity being a mental image, a referent in the world of objects or some kind of an abstract Platonic form). The meaning of a word is its use in language with its rules and grammar. To know the meaning of a word or, equivalently, to have the corresponding concept, is to be able to use it appropriately. But the appropriate use is not given by some definition, which must be antecedently available, comprising a set of necessary and sufficient conditions which specify when and how the word ought to be employed, but rather the appropriate use is learned in practice when the users of language are exposed to concrete examples of application. The uses of a particular word on different occasions and in different contexts, the different "facets" of the use (PG §36), bear similarities to each other, "overlapping and criss-crossing", and form a family of resemblances (PI §§66–67). Yet, no common thread runs through them all, and, so, no set of conditions can be used to fully define and bound a concept.[25] As a result, concepts for Wittgenstein are normally vague (RFM VII §70), fluid (PG §65), hazy (PG §76), fluctuating (PG §36), with blurred edges (PG §§71).[26] This does not mean, however, that they cannot be given sharp boundaries for specific purposes (PI §68–69) or that this rather loose understanding of concepts renders them useless or precludes the possibility of correct use (cf. PG §76, RFM I §116). For one, as Wittgenstein says, there is no single idea of exactness (PI §88); what counts as exact or inexact depends on what we are trying to do.[27] Also, it is not always an advantage to replace an indistinct picture by a sharp one.[28] Second, the fact that our concepts are not bounded by sharp definitional contours, that "a transition can be made from anything to anything" (PG §35), does not mean that the application of concepts is a matter of arbitrary decision, and it does not mean that there is no point in talking about correct use. It is true that Wittgenstein, in several places in his work, says that it is a matter of decision or stipulation whether a particular employment of a concept-word falls under the concept.[29] But nowhere does he say that it is a matter of *arbitrary* decision. Our concepts may not be bounded for us "by an arbitrary definition"[30] but are bounded by "natural limits" which correspond to whatever pertains to the role our concepts have in our life (RFM I § 116). Taking one or the other decision in border line cases has practical consequences which may get us into conflict with society or other priorities that we may have (ibid.). If, for instance, we extend the concept 'number', or the concept 'red', in unanticipated ways we need to give reasons and we need to consider the ramifications this move may have in a whole lot of activities. Wittgenstein's point seems to be that using language is not a matter of theoretically contemplating definitions which fix from without the determinate sense of words and dictate the correct course of action but a matter of practice which requires, among other things, to take responsibility for the judgments we make, which means in its turn to give reasons for what we do. This implies that what is correct to say or do is not determined by some standards set independently of the practices of human beings but rather by what these practices' priorities and goals are.[31]

Feyerabend was well acquainted with Wittgenstein's philosophy[32] and used it in attacking the formal theories of explanation and reduction in the sciences. Ernest Nagel (1979) had maintained that "the distinctive aim of the scientific enterprise is to provide systematic and responsibly supported explanations" (1979, p. 15)[33] and Carl Hempel, together with Paul Oppenheim (1948), provided the best known formulation of them: the deductive-nomological model. According to this model, an explanation consists of two parts: the explanandum (what is to be explained) and the explanans (what is used to do the explaining). The explanandum is a sentence describing either the occurrence of some individual event or the possession of some property by an object or some general regularity or law while the explanans is a set of two groups of sentences: one group contains sentences which represent universal laws and the other contains sentences which state antecedent conditions, i.e., singular statements which assert that certain events have occurred at indicated times and places or that given objects have certain properties (Nagel, 1979, p. 31).[34] Explanations have a deductive structure which means that the explanandum is a logical consequence of the explanans.

The reduction of individual theories to more inclusive ones is, according to Nagel, "an undeniable and recurrent feature of the history of modern science" in view of realizing "the ideal of a comprehensive theory which will integrate all domains of natural science" (Nagel, 1979, pp. 336–337). Reductions, just like explanations, have also a deductive structure. The laws and theories to be reduced (secondary science), for instance Newtonian mechanics, must be a logical consequence of the theory to which the reduction is made (primary science), for instance, Einstein's special and general theories of relativity. An obvious and indispensable requirement, says Nagel, is that the terms appearing in the statements which represent axioms, hypotheses or laws "[must] have meanings unambiguously fixed by codified rules of usage or by established procedures appropriate to each discipline" (ibid., p. 345). Otherwise the reduction cannot go through. Nagel acknowledges though, that, by this condition, it is possible that certain terms in the secondary science may be absent from the theoretical assumptions of the primary science. So, he states his condition of connectability, which requires that, in order for a reduction to proceed, some postulates need to be introduced to establish relations between the terms and expressions of the two sciences. These linkages may be logical connections, conventions created by fiat or factual hypotheses which need to be supported by evidence (ibid., pp. 353–355). With all this in place one theory can be derived from the other. The models of both explanation and reduction provide also a model for the progress of science. Science develops and knowledge is increased by constantly producing all the more comprehensive theories with enlarged and improved explanatory power.

In this context, conceptual change is just the continuous accumulation of better means (concepts, hypotheses, laws, theories) to reach the truth about the world.

Feyerabend (1981a) challenged both the deductive structure of explanation and reduction (on historical and logical grounds)[35] and the assumption it implies of meaning invariance, i.e., the assumption that meanings are invariant with respect to the processes of explanation and reduction. He maintained that the meaning of a term is given contextually,[36] i.e., it "is dependent upon the way in which the term has been incorporated into a theory" (ibid., p. 74) and claimed that elements of many pairs of theories (concepts, principles, laws, etc) are "incommensurable and therefore incapable of mutual explanation and reduction" (ibid., p. 77). The reason is that concepts of an earlier theory cannot be defined on the basis of primitive observational terms of the theory to which a reduction is attempted nor can there be found "correct empirical statements" to correlate corresponding terms and concepts (ibid., p. 76). Observation, and this is yet another influence of Wittgenstein's philosophy, was thought by Feyerabend, but also Hanson[37] and Kuhn, to be theory-laden, that is influenced and shaped by the categories and concepts of each theory. Feyerabend believed that the progress of science requires radical steps forward so, if the meanings of terms are preserved as science develops, the much desired revolutions in the interest of knowledge will not occur. Thus, meaning invariance, according to Feyerabend, is not only incompatible with actual scientific practice but also undesirable (1981a, p. 82). Finally, in an article that was first published in 1965 (1981b, p. 98) Feyerabend maintains that there is a change of meaning "either if a new theory entails that all concepts of the preceding theory have zero extension or if it introduces rules which cannot be interpreted as attributing specific properties to objects within already existing classes, but which change the system of classes itself". This is a view that, as we will see, features prominently in Kuhn's later philosophy.

At least the initial phase of Feyerabend's criticism may be considered internal to the philosophical tradition he was combating in the sense that it focused mostly on the philosophical shortcomings and inadequacies of the models that were put forward at the time. Toulmin (1961, 1972) and Kuhn (1970), more so than Feyerabend, attempted and effected a change of perspective. Toulmin questioned whether there is anything in common to the different explanatory sciences, comparing them to Wittgenstein's games (1961, p. 22), and urged for a more relevant philosophy of science, more relevant, that is, to its actual practice and history. He thought that what he called "Frege's method", which concentrated on idealized logical structures to escape from "the twin heresies of 'psychologism' and the 'genetic fallacy'" (1972, p. 58), "distracts us not only from the process of conceptual change, but also of questions about the external application of conceptual systems, as put to practical use" (ibid., p. 61).[38] Yet, although Toulmin was among the first to call attention to the evolution of science and its concepts, although he spoke of paradigms (borrowed from Wittgenstein's philosophy) and of profound change involving no common theoretical terms and problems (1961),[39] he was very much reluctant to endorse radical discontinuity in science. He contended that there is conceptual change without revolutions and that "intellectual discontinuities on the theoretical level of science conceal underlying continuities at a deeper, methodological level" (1972, pp. 105–106).

The figure most responsible for the change of perspective and the so-called historicist turn in philosophy of science in the 1960s was Thomas Kuhn. He laid emphasis on revolutions and radical conceptual change in science and acknowledged the implications of these claims. Kuhn held a PhD in physics from Harvard University but began his professional career as a historian of science teaching a General Education in Science course designed by the then president of Harvard, James Bryant Conant. His close reading of historical texts in this connection alerted him to the irreducible variability of scientific concepts and led him to question the idealized image of science which assimilated all possible theories to a standard model. In the first page of his celebrated book, *The Structure of Scientific Revolutions* (1970), he states his aim of sketching "[a] quite different concept of science that can emerge from the historical record of the research activity itself". By studying the details of particular historical cases Kuhn came to appreciate the significance of scientific education. He realized that what binds scientists together in a specific tradition, what gives their practice its character and coherence, is not a neutral, ubiquitous, formal description of theories which is based on some inter-subjectively avowed observation sentences, but exposure of students to concrete problem solutions, the paradigms or exemplars,[40] which may vary and which function as models for further research.[41] The process of initiation and training involves doing, rather dogmatically, "finger exercises", that is, learning, usually through textbooks, and then imitating, particular applications of concepts, particular ways of dealing with problems, particular techniques of using instruments and doing research. The consensus and the effectiveness of science are not earned theoretically but practically. Scientists do not need to concern themselves with abstract, explicit definitions, comprising necessary and sufficient conditions, in order to know how to apply a term. Nor do they need to reduce their practice to a set of abstract rules which capture what is essential in their field. Scientific education provides scientists with the ability, rather than the abstract knowledge of rules, to do successful research (1970, pp.43–51; cf. Kuhn, 1977).

Kuhn cites Wittgenstein and his idea of family resemblance to explain how different research problems and techniques are held together in a single tradition. They do not need to share a set of characteristics but are related between them in a network of resemblances overlapping and crisscrossing. In the case of concepts, such as, *game*, *chair*, *leaf*, *planet*, *mass*, *motion*, etc., again, the idea is that one does not need to know a set of attributes, the necessary and sufficient conditions, in order to apply the corresponding term. Now, this understanding of concepts — as abilities to use terms, which is a long way from the entity account involving a seepage of meaning from an observational basis through correspondence rules to an uninterpreted calculus — implies that when there is a change in the exemplars used in teaching there is going to be a change of concepts or, what amounts to the same thing, a change in the meaning of terms.

The change of exemplars is not forced upon scientists by the world as such nor is it brought about de novo. Kuhn emphasizes the indispensability of commitment to the tradition built around previously upheld theories as a condition of innovation and change. This is what he calls the "essential tension" implicit in scientific research (1977, pp. 227, 236). There is, on the one hand, firm, or even dogmatic, adherence to deeply ingrained patterns of research, and, on the other, a constant pursuit of novel ideas and discoveries. Scientists are pulled in both directions: they are traditionalists and iconoclasts at the same time (ibid., p. 227). According to Kuhn, only if scientists are well acquainted with the problems to be tackled and the techniques appropriate for use, can they be able to spot and evaluate anomalies which may arise in the course of their research. "[N]ovelty ordinarily emerges only for the man who, knowing with precision what he should expect, is able to recognize that something has gone wrong" (1970, p. 65). Tradition-bound research is called by Kuhn normal science. In this mode, scientists undertake to solve puzzles, that is, problems very similar to the textbook paradigms, which have solutions that are anticipated,[42] trying more to prove their own ingenuity rather than shatter the tradition and start a new one. Yet, their practice, conservative as it may be, paves the way to change, both on a regular basis — in the course of normal science — but also in revolutionary moments. When anomalies persist, when they become central to the investigation and when they preclude applications which are of practical importance, scientists need to reconsider their strong commitments and inherited beliefs. They proceed, then, to reconstruct their field in an effort to assimilate new solutions and new theories. This is not always achieved in a smooth way and what usually emerges is not a cumulative result. "Contrary to a prevalent impression, most new discoveries and theories in the sciences are not merely additions to the existing stockpile of scientific knowledge. To assimilate them the scientist must usually rearrange the intellectual and manipulative equipment he has previously relied upon, discarding some elements of his prior belief and practice while finding new significances in and new relationships between many others. Because the old must be revalued and reordered when assimilating the new, discovery and invention in the sciences are usually intrinsically revolutionary" (Kuhn, 1977, pp. 226–227).[43] Revolutionary shifts, which Kuhn sees as displacements of the conceptual networks through which scientists view the world (1970, p. 102), are rather rare but, he also notes, that "the historian constantly encounters many far smaller but structurally similar revolutionary episodes [which] are central to scientific advance" (1977, p. 226). So, scientific practice is a dynamic, developmental process punctuated occasionally by radical changes which produce theories that are incommensurable with the previous ones. This means that the new theories cannot be mapped onto the old, new relations are established between concepts and laws and new exemplars occupy the knots in the new framework. The two systems, old and new, lack a common core or a common measure.[44] Concepts in the new context, even when they continue to be named by the terms used in the previous theories, or even when there is quantitative agreement in calculations that involve them, still are viewed by Kuhn to be markedly different. "[T]the physical referents of ... the Einsteinian concepts are by no means identical with those of the Newtonian concepts that bear the same name. (Newtonian mass is conserved; Einstenian is convertible with energy. Only at low relative velocities may the two be measured in the same way, and even then they must not be conceived to be the same.)" (Kuhn, 1970, p. 102). The difference in the concepts of two successive theories lies in the different applications they have and the different connections they enter. There is no discussion of tracing a common meaning in some common observational content because terms in Kuhn's framework do not acquire meaning by being anchored to experience but by being taught in practice in specific applications.

EARLY RECEPTION OF THE HISTORICIST ACCOUNT OF CONCEPTUAL CHANGE

Feyerabend's and Kuhn's theses on conceptual change and incommensurability were received rather unfavorably by philosophers of science.[45] The main thrust of the criticism concerned the unpalatable consequences of incommensurability. First, it was claimed that if the incommensurability thesis "were true, no theory could contradict another" (Achinstein, 1968, p. 92). This can be shown by means of a historical example. The quantum theory of the atom, proposed by Niels Bohr in 1913, was supposed to contradict classical electromagnetic theory. According to the former theory, electrons orbiting around the nucleus (i.e., undergoing accelerated motion) did not radiate, in violation of the laws of the latter theory. If the term "electron" meant different things in the context of the two theories, however, there would be no contradiction between the quantum and the classical descriptions. A second, related difficulty is that if conceptual change were as radical as portrayed by Feyerabend and Kuhn, then two incommensurable theories would not even have a common subject matter. For instance, if the concepts of Newtonian mechanics and the concepts of relativity theory referred to different entities, they could not be alternative accounts of the same domain. Third, if the principles of a theory constituted the meanings of its terms, then those principles would have to be analytic statements. That is, they would have to be devoid of empirical content. A fourth difficulty concerned the process of learning a scientific theory. If the meaning of theoretical terms were theory-dependent, then "a person could not learn a theory by having it explained to him using any words whose meanings he understands before he learns the theory" (ibid., p. 7).

The root of these difficulties seemed to be Feyerabend's and Kuhn's claim that scientific concepts (or, equivalently, the meanings of scientific terms) were determined by the theoretical framework in which they were embedded. Several critics stressed the obscurity of this claim and pointed out that it was not supported by a full-fledged theory of meaning. Dudley Shapere was among the sharpest early critics of Kuhn and Feyerabend. In his critical review of *The Structure of Scientific Revolutions*, Shapere argued that "Kuhn has offered us no clear analysis of 'meaning' or, more specifically, no criterion of change of meaning" (Shapere, 1964, p. 390). He made a similar point against Feyerabend: "We are given no way of deciding either what counts as a part of the 'meaning' of a term or what counts as a 'change of meaning' of a term" (Shapere, 1981, pp. 41–42). Furthermore, the theoretical context of a term, which supposedly determined its meaning, was not fully specified. It was unclear, for example, whether the metaphysical beliefs of the creator of a theory play a role in determining the meaning of its terms (ibid., p. 42).

A similar problem was pointed out by Hilary Putnam. If the meaning of a term depends on its theoretical context, then are there parts of the context that may change without affecting the term's meaning (Putnam, 1975e, pp. 124–125)? Conversely, would every kind of theory change affect the meaning of its terms? Feyerabend acknowledged that certain minor variations of a theory would not impinge on the meanings of its terms. For example, the meaning of "force" would not change if we moved from classical mechanics to a similar theory that differs from classical mechanics only with respect to "the strength of the gravitation potential" (Feyerabend, 1981, p. 97).

As we saw in the previous section, Feyerabend attempted to respond to this difficulty by linking meaning with classification:

> a diagnosis of *stability of meaning* involves two elements. First, reference is made to rules according to which objects or events are collected into classes. We may say that such rules determine concepts or kinds of objects. Secondly, it is found that the changes brought about by a new point of view occur *within* the extension of these classes and, therefore, leave the concepts unchanged. Conversely, we shall diagnose a *change of meaning* either if a new theory entails that all concepts of the preceding theory have extension zero or if it introduces rules which cannot be interpreted as attributing specific properties to objects within already existing classes, but which change the system of classes itself. (ibid., p. 28)

However, this proposal also faced problems. First, for a new theory to entail "that all concepts of the preceding theory have extension zero", a common core of meaning must be shared by the two theories (Achinstein, 1968, p. 95; Shapere, 1981, p. 52). Second, Feyerabend's construal of meaning change as the outcome of classification change presupposes the absolute character of rules of classification. However, the existence of such rules in science is questionable. Scientific classifications often have a pragmatic character and they need not reflect the intrinsic properties of the entities classified. One may choose classificatory rules so as to make the existing system of classification immune to theory change (see Shapere, 1981, pp. 51–52).

A different line of attack against incommensurability focused on its incompatibility with the success of translation practices. Among the most prominent critics who followed this line were Donald Davidson and Hilary Putnam.[46] Davidson criticized incommensurability in a celebrated article where he denied the possibility of radically different systems of concepts or "conceptual schemes" (Davidson, 1984). He associated conceptual schemes with languages and claimed that two conceptual schemes could differ only if the languages that bear them were not intertranslatable. The difference of two conceptual schemes must, thus, have a linguistic manifestation: "two people have different conceptual schemes if they speak languages that fail of intertranslatability" (Davidson, 1984, p. 185). The impossibility of translation would preclude communication between two such speakers.

Furthermore, if there were texts written in a language incommensurable to our own, they would be impossible to translate and ipso facto to understand. The existence of such texts, however, is belied by the successful interpretive practice of historians, such as Kuhn himself. Kuhn has been able to decipher and convey the content of purportedly incommensurable concepts, found in past scientific texts, using the resources of contemporary language. The existence of incommensurability is called into question by that very interpretive success: "Kuhn is brilliant at saying what things were like before the revolution using — what else? — our post-revolutionary idiom" (ibid., p. 184). Thus, "Instead of living in different worlds, Kuhn's scientists may ... be only words apart" (ibid., p. 189).

Along the same lines, Putnam maintained that if the incommensurability thesis "were really true then we could not translate other languages — or even past stages of our own language — at all. And if we cannot interpret organisms' noises at all, then we have no grounds for regarding them as *thinkers*, *speakers*, or even *persons*" (Putnam, 1981, p. 114). Furthermore, incommensurability is at odds with historical analysis: "To tell us that Galileo had 'incommensurable' notions *and then to go on to describe them at length* is really incoherent" (ibid., p. 115).[47]

THE FIRST RESPONSE TO INCOMMENSURABILITY:
A FLIGHT TO REFERENCE

The first attempt to come to terms with the difficulties encountered by incommensurability by developing an alternative analysis of conceptual change was made by Israel Scheffler. Scheffler accepted the holistic account of meaning, which was shared by logical positivists and their historicist critics (Scheffler, 1982, pp. 45–46). He pointed out, however, an ambiguity of the word "meaning". On the one hand, the meaning of a word is "a matter of the concept or idea expressed", that is, it concerns "the connotation, intension, attribute, or sense associated with the word". On the other hand, the meaning of a word is "rather a matter of the thing *referred* to", that is, it concerns "the denotation, extension, application, or reference of the word" (ibid., pp. 54–55).

Scheffler argued "that, for the purposes of mathematics and science, it is sameness of reference that is of interest rather than synonymy [sameness of meaning], in accordance with the general principle that a truth about any object is equally true of it no matter how the object is designated." (ibid., p. 57). That is, a concept associated with a word may change without affecting the truth values of the statements containing the word, provided that its referent remains invariant. Furthermore, the stability of a term's referent makes possible a genuine disagreement between two users of the term who, nevertheless, associate different concepts with it. Finally, because of referential stability, conceptual change does not undermine the validity of scientific deductions. Thus, pace Feyerabend, Hempel's deductive-nomological model of explanation and Nagel's account of reduction qua deductive explanation remain applicable to actual cases of scientific explanation and scientific change (ibid., pp. 61–62).

Here it is important to point out that Scheffler did not rule out the possibility of referential variance. Rather his point was that conceptual change did not *necessarily* imply instability of reference. He did not spell out, however, his proposal to disentangle meaning and reference in terms of a developed theory of meaning. Such a theory, which would be developed by Hilary Putnam, would have to show how the reference of a term can be fixed without invoking the full concept associated with it.

MEETING THE HISTORICIST CHALLENGE: THE CAUSAL THEORY OF MEANING

The account of meaning that Putnam developed in the early 1970s was meant to be an alternative to both the logical positivist and the historicist views of meaning. In 1962 he had criticized the logical positivist distinction between observational and theoretical terms, arguing that it could not be explicated in terms of the distinction between observable and unobservable entities. Theoretical terms (e.g., "satellite") may refer to observable objects and observational terms (e.g., "particles too little to see") may refer to unobservable entities (Putnam, 1962, p. 218). Putnam's critique indicated that meaning should not be tied "too closely to the observable" (Ben-Menahem, 2005, p. 8). Furthermore, the historicist, contextual account of meaning was also problematic.[48] Historicists insisted on the theory-dependence of meaning. Furthermore, they stressed the ubiquitous presence of theory change in the historical development of the sciences. These two theses, along with the Fregean assumption that meaning determines reference, implied that the ontology of science has been in flux. For a scientific realist, as Putnam was at the time, that was an unacceptable consequence.

Putnam acknowledged "that meaning change and theory change cannot be sharply separated" (Putnam, 1975h, p. 255).[49] Furthermore, theories may not describe the world correctly and, therefore, "Meanings may not fit the world; and meaning change can be forced by empirical discoveries" (ibid., p. 256). Thus, the problem situation faced by Putnam was to come up with an account of meaning that would allow for meaning change, while neutralizing its *prima facie* relativist and anti-realist implications.

Putnam explicated the notion of meaning in terms of the notions of communication and teaching. "It is a fact ... that the use of words can be taught. If someone does not know the meaning of 'lemon', I can somehow convey it to him. ... in this simple phenomenon lies the problem, and hence the *raison d'être*, of 'semantic theory'" (ibid., p. 147). The meaning of natural kind terms, including those put forward in scientific theories, is not specified by a set of necessary and sufficient conditions that govern its application. Thus, it cannot be conveyed by "an analytic definition (i.e., an analytically necessary and sufficient condition). ... *Theoretical terms* in science have no analytic definitions" (ibid., p. 146). Furthermore, the meaning of a natural kind word, say "tiger", does not involve "the totality of accepted scientific theory about tigers, or even the totality of what I believe about tigers" (ibid., p. 147). If that were the case, then it would be impossible to teach anyone the meaning of a natural kind term he or she does not know. Rather, to get to know the meaning of such a term one needs to learn certain "core facts" about a "normal member of the kind" (ibid., p. 148). This is not sufficient, however, for learning the meaning of the term in question. One needs, in addition, to become acquainted with the reference of the term, that is, with the actual entities denoted by the term.

Putnam conceded that the meaning of scientific terms is, partly, theory-dependent. He suggested, however, that the reference of those terms is fixed not by theoretical beliefs, but through our causal interaction with the world.[50] For example,

> No matter how much our theory of electrical charge may change, there is one element in the meaning of the term 'electrical charge' that has not changed in the last two hundred years, according to a realist, and that is the reference. 'Electrical charge' *refers to the same magnitude* even if our theory of that magnitude has changed drastically. And we can identify that magnitude in a way that is independent of all but the most violent theory change by, for example, singling it out as the magnitude which is causally responsible for certain effects. (Putnam 1975b, p. ix)

Thus, our causal interaction with electrical charges plays a double role: First, it fixes the reference of "electrical charge"; and, second, it renders the reference in question immune to any revision of our theoretical beliefs about electrical charges. In general, theory change does not affect the reference of natural kind terms, which are used "to refer to a thing which belongs to a natural kind which does *not* fit the 'theory' associated with the natural kind term, but which was believed to fit that theory ... when the theory had not yet been falsified" (Putnam, 1975f, p. 143).

Putnam allowed for the possibility "that a concept may contain elements which are not correct" (Putnam, 1975g, p. 196). However, if the progress of science leads to the rejection of certain elements of a concept, its extension need not be affected: "concepts which are not strictly speaking true of anything may yet refer to something; and concepts in different theories may refer to the same thing" (ibid., p. 197). Different speakers need not associate the same concept with a term, say "electricity", in order to refer to the same entity. What they should share is " that each of them is connected by a certain kind of causal chain to a situation in which a *description* of electricity is given, and generally a *causal* description – that is, one which singles out electricity as *the* physical magnitude *responsible* for certain effects in a certain way" (ibid., p. 200).

But what exactly is a concept? Putnam evaded the question and focused instead on what it means to *have a* concept. Following Wittgenstein, he suggested that possessing a concept amounts to having certain perceptual and linguistic abilities: "an organism possesses a *minimal concept* of a chair if it can recognize a chair when it sees one, and ... it possesses a *full-blown concept* of a chair if it can employ the usual sentences containing the word *chair* in some natural language" (Putnam, 1975c, p. 3). Furthermore, "two people have the *same* concept ... [when they have] the same set of linguistic and nonlinguistic abilities in a certain respect" (ibid., p. 8). Given that concept possession is largely a matter of linguistic skills, it follows "that a great deal of philosophy should be *reconstrued* as about language ... In particular, all of the traditional philosophy about 'ideas', 'concepts', etc." (ibid., p. 9). It should, therefore, occasion no surprise that, in philosophy of science the problem of conceptual change has been approached, for the most part, through linguistic categories, such as meaning and reference. Putnam, for instance, explicitly identified meaning with "what it is to have a concept of something" (ibid., p. 16).

Nevertheless, according to Putnam, there is an important difference between concepts and meanings. The former are possessed by individuals, whereas the latter have a social character—they are possessed by a linguistic group (cf. Putnam, 1983, p. 75). Only certain people in a linguistic community, the relevant experts, have a mastery of the concepts associated with certain words. Only metallurgists, for instance, grasp fully the concept of gold. The meaning of 'gold', on the other hand, is possessed collectively by a whole community:

> everyone to whom gold is important for any reason has to *acquire* the word 'gold'; but he does not have to acquire the *method of recognizing* whether something is or is not gold. He can rely on a special subclass of speakers. The features that are generally thought to be present in connection with a general name — necessary and sufficient conditions for membership in the extension, etc. — are all present n the linguistic community *considered as a collective body*; but that collective body divides the "labor" of knowing and employing these various parts of the "meaning" of 'gold'. (Putnam, 1973, p. 705)

We think, however, that one still has the option to identify meanings with the concepts possessed by the relevant experts. This would imply that most of us have an inadequate mastery of the meaning of many of the words we use. But this is hardly a problem. There is no reason to pretend that a layman knows the meaning of a natural-kind term, when there are many situations in which he or she could not use this term correctly.

Moreover, Putnam argued strenuously that the concept we associate with a natural-kind term does not determine its reference. We have already seen that two speakers who associate different concepts with the same term may still refer to the same entity. Furthermore, two speakers may share the same concept and, nevertheless, refer to different things. Putnam exhibited this possibility by means of a thought experiment involving "twin earth", a fictitious planet that is identical with our earth in every respect save for the microscopic constitution of water. A speaker on earth and his counterpart on "twin earth" share the same concept of water (transparent, odorless, thirst-quenching liquid). They nevertheless refer to different things when they use the term "water". The speaker on earth refers to H_2O, whereas his counterpart refers to XYZ (ibid., pp. 701ff).

Natural-kind concepts do not determine the reference of the corresponding natural-kind terms because these terms have an "indexical" character. That is, they resemble words such as "I" or "this" whose reference depends on the spatial and temporal context in which they are used. The term "water", for instance, refers to "stuff that bears a certain similarity relation to the water *around here*" (ibid., p. 710).

Putnam developed a full-fledged account of meaning and reference in a paper entitled the "Meaning of 'Meaning'", where he articulated his insights about the indexical and social character of meaning and, especially, reference (Putnam, 1975h; cf. Floyd, 2005). To explicate the notion of meaning he introduced the notion of a stereotype associated with a natural kind, namely

> a standardized description of features of the kind that are typical, or 'normal', or at any rate stereotypical. The central features of the stereotype generally are *criteria* — features which in normal situations constitute ways of recognizing if a thing belongs to the kind or, at least, necessary conditions (or probabilistic necessary conditions) for membership in the kind. (Putnam, 1975h, p. 230)

Thus, possessing the main characteristics of the stereotype associated with a term is necessary for being able to use that term correctly. In actual scientific practice, however, those characteristics are not used as necessary and sufficient conditions. Rather they are employed as "*approximately* correct characterizations of some world of theory-independent entities" (ibid., p. 237). Furthermore, stereotypes are associated with "conventional ideas, which may be inaccurate. I am suggesting that just such a conventional idea is associated with 'tiger', with 'gold', etc., and, moreover, that this is the sole element of truth in the 'concept' theory" (ibid., p. 250). Recalling Putnam's discussion of concept possession, we may identify stereotypes with concepts. In his more recent work, Putnam suggested a similar view:

> I myself would regard possession of the *stereotype* — not the *theory* — that electrons are charged particles ("little balls" with trajectories and unit negative charge) as part of our concept of the electron. On my view, stereotypes are far more stable than theories, and contribute to the identity of our natural kind concepts *without* providing necessary and sufficient conditions for their correct applications. They cannot do the last because, in cases like this one, they are known to be "oversimplified". (Putnam, 1992, p. 445)

Thus, the deliberate simplification (or, we would add, idealization) of the stereotypic features is one more reason why these features cannot function as necessary and sufficient conditions.

Putnam made a further step away from the conception of meaning as a set of necessary and sufficient conditions. He disentangled meaning from analyticity. In traditional semantic theory the meaning of a natural kind term is specified by a set of features, whose attribution to the kind in question is a matter of analytic stipulation. The statement that members of the kind have these features is an analytic truth. Putnam, on the other hand, following Quine's well-known critique of the analytic-synthetic distinction (Quine, 1951), rejected the traditional view. Consider, for instance, the attribution of stripes to tigers:

> there is a perfectly good sense in which being striped is part of the meaning of 'tiger'. But it does not follow … that 'tigers are striped' is analytic. If a mutation occurred, all tigers might be albinos. Communication presupposes that I have a stereotype of tigers which includes stripes, and that you have a stereotype of tigers which includes stripes … But it does not presuppose that any particular stereotype be *correct*, or that the majority of our stereotypes remain correct forever. Linguistic obligatoriness is not supposed to be an index of unrevisability or even of truth; thus we can hold that 'tigers are striped' is part of the meaning of 'tiger' without being trapped in the problems of analyticity. (Putnam, 1975h, p. 256.

Thus, our meaning-constitutive (and *ipso facto* concept-constitutive) beliefs about natural kinds can be revised without change of subject matter. Our revised beliefs may still be about the "same things".[51]

If analytic definitions (or necessary and sufficient conditions) do not provide the means to understand meaning, then a novel account of meaning is needed. "The meaning of 'meaning'" provides such an account, according to which the meaning of a word is represented by a four-dimensional "vector" with the following components: "(1) the syntactic markers that apply to the word, e.g. 'noun'; (2) the semantic markers that apply to the word, e.g. 'animal', 'period of time'; (3) a description of the additional features of the stereotype, if any; (4) a description of the extension" (ibid., p. 269). The semantic markers consist of those features of the stereotype that "attach with enormous centrality to the [corresponding] words … form part of a widely used and important *system of classification*", and are "*qualitatively* harder to revise" than the rest (ibid., p. 267). In Putnam's view, "[t]he centrality guarantees that items classified under these headings virtually never have to be *re*classified" (ibid., pp. 267–268). Furthermore, the final component of a term's meaning is its extension, which is identified by means of a (fallible) description. Since the meaning of a term includes its extension, it follows that meanings should be distinguished from concepts (cf. Floyd, 2005, p. 23).

Putnam's account of meaning allows for conceptual change. The stereotype (the concept) we associate with a term may change under empirical pressure. However, conceptual change need not be accompanied by ontological shifts. Two successive scientific concepts may differ and, nevertheless, refer to the same thing(s). Thus, Putnam has offered us a way to take on board some of the historicist insights about the development of the sciences without, however, succumbing to their more radical relativist and anti-realist inclinations.

Putnam's promising approach to meaning and conceptual change has also encountered difficulties. Discussing these difficulties in detail would lead us too far astray. We will just sketch one of the most important.[52] The difficulty in question derives from the realist presuppositions of Putnam's account of meaning. As we have seen, the users of a natural kind term belong to a linguistic community which has "contact with the natural kind" (Putnam, 1975g, p. 205). There are two problems here. First, when the term in question denotes unobservable entities, such as the electron, it is unclear whether the required "contact" is available. Second, it has often been the case that words referring to putative natural kinds, such as "phlogiston" or "ether", turned out to be empty. In those cases the presumed "contact" was clearly missing. Thus, it would follow from Putnam's account of meaning that the users of those terms were not linguistically competent! Putnam realized that "it may seem counterintuitive that a natural kind word such as 'horse' is sharply distinguished from a term for a fictitious or non-existent natural kind such as 'unicorn', and that a physical magnitude term such as 'electricity' is sharply distinguished from a term for a fictitious or nonexistent physical magnitude or substance such as 'phlogiston'" (ibid., p. 206).

However, he did not seem to take into account that those who introduced and used those terms did so for similar reasons, namely to make sense of various observed phenomena. And that for some time theories based on 'electricity' and 'phlogiston' were equally viable accounts of their respective domains. It is unclear why our different (retrospective) judgments concerning the (non-)existence of phlogiston and electricity should lead us to different semantic stances towards the corresponding terms.

Despite its problems, Putnam's account of meaning has been one of the most articulate attempts to face the challenge that Feyerabend's and Kuhn's historicist accounts of conceptual change posed for the philosophy of science. Another such attempt was by Kuhn himself, who tried to come to terms with the difficulties faced by his early formulation of incommensurability. Kuhn's more recent work will be the subject of the next section.

KUHN'S EXPLICATION OF INCOMMENSURABILITY

Some of Kuhn's philosophical insights were an outgrowth of his experience as an interpreter of past scientific texts. One of those insights was incommensurability, which Kuhn regarded as the key notion of his philosophy of scientific development. During the 1980s and 1990s, he defended this notion against the criticisms that had been raised against it, and he attempted to explicate and develop it further (Kuhn, 2000).

As we have seen, two of those criticisms were particularly forceful. First, Kuhn's critics claimed that incommensurability implies incomparability and, therefore, renders rational theory-choice impossible. Second, incommensurability was construed as untranslatability and was declared to be at odds with the interpretive practices of historians of science. The purported incommensurability between past scientific theories and their contemporary descendants would imply that a translation of those theories to a modern scientific idiom is impossible. However, historians of science, such as Kuhn himself, have been able to translate past scientific texts, belonging to a discourse purportedly incommensurable to our own, to equivalents that are accessible to a modern audience. Thus, the incommensurability thesis is undermined by the very success of the historiography which it inspired.

Kuhn denied both of these critiques. First, he maintained that incommensurability does not imply incomparability. The term "incommensurability" was appropriated from geometry, where a comparison of incommensurable magnitudes is possible. The same is true of incommensurable theories. The fact that there is no common language in which the assertions of two incommensurable theories can be expressed does not preclude the comparison of the theories in question. Comparative theory-evaluation does not require the existence of such a common language.

Second, Kuhn resisted the identification of the interpretive practice of historians with a translation process. The aim of the historiographical enterprise is to understand, as opposed to translate, alien scientific texts. It is true that texts written in a language incommensurable to our own are impossible to translate. However, they are not impossible to understand, by acquiring from scratch the language in which they were written.

Having responded to criticism, Kuhn proceeded to develop a fuller account of incommensurability as a manifestation of a deeper mismatch between two linguistic structures. The language in which a scientific theory is formulated incorporates a taxonomic structure of natural kinds. These structures are subject to the so-called no-overlap condition. That is, no entity can belong to more than one natural kind. In Kuhn's words, "[t]here are no dogs that are also cats" (Kuhn, 2000, p. 92). The only case where this condition is not fulfilled is when one natural kind is part of another, more inclusive one. For example, cats are also mammals. Incommensurability is now conceived as the outcome of a violation of the no-overlap condition. Two incommensurable taxonomic structures contain overlapping natural kinds — kinds which have some members in common. The overlap has to be partial — the one kind must have members that do not belong to the other and vice versa. If, on the one hand, the overlap were complete then the two taxonomies would obviously coincide. If, on the other hand, there were no overlap at all, it would be possible to construct a more inclusive taxonomy incorporating each of the taxonomic structures in question. The natural-kind terms of this extended taxonomy could be used to express any assertion that can be formulated within each of the languages corresponding to the two more restricted taxonomies. In that case incommensurability would not arise.

When, however, two taxonomies partially overlap, it is not possible to subsume both of them under a wider taxonomic framework. Any framework that would subsume one of the taxonomies in question could not accommodate the other and vice versa. Such a framework would have to include overlapping natural kinds, which are ruled out by the no-overlap condition. In the absence of such a framework no language can be found that would provide a common ground between the taxonomies in question; hence incommensurability.

Taxonomic incommensurability can now be used to re-conceptualize scientific revolutions. These are episodes in the history of science where a whole taxonomic structure is replaced by its incommensurable successor, whose natural kinds partially overlap with some of the natural kinds that were hitherto in place. As a result of this overlap, the new taxonomy cannot subsume the old one. As an example, consider the transition from Ptolemaic to Copernican astronomy in the 16th century. In the Ptolemaic taxonomy of the heavens, planets were identified as those heavenly bodies which moved with respect to the fixed stars. They were seven: Moon, Mercury, Venus, Sun, Mars, Jupiter, and Saturn. In the Copernican taxonomic structure, on the other hand, planets were identified as those heavenly bodies which moved around the sun. They were six: Mercury, Venus, Earth, Mars, Jupiter, and Saturn. Obviously, there is a partial overlap between the Ptolemaic and the Copernican classificatory schemes. Because of this overlap some of the assertions of Ptolemaic astronomy regarding "planets" cannot be expressed in Copernican terms; hence the incommensurability between the Ptolemaic and the Copernican conceptual schemes.[53]

The reformulation of scientific revolutions in Kuhn's later writings goes as far as dimming the light on discontinuous change. Kuhn now speaks of two lexicons "used at two widely separated times" (Kuhn, 2000, p. 87), leaving aside and in the shadow the processes that made these lexicons possible and through which they came about. The philosopher studies two distant in time, frozen, taxonomic structures trying to detect congruence, compatibility and overlap, whereas the historian may try to uncover the micro-processes by which change is effected and which take place in the in-between transitional periods.

The emphasis given in Kuhn's later writings to some kind of continuity rather than abrupt change is also brought out in his analogy between revolutions in science and speciation in biological evolution (ibid., p. 98; see also Kuhn, 1970, pp. 171–173). In both cases, a slow, steady development driven from behind is occasionally marked by episodes which yield new specialties in science and new species in nature that branch off from the trunk of knowledge or the biological tree respectively. Breakdowns of communication in science are compared to reproductive isolation of populations in nature and are taken to be signals of crises (Kuhn, 2000, p. 100). Discourse, however, among scientists across the divide of incommensurable taxonomies still goes on, Kuhn admits, "however imperfectly" (ibid., p. 88), by using, for instance, metaphor and other linguistic tropes.

Focus on evolution and continuity rather than revolution and discontinuity in Kuhn's later writings may not have eliminated the idea of incommensurability, which has become local and has been understood as incongruity of clusters of partially overlapping conceptual frameworks, but has given rise to concerns regarding the Kuhnian project itself. Kuhn, supposedly, modified his philosophy to make more plausible the history of science which he saw as advancing through revolutions. If now evolution is substituted for revolution, "what point could there be in talking about Kuhnian revolutions at all?" (Machamer, 2007, p. 43). Kuhn's model was introduced as revisionist, upsetting the standard cumulative account of scientific development but, according to this critic, through its transformations, ended up looking very much like the one it displaced.

A second problem concerns the notion of local incommensurability. As we saw, in order to have local incommensurability between frameworks there needs to exist partial overlap between them. Two things can be said here: first, one may maintain that partial overlap between theories is likely to hold in most cases since theories develop out of earlier ones or, in case they are contemporaneous, they develop against each other (Fine, 1975, p. 30).[54] If this is true, then the thesis of incommensurability becomes trivialized. The second thing that can be said in relation to overlap is that instead of viewing it as a condition of incommensurability, one may view it as a means of eliminating it. Assuming certain common things, those falling under the area of overlap, may be of help when we try to trace and unpack the mismatching incommensurable clusters (ibid.). With some effort, based on this common ground, critics say, one may access the problematic areas and achieve communication and translation. Kuhn would have conceded, we think, that a partial overlap between incommensurable taxonomic structures may provide the common ground necessary for communication, albeit not for translation.

Another area of concern is taxonomic structure itself. Are the classificatory systems that we find in conceptual frameworks arbitrary, conventional, up to the scientific communities, or do scientists "carve nature at its joints"? What kind of similarities do objects which fall under a category share? Are these similarities detected or imposed? All these issues are related to the problem of realism. If classification is conventional, then the fear is that we lapse into idealism and constructivism. If similarities between objects are to be read off from actual instances, then abstract concepts with no observable extensions available need to be dealt with differently.[55]

Even if we grant that incommensurability amounts to a disparity between local areas of classificatory systems, still, the question remains whether there might be conceptual change that does not involve reorganization of lexical structure. Is all conceptual change a matter of taxonomic change? Kuhn's analysis of incommensurability is applicable to concepts that pick out observable objects, which can be identified by ostension. On the other hand, his analysis of the meaning of theoretical concepts (such as force, mass, charge, and field) has not been sufficiently developed. Those concepts refer to entities, properties, and processes that are not directly accessible and their meaning is learned in the context of the application of scientific laws. When those laws are revised, the meanings of the concepts they contain should change accordingly. However, the source of incommensurability in such cases is rather unclear (see Andersen & Nersessian, 2000; Nersessian, 2002d).

A different set of criticisms concentrates on the contribution of individuals to conceptual change. Kuhn has stressed the role of scientific communities in bringing about conceptual change, but his account, especially in its late formulation where he considers whether developed taxonomic structures map onto each other, does not examine how the restructuring of categories is motivated and how it takes place (Nersessian, 1998, 2002d). This criticism is reinforced by the literature on conceptual change in educational contexts, which has also stressed "the active role of the individual in understanding or constructing new knowledge" (Vosniadou, 2007, p. 3). And this brings us to our final section.

UNDERSTANDING THE FINE STRUCTURE OF CONCEPTUAL
CHANGE IN SCIENCE

Kuhn's later work on incommensurability has deepened considerably our understanding of the structure of conceptual revolutions in science. Its main drawback, as we see it, is that it focuses exclusively on the beginning and the final stages of radical conceptual change. Thus, it gives no account of the fine-grained processes, the nitty-gritty details of the transition between two incommensurable conceptual frameworks. This shortcoming is characteristic of most philosophical theories of conceptual change, with the exception of those offered by Dudley Shapere and Nancy Nersessian.

Shapere rejects both the necessary and sufficient conditions view of concepts and the idea that concepts are fully theory-dependent. Rather he considers scientific concepts as trans-theoretical, as providing a common ground between successive scientific theories. He accepts that concepts evolve, but he stresses the "chain-of-reasoning" connections between the successive versions of a concept. These connections guarantee the continuity of conceptual change:

> that continuity, or, more importantly, the chain of reasons which produced that continuity/... alone justifies our speaking of "the concept" or "the meaning" of ... [a] term, and our speaking of the term having "the same reference". (Shapere, 1984, p. xxxiv)

Thus, for Shapere, it is important to focus on the specific reasons that motivate conceptual change in order to understand its continuity.

Nersessian has developed Shapere's insight into a full-blown account of conceptual change in science (see, e.g., Nersessian, 1984, 1987, 1992, 1995). She has pointed out that the problem of conceptual change has two salient aspects (Nersessian, 2001). The first is about finding a representation of concepts that could capture both their synchronic characteristics and their diachronic development. Nersessian rejects the necessary and sufficient conditions view of concepts, arguing that it cannot do justice to the fact that concepts are evolving entities. If the meaning of a concept were given by a set of necessary and sufficient conditions, then the concept in question could not evolve; it could only be replaced by an altogether different one. Thus, the necessary and sufficient conditions view obscures the significant continuity that characterizes the evolution of scientific concepts. To highlight the continuity of conceptual change, Nersessian has proposed a representation of concepts in terms of a "meaning-schema":

> The meaning of a scientific concept is a two-dimensional array which is constructed on the basis of its descriptive/explanatory function as it develops over time. I will call this array a "meaning schema". A "meaning schema" for a particular concept, would contain, width-wise, a summary of the features of each instance and, length-wise, a summary of the changes over time. (Nersessian 1984, p. 156)

The features that comprise the meaning of a particular instance of a concept concern "'stuff', 'function', 'structure", and 'causal power' ... Here, "stuff" includes what it is (with ontological status and reference); 'function' includes what it does; 'structure' includes mathematical structure; and 'causal power' includes its effects" (ibid., p. 157). This matrix-like representation of scientific concepts portrays their complex structure and their dynamic, evolving character. Furthermore, it reveals the significant continuity between successive versions of a concept. Tracing the career of scientific concepts by means of "meaning-schemata", it becomes evident that they change in a continuous, albeit non-cumulative, fashion (see, e.g., Nersessian, 1987, p. 163; 1992, p. 36).

The second and most neglected part of the problem of conceptual change is to account for the mechanisms of concept formation and to understand how new concepts develop out of older conceptual frameworks. Recently, many historians and philosophers of science have shifted the focus of their analyses from the products of scientific activity (codified in published papers and textbooks) to the cognitive and material practices of scientists (science in action). Nersessian's approach to conceptual change is in tune with this turn to practice. She insists that conceptual change cannot be adequately understood by focusing exclusively on the products of scientific theorizing, that is, on fully articulated conceptual structures. Rather, it "is to be understood in terms of the people who create and change their representations of nature and the practices they employ to do so" (Nersessian, 1992, p. 9). These practices consist in problem solving. Developing an insight of Karl Popper, who viewed the history of science as a history of problem situations, Nersessian has argued that concept formation has to be understood in the context of evolving problem situations:

> Historical investigations establish conceptual change to be a problem-solving process that is extended in time, dynamic in nature, and embedded in social contexts. New concepts do not emerge fully grown from the heads of scientists but are constructed in response to specific problems by systematic reasoning. (Nersessian & Andersen, 1997, p. 113)

The resources and the constraints for the construction of novel concepts are provided by the scientific and socio-cultural context in which problem-solving activity is embedded. This activity encompasses a rich repertoire of reasoning strategies, going well beyond induction and deduction, which have been the main preoccupation of philosophers of science. Those heuristic strategies include drawing analogies, constructing visual representations, forming idealizations and abstractions, and inventing thought experiments (see Nersessian 1988, 1992). Nersessian has argued that these strategies can be viewed as instances of model-based reasoning, which has received extensive attention in cognitive science (Nersessian 1999, 2002a, 2002b, 2002c).[56] On the plausible assumption that the cognitive capacities of scientists do not differ substantially from those of "ordinary" people, it becomes possible to draw on the resources provided by cognitive science to analyze the forms of reasoning employed in creative scientific work. The resulting rapprochement between history and philosophy of science and cognitive science promises to be beneficial to both parties.

Let us close with indicating briefly how Nersessian's analysis of conceptual change may resolve one of the thorny philosophical problems that were brought to the fore by historicist philosophers of science, namely the problem of scientific rationality. Historicists and their critics thought that conceptual change undermined the rationality of scientific development. If, say, Newtonian "mass" and relativistic "mass" are not the same concepts, then how can one rationally compare Newtonian mechanics and relativity theory? This difficulty, however, is an artifact of the way the problem of conceptual change was framed, that is, as a problem concerning the relationship between the beginning and the final stages of a long process. If, on the other hand, one examines the fine structure of that process, the problem dissolves. As a matter of fact, scientists never faced a situation where they had to compare Newtonian mechanics and relativity theory. The transition from Newtonian "mass" to relativistic "mass" passed through various developments in electromagnetic theory, most notably through H. A. Lorentz's theory of electrons, all of which were rational in the sense that they were adequate responses to particular problem situations. The conceptual transition from Newtonian to relativistic physics was a gradual and reasoned process. Thus, conceptual change in science can be fully compatible with an account of science as a rational enterprise (see Nersessian, 1987, p. 163).

ACKNOWLEDGMENTS

We thank Stella Vosniadou and Nancy Nersessian for their helpful suggestions. Theodore Arabatzis would also like to acknowledge the generous support of the Max Planck Institute for the History of Science, where part of his work for this chapter was carried out.

NOTES

1. This goal consisted in unifying the language and the laws of the various branches of science by deriving, for instance, the laws of psychology and social science from the laws of physics and biology (see Carnap, 1981).
2. Carnap in his *Aufbau* (1969) called it "constructional system of concepts".
3. Schlick, for instance, claimed that content is, by definition (1981, p. 142), inexpressible and incommunicable (ibid., p. 137), whereas structure can be shared. This can be illustrated with the example of colour. Different people may have different images and impressions of particular colours but the system of colours can be represented in a publicly visible structure which can be shared by all. This structure was the three–dimensional colour solid in the shape of a double cone on which the whole system of colours was exhibited. Colour samples of hues were arranged on it according to hue, saturation and brightness, giving a spatial and synoptic presentation of colour complexity. With this device even a blind person familiar with the structure of space, "which to him is a certain order of tactual and kinaesthetic sensations" (ibid., p. 138), can acquire and have the system of colours. Visual or tactual content (as a matter of individual experience) is not important for understanding and communication. What is important is structure.
4. Carnap does not include in the theory of science the study of the actual scientific activity, its historical development, the individual conditions of scientists, the society in which science is practiced. He thinks that these issues have a place in the *Encyclopedia* (1938), the project the logical positivists had conceived to advance the understanding of science, but he assigns them to sociology, psychology, or history of science.
5. "The word 'concept' is used in various ways; its sense is sometimes psychological, sometimes logical, and sometimes perhaps a confused mixture of both" (Frege, 1979b, p. 88).
6. Frege also insisted on distinguishing the psychological laws of thought from the laws of logic (1979d, p. 149).
7. 'Begriffsschrift' has also been translated as 'ideography'. See Van Heijenoort (1980).
8. For a concept to have sharp boundaries means that "every object must fall under it or not, tertium non datur" (Frege, 1997b, p. 298). If a concept does not satisfy this requirement, it is meaningless (Frege, 1979c, p.122).
9. Frege compares thought to the kernel that has to be separated from the verbal husk (1979d, p. 142).
10. Frege (1980a, p. 7) spoke of "break[ing] the domination of the word over the human spirit by laying bare the misconceptions that through the use of language often almost unavoidably arise concerning the relations between concepts and by freeing thought from that with which only the means of expression of ordinary language constituted as they are, saddle it".
11. Leibniz called it "the alphabet of thought" (Leibniz, 1989, p. 6). It was supposed to aid reasoning and communication by calculations upon signs of concepts.
12. Frege's technical term 'Bedeutung' has also been translated as 'reference', 'denotation' or 'nominatum'. We are following here the most recent consensus to standardize the translation as 'meaning'. Two are the major reasons that are given: (1) This is the most natural English equivalent and captures, normally, Frege's early, non-technical, use of the term; (2) any other translation (for instance, 'reference') would mean that the translator proceeds to give a particular interpretation of the development of Frege's thought. For a thorough discussion of the issue see Beaney (1997, pp. 36–46).

    Frege made the distinction between sense and meaning to account for the informativeness of identity statements. While 'a=a' is a tautology and carries no information, 'a=b' is a statement that purportedly extends knowledge. If 'a=b' is true it might appear that it is no different from 'a=a'. By distinguishing between Sinn and Bedeutung, Frege could account for the difference in the cognitive value of the two equalities: the two names, a and b, have the same meaning, or designate the same Bedeutung, but they have a different sense.

13. For the exegetical and philosophical controversies regarding Sinn and Bedeutung in Frege's philosophy see Beaney's Introduction to *The Frege Reader* (1997).

14. According to Carnap the two pairs coincide in "ordinary (extensional) contexts" (Carnap, 1988, p. 124), i.e., contexts like sentences, whose truth value does not change if we substitute an expression which occurs in them with another. For instance, the sentence "The Morning Star is the planet Venus" continues to be true if we substitute the name 'The Evening Star' for the name 'The Morning Star', whereas substituting the 'The Evening Star' for the 'The Morning Star' in the sentence "John believes that the Morning Star is the planet Venus" does not mean that the sentence will have the same truth value (intensional context). Carnap also finds a correlation among his distinction between 'extension' and 'intension', the distinction between 'extension' and 'comprehension' in the Port-Royal Logic and John Stuart Mill's distinction between 'denotation' and 'connotation' (ibid., p. 126).

15. It should be noted that according to Frege concept words, just like any other words, have meaning only in the context of a proposition.

16. Carnap (1969, p. 8), just as Frege, traces his project back to Leibniz's idea of *ars combinatoria* and *characteristica universalis*.

17. The statements which connect theoretical concepts and postulates to experience have been called "coordinative definitions" by Reichenbach, "correspondence rules" and "semantic rules" by Carnap, "bridge principles" by Hempel, "dictionary" by Campbell and Ramsey, "coordinative definitions", "operational definitions", "epistemic correlations", "interpretative principles" (see Feigl, 1970, Hempel, 1970).

18. The logical positivists were indebted to Hilbert for the idea of implicit definitions (Friedman, 1999, p. 100).

19. Carnap says that the language of objects lends itself to realism while the language of concepts to idealism (Carnap, 1969, p. 10).

20. In a similar vein, Sellars (1973) considers the issue of change of belief vs. change of meaning and discusses the difference between conflicting beliefs involving the same concepts and conflicting beliefs involving different but similar concepts.

21. Notice that Carnap speaks of one unifying language of science. Toulmin (1972, p. 62) calls attention to what Carl Hempel means by 'the language of science': "the lower functional calculus with individual constants … universal quantifiers for individual variables, and the connective symbols of denial, conjunction, alternation and implication". Once again, notes Toulmin, "the philosopher's version of 'the language of science' turns out to be, not a mode of discourse ever employed in the actual work of professional scientists, but that very symbolism of 20th-century formal logic whose relevance needs to be demonstrated" (ibid.).

22. Bas van Fraassen (2002, p.117) makes a similar point: "Modern empiricism's notion of experience harbored a major historical tactic for denial of genuine conceptual change. If experience speaks with the voice of an angel, then we have a constant bedrock on which to found both discourse and rational belief".

23. Carnap admits that the distinction between observable and non-observable is not a sharp one (1936–37, p. 455).

24. Hempel (1990, pp. 225–226) notes however the difficulty of giving such definitions.

25. One of Wittgenstein's examples is the notorious concept of 'game' (PI §§ 66–71).

26. The references given are only indicative. Similar remarks can be found in many other places in Wittgenstein's work. One may compare here Wittgenstein's vague and fluid concepts to Waismann's open terms (1978, pp. 119–124). Waismann contends that most empirical concepts have an "open texture", i.e., "are not delimited in all possible directions" (ibid., p. 120) — the "essential incompleteness of an empirical description (ibid., p. 121), which means that their definitions are always corrigible. Waismann distinguishes open texture from vagueness, — "Vagueness can be remedied by giving more accurate rules, open texture cannot" — but understands vagueness rather differently from Wittgenstein.

Waismann calls a word vague "if it is used in a fluctuating way (such as 'heap' or 'pink')" (ibid., p. 120) while Wittgenstein thinks that normally all concepts are vague because they cannot be given precise definitions. So, even the word 'gold', which Waismann takes to be of an open texture but not vague in its actual use (ibid.), would be considered vague by Wittgenstein, in non scientific contexts, in the sense that its application cannot be delimited.

27. "Am I inexact when I do not give our distance from the sun to the nearest foot, or tell a joiner the width of a table to the nearest thousandth of an inch?" (PI §88).

28. Wittgenstein (PI §71) contrasts his own understanding of concepts to Frege's: "Frege compares a concept to an area and says that an area with vague boundaries cannot be called an area at all. This presumably means that we cannot do anything with it. –But is it senseless to say: 'Stand roughly there'? Suppose that I were standing with someone in a city square and said that. As I say it I do not draw any kind of boundary, but perhaps point with my hand – as if I were indicating a particular *spot*. And this is just how one might explain to someone what a game is. One gives examples and intends them to be taken in a particular way."

29. "I reserve the right to decide in every new case whether I will count something as a game or not" (PG §73; cf. PG §71).

30. Notice that here Wittgenstein, contrary to how we normally see things, attributes arbitrariness to the adoption of a definition.

31. A more thorough discussion of these issues would certainly have to take into account the complexities of the rule-following literature, exegetical and generally philosophical. A sample of the debates can be found in (Miller & Wright 2002).

32. Feyerabend had a brief encounter with Wittgenstein in Vienna but his plans to study with him at Cambridge were foiled by Wittgenstein's death in 1951. In 1952, he wrote a critical review of the *Philosophical Investigations*, more of a pastiche of paraphrase and comments, which was translated from the German by G.E.M. Anscombe herself (a leading philosopher and one of Wittgenstein's literary executors) and published in *Philosophical Review* Vol. 64, No 3 in 1955, 449–483.

33. Hempel (1948, p. 135) also thought that explanation is "one of the foremost objectives of all rational inquiry".

34. However, in case the explanandum is a general regularity, no singular antecedent conditions are needed in the explanans.

35. Feyerabend (1981a) argues that the history of actual scientific practice does not satisfy the requirements of the deductive-nomological model of explanation and that these requirements cannot be satisfied and should not be satisfied from the perspective of a "disinfected" or "sound" empiricism (ibid., pp. 47, 57, 76). His basic idea is that empiricism will admit and even require theories that are "factually adequate and yet mutually inconsistent" (ibid., p. 73) in order both to avoid dogmatism and maximize empirical content by encouraging the testing of theories against each other and not solely against their own empirical consequences. According to Feyerabend, the formal models of explanation and reduction do not take this version of the underdetermination thesis into account and require that theories be uniquely determined by facts and reduced to a single, comprehensive, theory.

36. Feyerabend explicitly connects contextual theory of meaning to Wittgenstein's philosophy but he wrongly criticizes Wittgenstein for allegedly replacing Platonism of concepts by Platonism of language-games (1981a, p. 74n68).

37. Hanson (1958, chapter 1) invokes Wittgenstein's philosophy constantly in his discussion of the theory-ladenness of observation. Feyerabend in his autobiography (1996, p. 140) cites three books that had influenced him in this respect: Bruno Snell's *The Discovery of the Mind*, New York: Dover (1982), first published in 1953, Heinrich Schäfer's *Principles of Egyptian Art*, Oxford: Griffith Institute (1987), first published in German in 1963, and Vasco Ronchi's *Optics, The Science of Vision*, New York: Dover Publications (1991) first published in 1957. In *Against Method* (1978, p. 133), he also cites Wittgenstein.

38. Toulmin feared that if we ignore the continuous evolution of science, "as philosophers, we may end, by replacing the living science which is our object of study by a formal and frozen abstraction, forget-

ting to show how the results of these formal enquiries bear on the intellectual and practical business in which working scientists are engaged" (1961, p. 109). And in his later work (1972, p. 59), he underscored the same point: "By analyzing our standards of rational judgement in abstract terms, we avoid (it is true) the immediate problem of historical *relativism*; but we do so only at the price of replacing it by a problem of historical relevance."

39. "Men who accept different ideals and paradigms have really no common theoretical terms in which to discuss their problems fruitfully. They will not even have the same problem: events which are 'phenomena' in one's man's eyes will be passed over by the other as 'perfectly natural'" (Toulmin 1961, p. 57).

40. Kuhn in *The Structure of Scientific Revolution* (1970) used the term paradigm in at least two different senses: one wide and one narrow. In the narrow sense a paradigm is a concrete exemplar or model. In the wide sense a paradigm is the tradition built around one or several exemplars. In his *Postscript to the Structure* (1970, pp. 174–210), he used two different terms to signify the difference in meaning: disciplinary matrix for the wide sense and exemplar for the narrow.

41. "[A] paradigm is what you use when the theory isn't there" (Kuhn, 2000a, p. 300).

42. "[T]he characteristic problems are almost always repetitions, with minor modifications, of problems that have been undertaken and partially resolved before" (Kuhn, 1977, p. 233).

43. In (1970, p. 85), Kuhn, citing the historian Herbert Butterfield, compares a science's reorientation after a paradigm change, to "handling the same bundle of data as before, but placing them in a new system of relations with one another by giving them a different framework".

44. Kuhn acknowledges, however, that "[d]uring the transition period there will be a large but never complete overlap between the problems that can be solved by the old and the new paradigm. But there will also be a decisive difference in the mode of solution. When the transition is complete, the profession will have changed its view of the field, its methods, and its goals" (1970, p. 85). As we will see, in his later writings, Kuhn stressed more strongly that incommensurability is only local.

45. For a good synopsis of the early criticisms of Kuhn's and Feyerabend's views of meaning, see Suppe 1977, pp. 200–208.

46. Cf. also Scheffler 1982.

47. Note that in his more recent work Putnam has distanced himself from Davidson's denial of conceptual schemes. See Putnam, 2004, p. 50.

48. It is worth noting that, at some point, Putnam had also subscribed to a contextual view of meaning. See Putnam, 1975d, pp. 40–41.

49. Interestingly enough, Putnam gives credit to Quine for the "realization" of the inter-dependence of theory and meaning.

50. Here Putnam's ideas overlapped with those of Saul Kripke (1980). Note, however, that Putnam's attitude towards the philosophically charged notion of causality has changed considerably since the 1970s. See Ben-Menahem 2005, p. 16.

51. By the way, this takes the bite out of some of the criticisms that were raised against Feyerabend's and Kuhn's views of meaning (see above, p. 354).

52. For some other difficulties faced by Putnam's theory of meaning we refer the interested reader to Enç, 1976, Nola, 1980, Kroon, 1985, Psillos, 1999, Stanford & Kitcher, 2000, Arabatzis, 2007.

53. Here we should point out that Hanne Andersen, Peter Barker, and Xiang Chen have recently developed an illuminating account of Kuhn's taxonomic approach to incommensurability, in terms of Lawrence W. Barsalou's frame representation for concepts (see Andersen, Barker, & Chen 2006).

54. The exceptions would be cases of complete overlap, where a theory is fully absorbed, as a limiting case, by its successor.

55. For a thorough discussion of these issues see Kuukkanen, 2006.

56. Space limitations prevent us from expanding on this point. We refer the interested reader to Nersessian's contribution to this volume, where she gives a detailed account of the role of model-based reasoning in conceptual change.

REFERENCES

Achinstein, P. (1968). *Concepts of science: A philosophical analysis.* Baltimore: The Johns Hopkins Press.

Andersen, H., & N. J. Nersessian (2000). Nomic concepts, frames, and conceptual change. *Philosophy of Science 67* (Proceedings), S224–S241.

Andersen, H., P. Barker, & X. Chen (2006). *The cognitive structure of scientific revolutions.* Cambridge: Cambridge University Press.

Arabatzis, T. (2007). Conceptual change and scientific realism: Facing Kuhn's challenge. In S. Vosniadou, A. Baltas & X. Vamvakoussi (Eds.), *Reframing the conceptual change approach in learning and instruction* (pp. 47–62). Amsterdam: Elsevier.

Beaney, M. (Ed.). (1997). *The Frege reader.* Oxford: Blackwell.

Ben-Menahem, Y. (2005). Introduction. In Y. Ben-Menahem (Ed.), *Hilary Putnam* (pp. 1–16). Cambridge: Cambridge University Press.

Carnap, R. (1936–37). Testability and meaning. *Philosophy of Science, 3,* 420–468; *4,* 1–40.

Carnap, R. (1959). The elimination of metaphysics through the logical analysis of language. In A. J. Ayer (Ed.), *Logical positivism* (pp. 60–81). New York: The Free Press.

Carnap, R. (1969). *The logical structure of the world (Der Logische Aufbau der Welt).* Translated by Rolf A. George. Berkeley: University of California Press.

Carnap, R. (1981). Logical foundations of the unity of science. In O. Hanfling (Ed.), *Essential readings in logical positivism* (pp. 112–129). Oxford: Blackwell.

Carnap, R. (1988). *Meaning and necessity.* Chicago: The University of Chicago Press.

Davidson, D. (1984). On the very idea of a conceptual scheme. In D. Davidson (Ed.), *Inquiries into truth & interpretation* (pp. 183–198). Oxford: Clarendon Press.

Enç, B. (1976). Reference of theoretical terms. *Nous, 10,* 261–282.

Feigl, H. (1970). The 'orthodox' view of theories. In M. Radner & S. Winokur (Ed.), *Minnesota studies in the philosophy of science Vol. IV* (pp. 3–16). Minneapolis: University of Minnesota Press.

Feyerabend, P. (1978). *Against method.* London: Verso.

Feyerabend, P. (Ed.). (1981a). Explanation, reduction and empiricism. In *Realism, rationalism and scientific method* (pp. 44–96). Cambridge: Cambridge University Press.

Feyerabend, P. (Ed.). (1981b). On the 'meaning' of scientific terms. In *Realism, rationalism and scientific method* (pp. 97–103). Cambridge: Cambridge University Press.

Feyerabend, P. (1996). *Killing time.* Chicago: The University of Chicago Press.

Fine, A. (1975). How to compare theories. Reference and change. *Nous, 9,* 17–32.

Floyd, J. (2005). Putnam's "The meaning of 'meaning'": Externalism in historical context. In Y. Ben-Menahem (Ed.), *Hilary Putnam* (pp. 17–52). Cambridge: Cambridge University Press.

Frege, G. (1979a). Boole's logical Calculus and the Concept-script. In H. Hermes, F. Kambartel, & F. Kaulbach (Eds.), *Gottlob Frege: Posthumous writings* (pp. 9–46). Translated by Peter Long & Roger White. Oxford: Blackwell.

Frege, G. (1979b). On concept and object. In H. Hermes, F. Kambartel & F. Kaulbach (Eds.). *Gottlob Frege: Posthumous Writings* (pp. 87–117). Translated by Peter Long & Roger White. Oxford: Blackwell.

Frege, G. (1979c). Comments on sense and meaning. In H. Hermes, F. Kambartel, & F. Kaulbach (Eds.), *Gottlob Frege: Posthumous writings* (pp. 118–125). Translated by Peter Long & Roger White. Oxford: Blackwell.

Frege, G. (1979d). Logic. In H. Hermes, F. Kambartel, & F. Kaulbach (Eds.), *Gottlob Frege: Posthumous writings* (pp. 126–151). Translated by Peter Long & Roger White. Oxford: Blackwell.

Frege, G. (1980a). Begriffsschrift, a formula language, modeled upon that of arithmetic, for pure thought. In J. Van Heijenoort (Ed.), *Frege and Gödel: Two fundamental texts in mathematical logic* (pp. 1–82). Cambridge, MA: Harvard University Press.

Frege, G. (1980b). *The foundations of Arithmetic: A logico-mathematical inquiry into the concept of number.* English translation by J. L. Austin. Oxford: Blackwell.

Frege, G. (1997a). On *Sinn* and *Bedeutung.* In M. Beaney (Ed.), *The Frege reader* (pp. 151–172). Oxford: Blackwell.

Frege, G. (1997b). Introduction to Logic. In M. Beaney (Ed.), *The Frege reader* (pp. 293–298). Oxford: Blackwell.

Frege, G. (1997c). Thought. In M. Beaney (Ed.), *The Frege reader* (pp. 325–345). Oxford: Blackwell.

Friedman. M. (1999). *Reconsidering logical positivism.* Cambridge: Cambridge University Press.

Hahn, H., Carnap. R., & Neurath, O. (1996). The scientific conception of the world. In S. Sarkar (Ed.), *The emergence of logical positivism. From 1900 to the Vienna Circle* (pp. 321–340). New York: Garland.

Hanson, N .R. (1958). *Patterns of discovery.* Cambridge: Cambridge University Press.

Hempel, C. (1970). On the 'standard' conception of scientific theories. In M. Radner & S. Winokur (Eds.), *Minnesota studies in the philosophy of science Vol. IV* (pp. 142–163). Minneapolis: University of Minnesota Press.

Hempel, C. (1990). Problems and changes in the empiricist criterion of meaning. In R. R. Ammerman (Ed.). *Classics of analytic philosophy* (pp. 214–230). Indianapolis, IN: Hackett.

Hempel, C. & Oppenheim, P. (1948). Studies in the logic of explanation. *Philosophy of Science, 15,* 135–175.

Kripke S. (1980). *Naming and necessity.* Cambridge, MA: Harvard University Press.

Kroon, F. W. (1985). Theoretical terms and the causal view of reference. *Australasian Journal of Philosophy, 63,* 143–166.

Kuhn, T. S. (1970). *The structure of scientific revolutions.* Chicago: The University of Chicago Press.

Kuhn, T. S. (1977). The essential tension: tradition and innovation in scientific research. In *The essential tension: selected studies in scientific tradition and change* (pp. 225–239). Chicago: The University of Chicago Press.

Kuhn, T. S. (2000). *The road since Structure: Philosophical essays, 1970–1993, with an autobiographical interview.* Chicago: The University of Chicago Press.

Kuhn, T. S. (2000a). A discussion with Thomas Kuhn. In James Conant & John Haugeland (Eds.), *The road since Structure* (pp. 255–323). Chicago: The University of Chicago Press.

Kuukkanen, J.-M. (2006). *Meaning change in the context of Thomas S. Kuhn's philosophy.* Unpublished PhD dissertation, University of Edinburgh, UK.

Leibniz, G. (1989). Preface to a universal character. In *Philosophical essays* (pp. 5–10). Translated by R. Ariew & D. Garber. Indianapolis, IN: Hackett.

Machamer, P. (2007). Kuhn's philosophical successes. In S. Vosniadou, A. Baltas, & X. Vamvakoussi (Eds.), *Re-framing the conceptual change approach in learning and instruc*tion (pp. 35–45). Amsterdam: Elsevier.

Miller, A., & Wright, C. (2002). *Rule-following and meaning.* Chesham, UK: Acumen.

Nagel, E. (1979). *The structure of science.* Indianapolis, IN: Hackett.

Nersessian, N. J. (1984). *Faraday to Einstein: Constructing meaning in scientific theories.* Dordrecht: Martinus Nijhoff.

Nersessian, N. J. (1987). A cognitive-historical approach to meaning in scientific theories. In N. J. Nersessian (Ed.), *The process of science: Contemporary philosophical approaches to understanding scientific practice* (pp. 161–177). Dordrecht: Martinus Nijhoff.

Nersessian, N. J. (1988). Reasoning from imagery and analogy in scientific concept formation. *PSA: Proceedings of the biennial meeting of the Philosophy of Science Association. 1988, Volume One: Contributed Papers,* 41–47.

Nersessian, N. J. (1992). How do scientists think? Capturing the dynamics of conceptual change in science. In R. N. Giere (Ed.), *Cognitive models of science, Minnesota studies in the philosophy of science 15* (pp. 3–44). Minneapolis: University of Minnesota Press.

Nersessian, N. J. (1995). Opening the black box: cognitive science and history of science. In A. Thackray (Ed.), *Constructing knowledge in the history of science. Osiris, 10,* 194–214.

Nersessian, N. J. (1998). Kuhn and the cognitive revolution. *Configurations, 6*(1), 87–120.

Nersessian, N. J. (1999). Model-based reasoning in conceptual change. In L. Magnani, N. J. Nersessian, & P. Thagard (Eds.), *Model-based reasoning in scientific discovery* (pp. 5–22). New York: Kluwer Academic/Plenum.

Nersessian, N. J. (2001). Concept formation and commensurability. In P. Hoyningen-Huene & H. Sankey

(Eds.), *Incommensurability and related matters, Boston studies in the philosophy of science 216* (pp. 275–301). Dordrecht: Kluwer.

Nersessian, N. J. (2002a). Maxwell and "the method of physical analogy": Model-based reasoning, generic abstraction, and conceptual change. In D. B. Malament (Ed.), *Reading natural philosophy: Essays in the history and philosophy of science and mathematics* (pp. 129–166). Chicago: Open Court.

Nersessian, N. J. (2002b). The cognitive basis of model-based reasoning in science. In P. Carruthers, S. Stich, & M. Siegal (Eds.), *The cognitive basis of science* (pp. 133–153). Cambridge: Cambridge University Press.

Nersessian, N. J. (2002c). Abstraction via generic modeling in concept formation in science. *Mind & Society, 3*, 129–154.

Nersessian, N. J. (2002d). Kuhn, conceptual change, and cognitive science. In T. Nickles (Ed.), *Thomas Kuhn* (pp. 178–211). Cambridge: Cambridge University Press.

Nersessian, N. J., & Andersen, H. (1997). Conceptual change and incommensurability: A cognitive-historical view. *Danish Yearbook of Philosophy, 32*, 111–152.

Neurath, O., Carnap, R., & Morris, C. (Eds.). (1938). *International Encyclopedia of Unified Science.* Chicago: University of Chicago Press.

Nola, R. (1980). Fixing the reference of theoretical terms. *Philosophy of Science, 47*, 505–531.

Psillos, S. (1999). *Scientific Realism: How Science Tracks Truth.* London: Routledge.

Putnam, H. (1973). Meaning and reference. *The Journal of Philosophy, 70*, 699–711.

Putnam, H. (1975a). What theories are not. In H. Putnam, *Mathematics, matter and method: Philosophical papers, volume 1* (pp. 215–227). Cambridge: Cambridge University Press.

Putnam, H. (1975b). Introduction: Philosophy of language and the rest of philosophy. In H. Putnam, *Mind, language and reality: Philosophical papers, volume 2* (pp. vii–xvii). Cambridge: Cambridge University Press.

Putnam, H. (1975c). Language and philosophy. In H. Putnam, *Mind, language and reality: Philosophical papers, volume 2* (pp. 1–32). Cambridge: Cambridge University Press.

Putnam, H. (1975d). The analytic and the synthetic. In H. Putnam, *Mind, language and reality: Philosophical papers, volume 2* (pp. 33–69). Cambridge: Cambridge University Press.

Putnam, H. (1975e). How not to talk about meaning. In H. Putnam, *Mind, language and reality: Philosophical papers, volume 2* (pp. 117–131). Cambridge: Cambridge University Press.

Putnam, H. (1975f). Is semantics possible? In H. Putnam, *Mind, language and reality: Philosophical papers, volume 2* (pp. 139–152). Cambridge: Cambridge University Press.

Putnam, H. (1975g). Explanation and reference. In H. Putnam, *Mind, language and reality: Philosophical papers, volume 2* (pp. 196–214). Cambridge: Cambridge University Press.

Putnam, H. (1975h). The meaning of 'meaning'. In H. Putnam, *Mind, language and reality: Philosophical papers, volume 2* (pp. 215–271). Cambridge: Cambridge University Press.

Putnam, H. (1981). *Reason, truth and history.* Cambridge: Cambridge University Press.

Putnam, H. (1983). Reference and truth. In H. Putnam, *Realism and reason: Philosophical papers*, volume 3 (pp. 69–86). Cambridge: Cambridge University Press.

Putnam, H. (1990). *Realism with a human face.* Edited and introduced by James Conant. Cambridge, MA: Harvard University Press.

Putnam, H. (1992). Truth, activation vectors and possession conditions for concepts. *Philosophy and Phenomenological Research, 52*, 431–447.

Putnam, H. (2004). *Ethics without ontology.* Cambridge, MA: Harvard University Press.

Quine, W. V. (1951). Two dogmas of empiricism. *The Philosophical Review, 60*, 20–43.

Scheffler, I. (1982). *Science and subjectivity.* Indianapolis, IN: Hackett.

Schlick, M. (1981). Structure and content. In O. Hanfling (Ed.), *Essential readings in logical positivism* (pp. 131–149). Oxford: Blackwell.

Sellars, W. (1973). Conceptual change. In G. Pearce & P. Maynard (Eds.), *Conceptual change. Synthese library* (Vol. 52, pp. 77–93). Dordrecht: D. Reidel.

Shapere, D. (1964). The structure of scientific revolutions. *The Philosophical Review, 73*, 383–394.

Shapere, D. (1981). Meaning and scientific change. In I. Hacking (Ed.), *Scientific revolutions* (pp. 28–59). Oxford: Oxford University Press.

Shapere, D. (1984). *Reason and the search for knowledge: Investigations in the philosophy of science. Boston Studies in the Philosophy of Science 78.* Dordrecht: Reidel.

Stanford, P. K., & Kitcher, P. (2000). Refining the causal theory of reference for natural kind terms. *Philosophical Studies, 97,* 99–129.

Suppe, F. (1977). The search for philosophic understanding of scientific theories. In F. Suppe (Ed.), *The structure of scientific theories* (pp. 3–241). Urbana: University of Illinois Press.

Toulmin, S. (1961). *Foresight and understanding.* New York: Harper.

Toulmin, S. (1972). *Human understanding. The collective use and evolution of concepts.* Princeton, NJ: Princeton University Press.

Van Fraassen, B. C. (2002). *The empirical stance.* New Haven, CT: Yale University Press.

Van Heijenoort, J. (Ed.). (1980). *Frege and Gödel: Two fundamental texts in mathematical logic.* Cambridge, MA: Harvard University Press.

Vosniadou, S. (2007). The conceptual change approach and its re-framing. In S. Vosniadou, A. Baltas, & X. Vamvakoussi (Eds.), *Re-framing the conceptual change approach in learning and instruction* (pp. 1–17). Amsterdam: Elsevier.

Waismann, F. (1978). Verifiability. In A. G. N. Flew (Ed.), *Logic and language* (pp. 117–144). Oxford: Blackwell.

Wittgenstein, L. (1958). *Philosophical investigations.* Translated by G.E.M. Anscombe. Oxford: Blackwell. [Abbreviated as PI]

Wittgenstein, L. (1978). *Remarks on the foundation of mathematics.* Translated by G.E.M. Anscombe. Oxford: Blackwell. [Abbreviated as RFM]

Wittgenstein, L. (1979). *Philosophical grammar.* Translated by A. Kenny. Berkeley: University of California Press. [Abbreviated as PG]

Wittgenstein, L. (1993). Wittgenstein's lectures in 1930–33. By G.E. Moore. In J. Klagge & A. Nordmann (Eds.), *Philosophical occasions* (pp. 46–114). Indianapolis, IN: Hackett.

14

Conceptual Change in the History of Science: Life, Mind, and Disease

Paul Thagard
University of Waterloo

INTRODUCTION

Biology is the study of life, psychology is the study of mind, and medicine is the investigation of the causes and treatments of disease. This chapter describes how the central concepts of life, mind, and disease have undergone fundamental changes in the past 150 years or so. There has been a progression from theological, to qualitative, to mechanistic explanations of the nature of life, mind, and disease. This progression has involved both theoretical change, as new theories with greater explanatory power replaced older ones, and emotional change as the new theories brought reorientation of attitudes toward the nature of life, mind, and disease. After a brief comparison of theological, qualitative, and mechanistic explanations, I will describe how shifts from one kind of explanation to another have carried with them dramatic kinds of conceptual change in the key concepts in the life sciences. Three generalizations follow about the nature of conceptual change in the history of science: there has been a shift from conceptualizations in terms of simple properties to ones in terms of complex relations; conceptual change is theory change; and conceptual change is often emotional as well as cognitive.

The contention that historical development proceeds in three stages originated with the 19th-century French philosopher, Auguste Comte, who claimed that human intellectual development progresses from a theological to a "metaphysical" stage to a "positive" (scientific) stage (Comte, 1970). The stages I have in mind are different from Comte's, so let me say what they involve. By the *theological* stage I mean systems of thought in which the primary explanatory entities are supernatural ones beyond the reach of science, such as gods, devils, angels, spirits, and souls. For example, the concept of fire was initially theological, as in the Greek myth of Prometheus receiving fire from the gods. By the *qualitative* stage I mean systems of thought that do not invoke supernatural entities, but which postulate natural entities not far removed from what they are supposed to explain, such as vital force in biology. Early qualitative concepts of fire include Aristotle's view of fire as a substance and Epicurus's account of fire atoms. By the *mechanistic* stage I mean the kinds of developments now rapidly taking place in all of the life sciences in which explanations consist of identifying systems of interacting parts that produce observable changes. The modern concept of fire is mechanistic: combustion is rapid oxidation, the combination of molecules. Much more will be said about the nature of mechanistic, qualitative, and theological explanations in connection with each of the central concepts of life, disease, and mind. I will show how resistance to conceptual change derives both from (1) cognitive difficulties in grasping the superiority of mechanistic explanations to the other two kinds and (2) emotional difficulties in accepting the personal implications of the mechanistic world view. First, however, I want to review the general importance of the topic of conceptual change for the history and philosophy of science.

HISTORY AND PHILOSOPHY OF SCIENCE

Historians and philosophers of science are concerned to explain the development of scientific knowledge. On a naïve view, science develops by simple accumulation, piling fact upon fact. But this view is contradicted by the history of science, which has seen many popular theories eventually rejected as false, including: the crystalline spheres of ancient and medieval astronomy, the humoral theory of medicine, catastrophist geology, the phlogiston theory of chemistry, the caloric theory of heat, the vital force theory of physiology, the aether theories of electromagnetism and optics, and biological theories of spontaneous generation. Rejection of these theories has required abandonment of concepts such as *humor, phlogiston, caloric,* and *aether*, along with introduction of new theoretical concepts such as *germ, oxygen, thermodynamics,* and *photon*. Acceptance of a theory therefore often requires the acquisition and adoption of a novel conceptual system.

We can distinguish different degrees of conceptual change occurring in the history of science and medicine (Thagard, 1992, 1999, p. 150):

1. Adding a new instance of a concept, for example, a patient who has tuberculosis.
2.. Adding a new weak rule, for example, that tuberculosis is common in prisons.
3. Adding a new strong rule that plays a frequent role in problem solving and explanation, for example, that people with tuberculosis have *Mycobacterium tuberculosis*.
4. Adding a new part-relation, for example, that diseased lungs contain tubercles.
5. Adding a new kind-relation, for example, differentiating between pulmonary and miliary tuberculosis.
6. Adding a new concept, for example, *tuberculosis* (which replaced the previous terms *phthisis* and *consumption*) or AIDS.
7. Collapsing part of a kind-hierarchy, abandoning a previous distinction, for example, realizing that phthisis and scrofula are the same disease, tuberculosis.
8. Reorganizing hierarchies by *branch jumping*, that is shifting a concept from one branch of a hierarchical tree to another, for example, reclassifying tuberculosis as an infectious disease.
9. *Tree switching*, that is, changing the organizing principle of a hierarchical tree, for example, classifying diseases in terms of causal agents rather than symptoms.

The most radical kinds of conceptual change involve the last two kinds of major conceptual reorganization, as when Darwin reclassified humans as animals and changed the organizational principle of the tree of life to be evolutionary history rather than similarity of features.

Thus, understanding the historical development of the sciences requires attention to the different kinds of conceptual change that have taken place in the non-cumulative growth of knowledge (see also Kuhn, 1970; Horwich, 1993; LaPorte, 2004; Nersessian, 1992). I will now describe the central changes that have taken place in the concepts of life, mind, and disease.

LIFE

Theology

Theological explanations of life are found in the creation stories of many cultures, including the Judeo-Christian tradition's book of Genesis. According to this account God created grass, herbs, and fruit trees on the second day, swarms of birds and sea animals on the fifth day, and living creatures on land including humans on the sixth day. Other cultures worldwide have different accounts of how one or more deities brought the earth and the living things on it into existence. These stories predate by centuries attempts to understand the world scientifically, which may only have begun with the thought of the Greek philosopher-scientist Thales around 600 B.C. The stories do not attempt to tie theological explanations to details of observations of the nature of life. Thus the first sub-stage of the theological stage of the understanding of life is a matter of myth, a set of entertaining stories rather than a detailed exposition of the theological origins of life.

During the 17th and 18th centuries, there was a dramatic expansion of biological knowledge based on observation, ranging from the discovery by van Leeuwenhoek of microorganisms such as bacteria to the taxonomy by Carl Linnaeus of many different kinds of plants and animals. In the 19th century, attempts were made to integrate this burgeoning knowledge with theological understanding, including the compellingly written *Natural Theology* of William Paley (1963). Paley argued that, just as we explain the intricacies of a watch by the intelligence and activities of its maker, so we should explain the design of plants and animals by the actions of the creator. The eight volumes of the Bridgewater Treatises connected divine creation not only to the anatomy and physiology of living things, but also to astronomy, physics, geology, and chemistry. Nineteenth-century natural theology was a Christian enterprise, as theologians and believing scientists connected biological and other scientific observations in great detail with ideas drawn from the Bible. Unlike the purely mythical accounts found in many cultures, this natural-theology sub-stage of theological explanations of life was tied to many facts about the biological world.

A third sub-stage of theological understandings of life is the relatively recent doctrine of intelligent design that arose in the United States as a way of contesting Darwin's theory of evolution by natural selection without directly invoking Christian ideas about creation. Because the U.S. Constitution requires separation of church and state, public schools have not been allowed to teach Christian ideas about divine creation as a direct challenge to evolution. Hence, in the 1990s there arose a kind of natural theology in disguise claiming to have a scientific alternative to evolution, the theory of intelligent design (e.g., Dembski, 1999). Its proponents claim that it is not committed to the biblical account of creation, but instead relies on facts about the complexity of life as pointing to its origins in intelligent causation rather than the mechanical operations of natural selection. U.S. courts have, however, ruled that intelligent design is just a disguised attempt to smuggle natural theology into the schools.

Qualitative Explanations of Life

Unlike theological explanations, qualitative accounts do not invoke supernatural entities, but instead attempt to explain the world in terms of natural properties. For example, in the 18th century, heat and temperature were explained by the presence in objects of a qualitative element called caloric: the more caloric, the more heat. A mechanical theory of heat as motion of molecules only arose in the 19th century. Just as caloric was invoked as a substance to explain heat, qualitative explanations of life can be given by invoking a special kind of substance that inhabits living things. Aristotle, for example, believed that animals and plants have a principle of life (*psuche*) that initiates and guides reproductive, metabolic, growth, and other capacities (Grene & Depew, 2004).

In the 19th century, qualitative explanations of life became popular in the form of *vitalism,* according to which living things contain some distinctive force or fluid or spirit that makes them alive (Bechtel & Richardson, 1998). Scientists and philosophers such as Bichat, Magendie, Liebig, and Bergson postulated that there must be some sort of vital force that enables organisms to develop and maintain themselves. Vitalism developed as an opponent to the materialistic view, originating with the Greek atomists and developed by Descartes and his successors, that living things are like machines in that they can be explained purely in terms of the operation of their parts. Unlike natural theology, vitalism does not explicitly employ divine intervention in its explanation of life, but for vitalists such as Bergson there was no doubt that God was the origin of vital force.

Contrast the theological and vitalist explanation patterns.

> *Theological explanation pattern:*
> Why does an organism have a given property that makes it alive?
> Because God designed the organism to have that property.
> *Vitalist explanation pattern:*
> Why does an organism have a given property that makes it alive?
> Because the organism contains a vital force that gives it that property.

We can now examine a very different way of explaining life, in terms of mechanisms.

Mechanistic Explanations of Life

The mechanistic account of living things originated with Greek philosophers such as Epicurus, who wanted to explain all motion in terms of the interactions of atoms. Greek mechanism was limited, however, by the comparative simplicity of the machines available to them: levers, pulleys, screws, and so on. By the 17th century, however, more complicated machines were available, such as clocks, artificial fountains, and mills. In his 1664 *Treatise on Man*, Descartes used these as models for maintaining that animals and the bodies (but not the souls) of humans are nothing but machines explainable through the operations of their parts, analogous to the pipes and springs of fountains and clocks (Descartes, 1985). Descartes undoubtedly believed that living machines had been designed by God, but the explanation of their operations was in terms of their structure rather than their design or special vital properties. The pattern is something like this:

> Mechanistic explanation pattern:
> Why does an organism have a given property that makes it alive?
> Because the organism has parts that interact in ways that give it that property.

Normally, we understand how machines work because people have built them from identifiable parts connected to each other in observable ways.

In Descartes' day, mechanistic explanations were highly limited by lack of knowledge of the smaller and smaller parts that make up the body: cells were not understood until the 19th century. They were also limited by the simplicity of available machines to provide analogies to the complexities of biological organisms. By the 19th century, however, the cell doctrine and other biological advances made mechanistic explanations of life much more conceivable. But it was still utterly mysterious how different species of living things came to be, unless they were the direct result of divine creation. Various thinkers conjectured that species have evolved, but no one had a reasonable account of how they had evolved.

The intellectual situation changed dramatically in 1859, when Charles Darwin published *On the Origin of Species*. His great insight was not the concept of evolution, which had been proposed by others, but the concept of natural selection, which provided a mechanism that explained how evolution occurred. At first glance, natural selection does not sound much like a machine, but it qualifies as a mechanism because it consists of interacting parts producing regular changes (for philosophical discussions of the nature of mechanisms, see Salmon, 1984; Bechtel & Richardson, 1993; Machamer, Darden, & Craver, 2000; Bechtel & Abrahamson, 2005). The parts are individual organisms that interact with each other and with their environments. Darwin noticed that variations are introduced when organisms reproduce, and that the struggle for existence that results from scarcity of resources would tend to preserve those variations that gave organisms advantages in survival and reproduction. Hence, variation plus the struggle for existence led to natural selection which leads to the evolution of species. Over the past 150 years, the evidence for evolution by natural selection has accumulated to such an extent that it ought to be admitted that evolution is a fact as well as a theory.

Why then is there continuing opposition to Darwin's ideas? The answer is that the battle between evolution and creation is not just a competition between alternative theories of how different species came to be, but between different world views with very different emotional attachments. Theological views have limited explanatory power compared to science, but they have very strong emotional coherence because of their fit with people's personal goals, including comfort, immortality, morality, and social cohesion (Thagard, 2005a). People attach strong positive emotional valences to the key ingredients of creationist theories, including supernatural entities such as God and heaven. In contrast, evolution by natural selection strikes fundamentalist believers as atheistic and immoral.

Although Darwin conceived of a mechanism for evolution, he lacked a mechanistic understanding of key parts of it. In particular, he did not have a good account of how variations occurred and were passed on to offspring. Explanation of variation and inheritance required genetic theory, which (aside from Mendel's early ignored ideas) was not developed until the first part of the 20th century. In turn, understanding of genetics developed in the second part of that century through discovery of how DNA provides a mechanism for inheritance. Today, biology is thoroughly mechanistic, as biochemistry explains how DNA and other molecules work, which explains how genes work, which explains how variation and inheritance work. The genomes of important organisms including humans have been mapped, and the burgeoning enterprise of proteomics is filling in the details of how genes produce proteins whose interactions explain all the operations required for the survival and reproduction of living things.

Hence, what makes things alive is not a divine spark or vital force, but their construction out of organs, tissues, and individual cells that are alive. Cells are alive because their proteins and processes enable them to perform functions such as energy acquisition, division, motion, adhesion, signaling, and self-destruction. The molecular basis of each of these functions is increasingly well understood (Lodish, Berk, Zipursky, Matsudaira, Baltimore, & Darnell, 2000). In turn, the behavior of molecules can be described in terms of quantum chemistry, which explains how the quantum-mechanical properties of atoms cause them to combine in biochemically useful ways. Thus, the development of biology over the past 150 years dramatically illustrates the shift from a theological to a qualitative to a mechanist concept of life. This shift has taken place because of an impressive sequence of mechanistic theories that provide deeper and deeper explanations of how living things work, from natural selection to genetics to molecular biology to quantum mechanics. This shift does not imply that there is only one fundamental level at which all explanation should take place: it would be pointless to try to give a quantum-mechanical explanation of why humans have large brains, as the quantum details are far removed from the historical environmental and biological conditions that produced the evolution of humans. It is enough, from the mechanistic point of view, that the lower-level mechanical operations are available in the background.

In sum, theoretical progress in biology has resulted from elaboration of progressively deeper mechanisms, while resistance to such progress results from emotional preferences for theological over mechanistic explanation. Similar resistance arises to understanding disease and mind mechanistically.

DISEASE

Theology

Medicine has both the theoretical goal of finding explanations of disease and the practical goal of finding treatments for them. As for life, early conceptions of disease were heavily theological. Gods were thought to be sometimes the cause of disease, and they could be supplicated to provide relief from them. For example, in the biblical book of Exodus, God delivers a series of punishments, including boils, on the Egyptians for holding the Israelites captive. Hippocrates wrote around 400 B.C., challenging the view that epilepsy is a "sacred disease" resulting from divine action. Medieval Christians believed that the black plague was a punishment from God. In modern theology, diseases are rarely attributed directly to God, but there are still people who maintain that HIV/AIDS is a punishment for homosexuality. But even if most people now accept medical explanations of the causes of disease, there are many who pray for divine intervention to help cure the maladies of people they care about. Hence, in religious circles the concept of disease remains at least in part theological.

Qualitative Explanations of Disease

The ancient Greeks developed a naturalistic account of diseases that dominated Western medicine until the 19th century (Hippocrates, 1988). According to the Hippocratics, the body contains four humors: blood, phlegm, yellow bile, and black bile. Health depends on having these humors in correct proportion to each other. Too much bile can produce various fevers, and too much phlegm can cause heart or brain problems. Accordingly, diseases can be treated by changing the balance of humors, for example by opening the veins to let blood out.

Traditional Chinese medicine, which is at least as ancient as the Hippocratic approach, is also a balance theory, but with *yin* and *yang* instead of the four humors. On the Chinese view, yin and yang are the two opposite but complementary forces that constitute the entire universe. Here is a summary (from Thagard & Zhu, 2003, pp. 83–84):

> Like everything else, the human body and its functions are all governed by the principle of *yin* and *yang*. Remaining healthy and functioning properly require keeping the balance between the *yin* and *yang* in the body. Diseases arise when there is inequilibrium of *yin* and *yang* inside the body. This principle is central to traditional Chinese medicine, and its application dominates the diagnosis, treatment and explanation of diseases. For example, a patient's high fever, restlessness, a flushed face, dry lips and a rapid pulse are *yang* symptoms. The diagnosis will be a *yin* deficiency, or imbalance brought by an excess of *yang* over *yin*. Once the *yin-yang* character of a disease is

assessed, treatment can restore the balance of *yin* and *yang*, for example by using *yin*-natured herbs to dampen and dissipate the internal heat and other *yang* symptoms.

Whereas the Hippocratic tradition used extreme physical methods such as blood-letting, emetics, and purgatives to restore the balance of the four humors, traditional Chinese medicine uses relatively benign herbal treatments to restore the balance of *yin* and *yang*. Unlike Hippocratic medicine, which has been totally supplanted by Western scientific approaches, traditional Chinese medicine is still practiced in China and is often favored by Westerners looking for alternative medical treatments.

Similarly, traditional Indian Ayurvedic medicine has attracted a modern following through the writings of gurus such as Deepak Chopra. On this view, all bodily processes are governed by three main *doshas: vata* (composed of air and space), *pitta* (composed of fire and water)*, and kapha* (composed of earth and water). Too much or too little of these elements can lead to diseases, which can be treated by diet and exercise. There is no empirical evidence for the existence of the *doshas* or for their role in disease, but people eagerly latch onto Chopra's theories for their promise that good health and long life can be attained merely by making the right choices. Just as creationism survives because it fits with peoples personal motivations, so traditional Chinese and Ayurvedic theories survive because they offer appealing solutions to scary medical problems.

The three balance theories described in this section are clearly not theological, because they do not invoke divine intervention. But they are also not mechanical, because they do not explain the causes of diseases in terms of the regular interaction of constitutive parts. They leave utterly mysterious how the interactions of humors, *doshas*, or *yin* and *yang* can make people sick. In contrast, modern Western medicine based on contemporary biology provides mechanistic explanations of a very wide range of diseases.

Mechanistic Explanations of Disease

Modern medicine began in the 1860s, when Pasteur and others developed the germ theory of disease. Bacteria had been observed microscopically in the 1670s, but their role in causing diseases was not suspected until Pasteur realized that bacteria are responsible for silkworm diseases. Bacteria were quickly found to be responsible for many human diseases, including cholera, tuberculosis, and gonorrhea. Viruses were not observed until the invention of the electron microscope in 1939, but are now known to be the cause of many human diseases such as influenza and measles (for a review, see Thagard, 1999).

The germ theory of disease provides mechanistic explanations in which bacteria and viruses are entities that interact with bodily parts such as organs and cells that are infected. Unlike vague notions like *yin*, *yang,* and *doshas*, these entities can be observed using microscopes, as can their presence in bodily tissues. Thus an infected organism is like a machine that has multiple interacting parts. The germ theory of disease is not only theoretically useful in explaining how many diseases arise, it is also practically useful in that antimicrobial drugs such as penicillin can cure some diseases by killing the agents that cause them.

As we saw for biological explanations, it is a powerful feature of mechanistic explanations that they decompose into further layers of mechanistic explanations. Pasteur had no idea how bacteria manage to infect organs, but molecular biology has in recent decades provided detailed accounts of how microbes function. For example, when the new disease SARS was identified in 2003, it took only a few months to identify the coronavirus that causes it and to sequence the virus's genes that enable it to attach themselves to cells, infect them, and reproduce. In turn, biochemistry explains how genes produce the proteins that carry out these functions. Thus the explanations provided by the germ theory have progressively deepened over the almost one and half centuries since it was first proposed. I have argued elsewhere that this kind of ongoing deepening is a reliable sign of the truth of a scientific theory (Thagard, 2007).

Not all diseases are caused by germs, but other major kinds have been amenable to mechanistic explanation. Nutritional diseases such as scurvy are caused by deprivation of vitamins, and the mechanisms by which vitamins work are now understood. For example, vitamin C is crucial for collagen synthesis and the metabolism and synthesis of various chemical structures, which explains why its deficiency produces the symptoms of scurvy. Some diseases are caused by the immune system becoming overactive and attacking parts of the body, as when white blood cells remove myelin from axons between neurons, producing the symptoms of multiple sclerosis. Other diseases such as cystic fibrosis are directly caused by genetic factors, and the connection between mutated genes and defective metabolism is increasingly well understood. The final major category of human disease is cancer, and the genetic mutations that convert a normal cell into an invasive carcinoma, as well as the biochemical pathways that are thereby affected, are becoming well mapped out (Thagard, 2003a, 2006).

Despite the progressively deepening mechanistic explanation of infectious, nutritional, autoimmune, and genetic diseases, there is still much popular support for alternative theories and treatments such as traditional Chinese and Ayurvedic medicine. The reasons for the resistance to changes in the concept of disease from qualitative to mechanistic are both cognitive and emotional. On the cognitive side, most people simply do not know enough biology to understand how germs work, how vitamins work, how the immune system works, and so on. Hence much simpler accounts of imbalances among a few bodily elements are appealing. On the emotional side, there is the regrettable fact that modern medicine still lacks treatment for many human diseases, even ones like cancer whose biological mechanisms are quite well understood. Alternative disease theories and therapies offer hope of inexpensive and noninvasive treatments. For example, naturopaths attribute diseases to environmental toxins that can be cleared by diet and other simple therapies, providing people with reassuring explanations and expectations about their medical situation. Hence resistance to conceptual change about disease, like resistance concerning life, is often as much emotional as cognitive. The same is true for the concept of mind.

MIND

Theology

For the billions of people who espouse Christianity, Islam, Hinduism, and Buddhism, a person is much more than a biological mechanism. According to the book of Genesis, God formed man from the dust of the ground and breathed into his nostrils, making him a living soul. Unlike human bodies, which rarely last more than 100 years, souls have the great advantage of being indestructible, which makes possible immortality and (according to some religions) reincarnation. Because most people living today believe that their souls will survive the demise of their bodies, they have a concept of a person that is inherently dualistic: people consist of both a material body and a spiritual soul.

We saw that Descartes argued that bodies are machines, but he maintained that minds are not mechanically explainable. His main argument for this position was a thought experiment: he found it easy to imagine himself without a body, but impossible to imagine himself not thinking (Descartes, 1985). Hence, he concluded that he was essentially a thinking being rather than a bodily machine, thereby providing a conceptual argument for the theological view of persons as consisting of two distinct substances, with the soul being much more important than the body. Descartes thought that the body and soul were able to influence each other through interaction in the brain's pineal gland.

The psychological theories of ordinary people are thoroughly dualist, assuming that consciousness and other mental operations belong fundamentally to the soul rather than the brain. Legal and other institutions assume that people inherently have the capacity for free will, which applies to actions of the soul rather than to processes occurring in the brain through interaction with other parts of the body and the external environment. Such freedom is viewed as integral to morality, making it legitimate to praise or blame people for their actions.

Notice how tightly the theological view of the mind as soul fits with the biological theory of creation. Life has theological rather than natural origins, and God is also responsible for a special kind of life: humans with souls as well as bodies. Gods and souls are equally supernatural entities.

Qualitative Explanations of Mind

Postulating souls with free will does not enable us to say much about mental operations, and many thinkers have used introspection (self-observation) to describe the qualitative properties of thinking. The British empiricist philosophers, Locke and Hume, claimed that minds function by the associations of ideas that are ultimately derived from sense experience. When Wilhelm Wundt originated experimental psychology in the 1870s, his observational method was still primarily introspective, but was much more systematic and tied to experimental interventions than ordinary self-observation.

Many philosophers have resisted the attempt to make the study of mind scientific, hoping that a purely conceptual approach could help us to understand thinking. Husserl founded phenomenology, an a priori attempt to identify essential features of thought and action. Linguistic philosophers such as J. L. Austin thought that attention to the ordinary uses of words could tell us something about the nature of mind. Analytic philosophers have examined everyday mental concepts such as belief and desire, under the assumption that people's actions are adequately explained as the result of people's beliefs and desires. Thought experiments survive as a popular philosophical tool for determining the essential features of thinking, for example when Chalmers (1996) uses them to argue for a non-theological version of dualism in which consciousness is a fundamental part of the universe like space and time.

Thought experiments can be helpful for generating hypotheses that suggest experiments, but by themselves they provide no reason to believe those hypotheses. For every thought experiment, there is an equal and opposite thought experiment, so the philosophical game of imagining what might be the case tells us little about the nature of minds and thinking. Introspective, conceptual approaches to psychology are appealing because they are much less constrained than experimental approaches and do not require large amounts of personnel and apparatus. They generate no annoying data to get in the way of one's favorite prejudices about the nature of mind. However, they are very limited in how much they can explain about the capacities and performance of the mind. Fortunately, mechanistic explanations based on experiments provide a powerful alternative methodology.

Mechanistic Explanations of Mind

Descartes thought that springs and other simple mechanisms suffice to explain the operation of bodies, but drew back from considering thinking mechanistically. Until the second half of the

20th century, these mechanical models of thinking such as hydraulic fluids and telephone switchboards seemed much too crude to explain the richness and complexity of human mental operations. The advent of the digital computer provided a dramatic innovation in ways of thinking about the mind. Computers are obviously mechanisms, but they have unprecedented capacities to represent and process information. In 1956, Newell, Shaw, and Simon (1958) developed the first computational model of human problem solving. For decades, the computer has provided a source of analogies to help understand many aspects of human thinking, including perception, learning, memory, and inference (see Thagard, 2005b, for a survey). On the computational view of mind, thinking occurs when algorithmic processes are applied to mental representations that are akin to the data structures found in the software that determines the actions of computer hardware.

However, as von Neumann (1958) noted early on, digital computers are very different from human brains. They nevertheless have proved useful for developing models of how brains work, ever since the 1950s. But in the 1980s there was an upsurge of development of models of brain-style computing, using parallel processing among simple processing elements roughly analogous to neurons (Rumelhart & McClelland, 1986). Churchland and Sejnowski (1992) and others have argued that neural mechanisms are computational, although of a rather different sort than those found in digital computers. More biologically realistic, computational models of neural processes are currently being developed (e.g., Eliasmith and Anderson, 2003). Efforts are increasingly made to relate high-level mental operations such as rule-based inference to neural structures and processes (e.g., Anderson, Bothell, Byrne, Douglas, Lebiere, & Qin, 2004). Thus neuroscience, along with computational ideas, inspired by neural processes provides powerful mechanistic accounts of human thinking.

Central to modern cognitive science is the concept of *representation*, which has undergone major historical changes. From a theological perspective, representations such as concepts and propositions are properties of spiritual beings, and thus are themselves non-material objects. Modern cognitive psychology reclassifies representations as material things, akin to the data structures found in computer programs. Most radically, cognitive neuroscience reclassifies representations as *processes,* namely patterns of activity in neural networks in the brain. Thus, the history of cognitive science has required *branch jumping,* which I earlier listed as one of the most radical kinds of conceptual change. It is too soon to say whether cognitive neuroscience will also require *tree switching,* a fundamental change in the organizing principles by which mental representations are classified.

We saw in discussing life and disease how mechanistic explanations are decomposable into underlying mechanisms. At the cognitive level, we can view thinking in terms of computational processes applied to mental representations, but it has become possible to deepen this view by considering neurocomputational processes applied to neural representations. In turn, neural processes — the behavior of neurons interacting with each other — can be explained in terms of biochemical processes. The study of mind, like the study of life and disease, is increasingly becoming molecular (Thagard, 2003a). That does not mean that the only useful explanations of human thinking will be found at the molecular level, because various phenomena are more likely to be captured by mechanisms operating at different levels. For example, rule-based problem solving may be best explained at the cognitive level in terms of mental representations and computational procedures, even if these representations and procedures ultimately derive from neural and molecular processes.

Indeed, a full understanding of human thinking needs to consider higher as well as lower levels. Many kinds of human thinking occur in social contexts, involving social mechanisms such as communication and other kinds of interaction. Far from it being the case that the social reduces to the cognitive which reduces to the neural which reduces to the molecular, sometimes what happens at the molecular level needs to be explained by what happens socially. For example, a social interaction between two people may produce very different kinds of neurotransmitter activity in their brains depending on whether they like or fear each other.

Of course, there is a great deal about human thinking that current psychology and neuroscience cannot yet explain. Although perception, memory, learning, and inference are increasingly subject to neurocomputational explanation, there are still puzzles such as consciousness where there are only sketches of mechanisms that might possibly be relevant. Such sketchiness gives hope to those who are opposed for various religious or ideological ideas to the provision of mechanistic explanations of the full range of human thought. From a theological perspective that assumes the existence of souls, full mechanistic explanation of thinking is impossible as well as undesirable. The undesirability stems from the many attractive features of supernatural souls, particularly their immortality and autonomy. Adopting a mechanistic view of mind requires abandoning or at least modifying traditional ideas about free will, moral responsibility, and eternal rewards and punishment. This threat explains why the last 50 years of demonstrable progress in mechanistic, neurocomputational explanations of many aspects of thought are ignored by critics who want to maintain traditional attitudes. Change in the concept of mind, as with life and disease, is affected not only by cognitive processes such as theory evaluation, but also by emotional processes such as motivated inference. In the next section I will draw some more general lessons about conceptual change in relation to science education.

CONCEPTUAL CHANGE

Of course, there are many other important concepts in the history of science besides life, mind, and disease, and much more to be said about other kinds of conceptual change (see, for example, Thagard, 1992). But, because the concepts of life, mind, and disease are central, respectively, to biology, psychology, and medicine, they provide a good basis for making some generalizations about conceptual change in the history of science that can be tested against additional historical episodes. The commonalities in ways in which these three concepts have developed are well worth noting.

In all cases, there has been a shift from conceptualizations in terms of simple properties to ones in terms of complex relations. Prescientifically, life could be viewed as a special property that distinguished living from non-living things. This property could be explained in terms of divine creation or some vital force. In contrast, the mechanistic view of biology considers life as a whole complex of dynamic relations, such as the metabolism and reproduction of cells. Life is no one thing, but rather the result of many different mechanical processes. Similarly, disease is not a simple problem that can be explained by divine affliction or humoral imbalance, but rather is the result of many different kinds of biological and environmental processes. Diseases have many different kinds of causes — microbial, genetic, nutritional, and autoimmune, each of which depends on many underlying biological mechanisms. Even more strikingly, mind is not a simple thing, the non-corporeal soul, but rather the result of many interacting neural structures and processes. Thus the conceptual developments of biology, psychology, and medicine have all required shifts from thinking of things in terms of simple properties to thinking of them in terms of complexes of relations. Students who encounter scientific versions of their familiar everyday concepts of life, mind, and disease need to undergo the same kind of shift. Chi (2005) describes the difficulties that arise for students in understanding emergent mechanisms, ones in which regularities arise from complex interactions of many entities. Life, mind, and disease are all emergent processes in this sense and therefore subject to the difficult learning challenges that Chi reports in other domains.

The shift in understanding life, mind, and disease as complex mechanical relations rather than as simple substances or properties is an example of what I earlier called branch jumping, reclassification by shifting a concept from one branch of a hierarchical tree to another. The tree here is ontological, a classification of the fundamental things thought to be part of existence. Life, for example, is no longer a kind of special property, but rather a kind of mechanical process. Mind is another kind of mechanical process, not a special substance created by God. Many more mundane cases of branch jumping have occurred as the life sciences developed, for example the reclassification in the 1980s of peptic ulcers as infectious diseases (Thagard, 1999).

Most radically, the shift from theological to qualitative to mechanistic conceptions of life, mind, and disease also involved tree switching, changing the organizing principle of a hierarchical tree. From a mechanistic perspective, we classify things in terms of their underlying parts and interactions. Darwin's mechanism of evolution by natural selection yielded a whole new way of classifying species, by historical descent rather than similarity. Later, the development of molecular genetics provided another new way of classifying species in terms of genetic similarity. Similarly, diseases are now classified in terms of their causal mechanisms rather than surface similarity of symptoms, for example as infectious or autoimmune diseases. More slowly, mental phenomena such as memory are becoming classified in terms of underlying causal mechanisms such as different kinds of neural learning (Smith & Kosslyn, 2007). Thus conceptual change in the life sciences has involved both branch jumping and tree switching.

Another important general lesson we can draw from the development of concepts of life, mind, and disease is that conceptual change in the history of science is theory change. Scientific concepts are embedded in theories, and it is only by the development of explanatory theories with broad empirical support that it becomes reasonable and in fact intellectually mandatory to adopt new complexes of concepts. The current scientific view of life depends on evolutionary, genetic, and molecular theories, just as the current medical view of disease depends on molecular, microbial, nutritional, and other well-supported theories. Similarly, our concept of mind should be under constant revision as knowledge accumulates about the neurocomputational mechanisms of perception, memory, learning, and inference. In all these cases, it would have been folly to attempt to begin investigation with a precise definition of key concepts, because what matters is the development of explanatory theories rather than conceptual neatness. After some theoretical order has been achieved, it may be possible to tidy up a scientific field with some approximate definitions. But if theoretical advances have involved showing that phenomena are much more complicated than anyone suspected, and that what were thought to be simple properties are in fact complexes of mechanical relations, then definitions are as pointless at later stages of investigation as they are distracting at early stages.

My final lesson about conceptual change in the history of science is that, especially in the sciences most deeply relevant to human lives, conceptual change is emotional as well as cognitive. The continuing resistance to mechanistic explanations of life, mind, and disease is inexplicable on purely cognitive grounds, given the enormous amount of evidence that has accumulated for theories such as evolution by natural selection, the germ theory of disease, and neurocomputational accounts of thinking. Although the scientific communities have largely made the emotional shifts necessary to allow concepts and theories to fit with empirical results, members of the general population, including many science students, have strong affective preferences for obsolete theories such as divine creation, alternative medicine, and soul-based psychology. Popular concepts of life, mind, and disease are tightly intertwined: God created both life and mind, and can be called on to alleviate disease. Hence conceptual change can require not just rejection of a single theory in biology, psychology, and medicine, but rather replacement of a theological world-view by a scientific, mechanist one. For many people, such replacement is horrific, because of the powerful emotional appeal of the God-soul-prayer conceptual framework. Hence the kind of theory replacement required to be bring about conceptual change in biology, psychology, and medicine is not just a matter of explanatory coherence, but requires changes in emotional coherence as well (for a theory of emotional coherence, see Thagard, 2000, 2003b).

From this perspective, science education inevitably involves cultural remediation and even psychotherapy in addition to more cognitive kinds of instruction. The transition from theological to qualitative to mechanistic explanations of phenomena is cognitively and emotional difficult, but crucial for scientific progress, as we have seen for the central concepts of life, mind, and disease.

REFERENCES

Anderson, J. R., Bothell, D., Byrne, M. D., Douglas, S., Lebiere, C., & Qin, U. (2004). An integrated theory of the mind. *Psychological Review, 111*, 1030–1060.

Bechtel, W., & Abrahamson, A. A. (2005). Explanation: A mechanistic alternative. *Studies in History and Philosophy of Biology and Biomedical Sciences, 36*, 421–441.

Bechtel, W., & Richardson, R. C. (1993). Discovering complexity. Princeton, NJ: Princeton University Press.

Bechtel, W., & Richardson, R. C. (1998). Vitalism. In E. Craig (Ed.), *Routledge encyclopedia of philosophy* (pp. 639–643). London: Routledge.

Chalmers, D. J. (1996). *The conscious mind.* Oxford: Oxford University Press.

Chi, M. T. H. (2005). Commonsense conceptions of emergent processes: Why some misconceptions are robust. *Journal of the Learning Sciences, 14*, 161–199.

Churchland, P. S., & Sejnowski, T. (1992). *The computational brain.* Cambridge, MA: MIT Press.

Comte, A. (1970). *Introduction to positive philosophy* (F. Ferré, Trans.). Indianapolis, IN: Bobbs-Merrill.

Dembski, W. (1999). *Intelligent design: The bridge between science and theology.* Downers Grove, IL: InterVarsity Press.

Descartes. (1985). *The philosophical writings of Descartes.* (J. Cottingham, R. Stoothoff, & D. Murdoch, Trans.). Cambridge: Cambridge University Press.

Eliasmith, C., & Anderson, C. H. (2003). *Neural engineering: Computation, representation and dynamics in neurobiological systems.* Cambridge, MA: MIT Press.

Grene, M., & Depew, D. (2004). *The philosophy of biology: An episodic history.* Cambridge: Cambridge University Press.

Hippocrates. (1988). *Hippocrates, vol. V* (P. Potter, Trans.). Cambridge, MA: Harvard University Press.

Horwich, P. (Ed.). (1993). *World changes: Thomas Kuhn and the nature of science.* Cambridge, MA: MIT Press.

Kuhn, T. S. (1970). *The structure of scientific revolutions* (2nd ed.). Chicago: University of Chicago Press.

LaPorte, J. (2004). *Natural kinds and conceptual change.* Cambridge: Cambridge University Press.

Lodish, H., Berk, A., Zipursky, S. L., Matsudaira, P., Baltimore, D., & Darnell, J. (2000). *Molecular cell biology* (4th ed.). New York: W. H. Freeman.

Machamer, P., Darden, L., & Craver, C. F. (2000). Thinking about mechanisms. *Philosophy of Science, 67*, 1–25.

Nersessian, N. (1992). How do scientists think? Capturing the dynamics of conceptual change in science. In R. Giere (Ed.), *Cognitive models of science* (Vol. 15, pp. 3–44). Minneapolis: University of Minnesota Press.

Newell, A., Shaw, J. C., & Simon, H. (1958). Elements of a theory of human problem solving. *Psychological Review, 65*, 151–166.

Paley, W. (1963). *Natural theology: Selections.* Indianapolis: Bobbs-Merrill.

Rumelhart, D. E., & McClelland, J. L. (Eds.). (1986). *Parallel distributed processing: Explorations in the microstructure of cognition*. Cambridge MA: MIT Press/Bradford Books.

Salmon, W. (1984). *Scientific explanation and the causal structure of the world*. Princeton, NJ: Princeton University Press.

Smith, E. E., & Kosslyn, S. M. (2007). *Cognitive psychology: Mind and brain.* Upper Saddle River, NJ: Pearson Prentice Hall.

Thagard, P. (1992). *Conceptual revolutions*. Princeton, NJ: Princeton University Press.

Thagard, P. (1999). *How scientists explain disease*. Princeton, NJ: Princeton University Press.

Thagard, P. (2000). *Coherence in thought and action*. Cambridge, MA: MIT Press.

Thagard, P. (2003a). Pathways to biomedical discovery. *Philosophy of Science, 70*, 235–254.

Thagard, P. (2003b). Why wasn't O. J. convicted? Emotional coherence in legal inference. *Cognition and Emotion, 17*, 361–383.

Thagard, P. (2005a). The emotional coherence of religion. *Journal of Cognition and Culture, 5*, 58–74.

Thagard, P. (2005b). *Mind: Introduction to cognitive science* (2nd ed.). Cambridge, MA: MIT Press.

Thagard, P. (2006). What is a medical theory? In R. Paton & L. A. McNamara (Eds.), *Multidisciplinary approaches to theory in medicine* (pp. 47–62). Amsterdam: Elsevier.

Thagard, P. (2007). Coherence, truth, and the development of scientific knowledge. *Philosophy of Science, 74*, 28–47.

Thagard, P., & Zhu, J. (2003). Acupuncture, incommensurability, and conceptual change. In G. M. Sinatra & P. R. Pintrich (Eds.), *Intentional conceptual change* (pp. 79–102). Mahwah, NJ: Erlbaum.

von Neumann, J. (1958). *The computer and the brain*. New Haven: Yale University Press.

IV

MECHANISMS FOR CONCEPTUAL CHANGE

15

Mental Modeling in Conceptual Change

Nancy J. Nersessian
Georgia Institute of Technology

INTRODUCTION

The nature and processes of "conceptual change" are problems that are of considerable interest to researchers across several disciplines occupied with developing understandings of science, learners, or cognitive development. Although the problems and methods to address them have different formulations in these areas, there is a long history in each of specifying the beginning and ending states of deep conceptual changes, such as what constitutes the nature of representational changes from Newtonian mechanics to the theory of relativity, or from a "naive" understanding of physical phenomena to a scientific understanding provided by physics or biology, or from individual early (possibly innate) representational structures to adult community representations of a whole range of phenomena, including of other humans, during processes of cognitive development.

A major outstanding problem in all of these areas is the nature of the processes — or "mechanisms" — through which concepts and conceptual structures change. In part because of similarities in features of conceptual changes across these areas, such as ontological shifts and degrees of "incommensurability," some, myself included, have proposed that the same or related processes are at work in the several kinds of conceptual change. Clearly one would expect differences between, for example, the practices used by scientists in constructing new concepts and students learning new (for them) concepts. For one thing scientists have articulated theoretical goals and sophisticated metacognitive strategies while children and students do not. However, in conceptual change processes, a significant parallel is that each involves problem solving. One way to think of learning science, for instance, is that students are engaged in (or need to be enticed into) trying to understand the extant scientific conceptualization of a domain. In this process, learning happens when they perceive the inadequacies of their intuitive understandings — at least under certain conditions — and construct representations of the scientific concepts for themselves. The impetus for a problem solving process can arise from many sources: acquiring new information, encountering a puzzling phenomenon, or perceiving an inadequacy in current ways of understanding.

Concepts provide a means through which humans make sense of the world. In categorizing experiences we sort phenomena, noting relationships, differences, and interconnections among them. A conceptual structure is a way of systematizing, of putting concepts in relation to one another in at least a semi — or locally — coherent manner. But a conceptual structure is complex and intricate and it is not possible to entertain it in its entirety all at once. Trying to understand new experiences or how a concept relates to others can reveal here-to-fore unnoticed limitations and problems in the representational capabilities of current conceptual structures and even reveal inconsistencies with other parts. Although how reflectively they engage in the process differs, scientists, learners, and developing children all engage in this kind of sense-making which suggests that to a greater or lesser extent conceptual change is a reasoned "change in view" (Harman, 1986).

Thinking of conceptual change in this way focuses attention on the nature of the reasoning scientists use in solving representational problems. Creating models as systems of inquiry is central in the problem solving practices of scientists. There is a large literature in history and philosophy of science that establishes that processes of constructing and manipulating analogical, visual, and simulative models play central role in episodes of conceptual change across the sciences. On the account of conceptual change in science I have been developing, reasoning through such models ("model-based reasoning") provides a significant means (not necessarily the *only* means) through which conceptual innovation and change occur (see, e.g., Nersessian, 1992a, 1992b, 1995, 1999, 2002b). Within both philosophy and cognitive science, the traditional view of reasoning is identified with logical operations performed on language-like representations. In contrast to these traditional conceptions, these modeling practices of scientists are not simply aids to logical reasoning but constitute a distinct form of reasoning. Loosely construed, a model is a representation of a system with interactive parts with representations of those interactions. Models are representations of objects, processes, or events that capture structural, behavioral, or functional relations significant to understanding these. What is required for something to be an instance of model-based reasoning is that 1) it involves the construction or retrieval of a model, 2) inferences are derived through manipulation of the model, and 3) inferences can be specific or generic, that is, they can either apply to the particular model or to the model understood as a model-type, representing a class of models.

To understand how model-based reasoning leads to conceptual change requires both detailed investigations of cases of their use in conceptual change and of their basis in human cognition — what I have called a "cognitive-historical" analysis. The latter requirement stems from a "naturalist" epistemology which holds that the problem-solving practices of scientists arise out of and are constrained by basic cognitive capacities exhibited also in mundane problem solving, though of course not from these alone. The normally functioning human cognitive apparatus is capable of mental modeling, analogy making, abstraction, visualization, and simulative imagining. The sciences, through individual and collective efforts, have bootstrapped their way from these basic capabilities to the current state of play through consciously reflective development of methods of investigation aimed at gaining specific kinds of understanding and insight into nature, such as quantitative understanding. Of course, the development of these methods has been and continues to be a complex interaction among humans and the natural and socio-cultural worlds in which they are embedded. Nevertheless, an important part of explaining how these investigative strategies fulfill their objectives requires examining the nature of mundane cognitive capabilities out of which they arise.

In this chapter I will focus on one capacity, that for mental modeling, in part because analogy, visualization, and simulation contribute to reasoning through mental modeling and in part because mental modeling is a central notion used in analyses of conceptual change across the literatures of studies of science, learning, and cognitive development. For an intuitive understanding of what it means to solve a problem through mental modeling, consider the situation where a large sofa needs to be moved through a doorway. The default approach to solving the problem is usually to imagine moving a mental token approximating the shape of the sofa through various rotations constrained by the boundaries of a doorway-like shape. In solving this problem, people do not customarily resort to formulating a series of propositions and applying logic or to doing trigonometric calculations. Note, too, that arriving at a problem solution is easier if it takes place in front of the doorway and the sofa, as opposed to in a furniture store and thinking about whether it is wise to purchase the sofa. In such mundane cases, the reasoning performed via mental modeling is usually successful, i.e., one figures out how to get the chair through the door, because the models and manipulative processes embody largely correct assumptions about every-day real-world phenomena. In scientific problem solving, where the situations are more removed from human sensory experience and the assumptions more imbued with theory, there is less assurance that a mental modeling process will be successful. More sophisticated and explicit knowledge of constraints relating to general principles of the science and mathematical equations will play a role in constructing and manipulating the mental models. There are four points to highlight that carry over from the mundane case in considering the case of science: 1) humans appear able to create representations from memory that enable them to imagine being in situations purely through mental simulation, 2) the imagining processes can take advantage of affordances in the environment can make problem solving easier, 3) the predictions, and other kinds of solutions arrived at through this kind of mental simulation are often correct — or good enough — in mundane cases, and 4) when solution fails a wide range of culturally available tools can be used, such as getting out the measuring tape and making the calculation.

Having wrestled with a considerable portion of the cognitive science literature on mental models, I have to concur with Lance Rips' observation that much use of the notion appears "muddled" (Rips, 1986), but I disagree with his conclusion that dismisses the viability of the notion entirely. A potentially quite powerful notion can be articulated and, as some researchers have contended, could provide a much-needed unifying framework for the study of cognition (see, e.g., Gilhooly, 1986; Johnson-Laird, 1980). My objective here is modest: to provide a much-needed clarification of reasoning through mental modeling; one that is consistent with the cognitive science research on mundane cases and is adequate as a cognitive basis for the scientific model-based reasoning practices exhibited in conceptual change, which can then be investigated further in empirical and theoretical research in cognitive science.

Thinking about the scientific uses has required extending my investigation beyond the literatures specifically on mental models to include research on imaginative simulation in mental imagery, mental animation, and perception-based representation. Further, within traditional cognitive science, the representations and processing involved in reasoning are held to take place "in the head," and reasoning is analyzed as detached from the material environments in which it occurs. Although it is possible that simple model-based reasoning might take place only "in the head," reasoning of the complexity of that in science is make extensive use of external representations. A wide range of data — historical, protocol, and ethnographic — establish that many kinds of external representations are used during scientific reasoning: linguistic (descriptions, narratives, written and verbal communications), mathematical equations, visual representations, gestures, physical models, and computational models. Thus even an analysis of *mental* modeling needs to consider the relations among the internal and external representations and processes in problem-solving. Here I consider the question of what might be the nature of the mental representation used in mental modeling such as to enable that internal and external representational coupling during reasoning processes.

THE MENTAL MODELS FRAMEWORK

The notion of a "mental model" is central to much of contemporary cognitive science. In 1943, the psychologist and physiologist Kenneth Craik hypothesized that in many instances people reason by carrying out thought experiments on internal models of physical situations, where a model is a structural, behavioral, or functional analog to a real-world phenomenon (Craik, 1943). Craik based his hypothesis on the predictive power of thought and the ability of humans to explore real-world and imaginary situations mentally. We will return to Craik's own view in a later section, after first considering its contemporary legacy. Craik made this proposal at the height of the behaviorist approach in psychology, and so it received little notice. The development of a "cognitive" psychology in the 1960s created a more hospitable environment for investigating and articulating the hypothesis. A new 1967 edition of Craik's book, with a Postscript replying to critics, fell on more fertile ground and has since had considerable impact on contemporary cognitive science. Since the early 1980s, a "mental models framework" has developed in a large segment of cognitive science. This is an explanatory framework that posits models as organized units of mental representation of knowledge employed in various cognitive tasks including reasoning, problem solving, and discourse comprehension.

What is a mental model? How is it represented? What kinds of processing underlie its use? What are the mental mechanisms that create and use mental models? How does mental modeling engage external representations and processes? These issues are not often addressed explicitly in the literature and where they are, there is as yet no consensus position that might serve as a theory of mental models. Thus, I have chosen the word "framework" to characterize a wide range of research. What the positions within this framework share is a general hypothesis that some mental representations of domain knowledge are organized in units containing knowledge of spatio-temporal structure, causal connections and other relational structures.

In the early 1980s, several, largely independent, strands of research emerged introducing the theoretical notions of "mental model" and "mental modeling" into the cognitive science literature. One strand introduced the notion to explain the effects of semantic information in logical reasoning (Johnson-Laird, 1983). Another strand introduced the notion to explain the empirical findings that in reasoning related to discourse comprehension, people seem to reason from a representation of the structure of a situation rather than from a description of a situation (so-called "discourse" and "situation" models; Johnson-Laird, 1982; Perrig & Kintsch, 1985). Both of these strands focused on the nature of the representations constructed in working memory during reasoning and problem-solving tasks. Yet another strand introduced the notion in relation to long-term memory representations of knowledge used in understanding and reasoning, in particular, about physical systems. This literature posited the notion to explain a wide range of experimental results indicating that people use organized knowledge structures relating to physical systems in attempting to understand manual control systems and devices in the area of human — machine interactions (see Rouse & Morris, 1986, for an overview) and in employing qualitative domain knowledge of physical systems to solve problems (Gentner & Stevens, 1983). Some of the early work relating to physical systems that began with psychological studies migrated into artificial intelligence (AI) where computational theories of "naive" or "qualitative" physics in particular were developed to explore issues of knowledge organization, use, access and control, such as in understanding and predicting the behavior of liquids (Hayes, 1979) or the motion of a ball in space and time (Forbus, 1983). Much of the pioneering research in third strand is represented in the edited collection, *Mental Models* (Gentner & Stevens, 1983) that appeared in the same year as Johnson-Laird's (1983) monograph of the same name which brought together the working memory strands.

Research within the mental models framework is extensive and varied. As an indication of the range, research includes: AI models of qualitative reasoning about causality in physical systems (see, e.g., Bobrow, 1985), representations of intuitive domain knowledge in various areas, such as physics and astronomy (see, e.g., Vosniadou & Brewer, 1992), analogical problem solving (see, e.g. Gentner & Stevens 1983), deductive and inductive reasoning (see, e.g., Holland, Holyoak, Nisbett, & Thagard, 1986; Johnson-Laird & Byrne, 1993), probabilistic inference (Kahneman & Tversky, 1982) "heterogeneous" or "multimodal" reasoning (Allwein & Barwise, 1996), modal logic (Bell & Johnson-Laird, 1998), narrative and discourse comprehension (see, e.g., Johnson-Laird, 1982; Perrig & Kintsch, 1985), scientific thought experimenting (Nersessian, 1991, 1992c), and cultural transmission (Shore, 1997). However, a consensus view has not developed among these areas of research. The preponderance of research into mental models has been concerned with specifying the content and structure of long-term memory models in a specific domain or with respect to specific reasoning tasks or levels of expertise, and not with addressing the more foundational questions raised above. Most importantly, clarification is needed on basic issues as to the nature of the format of the model and the processing involved in using a model.

Given that my focus is on mental modeling during reasoning processes, I consider here only the psychological accounts that hypothesize reasoning as involving the construction and manipulation of a model in working memory during the reasoning process and not those the accounts of the nature of representation in long-term memory, about which my account can remain agnostic. Of course, reasoning processes draw on long-term-memory representations and so the account developed of these can lead to insights into the nature of the stored representations that support reasoning and understanding. Additionally in conceptual change, the expectation is that reasoning would lead to changes in the content and structure of long-term memory representations. I also will not address accounts that are primarily computational since what Rips (1986) pointed out still holds true today: computational modeling of qualitative reasoning requires highly complex representations that in the end can do much simpler reasoning than humans can carry out. He considered this a reason for dismissing the very notion of mental modeling, whereas I would counter that the limitations of the computational models stem from the kinds of representations and processing used so far, and that these quite possibly differ from those used by people.

Working memory accounts of mental modeling include those concerned with reasoning and with narrative and discourse comprehension. The literatures on imaginative simulation in mental imagery, mental animation, and perception-based representation also provide insights relevant to developing an account of mental modeling. My strategy is to first address some general issue about representation and processing that we will need in discussing mental modeling, to briefly survey the accounts in the literatures noted, then to propose a synthesis of the several threads in the research to address simulative model-based reasoning as practiced by scientists, and finally to return to the implications of all this for conceptual change.

Format and Processing Issues

It has been a fundamental presupposition of cognitive science that humans think about real and imaginary worlds though internal representations. Although that assumption has been challenged by researchers in the areas of connectionism, dynamic cognition, and situated cognition, in this section I focus on the controversy about the nature of mental representation as it appears within the traditional cognitive science, where there are mental representations and "internal" and "external" are clear and distinct notions. Recently these founding assumptions were reiterated and elaborated upon by Alonso Vera and Herbert Simon (Vera & Simon, 1993) in response to criticisms. They specify a "physical symbol system" as possessing a memory capable of storing symbols and symbol structures and a set of information processes that form symbols and structures as a function of stimuli, which in humans are sensory stimuli. Sensory stimuli produce symbol structures that cause motor actions which in turn modify symbol structures in memory. Such a physical symbol system interacts with the environment by receiving sensory information from it and converting these into symbol structures in memory and by acting upon it in ways determined by those symbol structures. Perceptual and motor processes connect symbol structures with the environment, thus providing a semantics for the symbols. In the case of humans, then, all representation and processing is internal to the human mind/brain.

What is the nature of the symbols and the symbol structures? Since its inception, there has been a deep divide in the field of cognitive science between those who hold that all mental representation is language-like and those who hold that at least some representation is perceptual or imagistic in format. Herbert Simon reports that this divide "nearly torpedoed the effort of the Sloan Foundation to launch a major program of support for cognitive science" (Simon, 1977, p. 385). Volumes of research have since been directed towards and against each side of the divide, and even with significant clarification of the issues and considerable experimental work, the issue remains unresolved and most likely will continue to be until more is known about how the nature of the representation-creating mechanisms in the brain. The format issue is important because different kinds of representation — linguistic, formulaic, imagistic, analog — enable different kinds of processing operations.

Operations on linguistic and formulaic representations include the familiar operations of logic and mathematics. Linguistic representations, for example, are interpreted as referring to physical objects, structures, processes, or events descriptively. Customarily, the relationship between this kind of representation and what it refers to is truth, and thus the representation is evaluated as being true or false. Constructing these representations requires following a grammar that specifies the proper syntactical structures. Operations on such representations are rule-based and truth-preserving if the symbols are interpreted in a consistent manner and the properties they refer to are stable in that environment. Additional operations can be defined in limited domains provided they are consistent with the constraints that hold in that domain. Manipulation of a linguistic or formulaic representation of a model would require explicit representation of salient parameters including constraints and transition states. Condition — action rules of production systems provide an example, as do the equation-like representations of qualitative process models. In this latter case, simulative reasoning about physical systems occurs by changing the values of variables to create new states of the model. I will call representations with these characteristics "propositional," following the usual philosophical usage that refers to a language-like encoding possessing a vocabulary, grammar, and semantics (see, e.g., Fodor, 1975) rather than the broader usage sometimes employed in cognitive science which is co-extensive with "symbolic."

On the other hand, analog models, diagrams, and imagistic representations are interpreted as representing demonstratively. The relationship between this kind of representation, which I will call "iconic," and what it represents is similarity or goodness of fit (with isomorphism being the limit). Iconic representations are similar in degrees and aspects to what they represent, and are thus evaluated as accurate or inaccurate. Operations on iconic representations involve transformations of the representations that change their properties and relations in ways consistent with the constraints of the domain. Significantly, transformational constraints represented in iconic representations can be implicit, for example, a person can do simple reasoning about what happens when a rod is bent without having an explicit rule, such as "given the same force a longer rod will bend farther." The form of representation is such as to enable simulations in which the model behaves in accord with constraints that need not be stated explicitly during this process.

Dispersed throughout the cognitive science literature is another distinction pertinent to the format of mental models which concerns the nature of the symbols that constitute propositional and iconic representations — that between "amodal" and "modal" symbols (see, e.g., Barsalou, 1999). Modal symbols are analog representations of the perceptual states from which they are extracted. Amodal symbols are arbitrary transductions from perceptual states, such as those associated with a "language of thought." A modal symbol representing a cat would retain perceptual aspects of cats; an amodal symbol would have an arbitrary relationship to the cat in the way that, for example, the strings of letters of the words "cat" or "chat" or "Katze" are arbitrarily related to the perceptual aspects of cats. Propositional representations, in the sense discussed above, are composed of amodal symbols. Iconic representations can be composed of either. For example, a representation of the situation "the circle is to the left of the square, which is to the left of the triangle" could be composed of either modal tokens ❸ - ❺ - ❿ or amodal tokens, standing for these entities in much the way the letters C - S - T correspond to objects. Whether the mental symbols used in an iconic representation are modal or amodal has implications for how such representations are constructed and manipulated. Constructing a modal representation, for example, is likely to involve reactivation of patterns of neural activity in the perceptual and motor parts of the brain that were activated in the initial experience of something, thus manipulation of the representation is likely to involve perceptual and motor processing, whereas an amodal representation is typically held not to involve sensorimotor processing.

One difficulty in sorting through the mental modeling literature is that one can find all possible flavors in it: propositional, amodal iconic, and modal iconic mental models. Among the working memory accounts, Holland et al. (1986) maintain that reasoning with a mental model is a process of applying condition-action rules to propositional representations of the specific situation, such as making inferences about a feminist bank teller on the basis of a model constructed from representations of feminists and bank tellers. On Johnson-Laird's account mental models are not propositional, rather they are amodal iconic representations. Making a logical inference such as *modus ponens* occurs by manipulating amodal tokens in a spatial array that captures the salient structural dimensions of the problem and then searching for counterexamples to the model transformation. "Depictive mental models" (Schwartz & Black, 1996a) provide an example of modal iconic mental models. Depictive models are manipulated by using tacit knowledge embedded in constraints to simulate possible behaviors, such as in an analog model of a setup of machine gears. In both instances of iconic models operations on a mental model transform it in ways consistent with the constraints of the system it represents.

Although the jury is still out on the issue of the working memory representations the research that investigates reasoning about physical systems leads in the iconic direction, which, as I will now discuss, was the initial proposal by Craik.

"Craikian" Mental Modeling

The most influential account of mental modeling is that of Johnson-Laird (1983). On this account, a mental model is an iconic representation that is a structural, behavioral, or functional analog of a real-world or imaginary situation, event, object, or process. Johnson-Laird roots his view in the earlier proposal of Craik, however, his focus has been on mental modeling in the domains of deductive, inductive, and modal logics. This, coupled with his wanting to distinguish mental models from what is customarily understood as mental imagery have led him to underplay or not develop what I see as a central insight of Craik: reasoning about physical systems via mental simulation of analog representations. To account for simulative reasoning about physical systems and model-based reasoning in science in particular, requires more kinds of model manipulation than logical reasoning, which on Johnson-Laird's account involves moving amodal tokens in spatiotemporal configurations. Tacit and explicit domain knowledge of the physical system, such as causal knowledge, is needed in constructing models and creating new states and inferring outcomes via simulation.

Clearly, in the case of science, the knowledge required to carry out such a simulation is more complex, but I contend that it is this basic capability that underlies simulative model-based reasoning by scientists. There have been numerous reports by scientists and engineers of conducting mental simulations in solving problems. Kekule claimed to have imagined a circle of snakes, each biting the tale of the snake in front of it, and Einstein claimed to have imagined chasing a beam of light. Roger Shepard (1978) has listed many cases of famous scientists in his discussion of mental imagery. Eugene Ferguson's analysis of the role of visual thinking in engineering visualization and in *Engineering and the Mind's Eye* (Ferguson, 1983) provides several more, most notably Nicola Tesla's report that part of his process of designing devices was to imagine the devices and run them in his imagination over a period of weeks in order to see which parts were most subject to wear. Although the accounts given by historical scientists and engineers are retrospective, there is mounting experimental evidence from mundane and expert studies in support of the hypothesis of reasoning through mental simulation, as will be exemplified below.

The original Craikian notion emphasized the *parallelism* both in form and in operation in internal modeling: "By 'relation — structure' I do not mean some obscure non-physical entity which attends the model, but the fact that it is a physical working model which works in the same way as the process it parallels, in the aspects under consideration at any moment" (Craik, 1943, p. 51). By this I interpret him to mean that the internal model complies with the constraints of the real-world phenomena it represents, not that it is run like a "movie in the head," which signifies vivid and detailed visual representations "running" in real time. Craik based his hypothesis on the need for organisms to be able to predict the environment, thus he saw mental simulation as central to reasoning. He maintained that just as humans create physical models, for example, physical scale models of boats and bridges, to experiment with alternatives, so too the nervous system of humans and other organisms has developed a way to create internal "'small scale model[s]' of external reality" (p. 61) for simulating potential outcomes of actions in a physical environment. I interpret his use of quotation marks around "small scale models" to indicate that he meant it figuratively, and not that the brain quite literally creates, for example, an image of small-scale boat whose motion it simulates as in a movie. He does, however, appear to mean that the representations are modal or perception-based. Mental simulation occurs, he claimed, by the "excitation and volley of impulses which parallel the stimuli which occasioned them...." (p. 60). Thus the internal processes of reasoning result in conclusions similar to those that "might have been reached by causing the actual physical processes to occur" (p. 51). In constructing the hypothesis Craik drew on existing research in neurophysiology and speculated that the ability "to parallel or model external events" (p. 51) is fundamental to the brain.

Modern advocates of mental modeling also speculate that the capacity developed for simulating possible ways of maneuvering within the physical environment. It would be highly adaptive to possess the ability to anticipate the environment and potential outcomes of actions, so many organisms should have the capacity for mental simulation. Quite conceivably, then, the rat simulates its path through a familiar maze and performs the appropriate actions to get to the food at the end. Given that modern humans have linguistic capabilities, it should be possible to create mental models from both perception and description, which is borne out by the research on narrative and discourse comprehension that will be discussed below. Additionally, studies of expert/novice reasoning lend support to the possibility that skill in mental modeling develops in the course of learning (Chi, Feltovich, & Glaser, 1981). The nature and richness of models one can construct and one's ability to reason develops in learning domain-specific content and techniques. Thus, facility with mental modeling is a combination of an individual's biology and learning, and develops in interaction with the natural, social, and cultural realities in which one is embedded.

I will next bring together research on discourse and situation models, mental imagery, mental animation, and embodied mental representation as providing evidence in support of a Craikian notion of mental modeling.

Discourse and Situation Models

Reading, comprehending, and reasoning about stories would seem to epitomize thinking with language. Yet, there is a significant body of cognitive research that supports the hypothesis that the inferences subjects make from these activities are derived through constructing and manipulating a mental model of the situation depicted by the narrative, rather than by applying rules of inference to a system of propositions representing the content of the text. A major strategy of this approach is to differentiate the structure of the text from the structure of the situation depicted in the text and investigate which structure cognitive representations follow. Johnson-Laird in psycholinguistics and others in psychology, formal semantics, and linguistics have proposed cognitive representations in the form of working memory "discourse models" or a "situation models" are used in inferencing related to narratives. On this proposal, the linguistic expressions assist the reader/listener in constructing a mental model through which they understand and reason about the situation depicted by the narrative. That is, in reasoning, the referent of the text would be an internal model of the situation depicted by the text rather than a description. The central idea is that "discourse models make explicit the structure not of sentences but of situations as we perceive or imagine them" (Johnson-Laird, 1989, p. 471). The principal tenets of the theory, as outlined by Johnson-Laird, are as follows. As a form of mental model, a discourse model would embody a representation of the spatial, temporal, and causal relationships among the events and entities of the situation described by the narrative. In constructing and updating a model, the reader calls upon a combination of pre-existing conceptual and real-world knowledge and employs the tacit and recursive inferencing mechanisms of her cognitive apparatus to integrate the information with that contained in the narrative. In principle these should be able to generate the set of all possible situations a narrative could describe.

A number of experiments have been conducted to investigate the hypothesis that in understanding a narrative readers spontaneously construct mental models to represent and reason about the situations depicted by the text (Dijk & Kintsch, 1983; Franklin & Tversky, 1990; Johnson-Laird, 1983; Mani & Johnson-Laird, 1982; McNamara & Sternberg, 1983; Morrow, Bower, & Greenspan, 1989; Perrig & Kintsch, 1985; Zwann, 1999; Zwann & Radvansky, 1998). Although no instructions were given to imagine or picture the situations, when queried about how they had made inferences in response to an experimenter's questioning, most participants reported that it was by means of "seeing" or "being in the situation" depicted. That is, the reader sees herself as an "observer" of a simulated situation. Whether the view of the situation is "spatial" (i.e., a global perspective) or "perspectival" (i.e., from a specific point of view) is still a point of debate, though recent investigations tend to support the perspectival account, that is, the reference frame of the space appears to be that of the body (Bryant & Tversky, 1999; Glenberg, 1997b; Mainwaring, Tversky, & Schiano, 1996).

The interpretation given these experimental outcomes is that a situation represented by a mental model could allow the reasoner to generate inferences without having to carry out the extensive operations needed to process the same amount of background information to make inferences from an argument in propositional form. The situational constraints of the narrative are built into the model, making many consequences implicit that would require considerable inferential work in propositional form. For example, consider a case where a subject is asked to move an object depicted in a model. Moving an object changes, immediately, its spatial relationships to all the other objects. In simulative mental modeling, the reasoner could grasp this simply by means of the changes in the model and not need to make additional inferences. Such reasoning should be discernibly faster. Thus, the chronometric studies noted above provide additional experimental support that making inferences through simulation is faster than making logical inferences from propositions. Finally, reasoning through a model of a situation should restrict the scope of the conclusions drawn. For example, moving an object in a specified manner both limits and makes immediately evident the relevant consequences of that move for other objects in the situation detailed by the narrative. Further support is thus provided by demonstrations in this literature that it is much more difficult to make inferences — and sometimes they are not made at all — when participants are required to reason with the situation represented in propositional form.

Mental Spatial Simulation

There is an extensive literature that provides evidence that humans can perform various simulative transformations in imagination that mimic physical spatial transformations. The literature on mental imagery establishes that people can mentally simulate combinations, such as with the classic example where subjects are asked to imagine a letter B rotated 90 degrees to the left, place an upside triangle below it and remove the connecting line and the processes produces an image of a heart. People can perform imaginative rotations that exhibit latencies consistent with actually turning a mental figure around, such as when queried as to whether two objects presented from different rotations are of the same object (Finke, 1989; Finke, Pinker, & Farah, 1989; Finke & Shepard, 1986; Kosslyn, 1980, 1994; Shepard & Cooper, 1982; Tye, 1991), and there is a correlation between the time it takes participants to respond and the number of degrees of rotation required. Further, rotational transformations of plane figures and 3-dimensional models are evidenced. As Stephen Kosslyn (1994, p. 345) summarizes, psychological research provides evidence of rotating, translating, bending, scaling folding, zooming, and flipping of images. The combinations and transformations in mental imagery are hypothesized to take place according to internalized constraints assimilated during perception (Shepard, 1988). Kosslyn also notes that these mental transformations are often accompanied by twisting and moving one's hands to represent rotation, which indicates motor as well as visual processing (see also, Jeannerod, 1993, 1994; Parsons, 1994). Other research indicates that people combine various kinds of knowledge of physical situations with imaginary transformations, including real-time dynamical information (Freyd, 1987). When given a problem about objects that are separated by a wall, for instance, the spatial transformations exhibit latencies consistent with the participants having simulated moving around the wall rather than through it, which indicates at least tacit use of physical knowledge that objects cannot move through a wall (Morrow et al., 1989). This kind of knowledge is evidenced in other studies, such as in which participants are shown a picture of a person with an arm in front of the body and then one with the arm in back, and they report imagining rotating the arm around the body, rather than through it, and the chronometric measurements are consistent with this (Shiffrar & Freyd, 1990).

Although physical knowledge other than spatial appears to be playing a role in such imaginings, it has not been explored systematically in the mental imagery literature. The kinds of transformations considered thus far are spatial: structural/geometrical/topological transformations. I refer to the literature on imagery not to make the claim that mental models are like images, but because this literature provides significant evidence for the hypothesis that the human cognitive system is capable of transformative processing in which spatial transformations are made on iconic representations through perceptual and motor processes. Indeed, there is significant evidence from neuropsychology that the perceptual system plays a role in imaginative thinking (see, e.g., Farah, 1988; Kosslyn, 1994). Again, this makes sense from an evolutionary perspective. The visual cortex is one of the oldest and most highly developed regions of the brain. As Roger Shepard, a psychologist who has done extensive research on visual cognition, has put it, perceptual mechanisms "have, through evolutionary eons, deeply internalized an intuitive wisdom about the way things transform in the world. Because this wisdom is embodied in a perceptual system that antedates, by far, the emergence of language and mathematics, imagination is more akin to visualizing than to talking or to calculating to oneself" (Shepard. 1988, p.180). Although the original ability to envision, predict, and inference by imagining developed as a way of simulating possible courses of action in the world, as humans developed, this ability has been "bent to the service of creative thought" (Shepard, 1988, p.180). Understood in this way, the mundane ability to imagine and visualize underlies some of the most sophisticated forms of human reasoning as evidenced in creative reasoning in science. To stress once again, though, the representational format of mental imagery should not be conflated with that of external pictorial representations. As various researchers have shown, such as with Gestalt figures (Chambers & Reisberg, 1985), internal representations appear more sketchy and less flexible in attempts at reinterpretation. Furthermore, congenitally blind individuals can carry out some classic imagery tasks, though the source of such transformational knowledge would be haptic perception and the imagery possibly kinesthetic in nature (Arditi, Holtzman, & Kosslyn, 1988; Kerr, 1983; Marmor & Zaback, 1976).

Mental Animation

There is a growing literature in psychology and neuroscience that investigates the hypothesis that the human cognitive system possesses the ability for *mental animation* in problem solving tasks. This ability would be central in Craikian mental modeling. This kind of simulative model-based reasoning both in mundane thinking and in science is likely to go beyond just making spatial transformations and extend to the kinds of transformations of physical systems requiring causal and other behavioral knowledge. Indeed, Shepard extended his claim about the nature of the information humans internalize about how things transform in the world to include behavioral constraints, and attempted to develop an account of the psychokinetic laws of such transformations (Shepard, 1984, 1994). There is also a significant body of research on infant cognition that has established that days old infants have an acute sensitivity to causal information. Infants gaze longer and show more interest in events that appear to contradict causality (Spelke, 1991; Spelke, Phillips, & Woodward, 1995).

Recent investigations of physical reasoning have moved beyond spatial and temporal transformations to examining the role of causal and behavioral knowledge in mental simulation. The ability to mentally animate is highly correlated with scores on tests of spatial ability (Hegarty & Sims, 1994). However, as Mary Hegarty, too, stresses the mental representations underlying animation need not be what are customarily thought of as "mental images." Images are often taken to be vivid and detailed holistic representations, such as in a photograph or in a movie, where simulation would take place all at once. However, the imagery literature supports the notion that imagery most often is largely sketchy and schematic and that animation of an image can be piecemeal, as supported by her research. Kosslyn's highly elaborated neuroscience account of imagery (Kosslyn, 1994), argues that transformations of the image most likely take place outside of the visual buffer through connections with long term memory representations, with the image in the buffer being "refreshed" with the updated transformation.

Much of this research has its origin in thinking about diagrammatic representations in reasoning, specifically, inferring motion from static representations. It thus provides insights into the relations between internal and external representations that we will follow up on in a later section. One indication of interaction is that participants in these kinds of studies often use gestures, sometimes performed over the diagram, that simulate and track the motion (see, e.g., Clement, 1994, 2003; Golden-Meadow, Nusbaum, Kelly, & Wagner, 2001; Hegarty & Steinhoff, 1994). Prominent research on mental animation includes Hegarty's (Hegarty, 1992; Hegarty & Ferguson, 1993; Hegarty & Just, 1989) investigations of reasoning about the behavior of pulley systems and Daniel Schwartz's (Schwartz, 1995; Schwartz & Black, 1996a, 1996b) studies focusing on gear rotations. These studies, respectively, provide evidence that people are able to perform simulative causal transformations of static figures provided with the initial set up of the pulleys and the of gears. Several findings are important here. Protocols of participants indicate that they do not mentally animate the pulley systems all at once as would appear to happen in the real world experience of it, but animate in segments in the causal sequence, working out in a piecemeal fashion the consequences of previous motion for the next segment. The response time for the participants in the gear problems indicates they, too, animated in sequence, and when given only one set of gears, their response time was proportional to the rate of the angle of rotation. Participants perform better when given more realistic representations of gears, than highly schematic ones, such as those of just circles with no cogs. In the realistic case, they seem to use physical knowledge, such as friction, directly to animate the model, whereas in the schematic case they revert to more analytic strategies such as comparing the size of the angles gears of different sizes would move through. Schwartz's research also indicates that mental animation can make use of other non-visual information such as of viscosity and gravity. When participants are well trained in rules for inferring motion, however, they often revert to these to solve the problem more quickly (Schwartz & Black, 1996). Mental animation, on the other hand, can result in correct inferences in cases where the participant cannot produce a correct description of the animation (Hegarty, 1992). Further, people can judge whether an animation is correct even in cases where the self-produced inference about motion is incorrect (Hegarty, 1992).

Although not much research has been conducted with scientists, what there is indicates that they, too, "run" mental models in problem solving (Clement, 1994; Trafton, Trickett, & Mintz, in press). As with the gear and pulley studies, that research provides evidence of significant interaction between the internal and external representations in the mental simulation. Though it is some distance from employing causal transformations of rotating gears or pulleys to employing the kinds of transformations requiring knowledge contained in a scientific theory, the mental animation research supports the position that the scientific practices originate in and develop out of mundane imaginative simulation abilities.

Internal–external Coupling

As noted previously, mental modeling is often carried out in the presence of real-world resources, including representations such as diagrams and objects such as sofas. How might the mental capability interface with relevant resources in the external world? Much of the research on this question is directed towards diagrams and other kinds of visual representations. Research by Jiajie Zhang (Zhang, 1997; Zhang & Norman, 1995), for instance, analyzes diagrams as external representations that are coupled as an information source with the individual solving problems. Recently, Hegarty has argued that the corpus of research on mental animation in the context of visual representations leads to the conclusion that internal and external representations are best seen as forming a "coupled system" (Hegarty, 2005). In considering the relation between mental modeling and external physical models I have argued that we need to conceptualize cognitive capacities as encompassing more than "natural" biological capacities (Nersessian, 2002a). "Cognitive capacities" can encompass various kinds of external representations such as text, visual representations, and physical simulation devices, such as those evidenced in ethnographic research on cognitive practices in biomedical engineering where technological artifacts instantiate models of *in vivo* phenomena to carry out *in vitro* simulations (Nersessian, 2005; Nersessian, Kurz-Milcke, Newstetter, & Davies, 2003).

On the traditional cognitive science view, reasoning uses information abstracted from the external environment and represented internally and processed internally. External displays of various sorts of information in the world might assist working memory by, for example, co-locating information that gets abstracted (Larkin, 1989; Larkin & Simon, 1987), but all cognitive processing is internal to the individual mind. The traditional view is under challenge by several current research strands that re-construe the notion of representation and processing such some information remains in the environment and that processing is within the coupled system linking internal and external worlds. A major open problem for the coupled system view is an account of the nature of the cognitive mechanisms through which the internal and external worlds mesh, and this is an empirical question. On the one hand, given that some mental simulation can take place in the absence of external stimuli, the mechanisms need to be such as to take stored information and process it in such a way as to allow for the possibility of making at least some of the same inferences as if the real-world stimuli were present. On the other hand, as Daniel Dennett has noted succinctly, "[j]ust as you cannot do very much carpentry with your bare hands, there's not much thinking you can do with your bare mind" (Dennett, 2000, p.17). Thus, even in the absence of an account of "mechanisms," there has been considerable theorizing over the last twenty years in the direction of how aspects of the environment might enter directly into cognitive processes, rather than simply scaffolding them.

"Environmental perspectives" (Nersessian, 2005) make human action the focal point for understanding cognition and emphasize that cognition occurs in complex social, cultural, and material environments. Although not all strands of research contributing to these perspectives have taken the system view of cognition, each can be considered as contributing support for the argument in its favor. This research comprises the notions that cognition is "embodied" (perception-based accounts of representation such as (Barsalou, 1999; Glenberg & Langston, 1992; Glenberg, 1997b; Johnson, 1987; Lakoff, 1987; Lakoff & Johnson, 1998); "enculturated" (co-evolution of cognition and culture such as (Donald, 1991; Nisbett et al., 2001; Shore, 1997; Tomasello, 1999); "distributed" (occurring across systems of humans and artifacts such as (Hutchins, 1995a; Norman, 1988; Zhang & Norman, 1995; Zhang, 1997), or "situated" (located in and arising from interactions within situations such as (Clancey, 1997; Greeno, 1989, 1998; Lave, 1988; Suchman, 1987).

One mantra of the distributed and situated research is that cognition is not only "in the mind" or "in the world" but "in the system" such that an individual's mental activities comprise interactions with other material and informational systems (including other humans). To accommodate this insight, the distributed cognition perspective proposes analyses of cognitive processing that incorporate the *salient* resources in environment in a non-reductive fashion (see, e.g., Hutchins, 1995a, 1995b; Norman, 1991). Salient resources are, broadly characterized, those factors in the environment that can affect the outcome of a cognitive activity, such as problem solving. These cannot be determined *a priori* but need to be judged with respect to the instance. For ship navigators, for example, the function of a specific instrument would be salient to piloting the ship, but not usually the material from which the instrument is made. For physicists, whether one sketches on a black board or white board or piece of paper is likely irrelevant to solving a problem, but sketching on a computer screen has the potential to be salient because the computer adds resources that can affect the outcome.

The artifacts of a culture that participate in systems that perform cognitive functions are referred to as "*cognitive artifacts*" and determining these within a specific system is a major part of the analytical task for environmentalists. Hutchins has studied the cognitive contributions of artifacts employed in modern navigation, such as the alidade, gyrocompass, and fathometer. Various kinds of external representations are candidate cognitive artifacts, and much research has focused on visual representations, especially diagrams. In addition to the mental animation literature discussed above, there is an extensive literature on diagrammatic representations that reinforces the "coupled system" notion, such as that of Zhang and Norman referenced earlier. They have studied problem solving with isomorphic problems to ascertain potential cognitive functions of different kinds of visual representations and have found that external representations differentially facilitate and constrain reasoning processes. The format of the external representation, for example, can change the nature of the processing task, as when the tic-tac-toe grid is imposed on the mathematical problem of "15." Specifically, they argue that diagrams can play more than just a supportive role in what is essentially an internal process; rather, these external representations can be coupled directly as an information source with the person without requiring the mediation of an internal representation of the information provided in them. Not all external representations are equally facilitating, though, as Bauer and Johnson-Laird (Bauer & Johnson-Laird, 1993) show in their study of diagrams in mental modeling tasks. Intriguingly, diagrams with information represented in amodal iconic format appear to provide no facilitation, but diagrams in modal format — perceptually resembling the objects being reasoned about — do significantly enhance problem solving, as was evidenced also in the mental animation research.

In research on problem solving with diagrammatic representations in formal logic, Keith Stenning and colleagues have argued that they restrict the internal problem space so as to constrain the kinds of inferences that can be made (Stenning, 2002; Stenning & Oberlander, 1995). Recently, Trafton and colleagues (Trafton et al., in press) have been investigating scientists' interactions with computer visualizations, which offer more and greater ease of possibilities for manipulation during problem solving. They have found that in the presence of external computer visualizations, scientists tend to do considerable mental manipulation interactive with the visualization represented before them, instead of either just creating a mental image or making direct adjustments to the image on the computer screen. Their manipulations and comparisons seemed to be aimed at constructing a mental model constrained by the computer visualization and though which to understand the implications of the visualization.

The ethnographic studies my research group has been conducting examine the role of representations in the form of physical devices used by biomedical engineers for simulating *in vivo* biological processes. Within the cognitive systems in the laboratory these physical devices instantiate part of the current community model of the phenomena and allow simulation and manipulation of this understanding. One researcher aptly referred to the process of constructing and manipulating these *in vitro* physical models as "putting a thought into the bench top and seeing whether it works or not." These instantiated "thoughts" allow researchers to perform controlled simulations of an *in vivo* context, for example, of the local forces at work in the artery. We interpret such simulative model-based reasoning as a process of co-constructing and manipulating the "internal" researcher models of the phenomena and of the device and the "external" model that is the device, each incomplete. Here simulative model-based reasoning consists of processing information both in memory and in the environment (see also, Gorman, 1997; Greeno, 1989).

Although the capacity for making inferences might be ascribed to the traditionally conceived "mental" part, the internal and external representations and processes involved in simulative model-based reasoning are best understood as a coupled system, and thus the ascription of "mental" might better be construed as pertaining more to the property that inferences are generated from it than to it as a locus or medium of operation. Components of the inferential system would include both one or more people and artifacts (Osbeck & Nersessian, 2006). For simplicity, here, I will continue to use "mental modeling" as referring to the human locus of operation.

One way to accommodate the hypothesis of coupling between external and internal representations is to expand the notion of memory to encompass external representations and cues; that is, to construe specific kinds of affordances and constraints in the environment, literally, as memory in cognitive processing. If memory is so distributed, then we can conceive of the *problem space* not in the traditional way as internally represented, but as comprising internal and external resources (Nersessian, 2005; Nersessian et al., 2003; Nersessian, Newstetter, Kurz-Milcke, & Davies, 2002). The evolutionary psychologist Merlin Donald (Donald, 1991) has argued that evolutionary considerations lead to the view that human memory encompasses internal and external representation. Donald uses a wide range of evidence from anthropology, archeology, primatology, and neuroscience to argue his case. He maintains that this evidence establishes that external representations have been and continue to be indispensable in complex human thinking, and their development was central to the processes of cultural transmission. Donald's analysis of the evolutionary emergence of distinctively human representational systems starts from the significance of mimesis — or re-creation such as using the body to represent an idea of the motion of an airplane — in the developments of such external representations as painting and drawing (40,000 years ago), writing (6,000) and phonetic alphabets (4,000). The artifacts that contribute to remembering are social and cultural constructs designed by human communities that rely on them in supporting remembering. Donald argues for a distributed notion of memory as a symbiosis of internal and external representation on the basis of changes in the visuo-spatial architecture of human cognition that came about with the development of external representation. On this notion affordances and constraints in the environment are *ab initio* part of cognitive processing.

Recasting cognition such that the relationship between the internal and external worlds form a coupled cognitive-cultural system, presents the challenge for cognitive science to determine the mechanisms of representation and processing that would enable this coupling. Part of this problem is to address format and processing issues with respect to the human components of the system. Here Greeno's criteria that the internal representations in mental modeling processes to be such that "we interact with them in ways that are similar to our interactions with physical and — probably — social environments," (Greeno, 1989, p. 313) and thus be such that they are "acquired with significant properties of external situations and one's interactions with the situations .... such that at least some of the properties are known implicitly in something like the way that we know how to interact with [external] environments" (p. 314) echo the earlier views of Craik, as do the analyses of Shepard (Shepard, 1984, 1988, 1994) on the internalization of physical constraints. Human representations need also to be such that they interface smoothly with other system representations in problem solving processes. One plausible way for the interfacing to be smooth is for human representations to have modal aspects such that perceptual and motor mechanisms would be employed in processing.

Embodied Representation: "Perceptual" Mental Models

What might the format of the representation of a "Craikian" mental model be? For Johnson-Laird's analysis of logical reasoning, the working memory constructs are iconic representations.

Perhaps for logical reasoning it suffices that the information in a mental model is represented amodally. Model-based reasoning about physical systems, however, needs to allow for the possibility of simulations of physical entities, situations, and processes that go beyond manipulating amodal tokens in a spatial array. Following Craik's notion of parallelism in the form and operation of used in reasoning, working memory models of physical systems would be perception-based representations. Considerable knowledge would be needed such a mental simulation, not just what can be derived from perception as it is usually understood as separate from conceptual understanding. The behaviors of the parts of the model, for example, need to be connected to knowledge of how these function, although much of this can be tacit. For example, people can usually infer how water will spill out of a cup without being able to make explicit or describe the requisite knowledge. Although we have only been considering mental modeling as a working memory process, of course information from long term memory plays a role in this process, some of which is likely to be represented in propositional form. Thus, as with mental imagery (Kosslyn, 1994), mental modeling representations need to maintain a connection to long-term memory representations, and so an account is needed of how information might be stored so as to connect to working memory representations.

It is a common sense observation *that* humans do have some means of storing knowledge and of calling it selectively into use, but the format of that information remains an open question. In this section I want to draw on research on *embodied* representations to propose that the format of the information contained in working memory representation is modal and most likely also the information to which the models are connected in memory that enable simulation has a modal aspect. This would be the most efficient way for the internal–external representational coupling to work. The embodied representation research focuses on the implications of the interaction of the human perceptual system with the environment for internal representation and processing, generally. Proponents contend that a wide range of empirical evidence shows perceptual content is retained in all kinds of mental representations, and that perceptual and motor mechanisms of the brain play a significant role in many kinds of cognitive processing traditionally conceived as separate from these, including memory, conceptual processing, and language comprehension (see, e.g., Barsalou, 1999, 2003; Barsalou, Simmons, Barbey, & Wilson, 2003; Barsalou, Solomon, & Wu, 1999; Catrambone, Craig, & Nersessian, 2005; Craig, Nersessian, & Catrambone, 2002; Glenberg, 1997b; Johnson, 1987; Kosslyn, 1994; Lakoff, 1987; Solomon & Barsalou, 2004; Yeh & Barsalou, 1996).

One extensive area of research concerns the representation of spatial information in mental models. This research leads to the conclusion that internal representation of spatial configurations does not provide an "outsider" 3-D Euclidian perspective — the "view from nowhere" — but provides an embodied that is relative to the orientation of one's body and to gravity. In early research Irwin Rock hypothesized that there is a "deeply ingrained tendency to 'project' egocentric up-down, left-right coordinates onto the [imagined] scene" (Rock, 1973, p. 17). This hypothesis is borne out by recent research (see, e.g., Bryant & Tversky, 1999; Bryant, Tversky, & Franklin, 1992; Franklin & Tversky, 1990; Glenberg, 1997a; Perrig & Kintsch, 1985). In particular, Barbara Tverksy and colleagues have found that mental spatial alignment corresponds with bodily symmetry — up-down, front-back, and gravity — depending on how the participant is oriented in the external environment. When asked to imagine objects surrounding an external central object, mental model alignment depends on whether the object had the same orientation as the observer. Arthur Glenberg argues that this bodily orientation is tied to preparation for *situated action* paralleling that which would occur in real-world situations (Glenberg, 1997a).

A second line of research focuses on concept representation. From an embodied cognition alternative, as expressed by George Lakoff and Mark Johnson, a "concept is a neural structure that is actually part of, or makes use of, the sensorimotor system of our brains" (Lakoff & Johnson, 1998, p. 20). Lawrence Barsalou has been formulating a theory (first fully articulated in Barsalou, 1999) of the human conceptual system that calls into question the traditional understanding of concept representation as amodal. A wide range of research dovetails in thinking about embodiment and representation, but I will focus largely on the recent work of Barsalou and colleagues because they argue for the perceptual basis of concept representation through drawing together evidence from much of that research, as well as through experiments specifically designed to test the hypothesis. Since my goal is not to argue that Barsalou's theory is "right" — but rather to advocate that it goes in the right direction for further articulating the kind of account of simulative model-based reasoning the science case requires — I present only the broad outlines.

Barsalou argues that there is an extensive experimental literature that can be read as supporting the contention that mental representations retain perceptual features, or are modal, and that many cognitive functions involve re-enactment or "simulation" of perceptual states. These include perceptual processing, memory, language, categorization and inference. He makes a compelling experimental case for the broad claims of the theory from evidence drawn from existing behavioral and neuroscience research, and behavioral tasks designed specifically to test its implications (summarized in Barsalou, 2003). The experiments he and his colleagues have designed to test the implications of the theory primarily involve property generation and property verification tasks. They distinguish between the alternatives of simulating the referent of a word (modal version) and looking up a word in a semantic network or frame (amodal version). The participants are given either a neutral condition with no instructions on how to do the task or an imagery condition where they are asked to visualize or imagine the referent. On the amodal version, the neutral condition should produce patterns of response different from the imagery condition. Across a wide range of terms, these experiments show a similar pattern of responses between the two conditions, favoring the modal version. Other significant experiments involve manipulating perceptual variables, such as occlusion. For example, in property generation experiments, participants listed twice as many internal features of objects when they were presented with modified object terms such a "rolled up lawn" (e.g., "roots") as opposed to "lawn," ½ watermelon (e.g., "seeds"), and glass car (e.g., "seats") (Barsalou et al., 2003; Barsalou et al., 1999). Experiments using fMRI in the neutral condition provide evidence of activity in sensorimotor areas of the brain during the property generation task, whereas on the traditional separation of cognition and perception (amodal version), there should be no activation in sensorimotor areas when representing a concept (Simmons, Hamann, Nolan, Hu, & Barsalou, 2004).

On Barsalou's modal account, cognitive processing employs "perceptual symbols" ("modal iconic" representations on our earlier classification) which are neural correlates of sensorimotor experiences (Barsalou, 1999). These symbols "result from an extraction process that selects some subset of a perceptual state and stores it as a symbol" (Barsalou & Prinz, 1997, p. 275). The relationship between the symbols and what they represent is analogical, i.e., that of similarity, as opposed to arbitrary. The perceptual symbols form a common representational system that underlies both sensorimotor and conceptual processing. Because the conceptual system uses perceptual and motor mechanisms, concept representations are distributed across modality specific systems. These representations possess simulation capabilities; that is, perceptual and motor processes associated with the original experiences are re-enacted when perceptual symbols are employed in thinking. Concepts are separable neural states underlying perception and constituting the units of long-term memory representation, which in turn can be organized into knowledge units such as schemas, mental models, or frames.

Coupling among various representations takes place in categorization processes, including the construction of ad hoc categories, to form "perceptual symbol systems." One strong objection against perceptual representations has been that they cannot accommodate properties known to hold of conceptual systems, such as the potential to produce an infinite number of conceptual combinations and the capability to distinguish types from tokens and to represent abstract concepts. The need to accommodate these known possibilities of conceptual representations led to the traditional propositional (amodal) account, rather than direct empirical evidence in favor of it. However, there are several notorious problems with the amodal account, including the "symbol grounding problem," that is, the problem of how are the arbitrary transductions mapped back onto perceptual states and entities in the world (Harnard, 1990; Searle, 1980). Barsalou (1999) and, later, Jesse Prinz (Prinz, 2002) provide arguments that, in principle, perceptual symbol systems can exhibit all the salient characteristics of propositional systems. The (mis-)perception that they cannot stems from the tendency to conflate perceptual representations with *recording systems* in which images are captured but are not interpreted (Haugeland, 1991). The human conceptual system is interpretive and inferential. Perceptual symbols are not holistic representations of their real-world counterparts and their componential, schematic, and dynamic nature allows for combination, recombination, and abstraction. Barsalou stresses that the human conceptual system should not be understood by means of an analogy to a recording system. Perceptual symbols are schematic extractions from perceptual processes that allow for infinite possibilities of imaginative recombination. Further, one should not expect simulations to be as detailed or vivid as the original perceptions. In conducting a perceptual simulation, one needs neither to be consciously aware of mental imagery, which requires extra cognitive effort to produce, or of the simulation process. Performing a perceptual simulation is not akin to "running" a kind of motion picture in the head.

Concept representation is likely to have both modal and amodal aspects. However, the modal aspects serve the requirements of simulative mental modeling we have been discussing — both the simulation needs and the need for interfacing between external and internal representations. There are many open questions about modal representation for which only partial solutions have been suggested, such as: How do abstract concepts become represented? How does "translation" take place across modalities? How does integration take place? How are perceptually dissimilar instances of a concept recognized and categorized? But there are many open questions about amodal representation as well, and, significantly, as Barsalou points out, there little direct empirical evidence in favor of a fully amodal view. In sum, Barsalou and other proponents of embodied cognition do make a compelling case that at the very least a more tempered conclusion is warranted in the present circumstances, and this is sufficient for our needs: "The conceptual system appears neither fully modular nor fully amodal. To the contrary, it is non-modular in sharing many important mechanisms with perception and action. Additionally, it traffics heavily in the modal representations that arise in sensory-motor systems" (Barsalou, 2003, p. 27). Thus, how modal representations could contribute to various cognitive processes, such as mental modeling, merits investigation.

A "perceptual mental model" (which Craik seems to have in mind) would facilitate the interfacing between the internal and external representations of a coupled system in simulative reasoning. Recall that on Craik's speculation, mental simulation occurs by the "excitation and volley of impulses which parallel the stimuli which occasioned them...." (Craik, 1943, p. 60), with simulative reasoning processes resulting in conclusions similar to those that "might have been reached by causing the actual physical processes to occur" (p. 51). On the perceptual symbol theory, too, the human conceptual system is predicated on a form of re-enactment, where working-memory-specific concept representations are constructed for the purpose of supporting situated action. One important implication of the modal view of category representation is that, rather than being context free, object representations include situational information that is active in conceptual processing. There is abundant empirical evidence from psychological experiments favoring this implication (Yeh & Barsalou, 1996). This supports the idea that the conceptual system is held to be "organized around the action-environment interface" (Barsalou, 2003, p.12). In situated action, "a concept is a skill that delivers specialized packages of inferences to guide an agent's interactions with specific category members in particular situations. Across different situations, different packages tailor inferences to different goals and situational constraints" (Barsalou, 2003, p. 27). Thus, for the human component of a coupled system to have a concept is to possess a skill for constructing an infinite number of simulations tailored to ones immediate goals and needs for action.

Conceiving of model-based reasoning about physical systems as a form of "situated action," allows the reasoning to be fully imaginative or to be carried out in conjunction with real-world action, such as looking at the sofa and the doorway when reasoning, drawing a sketch or diagram, or using a physical device to simulate a model. This notion of mental modeling would meet the criteria, that is, people should be able to interact with the internal representations "in ways that are similar to our interactions with physical and — probably — social environments" (Greeno, 1989, p. 313). Perceptual mental models are built on representations "acquired with significant properties of external situations and one's interactions with the situations ... such that at least some of the properties are known implicitly in something like the way that we know how to interact with [external] environments" (p. 314). So, affordances and constraints of situational information would be at play even in the solely imaginative cases of mental modeling where only one's conceptual understanding is used. Just how the mental models would be "run" in simulative reasoning is an open research question requiring more knowledge about the cognitive and neural mechanisms underlying such processes. But it cannot be assumed *a priori* that these reduce to the same kinds of computations possible for a computer. And, even if deductive and inductive reasoning were to use amodal representations, it is possible that simulative reasoning about physical systems could involve modal representations and perceptual — motor processes, enabling direct and effective use of affordances and constraints of representations external to humans in the system. The mental model and the real-world resources form a coupled system by which inferences are made. In this way the problem solver does not simply "use" external representations, rather they are incorporated directly into the *cognitive* processing.

Conclusion: Model-based Reasoning in Conceptual Change in Science

I have argued here that the capacity for mental modeling provides a cognitive basis for model-based reasoning evidenced in conceptual changes in the sciences. It is a fundamental form of human reasoning that is likely to have evolved as an efficient means of navigating the environment, of anticipating situations, and of solving problems in matters of significance to existence. Humans have extended its use to more esoteric situations, such as constructing and reasoning with scientific representations. A mental model is a conceptual system representing the physical system that is being reasoned about. It is an abstraction — idealized and schematic in nature — that represents a physical situation by having surrogate objects or entities and properties, relations, behaviors, or functions of these that are in correspondence with it. In mundane reasoning situations, mental models are likely homomorphic (many-one), but in scientific reasoning, the intended relation is isomorphic (one-to-one with respect to salient dimensions). Mental models embody and comply with the constraints of the phenomena being reasoned about, and enable inferences about these through simulation processes. Inferences made in simulation processes create new data that play a role in evaluating and adapting models. In reasoning processes, mental models interact with other representations — external diagrams, written equations, verbal representations such as written or oral descriptions or instructions, and gestural representations provide examples of these. The notion of interaction among internal and external resources during reasoning as "representational coupling" leads to the notion that mental models have significant modal aspects ("perceptual mental models"), though a conclusive argument cannot be made in either the modal or amodal literatures.

Simulative mental modeling can lead to potential empirical insights, as in thought experimenting (Nersessian, 1992b), by creating new states or situations that parallel those of the real world. In mundane cases at least tacit knowledge of constraints is needed, such as that the chair cannot simply pass through the wood of the door frame or that the frame of the sofa will not bend or be capable of squishing as does a cushion. In the case of science, implicit and explicit knowledge of constraints relating to general principles of the domain and mathematical equations play a role. This knowledge such as of causal coherence and mathematical consistency is likely to be represented in different informational formats. A cognitive science account is still needed of how conceptual, and in general, domain knowledge is utilized in mental modeling, how abstraction and model construction take place, and how the mental processes interface with the external world.

How might reasoning through mental modeling lead to conceptual change? A central problem is that given that conceptual innovation starts from existing representations, how is possible for a genuinely novel representation to be created? In earlier work I have proposed that a significant method of conceptual innovation and change in science involves iterative processes of constructing, evaluating, and revising models that exemplify features of the phenomena under investigation. These models do not serve simply as aids to reasoning but are the means through which one reasons to the new conceptual representations. The model construction and manipulation processes, which include analogical, imagistic, and simulative processes, abstract and integrate information from multiple sources specific to the problem-solving situation so as to allow for truly novel combinations to occur, that is, for a model in which here-to-fore unrepresented structures or behaviors emerge. The consequences of the novel combinations can be explored imaginatively, through physical realizations, and through manipulations possible by expression in other representational formats, such as mathematics and language. Selective abstraction is needed for this kind of representation building. Take, for example, the case of Maxwell's construction of the field representation of electromagnetism. In using continuum mechanics as an analogical source domain, he was able to narrow the source further to that of elastic fluids by guiding the selection with constraints from the electromagnetic target domain. The selection of relevant structures from the domain of elastic fluids was in turn guided by the constraints that a model would need to be capable of rotational motion (creating "vortices") and result in certain kinds of geometric configurations so as to give rise to observed lines of force, and thus the resulting model was a hybrid of constraints from both domains. Such hybrid representations possess their own, emergent, constraints that figure into the analytical mix. Maxwell's initial hybrid model, for instance, led to the constraint of friction between vortices when in motion. It is likely that he recognized the friction constraint though attempting to simulate the model imaginatively. In such a simulation one could see the vortices touching and infer friction between them. Following out the problem of accommodating the model constraint of friction led him to another source domain, machine mechanics, a new representational resource, the "idle-wheel," and then another hybrid model which proved capable of representing additional electromagnetic constraints as well as possessing emergent constraints.

Many abstractive processes enable model construction, including, idealization, limiting case, and generic abstraction. These provide ways of generating and accommodating constraints from multiple domains. "Generic" abstraction, for instance, captures the idea that in reasoning it is possible to make inferences not only about the specific model, but also about the class of models at different levels of abstraction, for example, reasoning about a specific spring or reasoning about it as representative of the class of simple harmonic operators. The Maxwell case provides an exemplar of what is powerful about this mode of abstractive reasoning. Starting from thinking about specific connecting mechanisms, such as idle wheels, and abstracting to what the dynamical relations between idle wheels and vortices have in common with the category of "general dynamics relational structures that capture the motion of a connected system in which one part imparts motion to another in a continuous fashion," Maxwell arrived at a continuous-action representation of the transmission of forces, that is, a concept of "field" — a here-to-fore unrepresented structure in physics.

Finally, a significant way in which conceptual change in science is unlike that in learning and cognitive development is that it occurs also across communities. The community of physicists, for instance, experiences a conceptual change from understanding "force" to represent actions-at-a-distance to representing continuous-action in the space surrounding charges and bodies and through the space between them or understanding "mass" to represent an invariant quantity to understanding it to represent something that varies with speed. Most philosophical and sociological explanations of conceptual change operate at the level of how scientists choose among alternative conceptual structures or how one structure comes to replace another in a community. Thomas Kuhn, for example, in his post-*Structure* writings repudiated his "gestalt switch" metaphor as characterizing conceptual change for precisely the reason that he argued that he intended to be addressing the level of community change while the metaphor operates at the level of individuals. However, for there to be a community phenomenon, a story needs to be told at the individual level as well (Kuhn was likely also addressing this in his last work on the unfinished follow-on book to *Structure*). That is, what is the nature of cognitive processes used by individual scientists that generate new concepts and conceptual structures, making them available for communities to choose among, if that is what happens in the community? It is this story that has the potential to contribute to accounts of conceptual change in learning and in cognitive development.

ACKNOWLEDGMENTS

This research was supported in part by grants from the National Science Foundation (REC0109773 & REC0450578), the National Endowment for the Humanities, and Radcliffe Institute for Advanced Study.

REFERENCES

Allwein, G., & Barwise, J. (1996). *Logical Reasoning with Diagrams*. New York: Oxford University Press.

Arditi, A., Holtzman, J. D., & Kosslyn, S. M. (1988). Mental imagery and sensory experience in congenital blindness. *Neuropsychologia, 26*(1–12).

Barsalou, L. W. (1999). Perceptual symbol systems. *Behavioral and Brain Sciences, 22*, 577–609.

Barsalou, L. W. (2003). Situated simulation in the human conceptual system. *Language and Cognitive Processes, 18*, 513–562.

Barsalou, L. W., & Prinz, J. J. (1997). Mundane creativity in perceptual symbol systems. In T. Ward, S. M. Smith & J. Vaid (Eds.), *Creative Thought: A Investigation of Conceptual Structures and Processes* (pp. 267–307). Washington, DC: American Psychological Association.

Barsalou, L. W., Simmons, W. K., Barbey, A. K., & Wilson, C. D. (2003). Grounding conceptual knowledge in modality-specific systems. *Trends in Cognitive Science, 7*, 84–91.

Barsalou, L. W., Solomon, K. O., & Wu, L. L. (1999). Perceptual simulation in conceptual tasks. In M. K. Hiraga, C. Sinha & S. Wilcox (Eds.), *Cultural, typological, and psychological perspectives in cognitive linguistics: The proceedings of the 4th annual conference of the International Cognitive Linguistics Association* (Vol. 3, pp. 209–228). Amsterdam: John Benjamins.

Bauer, M. I., & Johnson-Laird, P. N. (1993). How diagrams can improve reading. *Psychological Science, 4*, 372–378.

Bell, V. A., & Johnson-Laird, P. N. (1998). A model theory of modal reasoning. *Cognitive Science, 22*(1), 25–51.

Bobrow, D. G. (Ed.). (1985). *Qualitative Reasoning About Physical Systems*. Cambridge, MA: MIT Press.

Bryant, D. J., & Tversky, B. (1999). Mental representations of perspective and spatial relations from diagrams and models. *Journal of Experimental Psychology: Learning, Memory, and Cognition, 2*, 137–156.

Bryant, D. J., Tversky, B., & Franklin, N. (1992). Internal and external spatial frameworks for representing described scenes. *Journal of Memory and Language, 31*, 74–98.

Catrambone, R., Craig, D. L., & Nersessian, N. J. (2005). The role of perceptually represented structure in analogical problem solving. *Memory and Cognition, 34*, 1126–1134.

Chambers, D., & Reisberg, D. (1985). Can mental images be ambiguous? *Journal of Experimental Psychology: Human Perception and Performance, 11*(3), 317–328.

Chi, M. T. H., Feltovich, P. J., & Glaser, R. (1981). Categorization and representation of physics problems by experts and novices. *Cognitive Science, 5*, 121–152.

Clancey, W. J. (1997). *Situated Cognition: On Human Knowledge and Computer Representations*. Cambridge: Cambridge University Press.

Clement, J. (1994). Use of physical intuition and imagistic simulation in expert problem solving. In D. Tirosh (Ed.), *Implicit and Explicit Knowledge* (pp. 204–242). Norwood, NJ: Ablex Publishing.

Clement, J. (2003). Imagistic simulation in scientific model construction. In D. Alterman & D. Kirsch (Eds.), *Proceedings of the Cognitive Science Society 25* (pp. 258–263). Hillsdale, NJ: Erlbaum.

Craig, D. L., Nersessian, N. J., & Catrambone, R. (2002). Perceptual simulation in analogical problem solving. In L. Magnani & N. J. Nersessian (Eds.), *Model-Based Reasoning: Science, Technology, Values* (pp. 167–190). New York: Kluwer.

Craik, K. (1943). *The Nature of Explanation*. Cambridge: Cambridge University Press.

Dennett, D. C. (2000). Making tools for thinking. In D. Sperber (Ed.), *Metarepresentations: A Multidisciplinary Perspective* (pp. 17–29). New York: Oxford University Press.

Dijk, T. A. v., & Kintsch, W. (1983). *Strategies of Discourse Comprehension*. New York: Academic Press.

Donald, M. (1991). *Origins of the Modern Mind: Three Stages in the Evolution of Culture and Cognition*. Cambridge, MA: Harvard University Press.

Farah, M. J. (1988). Is visual imagery really visual? Overlooked evidence from neuropsychology. *Psychological Review, 95*, 307–317.

Ferguson, E. S. (1983). *Engineering and the Mind's Eye*. Cambridge, MA: MIT Press.

Finke, R. A. (1989). *Principles of Mental Imagery*. Cambridge, MA: MIT Press.

Finke, R. A., Pinker, S., & Farah, M. (1989). Reinterpreting visual patterns in mental imagery. *Cognitive Science, 13*, 51–78.

Finke, R. A., & Shepard, R. N. (1986). Visual functions of mental imagery. In K. R. Boff et al. (Eds.), *Handbook of Perception and Human Performance* (pp. 37.31–37.55). New York: Wiley.

Fodor, J. A. (1975). *The Language of Thought*. New York: Thomas Y. Crowell.

Forbus, K. (1983). Reasoning about space and motion. In D. G. a. A. Stevens (Ed.), *Mental Models* (pp. 53–74). Hillsdale, NJ: Erlbaum.

Franklin, N., & Tversky, B. (1990). Searching imagined environments. *Journal of Experimental Psychology, 119*, 63–76.

Freyd, J. J. (1987). Dynamic mental representation. *Psychological Review, 94*, 427–438.

Gentner, D., & Stevens, A. L. (1983). *Mental Models*. Hillsdale, NJ: Erlbaum.

Gibson, J. J. (1979). *The Ecological Approach to Visual Perception*. Boston: Houghton Mifflin.

Gilhooly, K. J. (1986). Mental Modeling: A Framework for the Study of Thinking. In J. Bishop, J. Lochhead & D. Perkins (Eds.), *Thinking: Progress in Research and Teaching* (pp. 19–32). Hillsdale, NJ: Erlbaum.

Glenberg, A. M. (1997a). Mental models, space, and embodied cognition. In T. Ward, S. M. Smith, & J. Vaid (Eds.), *Creative Thought: An Investigation of Conceptual Structures and Processes* (pp. 495–522). Washington, DC: American Psychological Association.

Glenberg, A. M. (1997b). What memory is for. *Behavioral and Brain Sciences, 20*, 1–55.

Glenberg, A. M., & Langston, W. E. (1992). Comprehension of illustrated text: Pictures help to build mental models. *Journal of Memory and Language, 31*, 129–151.

Golden-Meadow, S., Nusbaum, H., Kelly, S. D., & Wagner, S. (2001). Explaining math: Gesturing lightens the load. *Psychological Science, 12*(6), 332–340.

Gorman, M. (1997). Mind in the world: Cognition and practice in the invention of the telephone. *Social Studies of Science, 27*, 583–624.

Greeno, J. G. (1989). Situations, mental models, and generative knowledge. In D. Klahr & K. Kotovsky (Eds.), *Complex information processing* (pp. 285–318). Hillsdale, NJ: Erlbaum.

Greeno, J. G. (1998). The situativity of knowing, learning, and research. *American Psychologist, 53*, 5–24.

Harman, G. (1986). *Change in View*. Cambridge, MA: MIT Press.

Harnard, S. (1990). The symbol grounding problem. *Physica D, 42*, 35–46.

Haugeland, J. (1991). Respresentational genera. In W. Ramsey, S. Stitch & D. E. Rumelhart (Eds.), *Philosophy and Connectionist Theory*. Hillsdale, NJ: Erlbaum.

Hayes, P. J. (1979). The naive physics manifesto. In D. Mitchie (Ed.), *Expert Systems in the Micro-Electronic Age*. Edinburgh: Edinburgh University Press.

Hegarty, M. (1992). Mental animation: Inferring motion from static diagrams of mechanical systems. *Journal of Experimental Psychology: Learning, Memory, and Cognition, 18*(5), 1084–1102.

Hegarty, M. (2005). Mechanical reasoning by mental simulation. *Trends in Cognitive Science, in press.*

Hegarty, M., & Ferguson, J. M. (1993). *Strategy change with practice in a mental animation task.* Paper presented at the Annual Meeting of the Psychonomic Society, Washington, DC.

Hegarty, M., & Just, M. A. (1989). Understanding machines from text and diagrams. In H. Mandl & J. Levin (Eds.), *Knowledge Acquisition from Text and Picture*. Amsterdam: North Holland: Elsevier Science.

Hegarty, M., & Sims, V. K. (1994). Individual differences in mental animation from text and diagrams. *Journal of Memory and Language, 32*, 411–430.

Hegarty, M., & Steinhoff, K. (1994). *Use of diagrams as external memory in a mechanical reasoning task.* Paper presented at the Annual Meeting of the American Educational Research Association, New Orleans, LA.

Holland, J. H., Holyoak, K. J., Nisbett, R. E., & Thagard, P. R. (1986). *Induction: Processes of Inference, Learning, and Discovery*. Cambridge, MA: MIT Press.

Hutchins, E. (1995a). *Cognition in the Wild*. Cambridge, MA: MIT Press.

Hutchins, E. (1995b). How a cockpit remembers its speed. *Cognitive Science, 19*, 265–288.

Jeannerod, M. (1993). A theory of representation-driven actions. In U. Neisser (Ed.), *The Perceived Self* (pp. 68–88). Cambridge: Cambridge University Press.

Jeannerod, M. (1994). The representing brain: Neural correlated of motor intention and imagery. *Brain and Behavioral Sciences, 17*, 187–202.

Johnson, M. (1987). *The Body in the Mind: The Bodily Basis of Meaning, Imagination, and Reason*. Chicago: University of Chicago Press.

Johnson-Laird, P. N. (1980). Mental models in cognitive science. *Cognitive Science, 4*, 71–115.

Johnson-Laird, P. N. (1982). The mental representation of the meaning of words. *Cognition, 25*, 189–211.

Johnson-Laird, P. N. (1983). *Mental Models*. Cambridge, MA: MIT Press.

Johnson-Laird, P. N. (1989). Mental models. In M. Posner (Ed.), *Foundations of Cognitive Science* (pp. 469–500). Cambridge, MA: MIT Press.

Johnson-Laird, P. N., & Byrne, R. (1993). Precis of the book, Deduction with peer review commentaries and responses. *Brain and Behavioral Sciences, 16*, 323–380.

Kahneman, D., & Tversky, A. (1982). *Judgement Under Uncertainty: Heuristics and Biases*. New York: Cambridge University Press.

Kerr, N. H. (1983). The role of vision in "visual imagery". *Journal of Experimental PSychology: General, 112*, 265–277.

Kosslyn, S. M. (1980). *Image and Mind*. Cambridge, MA: Harvard University Press.

Kosslyn, S. M. (1994). *Image and Brain*. Cambridge MA: MIT Press.

Kuhn, T. (1970). *The Structure of Scientific Revolutions* (2nd ed.). Chicago: University of Chicago Press.

Lakoff, G. (1987). *Women, Fire, and Dangerous Things: What Categories Reveal about the Mind*. Chicago: University of Chicago Press.

Lakoff, G., & Johnson, M. (1998). *Philosophy in the Flesh*. New York: Basic Books.

Larkin, J. H. (1989). Display-based problem solving. In D. Klahr & K. Kotovsky (Eds.), *Complex Information Processing: The Impact of Herbert A. Simon* (pp. 319–342). Hillsdale, NJ: Erlbaum.

Larkin, J. H., & Simon, H. A. (1987). Why a diagram is (sometimes) worth ten thousand words. *Cognitive Science, 11*, 65–100.

Lave, J. (1988). *Cognition in Practice: Mind, Mathematics, and Culture in Everyday Life*. New York: Cambridge University Press.

Mainwaring, S. D., Tversky, B., & Schiano, D. J. (1996). Effects of task and object configuration on perspective choice in spatial descriptions. In P. Olivier (Ed.), *AAAI Symposium* (pp. 56–67). Stanford, CA: AAAI Press.

Mani, K., & Johnson-Laird, P. N. (1982). The mental representation of spatial descriptions. *Memory and Cognition, 10*, 181–187.

Marmor, G. S., & Zaback, L. A. (1976). Mental rotation by the blind: Does mental rotation depend on visual imagery? *Journal of Experimental Psychology: Human Perception and Performance, 2*, 515–521.

Maxwell, J. C. (1890). *The Scientific Papers of James Clerk Maxwell*. Edited by W. D. Niven(2 vols.). Cambridge: Cambridge University.

McNamara, T. P., & Sternberg, R. J. (1983). Mental models of word meaning. *Journal of Verbal Learning and Verbal Behavior, 22*, 449–474.

Morrow, D. G., Bower, G. H., & Greenspan, S. L. (1989). Updating situation models during narrative comprehension. *Journal of Memory and Language, 28*, 292–312.

Nersessian, N. J. (1991). Why do thought experiments work? In *Proceedings of the Cognitive Science Society 13* (pp. 430–438). Hillsdale, NJ: Erlbaum.

Nersessian, N. J. (1992a). Constructing and instructing: The role of 'abstraction techniques' in developing and teaching scientific theories. In R. Duschl & R. Hamilton (Eds.), *Philosophy of Science, Cognitive Science, & Educational Theory and Practice* (pp. 48–68). Albany, NY: SUNY Press.

Nersessian, N. J. (1992b). How do scientists think? Capturing the dynamics of conceptual change in science. In R. Giere (Ed.), *Minnesota Studies in the Philosophy of Science* (pp. 3–45). Minneapolis: University of Minnesota Press.

Nersessian, N. J. (1992c). In the theoretician's laboratory: Thought experimenting as mental modeling. In D. Hull, M. Forbes & K. Okruhlik (Eds.), *PSA 1992* (Vol. 2, pp. 291–301). East Lansing, MI: PSA.

Nersessian, N. J. (1995). Should physicists preach what they practice? Constructive modeling in doing and learning physics. *Science & Education, 4*, 203–226.

Nersessian, N. J. (1999). Model-based Reasoning in Conceptual Change. In L. Magnani, N. J. Nersessian & P. Thagard (Eds.), *Model-Based Reasoning in Scientific Discovery* (pp. 5–22). New York: Kluwer.

Nersessian, N. J. (2002a). The cognitive basis of model-based reasoning in science. In P. Carruthers, S. Stich & M. Siegal (Eds.), *The Cognitive Basis of Science* (pp. 133–153). Cambridge: Cambridge University Press.

Nersessian, N. J. (2002b). Maxwell and the "method of physical analogy": Model-based reasoning, generic abstraction, and conceptual change. In D. Malament (Ed.), *Reading Natural Philosophy: Essays in the History and Philosophy of Science and Mathematics* (pp. 129–165). Lasalle, IL: Open Court.

Nersessian, N. J. (2005). Interpreting scientific and engineering practices: Integrating the cognitive, social, and cultural dimensions. In M. Gorman, R. D. Tweney, D. Gooding & A. Kincannon (Eds.), *Scientific and Technological Thinking* (pp. 17–56). Hillsdale, N J: Erlbaum.

Nersessian, N. J., Kurz-Milcke, E., Newstetter, W., & Davies, J. (2003). Research laboratories as evolving distributed cognitive systems. In D. Alterman & D. Kirsch (Eds.), *Proceedings of the Cognitive Science Society 25* (pp. 857–862). Hillsdale, NJ: Erlbaum.

Nersessian, N. J., Newstetter, W., Kurz-Milcke, E., & Davies, J. (2002). A mixed-method approach to studying distributed cognition in evolving environments. In *Proceedings of the International Conference on Learning Sciences* (pp. 307–314). Hillsdale, NJ: Erlbaum.

Nisbett, R., Peng, K., Choi, I., & Norenzayan, A. (2001). Culture and systems of thought: holistic v. analytic cognition. *Psychological Review, 108*(2), 291–310.

Norman, D. A. (1988). *The Psychology of Everyday Things*. New York: Basic Books.

Norman, D. A. (1991). Cognitive artifacts. In J. M. Carroll (Ed.), *Designing Interaction*. Cambridge: Cambridge University Press.

Osbeck, L., & Nersessian, N. J. (2006). The distribution of representation. *The Journal for the Theory of Social Behaviour, 36*,141–160.

Parsons, L. (1994). Temporal and kinematic properties of motor behavior reflected in mentally simulated action. *Journal of Experimental Psychology: Human Perception and Performance, 20*, 709–730.

Perrig, W., & Kintsch, W. (1985). Propositional and situational representations of text. *Journal of Memory and Language, 24*, 503–518.

Prinz, J. J. (2002). *Furnishing the Mind: Concepts and Their Perceptual Basis*. Cambridge, MA: MIT Press.

Rips, L. (1986). Mental muddles. In H. Brand & R. Hernish (Eds.), *The Representation of Knowledge and Belief* (pp. 258–286). Tucson: University of Arizona Press.

Rock, I. (1973). *Orientation and Form*. New York: Academic Press.

Rouse, W. B., & Morris, N. M. (1986). On looking into the black box: Prospects and limits in the search for mental models. *Psychological Bulletin, 100*(3), 349–363.

Schwartz, D. L. (1995). Reasoning about the referent of a picture versus reasoning about a the picture as the referent. *Memory and Cognition, 23*, 709–722.

Schwartz, D. L., & Black, J. B. (1996a). Analog imagery in mental model reasoning: Depictive models. *Cognitive Psychology, 30*, 154–219.

Schwartz, D. L., & Black, J. B. (1996b). Shuttling between depictive models and abstract rules: Induction and fall back. *Cognitive Science, 20*, 457–497.

Searle, J. (1980). Minds, brains, and programs. *Behavioral and Brain Sciences, 3*, 417–424.

Shepard, R. N. (1984). Ecological constraints on internal representation: Resonant kinematics of perceiving, imagining, thinking, and dreaming. *Psychological Review, 91*, 417–447.

Shepard, R. (1988). Imagination of the scientist. In K. Egan & D. Nadaner (Eds.), *Imagination and the Scientist* (pp. 153–185). New York: Teachers College Press.

Shepard, R. N. (1994). Perceptual-cognitive universals as reflections of the world. *Psychonomic Bulletin and Review, 1*, 2–28.

Shepard, R. N., & Cooper, L. A. (1982). *Mental Images and their Transformations*. Cambridge, MA: MIT Press.

Shiffrar, M., & Freyd, J. J. (1990). Apparant motion of the human body. *Psychological Science, 1*, 257–264.

Shore, B. (1997). *Culture in Mind: Cognition, Culture and the Problem of Meaning*. New York: Oxford University Press.

Simmons, W. K., Hamann, S. B., Nolan, C. L., Hu, X., & Barsalou, L. W. (2004). *fMRI evidence for the role of word association and situation simulation in conceptual processing*. Paper presented at the Meeting of the Society for Cognitive Neuroscience, San Francisco.

Simon, H. A. (1977). *Models of Thought*. Dordrecht: D. Reidel.

Solomon, K. O., & Barsalou, L. W. (2004). Perceptual simulation in property verification. *Memory and Cognition, 32*, 244–259.

Spelke, E. S. (1991). Physical knowledge in infancy: Reflections on Piaget's theory. In S. Carey & R. Gelman (Eds.), *The Epigenesis of Mind: Essays on Biology and Cognition* (pp. 133–169). Hillsdale, NJ: Erlbaum.

Spelke, E. S., Phillips, A., & Woodward, A. L. (1995). Spatio-temporal continuity, smoothness of motion and object identity in infancy. *British Journal of Developmental Psychology, 13*, 113–142.

Stenning, K. (2002). *Seeing Reason: Image and Language in Learning to Think*. London: Oxford University Press.

Stenning, K., & Oberlander, J. (1995). A theory of graphical and linguistic reasoning. *Cognitive Science, 19*, 97–140.

Suchman, L. A. (1987). *Plans and Situated Actions: Tthe Problem of Human-Machine Communication.* Cambridge: Cambridge University Press.

Tomasello, M. (1999). *The Cultural Origins of Human Cognition.* Cambridge, MA: Harvard University Press.

Trafton, J. G., Trickett, S. B., & Mintz, F. E. (in press). Connecting internal and external representations: Spatial transformations of scientific visualizations. *Foundations of Science.*

Tye, M. (1991). *The Imagery Debate.* Cambridge, MA: MIT Press.

Vera, A., & Simon, H. (1993). Situated cognition: A symbolic interpretation. *Cognitive Science, 17*, 4–48.

Vosniadou, S., & Brewer, W. F. (1992). Mental models of the earth: A study of conceptual change in childhood. *Cognitive Psychology, 24*, 535–585.

Yeh, W., & Barsalou, L. W. (1996). The role of situations in concept learning. In G. W. Cottrell (Ed.), *Proceedings of the Cognitive Science Society 18* (pp. 469–474). Hillsdale, NJ: Erlbaum.

Zhang, J. (1997). The nature of external representations in problem solving. *Cognitive Science, 21*(2), 179–217.

Zhang, J., & Norman, D. A. (1995). A representational analysis of numeration systems. *Cognition, 57*, 271–295.

Zwann, R. A. (1999). Situation models: the mental leap into imagined worlds. *Current Directons in Psychological Science, 8*, 15–18.

Zwann, R. A., & Radvansky, G. A. (1998). Situation models in language comprehension and memory. *Psychological Bulletin, 123*, 162–185.

16

The Role of Explanatory Models in Teaching for Conceptual Change

John Clement
University of Massachusetts at Amherst

INTRODUCTION

In the space allowed for this chapter, I will concentrate on model based, cognitive strategies for fostering conceptual change as an outcome in individual students. Most recent strategies will involve considering the roles that group discussions and co-construction with a teacher can play, and so there the approach is socio-cognitive. Other recent studies in the literature address other social, cultural, metacognitive, and motivational factors that have very important influences on conceptual change. For example, in their chapters in this book, Smith and Wiser discuss students' metacognitive difficulties in understanding the nature and function of models; and Sinatra and Mason discuss these as well as motivational issues. While all of these research areas are very important, we still need to address an enormous gap that remains at the core of conceptual change theory: we do not have an adequate cognitive model of the basic conceptual change process; we do not have a good understanding of how flexible models are constructed. These are the long-term questions motivating this chapter. Most of the classical theory of conceptual change in science education (Posner, Strike, Hewson, & Gertzog, 1982, Strike & Posner, 1992) is either about *conditions* for change (e.g., dissonance), *effects* of change (e.g., a more plausible conception, developmental stages of conceptions), or *factors* that make it easier or more difficult (e.g., the presence of a persistent preconception). What is missing is a fuller specification of *mechanisms* of change — causal descriptions of processes that produce conceptual change. Many suspect that models and analogies can play a central role in conceptual change. But there is little consensus on a definition for the term *model* itself. The term is used for such a wide variety of different entities that one wonders how useful the broad concept can be, meaning that there is a need to narrow in on the most fundamental type of model in science learning in order to attain focus. And we are hard pressed to describe something as basic as the relationship between analogies and models in science learning — a clear description of this has been elusive and difficult to formulate. Historians of science such as Hesse (1966) and Harre (1972) understood that this relationship is complex and subtle in science itself, so we should expect no less in the area of student learning. Thus, there is still much work to do within the basic cognitive core of conceptual change theory as well as outside the core.

CONCEPTUAL VOCABULARY

Conceptual Change and Mental Models

The term *conceptual change* has been used in a variety of ways. Thagard (1992) describes a spectrum of possible degrees of change, from changes in relatively surface-level details, or small revisions, to radical shifts in core concepts. A definition of conceptual change that fits well with Thagard's spectrum is learning in cases where new cognitive structure is created — a change that is structural or relational in character rather than a change in surface features. This could occur via the construction of a new structure or a modification or replacement of an old structure. This broad definition will suffice for discussing most of the literature. But the need to broaden it even further will be discussed in the section on types of conceptual change later in the chapter.

Developing a stable vocabulary with which to talk about *models* is one of the major challenges in this area. In its widest use in the literature, the term *mental model* is almost too large a category to be useful, essentially meaning any knowledge structure that represents a number of relationships between interconnected entities in a system (possibly including perceptual/spatial relationships), as opposed to a list of isolated facts. Gilbert, Boulter, and Rutherford (1998) point out that models focus the user on certain features in a system. Here I will use the term mental model in the broad sense to mean a (mental) representation of a system that focuses the user on certain features in the system and that can predict or account for its structure or behavior (Clement, 1989). I will make some minimal assumptions about useful models. Models are often idealized; one might say they are always simplified, since we cannot comprehend every microscopic detail of entities in the world. A useful model represents the important interrelationships in a system as opposed to merely a collection of isolated facts, and thereby allows a model to account for many events, making it an efficient kind of knowledge representation. This corresponds more or less to Nancy Nersessian's (chapter 15, this volume) definition of mental model: "A mental model is a conceptual system representing the physical system that is being reasoned about. It is an abstraction — idealized and schematic in nature — that represents a physical situation by having surrogate objects and properties, relations, behaviors, or functions of these that are in correspondence with it." I want to be careful, however, to take "abstraction" here to mean something with a degree of generality — as opposed to something completely non-concrete or non-imagistic — because I want to include the possibility of schematic, imagistic models that are concrete in the sense of being perception-like, but that are abstract in the sense of being schematic and general.

For example, people can have a mental model at many different levels of depth for, say, an old style 3-speed bicycle. Some may include a schematic image of a chain, bearings, and cables for brakes, internal gear shift mechanism, and gyroscopic action of the wheels, but other individuals are missing one or all of these elements (Piaget, 1930). These models are abstract in the sense of being simplified, schematic, and somewhat general, in that they apply to millions of bikes, but they still may be concretely imageable. *External models*, such as diagrams, may serve to record features of a mental model, and may allow one to develop a model too complex to be stored or envisioned at once in working memory.

Scientific Models

Minimal criteria for considering a mental model to be a *scientific model* include the requirement for a certain level of precision; the requirement for a basic level of plausibility that rules out, for example, occult properties; and a requirement that, if possible, the model be internally consistent (not self-contradictory). Under this broad definition, analogies, such as thinking about water wave reflection for light reflection, or a mechanical thermostat for the body's temperature regulation system, can also be scientific models when they are used in an attempt to predict or account for the behavior or structure of the system.

Explanatory vs. Non-Explanatory Models

Harrison and Treagust (1996) discuss a pantheon of types of models, including the scale model, analogical model, mathematical model, chemical formula, theoretical model, a standard (something to be imitated), maps and diagrams. To complement this pantheon I have found it helpful to make two orthogonal distinctions to help focus theory on a narrower "space" of models. Along one dimension lies the familiar distinction between qualitative and quantitative models. The other dimension requires more introduction. In a study of experts Clement (1989), found that the idea of an *explanatory model* helped to account for what was missing in subjects who were unsatisfied with their own understanding of a system, even though they could predict the behavior of the system. Such subjects were able to make a confident prediction at a behavioral level based on certain analogies and extreme cases, but they still appeared to lack an explanatory model that could provide them with a satisfying explanation for the behaviors. Historians of science, such as Campbell (1920), Hesse (1966), and Harre (1972), have developed important distinctions between explanatory models, empirical law hypotheses, and formal principles; these form the vertical dimension depicted in Table 16.1. These historians believe that hypothesized, theoretical, qualitative models (I will call these explanatory models), such as molecules, waves, and fields, are a kind of hypothesis separate from empirical patterns or observational descriptions of behavior. As a special kind of scientific model, an explanatory model is not simply a condensed summary of empirical observations, but is rather an invention that contributes new theoretical terms and images that are part of the scientist's view of the world, and which is neither given in, nor implied by, the data. Campbell gives the example that merely being able to make predictions from the empirical gas law stating that PV is proportional to RT is not the same as understanding *why* the system behaves as it does in terms of an explanatory model of molecules in motion. Thus the gas law is a scientific model but not an explanatory model. The explanatory elastic particle model provides a description of a hidden, non-observable mechanism that explains *how* the gas works and answers *why* questions about the causes underlying observable changes in temperature and pressure. The precision of such a model can be extended by adding a mathematical description of relations between variables in the model. These distinctions helped me explain how an expert could develop predictive knowledge at the Empirical Law Level in Table 16.1, yet be unsatisfied that they understood a system at the Explanatory Model Level. Level 4 contains formal theoretical principles, such as the Laws of Thermodynamics or Newton's laws, that consolidate general features of the mechanisms from the Explanatory Model Level and state them as part of a formal deductive system. Note that knowledge at any of the four levels in Table 16.1 can be qualitative or quantitative; so that this is a separate dimension from the levels shown there. Beyond these basic features, scientists often prefer explanatory models that are general, visualizable, simple, and that contain familiar entities (Nagel, 1961). More extensive sets of evaluatory criteria for a "good" explanatory model are discussed by Kuhn (1977) and Darden (1991). For a discussion of studies of other kinds of models, such as graphs, charts, and maps (e.g., Lehrer & Schauble, 2003; Raghavan & Glaser, 1995), familiarity with which may be an important prerequisite for preparing young children to work with explanatory models, see Jonassen (chapter 26, this volume).

Why Focus on Explanatory Models?

Authors such as Machamer, Darden, and Craver (2000), Campbell (1920), Harre (1972), Nagel (1961), and Hesse (1966) have argued that qualitative explanatory models, or mechanisms, are at the central core of most theories, and that to develop successful explanatory models is a central goal of most sciences. Such a model is seen as the means by which a theory takes on meaning, and, if used flexibly, it gives the theory the power to explain and make predictions for new cases that the subject has not seen. On this account, significant changes in an explanatory model are one of the most important types of conceptual change (Lawson, Clark, Meldrum, Falconer, Sequist, & Kwon, 2000).

In the next several sections, I will review some major approaches to instruction for producing conceptual change in science. I will put more emphasis on literature from science education, since Jonassen (this volume) has emphasized findings on models from educational psychology. I begin with the simplest one, that of presenting an explanatory model.

The Strategy of Presenting Models

Perhaps the most direct strategy is that of *presenting* descriptions of models in a concise and clear way. For example, studies by Mayer (1989, 2003) have tended to do this via schematic diagrams and text, finding, in many cases, that for presented explanations of mechanical systems (e.g., how car brakes work), the inclusion of a clear and simple diagram can yield a significant improvement in conceptual understanding (but usually not in factual knowledge), especially for students who have low spatial ability. Work by Hegarty, Kriz, and Cate (2003) indicates that learners can be induced to mentally animate static diagrams of dynamic processes. However, while encouraging, these studies have not tended to focus on areas where persistent misconceptions are found, or to measure understanding with distractors designed to detect such misconceptions. Lowe (1993) found that the mental representations derived by experts and novices from abstract technical diagrams (weather maps) depended on their ability to process the material in terms of dynamic relations between the components of the diagrams. Those who lacked prerequisite concepts did not comprehend the presented diagrams. In a related vein, Gabel (1999) found that adding the use of physical block models of molecules to chemistry lessons increased middle school students' comprehension of chemistry reactions and principles. Such studies indicate that a focus on communicating the visual aspects of explanatory models can make a positive difference in instruction.

Other studies, however, have shown that a limitation of presentation approaches is that they do not adequately deal with the problem of persistent misconceptions in the sciences. A set of "disaster studies" in physics in the early eighties, too numerous to review here, provided a wake up call to the physics education community, and similar results have been produced to some extent in biology and chemistry. These results indicated that even though college physics students, including engineering majors, were often able to learn to solve quantitative problems using algebraic formulas, they had great difficulty with many qualitative conceptual problems. These "disaster problems" were predominantly about explanatory models such as forces, models which had been presented to the students. This suggests that superficial knowledge at Level 4: Formal Theoretical Principles, in Table 16.1, does not imply understanding at Level 3: Explanatory Models, and it highlights the sometimes unrecognized importance of Level 3 in science education.

TABLE 16.1
Four Levels of Knowledge Used in Science

	Levels	*Example: Study of Gases*
THEORIES	4. Formal Theoretical Principles	Principles of Thermodynamics
	3. Explanatory Models	Colliding elastic particle model
OBSERVATION	2. Qualitative or Mathematical Descriptions of Patterns in Observations, including Empirical Laws	PV = kT (refers to patterns of observations of measuring apparatus)
	1. Primary-Level Data: Observations	Measurement of a single pressure change in a heated gas

DISSONANCE PRODUCING STRATEGIES

Dissonance Strategies

Teaching by Direct Contrast

Although I have chosen to define the concept of conceptual change more broadly, the problem of producing change in persistent misconceptions is especially interesting and challenging. The most direct approach to dealing with misconceptions in instruction is to refer intentionally to misconceptions during instruction and to contrast them with the scientists' view. Guzetti, Snyder, Glass and Gamas (1993) reviewed a number of studies of refutational texts — documents in which typical misconceptions are refuted directly in juxtaposition to the scientific view — and found that, overall, there was evidence of a positive effect. A related but somewhat milder approach is to draw out students' conceptions, relate them to observations, then hold up the target model in comparison. McCloskey, Washburn, and Felch (1983) found positive effects from asking high school mechanics students to explain their conceptions of force and motion and then contrasting these with the scientific view. This is called "contrastive teaching" by Schecker and Niedderer (1996), who believe that the student's original conception may not disappear, but that students can become aware of the difference between the two points of view.

Discrepant Events

Instead of contrasting a student model with the correct model directly, others have attempted to create more subtle forms of "participative dissonance," where information is provided that allows the student to discover a conflict with his or her own current model. Discrepant events are empirical experiments, data summaries, or demonstrations that provide data that could promote dissonance with students' preconceptions. Early studies reporting some success in using this technique have appeared in physics (Stavy & Berkovitz, 1980; Rowell and Dawson, 1985; Arnold & Millar, 1987), chemistry (Hand & Treagust, 1988), and biology (Dreyfus, Jungwirth, & Eliovitch, 1990), and some of the studies reporting significant differences in gains in favor of experimental groups using discrepant event strategies over control groups are Zietsman and Hewson (1986) and Licht (1987).

A simplified picture of dissonance strategies can be diagramed as shown in Figure 16.1a, with time moving from left to right. After dissonance is produced, Misconception 1 is either discarded (symbolized by the X) or suppressed in certain contexts (shown as a dotted line). Another Conception M2 then takes its place. Chiu, Chou, and Liu, (2002) reported significantly more radical conceptual change in experimental tutoring sessions than in a control group. In transcript analyses, they found evidence that producing cognitive dissonance in students by having them first explain their own concepts and only then presenting conflicting evidence appeared to be an important strategy (among others) for fostering understanding and preventing students from memorizing answers by rote. In a recent study of ninth graders learning about causes of the seasons, Tsai and Chang (2005) found significant gain differences in favor of groups that were encouraged to explain the seasons in their own terms (e.g., summer occurs when the earth is closest to the sun), after which they were presented with discrepant evidence (e.g., the earth is farther in the summer). Again, they interpret this as a way to prevent rote memorization, since the control group's answers were more evenly matched to the experimental group's immediately after instruction, but deteriorated on delayed post tests.

Some authors recognize that the purpose of a discrepant event is not just to promote dissonance with existing conceptions, but also to introduce a controversial question into a class in order to promote active discussion. Working from a theory of optimal dissonance for learning motivation, Inagaki and Hatano (1977) showed that student comprehension can be heightened by asking each student to commit to a prediction for an experiment or event to be discussed. This view of the role of dissonance is more complex than a simple conflict theory.

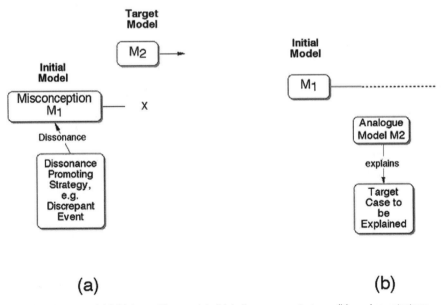

(a)   **(b)**

FIGURE 16.1   (a) Initial cognitive model of (a) dissonance strategy; (b) analogy strategy.

Other Dissonance Producing Strategies

Dissonance can come from a variety of sources in addition to discrepant events. Another source is student-student dissonance, between students' spontaneous ideas about a predicted phenomenon (Scott, 1992). Other studies using this approach include Dreyfus, Jungwirth, & Eliovitch (1990); Niedderer (1987); Hewson & Hennessey (1992); and Posner, Strike, Hewson, and Gertzog (1982). Jonassen (chapter 26, this volume) also reviews other dissonance studies.

Critiques of Dissonance Strategies

In summary, a positive characteristic of the studies cited above is that they embodied new recognition of the persistence of some student misconceptions, and corresponding recognition of a need to design instruction in a way that could deal with these misconceptions. Other studies however, argue that using discrepant events alone does not always work, for several possible reasons:

- *Lack of effect of single discrepant event*: Chinn and Brewer (1998) have catalogued a variety of student reactions to discrepant information, including cases where they ignore it or do not place it in conflict with their previously stated beliefs.
- *Affective critique:* In the Dreyfus et al. study cited above, the authors noted that, while the brighter, more successful students reacted enthusiastically to "cognitive conflicts," the unsuccessful students developed negative attitudes and tried to avoid conflicts. Stavy (1991) suggested avoiding conflict to prevent students' loss of confidence and possible regression.
- *Omission critique*: From a theoretical standpoint, using conflict strategies alone appears not to deal with building up a complex new explanatory model once the old model is called into question (Chan, Burtis, & Bereiter, 1997). In other words, one can ask, where does M2 in Figure 16.1 come from once M1 has been discounted? Can one always rely on students to simply invent M2 as the targeted scientific model?
- *Replacement critique*: Other theoretical objections have been posed by authors such as Smith, diSessa, and Roschelle (1993), who worry that:

Instruction designed to confront students' misconceptions head-on … seems destined to undercut students' confidence in their own sense-making abilities….

In focusing only on how student ideas conflict with expert concepts, the misconceptions perspective offers no account of productive ideas that might serve as resources for learning. Since they are fundamentally flawed, misconceptions themselves must be replaced. (p. 18)

Instead, they argue for more continuous approaches to teaching that engender developmental continuity. diSessa (1988) and his colleagues, such as Hammer (1996), as well as Clement, Brown and Zietsman, (1989), and Minstrell and Krauss (2005), have also advocated an increased focus on students' useful conceptual resources, in contrast to an exclusive focus on misconceptions.

Controversy

Thus, the literature on dissonance-producing strategies raises an interesting controversy. Some positive results have been documented using these strategies, but other studies question whether this can lead to some students becoming discouraged, or mistrusting their own intuitions or scientific reasoning skills. Because there are various types and sources of dissonance, these mixed results would seem to indicate the need for further research that investigates the effect of different types or levels of dissonance.

Instruction Using Analogies

Some authors have pointed to the use of analogies as a more positive approach to fostering conceptual change. Dupin and Johsua (1987) found that students studying electricity showed very limited change in the belief that current is "used up" in a bulb in a DC circuit after they were confronted with what the teacher hoped would be a discrepant event: data showing that the current was the same on each side of the bulb. However, when an analogy between electron flow in series circuits and a train running on a circular track was discussed with the students, a significant number changed to a constant-current point of view. Thus, this study pointed both to a possible limitation of discrepant events and to the positive effect of an analogy.

Theoretical Potential of Analogies

Analogies are seen by some as an alternative to conflict (Stavy, 1991) and replacement. They are one approach to meeting the call cited at the end of the previous section above for more use of students' positive preconceptions and other resources. Since some useful reviews of instructional analogies already exist (Dagher, 1994, 1995; Duit, 1991; Glynn, 2003), and my main purpose with regard to analogies is eventually to discuss their relationship to explanatory models, I will not review the extensive literature on analogical reasoning here. However, I do want to give a few examples as background for discussing the relationship between analogies and explanatory models. Analogies can be introduced in text or lectures, but many science education researchers advocate developing them interactively in class discussions. Analogies are said to tap existing knowledge in the learner that is similar enough to a target conception to allow some relational information to be inferred in the target (Gentner, 1983; Gorsky & Finegold, 1994; Royer & Cable, 1976; Simons, 1984; Stavy, 1991; Stepich & Newby, 1988).

The intended effect of analogies in instruction can be diagramed as shown in Figure 16.1b, where prior knowledge in the base of the analogy is tapped in order to make inferences about relationships in a target problem. Analogies make explicit use of students' prior knowledge in a positive way. This represents an important shift from focusing on student prior knowledge only as problematic misconceptions. Analogy also holds out hope for efficient global change that is more than small revision, since one may be able, theoretically, to "import" a whole set of interconnected relations from the base of the analogy to the model.

Classroom Learning Trials

A number of authors have measured learning gains associated with instruction that uses analogies, including Bulgren, Deschler, Schumaker, and Lenz (2000), Glynn. (1991), Mason (1994), Venviille and Treagust (1996), Dupin and Johsua (1989), Minstrell (1982), Brown (1992, 1994), Brown and Clement (1992), and Clement (1993). Glynn (1991) introduced a six-step strategy he called a "Teaching with Analogies (TWA)" approach that includes steps for mapping similarities between the analogue and target explicitly, and indicating where the analogy breaks down. When these steps are taken in interactive discussion, this strategy goes well beyond that of presenting the analogy in lecture.

Limitations of Analogies

Others, however, have sounded caution on the limitations of using analogies, several of which are summarized in Table 16.2 (Yerrick, Doster, Nugent, Parke, Crawley, 2003; Else & Clement, 2008a). For example, Harrison and Treagust (1996), in a study of the effectiveness of analogies used in eight- to tenth-grade classrooms, write: "It appears that many students do not interpret teacher metaphors and analogies in the intended manner. Rather, they transfer attributes from the teachers' analog to the target . . . in a literal and undifferentiated sense." (p. 511) Although they found some positive effects of analogies, they found that some students preferred less accurate models of atoms over others and that many students thought that atoms were alive and divide like cells. They believe that these 'dangerous' features came from analogical models used in instruction, concluding that their study "has illustrated the negative outcomes that arise when students are left to draw their own conclusions about analogical models." Duit, Roth, Komorek, and Wilbers (2001) sounded a similar theme in a study where they examined a set of ninth-grade lessons on quantum and catastrophe theory phenomena in which students were encouraged to generate their own analogies. The "discuss the limitations" step in Glynn's TWA strategy described above, is designed to avoid difficulty 3 in Table 16.2. However, even when that strategy is heeded, students may still "over-transfer" (Else & Clement, 2008).

Finding a Good Base

Clement et al. (1989), diSessa (1988), and Hammer (1996) have called for the systematic study of students' positive preconceptions, or "anchors," to address problem 1 in Table 16.2. Clement et al. (1989) found that different examples of what appears to experts to be the same physical principle varied strongly with respect to whether students could understand them as examples of the principle. This means that one has to be quite careful in choosing examples for the base of an analogy, i.e. base examples need to be tested with students. Duit et al. (2001) confirmed this in the case of certain analogies for quantum effects where the base was poorly understood by certain students. Clement et al. (1989) documented that other examples, however, are interpreted correctly by the vast majority of students and therefore can provide good starting points, or "anchors," for instruction, concluding that many preconceptions are not misconceptions. On the other hand, in areas where students have insufficiently developed anchoring intuitions about the base, those intuitions may need to be developed by real or simulated experiences. Examples are Arons' (1990) activity of having students push large objects in a low friction environment, McDermott's (1984) use of air hoses to accelerate dry ice pucks, diSessa, Horwitz, and White's use of dynaturtle (White, 1993), and Steinberg's (2004) use of air pressure experiments to develop intuitions to be applied later to analogous electrical circuits.

TABLE 16.2
Possible Limitations and Difficulties in Using Analogies in Instruction

1. The base (anchor) may not be understood sufficiently
2. The base may be too far from the target for the student to see the mapping or to see its applicability to the target
3. The student may transfer too much from base to target
4. The analogous case may not contain all of the relations needed to develop the target model

Bridging Strategy

A strategy called *Bridging analogies*, which uses multiple analogies, has been developed to try to overcome difficulty 2 in Table 16.2 (Clement et al, 1987; Brown & Clement, 1989; Clement, 1993). The strategy is used in about a dozen mechanics lessons in Camp and Clement (1994). For example, they built on their tutoring study research and work by Minstrell (1982) to construct a lesson on normal forces. A common misconception in this area is that a table cannot push up on a book. Students say the table is only in the way, serving as a barrier that keeps the book from falling, but do not see it as a force-producing entity. The physicist, on the other hand, views the table as elastic — deforming a tiny amount in response to the force from the book and providing an equal and opposite force upward to keep the book from falling. In the lessons, first, an *anchoring example* of a hand pushing down on a spring was used, which draws out a physical intuition in the student that is in agreement with accepted physical theory (most students agreeing that the spring pushes up on the hand). Then, a chain of bridging analogies was used, as shown in Figure 16.2, to gradually transfer the student's intuition, from the anchoring example of the hand on the spring to a near case of the book on a foam pad, then to the book on a thin flexible board, and finally to the far case of a book on a table. The teachers taught Socratically during this 25-minute session, posing questions about each example, summarizing and paraphrasing student comments, and keeping the discussion from wandering off track, but not revealing their own views. This led to some unusually animated discussions in some classes. Students were asked to evaluate and vote on the analogy relations between the examples. This process exemplifies the type of change emphasized by diSessa (1988), that of changing the domain of application, or applicability conditions, of a concept. In this case, the domain of the "Springiness" conception is expanded gradually via the progression of examples in order eventually to encompass the unintuitive case of tables and other rigid objects.

Brown (1992a) conducted a study in which high school chemistry students who had not had physics were asked to "learn aloud" individually as they worked through a textual presentation of the bridging analogies strategy for the book on the table lesson. Students taught with this method had significantly higher pre-post gains than students in a control group. One of the retrospective comments by students that supports the latter view of the source of effectiveness of bridging is the following: "Out of context you just compare the spring and the table — it wouldn't help, but you sort of built a way up from the spring, which is obvious, to a flexible board, to a not so flexible board, to foam rubber, to a table, which is pretty good." This quotation is consistent with an "extending the domain of application of a 'springiness' schema" view of the role of bridging cases here. The control group in this case read a passage of equivalent length from a well-known innovative physics textbook which presented many concrete examples of Newton's Third Law

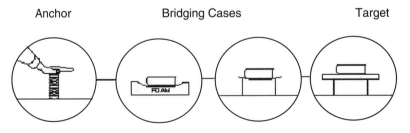

Anchor   Bridging Cases   Target

FIGURE 16.2   Chain of bridging analogies transferring intuition from anchor to target.

after stating the law. This passage focused on citing many examples rather than on developing bridging analogy relations and models with a few carefully selected examples. It was as if the control text were aiming to have the student reinforce or induce a very general and abstract principle from a large set of unordered examples. In contrast, the superior performance of the experimental group was used to argue that the transfer of a concrete, dynamic model in a systematic, stepwise manner from the anchor toward the target is more effective.

Summary

A number of studies have documented promising gains from analogy-based instruction. However, other studies have exposed various problems that can arise, as shown above in Table 16.2. Identifying the conditions under which analogies succeed and fail is therefore an important problem for future research. The use of analogies is usually considered to be a strategy that is more constructive than disconfirmatory. A remaining potential general criticism of the use of analogy on its own, in addition to the criticisms in Table 16.2, is that building up a model using an analogy may do nothing to counteract a persistent prior misconception (shown as the persisting M1 in Figure 16.1b). Later on, the prior misconception may reassimilate the target T, causing the student to revert to their previous misconception. This suggests the strategy of combining analogies and dissonance producing situations, discussed in the next section.

Combined Strategy: Using Analogies And Dissonance Together

Minstrell (1982) and curricula by Camp and Clement (1994) and Steinberg (2004) have taken a position that embraces both the use of dissonance and the use of analogies, as summarized by the concept diagram shown in Figure 16.3. They were impressed with both (a) the depth of the persistence problem for misconceptions in many areas of physics, and (b) the importance of building on student's intuitions wherever possible (diSessa 1988; Clement et al., 1989). This combined strategy works to resolve what I call the Prior Knowledge Paradox: constructivist theory tells us to build on what the student knows, but conceptual change research tells us that a significant part of what the student knows is in conflict with scientists' views. The paradox can be resolved if one recognizes that both kinds of knowledge can coexist in students, and that one can use analogies that tap positive preconceptions to help students deal with misconceptions.

A number of the lessons designed by Camp et al. (1994) used both analogies and discrepant events, as shown in Figure 16.3. For example, the normal forces lesson included not only bridging analogies discussed earlier but also a discrepant event where a light beam reflected from a mirror flat on the teacher's desk to a wall is deflected downward along the wall when a person stands on the desk. This experiment provides dissonance for students who believe that desks are rigid objects that cannot deform to provide an elastic force. After establishing the existence of a normal force in the first lesson, the equality of forces in such cases was addressed using similar techniques in a second lesson. In comparison with control groups, this lesson unit has shown large significant gain differences greater than one standard deviation in size, as measured by pre- and post-tests on problems that deal with students' preconceptions. Some students changed their position toward the scientific view during each major section of the lesson, e.g., after the anchor, bridge, microscopic model presentation, and discrepant event sections, leading the author to hypothesize that each technique was helpful to some subset of students in changing the applicability conditions of the "springiness" schema so that it could also apply it to solid objects like tables (Clement, 1993). Thus there was evidence that a discrepant event in this lesson helped a number

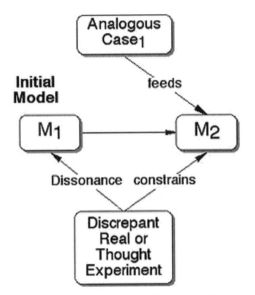

FIGURE 16.3   Combined strategy using analogies and dissonance together.

of the students increase their acceptance of the concept, providing evidence that using analogies and discrepant events in combination is an effective strategy for some instructional situations. Large significant gain differences were also realized in three other topic areas in mechanics where lessons combined analogies and discrepant events (Clement et al., 1987; Brown & Clement, 1991; Clement, 1993). Additional examples of using analogies and dissonance producing tactics together will be discussed in the next section, on model evolution. These studies appear to challenge the dichotomy between a dissonance approach and an approach that begins with students' positive preconceptions, by doing both of these in the same lesson.

MODEL EVOLUTION PROCESSES

Multiple Analogies Foreshadow Model Evolution

Kuhn's (1970) description of science as going through revolutions was challenged by Toulmin (1972) who cited examples of historical change processes that appeared to be a more gradual kind of evolution. Both ideas have been used as metaphors for conceptual change in students (Novak, 1977). Approaches that build up a model in stages by using successive analogies foreshadow a model evolution approach since they involve gradual improvement of the student's model. Harrison and De Jong (2005) describe the use of multiple analogies in chemistry, and Spiro et al. (1991), and Glynn and Duit (1995) describe the use of multiple analogies to gradually build up a student's conception of biological systems such as muscle fibers or the eye, respectively. Chiu and Lin (2005) found that multiple analogies were significantly more effective than single analogies when they were complementary analogies (that spoke to different aspects of the target); when multiple analogies used were similar to each other, they were no more effective than single analogies.

Model Evolution through Successive Modifications

This raises the issue of an evolution/revolution debate by posing the question as to whether new explanatory models should be (1) evolved incrementally, by starting from and modifying the student's own ideas, to foster engagement and ease of modification, or (2) introduced all at once in order to display their coherence and superior explanatory power by contrast in a more revolutionary manner. The three studies cited earlier at the beginning of the section on Dissonance Producing Strategies can be interpreted as advocating a more revolutionary perspective, as examples of contrastive teaching.

On the other hand, Buckley (2000) traced the work of the most successful student in a class who was given many kinds of information resources and who was told to work without direct instruction on learning how the circulatory system works. She characterized this student as the one who was best able to maintain a partial, initially incomplete and faulty, explanatory model of the system that grew and became more sophisticated as new elements were incrementally added or eliminated. Not only did the student's partial model act as a central place where she added new information coherently, but new *predictions* she made from her model generated questions that motivated her to learn more about circulation. This paper weighs in on the side of an evolutionary approach by documenting the potential for engaging and maintaining student reasoning during learning by starting from mostly familiar concepts in a partial model and pursuing a series of implications and improvements. It is unusual in documenting a very student directed approach.

Most of the teaching strategies previously described in this chapter are utilized in the diagram in Figure 16.4, which makes explicit a model evolution approach for teaching models of electric circuits, as described in Steinberg and Clement (1997) and Clement and Steinberg (2002). They conducted a case study of model construction in which they used detailed transcripts from tutoring sessions to acquire fine grained data on a series of substantial changes in a student's model of circuits. The middle row of Figure 16.4 shows highlights in the progression of the student's model, with analogies being introduced from above and discrepant events from below. Their case study evidence supports the conclusion that a cycle of small incremental steps involving dissonance and then constructive activity aided this student in gradually building a more complex model. For example, students who associate power only in circuits with a battery experience dissonance when they light a bulb (temporarily) by discharging a very large capacitor in a circuit with no battery. An analogy between a discharging capacitor that is releasing charge and a pressurized tire that is releasing air helps to begin building up a model that can explain this.

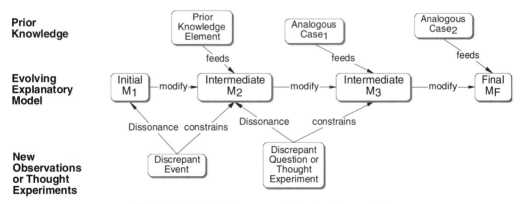

FIGURE 16.4   Evolution approach for teaching models.

Thus, the model undergoes a *series of successive refinements*. Only two intermediate models are shown in Figure 16.4, but in practice there can be many more. Most intermediate student models in a topic area are partly correct and partly faulty. The teacher then tries to retain the positive pieces, and to promote conflict with each faulty piece, one step at a time, while recruiting elements from prior knowledge (often via analogy) to help repair that part of the model.

The idea of building up the student's model gradually through revisionary change is also discussed by Treagust et al. (1996), Dupin and Johsua (1989), and Minstrell and Krauss (2005). It is implicit in the open discussions of lab results advocated by Wells, Hestenes, and Swackhamer, (1995), who have developed important ways of training physics teachers to postpone evaluation of student ideas in order to facilitate such discussions. Scott (1992) and Niedderer and Goldberg (1996) highlight the importance of the very closely related idea of a *learning pathway* of intermediate states seen as stepping stones between preconceptions and target conceptions (see review by Niedderer, 2001). They point out that such intermediate states can develop from student ideas that are unanticipated, requiring teaching or tutoring studies, not just task analysis, to determine good pathways. Niedderer views intermediate knowledge states that appeal to many students as 'attractors.' For curricula resulting from such studies, Clement (2008a) distinguishes between a planned learning pathway specified ahead of time in a lesson plan and an implemented learning pathway that results from the teacher using the plan with real students adaptively. As students introduce unanticipated ideas and details, the implemented pathway is bound to be longer and somewhat different from the planned pathway. Nevertheless, the planned pathway is seen as a valuable source of focus. An extended version of this idea applied in higher level planning to multi-year time spans has been dubbed a "learning progression" in articles such as Smith, Wiser, Anderson, Krajcik (2006) as an important principle for developing teaching standards.

Multiple Short Cycles Needed for Complex Models

Concerning Figure 16.4, Clement and Steinberg (2002) write that the small step sizes of the revisions were made possible by the careful choice on the part of the tutor of coordinated "small" analogies and "small" discrepant events. They theorize that this makes it possible for the student to participate in suggesting model revisions that are small enough to make immediate sense, allaying concerns expressed earlier about possible negative effects of too much dissonance. Brown (1992a) and Steinberg (2008) documented large gains over control groups using a curriculum on circuits of this kind, including disproportionately large confidence gains in female students. Others who have focused on the explicit development of a series of intermediate models are White (1989), Gilbert et al. (1998), Gobert and Buckley (2000) and Niedderer and Goldberg (1996). In a very different context, White (1993) used a series of more than 40 short, computer simulation "hit the target" games to successfully teach, one step at a time, a qualitative appreciation of Newtonian force and motion ideas in a virtual frictionless environment.

Successive Refinement Cycles

The description in Figure 16.4 was also influenced by expert studies. On the basis of expert protocols, Clement (1981, 1989) proposed that models can be constructed via an extended evolutionary cycle of criticism and revision. For example, the 1989 study traces a series of five evaluation and revision cycles as an expert constructs a model while solving an explanation problem. This cycle of model generation, evaluation, and modification is referred to as a GEM cycle. Experts engaging in theory formation and assessment cycles using analogies have also been discussed by Holland, Holyoak, Nisbett, and Thagard (1986), and Darden (1991). Nersessian

(1992, 2002) documents the cyclical progressive revision process taken by Maxwell during his construction of several visualizable models of the electromagnetic field, just prior to formulating his famous field equations. In these studies as well, we see that dissonance can be part of an evolutionary cycle.

The Role of Dissonance in Model Evolution

In the following, I highlight some ways in which dissonance is hypothesized to contribute to evolution.

1. *Model evaluation.* The fostering of dialectic discussions requires the careful development of a spirit of inquiry in the classroom, where students' ideas are valued. On the other hand, model evolution techniques do require model evaluation and criticism, suggesting the importance of dissonance strategies. Minstrell (1982) discusses strategies for distancing ownership of ideas away from individual students to make criticism non-threatening. Also, students have been observed using discrepant questions and thought experiments to create dissonance themselves, although this may happen only after students are used to discussing models (Nunez-Oviedo, Clement, & Rea-Ramirez, 2008; Stephens & Clement, 2006). There is some evidence that students' preconceptions in different areas vary in how persistent they are (Gorsky and Finegold, 1994), ranging from being easily discarded (see Nunez-Oviedo et al., 2008; Zietsman & Hewson (1986)) to very deep-seated (see Clement, 1982, 1993; Hestenes et al., 1992). In low persistence cases at least, mild forms of dissonance can be used in conjunction with other positive teaching strategies to produce model evolution. Thus, the use of dissonance to deal with misconceptions need not necessarily be associated with strong, confrontational methods (Rea-Ramirez & Clement, 1998).

2. *Positive effects of dissonance.* Clement and Steinberg (2002) point out that discrepant events can be designed not only to generate dissonance with the students' old model, but also to provide a framework of constraints for guiding construction of the new model, thereby making a positive as well as negative contribution to conceptual change. In Figure 16.4, the discrepant event is shown both generating dissonance with M2 and constraining the development of M3. Clement and Rea-Ramirez (1998) called this a "Dual effect." In a study of ninth graders learning models of heat transfer, She (2004) found that carefully designed discrepant events or questions did help students detect problems in their existing models and also appeared to provide constraints and motivation for constructing the next step in their evolving model. Nersessian (2002) has described similar constraint-based modeling processes in her analysis of Maxwell's thought experiments, and Clement (2008c) describes such processes in experts thinking aloud. Thus instead of limiting ourselves to the choice between "confrontation" and "no confrontation," vaguely defined, there are a variety of sources of dissonance of different strengths, and this suggests intermediate strategies that should be articulated and tested.

Evidence from Curriculum Trials for Effective Model (and Concept) Evolution

Other studies have provided evidence that model evaluation and modification cycles can be used effectively in biology (Barker & Carr, 1989a,b; Nunez-Oviedo & Clement, 2007; Hafner & Stewart, 1995), chemistry (Khan, Stillings, Clement, & Tronsky, 2002) Fretz et al. (2002), heat (Linn, Bell, & Hsi, 1998), electricity (Steinberg, 2008; Clement & Steinberg, 2002), thermal equilibrium (She, 2004), and mechanics (White, 1989, 1993; Zietsman & Clement, 1997). At an even more fine-grained level than intermediate models, Brown and Clement (1992) describe large gains over controls for mechanics lessons that teach students a set of intermediate *concepts* of inertia, such as "keeps going tendency" and "holdback tendency," before leading the students to modify and combine the concepts into a single expert concept.

Instructional Implications: Teacher Directed or Student Directed?

I have said very little about how open to novel student ideas the modeling process should be, because teachers and projects vary tremendously on this dimension. Requesting student participation in the model generation, evaluation, and revision process does open up the conversation and make it more student active and student centered, but teachers and students using such approaches need to become comfortable with the idea of discussing intermediate models that are partially incorrect, prior to students developing a more sophisticated model. An intermediate position has the teacher fostering *co-construction* by stimulating inferences — the teacher has some input to the construction, but is also striving to stimulate student input (Hammer, 1996; Minstrell & Krauss, 2005). An extended discussion of co-construction strategies is given in Clement and Rea-Ramirez (2008).

For example, getting students to speculate on and generate models of systems like the pulmonary system is not hard, even at the middle school level. But students may generate a variety of ideas for model elements, some of which are at odds with the scientific view (air goes from the mouth to the heart), more or less compatible with the scientific view (air goes into your lungs), and partially correct (lungs are like hollow balloons that expand and contract). Five or fifteen contributions can lead to a large variety of ideas, or what Easley (1990) termed *conceptual splatter*. Clement (2008b) describes the challenge this poses: a teacher must decide which idea to deal with first in order to keep students in a reasoning zone. There is a need to set an agenda, to decide how to draw on the positive portion of the students' ideas, and this requires that teachers think on their feet, based on what models the students have generated. Nunez-Oviedo et al. (2007), Williams (2006), and Williams and Clement (2006) have tracked how a skilled teacher can guide discussions to produce model evolution in the presence of such multiple difficulties. The skills used pose an additional challenge for teachers and teacher education. Inagaki, Hatano, and Morita, (1998) suggests that one way to reduce the load on the teacher is to have students vote on a limited number of choices-- those that have been researched ahead of time and shown to have many advocates. Electronic response systems (Dufresne, Gerace, Leonard, Mestre, & Wenk, 1996) may facilitate this.

Theoretical Implications

One can extrapolate to form several theoretical hypotheses from the ideas about model evolution reviewed above:

- While it is not likely that all science models require an evolutionary approach with many GEM cycles for learning to occur, such strategies may be especially needed whenever target models are complex or multiple misconceptions are present.
- The intermediate steps used in model evolution are reminiscent of the "bridging analogies" approach discussed earlier. However, the intermediate steps represented in Figure 16.2 are separate analogous *cases* that are potentially observable (e.g., a book on foam rubber), whereas the intermediate models in Figure 16.4 are non-observable, explanatory

models (e.g., more and more adequate models of what drives currents in circuits). Figure 16.2 shows a chain of analogical connections whereas Figure 16.4 shows changes in the model itself via successive modifications. Both processes have intermediate elements, but they play different cognitive roles.

• In their call for small step model revision starting from students' ideas, model evolution approaches support the idealistic positions of diSessa (1988), Smith et al. (1993) and Clement, et al. (1989) and contrast with a global replacement approach. However, model evolution in small step sizes is also an interesting idea theoretically, because it challenges the distinction between a substantial conceptual change (in the extreme, a revolution) and a minor revision; a long series of small changes in a model could result, in theory, in a very substantial global change.

Types of Conceptual Change and the Need for Multiple Teaching Strategies

Dagher (1994) sorted researchers' investigations of conceptual change according to where they fell on Thagard's (1992) spectrum of types of conceptual change. I will attempt to paint a somewhat larger spectrum in an attempt to represent the variety of conceptual change types needed in instruction. Types of conceptual change are listed in the left hand column of Table 16.3. In particular:

• A small change in a single feature of a model, as in Thagard's (1992) "adding a weak rule", can be considered a Minor Model Revision and can sometimes be accomplished by students who have had minimal prompting.
• diSessa (1988) and Smith et al. (1993) provide examples where the content of a conception remains largely the same but the Domain of Applicability is changed or expanded significantly so that it applies to new cases.

TABLE 16.3
Types of Conceptual Change in Explanatory Model Development

CC Process	Example of Author	Outcome
Paradigm Shift	Kuhn	Collection of ideas that differs drastically from original in multiple ways
8) Branch Jumping and Tree Switching	Thagard, Chi	Replace concept w. ontologically different type of concept
7) Fundamental Concept Differentiation or Integration	Carey, Wiser	Fundamental concept split or concepts united
6) Construct New Initial Model	Mayer	Initial Model formed, with assumption that it has not grown out of an earlier model
5) Synthesis or Combination	Vosniadou, Collins and Gentner	Conjoined Models
4) Major Model Modification	Clement, Steinberg	Add, remove, or change element to produce Modified Model
3) Abstraction	Gentner, Holyoak, Nersessian	General Schema formed from exemplars
2) Change in Domain of Applicability	diSessa	Model with new applicability conditions and exemplars
1) Minor Model Revision	Rumelhart and Norman's "tuning"	Adjusted Model

- Gentner (1983) and Holyoak and Thagard (1989) speak of an inductive process of Abstraction whereby a general schema can be formed by stripping away differences between two or more analogous exemplars. In a related process, Nersessian (1992) writes of scientists forming abstract models with surface features removed.

- Clement and Steinberg (2002) document examples of Major Model Modification, such as the change from a focus on pressure to a focus on pressure *differences* as the cause of flows (representing voltage differences as the cause of current flow in electric circuits).

- Vosniadou and Brewer (1992) document a process of synthesis whereby subjects form a hybrid model that combines a prior model with a newly learned model. This process may be related to what Collins and Gentner (1987) described as "pasting component models together" and what Clement (1994) refers to as "compound simulation".

- Through a process of abduction, receiving a presentation (Mayer, 1989), or both, some authors believe that a new initial model can be learned by a process of constructing a model from known pieces or by transmission.

- Researchers have documented cases of Concept Differentiation or Integration that present major challenges to students, such as the differentiation of heat from temperature (Wiser & Carey, 1983) or the integration of acceleration and deceleration into a single concept.

- Some researchers believe it is particularly difficult to replace a conception that has the characteristics of one philosophical/ontological category with a conception that has the characteristics of a different category; e.g., changing the conception of *heating as substance transfer* to one of *heating as energy transfer* (Chi, 1992; Thagard, 1992).

Listed at the top of Table 16.3 is a process that would occur on a larger time scale than an individual conceptual change, and so in some contexts it might be placed on a different dimension than the others. A paradigm shift, such as the shift from Aristotelian to Newtonian mechanics, involves deep changes in many concepts, and therefore one would not expect it to be possible via a single, or even a few, conceptual changes. Therefore a dotted line is shown between it and the other processes. Students' naïve views of mechanics are not identical to Aristotle's, and there is a question of whether the shift from naïve physics to Newtonian physics constitutes a paradigm shift, depending on whether one considers naïve physics to be a paradigm. However there is substantial evidence that it is a huge shift that meets stiff resistance. One may need to warn students that the Newtonian view may not make sense immediately until they have attained a critical mass of new concepts, including velocity, acceleration, force, weight, inertial mass, friction force, relative motion, vector addition of velocities, addition of forces, and net force.

Some have endeavored to draw a cutoff line in various places across Table 16.3 and to reserve the term *conceptual change* only for processes above the line. I am going to resist that impulse here. All of these types could be seen as conceptual change in certain cases — that is, as a significant change in conceptual understanding. I therefore concur with the preference for including smaller changes in structure as one type of conceptual change, broadly defined. As Dagher (1994) puts limiting worthwhile science to revolutionary science. This is partly because teachers are not so much interested in whether a change is large enough to be "officially certified" as they are in being able to foster progress toward understanding. This is especially true in the context of this chapter where the focus is on change in an explanatory model (i.e., explanatory structure). Even a small change in explanatory structure may be quite important. In addition, it is possible that a series of smaller changes can add up to a large structural change, making the drawing of a sharp boundary line difficult.

Also, it appears that change of any type in Table 16.3 could meet with more or less resistance from an existing preconception, depending on the strength of that preconception. Thus, it is possible that what looks like a small change from a philosophical or linguistic point of view (near the bottom of Table16.3) is actually a huge change from the student's point of view. For example, the idea that air has a small, but significant, weight would seem to be a small attribute change, yet it is very counterintuitive for most middle school students. Thagard's taxonomy itself did not deal with resistance in this sense. I will treat it as a separate dimension that can apply to any of the types of conceptual change. Chiu et al. (2002) describe how different portions of a chemistry unit varied in difficulty according to the kinds of conceptual change involved, roughly consistent with their type in Table 16.3.

Change in applicability conditions is one type of change that may not fit the definition of conceptual change given at the beginning of this chapter, "learning in cases where new cognitive structure is created." We can change the definition to include this type but to go beyond that provides an interesting challenge for theory in this area (diSessa, 1988).

Table 16.3 is also conceptualized as representing a dimension different from processes of *model evaluation*, including processes of model confirmation or disconfirmation, and model competition. Generation, evaluation, and modification cycles (GEM cycles) were discussed in the earlier section on model evolution approaches to instruction as a larger pattern. Any model resulting from a conceptual change should be evaluated intuitively according to whether it makes sense, but also by more established criteria (cf. Darden, 1991). Such processes have been documented during instruction by Linn et al., (1998) and Nunez-Oviedo et al. (2007) among others. These vary from those using more formal schemes derived from Toulmin (1972) for tracking arguments to less formal schemes (see also Duschl & Osborne, 2002). Model evaluation is an important process skill that is partly intuitive, but that also needs to be refined significantly (Hammer & Elby, 2002; Clement, 2008c). Model competition processes have been documented in science by Kuhn (1970), Giere (1988), and Thagard (1992), in scientists' think alouds by Clement (1989, in press), and in instruction by Linn et al. (1998), Tabak, Sandoval, Smith, Agganis, Baumgartner, and Reiser (1995), Taber (2001), and Nunez-Oviedo and Clement (2007). This process operates to comparatively evaluate models generated by any of the other processes in the table.

Need For Multiple Teaching Strategies

My own opinion, having worked on two, large, model-based curriculum projects in mechanics and in the biology of respiration, is that all types of change listed in Table 16.3 are applicable at times as descriptors of student learning processes. Many of the types of change could be involved in a single unit of instruction. This view contrasts with those in the first three sections of this chapter, which focused on interventions primarily using one predominant strategy. Also, this possible variation in learning processes, from very easy to very difficult within a single unit, means that progress may be quite uneven; as a result, teachers are probably not fully prepared to appreciate the range of difficulty that can be present within a unit.

For example, the "Book on the Table" lesson, discussed earlier, aims at more than one type of conceptual change, i.e., a change in applicability conditions (expansion of the domain of exemplars for the "springiness" p-prim) and the construction of a new hidden explanatory model (molecules with springy bonds). In this lesson, one can also see evidence for several types of teaching strategies, including requests for explanation, use of analogies, use of a discrepant event, and the presentation of an explanatory model. Brown (1994) found in a tutoring study, using a lesson of this kind, that different students picked different strategies when asked what they had learned from the most. This and the recognition that there are many types of conceptual change as represented n Table 16.3 argues that using multiple teaching strategies is an important technique for reaching students, and this is exemplified further in Figure 16.5. This type of diagram is described in Clement and Rea-Ramirez (2008) and depicts strategies used in a videotaped teaching session where the teacher was piloting a new curriculum unit on pulmonary respiration with a group of four middle school students. She first asked the students to draw their initial ideas about the structure of the lungs. In Figure 16.5, the developing student model is shown from left to right across the middle. The student contributions are across the top, while teacher inputs and teaching strategies are across the bottom. The teacher promoted student model construction with teaching strategies such as requests for explanation, discrepant questions, analogies, a discrepant event, the teacher giving students a presentation about a feature of the model, an animation showing O2 diffusing to blood cells from alveoli, and the exploration of a physical model (string wrapped around artificial grapes on a vine to represent blood vessels and alveoli). Throughout the process, the teacher encouraged the students to question and revise their own and other students' models by modifying their drawings of the lungs and alveoli.

This lesson unit employs a number of teaching strategies in addition to the use of discrepant events and analogy, expanding the image of conceptual change teaching that was depicted in Figure 16.4 to one that includes multiple methods for supporting or feeding model evolution. This unit also used different degrees of student (as opposed to teacher) idea generation in different places. The ratio of student to teacher idea generation that is possible is likely to depend on what cognitive resources are available to students for each given topic. In some places here, the primary generator of ideas was the group of students, and in other places, it was the teacher. Figure 16.5 adds to our image of what Model Evolution via Co-construction can look like, with both student and teacher inputs to the developing model, making it a social construction. Note that some strategies are seen as producing dissonance with the current model, whereas others simply speak to a gap in the model.

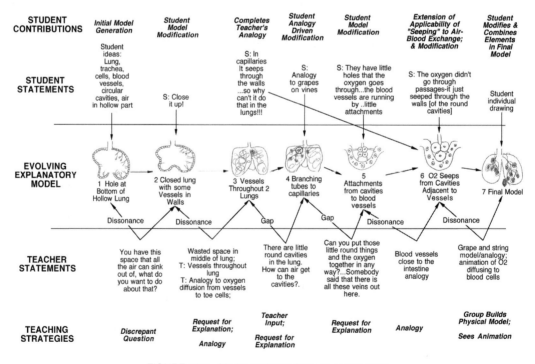

FIGURE 16.5   Model evolution from co-construction.

Tsai and Chang (2005), in their study of learning the causes of the seasons, designed their lesson around a "conflict map" diagram that shows not only discrepant information to be introduced, but also multiple kinds of evidence supporting the scientific model of the seasons. When included in a curriculum, such multiple strategy diagrams should help teachers focus on the conceptual goals and major cognitive strategies of the lesson (see also Camp & Clement, 1994). Achieving focus is no mean feat when operating within the distractions of a real classroom and the somewhat unpredictable course of a large group discussion.

Figure 16.5 is organized around a model modification framework as the major type of conceptual change in Table 16.3 being pursued at that point in the curriculum. It is interesting that "analogy" does not appear in Table 16.3 as a type of conceptual change. Rather, it is considered here to be one of many types of teaching strategies at a finer grain size level, shown in the bottom row of Figure 16.5, which can facilitate the conceptual changes in Table 16.3.

Comment on Process Goals

This chapter is focused on methods for achieving content goals of conceptual understanding, but this focus can quickly lead one to needing students to become engaged in scientific thinking that speaks to certain process goals. The teaching strategies already described fulfill some process goals already, but approaches that also emphasize process goals for their own sake would need to add additional investigation activities. It is possible that certain deep process goals, such as skills for managing self directed inquiry cycles, are better pursued in separate types of activities from those dealing with persistent misconceptions, as opposed to trying to combine them in the same activity. This is another question for future research.

Section Summary

I have posed the possibility that all of the types of conceptual change in Table 16.3 could be involved in the learning process when a student is developing the model of any complex system such as the conversion of energy in the human body. Recognizing the possibility of model evolution and the variety of teaching strategies that can be involved in its many steps, leads one to appreciate the need for multiple teaching strategies rather than simplistic one- or two-strategy models of teaching. It can be hypothesized that topics where misconceptions are persistent or target conceptions are complex will probably require a greater number and variety of teaching strategies. Also, it stands to reason that specialized teaching strategies are possible for each type of conceptual change, giving us another agenda for research. I examine this possibility for the case of analogies in the next section.

THE RELATIONSHIP(S) BETWEEN ANALOGIES AND EXPLANATORY MODELS

An Analogy Can Contribute to Building a Model

The distinction between analogies, explanatory models, and other types of models has been blurred in much of the literature, but once it is established, it makes possible a further clarification of the different types of special contributions that analogies can make to explanatory model construction. Unlike Figure 16.1b, Figures 16.4 and 16.5 separate the analogous case from the explanatory model, allowing one to see analogy as participating in the revision of the student's prior model; i.e., analogy as one source of ideas for improving a model rather than as identical to, or the sole source of, a model. These are subtle, but very important, shifts in one's view of the role of analogies. It suggests that the teacher should not rely on an analogy as the only source for model development, but rather as one (albeit an important) source in an instructional sequence that promotes model evolution (Spiro, Feltovich, Coulson, & Anderson, 1991; Steinberg & Clement, 1997). In this section, I will expand on this role as the most important one that analogy can play in conceptual change, and I will compare it with other roles.

One of the possible theoretical reasons for using an organizing analogy, such as air pressure for electric potential in circuits, is that it may be very efficient in producing a large conceptual change "all at once" by importing a whole relational structure from a different domain. I call this the "big bang" or "Eureka" theory of analogy in instruction. In theory, one could hope that the air pressure analogy would cause rapid, large-scale conceptual change, from battery-driven, source-sink model to a current-flow model driven by potential differences. In fact though, Clement and Steinberg (2002) found that each implication of the global air pressure analogy must be explored and examined for each type of circuit element or junction. This means that this model is still constructed in small pieces, as depicted in Figure 16.4, and each piece involves working through its own particular kind of evaluation (via dissonance) and revision cycles in the face of common difficulties. The global analogy of air pressure and flow, in this case, takes weeks to develop fully; it does not necessarily save time, but it appears to increase depth of understanding significantly (Steinberg, 2007). Not all analogies are this global and complex, but Else, Clement, and Rea-Ramirez (2008) and Harrison and Treagust (1993) have emphasized that teachers in other areas can underestimate the time and care needed to develop an analogy properly, especially for younger students. These studies indicate that analogies can be viewed inappropriately, as a quick fix for student learning, and that it is better to view them as a strategy for in-depth learning of a more encompassing explanatory model and to use them only when time is allocated for that.

Learning From Analogies Via Enrichment Vs. Abstraction

A widely accepted view considers that an analogy is beneficial because it helps the student view the target in a more abstract way. In that view, by helping the student focus on the shared relational structure between the base and the target and downplaying the significance of the actual objects and surface level object attributes, the analogy is thought to help lend abstract relational structure to the previously poorly structured target situation (Gentner, 1983; Gick & Holyoak, 1980, 1983; Holland, Holyoak, Nisbett, & Thagard, 1986; Holyoak & Thagard, 1989). The learner is left with a mental representation of the target in which objects and object attributes are less salient and abstract relational structure is more salient.

By contrast, in the successful intervention in the book on the table study described earlier (Brown & Clement, 1989), the "atomic bonds as springs" analogy appeared to help *enrich* the students' conceptions of the target situations, rather than (or at least in addition to) helping them view the situations more abstractly. In this intervention, the concrete idea of elastic springs is projected into the microscopic realm to form an explanatory model of spring-like bonds between atoms. The student learns about a new, concrete mechanism that explains what is happening inside the targeted table system. It was hypothesized that this enrichment of the target with new objects, object attributes, and casual relations (e.g., microscopic bonds, flexibility and bending causing forces) is a very important means for conceptual re-structuring. Here, the dimensions of concreteness and generality become separated; the concreteness of the imagined mechanism does not imply a lack of generality. General, schematic models can be sparse in detail but still quite concrete in being dynamically imaged. As another example, the idea of swarms of moving molecules in a gas is concretely imageable, but the model is very schematic and general in the sense of being widely applicable. The fact that this model is hidden from observation does not mean that it is not concrete. In this view, the move in Table 16.1 from the observation pattern relations at Level 2, between temperature and pressure, to the explanatory model relations at Level 3, between molecular speed and impact on the walls of the container, is not a move from concrete to non-concrete imagery; rather, it is a move from one set of concrete images at the empirical level to another set of concrete images at the theoretical level. In this view, analogies and models can be a source of enrichment rather than a source of abstraction.

Brown (1993) argued that analogies can help students "refocus core intuitions" by helping them to enrich their representation of the target. On the basis of in-depth interviewing data with students learning electricity via the pressure analogy, he argues that analogies can sometimes change the way the student's "core intuitions" are projected into a target domain. This can be very important for sensemaking and retention, since other strong intuitions can be responsible for "unseating" newly learned models (see also Brown and Hammer, chapter 6, in this volume).

Contrasting Diagrams

Thinking about model learning in biology offers a fresh perspective on the issue of abstraction, since abstraction is, in general, more pronounced in physics than in biology, where elaborated structures are a major focus. The models in Figure 16.5 are somewhat abstract in that they are simplified, schematic representations of living organs of biomass. Rather than seeing increasing abstraction as central to all model construction activity, however, in images of model evolution like those in Figure 16.5, conceptual change appears as the gradual revision and *enrichment* of initially simplistic models, a trend that can be considered in the opposite direction from abstraction. The use of concrete, scale models of molecules and of the solar system would seem also to work in this direction by adding more and more schematic, but concrete, structure.

On Analogies vs. Explanatory Models

It is common to make such statements as "The billiard table is an 'analogue model' of the gas." The previous sentence is acceptable if "analogue model" refers to "scientific model in the broadest sense"— in which case any constructed representation that can be used to think about the gas qualifies. But the sentence is not acceptable in the present framework if "analogue model" means an *explanatory* model. A scientist's elastic-particle model of a monotonic gas is not the same as a billiard table. Certain elements have been added (tiny size, perfect elasticity, 3-dimensional motion, constant motion, etc.) and subtracted (colors, external cause of motion, etc.) from the original analogous case. We do not think of there actually being billiard balls inside of gases. I would prefer to say that the *analogous case* of the pool table can be used as a starting point for developing an *explanatory model* of a gas as a swarm of elastic particles. I will call this kind of analogous case a *proto-model*. By using different names for these two entities, their relationship can be discussed, something that is not often done in the literature.

How analogous cases as proto-models can support explanatory model construction, not just provide a correct prediction for the target problem: Harre's view   Hesse (1967) and Harre (1972) distinguish between the following:

1. An analogous case that shares only its abstract form with the target (Hesse cites hydraulic models of economic systems as one example). Such a case may happen to behave like the

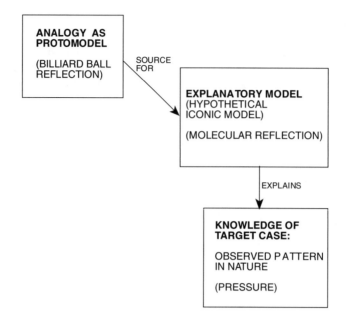

FIGURE 16.6   Three-element view of the relation between target, analogous case, and explanatory model.

target case and therefore provide a way of predicting what the target will do. But it does not explain how the target works. I call this an *expedient* analogy.

2. A model that has become, in Harre's terms, a "candidate for reality." In this case, a set of material — but hidden — features, in addition to the abstract form, is hypothesized to be the same in the model and the target situation. (These features are often unobservable in the target at the time). The example used earlier was the elastic particle model for gasses, in which a gas is hypothesized not only to behave like particles bouncing around, but to actually consist of something very much like tiny particles bouncing around. I refer to the latter kind of model as explanatory.

Thiele and Treagust (1994) observed a number of expedient analogies in their study of chemistry teachers use of analogies, such as: activation energy is like a pole vaulter attempting a vault; and competing forward and reverse rates of a reaction is like a person walking up a down escalator. Here I call these expedient analogies because, although they are instructive, they do not introduce material elements as starting points for constructing an explanatory model.

Triangular Relation in Model Construction

An analogy can be viewed as involving two main elements: the target case and the analogous case. However, the above considerations mean that it is often desirable to take a three-element view of the relation between target, analogous case, and explanatory model, as in Figure 16.6. Pressure in a car cylinder can be explained roughly by analogy to a billiard table, but greater power comes from the development and refinement of an explanatory model, which can be thought of as our best estimate of nature's hidden mechanism in the gas. Clement (2008c) argues that such a model is neither deduced from axioms nor induced as a pattern from repeated experiences. Rather, it is abducted as a construction pieced together from various sources, including the analogy, designed in such a way as to provide an explanation for the target phenomenon.

As mentioned, Clement and Steinberg (2002) tracked the learning of a high school student as she was introduced to electric circuit concepts via an air pressure analogue. There is evidence that this was a proto-model since one can see how concrete features of air pressure differences causing air flow are transferred by her to the explanatory model as a starting point for thinking about how differences in "electric pressure" (voltage) cause current flow.

Roles of Analogy

The distinctions developed in the sections above allow one to discriminate between several purposes for analogies, as shown in Table 16.4. In this view, analogies have more purposes than are commonly recognized. These analogy types have been distinguished in expert protocols in Clement (2008), and a few examples exist in the literature, but explicit comparisons of their uses in educational contexts is a task for future research.

Using an Analogue as a Proto-Model

Earlier, I raised questions about the limitations of analogies as a lone strategy in Figure 16.1b, saying that it might not deal with the student's prior model M1. Figure 16.4 depicts an improved strategy by showing how analogy can play the role of a proto-model as one source of material to help modify model M1. For example, a case of lower than ambient pressure such as a vacuum cleaner can be incorporated into an existing "pressure" model of electric potential to introduce the concept of negative voltage at one end of a battery. The intention is not to import the entire vacuum cleaner idea into the model but primarily to contribute the "lower than ambient pressure" idea. Their use in this contributory way is not "watered down" science, because a number of historians of science have described analogies as providing contributory elements during model evolution, such as Darden (1991), Nersessian (2002), Holland et al. (1986), Millman and Smith (1997), and Gruber (1981).

Figure 16.4 can also be used to contrast this role for analogies with that of a bridging analogy or "domain expander" illustrated in Figure 16.2. In Figure 16.2 the bridging analogies are cases that are compared with each other and the target case. In Figure 16.4 the proto-model analogy is not just a case to be compared with the target but contributes a subschema that is incorporated into the explanatory model itself.

One can now hypothesize that analogies playing the roles in Table 16.4 may contribute selectively to different processes of conceptual change shown in Table 16.3. For example, the expedient analogue of a pole vaulter might be used to introduce the idea of activation energy for a reaction, but this does not really give an *explanation* for the relationship; therefore, its contribution to explanatory modeling is marginal. A domain-expanding, bridging analogy would naturally contribute to type (2) in Table 16.3, conceptual change via changing the domain of applicability for a concept. Using analogous cases as exemplars for abstraction naturally can contribute to (3) forming a general schema by abstraction. A proto-model analogue would serve as a starting point for (6) constructing a new initial model, or for adding a new component in (4) a major model modification. This mapping between types of analogies and types of conceptual change is not presently discussed in the literature, to my knowledge, and it suggests that different techniques for using analogies are needed for different types of change.

A Focus on Modelling

One thing these distinctions can buy us is focus — the ability to focus on the development of the explanatory model as the most important content goal of science instruction. The central

TABLE 16.4
Four Types and Purposes of Analogy

Analogous Case as Exemplar for Induction or Abstraction. Example: several exemplars of acceleration may be given in order to develop the concept of acceleration. The exemplars are analogous to each other and may help students form an abstract concept of acceleration. Some may prefer to refer to this process as induction from exemplars rather than induction from analogy.

Expedient Analogy. Example: the behavior of an LRC circuit is analogous to the behavior of a weight oscillating on a spring, including the concepts of oscillation, amplitude, and damped oscillation. But there is no deep causal connection where elements of one system can be used as an explanatory model for the other in the sense of a mechanism viewed as actually operating in the other.

Domain-Expanding Analogy. Example: bridging analogies were used to expand the domain of application of the springiness idea in the book on the table lesson. (The form of this is shown in Figure 16.2.) An analogy can be formed between two examples at the same level — that is, an anchoring analogous case and a target (e.g., the spring and the table) — which can encourage a student to stretch the domain of application of a correct intuition and apply it to the target example.

Analogue as Proto-Model. Example: using billiards as a starting point for the elastic particle model (shown in Figure 16.6) or using a camera as a starting point for developing an explanatory model of how the eye works (Glynn, 1991). Here, the anchoring, analogous case is used as a starting point, or building block, for adding to an explanatory model. The model is at a deeper, hidden, explanatory level than the observable target phenomenon, and the analogous case provides a piece of, or starting point for, developing the model. In contrast to analogy type one above, here the analogous case is not an exemplar of the explanatory model; e.g., a billiard table is not an exemplar of a gas.

---

row in Figure 16.5 represents this development. The model, as a schematic, general, and flexible knowledge structure, is a more important outcome than the knowledge of any one analogy or case. Rather than being an endpoint in themselves, analogies are seen as one of several sources of ideas for initiating or developing an evolving explanatory model. Personally, I believe this to be the way to describe the most important role of analogy in science instruction. (Zietsman and Clement (1997) found that some *extreme cases* can play a similar role in supporting model construction. This is in opposition to the prevailing theory that the only major role of extreme cases is to provide a confident extra data point for inducing a pattern or testing a theory.)

This is consistent with Glynn's call for teachers to be explicit about the parts of an analogy that do not map to the target. Mason (1994) documents fifth-grade students abilities to discuss the shortcomings of an analogy between postmen delivering letters and the blood cells delivering oxygen to other cells, which she sees as indicative of their increasing metacognitive awareness of the purpose of an analogy. When an analogy is viewed as one stepping stone in a longer process of model evolution, the "dangerous" disanalogous aspects can become valuable points for discussion that highlight distinctive features of the explanatory model, that contrast to those in the analogy.

What, if anything, is transferred from an analogy to an explanatory model? Clement and

Steinberg (2002) and Clement (2003) hypothesize that it can include schema elements capable of generating dynamic imagery, citing, for example, case study evidence in which particular gestures for both pressure and flow appeared during their subject's work with the air pressure analogy and then reappeared during her work on instructional problems on circuits. They speak of this as transfer of imagery or "transfer of runnability" (Clement & Steinberg, 2002, p. 429). Hesse's idea that explanatory models involve mechanisms thought to have some material similarity to the hidden structure of the target is consistent with the idea that a central component of an explanatory model is an imagistic, or analog representation that preserves some of the structure of what it represents. The roles of imagery in analogy and explanatory model construction are large and important topics that I have not had space for in this chapter. It is examined in Hegarty et al. (2003), Nersessian (2002), and Clement (2003, 2004, 2006, 2008c).

In sum, analogies can play a narrower role in instruction for explanatory model construction than is assumed by some, in the sense that they are only one of many strategies needed for model construction (Figure 16.5). And in contrast to the prediction of the "big bang" theory of producing fast and large conceptual change via analogy, instructional analogies can require extended and careful development. Conversely, analogies can play a wider, more varied, more important role in instruction than is commonly assumed, in the sense that they may have more varied purposes than commonly recognized. It may be that different techniques are needed for using analogies for different purposes, such as those in Table 16.3 and Table 16.4. This provides an important agenda for future research.

CHAPTER CONCLUSION: THE ROLE OF EXPLANATORY MODELS IN TEACHING FOR CONCEPTUAL CHANGE

This chapter began by asking several basic questions deemed crucial to making further progress on an applied theory of conceptual change that proposes mechanisms of change. What is an explanatory model? What are some basic strategies that have been used to promote conceptual change in such models? What is the relationship between explanatory models and analogies? The tables and figures in this chapter form the basis for a summary of conclusions from each major section:

- As hypothesized hidden mechanisms, explanatory models are a separate form of knowledge from qualitative or quantitative patterns in observations (as shown in Table 16.1).
- The theoretical perspective of this chapter regards explanatory models as *the qualitative core of meaning for scientific theory* and *the center of sense making for students*. It suggests refocusing curriculum development and instruction so that explanatory models are the central organizers for content goals.
- A variety of studies conclude that model presentation, dissonance, and analogy strategies can lead to positive results in conceptual change teaching.
- However, other studies show that each method can sometimes fail to produce widespread change when used alone.
- This has led to some studies of the successful use of analogies and dissonance together in a *Combined Strategy* (as depicted in Figure 16.3).
- Figure 16.4 depicts the important approach of *model evolution* that has been used in several innovative curricula. So far, only a limited number of studies have been done on such approaches, but the initial results are promising. Repeated *model criticism and revision* processes are part of this approach.

- Each revision can also utilize other contributing strategies besides dissonance promoters and analogies, *expanding the image of conceptual change teaching to one that includes multiple methods for supporting model evolution as a central approach* as depicted in Figure 16.5. It was hypothesized that for classes where the primary goal is efficient learning of conceptual content with understanding, gradual model evolution enables teacher-student co-construction, with both contributing ideas. This was described as a middle road between lecture and open-ended discovery learning.

- Building on Thagard's theory of types and the work of other authors, Table 16.3 portrays a *large variety of types of conceptual change* of impressive breadth and variety of processes that have been identified by different researchers. Theoretically, all can apply to changes in an explanatory model as the narrower focus of this chapter. I have argued here for an eclectic view, that all the types are important for the construction of explanatory models in the classroom — including types that produce small changes or produce only an initial partially incorrect model.

- Using these ideas, an idealized image of an approach to curriculum development begins from the identification of students' preconceptions and the description of structures within the target model. A planned sequence of developing intermediate models, or planned *learning pathway* (shown in the central row of Figure16.5), can serve in a curriculum as a guiding sequence of goals to focus on. This prepares the way for research based lesson or unit planning by first identifying the type of conceptual change being sought from those in Table 16.3, for a step in the pathway, then choosing teaching strategies at a finer grain size, such as those in the bottom row of Figure 16.5, to facilitate the conceptual change. Within a lesson, maintaining class discussions, or using student *"voting"* techniques and other ongoing assessments are ways to give the teacher enough feedback to decide how to keep students in a "reasoning zone" — to decide when to let discussion take its course, when to add more strategies for the present goal, and when to move on to the next goal. Such decisions may also depend strongly on the sensed level of persistence in preconceptions in that area. This kind of teaching that responds to students' ideas, contrasts sharply with teaching that simply uses a lesson plan as a series of topics (i.e., facts) to be covered or activities to be completed. To succeed, these cognitive considerations need to be combined with other considerations not dealt with in this chapte — such as ways to foster: social dynamics of large and small group learning, larger integrative and motivational contexts, students learning about the nature of models and science learning, and ongoing metacognitive self-assessment.

- A theory positing *four basic purposes for analogy* was developed on the basis of expert studies and teaching studies. For each of these types, the relationship between the analogy and the final explanatory model is different. Two purposes were identified as especially important for explanatory model construction: analogies used for domain expansion and analogies used as proto-models. Both of these processes can use analogy as a first step that gets conceptual change started. Subsequent model revision going beyond the original analogy, however, is deemed essential, and multiple analogies may be needed for this purpose. This contrasts with a view of analogy as a simple short cut to understanding, and indicates that specialized teaching strategies may be important for different types of analogies to succeed. These considerations may eventually help us explain why previous studies have found mixed results in using analogies.

I believe that organizing learning processes in levels that work at larger and smaller time scales will be an important component in developing a more adequate theory of conceptual change instruction. As an approximate but possibly useful method of organization, one can envision four levels of processes, three of which have been discussed in this chapter as participating in instruction (not to be confused with the four types of knowledge in Table 16.1 as a different dimension). At the highest (fourth) level for example, model competition and model evolution (including evaluation) processes occur over longer periods of days; at the next (third) level, a large variety of types of individual conceptual changes shown in Table 16.3 can participate in model evolution[1]; and various teaching strategies (at a second level) such as those shown at the bottom of Figure 16.5 can facilitate such conceptual changes. I have not had room to discuss tactics at a finer first level operating over very short time scales of seconds in this chapter, such as the dialog facilitating tactics discussed by van Zee and Minstrell (1997). (Further discussion of a larger number of levels of cognitive strategies and tactics, is given in Clement, 2008b).

Filling in other processes and describing the relationships between these levels then outlines an important agenda for future research. Ideally, we might be able to suggest a mapping from instructional strategies at level two to the larger conceptual change process they serve at level three. An example in this chapter is the attempt to differentiate and identify four different types of analogy processes based on the different types of conceptual change they can produce. Similarly, in future research, we may be able to map other teaching strategies to different types of conceptual change. One can then imagine a form of top down curriculum planning that could occur, starting from research on students' preconceptions and a learning pathway specifying the type of conceptual change that needs to happen at each juncture.

It appears that a curriculum designer or teacher trying to decide how to teach a unit is going to encounter the need for many types of conceptual change. If we can understand what these types are, and what teaching strategies are particularly important for each, it will be a powerful advance in our theory of conceptual change instruction.

NOTE

1. An exception to the time scale ordering in this scheme should be noted for tree switching or paradigm shifts, which describe processes that can take long periods of time.

REFERENCES

Arnold, M., & Millar, R. (1987). Being constructive: An alternative approach to the teaching of introductory ideas in electricity. *International Journal of Science Education*, 9(5), 553–563.

Arons, A. B. (1990). *Teaching introductory physics*. New York: Wiley.

Barker, M., & Carr, M. (1989a). Teaching and learning about photosynthesis. Part 1: An assessment in terms of students' prior knowledge. *International Journal of Science Education*, 11(1), 49–56.

Barker, M., & Carr, M. (1989b). Teaching and learning about photosynthesis. Part 2: A generative learning strategy. *International Journal of Science Education*, 11(2), 141–152.

Brown, D. E. (1992a). Teaching electricity with capacitors and causal models: Preliminary results from diagnostic and tutoring study data examining the CASTLE project. Paper presented at the annual meeting of the National Association for Research in Science Teaching, Boston, MA.

Brown, D. E. (1992b). Using Examples and analogies to remediate misconceptions in physics: Factors influencing conceptual change. *Journal of Research in Science Teaching*, 29(1), 17–34.

Brown, D. E. (1993). Refocusing core intuitions: A concretizing role for analogy in conceptual change. *Journal of Research in Science Teaching*, 30(10), 1273–1290.

Brown, D. E. (1994). Facilitating conceptual change using analogies and explanatory models. *International Journal of Science Education*, 16(2), 201–214.

Brown, D., & Clement, J. (1989). Overcoming misconceptions via analogical reasoning: Factors influencing understanding in a teaching experiment., *Instructional Science*, *18*, 237–261.

Brown, D., & Clement, J. (1992). Classroom teaching experiments in mechanics. In R. Duit, F. Goldberg, & H. Niedderer (Eds.), *Research in physics learning: Theoretical issues and empirical studies* (pp. 380–397). Kiel: IPN.

Buckley, B. C. (2000). Interactive multimedia and model-based learning in biology. *International Journal of Science Education*, *22*(9), 895–935.

Bulgren, J. A., Deschler, D. D., Schumaker, J., & Lenz, B. K. (2000). The use and effectiveness of analogical instruction in diverse secondary content classrooms. *Journal of Educational Psychology, 92*(3), 426–441.

Camp, C., & Clement, J., (1994). *Preconceptions in mechanics: Lessons dealing with conceptual difficulties*. Dubuque, IA: Kendall Hunt.

Campbell, N. (1920). *Physics: The elements*. Cambridge: Cambridge University Press. Republished in 1957 as *The foundations of science*. New York: Dover.

Chan, C., Burtis, J., & Bereiter, C. (1997). Knowledge building as a mediator of conceptual change. *Cognition & Instruction, 15*(1), 1–40.

Chi, M .T .H. (1992). Conceptual change within and across ontological categories: Examples from learning and discovery in science. In R. N. Giere (Ed.), *Minnesota studies in the philosophy of science, Vol. XV: Cognitive models of science* (pp. 129–186). Minneapolis: University of Minnesota Press.

Chi, M. T., & Roscoe, R. D. (2002). The processes and challenges of conceptual change. In M Limon & L. Mason (Eds.), *Reconsidering conceptual change: Issues in theory and practice* (pp. 3–27). Dordrecht, The Netherlands: Kluwer.

Chinn, C. A., & Brewer, W. F. (1998). An empirical test of taxonomy of responses to anomalous data in science. *Journal of Research in Science Teaching*, *35*(6), 623–654.

Chiu, M.-H., Chou, C.-C., & Liu, C.-J. (2002). Dynamic processes of conceptual change: analysis of constructing mental models of chemical equilibrium. *Journal of Research in Science Teaching*, *39*(8), 688–712.

Chiu, M.-H., & Lin, J.-W. (2005). Promoting fourth graders' conceptual change of their understanding of electric current via multiple analogies. *Journal of Research in Science Teaching*, *42*(4), 429–464.

Clement, J. (1982). Students' preconceptions in introductory mechanics. *The American Journal of Physics*, *50*(1), 66–71.

Clement, J. (1988). Observed methods for generating analogies in scientific problem solving. *Cognitive Science*, *12*, 563–586.

Clement, J. (1989). Learning via model construction and criticism: Protocol evidence on sources of creativity in science. In J. Glover, R., Ronning, & C. Reynolds. (Eds.), *Handbook of creativity: Assessment, theory and research*. (pp. 341–381). New York: Plenum.

Clement, J. (1993). Using bridging analogies and anchoring intuitions to deal with students' preconceptions in physics. *Journal of Research in Science Teaching*, *30*(10), 1241–1257.

Clement, J. (1994). Use of physical intuition and imagistic simulation in expert problem solving. D. Tirosh, (Ed.), *Implicit and explicit knowledge* (pp. 204–244). Norwood, NJ: Ablex.

Clement, J. (1998). Expert novice similarities and instruction using analogies. *International Journal of Science Education, 20*(10), 1271–1286.

Clement, J. (2000). Analysis of clinical interviews: Foundations and model viability. In R. Lesh & A. Kelly (Eds.), *Handbook of research methodologies for science and mathematics education* (pp. 341–385). Hillsdale, NJ: Erlbaum.

Clement, J. (2003). Imagistic simulation in scientific model construction. In R. Alterman & D. Kirsh (Eds.), *Proceedings of the Twenty-Fifth Annual Conference of the Cognitive Science Society, 25* (pp. 258–263). Mahwah, NJ: Erlbaum.

Clement, J. (2004). Imagistic processes in analogical reasoning: Conserving transformations and dual simulations. In K. Forbus, D. Gentner, & T. Regier (Eds.), *Proceedings of the Twenty-Sixth Annual Conference of the Cognitive Science Society, 26* (233–238). Mahwah, NJ: Erlbaum.

Clement, J. (2006). Thought experiments and imagery in expert protocols. In L. Magnani (Ed.), *Model-based reasoning in science and engineering* (pp. 151–166). London: College Publications.

Clement, J. (2008a). Six levels of organization for curriculum design and teaching. In J. Clement & M. A. Rea-Ramirez (Eds.), *Model based learning and instruction in science* (pp. 255–272). Dordrecht, The Netherlands: Springer.

Clement, J. (2008b). Student/teacher co-construction of visualizable models in large group discussion. In J. Clement & M. A. Rea-Ramirez (Eds.), *Model based learning and instruction in science* (pp. 11–22). Dordrecht, The Netherlands: Springer.

Clement, J. (2008c). *Creative model construction in scientists and students: The role of imagery, analogy, and mental situation*. Dordrecht: Springer.

Clement, J., Brown, D., & Zietsman, A. (1989). Not all preconceptions are misconceptions: Finding anchoring conceptions for grounding instruction on students' intuitions. *International Journal of Science Education, 11,* 554–565.

Clement, J., & Rea-Ramirez, M. (1998). The role of dissonance in conceptual change, *Proceedings of National Association for Research in Science Teaching,* San Diego, CA.

Clement, J., Rea-Ramirez, M. A. (Eds.). (2008). *Model based learning and instruction in science*. New York: Springer.

Clement, J., & Steinberg, M. (2002) Step-wise evolution of models of electric circuits: A "learning-aloud" case study. *Journal of the Learning Sciences, 11*(4), 389–452.

Clement, J., Zietsman, A., & Monaghan, J. (2005). Imagery in science learning in experts and students. In J. Gilbert (Ed.), *Visualization in science education*. Dordrecht: Springer.

Collins, A., & Gentner, D. (1987). How people construct mental models. In D. Holland & N. Quinn (Eds.), *Cultural models in thought and language* (pp. 243–265). Cambridge: Cambridge University Press.

Dagher, Z., R. (1994). Does the use of analogies contribute to conceptual change? *Science Education, 78*(6), 601–614.

Dagher, Z. R. (1995). Review of studies on the effectiveness of instructional analogies in science. *Science Education, 79*(3), 295–312.

Darden, L. (1991). *Theory change in science: Strategies from Mendelian genetics*. New York: Oxford.

diSessa, A. A. (1988). Knowledge in pieces. In G. Forman & P. B. Pufall (Eds.), *Constructivism in the computer age* (pp. 49–70). Hillsdale, NJ: Erlbaum.

Dreyfus, A., Jungwirth, E., & Eliovitch, R. (1990). Applying the "cognitive conflict" strategy for conceptual change --some implications, difficulties, and problems. *Science Education, 74*(5), 555–569.

Driver, R. (1983). *The pupils as scientist?* Milton Keynes: Open University Press.

Dufresne, R. J., Gerace, W. J., Leonard, R., Mestre, J. P., & Wenk, L. (1996). Classtalk: A classroom communication system for active learning. *Journal of Computing in Higher Education, 2*(7), 3–47.

Dunbar, K. (1999). The scientist in vivo: How scientists think and reason in the laboratory. In L. Magnani, N. Nersessian, &P. Thagard (Eds.), *Model-based reasoning in scientific discovery*. New York: Plenum Press.

Duit, R. (1991). On the roles of analogies and metaphors in learning science. *Science Education, 75,* 649–672.

Duit, R., Roth, W.-M., Komorek, M., & Wilbers, J. (2001). Fostering conceptual change by analogies: Between Scylla and Charybdis. *Learning and Instruction, 11*(4-5), 283–303.

Dupin, J. J., & Johsua, S. (1989). Analogies and "modeling analogies" in teaching: Some examples in basic electricity. *Science Education, 73*(2), 207–224.

Duschl, R. A., & Osborne, M. (2002). Supporting and promoting argumentation discourse in science education. *Studies in Science Education, 38,* 39–72.

Easley, J. (1990). Conceptual splatter in peer dialogues in selected Japanese and U.S. first-grad mathematics classes. In L. Steffe & T. Wood (Eds.), *Transforming children's mathematics education*. Hillsdale, NJ: Erlbaum.

Else, M., Clement, J., & Rea-Ramirez, M. A. (2008). Using analogies in science teaching and curriculum design: Some guidelines. In J. Clement & M. A. Rea-Ramirez (Eds.), *Model based learning and instruction in science*. (pp. 215–233). New York: Springer.

Fretz, E. B., Wu, H.-K., Zhang, B. H., Davis, E. A., Krajcik, J. S., & Soloway, E. (2002). An investigation of software scaffolds supporting modeling practices. *Research in Science Education, 32*(4), 567–589.

Gabel, D. (1999). Improving teaching and learning through chemistry education research: a look to the future. *Journal of Chemical Education, 76*(4) 548–554.

Gentner, D. (1983). Structure-mapping: A theoretical framework for analogy. *Cognitive Science, 7,* 155–170.

Glynn, S. M. (1991). Explaining science concepts: A teaching-with-analogie model. In S. M. Glynn, R. H. Yeany, & B. K. Britton (Eds.), *The psychology of learning science* (pp. 219–240). Hillsdale, NJ: Erlbaum.

Glynn, S. M. (2003). Teaching science concepts: Research on analogies that improve learning. In D. F. Berlin & A. L. White (Eds.), *Improving science and mathematics education: Insights for a global community* (pp. 179–192). Columbus, OH: International Consortium for Research in Science and Mathematics Education.

Glynn, S. M., & Duit, R. (1995). Learning science meaningfully: Constructing conceptual models. In S. M. Glynn & R. Duit (Eds.), *Learning science in the schools: Research reforming practice.* Mahwah, NJ: Erlbaum.

Gick, M. L., & Holyoak, K. J. (1980). Analogical problem solving. *Cognitive Psychology, 12,* 306–355.

Gick, M. L., & Holyoak, K. J. (1983). Schema induction and analogical transfer. *Cognitive Psychology, 15,* 1–38.

Giere, R. (1988). *Explaining science: A cognitive approach.* Chicago: Chicago University Press.

Gilbert, J. K., Boulter, C., & Rutherford, M. (1998). Models in explanations, part 2: Whose voice? Whose ears? *International Journal of Science Education, 20,* 187–203.

Gobert, J., & Buckley, B. (2000). Introduction to model-based teaching and learning in science education. *International Journal of Science Education, 22*(9), 891–894.

Gorsky, P., & Finegold, M. (1994). The role of anomaly and of cognitive dissonance in restructuring students' concepts of force. *Instructional Science, 22,* 75–90.

Gruber, H. E. (1981). *Darwin on man: A psychological study of scientific creativity.* Chicago: University of Chicago Press.

Guzzetti, B. J., Snyder, T. E., Glass, G. V., & Gamas, W. S. (1993). Promoting conceptual change in science: a comparative meta-analysis of instructional interventions from reading education and science education. *Reading Research Quarterly, 28*(2), 116–159.

Hafner, R., & Stewart, J. (1995). Revising explanatory models to accommodate anomalous genetic phenomena: Problem solving in the "context of discovery." *Science Education, 79*(2), 111–146.

Hammer, D. (1996). More than misconceptions: Multiple perspectives on student knowledge and reasoning, and an appropriate role for education research. *American Journal of Physics, 64*(10), 1316–1325.

Hammer, D., & Elby, A. (2002). Tapping epistemological resources for learning physics. *Journal of the Learning Sciences, 12,* 53–90.

Hand, B. M., & Treagust, D. (1988). Application of a conceptual conflict teaching strategy to enhance student learning of acids and bases. *Research in Science Teaching, 18,* 53–63.

Harre, R. (1972). *The philosophies of science.* Oxford: Oxford University Press.

Harrison, A., & De Jong, O. (2005). Exploring the use of multiple analogical models when teaching and learning chemical equilibrium. *Journal of Research in Science Teaching, 42*(10), 1135–1159.

Harrison, A. G., & Treagust, D. (1993). Teaching with analogies: A case-study in grade 10 optics. *Journal of Research in Science Teaching, 30*(10), 1291–1307.

Harrison, A. G., & Treagust, D. F. (1996). Secondary students mental models of atoms and molecules: implications for teaching science. *Science Education, 80,* 509–534.

Hegarty, M., Kriz, S., & Cate, C. (2003). The roles of mental animations and external animations in understanding mechanical systems. *Cognition and Instruction, 21*(4), 325–360.

Hesse, M. (1966). *Models and analogies in science.* South Bend, IN: Notre Dame University Press.

Hesse, M. (1967). Models and analogies in science. In P. Edwards (Ed.), *The encyclopedia of philosophy.* New York: Free Press.

Hestenes, D., Wells, M., & Swackhammer, G. (1992). Force concept inventory. *The Physics Teachers, 30*(3), 141–158.

Hewson, P. W. (1981). A conceptual change approach to learning science. *European Journal of Science Education, 3*(4), 383–396.

Hewson, P., & Hennessey, W. (1992). Making status explicit: A case study of conceptual change. In R. Duit, F. Goldberg, & H. Niedderer (Eds.), *Research in physics learning: Theoretical issues and empirical studies* (pp. 176–187). Kiel: IPN.

Hoffman, J. L., Wu, H.-K., Krajcik, J. S., & Soloway, E. (2003). The nature of middle school learners' science content understandings with the use of on-line resources. *Journal of Research in Science Teaching, 40*(3), 323–346.

Holland, J., Holyoak, K., Nisbett, R., & Thagard, P. (1986). *Induction: Processes of inference, learning, and discovery*. Cambridge: MIT Press.

Holyoak, K., & Thagard, P. (1989). A computational model of analogical problem solving. In S. Vosniadou and A. Ortony (Eds.), *Similarity and analogical reasoning* (pp. 199–241). New York: Cambridge University Press.

Inagaki, K., & Hatano, G. (1977). Amplification of cognitive motivation and its effects on epistemic observation. *American Educational Research Journal, 14*(4), 485–491.

Inagaki, K., Hatano, G., & Morita E. (1998). Construction of mathematical knowledge through whole-class discussion. *Learning and Instruction, 8*(6), 503–526.

Khan, S., Stillings, N., Clement, J., & Tronsky, N. (2002). The impact of an instructional strategy using computer simulations on inquiry skills in chemistry. Presented at the National Assn. of Research in Science Teaching, April 2002, New Orleans, LA.

Kuhn, T. (1970). *The structure of scientific revolutions* (2nd ed.). Chicago: University of Chicago Press.

Kuhn, T. (1977). Objectivity, value judgment, and theory choice. Reprinted in Kuhn, *The essential tension* (pp. 320–339). Chicago: University of Chicago Press.

Lawson, A. E., Clark, B., Meldrum, E. C., Falconer, K. A., Sequist, J. M., & Kwon, Y. J. (2000). Development of scientific reasoning in college biology: Do two levels of general hypothesis-testing skills exist? *Journal of Research in Science Teaching, 37*(1), 81–101.

Lehrer, R., & Schauble, L. (2003). Origins and evolution of model-based reasoning in mathematics and science. In R. Lesh & H. M. Doerr (Eds.), *Beyond constructivism: Models and modeling perspectives on mathematics problem solving, teaching, and learning* (pp. 59–70). Mahwah, NJ: Erlbaum.

Licht, P. (1987). A strategy to deal with conceptual and reasoning problems in introductory electricity education. In J. Novak (Ed.), Proceedings of the 2nd International Seminar *Misconceptions and Educational Strategies in Science and Mathematics*, Vol. II (pp. 275–284). Ithaca, NY: Cornell University.

Linn, M., Bell, P., & Hsi, S. (1998). Using the internet to enhance student understanding of science: The knowledge integration environment. *Interactive Learning Environments, 6*(1-2), 4–38.

Lowe, R. (1993). Constraints on the effectiveness of diagrams as resources for conceptual change. In W. Schnotz, S. Vosniadou, & M. Carretero (Eds.), *New perspectives on conceptual change* (pp. 223–245). New York: Pergamon.

Machamer, P., Darden, L., & Craver, C. F. (2000). Thinking about mechanisms. *Philosophy of Science, 67*, 1–25.

Mason, L. (1994). Cognitive and metacognitive aspects in conceptual change by analogy. *Instructional Science, 22*(3), 157–187.

Mayer, R. E. (1989). Models for understanding. *Review of Educational Research, 59*(1), 43–64.

Mayer, R. E. (2003). The promise of multimedia learning: Using the same instructional design methods across different media. *Learning and Instruction, 13*, 125–139.

McCloskey, M., Washburn, A., & Felch, L. (1983). Intuitive physics: The straight-down belief and its origin. *Journal of Experimental Psychology, 9*(4), 636–649.

McDermott, L. (1984). Research on conceptual understanding in mechanics. *Physics Today. 37*, 2–32.

Millman, A. B., & Smith, C. L. (1997). Darwin's use of analogical reasoning in theory construction. *Metaphor and Symbol, 12*(3), 159–187.

Minstrell, J. (1982). Explaining the 'at rest' condition of an object. *The Physic Teacher, 20*, 10–14.

Minstrell, J., & Krauss, P. (2005). Guided inquiry in the science classroom. In M. S. Donovan & J. D. Bransford, (Eds.), *How students learn: Science in the classroom* (pp. 475–514). Washington, DC: National Academies Press.

Nagel, E. (1961). *The structure of science*. New York: Harcourt, Brace, and World.

Nersessian, N. (1992). Constructing and instructing: The role of 'abstraction techniques' in creating and learning physics. In R. Duschl & R. Hamilton (Eds.), *Philosophy of science, cognitive psychology and educational theory and practice* (pp. 48–68). New York: State University of New York Press.

Nersessian, N. (2002). The cognitive-basis of model-based reasoning in science. In P. Carruthers, S. Stitch, & M. Siegal (Eds.), *The cognitive basis of science* (pp. 133–153). Cambridge: Cambridge University Press.

Newby, T. J., Ertmer, P. A., & Stepich, D. A. (1995). Instructional analogies and the learning of concepts. *Educational Technology Research and Development, 48*(1), 5–18.

Niedderer, H. (1987). A teaching strategy based on students' alternative frameworks theoretical conceptions and examples. In *Proceedings of the Second International Seminar. Misconceptions and Educational Strategies in Science and Mathematics* 2 (pp. 360–367). Itaca, NY: Cornell University.

Niedderer, H. (2001). Physics learning as cognitive development. In R. H. Evans, A. M. Andersen, & H. Sørensen: *Bridging research methodology and research aims*. The Danish University of Education. Available at: http://didaktik.physik.uni-bremen.de/niedderer/personal.pages/niedderer/Pubs.html#lpipt

Niedderer, H., & Goldberg, F. (1996). Learning processes in electric circuits. Paper present at Annual meeting of the National Association for Research in Science Teaching.

Novak, J. D. (1977). *The philosophical basis for education*. Ithaca: Cornell University Press.

Nunez, M., Ramirez, M., Clement, J., Else, M. (2002). Teacher-student co-construction in middle school life science. *Proceedings of the AETS 2002 Conference*, January, Charlotte, NC.

Nunez-Oviedo, M. C., Clement, J., & Rea-Ramirez, M. A. (2007). Developing complex mental models in biology through model evolution. In J. Clement & M. A. Rea-Ramirez (Eds.), *Model based learning and instruction in science* (pp. 173–193). New York: Springer.

Nunez-Oviedo, M. C. & Clement, J. (2008). A competition strategy and other discussion modes for developing mental models in large group discussion. In J. Clement & M. A. Rea-Ramirez (Eds.), *Model based learning and instruction in science*. Dordrecht, The Netherlands: Springer.

Piaget, J. (1930). *The child's conception of physical causality*. London: Kegan Paul.

Posner, G. J., Strike, K. A., Hewson, P. W., & Gertzog, W. A. (1982). Accommodation of a scientific conception: Toward a theory of conceptual change. *Science Education, 66*(2), 211–227.

Raghavan, K., Glaser, R. (1995). Model-based analysis and reasoning in science: The MARS curriculum. *Science Education, 79*(1), 37–61.

Rea-Ramirez, M., & Clement, J. (1998). In search of dissonance: The evolution of dissonance in conceptual change theory. *Proceedings of National Association for Research in Science Teaching*, San Diego, CA.

Rea-Ramirez, M. A., Nunez-Oviedo, M. C., & Clement, J., (2004). *Energy in the human body: A middle school life science curriculum*. Amherst: University of Massachusetts.

Rowell, J. A., & Dawson, C. J. (1985). Equilibrium, conflict and instruction: A new class-oriented perspective. *European Journal of Science Education, 5*, 203–215.

Royer, J. M., & Cable, G. W. (1976). Facilitated learning in connected discourse. *Journal of Research in Science Teaching, 30*(8), 919–934.

Schecker, H., & Niedderer, H. (1996). Contrastive teaching: A strategy to promote qualitative conceptual understanding of science. In D. F. Treagust, R. Duit, & B. J. Fraser (Eds.), *Improving teaching and learning in science and mathematics* (pp. 141–151). New York: Teachers College Press.

Schoenfeld, A. H. (1998). Toward a theory of teaching-in-context. *Issues in Education, 4*(1), 1–94.

Schnotz, W., & Preuß, A. (1999). Task-dependent construction of mental models as a basis for conceptual change. In W. Schnotz, S. Vosniadou, & M. Carretero (Eds.), *New perspectives on conceptual change* (pp. 193–221). Amsterdam: Pergamon.

Scott, P. H. (1992). Conceptual pathways in learning science: A case study of the development of one student's ideas relating to the structure of matter. In R. Duit, F. Goldberg, & H. Niedderer (Eds.), *Research in physics learning: Theoretical issues and empirical studies* (pp. 203–224). Kiel: IPN.

Scott, P. H., Asoko, H. M., & Driver, R. (1992). Teaching for conceptual change: A review of strategies. In R. Duit, F. Goldberg, & H. Niedderer (Eds.), *Research in physics learning: Theoretical issues and empirical studies* (pp. 310–329). Kiel: IPN.

She, H.-C. (2004). Fostering radical conceptual change through dual-situated learning model. *Journal of research in science teaching, 41*(2), 142–164.

Simons, P. R. J. (1984). Instructing with analogies. *Journal of Educational Psychology, 76,* 513–527.

Smith, C., Wiser, M., Anderson, C., & Krajcik, J. (2006). Implications of research on children's learning for standards and assessment: A proposed learning progression for matter and the atomic-molecular theory. *Measurement: Interdisciplinary Research and Perspectives, 4*(1&2), 1–98.

Smith, J. P., diSessa, A. A., & Roschelle, J. (1993). Misconceptions reconceived: A constructivist analysis of knowledge in transition. *Journal of the Learning Sciences, 3*(2).

Spiro, R. J., Feltovich, P. J., Coulson, R. I., and Anderson, D. K. (1991). Multiple analogies for complex concepts: Antidotes for analogy-induced misconception in advanced knowledge acquisition. In S. Vosniadou & A. Ortony (Eds.), *Similarity and analogical reasoning* (pp. 498–531). Cambridge, Cambridge University Press.

Stavy, R. (1991). Using analogy to overcome misconceptions about conservation of matter. *Journal of Research in Science Teaching, 28*(4), 305–313.

Stavy, R., & Berkovitz, B. (1980). Cognitive conflict as a basis for teaching quantitative aspects of the concept of temperature. *Science Education, 64*(5), 679–692.

Steinberg, M. (2004). *Electricity visualized — The CASTLE project.* Roseville, CA: PASCO Scientific.

Steinberg, M. (2008). Target model sequence and critical learning pathway for an electricity curriculum based on model evolution. In J. Clement & M. A. Rea-Ramirez (Eds.), *Model based learning and instruction in science* (pp. 79–102). Dordrecht, The Netherlands: Springer.

Steinberg, M., & Clement, J. (1998). Constructive model evolution in the study of electric circuits. In Proceedings of the International Conference *From Misconceptions to Constructed Understanding.* Ithaca, NY: Cornell University Press.

Steinberg, M., & Clement, J. (2001). Evolving mental models of electric circuits. In H. Behrendt, Dahncke, H., Duit, R., Graber, W., Komerek, M., Kross, A., & Reiska, P. (Eds.), *Research in science education—Past, present, and Future* (pp. 235–240). Dordrecht, The Netherlanads: Kluwer.

Stephens, L. & Clement, J. (2006). Depictive gestures as evidence for dynamic mental imagery in four types of student reasoning. *Proceedings of the Physics Education Research Conference*, Syracuse, New York.

Stepich, D. A., & Newby, T. J. (1988). Analogical instruction within the information processing paradigm: Effective means to facilitate learning. *Instructional Science, 17,* 129–144.

Strike, K. A., & Posner, G. J. (1992). A revisionist theory of conceptual change. In R. Duschl, & R. Hamilton (Eds.), *Philosophy of science, cognitius psychology and educational theory and practice* (pp. 147–176). Albany: State University of New York Press.

Tabak, I., Sandoval, W. A., Smith, B. K., Agganis, A., Baumgartner, E., & Reiser, B. J. (1995). Supporting collaborative guided inquiry in a learning environment for biology. Paper presented at the Proceedings of CSCL '95: *The First International Conference on Computer Support for Collaborative Learning.* Available at: http://citeseer.ist.psu.edu/tabak95supporting.html

Taber, K. S. (2001). Shifting sands: a case study of conceptual development as competition between alternative conceptions. *International Journal of Science Education, 23*(7), 731–753.

Thagard, P. (1992). *Conceptual revolutions.* Princeton, NJ: Princeton University Press.

Toulmin, S. (1972). *Human understanding: An inquiry into the aims of science.* Princeton, NJ: Princeton University Press.

Tregust, D., Harrison, A., Venville, G., & Dagher, Z. (1996). Using an analogical teaching approach to engender conceptual change. *International Journal of Science Education, 18,* 213–229.

Tsai, C.-C., & Chang, C.-Y. (2005). Lasting effects of instruction guided by the conflict map: Experimental study of learning about the causes of the seasons. *Journal of Research in Science Teaching, 42*(10), 1089–1111.

van Zee, E., & Minstrell, J. (1997). Reflective discourse: Developing shared understandings in a physics classroom. *International Journal of Science Education, 19,* 209–228.

Vosniadou, S., & Brewer, W. F. (1992). Mental models of the earth: A study of conceptual change in childhood. *Cognitive Psychology, 24,* 535–585.

Vosniadou, S., & Ioannides, C. (1998). From conceptual development to science education: A psychological point of view. *International Journal of Science Education, 20*(10), 1213–1230.

Wells, M., Hestenes, D., & Swackhamer, G. (1995). A modeling method for high school physics instruction. *American Journal of Physics, 63*, 606–619.

White, B. Y. (1989). The role of intermediate abstractions in understanding science and mathematics. In *Proceedings of the Eleventh Annual Conference of the Cognitive Science Society.* Ann Arbor, Michigan.

White, B. Y. (1993) ThinkerTools: Causal models, conceptual change, and science education. *Cognition and Instruction, 10,* 1–100.

Williams, E. G. (2006). Teacher moves during large-group discussions of electricity concepts: Identifying supports for model-based learning. Proceedings of the Annual Meeting of the National Association for Resreach and Science Teaching – San Francisco, CA, April.

Williams, G., & Clement, J. (2006). Strategy levels for guiding discussion to promote explanatory model construction in circuit electricity. Proceedings of the Physics Education Research Annual Conference, Syracuse University, Syracuse, New York, July 22–26.

Wiser, M., & Carey, S. (1983). When heat and temperature were one. In D. Gentner & A. Stevens (Eds.), *Mental models* (pp. 267–297). Mahwah, NJ: Erlbaum.

Yerrick, R., Doster, E., Nugent, J. S., Parke, H. M., & Crawley, F. E. (2003). Social interaction and the use of analogy: An analysis of preservice teachers' talk during physics inquiry lessons. *Journal of Research in Science Teaching, 40*(5), 443–463.

Zietsman, A., & Clement, J. (1997). The role of extreme case reasoning in instruction for conceptual change. *Journal of the Learning Sciences, 6*(1), 61–89.

Zietsman, A. I., & Hewson, P. W. (1986). Effect of instruction using microcomputer simulations and conceptual change strategies on science learning. *Journal of Research in Science Teaching, 23,* 27–39.

17

Conceptual Change through Collaboration

Naomi Miyake
Chukyo University

People know many things but do not always understand all of them very deeply. Many know what a sewing machine does, for example, but few could give a satisfactory mechanical explanation when asked how it makes its stitches. Yet, it is also true that we sometimes engage in conversation about a phenomenon none of us "understands" at first and eventually find some plausible explanation, by exchanging proposals and scrutinizing them collaboratively. This chapter characterizes such a social, collaborative endeavor as a cause of conceptual change in its broader sense, proposes cognitive mechanisms for how it is possible, and relates the research on how to support such collaborative conceptual change to emerging research questions in learning sciences.

INTRODUCTION

Even though we are surrounded with many scientific facts and phenomena in our daily life, our explanatory knowledge of them could be quite superficial. Keil explored this folk scientific knowledge by asking people a somewhat deeper level of question than taken for granted, and found out that we are in general overconfident (Keil, 2003). When asked how a helicopter flies, we think we know the answer, until we are asked to give a detailed, step-by-step explanation. Rozenblit and Keil (2002) distinguish explanatory knowledge from knowledge about facts, procedures, and narratives, and claim that people's folk knowledge is especially elusive when we are surrounded with an environment that supports real-time explanations interactively, with visible mechanisms. In everyday situations, we are often surrounded with real things we could test, if we opt to do so, which gives us a strong illusion that we understand, or that we have a "concept" of the target. Though Rozenblit and Keil did not report whether these shallow concepts could be changed easily, their data demonstrate that at least some meta-cognitive intervention could raise the participants' awareness about this shallowness. After they read experts' explanations about the phenomena, the participants' self evaluation was more realistic. If they had had a chance to talk among themselves, with some real machines at hand, they could have changed their folk concepts to some extent, toward a scientifically deeper understanding.

Cognitive processes of comprehension have been studied mainly on individual subjects. The process has also been denoted as "difficult." Among many who report on this difficulty, Clement

(1982) offers one of the most often cited illustrations. In this study, expert physicists were asked to justify their answers. The study documents that each took a long and twisted route to reconstruct the conceptual view, after they solved the problems.

Up to the mid-1980s, these processes were studied under such topics as mental models, analogical understanding, comprehension process and the like. The focus of research on understanding has been further sharpened by newly developed research on conceptual change, after the construct was brought to the attention of developmental researchers (e.g., Carey, 1985). The construct contributed to refining distinctions between naïve, everyday construction of knowledge and the construction of more scientific concepts, both in cognitive developmental research as well as research in practice. The refinement also encouraged new integration of a socio-cultural, collaborative approach to comprehension studies and their more traditional, individual-oriented, laboratory-based counterparts. The scope of this conceptual change research has recently grown to include instruction-induced, intentional change of scientific concepts (Vosniadou, 2003, 2007; Sinatra & Pintrich, 2003), bringing its studies closer to yet another neighboring research field of learning sciences.

This shift brought about a new perspective on the notorious "difficulty" of conceptual change. Such change is difficult, yet it is also true that we occasionally engage in social exchange, conversation, and collective reflection during our daily life. These social activities seem to lead us to better understandings of the phenomenon at hand, to some conceptual change. Adults may be asked by children why something works in the way it does, find they cannot give a satisfactory answer, and then engage in exploratory conversation to figure out the answer. Children of similar ages could get together to wonder over some phenomenon, try to give different exploratory ideas, and discuss their plausibility, until they settle on a most promising conjecture. These are examples of collaborative reflection, which could bring the conceptual change within reach of our daily experiences.

Let us point out some illustrative cases. Greeno and MacWhinney reported an analysis of an interaction among high-school physics teachers who tried to explain why objects in the earth's gravitational field with different masses (e.g., 1 and 10 pounds) fall at the same speed. Their specific problem was to understand why objects differing in mass could have equal acceleration, when the scientific formula, $f = ma$, indicates that the "mass matters." During the discussion, one teacher proposed to equate the larger ball as "ten small balls," which triggered the other members' conceptual change. Eventually, they understood the constant gravitational pull as an aggregate force on the 10-pound ball equal to ten times that on the 1-pound ball (Greeno & Mac-Whinney, 2006). Greeno and MacWhinney depicted this shift on the amended semantic network representation as a merging of two different networks.

Schwartz (1995) also demonstrated that dyads could turn their primitive external representations into abstract ones through joint work more often than individuals. He observed a pair of middle school students who constructed visualizations on the topic of biological transmissions. One student drew a picture of a monkey and a tree, with the letter H connected to the monkey by an arrow. Its meaning remained ambiguous because she did not explain it. The second student looked at the first student's representation and drew a picture of a banana with an arrow from the monkey, which confused the first student, because it turned out that she had intended to use the arrow as a label (H denoting the monkey), not to indicate transmission (who eats what). They negotiated over these externalized objects and jointly developed a representation where an arrow represented the transmission, not a connector of a letter to an object. This way, the dyad developed a more abstract, elaborate use of the notations.

It has also been known that in classroom conversation analyses, teachers' appropriation (Newman et al., 1989) and/or "revoicing" of pupils' utterances sometimes evoke discussions that lay ground for a conceptual change in children (Strom, Kemeny, Lehrer, & Forman, 2001; O'Conner & Michaels, 1996).

Taking these everyday, socio-cultural factors seriously, Inagaki and Hatano advocated that the intentional processes for conceptual change need to be studied as integration of intra-mental, individual knowledge construction and inter-mental, socio-culturally constrained development (Hatano & Inagaki, 2003; Hatano, 2005). Some contributed extensive protocol analyses to explicate what happens during such integration, in problem-solving and comprehension activities (e.g., Miyake, 1986), as well as in learning (e.g., Roschelle, 1992).

The aim of this chapter is to give an overview on research related to mechanisms and their applications of intentional conceptual change, with particular focus on the roles of collaboration and reflection. Because I concentrate on research on interaction, I tried to cite actual transcripts and protocols as much as possible. This chapter consists of three sections. The first section introduces descriptive research with rich protocols to document that simple conversation could lead to relatively substantial conceptual change. In the second section, I will introduce two research studies that reveal underlying mechanisms of how collaborative reflection contributes to change concepts, through detailed protocol analyses. Simply put, there are two lines of research, using different units of analyses. One line focuses more on the process of convergence among the participants by taking a pair or a group as its unit of analysis. The other line emphasizes more of the divergent, individualistic concept formation through social interaction, by taking each individual as the unit. Although there are some core similarities between these accounts, they yield some different predictions about collaborative processes in general and their individual outcomes in particular. I will present some evidence that speaks to these differences in this section.

In the third section, I will review educational application research using the mechanisms of collective reflection explained in the second section. I will introduce emerging research topics from learning sciences and Computer Supported Collaborative Learning (CSCL). CSCL has demonstrated some substantial success in implementing innovative educational curricula for inducing intentional growth of scientific understanding (you can get a glimpse of the field in the *Cambridge Handbook of the Learning Sciences*, 2005; for more detailed reports please go to academic journals like the *Journal of the Learning Sciences*, *Learning & Interaction*, *International Journal of CSCL*, and *Cognition & Instruction*). I will introduce some studies on tested collaborative designs, including Hatano and Inagaki's work on a Japanese science education practice called Hypothesis-Experimental-Instruction (HEI).

To conclude, I will introduce some new directions of the field, the need for taking a longer-term perspective to support life-long learning for sustained conceptual change, and for scaffolding the learners to be able to integrate learning outcomes from different learning situations. This direction is strongly called for, to help both children and adults grow intellectually, to succeed not just in acquiring one set of scientific concept in one domain but several, and in integrating them well to make more clever judgments in their daily lives.

EVERYDAY COLLABORATIVE CONCEPTUAL CHANGE

In the mid-1980s, cognitive science proposed frameworks to understand the basic characteristics of human comprehension of everyday phenomena. While physics professionals rely on quantitative, formal expressions, it was claimed that lay people use more qualitative, intuitive understandings, often in the forms of mental models. It was not that the qualitative reasoning was easy, but it apparently opened up new research topics on how lay people reason. The research was sometimes done in interactive settings, which makes its intermediate steps accessible both for self-reflection and for research.

Multiple and Fragmented, Yet Progressive Mental Models

One example is Williams, Hollan, and Stevens (1983), who analyzed protocols taken from a young adult who tried to answer questions on how a heat-exchanger (a radiator) works. When the question was easy, the subject quickly constructed a simple model relying on his experiential knowledge of an ordinary object whose function he could take for granted (which they called an "autonomous object"). When the question was more complicated, he constructed another model, with more everyday knowledge, without destroying the first one. If juxtaposed, those models were incompatible with each other. From these analyses, Williams et al. proposed that lay people could hold fragmented and multiple mental models supporting their mechanical understandings of their surrounding physical phenomena. They also claimed the models could flexibly shift from a simpler one to a more complex one, according to the needs at hand. Let us see how they justified these claims.

In the experiment, the function of the heat exchanger of a big ship was explained to the subject as cooling down a hot fluid like oil, to lubricate and cool the ship engine. The heat is removed by a cold fluid, usually a river or seawater. The subjects were then asked to reason and think aloud about its mechanisms by referring to parameters like the flow of the hot fluid $f1$ and the cold fluid $f2$, with the inlet and outlet temperatures of the hot fluid ($T1$ and $T2$) and those of the cold fluid ($T3$ and $T4$).

While answering a series of questions ranging from an easy one ("What would happen to $T2$ if $T1$ were to increase, and why?") to a difficult one ("Let us say $T2$ increased. What might be the cause of this? Why? How could you tell if you could only look at temperature parameters, but no fluid flows?"), it was observed that the subject created three different models, partially using his experiential knowledge. Each model was progressively more powerful in terms of its ability to answer more difficult questions. The subject's initial reasoning was drawn from a simple container model. In his trial to predict what would happen to $T4$ (temperature at hot fluid outlet) when $T1$ (temperature at cold inlet) increases, he answered, "If $T1$ is hotter, then that's pumping more heat into the whole system." When asked for a justification of his reasoning, he introduced a more elaborate model that presumes a complex topology of fluid regions and a heat transfer mechanism with constant heat flow. Such a model was evident in his explanations as "$T2$ would increase also…because I guess the first cut is that the heat exchanger is going to drain off a fixed amount of heat from the, from this liquid." While trying to answer some subsequent questions, he discovered a bug in this model and modified the heat transfer mechanism to account for heat flow dependent on the temperature differential between the hot and cold fluid regions. The important point is that each succeeding model either makes more predictions than the preceding one or provides correct predictions where the prior model made erroneous answers. By analyzing these processes, Williams et al. (1983) claim,

> We assume that the subject starts with a set of basic heuristics for creating mental models. These heuristics may evolve out of the subject's experiential knowledge. They include the notion of what an autonomous object is, what the permissible interactions among objects might be, and a means of employing the internal calculus of the objects. The subject appears to be driven by our questions to produce models that are locally successful. When he is unable to answer a question or determines that an answer a model produces is incorrect, in that it violates experiential knowledge or is inconsistent with a higher order model, he seeks to revise the calculus of the model or to construct a new model. (p. 150)

Two things are relevant to our discussion here. For one, even though it is not often documented at this level of detail, we observe and experience this progressive construction of mental models, which would sometimes turn into a scientific understanding of the phenomenon. Parts of the models come from our experiences, and multiple and fragmented models coexist in our daily reasoning. Also as Williams et al. (1083) claim, this process appears to be a product of social interaction, induced by the experimenter's questioning, plus the subject's willingness, or motivation, to develop his own understanding. Together, this mental model research provides us with an illustrative case of relatively flexible conceptual change, in everyday-like collaborative situations.

Children's Spontaneous Conceptual Change through Collaboration

If this kind of progressive conceptual change is a prevailing everyday phenomenon, it could occur at younger ages. Motoyoshi, an experienced daycare teacher, reports a case of collaborative conceptual change of 5-year-olds on reasons why water freezes (Motoyoshi, 1979, in Japanese). In her daycare center, it was customary for the 5-year-olds to play with ice in the garden pool during the winter by stepping on it. One day, Yusuke, a boy, noticed and commented that the ice was only covering the surface. They had to give up playing on it. Next day, they found there was no ice in the pool. They started to discuss how the water froze. "We don't have ice. Is it because it did not rain?" "No. I know there is ice in the pool on clear days, too." "Then why is there no ice in the pool today?" This kind of conversation led them to "experiment" by leaving water in various containers at different locations of the daycare center when they went home. The night was cold and clear. Next morning, they found the water in all the containers was frozen, confirming that rainfall did not have anything to do with freezing. They also found that some containers had thicker ice than others. They noticed for example that two containers put inside had much thinner ice, but at this time there was no discussion about the relationship with the thinness and the location.

They continued doing this experiment, using different containers at different locations for several days, noticing various outcomes of thick and thin ice, sometimes in the same type of container ("Hey, why is the thickness of ice different between my container and Yuriko's? We both used the same blue plastic bucket."), sometimes at different locations, etc. After this chaotic period, one child suggested using different containers but putting them all at the same location. Next morning, there was no ice. The children became suspicious that "putting them all at one place would prevent the water from freezing," but decided to try the same setting one more day, to make sure. The water froze next morning, except for one container. The child whose container did not freeze started to cry, but the other kids noticed that it was the only container with its lid on. The finding encouraged the kids to systematically reflect on their experiences and reason like "when I put my container inside, the water did not freeze; when I put it outside, it froze." After this discussion, the kids talked among themselves and decided to proceed much more systematically. They selected where to put their containers so that they could "test" their ideas. The next two days were too warm for the water to freeze, but the children persisted with the experiment. On the third morning, six containers put outside on the north veranda of the building all had ice, while there was no ice in other containers.

All in all, the experiment lasted for nine days. The children collectively came up with many observations and reasons about why and when the water freezes.

"The water does not freeze every day."
"The water seems to freeze more often on cold days."
"The water inside tends not to freeze; water outside often freezes."
"The water in a thin, metal container freezes into thick ice."

"The water in a Styrofoam container does not freeze easily."

"When we put lots of water in a bucket, only its top part freezes. The bottom could be warmer."

"Freezing does not have anything to do with rain."

"The north, darker side of the building is good for making ice."

"The water in the bottle buried in the sandbox never froze."

The children felt fairly satisfied, but some continued on to invent a new game of competing to see whose ice would melt faster by bringing the containers into the sunlight. This brought out new wonders. "The thick ice in the thin metal container melts quickly (even though it was thick). Why?" "It was difficult to make ice in the Styrofoam container, but once made, the ice did not melt easily, that is strange." These findings all contradicted their "theory," causing them to think deeper.

This episode exemplifies that some persistent, collaborative daily experiences could bring out some scientific conceptual change, even at the age of five. It is also noteworthy that the activities were social, strongly supported by the relationship among the children, as well as by the atmosphere created by the teacher. The teacher did not direct them to do things, but apparently encouraged them to keep discussing and exchanging their experiences, which was crucial for the persistency of their activities.

Distinguishing Successful Collaboration from Unsuccessful Collaboration

Because not all collaboration works successfully, it is worth comparing successful and unsuccessful cases. Stenning, Greeno, Hall, Sommerfeld, and Wiebe (2002) analyzed the same set of successes and failures in collaborative activities where three junior high school students tried to understand population dynamics by modeling. To do this analysis, they adopted three different viewpoints, i.e., fundamental semantic analyses of heterogeneous representations (Stenning & Sommerfeld, 2000) and two types of interactional analyses, on discourse structures (Greeno, Sommerfeld, & Wiebe, 2000) and on coordination of representations (Hall, 2000).

In the successful case, the question was how many mice there would be in the eighth season from 20 original adults with a birthrate of 4 per couple. Student M first computed the solution as 320 by doubling 20 and then by multiplying 40 by 8 (seasons). However, following a suggestion by student K, he added the number of initial adults to get 340 and attempted to draw a graph on the worksheet. The following conversations took place in the process. (Numerals represent protocol lines in the paper and the letters signify the students' initials.)

173: M: Ok (points up with pencil), in the first season came out (pencil beats on table) forty babies (looking at L; L and K looking at M)

174: L: Uh huh (stands, leans against table)

175: M: And then but there's that (pen circles on table) twenty original.

176: K: Oh, so there's sixty mice altogether, ok. (looks up, nodding)

177: L: Oh yeah, ok.

178: M: So that's sixty. (returns to graph and ruler)

179: K: Ok. (nodding, glances at camera and returns gaze to L)

180: M: (marking graph) See now the first season is over here…

181: L: And the second season, that's (an) increase, so then its (forty and 3sec) Wait a minute!

182: K: Sixty…that's equal (inaudible, looks at L then M) is that a hundred and forty?

183: M: And then sixty plus… (looks at M) it's gonna be a hundred.
184: L: (leans in over M's graph, looking directly at K) WAIT a minute! It's forty (kneels down), and then it's like…(hands up, form triangle over table surface, fingertips touching) like forty, right? (looks at K)
185: K: (leans forward, looking at L) Mm hm.
186: L: And then you have to pair those up (brings palms together) and then they have kids (hands flatten and spread apart over table surface)
187: M: (looks up at L, mouth drops open)
188: K: Pair the f-
189: M: (looks at camera, eyes widen) OH, yeah, huh? (smiles and looks over at L)
190: L: (looking at M, laughing, hands still spread open on table top)
191: K: So that means
192: M: We were doing it (looks at K with wide smile)
193: K: Ok, ok. (nodding, R hand beats down on table) That goes (back)
194: L: (laughing) That's a lot of mice (sits back on heels; looks up at camera, smiling)
195: K: Ok, back up.
196: M: (rips the graph sheet off pad)
197: K: Gosh, they'd be repro- Oh my gosh, that's a lot of nasty mice. OK. (pp. 13–14)

According to Stenning and Sommerfeld (2000), the reason this exchange successfully led the triad to correct solution is as follows.

> The graphing practices during this trial involved step-by-step plotting of points. Those external-ized points were studied collaboratively as intermediate results, which helped them reconsider their calculations in the context of the step-by-step sequence of events in mice reproduction, lead-ing them to reconstruct their knowledge. (p. 14)

In the second case where the collaboration failed, the problem was "Begin by raising ten guppies and determine the size of the tank that would be sufficient to hold the offspring they produce during a two-year period." Student M mistakenly attempted to enter the "survival rate" rather than "birthrate" into the computer and worksheet. Student L then said, "The number of guppies born differs from the number of guppies that survive." She subsequently pointed out that the term "survival rate" was incorrectly used by student M, but this point was rejected.

There are many factors that distinguish these two cases. Stenning and Sommerfeld (2000) considered the difference from the viewpoint of "mixed reasoning." This seemed to depend on the availability of different representations. In Case 1, the students used a graph in addition to language, gesture and numerical expressions. Case 2 did not provide them with the same richness of expressions.

So the richness that supports mixed reasoning appears to matter. Greeno et al. (2000) ex-plained the same two cases from the viewpoint of their "threshold theory." For a change in per-spectives, they claim that any question, objection, or alternative must exceed a "threshold" to be taken up by other members. While student M tried to solve the problem with a formula "unit volume x unit number = total number" in Case 1, student L raised a persuasive objection by in-troducing a status model (lines 184 to 194), enabling the group to change the solution policy by exceeding the threshold. However, it was difficult to apply any status model in Case 2 to explain the difference between the birthrate and survival rate and the objection raised did not exceed the threshold. According to this explanation, the explicitness of the comparison between a normative, status model and the topic of discussion at hand appears to matter (Hall, 2000). The researchers involved in these analyses suggest that it is prudent to identify the success factors from different perspectives because successful collaboration is an outcome of very complex interaction among many factors.

We have seen so far some compelling cases where people engage in conversational activities or social exchange to change their concepts. Exactly how does this happen?

MECHANISMS FOR CONCEPTUAL CHANGE THROUGH COLLABORATIVE REFLECTION

To analyze mechanisms for collaborative conceptual change, we could use two different units for analysis. One is the pair or the group as a whole, combined unit. The other is each individual as the basic unit, to examine how the cognitive processes of each intertwine to make the whole. Adherents of the former unit often claim that the overall outcome of collaboration is "convergence." Adherents of the latter unit tend to focus more on the divergent nature of the collaborative outcome, as well as of the process. On the surface, the two approaches are contradictory. In reality, they are complementary. The former emphasizes "the pair (or the group)" as a whole to provide a uniform explanation about the "shared" (or "joint") collaborative process. The latter describes more detailed interaction by focusing on each participant's intra-mental exchange between externalized and internalized ideas of individual thoughts, which are profoundly influenced by the inter-mental exchange with other's perspectives through social interaction. In this section, I will explain these two approaches in some detail. My aim is to integrate these views and identify important characteristics when we wish to design supportive environments for collaborative conceptual change.

The Convergence-Oriented Approach

Let us examine the analyses of Roschelle and his colleagues as one of the most prominent examples of the convergence-oriented approach (Roschelle, 1992; Teasley & Roschelle, 1993).

> ... the crux of collaboration is the problem of convergence: How can two (or more) people construct shared meanings for conversations, concepts, and experiences? ... The central claim is that a process (described by four primary features) can account for students' incremental achievement of convergent conceptual change. (Roschelle, 1992, p. 235)

In this paper, he proposes to integrate prior research about scientific collaboration (c.f., Latour, 1986; Nerserssian, 1988), social constructivist studies (c.f., Newman, Griffin, & Cole, 1989), and "situated actions" in the relational theory of meaning (Barwise & Perry, 1983) in order to analyze students' convergent conceptual change. He claims that there are four primary features in the proposed process.

1. The construction of a "deep-featured" situation at an intermediate level of abstraction from the literal features of the world.
2. The interplay of metaphors in relation to each other and to the constructed situation.
3. An iterative cycle of displaying, confirming, and repairing situated actions.
4. The application of progressively higher standards of evidence for convergence.

To support this, he analyzed protocols taken from a pair of students of an urban high school, Carol and Dana (not their real names), while they studied the basics of Newtonian physics. They

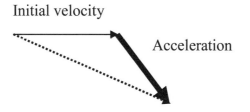

FIGURE 17.1   The schematic drawings shown in the Newtonian window of the Envisioning Machine.

had not previously studied physics. They worked on a computerized scaffold called the Envisioning Machine (Roschelle, 1991). They were asked to manipulate the position, velocity, and acceleration of the particle drawn with arrows in the Newtonian world (window) so that it makes the same motion as the ball in the separate, Observable window. Figure 17.1 schematically depicts the Newtonian window.

Their task was to answer a series of questions on figuring out what would happen to the initial velocity when some acceleration is added. They worked on this task for two after-school sessions, for two hours in total. Roschelle (1991) extracted five episodes from the 15-minute interaction of the second session, and analyzed their language and gestures to see whether he could identify the four features mentioned above.

Their progress through the episodes could be summarized as follows. Prior to the first Episode (Episode 1), both Carol and Dana had misconceptions of "acceleration pulls the material point," which, according to Roschelle (1992, pp. 241–243), is a common misunderstanding among high school students. During Episode 1, Carol changed her concept to "acceleration pulls the tip of the initial velocity" by using the "pulling metaphor." Dana converged to it in transcending from Episode 1 to 2. In Episode 3 Dana started to use the "adding metaphor," which was immediately shared by Carol, thus causing both to change their concept through Episode 4. In Episode 5, they converged to the shared "traveling along metaphor" that let them correctly solve the problem (Roschelle, 1992, pp. 235–276).

Now let us follow some of the analyses in detail to see exactly what is meant by "convergence" in the convergence perspective.

Shortly after they started, they could only talk about the movements in the display with ambiguous, everyday terminology, like "lengthen" and "pull" (D for Dana; C for Carol; the numbers to the left are the line numbers of their protocol).

1. D: But what I don't understand is how the lengthening, the positioning of the arrow…
2. C: Ooh, you know what I think it is? It's like the line. Fat arrow (acceleration) is the line of where it pulls that (tip of the initial velocity line) down. Like see how that makes this dotted line (trace). That was the black arrow (acceleration). It (acceleration) pulls it (velocity).

Roschelle (1992, p. 245) interprets this as "Carol brought the three lines to the foreground and gave them abstract interpretations as deep features — initial velocity, final velocity, and acceleration. She developed an explanation of the configuration by refer [sic] to the metaphor of pulling." This achieves the first feature listed above.

Up to this point, the achievement is mostly Carol's, not yet shared by the other member. This conversation continued.

3. D: You're saying this (dotted line) is the black arrow?
4. C: Yeah.
5. D: And it pulls it the other arrow [points to velocity line with mouse curser] like
6. C: like on its hinge. It pulls the other arrow on the hinge down to the tip of the black arrow.

In this follow up, Roschelle concludes that Dana "shares" her description with Carol, indicating the onset of their convergent conceptual change, or the first cycle of features 2, 3, and 4 listed above. I might point out that on line 5 Dana uses the verb "pull" like Carol just did in line 2, as an indicator of her trial to construct a mental model similar to the one just proposed by Carol. Though Roschelle does not rely on this level of analysis, this gives some side-support to his argument.

Roschelle analyzed four more episodes like this, through which both Carol and Dana cyclically achieved features 2, 3, and 4 listed above. In the third episode, the two students diverged from each other in terms of their understanding about the speed of acceleration, but they successfully repaired the bug in the fourth episode, as shown in the following exchange.

38. D: So I am saying, OK =
39. C: =I bet if I leave it (the acceleration line) like that [creates a hypothetical situation to test her theory and displays how it works on the screen] it's going to make this [resultant] angle =
40. D: = Right that's what I'm saying.
         (= equal sign indicates there was no interval between the end of a prior utterance and the start of the next.)

Roschelle (1992) claims that this is a clear case of joint repair, because Carol could demonstrate her way of understanding (scientifically correct one) following Dana, who immediately identified Carol's demonstration as what she was trying to say. In their fifth episode, they used the Envisioning Machine to confirm their conception, made correct predictions about the answer to the question they were tackling. In their post interview when the experimenter asked for an explanation of what they had learned, they took turns completing their explanations. They then introduced a question, not asked by the experimenter but created by them and that had remained unsolved while they had been testing their conception, to which both could give the correct answer. Taking into account all these concrete pieces of evidence, Roschelle claims that "(a) conceptual change occurred and (b) individual interpretations converged toward shared knowledge" (p. 264). This process could be paraphrased as follows.

1. They externalized their initial ideas into verbal explanations, gestures, and manipulation of the Envisioning Machine display.
2. Each tried to understand the representations, as well as to modify their externalizations.
3. While they did this, their explanations became more abstract.

The episodes and the analyses are both convincing, to the point that the collaborative endeavor led the pair, as a whole, to change their everyday misconception of acceleration into a more scientific one. The convergence framework thus claims that collaboration induces conceptual change of a pair (or a group) as the unit of analysis.

What is not clear yet is the exact mechanism of why and exactly how this convergence occurred. There were 14 pairs in this experiment, out of which only six exhibited all four features of conceptual change. This is not a problem for the framework because it does not claim that collaboration always induces conceptual change. A remaining problem may be that the framework does not explain whether each individual outcome could be different from the others. Because individuals tend to diverge, Roschelle argues that the question is how convergent conceptual change could ever occur. As Roschelle put it,

> Carol and Dana received no prior instruction on scientific descriptions or conceptions of motion. Nor can one attribute their learning directly to the structure of the computer simulation, as students who experience the same simulation construct widely divergent ideas (Roschelle, 1991). As a result, the means for convergent conceptual change therefore appears incommensurate with the outcome: How could Carol and Dana converge on a deep new conception with only figurative, ambiguous, and imprecise language and physical interactions at the disposal? (p. 239)

Roschelle's answer is, as we have been suggesting, that "convergent conceptual change is achieved incrementally, interactively, and socially through collaborative participation in joint activity" (p. 238). In other words, when he took the pair as a whole and analyzed their language as each complementing the other, there emerged the convergent pattern of the conceptual change in the targeted direction.

Yet, the other possible solution to this problem would be to analyze each individual's language, to see whether there really was any convergence reached by each. They might not have converged on their individual conceptual levels.

It is clear that each influenced the other, with their language as well as with the Envision Machine display they created. Each could have gone through substantial individualistic conceptual change, in divergent forms. Each might have developed her specific concept, more abstract in quality than her initial ideas, yet with varying degrees of similarity to the target scientific concept.

In order to check the validity of this possibility, we analyzed some of the wordings Carol and Dana used individually. The resultant pattern was lopsided: among the 14 key expressions we selected, only three were "shared" or frequently used by both. Carol used the verb "pull" six times, while Dana used it only once when she paraphrased Carol's explanation (see line 5 above). Dana used "lengthen" three times, but Carol never used it. Carol tended to use "the fat arrow (acceleration)" as the subject that "pulls" the tip of "the thin arrow (velocity)" as its object, suggesting that she created a rather dynamic mental model. Dana preferred to use terms "lengthen" and "add on" as her relational verbs, and "the thin arrow" as its subject and "the fat arrow" as the object. Dana's language thus implies that she had a rather static geometrical model around the velocity, which she could either "lengthen" or "add on" with the amount given in the acceleration (c.f., Shirouzu & Miyake, 2002).

Each model could have belonged to each individual to the very end of their collaboration, where they could "complement" each other's explanation (as Roschelle, 1992, suggests). While this complemented whole could represent their "common" ground, it does not guarantee the "shared" conceptual change for both. It could even be said that the complementing action was possible because the explanations given by one member were almost never complete to the other, and the incompleteness invited the latter to provide the missing pieces from her repertoire. We cannot justify this because we do not have access to all the data and because we do not know what concepts Carol and Dana achieved at the end of the intervention either. However, it points to the importance of analyzing the collaborative process by taking each individual as the smaller unit of analysis. It would give a different answer to Roschelle's question. It could also provide a different answer to the collaborative conceptual change mechanism.

The Constructive Interaction Framework

Miyake and her colleagues' work (Miyake, 1986; Shirouzu, Miyake, & Masukawa, 2002) provides an illustrative case of analyzing interaction for conceptual change with each individual as the unit of analysis. In her 1986 study, the subjects were instructed to "talk together to figure out how a sewing machine makes its stitches." Her main concern was to verify her proposal of the iterative process of understanding. She used pairs of subjects because the other aim of her study was to explore a new method called "constructive interaction" to study the comprehension process in general. At the time, there was a heated discussion about whether verbal protocols are data (Nisbett & Wilson, 1977; Ericsson & Simon, 1980, 1984). One unnatural aspect of the traditional protocol is that the subject is forced to talk out loud when he/she would normally be silent. She proposed the constructive interaction method in order to circumvent this problem.

Through individual-based interaction analyses, she found that the joint problem-solving situation consists of each individual's independent processes. Both the language they used and their final mental models differed from one participant to the other. Because they work on their own problems in their own way, it is reasonable to assume they do not have easily accessible checking mechanisms to validate their solutions. She claimed that this is where the virtues of the interaction are found. Because each participant works from a different starting schema, what is obvious and natural to one may not be so to the other. This difference was often identified in her data as questions and criticisms. Studying their patterns, she concluded that the socially interactive or joint problem solving has a high potential to elicit conceptual change for each participant in different ways.

She also maintained that there is a role shift of task-doing and monitoring associated with the difference, as a possible cause for their concepts to change into more abstract scientific forms. Miyake and her colleagues expanded this view on the role-shift by examining the effects of the externalized objects and the perspectives taken by the monitors on the externalized objects (Shirouzu et al., 2002). Their task called for integrating various solutions to an arithmetic problem using a square sheet of paper. They found that pairs tended to reach an abstract solution more often than solos on this task. In the protocol of the pairs, they could trace the role exchange contributing to each taking a slightly broader, monitoring perspective than the other.

Let us go through some of the details of these studies to validate their claims.

HOW DOES A SEWING MACHINE MAKE A STITCH? — A CASE OF FINDING A NEW CONCEPT

When people try to understand complex physical devices like a sewing machine, they proceed in an iterative fashion. They seem to reach several points at which they claim to "understand" the device. Each point of understanding is incomplete and requires a new level of understanding. This iterative cycle happens during each individual's conceptual change, depending on the individual's prior, experience-based understanding, as well as the goal of how deeply one needs to, or wishes to, understand the target. The first aim of Miyake (1986) was to examine this iterative process of understanding (the other aim was to examine the experimental method she called "constructive interaction"). To do this, she prepared two frameworks: the function-mechanism hierarchy to identify the levels of understanding of the sewing mechanism, and another framework to capture the nature of the cycling of understanding and non-understanding. With these she examined whether her protocol reveals that her subjects actually traced down the understanding levels by going through the understanding cycles.

The Function-Mechanism Hierarchy

The hierarchy has several levels corresponding to psychological "levels" of understanding. The term "function" refers to the description of the task performed at any given level, corresponding to what Williams, Hollan, and Stevens (1983) called an "autonomous object." A functional description says, essentially, that "such and such happens," but it does not explain how. The term "mechanism" is used to describe the "how." The explanation is comprised of functions connected together with simple relationships. There is a dovetailing of functions and mechanisms: the function at one level requires the mechanism at the next lower level to explain it. The distinction of levels here is relative, not absolute. Miyake (1986) explains that she used six levels simply because that was all that was required by the data from her studies.

She identified six levels on the sewing machine problem as needed to analyze the data. At the top level, level 0, the function of a sewing machine is to make stitches. To achieve that function, the level 1 mechanism has as its function the intertwining of two threads. In level 2, a stitch is made when the needle pushes a loop of the upper thread through the material to the underside. The upper thread is then looped entirely around the lower thread. The looping "function" creates a topological puzzle, requiring one lower level "mechanism" for the upper thread to go around the free end of the lower thread. Determining this mechanism creates the major difficulty in understanding how the machine works. The answer is that the upper thread can go around the whole bobbin because the bobbin itself serves as a free end. Grasping this mechanism is level 3 understanding. However, the statement "the upper thread can go around the whole bobbin" still does not show complete understanding, because one can still ask how a bobbin can serve as a free end when it must also be attached to the body of the machine. In level 4, the actual path of the upper loop comes into focus, thus conceptually shifting the role of the bobbin from a free-end provider to a provider of a space in the back. Lastly, the physical configuration of the bobbin parts comes into focus at level 5. This Function Mechanism hierarchy is shown in Table 17.1.

TABLE 17.1
The Function-Mechanism Hierarchy for the Sewing Machine Stitch Problem. A Function is Bracketed in []. A Mechanism Consists of Several Functions, Concatenated with + Signs, as []+[]+[]...

Level 0	*[Stitch]*								
1			[Thread comes from above]	+	[Thread 1 intertwines, can pick up thread 2]	+	[Thread 2 comes from below]		
2	[Nedle makes loop of upper thread]	+	[Needle pulls down loop]	+	[Bottom thread goes through loop]	+	[Bottom thread comes from below]	+	[Needle pulls up loop]
3	[Hook catches loop]	+	[Hook pulls down loop]	+	[Loop goes around bobbin]	+	[Hook releases loop]		
4	[Bobbin is clear on front]	+	[Hook separates loop]	+	[Bobbin structure provides back space]	+	[Side 1 of loop passes bobbin back]	+	[Side 2 of loop passes bobbin front]
5	[Bobbin is on case]	+	[Case clams on holder]	+	[Holder is held by collar]	+	[Collar is part of hook_shaft]	+	[Hook_shaft is fixed to machine]

Understanding and Non-Understanding

Miyake (1986) proposed that the process of understanding follows the function-mechanism hierarchy, with each level guiding the steps to be followed for understanding to proceed. When a function in a level n mechanism is identified and questioned (i.e., one puzzles over how that function gets done), this opens up the search for a level n + 1 mechanism. A mechanism is then proposed as a tentative solution. This proposal can be criticized, and if it passes this criticism, it is stated as confirmed. Thus, at each level, understanding proceeds through steps of identifying and questioning a function at level n, followed by searching, proposing, criticizing, and confirming the corresponding mechanism at level n + 1. The mechanism at level n + 1 can then be decomposed into its functions, and those one-level lower functions, when questioned, could then lead to search of a level n + 2 mechanism.

She also assumed that when people are engaged in the steps of "identify," "propose," and "confirm," they think they understand the phenomenon at hand. When they "search," "criticize," and "question" they feel they do not understand. Roughly, when one finds an explanation in a level n + 1 mechanism for a level n function, it is felt to be understood; when a function of level n is questioned and one starts searching for its mechanisms, this gives a sense of non-understanding. Thus, going through the steps and going down the levels produces an alternation of feelings of understanding and non-understanding.

Results of the Protocol Analysis

Miyake (1986) analyzed three pairs of subjects on the sewing machine interactions, Pair A, B and C (each member of the pairs will be denoted with numbers, as A1 and A2 formed Pair A). All subjects reached a level 5 mechanism. In terms of the understanding process, the analyses confirmed her framework. Her subjects identified a questionable function on each level, questioned how it happened and started to find a possible mechanism at one level below. Their senses of understanding and non-understanding alternated. Their language revealed their conceptual viewpoints that tended to be stable while they understood and tended to shift often while they did not understand. In addition, her analyses of individual protocols in terms of how each descended the levels revealed some fundamental mechanisms of both individualistic as well as socially supported constructive interaction to achieve conceptual change.

Individualistic Aspects of Interaction

While all the subjects solved the task, each took a different course. They were often on different levels while exchanging proposals: for Pair A, out of their 91 turn takings, A1 and A2 were on different levels 31 times (36.3%). This discrepancy was greater at the beginning. In the first one-third, when they were talking just with paper and pen, they were out of synchrony 57.7% of the time. When interviewed about this after the experiment, they were unaware of this discrepancy at all.

Their final models were different also. If we compare expressions of their level 5 mechanisms, they were not very similar. For instance, while A1 reached a more standard model you might find in a book, A2's solution was built on an analogy with a spoke-less bicycle wheel. The difference was also revealed in the drawings used by A1 and A2 both during and at the very end of their interaction. At the end of the experiment, they were asked to explain how the sewing machine works "as if to a person who does not know anything." They took different points of view in their explanations. A1 drew a cross-sectional view, as he had been doing throughout the interaction. A2 drew a front view, even though the drawing he most often dealt with in the interaction was A1's cross-sectional view. This difference again showed up 6 months later, when they were asked to do this same task.

This may reflect the norm of conversation that people do not really talk to one other (e.g., Hobbs & Evans, 1980). It was also true though, as their post-experiment interview revealed, that they felt they had talked with each other quite cooperatively, worked together to find "the" answer, and were satisfied with their achievement at the end. For all pairs, one person gave a more extensive mechanism while the other gave a much simpler one. This may be an artifact because if one participant gives an extensive answer, there is no need for the other to repeat it, except for the most important or different parts. In this sense, differences observed are those the subjects cared enough to express. Yet in actuality their solutions were different, more so than they appeared to notice themselves.

Criticisms Provide Validation Checking Mechanisms

Even when the starting and ending of interactions are individualistic, there is the virtue of working together. People interpret the problem or situation in their own ways. They find their own satisfactory solutions. The interaction provides a mechanism to validate their individualistic solutions. Because each participant works from a different starting schema, what is obvious and natural to one may not be so to the other. This leads to "criticisms."

In the sewing machine protocol, Miyake observed 41 criticisms in all. Self-criticizing accounted for only 12% of the incidents (5 out of the total of 41), implying that validation checking is hard within an individual system. Criticizing the level on which both participants were working is also rare (four times). Most of the criticisms were "downward," where the person who is criticizing has less understanding than the other (22 times). It could mean that the criticizer could not understand the proposed mechanism. The important point is, however, that these criticisms did force the other person, the one with more understanding, to keep searching for better mechanisms, or better explanations of what s/he wants to propose. Out of 22 observed downward criticisms, 10 pushed the partner to search deeper for their answers.

It seems, therefore, that criticism could occur when the two people are at different levels and have different focuses. This difference appears to stimulate both participants to search for better understanding.

MOTIONS — THE ROLE OF THE MONITORS

Miyake (1986) also analyzed "motion," suggestions of a new way to approach the problem. Near the end of the Pair A interaction, A2 suggested taking off the bottom panel of the machine, so that they could get a better view of the backside of the bobbin. This suggestion moved them to their final conclusions.

She could identify two different types of motions. Motions can be closely related to the topic under discussion at the time or can be divergent from the topic. While suggesting going back to the machine for more observation is topic related, suggesting taking off the bottom panel for a better view is topic-divergent. When she compared members in each pair, topic-related motions were generated more by the "task-doers," or the people who were leading the problem solving at the moment. Observers who were monitoring the process tended to give more topic-divergent motions. If task-doers were more engaged with a local focus, observers could have had a more global focus, not yet being able to or not having to narrow their focus to match that of the task-doers. Topic-divergent motions might have their origins in this global focus that was not easily available to the doers. Moreover, some topic-divergent motions worked constructively. Out of the total of 17 divergent motions, six were followed by some change in the course of the problem solving. Thus, in two-person, constructive interactions, the person who has more to say about the current topic takes the task-doer's role, while the other becomes an observer, monitoring the situation. The observer can contribute by criticizing and giving topic-divergent motions, which are not the primary roles of the task-doer.

Active Use of External Resources

In another study, Shirouzu et al. (2002) expand the notion of role-exchange and offer an explanation of how it can contribute to abstract and flexible problem solving. They asked their subjects to obtain three-fourths of two-thirds, or its reverse, of a square sheet of origami. There are mathematical and non-mathematical solutions to this problem. The mathematical solution is to solve it by calculation, as $2/3 \times 3/4$, while non-mathematical solutions do not involve any calculations. They compared the Solo subjects and the Pair subjects to do this and found that both solved this non-mathematically nearly 90% of the time. When they asked them to solve the reverse problem the second time (that is, getting three-fourths of two-thirds first, then two-thirds of three-fourths second, or vice versa), the Solos tended to use the same strategy, while the Pairs tended to shift it to an arithmetic solution.

The solution strategies adopted by the subjects affected their solution paths. Let us explain this with the problem of getting two-thirds of three-fourth. When they used the non-mathematical strategy, the subjects tended to follow a two-step solution of obtaining the three-fourth first and then delineating the two-thirds in the obtained three-fourths. With the same non-mathematical strategy, some could apply a one-step solution of perceiving the three parts in the already-obtained three-fourths and directly taking two out of the three. Others adopted the mathematical strategy, though fewer in number. They solved the problem by multiplying the two-thirds with three-fourths and obtaining one-half as the answer.

Whichever path they took, the objective reflection on the correct answer would have the subjects realize the mathematical solution, which, in this case, is quicker and requires less effort. The Solo subjects did not seem to realize this. This objective reflection can be identified by the shift of strategies from externally oriented, two-step solution path to the mathematical one. When tested first to get the two-thirds of three-forths, and then its reverse immediately thereafter, Solos did not change their solution paths (nearly 85% stayed on, possibly showing some bias toward confirmation). In contrast, over 70% of the Pairs converted their non-arithmetic solution paths to the arithmetic one.

Shirouzu et al. (2002) interpreted these results to make the following claims. First, human beings use external resources actively, and they react to their own doings rather subjectively; that is, they actively leave traces while solving a problem, in which they only see what they expect to find in such traces. When working alone, they are not always able to assume objective perspectives. This is where having another person could contribute to changing the perspectives.

Second, the roles of performing and monitoring tasks are often frequently exchanged during collaborative joint problem solving. The monitor has opportunities to observe emerging events in the situation from a perspective slightly different or slightly more objective from that of the doer. Thus in a collaborative situation, these two factors, the active use of and the subjective perspective on external resources and frequent role exchanges, interact and produce solutions that evolve from highly individualistic and situated to more abstract and flexible alternatives. Objective comments made by the observer regarding the traces and the process often refer to broader conditions than the focus of the task-doer, since the monitor does not necessarily share the original solution path of the doer. This contributes to increases in the variety of solutions to be reflected upon, which vary not just in type but also in the degree of abstraction. Such reflection often led the paired subjects to adopt the abstract mathematical solution strategy in their second trials. During collaboration, participants have the advantage to integrate various solutions differing in the degree of abstraction, which is a natural outcome of the interaction between the task-doer's plans and the monitor's re-interpretation.

This set of findings should be relevant to understanding the design principles for effective collaboration for scientific conceptual change. This mechanism offers an explanation of why there could be different learning outcomes from paired learners. It is because the abstraction level for each participant depends on the degree of the integration of the shared task-doing and the monitoring, during and after the interaction. This also explains why a more knowledgeable participant, or the person who preceded the other in his/her understanding, could still benefit from the interaction. This model implies that for the design of collaborative conceptual change it is important to encourage perspective exchanges and to secure ample chances for each individual learner to reflect upon the shared resources. The model is not necessarily the one widely shared among ordinary learners. They do not always grasp the value of interaction according to this model and may complain, when put in collaborative environments without much preparation, that the more capable participants may not learn much. The model provides explanations why this is not so. To make a collaborative curriculum successful, sharing this piece of knowledge among the learners, teachers, and the designers as well is often the key. Let us move on to study explicit support for intentional conceptual change in learning situations.

COGNITIVE AND SOCIO-CULTURAL ACCOUNTS OF CONCEPTUAL CHANGE IN THE CLASSROOM

Hatano and Inagaki (1991) introduced to the world a Japanese collaborative practice called Hypothesis-Experiment-Instruction (HEI) for science education. They studied this method in relation to motivation for comprehension and collective comprehension activity.

The HEI standard procedure consists of the following steps (Itakura, 1997).

1. Students are presented with a problem with three or four answer alternatives. The alternatives take the form of directly testable predictions, representing naive interpretations, models, or theories that students tend to possess. The problem specifies how to confirm which alternative is right. Either one of the students or the teacher reads the problem with the alternatives to make sure everybody understands. The teacher sometimes shows the experiment settings (with care not to reveal the outcome) to confirm the students' understanding of the problem.
2. Students are asked to choose one answer by themselves.
3. Students' responses, counted by a show of hands, are tabulated on the blackboard by the teacher.
4. Students are encouraged to explain their choices to the class.
5. Students are encouraged to question and discuss the above explanations until they feel they have completed the discussion.
6. Students are asked to choose an alternative once again. They may change their choices.
7. Students observe an experiment conducted by the teacher or read a given passage, to determine whether their choices were correct.
8. Students write down what the result was, with comments.

In the HEI practice, there are some shared "rules of thumb" to follow these steps. Children may change their choices any time. They are also allowed to stay silent. If there is not much discussion and the kids feel they are ready to test their choices, the class can move directly on to the concluding experiment. It is the norm for the teacher to keep the class atmosphere as flexible and forgiving as possible so that the students observe the epistemic agency themselves.

Though the last step asks the pupils to write down the result of the day, with comments, this does not require them to write any particular thing in scientific diction. They could just say bravo because they were right, or they could write nothing. This makes it difficult to keep a good record of the understanding status of the kids from the researcher's point of view. For HEI, however, Itakura maintains it is more important to preserve the autonomy for each student "to think scientifically" without enforcing them to think or write in a dogmatic way.

The key in HEI is that the experiment comes in a carefully prepared series so that the students could naturally relate the outcomes to form a "theory." Itakura maintains that a hypothesis (e.g., metal conducts electricity) cannot be confirmed by a single experiment, but has to be validated by integrating several consecutive experiment outcomes (for example, by inserting several different things like a coin, lead galena, ferrite magnet, a 10,000 yen bill, a colored pencil, etc., in the middle of a copper line connecting batteries and a light bulb, they could accumulate results to differentiate what makes the bulb light and what does not). It is the job of each student to infer an abstract "theory." A number of studies in science education have shown that presenting an unexpected, surprising, or anomalous piece of information is not effective in inducing conceptual change (e.g., Vosniadou & Ioannides, 1998). Itakura's HEI responds to these results well, by arranging the experiments to build expectations among the students to integrate the results. Because this succession of the experiments is built into HEI, there is no need (or it is even regarded detrimental) for students to prepare for the class. For the same reason, there is no encouragement for summing up, giving explanations, or encouraging discussion about the outcomes.

This pattern of practice makes it difficult to examine carefully the effects of the whole class discussion. Inagaki and Hatano studied this in an experimental set up (Inagaki & Hatano, 1968; Hatano & Inagaki, 1991, 2003). In one such study (Hatano & Inagaki, 1991), students in the fourth grade received a science lesson concerning the conservation of weight when sugar is dissolved into water. Students were randomly divided into experiment and control groups (44 and 43 students, respectively) based on their performance on the target task in a pretest. Two-thirds of the members in each group were non-conservers. Students in both conditions were given a problem with three answer alternatives. Suppose that two lumps of sugar and a glass of water on one tray of a scale and a weight in the other tray are balanced on a scale. The two lumps of sugar are put into the glass of water and dissolved completely after stirring. Now, does the glass of water with dissolved sugar (a) become heavier than the weight, (b) become lighter than the weight, or (c) remain balanced with the weight?

In the experiment condition, all of the steps up to step 7 of HEI (step 8 was omitted in this experiment) were followed in groups of about 20 students each, whereas in the control condition, steps 4, 5, and 6 were omitted. Thus, the difference between the conditions was in the extent of the exchange of ideas among the students, more specifically, of the information about which students (or how many students) supported each of the alternatives and how they justified their choices, not in the amount of authoritative information given. Immediately before step 7, the students in both conditions were asked to rate their interest in observing the experiment using a four-point scale (from very eager to see the experiment to not eager to do so). After step 7, both groups of students were given a posttest consisting of the conservation of weight of sugar and other substances. Their data indicated that cognitive motivation was amplified through the discussion. The students in the experiment condition exhibited greater interest in observing the experiment after the discussion (and immediately before the experiment) than those in the control condition. The conservation level of the students was similar between the experiment and the control groups. However, when they were asked to give explanations, 26% of the experiment group students gave atomistic, or quasi-atomistic, explanations, whereas none of the control students could give such answers.

Hatano and Inagaki (1991) identify the following features of the whole-class discussion as contributing factors for fostering the observed conceptual change. First, students' enduring comprehension activity was propelled by their social motivation as well as cognitive or "epistemic" motivation. Second, this partisanship made students' comprehension activity more effective because it served to divide the task into several manageable parts. For example, their tasks were divided into making reasonable answers and estimating others opinions. They claim, from these observations,

> It is reasonably clear that explanations offered in group discussion could be assimilated, or more accurately, reconstructed, when the students were given external feedback informing them which alternative was correct. … The analysis of group protocols strongly suggests that its effectiveness derives primarily from social amplification of individual motivation for comprehension and also from the division of labor created by group discussion. (Hatano & Inagaki, 2003, pp. 420–421)

If the single class in their experiment exhibited this strong tendency toward conceptual change, what are the real effects on the students who engage in a series of HEI practice? Because of the way the practice is constructed and because of the common style of classroom management, the same child often stays with the same teacher for 1 year to 2 to 3 years, learning all the subjects from her. These cases provide us with a chance to see the pragmatic effects of HEI. Though not much rigorous research has been reported, there are ample episodes demonstrating the effects. One teacher who practiced the HEI for 10 years reports the sustainability of the conceptual change. He kept teaching the concept of weight in terms of the molecular construction for 8 years. In the 8th year, he tested the graduates on their understanding and got the results shown in Table 17.2 (Shoji, 1988, in Japanese). One would say it is not surprising to see that the 80% of the high school students tested answered correctly the weight problem that is solvable by the students in the fourth grade. The numbers are yet telling the effects of the HEI practice because the percentage is 15% lower for young adults of the same age who did not experience HEI on this "easy" problem.

TABLE 17. 2
Follow-up Study on Retention Rate of the Concept of Weight between HEI Graduates (Who Experienced HEI at 4th Grade) with Non-HEI Graduates (with No HEI Experiences)

Grade	After HEI	HEI graduates	Non HEI graduates	Difference in %
Elementary 4th	0.5 year	70.9	-	-
5th	1.5 years	77.3	-	-
6th	2.5 years	79.0	-	-
Middle 1st (7th)	3.5 years	74.4	57.5	16.9
Middle 2nd (8th)	4.5 years	81.9	67.3	14.6
Middle 3rd (9th)	5.5 years	82.2	59.8	22.4
High 1st (10th)	6.5 years	80.6	63.7	16.9
High 2nd (11th)	7.5 years	82.3	67.4	14.9

Another gain from the HEI practice should be social because, as Hatano and Inagaki suggest, it is well structured to foster the sense of collaborative learning through discussion. There are numerous episodes demonstrating that the students like the class and develop exploratory minds, which also lasted for a longer period of time than usually known. They also seem to gain social skills required to work collaboratively on their own when necessary. Hatano and Inagaki report (1991) a case where five fifth graders jointly wrote an essay reflecting on and summarizing how their ideas about molecules had evolved mainly through participating in HEI. They had had a series of HEI lessons over the preceding 3 years on topics concerning solid bodies and their weight, and felt that the essay would be useful for new classmates who had not participated in those lessons. The essay reveals the stability of their comprehension.

> Let us tell you the history of how we have understood the perspectives of 'molecules.' We want to do this because we think what we learned in the fourth grade in the Hypothesis Experiment classes could be important for our classmates who did not learn those lessons. In science classes, we often think "what would be the answer if we take the molecular perspective," but this is not easily shared by our classmates.... We clearly understood this perspective when we studied crystallization after dissolution. We made models of crystals and imitated molecular movements. It was so much fun! We will never forget the excitement we felt at those lessons throughout our lives. When we understood that many seemingly different things can be answered by thinking of them in terms of molecules, we felt like the sky was clear, as in the sunniest day. We then deepen our understanding through lessons on classes on the three states of water, solid, liquid and gas.... (Obara, 1971, pp. 108–109; translated by the author)

The classmates without the HEI lessons read this essay, according to Obara, their teacher, and started habits of discussing subjects in their classes. These episodes are quite promising. In order to see how the HEI experience at a certain grade prepares the students to learn better in their subsequent classes, longer-term, more systematic scientific research is needed.

CSCL: A NEW FIELD OF RESEARCH SUPPORTING CONCEPTUAL CHANGE THROUGH COLLABORATION WITH TECHNOLOGY

Computer Support for Collaborative Learning (CSCL) is an emerging field of research and practice on learning, to which the studies on conceptual change have much to contribute (Stahl, Koschmann, & Suthers, 2006; Miyake, 2007). Current CSCL regards one of the aims of learning as serious scientific conceptual change, often attained through collaboration. Each learner, as an "epistemic agent" (Scardamalia & Bereiter, 1994), is responsible for creating his/her own knowledge through social interaction with other human beings, by interacting with physical objects, in social as well as in everyday situations. The goals of such learning have also been described as achieving "adaptive" or generalizable expertise (Hatano & Inagaki, 1986).

In order to help support the new type of learning, research in CSCL requires recording and analyzing the processes of learning (Granott & Parziale, 2002), with greater detail for a much longer period than conventional, laboratory-based learning studies. Currently, computers and computer-controlled recording and analyzing tools are most promising to meet such requirements.

Computers are also an indispensable component in CSCL to help support collaborative conceptual change. Based on theoretical research on how collaboration works, CSCL calls for such principles as making initial thoughts visible, scaffolding generations of different ideas, and engaging learners in collaborative reflection for developing their ideas further. To design effective collaborative learning environments by implementing these requirements, computers are also quite promising tools, when coupled with carefully thought-out learning activities. Let me illustrate how some design principles are implemented in learning activities.

Making Thinking Visible

Writing is perhaps the most orthodox way to make one's thinking visible. When writing is done collaboratively, it also strongly supports constructive reflection. Knowledge Forum (Scardamalia & Bereiter, 1994, 2006) is one of the oldest and the most successful knowledge building environments relying on collaborative writing. Based on their basic research on writing, Scardamalia and Bereiter (1994) maintain there are two types of writing, "knowledge reformation" and "knowledge telling," of which only the former is related to knowledge building. They have created a networked knowledge-building environment where the students write notes on shared problems in different subject areas over a substantial period of time. They are encouraged by the system to write not just what they find out, but also what they need to know, and comments on other students' notes. As the notes accumulate, the system also encourages them to "rise above" the current discussion so that they can start working on abstracted levels of knowledge construction, or scientific conceptual change. Students are treated as "epistemic agents" responsible for changing their own knowledge and sustaining the intellectual community they belong to.

Many CSCL tools aim at "making scientific reasoning visible" (Linn & Hsi, 2000), as a way to support collaborative scientific conceptual change. The SenseMaker (Bell, Davis, & Linn, 1995) requires the students to find evidential facts and categorize them to make explicit how they reason to claim some scientific position (e.g., the light could travel forever) against some other position (e.g., the light dies out at some point). They keep these categories visually displayed while debating their positions so that the listeners could "point" to the pieces of evidences for furthering discussion if needed. This also helps teachers to analyze their students' current understanding and how it would develop.

Increasing the Variability of Perspectives

When thinking can be made visible, it is also desirable to increase its variability. HIE does this by providing a width of alternatives worth considering under the given problem.

The Jigsaw method, first developed by social psychologists for "teaching cooperativeness as a skill" (Aronson & Patnoe, 1997, p. 14), also helps increase the diversity of perspectives on a shared task (e.g., Brown, 1997). It is highly flexible, modifiable to facilitate many different types of collaboration, which Miyake and her colleagues have been exploring (c.f., Miyake et al., 2001). The Jigsaw can, for instance, be quite dynamic, to let a college class of around 60 students collaboratively cover 20 to 30 learning materials, each representing classic research in three different domains of cognitive science. The students are supported to collaboratively read, explain, exchange, and discuss the materials to integrate them, so that each participating student would be able to verbally explain the integrated "concepts" of the target discipline, with necessary evidential pieces of knowledge from the relevant research. Knowledge integration is explicitly scaffolded by successively enlarging the scope of materials each has to cover: they start with one, exchange it with someone else and integrate those two, then exchange those two with someone else who could also explain two to integrate four, and so forth. Some assessment analyses of this type of activities have revealed (1) fair amount of retention of the learning material concepts 4–6 months after the end of the course, (2) explicit knowledge integration surrounding each student's personal needs, and 3) some conscious acquisition of learning skills such as asking specific, content-driven questions (Miyake, 2005a, 2005b; Miyake, Shirouzu, & Chukyo Learning Science Group, 2005; Miyake & Shirouzu, 2006).

Soliciting Learning-Effective Role Exchanges

How to solicit learning-effective role exchange is yet another research topic related to conceptual change in CSCL. Palincsar and Brown (1984) devised an interactive support for reading for students who were quite behind their required reading levels. They focused on gaining the metacognitive, self-guiding questions while reading. The teacher coaches students by asking questions, and then they turn the roles so that the students have to ask questions of teachers, and then of other students, to grow the sense of when to ask what of themselves to guide their own readings. This guidance is somewhat ritualistic, but the students were found to gain some robust metacognitive skills that they could use long after the treatment. Expanded versions of this method have been implemented in computerized environments.

An intriguing and very promising extension of this approach is the notion of "Teachable Agents" (Biswas, Schwartz, Leelawong, Vye, & TAG-V, 2005; Schwartz et al., 2007). This is a rather straightforward implementation of one of the oldest beliefs of effective teaching, "people learn best when they teach." Students teach a computer agent by identifying important components and the causal relationships as links like "increase" and "decrease" among them, on which the system creates a relational map. Based on this structured database, the agent can answer questions and explain her answers by tracing through the links. In one of their recent studies, Schwartz et al. (2007) had fourth- to fifth-grade children work with the agents for about a month learning the oxygen cycle. In one situation, the students teach the agent. They ask their agent questions and see if it gets them right or wrong. In another situation, students are told they are making a concept map, and they have to ask a mentor agent if the map is right or wrong. At the end of 1 month, everyone looks about the same. One month later, they asked the students to learn a new topic, the nitrogen cycle. As a result, the students who had taught the agent learned more. Moreover, when they look at the students' explanations of why, it turns out that the group who used the teachable agent initially was more likely to check the coherence of their understanding when they were learning the nitrogen cycle. Schwartz et al. propose to interpret this as suggesting that the reciprocal, collaborative type of "learning through teaching" could help the students develop some cognitive resource for further learning (c.f., Schwartz & Martin, 2004).

FUTURE CHALLENGES

To conclude, let me point out some future challenges for putting the conceptual change studies into real learning settings. One is the problem of assessment and communicating the research findings of long-term, large-scale learning projects, with rich and complex data. The other challenge is, as the HEI practice has hinted, setting longer term goals for learning. This also involves redefining transfer, or learning goals, for sustainable learning and creating changes in society (c.f., Bransford & Schwartz, 1999).

There is a hidden agenda in our modern conception of learning — especially as embodied in education — that the learning experiences gained in one "learning situation" are naturally built-upon, expanded, and integrated with experience from other learning situations. However, this implicit learning assumption has not been as substantially researched or discussed as is warranted by its importance. Furthermore, little support has been implemented to guide integration across such learning experiences.

Short-term assessments of learning performance may not be as predictive as we would hope of cross-situational uses of concepts, skills and other achievements in the realism of longer time frames. This concern is clearly related to how outcomes from different settings of learning are, or should be, portable to other situations, be dependable when the need arises to use them in different situations, and prove sustainable in terms of providing preparation for further learning. Examination of these issues could open additional dialogues about redefining the "transfer of learning" theoretical construct, and related concepts such as "generative learning," and "preparing for future (PFL)" learning.

There are some emerging trends in the studies of cumulative quality of experience. For example, in a series of studies of about a month with high school students, Schwartz and his colleagues (c.f. Schwartz & Martin, 2004) had middle school students go through cycles of learning about statistics, and then gave them PFL assessments. The results were very positive — the students could both learn new ideas without being explicitly told what to do and they could flexibly develop their own ways to solve new classes of problems (e.g., they were taught about variance, and later many figured out how to compute covariance more easily than those who were trained to just solve similar problems mechanically, given a suitably structured problem). They checked back a year later to see if the students remembered, which they did (compared to college students who had taken a semester of statistics and could remember nothing, nor could they explain "the verbal principle"). The study to follow up to see whether they had continued to grow is yet to come.

CONCLUSIONS

In this chapter, I have proposed that the basic form of conceptual change, particularly the type closely related to everyday learning, is the interaction among inner and outer resources of a learner; the inner being the accumulated and structured knowledge that humans have and the outer being the physical and social environments in which humans live. Initial solutions to problems in the outer world may depend heavily on (or may take full advantage of) what is available in the external and social environment at the given time and space. Different solutions may evolve with the same problem being solved in slightly different situations, particularly so in divergent social groups. People then sort these solutions, to integrate those that are most relevant and promising into a "schema" or some abstracted representation of the solutions, which becomes the solid source for further change of the concepts into scientific ones.

I have also emphasized that collaboration with others is a very assuring source of the variability desirable for natural conceptual change. This is a highly plausible course of learning (though not necessarily an easy one), and studies on the interaction of its process should lead us to a better design of environments that will facilitate productive conceptual change, in school and out, for all the members of the knowledge-creating society.

ACKNOWLEDGMENTS

The writing of this chapter was partly supported by SORST/JSP 2005–2007 and JSPS Grant-in-Aid 15200020 (2004–2006). The author expresses her sincere gratitude to Giyoo Hatano, to whom this volume is dedicated, who encouraged her to write this chapter. She deeply regrets his death.

REFERENCES

Aronson, E., & Patnoe, S. (1997). *The jigsaw classroom: Building cooperation in the classroom.* New York: Longman.

Barwise, J., & Perry, J. (1983). *Situations and attitudes.* Cambridge, M.A: The MIT Press.

Bell, P., Davis, E. A., & Linn, M. C. (1995). The knowledge integration environment: Theory and design. In J. L. Schnase & E. L. Cunnius (Eds.), *Proceedings of the Computer Supported Collaborative Learning Conference '95* (pp. 14–21). Hilsdale, NJ: Erlbaum.

Biswas, G., Schwartz, D. L., Leelawong, K., Vye, N., & TAG-V (2005). Learning by teaching: A new agent paradigm for educational software. *Applied Artificial Intelligence, 19,* 363–392.

Bransford, J., & Schwartz, D. (1999). Rethinking transfer: A simple proposal with multiple implications. In A. Iran-Nejad & P. D. Pearson (Eds.), *Review of research in education* (pp. 61–100). Washington, D.C.: American Educational Research Association.

Brown, A. (1997). Transforming schools into communities of thinking and learning about serious matters. *American Psychologist, 52,* 399–413.

Carey, S. (1985). *Conceptual change in childhood.* Cambridge, MA: MIT Press.

Clement, J. (1982). Student's preconceptions in introductory mechanics. *American Journal of Physics, 50,* 66–71.

Ericsson, K. A., & Simon, H. A. (1980). Verbal reports as data. *Psychological Review, 87,* 215–251.

Ericsson, K. A., & Simon, H. A. (1984). *Protocol analysis: Verbal reports as data.* Cambridge, MA: The MIT Press.

Granott, N., & Parziale, J. (2002). *Microdevelopment: Transition processes in development and learning.* New York: Cambridge University Press.

Greeno, J. G., & MacWhinney, B. (2006). Perspectives in reasoning about quantities. In R. Sun (Ed.), *Proceedings of the 28th annual conference of the Cognitive Science Society* (p. 2495). Mahwah, NJ: Erlbaum.

Greeno, J. G., Sommerfeld, M. C., & Wiebe, M. (2000). Practices of questioning and explaining in learning to model. In L. R. Gleitman & A. K. Joshi (Eds.), *Proceedings of the 22nd annual conference of the Cognitive Science Society* (pp. 669–674). Mahwah, NJ. Erlbaum.

Hall, R. (2000). Work at the interface between representing and represented worlds in middle school mathematics design projects. In W. D. Gray & C. Shunn (Eds.), *Proceedings of the 22nd annual conference of the Cognitive Science Society* (pp. 675–680). Mahwah, NJ: Erlbaum.

Hatano, G. (2005). Neo-Vygotskian theory of learning: Importance of converging intra-mental and inter-mental analyses of conceptual change. Invited talk presented at CSCL05, Taipei, Taiwan.

Hatano, G., & Inagaki, K. (1986). Two courses of expertise. In H. Stevenson, H. Azuma, & K. Hakuta (Eds.), *Child development and education in Japan* (pp. 263–272). New York: Freeman & Co.

Hatano, G., & Inagaki, K. (1991). Sharing cognition through collective comprehension activity. In B. Resnick, J. M. Levine, & S. D. Teasley (Eds.), *Perspectives on socially shared cognition* (pp. 331–348). Washington D.C.: American Psychological Association.

Hatano, G., & Inagaki, K. (2003). When is conceptual change intended? A cognitive-sociocultural view. In G. M. Sinatra & P. R. Pintrich (Eds.), *Intentional conceptual change* (pp. 407–427). Mahwah, NJ: Erlbaum.

Hobbs, J. R., & Evans, D. A. (1980). Conversation as planned behavior. *Cognitive Science, 4,* 349–377.

Inagaki, K., & Hatano, G. (1968). Ninchi-teki kansatsu ni okeru naihatsu-teki doukizuke (Intrinsic motivation in cognitive observation). *Kyoiku Shinrigaku Kenkyu (The Japanese Journal of Educational Psychology), 16,* 191–202. [in Japanese]

Itakura, K. (1997). Kasetsu-Jikken-Jugyo no ABC, Dai 4 han. (*The ABC of the Hypothesis-Experiment-Instruction: Invitation to enjoyable classes, Ver. 4.*) Tokyo: Kasetsu-Sha. [in Japanese]

Keil, F. C. (2003). Folkscience: coarse interpretations of a complex reality. *Trends in Cognitive Science, 7,* 368–373.

Latour, B. (1986). Visualization and cognition: Thinking with eyes and hands. *Knowledge and Society: Studies in the Sociology of Culture, 6,* 1–40.

Linn, M. C., & Hsi, S. (2000). *Computer, teachers, peers*. Mahwah, NJ: Erlbaum.

Miyake, N. (1986). Constructive interaction and the iterative process of understanding. *Cognitive Science*, *10*, 151–177.

Miyake, N. (2005a). Multifaceted outcome of collaborative learning: Call for divergent evaluation. Paper presented at the meeting of the 13th international conference on computers in education (ICCE2005), Singapore.

Miyake, N. (2005b). How can Asian educational psychologists contribute to the advancement of learning sciences? Invited talk at the meeting of the Korean society of educational psychology 2005 International Conference, Seoul, Korea.

Miyake, N. (2007). Computer supported collaborative learning. In R. Andrews & C. Haythornthwaite (Eds.), *The handbook of elearning research* (pp. 248–265). London: Sage.

Miyake, N., Masukawa, H., & Shirouzu, H. (2001). The complex jigsaw as an enhancer of collaborative knowledge building. *Proceedings of European perspectives on computer-supported collaborative learning* (pp. 454–461). Maarstricht, The Netherlands.

Miyake, N., & Shirouzu, H. (2006). A collaborative approach to teach cognitive science to undergraduates: The learning sciences as a means to study and enhance college student learning. *Psychologia*, *18*(2), 101–113.

Miyake, N., Shirouzu, H., & Chukyo Learning Science Group. (2005). The dynamic jigsaw: repeated explanation support for collaborative learning of cognitive science. Paper presented at the meeting of the 27th annual meeting of the cognitive science society, Stresa, Italy.

Motoyoshi, M. (1979). *Watashi no seikatsu hoiku ron* (*My theory of everyday daycare*). Tokyo: Frobel Kan. [in Japanese].

Nerserssian, N. J. (1988). Reasoning from imagery and analogy in scientific concept formation. *PSA*, *1*, 41–47.

Newman, D., Griffin, M., & Cole, M. (1989). *The construction zone: Working for cognitive change in school*. Cambridge: Cambridge University Press.

Nisbett, R. E., & Wilson, T. D. (1977). Telling more than we can know: Verbal reports on mental processes. *Psychological Review*, *84*, 231–259.

Obara, T. (1971). Childen's naïve molecular theoretic ideas. *Kagaku-Kyouiku-Kenkyu* (*Studies in Science Education*), *3*, 99–110. [in Japanese].

O'Conner, C., & Michaels, S. (1996). Shifting participant frameworks: Orchestrating thinking practices in group discussion. In D. Hicks (Ed.), *Discourse, learning and schooling* (pp. 63–103). New York: Cambridge University Press.

Palincsar, A. S., & Brown, A. L. (1984). Reciprocal-teaching of comprehension fostering and monitoring activities. *Cognition and Instruction, 1,* 117–175.

Roschelle, J. (1991). Students' construction of qualitative physics knowledge: Learning about velocity and acceleration in a computer microworld. Unpublished doctoral dissertation, University of California, Berkeley.

Roschelle, J. (1992). Learning by collaboration: convergent conceptual change. *The Journal of the Learning Sciences, 2*, 235–276.

Rozenblit, L., & Keil, F. (2002). The misunderstood limits of folk science: an illusion of explanatory depth. *Cognitive Science, 26,* 521–562.

Scardamalia, M., & Bereiter, C. (1994). Computer support for knowledge-building communities. *Journal of the Learning Sciences, 3,* 265–283.

Scardamalia, M., & Bereiter, C. (2006). Knowledge building: Theory, pedagogy, and technology. In K. R. Sawyer (Ed.), *The Cambridge handbook of the learning sciences* (pp. 97–115). New York: Cambridge University Press.

Schwartz, D. L. (1995). The emergence of abstract representations in dyad problem solving. *The Journal of the Learning Sciences, 4,* 321–354.

Schwartz, D. L., Blair, K. P., Biswas, G., Leelawong, K., & Davis, J. (2007). Animations of thought: Interactivity in the teachable agents paradigm. In R. Lowe & W. Schnotz (Eds.), *Learning with Animation: Research and implications for design* (pp. 114–140). New York: Cambridge University Press.

Schwartz, D. L., Brophy, S., Lin, X. D., & Bransford, J. D. (1999). Software for managing complex learning: An example from an educational psychology course. *Educational Technology Research and Development, 47,* 39–59.

Schwartz, D. L., & Martin, T. (2004). Inventing to prepare for learning: The hidden efficiency of original student production in statistics instruction. *Cognition & Instruction, 22,* 129–184.

Shirouzu, H., & Miyake, N. (2002). Learning by collaborating revisited: Individualistic vs. convergent understanding. *Proceedings of the 24th conference of the Cognitive Science Society*, 1039.

Shirouzu, H., Miyake, N., & Masukawa, H. (2002). Cognitively active externalization for situated reflection. *Cognitive Science, 26,* 469–501.

Shoji, K. (1988). *Kasetsu-Jikken-Jugyou no ro*nri (*Logic of the hypothesis-experiment-instruction*). Tokyo: Meiji-Tosho. [in Japanese].

Sinatra, G. M., & Pintrich, P. R. (2003). *Intentional conceptual change*. Mahwah, NJ: Erlbaum.

Stahl, G., Koschmann, T., & Suthers, D. D. (2006). Computer-supported collaborative learning. In K. R. Sawyer (Ed.), *The Cambridge handbook of the learning sciences* (pp. 409–425). New York: Cambridge University Press..

Stenning, K., Greeno, J. G., Hall, R., Sommerfeld, M., & Wiebe, M. (2002). Coordinating mathematical with biological multiplication: Conceptual learning as the development of heterogeneous reasoning systems. In P. Brna, M. Baker, K. Stenning, & A. Tiberghien (Eds.), *The role of communication in learning to model* (pp. 3–48). Mahwah, NJ: Erlbaum.

Stenning, K., & Sommerfeld, M. (2000). Heterogeneous reasoning in learning to model. *Proceedings of the 22nd conference of the Cognitive Science Society,* 493–498.

Strom, D., Kemeny, V., Lehrer, R., & Forman, E. (2001). Visualizing the emergent structure of children's mathematical argument. *Cognitive Science, 25,* 733–773.

Teasley, S. D., & Roschelle, J. (1993). Constructing a joint problem space: The computer as a tool for sharing knowledge. In S. Lajoie & S. Derry (Eds.), *Computers as cognitive tools* (pp. 229–258). Hillsdale, NJ: Erlbaum.

Vosniadou, S. (2003). Exploring the relationships between conceptual change and intentional learning. In G. M. Sinatra & P. R. Pintrich (Eds.), *Intentional conceptual change* (pp. 377–406). Mahwah, NJ: Erlbaum.

Vosniadou, S. (2007). Conceptual change and education. *Human Development*, *50*, 47–54.

Vosniadou, S., & Ioannides, C. (1998). From conceptual development to science education: A psychological point of view. *International Journal of Science Education*, *20*, 1213–1230.

Williams, M. D., Hollan, J. D., & Stevens, A. L. (1983). Human reasoning about a simple physical system. In D. Gentner & A. L. Stevens (Eds.), *Mental models* (pp. 131–153). Hillsdale, NJ: Erlbaum..

18

Dynamic Transfer and Innovation

Daniel L. Schwartz and Sashank Varma
Stanford University

Lee Martin
University of California at Davis

Conceptual change occurs when people learn a new way to think about a class of situations. There are gradations of conceptual change from the simple accumulation of enriching examples to total conceptual replacement (e.g., Tyson, Venville, Harrison, & Treagust, 1997). The history of science provides instances of grand conceptual change, for example, the discovery that disease is due to germs (Thagard, 1996). Developmental psychology has also noted a number of recurrent conceptual changes, for example, children's developing notion of "alive" (Carey, 1985). Adults too, can experience conceptual change, for example, when becoming parents.

Transfer occurs when people use learning from one situation in another. For example, individuals may transfer learning from school to kitchen and from algebra to chemistry. Transfer is relevant to conceptual change, because new ideas build on a foundation of prior learning. Yet, at the same time, people need to go beyond their original learning to accomplish a conceptual change. The product cycle of Intel, for example, requires a new product release every three months (COSEPUP, 2006). If the chip designers at Intel could not transfer in their prior learning to facilitate the design of new chips, Intel would be too inefficient to keep up with its competitors. At the same time, if the chip designers did not go beyond their prior knowledge, there would be no innovative product designs. Understanding transfer's relation to conceptual change may help create conditions that foster innovation.

Transfer research addresses two challenges for conceptual change: the *knowledge problem* and the *inertia problem*. The knowledge problem asks how prior knowledge can make innovative new knowledge. Through what processes can old concepts of one sort possibly create new concepts of another sort? The transfer literature proposes two different solutions called *similarity transfer* and *dynamic transfer*. In similarity transfer, people apply well-formed concepts from one situation to explain another situation in a novel way. For example, people often use causal explanations for the "sophomore slump" in sports, where rookies who excel in their first season do worse the next year (e.g., early success led to complacency). By transferring in their knowledge of statistics, people may reconceptualize the drop in performance as an instance of regression to the mean. In dynamic transfer, the context helps people coordinate component abilities to create a novel concept in the first place. Thelen and Smith (1994), for example, describe how infants learn to coordinate their physical actions of looking and reaching, which leads to the development of object permanence (the appreciation that an object is still there even though one may not see it). We describe the two forms of transfer more fully below.

While the knowledge problem asks how people change concepts, the inertia problem addresses why people do not always do so. Transfer is a double-edged sword for change. People can transfer in prior learning to support change, but they can also transfer in routines that prevent change. In Luchins and Luchins' (1959) classic studies of *einstellung*, or rigidity of behavior, people learned a complex method for measuring water using several jars in sequence. Once they had mastered the multi-jar method, they received simpler problems that could be solved more efficiently with only one or two jars. People transferred the complex method and never considered searching for an alternative.

The inertia problem highlights the tension between using, yet going beyond prior learning. An excellent example comes from children learning fractions. Children could hardly learn to compare two-out-of-three wins versus four-out-of-seven wins, if they had never learned about natural numbers. New ideas do not arise in a vacuum. At the same time, children have difficulty interpreting "2/3" as a ratio. Instead, they interpret the "2" and "3" as natural numbers (Kerslake, 1986). They overrely on their well-practiced and well-understood natural number schema.

The inertia problem asks what conditions lead people to transfer for change rather than repetition. Before people have made a conceptual innovation, it is hard to know whether it is worth pursuing — people cannot know the concept before they have it. Moreover, people's prior learning typically yields routines that are good enough for getting by. Consequently, people often do not recognize, seek, or risk alternatives. Similarity and dynamic transfer provide different routes by which people can overcome the problem of inertia. In the final section of the chapter, we consider the inertia problem in the context of creating educational experiences that can help people transfer the idea of being innovative.

To develop the relation between transfer and innovation, the chapter relies on two sets of empirical examples. One set involves mathematics. We choose mathematics because it has been an important focal point for testing theories of transfer. Mathematics, like logic, is general and widely applicable across many domains, but people do not always transfer mathematics when relevant. Moreover, the development of mathematical reasoning depends on many conceptual changes, such as the shift from counting whole quantities to working with ratios. Thus, mathematics is an ideal content area for examining the mechanisms of transfer for innovation. Our second set of examples involves tools, including physical and representational tools. Whereas mathematics leads us to focus on conceptual innovations, tools lead us to focus on material innovations.

The first section sketches the relations between innovation, conceptual change, and transfer. The second section offers a brief review of similarity transfer, which has been the primary focus of transfer research. From there, the chapter moves into new terrain. The third section consolidates a number of findings to introduce dynamic transfer and argue for its relevance to both transfer and conceptual change. The final section discusses the inertia problem by introducing a representation of context that helps delineate different trajectories that do and do not lead to conceptual change.

INNOVATION AND TRANSFER

Transfer is unique among the many approaches to conceptual change, because transfer is intimately concerned with the context of cognition. Transfer research tries to explain why people can retrieve and change their ideas in some contexts, but not others. In his illuminating discussion on the evolving concept of disease, Thagard (1996) concludes, "A full theory of conceptual change must integrate its representational, referential, and social aspects" (p. 477). By referential, Thagard means how concepts interact with context, as opposed to how concepts are represented. Here, we address the referential aspects of conceptual change. In fact, we broaden the discussion of conceptual change to include structural changes to the environment, which can feed back and change people's mental representations. To avoid diluting the term *conceptual change*, we adopt the broader term *innovation*, which can refer to new ideas and new material structures.

The strength of the transfer literature for innovation is in its explication of how people and contexts interact to achieve an innovation. Unlike the conceptual change literature, a precise definition of a conceptual change or innovation is not central to the transfer literature. Nevertheless, it is useful to have a working definition, so we propose *prior inconceivability* and *generativity* as criteria for innovations.

Prior inconceivability means that the changes that result from an innovation could not be prefigured prior to the change. For example, for children who have already learned two-digit addition, learning three-digit addition is a conceivable extension. For children who have only learned addition, comparing ratios is incomprehensible. Learning to do so would constitute an innovation. Generativity means that innovations can extend beyond the specific situations and problems that led to their initial development. For example, a fully developed concept of ratio can extend to quantities that did not appear in the conditions of original learning — from fractions to proportions and percentages.

The term *innovation* can refer to an outcome or to a process. Innovative outcomes come at two scales. Grand innovations are those which are novel on a global scale, and which were previously unknown to most everyone, such as the telephone and the theory of evolution. Petite innovations are local and new to a given person. Over history, many different people can achieve the same petite innovation. For example, most children learn that the amount of water in wide glass does not change when poured into a narrow glass, even though the visual height changes. The prevalence of this "conservation" concept does not diminish the innovative value of the concept for any one child.

The process of innovation refers to the mechanisms involved in restructuring thought or the environment. The process of innovation applies to both grand and petite innovations. This is important, because grand innovations are rare events, and their low frequency and unpredictability make it hard to develop an empirically grounded account of innovation (Johnson-Laird, 1989). However, because petite innovations regularly recur across people, it is possible to study the processes of these innovations. Ideally, findings from research on petite innovations can help create conditions for grand innovation. One important goal of education is to make the next generation of innovators — innovators who can make petite innovations in response to a rapidly changing world, and those who can make grand innovations that rapidly change the world.

Transfer mechanisms are relevant to the process of innovation, because they enable the application of prior learning for the purposes of innovation. The main body of transfer research has not examined how mechanisms of transfer support innovation. Detterman (1993), for example, defined transfer as "the degree to which a new behavior will be repeated in a new situation" (p. 4). Replicating a behavior is quite different from innovating a new one. Transfer research has typically focused on the transfer of prior knowledge or behavior to improve speed and accuracy on a novel task (Schwartz, Bransford, & Sears, 2005). Bassok and Holyoak (1989), for instance, taught students an algorithm to compute arithmetic progressions. Half of the students learned the algorithm as a math lesson and half as a physics lesson. Students who received the algorithm in the math lesson were more likely to transfer it to a new problem domain (e.g., finances). Students who did not transfer the algorithm could still solve the new problem. They were just slower, because they used an iterative technique. Their use of an inefficient method indicated they had failed to transfer. Asking how people become more efficient by repetition is different from asking how people innovate by building on prior knowledge. Nevertheless, there is research on transfer that is relevant to innovation, which we describe next.

SIMILARITY TRANSFER AND THE KNOWLEDGE PROBLEM

Processes of Innovation and Similarity Transfer

In similarity transfer, people already possess well-formed prior knowledge developed for one situation, and they use this knowledge to understand a different situation in a new way. For example, scientists might learn to view traffic congestion in terms of their knowledge of fluid dynamics. The conceptual change does not occur to their existing knowledge of fluid dynamics; rather, they change their concept of freeway congestion. We call this similarity transfer, because the key move involves recognizing that two situations or ideas are similar, even though they may not appear so at first.

Similarity transfer occurs when people realize that what they learned for one situation can be used for another situation. Similarity transfer depends on well-formed prior knowledge. Many purported demonstrations of failed transfer actually were not failed transfer — people never learned the concepts or skills to start with, so there was no way they could fail to transfer. A genuine failure of similarity transfer occurs when people have "inert knowledge" (Whitehead, 1929). Inert knowledge is a description of the situation where people have relevant knowledge but do not spontaneously apply it. The field has made several important discoveries about the types of experiences and knowledge structures that help people avoid inert knowledge. These include the opportunity to discern commonalities and differences using multiple examples (e.g., Gick & Holyoak, 1983; Schwartz & Bransford, 1998), explicate the general principal behind the examples (e.g., Brown & Kane, 1988), and experience the problem for which the transferable knowledge would be the solution (e.g., Bransford, Franks, Vye, & Sherwood, 1989).

In similarity transfer, people have knowledge gained in one context that is sufficient for application to another. The question is whether they will use that knowledge in the new context. To make the transfer, people need to detect the similarity between one situation and another. One type of similarity occurs at the level of perceptual *surface features* or "identical elements" (Thorndike & Woodworth, 1901). Chi, Feltovich, and Glaser (1981), for example, reported that undergraduates taking introductory physics classified problems by surface features (e.g., pulley problems, spring-mass problems). A focus on surface features can cause individuals to transfer the wrong ideas across problems. For example, the undergraduates would likely *fail* to transfer solutions across spring and pulley problems, because they see them as unrelated. They are also likely to exhibit the *negative* transfer of a solution from one pulley problem to another, even if the problems do not involve the same principles (cf., Ross, 1989).

A second type of similarity involves identical relations or *deep features*. For example, in contrast to undergraduates, the physics graduate students in Chi, Feltovich, and Glaser's (1981) study classified spring and pulley problems according to the underlying principles needed to solve the problems. The graduate students could appreciate that the relations between the objects within each problem involved the same principles, even though they looked quite different. When people can recognize relational or structural similarities, they are able to make the transfer across situations that have surface level differences. For example, they can transfer principles from pulley to spring problems (when appropriate).

Similarity transfer, particularly when the nature of the similarity is relational, can support innovation. The most extensively studied use of similarity transfer for innovation comes from studies of *analogical transfer* (for representative studies on analogical transfer see Gick & Holyoak, 1983; Reed, Ernst, & Banerji, 1974). Kepler managed to develop his theory of planetary motion by drawing an analogy from the light of the sun (Gentner, Brem, Ferguson, Markman, Levidow, Wolff, & Forbus, 1997). He posited that the sun projected a force to the planets in a similar manner that light emanated from the sun. From there, he further drew an analogy between the amount of light that reached a planet through its movement and the amount of force that kept it in place. This is an example of a grand innovation. Kepler's introduction of the concept of force explained elliptical orbits. Kepler's innovation was also generative. His theory could predict orbits of planets wherever they might be, so it went beyond the specific instances he worked with.

Researchers often distinguish *near* and *far* transfer, which is another way of stating the experienced similarity of two situations (for factors that affect experienced similarity, see Barnett & Ceci, 2002). Generally speaking, transfer based on surface features is considered near, and transfer based on deep features is considered far. Innovations, almost by definition, depend on far transfer. If the transfer were too near, then it would not illuminate a different situation in a novel way.

Another useful distinction involves *spontaneous* and *prompted* transfer. Instructors can often prompt far transfer by introducing analogies that help students innovate new (to them) concepts. For example, an instructor might use the analogy of water in a pipe to explain the invisible processes of electricity. In contrast, spontaneous transfer occurs when people make the analogy themselves without any external support. Using an analogy to help explain a concept to someone else is quite different from learners spontaneously generating the analogy on their own. Spontaneous, self-directed transfer across highly different domains or contexts is infrequent (Detterman, 1993). It took Kepler a lifetime to work out the analogy between light and gravity.

One possible reason that spontaneous and innovative far transfers are infrequent is that people often do not have enough knowledge about a second domain. Scholars, for example, often have very precise knowledge about the topic for which an innovation would be useful. However, they may not have sufficient expertise in any other domains to generate candidate analogies. The analogies they can generate from other domains will not have sufficient precision and structure to map into the complexity of the situations they are trying to explain.

If we expand the unit of analysis for similarity transfer beyond the individual, we find more instances of innovation. Biologists, for example, have extremely detailed knowledge about the problems they need to solve and the constraints on what would make a good solution. Dunbar (1997) found that biology labs have computer programs that help scientists generate candidate analogies. The biologists enter specific characteristics of the biological compounds and interactions they are trying to understand, and the computer program generates homologs (i.e., other biological structures that have similar properties), and the biologist can draw the analogy between the homologs to see if they work. A second example comes from companies that use on-line programs to solicit analogies from different disciplines (Feller, Fitzgerald, Hissam, & Lakhani, 2005). For example, a pharmaceutical company might post a drug compound that has side effects they cannot explain. People from other disciplines can look at the posting. If they can generate a solution, the company might pay them for it. For example, a mathematician might recognize the drug problem as an instance of mathematical knot theory.

Similarity Transfer as a Measure of Innovative Outcomes

The term *transfer* has two uses. Thus far, we have described transfer as a mechanism that leads to an innovative process. Transfer can also mean a transfer task specifically designed to measure outcomes.[1] Transfer tasks are useful because they can measure the generality of an innovative outcome or conceptual change. For example, if a child shows conservation of liquid, measures of transfer allow us to ask whether the conservation concept extends to the conservation of solids (e.g., a ball of clay that thins as it stretches).

Similarity transfer uses a specific task structure to measure learning outcomes. Bransford and Schwartz (1999) called this type of measure Sequestered Problem Solving (SPS). In SPS assessments of transfer, people receive a new problem without any resources or interactive opportunities to learn. The assessment detects the robustness and generality of people's learning. SPS measures provide a useful index for evaluating a purported conceptual change. We consider two kinds of conceptual change — *global* and *domain-specific*.

Global conceptual changes are the result of broad cognitive reorganizations that necessarily transfer across all relevant situations. A simple analogy can be drawn to the literature on perceptual development. As infants develop binocular vision over the first weeks of life, their brain reorganizes to see the world in depth, and children subsequently see depth in all contexts. Similar arguments have been made about conceptual changes that involve reasoning. Piaget (1952), in particular, argued that children go through a series of stages that involve increasingly complex reasoning structures. Once children achieve a particular stage in their reasoning, they will see the world in those terms. For example, one important development is the ability to conserve quantities. An example of conservation involves knowing that an amount of clay does not change, even as one stretches it from a ball into a long rope. To test the claim that the ability to conserve is a global change, one would use SPS measures to see if children transfer conservation across a number of diverse tasks, such as when water is poured from a wide glass into a narrow one. If children fail to transfer conservation across problems, then the claim that there is a global conceptual change fails.

Transfer tasks can also illuminate domain-specific changes. Researchers can learn about the generality and precision of a concept by seeing how far it transfers. For example, very young children develop a rudimentary concept of aliveness (Keil, 1989), an instance being the development of the distinction between inanimate and dead (Carey, 1985). What is the nature of children's concepts? Some authors propose that children's early concepts have a theoretical quality, in the sense there are causal coherence, underlying abstractions, and sensitivity to negative evidence (Gopnick & Meltzoff, 1997). Okita and Schwartz (2006) examined this proposition by using SPS transfer tasks. They asked 3- to 5-year-olds questions that probed whether robotic dogs were alive. It was an SPS assessment because the children had no opportunity to learn during the assessment, for example, by interacting with the robots to get further information. The researchers showed children a dancing robotic dog and asked questions including whether it felt hunger, whether it would run away if there were a fire, whether it could "wake-up" without a remote control, and so forth.

Three-year-old children extended the concept of alive to the robotic dogs by giving the same answers they give for regular dogs. These younger children also extended the concept of alive to stuffed animals. In contrast, 5-year-olds did not extend all aspects of alive to the robotic dogs or stuffed animals. They believed the robotic dogs needed a remote control and would not grow, but they still thought the robotic dogs felt hunger and would wake up in a fire. These older children were also less likely to indicate attributes of aliveness for stuffed animals. By measuring what children spontaneously transferred to make sense of the robotic dogs, the researchers found that children began with an undifferentiated concept of alive that did not exclude anything with surface features resembling dogs. Thus, the concept was not a theory in the sense of being applied differentially to empirical situations. Moreover, with development, the children's concept of alive changed in piecemeal fashion, rather than exhibiting the coherence of a true theory. The researchers concluded that children's concept of alive was more script-like than theory-like. That is, children recalled interaction scripts with living things, and this led to the organization of their attributions of alive. For example, older children knew the script for using remote controls, so they merged this script into their other scripts for interacting with pets (e.g., feeding them).

Similarity measures of transfer that use SPS assessments can reveal the nature of people's concepts and the outcomes of intellectual innovation. However, SPS assessments are not ideal for measuring the process of conceptual change, because they do not include opportunities to learn and change during the assessment. Below, we describe a different measure of transfer that is more suited to evaluating the process of innovation.

DYNAMIC TRANSFER AND THE KNOWLEDGE PROBLEM

The Processes of Innovation and Dynamic Transfer

Dynamic transfer tries to explain how prior knowledge can create concepts that did not previously exist. While similarity transfer explains how people map well-formed concepts to structure new situations, it does not explain how initial concepts develop in the first place. In dynamic transfer, people bring component competencies and situations into coordination to learn a new concept. Dynamic transfer is one of many different mechanisms by which people learn new ideas. Dynamic transfer has not been the focus of traditional transfer research, which has instead focused on similarity transfer. Although dynamic transfer is different from traditional investigations of transfer and seeks to explain different phenomena, we still maintain the label transfer for three reasons. The first is that it depends on reusing prior knowledge in new contexts, which is the hallmark of transfer. The second reason is that the term is already in use by physics educators who have been working on the challenge of changing students' intuitive physical concepts into normative physics concepts (e.g., Dufresne, Mestre, Thaden-Koch, Gerace, & Leonard, 2005; diSessa & Wagner, 2005; Hammer, Elby, Scherr, & Redish, 2005; Mestre, 1994; Rebellow, Zollman, Allbaugh, Englehardt, Gray, Hrepic, & Itza-Ortiz, 2005). The third reason is that there are a number of critics of similarity transfer who have urged a broader consideration of how the environment, which includes social and physical aspects, helps people coordinate productive actions (e.g., Carraher & Schliemann, 2002; Greeno, Smith, & Moore, 1993; Hutchins, 1995; Pea, 1993; Suchman, 1987). We agree with these investigators that similarity transfer does not address these considerations, but we do not think this is sufficient reason to abandon the many important findings and theories from similarity transfer. By juxtaposing dynamic and similarity transfer, we want to emphasize that they are not mutually exclusive or opposing theoretical camps. They are simply different mechanisms of innovation, and both can be at play in the same innovation, as we describe in the final section on learning to be innovative.

There are a number of distinctions between similarity and dynamic transfer. The first involves the prior knowledge that precipitates the transfer. Similarity transfer depends on well-formed prior knowledge, so people can re-conceptualize the new situation in terms of the prior knowledge. In contrast, dynamic transfer depends on component knowledge, skills, or abilities that become well-formed during the process of transfer.

The second distinction involves the crux move in achieving the transfer. In similarity transfer this involves seeing that "this is like that," while dynamic transfer involves seeing that "this goes with that." Similarity transfer hinges on detecting the similarity between situations so people can apply their ideas. Dynamic transfer hinges on coordinating systems that may be quite dissimilar.

The third distinction involves the role of the context in causing transfer. In similarity transfer, the environment cues the retrieval of intact prior knowledge. In dynamic transfer, the environment coordinates different components of prior knowledge through interaction. It is important to note that similarity transfer includes a period of "mapping" — once people have a candidate analogy, they figure out which parts of the analogy work for the target situation (Gentner et al., 1997). Mapping differs from coordination; dynamic coordination depends on an environment that provides feedback and/or structuring resources to join ideas together. In contrast, mapping similarities can occur in thought alone.

Before discussing dynamic transfer in more detail, we offer two examples. The interactive process of dynamic transfer often has the quality of trial and error, and it can look highly inefficient. However, when coupled with the right resources, the interactions may result in a coordination that can be an innovation. In the first example, interactions with the material world lead to an innovation in symbolic thought. In the second example, interactions with symbols lead to an innovation in thinking about the material world.

Two Examples of Dynamic Transfer

Our first example of dynamic transfer involves 9- and 10-year-old children learning to add simple fractions like 1/4 + 1/2 (Martin & Schwartz, 2005). Half of the children learned using pie pieces and half learned with tile pieces, as shown in Figure 18.1. After instruction, both groups could solve the problems using their respective materials, but they could not solve the problems in their heads. For the transfer task, the children received similar fraction addition problems, but they had to use novel materials (e.g., beans, fraction bars). The question was how the children from the two conditions would transfer their prior learning to work with the new materials. The Tile students exhibited a successful dynamic transfer, and the Pie students exhibited a failed similarity transfer.

Figure 18.2 provides a schematic of the two courses of transfer for the Tile and Pie children. The vertical dimension indicates how frequently children gave accurate verbal answers; for example, given the problem 1/2 + 1/4, they state "three-fourths." The horizontal dimension indicates how frequently the children arranged the physical materials correctly; for example, for 1/2 + 1/4, the children arrange the one-half as two groups with two pieces each. The arrows indicate the average trajectory of learning over time for the two groups.

The Tile children showed a stable trajectory that ended in the top right corner of near-perfect verbal and physical performance. The Tile children first improved in how they structured the physical materials, before they began to give the correct symbolic answers. They exhibited a dynamic transfer, because their interactions with the environment helped them slowly coordinate their (verbal) understanding. In contrast, the Pie children did not reach high levels of accuracy on either dimension, nor were they stable: they often regressed from one trial to the next. In addition, unlike the Tile children, the Pie children were better at giving verbal answers than arranging the

FIGURE 18.1   Pie wedges and tiles often used to teach children fractions. The pies exhibit a part-whole structure. In contrast, to turn the three tiles into three-fourths, it is necessary to impose structure, for example, by adding a fourth tile to the side.

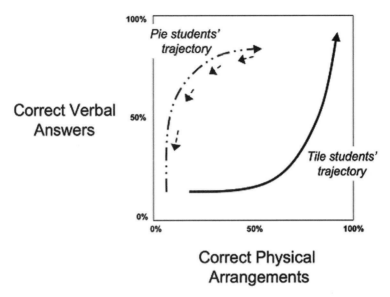

FIGURE 18.2   Two trajectories of transfer (adapted from Martin & Schwartz, 2005).

materials. What explains the poor performance of the Pie children? During their initial learning, they had implicitly relied on the part-whole structure of the pies, and the new materials did not exhibit the circular whole. These children could not make a dynamic transfer through interaction, because they had never explicitly learned to impose a whole to turn discrete elements into fractions — they always got the whole "for free" when working with the pies. So, instead of completing a dynamic transfer, they attempted a similarity transfer by trying to remember how they solved similar prior problems, and they could not use the structure of the novel materials to help them learn.

Our second example involves a dynamic transfer where children interact with the symbols of mathematics. Figure 18.3 provides an instance of a balance scale problem used in the research (Schwartz, Martin, & Pfaffman, 2005). The children needed to answer how the balance scale behaves when the hand lets go. Children under 12 typically solve the problem by focusing on the weights or distances, but not both. For example, they might say that it will tilt to the left, because there are more weights on the left side, or it will tilt to the right, because the weights are farther out on the right side. The children do not coordinate the two dimensions of weight and distance simultaneously, and therefore, they cannot infer that the scale will balance. Learning to

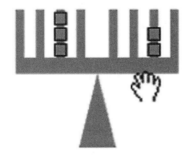

FIGURE 18.3   A balance scale problem. When the hand is removed, will the balance scale tilt left or right, or will it balance?

think about two dimensions simultaneously heralds an important innovation in how children can reason about many complex situations.

Children from 9- to 11-years-old solved a series of increasingly complicated problems. For each problem, they made a prediction about what would happen, and they had to type in a justification for their prediction. They then saw the correct answer. The critical manipulation was that half of the children were told to justify their answers using words. The other half of the children were told to justify their answers using math. The motivation behind this contrast was that the Math children might transfer in their knowledge of math to help coordinate and structure their thinking about the scale. The idea that the developing child, like a scientist, might be able to use mathematics, diagrams, and other explicit representations to discover and organize complex empirical relations comes from Vygotsky's (1987) foundational insight that cultural forms mediate development. The current experimental manipulation examined the significance of mathematics, a cultural form, in helping children develop complex physical knowledge about balance.

Children in the Word condition did not make much headway. They typically justified an answer based on one dimension, for example, "More weight." If they saw they had the wrong answer, they would switch to the other dimension, for example, "More distance." The Math children, in contrast, progressively learned to consider both dimensions simultaneously. Here is a prototypical sample of responses for a 10- to 11-year-old. At first, the child justified her answer with "$3 > 2$," focusing on only one dimension. Later, on a new problem, the child wrote, "$3 + 3 = 4 + 2$." She was considering both dimensions of information and all four of the relevant parameters simultaneously (two weights and two distances). When she saw that she made the wrong prediction, her justification shifted to "$3 - 3 < 4 - 2$." Mathematics provided candidates for structuring the problems, so she could switch from addition to subtraction. After a few more struggles, this child discovered that multiplication works, and she was able to solve all the subsequent problems (e.g., $4 \times 3 = 3 \times 4$).

In a posttest, the Word children performed just like other children their age. Only 36% of the 10- to 11-year-old Word children tried to solve the problems by considering both dimensions. In contrast, 95% of the 10- to 11-year-old Math children considered both dimensions in their answers. Results from the 9-year-old Math children are particularly relevant for distinguishing similarity and dynamic transfer. Very few of the 9-year-olds discovered the correct solution, so they never developed a mathematical formula for solving the problem. This means they never succeeded in seeing the similarity between the balance scale and multiplication structures. Nevertheless, 86% of the Math 9-year-olds reasoned about two dimensions simultaneously on the posttest. A common line of reasoning for these children was, "This side has more weight, but this side is closer." Even though the younger children did not find the similarity between multiplication equations and the balance scale, in the process of dynamically transferring math, they learned a more complex, qualitative way to approach this physical system.

Examples of Coordination and Innovation

A nagging question for conceptual change asks, "Where do new concepts come from?" Theories of similarity transfer have difficulty answering this question. Through the mechanisms of similarity transfer, new concepts arise by building bridges between existing concepts, allowing one concept to inform another. However, if we only entertain similarity transfer, then all new concepts are links between existing concepts, and it is impossible to break out of this closed system to create something genuinely new. Theories of dynamic transfer are better suited to answer the question of where new concepts come from, as the coordination of different systems or bodies of knowledge can yield innovations that are more than the sum of their parts. Dynamic transfer can create new "coordination classes" (diSessa & Wagner, 2005). By examining how basic components can combine to give rise to more complex concepts, we can begin to understand how new concepts arise. We provide examples from three domains: machine learning, animal learning, and human learning.

A suggestive example comes from early work on connectionist networks. Connectionist networks showed impressive learning, but they soon ran into a problem that required the network to undergo a "conceptual change." Early models used two layers of nodes. When a stimulus is presented to the input nodes, the network gives the response on the output nodes. The network learns by adjusting the strength of the associations among the input and output nodes. These two-layer networks could learn to reason about conjunctions and disjunctions of stimuli, but they could not simultaneously learn to handle exclusive disjunctions (A or B, but not both; Papert, 1988). No amount of learning enabled the connectionist networks to make the conceptual change necessary to reason about exclusive disjunctions. Later, researchers solved the problem by interspersing a third (so-called "hidden") layer to coordinate the input and output layers (Rumelhart, Hinton, & Williams, 1986). With the added layer and appropriate feedback during learning, the system learned to compute conjunctions, disjunctions, and exclusive disjunctions. Thus, by coordinating the two layers with a third layer that had the same structure as the first two layers, the system was able to exhibit a "conceptual change."

A second example comes from work with Macaque monkeys. Macaques do not exhibit tool use in the wild. They have no "innate" concept of tool. Ishibashi, Hihara, Takahashi, Heike, Yokota, and Iriki (2002) successfully trained a monkey to use a small rake to retrieve food. Afterwards, the scientists gave the monkey a transfer task. The monkey received a rake that was too short to reach the food, but it was long enough to reach a longer rake that could not be grabbed directly. The monkey used the short rake to grab the long rake, and then used the long rake to grab the food. The monkey had developed a sufficiently general "concept" of "reaching-tool" that it could think to see whether the long rake could achieve the goal. When the scientists examined the brain of the monkey, they found a set of rich neuronal projections that connected visual and motor regions. Macaques do not normally have such extensive projections (though humans do). However, they do have a latent gene that can express the neurotransmitters for growing such projections, enabling the coordination of these brain regions. The external pressure of trying to use the tool to retrieve the food caused the gene to express itself, and enabled the monkey to coordinate its visual and motor systems. The monkey coordinated two pre-existing neural systems to develop a "concept" of tool.

A third example comes from Case and colleagues who examined how children developed a robust concept of natural numbers (e.g., Case & Okamoto, 1996). He theorized that young children need to coordinate a number of distinct systems. For example, infants (and animals) have the ability to make magnitude comparisons of perceptual input such as loud and soft, bright and dim. Infants (and some animals) also demonstrate another perceptual system that individuates small sets of objects (subitizing; Trick & Pylyshyn, 1994). Case proposed that systems like these served as the building blocks of the concept of number, such that a child can understand that 5 is a greater magnitude than 3, and that 5 refers to the count of objects in a set. Case hypothesized that some children have not coordinated these distinct systems into a central conceptual structure of number. Although each system was relatively robust in isolation, the lack of integration prevented children from having a solid concept of number, which in turn led to mathematical difficulties. For example, Griffin, Case, and Siegler (1994) found children who could add 2 + 4 but did not know that the answer 6 was larger than the addends. These children were at risk for school failure, because they had not developed an integrated concept of number.

Based on his hypothesis, Case and colleagues created a curriculum called RightStart where students played a number of board games designed to help coordinate different systems that feed into the adult concept of number. For example, the children would count a number of steps on the game board and compare the total number of steps with another value, which helped them relate the ordinal (fifth step) and cardinal (five total) meanings of number. The at-risk children who played these games for several months ended up equivalent to their peers who were not at risk. Interestingly, matched children who completed more traditional remediation did not show strong gains in their core concept of number. By hypothesis, this is because they did not coordinate different aspects of number. For example, children in traditional math programs simply counted but did not compare magnitudes of the counts in the same activity. More recent brain-based research is further exploring the hypothesis that the development of the concept of number depends on coordinating different perceptual systems (e.g., Butterworth, 1999).

In each of the three preceding examples, innovations in thought resulted from the coordination of lower-level systems. We view these as examples of dynamic transfer, because they unified competencies originally developed for another purpose or historical context. Some might object to viewing these as examples of transfer, because transfer often refers to the transfer of knowledge (as opposed to systems). However, this difference is simply one of disciplinary perspective. In Case's formulation, he did not describe the component abilities that feed into the concept of number as perceptual systems. Rather, he described them as ordinal and cardinal knowledge about quantity. Dynamic transfer involves the coordination of different sources of functional behavior, whether they are mental, social, and physical systems or different types of knowledge states and abilities.

The Significance of Interactive Experiences for Innovation and Dynamic Transfer

Dynamic transfer depends on the environment to support coordination. We highlight four characteristics of environments and how they can support innovation. We emphasize characteristics of the environment to rebalance the transfer literature, which has tended to emphasize internal processes of transfer. Nevertheless, it is important to remember throughout this discussion that we cannot fully ascribe the processes of dynamic transfer to the structure of the environment. People need to engage the environment in ways that lead to innovation. If people have performance goals that stress immediate efficiency, they can block useful exploration into the larger structure of the situation and minimize learning (Vollmeyer, Burns, & Holyoak, 1996). In contrast, a playful attitude allows people to explore new ways of interaction that can yield innovations. Hatano and Inagaki (1986) argued that if the risk attached to the performance of a procedure is minimal, people are more inclined to experiment and adapt new ways of doing things, noting that "when a procedural skill is performed primarily to obtain rewards, people are reluctant to risk varying the skills, since they believe safety lies in relying on the 'conventional' version" (p. 269). Adaptive experts may recuse themselves from high-pressure situations, so they can work out new ways of doing things at lower risk. Examples include superstar athletes who continue to change their repertoire in the off-season or professors who take sabbaticals to learn new skills. More generally, the structure of the environment is a necessary component for dynamic transfer, but people still need to transfer in attitudes, values, and other remnants of prior experience that determine whether they will engage (or change) the environment in productive ways. We say more about this when we turn to the inertia problem.

Distributed Memory

The first reason the environment of interaction is valuable is that people have limited working memories, and it is hard to coordinate a jumble of concepts without distributing some of the work to the environment. This is not to say that people cannot do important intellectual work without interacting in the environment. Self-explanation, for example, is a powerful way for people to check for inconsistencies in their understanding (Chi, de Leeuw, Chiu, & LaVancher, 1994). Thought experiments, such as Maxwell's demon, Schrödinger's cat, and Searle's Chinese room, are an example of this. People also have powerful imaginations that enable them to reconfigure spatial relations into novel structures (Finke, 1990). Kekule famously proposed the structure of the benzene ring after imagining a snake seizing its own tale. Even so, it is difficult to use purely internal processes to coordinate new ideas during dynamic transfer. An important property of the external world is that it can store intermediate structures. Architects, for example, sketch designs to help the process of conceptualizing a new design (Goel, 1995). We suspect that one of the important conceptual changes in meta-cognition involves learning when and how to use the environment to amplify thinking and memory in ways that lead to innovation.

An example of how alleviating memory demands supports discovery comes from research by Zhang and Norman (1994). These authors had people solve variants of the Tower of Hanoi puzzle, which involves moving a stack of disks, one-by-one, from one peg to another. Zhang and Norman created variants of the Tower of Hanoi task that eased the burden of remembering the rules of the task. For example, one rule is that a larger disk cannot be placed on a smaller one. By replacing the disks of different sizes with cups of different sizes, people did not have to remember the abstract verbal rule, because the environmental constraints (cups fitting into each other) enforced the rule. Participants who received the cup version of the task were more effective at innovating an efficient algorithm for solving the Tower of Hanoi problem.

Distributed memory is a particularly powerful support for innovation in young children. Piaget (1976) conducted the first developmental research with the Tower of Hanoi task. He found that 5- and 6-year-old children could not solve simple problems involving as few as two disks. Klahr and Robinson (1981) reasoned that this was due to the challenge of remembering the task rules. They constructed a version of the Tower of Hanoi quite similar to Zhang and Norman's (1994), for example, replacing disks with cups so that the children did not have to remember the ordering rules. As a result, 6-year-old children were able to innovate solutions for problems with as many as three cups requiring as many as five moves.

External changes that leave a trail also support backtracking. Similarity transfer, as the act of an individual mind, often has an all-or-nothing quality. If people make a far transfer that does not succeed, they can learn why the analogy did not work. But, they need to start over looking for a new analogy. In contrast, dynamic transfer is an iterative process: a sequence of near transfers that accumulate into innovations. When the process of dynamic transfer hits a dead end, people can backtrack, unrolling near transfers by looking at a record in the environment, until a choice point is reached and another possible trajectory revealed and pursued. For example, the Math children who were learning the balance scale often made faulty predictions, even late in the learning session. When a prediction failed, they changed their justifications. They did not start over by considering only weight or distance. They maintained their use of two dimensions of information and changed the mathematical operators.

Alternative Interpretations and Feedback

The second reason that interactive experiences are valuable is that they can help people let go of pre-existing ideas that can block innovation. One obstacle to innovation is that prior interpretations can transfer in and interfere with developing new interpretations. Bruner and Potter (1964), for example, asked people to view pictures of common objects (e.g., a dog, silverware). The pictures were initially blurry and the experimenters slowly brought them into focus. The researchers measured how much focus the participants required before they could name the object

FIGURE 18.4   Duck/rabbit image used in many experiments (e.g., Chambers & Reisberg, 1985).

of the picture. The researchers found that a high level of initial blurriness and a slow rate of focusing interfered with people's abilities to identify the pictures. Under these conditions, participants needed more focus before they could name the picture. The authors' explanation was that people formed interpretations of the initial pictures and had a hard time letting go of them. The blurrier the initial photo, the worse their initial interpretations. Moreover, the slower the focusing, the more entrenched participants became in their original interpretation. This study is often cited by philosophers of science as evidence that existing hypotheses can blind scientists to novel interpretations of the data (e.g., Greenwald, Pratkanis, Leippe, & Baumgardner, 1986). Here, it illustrates how initial interpretations can interfere with the development of alternative ways of seeing.

Interactions with the environment generate feedback and variability that can help people shake free of their initial interpretations. Chambers and Reisberg (1985) studied how prior interpretations can interfere with developing new ones. The researchers asked people to look at a picture that can be seen as a duck or a rabbit (e.g., Figure 18.4). Once people had an interpretation, they closed their eyes. Chambers and Reisberg asked the people if they could come up with a second interpretation. Could they overcome their original interpretation (e.g., duck) and see a second interpretation (e.g., rabbit)? Not a single participant over several studies could do the reinterpretation. They were stuck with their first interpretation. However, if people are allowed to open their eyes and jiggle the picture a bit, they can find the alternative interpretation.

A second example of the value of interaction comes from a study by Martin and Schwartz (2005). They asked 9-year-olds to solve equivalent fraction problems, for example, "What is one-fourth of eight?" Children received eight small plastic tiles and had to indicate their answers. When children could only look at the pieces without touching, they tended to indicate one and/or four pieces as the answer. They mapped the pieces in one-to-one fashion to the numerals "1" and "4" of the fraction 1/4. They were interpreting the problem with their prior concept of natural number. However, when children could push the pieces around, they were nearly four times more successful. By moving the pieces, the children began to notice grouping structures. They discovered new mathematical interpretations of the tiles, including that it is possible to make "4" groups where each ("1") group has two pieces. The children were on their way to innovating a new understanding of rational number.

Candidate Structure

The third reason interactivity is highly important for innovation is that the environment constrains and structures possible actions. This point was made forcibly by Simon (1969), who introduced the metaphor of an ant walking on a beach to a food source. To the external observer, the ant appears to be engaged in a sophisticated representational process of navigation while keeping in mind the goal of obtaining food. Simon, however, proposed that the ant had no such representation. Instead, the ant had a few simple rules of behavior that led to complex behaviors due to the complexity of the beach.

Unlike ants, people can learn from interacting with complex, well-structured environments. This is one of the core ideas behind scaffolding. A scaffold permits people to engage in the structure of a mature performance. Through this engagement, people appropriate or internalize the structure of the environment. Ideally, they learn the structure well enough that the scaffolds can be removed and people do not become dependent on them. If the structures of the environment are new to the learner, they can yield petite innovations. The benefits of structuring environments are not limited to physical environments. As noted above, children used symbolic mathematics to generate candidate structures for predicting the behavior of a balance scale. Without the candidate structures of mathematics, the children could not coordinate the two dimensions of weight and distance.

New structures can also be imported into people's environments, and people can learn to innovate new ways of interacting with those artifacts. Lin (2001), for example, describes the case of teacher in Hong Kong who decided to use a form of instruction imported from the United States. The teacher used an extended mathematics problem-solving task based on a 20-minute video narrative called *The Adventures of Jasper Woodbury* (CTGV, 1997). To solve the problem in the video, students often have to work for several days, and they work in groups. This manner of instruction was foreign to the Hong Kong teacher, who had not used group learning and who had always taught modular units that ended with each class. As the students worked on the problem, the teacher confronted a number of problems: students turned out to be competitive in groups; the extended nature of the problem disrupted her classroom routines; and the teacher was concerned about losing authority as the students worked on the problem without her direct guidance. The structure of the novel instructional materials was disruptive, but, over time, the teacher found innovative solutions that built on the materials' structure and that helped her to restructure the classroom and how she thought about the importance of teaching social skills.

A Focal Point for Coordination

Finally, interactivity provides a natural focal point for coordinating different sources of knowledge. One powerful example of coordination taking place in the environment comes from the study of so-called "split-brain" patients who have had the neural connections between the right and left hemispheres of their brains severed as a treatment for severe epilepsy. Although this procedure creates two highly isolated cognitive systems within a single individual, some patients who have had this procedure can function quite normally in everyday life. One reason for their success may be their ability to use the external world to coordinate thinking in their isolated hemispheres. Kingstone and Gazzaniga (1995) report that one split-brain patient almost fooled them into thinking there was covert communication between his two hemispheres. When they presented the words "bow" and "arrow" to opposite hemispheres (via opposite visual fields), the patient was able to produce a coordinated drawing of a bow and arrow. Although this seemed like neural communication between the hemispheres, it was actually occurring through the drawing surface itself, as each hemisphere had access to the emerging drawing on the page. The patient substituted the external world for neural pathways as the focal point of coordination.

Although less dramatic, neurologically normal people can find themselves in a similar situation as the split-brain patients. Innovations depend on integrating knowledge, but people often lack the structures necessary to relate the knowledge. With insufficient resources to make progress "inside the head," coordination of mental systems often must occur outside the brain. Consequently, external interactions are central to this coordination. Sometimes, connections made in the external world can be internalized so that environmental supports are no longer needed. We can return to the example of children's early number learning reported by Case and colleagues (Griffin, Case, & Siegler, 1994). The simple board games were designed so that children had to coordinate ordinal and cardinal conceptions of number. For example, imagine a game where children roll a die that shows a "6." The children have to count out six spaces in order to reach a particular position. As they land on each space, they pick up a chip. When they reached the final space, they have to decide if they have more chips than another student who rolled a "5" and ended up on the fifth space. In this example, the environment is designed to help the child coordinate the cardinal value of the digit "6" (total amount) with its ordinal value (sixth step). Interactive focal points can bring different pockets of knowledge into alignment, and for the children learning math, it leads to an understanding of number where ordinal and cardinal properties are related to one another.

Dynamic Transfer as a Measure of Innovative Experiences

Innovation can present a problem for educational settings. Innovative processes are often slow and filled with trial and error. In the balance scale study, the children were trying almost any type of mathematical operation to find an answer. Moreover, innovative processes often fail to yield an innovative outcome. Many of the younger children never learned to use multiplication to solve the balance scale problems. These perceived inefficiencies raise challenges for educational practice. For example, discovery curricula can look inefficient, which leads to objections like "Wouldn't it just be more efficient to tell students the answer?" At the same time, schools should be an ideal setting for designed experiences in innovation, which learners can then transfer to life beyond school.

The relation of education to innovation hinges on the types of assessments used to measure the benefits of particular experiences. Sequestered Problem Solving (SPS) assessments of transfer are excellent for detecting the scope of a successful innovation. However, they are not ideal for evaluating innovative experiences that do not come to fruition with an innovative outcome. An alternative approach is to use Preparation for Future Learning (PFL) assessments (Bransford & Schwartz, 1999). PFL assessments measure dynamic transfer; students have an opportunity to learn during the assessment with the support of useful external resources. In a PFL assessment, using the environment to learn during a test does not contaminate the test results or mean the student has been cheating. Instead, the assessment asks whether people can learn with the help of the environment.

One example of a PFL assessment that detected the benefits of innovative experiences comes from classroom research on learning statistics (Schwartz & Martin, 2004). Over multiple class periods, ninth-grade students received numerous opportunities to innovate ways to graph and measure variability. Consider a task where students had to innovate a way to measure variability. Students received the grids shown in Figure 18.5. Each black circle indicates where a pitching machine threw a ball when aimed at the X in the center. The students' task was to find a method to compute a reliability index for each machine, so people might decide which one they would like to buy. The goal was not for the students to invent the canonical solutions for measuring variability (though that would have been a fine outcome). Instead, the goal was for the students to have the opportunity to innovate in a well-structured environment. Students were explicitly told they were inventing a solution so they would engage the environment with an innovative mindset.

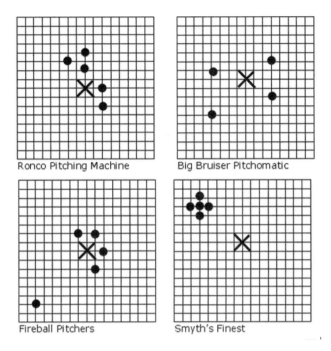

FIGURE 18.5 Pitching machine task (Schwartz & Martin, 2004).

Notice that the task includes the four elements of environments useful for supporting innovation. Students worked in pairs and they could draw on the sheets to test out ideas, thus the task is designed to help them distribute their cognition. The pitching grids create "contrasting cases" to help students generate alternative interpretations. For example, the lower right-hand grid shows a number of tightly clustered pitches that are far from the target. This helps students distinguish variability and error. The task requires students to use the candidate structures of symbolic mathematics to help them innovate. So, rather than simply ask the students to rank the reliability of the four pitching machines, they have to use the structure of mathematics to help them coordinate the different aspects of variability (e.g., sample size, density, distance from the mean, etc.). The visual structure of the grids naturally creates a point of coordination for organizing discussions and tentative solutions. For example, one student kept his finger on the ball of one pitching grid, while talking about another.

For tasks like these, very few students innovate the conventional solution. This fact returns us to the question of whether there is any value in engaging innovative processes even though they may not yield an innovative outcome. This is where PFL measures can be helpful: they can measure the extent to which innovative experiences prepare students to appreciate an innovative (to them) solution when it appears. The second phase of this experiment tackled this question. The target innovation was to learn to make comparisons across unlike distributions by normalizing data, as one done does when comparing the performance of athletes from different eras, even though they may have used different equipment.[2]

On the last day of 2 weeks of instruction, students were divided into two instructional conditions. Students in the Invent-a-Measure condition received raw data and tried to innovate a way to compare specific individuals from different distributions (e.g., given two groups of students who took different exams, which student got the highest relative score). No students innovated a satisfactory solution. Students in the Tell-and-Copy condition received the same data, but they learned and practiced a graphical procedure for solving the problems. A few days later,

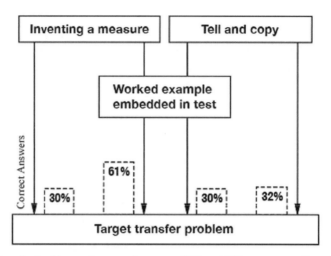

FIGURE 18.6   The effects of innovative experiences on SPS and PFL measures of learning (adapted from Schwartz & Martin, 2004).

all students completed a long paper-and-pencil test that covered 2 weeks of instruction. The last problem on the test involved comparing athletes from different eras, which requires finding and using normalized scores. The students had not compared athletes during the instruction. Moreover, the target problem only provided summary statistics, whereas the students in both conditions had worked with raw data. Thus, it did not share surface features with the instruction, and it made a difficult transfer problem.

The two instructional conditions were further subdivided into two test conditions. Half of the students in each condition had a worked example embedded in the middle of their test (the PFL condition), and the other half did not (the SPS condition). The worked example held the keys for how to solve normalizing problems. Students in the PFL conditions had to copy the worked example as part of the test, which they did quite accurately. The question was whether they would learn from the worked example, and then apply this learning to solve the target problem at the end of the test. Figure 18.6 summarizes the design of the study and shows the results.

As measured by the SPS assessment, the innovative experiences of the Invent-a-Measure condition did not yield any special benefits over the Tell-and-Copy condition. It was the PFL assessment that revealed the benefits of the innovative experiences: the students learned from the worked example, as indicated by their performance on the target transfer problem. In contrast, the Tell-and-Copy students who received the worked example showed little benefit. The results from this study indicate that innovative experiences can prepare students to learn, even if students never innovate the correct outcome themselves, and that PFL assessments can detect the fruits of the innovation process. This is useful, because it helps to overcome the worry that innovative experiences, while fun for students, may not have any particular value. It also shows that dynamic transfer measures, which include opportunities to learn at transfer, can be more sensitive to important types of prior learning than standard similarity-based transfer measures that do not permit learning during the assessment. In this case, the PFL assessment showed that the innovation experiences prepared students for the conceptual change that it is possible to compare unlike entities.

Unlike much of life, education can design innovation experiences that maximize productive processes and minimize loses. Sears (2006), for example, compared college students learning the Chi-Square statistic. The students received two kinds of instruction: once group read how to solve a series of contrasting cases involving the Chi-Square statistic; the other tried to innovate a solution to handle the contrasting cases, and then they were shown how to solve the problems. Only the instructional goal differed; the students received the exact same materials and the same amount of time on task. The only difference was whether the students learned how to compute Chi-Square before or after they received the series of contrasting cases. There was a second, orthogonal factor: half of the students in each group worked in pairs, and half worked individually. On a subsequent SPS measure of how well the students had learned Chi-Square, all the conditions performed quite well with no differences. Thus, the designed innovation experience did not hurt the students, so long as they ultimately received the correct procedure. A different pattern of results showed up on a PFL assessment that involved learning Cohen's Kappa, which is a variant of Chi-Square. The students who innovated around Chi-Square made the dynamic transfer to Cohen's Kappa more frequently. Notably, the group work enhanced the effects of innovation experiences on the PFL assessment relative to working alone, but group work made no difference for the students who had simply solved (but not innovated solutions to) the Chi-Square problems. This makes sense. Groups working on standard, efficiency-driven tasks tend to partition and "hand off" results to one another for checking. In contrast, well-functioning groups engaged in innovation are more likely to negotiate one another's ideas and learn from one another. Said another way, their discourse environment offers distributed memory, alternate interpretations, multiple candidate structures, and a focal point for coordinating their efforts — characteristics that we have argued support dynamic transfer for innovation.

THE INERTIA PROBLEM

A natural threat to innovation is the tendency to assimilate situations into one's pre-existing routines. People may treat new situations like old ones, instead of changing their ideas or actions. The great strength of transfer is that people can reuse what they know to help them handle a new situation. The great risk of transfer is that people may have sufficient prior knowledge that they can operate efficiently enough in the situation. There is minimal impetus to overcome inertia and innovate a new way of doing or thinking about things. In the prior example of people learning to pour between jugs, the complex method was good enough to get the job done, and people did not seek out a potentially more effective solution. Instead of transferring for innovation, people often transfer for repetition. In many situations, repetition is a good thing, and constant innovation would be insufferable.

There is a second source of the inertia problem. Even if people do recognize a situation might be worth a bit of innovation, there is no guarantee that the effort to innovate will yield an innovative outcome. Moreover, the process of innovation typically requires a "productivity dip" as people become temporarily less efficient. Fullan (2001) discusses the "implementation dip" that occurs when people deploy an innovation, for example, in a business setting. The productivity dip refers to the loss of effectiveness while making the innovation itself.

An example of a productivity dip comes from the U-shaped curve in the acquisition of past tense (Ervin & Miller, 1963). Early on, children correctly use regular and irregular past tense forms, for example, "talked" and "bought" and "gave." At this stage, children have memorized the past tense for each word on a case-by-case basis. In the next stage, children make a conceptual innovation by switching from their ad hoc system to a rule that might be summarized as, *add "-ed" to a verb to make it past tense*. At this stage, children are able to convert novel words into the past tense, but they also add "-ed" to irregular verbs that they previously said correctly. For example, they might say "buyed" or "gived." They overgeneralize the newly acquired rule. It is only after some time that they learn to apply the past tense rule to some words and to use irregular forms for other words.

How do people overcome the inertia of their prior learning so they engage in innovation? Since at least Piaget (1952), the supposition has been that efforts towards innovation are fault-driven. People detect an internal contradiction or an external impasse, and this causes them to search for a new way to resolve the problem. This account is consistent with the scientific practice of rectifying theories given falsifying data. A fault-driven account claims that at a minimum transfer supports innovation because people need to transfer in prior learning to recognize there is a fault (cf. Popper, 1968).

Fault-driven transfer for innovation, however, cannot be the complete story. In some cases, people may not experience any fault in performance, but they will still try to coordinate new information with their prior learning, and this will yield new conceptions. Vosniadou and Brewer (1992) showed that children integrate their experience of a flat world with overheard verbal facts, for example, that the world is round. As a result, they innovate hybrid models of the earth (e.g., a flat earth inside a round bowl). This is true even though their existing concept of a flat world does not lead to performance problems in their everyday lives. In the preceding case of language learning, children change their concept of past tense, even though the change leads to more errors in the short term. They are undeterred by the productivity dip.

Trajectories Through a Space of Innovation

Similarity and dynamic transfer provide different processes by which people interact with their context to overcome the inertia problem, or not. We describe how the two processes can work together, and how educational experiences can help people transfer the idea of being innovative. First, however, we treat each mechanism separately. Figure 18.7 anchors the discussion of how transfer and context interact with respect to innovation.

Figure 18.7 uses a spatial metaphor to create a space of innovation. The vectors represent a sample of the trajectories people can follow over time; they range from genuine innovation to mere improvements in efficiency to outright failure. Movement up the gradient represents the process of adaptation over time. The height of the gradient at any point captures the adaptiveness of the outcomes at that point in time. (Adaptiveness can be gauged according to different definitions — time, cost, happiness, cultural mandates. The basic abstraction stays the same.) Over time, some trajectories reach higher levels of adaptiveness that constitute innovations. Other

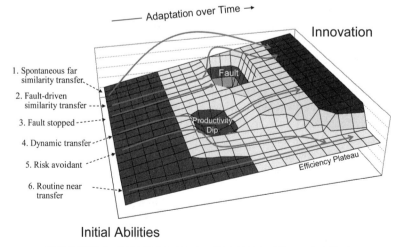

FIGURE 18.7   Trajectories of innovation (see text for explanation).

trajectories achieve more efficient routines, but they do not yield the long-term adaptive benefits gained by innovations. The "fault" and "productivity dip" zones indicate that people become locally less adaptive in those areas. The gradient representation is inspired by work in artificial intelligence. Higher peaks represent more innovative outcomes. However, a steeper rise is more difficult to climb, because it implies a faster rate of adaptation. The trajectories of Figure 18.7 do not cover the complete range of ways people traverse the space of innovation (different endeavors will have their own terrains), but they help to clarify different transfer solutions to the inertia problem.

In similarity transfer, people apply prior learning whole cloth to a new situation. The challenge for similarity transfer is whether the existing knowledge and the new situation are close enough in the innovation space that the similarity will be noticed and leveraged. Trajectory 1 represents a spontaneous, far transfer that yields an innovation. The figure illustrates why spontaneous far transfer is rare: it depends on an unprovoked, prospective leap far beyond one's position in the space. There is no impetus to do so, unless people can prefigure the innovative outcome of the transfer. And if it fails, people have learned little about the terrain over which they jumped.

Trajectory 2 represents fault-driven similarity transfer. A sequence of near transfers advances up the slope of innovation, until there is a fault that blocks further incremental progress. For example, engineers might work on creating fruit pickers. They transfer techniques of making gentle claws in a series of near transfers that handle increasingly delicate fruit, for example, from melons to oranges to nectarines. However, a situation presents a fault that cannot be traversed by a near transfer. For example, it turns out that their various claws keep puncturing and crushing tomatoes. The engineers might go down the chasm and perseverate on the near transfer of making gentler claws, but the continued loss of adaptiveness may be too great. In the terms of artificial intelligence, hill-climbing algorithms do not descend into valleys. Instead, the engineers might intentionally search for an innovative analogy. They might draw the analogy to work they had done on claws for lifting boxes. They remember they made the boxes thicker. Given this prior learning, they might jump to the innovation of changing the thickness of the tomato through genetic engineering instead of working on softer and softer claws.

Trajectory 3 shows people stopping at the sign of a major fault. Prior knowledge fails to adapt to the demands of a new situation. Rather than moving forward, people disengage from the problematic situation and the process of adaptation stops. This is not inherently bad; dead ends can signal ill-conceived plans. In some cases, however, people disengage when there might be other paths available given perseverance. The transfer literature would be enriched if it examined the types of dispositions and social supports that can help people avoid the tendency to transfer in the belief that efforts to persevere are fruitless (e.g., Blackwell, Trzesniewski, & Dweck, 2007). Barron (2004) studied interest development in technology and found that some children who exhibit perseverance in innovation have parental models that reveal the other side of fault situations. Their parents provide models of the valued outcomes that expertise in computer science can yield.

Trajectory 4 shows dynamic transfer. Dynamic transfer is the product of a sequence of interactions with a well-structured environment that may include tools, representations, other people, and so forth. People make a number of small dynamic transfers that eventually yield the stable coordination that constitutes an innovation, as in the case of the children learning the balance scale. The children slowly worked through different applications of math until they ended up with a stable way to coordinate two dimensions of information.

Dynamic transfer cannot jump across the productivity dip (or a fault) with a far transfer. Dynamic transfer depends on coordination with the environment for learning; it cannot fly across the environment with an abstraction. Nevertheless, the ease of the near transfers can lead people into the productivity dip. In fault-driven learning, it is necessary to recognize the fault. This is not the case with dynamic transfer, which depends on coordination rather than fault detection. Therefore, the temporary loss of adaptiveness does not have to be registered for continued learning. People can continue forward without noticing (or caring) that there has been a loss of productivity. We saw an example of this earlier in the productivity dip that children traverse when acquiring the past tense. Interestingly, connectionist models of past-tense acquisition are consistent with Trajectory 4. They demonstrate that small, local, and quantitative changes of the kind licensed by dynamic transfer can lead to innovations — qualitative changes in how knowledge of inflectional forms is organized (e.g., Plunkett & Marchman, 1996).

Dynamic transfer provides a less arduous route to innovation than similarity transfer, because people do not have to make a leap of innovation and because they may not register the productivity dip. Of course, there are situations where the environment is not conducive to entering the productivity dip, and people will avoid it. Children learn the past-tense rule because they are in an environment that encourages on-going interaction and tolerates dips in efficiency. In contrast, Trajectory 5 represents a situation of high risk or pressure to perform in the short term. In this trajectory, people balk at the productivity dip, because any loss of effectiveness can be problematic. One option is to stop adapting. Here, we show the second alternative, which is to take a shallow gradient that does not involve a short-term loss in effectiveness. This trajectory ultimately merges with the final trajectory in our inventory.

Trajectory 6 represents a series of near similarity transfers, where people generalize and fine-tune their abilities across situations. This leads to an improvement in efficiency, but not a genuine innovation. This shallow region of the space is traversed until a plateau is reached. People achieve a level of "routine expertise" that enables them to accomplish familiar tasks in familiar and efficient ways (Hatano & Inagaki, 1986).

Transferring the Idea of Dynamic Transfer

Given the space of innovation, we can hypothesize how people learn to be innovative. Our proposal is simple and involves a combination of similarity and dynamic transfer. The similarity transfer involves recognizing that similar situations have been solved by engaging in dynamic transfer. People learn that it is worth taking the temporary productivity dip associated with dynamic transfer, and they learn techniques that can help them make the dynamic transfer. We first describe a study that shows that specific educational experiences correlate with dynamic transfer. We conclude with a final study on transferring the very idea of being innovative through dynamic transfer.

In a study designed to demonstrate that educational experiences can correlate with dynamic transfer, college students completed a diagnosis task (Martin & Schwartz, under review). The students received 12 reference cases, each on a separate sheet of paper. Each sheet indicated the symptoms and diagnosis for one patient. The students had to use the reference cases to help diagnose a series of 10 new patients. For each new patient, they ordered medical tests to reveal symptoms, and when ready, they made their diagnosis. The primary question was whether the students would make representations of the reference cases to help with diagnosis, for example, creating tables or decision trees. Or, would they simply shuffle through the reference cases to diagnose each new patient? Stepping back to make a representational tool before diagnosing the patients would involve a short-term productivity dip compared to just diving into the diagnosis task. The study compared undergraduate and graduate students. The graduate students were drawn from disciplines that involved complex information management (e.g., computer science, engineering, biology), but none of them had completed diagnoses like these.

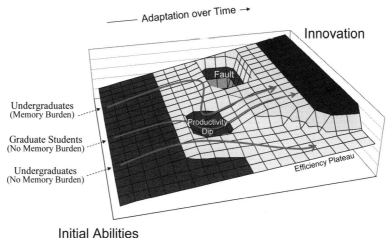

FIGURE 18.8   Three trajectories in a medical diagnosis task.

All of the graduate students made visual representations of the reference cases, and spent roughly 15 minutes before they tried to diagnose their first patient. All told, they achieved 94% accuracy. The graduate students made a dynamic transfer. They used their general knowledge of data management to fashion representations tailored to the specifics of diagnosis, and half of them changed their representations as they became more familiar with the task. In contrast, less than 20% of the undergraduates made any sort of representation to help solve the problems. They began diagnosing the new patients within two minutes of receiving the reference cases. Even so, they achieved 91% accuracy in their diagnoses by shuffling through the reference cases to help diagnose each new patient. The study also included a third condition. Undergraduates completed the same set of diagnoses, but they had to set aside the reference cases each time they tried to diagnose a new patient. This imposed a heavy memory burden. Under these conditions, 88% of the undergraduates took the time to make representations. Thus, the (otherwise similar) undergraduates who had continuous access to the cases knew how to make representations. They simply did not bother to do so. In contrast, the graduate students found it worthwhile to make representations. Their experiences in school were associated with their tendency to engage in dynamic transfer and its associated productivity dip.

Figure 18.8 provides a summary of the trajectories of the three conditions. The undergraduates who did not have a memory burden avoided the productivity dip of making a representation. They engaged the task directly and did well enough, though their approach would become relatively inefficient given more diagnoses. (Once they completed their representations, those students who made representations were faster for each individual diagnosis and ordered more informative tests.) In contrast, the undergraduates who had the memory burden encountered a fault condition. They could not remember all the information from the reference cases. They made a similarity-based transfer along the lines of, "in situations of high memory load, it is worth making an external representation." This drove them into the productivity dip, where they dynamically transferred in their knowledge of representations and adapted it to the particular task. The graduate students also entered the productivity dip to make the dynamic transfer. They had sufficient prior experiences with data management that they did not need to experience a fault to engage in the dynamic transfer of creating and revising representations.

Transferring the Idea of Innovating

The graduate students suggest that it is possible for people to learn to engage in dynamic transfer, even when it is not necessary for immediate efficiency. For these graduate students, making a visual representation to help solve these problems hardly seems like a process of innovation (e.g., see Novick & Morse, 2000). But, for people who have less experience, it would constitute a process of innovation. The next study demonstrates that educational experiences can lead to people to transfer the very idea of innovating through a dynamic transfer.

In this study, seventh-grade students received a pretest hidden in a regular class activity that involved problems where a visual representation of causal chains would be helpful (Schwartz, 1993). The problems were something like, "X can communicate the disease to Y. Q can get the disease from R. F gets infected by Y. If X has the disease, what else can get the disease?" On the pretest, none of the children tried to construct a visual representation to help solve the problems. Two weeks later, the students completed several cycles where they explicitly invented visual representations to solve complex problems, none of which involved causal chains. After each invention effort, they were shown the representations that experts might use to solve the problem (e.g., a matrix, a Cartesian graph). This way they had a chance to experience the innovative process of visualization, and they had a chance to experience the outcome of a good visualization. Two weeks after the instructional intervention, the students received a posttest similar to the pretest; it involved causal chains, and it was embedded in a regular class activity. The key finding was that half of the students tried to invent new visual representations to help solve the problems on the posttest, compared to none at the pretest. Even though they had not used visualizations for problems of this structure, they recognized that the problems were quite complex, and they made the similarity transfer that visualizations could help. They then engaged in the dynamic transfer of trying to innovate a visual representation that could help solve the problem. They demonstrated a conceptual change in the sense that before the instruction they would engage a task as given, and after, they learned the concept that trying to invent a visual representation can help manage information complexity.

Together, the preceding two studies suggest that appropriate experiences can lead people to transfer the idea of innovating. It is notable that the studies involved innovations for a specific class of problems (complex information management) using a specific external representational tool (visualizations). The children did not demonstrate a general disposition to innovate, for example, by brainstorming. To our knowledge, they also did not suddenly become more creative or innovative at home.

It is an important open question whether innovation can be a general, meta-cognitive mindset that transfers to many situations, or whether it is more confined to a specific set of techniques that are more or less appropriate for specific situations. We are not sanguine about "creativity programs" that try to train business people or children to be creative in general. As the literature on transfer has repeatedly shown, people do not transfer universally applicable skills like logical reasoning (e.g., Nisbett, Fong, Lehman, & Cheng, 1987). Instead, the ability to transfer and innovate grows from experiences where people gain insight into important environmental structures and their possibilities for interaction.

ACKNOWLEDGMENTS

This material is based upon work supported by the National Science Foundation under Grants No. BCS-0214549 and SLC-0354453. Any opinions, findings, and conclusions or recommendations expressed in this material are those of the authors and do not necessarily reflect the views of the National Science Foundation.

NOTES

1. There has been some confusion about transfer, because researchers slip between its meaning as an outcome measure and as a mechanism. This is natural, because people draw inferences about the mechanisms of transfer by looking at measures gathered from transfer tasks. However, as many authors have proposed (e.g., Lobato, 2003), if people fail on a researcher-designed measure of transfer, it does not mean there were not mechanisms of transfer at play that led the people to give their answer. It just means the hypothesis that the experimental manipulation would promote transfer for a specific outcome failed.

2. One computes how far each athlete's performance exceeds the mean of their respective era, and then divides those values by the variability of the era. These measures indicate how far each athlete outstripped others at the time, and these measures can be compared.

REFERENCES

Barnett, S. M., & Ceci, S. J. (2002). When and where do we apply what we learn? A taxonomy for far transfer. *Psychological Bulletin, 128,* 612–637.

Barron, B. (2004). Learning ecologies for technological fluency: Gender and experience differences. *Journal of Educational Computing Research, 31*, 1–36.

Bassok, M., & Holyoak, K. J. (1989). Interdomain transfer between isomorphic topics in algebra and physics. *Journal of Experimental Psychology, 15*, 153–166.

Blackwell, L. S., Trzesniewski, K. H., & Dweck, C. S. (2007). Implicit theories of intelligence predict achievement across an adolescent transition: A longitudinal study and an intervention. *Child Development, 78*, 246–263.

Bransford, J. D., & Schwartz, D. L. (1999). Rethinking transfer: A simple proposal with multiple implications. In A. Iran-Nejad & P. D. Pearson (Eds.), *Review of Research in Education, 24*, 61–100.

Bransford, J. D., Franks, J. J., Vye, N. J., & Sherwood, R. D. (1989). New approaches to instruction: Because wisdom can't be told. In S. Vosniadou & A. Ortony (Eds.), *Similarity and analogical reasoning* (pp. 470–497). New York: Cambridge University Press.

Brown, A. L., & Kane, M. J. (1988). Preschool children can learn to transfer: Learning to learn and learning from example. *Cognitive Psychology, 20*, 493–523.

Bruner, J. S., & Potter, M. C. (1964). Inference in visual recognition. *Science, 144*, 424–425.

Butterworth, B. (1999). *The mathematical brain*. London: MacMillan.

Carey, S. (1985). *Conceptual change in childhood*. Cambridge, MA: MIT Press.

Carraher, D. W., & Schliemann, A.D. (2002). The transfer dilemma. *Journal of the Learning Sciences, 11*, 1–24.

Case, R., & Okamoto, Y. (1996). The role of central conceptual structures in the development of children's thought. *Monographs of the Society for Research in Child Development, 61*, 1–265.

Chambers, D., & Reisberg, D. (1985). Can Mental Images Be Ambiguous? *Journal of Experimental Psychology: Human Perception and Performance, 11*, 317–328.

Chi, M. T. H., de Leeuw, N., Chiu, M-H., & LaVancher, C. (1994). Eliciting self-explanations improves understanding. *Cognitive Science, 18*, 439–477.

Chi, M. T. H., Feltovich, P., & Glaser, R. (1981). Categorization and representation of physics problems by experts and novices. *Cognitive Science, 5*, 121–152.

COSEPUP [Committee on Science, Engineering, and Public Policy]. (2006). *Rising above the gathering storm: Energizing America for a brighter economic future*. Washington DC: The National Academies Press.

CTGV [Cognition and Technology Group at Vanderbilt]. (1997). *The Jasper Project: Lessons in curriculum, instruction, assessment, and professional development.* Mahwah, NJ: Erlbaum.

Detterman, D. L. (1993). The case for the prosecution: Transfer as epiphenomenon. In D. K. Detterman & R. J. Sternberg (Eds.), *Transfer on trial: Intelligence, cognition, and instruction* (pp. 1–24). Norwood, NJ: Ablex.

diSessa, A. A., & Wagner, J. F. (2005). What coordination has to say about transfer. In J. P. Mestre (Ed.), *Transfer of learning from a modern multidisciplinary perspective* (pp. 121–154). Greenwich, CT: Information Age.

Dufresne, R., Mestre, J., Thaden-Koch, T., Gerace, W., & Leonard, W. (2005). Knowledge representation and coordination in the transfer process. In J. P. Mestre (Ed.), *Transfer of learning from a modern multidisciplinary perspective* (pp. 155–216). Greenwich, CT: Information Age.

Dunbar, K. (1997) How scientists think: On-line creativity and conceptual change in science. In T. B. Ward, S. M. Smith, & J. Vaid (Eds.), *Conceptual structures and processes: Emergence, discovery, and change* (pp. 461–493). Washington, D.C.: American Psychological Association Press.

Ervin, S. M., & Miller, W. R. (1963). Language development. In H.W. Stevenson (Ed.), *Child psychology: The sixty-second yearbook of the National Society for the Study of Education, Part 1* (pp. 108–143). Chicago: University of Chicago Press.

Feller, J., Fitzgerald, B., Hissam, S., & Lakhani K. R. (Eds.). (2005). *Perspectives on free and open source software.* Cambridge, MA: MIT Press.

Finke, R. (1990). *Creative imagery: Discoveries and inventions in visualization.* Hillsdale, NJ: Erlbaum.

Fullan, M. (2001). *Leading in a culture of change.* San Francisco, CA: Jossey-Bass

Gentner, D., Brem, S., Ferguson, R. W., Markman, A. B., Levidow, B. B., Wolff, P., & Forbus, K. D. (1997). Analogical reasoning and conceptual change: A case study of Johannes Kepler. *Journal of the Learning Sciences, 6,* 3–40.

Gick, M. L., & Holyoak, K. J. (1983). Schema induction and analogical transfer. *Cognitive Psychology, 15,* 1–38.

Goel, V. (1995). *Sketches of thought.* Cambridge, MA: MIT Press.

Gopnik, A., & Meltzoff, A. N. (1997). *Words, thoughts, and theories.,* Cambridge MA: Bradford MIT Press.

Greeno, J. G., Smith, D. R., & Moore, J. L. (1993). Transfer of situated learning. In D. K. Detterman & R. J. Sternberg (Eds.), *Transfer on trial: Intelligence, cognition, and instruction* (pp. 99–167). Norwood, NJ: Ablex.

Greenwald, A. G., Pratkanis, A. R., Leippe, M. R., & Baumgardner, M. H. (1986). Under what conditions does theory obstruct research progress? *Psychological Review, 93,* 216–229.

Griffin, S. A., Case, R., & Siegler, R. S. (1994). Rightstart: Providing the central conceptual prerequisites for first formal learning of arithmetic to students at risk for school failure. In K. McGilly (Ed.), *Classroom lessons: Integrating cognitive theory and classroom practice* (pp. 25–49). Cambridge, MA: MIT Press.

Hammer, D., Elby, A., Scherr, R. E., & Redish, E. F. (2005). Resources, framing, and transfer. In J. P. Mestre (Ed.), *Transfer of learning from a modern multidisciplinary perspective* (pp. 89–120). Greenwich, CT: Information Age.

Hatano, G. & Inagaki, K. (1986). Two courses of expertise. In H. Stevenson, H. Azuma, & K. Hakuta (Eds), *Child development and education in Japan* (pp. 262–272). New York: Freeman.

Hutchins, E. (1995). *Cognition in the wild.* Cambridge, MA: MIT Press.

Ishibashi, H., Hihara, S., Takahashi, M., Heike, T., Yokota, T., & Iriki, A. (2002). Tool-use learning selectively induces expression of brain-derived neurotrophic factor, its receptor trkB, and neurotrophin 3 in the intraparietal multisensorycortex of monkey. *Cognitive Brain Research, 14,* 3–9.

Johnson-Laird, P. N. (1989). Analogy and the exercise of creativity. In S. Vosniadou & A. Ortony (Eds.), *Similarity and Analogical Reasoning* (pp. 313–332). New York: Cambridge University Press.

Keil, F. C. (1989) *Concepts, kinds, and cognitive development.* Cambridge, MA: MIT Press.

Kerslake, D. (1986). *Fractions: Children's strategies and errors.* Berkshire, England: NFER-Nelson.

Kingstone, A., & Gazzaniga, M. S. (1995). Subcortical transfer of higher order information: More illusory than real? *Neuropsychology, 9,* 321–328.

Klahr, D., & Robinson, M. (1981). Formal assessment of problem-solving and planning processes in pre-school children. *Cognitive Psychology, 13*, 113–148.

Lin, X. D. (2001). Reflective adaptation of a technology artifact: A case study of classroom change. *Cognition & Instruction, 19*, 395–440.

Lobato, J. (2003). How design experiments can inform a rethinking of transfer and vice versa. *Educational Researcher, 32*, 17–20.

Luchins, A. S., & Luchins, E. H. (1959). *Rigidity of behavior: A variational approach to the effect of einstellung*. Eugene: University of Oregon Books.

Martin, L., & Schwartz, D. L. (under review). Prospective adaptation in the use of external representations. Manuscript submitted for publication. Stanford University, CA.

Martin, T., & Schwartz, D. L. (2005). Physically distributed learning: Adapting and reinterpreting physical environments in the development of the fraction concept. *Cognitive Science, 29*, 587–625.

Mestre, J.P. (1994, February). Cognitive aspects of learning and teaching science. In S.J. Fitzsimmons & L.C. Kerpelman (Eds.), *Teacher enhancement for elementary and secondary science and mathematics: Status, issues and problems* (pp. 3–53). Washington, D.C.: National Science Foundation (NSF 94-80).

Nisbett, R. E., Fong, G. T., Lehman, D. R., & Cheng, P. W. (1987). Teaching Reasoning. *Science, 238*, 625–631.

Novick, L. R., & Morse, D. L. (2000). Folding a fish, making a mushroom: The role of diagrams in executing assembly procedures. *Memory & Cognition, 28*, 1242–1256.

Okita, Y. S., & Schwartz, D. L. (2006) Young children's understanding of animacy and entertainment robots. *International Journal of Humanoid Robotics, 3*, 393–412.

Papert, S. (1988). One AI or many. *Daedalus, 17*, 1–13.

Pea, R. D. (1993). Practices of distributed intelligence and designs for education. In G. Salomon (Ed.), *Distributed cognitions* (pp. 47–87). New York: Cambridge University Press.

Piaget, J. (1952). *The origins of intelligence in children* (M. Cook, Trans.). New York: International Press.

Piaget, J. (1976). *The grasp of consciousness*. Cambridge, MA: Harvard University Press.

Plunkett, K., & Marchman, V. A. (1996). Learning from a connectionist model of the acquisition of the English past tense. *Cognition, 61*, 299–308.

Popper, K. R. (1968). *The logic of scientific discovery*. New York: Harper and Row.

Rebellow, N. S., Zollman, D. A., Allbaugh, A. R., Englehardt, P. V., Gray, K. E., Hrepic, Z., & Itza-Ortiz, S. F. (2005). Dynamic transfer: A perspective from physics education research. In J. P. Mestre (Ed.) *Transfer of learning from a modern multidisciplinary perspective* (pp. 217–250). Greenwich, CT: Information Age.

Reed, S. K., Ernst, G. W., & Banerji, R. B. (1974). The role of analogy in transfer between similar problem states. *Cognitive Psychology, 6*, 436–450.

Ross, B. (1989). Remindings in learning and instruction. In S. Vosniadou & A. Ortony (Eds.), *Similarity and analogical reasoning* (pp. 438–469). New York: Cambridge University Press.

Rumelhart, D. E., Hinton, G. E., & Williams, R. J. (1986). Learning representations by back-propagating errors. *Nature, 323*, 533–536.

Schwartz, D. L. (1993). The construction and analogical transfer of symbolic visualizations. *Journal of Research in Science Teaching, 30*, 1309–1325.

Schwartz, D. L., & Bransford, J. D. (1998). A time for telling. *Cognition & Instruction, 16*, 475–522,

Schwartz, D. L., Bransford, J. D., & Sears, D. (2005). Efficiency and innovation in transfer. In J. P. Mestre (Ed.), *Transfer of learning from a modern multidisciplinary perspective* (pp. 1–52). Greenwich, CT: Information Age.

Schwartz, D. L., & Martin, T. (2004). Inventing to prepare for learning: The hidden efficiency of original student production in statistics instruction. *Cognition & Instruction, 22*, 129–184.

Schwartz, D. L., Martin, T., & Pfaffman, J. (2005). How mathematics propels the development of physical knowledge. *Journal of Cognition and Development, 6*, 65–88.

Sears, D. A. (2006). Effects of innovation versus efficiency tasks on collaboration and learning. (Doctoral dissertation, Stanford University, 2006). Dissertation Abstracts International, 67, 1652A.

Simon, H. A. (1969). *The sciences of the artificial.* Cambridge, MA: MIT Press.

Suchman, L. (1987). *Plans and situated actions: The problem of human machine communication.* New York: Cambridge University Press.

Thagard, P. (1996). The concept of disease: Structure and change. *Communication and Cognition, 29,* 445–478.

Thelen, E., & Smith, L.B. (1994). *A dynamic systems approach to the development of cognition and action.* Cambridge, MA: The MIT Press.

Thorndike, E. L., & Woodworth, R. S. (1901). The influence of improvement in one mental function upon the efficacy of other functions. *Psychological Review, 8,* 247–261.

Trick, L. M., & Pylyshyn, Z. W. (1994). Why are small and large numbers enumerated differently? A limited-capacity preattentive stage in vision. *Psychological Review, 101,* 80–102.

Tyson, L. M., Venville, G. J., Harrison, A. L., & Treagust, D. F. (1997). A multidimensional framework for interpreting conceptual change events in the classroom. *Science Education, 81,* 387–404.

Vollmeyer, R., Burns, B. D., & Holyoak, K. J. (1996). The impact of goal specificity on strategy use and the acquisition of problem structure. *Science, 20,* 75–100.

Vosniadou, S., & Brewer, W. F. (1992). Mental models of the earth: A study of conceptual change in childhood. *Cognitive Psychology, 24,* 535–85.

Vygotsky, L. S. (1987). *The collected works of L. S. Vygotsky.* R. Rieber & A. Carton (Eds.). New York: Plenum.

Whitehead, A. N. (1929). *The aims of education.* New York: MacMillan.

Zhang, J., & Norman, D. A. (1994). Representations in distributed cognitive tasks. *Cognitive Science, 18,* 87–122.

V
THE CONTEXT AND THE LEARNER

19

The Contextuality of Knowledge: An Intentional Approach to Meaning Making and Conceptual Change

Ola Halldén, Max Scheja, and Liza Haglund
Stockholm University

INTRODUCTION

Looking across the research on learning and conceptual change, it would probably be fair to say that there has been a tendency in the research to adhere to what Rommetveit (1978) has called a 'negative rationalism'. Such negative rationalism is characterised by a predominant focus on students' shortcomings, difficulties and general fallibility in relation to learning tasks confronting them in various settings. At a recent research meeting held in Britain, Perkins (2005) used the phrase 'theories of difficulty' to label and characterise a good portion of the research concerned with learning and development in educational settings. This phraseology captures fittingly the main thrust of the work carried out within the Alternative Framework Movement (Gilbert & Watts, 1983) and other research concerned with students' cognitive development and learning: to study obstacles for student learning. As Säljö (1991a) has pointed out in his critique of constructivist research on children's counting competencies, by adopting such a negative perspective on human learning and development we run the risk of constraining our thinking and hampering the discourse on cognition and learning:

> Children (and adults) are constantly portrayed as lacking in abilities and s[i]tuationally appropriate and perfectly rational modes of quantifying and handling problems [...] are marginalized in the experiment (or in the formal setting). Other modes of reasoning, usually academic and formally elegant, are given priority as if they were "better", irrespective of what the actor is attempting to achieve. (Säljö, 1991a, p. 123)

This normative critique asserts that research systematically tends to underestimate the competencies of the learner. However, constructivist research programmes have also been critiqued on methodological grounds. In particular, it has been argued that knowledge should be viewed as contextualised within discursive practices and that it is misleading to describe beliefs, conceptions, or conceptual structures in isolation from such discursive practices; knowledge is always situated, and so any attempt to account for an individual's knowledge structures must take this situatedness into account (Resnick, 1991). It is difficult to raise objections against such a methodological claim. However, sometimes, this critique takes the form of an ontological statement, saying that knowledge is socially constructed and transpires only in social practices (Lave, 1991). That is to argue for the social character of knowledge, for verbal communication as being a continuous process of joint construction of meanings (Marková, 1990, p. 136). From such a vantage point, interviewing provides an example of such joint construction of meaning. According to Fontana and Frey (2005), interviewing is 'inextricably and unavoidably historically, politically, and contextually bound' (p. 695), and is best described as a 'negotiated text' (p. 716). The outcome of an interview depends as much on the interviewer as on the interviewee, and on their interaction within a socio-historical setting at a particular point in time. So, interviews are not neutral tools for collecting data but rather 'active interactions between two (or more) people leading to negotiated, contextually based results' (Fontana & Frey, 2005, p. 698).

Any research programme seriously intent on contributing to the theoretical discourse on cognition and learning would need to explicate its position in respect of the concern for negative rationalism mentioned above. It would also have to employ methods for studying conceptual frameworks that can stand up against the methodological critique put forward by the sociocultural research paradigm. This chapter makes an effort to present such a theoretical stance, drawing on earlier conceptualisations and findings from a number of research projects that have considered the nature and process of conceptual change across a variety of settings. This does not mean that the research programme proposed here adheres to the ontological claims made within sociocultural approaches. On the contrary, it holds on firmly to the idea that people harbour beliefs and that these beliefs form structures, and the aim of this chapter is to propose a method for interpretation that renders the description of such belief structures an intellectually sound enterprise.

Departing from Piaget's early work, the chapter begins by describing a basic constructivist model for conceptual change. It then proceeds to consider two different, but related, strands of research growing out of constructivist research on students' alternative frameworks — one focused on the nature of alternative frameworks, and the other focused on the process of conceptual change. Against the background of this brief overview, we offer an alternative view on conceptual change which takes into account the intentional character of learning. In essence, this alternative view continues the early work by Marton and Säljö (1976a, 1976b; see also Marton, Hounsell, & Entwistle, 1997) which emphasised a content-related view of learning, that is, that learning always involves someone learning something, a particular content, and that the outcome of student learning is functionally related to what the students are trying to achieve in relation to a particular learning task in a particular teaching-learning environment.

A BASIC MODEL FOR CONCEPTUAL CHANGE

In the early 20th century, when Piaget published his works on children's conception of the world and the moral reasoning in the child (Piaget, 1929, 1932), his focus was *not* on the deficiencies in the child's reasoning but rather on *how* the child set about reasoning. Piaget's objective was not to test the child's abilities or to differentiate among children with regard to their abilities. Rather, he sought to describe their shared meanings and the processes by which they constructed meaning from their experiences. So the question of interest was not what was lacking in the child's reasoning, but rather what this reasoning was like. In a sense, Piaget gave children a voice of their own; it was the children's conceptions of the world that were put to the fore and explored.

Piaget (1970) was interested in the growth of intelligence as a common feature of human beings and, in his earlier writings, the construction of our view of the world. In *The Child's Con-*

FIGURE 19.1   A linear model of conceptual change.

ceptions of the World (Piaget, 1929), this interest reflects itself in studies of how children change their conceptions of phenomena like dreams, thoughts, the origin of the moon, cause and the nature of the night. The pattern of conceptual change thus described was that of a conception (A) being exchanged for another conception (B) (see Figure 19.1).

This model describes a linear and hierarchical conceptual development in which primitive conceptions are successively replaced by more advanced conceptions, ultimately resulting in a conceptual repertoire corresponding to that held by a particular culture in a particular society at a given time. Research carried out within such a linear model often displays negative rationalist tendencies; there are rights and wrongs, and the concern is to explore how the individual proceeds from the wrong conception to the correct one, that is, to ascertain how the individual exchanges primitive conceptions for more advanced and culturally endorsed ones. So far, the model describes a process in which the individual is socialised into an existing culture of shared meanings. However, the aim of Piaget's studies was primarily to explore the development in the child from an initial practical solipsism to the gradual construction of a world that includes her or himself as an element. So, the focus in these studies by Piaget was not on the erroneous conceptions in themselves, but rather on the underlying structures producing these conceptions. For example, a small child often has difficulties in distinguishing between the self and events in the surrounding world. This results in a continuing process in which the child incorporates events which appear to exist in the world, dreams for instance, into her or his self, and a counter-directed process in which omnipotent egocentric ideas, such as the creation of nature, are gradually alienated into the external world.

However, there is also a normative side to this matter. The discrepancies between how children usually view the world and what may be regarded as culturally accepted views beg the question how it is possible to help children to abandon their naïve conceptions in favour of more advanced and culturally accepted conceptions. Piaget's aim was to describe this process as an aspect of human cognition and development. Educational science, however, took it upon itself to address the normative side of the matter, focusing on how it is possible to influence this process so as to facilitate conceptual change in line with the conceptual understanding communicated in the teaching. The 1970s saw a rapid growth of research on conceptual change in the sciences aimed at resolving this question. When Driver and Easley (1978) published their seminal paper on conceptual development in adolescent students, they pointed out that when students come up with erroneous answers to questions posed in school, these answers should not primarily be seen as misunderstandings; they could equally well be seen as coming from a perspective alternative to that used by the teacher. A central distinction was thus made between misconceptions, on the one hand, and alternative frameworks, on the other. While misconceptions could be seen as incorrect ideas resulting from misunderstandings of theories or models presented in the teaching, alternative frameworks could be viewed as students' "autonomous frameworks for conceptualising the physical world" (Driver & Easley, 1978, p. 62). Such alternative frameworks would prompt learners to describe and explain events in ways alternative to those endorsed in the science classroom. Moreover, alternative frameworks could also lead students to interpret information communicated in the teaching in ways other than intended. When we study history we are always trying to understand a culture and a way of perceiving the world that differ from our personal viewpoint. Similarly, students studying science are trying to grasp a scientific culture or a particular way of perceiving the world that may differ from their already established ways of viewing the world around them. The students are, as it were, approaching "one framework of ideas from within another" (Lee, Dickinson, & Ashby, 1998, p. 234). For the teacher, the problem becomes one of helping the learner adopt the most appropriate point of view and to acquire a scientifically valid conceptual understanding of the topics studied. In other words: the teacher's task is to help the learner switch from the inadequate concept (A) to the scientifically approved concept (B) (see Figure 19.1).

Two interdependent lines of research were to be developed from this idea. One was all about mapping the As, as it were, that is, about describing the learners' alternative frames of reference. The other was about trying to describe and explain the process of conceptual change. These two strands of research are interdependent in the sense that mappings are construed with the aim of accounting for the process, and when the processes are described, they point towards specific kinds of mappings. However, for the purposes of this chapter we will describe them as two separate research strands.

RESEARCH ON THE NATURE OF ALTERNATIVE FRAMEWORKS

The 1980s and 1990s saw a rapid growth of research describing learners' conceptions of central concepts within the natural sciences (for a bibliography, see Duit, 2006). For instance, Watts (1983) described eight different ways of understanding meanings of force in physics, and Stewart (1982, 1983) documented different ways of understanding heredity in biology. Brumby (1979, 1984) foregrounded interpretations of the concept of natural selection, and Deadman and Kelly (1978) explored students' understandings of evolution and heredity prior to instruction. While there was an abundance of research being carried out within the natural sciences, the research on alternative frameworks within the humanities and the social sciences was languishing. Of course, there were studies looking at naïve conceptions, but this research was primarily concerned with describing phases or stages in learners' conceptual development (e.g., Berti, 1994; Furnham, 1994; Torney-Purta, 1994). However, in parallel with the alternative framework movement, there were other studies focusing on the learning and teaching of history. For instance, Dickinson, Gard, and Lee (1986) explored how the notion of evidence was used in history and in a class-room setting, respectively. Halldén (1986, 1993, 1994, 1998) also used history as an example in exploring student learning with the explicit aim of discussing the notion of alternative frameworks. In parallel with Halldén's approach, Marton (1981) and colleagues developed a conceptualisation of learning involving rich empirical descriptions of students' conceptions of learning material in relation to teaching and learning in school and higher education. Within this phenomenographic (Marton, 1981, 1992) research tradition, Dahlgren (1978) explored students' approaches to studying and learning economics. The findings showed that students, regardless of their having taken a basic course in economics involving teaching of the fundamental principle that 'price' is a function of supply and demand for a certain article of trade, insisted on explaining, for instance, the price of a bun as a result of the cost for producing that bun.

Alternative frameworks have been described in several different ways. For instance, Osborne, Bell, and Gilbert (1983) talked about 'children's science', meaning "the views of the world and meanings for words that children tend to acquire before they are formally taught science" (p. 1). Posner, Strike, Hewson, and Gertzog (1982) described a 'conceptual ecology', characterised by: Anomalies, analogies and metaphors, epistemological commitments, metaphysical beliefs and concepts and other knowledge (Posner, Strike, Hewson, & Gertzog, 1982, p. 214f; cf. also Strike & Posner, 1982, 1992). So conceptions have been seen as something embedded in a larger conceptual system. Such systems have been explicated in various ways. In proposing that conceptions are embedded in theories, Vosniadou (1994) described a hypothetical conceptual structure involving a framework theory built on ontological and epistemological presuppositions, and a specific theory, comprising information about the target conceptions. On this basis, students form specific beliefs or mental models in order to solve specific problems in practical situations.

An alternative way of describing conceptual structure was offered by Tiberghien (1994) who suggested that alternative frameworks involve different levels. Using a view of modelling in physics, Tiberghien (1994) distinguished between a theory level, a model level and a level of experimental field of reference. The theory level describes paradigms, principles, laws and so forth. The model level involves formalisms, relations between physical quantities and qualitative aspects associated with observable phenomena. The level of experimental field of reference, finally, involves experimental facts, experimental devices, measurements and similar phenomena. Along a similar theoretical vein, Caravita and Halldén (1994) suggested that alternative frameworks may be understood in relation to three different levels: A theoretical, a conceptual and an empirical, stressing that differences between common-sense beliefs and the descriptions and explanations given in science may occur at all three levels simultaneously.

In the wake of this research on the structure of conceptual systems, a debate arose on the context dependence of alternative conceptions. In studying students' beliefs of whether acquired characteristics are inherited or not, Engel Clough and Driver (1986) demonstrated that students' beliefs were dependent on whether they were talking about the Arctic fox or caterpillars. Later, Taber (2000) argued that there are several alternative and stable conceptions that can be used in similar situations, and that it is:

> possible to study conceptual development in terms of the changing extent to which the alternatives are selected over time as the learner develops both the conceptual frameworks themselves, and judgements about the contexts in which they are best applied. (Taber, 2000, p. 414)

This view of 'multiple alternative frameworks' has received support from a range of research studies, showing how students tend to use a variety of understandings in tackling learning tasks in a variety of different settings, and that such variations in ways of understanding learning tasks may be found both within and between students in various educational settings (see e.g., Caravita & Halldén, 1994; Halldén, 1999; Maloney & Siegler, 1993; Petri & Niedderer, 1998; Taber, 1995, 1997; Taber & Watts, 1997; Tytler 1998; Watson, Prieto, & Dillon, 1997; cf. Jovchelovitch, 2002).

QUESTIONING THE NOTION OF ALTERNATIVE FRAMEWORKS

While most of the research has proposed elaborations, refinements and clarifications within this idea of stable alternative frameworks, there have also been attempts to radically shift the theoretical position and move away from the notion of alternative frameworks altogether. DiSessa (1988), for instance, has proposed that learners' knowledge is better understood as 'knowledge in pieces'.

However, the most serious critique of alternative framework research has come from the sociocultural theory of learning. In critically reviewing and appraising the research on cognitive development and learning, sociocultural commentators have levelled critique against constructivist research in general — including research on alternative frameworks and conceptual change — for not paying sufficient attention to the communicative and situational aspects of learning. Findings from a range of studies carried out within the sociocultural research tradition have demonstrated the strong impact that the learning environment has on learning in instructional settings. Säljö (1991b), for example, has shown that students' abilities to solve problems vary as a direct result of how learning tasks are presented, which suggests that conceptions should be seen not as fixed cognitive entities, but rather as socially constituted through continuous interaction with the teaching-learning environment (see also Säljö, 1994; Säljö, Schoultz, & Wyndhamn, 2001; Säljö & Wyndhamn, 1990; Wyndhamn, 1993). This criticism of research for not taking sufficient account of contextual influences on learning has not only struck the research on conceptual change. Phenomenographic research (Marton, 1981; Marton & Booth, 1997) has also been criticised for not giving sufficient attention to how situational aspects might influence learners' conceptions of aspects of various phenomena, and thus for giving a decontextualised account of students' conceptions (Säljö, 1994; cf. also Bowden, 1995). Moreover, Säljö (1997) has argued that using research interviews as the primary source of information about individuals' mental lives does not really provide access to people's conceptions, but rather to specific discourses as they unfold in particular communicative practices, notably, the interview. In particular, Säljö (1997) levelled critique against the common practice of viewing answers given by interviewees in interviews as indicators of existing conceptions or 'ways of experiencing' the world; such a view, he argued, obstructs alternative interpretations of functional mechanisms of why people talk the way they do.

> This circularity prescribes a logic to the research process that in unnecessary ways restricts the potential significance of its outcome: we could learn much more about actors' definitions of the world if we viewed their accounts primarily as attempts at communicating in situated practices rather than as ways of experiencing. (Säljö, 1997, p. 188)

So, it is important to realise that the interview, as indeed any form of institutionalised communication, involves specific social constraints which influence the interaction between interviewer and interviewee and thus shape both the form and the content of their interchange (Säljö, 1997; Jönsson, Linell, & Säljö, 1991). Indeed, the dynamics of a dialogue between interlocutors forms "part of a continuous process in verbal communication in which the speaker and the listener jointly construct the meaning of a linguistic item" (Marková, 1990, p. 136). And even though dialogues are reciprocal by their very nature, they are also inherently asymmetrical (Marková & Foppa, 1991, p. 260). Therefore, in obtaining information about cognitive processes from interviews or other dialogically generated data, a crucial task will be to account both for situational influences and for the cognitive content of the dialogue. In other words, to arrive at a more complete understanding of the phenomenon under study any interpretation of data has to take into account cognitive as well as situational aspects of that phenomenon.

Critique of this kind has sparked discussion about the theoretical status of the construct of alternative frameworks (the A in Figure 19.1) and how this theory should be brought to bear on issues relating to teaching and learning.

RESEARCH ON THE PROCESS OF CONCEPTUAL CHANGE

As mentioned earlier, the other strand of research growing out of considerations of how learners' conceptual development may be facilitated focused on the process of conceptual change; in other words, on the transformative properties of the arrow in Figure 19.1. Drawing on Piagetian developmental psychology, the history of science and the notion of conceptual ecology, Posner and coworkers (1982) argued that there are four necessary conditions that need to be fulfilled in order for conceptual change to occur: there has to be (1) an initial dissatisfaction with an existing conception, (2) a new and intelligible conception must present itself; (3) this conception must be plausible, and (4) also suggest possibilities for a fruitful research programme. Posner and coworkers (1982) described the process of conceptual change as an entirely rational process with the learner acting like a 'little scientist'.

In the beginning of the 1980s, Gilbert and Watts (1983) reviewed the research within the alternative framework movement and described three different models for conceptual change in relation to three different perspectives on the concept of 'conception': (1) The 'Stepped-Change Model', involving an all-or-nothing view on conceptions as a set of 'logical atoms' that the individual either has or does not have, (2) the 'Smooth-Change Model' which took a linear view of conceptual change involving gradual changes over an extended period of time, and finally (3) the 'Catastrophe Theory Model', the model preferred by Gilbert and Watts (1983), drawing on a comprehensive view of conceptual change allowing both gradual changes in conceptions and more instantaneous change processes to occur. A central idea in this model was that it allowed a cost-benefit analysis in relation to conceptual change: what do I gain if I acquire a new concept and what do I lose if I abandon my established way of conceptualising the phenomenon in question?

Despite the apparent differences in views on how conceptual change occurs, these models have something in common: they outline a profile of conceptual change as a process moving from a conception (A) to a conception (B), but reveal little about the active components of this process; the models do not reveal much about what is involved in conceptual change or what obstacles there might be for conceptual change to occur.

As previously mentioned, Vosniadou (1994) described a conceptual structure comprising a framework theory built on ontological and epistemological presuppositions together with a related set of beliefs, a specific theory, about the target conception, that is, the conception that is supposed to change. Conceptual change, then, may involve a gradual suspension and revision of the presuppositions of the framework theory ultimately allowing restructuring of beliefs within the specific theory resulting in a conceptual change. This can make the process of conceptual change a relatively slow process sometimes involving the construction of *synthetic models* as intermediate steps towards genuine conceptual change. So, from this perspective, the core problem of conceptual change is not the direct transition from a conception A to another conception B. Rather, "It is the presuppositions that are difficult to change and resistant to instruction and not the misconceptions *per se*" (Vosniadou, 1994, p. 65). Undoubtedly, this is still a causal model of conceptual change, but it is perhaps better described in a 'non-linear' fashion (cf. diSessa, 2002):

$$A \rightsquigarrow B$$

Quite a different way of looking at the process of conceptual change was introduced by diSessa and Sherin (1998), who described 'conceptions', in terms of *coordinating classes*, as "systematically connected ways of getting information from the world" (p. 1171). In fact, they did away with the concept of 'conception' altogether and talked about different ways of 'seeing' the world. Taking their theory to be a theory of perception, it implies that we are not bound by discursive practices and cultural tools in explaining the surrounding world. Nor are we bound by previously established conceptual structures. We are, however, constrained by particular strategies for obtaining information and particular strategies for seeing. In taking this view, diSessa and Sherin (1998) moved away from much of the prior work on conceptual change, proposing that the core problem of conceptual change is "shifting the means of seeing" (p. 1171). diSessa and Sherin's (1998) theory brings to the fore the processes involved in concept formation when students are presented with scientifically relevant learning tasks. Rather than focusing on erroneous conceptions as a barrier to acquiring new conceptions, diSessa and Sherrin (1998) introduced more of a systems theory approach pointing up the role of coordination activities in the learner. And in connecting the students' performances in relation to learning tasks and the processes apparently guiding those performances this theory makes an original alternative to the research perspectives adopted within the alternative framework movement which, as has been argued above, often hold an A → B view of the process of conceptual change.

This summary of research on alternative frameworks and the process of conceptual change illustrates some of the variations and tensions in theoretical approaches and conceptualisations. However, looking across the different research strands also reveals a pervading pattern implying a *causal view of conceptual change*. Almost invariably the research seeks to explain deficiencies in the conception A that force the learner to conceptual change, or to explain difficulties in achieving an understanding of B (conceptual change), by referring to constraining conditions within or around A (see Figure 19.1). However, if we view learners as individuals who intentionally try to realise certain goals, the shortcomings observed in A do not become antecedents in a causal relationship. Rather, they become arguments in a *teleological* explanation of why learners explain things as they do. In taking the intentional character of learning into account, the present research builds on and follows through on the research initiative originally proposed by Marton and Säljö (1976a, 1976b) in their influential studies on the relations between learning processes and learning outcomes. Next, an attempt will be made to clarify this intentional view on learning and conceptual change.

A DISTINCTION BETWEEN 'TASK' AND 'PROBLEM'

In a series of early research studies (Halldén, 1982; Wistedt, 1987), the observation was made that students who were assigned learning tasks by their teacher often ended up working on different problems than the ones the teacher had expected them to work on (cf. Bennet, Desforges, Cockburn, & Wilkinson, 1984; Doyle, 1979a, 1979b). Essentially, it seemed as if the students were trying to learn something different from what they were being taught. Extensive analyses of how the students tackled various tasks in different subjects made it clear that the difficulties that they had in coping successfully with subject-matter requirements could be understood with reference to the students' personal interpretations of tasks that confronted them in various settings. Accordingly, an explicit distinction was introduced between 'task' and 'problem', defining task as: "what is presented to the [students] by the teacher with the intention that they are to do something and/or that they are to learn something" (Halldén, 1988, p. 125) and problem as the student's personal "interpretation of the task given" (Halldén, 1988, p. 125). Methodologically, this distinction between task and problem described a shift from a teacher-oriented to a student-oriented perspective on the learning that occurs in a particular teaching-learning environment (Entwistle, 1996; Entwistle & Ramsden, 1983). Moreover, and importantly, this distinction involved the recognition that students who were confronted with the same learning task might end up working on what amounts to different problems. While much of the previous research had been focused on students' mistakes and difficulties — thus adhering to what Rommetveit (1978) called the "negative scholarly rationalism" — an important question became what sort of learning activities that students do, in fact, engage in when they are confronted with learning tasks in different settings, and what these activities imply in terms of opportunities for students' learning.

Two studies (Halldén, 1999; Scheja, 2006) on students' conceptions of statistical probability provide an example of this research stance. In both studies, a sample of undergraduates taking a basic course in education were invited to participate in a problem session presenting them with the following task, originally used by Kahneman and Tversky (1982) in their investigations into decision making and judgement under uncertainty:

Linda is 31-years-old, single, outspoken, and very bright. She majored in philosophy. As a student, she was deeply concerned with issues of discrimination and social justice, and also participated in anti-nuclear demonstrations.

Which of the following two statements about Linda is more probable.

A) Linda is a bank-teller.
B) Linda is a bank-teller and is active in the feminist-movement. (p. 496)

When the students had studied the task and decided on one of the two alternatives, they were also encouraged to comment on their choices. For a statistician, the obvious answer would be that A is the more probable statement since it is a principle of probability theory that the probability of a particular statement or an event P (e.g., that Linda is a bank-teller) is always higher than the probability of P in conjunction with another statement Q (e.g., that Linda is a bank-teller *and* is active in the feminist-movement). In both studies, and in the original study by Kahneman and Tversky (1982), the majority of the students responded that B was the more probable statement. Looking solely at the quantitative distribution of the students' responses, one way of accounting for this fallacy would be to see it as a result of shortcomings in the students' knowledge of probability theory. However, while this is often the conclusion drawn, the later studies by Halldén (1999) and Scheja (2006) went beyond the quantitative pattern of responses to produce an alternative explanation of the outcome, an explanation taking into account the students' reasons for picking one statement before the other. By way of example, some students had great difficulty in choosing between the two statements. One student, who picked B, described the dilemma as follows:

First, I thought [about choosing] A, according to the rules for determining the probability of a true statement, but then I thought I was supposed to draw conclusions from the text describing Linda, and so I chose B. But now I realize I was wrong! (Halldén, 1999, p. 57)

For this student, the task seemed to present two very different notions of 'probability'. The task may be seen as a problem of statistical probability, in which case the rules of probability theory may be applied. Or, it may be seen as a problem involving the construction of a 'good-reason assay', that is, a rationale through which information about a person (here 'Linda') can be used to reach a probable, in terms of being sensible or realistic, conclusion about that person, given the circumstances (e.g., that 'Linda is a bank-teller and is active in the feminist movement'). In everyday life individuals often make decisions about probability by construing a good-reason assay and look for the rationality in observed behaviours (for an explication of this argument, see Halldén, 1999 and Scheja, 2006). The student in the excerpt above gave her answer according to her interpretation of what she thought she was supposed to do. This conclusion may seem trivial, but is nevertheless of crucial importance for understanding the personal rationality guiding the student's learning activity in relation to the task. The student tackled the task in view of her own understanding of the setting in which the task was presented; she thought she was supposed to draw conclusions from the information presented in the task, including the description of 'Linda', and so tried to produce a good-reason assay arguing for the alternative that best mapped onto that description. So far, it would seem that the reasons for the student's picking statement B rather than statement A may be explicated solely with reference to the 'social rules' or the discursive practice pervading the setting in which the task was presented. However, a close reading of the transcript makes it clear that the student did not draw exclusively on her knowledge (or lack of knowledge) about the situation or of the social practice as such ("But now I realize I was wrong!"). Her interpretation of the task also included a variation in ways of looking at probability as, on the one hand, a construct of probability theory and as a historical account relying on the presumed rationality embodied in the description of the person 'Linda', on the other. This analysis makes it clear that the student's understanding of the task as a problem to be solved involves not just an adjustment to perceived discursive requirements, but it also involves the actualisation of a repertoire of beliefs among which the student picks the belief that is perceived as being the most appropriate in the setting.

So, in solving the task the student considers the discursive requirements of the setting in which she finds herself and, in doing so, draws on her previous repertoire of beliefs and experiences to evaluate which sort of knowledge would fit the perceived requirements of that setting. From this deliberation a particular strategy for action is formed, which manifests itself in a particular way of tackling the learning task. Such a rationale for explaining students' activities has some affinity with how von Wright (1971) explained the interpretation of an action. To understand why people act the way they do in various situations it is necessary to ascribe meaning to their behaviour, that is, to regard it as intentional. It is in the light of a person's intentions that her behaviour becomes meaningful, can be understood in terms of action. From such an intentional perspective, to explain an action involves identifying circumstances within or around the agent that can clarify why the act was undertaken. In short: "Behavior gets its intentional character from being seen by the agent himself or by an outside observer in a wider perspective, from being set in a context of aims and cognitions" (von Wright, 1971, p. 115, cf. von Wright, 1979, 1980). Setting students' behaviour into an explanatory framework involving aims and cognitions evokes two kinds of contexts: one involving the students' beliefs about how to reach certain ends and another comprising their beliefs about the type of situation and demands put on them by that particular setting, as well as beliefs about opportunities for acting in these circumstances (Figure 19.2).

This model, and the thinking that flows from it, has proven helpful in explaining variations in students' ways of dealing with learning tasks across a variety of course settings (e.g., Halldén, 1999; Lundholm, 2005; Nilsson, 2006; Petersson, 2005; Ryve, 2006; Scheja, 2002; Wistedt, 1994a, 1994b). By focusing on students' idiosyncratic ways of understanding learning tasks con-

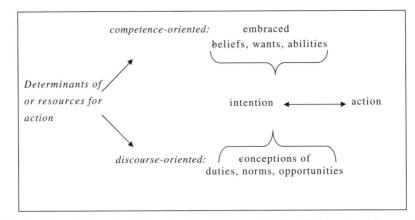

FIGURE 19.2   A model for rationalising action (modified from Halldén, 1999, and based on von Wright, 1971, 1974, 1979, and 1980. Reprinted with permission from Elsevier).

fronting them in various settings, it is possible to rationalise their way of dealing with these tasks with reference to their *competence-oriented* and *discourse-oriented resources* for acting on these tasks. Competence-oriented resources refer to the abilities, wants and desires, as well as to the beliefs that an individual holds, irrespective of situation. But any interpretation of students' activities also has to take into account how the students perceive the situation in hand. Accordingly, discourse-oriented resources allow explanation of students' ways of acting on a learning task with reference to their conceptions of duties, norms and opportunities. This is performed in a way which takes into consideration the students' beliefs about the actual setting as well as cultural norms for acting in that particular setting (Halldén, 1999). In view of this explication of the model, it may be argued that it incorporates, not only a cognitive dimension, but also a dimension of discursive practice, albeit without explicitly addressing the matter of participation and the discursive nature of human communication brought to the fore in sociocultural theory (e.g., Rogoff, 2003; Rommetveit, 1988).

To recap, the theoretical stance described here offers an explanatory framework for rationalising students' actions which takes account of both cognitive and sociocultural dimensions of the interaction with a particular teaching-learning setting. Students' ways of dealing with learning tasks, or more broadly, with their studies, can be explained by describing their personal understanding of the conceptual aspects of learning material, that is, with reference to competence-oriented resources. But it can also be explained with reference to discourse-oriented resources, in terms of the students' understanding of the situational constraints for dealing with their studies. In fact, competence-oriented and discourse-oriented resources can be seen as providing complementary perspectives for analysing individual students' understanding of topics brought to the fore in a teaching-learning environment (Scheja, 2002).

So, for the researcher, the concepts of competence-oriented and discourse-oriented resources of action become important analytical categories that can help to procure a nuanced understanding of the object of study. In particular, the model described above allows reflection on the data from different viewpoints: from a cognitive outlook focusing on students' wants, beliefs and desires in relation to the content of a learning task, and from a sociocultural viewpoint focusing on the constraints and affordances for acting in a certain setting, as these are perceived by the students' in the circumstances (Figure 19.3).

This description of the analytical activity of the researcher, shown in Figure 19.3, in terms of a movement between different aspects of interpretation resembles the process of learning as it has been described in research on concept formation, where learners construct their conceptual

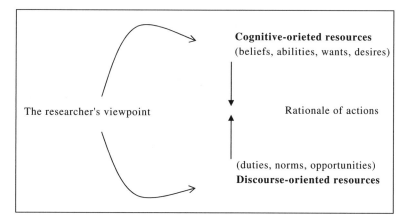

FIGURE 19. 3   The variation in viewpoints involved in the rationalisation of an action.

understanding of a given task with reference to interpretations at a meta level of the subject matter as a whole (Halldén, 1988, pp. 134ff.). By analogy, the researcher, too, must construct her or his knowledge of what is to be explained, and in doing so must draw on both cognitive and sociocultural data in order to form valid explanations of students' learning activities. Thus it is by shifting between these two different realms for interpretation, the cognitive and the sociocultural, that it is possible to reach an understanding of the meaning-making processes in which individuals involve themselves.

COHERENCE AS A PREREQUISITE FOR INTERPRETATION

Of course, these considerations of the researcher's role in rationalising individuals' meaning-making processes raise questions relating to the ontological assumptions underlying an interpretive act of the kind described above. Arguments for systematically ascribing rationality to individuals' behaviours can be found in contemporary philosophical discussions about 'radical interpretation'. It has, for instance, been argued that any effort that tries to make sense of other people's utterances must rest on an assumed maxim of coherence that forms part of a wider *principle of charity* (Davidson, 2001). In essence, this principle implies that the researcher, to make sense of individuals' ways of acting on a particular situation has to assume that these actions rely on a certain degree of coherence and cogency. In other words, the researcher has to assume that it is possible to understand other individuals. In fact, Davidson (2001) described interpretation as an adjustment between what seems to stand out as salient features for individuals and the coherence in their meaning-making processes. This implies that individuals, to some extent, overlap in how they view the world, and that this shared world-view enables intersubjectivity and mutual understanding. Salience, then, is to be regarded as a relational phenomenon; what is perceived as salient for an individual is contingent upon the situation in hand and on prior experiences (cf. Roth, 2001).

So, in research on individuals' meaning-making processes, the challenge becomes one of 'optimizing agreement' between the individual's view and the interpretation proposed as an explication of the meaning-making activities that the individual engages in. Assuming coherence and cogency can thus be seen as a prerequisite of maximizing the intelligibility of an individual's actions. Such an assumption provides a common background against which deviations from the assumed coherency may first be recognised, and then rationalised by being set in a context of individual intentions and cognitions explicating the observed meaning-making processes from the individual's own point of view. Formally, such an intentional explication may be captured in the form of a practical syllogism (for examples, see Halldén, Haglund, & Strömdahl, 2007; Scheja, 2002).

To simply assume coherence may be regarded as a bit straightforward, considering the lively debate on coherence in conceptual structures (cf. e.g., diSessa, chapter 2, this volume; Engel Clough & Driver, 1986; Taber, 2000; Tytler, 1998). But this debate has focused exclusively on the conceptualisations of, for instance, science concepts. The main question has had to do with to what extent laypeople coherently use conceptualisations alternative to those used in science. However, in the present chapter, the question of coherence relates to the coherence within individuals' conceptual structures and between such structures and the individuals' interpretations of the situation to hand. In short, instead of focusing on coherence across situations the research stance presented here is concerned with the coherence identified within particular situations. Below, an attempt will be made to clarify this theoretical position drawing on ongoing empirical research into the process of conceptual change. These examples will serve to illustrate, not just our theoretical stance, but also what this position can add to the research in terms of explaining the process of conceptual change.

INFERRING CONCEPTIONS FROM ACTIONS — CREATING RELATIONSHIPS

In an ongoing study aimed at describing 4- and 5-year-old children's emerging understanding of the word 'earth' (Larsson, Haglund, & Halldén, 2007), an attempt has been made to identify what kinds of problem children encounter. Besides referring to earth as 'soil', the children seem to perceive the earth as a circular object up in the sky. Thus, the connotations evoked by 'earth' seem to emanate, not from physical experience, but rather from experiences that the children have gained in their social lives. In addressing the problem of where people live across the earth, the children talked about earth as 'ground'. So, in the interviews the children were talking on the one hand about the 'earth' in the sky and about the 'earth' on the ground where people live, on the other. However, they used different labels to refer to these two 'earths'. Some of the children, apparently realising that people live on the earth located in the sky, had to try to unite the two meanings of 'earth'. In doing so, they were confronted with several problems. For instance, if people live on top of a spherical body they might easily fall off (cf. Vosniadou, 1994; Vosniadou, Skopeliti, & Ikospentaki, 2005). There was also the question of how it is possible to breathe on an earth located high up in the sky or in space. Some of the children who were faced with these problems tried to solve them by creating a picture of the earth as inhabiting people on a circular disc surrounded by a hollow sphere (this model has been reported in several studies on children's conception of the earth, see e.g., Nussbaum, 1979, 1985; Vosniadou, 1994). This hollow sphere model of the earth solved the initial problem of grasping the earth as being at the same time a circular body in the sky and the 'ground' where people live and lead their lives. It also solved related problems of what is up and what is down on the earth, as well as the problem of the availability of oxygen or air. This *compounded model* (Halldén, Petersson, Scheja, Ehrlén, Haglund, Österlind, & Stenlund, 2002; Larsson, Haglund, & Halldén, 2007) can be seen as an alternative to the synthetic model described by Vosniadou (1994). The compounded model is not a synthesis between an initial model and a scientific model but rather a model that collects information from a range of different sources and incorporates this information into a coherent system. It should also be noted that such a model does not prescribe a recipe for a correct modelling of the earth. It is simply a way for an individual to create coherence and meaning from a range of different, and sometimes contradictory, facts. In respect of questions relating to the shape of the earth, the compounded model meets the requirements both of flat models of the earth, such as maps, and astronomical models of the earth, the globe for example. In process terms the model captures a conceptual transformation that can be described in terms of two conceptions A and B being combined into a compounded conception AB (Figure 19.4).

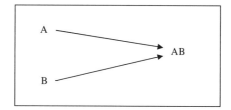

FIGURE 19.4   Two conceptions are combined into one conception.

In a sense, this model illustrates Vosniadou's point (1994) that new information "[…] is assimilated into the existing conceptual structure creating synthetic models or misconceptions" (Vosniadou, 1994, p. 56). The creation of a compounded, or synthetic model makes it possible to assimilate new information into this model. But the process of constructing a compounded model is rather a question of accommodation in the Piagetian sense of the word (Piaget, 1970); the model is an original product of the child's constructing activity which enables further assimilation of new information. So, the construction of a compounded model is prompted by an intention to relate disparate pieces of information to make sense of the world. The model can be seen as the child's invention used to solve specific problems that do not always have their roots in presuppositions. Ultimately, this meaning-making process, involving the connection of disparate pieces of information to one another in an attempt to make sense of the world, is an essential ingredient in learning and understanding.

The above provided an example of relating two contradictory bits of information to each other. However, to be able to relate more complex amounts of data to one another it is also necessary to construct some sort of coherent whole which can act as a frame of reference for these relating processes. Half a century ago, Miller (1956) argued that an individual's memory capacity is limited to bits of information ranging between five and nine. To further extend this capacity, it is necessary to organise different bits of information into units or chunks. Since the memory span is a fixed number of chunks, it is possible to increase the number of bits of information that it contains by continuously creating larger chunks. It follows that to effectively make use of one's memory capacity and to fathom the events of an increasingly complex surrounding world, it is necessary to construct personal contexts for the information. Another study (Wang, 2007) carried out within our research group provides an illustration of this process of constructing coherent wholes of information belonging to different problem areas.

The study, which focused on student's understandings of environmental problems and the intensified greenhouse effect in 'green schools' in China, illustrates how the teaching in these schools confronts the student with information about pollution, the intensified greenhouse effect, the depletion of the ozone layer, the melting of the ice at the poles, technical information on why the ozone layer is destructed, and so forth. The challenge for these students is not to relate two parameters to each other, but rather to make meaning of a huge amount of information derived from a variety of different conceptual contexts and used in several different communicative genres (Mäkitalo, Jakobsson, & Säljö, in press). The study illustrates how the students try to relate these quite diverse information bits and events to one another. And, in being asked to explain what is meant by the intensified greenhouse effect the students make an effort to construct models which allow the incorporation of most of the information given, into an all embracing model. One such model is described in an interview with a girl called Zhu. Zhu's modelling of the intensified greenhouse effect consists of holes in the atmosphere, as a result of the depletion of the ozone layer; these holes allow the sun light to reach the earth and to heat it up. The model also implies impossibility for the heat to escape out into space from other places on the earth where there are no holes in the atmosphere, because of the pressure of the atmosphere itself. Moreover, the melting of the ice at the poles means that the earth suffers the loss of the ice's cooling effect. A similar description of "holes" in the atmosphere was provided by a boy, Hao, who pointed out that the gases that destroy the ozone layer stay at the polar regions because "the north and the south poles are at the tops of the earth" and that is why the ozone layer is thinnest at the polar regions and the sun is able to shine right through at the earth.

Clearly these students were constructing compounded models, although these compounded models brought together more disparate information than was the case with the children's modelling of the earth. Moreover, the modelling of the intensified greenhouse effect illustrated above could hardly be regarded as a compromise or mesh of scientifically endorsed and naïve models. Of course, it may be argued that these apparently erroneous ideas should not be regarded as models in the first place, but are perhaps better described as aspects of *romancing* in Piagetian sense of the word (Piaget, 1929). Nevertheless, they illustrate a particular way of constructing meaning from a great deal of facts and this meaning-making process may potentially be seen as a step towards a more complete, and perhaps scientifically valid, conceptualisation of the phenomena involved. The point we wish to make here is, that regardless of how correct or erroneous these models were in relation to a given school norm or in relation to academic science, they nevertheless made sense from the individual's point of view, and carried with them a personal rationality imbued in the coherence offered by the compounded models.

A recent investigation into a group of students' studying history provides yet another example of how individuals' meaning-making processes involve the creation of compounded models. In their efforts to contextualise the vast amount of information presented during a visit at a museum, the students conformed either to a narrative or to a structural view (Björk, 1983) on historical description (Haglund & Halldén, 2007). In particular, the students seemed to construct alternative ways of accounting for the information provided — alternative in relation to the models sought after in the teaching. The analysis of data made it clear that for the students the challenge was about structuring the information provided and to group it into one or several contexts for interpretation that would render the information meaningful.

In sum, the examples presented above provide an illustration of how relationships are created between disparate and sometimes contradictory pieces of information by relating these bits and pieces to a coherent whole. Essentially, this is a description not only of alternative frameworks but also of the construction of such alternative frameworks. Importantly, a compounded model of the sort described here does not imply a compromise being made between common-sense thinking and scientifically approved models. Since the learner does not have access to the complete scientific model in the first place, there can be no real compromise. Rather, the compounded model is a solution to problems that the learner faces in relation to being presented with disparate or contradictory information. Thus, the compounded model is the construction of a common context that be used for understanding and explaining a variety of information.

In effect, the compounded model can be looked upon as an explication of the competence oriented resources in Figure 19.3. It describes what makes assimilation (Piaget, 1952) or enrichment (Vosniadou, 1994) possible and points up the resources on which the learner draws on in acting on a particular situation. As mentioned earlier, such a model can be described as involving different levels (Caravita & Halldén, 1994). There is an empirical level that states what is seen as data or evidence in a description or an explanation; this empirical level thus defines what there is to be noticed or potentially to be seen. Going back to the study on students' conceptions of probability exemplified above, it can be noted that the personal details provided by the task description on the person 'Linda' are not really relevant in calculating the probability of the two statements; the information needed to reach a probability theoretical solution is rather the number of propositions made about Linda. It follows that the empirical level is constituted by a conceptual level determining what should be regarded as salient features at the empirical level. However, and as pointed out earlier, conceptions are linked to one another according to overarching principles and beliefs to be found at a theoretical or meta-level. To illustrate, in a study (Halldén, 1998) on students' understanding of the Darwinian theory of evolution it was found that students' difficulties in understanding and giving scientific explanations of, for instance, natural selection had to do with their views on what really counts as a scientific explanation (Halldén, 1998; for examples from the understanding of history see Halldén, 1986, 1998; compare the idea of presuppositions in Vosniadou, 1994). This differentiation between levels of frameworks has important implications for the conceptualisation of conceptual change. Radical conceptual change or restructuring, as opposed to enrichment (Vosniadou, 1994), would involve changes at all three levels simultaneously. Conceptual change is likely to occur when reflection at the theoretical level and tentative interpretations made at the empirical level are calibrated and brought together into a coherent conceptual pattern (Halldén, 1999) transferring the learner into an entirely new or different conceptual context (cf. Ehrlén, 2008; Österlind, 2005; cf. also Entwistle, 2007, for a related discussion on 'knowledge objects').

The stability of compounded models will not be dwelt on further here. It is still an empirical question to what extent such models are momentary constructions in a specific situation and to what extent they form stable representations used for explaining phenomena in different situations.

EXPLICATING COHERENCE AS A PREREQUISITE FOR INTERPRETATION

Earlier it was mentioned that, from a methodological point of view, assuming coherence and cogency is a prerequisite of understanding an individual's meaning-making processes. In particular, it is by setting an individual's utterances and behaviour in a context of aims and cognitions that it is possible to explicate this behaviour in terms of meaning-making processes that make sense in the circumstances. So, methodologically, to arrive at such an understanding of an individual's meaning-making activities, it is necessary to put these activities into context. Moreover, meaning making itself, in the sense it has been exemplified here, involves putting bits and pieces into context. So, in modelling the process of conceptual change, the notion of context seems to take on added importance. The concept of context, as it is used here, refers, not to the physical or discursive situation in which individuals find themselves, but to the individuals' personal framings of that situation — framings within which they think about learning material, for example science concepts (cf. Cobb, 1986, 1990). This constructivist definition of context allows the study of meaning making in terms of individuals' contextualisations of information that is presented in a particular setting. The compounding of information into broad, but seemingly coherent, models illustrates this contextualisation process and also points to the variation of contexts potentially involved in such a process.

In relation to the study of meaning making and conceptual change, different forms of context have been brought to the fore. First, there is the conceptual context which involves individual beliefs about, for instance, science concepts. An individual's notion of a science concept, of course, may differ a great deal from the ideas captured in the scientific definition of that concept. The concept of force, for example, has its place within a scientific framework that gives a particular meaning to force as something that changes the direction or velocity of an object. An individual's conception of force, however, may be something that makes an object move. The difference between these accounts falls back on how the concept in question is contextualised by an individual in a particular situation. The situation is important because it can provide the individual with cues for how the information presented, for instance in a teaching-learning setting, should be dealt with. So, apart from a conceptual context, there is also a situational context that can influence how an individual understands and deals with a particular piece of information. The study presented earlier, in which students were confronted with the task of deciding on the probability of two statements in relation to a description of a person 'Linda', provides a clear example. In deciding on one of the alternatives the student considered the situational framing of the task to be an important indication of how the task should be tackled.

Above it was described (Figure 19.3) from a methodological point of view how competence-oriented and discourse-oriented resources can be used as complementary perspectives in trying to arrive at an understanding of individuals' meaning-making activities. Similarly, from an empirical viewpoint the conceptual and situational contexts that individuals form as a result of trying to make sense of diverse pieces of information can be seen as working together in shaping the individuals' understandings of topics brought to the fore in different settings (Scheja, 2002). This combination of conceptual and situational contexts suggests a multidimensional structure of an individual's meaning-making process in relation to tackling learning tasks in an instructional setting. In line with the distinction introduced earlier, between task and problem, students may be confronted with the one and the same learning task, but may end up working on quite different problems as a result of having — both situationally and conceptually — contextualised the task in different ways. An investigation into mathematics learning (Wistedt, 1994b) is illustrative in this regard. In the study 11-year-old students were asked, in groups of three to four students, to divide a piece of wood into three equally big pieces and to express this division in decimal form. From the analyses of the students' interactions, it was clear that some students had contextualised the task as an everyday problem of dividing a real piece of wood, where 'equally big pieces' was interpreted as 'equally big, so the difference doesn't show'. Others had contextualised the task as a theoretical problem where 'equally big' took on quite a different and more abstract meaning, leading the students towards considering the problem of infinity. This example illustrates the shaping of a problem context in which situational and conceptual contextualisations provide a frame of reference for thinking about a perceived problem. From the researcher's viewpoint, in the interpretation of data several different contexts need to be taken into account: the hypothesized conceptual structure of the individual — the conceptual context — and the individual's perception of the actual setting — the situational context. Of course, the situational context may also include cultural norms and presuppositional beliefs that the individual acts on habitually (Ehrlén, in press a; Halldén, 1999). However, it is also necessary to take the problem context into consideration, that is, the context in which individual learners situate a particular problem that they set themselves to solve. By studying these individually constructed contexts, it is possible to achieve an understanding of the rationality of the learners' actions from the viewpoint of the learners' themselves.

COMPOUNDED MODELS AND DIFFERENTIATION

To return to the question of the process of conceptual change, above it was illustrated how individuals, confronted with information from a variety of different sources, form compounded models in an attempt to bring coherence to this jumble of information (Figure 19.4). Needless to say, however, this process of combining conceptions into compounded models only accounts for part of the process of conceptual change. In what follows, and drawing on the constructivist notion of context explicated above, we would argue that if conceptual compounding reflects one step in the meaning-making process, another important step involves *differentiation* within and between such compounded models.

Looking at the now rather well-researched problem of conceptions of the earth, the problem addressed in research up till now has been not how children come up with a hollow-sphere model, but rather why it is so difficult for them to abandon the hollow sphere in favour of the more scientifically accurate spherical model. The hollow-sphere model covers what is culturally accounted for by, for instance, maps that can be used to navigate in a city, globes that can be used in calculations of long distance trips, or as a model for the earth as an astronomical body. Similarly, looking at the research on conceptions of the intensified greenhouse effect, the problem addressed by the research has been not why students blend ideas about the depletion of the ozone layer with ideas about the greenhouse effect, but rather how this merger acts as an obstacle for students in achieving a scientifically valid understanding of the intensified greenhouse effect. The examples provided in this chapter serve to illustrate how learners who are confronted with learning material in a particular setting, try to put this information into context, and, as a result, construct conceptual contexts for interpretation. Sometimes these conceptual contexts may be deemed inadequate in relation to the demands put on the students by the teaching-learning environment. However, the point is that students, as part of their development of a conceptual understanding, differentiate between different contexts, and realise that while it is possible to use one single model to account for a range of different phenomena, it may be preferable and more effective to use two models, for example in relation to the earth, or several different models to account for, for instance, the ozone layer, the intensified greenhouse effect, and environmental pollution.

DIFFERENTIATION BETWEEN CONTEXTS

What has just been described basically amounts to a model of conceptual change in which individuals who are confronted with information in a particular setting, contextualise this information in ways that enable them to (1) combine information of the conceptions provided into a single compounded model and (2) differentiate between available contexts for interpretation and use ways of conceptualising the information that correspond to these different contexts and to the current situation in hand (Figure 19.5).

As illustrated by the empirical examples provided in this chapter, this process of compounding and differentiating involves a process of deliberation where the individual draws on cognitive-oriented and discourse-oriented resources, involving both personal beliefs about how the information should be understood and the social framing—such as discursive rules, norms and opportunities — that may support this contextualisation process.

On the face of it, this way of describing conceptual change as a process involving deliberation may conjure up an image of an intentional conceptual change in terms of deliberate attempts to radically change from one conceptual system to another (e.g., Sinatra & Pintrich, 2003). It should, however, be noted that the model proposed here involves intentionality not as a motivational and psychological background factor prompting an individual's actions, but rather as an analytical construct ascribed to the individual's actions and inferred from the ways in which the individual tackles the situation in hand. To put it differently, intentions here are not to be viewed as 'prior intentions' (Searle, 1969, 1983) in a causal chain of events, but as 'intentions in action' (Searle, 1969, 1983) inferred within a teleological explanative framework (Davidson, 2001; von

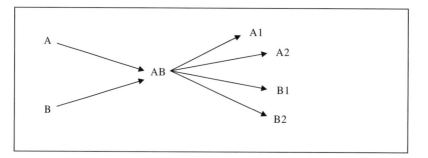

FIGURE 19.5   The process of conceptual change as a process of compounding and differentiating contexts.

Wright, 1971). It is by ascribing individuals' behaviours (e.g., utterances), an intentionality that makes these behaviours meaningful and reasonable in the circumstances, that it is possible to arrive at an understanding of what these individuals are trying to achieve.

Such an approach differs from a sociocultural research stance in that it focuses on the individual and the individual's apparent interpretation of the setting, not — as in most sociocultural analyses — on the setting itself or on the discursive practices constituting that setting. And while sociocultural research strives to account for activities occurring within such discursive practices in terms of ways of talking or of engaging in tool-mediated action (Wertsch, 1998, cf. also Vosniadou, Skopeliti, & Ikospentaki, 2005 with regard to their critique of sociocultural research), the intentional approach proposed here puts an effort into inferring conceptions and conceptual structures from individuals' ways of acting in a particular setting.

Moreover, and importantly, an intentional approach of the kind described here obviates at least some of the critique from sociocultural research concerning the difficulty in gaining access to people's conceptions of the world (Säljö, 1997). The research stance proposed here focuses on individuals' learning activities in a particular setting, and on the meanings that can be ascribed to those activities. In view of this focus on meaning making, the intentional approach is perhaps best described not as a psychology but rather as methodology for understanding and explaining individuals' meaning-making activities and conceptual change. However, as illustrated by the empirical examples presented above, the application of this methodology nevertheless has generated findings that point towards a theoretical model offering a view of the process of conceptual change alternative to those typically followed in research on conceptual change.

CONCLUDING REMARKS

At the outset of this chapter, it was argued that much of the research on learning and conceptual change has adhered to a negative rationalism (Rommetveit, 1978) focusing on students' shortcomings and difficulties. The chapter has outlined a methodology which does not seek to judge students' reasoning in terms of how well they do in relation to a given task. In contrast, the intentional approach proposed here actively moves away from a negative rationalist view, towards what might be called a 'positive pedagogy' focusing on learners' potentiality for learning through exploring the opportunities for learning that arise in the learners' interaction with the learning material and with their surroundings. Adopting an approach to conceptual change which emphasizes potentiality rather than fallibility has important implications for teaching. From such a perspective, guiding students' efforts to develop conceptual understanding in different subject areas does not mean accepting or ignoring apparent mistakes or misconceptions. It means taking them seriously enough to look for ways to help students extend and develop these efforts within contexts that allow important salient features of the learning material to be recognised as crucial ingredients in understanding those concepts. Such a perspective, which reveals students' ways of contextualising concepts and learning tasks, enables teachers to engage not only with students but also with students' efforts to understand. In that sense it also provides a crucial pathway for linking the students' personal conceptions to ways of thinking endorsed within the discipline.

REFERENCES

Bennet, N., Desforges, C., Cockburn, A., & Wilkinson, B. (1984). *The quality of pupil learning experiences*. Mahwah, NJ: Erlbaum.

Berti, A. E. (1994). Children's understanding of the concept of the state. In M. Carretero & J. F. Voss (Eds.), *Cognitive and instructional processes in history and the social sciences* (pp. 49–76). Mahwah, NJ: Erlbaum.

Björk, R. (1983). *Den historiska argumenteringen. Konstruktion, narration, och kolligation. Förklaringsresonemang hos Nils Ahnlund and Erik Lönnroth* [*The historical argumentation. Construction, narration and colligation*]. Stockholm: Almqvist & Wiksell.

Brumby, M. N. (1979). Students' perceptions and learning styles associated with the concept of evolution by natural selection, Doctoral diss., University of Surrey.

Brumby, M. N. (1984). Misconceptions about the concept of natural selection by medical students. *Science Education, 68*, 493–503.

Bowden, J. (1995). Phenomenographic research. Some methodological issues. *Scandinavian Journal of Educational Research, 15*, 144–155.

Caravita, S., & Halldén, O. (1994). Reframing the problem of conceptual change. *Learning and Instruction, 4*, 89–111.

Cobb, P. (1986). Context, goals, beliefs, and learning mathematics. *For the Learning of Mathematics, 6*, 2–9.

Cobb, P. (1990). Multiple Perspectives. In L. P. Steffe & T. Wood (Eds.), *Transforming children's mathematics education* (pp. 200–215). Mahwah., NJ: Erlbaum.

Dahlgren, L-O. (1978). Effects of university education on the conception of reality. Paper presented at the 4th International Conference on Improving University Teaching. July 26–29, 1978, Aachen, Germany.

Davidson, D. (2001). *Inquiries into truth and interpretation* (2nd ed.). Oxford: Oxford University Press.

Deadman, J. A., & Kelly, P. J. (1978). What do secondary school boys understand about evolution and heredity before they are taught the topics? *Journal of Biology Education, 12*, 7–15.

Dickinson, A. K., Gard, A., & Lee, P. J. (1986). Evidence in history and the classroom. In A. K. Dickinson & P. J Lee (Eds.), *Historical teaching and historical understanding* (pp. 1–20). London: Heineman.

diSessa, A. A. (1988). Knowledge in pieces. In G. Forman & P. Pufall (Eds.), *Constructivism in the computer age* (pp. 49–70). Mahwah, NJ: Erlbaum.

diSessa, A. A. (2002). Why conceptual ecology is a good idea. In M. Limon & L. Mason (Eds.), *Reconsidering conceptual change – issues in theory and practice* (pp. 29–60). Dordrecht; Kluwer.

diSessa, A. A., & Sherin B. L. (1998). What changes in conceptual change?, *International Journal of Science Education, 20*, 1155–1191.

Doyle, W. (1979a). Classroom tasks and students' abilities. In P. L. Peterson & H. L. Walberg (1979), *Research on teaching: Concepts, findings and implication* (pp. 183–209). Berkeley, CA: McCutchan.

Doyle, W. (1979b). Making managerial decisions in classroom. In. D. L. Duke (Ed), *Classroom management*. The seventy-eight yearbook of the national Society for the study of Education (pp. 42–74). Chicago: University of Chicago Press.

Driver, R., & Easley, J. (1978). Pupils and paradigms: a review of literature related to concept development in adolescent science students. *Studies in Science Education, 5*, 61–84.

Duit, R. (2006). *Bibliography: Students' and teachers' conceptions and science education database (2006).* University of Kiel, Kiel, Germany. Retrieved on 5 June 2006 from http://www.ipn.uni-kiel.de/aktuell/stcse/stcse.html.

Ehrlén, K. (2007). Children's understanding of globes as a model of the earth: A problem of contextualizing. *International Journal of Science Education, 30*(2), 222–238.

Ehrlén, K. (2008). Drawings as representations of children's conceptions. *International Journal of Science Education*, 1–17 [iFirst Article].

Engel Clough, E., & Driver, R. (1986). A study of consistency in the use of students' conceptual frameworks across different task contexts. *Science Education, 70*, 473–496.

Entwistle, N. (1996). Recent research on student learning and the learning environment. In J. Tait & P. Knight (Eds.), *The management of independent learning*. London: Kogan Page.

Entwistle, N. (2007). Conceptions of learning and the experience of understanding: Thresholds, contextual influences, and knowledge objects. In S. Vosniadou & A. Baltas (Eds.), *Philosophical, historical and psychological approaches to conceptual change* (pp. 123–143). Amsterdam: Elsevier.

Entwistle, N., & Ramsden, P. (1983). *Understanding student learning.* London: Croom Helm.

Fontana, A., & Frey, J. (2005). The interview: From neutral stance to political involvement. In N. K Denzin & Y. S. Lincoln (Eds.), *The Sage handbook of qualitative research* (pp. 695–727). London: Sage Publications.

Furnham, A. (1994). Young people's understanding of politics and economics. In M. Carretero & J. F. Voss (Eds.), *Cognitive and instructional processes in history and the social sciences* (pp. 17–48). Mahwah, NJ: Erlbaum.

Gilbert, K. G., & Watts, D. M. (1983). Concepts, misconceptions and alternative conceptions: Changing perspectives in science education. *Studies in Science Education, 10,* 61–98.

Haglund, L., & Halldén, O. (2007). Making meaning of historical events. Submitted manuscript.

Halldén, O. (1982). *Elevernas tolkning av skoluppgiften* [*The learners' interpretation of the school task*]. Doctoral diss., Stockholm University, Department of Education.

Halldén, O. (1986). Learning history. *Oxford Review of Education, 12,* 53–66.

Halldén, O. (1988). Alternative frameworks and the concept of task. Cognitive constraints in pupils' interpretations of teachers' assignments. *Scandinavian Journal of Educational Research, 32,* 123–140.

Halldén, O. (1993). Learners' conceptions of the subject matter being taught: A case from learning history. *International journal of Educational Research, 19,* 317–325.

Halldén, O. (1994). Constructing the learning task in history instruction. In J. Voss, & M. Carretero (Eds.), *Cognitive and instructional processes in history and the social sciences* (pp. 187–200). Mahwah, NJ: Erlbaum.

Halldén, O. (1998). Personalization in historical descriptions and explanations. *Learning and Instruction, 8,* 131–139.

Halldén, O. (1999). Conceptual change and contextualisation. In W. Schnotz, S. Vosniadou, & M. Carretero (Eds.), *New perspectives on conceptual change* (pp. 53–65). Mahwah, NJ: Erlbaum.

Halldén, O., Haglund, L., & Strömdahl, H. (2007). Conceptions and contexts. On the interpretation of interviews and observational data. *Educational Psychologist, 42,* 25–40.

Halldén, O., Petersson, G., Scheja, M., Ehrlén, K., Haglund, L., Österlind, K., & Stenlund, A. (2002). Situating the question of conceptual change. In M. Limon, & L. Mason (Eds.), *Reconsidering conceptual change — issues in theory and practice* (pp. 137–148). Dordrecht: Kluwer.

Jönsson, L., Linell, P., & Säljö, R. (1991). Formulating the past: On remembering in police interrogations. *Multidisciplinary Newsletter for Activity Theory, 9, 10,* 5–11.

Jovchelovitch, S. (2002). Re-thinking the diversity of knowledge: Cognitive polyphasia, belief and representation. *Psychologie & Societé, 5,* 121–138.

Kahneman, D., & Tversky, A. (1982). On the study of statistical intuitions. In D. Kahneman, P. Slovic, & A. Tversky (Eds.), *Judgment under uncertainty: heuristics and biases* (pp. 493–508). New York: Cambridge University Press.

Larsson, Å., Haglund, L., & Halldén, O. (2007). On the emergence of a conception: Metaphors and models in conceptual change. *Submitted manuscript.*

Lave, J. (1991). Situating learning in communities of practice. In L. Resnick, J. Levine, & S. Teasley (Eds.), *Perspectives on socially shared cognition* (pp. 63–82). Washington, DC: American Psychological Association.

Lee, P. J., Dickinson, A., & Ashby, R. (1998). Researching children's ideas about history. In J. F. Voss & M. Carretero (Eds.), *Learning and reasoning in history. International review of history education, Vol. 2* (pp. 227–251). London: Woburn Press.

Lundholm, C. (2005). Learning about environmental issues: Postgraduate and undergraduate students' interpretations of environmental contents in education. *International Journal of Sustainability in Higher Education, 6,* 242–253.

Mäkitalo, Å., Jakobsson, A., & Säljö, R. (in press). Learning to reason in the context of socioscientific problems: exploring the demands on students in 'new' classroom activities. In K. Kumpulainen & M. Cesar (Eds.), *Investigating classroom interaction: Methodolgical choices and challenges.* London: Sense Publishers.

Maloney, D. P., & Siegler, R. S. (1993). Conceptual competition in physics learning. *International Journal of Science Education, 15,* 283–295.

Marková, I. (1990). A three-step process as a unit of analysis in dialogue. In I. Marková, & K. Foppa (Eds.), *The dynamics of dialogue* (pp. 129–146). London: Harvester Wheatsheaf.

Marková, I., & Foppa, K. (1991). Conclusion. In I. Marková, & K. Foppa (Eds.), *Asymmetries in dialogue* (pp. 259–273). London: Harvester Wheatsheaf.

Marton, F. (1981). Phenomenography — describing conceptions of the world around us. *Instructional Science, 10*, 177–200.

Marton, F. (1992). Phenomenography and "the art of teaching all things to all men". *Qualitative Studies in Education, 5*, 253–267.

Marton, F., & Booth, S. (1997). *Learning and awareness.* Mahwah, NJ: Erlbaum.

Marton, F., Hounsell, D., & Entwistle, N. (Eds.) (1997). *The experience of learning. Implications for teaching and studying in higher education* (2nd ed). Edinburgh: Scottish Academic Press.

Marton, F., & Säljö, R. (1976a). On qualitative differences in learning I. Outcome and process. *British Journal of Educational Psychology, 46*, 4–11.

Marton, F., & Säljö, R. (1976b). On qualitative differences II. Outcome as a function of the learner's conception of the task. *British Journal of Educational Psychology, 46*, 115–127.

Miller, G. A. (1956). The magical number seven plus or minus two: Some limits on our capacity for processing information. *Psychological Review, 63*, 81–97.

Nilsson, P. (2006). Exploring probabilistic reasoning. A study of how students contextualise compound chance encounters in explorative settings. Doctoral diss., Växjö University, Växjö: Växjö University Press.

Nussbaum, J. (1979). Children's conceptions of the earth as a cosmic body: A cross age study. *Science Education, 63*, 83–93.

Nussbaum, J. (1985). The earth as a cosmic body. In R. Driver, E. Guesne, & A. Tiberghien (Eds.), *Children's Ideas in Science.* Milton Keynes, UK: Open University Press.

Osborne, R. J., Bell, B. F., & Gilbert, J. K. (1983). Science teaching and children's views of the world. *European Journal of Science Education, 5*, 1–14.

Österlind, K. (2005). Concept formation in environmental education: 14-year olds' work on the intensified greenhouse effect and the depletion of the ozone layer. *International Journal of Science Education, 27*, 891–908.

Perkins, D. (2005). *Teaching to encourage thinking dispositions and understanding.* Paper presented at the British Journal of Psychology Conference. Edinburgh, Scotland, 19–20 May, 2005.

Petersson, G. (2005). Medical and nursing students' development of conceptions of science during three years of studies in higher education. *Scandinavian Journal of Educational Research, 49*, 281–296.

Petri, J,. & Niedderer, H. (1998). A learning pathway in high-school level quantum atomic physics. *International Journal of Science Education, 20*, 1075–1088.

Piaget, J. (1929/1951). *The child's conception of the world.* Savage, MD: Littlefield Adams Quality Paperbacks.

Piaget, J. (1932/1965). *The moral judgement of the child.* London: Free Press.

Piaget, J. (1952). *The origins of intelligence in children* (2nd ed.). New York: International Universities Press.

Piaget, J. (1970). *Genetic epistemology.* New York: Columbia University Press.

Posner, G. J., Strike, K. A., Hewson, P. W., & Gertzog, W. A. (1982). Accommodation of a scientific conception: toward a theory of conceptual change. *Science Education, 66*, 211–227.

Resnick, L. B. (1991). Shared cognition: Thinking as social practice. In L. B. Resnick, J. Levine, & S. Teasley (Eds.), *Perspectives on socially shared cognition* (pp. 1–20). Washington, DC: American Psychological Association.

Rogoff, B. (2003). *The cultural nature of human development.* Oxford: Oxford University Press.

Rommetveit, R. (1978). On the negative rationalism in scholarly studies of verbal communications and dynamic residuals in the construction of human intersubjectivety. In M. Brenner, P. Marsh, & M. Brenner (Eds.), *The social contexts of method* (pp. 16–32). London: Croom Helm.

Rommetveit, R. (1988). On literacy and the myth of literal meaning. In R. Säljö (Ed.), *The written world: Studies in literate thought and action* (pp. 13–40). Berlin: Springer-Verlag.

Roth, W. M. (2001). Situation Cognition. *The Journal of Learning Sciences, 10*, 27–61.

Ryve, A. (2006). Approaching mathematical discourse. Two analytical frameworks and their relation to problem solving interactions. Doctoral diss., Mälardalen University, Sweden.

Säljö, R. (1991a). Piagetian controversies, cognitive competence, and assumptions about human cognition. *Educational Psychology Review, 3*, 117–126.

Säljö, R. (1991b). Learning and mediation: fitting reality into a table. *Learning and Instruction, 1*, 261–272.

Säljö, R. (1994). Minding action: conceiving of the world versus participating in cultural practices. *Journal of Nordic Educational Research, 14*, 71–80.

Säljö, R. (1997). Talk as data and practice — a critical look at phenomenographic inquiry and the appeal to experience. *Higher Education Research & Development, 16*, 173–190.

Säljö, R., & Wyndhamn, J. (1990). Problem-solving, academic performance, and situated reasoning. A study of joint cognitive activity in the formal setting. *British Journal of Educational Psychology, 60*, 245–254.

Säljö, R., Schoultz, J., & Wyndhamn, J. (2001). Heavenly talk. A discursive approach to conceptual knowledge and conceptual change in children's understanding of elementary astronomy. *Human Development, 44*, 103–118.

Scheja, M. (2002). Contextualising studies in higher education: First year experiences of studying and learning in engineering. Doctoral diss., Stockholm University, Department of Education.

Scheja, M. (2006). Contextual variation and conceptual understanding in higher education. Paper presented at the SIG symposium on conceptual change, 14–17 May in Stockholm, Sweden.

Searle, J. R. (1969). *Speech acts*. Cambridge: Cambridge University Press.

Searle, J. R. (1983). *Intentionality*. Cambridge: Cambridge University Press.

Sinatra, G. M., & Pintrich, P. R. (Eds.). (2003). *Intentional conceptual change*. Mahwah, NJ: Erlbaum.

Stewart, J. H. (1982). Difficulties experienced by high school students when learning basic Mendelian genetics. *The American Biology Teacher, 44*, 80–89.

Stewart, J. H. (1983). Student problem-solving in high school genetics. *Science Education, 67*, 731–749.

Strike, K. A. & Posner, G. (1982). Conceptual change and science teaching. *European Journal of Science Education, 4*, 231–240.

Strike, K. A., & Posner, G. (1992). A revisionist theory of conceptual change. In R. Duschl, & R. Hamilton (Eds.), *Philosophy of science, cognitive psychology, and educational theory and practice* (pp. 147–176). Albany: State University of New York.

Taber, K. S. (1995). Development of Student Understanding: A Case Study of Stability and Lability in Cognitive Structure. *Research in Science & Technological Education, 13*, 87–97.

Taber, K. S. (1997). Understanding chemical bonding — The development of A level students' understanding of the concept of chemical bonding. Ph.D. thesis, University of Surrey.

Taber, K. S. (2000). Multiple frameworks? Evidence of manifold conceptions in individual cognitive structure. *International Journal of Science Education, 22*, 399–417.

Taber, K. S., & Watts, M. (1997). Constructivism and concept learning in chemistry — Perspectives from a case study. *Research in Education, 58*, 10–20.

Tiberghien, A. (1994). Modelling as a basis for analysing teaching-learning situations. *Learning and Instruction, 4*, 71–88.

Torney-Purta, J. (1994). Dimensions of adolescents' reasoning about political and historical issues: Ontological switches, developmental processes, and situated learning. In M. Carretero, & J. F. Voss (Eds.) *Cognitive and instructional processes in history and the social sciences* (pp.103–122). Mahwah, NJ: Erlbaum.

Tytler, R. (1998). Children's conceptions of air pressure: Exploring the nature of conceptual change. *International Journal of Science Education. 20*, 929–958.

von Wright, G. H. (1971). *Explanation and understanding*. Ithaca, New York: Cornell University Press.

von Wright, G. H. (1974). Lecture given at Stockholm University, March 5, 1974.

von Wright, G. H. (1979). Reasons, action, and experience. In H. Kohlenberger (Ed.), *Essays in honour of Raymond Klibanshy* (pp. 107–119). Hamburg: Felix Meiner Verlag.

von Wright, G. H. (1980). *Freedom and determination. Acta Philosophica Fennica, 1*(31), 1–8.

Vosniadou, S. (1994). Capturing and modeling the process of conceptual change. *Learning and Instruction, 4,* 45–70.

Vosniadou, S., Skopeliti, I., & Ikospentaki, K. (2005). Reconsidering the role of artefacts in reasoning: Children's understanding of the globe as a model of the earth. *Learning and Instruction, 15,* 333–351.

Wang, L. (2007). An investigation of students' understanding of the intensified greenhouse effect: Its cause and effect. Submitted for publication.

Watson, R., Prieto, T., & Dillon, J. S. (1997). Consistency of students' explanations about combustion. *Science Education, 81,* 425–444.

Watts, D. M. (1983). A study of schoolchildren's alternative frameworks of the concept of force. *European Journal of Science Education, 5,* 217–230.

Wertsch, J. V. (1998). *Mind as action.* Oxford: Oxford University Press.

Wistedt, I. (1987). *Rum för lärande [Latitude for learning].* Doctoral diss., Stockholm University, Department of Education.

Wistedt, I. (1994a). Everyday common sense and school mathematics. *European Journal of Psychology of Education, 9,* 139–147.

Wistedt, I. (1994b). Reflection, communication and learning mathematics: A case study. *Learning and Instruction, 4,* 123–138.

Wyndhamn, J. (1993). *Problem-solving revisited: on school mathematics as a situated practice.* (Linköping studies in arts and science, 98). Linköping: Linköping University.

20

The Idea of Phenomenography and the Pedagogy of Conceptual Change

Ference Marton
Göteborg University

Ming Fai Pang
The University of Hong Kong

A particular view of conceptual change is presented in this chapter, and its implications for teaching for conceptual change are illustrated through a detailed example of how young students make sense of price and pricing and how they become able to make better sense of the same. In the first part of the chapter, we characterize our approach to conceptual change. The second part of the chapter is one single example dealt with in considerable detail, followed by the third part in which theoretical issues are reflected in the main example. The way of presenting our research approach is operational: we want to show how we do it.

THE THEORY

The Idea of Conceptual Change

Two kinds of changes that are often described in research are changes due to learning and changes due to development. Change in learning frequently means that there is something someone cannot do. Then, after a period of learning, they can do it — at least to a certain extent. So, the change is from "nothing" to "something". For example, in the infancy of research on learning, Hermann Ebbinghaus presented lists (or pairs) of meaningless syllables, which the learners could not possibly recall without even having seen them, but mastered after a sufficient number of trials (Ebbinghaus, 1964). In the same way, one cannot swim or ride a bicycle until one has learnt to do so.

In research on development, on the other hand, the same task is given to children at different points in time, and comparisons are made between the different ways in which children handle that task at the different points in time. In this case, change goes from "something" (handling the task in one way) to "something" (handling the task in another way). Piaget studied, for instance, children's different ways of handling tasks including transformation of form and conservation of number, mass, volume, etc. When the same amount of liquid is poured from a narrow but high glass (A) to a wide but low glass (B), at first, the child might focus on height only and say that there is less in B, or they might focus on width only and say that there is more in B (see, for instance, Gruber & Voneche, 1977). Later on, the child focuses on both height and width, saying "it's the same in both", thus conserving the amount of liquid.

According to this line of reasoning, there seem to be two kinds of tasks. In one case, there are specific experiences needed for mastering the tasks, and therefore the learner starts from scratch[1] and by having the necessary experiences manages to master the tasks (for instance, such as re-calling meaningless syllables, learning to swim, to ride the bike or to speak a new language). In the other case, the necessary experiences for mastering the task are of such a general nature that it seems reasonable to give it to any child at a certain age level, without any recognized need for specific experiences, such as in the case of the Piagetian experiment just quoted.

Now, the school as a societal institution has a responsibility for arranging specific experi-ences in order to bring about specific capabilities in the students. This is why schools are mainly discussed in terms of learning rather than development.

Let us illustrate this by means of a problem in economics, which is a regular subject at the secondary school level in Hong Kong. The object of learning (i.e., what students are supposed to learn) is "to determine the price when demand and supply curves are given" (see Figure 20.1).

After having covered the topic, students are expected to be able to "identify how the price will be determined by the shifts of demand and supply curves" by examining the graphs.

Of course, you cannot ask students this question if they have never studied economics, as it demands specific technical knowledge, which can only be acquired through specific experiences. At the same time, there is something it does not demand, which a similar problem in life outside the school might have demanded. The problem takes for granted the aspects of the situation that are essential for solving the problem, and in this way the conceptual aspects of the problem be-come hidden. The student does not have to discern demand and supply as the critical features of the situation; they are given. In real life, on the other hand, you have to find out what has to be considered in order to determine the price. Then, you have to discern what is critical and also use the technical tools to achieve your aim (to find "the right" price). In this case, the task has two levels: a conceptual/developmental level and a technical/learning-related level. In school, often only the latter is represented.

Refer to the diagram below. E_0 is the initial equilibrium point of the toy market in the U.S. After a sharp increase in the price of raw materials and a boom in the US economy, the new equilibrium point will be

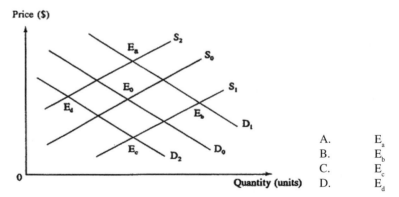

FIGURE 20.1   A question extracted from the Hong Kong Certificate of Education Examination in 1994.

Compare the above question with the question Dahlgren (1978, 1979) asked university students and young children. "Why does a bun cost 1 krona?" In this case, the relevant aspects of the situation are not given, but chosen by the interviewees themselves: They may — or may not — refer to features of the market, such as demand and supply, or they may focus on features of the bun instead, if it is appealing, big, newly baked.

It should be obvious that the dividing line between learning and development is relative to the nature of experiences of children in a certain culture (what is part of their life-world in one culture may not be in another). Still, a main contribution of the conceptual change movement has been, in our view, the introduction of a developmental perspective in institutional learning. This means that in research on conceptual change, conceptual (non-technical) questions are asked about things that the students are supposed to learn about and the conceptual aspects of which are frequently taken for granted. These questions resemble those that are asked in developmental research as they are meaningful even without specific school experiences. In the next part of the chapter, we give an example of a task of that kind, showing what insights we can gain from the students' ways of handling it.

The Idea of Phenomenography

The object of research of phenomenography is the qualitatively different ways in which people are aware of the world, and the ways in which they experience various phenomena and situations around them. Instead of adopting a first-order perspective, and trying to describe phenomena "as they are", phenomenography takes a second-order perspective, which focuses on how the phenomena are perceived by people.

Fundamental to the phenomenographic approach is its interest in the understanding of human experience, conceptualised as a form of human-world relationship. Human experience is intentional. You cannot experience without something being experienced. The epistemological stance of phenomenography builds on the principle of intentionality advocated by Brentano (see Spiegelberg, 1982).

Phenomenography holds a non-dualist view of human consciousness in which human beings and the world are inseparable. The world will not be the same world in the absence of the experiencing person, and reciprocally the person will not be the same person if the world that they are experiencing does not exist. One's experience of the world is thus consisting of functional entities describing both the experiencing person and the phenomenon to be experienced.

Premised on the principle of intentionality and the non-dualistic stance, phenomenography describes conceptions or ways of experiencing as human experiences in the sense that they are human-world relationships. This is in stark contrast to other approaches such as the cognitivist and constructivist, which describe conceptions in terms of the general cognitive functioning of the individual, implying that the cognitive act of understanding can be described in terms of psychological entities within an individual and can be fully accounted for by the conditions of cognition or internal mechanisms.

Based on a large number of empirical studies, phenomenographers assert that people's ways of experiencing or seeing a phenomenon, whilst qualitatively distinct, are limited in number. This assertion can be explained by the notion that for a phenomenon to be seen as such, it must contain a limited number of discernible aspects, and the discernment of these aspects in turn brings about a certain way of experiencing. If this condition does not hold, it means that different persons would experience a particular phenomenon in different ways at different times. People would not be able to identify that particular phenomenon at all and thus not be able to communicate with each other effectively as every one of us would have been living in a different world.

The main outcome of phenomenographic research is an "outcome space", which comprises a set of related categories of description of a specific phenomenon in question. Each category of description denotes a distinctively different way of experiencing or seeing the phenomenon, which is generalisable across different situations in which the same phenomenon occurs (Marton, 1981). The outcome space shows the relationship among the various categories of description according to their logical complexity and inclusiveness and describes the variation in the possible ways in which a phenomenon is experienced.

The interest in logical relationships between categories of description is a distinctive feature of our approach to conceptual change. The idea is that the qualitatively different meanings of a certain phenomenon can be characterised by the same set of dimensions of variation. As they are different meanings of the same phenomenon, it seems reasonable that they are logically related to each other.

A huge volume of studies have been conducted to investigate people's conceptions in various content domains. They include the Lybeck (1981) study of the student understandings of proportionality; the Johansson, Marton, and Svensson (1985) study of student understandings of mechanics; the Neuman (1987) study of how young children deal with arithmetic problems; the Lybeck, Marton, Strömdahl and Tullberg (1988) study of student understandings of the mole concept in Chemistry; and the Renström (1988) study of student conceptions of the nature of matter. There have also been a parallel series of phenomenographical studies which focused on investigating learners' conceptions of what learning is (e.g., Säljö, 1982; Pramling, 1983; Marton, Beaty, & Dall'Alba, 1993). Furthermore, the phenomenographic research method has been used to the study of phenomena outside the educational context, such as the Theman's (1983) study of people's understandings of political power, Wenestam's (1982) study of conceptions of death, and the Marton, Fensham, and Chaiklin (1994) study of Nobel laureates' views of scientific intuition.

Most studies in this strand of research orientation take as their point of departure the question "what are the different ways of experiencing the phenomenon?" Phenomenography in this sense is descriptive and methodologically oriented. The variation between different ways of seeing something is experienced and described by the researcher.

In addition to further development of the methodological aspects of phenomenography (Dall'Alba & Hasselgren, 1996; Bowden & Walsh, 2000; Bowden & Green, 2005), there have been substantial empirical advancements in the mapping of people's conceptions in many different domains, such as information systems (Bruce, 1997; Limberg, 1998; Lupton, 2004), computer science (Booth, 2001; Berglund, 2004), medical and other health sciences (Barnard, McCosker, & Gerber, 1999; Sjöström & Dahlgren, 2002) and academic work in general (Trigwell, Martin, Benjamin, & Prosser, 2000; Brew, 2001; Åkerlind, 2003), in addition to others.

Conceptions of Economic Phenomena

This part of the chapter provides a background to the second part in which we focus on a study of children's conceptions of price. In addition, some earlier studies of conceptions of economic phenomena will be dealt with in more detail. There have been some key studies investigating student learning of various economic concepts. The first study by Dahlgren (1975) identified the various conceptions that university students held about the economic concepts contained in a textbook. It concluded that the description of the outcome of student learning in terms of the various conceptions of its content is the proper level of inquiry in research on non-verbatim learning.

The Dahlgren (1978) study was aimed at studying the effects of a university course in economics on students' conceptions of economic aspects of their everyday life. The categories of description arrived at represented qualitatively different conceptions of particular phenomena, and each conception constituted a particular way of experiencing the phenomenon in question. Take the concept of price as an illustration. Two qualitatively different ways of experiencing were identified. Answers belonging to Category A indicated a conception of price as an entity which was determined by a system in which price is a function of interaction between consumers and producers in the market. Category B revealed a more product-oriented conception of price, as these answers stated that the price represented the production costs and reasonable profits on the various constituents. The study concluded that the effects of the course on students' conceptions were limited — students merely learnt the technical jargon without any real transformations taking place in the conceptions that they held.

Dahlgren (1979) then carried out a similar study on the conceptions of price held by nursery and primary school children. He derived a very similar outcome space as that of the previous study, which included an additional sub-category for Category B in which price is seen as a function of the physical characteristics of the commodity. It is noteworthy that the conceptions were found to be a function of the questions asked and were very context-dependent, as many students expressed different conceptions for different questions. On the whole, the emphasis of these three studies was on the description of the qualitatively different ways of experiencing certain economic phenomena, and the major results were the categories of description and thus the outcome spaces formulated.

The Pong (2000) study made explicit reference to Dahlgren's works, and the categories of description which were found echoed Dahlgren's finding that the conception of price can be classified into two broad categories: one focusing on the object itself, and the other focusing on the market system. This study further provided more sub-categories of the conception of "the market", namely, those related to demand conditions, supply conditions, and the opposing forces of demand and supply in the market. It also explained the formation of particular conceptions in terms of the aspects which were simultaneously focused on by the student and conceptions which were depicted as dynamic states of awareness. This new way of understanding how conceptions are formed allowed phenomenography to develop in such a way that in order to help students to develop a certain way of experiencing, a certain pattern of variation and invariance was regarded as the sine qua non of learning.

Characterising a Way of Experiencing

In phenomenography, there was an important development which aimed to characterise particular ways of experiencing or seeing. To this end, it is pertinent to develop an understanding of what it means to experience a phenomenon in a particular way. Phenomenography examines not only what constitutes a way of experiencing something, but also explores the differences between ways of experiencing the same thing, and how those differences evolve.

Marton and Booth (1997) advanced the theory of variation in order to address these concerns, which marked the advent of the "new" phenomenography (see Marton & Pang, 1999). In this theory, Marton and Booth (1997) argued that a way of experiencing something is related to one's structure of awareness, which is defined in terms of the critical aspects of that something as discerned and focused upon by the experiencer simultaneously. Learning is associated with a change in discernment, which entails a change in the aspect(s) of the phenomenon in the focal awareness of the learner, which implies a change in one's way of experiencing the phenomenon. Learning is related to discernment, variation, and simultaneity (Marton & Booth, 1997; Marton & Pang, 1999; Pang, 2003).

One cannot discern an aspect of a phenomenon without experiencing variation in a dimension which corresponds to that aspect. When certain aspects of a phenomenon vary while other aspects are kept invariant, those varying aspects are discerned. In other words, without experiencing the different values relating to a particular aspect of a phenomenon in separate instances, one would not be able to discern the common aspect across the instances encountered. To exemplify, one would not be able to discern the aspect of emotion should there be only hatred in the world; or the aspect of season should there be winter throughout the year. Every aspect of a phenomenon can be a dimension of variation, and the capability to discern a critical aspect is seen as a function of the variation that is experienced in that dimension.

The experience of variation implies that one is aware of the critical aspects of the phenomenon simultaneously either at different points in time, diachronically, or at one specific time, synchronically. An example of experiencing diachronically is when one notices the height of a person that is especially tall or short. This one does against the backdrop of one's previous experience of variation in height, and to experience that variation one has to experience simultaneously (in the diachronic sense) people of different height whom one came across at different points in time.

To have a simultaneous experience of an aspect of a phenomenon across time, this aspect must come to the 'figural' or be highlighted in a person's focal awareness, and the experiencer has to discern it as an aspect. For instance, to experience the colour of hair of a person, the dimension of colour of hair must be discerned. Through the diachronic experience of simultaneity, the different 'values' (i.e., blonde, brown, black, grey, etc.) of this aspect are synthesised to constitute a dimension of variation, and discernment depends on experienced variation of this dimension. Without discernment, one would not have simultaneous experience, in the sense of experiencing different instances of an aspect at different points in time (i.e., diachronically).

To experience or see a phenomenon in a particular way, one must discern certain aspects which correspond to the dimensions of variation of that phenomenon at one point in time, synchronically. For instance, to develop a way of understanding the Archimedes' principle, one must be able to discern the weight of a body immersed in water as compared to its weight when not immersed, and of the weight of the water displaced simultaneously. Thus, a particular way of experiencing or seeing something thus represents a set of related aspects or dimensions of variation which are discerned and focused upon synchronically. The limited number of qualitatively different ways of experiencing something can thus be characterised in terms of the discernment of aspects, the simultaneity of discerned aspects and the potential for variation in the discerned aspects of the phenomenon in question, which reflects the differences in the structure and organisation of awareness.

For instance, Ueno, Arimoto, & Fujita (1990) argued that "variation in the frame of reference" could enhance student learning of the concept of motion. The fundamental difference between the Newtonian and Aristotelian view of motion was whether or not the frame of reference was discerned by the learner as a dimension of variation. Those who held the taken-for-granted perspective of "objects-at-rest" discerned the Aristotelian view, whilst those who regarded the frame of reference as a dimension of variation had a better chance of discerning the Newtonian view. Similarly, Bowden, Dall'Alba, Laurillard, Martin, Marton, Masters, Ramsden, Stephanou, and Walsh, (1992) contended that many of the alternative conceptions of force could be explained by the different aspects of the object which were focused upon by the learner. They argued that to enhance an understanding of "force" in Newtonian physics, the aspect of "velocity" but not "motion" of the object should be directed at the learner's focal awareness.

To summarise, the development of the "new" phenomenography has provided "a way of experiencing" an ontological status, implying a shift in the primary emphasis of phenomenography from methodological to theoretical concerns. It involves the study of variation not only between different ways of experiencing something as seen by the researcher, but also among the critical aspects of the phenomenon as experienced or seen by the experiencer.

DESCRIBING AND ANALYSING CLASSROOM TEACHING

According to Marton and Pang (2006), certain patterns of variation and invariance are considered to be the necessary conditions for certain forms of learning. It is therefore of utmost importance to ascertain the patterns of variation and invariance that teachers bring about and the ways in which this is achieved. Phenomenography has further developed to make use of the theory of variation to describe and analyse how teachers handle particular objects of learning and how the differences in their ways of dealing with those objects of learning are reflected in the differences in the student learning outcomes of their classes.

Runesson (1999) employed the theory of variation to analyse classroom teaching and to study the different ways that teachers dealt with the mathematical topic of fractions and percentages in Sweden. The results showed that although teachers seemed to have taught the same topic in very similar ways, there existed some fundamental and systematic differences in the aspects that they focused on, in terms of what they varied and what they kept invariant. In the lessons, different teachers were found to have thematised different aspects of the content, putting other aspects into their peripheral awareness, and opened up different dimensions of variation in order for students to discern the critical aspects of the phenomenon. The implication of the study was that for learning to take place, teachers should find out the critical aspects of the phenomena that are being handled and of pupils' learning simultaneously, against a backdrop of experienced variation of the aspects concerned, and introduce variation in those critical aspects systematically.

Rovio-Johansson (1999) also made use of the theory of variation to examine the nature of good teaching, but with particular reference to teaching at university level. The aim of this study was to investigate the different ways in which teachers handled a specific concept in Management Accounting and the different ways in which students experienced the content of the lectures. Three teachers were observed while teaching concepts about cost accounting, budgeting, and standard costing and variance analysis in three lectures. The study showed that the teachers introduced variation in different aspects of the concepts, thus providing different learning conditions and experience to students. As a consequence, the awareness of the students was brought to bear upon different objects of learning as moulded by the teachers. Students' ways of being aware of the object of learning were found to be very much influenced by the very pattern of variation and invariance introduced by the teachers during the lessons.

This way of applying the theory of variation of phenomenography to the analysis of classroom teaching was then widely used in a number of studies in Hong Kong to investigate the good practices of Chinese and English language teaching in primary schools (see Marton & Morris, 2002). In the studies, teachers were paired up to teach the same topic so that comparisons could be made to reveal potential differences in the patterns of variation and invariance of their teaching. The theory of variation was used to examine how a space of learning was jointly created by both the teachers and the learners: that is, what aspects of the object of learning the teachers varied to enhance the possibilities of discernment. The space of learning describes what learners can possibly experience and learn in a specific setting from the perspective of what is intended to be learnt. It becomes the key issue to be considered in the analysis of teaching, as it defines the conditions or potential for learning in the classroom.

As seen from the above studies, in terms of analysing and describing classroom teaching the analytical framework derived from the theory of variation of phenomenography was very useful and insightful, as it empowered the researchers and the teachers to look at classroom teaching from a new perspective, in terms of what varies and what is kept invariant. It could be applied to evaluate the elements that are crucial for high-quality teaching, such as the macro-level variations in terms of the structure of lessons and the micro-level variations in terms of the specific ways of handling a particular dimension of the object of learning. In other words, teaching quality can be examined by looking into the nature of the space of learning co-constituted by teachers and students in the lessons.

Bringing Learning About

The foundation for phenomenographic research tradition is pedagogical, which attempts to identify, formulate and tackle certain types of research questions about learning and understanding in educational environments. The question that we are interested in has evolved to be "how can we bring about different ways of experiencing something?" Phenomenography has moved to a new stage of development, in which the researcher(s) in collaboration with educational practitioners attempt to utilise the results of phenomenographic studies conducted, in conjunction with the theory of variation, to bring learning about.

The object of study becomes how to make use of the theory of variation to design learning environments which create specific/particular patterns of variation and invariance and which thereby improve student learning, i.e., seeing the phenomenon in question in a new light. This is to help learners discern certain aspects of the phenomenon that were previously not focused on or that were taken for granted and to bring those aspects into view. Ultimately, the aim of the theory of variation is to improve classroom teaching and to facilitate learning.

In using the theory of variation, the role of the teacher is to design learning experiences in such a way as to help students to discern the critical aspects of the object of learning with the use of variation as a pedagogical tool. In relation to every object of learning, certain patterns of variation and invariance in the learning environment are implied. By consciously varying certain critical aspect(s) of the phenomenon in question, whilst keeping other aspects invariant, a space of variation is created that can bring the learner's focal awareness to bear upon those critical aspects and thereby make it possible for the learners to experience the object of learning.

To achieve this, the notion of "learning study" (Pang & Marton, 2003, 2005) was introduced. A learning study has two aspects: first, it aims to develop innovative learning environments and to undertake research studies of theoretically grounded innovations. Second, it aims to pool teachers' valuable experiences in handling the object of learning to improve teaching and learning. At the heart of the learning study approach are two factors: the object of learning, i.e., the capability that the study is expected to contribute to developing, and the theoretical framework of learning, i.e., phenomenography and the theory of variation, in our case, which guide the design of instruction to achieve the object of learning in a more consistent and systematic way.

Take the learning study conducted by Pang (2002) as an illustration. The object of learning chosen for the study was to help students at Grade 10 to develop the capability to see the phenomenon of the incidence of a sales tax in an economic way, i.e., realizing that the distribution of tax burden between buyers and sellers depends on the relative elasticity of demand and supply. Two groups of five economics teachers were involved in the study. Each group worked out a set of shared lesson plans for teaching the same topic for a series of four lessons, with the aim of achieving an agreed object of learning. One group of teachers, the lesson study group which follows the lesson study model, drew on their own experiences and intuition as well as the findings from the pilot study. The other group, the learning study group, followed the same procedure, except that they were introduced to the theory of variation, which they used as a tool for developing their lesson plans.

All the lessons were videotaped and subsequently analysed in terms of their enacted objects of learning, i.e., what is possible to learn. After the lessons, all 356 students were required to complete a written task, and five students from each class were chosen randomly for interviews. This was to evaluate student understanding of the topic concerned. Based on the data obtained, both inter- and intra-group comparisons were conducted in order to explore the relationship between the enacted objects of learning and student understanding.

The results showed that there was a spectacular difference in the learning outcome between the two groups: more than 70% of the students taught by the learning study group demonstrated the desired way of understanding the economic phenomenon, but less than 30% of the students taught by the lesson study group did so. This difference in learning outcomes were found to be systematically related to differences in how the object of learning was dealt with in terms of the patterns of variation and invariance constituted in the lessons.

Similar design was used in another learning study in economics (reported earlier in Marton & Pang, 2006). In this study, the object of learning was "the effect of a simultaneous change in demand and supply on price". In order to develop a powerful understanding of how the price of a product will change as a result of a simultaneous change in demand and supply, the relative magnitude of the changes in demand and supply must be discerned.

The students' mastery of this concept of the two groups after a series of three lessons was compared and the difference in learning outcomes in the post-test written task was striking. About 84.4% of the students who were taught by the learning study group showed that they managed to take into account the relative magnitude of change in demand and supply when looking at the price change. In the lesson study group, 22.8% of the students reached this level of understanding. Observations of what was happening in the classrooms showed subtle but decisive differences correlated with the differences in outcome. These differences were interpreted in terms of the theory of variation, through scrutinizing how the object of learning is handled in the classroom, in terms of variation and invariance, i.e., how the teachers jointly constituted an appropriate pattern of variation and invariance together with their students to draw students' focal awareness to the critical aspects of the object of learning. Both kinds of results, those indicating the power of the theory of variation and those indicating the systematic relationship between classroom teaching and student learning, are supported by a great number of previous studies (e.g., Marton & Morris, 2002; Marton & Tsui, 2004).

Phenomenography vs. Other Approaches to Conceptual Change

Although the interest in logical relationship between categories of description may be a feature distinguishing our own approach to conceptual change from other approaches, we would like to argue that researchers with different theoretical approaches to conceptual change to a great extent would make similar distinctions in data originating from different ways of dealing with the same problem or answering the same question. The same set of data is likely to be separated into different categories regardless of theoretical orientation, and moreover, into largely same set of categories. What differs is what the various categories signify, in what terms the very idea of meaning is made sense of, or in what way the question "What changes in conceptual change?" is answered.

One of the most important differences between our own theoretical approach to conceptual change and some of the other well known theoretical approaches is that the other theories (such as Vosniadou, 1994; diSessa, 1993; Chi, 1992) presuppose a mental representation: from what learners say and do, we can infer a meaning which is somehow represented in the learners' minds. The learner thus *has* something that may be replaced, changed or added to. This means that even if other researchers derived the same categories as we did, these categories would for them refer to the mental representations of price that students have in their minds.

From a pedagogical point of view, however, it might be more interesting to know what the learners can "see" or experience than what they have in their minds. What does it take to know why certain things are expensive and others cheap", for instance? Is it primarily "knowing that" or "knowing how"? (cf. Ryle, 1949) We would suggest in accordance with Broudy (1988) that it is primarily "knowing with", or even better: "seeing with". A conceptual entity like "price as a function of demand and supply" is understood best as a powerful tool for seeing a certain class of phenomena. The learner has to discern variation in the price of, demand for, and supply of, a product. This means that we are not trying to look into the minds of the learners to figure out what kind of mental representations reside there; rather, we are trying to see what the learners *see*. "What the learners see" amounts to what they discern and focus on simultaneously.

Our line of reasoning goes like this: What does it take to see something in a certain way? The point of departure is that there is potentially more information in everything we encounter than we can possibly receive. This is why attention must necessarily be selective (Gibson & Gibson, 1955). If we were able to extract all the information there is in a certain situation, we would, of course, see it in the same way. But we do not. In our own research tradition, it has been shown in countless studies that whatever people encounter, they see it in a number of qualitatively different ways (Marton & Booth, 1997). We can argue that although each answer to a certain question might be unique, on another level we find a limited number of qualitatively different ways of responding to the question. That other level is the level of meaning or the level of "ways of seeing". We thus make a distinction between "the meaning" and "the expression": the same meaning can be expressed in different ways. Furthermore, meaning is defined in terms of what is discerned and focused on simultaneously.

Perception is seen as discernment (and not construction, for instance), and our concern is primarily *the differences* between different "ways of seeing". Above all, our answer to the question "What changes in conceptual change?" is different from the answers suggested by other theorists. In our view it is the world experienced, the world seen, the world lived that changes. The change is outside the individual (as seen from their own perspective) so to speak; it is in the world that surrounds them. But to the extent that the world remains the same to an observer, the learner must have changed in order to see the same world differently. Yes, indeed, the learner demonstrates that they are not only capable of seeing something in one way (as they did on the first occasion), but also capable of seeing the same thing in another way (as they do on the second occasion). Well, once more, how can we define a way of seeing? As we have said, "a way of seeing something" can be defined in terms of what features are discerned and focused on simultaneously, but what does it take "to discern a feature"? According to the line of reasoning developed elsewhere (see Marton & Tsui, 2004), discerning a feature amounts to noticing certain kinds of differences, and noticing certain kinds of differences amounts to making certain distinctions. Therefore, the learner shows that they are capable of seeing something in a certain way by making certain distinctions. We do not ask the question: Do they really see something in the way they claim seeing it? Instead, we ask the question: What way of seeing something is expressed by making certain distinctions. In this way we can describe the different ways in which other people are capable of seeing something. We can describe what they (possibly) see. We can describe the seen, experienced, lived world, which is actually our object of research. People do not see, or experience, mental representations; they see, or experience, things in the world, and so if we want to describe their experiences, we have to describe how the world appears to them. Accordingly, what it is that changes in conceptual change is the world perceived and the learner's capability of perceiving it. But these two things are actually two sides of the same thing: the experience of the world and the experienced world.

Now, someone might argue that the capability of experiencing something in a certain way is a function of mental representation in the learner's mind. However, the idea of mental representation is an answer to the question: "In what form must past experiences be stored for the learner to be able to make use of them to handle novel situations in powerful ways?" This is a reasonable question, but it is not our question. Our question is "How must the learner experience a certain situation in order to handle it in a powerful way?" There is a specific answer to this question in each specific case. Because of shortage of space, we are going to deal with this question in terms of specific examples only here (for more general treatments, see Marton & Tsui, 2004; Marton & Booth, 1997). The *nature of the difference* between different ways of experiencing the same situation is, however, theoretically defined; the theory specifies the kind of differences that we may find empirically in different cases.

The phenomenographical approach to conceptual change focuses on the anatomy of the experience itself, rather than on the anatomy of the mind underlying the experience. This is why different approaches might agree on what different meanings or experiences the learners express but differ as to how those different meanings are theoretically and hence pedagogically, conceptualized.

As we mentioned above, we are looking for changes outside the learners so to speak, in the world which they experience, in the world in which they live. In this sense, our approach belongs to the phenomenological tradition aimed at revealing the structure and content of human experience, awareness, consciousness (see Spiegelberg, 1982). The phenomenological movement was to begin with a philosophical undertaking, a first person project, in which the philosopher studies human experience and consciousness through reflecting on their own experience and consciousness. One of the basic tenets of phenomenology is that human experience is always intentional: experience is always the experience of *something*. We are always directed to beings and things in what philosophers call the *natural attitude:* we see beings and things without thinking that what is available to us is our *experience* of beings and things.

In a phenomenological first person investigation, the researcher–philosopher makes a reflexive move and directs his attention to his *own* acts of relating to the world. We can say that this is a transformation from focusing on the content of consciousness — beings and things — in the natural attitude to focusing on the acts of consciousness in — what philosophers call — *the phenomenological attitude*.

Phenomenography, however, is empirical. Here, the researcher's focus is neither on the beings and things in the world, nor on their own acts of relating to beings and objects, but on *other people's* acts of relating to beings and things. This is what we call the second order perspective, which represents an empirical turn in relation to phenomenology that has also been taken in many other research approaches (see, for instance, Giorgi, 1995; Petitot, Varela, Pachoud, & Roy, 1999).

Some Pedagogical Implications

However, if researchers adopting different approaches still describe differences in meaning in similar ways, does it really matter that the nature of these differences is characterised in varying ways, in varying theoretical contexts? Well, differences in how differences are characterised are highly important in one respect at least, and that is in their pedagogical implications. Our own way to characterise differences in meaning does suggest a particular pedagogical approach in which we not only want to study and describe conceptual change, but also want to bring it about.

First of all, what kind of capability do we want to nurture? We want students to develop more powerful ways of seeing, and we consider the conceptual resources of science, economics, and the like as tools for making sense of the world around us, or tools "to see with" (Broudy, 1988). Above, we defined a way of seeing in terms of aspects of a situation discerned and focused on simultaneously. An aspect of a situation is a value in a dimension of variation. "High demand for a certain product", for instance, is a value in the dimension of variation (in demand), and discerning such an aspect amounts to opening up a dimension of variation, which is experienced against the tacit background of other possible values in the same dimension of variation. Discerning the aspect "high demand" in a situation implies an awareness that the demand could have been lower or even higher. The thesis is that we cannot discern anything without experiencing explicit or implicit variation. Now, if we are right in this, we must create the necessary conditions for discernment by letting the students experience variation in relevant aspects, and in order to experience variation, there must be variation to experience. However, if many things vary at the same time, you may not be able to discern any of them, and so by creating certain patterns of variation and invariance, we can create the necessary conditions for discerning a particular aspect of a phenomenon or situation. If only demand varies, you can discern demand; if only supply varies, you can discern supply, but if both demand and supply vary initially, you cannot discern either of them. However, if you discern one first and then the other and both vary subsequently, you can discern and experience both at the same time. Let us now see how this framework was applied in an attempt to enable 10-year-old students to make sense of price-related situations in terms of demand and supply at the same time.

THE EXAMPLE

The Price of a Hot Dog

We have pointed out that it would not be reasonable to put the above question on price to anyone who has not been taught anything about economics. But if we formulate the more difficult conceptual question, we can, paradoxically, even ask Primary 4 (10-year-old) students. This is exactly what Pang, Linder, and Fraser (2006) did. Two forms of the same question were:

> Have you ever tried the hot dogs sold in our school tuck shop? Do you know how much they are sold for? Maybe you know or you don't know. Anyway, just for your information, hot dogs are now sold for HK\$4.50.
>   Suppose that you were the new owner of the tuck shop. What price would you set for a hot dog? Would you set the current price or a different price? What would you consider when you set the price?[2]

The purpose in asking this question was to generate data to be used as input for an attempt to develop the students' capability of handling problems of price in terms of demand and supply. Describing the students' ways of handling problems (or more correctly: differences in their ways of handling problems of price) would be useful, we thought, when it came to developing their ways of handling such problems.

Our approach to conceptual change focuses very much on differences in meaning, regardless of whether these differences are differences within or between individuals. We are thus not primarily interested in differences between individuals, and we do not make any assumptions about the stability or generalisability of the meanings expressed by them. We are simply interested in what different meanings of a certain phenomenon (in this case: price) can be found.

So, how do we find these differing meanings?

The answers given by the students are our "pool of meaning". At the word level, all the answers are different, but we are looking for answers that differ at the word level, but not in terms of meaning, and which differ from other answers both at the word level and in terms of meaning. We are looking for *critical differences* between answers. These differences are supposed to be critical in relation to the object of learning (what the students are expected to learn — in this case to handle price in terms of demand and supply). The object of learning is not defined as clearly in the beginning of the analysis as it is later on. In a way the object of learning gets defined through our efforts to relate different answers to it.

Let us now consider eight answers given to the above question:

Quote 1:

No, I would sell hot dogs for $3.50 each. I would consider the size of the hot dog. (S63)

Quote 2:

If I were the owner, I would set the price at $5.0. This is because the economic conditions are not good at the moment. Some of the students' parents have lost their jobs and they are not able to give pocket money to their children. Also, I think that the price of biscuit sticks is not that high. Therefore, I would set the price at $5.0. If the price is too high, I would try to lower it to the level which is deemed appropriate. At such a low price, I think there would be many people who want to buy it. (S12)

Quote 3:

I would sell it for $15 because I could earn more money. As you know, a box of soft drink is sold for $3.0 in the Tuck Shop. The biscuit stick is a new product on the market. If I reduced the supply by 30 boxes, that means I would just supply 10 boxes a day, then the students would rush for it. If I increased the supply by 50 boxes, then the students might not go for it. So, I would reduce the supply so that I would earn more. (S26)

Quote 4:

During recess, I used to go to the Tuck Shop to buy the biscuit sticks, but I think the price is too low. If I were the owner, I would sell it at 7.50, because this tuck shop is the only food shop within this school. Also, I would consider whether the students could afford to buy the biscuit sticks at this price. (S102)

Quote 5:

I would set the price at 6.0. I would see how many sticks of biscuits there were inside the box when I set the price. (S33)

Quote 6:

I would decide to sell it for $4 because the quantity of biscuit sticks could not be too many or too few. Also, our Discipline Master Mr. Chow allows students to bring in at most $10 to school. Therefore, their purchasing power is not that high. However, if my supply is very large, then I should lower the price. (S09)

Quote 7:

No, I would sell it at $3. Because the economy is going down, most parents would give only $1–$5 pocket money to their children. If you set the price at $4.5, that means if the student buys a hot dog, he would have 50 cents left. They are not able to buy other food or drinks. (S56)

Quote 8:

I would set the price at $6 or $10. If I have too much inventory, I would sell the biscuit stick at $6. This is because when I have so much stock, I need to set a lower price to sell all the goods. On the other hand, if I have little inventory, I would sell it for $10 so that I would earn more profit. I might even tell the customers that whoever offers me the highest bid, I would give the goods to him or her. (S152)

The variation even between these eight answers may appear bewildering, but we had 324 answers altogether from two occasions. By examining the answers again and again and comparing them in terms of how they differed from the object of learning (dealing with price in terms of demand and supply) and from each other, we started to distinguish different groups of quotes. Observed differences between answers constituted conjectures about critical differences, which we tried out on the entire material.

We might actually notice that the question asked (about hot dogs or biscuit sticks) implies a potential variation in price, and the student might decide to stick to the current price, raise it or lower it. They make a judgement in this respect and refer to something else which also may vary in one way or in another. This "something else" is used by students as an explanatory construct for how they set the price. Working our way through the data we came to the conclusion that the students' answers could be divided into four groups: Group 1 (Quotes 1 and 5); Group 2 (Quotes 2 and 7); Group 3 (Quotes 3 and 8) and Group 4 (Quotes 4 and 6).

We find a striking difference between the two quotes in Group 1 and the other quotes. In the case of the Group 1 responses, students see price as a function of the characteristics of the product (*size* of hot dog, *number* of sticks in the biscuit box), while in all the other quotes (Groups 2, 3 and 4), price is seen as a function of market conditions (demand and/or supply). Therefore, this difference is between a focus on the product itself on the one hand, and a focus on the market on the other. In the former case, the students *open up variation in the characteristics of the product*: the price of the hot dog depends on its size, or the price of the biscuit sticks depends on how many there are in the box.

The question that was asked assumed hot dogs of a certain quality and size, and biscuit boxes with a certain number of sticks in them. Why then do some of the students start talking about hot dogs of different sizes and biscuit boxes with different numbers of sticks? Our interpretation is that as the price might vary, the students feel that they have to link variation in price to something else that varies, and they certainly have experiences of bigger hot dogs being more expensive than smaller ones and many biscuit sticks costing more than a few.

All the other students, however, seem to assume that the size of the hot dog and the number of biscuit sticks are the same, and to the extent that price varies, this variation has to be explained by means of something else that varies.

In the second group, this something is the demand for hot dogs and biscuit sticks and the demand supported by purchasing power: what do the potential customers want to buy and what can they afford to buy. Greater willingness to buy and greater ability to do so leads to higher prices, while less willingness to buy or lower ability to do so leads to lower prices. The meaning of price expressed in the quotes in this group is: price is a function of *willingness to buy and purchasing power*, i.e., price is a function of demand.

In the third group, a certain level of demand is implicitly assumed and what varies is how much of the product is available. If there is plenty of it, the price should go down, while if there is a shortage, the price can be increased. In this case, price is seen as a function of *the availability of the product*, or to put it slightly differently, price is a function of supply.

In the fourth group, the students are aware of the fact that not only variation in one respect, but actually variation in both of the respects mentioned above can affect price, and usually does. In this group, price is seen as a function of the potential customers' *willingness to buy and their purchasing power as well as the availability of the goods*. In other words, price is a function of demand and supply at the same time.

TABLE 20.1
Patterns of Experienced Variation and Invariance that Correspond to Different Ways of Seeing Price

Category	Features of product	Demand	Supply	Price
A	v	i	i	v
B1	i	v	i	v
B2	i	i	v	v
C	i	v	v	v

We have thus described the variation in the meaning of price in terms of the categories corresponding to the four groups of quotes. At the same time, these four categories can be distinguished from each other in terms of two dimensions of variations (namely demand and supply), two respects in which the students may or may not express variation through their answers. By means of variation in one or several dimensions of the product or of its market conditions, they are trying to discuss potential variations in price — expressed by the questions.

We can represent these differences in meaning as a function of differences in what varies (v) and what is invariant (i) (see Table 20.1).

According to Table 20.1, there is a hierarchical relationship between category C and categories B1 and B2: B1 points to demand, B2 to supply, while C includes both.

Learning about Price

This study (reported earlier in Pang, Linder, & Fraser, 2006) was a so-called "learning study". A "learning study" (e.g., Pang & Marton, 2003) is a hybrid between a design experiment, or design-based research as characterised by Brown (1992), Collins (1992) and Kelly (2004) on the one hand, and a Japanese lesson study as characterised by Yoshida (1999) and Stigler and Hiebert (1999) on the other. Theoretical grounding and systematic evaluation point to the former, while collaborative designing of the lesson(s) and teachers' ownership of the attempt to improve learning by means of successive revisions of the lesson design point to the latter.

In a learning study, a group of teachers comes together to develop instructional means for making it possible for students to appropriate a specific object of learning. An object of learning is a specific insight, skill, or capability that the students are expected to develop. The teachers, who work in collaboration with a researcher, choose a particular object of learning and plan the lesson(s) together. They draw upon their previous experiences in handling this object of learning; past research in relevant areas; the particular framework that they use to identify the necessary conditions for this object of learning; and, above all, the study of the extent to which the object of learning and/or its prerequisites have been appropriated by the students before the lesson.

A learning study could, in principle, have any theory of learning and teaching as its fundament, but in the studies described in this chapter, our own "variation framework" (here corresponding to "the pedagogical implications of phenomenography") has been used. The teachers pay great attention to the way in which the specific object of learning will be dealt with, in terms of the aspects of the object of learning that will vary and those that will remain invariant. The focus on what varies and what is invariant derives from the variation framework the teachers are making use of, and the choice of other factors such as teaching arrangements, forms of representation, etc. is subordinate to the teachers' design of the pattern of variation and invariance.

One of the teachers first carries out the lesson, while the other members observe. Usually, the lesson is video-recorded, and what the students have learned is probed by written questions and interviews. The lesson is analysed in terms of whether it is possible to appropriate the object of learning through the pattern of variation and invariance that is jointly constituted by the teacher and students. This is the basic tenet of the variation framework (see e.g., Marton & Booth, 1997) that underlies this study. From the student answers given before and after the lesson, the gains and the absence of gains can then be related to what has happened in the classroom.

In the post-lesson evaluation meeting, the group may come up with some suggestions to improve the design and implementation of the lesson(s). Another teacher then carries out the new version of the plan following the same procedures. The cycle will continue until all the group members have tried out the plan, and the study is always concluded by documentation.

The present learning study involved five Primary 4 General Studies teachers and 11 organised meetings.

Ascertaining Students' Existing Understanding

The exploration of the students' understanding of price described above was actually the first phase of this intervention study carried out to inform the teachers about the students' ways of understanding in relevant respects. The distribution of the 162 Primary 4 students across the categories can be seen in Table 20. 2.

The teachers found that it was prevalent for students to explain the phenomenon of price by focusing on the demand-side factors and ignored the supply side of the situation. Some students did the reverse and focused on supply, and a few others took both demand and supply into consideration.

After carefully examining students' qualitatively different ways of experiencing the phenomenon of price as shown in the pre-test, two critical differences were identified. The first was between seeing price in terms of features of the product itself and seeing price in terms of market conditions (such as demand and supply). The second was between seeing price in terms of either demand or supply and seeing price in terms of both demand and supply simultaneously. The pedagogical implication of this was that variation had to be introduced first in the dimension of demand, with supply and the product invariant, then in the dimension of supply, with demand and the product invariant, followed by simultaneous variation in both supply and demand (with invariant product). Finally, the last condition could then be repeated by different kinds of products.

Another major reason for setting the pre-test was to set a comparison baseline that the students' learning outcomes (measured by the same test) after the learning study could be compared with. As seen from Table 20.2, only 6.8% of the students came to class with the way of conceptualising price that the lesson aimed at — that is, taking into account both the demand-side and the supply-side factors. All teachers involved agreed that it was a fairly advanced concept for students at this level.

TABLE 20.2
Distribution of Conceptions for the Pre-Test

Conception	Occurrence	Percentage
A: Object	12	7.4%
B: Demand	92	56.8%
C: Supply	11	6.8%
D: Demand & Supply	11	6.8%
Unclassified[4]	36	22.2%

Designing the Lesson

When designing the lesson, the teachers drew on the pre-test results, their previous experiences in dealing with this object of learning and the research findings of relevant phenomenographic studies (for instance, Dahlgren, 1978, 1979; Pong, 2000). Based on their understanding of the theory of variation, the teachers made *conscious and systematic* use of variation and invariance, i.e., they planned to systematically vary one or two aspects while keeping the other aspects invariant. The uses of variation and invariance in the lesson were as follows.

The teacher starts off with the introduction of an auction to raise funds for the school's construction project. They explain the procedures and regulations of the auction, divide the class into groups of six students and allocate each group HK$200 of auction money. The teacher then displays the auctioned items with the base prices shown, and this is followed by the actual auction. Each group of students is reminded to note down the auctioned prices and to discuss among themselves why some goods reach higher prices than others. Subsequently, some students are invited to share their views with the whole class.

Anticipating that some students would account for the higher prices by referring to keener competition amongst groups, the teacher introduces a new scenario in which the quantity of each auctioned item is reduced by one while allocating the same amount of auction money to each group. *By varying the supply of the auctioned items and maintaining the demand and the features of the products invariant*, the teacher directs students' focal awareness to the dimension of supply.

In the next round, to bring students' focal awareness to bear upon the dimension of demand, *the teacher varies the demand (through varying the purchasing power of the students), while keeping the supply and the features of the products invariant.* The teacher deliberately reduces the auction money of each group by HK$100, and thus their purchasing power and demand for goods are reduced.

According to the variation framework, in order to enable the students to focus on demand and supply at the same time, simultaneous variation in the dimensions of demand and supply should be introduced, *keeping the features of the products invariant.* However, the participating teachers thought that the lesson would be more interesting if a new trendy item could be brought in. So, it was decided that the teachers would ask every student to individually complete the following question which embodies the simultaneous variation in demand and supply *in a new context* (i.e., with another product):

> As you know, the dinosaur machine is now selling for $80 in toyshops. Suppose that you are the owner of a large toyshop, which is the sole supplier of the new model, which has not been publicly released and is issued as a limited version. At the same time, you observe that the Hong Kong economy has been recovering very well over this period of time. Given these conditions, what price will you set for this new model? Why?

The students are guided to consider the variation in the supply of the product as well as the variation in the purchasing power of people (demand for the product) at the same time. The pattern of variation and invariance is summarized in Table 20.3.

Carrying Out the Lesson

Afterwards, all five teachers implemented the plan in a fairly faithful manner. The researcher and all other teachers involved observed each of the classes. Immediately after each trial, the teacher/researcher team conducted a meeting to evaluate the lessons. All lessons were video-recorded for later analysis.

TABLE 20.3
Patterns of Variation and Invariance (Temporal Sequence)

Supply	Demand	Features of the Product	Price
i	i	i	i
v	i	i	v
i	v	i	v
v	v	v	v

Describing the Outcomes of Learning

Comparison Between the Pre- and Post-test Results

A post-lesson study was conducted to ascertain how well the students had developed the target capability. The same question was used in the post-test as in the pre-test, except that the product in question changed from hot dogs to biscuit sticks. The students' ways of experiencing the phenomenon were identified and then categorized in accordance with the categories of description described earlier.

As shown in Table 20.4, considerable gains in students' learning outcomes were found. Around 26% of the students' answers in the post-test fell into Category C, corresponding to the object of learning agreed upon by the teachers. This was noticeably higher than the percentage for the same category in the pre-test, which amounted to only 6.8%. The difference is statistically significant (Chi-square = 151.643, for df = 25, p < 0.001). It is noteworthy that compared with Dahlgren's study (1978) in which a majority of university undergraduates, after attending the first-year economics course, could not explain a daily-life economic phenomenon such as how the price of a bun is determined, using some fundamental economic concepts like supply and demand, the results obtained in this study with the 10-year-old Primary 4 students were fairly encouraging.

Considering the results, the theory of variation may be argued to be a powerful tool in promoting student learning of the notion of market price. Furthermore, as we will show in the next section, differences between the learning outcomes of different classes were linked to differences in how the object of learning was handled in terms of variation and invariance, i.e., how the teachers constituted patterns of variation and invariance to draw students' attention to the critical aspects of the object of learning.

TABLE 20.4
Comparison of the Conceptions Displayed by Students
in the Pre-Test and Post-Test

Conception	Pre-test (162 students)	Post-test (162 students)
A: Object	7.4%	6.8%
B1: Demand	56.8%	52.5%
B2: Supply	6.8%	5.6%
C: Demand & Supply	6.8%	25.9%
Unclassified	22.2%	9.0%

Chi-square = 151.643 (df = 25), p = 0.000

TABLE 20.5
Students Expressing Conception C in Each Class after Each
Consecutive Lesson in the Pre-Test and Post-Test

Class	Pre-test	Post-test
4A	3.0%	9.1%
4B	10.3%	61.5%
4C	3.2%	12.9%
4D	7.1%	14.3%
4E	9.7%	22.6%

Comparison between Different Classes

Table 20.5 shows that there were gains in all classes in terms of the percentage of students who demonstrated the target understanding of "price", i.e., Conception C. The outstanding performance of Class 4B (with about a 51.3% increase) compared to other classes caught our attention, and thus we tried to investigate what had actually taken place in Class 4B to account for this difference in results.

When scrutinizing the classroom teaching of 4B, we found that the teacher, together with the students, had constituted an unplanned pattern of variation and invariance during the lesson. According to the lesson plan, to help students to discern and focus on demand, the teacher deliberately reduced the auction money allocated to each group while keeping the supply and features of the product invariant. However, something unexpected happened. Instead of recording expected lower prices for the various items because of a fall in the purchasing power of the groups, the price of one of the items was found to be higher ($190) than the price of the same item obtained in the first round ($110). To deal with this anomaly, the teacher spontaneously increased the supply, offering two more of the same item for auctioning, and a group of students succeeded in getting it at the base price ($20). The price of the auctioned item thus fell sharply from $190 to $20, as a function of the further drop in purchasing power due to the using up of auction money by most groups and the unexpected increase in supply of the item as initiated by the teacher.

Although the activity might not have been in line with the original intention, it allowed simultaneous variation in both the dimension of demand (a decrease in purchasing power when compared with the first round as the auction money was reduced by HK$100, and a further decrease in purchasing power because most groups had used up their auction money) and the dimension of supply (an increase in supply as two more of the same item were offered for auctioning) to come into play, *while the product was invariant.* As we pointed out above, in the original lesson design the product was unfortunately changed when simultaneous variation in demand and supply was introduced. Such a simultaneous variation with the same product resulted in drawing the students' attention to the effect of the demand-supply interaction on the price of a product, which was, however, not found in other classes, in which no additional auction was introduced with any of the auctioned products. This was probably the reason why students in Class 4B were better at discerning and simultaneously focusing on demand and supply when determining the price of a product.

Conclusions from the Study

In this study, we could see how the teachers determined the critical differences between different meanings of the direct object of learning (price) before it was taught, and how they made use of this variation, alongside the theoretical framework, in planning the lesson. The same theoretical framework was also used when interpreting differences in learning outcomes due to differences between the lesson plan and what actually happened when the lesson plan was carried out.

THE THEORY IN THE EXAMPLE

The Relationship Between Student Learning and Classroom Teaching

One of the most important aspects of the study just described is that we were using a theoretical framework to interpret changes and differences in student learning in terms of the teaching and classroom interaction that students had participated in. In a recent article, Nuthall (2004) discussed the failure of educational research to bridge the theory-practice gap, as reflected in the missing link between student learning and classroom teaching. He argues — with Kennedy (1999) — that teachers feel that student outcomes are "unpredictable, mysterious and uncontrollable" (p. 528). He also quotes Prawat (1992), who claims that most teachers believe that "student interest and involvement constitutes both necessary and sufficient condition for worthwhile learning" (p. 389). Educational research does not contribute much towards counteracting such beliefs as it does not provide teachers with tools for interpreting success and failure in teaching, nor for improving their practice. In order to do the latter, we would need better ideas of the consequences of their actions, Nuthall argues. He points to the need for an explanatory theory specifying "an underlying mechanism or process that connects, in a direct and unavoidable way, a cause with its effect" (p. 277).

There is nothing that the teacher does, however, that can "cause" learning in an "unavoidable way". Having a certain experience may imply a certain learning effect, but, even if you can say that having a certain experience is a necessary and sufficient condition for a certain kind of learning, you can never claim that something you (as a teacher) do makes a necessary and sufficient condition for a third party (a student, for instance) to have a certain experience.

On the other hand, we can specify the conditions which are necessary for a certain experience (even if they are not sufficient). If life does not provide one with an opportunity to experience an elephant, one cannot possibly experience an elephant. If elephants are the only animals that have crossed one's path, one cannot possibly separate the category "elephant" from the category "animal". A student who has only come across Pythagoras's theorem cannot possibly separate "mathematical proof" from Pythagoras's theorem. Nobody can discern "demand" and "supply" without having encountered different prices of the same product.

The point we are making in this chapter is that what varies and what is invariant in the classroom is of decisive importance for what students can possibly experience and hence learn. What varies and what is invariant have to do with how the content — or rather the object of learning — is dealt with in the classroom. They constrain what can possibly be learned. The way in which the object of learning is dealt with may or may not provide students with the necessary conditions for appropriating that specific object of learning.

A certain pattern of variation and invariance is, of course, not the only necessary condition for a certain kind of learning to take place. There are actually countless others (and here is one of the main differences between research in education and research in science). Above all, there are material conditions that have to be met (visibility, hearability, temperature, etc.); there are necessary conditions which have to do with the teachers, or with the students; there are necessary conditions which have to do with how learning is organized (there must be a certain space for learners' active involvement). However, even when the necessary conditions are met in classrooms, there are still differences in learning outcomes. In our studies carried out in materially well-developed societies such as Hong Kong (e.g., Lo, Pong, & Chik, 2005), Sweden (e.g., Holmqvist, Gustavsson, & Wernberg, in press), and the U.K. (e.g., Thabit, 2006), we found that what varied critically between classrooms — in the sense of being related to variation in learning outcomes, was the way in which a particular object of learning is dealt with. In order to discover this empirical fact, you need to compare how the very same object of learning is dealt with in different classrooms. This is rarely done, but this is exactly what we did, and this is why we managed to find the actual relationship between learning and teaching.

Furthermore, we found that differences in how the object of learning is dealt with can be described in terms of what varies and what is invariant, and it is differences in this respect which are essential when it comes to understanding differences in learning outcomes.

The Object of Learning

Our points of departure are the questions: What are the students expected to learn? What have they learned before being taught? What is made possible for them to learn in the classroom? What have they learned by being taught? There is an obvious focus on the "what" of learning. This "what" corresponds to "the object of learning". What is then "the object of learning"? Let us briefly elaborate.

There is something we might refer to as "the content of learning". In our study above, this content was "price as a function of demand and supply". This is what the students were supposed to focus on during the lesson. We call this the direct object (that is, content) of learning. But what were the students supposed to be able to do with the content? Were they supposed to be able to recall the statement "price is a function of demand and supply"? Or were they supposed to be able to determine the correct price of a product for a given supply and a given demand curve (cf. the public examination example above)? Therefore, in addition to the content, *the direct object of learning*, the object of learning has another component which has to do with the nature of capability, what the students are supposed to be able to do with the direct object of learning. We call this additional component *the indirect object of learning*. In our above study, the indirect object was something like "being able to see a situation in terms of …". The direct and indirect objects of learning together define the object of learning, which in this case is: "being able to see price-related situations in terms of demand and supply".

This was the object of learning in the study. But it answers only the first of several questions: "What are the students expected to learn?" The answer — which we have just given — (being able to see price-related situations …) is the *intended* object of learning, corresponding to the far more common expression "learning objective". Our intended object of learning is one type of — and one way of describing — the learning objective. In this special case, we imagine the learner encountering a "price-related situation" (for instance, a sale, where the price of a mountain-bike is reduced from $1000 to $500) and making sense of it in terms of demand and supply (for instance, as "There are too many bikes of this old model left and there are not many people willing to buy it for $1000"), instead of seeing price as an inherent feature of the bike (for instance, as "Now I can earn $500 if I buy that bike"). The idea is that the student will see variation in price in terms of variation (possible differences) in demand and supply.

The intended object of learning in this particular case can thus be characterised:

Product	Demand	Supply	Price
i	v	v	v

So, this is what the students should learn (the intended object of learning), but what about *what they actually learn*? Both what they have actually learned before the lesson and what they actually learn during the lesson we call *"the lived object of learning"*, and in order to distinguish between these two lived objects of learning, we add (1) to the former and (2) to the latter.

As far as the "lived object of learning (1)" in the above study was concerned, there were actually four different answers to the question "what have they learned already?" They might think of price as a function of features of the product, of demand, of supply or of demand and supply at the same time. In accordance with Table 20.1, we can characterise these four ways of seeing price-related situations:

Product	Supply	Demand	Price
v	i	i	v
i	i	v	v
i	v	i	v
i	v	v	v

As we can see, concerning the fourth category, which was identical with the intended object of learning, a few students had reached it already before being taught.

Next, we want to characterise what was possible to learn. The way the direct object of learning was dealt with in the classroom was also characterised in terms of what varied and what was invariant. This was also a form of the object of learning, namely the *enacted object of learning*, referring to what was possible to learn. Here we did not have four different patterns but a succession of four patterns which together constituted the enacted object of learning. According to the design developed by the group of teachers, after introducing the scenario, variation would be introduced in demand, then in supply and finally in both demand and supply. The products were supposed to remain invariant during the whole series:

Product	Supply	Demand	Price
i	i	i	v
i	i	v	v
i	v	i	v
i	v	v	v

As we pointed out earlier, this pattern was brought out only in the class with the highest results — by accident. In all the classes, the products were unfortunately changed in the last stage, and thus the pattern was:

Product	Supply	Demand	Price
i	i	i	v
i	i	v	v
i	v	i	v
v	v	v	v

When the teaching was completed, the students were probed again to get an answer to the question "What have they learned by being taught?" The answer to this question is "The lived object of learning (2)" described in terms of the same four categories as were used to characterise the "lived object of learning (1)" (cf. Table 20.1).

The most remarkable feature of this model of description is, in our view, that goal (intended object of learning), teaching (enacted object of learning) and results (lived object of learning) are described in the same terms, in commensurable ways. This enables us to examine the relationship between the differences in the intended and enacted objects of learning and the relationship between the differences in the enacted object of learning and student learning in a more systematic and consistent manner, when the intended/enacted objects of learning are described in terms of the different planned/observable patterns of variation and invariance co-constituted by the teachers and students in the different classrooms and when the lived objects of learning are described in terms of different patterns of variation and invariance experienced and expressed by the students through their ways of dealing with the problems used as criteria of learning.

Critical Features and Critical Differences

In this chapter, we have tried to illustrate how conceptual change can be brought about, when conceptual change is considered to be a change between different ways of seeing (and handling) a certain class of situations. The method is straightforward enough:

1. Find the critical differences in the lived object of learning.
2. Make it possible for the learners to appropriate that object of learning by means of constituting a certain pattern of variation and invariance.

In the example study, the object of learning was to understand price in terms of demand and supply. Can we argue that our theoretical framework and our empirical study might provide teachers who take on the same object of learning with powerful resources for teaching, which they would not have had without our research? Do we have anything to offer which goes beyond knowing economics and being familiar with general methods of teaching which are considered to be effective, such as pedagogical strategy, for instance, perhaps in the form of an auction, as in the study? Well, the potential theoretical contribution to future attempts to teach the same object of learning is that "understanding price in terms of demand and supply" is specified as "being able to discern demand and supply and focus on them simultaneously". Furthermore, we argue that the learner can discern and learn to discern a certain feature (such as demand or supply) of a certain class of situations if there is variation in that respect against the background of invariance in other respects.

The potential contribution of our empirical study (Pang, Linder, & Fraser, 2006), together with other similar empirical studies (Dahlgren, 1978; Thomas, 1983; Wood, 2000; Pang, 2002), is the pointing out of the critical differences in the lived object of learning. These are differences between hierarchically structured categories denoting different ways of seeing price and pricing in the specific example. Such differences we find in Table 20.1 between category A and categories B1 and B2, and between the latter and category C. The first distinction (critical difference) is between seeing price in terms of characteristic of the product on the one hand, and in terms of market conditions (such as demand and supply) on the other. The second distinction (critical difference) is between seeing price in terms of either demand or supply on the one hand and in terms of both demand and supply simultaneously on the other. The implication of this is that variation has to be introduced first in demand, while supply and product are invariant, and then in supply, with demand and product invariant, followed by simultaneous variation in both, with the product invariant. The last condition can then be repeated by different kinds of product (although this was not done in the study). In the description of the study, we can see that the better approximation to such a structure, the better results.

Finally

We have used the expressions "critical features" and "critical differences", and the two are closely related to each other. In order to handle a certain task, the learner has to take into consideration certain *critical features*[3] at the same time, such as "demand" and "supply" in the example study.

The concept of price, in economics, is considered as a function of the critical features. Economics (i.e., disciplinary knowledge) thus tells us what the critical features are. What "taking into consideration at the same time" means, on the other hand, is suggested by our theoretical framework, which says that a critical feature has to be discerned and that you can only discern it if you experience variation in that respect. Hence the teacher has to help the students to discern the critical features by constituting necessary patterns of variation and invariance. What features learners discern and focus on makes up their way of seeing, the phenomenon that is the object of learning (the meaning of it they express). Differences between ways of seeing (experiencing) the object of learning are critical for how to handle it in teaching.

Critical features are what learners are supposed to see (discern and focus on), and critical differences are differences between conceptions which the teachers have to attend (discern and focus on). These critical differences can be described in terms of patterns of variation and invariance in critical features. While the teachers' awareness of critical features is part of their content knowledge, their awareness of critical differences is part of their pedagogical content knowledge.

In many phenomenographic studies which explore people's qualitatively different ways of seeing the direct object of learning, such critical differences have been identified. These are the potential contributions to teachers' pedagogical content knowledge from phenomenographic research. By introducing the variation framework, we have been able to interpret the earlier findings in terms of patterns of experienced variation and invariance (taken-for-grantedness). At the same time, we have become able to develop instructional strategies for going beyond describing conceptual change, by actually bringing it about intentionally. This has been our path from the idea of phenomenography to the pedagogy of conceptual change.

ACKNOWLEDGMENTS

We would like to express our gratitude to the Swedish Research Council and the Hong Kong Research Grants Council for financial support to our writing of this chapter.

NOTES

1. Although other, but somehow related, past experiences might affect the likelihood of success.
2. The question was asked in this form the first time the students encountered it. At a later occasion the question was asked again with "hot dogs" replaced by "biscuit sticks". The answers below refer to either of these two forms.
3. Corresponding to a dimension of variation with different values. For instance, colour is a dimension of variation and different colours, such as blue, red, green...are values. At the same time a dimension of variation with a certain value, such as red, is an aspect of an object.
4. Because of the brevity of the written answers or the incoherent lines of thought expressed by the young students of Primary 4, it was sometimes difficult to classify their answers meaningfully. Moreover, although some of the answers in this category were quite reasonable, they did not look at the notion of price from an economic point of view, and thus they were not included in our system of categories.

REFERENCES

Åkerlind, G. S. (2003). Growing and developing as a university teacher — Variation in meaning. *Studies in Higher Education, 28*(4), 375–390.

Barnard, A., McCosker, H., & Gerber, R. (1999). Phenomenography: A qualitative research approach for exploring understanding in health care. *Qualitative Health Research, 9*(2), 212–226.

Berglund, A. (2004). A framework to study learning in a complex learning environment. *Research In Learning Technology Journal, 12*(1), 65–79.

Booth, S. (2001). Learning computer science and engineering in context. *Computer Science Education, 11*(3), 169–188.

Bowden, J., Dall'Alba, G., Laurillard, D., Martin, E., Marton, F., Masters, G., Ramsden, P., Stephanou, A., & Walsh, E. (1992). Displacement, velocity and frames of reference: Phenomenographic studies of students' understanding and some implications for teaching. *American Journal of Physics, 60*, 262–269.

Bowden, J., & Green, P. (Eds.). (2005). *Doing developmental Phenomenography.* Melbourne: RMIT University Press.

Bowden, J., & Walsh, E. (Eds.). (2000). *Phenomenography.* Melbourne: RMIT University Press.

Brew, A. (2001). Conceptions of research: A phenomenographic study. *Studies in Higher Education, 26*(3), 271–285.

Broudy, H. S. (1988). *The uses of schooling.* London: Routledge.

Brown, A. L. (1992). Design experiments: Theoretical and methodological challenges in creating complex interventions in classroom settings. *The Journal of the Learning Sciences, 2*(2), 141–178.

Bruce, C. (1997). *The seven faces of information literacy.* Blackwood: Auslib Press.

Chi, M. T. H. (1992). Conceptual change in and across ontological categories: Examples from learning and discovery in science. In R. Giere (Ed.), *Cognitive models of science* (pp. 129–160). Minneapolis: University of Minnesota Press.

Collins, A. (1992). Toward a design science of education. In E. Scandlon & T.D. Shea (Eds.), *New directions in educational technology* (pp. 15–22). Berlin: Springer.

Dahlgren. L. O. (1975). *Qualitative Differences in Learning as a Function of Content-oriented Guidance.* Göteborg, Sweden: Acta Universitatis Gothoburgersis.

Dahlgren, L. O. (1978). *Effects of university education on the conception of reality.* Reports from the Institute of Education (65). Goteborg: The Institute of Education, University of Goteborg.

Dahlgren, L. O. (1979). *Children's Conception of Price as a Function of Questions Asked.* Göteborg: The Institute of Education, University of Goteborg.

Dall'Alba, G., & Hasselgren, B. (1996). *Reflections on phenomenography. Toward a Methodology.* Göteborg: Acta Universitatis Gothoburgensis.

diSessa, A. (1993). Toward an epistemology of physics. *Cognition and Instruction, 10*, 105–225.

Ebbinghaus, H. (1964). *Memory. A contribution to experimental psychology.* New York: Dover (original work published, 1885)

Gibson, J. J., & Gibson, E. J. (1955). Perceptual learning: Differentiation or enrichment? *Psychological Review, 62*(1), 32–41.

Giorgi, A. (1995). Phenomenological Psychology. In J. A. Smith, R. Harre, & L. V. Langenhove (Eds.), *Rethinking psychology,* (pp. 24–42). London: Sage.

Gruber, H. E., & Voneche, J. J. (1977). *The essential Piaget. An interpretative reference and guide.* New York: Basic Books.

Holmqvist, M., Gustavsson, L., & Wernberg, A. (in press). Variation Theory — A tool to improve education. In Kelly, A. E., & Lesh, R. (in press). *Handbook of design research methods in education.* Mahwah, NJ: Erlbaum.

Johansson, B., Marton, F., & Svensson, L. (1985). An approach to describing learning as change between qualitatively different conceptions. In A. L. Pines & L.H.T. West (Eds.), *Cognitive structure and conceptual change* (pp. 233–257). New York: Academic Press.

Kelly, A. E. (2004). Design research in education: Yes, but is it methodological? *The Journal of the Learning Sciences, 13*(1), 115–128.

Kennedy, M. M. (1999). A test of some common contentions about educational research. *American Educational Research Journal, 36,* 511–541.

Limberg, L. (1998). *Att söka information för att lära. En studie av samspel mellaninformationssökning och lärande.* Borås: Valfrid.

Lo, M. L., Pong, W. Y., & Chik, P. M. (Eds.). (2005). *Learning studies: Catering for individual differences.* Hong Kong: Hong Kong University Press.

Lupton, M. (2004). *The learning connection: Information literacy and the student experience.* Adelaide: Auslib press.

Lybeck, L. (1981). *Arkimedes i klassen. En amnespedagogisk berattelse (Archimedes in the classroom. A narrative on the didactics of subject matter).* Göteborg: Avta Universitatis Gothoburgensis.

Lybeck, L., Marton, F., Strömdahl, H., & Tullberg, A. (1988). The phenomenography of the 'mole concept' in Chemistry. In P. Ramsden (Ed.), *Improving learning: New perspectives* (pp. 81–108). London: Kogan Page.

Marton, F. (1981). Phenomenography — describing conceptions of the world around us. *Instructional Science, 10,* 177–200.

Marton, F., Beaty, E., & Dall'Alba, G. (1993). Conceptions of learning. *International Journal of Educational Research, 19,* 277–300.

Marton, F., & Booth, S. (1997). *Learning and awareness.* Mahwah, NJ: Erlbaum.

Marton, F., Fensham, P., & Chaiklin, S. (1994). A Nobel's eye view of scientific intuition: Discussions with the Nobel prize-winners in Physics, Chemistry, and Medicine (1970–1986). *International Journal of Science Education, 16,* 457–473.

Marton, F., & Morris, P. (Eds.). (2002). *What matters? Discovering critical conditions of classroom learning.* Göteborg: Acta Universitatis Gothoburgensis.

Marton, F., & Pang, M. F. (1999). Two faces of variation. Paper presented at the 8th European Conference for Learning and Instruction, Goteborg, Sweden, August 24–28.

Marton, F., & Pang, M. F. (2006). On some necessary conditions of learning. *The Journal of the Learning Sciences, 15*(2), 193–220.

Marton, F., & Tsui, A. B. M. (Eds.). (2004). *Classroom discourse and the space of learning.* Mahwah, NJ: Erlbaum.

Neuman, D. (1987). *The origin of arithmetic skills: A phenomenographic approach.* Göteborg: Acta Universitatis Gothoburgensis.

Nuthall, G. (2004). Relating classroom teaching to student learning: A critical analysis of why research has failed to bridge the theory-practice gap. *Harvard Educational Review, 74*(3), 273–306.

Pang, M. F. (2002). Making learning possible: The use of variation in the teaching of school economics. Unpublished PhD thesis, The University of Hong Kong.

Pang, M. F. (2003). Two faces of Variation — On continuity in the phenomenographic movement. *Scandinavian Journal of Educational Research, 47*(2), 145–156.

Pang, M. F., Linder, C., & Fraser, D. (2006). Beyond Lesson Studies and Design Experiments – Using theoretical tools in practice and finding out how they work. *International Review of Economics Education, 5*(1), 28–45.

Pang M. F., & Marton, F. (2003). Beyond "lesson study" — Comparing two ways of facilitating the grasp of economic concepts. *Instructional Science, 31*(3), 175–194.

Pang, M. F., & Marton, F. (2005). Learning theory as teaching resource: Another example of radical enhancement of students' understanding of economic aspects of the world around them. *Instructional Science, 33*(2), 159–191.

Petitot, J., Varela, F.J., Pachoud, B., & Roy, J. (1999). *Naturalizing phenomenology. Issues in contemporary phenomenology and cognitive science.* Stanford, CA: Stanford University Press.

Pong, W. Y. (2000). Widening the space of variation - inter-contextual and intra-contextual shifts in pupils' understanding of two economic concepts. Unpublished PhD thesis, The University of Hong Kong.

Pramling, I. (1983). *The child's conception of learning.* Göteborg: Acta Universitatis Gothoburgensis.

Prawat, R. S. (1992). Teachers' beliefs about teaching and learning: A constructivist perspective. *American Journal of Education, 100,* 354–395.

Renström, L. (1988). *Conceptions of matter: A phenomenographic approach* (Göteborg Studies in Educational Sciences 69). Göteborg: University of Göteborg.

Rovio-Johansson, A. (1999). *Being good at teaching: Exploring different ways of handling the same subject in higher education.* Göteborg: Acta Universitatis Gothoburgersis.

Runesson, U. (1999). *Variationens Pedagogik* (*Pedagogic Variations*). Göteborg: Acta Universitatis Gothoburgersis.

Ryle, G. (1949). *The concept of mind.* London: Hutchinson.

Säljö, R. (1982). *Learning and understanding.* Göteborg: Acta Universitatis Gothoburgensis.

Sjöström, B., & Dahlgren, L. O. (2002). Applying phenomenography in nursing research. *Journal of Advanced Nursing, 40*(3), 339–345.

Spiegelberg, H. (1982). *The Phenomenological Movement: A Historical Introduction* (3rd ed.). Martinus Nijhoff: The Hague.

Stigler, J. W., & Hiebert, J. (1999). *The teaching gap: Best ideas from the world's teachers for improving education in the classroom.* New York: The Free Press.

Thabit, A. (2006). Dimensions of variation as an analytical tool for characterising pupils' learning of elementary algebra. Unpublished doctoral thesis, Oxford University.

Theman, J. (1983). *Uppfattningar av politisk makt* (*Conceptions of Political Power*). Göteborg: Acta Universitatis Gothoburgersis.

Thomas, L. M. (1983). 12–16-year-old pupils' understanding of economics. Unpublished Ph.D. Thesis, University of London.

Trigwell, K., Martin, E., Benjamin, J., & Prosser, M. (2000). Scholarship of teaching: A model. *Higher Education Research and Development, 19*(2), 155–168.

Ueno, N., Arimoto, N., & Fujita, G. (1990). Conceptual models and points of view: Learning via making a new stage. Paper presented at the Paper presented at AERA, Boston.

Vosniadou, S. (1994). Capturing and modelling the process of conceptual change. *Learning and Instruction, 4*, 45–69.

Wenestam, C. G. (1982). Children's reactions to the word "death". Paper presented at the AERA annual meeting, New York.

Wood, K. (2000). The experience of learning to teach: changing student teachers' ways of understanding teaching. *Journal of Curriculum Studies, 32*(1), 75–93.

Yoshida, M. (1999). Lesson Study: A case study of a Japanese approach to improving instruction through school-based teacher development. Unpublished PhD thesis, University of Chicago.

21

Beyond Knowledge:
Learner Characteristics Influencing
Conceptual Change

Gale M. Sinatra
University of Nevada

Lucia Mason
University of Padova

For the past several decades, researchers studying conceptual change have demonstrated in numerous studies that learning presents unique challenges when students have their own naïve theories or preconceived notions about the world around them (see, for example, Anderson, Reynolds, Schallert, & Goetz, 1977; Carey, 1985; Chinn & Brewer, 1993; Piaget, 1952; Spelke, 1991; Vosniadou & Brewer, 1987). These challenges distinguish learning for conceptual change from knowledge acquisition conceptually and pedagogically in significant ways. Further, it is precisely these distinctions that make the area of conceptual change research fruitful for providing insights into the nature of learning itself.

Prior to the emergence of explanatory models of conceptual change, researchers studying knowledge acquisition recognized that students responded differently in learning situations when their preexisting knowledge conflicted with the information conveyed in their textbooks and classrooms. However, this represented an interesting learning paradox. That is, how could background knowledge — well established in the psychological literature as a facilitator of learning — serve as a barrier to learning when students had everyday experiences with the phenomena? Progress on understanding the apparent paradox of background knowledge serving both as a facilitator and a barrier to learning was modest until models of conceptual change were introduced (Chi, 1992; Posner, Strike, Hewson, & Gertzog, 1982; Vosniadou & Brewer, 1992).

Cognitive developmental approaches to conceptual change helped to explain how learners constructed an understanding of the natural world through both maturation and experience. Vosniadou and Brewer's (1992, 1994) classic study of children's developing conceptions of astronomical bodies illustrates how teaching young children about the shape of the earth is not simply a knowledge acquisition task. Vosniadou and Brewer (1992) demonstrated that children's conceptions of the earth are coherent, explanatory, robust, and difficult to change in favor of a scientific notion of a spherical earth. This study and dozens more demonstrated that learning about topics from the natural world requires going beyond classic knowledge acquisition processes; it also requires overcoming significant conceptual and affective obstacles. Models of conceptual change have evolved to help explain these challenges.

Early accounts of learning for conceptual change documented how children's conceptions were different from those of scientists (Clough, & Driver, 1985; Eaton, Anderson, & Smith, 1984; Posner et al., 1982; West & Pines, 1985). However, these views gave little recognition to the affective, situational, and motivational factors that often play a determinative role in whether or not a new conception will be adopted. These perspectives were labeled "cold conceptual change" due to their focus on rational, cognitive factors to the exclusion of extra-rational or "hot" constructs (Pintrich, Marx, & Boyle, 1993).

Recently, however, there has been a "warming trend" in conceptual change research (Sinatra, 2005). Since Pintrich et al.'s (1993) revolutionary article, "Beyond cold conceptual change: The role of motivational beliefs and classroom contextual factors in the process of conceptual change," there have been an increasing number of researchers characterizing conceptual change as social, contextual, motivational, and affective in nature (see, for example, Dole & Sinatra, 1998; Gregoire, 2003, and Murphy & Mason, 2006). These models seek to characterize the role of hot constructs that affect conceptual change beyond those effects due to background knowledge.

The recent emphasis on understanding social and contextual aspects of conceptual change is critical to developing an adequate understanding of knowledge change. However, in our zeal to capture these previously overlooked social, motivational, and contextual factors, cognitive aspects of the conceptual change process have recently been deemphasized. We caution that conceptual change researchers should avoid falling into the trap of adopting a "replacement" view of theoretical progress. Just as conceptual change researchers recognize that students' conceptions are usually not replaced but restructured, so too should our theories evolve and refine, not necessarily replace previous perspectives.

With this in mind, we argue that conceptual change researchers should avoid considering socio-cultural views of learning as replacements for cognitive-information processing views of learning. Rather, for the most comprehensive view of the conceptual change process, we posit that attention must be paid to the observations from both perspectives. Each provides useful descriptions of some aspects of the nature of human learning in general, and learning for conceptual change in particular. Great debates in psychology, such as nature versus nurture, are often resolved by evidence revealing the import of both factors working in interaction. We posit that contrasting depictions of conceptual change as cognitive, individual, psychological, and occurring without conscious attention — or as affective, contextualized, social, cultural, and intentional may not be providing competing explanations of the same phenomena but rather offering explanations of critical but different facets of conceptual change.

AN INTERACTIVE APPROACH TO CONCEPTUAL CHANGE

We contend that a multi-faceted, theoretically complex, and interactive view of conceptual change is emerging. Key to understanding this new view is an examination of the role learner characteristics play in that interaction. Research examining how learner characteristics beyond those attributable to background knowledge affect the conceptual change process has seen a recent flurry of activity. A major objective of this chapter is to review recent research designed to understand the interaction of these learner characteristics within the conceptual change process. But first, it is necessary to understand the theoretical grounding for the multifaceted, interactive picture of conceptual change that is coming into focus.

Cognitive theory and research suggest that human cognition is organized into levels of awareness. These levels range from automatic processing of information without conscious attention (what some call algorithmic processing) to consciously aware, goal-directed, and intentional processing along a continuum of levels of awareness (for various characterization of a levels view see Anderson, 1990, 1991; Craik & Lockhart, 1972; Newell, 1990; Stanovich, 1999). These levels of awareness represent and analyze different types of information. This structure of the human cognitive architecture allows for efficient processing given our limited resources (Bargh & Chartrand, 1999).

Toward the automatic end of the continuum of awareness is algorithmic processing. The algorithmic level of awareness performs computations necessary for carrying out basic information processing tasks automatically, quickly, accurately, and almost effortlessly (Speelman, 1998). Conceptual change that occurs incidentally or implicitly without the conscious attention of the learner would be characterized as toward the algorithmic or automatic end of the continuum of awareness. This type of conceptual change occurs when one experiences the "aha" phenomena. That is, when the new information "clicks" into place and knowledge is restructured without apparent conscious deliberation, and without purposive regulation of learning goals directed toward resolving cognitive conflict, or without specific intentions to change one's view.

In contrast to this form of conceptual change, some aspects of conceptual change have been characterized as initiating from the intentional end of the continuum of awareness (Sinatra & Pintrich, 2003). Sinatra and Pintrich (2003) defined intentional conceptual change as "goal-directed and conscious initiation and regulation of cognitive, metacognitive, and motivational processes to bring about a change in knowledge" (p. 6). Unlike change initiating from the algorithmic end of the continuum of awareness (or non-intentional conceptual change) intentional conceptual change is under the learner's conscious control.

It is our view that understanding the role of learner characteristics which can be brought to bear on functions at the intentional level of awareness may resolve (at least in part) the apparent learning paradox described earlier. That is, students with similar background knowledge may have different learning goals, motivations, and intentions to learn (or to not learn) new conceptions.[1] Pintrich et al. (1993) explained how constructs such as mastery goals, epistemological beliefs, personal interest, importance, values, achievement goals, self-efficacy, and control beliefs can play a determinative role in intentional conceptual change. Research on learner characteristics that play a key role at the intentional level of awareness in conceptual change has begun to explore how these constructs can determine the likelihood of change, over and above background knowledge and algorithmic level processes. It is the importance of these characteristics for understanding the multifaceted, interactive, theoretically complex nature of change that we emphasize in this chapter. We turn now to a review of these characteristics with an eye toward understanding the powerful influence of learner characteristics on conceptual change.

LEARNER CHARACTERISTICS AND INTENTIONAL CONCEPTUAL CHANGE

Learner characteristics that can act at the intentional level of awareness in conceptual change include personal interest, importance, utility value, achievement goals, self-efficacy, and control beliefs according to Pintrich et al. (1993). Following the warming trend (Sinatra, 2005), many of these characteristics have become important in recent theoretical models of conceptual change (see, for example, Dole & Sinatra, 1998; Gregoire, 2003; and Murphy & Mason, 2006). Although increased attention has been paid to understanding the role these characteristics play in conceptual change in recent years, it is important to note that empirical studies investigating the relationship between these factors and conceptual change are still relatively rare. Therefore, we discuss only factors that have been the focus of recent empirical research on conceptual change which highlight the impact of students' motivation and affect on conscious, deliberate, and self-regulated intentional knowledge change. We also draw implications from this research for the interactive nature of conceptual change and the pedagogies that support change. Other learner characteristics are reviewed in other chapters in this volume and likely there are many learner characteristics of import that have yet to be identified by conceptual change researchers that may also act at the intentional level of awareness.

Achievement Goals

The construct of achievement goals captures the process of energizing and directing behavior in achievement situations (e.g., the classroom or workplace). Achievement goals are described as explaining the why and how of student involvement in a task or activity (Ames, 1992). For example, the student who studies a subject in depth may have the achievement goal of understanding for personal interest or because she deems the information important to her future profession. The achievement goal of another student may be to obtain an excellent evaluation which can be proudly shown to his classmates or parents. Both students involve themselves in study activities, but they are oriented toward different achievement goals.

A number of scholars contributed to an extensive analysis of this construct in the 1980s (e.g., Ames, 1984; Dweck & Leggett, 1988; Elliot & Dweck, 1988; Maehr, 1984; Nicholls, 1984) which led to the well-known conceptual distinction between mastery and performance goals. Students who adopt mastery goals engage in school work to understand and learn. They focus on the content to be mastered and use more complex information processing strategies to help them learn the information. In contrast, students who adopt performance goals seek to demonstrate their ability and self-worth to others, or to avoid demonstrating their incompetence. Therefore, aspects of the self rather than the task become the focus of their concern. Achievement goals have a number of well documented effects. For example, mastery oriented students tend to attribute failure to insufficient effort, they are not bothered by mistakes, they consider challenging tasks as opportunities to learn, and they persist in learning activities. In contrast, performance oriented students have been shown to engage in maladaptive behaviors such as attributing failure to insufficient ability, considering mistakes as a threat to the self, avoiding challenging tasks, and failing to persist.

According to normative models of achievement goals, mastery goals are associated with better learning, self-regulatory behavior, and positive affect. Performance goals are instead related to superficial learning, low self-regulation, and negative affect (Dweck & Leggett, 1988; Pintrich, 2000; Smiley & Dweck, 1994). In particular, research has shown a clear relationship between mastery goals and higher levels of cognitive engagement; whereas performance goals have been associated with lower levels of cognitive engagement (Pintrich, 2000; Pintrich & Schrauben, 1992). Indeed, a number of correlational studies have shown a positive relationship between self-reported use of deep processing and metacognitive strategies and mastery goals for junior high school and college students (e.g., Nolen, 1988; Pintrich & Garcia, 1991; Wolters, Yu, & Pintrich, 1996). Experimental studies have also documented that students who are more task focused perform better in tasks requiring deeper processing (e.g., Elliot, McGregor, & Gables, 1999; Graham & Golan, 1991). These results have been demonstrated in a variety of domains. For example, research on learning in science, specifically physics, has demonstrated that having understanding as a goal led to deeper processing of the material (Hammer, 1994).

Until recently, few studies have documented empirically the role of achievement goals in the conceptual change process. Linnenbrink and Pintrich (2002) carried out two studies examining college students' changing understandings of projectile motion which demonstrate the role of student characteristics in the interactive, multi-faceted process of knowledge restructuring.

Based on prior research, Linnenbrink and Pintrich (2002) hypothesized that students who adopted a mastery goal would use more metacognitive, self-regulatory strategies which would lead to deeper levels of engagement with the information. Deeper engagement would in turn allow students to detect discrepancies between their existing conceptions and the new information. Thus, these students would be more likely to experience conceptual change. Conversely, the researchers hypothesized that students with performance goals would be less likely to experience conceptual change because they may have difficulty admitting their existing ideas were incorrect, since they tend to focus on how they appear to others.

Students were randomly assigned to two conditions where mastery or performance goals were induced experimentally prior to reading a refutational text on Newtonian physics. Although the goal induction met with limited success, results from correlational analyses in Study I showed that a self-reported focus on understanding and learning, that is, adopting mastery goals, was related to a change in understanding. This finding was particularly apparent for students who had low prior knowledge of the topic, revealing the potential interactive effect of these characteristics with students' knowledge. Performance goals did not promote conceptual change, but at the same time, they did not impede it.

The researchers tried to replicate their findings in a second study. Study II also revealed that mastery goals led to a change in physics understanding. However, in this study, this finding was not related to the level of students' prior knowledge as in the previous study. In addition, regression analyses showed that mastery goals were associated with elaborative strategies, as well as with a lessening of negative affect. Linnenbrink and Pintrich (2002) maintained that lowering negative affect mediated the influence of this type of achievement goal in the conceptual change process (Linnenbrink & Pintrich, 2002), possibly by reducing the distracting effects of anxiety on learning.

These two studies reveal how specific characteristics of students, such as the type of goals they adopt and their mood during instruction, affect conceptual change either directly via the use of elaborative strategies or indirectly by decreased negative affect. These studies illustrate how students' intentions, expressed through the implementation of a mastery goal, can play a pivotal role in the process of conceptual change.

These findings are promising because they illustrate how learners can be active participants in their own knowledge restructuring. However, the role learner characteristics play is unfortunately quite complex. Some authors (Harackiewicz, Barron, Pintrich, Elliot, & Thrash, 2002; Harackiewicz & Elliott, 1993; Harackiewicz & Sansone, 1991) have questioned whether performance goals are truly maladaptive. Some studies have shown their effects to be insignificant (Linnenbrink & Pintrich, 2002), or even positive in certain cases.

In a study of high school students' conceptual change in physics, the multidimensional nature of motivation emerged (Hynd, Holschuh, & Nist, 2000). Students who learned the new information through conceptual change reported slightly higher motivations than students who did not move toward the scientific view. Interestingly, students' motivations appeared to be grounded not only in intrinsic aspects, such as interest that focuses attention on the content, but also on extrinsic aspects, such as attaining good grades to meet future goals. The authors interpreted this finding by positing that grades are not merely rewards, they are also a means for pursuing important goals, such as admission to college or winning a scholarship. Therefore, the effects of grades on motivation are not clear cut, but rather tied to students' feelings of self-worth in relation to future goals, as they are internalized by the students. In addition, when asked to discuss the strategies used to understand physics, the students who experienced conceptual change mentioned cognitive effort more often than strategies. In contrast, the students who did not learn the counterintuitive concepts mentioned strategies they used more than cognitive effort (Hynd et al.,

2000). This research illustrates the complexity of the learning environment and the importance of understanding which learner characteristics are coming into play in a particular situation.

The positive influence of performance goals has been confirmed in a cross-cultural study involving American and Chinese high school students (Qian & Pan, 2002). A significant positive correlation between performance goals and conceptual change indicated that students who were more inclined to change their conceptions about projectile motion were also those who focused on the self. In this study, strong performance goals sustained persistence through the demanding process of conceptual change. More recently, it has been proposed that mastery goals coupled with performance goals can form a better achievement profile than mastery goals in combination with the absence of performance goals (Elliot, 2005). Therefore multiple achievement goals may lead to better learning performance than a single goal (Linnenbrink & Pintrich, 2003).

Finally, it should be pointed out that over the last decade of theorizing on achievement motivation, a distinction between approach and avoidance motivation has emerged (Elliot, 1999, 2005). The former describes both mastery and performance goals as they focus on potential positive results, the latter describes avoidance goals, which focus on heading off a potential negative outcome. In her model of teacher belief change, Gregoire (2003) posits that avoidance goals may be adopted when a message is perceived as threatening.

In a recent study Mason, Boldrin, and Vanzetta (2006) examined the effects of achievement goals on conceptual change when learning about magnets. Goals were examined in relation to beliefs about the certainty, development, justification, and source of scientific knowledge. Pre- to post-test comparisons revealed a significant interaction between goals and beliefs about the nature of scientific knowledge. Students who had less advanced beliefs about scientific knowledge benefited more from reading a text if they had mastery goals than students who were less mastery oriented. Performance goals were not associated with conceptual change. Like Linnenbrink and Pintrich (2002), students who were more mastery oriented reported more positive affect during reading than those who were less oriented toward understanding.

Although research on the role of goals in intentional conceptual change has just begun, it is already clear that goals are important in learning and that their role in the process of knowledge restructuring warrants greater investigation. Achievement goals well illustrate the highly interactive, theoretically complex nature of conceptual change. Students formulate and act on goals they develop within a socio-cultural and classroom context (Elliott & Moller, 2003; Qian & Pan, 2002). Goals impact the types of strategies students employ during learning (for example, the use of either shallow and superficial or deep and metacognitive strategies). Cognitive factors such as the depth and breath of students' content knowledge and the degree to which domain-specific study strategies can be automatically activated and employed, determine the degree to which students can successfully execute their intended learning strategies. Goals may prove to be the linchpin to unlocking this nuanced interaction between levels of awareness, knowledge, and the intentional reconstruction of knowledge.

EPISTEMIC MOTIVATION AND BELIEFS

Epistemic motivation refers to motivations that are not focused on the self but rather on knowledge as an object (Kruglanski, 1989). Pintrich et al. (1993) identified epistemic motivation as one of the key learner characteristics likely implicated in the knowledge restructuring process. This characteristic is related to the broader view of motivated social cognition (Kruglanski, 1989; Kruglanski & Webster, 1996) that examines the interplay between cognition and motivation and explores the "pervasive role that affect and motivation play in attention, memory, judgment, decision making, and human reasoning, as well as highlighting the cognitive, goal-directed aspects of most motivational phenomena" (Jost, Glaser, Kruglanski, & Sulloway, 2003, p. 342).

Kruglanski and colleagues have discussed two epistemic motivations, seeking closure and avoiding closure, which can produce a wide range of effects on the knowledge construction process. Need for closure refers to the desire for definitive knowledge on a topic and the need to avoid ambiguity and uncertainty (Kruglanski, 1989, 1990). The need for closure can be evoked in a particular situation (such as time pressure for decision making) or may operate as a stable dispositional trait across a variety of situations and contexts. Need for closure has been shown to relate to a tendency to seize on information prematurely, effectively "freezing" the decision making process, resulting in relative closed-mindedness on the issue (Kruglanski & Webster, 1996).

In contrast, the epistemic motivation of avoiding closure refers to the need to seek new information, question current ideas, and solve discrepancies and problems. "Unfreezing" of cognition implies continued searching for information and generation and testing of hypotheses — cognitive processes that are assumed to underlie successful knowledge restructuring. According to Kruglanski and colleagues, "there are situational and dispositional factors that may encourage a general cognitive-motivational orientation toward the social world that is either open and exploratory or closed and immutable" (Jost et al., 2003, p. 348).

Hatano and Inagaki (2003) used the construct of epistemic motivation in describing the conditions necessary for intentional conceptual change. They described how students must first be provided with experiences that make the inadequacies of their current conceptions evident. They argued that anomalous data can create cognitive conflict and induce epistemic motivation to understand, or to a revise one's understanding about a phenomenon or event. Hatano and Inagaki (1991) emphasized that such individual motivation should be heightened by a sociocultural environment that values dialogical interaction in the form of group discussion or reciprocal teaching, in which different conceptions can be critically examined and evaluated in the service of intentional revision of knowledge.

Epistemic motivations are closely related to cognitive styles or dispositions such as actively open-minded thinking (Stanovich, 1999) and need for cognition (Cacioppo, Petty, Feinstein, & Jarvis, 1996), which have been investigated by conceptual change researchers. Sinatra and colleagues (Sinatra, Southerland, McConaughy, & Demastes, 2003; Sinatra, Southerland, Broughton, & Lassus, in submission) have explored how college students' background knowledge, beliefs, and cognitive dispositions relate to their acceptance of scientific theories. In a series of three studies, participants read passages presenting controversial theories about photosynthesis, bird evolution, and human evolution and rated their acceptance of the ideas presented in the text as well as the general scientific theories. The researchers predicted that students who held a more constructivist view of knowledge and who enjoyed effortful, critical and open-minded thinking would be more likely to accept scientific theories such as human evolution than students with more static views of knowledge who were less interested in deep, critical thinking.

In all three studies, students' beliefs and thinking dispositions predicted acceptance of human evolution. Knowledge, however, was only a significant predictor of acceptance when students' level of knowledge was high (an average of nearly seven college biology courses). The researchers concluded that for students with limited biology knowledge, beliefs and dispositions serve much like epistemic motivations. That is, they play the determinative role in acceptance of emotionally laden socially embedded topics, like human evolution. They also concluded that for knowledge to overcome motivations in decision making about scientific theories, students must undergo "epistemic conceptual change" (Sinatra, et al. in submission). That is, students must develop sufficient expertise in a domain that they develop an appreciation of the complex and evolving nature of knowledge in that domain (Alexander & Sinatra, 2007).

Epistemic beliefs, beliefs about the nature of knowledge and knowing (Hofer & Pintrich, 1997), have also been shown to relate to conceptual change. Qian and Alvermann (1995) demonstrated that epistemic beliefs can have a directly impact on the process of knowledge restructuring. They examined the relationship between high school students' epistemic beliefs, motivational goals, and conceptual change. Their research showed that students who viewed knowledge as simple and certain were less likely to reason effectively and experience conceptual change.

Windschitl and Andre (1998) examined undergraduate introductory biology students' epistemic beliefs and their understandings of the human cardiovascular system, a topic about which many students hold misconceptions. They found that students' epistemic beliefs predicted the likelihood of conceptual change. Students with more constructivist epistemic beliefs — that is beliefs that knowledge is both socially and personally constructed and thus ever changing experienced more change in their ideas about the circulatory system than those with more static views of knowledge. They also found that students with more constructivist epistemic beliefs performed better when they were in instructional conditions that allowed them to construct and test their own hypotheses. Conversely, students with more static views of knowledge did more poorly in this instructional setting than in more structured traditional instructional settings.

Mason (2000) investigated epistemic beliefs in relation to anomalous data in theory change on two controversial topics: One was scientific, the extinction of dinosaurs, and the other historical, the construction of the great pyramids in Giza (Egypt). The findings indicated that eighth graders' acceptance of anomalous data made the most significant contribution to their theory change. In addition, acceptance of anomalous data was associated with the belief about the stability (certain/evolving) and source (handed down by authority/derived from reason) of knowledge, although not strongly, for the scientific topic. The more students believed in the changing knowledge, derived from reason, the more likely they were to accept anomalous data and change their theory.

Nussbaum, Sinatra, and Poliquin (in press) hypothesized that instruction in the criteria of developing a scientific argument, along with constructivist epistemic beliefs would produce deeper intentional conceptual change. They found that college students who received argumentation instruction developed better arguments than those who did not. In regards to epistemic belief, evaluativists, who according to Kuhn, Cheney, and Weinstock (2000) hold reasoned justifications for their knowledge, engaged more with their partners, raised more alternative ideas, solved more physics problems accurately, and demonstrated a reduction in misconceptions compared to other belief groups.

The role of epistemic beliefs in relation to the text structure in the learning of natural selection and biological evolution was investigated by Mason and Gava (2007). Eighth graders in the experimental condition read a refutational text, and those in the control condition read a normal expository text. Findings from pre- to immediate and delayed post-tests showed that reading the refutational text and holding more sophisticated epistemic beliefs led to generate greater conceptual change. Moreover, a significant interaction between the two factors advantaged students who read the refutational text and believed more in complex and uncertain knowledge. Learners' metaconceptual awareness of changes in their own conceptions was also related to both variables.

Stathopoulou and Vosniadou's (2007) study with tenth graders also indicated that physics-related epistemic beliefs are necessary, although insufficient, for conceptual understanding in physics. Only students with highly constructivist epistemic beliefs achieved a deep understanding of Newtonian dynamics.

Epistemic motivations and beliefs, like achievement goals, are developed within a socio-cultural context and can serve to facilitate or inhibit conceptual change. Alexander and Sinatra (2007) posit that beliefs about knowledge and knowing are likely more domain-specific than previously realized. As noted, students develop a view of knowledge as complex and nuanced when they develop sufficient expertise in the domain to realize its complexity. A modest but compelling set of studies have begun to suggest that epistemic beliefs interact with learners' content knowledge and processing capabilities in important ways that warrant further study. It has been argued that epistemic beliefs, when brought to the level of learners' awareness, can promote epistemic conceptual change (Sinatra, 2005). There is emerging evidence that as students develop a view of knowledge as constantly changing, they themselves become more open to changing their conceptions of scientific phenomena (Sinatra et al., 2003; Mason, 2003).

Interest

Interest is one of the student characteristics identified by Pintrich et al. (1993) as a potential for motivating conceptual change. Studies on interest as a motivational variable draw a conceptual distinction between individual and situational interest (Alexander, 1997, 1998; Hidi & Baird, 1986; Renninger, Hidi, & Krapp, 1992; Tobias, 1994). Individual interest is a relatively stable student characteristic described as an evaluative orientation towards an object or domain. In contrast, situational interest is generated by certain conditions and/or environmental stimuli such as novelty and intensity, which contribute to the "interestingness" of a situation (Schraw & Lehman, 2001). According to Schiefele (1991, 1998), two aspects of interest as an individual preference for a certain class of objects can be identified. One aspect includes the attribution of personal significance to an object ("It is important to me"), the other refers to the positive affect (feelings) associated with it ("I feel stimulated").

The type of interest that has been investigated particularly in relation to learning from text is topic interest. It can be considered as both individual and situational (Hidi, 2000). Topic interest can be an expression of individual interest when a person has positive feelings about the topic, finds it of value, and seeks information about it. At the same time, it can be an expression of situational interest as it may be related to certain characteristics of the situation that trigger a person's cognitive and affective response.

The role of topic interest in learning has been demonstrated in a number of studies. It was found to be significantly related to recall of idea units, elaborations, and main ideas, independent of preexisting knowledge (Schiefele, 1996; Schiefele & Krapp, 1996). Highly interested senior high school students understood a text more deeply, whereas low interest readers assimilated it superficially, regardless of their degree of prior knowledge. A study by Alexander, Kulikovich, and Schulze (1994) revealed that college students' domain knowledge and topic interest were both significant predictors of comprehension of a technical physics text. Alexander and Murphy (1998) also showed that strong interest in a domain and willingness to pursue understanding discriminated highly successful from less successful college students. A study by Boscolo and Mason (2003) revealed that topic interest contribution increased relative to the degree of the learner's topic knowledge. When topic knowledge is high, topic interest may help students develop a deeper level of understanding of the text. Moreover, the beneficial effect of topic interest was evidenced in high school students' comprehension of a dual-position text on the controversial topic of genetically modified food. Highly topic-interested readers gave more accurate and richer answers about the conflicting perspectives presented in the text than low and moderately topic-interested readers (Mason & Boscolo, 2004).

The influence of potential situational interest sources — ease of comprehension, text cohesion and vividness, engagement, emotiveness, and prior knowledge — on text comprehension has also been revealed. The most effective sources were found to be ease of comprehension and vividness (Schraw, Bruning, & Svoboda, 1995). More recently, the concreteness of a text, rather than its seductive details, seemed to be a considerable resource for improving text learning and remembering (Sadoski, 2001).

Whereas several studies have demonstrated the effect of topic interest on text comprehension, only a few have focused on the relationship between interest (individual or situational) and conceptual change. These studies have revealed that interest may not always be a resource for conceptual change. In a study of high school students' understanding of genetics, Venville and Treagust (1998) reported some contradictory data. Students interested in the topic produced either high or very low levels of conceptual change. It should be underlined, however, that students' high interest was in human heredity and not in the microscopic aspects of genetics to be learned. Murphy and Alexander (2004) found that college students with high topic interest were less likely to alter their beliefs. The high correlation between interest and prior knowledge seen in these studies could explain the apparently contradictory findings. As pointed out by Dole and Sinatra (1998) in their model, individuals with high knowledge may show more resistance to change.

There is research demonstrating a positive effect of interest in intentional conceptual change. Andre and Windschitl (2003) conducted a series of studies on conceptual change about electrical circuits. College students' interest in the subject matter of physics and electricity was assessed together with their experience with electric circuits and verbal ability (Chambers & Andre, 1995, 1997). In the first study, interest in the subject matter and experience were related to post-test performance. Conceptual understanding was positively related to interest in the subject matter, regardless of whether a traditional or conceptual change text was read. In the second study, interest contributed again to conceptual understanding of electrical circuits, significantly and independently. Since in these studies pre-test measures were not available, in the third study both pre- and post-reading learning measures were taken into account together with interest, experience, and verbal ability. A path analysis revealed that interest contributed indirectly to conceptual change through the mediated effect of prior experience. In addition, interest also influenced students' post-test performance independently of its effect on experience. Topic interest can therefore affect conceptual change both directly and indirectly, through experience and knowledge (Andre & Windschitl, 2003).

In a recent study of fifth graders' conceptual change about light and vision, topic interest was examined in relation to beliefs about scientific knowledge (Mason, Gava, & Boldrin, in press). Students read either a traditional text or refutational text on the content to be learned which challenged alternative conceptions and showed the value of the scientific view. Topic interest was found to be a resource for change, as highly interested students changed their alternative conceptions more often than less interested students. In addition, topic interest interacted significantly with epistemological beliefs and the type of text. High interest and more constructivist beliefs about scientific knowledge, along with the instructional variable of a refutational text, proved to be a powerful combination that led to the best performance both at the immediate and delayed post-tests (Mason et al., in press).

The beneficial effect of interest on the knowledge restructuring process can be explained in light of the issues offered by recent literature on interest (e.g., Ainley, Hidi, & Berndorff, 2002). Interest directs the attentional resources of arousal, selective attention, and concentration. More interest in a topic is associated with increased attentional resources devoted to learning that information (Schiefele & Rheinberg, 1997). Spontaneous selective attention (Hidi, 1990), without deliberate effort, may also be involved (Shirey, 1992) in the cognitive processing of interesting information. Moreover, concentration or spontaneous prolonged attention may lead students to use their personal resources maximally and persist in the task (Voss & Schauble, 1992). Further, cognitive resources, "liberated" by interest, can therefore be devoted to cognitive processing. All together, arousal, selective attention, and concentration sustain deep or systematic processing of the content to be learned, a key factor in intentional conceptual change.

Like goals, interest seems to have the potential to direct attention toward the information to be learned, thereby bootstrapping the conceptual change process. Some research suggests that topic interest can be a catalyst for change. And yet, interest may be associated with commitment to one's current views and may create motivation to maintain one's current beliefs. This learner characteristic may be a "double edged sword" in terms of its connection to conceptual change and well illustrates the complex interactive nature of the knowledge restructuring process. Self-efficacy is another characteristic that may play conflicting roles in knowledge restructuring.

Self-Efficacy

Self-efficacy beliefs were defined by Bandura as individuals' beliefs about their performance capabilities in particular domains or tasks or "judgments on how well they will be able to perform in given situations" (1986, p. 392). The construct does not refer to individuals' global self-concept but rather to self-judgments about functioning in general academic domains (such as mathematics, foreign languages, or history) or specific tasks, such as solving word problems in mathematics. The predictive power of self-efficacy beliefs has been documented extensively in multiple areas of academic achievement, from mathematical learning (Pajares & Miller, 1994; Schunk, 1998) to writing (Pajares, 2003; Pajares & Johnson, 1996; Pajares & Valiante, 1999) to reading (Shell, Colvin, & Bruning, 1995; Schunk, 2003) to science learning (Pajares, Britner, & Valiante, 2000). Self-efficacy beliefs have also been shown to relate to such diverse areas as self-regulation (Zimmerman & Martinez-Pons, 1990) and career choice (Hackett, 1995).

The association of high self-efficacy beliefs with increased effort and persistence in difficult tasks and resilience in the face of obstacles and adverse situations has been offered as the explanation of the potential of self-efficacy to promote learning new and difficult content. The activation of appropriate knowledge and strategies to process new information has also been hypothesized as the mechanism driving the self-efficacy effect (Pintrich et al., 1993; Renninger, 1992; Schunk & Pajares, 2005).

Furthermore, self-efficacy is associated with positive emotional reactions. A high degree of confidence in one's own capabilities creates a feeling of comfort and calm, while low confidence is associated with anxiety and stress (Schunk & Pajares, 2005). Adaptive cognitions, motivations, and positive affect all seem to suggest that a self-confident learner would be more likely to engage in intentional conceptual change.

Pintrich (1999; Pintrich et al., 1993; Linnenbrink & Pintrich, 2003) cautioned, however, that there are two possible implications of the self-efficacy construct in the study of conceptual change. The first is that self-efficacy may create confidence in students' capabilities to gain a better understanding of an examined phenomenon and to learn through changing their ideas. In this case, higher self-efficacy would be facilitative of conceptual change. In contrast, the second possibility is that self-efficacy may foster students' sense of confidence in their ideas and perspectives. In this case higher self-efficacy could lead to increased resistance to changing those ideas. So, confidence in one's ideas may serve as an obstacle to learning for conceptual change, or confidence in oneself as a learner who is capable of thinking and reasoning about a topic may serve as a resource for overcoming alternative conceptions.

There is scarce empirical evidence to discern which of these two roles self-efficacy plays in the knowledge restructuring processes. In revising their well known model describing the conditions necessary for successful conceptual change, Strike and Posner (1992) explored the influence of a student's conceptual ecology. In addition to epistemic views, motivational factors such as self-efficacy and achievement goals were also examined as part of a single factor defined as learning attitude. A significant positive correlation emerged between students' learning attitudes (which included confidence in their ability to learn science meaningfully) and conceptual change in physics, providing modest evidence in favor of the facilitative role of efficacy beliefs.

The complex influence of self-efficacy on conceptual change processes can be illustrated through the analysis of a qualitative case study of a 6-year-old child's conceptual change (Maria, 1998). More specifically, Maria (1998) chronicled the change in her granddaughter's thinking in response to her instruction on basic earth concepts. The child began the instructional sessions with little confidence in her own explanations, as indicated by her frequent questioning if her answers were correct. Then, she gained enough confidence to reject the scientific ideas which were in conflict with her own. Over the course of many sessions, however, the confidence in her ideas lowered but at the same time, her confidence in herself as a learner remained high. These two aspects of self-efficacy allowed her to eventually engage in a successful process of change in her conceptions about the earth and gravity. More studies that investigate both confidence in one's conceptions and confidence in one's ability to learn in specific domains are needed to shed light on the double-edged sword of self-efficacy in the conceptual change processes.

In the previously mentioned study carried out by Qian and Alvermann (1995) on the relationship between epistemic beliefs and conceptual change, the role of learned helplessness (Dweck, 1975), which is the opposite of self-efficacy, was also examined. Findings showed that high school students, who learned to believe that obstacles and difficulties are insurmountable because of their low ability, were less likely to abandon their naïve conceptions about motion.

The interactive nature of learning for conceptual change clearly emerges when we consider the multiple roles of self-efficacy. Both students' perceptions of their capabilities to accomplish a task and confidence in their current conceptions may impact knowledge restructuring processes and produce different learning outcomes.

Affect and Emotions

There has been increasing interest in the role affect plays in the conceptual change process. Unfortunately, researchers do not seem to agree on a common definition of affect (Linnenbrink & Pintrich, 2004). Affect is often imprecisely used as a general term to refer to both states and traits of moods and/or emotions. Often the valance (positive or negative) is not properly taken into account. In cognitive and educational research, the term *affect* can refer to a host of "hot" constructs that extend beyond "cold" cognitive views of learning, but often specificity or precise definitions are lacking.

One perspective that distinguishes affect, mood, and emotion comes from Rosenberg (1998). According to this view, affective traits are predispositions towards emotional responses that tend to remain stable throughout one's lifetime (Rosenberg, 1998). Affective traits influence affective states, those more situational and temporary responses. Moods and emotions are affective states; that is, they are only temporary. Moods may last for up to a few days, and emotions are even more fleeting, typically occurring in response to a specific person or event (Linnenbrink & Pintrich, 2004). Rosenberg (1998) describes emotions as "brief, psychophysiological changes that result from a response to a meaningful situation in one's environment" (p. 250). Emotional responses are quick, automatic, and often occur unconsciously. However, emotions can also occupy the foreground of one's cognition, overwhelming conscious thoughts.

Pekrun and his colleagues (Pekrun, Goetz, Titz, & Perry, 2002) describe emotions that relate specifically to academic learning and classroom instruction. Academic emotions describe students' responses to studying, test taking, and other classroom activities, and therefore, may be very relevant to conceptual change learning. Pekrun et al. (2002) describe a two-dimensional model of emotions that includes the valence of the emotion (either positive or negative) and the activation level (either activating or deactivating). Positive activating emotions include enjoyment, pride, and hope, whereas negative activating emotions include anxiety, anger, and shame. Positive deactivating emotions would be feelings such as relief, whereas negative deactivating emotions include boredom and hopelessness.

Positive activating emotions have a positive effect on academic achievement by increasing motivation, critical thinking, elaboration, and metacognitive strategy use. In contrast, negative deactivating emotions diminish motivation, direct attention away from the task, and can result in superficial cognitive processing. Positive deactivating emotions may temporarily reduce cognitive processing, but over the longer term, positive responses may increase motivation to continue putting forth cognitive effort towards the task. Negative activating emotions such as anxiety and shame can also be beneficial to academic achievement because they may increase the students' motivation to carefully process the information in order to ultimately succeed with the learning task.

Clearly creating a classroom environment that fostered positive activating emotions would be recommended for promoting conceptual change, although Pekrun's model of academic emotions suggests that both positive and negative activating emotions have the potential to promote conceptual change if the emotions serve to increase motivation, focus attention, or promote deeper processing or elaboration.

Empirical research on the influence of emotional responses on conceptual change is even scarcer than research on motivational effects. In the first of the two studies described above by Linnenbrink and Pintrich (2002), mastery oriented students reported more positive affect (e.g., good mood, happiness, enjoyment) than negative affect (bad mood, frustration, anxiety) in comparison with performance oriented students. In the second study negative affect significantly related to lower degrees of conceptual change. However, as pointed out by the authors (Linnenbrink & Pintrich, 2002), these studies rely on self-reported measures of affect which are problematic. It is possible that students do not report their own affect accurately, or that their perception of their performance at post-test alters their reported affective state. Moreover, the measure was not intended to measure mood or emotions, but rather positive and negative feelings.

Regarding the mechanisms underlying the impact of affect on the knowledge construction and revision process, Linnenbrink and Pintrich (2004) emphasized that they are not yet clear. The authors posited that affect may influence encoding and retrieval of information as well as its processing. As noted, positive emotions may facilitate conceptual change if they support deep processing. However, if alternative prior knowledge is associated with a positive mood, it can make the change process more difficult. Negative emotions can also hinder learning for conceptual change if they lead to a focus on task details, rather than the content to be learned. However, it has been suggested that negative emotions arising from the experience of cognitive conflict may also promote knowledge restructuring. Cognitive conflict is considered one of the more effective instructional strategies for enhancing conceptual change. Some negative emotions may be associated with cognitive conflict as students recognize that their current conceptions are not in accord with the new conception. To some extent, negative emotions may accompany metacognitive awareness of the need for knowledge restructuring (Linnenbrink & Pintrich, 2004).

In her model of teacher belief change, Gregoire (2003) emphasizes the emotional influences on the process of change. More specifically, she explains the role anxiety and fear play when teachers encounter reform messages. When teachers receive a complex message that challenges traditional instruction in favor of a reform, they may appraise it with a feeling of anxiety. Anxiety is experienced when an individual perceives that the situation at hand exceeds her or his personal resources for coping. However, anxiety per se is not always negative. It can lead to better learning if it is perceived as an opportunity for growth and change. The perceived challenge becomes an emotionally positive experience if it is tempered by efficacy beliefs. In other words, if a teacher believes in her capability to help students learn by implementing the reform initiative described in the message, then the teacher is more likely to process the complex message. If the anxiety generated by the message is not associated with positive self-efficacy, the teacher is more likely to perceive it as a threat. This response leads the teacher to avoid the reform message. If the message is never processed deeply, then the deliberate processing necessary for belief change will not occur.

As suggested by these preliminary perspectives on emotions, learning, and conceptual change, emotions like self-efficacy, may play either a facilitative or inhibitory role in the change process. The complexity of affective constructs makes them a challenging but potentially fruitful area for further research.

A SYNTHESIS: ON THE IMPACT OF LEARNER CHARACTERISTICS ON CONCEPTUAL CHANGE

We have sought to describe what we believe to be the multi-faceted and highly interactive nature of the conceptual change process, with particular emphasis on the role learner characteristics other than knowledge play in determining whether or not knowledge restructuring occurs. Learner characteristics tend to impact conceptual change when: (1) prior knowledge conflicts with to be learned information, (2) there is a high level of commitment to that knowledge, and (3) there are activated emotions associated with that commitment.

Learners' background knowledge is always important in any learning situation. However, in many circumstances, learners may have little relevant topic knowledge, or the knowledge they have may not conflict with the new information. For example, if a student new to chemistry is learning the symbols in the periodic table, most likely the majority of the symbols are new to her. Coming to accept that B is the chemical symbol for Boron presents no difficulty, conflict, or learning challenge for our learner. However, in conceptual change situations, students have a great deal of relevant topic knowledge developed through years of experience. For example, if the topic is the speed with which objects of different weight fall, our learner has much relevant experience with the topic. Since she was an infant, our learner has been observing objects fall to the earth in a variety of circumstances. Some objects, such as leaves from the trees in late September, seem to float gently and slowly to the ground. While others, like ice cream from a cone on a hot July day, seem to fall to the ground in the blink of an eye. Learners bring the wealth of their prior experiences with them and this creates potential conflicts with scientific views.

In addition to experience, there is increasing evidence from cognitive developmental research that children are endowed through evolutionary history with conceptions of the physical and social world around them. Characterized as naïve physics, naïve biology, and naïve psychology (Vosniadou, 2007; Geary, in press), these theories or frameworks assure that some information critical to an individual's survival is learned quickly and effortlessly. According to Vosniadou (2007), these frameworks come about because there are domain-specific constraints that serve as predispositions to interpret the world in particular ways. These predispositions serve as the basis for future learning and explain why conceptions that conflict with naïve frameworks are harder to accept than others.

Not only do learners in a conceptual change situation have relevant prior knowledge, they may also have a high degree of commitment to their ideas. For learners who have a high level of prior knowledge that differs from the new conception, learning may not be challenging if the learner has no commitment to that prior conception. So for example, it may not be difficult to accept the idea that botanists would consider a tomato to be a fruit because it grows on a vine, even though prior experience leads you to believe that it is a vegetable. If you do not have any deep commitments to the tomato's status (other than that you like them raw in your salads and cooked on your pasta), accepting a change in a tomato's classification from vegetable to fruit may present little challenge.

In contrast, there are many ideas to which learners are deeply committed. The notions that the earth is flat or that objects fall to the ground at different rates may be based on naïve physics understandings and on everyday experiences ingrained over a lifetime. Strongly committed ideas are highly resistant to change in part due to this commitment (and in part due to their likely rich interconnections with other ideas). Resistance creates various barriers to learning that range from outright rejection of the new idea to deliberate revision of the conception to fit with preexisting notions (see Chinn & Brewer, 1993).

Finally, for some topics, such as the notion that humans are divine, supernaturally created beings, learners may have deeply emotional commitments. Such commitments change how learners interact with information they perceive as a threat to their views. The feeling of perceived threat is not confined to religious beliefs but can be a characteristic of any beliefs to which a learner has an affective commitment (see Gregoire, 2003, for a description of teachers' commitments to their instructional beliefs).

The degree of commitment to one's knowledge and beliefs and the activation level and type of emotion or affective trait tied to that commitment stems in part from the socio-cultural context in which knowledge is embedded. Jovchelovitch (2007) describes how knowledge representations are "… at once epistemic, social and personal and it is the appreciation of these three dimensions that can explain why representations are not a copy of the world outside but a symbolic construction of it" (p. 26). Jovchelovitch's (2007) perspective of "knowledge in context" reminds us of the dynamic interactive nature of knowledge construction and reconstruction and demands a multifaceted explanation of conceptual change that is both cognitive and social in nature.

INSTRUCTIONAL IMPLICATIONS

The multifaceted interactive nature of conceptual change, and the powerful role of learner characteristics, suggests there is a need to tailor instruction to match facets of the change process that present barriers to change. To be successful, conceptual change pedagogy must first include a determination of the full range of possible barriers to change. Instruction can then be targeted to confront barriers from multiple fronts. If learners hold misconceptions or alternative conceptions, these must be identified. The learners' level of commitment to their prior conceptions must also be determined. Next, the activation level and type of emotions or affective traits or states tied to their prior knowledge should also be determined. This may sound overwhelming and unachievable, but in fact, there are several instruments available to ascertain misconceptions (see, for example, Glynn & Duit, 1995; White & Gunstone, 1992), determine the strength and commitment to ideas (Stanovich, 1998; Stanovich & West, 1997) and characterize epistemic views (Wood & Kardash, 2002; Kuhn et. al., 2000). Lacking these resources or the time or expertise to analyze the results, carefully crafted teacher-led discussions can bring students' misconceptions and strong beliefs and emotions to the surface quite readily.

Once possible barriers are identified, instruction must be geared toward overcoming the particular barriers blocking change. Such interventions should be tailored for both the nature of the barrier and the topic. Minor conceptual misunderstandings about a tangential aspect of a phenomena and major misconceptions about a central tenet of a scientific theory require different instructional approaches. So, for example, whereas refutation text may work to overcome a relatively minor misconception, argumentation pedagogy may be needed to promote a change in students' thinking about a controversial topic (Nussbaum & Sinatra, 2003).

As the barriers to change increase in terms of their strength or level of resistance, the nature of the instruction must also adjust to fit the level of resistance. Students' degree of commitment to their own ideas suggests certain instructional approaches would be more successful than others. Deep commitments to an alternative conception based in naïve physics, naïve biology, or naïve psychology and developed through extensive interactions with the physical, biological, and emotional world require pedagogical approaches that demand high engagement (Dole & Sinatra, 1998) such as experimentation, inquiry, or problem-based learning (Hennessey, 2003; Kolodner, Camp, Crismond, Fasse, Gray, Holbrook, Puntambeaker, & Ryan, 2003; White & Frederiksen, 1998).

Emotionally-based commitments to deeply held personal beliefs, affective traits or epistemic beliefs that create resistance to change, or motivations or dispositions toward maintaining one's views would require instruction to be "ratcheted up" to another level of engagement. In these circumstances, argumentation-based pedagogies such as collaborative argumentation (Nussbaum & Sinatra, 2003) or the use of persuasive pedagogies (Murphy, 2001; Sinatra & Kardash, 2004) may be more effective in promoting change.

The nature of the topic itself has significant implications for selecting an instructional approach as well. Some topics may be more inherently interesting than others (Schiefele, 1991). Some topics bring naïve frameworks more to the fore than others. Further, there are topics that present greater challenges for conceptual change due to the level of controversy engendered by the topic itself (Kardash & Scholes, 1996).

The classroom climate may need to be changed as well if deeply held conceptions and beliefs are to be broached pedagogically. For example, the evaluation and reward structure may need to be changed from a focus on performance goals toward promoting a mastery goal orientation. Structures and systems must be in place allowing students to feel safe to discuss alternative points of view without fear of social or academic consequences. Ultimately, students must feel unthreatened by expressing their own opinions and free to form appropriate arguments against their peers', teachers', or textbooks' espoused views.

Finally, according to Alexander's Model of Domain Learning (Alexander, Jetton, & Kulikowich, 1995), students need to move away from the acclimation stage, where they are taking their initial forays into learning about a domain and move toward the proficiency stage where they are developing expertise before they have sufficient knowledge with which to reason (Sinatra et al., 2003). Sufficient content knowledge is necessary to reason and think critically about their views. At the same time, students may need to be taught the type of learning strategies characteristic of the proficient learner (Alexander et al., 1995).

IMPLICATIONS FOR THEORIES OF CONCEPTUAL CHANGE

We have tried to paint a picture of the conceptual change process as complex, interactive, and at once cognitive, affective, and social. Key to understanding this multifaceted view is an examination of the role learner characteristics play in the interaction. We believe theories and models of conceptual change must account for the complexity of the process. Models that are strictly cognitive or strictly social will not ultimately succeed in explaining the complexity of learning that is conceptual change (Mason, 2007).

Different theoretical perspectives on conceptual change can each be viewed as offering explanations of change at various levels of awareness, stages of development, or points along the individual to social continuum. A view of conceptual change as multifaceted affords an opportunity to bridge the gap between what is oft seen as competing explanations of the change process. Different perspectives broaden our understanding of the nature of change itself and how knowledge restructuring can be facilitated. Ultimately, conceptual change theories and models that embrace the complexity inherent in the knowledge restructuring process will have profound implications for all forms of learning.

NOTE

1. Clearly, learner characteristics impact conceptual change at more than one level of awareness. However, we discuss their impact at the intentional level because it is at this level that they come under the conscious control of the learner and therefore have the most opportunity to affect change.

REFERENCES

Ainley, M., Hidi, S., & Berndorff, D. (2002). Interest, learning, and the psychological processes that mediate their relationship. *Journal of Educational Psychology, 94,* 545–561.

Alexander, P. A. (1997). Mapping the multidimensional nature of domain learning: The interplay of cognitive, motivational, and strategic forces. In M. L. Maehr & P. R. Pintrich (Eds.), *Advances in motivation and achievement* (Vol. 10, pp. 213–250). Greenwich, CT: JAI Press.

Alexander, P. A. (1998). The nature of disciplinary and domain learning: The knowledge, interest, and strategic dimensions of learning from subject-matter text. In C. Hynd (Ed.), *Learning from text across conceptual domains* (pp. 263–287). Mahwah, NJ: Erlbaum.

Alexander, P. A., & Murphy, P. K. (1998). Profiling the differences in students' knowledge, interest, and strategic processing. *Journal of Educational Psychology, 90,* 435–447.

Alexander, P. A., & Sinatra, G. M. (2007). First steps: Scholars' promising movements into a nascent field of inquiry. In S. Vosniadou, A. Baltas, & X. Vamvakoussi (Eds.), *Re-Framing the Problem of Conceptual Change in Learning and Instruction* (pp. 221–236). Oxford, UK: Elsevier Science.

Alexander, P. A., Jetton, T. L., & Kulikowich, J. M. (1995). Interrelationship of knowledge, interest, and recall: Assessing a model of domain learning. *Journal of Educational Psychology, 87*(4), 599–575.

Alexander, P. A., Kulikowich, J. M., & Schulze, S. K. (1994). The influence of topic knowledge, domain knowledge, and interest on the comprehension of scientific exposition. *Learning and Individual Differences, 6,* 379–397.

Ames, C. (1984). Competitive, cooperative, and individualistic goal structures: A cognitive-motivational analysis. In C. Ames & R. Ames (Eds.), *Research on motivation in education* (Vol. 3, pp. 177–207). New York: Academic Press.

Ames, C. (1992). Classrooms: Goals, structures, and student motivation. *Journal of Educational Psychology, 84,* 261–271.

Anderson, J. R. (1990). *The adaptive character of thought.* Hillsdale, NJ: Erlbaum.

Anderson, J. R. (1991). Is human cognition adaptive? *Behavioral and Brain Sciences, 14,* 471–517.

Anderson, R. C., Reynolds, R. E., Schallert, D. L., & Goetz, E. T. (1977). Frameworks for the comprehension of discourse. *American Educational Research Journal, 14*(4), 376–381.

Andre, T., & Windschitl, M. (2003). Interest, epistemological belief, and intentional conceptual change. In G. M. Sinatra & P. R. Pintrich (Eds.). *Intentional conceptual change* (pp. 173–193). Mahwah, NJ: Erlbaum.

Bandura, A. (1986). *Social foundation of thought and action: A social cognitive theory.* Englewood Cliffs, NJ: Prentice-Hall.

Bargh, J. A., & Chartrand, T. L. (1999). The unbearable automaticity of being. *American Psychologist, 54*(7), 462–479.

Boscolo P., & Mason, L. (2003). Prior knowledge, text coherence, and interest: How they interact in learning from instructional texts. *Journal of Experimental Education, 71*, 126–148.

Cacioppo, J. T., Petty, R. E., Feinstein, J., & Jarvis, W. (1996). Dispositional differences in cognitive motivation: The life and times of individuals varying in need for cognition. *Psyhcological Bullettin, 119*, 197–253.

Carey, S. (1985). *Conceptual change in childhood*. Cambridge, MA: MIT Press.

Chambers, S. K., & Andre, T. (1995). Are conceptual change approaches to learning science effective for everyone: Gender, prior subject matter interest, and learning about electricity. *Contemporary Educational Psychology, 20*, 377–391.

Chambers, S. K., & Andre, T, (1997). Gender, prior knowledge, interest, and experience in electricity and conceptual change text manipulations in learning about direct current. *Journal of Research in Science Teaching, 34*, 105–123.

Chi, M. T. H. (1992). Conceptual change within and across ontological categories: Examples from learning and discovery in science. In R. N. Giere (Ed.). *Minnesota Studies in the Philosophy of Science: Vol. XV. Cognitive models of science* (pp. 129–186). Minneapolis: University of Minnesota Press.

Chinn, C. A., & Brewer, W. F. (1993). The role of anomalous data in knowledge acquisition: A theoretical framework and implications for science instruction. *Review of Educational Research, 63*(10), 1–49.

Clough, E. E., & Driver, R. (1985). Secondary students' conceptions of the conduct of heat: Bringing together scientific and personal views. *Physics Education, 20*, 176–182.

Craik, F. I. M., & Lockhart, R. S. (1972). Levels of processing: A framework for memory research. *Journal of Verbal Learning and Verbal Behavior, 11*, 671–684.

Dole, J. A., & Sinatra, G. M. (1998). Reconceptualizing change in the cognitive construction of knowledge. *Educational Psychologist, 33*(2/3), 109–128.

Dweck, C. S. (1975). The role of expectations and attributions in the alleviation of learned helplessness. *Journal of Personality and Social Psychology, 31*, 674–685.

Dweck, C. S., & Leggett, E. L. (1988). A social-cognitive approach to motivation and personality. *Psychological Review, 95*, 256–273.

Eaton, J. F., Anderson, C. W., & Smith, E. L. (1984). Students' misconceptions interfere with learning: Case studies of fifth grade students. *Elementary School Journal, 64*, 365–379.

Elliot, A. J. (1999). Approach and avoidance motivation and achievement goals. *Educational Psychologist, 34*, 149–169.

Elliot, A. J. (2005). A conceptual history of the achievement goal construct. In A. J. Elliot & C. S. Dweck (Eds.), *Handbook of competence and motivation* (pp. 52–72). New York: Guilford.

Elliot, A. J., McGregor, H. A., & Gables, S. (1999). Achievement goals, study strategies, and exam performance: A mediational analysis. *Journal of Educational Psychology, 91*, 549–563.

Elliott, E. S., & Dweck, C. S. (1988). Goals: An approach to motivation and achievement. *Journal of Personality and Social Psychology, 54*, 5–12.

Elliott, E. S., & Moller, A. (2003). Performance-approach goal: Good or bad forms of regulation? *International Journal of Educational Research, 39*, 339–356.

Geary, D. C. (in press). An evolutionarily informed education science. *Educational Psychologist*.

Glynn, S. M., & Duit, R. (Eds.). (1995). *Learning science in the schools*. Mahwah, NJ: Erlbaum.

Graham, S., & Golan, S. (1991). Motivational influences on cognition: Task involvement, ego involvement, and depth of processing. *Journal of Educational Psychology, 83*, 187–194.

Gregoire G., M., Ashton, P., & Algina, J. (2004). Changing preservice teachers' epistemological beliefs about teaching and learning in mathematics: An intervention study. *Contemporary Educational Psychology, 29*(2), 164–185.

Gregoire, M. (2003). Is it a challenge or a threat? A dual-process model of teachers' cognition and appraisal processes during conceptual change. *Educational Psychology Review, 15*, 147–179.

Hackett, G. (1995). Self-efficacy in career choice and development. In A. Bandura (Ed.), *Self-efficacy in changing societies* (pp. 232–258). New York: Cambridge University Press.

Hammer, D. (1994). Epistemological beliefs in introductory physics. *Cognition and Instruction*, *12*, 151–183.

Harackiewicz, J. M., & Sansone, C. (1991). Goals and intrinsic motivation: You *can* get there from here. In M. L. Maehr, & P. R. Pintrich (Eds.), *Advances in motivation and achievement* (Vol. 7, pp. 21–49). Greenwich, CT: JAI Press.

Harackiewicz, J. M., & Elliott, A. J. (1993). Achievement goals and intrinsic motivation. *Journal of Personality and Social Psychology*, *65*, 904–915.

Harackiewicz, J. M., Barron, K. E., Pintrich, P. R., Elliot, A. J., & Thrash, T. M. (2002). Revision of achievement goal theory: Necessary and illuminating. *Journal of Educational Psychology*, *94*, 638–645.

Hatano, G., & Inagaki, K. (1991). Sharing cognition through collective comprehension activity. In L. B. Resnick, J. M. Levine, & S. D. Teasley (Eds.), *Perspectives on socially shared cognition* (pp. 331–348). Washington, DC: American Psychological Association.

Hatano, G., & Inagaki, K. (2003). When is conceptual change intended? A cognitive-sociocultural view. In G. M. Sinatra & P. R. Pintrich (Eds.), *Intentional conceptual change* (pp. 407–427). Mahwah, NJ: Erlbaum.

Hennessey, M. G. (2003). Metacognitive aspects of students' reflective discourse: Implications for intentional conceptual change teaching and learning. In G. M. Sinatra & P. R. Pintrich (Eds.), *Intentional conceptual change* (pp. 103–132). Mahwah, NJ: Erlbaum.

Hidi, S. (1990). Interest and its contributions as a mental resource for learning. *Review of Educational Research*, *60*, 549–571.

Hidi, S. (2000). An interest researcher's perspective: The effects of intrinsic and extrinsic factors on motivation. In C. Sansone & J. M. Harackiewicz (Eds.), *Intrinsic and extrinsic motivation* (pp. 309–339). San Diego, CA: Academic Press.

Hidi, S., & Baird, W. (1986). Interestingness — A neglected variable in discourse processing. *Cognitive Science*, *10*, 179–194.

Hofer, B. K., & Pintrich, P. R. (1997). The development of epistemological theories: Beliefs about knowledge and knowing and their relation to learning. *Review of Educational Research, 67*(1), 88–140.

Hynd, C. (1998). Conceptual change in a high school physics class. In B. Guzzetti & C. Hynd (Eds.), *Perspectives on conceptual change: Multiple ways to understand knowing and learning in a complex world* (pp. 27–36). Mahwah, NJ: Erlbaum.

Hynd, C., Holschuh, J., & Nist, S. (2000). Learning complex scientific information: Motivation theory and its relation to student perception. *Reading and Writing Quarterly: Overcoming Learning Difficulties, 36*(1), 23–58.

Jost, J. T., Glaser, J., Kruglanski, A. W., & Sulloway, F. J. (2003). Exceptions that prove the rule: Using a theory of motivated social cognition to account for ideological incongruities and political anomalies: Reply to Greenberg and Jonas. *European Journal of Social Psychology, 33*, 13–36

Jovchelovitch, S. (2007). *Knowledge in context*. Cambridge: Cambridge University Press.

Kardash, C. M., & Scholes, R. J. (1996). Effects of preexisting beliefs, epistemological beliefs, and need for cognition on interpretation of controversial issues. *Journal of Educational Psychology*, *88*(2), 260–271.

Kolodner, J. L., Camp, P. J., Crismond, D., Fasse, B., Gray, J., Holbrook, J., Puntambeaker, S., & Ryan, M. (2003). Problem-based learning meets case-based reasoning in the middle-school science classroom: Putting learning by design-super (TM) into practice. *Journal of the Learning Sciences, 12*, 495–547.

Kruglanski, A. W. (1989). *Lay epistemics and human knowledge: Cognitive and motivational bases*. New York: Plenum.

Kruglanski, A. W. (1990). Lay epistemic theory in social cognitive psychology. *Psychological Inquiry, 1*, 181–197.

Kruglanski, A. W., & Webster, D. M. (1996). Motivated closing of the mind: "Seizing" and "Freezing." *Psychological Review, 103*, 263–283.

Kuhn, D., Cheney, R., & Weinstock, M. (2000). The development of epistemological understanding. *Cognitive Development*, *15*, 309–328.

Linnenbrink, E. A., & Pintrich, P. R. (2002). The role of motivational beliefs in conceptual change. In

M. Limón & L. Mason (Eds.), *Reconsidering conceptual change: Issues in theory and practice* (pp. 115–135). Dordrecht, The Netherlands: Kluwer Academic.

Linnenbrink, E. A., & Pintrich, P. R. (2003). Achievement goals and intentional conceptual change. In. G. M. Sinatra & P. R. Pintrich (Eds.), *Intentional conceptual change* (pp. 347–374). Mahwah, NJ: Erlbaum.

Linnenbrink, E. A., & Pintrich, P. R. (2004). Role of affect in cognitive processing in academic contexts. In D. Y. Dai & R. J. Sternberg (Eds), *Motivation, emotion, and cognition* (pp. 57–88). Mahwah, NJ: Erlbaum.

Maehr, M. L. (1984). Meaning and motivation. In R. Ames & C. Ames (Eds.), *Research on motivation in education: Student motivation* (Vol. 1, pp. 115–144). New York: Academic Press.

Maria, K. (1998). Self-confidence and the process of conceptual change. In B. Guzzetti & C. Hynd (Eds.), *Perspectives on conceptual change* (pp. 7–16). Mahwah, NJ: Erlbaum.

Mason, L. (2000). Role of anomalous data and epistemological beliefs in middle students' theory change on two controversial topics. *European Journal of Psychology of Education, 15,* 329–346.

Mason, L. (2003). Personal epistemologies and intentional conceptual change. In. G. M. Sinatra & P. R. Pintrich (Eds.). *Intentional conceptual change* (pp. 199–236). Mahwah, NJ: Erlbaum.

Mason, L. (2007). Introduction: Bridging the cognitive and sociocultural approaches in research on conceptual change. Is it feasible? *Educational Psychologist, 41*(1), 1–7.

Mason, L., & Boscolo, P. (2004). Role of epistemological understanding and interest in interpreting a controversy and in topic-specific belief change, *Contemporary Educational Psychology, 29*(2), 103–128.

Mason, L., & Gava, M. (in press). Effects of epistemological beliefs and learning text structure on conceptual change. In S. Vosniadou, A. Baltas, & X. Vamvakoussi (Eds.), *Re-Framing the problem of conceptual change in learning and instruction* (pp. 165–196). Oxford: Elsevier Science.

Mason, L., Boldrin, A., & Vanzetta, A. (2006). Epistemological beliefs and achievement goals in conceptual change learning. Paper presented at the 4th Symposium of the SIG "Metacognition" of the European Association for Research on Learning and Instruction. Stockholm, Sweden.

Mason, L., Gava, M., & Boldrin, A. (in press). On warm conceptual change: The interplay of text, epistemological beliefs, and topic interest. *Journal of Educational Psychology.*

Murphy, P. K. (2001). Teaching as persuasion: A new metaphor for a new decade. *Theory into Practice, 40*(4), 224–227.

Murphy, P. K., & Alexander, P. A. (2004). Persuasion as a dynamic, multidimensional process: A view of individual and intraindividual differences. *American Educational Research Journal, 41,* 337–363.

Murphy, P. K., & Mason, L. (2006). Changing knowledge and beliefs. In P. A. Alexander & P. H. Winne (Eds.), *Handbook of educational psychology* (pp. 305–324). Mahwah, NJ: Erlbaum.

Newell, A. (1990). *Unified theories of cognition.* Cambridge, MA: Harvard University Press.

Nicholls, J. G. (1984). Achievement motivation: Conceptions of ability, subjective experience, task choice, and performance. *Psychological Review, 91,* 328–346.

Nolen, S. B. (1988). Reasons for studying: Motivational orientations and study strategies. *Cognition and Instruction, 5,* 269–287.

Nussbaum, E. M., & Sinatra, G. M. (2003). Argument and conceptual engagement. *Contemporary Educational Psychology, 28,* 384–395.

Nussbaum, E. M., Sinatra, G. M., & Poliquin, A. (in press). Role of epistemological beliefs and scientific argumentation in promoting conceptual change. *International Journal of Science Education.*

Pajares, F. (2003). Self-efficacy beliefs, motivation, and achievement in writing: A review of the litearature. *Reading and Writing Quarterly, 19,* 139–158.

Pajares, F., & Miller, M. D. (1994). The role of self-efficacy and self-concept beliefs in mathematical problem-solving: A path analysis. *Journal of Educational Psychology, 86,* 193–203.

Pajares, F., & Johnson, M. J. (1996). Self-efficacy beliefs and the writing performance of high school students. *Psychology in the Schools, 33,* 163–175.

Pajares, F., & Valiante, G. (1999). Grade level and gender differences in the writing self-beliefs of middle school students: A function of gender orientation? *Contemporary Educational Psychology, 26,* 366–381.

Pajares, F., Britner, S. L., & Valiante, G. (2000). Writing and science achievement goals in middle school students. *Contemporary Educational Psychology, 25*, 406–422.

Pekrun, R., Goetz, T., Titz, W., & Perry, R. P. (2002). Academic emotions in students' self-regulated learning and achievement: A program of qualitative and quantitative research. *Educational Psychologist, 37*(2), 91–105.

Piaget, J. (1952). The *origins of intelligence in children*. New York: International Universities Press.

Pintrich, P. R. (1999). Motivational beliefs as resources for and constraints on conceptual change. In W. Schnotz, S. Vosniadou, & M. Carretero (Eds.), *New perspectives on conceptual change* (pp. 33–50). Amsterdam, The Netherlands: Pergamon.

Pintrich, P. R. (2000). The role of goal orientation in self-regulation learning. In M. Boekaerts, P. R. Pintrich, & M. Zeidner (Eds.), *Handbook of self-regulation: Theory, research and applications* (pp. 451–502). San Diego, CA: Academic Press.

Pintrich, P. R., & Garcia, T. (1991). Student goal orientation and self-regulation in the college classroom. In M. L. Maehr & P. R. Pintrich (Eds.), *Advances in motivation and achievement: Goals and self-regulatory processes* (Vol. 7, pp. 371–402). Greenwich, CT: JAI Press.

Pintrich, P. R., & Schrauben, B. (1992). Students' motivational beliefs and their cognitive engagement in classroom academic tasks. In D. Schunk & J. Meese (Eds.), *Student perceptions in the classroom* (pp. 149–183). Hillsdale, NJ: Erlbaum.

Pintrich, P. R., & Sinatra, G. M. (2003). Future direction for theory and research on intentional conceptual change. In. G. M. Sinatra & P. R. Pintrich (Eds.). *Intentional conceptual change* (pp. 429–441). Mahwah, NJ: Erlbaum.

Pintrich, P. R., Marx, R. W., & Boyle, R. B. (1993). Beyond cold conceptual change: The role of motivational beliefs and classroom contextual factors in the process of conceptual change. *Review of Educational Research, 63*, 167–199.

Posner, G. J., Strike, K. A., Hewson, P. W., & Gertzog, W. A. (1982). Accommodation of a scientific conception: Towards a theory of conceptual change. *Science Education, 67*(4), 489–508.

Qian, G., & Alvermann, D. (1995). Role of epistemological beliefs and learned helplessness in secondary school students' learning science concepts from text. *Journal of Educational Psychology, 87*, 282–292.

Qian, G., & Pan, J. (2002). A comparison of epistemological beliefs and learning from science text between American and Chinese high school students. In B. K. Hofer & P. R. Pintrich (Eds.), *Personal epistemology. The psychology of beliefs about knowledge and knowing* (pp. 365–385). Mahwah, NJ: Erlbaum.

Renninger, K. A. (1992). Individual interest and development: Implications for theory and practice. In K. A. Renninger, S. Hidi, & A. Krapp (Eds.), *The role of interest in learning and development* (pp. 361–395). Hillsdale, NJ: Erlbaum.

Renninger, K. A., Hidi, S., & Krapp, A. (Eds.). (1992). *The role of interest in learning and development*. Hillsdale, NJ: Erlbaum.

Rosenberg, E. L. (1998). Levels of analysis and the organization of affect. *Review of General Psychology, 2*, 247–270.

Sadoski, M. (2001). Resolving the effects of concreteness on interest, comprehension and learning important ideas from text. *Educational Psychology Review, 13*, 263–281.

Schiefele, U. (1991). Interest, learning, and motivation, *Educational Psychologist, 26*, 299–323.

Schiefele, U. (1996). Topic interest, text representation, and quality of experience. *Contemporary Educational Psychology, 12*, 3–18.

Schiefele, U. (1998). Individual interest and learning: What we know and what we don't know. In L. Hoffmann, A. Krapp, K. A. Renninger, & J. Baumert (Eds.), *Interest and learning* (pp. 91–104). Kiel, Germany: IPN.

Schiefele, U., & Krapp, A. (1996).). Topic interest and free recall of expository text. *Learning and Individual Differences, 8*, 141–160.

Schiefele, U., & Rheinberg, F. (1997). Motivation and knowledge acquisition: Searching for mediating processes. In M. L. Maehr & P. R. Pintrich (Eds.), *Advances in motivation and achievement* (Vol. 10, pp. 251–301). Oxford: Elsevier Science.

Schraw, G., & Lehman, S. (2001). Situational interest: A review of the literature and directions for future research. *Educational Psychology Review, 13* (1), 23–52.

Schraw, G., Bruning, R., & Svoboda, C. (1995). Sources of situational interest. *Journal of Reading Behavior, 27*, 1–17.

Schunk, D. H. (1998). Teaching elementary students to self-regulate practice of mathematical skills with modeling. In D. Schunk & B. J. Zimmerman (Eds.), *Self-regulated learning: From teaching to self-reflective practice* (pp. 137–159). New York: Guilford.

Schunk, D. H. (2003). Self-efficacy for reading and writing: Influence of modeling, goal setting, and self-evaluation. *Reading and Writing Quarterly: Overcoming Learning Difficulties, 19*, 159–172.

Schunk, D. H., & Pajares, F. (2005). Competence perception and academic functioning. In A. J. Elliot & C. S. Dweck (Eds.), *Handbook of competence and motivation* (pp. 85–104). New York: Guilford.

Shell, D., Colvin, C., & Bruning, R. (1995). Self-efficacy, attribution, and outcome expectancy mechanisms in reading and writing achievement: Grade level and achievement-level differences. *Journal of Educational Psychology, 87*, 386–398.

Shirey, L. L. (1992). Importance, interest, and selective attention. In K. A. Renninger, S. Hidi, & A. Krapp (Eds.), *The role of interest in learning and development* (pp. 281–296). Hillsdale, NJ: Erlbaum.

Sinatra, G. M. (2005). The "warming trend" in conceptual change research: The legacy of Paul R. Pintrich. *Educational Psychologist, 40*(2), 107–115.

Sinatra, G. M., & Kardash, C. M. (2004). Teacher candidates' epistemological beliefs, dispositions, and views on teaching as persuasion. *Contemporary Educational Psychology, 29*, 483–498.

Sinatra, G. M., & Pintrich, P. R. (Eds.). (2003). *Intentional conceptual change.* Mahwah, NJ: Erlbaum.

Sinatra, G. M., Southerland, S. A., McConaughy, F., & Demastes, J. (2003). Intentions and beliefs in students' understanding and acceptance of biological evolution. *Journal of Research in Science Teaching, 40*(5), 510–528.

Smiley, P. A., & Dweck, C. S. (1994). Individual differences in achievement goals among young children. *Child Development, 65*, 1723–1743.

Speelman, C. (1998). The automaticity of discourse comprehension. In K. Kirsner, C. Speelman, M. Maybery, O'Brien-Malone, A., M. Anderson et al. (Eds.), *Implicit and explicit mental processes* (pp. 187–200). Mahwah, NJ: Erlbaum.

Spelke, E. (1991). Physical knowledge in infancy: Reflections on Piaget's theory. In S. Carey & R. Gelman (Eds.), *Epigenesis of mind* (pp. 133–170). Hillsdale, NJ: Erlbaum.

Stanovich, K. E. (1998). Individual differences in rational thought. *Journal of Experimental Psychology: General, 127*, 161–179.

Stanovich, K. E. (1999). *Who is rational? Studies of individual differences in reasoning.* Mahwah, NJ: Erlbaum.

Stanovich, K. E., & West, R. F. (1997). Reasoning independently of prior belief and individual differences in actively open-minded thinking. *Journal of Educational Psychology, 89*, 342–357.

Stathopoulou, C., & Vosniadou, S. (2007). Exploring the relationship between physics-related epistemological beliefs and physics understanding. *Contemporary Educational Psychology, 32*(3), 255–281.

Strike, K. A., & Posner, G. J. (1992). A revisionist theory of conceptual change. In R. A. Duschl & R. J. Hamilton (Eds.), *Philosophy of science, cognitive psychology, and educational theory and practice* (pp. 147–176). Albany: State University of New York Press.

Tobias, S. (1994). Interest, prior knowledge, and learning. *Review of Educational Research, 64*, 37–54.

Venville, G. J., & Treagust, D. F. (1998). Exploring conceptual change in genetics using a multidimensional interpretive framework. *Journal of Research in Science Teaching, 35*, 1031–1055.

Vosniadou, S. (2007). Conceptual change as cognitive activity in socio/cultural context. *Educational Psychologist, 42*(1), 55–73.

Vosniadou, S., & Brewer, W. F. (1987). Theories of knowledge restructuring in development. *Review of Educational Research, 57*, 51–67.

Vosniadou, S., & Brewer, W. F. (1992). Mental models of the earth: A study of conceptual change in childhood. *Cognitive Psychology, 24*, 535–585.

Vosniadou, S., & Brewer, W.F. (1994). Mental models of the day/night cycle. *Cognitive Science, 18*, 123–183.

Voss, J. F., & Schauble, L. (1992). Is interest educationally interesting? An interest-related model of learning. In K. A. Renninger, S. Hidi, & A. Krapp (Eds.), *The role of interest in learning and development* (pp. 101–120). Hillsdale, NJ: Erlbaum.

West, L. H. T., & Pines, A. L. (1985). *Cognitive structure and conceptual change*. Orlando, FL: Academic Press.

White, B. Y., & Frederiksen, J. R. (1998). Inquiry, modeling, and metacognition: Making science accessible to all students. *Cognition and Instruction, 16*, 3–118.

White, R., & Gunstone, R. (1992). *Probing understanding*. London: The Falmer Press.

Windschitl, M., & Andre, T. (1998). Using computer simulations to enhance conceptual change: The roles of constructivist instruction and student epistemological beliefs. *Journal of Research in Science Teaching, 35*(2), 145–160.

Wolters, C. A., Yu, S. L., & Pintrich, P. R. (1996). The relation between goal orientation and students' motivational beliefs and self-regulated learning. *Learning and Individual Differences, 8*, 211–238.

Wood, P., & Kardash, C. M. (2002). Critical elements in the design and analysis of studies of epistemology. In B. K. Hofer & P. R. Pintrich (Eds.), *Personal epistemologies: The psychology of beliefs about knowledge and knowing* (pp. 231–260). Mahwah, NJ: Erlbaum.

Zimmerman, B. J., & Martinez-Pons, M. (1990). Student differences in self-regulated learning: Relating grade, sex, and giftedness to self-efficacy and strategy use. *Journal of Educational Psychology, 82*, 51–59.

22

The Role of Knowledge, Beliefs, and Interest in the Conceptual Change Process: A Synthesis and Meta-Analysis of the Research

P. Karen Murphy
The Pennsylvania State University

Patricia A. Alexander
University of Maryland

INTRODUCTION

Over the last 20 years, research in cognitive and educational psychology has revealed that constructs such as learners' knowledge, beliefs, and interests play powerful roles in the acquisition and modification of concepts in academic domains such as astronomy or physics (e.g., Schur, Skuy, Zietsman, & Fridjhon, 2002; Wiser & Amin, 2001). The theoretical notion of the "Matthew effect" (Stanovich, 1984), for instance, holds that those who are cognitively and motivationally richer thrive within the instructional setting, while those with cognitive or motivational deficits fall farther behind. Further, entire theories, such as self-efficacy or attribution theory, are built on the assumption that learners' beliefs about their ability to perform particular tasks or their explanations for past successes or failures are significant predictors of subsequent performances (Bandura, 1977; Pajares, 1997).

Yet, one need not look beyond the chapters in this volume to find solid evidence that learners' knowledge, beliefs, and motivations are inextricably entwined with conceptual formation and reformation. For instance, the contribution of Michelene Chi (chapter 3, this volume) speaks directly to conceptual change as ontological shifts, while Marcia Linn (chapter 27) examines knowledge integration as key to the change process. Moreover, in chapter 21 by Sinatra and Mason, we are introduced to predominant models of conceptual change, many of which endeavor to chart the interactions among knowledge and motivation (e.g., Dole & Sinatra, 1998) or beliefs and knowledge (e.g., Vosniadou, 1994). The presence of learner knowledge, beliefs, and motivations are well positioned within each of those well-respected and often discussed models.

Thus, it is not our intention to question conventional wisdom regarding the intimate relation between knowledge, beliefs, and motivations and the nature of conceptual change. Rather, we begin this chapter under the assumption that conceptual change is reflected in minor to major transformations in learners' knowledge, beliefs, and interests. In fact, we build on that assumption by exploring the degree to which conceptual change is evidenced in documented modifications in three classes of variables: subject-matter knowledge, domain or topic beliefs, and learner interests.

Specifically, as a way to understand those cognitive and motivational outcomes better, we undertook a systemic examination of conceptual change research reported within the last five years. The definitions of subject-matter knowledge, domain beliefs, topic beliefs, and learner interests that are central to the ensuing analysis and discussion are based on more than two decades of theory and research in text-based learning and expertise development (e.g., Alexander, Jetton, & Kulikowich, 1995; Alexander, Schallert, & Hare, 1991; Alexander, Sperl, Buehl, Fives, & Chiu, 2004). Consistent with this theoretical framing, domain and topic knowledge and ensuing beliefs are presumed to differ with regard to their specificity within a given subject-matter area with *domain* signifying broader knowledge or beliefs about the subject-matter area itself (e.g., history or physics) and *topic* representing one's knowledge or beliefs about a particular concept or topic associated with that area (e.g., chromosomal structures or velocity).

Moreover, we proceed under the assumption that conceptual change is a latent variable. That is to say, conceptual change is a theoretical variable that cannot be directly observed or measured but is presumed to exert influence on other observable variables such as learning or achievement (Kulikowich & Hancock, in press). Consequently, as will become evident in this review, conceptual change becomes operationalized as modifications or transformations in related variables, including participants' knowledge or beliefs. Thus, our overarching goal was to ascertain, through meta-analytic procedures, the quantifiable effects of approaches to conceptual change on learners' knowledge, beliefs, and interest.

Given that more than half of the studies informing our understanding of the role of knowledge, beliefs, and interest in the conceptual change process did not meet the requirements for meta-analysis, we felt that it was also essential to examine the relevant literature thematically, as well as statistically. In addition, we recognize that one cannot consider the power or significance of variables outside of the context of those studies and their specific features. Thus, in order to address our broad question about the role of knowledge, beliefs, and interest in the change process, we also describe particular design features of this empirical literature, such as the domains or topics studied or the ethnicity, ages, or abilities of participants. Drawing on those design features and the major findings of the identified works, we then turn our attention to three significant trends that arose from the synthesis of the identified literature. Those trends shed light on the researchers' conceptualizations and operationalizations of concepts and conceptual change, as well as the conditions under which transformations in learners' knowledge, beliefs, and interest were documented.

THE LITERATURE BASE

The statistical results and the subsequent analyses of trends we share here were the products of an extended literature review. To ensure that we conducted an adequate and defensible review, we first cast a wide net and then systematically narrowed the resulting pool to the most relevant works. We generated that initial pool by conducting a search of several databases including PsycINFO, ERIC, and Education Abstracts.

First, we broadly searched the literature reported in the last five years by identifying any works within the electronic databases that referenced conceptual change either in title, abstract, or listing of key concepts. Our decision to focus the review efforts on the last five years was based on both practical and theoretical considerations. Practically speaking, we felt that the resulting pool from this period would afford us an adequate picture of the role that knowledge, beliefs, and interest play in the change process without proving unwieldy. Theoretically, we considered the last 5 years to be an especially fertile period for examining these variables due to the burgeoning attention to belief and interest factors within the educational literature, including the studies of conceptual change (e.g., Chinn & Malhotra, 2002).

Our inspection of the electronic databases resulted in an initial pool of 67 studies. With this initial pool in hand, we proceeded to narrow the studies to those that we believed could best inform our overarching goal. With our goal and the literature as a guide, we established seven additional criteria that determined the inclusion or exclusion of each of the 67 works.

Specifically, beyond mentioning conceptual change in title, abstract, or key concepts, studies to be included in our synthesis and meta-analysis had to:

1. investigate a targeted construct (i.e., knowledge, beliefs, and interest);
2. be empirical in nature; that is, no research summaries or strictly theoretical analyses were considered;
3. be fully retrievable from the archived source so that descriptive statistics and design features could be charted; thus, no summary of conference proceedings or dissertation abstracts were included;
4. undergo peer review; consequently no dissertations or theses were analyzed;
5. involve K–12 students' conceptual change in total or in part;
6. incorporate some learning outcome; and,
7. be reported in English (due to our language limitations).

By applying these criteria, we selected 41 documents for further investigation. Two of the selected articles (i.e., Chinn & Malhotra, 2002; Lee & Law, 2001) consisted of 4 experiments each, bringing the full literature base to 47 independent experiments or studies. To guide the synthesis and meta-analysis, we developed a 52-item manual for coding a range of information relative to each study. Among the data collected from each study were: sample characteristics (e.g., number of students and teachers, age, or socioeconomic status), research design characteristics (e.g., single group/multiple group or student assignment to conditions), subject-matter area and topic of the study, the purposes or objectives and major findings, and characteristics of any subsamples in the study (e.g., by ability).

We also coded relevant information (e.g., definitions) pertaining to our constructs of interest (i.e., knowledge, beliefs, interest, concept, and conceptual change), dependent measure characteristics (e.g., nature of the measure), catalysts for conceptual change (e.g., refutation texts or oral arguments), and effect size data. Also included in the Coding Manual was an effect size flow chart to be used during coding. The manual was used to train research assistants who assisted in the coding. Following training to criterion of 90%, all interrater agreements exceeded 94% with differences resolved through conference. Interestingly, the major area of contention was related to codings for the construct of conceptual change. This problem arose because researchers used proxy variables (e.g., topic knowledge) as a means of operationalizing conceptual change. To address this problem, we reviewed all studies a second time to more clearly specify what counted as conceptual change.

As might be expected, not all of the 47 experiments resulted in or reported data that were analyzable by meta-analytic techniques. For example, multiple studies reported qualitative syntheses from student interviews (e.g., Boo & Watson, 2001; Mazens & Lautrey, 2003; Park & Han,

2002), while other studies reported quantitative findings from analyses that could be submitted to meta-analytic techniques (e.g., Mason & Boscolo, 2004). Subsequently, 20 of the original 47 studies provided data that could analyzed via meta-analysis.

In addition, for the meta-analytic portion of our codings, we established certain rules for preparing the data. One of those rules pertained to sample size since the number of participants in the included studies varied dramatically from 4 to 396. In this instance, data were unbiased to control for the effects of small sample sizes and weighted so that large samples exerted greater influence in analysis. The second rule concerned the basis for calculating effect sizes. Specifically, we decided to report effect sizes on the total scale scores of measures rather than subscale scores. This procedure resulted in a total of 68 effects sizes entered into analysis. Third, we chose to report effect sizes for total samples in studies rather than identified subsamples. The one exception to this rule was the Mason and Boscolo (2004) study for which data from subsamples were based on post hoc assessments of students' epistemic sophistication.

CHARTING TRENDS IN CONCEPTUAL CHANGE RESEARCH

Given that only a subset of the articles met the criterion for the meta-analysis, we felt that it was very important to begin by synthesizing across the larger set of studies. There is much to be learned by inspecting and dissecting conceptual change studies in terms of their design features (e.g., domains explored or variables targeted) and their major findings. For that reason, we undertook a detailed synthesis of the 47 studies located through our extensive literature search. For the purposes of this study, we highlight three interrelated trends that we regard as especially pervasive or particularly powerful within our identified literature base. The first trend pertains to the characteristics of the identified studies in terms of their design features. The second trend centers on the definitional ambiguities and vagaries that we encountered in this analysis. Finally, we look across the identified literature to consider the continuities or discontinuities between theoretical models of conceptual change and the empirical research conducted to support or substantiate such models.

The Who, What, and Where of Conceptual Change Research

Who gets studied? Even a cursory examination of Table 22.1 points to some trends evident in the design and execution of conceptual change research. Our intention herein was to investigate the conceptual change literature at the level of K–12 because we felt that much of the existing research dealt with individuals at the university or tertiary levels of education. Our goal was to look at children or youth in hopes of understanding effects on knowledge, beliefs, and interests during more formative years of cognitive change. We were pleased to locate a few studies that considered concept formation and reformation among young children ages 6–8 (e.g., Hayes, Goodhew, Heit, & Gillan, 2003; Ross, Medin, Coley, & Atran, 2003). Nonetheless, the vast majority of the studies we identified focused on learners above the age of 10 and frequently of high-school age. It should also be remembered that our intention to stay within the K–2 school range resulted in the exclusion of a number of studies with college-aged students as participants. Indeed, this was our largest category of exclusion.

There are likely theoretical as well as practical reasons for the tendency of researchers to select older students for their studies of conceptual change. For instance, it might be presumed that children must achieve a certain level of cognitive and linguistic maturity in order to form certain conceptions and be able to communicate their understandings of those concepts within an

TABLE 22.1

Summary Table of Article Features and Findings for Each Study

Author (Year)	Sample Size	Mean Age	Topic	Major Findings
Pozo & Crespo (2005)	278	15	matter	*Consistent use of intuitive representations as opposed to scientific ones. *These results confirm consistency across intuitive representations and confirm the use of implicit theories. *Most of the employed properties of matter were macroscopic (observable, embodied theory).
Smith, Solomon, & Carey (2005)	50	10	divisibility of number and matter	*Children's spontaneous acknowledgement of the existence of numbers between 0 and 1 was strongly related to their induction that numbers are infinitely divisible (i.e., can be repeatedly divided without ever getting to zero). *The conceptualization of infinite divisibility was strongly related to having a model of fraction notation based on division and to judgment of the relative magnitudes of fractions and decimals. *The results support a conceptual change account of knowledge acquisition involving two-way mappings between the domain of number and physical quantity.
Mason & Boscolo (2004)	65	16.5	genetically modified food	*Epistemic understanding and topic interest, to some extent, affect the conceptual understanding and critical interpretation of a controversy. *Covariates of prior knowledge and initial topic beliefs did not correlate with the text conclusions written by students. *Students with advanced epistemic beliefs scored higher in their answers to the open-ended questions than those with less advanced epistemic development. *Highly interested students outperformed low-interest students in knowledge acquisition. *Students shifted to a more neutral stance as a result of reading. *More belief revision was evidenced by those with more advanced epistemic understandings. *No interaction between epistemological understanding and topic interest was evidenced.
She (2004)	27	15	heat transfer	*The Dual-Situated Learning Model has great potential to foster radical conceptual change in learning about heat transfer. *Radical conceptual change can definitely be achieved and does not necessarily involve a slow or gradual process.
Alsparslan, Tekkaya, & Geban (2003)	68	16.5	respiration	*Results indicated that students' science process skills accounted for a significant portion of variation in respiration concepts achievement. *The conceptual change instruction produced significantly greater achievement in the understanding of respiration concepts. *A significant difference between the performance of females and males in favor of females was found, but there was no significant interaction between treatment and gender difference.
Cheng & Shipstone (2003)	16	999	electric circuit theory	*The program devised helped students to develop useful concepts of current and voltage, to acquire a more integrated understanding of circuit behavior and overcome their tendencies towards localized and sequential reasoning. *The approach provided learners with a valuable aid for problem solving.

(continued)

TABLE 22.1
Continued

Author (Year)	Sample Size	Mean Age	Topic	Major Findings
Diakidoy, Kendeou, & Ioannides (2003)	215	12	energy	*Students who read the refutation text outperformed students who received standard instruction only. *The influence of the expository text was negligible and generally comparable to that of standard instruction.
Edens & Potter (2003)	184	10.5	law of conservation of energy	*A statistically significant difference on a posttest conceptual understanding measure was found between students who generated descriptive drawings and those who wrote in a science log. *Students who copied an illustration also scored higher than the writing group, but not at a significant level. *The quality and number of concept units present in the drawing/writing log were significantly correlated with posttest and delayed test scores.
Hayes, Goodhew, Heit, & Gillan (2003)	132	6	shape of the earth	*Both instruction methods produced increases in factual knowledge. *Only children receiving instruction about two core beliefs, however, showed an increased rate of acceptance of a spherical earth model at posttest. *Findings show that instruction that challenges diverse aspects of naïve scientific beliefs is more likely to produce conceptual change.
Mazens & Lautrey (2003)	89	7.7	physics: sound	*Younger children considered sound to be more like an object than older children. *Substantiality was attributed to sound more often than were weight and performance. *Based on substantiality data, four mental models were identified (i.e., sound cannot pass through other objects unless there are holes, sound can pass through solids if it is harder than they are, sound is immaterial, and sound is a vibratory process). *Conceptual change in knowledge about sound does not happen through sudden transfer of the concept from the ontological category of matter to the ontological category of processes, but rather through a slow and gradual process of belief revision, in the course of which various properties of matter area banded in a hierarchical order.
Oliva (2003)	155	16	mechanics	*Students with the highest level of formal reasoning change their alternative conceptions more easily when these display a higher level of initial structuralization. *Students showing concrete reasoning do so more easily when their conceptions are less structured.
Ross, Medin, Coley, & Atran (2003)	242	8	folkbiological induction	*Only urban children showed evidence for early anthropocentrism, suggesting that the co-mingling of psychology and biology may be a product of an impoverished experience with nature. *In comparison to urban majority culture children, even the youngest rural children generalized in terms of biological affinity. *In addition, all ages of Native American children and the older rural majority culture children (unlike urban children) gave clear evidence of ecological reasoning.

Study	n	Age/Grade	Content	Findings
Tsai (2003)	190	14	electric circuits	*Conflict maps could help students overcome alternative conceptions about simple series electric circuits.
von Aufschnaiter & von Aufschnaiter (2003)	27	17	physics	*Students' meanings always refer to a narrow area of content, are developed bottom-up with respect to complexity, and show time-dependent dynamics in which maxima of 30 seconds and 5 minutes are important time scales.
Bigozzi, Biggeri, Boschi, Conti, & Fiorentini (2002)	79	9.5	physical prop.	*Participants in the experimental group were able to give reasons as to why the scientific phenomena they studied occurred. *They were better able to explain these newly acquired concepts, producing spontaneously large amounts of metaphors and analogies, while they tried to understand, record, and discuss what they had observed.
Chinn & Malhotra (2002) Study 1	228	10	rocks dropped	*In the four experiments, conceptual change was blocked most strongly at observation. *The students had difficulty making accurate observations, but they did not simply observe what they expected to observe. *The students usually aligned their conceptions with their observations, evidencing an implicit epistemology in which they distinguished conceptions from evidence and changed beliefs in response to evidence. *Providing explanations to students promoted conceptual change.
Chinn & Malhotra (2002) Study 2	26	11	forward movement, current, falling objects	*In the four experiments, conceptual change was blocked most strongly at observation. *The students had difficulty making accurate observations, but they did not simply observe what they expected to observe. *The students usually aligned their conceptions with their observations, evidencing an implicit epistemology in which they distinguished conceptions from evidence and changed beliefs in response to evidence. *Providing explanations to students promoted conceptual change.
Chinn & Malhotra (2002) Study 3	138	11	temperature, combustion, falling objects	*In the four experiments, conceptual change was blocked most strongly at observation. *The students had difficulty making accurate observations, but they did not simply observe what they expected to observe. *The students usually aligned their conceptions with their observations, evidencing an implicit epistemology in which they distinguished conceptions from evidence and changed beliefs in response to evidence. *Providing explanations to students promoted conceptual change.
Chinn & Malhotra (2002) Study 4	89	12	temperature, current	*In the four experiments, conceptual change was blocked most strongly at observation. *The students had difficulty making accurate observations, but they did not simply observe what they expected to observe. *The students usually aligned their conceptions with their observations, evidencing an implicit epistemology in which they distinguished conceptions from evidence and changed beliefs in response to evidence. *Providing explanations to students promoted conceptual change.

(continued)

TABLE 22.1
Continued

Author (Year)	Sample Size	Mean Age	Topic	Major Findings
Chiu, Chou, & Liu (2002)	30	16	chemical equilibrium	*The Cognitive Apprenticeship group significantly outperformed the non-Cognitive Apprenticeship group. *The students in the Cognitive Apprenticeship group were capable of constructing the mental models of chemical equilibrium, including dynamic, random activities of molecules and interactions between molecules in the microworld, whereas the students in the non-Cognitive Apprenticeship group failed to construct similar correct mental models of chemical equilibrium.
Eryilmaz (2002)	396	16.8	force & motion	*Conceptual change discussion was an effective means of reducing the number of misconceptions students held about force and motion. *The conceptual change discussion was also found to be effective in improving students' achievement in force and motion.
Park & Han (2002)	49	14	force and motion	*Twenty-six of the 27 students could find the direction of force correctly by using deduction. *Logical thinking could help students change their prior ideas regarding abstract concepts like force. *This change does not occur automatically. *Four factors are present which prevent students' deductive reasoning. *By introducing explanatory strategies to promote the use of deductive reasoning, students could obtain a logically valid conclusion and change their prior ideas.
Pnevmatikos (2002)	132	999	religion	*Ten different types of drawings were extracted. *Among children's drawings were found changes which imply, in terms of Thagard (1992) not only belief revision, but also a conceptual change. *Hierarchy reinterpretation, in which the concept of God changes from the part of the cosmos to the creator (ontologically different from the creatures), was not observed among the primary school children. *The development of the different hierarchies constructed on the basis of children's drawings seem to follow the developmental changes, which took place in the history of Greek religions.
Schur, Skuy, Zietsman, & Fridjhon (2002)	32	15	astronomy	*A pre-test mean score of the control group remained virtually the same at the post-test, while the experimental group post-test score improved considerably. *A significant post-test difference was yielded between the experimental and control groups in general scientific knowledge in Section 1, but not Section 2. *A significant difference was yielded between the experimental and control groups in the degree of change they underwent in their notions of the concept of Earth. *The experimental group improved considerably more than the control group on solving cognitive-rich scientific problems. *The Thinking Journey approach was relatively effective in promoting a process of positive change in the students' conceptualization of Earth, improving their knowledge of astronomy, enhancing their general scientific knowledge, and developing their cognitive functioning and problem solving abilities.

Study			Topic	Findings
She (2002)	20	15	air pressure & buoyancy	*The notion of buoyancy required more dual-situated learning events for conceptual change to occur than that for air pressure. * After dual-situated learning event 1, all students changed to beliefs that air inside the syringe could be compressed. * After the dual situated learning event 2, about 95% began to believe that air exerted pressure on all sides of the foam rubber, making it smaller on all sides. * After the use of dial situated learning event 3, all students began to believe that the solid object would sink while the boat-shaped object would float. * After dual situated learning event 4, 45% of students with misconceptions changed to believe that sample cans would float at higher concentration of salt water. * About 30% believed that the empty can would float because its density was lower than that of salt water. * After event 5, 80% began to believe that the boat-shaped object would have greater displacement of water that the solid one. *60% explained that the object that floated exerted greater buoyancy, thus displacing greater volume of water.
Biemas, Deel, & Simons (2001)	10	11.5	physical geography, equator, earth rotation, rain	*Both qualitative and quantitative differences were found between successful and less successful students. *During the training sessions, qualitative and quantitative differences in cognitive learning activates showed up when students were performing the second CONTACT-2 step on "comparing and contrasting preconceptions with new information," and that these differences continued to exist (at least) until students were doing the corresponding learning performance post-test.
Boo & Watson (2001)	48	17	chemical reactions	*Results show that students made some progress in their understanding of the concept of chemical reaction, but some fundamental misconceptions remained.
Chan (2001)	108	16.5	biological evolution	*Peer collaboration resulted in some mixed findings, suggesting that peer effects may very depending on collaborative interactions. *In-depth analyses of collaborative interactions indicated two discourse patterns: "surface" moves included rating, ignoring, rejecting and patching to eliminate differences; "problem-centered" moves involved problem recognition, formulation of questions, and construction of explanations. *Comparisons between successful and unsuccessful learners showed significant differences in their proportional use of surface and problem-centered moves. *External conflict did not lead to deeper discourse and more conceptual change; students may need to experience meaningful conflict.
Chinn & Brewer (2001)	168	999	geology & paleontology	*Patterns in undergraduates' written data evaluations support the predictions of the models-of-data theory. *One hundered seven responses (61%) could be readily interpreted as denials of particular links in the models provide particularly strong support for the models-of-data theory framework. *The models-of-data theory predicts that when people cannot offer specific alternative causes, they may simply assert that alternative causal factors may exist, and 37 of the 93 causal criticisms were such assertions. *Undergraduates were more likely to discount data that contradicted their beliefs than to discount data that supported their beliefs. *Although high-credibility anomalous data promote greater acceptance than low-credibility anomalous data, 65% of the participants found ways to discount even high-credibility data.

(continued)

TABLE 22.1
Continued

Author (Year)	Sample Size	Mean Age	Topic	Major Findings
Chiu, Kessel, Moschkovich, & Munoz-Nunez (2001)	1	14	linear functions & graphs	*Paul used each strategy component out of sequence at least once. So, these strategy components were relatively independent of one another. *Paul used four major complex strategies to solve the y-intercept problems. *The student did not erase his original conception or replace it with a conception supported by instruction, but instead refined his initial strategies and conceptions.
Diakidoy & Kendeou (2001)	63	10.5	shape of earth & d/n cycle	*Fifth-grade students who received the experimental instruction of target astronomy concepts demonstrated significant improvement in their understanding and learning of these concepts as opposed to students who received standard, textbook-based instruction.
Duit, Roth, Komorek, & Wilbers (2001)	25	16	non-linear physics systems	*Students generated only a small number of spontaneous comparisons with familiar phenomena to explain the behavior of the magnetic pendulum. Most comparisons were based on surface-level associations. *The elementary analogies assist some students in spontaneously constructing an understanding of the magnetic pendulum's chaotic behavior. Providing additional support for constructing appropriate observation sentences of bases and targets that allow a mapping of the key features can increase the proportion of students who construct analogical relations. *Students' small group interactions appear to support the construction of canonical observational descriptions and desired analogies. *Parallel construction of relevant observational descriptions of base and target phenomena usually does not occur spontaneously. However, given sufficient small-group discussion time and specific hints, many students do construct the desired analogy. *Students frequently switched perspectives. That is, students tested conjectures based on observational sentences about one system in the other system. Students were making use of the symmetrical nature of the analogical relation without being guided to this possibility by the teacher.
Harrison & Treagust (2001)	11	17	chemistry-atoms & molecules	*The case studies support an argument that high scores on achievement tests are unreliable indicators of conceptual learning and recommend that teachers and researchers pay more attention to qualitative indicators of learning, such as students' conceptual status, modeling level, and intellectual position.
Lee & Law (2001) Study 1	6	17	circuitry concepts	*A large difference in test performance was found among the group of students. *Interviews revealed students still held a number of alternative conceptions frequently documented in the research literature, even after formal instruction. *Five of six students still believed that the battery was the source of current and treated the current flowing from the battery as being unaffected by changes in the external circuit. *Frequently, students struggling with some conceptual conflicts between the learned ideas and their intuitive concepts displaced the learned concept with the alternative conceptions.

Lee & Law (2001) Study 2	9	15.5	circuitry concepts	*Students with higher test scores tend to consider a circuit as a system, where a change at any one point affects the parameters in the rest of the circuit. *Students with lower scores tend to reason about the circuit by analyzing it segment by segment and do not see it as a whole system. *Co-construction of meaning occurred during students' interactions (discussions), and they were able to revise their analogies to provide an underlying mechanism. *Both groups were able to refine their analogies through group discussion and to move towards CBI reasoning. *Students can produce and use self-generated analogies in explaining some simple circuit phenomena and communicating their understanding to others. *Through socio-cognitive interactions in group discussions, students can develop a better understanding of circuit phenomena. *Using POE tasks involving two different circuit arrangements or a change in the circuit setting, students can be encouraged to modify their analogies and to move towards CBI reasoning. *The POE tasks used only encouraged students to focus on current and not on voltage, even for the six secondary students who had learned this concept before.
Lee & Law (2001) Study 3	9	15.5	circuitry concepts	*Guiding students to focus on variation of voltage in circuits with different battery configurations encourages students to think in terms of processes and to use a systems approach in reasoning about circuit phenomena. However, for students to more successfully towards using CBI reasoning, knowledge of Ohm's Law is also crucial.
Lee & Law (2001) Study 4	6	15	circuitry concepts	*All alternative conceptions found in study 1 were also found among this group. *All students used sequential reasoning in explanations. *Students tended to use the words 'electricity' and 'electric current' interchangeably. *Students tended to associate 'electricity' with energy consumption and this concept possesses the attributes of the matter ontology. *As the sequence of lessons progresses, students exhibited the ability to give up sequential reasoning and became aware that the circuit configuration is as important as the number of circuit elements. *The pre-test indicated students' performance was rather poor, with five of six students getting only less than 20% correct and none reaching 40%. The post-test minimum score achieved was 56% and half of the students gained a perfect score. *The teaching strategy used has been successful in promoting conceptual change. *All six students achieved significant improvements in test performance after the teaching intervention.

(continued)

TABLE 22.1
Continued

Author (Year)	Sample Size	Mean Age	Topic	Major Findings
Mason (2001a)	12	10	process of decay and cycling of matter	*Some of the alternative conceptions found in previous studies were found in the beginning of the intervention. *Students were able to discuss a specific knowledge object in a group, reaching high levels of reasoning and arguing. *In almost all discussion, participants who shared the cognitive burden of collaborative thinking progressed level toward the scientific perspective to be understood. *Reasoning and arguing in group discussions indicate that through steps of critical opposition and co-construction, the learners negotiated and renegotiated meanings and ideas to construct on an interpsychological plane of new common knowledge on which more advanced explanations of the examined phenomena were based. *Writing allowed students to express their current ideas about the science topics in a formal that they could look at and think about. *Participants individually progressed in understanding the process of decay, the goal concept, although not all reached the same level of scientific understanding.
Mason (2001b)	126	14	controversial topics	*The results showed the 24 categories of reasons given by participants, who were much younger than those involved in the study by Chinn & Brewer, fit into their revised taxonomy, which consists of eight responses (with the exception of the response "ignoring").
Mikkila-Erdmann (2001)	209	10.5	photosynthesis	*Children who studied the conceptual change text design performed statistically better than the traditional text group on questions which demanded construction of an adequate mental model of photosynthesis. *High prior knowledge learners profited from conceptual change text design in questions which were constructed to measure inferential text comprehension. *Both high and low prior knowledge learners benefited from the conceptual change text design in answering the critical distinction questions. *Both low pretest score learners and high pretest score learners profited from the conceptual change text design when measured by generative questions which required construction of a mental model of photosynthesis and can thus be considered a criterion for conceptual change. *Results indicate that the conceptual change text helped learners to go through conceptual change concerning photosynthesis. *The traditional text worked well in questions which are typical "school questions," requiring fact-finding and text comprehension mainly on the level of the text base.
Nieswandt (2001)	81	15	chemistry	*Results show some erosion of students' everyday conceptions in favor of scientific conceptions, especially in their understanding of changes of properties of a substance as an indication that a new substance has been created. *Some students' notions can be described as a mixture of everyday descriptions and scientific explanations. These students are "on the way" to the scientific concept but have not fully understood and accepted it during the project. *More than 50% of students at the end of the trial use scientific explanation for items that deal with the changing of properties.

Palmer (2001)	53	16	force of gravity, action & reaction	*The majority of students had a mixture of scientifically acceptable conceptions and alternative conceptions. *Explanations indicated that they were using an "if…then" type of reasoning which linked the two conceptions. This is referred to as a personal conditional. *Through using a personal conditional, a student will invoke one conception in some contexts and another conception in other contexts. Their responses will therefore have internal coherence, but will be inconsistent from the point of view of an observer.
Reiner (2001)	28	15	ecology- food chain	*Conceptual change does not necessarily result in changes in the classroom conceptual environment. *Though more than half of the students changed their responses, ontological beliefs were hardly changed. *Changes in students' responses apparently cancelled each other; thus from the classroom point of view, only a minor change was identified in the overall conceptual environment. *The social-conceptual tension involved in conceptual change is not necessarily changed.
Sungur, Tekkaya, & Geban (2001)	49	16.5	human circulatory system	*Science process skill, the treatment, and previous learning in biology each made a statistically significant contribution to the variation in students' understandings of the human circulatory system. *The conceptual change texts accompanied by concept mapping instruction produced a positive effect on students' understanding of concepts. *The mean scores of experimental and control groups showed that students in the experimental group performed better with respect to the human circulatory system. The average percent of correct responses of the experimental group was 59.8% and that of the control group was 51.6% after treatment.
Vosniadou, Ioannides, Dimitrako-poulou, & Papademetriou (2001)	41	11	mechanics	*Significant differences were found between the experimental and control groups in post-test comparisons, confirming the hypothesis that the experimental learning environment would result in cognitive gains for the participating students. *It is clear that at least some of the conceptual understanding gains found in the experimental class could be related to the teacher asking complex questions that require complex explanations, which the students provide to the teacher. *Complex exchanges in the experimental class dialogue usually take place when the students are explaining their point of view, or when the teacher is obliged to explain what he means, because there is no established common language between him and the children. *Another case where complex dialogue is generated is when the teacher uses empirical observations to lead children to induce theoretical abstractions. *The experimental class teacher's purposes seem to be that of making the children understand certain counterintuitive ideas about forces, as they are understood within current scientific theory. His underlying theory of learning is that learning consists of the enrichment and reorganization of existing knowledge structures.

(continued)

TABLE 22.1
Continued

Author (Year)	Sample Size	Mean Age	Topic	Major Findings
Windschitl (2001)	14	14	human cardiovascular system	*Teacher-based assertiveness ratings of individuals were not significant predictors of their conceptual change score. However, the assertiveness ratings of individuals' partners were a significant negative predictor of the individuals' conceptual change scores. *Assertive pair members were more likely than their less assertive partners to: articulate perceived relationships that were evident to them in the simulated environment, suggest 'what if' scenarios, and direct partners to take certain actions. *Less assertive members often acquiesced to directives given by their partners. *Less assertive members were not less methodical or disinterested with the learning task, but tended to focus on the stepwise completion of the exercises, with few expressions about why or how phenomena took place in the simulated environment.
Wiser & Amin (2001)	14	14	thermal physics	*The metaconceptual lessons helped students capitalize on what they had learned from the models and direct instruction. *Students' pre-metaconceptual intuitive distinctions between (heat) energy & heat were clarified and formalized, but also radically restructured: heat became hotness, a perceptual entity, and (heat) energy became heat, the only physical entity in objects. *The two new entities became causally linked instead of simply correlated (as in Lesson 2), or coalesced (as in Lesson 3). *Having assimilated the ontological changes, students could reinterpret information in the models in terms of heat and temperature.

experimental situation. It could also be that certain interventions, such as texts or oral explanations, are more appropriate for older students who have the linguistic skills to gain from such interventions. Practically speaking, it might also be that the concepts, topics, or domains of interest to researchers do not become the focus of formal education until middle school, high school, or college. We do not expect young children to know much about chemical equilibrium (Chiu, Chou, & Liu, 2002), for instance, but would except that children would have certain folk beliefs about living things (Ross et al., 2003). These theoretical and practical issues aside, the conceptual change literature remains in need of a more developmental perspective, as well as investigations that permit the modeling of initial conceptual formations as much as later reformations.

Beyond the age of participants, there were other characteristics of the students that we analyzed, although with much less success. Specifically, we attempted to code the ethnicity, geographic venue (e.g., urban or rural), socioeconomic status, and ability levels of participants. Regrettably, such demographic information was typically unspecified by researchers. For instance, it seemed that researchers mentioned the students' ethnicity or geographic venue in those studies with largely minority samples (15 studies) or participants drawn from urban areas (19 studies). The socioeconomic status was undocumented for 40 of the 47 experiments, and the ability level of students could not be ascertained in 35 cases. Moreover, we were pleased to see that rather equivalent numbers of females (50.88%) and males (49.12%) were represented in those studies reporting the gender of participants. Unfortunately, gender of the participants was only reported in 25 of the 47 studies. Having richer demographics on study participants could serve to uncover significant patterns in the nature of concept formation and information.

Conceptual Change as a Domain-specific or Domain-general Phenomenon

Related to the call for a more developmental model of the conceptual change process is the need for a broader view of change that is not dependent on scientific domains or concepts. Yet, scanning the list of investigations in Table 22.1 confirms that conceptual change, as a field of inquiry, tends to be nested within scientific domains, particularly the physical sciences. Of the 47 studies tabled, only 2 dealt with ill-structured domains or topics: religion (Pnevmatikos, 2002) and folkbiological induction (Ross et al., 2003). In addition, only 2 other studies focused on content that was not specifically scientific in nature (linear functions/graphs: Chiu, Kessel, Moschkovich, & Muñoz-Nuñez, 2001; divisibility of number and matter: Smith, Solomon, & Carey, 2005).

Here again, several plausible reasons can be offered as to why this domain-specificity has occurred. For one, as Murphy and Mason (2006) have suggested, the study of conceptual change has largely been the study of knowledge change. Although belief and motivational variables are beginning to make an appearance in this arena, beliefs are more often relegated to the persuasion literature, and interest remains largely the focus of learning theory and research. For another, it appears to be easier to identify misconceptions or naïve theories within domains like biology or physics that are more well-structured than in fields like history or reading, where "correct" or "scientifically-valid" positions are elusive (Alexander, 1998, 2006; Murphy & Mason, 2006; Southerland, Sinatra, & Matthews, 2001). It would seem that the conceptual change research would be enriched by stepping outside of this scientific "comfort zone" to investigate the change process in a range of academic domains, including those for which more data-based or justifiable outcomes are more difficult to substantiate.

An International Investment

One of the trends that proved pleasantly surprising to us was the strong international presence in the study of conceptual change. Twenty countries were represented among the 47 studies analyzed. Further, those countries came from all corners of the globe, from Australia (3 studies) to Singapore (1) and from Finland (1) to Greece (1). The largest number of experiments were reported for the United States (12), followed by Hong Kong (4), Italy (4), and Taiwan (4). We believe that this international focus bodes well for the future of conceptual change research.

Conceptual Clarity

Earlier in this chapter we described our efforts to code the form of knowledge, beliefs, or interest investigated in each of the 20 studies submitted to meta-analysis. In our opinion, those efforts established the need for greater specificity and consistency in the terminology used by conceptual change researchers. As we have done elsewhere (Alexander et al., 1991; Murphy & Alexander, 2000), we indicated in this review whether specific terms used by researchers to identify or classify their variables of interest (e.g., concepts, epistemic beliefs, or domain knowledge) were explicitly (E) or implicitly (I) defined, or not defined in either manner (X). Further, in those cases where terms were implicitly defined, we marked whether one could derive some sense of the intended meaning by certain words or phrases favored by the researchers (C), from particular references to key researchers or studies they incorporated in their writings (R), or by the measures the researchers selected to operationalize their chosen variables (O). Due to space limitations, only the results for the 20 articles included in the meta-analysis are reported in Table 22.2 as exemplars. It is important to note that our analysis is based on all 47 articles, and not just those included in the meta-analysis.

What we learned from this coding process was that one of the most central and pervasive terms within the conceptual change literature was rarely explicitly defined and only infrequently implicitly defined. That term is *concept*. Even the term *conceptual change* proved difficult for us to code, as we suggested. In that case, researchers frequently incorporated some explicit definition of conceptual change within their studies. However, those definitions often varied markedly as a consequence of the theoretical models or frames from which they derived. For instance, Mazens and Lautrey (2003) drew on Vosniadou's mental model research (with Brewer, 1992) and defined conceptual change as occurring when "an initial mental model is invalidated" (p. 161). Interestingly, these same researchers later referred to the developmental work of Carey (1985) and then defined conceptual change as conceptual differentiation, coalescence, or change in type or principle. As this particular case suggests, the same term or phrase could be variably defined — even within the same article. Consequently, it was not always apparent what researchers specifically meant by conceptual change or whether it would be possible to construct some definition of this process that would prove acceptable across varying theoretical frameworks.

It was not just that definitions were absent or vague. And, it was not solely that varied definitions were offered from the same key constructs. There were also instances when different terms were seemingly applied to the same ideas. One example of this was the researchers' use of topic knowledge or concept knowledge to signify quite similar forms of content found within a lesson or text. Another interesting finding pertained to the researchers' employment of the term beliefs. In the literature we reviewed, those talking generally about learners' beliefs or specifically about individuals' beliefs about given domains or topics typically described these as initial, preinstructional, or nonscientific understandings (e.g., Chinn & Brewer, 2001). Such a description varies from the treatment of beliefs in the social psychology literature (see Murphy & Mason, 2006 for extended review) where beliefs usually refer to those thoughts or ideas that cannot be verified by external evidence.

In contrast, conceptual change researchers appear to rely on a conception of beliefs that likely emerged from philosophy or philosophy of science (Southerland et al., 2001). What is

TABLE 22.2

Definitions of Constructs for Articles Included in the Meta-Analysis

Author (Year)	N	Age*	Topic	Construct Category	Construct	Definitional Clarity E/I(C,O,R)	Definition
Mason & Boscolo (2004)	65	16.5	genetically modified food	belief	epistemic beliefs	E	"…beliefs about the organization and source of knowledge; its truth value and justification criteria of assertions…" p. 104 (Hofer & Pintrich, 1997, 2002)
				belief	topic beliefs	I(C)	beliefs about the topic
				interest	individual interest	E	"Individual interest is a relatively stable evaluative orientation toward a domain" pp. 107). (e.g., Alexander, 1997, 1998; Hidi & Baird, 1986; Renninger, Hidi, & Krapp, 1992)
				interest	text-based interest	E	a readers interest in the specific content of a dual-position text regarding that topic
				knowledge	prior knowledge	I(R)	Alexander, Kulikowich, & Schulze (1994)
				knowledge	topic knowledge	I(C)	Alexander, Kulikowich, & Schulze (1994)
Alsparslan, Tekkaya, & Geban (2003)	68	16.5	respiration	concept	misconception	E	"refers to students' conceptions that are different from scientific conceptions
				knowledge	conceptual knowledge	I(C)	seems to refer to a topic-size unit of knowledge (e.g., respiration, circulatory system, photosynthesis
				knowledge	declarative knowledge	I(C)	appears to be declarative knowledge; knowledge; knowledge of facts
Diakidoy, Kendeou, & Ionnides (2003)	215	12	energy	concept	concept	I(C)	similar in size to a topic (i.e., energy)
				knowledge	declarative knowledge	I(C)	same as other group
				knowledge	declarative knowledge	I(C)	understanding about the concept

(continued)

TABLE 22.2
Continued

Author (Year)	N	Age*	Topic	Construct Category	Construct	Definitional Clarity E/I(C,O,R)	Definition
Hayes, Goodhew, Heit, & Gillan (2003)	132	6	shape of the earth	belief	erroneous beliefs	E	based upon misconceptions: 1) resolving the apparent contradiction between spherical shape of the earth and its flat appearance; 2) failure to appreciate the influence of gravity (pp. 254–255)
				belief	scientific beliefs	X	
				concept	concept	X	
				concept	conceptual framework	E	"intuitive theories in an attempt to explain the natural phenomena that they observe" (p. 254; see Wellman & Gelman, 1998)
				knowledge	conceptual knowledge	I(O)	Vosniadou & Brewer's (1992) structured interview used proxy
Tsai (2003)	190	14	electric circuits	concept	concept	I(R)	Pintrich et al., 1993
				concept	misconception	I(O)	content of idea networks and responses as coded from interview data
				knowledge	declarative knowledge	I(O)	concept map used by treatment group to explore idea networks about electric circuits. Data comes from in-depth interviews with selected students (24 per group). Interviews were coded for ideas
				knowledge	explanatory knowledge	I(O)	what students share during interviews
Chinn & Malhotra (2002)	228	10	rocks dropped	belief	topic beliefs	I(C)	relations between predictions and observations of the speed at which rocks of different weights fall — Observational Report
				belief	topic beliefs	I(C)	"beliefs about empirical regularities" (p. 329)
				concept	preinstructional conceptions	X	
				concept	scientific conceptions	X	
				knowledge	scientific knowledge	I(R)	Woodward (1989)

Study	N	Age	Topic				Description
	26	11	forward movement, current, falling objects	belief	topic beliefs	I(C)	"beliefs about empirical regularities" (p. 329)
	138	11	temperature, combustion, falling objects	belief	topic beliefs	I(C)	"beliefs about empirical regularities" (p. 329)
	89	12	temperature, current	belief	topic beliefs	I(C)	"beliefs about empirical regularities" (p. 329)
Chiu, Chou, & Liu (2002)	30	16	chemical equilibrium	belief	ontological categories	X	
				knowledge	domain knowledge	I(O)	13 items about concepts of chemical equilibrium
Eryilmaz (2002)	396	16.8	force & motion	belief	intuitive beliefs	E	"students develop on their own before taking the first course in physics" (p. 1001). Also called preconceptions, alternative conceptions, misconceptions, children's science, common sense concepts, spontaneous knowledge
				concept	misconceptions	E	"refers only to those beliefs students have that contradict accepted scientific theories" (p. 1001)
				concept	misconceptions	I(O)	Force Misconception Test -misconceptions about force and motion
				concept	preconceptions	E	"used to indicate all beliefs students have before enrolling in their first formal physics course" (p. 1001)
				knowledge	topic knowledge	I(O)	Force Achievement Test - achievement in force and motion
Schur, Skuy, Zietsman, & Fridjhon (2002)	32	15	astronomy	concept	initial conceptions	E	"The initial concept stems from the everyday perception of the environment that people living on the earth have when they look around them" (pp. 49–50)
				concept	scientific concepts	E	"the scientific concept relates to the Earth as a whole" (p. 50)
				knowledge	domain knowledge	I(O)	General scientific knowledge questions of the ISSET - Section 1, Section 2
				knowledge	topic knowledge	I(O)	Astronomy questions of the ISSET, Science Test 1, Test 2

(continued)

TABLE 22.2
Continued

Author (Year)	N	Age*	Topic	Construct Category	Construct	Definitional Clarity E/I(C,O,R)	Definition
She (2002)	20	15	air pressure & buoyancy	belief	ontological beliefs	I(R)	Chi et al. 1994
				concept	concept	X	
				knowledge	conceptual knowledge	X	
				knowledge	procedural knowledge	I(R)	Duschl et al. (1992). Radical restructuring requires the learner to acquire new procedural knowledge with which to reevaluate existing knowledge before changes can occur.
Diakidoy & Kendeou (2001)	63	10.5	shape of earth & d/n cycle	belief	beliefs	E	"...absolute truths and not as alternative conceptions that require verification" (p. 4). (Vosniadou, 1991)
				concept	initial conceptions	X	
				concept	scientific conceptions	X	
Lee & Law (2001)	6	17	circuitry concepts	knowledge	prior knowledge	I(O)	knowledge items from Vosniadou and Brewer (1992)
				concept	concept	E	intuitive conceptions, misconceptions, alternative conceptions, children's science — "students have already acquired considerable knowledge and ideas about the natural and technological world before any formal instruction had taken place" (p. 111)
Mikkila-Erdmann (2001)	209	10.5	photosynthesis	knowledge	prior knowledge	I(C)	prior understandings or misconceptions
				knowledge	scientific knowledge	I(C)	
Nieswandt (2001)	81	15	chemistry	concept	everyday conception	I(R)	preinstructional knowledge, misconceptions (Driver & Easley, 1978), preconceptions (Driver & Easley, 1978), alternative frameworks (Driver & Erickson, 1983), children's science (Osborne & Freybert, 1985). In this article, they are called "Everyday Conceptions"

Study		Topic			Code	Description
Reiner & Eliam (2001)	28	ecology — food chain	belief	deep structure belief	I(C)	beliefs that form the backbone of understanding
	15		belief	ontological beliefs	I(C)	"deep, basic, and often tacit. They serve as anchors for assimilation and construction of new beliefs" (p. 552)
			concept	concept	X	"surface features of students' reasoning" (p. 552)
			concept	students concepts	E	
Sungur, Tekkaya, & Geban (2001)	49	human circulatory system	concept	misconception	E	(also called alternative conceptions, naïve theories, children's science) — "students' conceptions that are different from scientific conceptions" (p. 91)
	16.5		concept	scientific conceptions	I(O)	Human Circulatory System Concepts Test — 16 item, multiple choice. Distracters reflected common misconceptions
			knowledge	knowledge	X	
Vosniadou, Ioannides Dimitrakopoulou Papademetriou (2001)	41	mechanics	belief	beliefs	I(R)	Vosniadou & Brewer (1992). Two kinds of beliefs: those based on superficial observation and those deeply entrenched presuppositions
	11		belief	ontological beliefs	I(C)	understanding of relations of objects in the world (p. 385); how the physical world operates (p. 387)
			concept	concept	I(C)	differentiated between intuitive concepts and scientific concepts
			knowledge	conceptual knowledge	I(O)	8 items asking students to select from choices what is happening in a picture in relation to the concepts of energy and force
			knowledge	knowledge base	E	"...consists of a number of interrelated observations, beliefs, and presuppositions that form a relatively coherent explanatory framework" (p. 388)
			knowledge	prior knowledge	I(C)	what students know
			knowledge	scientific knowledge	X	
			knowledge	subject-matter knowledge	X	

(continued)

TABLE 22.2
Continued

Author (Year)	N	Age*	Topic	Construct Category	Construct	Definitional Clarity E/I(C,O,R)	Definition
Windschitl (2001)	90	14	human cardiovascular system	concept	alternative conception	X	
				knowledge	prior knowledge	I(O)	22 multiple choice content items
Wiser & Amin (2001)	4	14	thermal physics	concept	everyday conceptions	E	"Before formal instruction, students conceptualize thermal phenomena in fundamentally different ways from scientists (Duit, 1994; Lewis & Linn, 1994; Wiser, 1995)" (p. 335)
				concept	misconception	E	"...resulting from wrongly assimilating information into pre-existing beliefs" (p. 334)
				concept	naïve conceptions	X	
				knowledge	scientific knowledge	X	

Note: Within the Definitional Clarity column, E = explicit, I = implicit, C = conceptual, R = reference, O = operational, and X = no definition.

important about this conceptual change versus social psychology distinction is not just the definition of beliefs, but the process by which such beliefs *become* knowledge. For conceptual change
researchers, beliefs can be understood as initial understandings that are not necessarily true or
justified. Such beliefs lack the necessary requirements (i.e., truth and justification) to be considered knowledge from an epistemic perspective (Murphy, Alexander, Greene, & Edwards, in
press). It became apparent to us that many conceptual change researchers hold to the premise that
the epistemic ascent from beliefs to knowledge occurs through the process of conceptual change
(e.g., Chinn & Malhotra, 2002; Mason 2001a, 2001b; Vosniadou, Ioannides, Dimitrakopoulou,
& Papademetriou, 2001).

Simply put, conceptual change is a process through which students' initial understandings
or beliefs are altered to more closely align with scientifically-held understandings (e.g., Oliva,
2003; Chiu et al., 2002). At times, this process of ascent to knowledge is gradual (Vosniadou,
1994; Vosniadou et al., 2001), and other times this process is thought to be more rapid (She, 2002,
2004). In essence, in the reviewed studies, the epistemic requirement for beliefs to be considered
knowledge was for those beliefs to be justified with scientific evidence — evidence obtained
through a reliable scientific method. Rooted in the philosophical literature, we have referred to
this type of epistemic position as a reliabilist framework (Murphy et al., in press). Essentially,
the reliabilist, beliefs are warranted if they are formed by a process that generally produces true
beliefs rather than false ones.

Although the understanding that conceptual change is a process through which intuitive beliefs are modified to align with scientifically-held understandings was espoused in 17 studies, this
was not the only perspective of conceptual change offered in the reviewed articles. We deduced
at least 3 other major perspectives toward the nature of conceptual change. Among those was the
perspective that conceptual change is predominantly a process through which existing knowledge
structures are purposefully reorganized by individuals as they become increasingly aware of the
incompatibility between their own understanding and the more scientifically-held process (e.g.,
Biemas, Deel, & Simons, 2001; Mikkila-Erdmann, 2001; Pnevmatikos, 2002). This perspective
of conceptual change was espoused in 12 of the reviewed articles. Similarly, there was a smaller
number of articles ($n = 4$) in which conceptual change was described as a particular form of
restructuring; that is, reassignment of a concept from one ontological category to another ontological category (e.g., Lee & Law, 2001; Nieswandt, 2001; von Aufschnaiter & von Aufschnaiter,
2003). For example, a student might understand energy as a process more than as a solid, which
could understood as an ontological shift.

These were also two studies in which conceptual change was viewed more as a developmental process through which the meaning and structure of the underlying concepts (e.g., dog
or death) changed as a result of maturation (e.g., Smith et al., 2005). There were four additional
studies in which conceptual change was not defined or defined only by reference (e.g., Mason &
Boscolo, 2004; Windschitl, 2001). In raising this issue, it is not our intention to suggest that one
of these interpretations of conceptual change is somehow better or more efficacious as a mechanism for undergirding change. Rather, we see these differences as a critical issue for conceptual
change researchers in that it is difficult to compare perspectives when definitions of the underlying process vary.

As such, when it came to calculating effect sizes, we chose to sort by whatever label researchers used for the knowledge or beliefs they studied, even though there was ambiguity and
overlap in those labels. However, drawing on this body of work and the extant literature, we
have attempted to extract workable definitions for key conceptual change terminology (see Table
22.3). These definitions represent similarities emerging during our review of the literature. When
possible, we have used direct quotes from original works and provided additional supporting

TABLE 22.3
Working Definitions of Key Belief, Knowledge, Interest, and Concept Constructs

Term	Conceptual Definition
Belief	nonscientific views or preconceptions (Chan, 2001), some of which are based on superficial observations and others which are more deeply entrenched (Vosniadou, Ioannides, Dimitrakopoulou, & Papademetriou, 2001)
Epistemic beliefs	"beliefs about the organization and source of knowledge; its truth value and justification criteria of assertions" (Mason, 2001b; Mason & Boscolo, 2004, p. 104)
Erroneous beliefs	based upon misconceptions (Hayes, Goodhew, Heit, & Gillan, 2003). [Synonym: intuitive beliefs (Eryilmaz, 2002)]
Ontological beliefs	understanding of relations of objects in the world and how the physical world operates (Vosniadou, Ioannides, Dimitrakopoulou, & Papademetriou, 2001); such beliefs are "..deep, basic, and often tacit" and "..serve as anchors for assimilation and construction of new beliefs" (Reiner & Eilam, 2001, p. 552; Chi, 1992)
Topic beliefs	beliefs that students hold relative to some topic (e.g., reason for dinosaur extinction) or one's understanding on an alternative theory (Chinn & Brewer, 2001; Chinn & Malhotra, 2002; Mason & Boscolo, 2004; She, 2004)
Concept	"...an idea that is stable over time, the result of a constructive process, connected to other aspects of a students' knowledge system, robust when confronted with other conceptions, and widespread…a conception is a definite idea" (Chiu, Kessel, Moschkovich, & Muñoz-Nuñez, 2001, p. 219; Smith, diSessa, & Roschelle, 1993; Osborne & Wittrock, 1983). "Students' conceptions are organized by forming a hierarchical network in which certain structures fit inside others, according to an order that ranges from greater to lesser generalizability" (Oliva, 2003, p. 542; Vosniadou, 1994; Pozo & Gómez Crespo, 1998; Smith, Solomon, & Carey, 2005)
Intuitive conceptions	understandings formed as a result of students interactions with the world….influence how they interpret and construct new conceptions (Schur, Skuy, Zietsman, & Fridjhon, 2002; Vosniadou & Brewer, 1992). [Synonyms: alternative conceptions (Boo & Watson, 2001, p. 568), preinstructional conceptions (Duit, Roth, Komerek, & Wilbers, 2001), preconceptions (Biemas, Deel, & Simons, 2001; Eryilmaz, 2002; Park & Han, 2002), everyday conceptions (Nieswandt, 2001; Wiser & Amin, 2001)]
Conceptual framework	"intuitive theories in an attempt to explain the natural phenomena that they observe" (Hayes, Goodhew, Heit, & Gillan, 2003, p. 254; see Wellman & Gelman, 1998)
Misconception	refers to students' understandings, conceptions, or beliefs that are different from scientific conceptions (Alsparslan, Tekkaya, & Geban, 2003; Eryilmaz, 2002; Mazens & Lautrey, 2003; Sungur, Tekkaya, & Geban, 2001)
Conceptual Change	"…what happens in the student's mind as he modifies his preconceptions to reach consonance with the accepted scientific conceptions" (Bigozzi, Biggeri, Boschi, Conti & Fiorentini, 2002); usually occurs as individuals attempt to reconcile their beliefs with scientific information presented during instruction (Diakidoy & Kendeou, 2001)
Interest*	"Signifies the processes by which the underlying needs or desires of learners are energized" (Alexander, Murphy, Woods, Duhon, & Parker, 1997, p. 128)
Individual interest	"...is a relatively stable evaluative orientation toward a domain" (Mason & Boscolo, 2004, p. 107; Alexander, 1997, 1998; Renninger, Hidi, & Krapp, 1992)
Situational interest*	"A transitory, short-lived interest that pertains to the specific characteristics of an event or object within the immediate situation or context" (Murphy & Alexander, 2000, p. 28)
Text-based interest	a reader's interest in the specific content of a text regarding that topic (Mason & Boscolo, 2004)
Knowledge	understandings one constructs (von Aufschnaiter & von Aufschnaiter, 2003) often as a result of conceptual change (Chan, 2001).

Term	Conceptual Definition
Declarative knowledge	understandings about a concept or topic, particularly those that are factual (Alsparslan, Tekkaya, & Geban, 2003; Diakidoy, Kendeou, & Ionnides, 2003)
Domain knowledge	"a body of knowledge that identifies and interprets a class of phenomena assumed to share certain properties and to be of a distinct and general type" (Mazens & Lautrey, 2003, p. 160)
Prior knowledge	"...can be described as all knowledge learners have when entering a learning environment, and which is potentially relevant for constructing new knowledge" (Biemas, Deel, & Simons, 2001, p. 266). [Synonyms: naïve knowledge (Mazens & Lautrey, 2003) or intuitive knowledge (Pozo & Gómez Crespo, 2005)]
Topic knowledge	topic-focused declarative and procedural understanding relative to a specific text or lesson (Cheng & Shipstone, 2003; Bigozzi, Biggeri, Boschi, Conti, & Fiorentini, 2002)

Note: Those terms marked with an asterisk (*) were not defined in any way in the reviewed articles. As such, definitions were quoted from supplemental peer-reviewed articles.

citations. When possible, we also listed commonly used synonyms for each construct. We make no claim that this attempt represents the definitive meanings of these select terms, but we do feel that these definitions are a useful starting point to bring needed conceptual clarity to the study of conceptual change.

Theoretical Modeling vis-à-vis Empirical Research

Within this volume, Sinatra and Mason have overviewed leading models of conceptual change, comparing and contrasting the various components and predictive paths of each. In general, those models richly depict the cognitive and motivation forces that contribute to the latent construct called conceptual change. Although those theoretical models differ in the specific variables they incorporate or in the paths of change they specify, all acknowledge the complexity and dynamism that are part of the change process.

However, when the empirical research analyzed in this chapter is juxtaposed to those theoretical models, significant discontinuities emerge. Simply stated, prevailing models of conceptual change are presumed to depict the nature or process of change broadly. Whether we are discussing the Conceptual Change Model of Posner, Strike, Hewson, and Gertzog (1982) or the Cognitive Reconstruction of Knowledge Model (CRKM) of Dole and Sinatra (1998), we are presented with generic models that speak to conceptual change in (a) any content (b) for all learners (c) at any point in their academic development. Such is the nature of general theoretical models.

The characteristics of the empirical research on conceptual change, in contrast, offer a different reality. Where the theoretical models are generic in nature, research remains domain-specific. Even more to the point, as highlighted previously, empirical research in conceptual change tends to be predominately science specific. Further, while theoretical models, especially the more recent ones like the CRKM, pay homage to non-knowledge factors such as need for cognition (Petty & Cacioppo, 1986), the empirical research remains largely the study of knowledge change. Finally, whereas theoretical models assume a process of change that encompasses individuals of varying ages and abilities, the empirical research relies mainly on data from older children through young adults to ascertain the nature of conceptual change.

Similarly, beliefs seem to play a substantively different role in the theoretical models than they do in the empirical research. Specifically, many prominent models of conceptual change (e.g., Conceptual Change Model: Posner et al., 1982; or Framework Theory: Vosniadou, 1994) attest to the primary role of ontological presuppositions and epistemic beliefs in the formation of initial understandings. For example, Posner et al. (1982) suggested that students' ontological and epistemic beliefs play a fundamental role in conceptual ecology or the conditions necessary for conceptual change. Similarly, Vosniadou (1994) explains that learners' ontological presuppositions provide an initial framework through which they interpret their experiences. Despite the foundational role of beliefs in these prominent models, few researchers investigated the role of beliefs in their conceptual change studies. It is likely that empirical investigations focusing on these belief constructs in conjunction with knowledge will better inform the field's understanding of the conceptual change process (e.g., Mason & Boscolo, 2004).

At this point, one might rightly question whether continuity should even be expected between theoretical models of conceptual change and empirical studies of this phenomenon. After all, theoretical models are, by their very nature, abstract representations of highly complex and intangible constructs and relations. Theorists must be free to speculate about constructs and processes that are not fully or directly testable. Still, we would expect that research drawn from such theoretical frameworks bear strong resemblances to their conceptual parents. It is one thing to initiate a program of research on conceptual change within the physical sciences, but it is another to remain largely nested in such domains over decades of empirical inquiry. It is one thing to theoretically acknowledge the power of beliefs or motivation to influence conceptual change, but it is another to design studies that routinely incorporate variables other than subject-matter knowledge.

For these reasons, we would hope that the empirical research within conceptual change will continue to grow and mature in a manner that moves it closer to the theoretical frames and models that guide researchers in their quests to understand this fundamental process. We appreciate that this will be a difficult task, in part because we remain statistically and methodologically limited in our endeavors. Yet, given the collective expertise represented in this field, and apparent in this volume, and in light of the significance of understanding the nature of conceptual formation and reformation for all learners in all domains, we believe that the task is well worth the effort.

CALCULATING EFFECT SIZES FOR KNOWLEDGE, BELIEFS, AND INTEREST

In addition to the conceptual trends evident in this body of research, we also wanted to calculate the effect sizes for learners' knowledge, beliefs, and interest. Those effect sizes were associated with various instructional catalysts (e.g., text, discussion, or argumentation) to change (Table 22.4). As noted, we could not study effects for conceptual change directly since this latent construct was represented by more measurable proxy variables. Although models of conceptual change, such as those overviewed by Sinatra and Mason (chapter 21, this volume), incorporate knowledge, beliefs, and motivations as influential forces in the change process, researchers looked for evidence of concept formation and reformation in observable shifts in those same variables.

As we engaged in this meta-analysis, we came to certain critical realizations about these proxy variables. First, although the construct of interest proved informative as part of the research synthesis, we found it necessary to drop it as a variable in the meta-analysis. The reason was that only one of the 20 investigations in the meta-analysis directly tracked changes in learners' interest (Mason & Boscolo, 2004). However, the effect size for those data could not be calculated due to the cross-tabular form in which those data were presented in the text. Consequently, the meta-analysis deals only with subject-matter knowledge and beliefs. Second, forms of subject-matter knowledge (e.g., concept knowledge, topic knowledge, or domain knowledge) were, by far, the proxy variables of choice in the empirical research on conceptual change — an observation we discuss further among our defining trends. Therefore, forms of subject-matter knowledge clearly dominate our summary of effect sizes displayed in Table 22.4.

TABLE 22.4
Effect Sizes for Constructs by Conceptual Change Approach

Construct	Conceptual Change Catalysts	Effect Size (#ES Contributing)	Studies Contributing
Belief			
Topic Belief	Text	.456 (3)	Mason & Boscolo (2004)
	Explanations	1.336 (12)	Chinn & Malhotra (2002), Studies 3 & 4
	Predictions	.439 (9)	Chinn & Malhotra (2002), Studies 1 & 2
Knowledge			
Concept Knowledge	Text	.589 (2)	Alsparslan, Tekkaya, & Geban (2003); Sunger, Tekkaya, & Geban (2001)
	Discussion combined with hands-on experiments	1.362 (1)	Vosniadou, Ioannides, Dimitrakopoulou, & Papademetriou (2001)
	Cognitive Apprenticeship approach with hands-on experiments	1.032 (6)	Chiu, Chou, & Liu (2002)
	Conceptual assignments where students observe and explain a phenomenon	−.024 (1)	Eryilmaz (2002)
	Group discussions about specific science phenomena	.208 (1)	Eryilmaz (2002)
	General knowledge change from teaching units designed to confront erroneous prior knowledge	1.499 (2)	Nieswandt (2001)
	Hands-on laboratory experiments	1.409 (2)	Lee & Law (2001); Reiner & Eilam (2001)
	Instruction in induction and scientific reasoning using videos	.243 (2)	Hayes, Goodhew, Heit, & Gillan (2003)
	Misconception change from teaching units designed to confront erroneous prior knowledge	−.597 (2)a	Nieswandt (2001)
Declarative Knowledge	Text	.467 (3)	Alsparslan, Tekkaya, & Geban (2003); Diakidoy, Kendeou, & Ioannides (2003)
	Conflict map use	.492 (1)	Tsai (2003)
Domain Knowledge	Cognitive Apprenticeship approach with hands-on experiments	2.228 (2)	Chiu, Chou, & Liu (2002)
	Exploratory Astronomy Curriculum consisting of observations of the physical environment from different perspectives	.792 (2)	Schur, Skuy, Zietsman, & Fridjhon (2002)
	Instruction in induction and scientific reasoning using videos	.917 (2)	Hayes, Goodhew, Heit, & Gillan (2003)

(continued)

TABLE 22.4
Continued

Construct	Conceptual Change Catalysts	Effect Size (#ES Contributing)	Studies Contributing
Topic Knowledge	Text	.239 (4)	Mikkila-Erdmann (2001)
	Exploratory Astronomy Curriculum consisting of observations of the physical environment from different perspectives	1.157 (5)	Schur, Skuy, Zietsman, & Fridjhon (2002)
	Conceptual assignments where students observe and explain a phenomenon	.063 (1)	Eryilmaz (2002)
	Group discussions about specific science phenomena	.178 (1)	Eryilmaz (2002)
	Explanations and demonstrations of science phenomena	1.291(2)	Diakidoy & Kendeou (2001)
	Metaconceptual lessons addressing the existence of two conflicting conceptions	.918 (2)	Wiser & Amin (2001)
	Pairs of students working to resolve health problems in scenarios	.819 (1)	Windschitl (2001)
	Dual-situated learning events designed to challenge prior conceptions	.762 (1)	She (2002)

Note: Hedge's g effect sizes are presented. [a]Negative effect size represents a decrease in students' misconceptions.

Finally, the boundaries between specified forms of subject-matter knowledge, such as conceptual versus topic knowledge, were often vaguely specified within the identified literature. However, for the sake of the meta-analysis, we chose to sort the variables as they were designated by the researchers and elected to deal with the definitional problems as part of the research synthesis. The one exception to this decision rule was for those outcomes that researchers labeled as "conceptual change." Because conceptual change is a latent variable, those outcomes were more accurately categorized as measures of knowledge or beliefs. Thus, we followed the specifications in our coding manual to recategorize all data initially marked as conceptual change by study authors.

It should be stated that the studies considered in both the synthesis and meta-analysis typically included multiple indicators of conceptual change. For example, in Chiu et al. (2002) experiments around the topic of chemical equilibrium, the researchers not only examined the effects of a cognitive apprenticeship on high school students' beliefs but also their domain knowledge. Similarly, Schur et al. (2002) investigated the effects of the Experimental Astronomy Curriculum or EAC on students' concept, topic, and domain knowledge.

Topic Beliefs

The organization of Table 22.4 reveals not only the form of knowledge or beliefs studied in the conceptual change literature, but also the method or approach used to instigate conceptual formation or reformation among K–12 students. Thus, we find that 5 experiments and 24 scale measurements contributed to the effect size data on belief change. All those outcomes dealt with beliefs about specific academic topics such as genetically modified foods (Mason & Boscolo, 2004), temperature, or falling bodies (Chinn & Malhotra, 2002).

Further, researchers used three methods as catalysts for those topic belief changes: text, explanations, and prediction techniques. For example, Chinn and Malhotra (2002) examined the effects of data-based and explanation-based instruction on students' beliefs about forward movement and the nature of falling objects. Overall, the use of dual position texts (Mason & Boscolo, 2004) and the formation of predictions (Chinn & Malhotra, 2002) were moderately effective at altering students' naïve beliefs about a given academic topic. By comparison, data-based or explanation-based instruction like those employed by Chinn and Malhotra (2002) were found to exert strong effects on K–12 students' topic beliefs.

Concept, Declarative, Domain, and Topic Knowledge

Much of the researchers' focus in the empirical study of conceptual change was in ascertaining the effects of textual or other types of instructional interventions on students' knowledge base. At times that focus was specifically at the concept level. The empirical question was whether researchers could demonstrate a marked growth in the accuracy or sophistication of students' concept knowledge by introducing well-crafted refutational texts, posing questions, conceiving instruction as a cognitive apprentice, or using hands-on activities. With declarative knowledge, the empirical interventions targeted factual understandings within particular domains, whereas topic knowledge involved a number of related understandings pertaining to a designated topic associated with a text or specific lesson (e.g., electric circuit theory). At the broadest level, conceptual change researchers explored knowledge effects at the level of an academic domain; that is, a specified field of study such as physics, geometry, or biology.

Looking across these differing forms of knowledge, it would seem that certain catalysts had weak and even negative effects on students' knowledge. For example, relying on videos or conceptual assignments to modify students' knowledge base was, at best, a weak approach to conceptual change. In the case of concept knowledge, such techniques even resulted in a weak, negative effect (Eryilmaz, 2002). Conversely, it appeared that using hands-on activities (e.g., Lee & Law, 2001; Reiner & Eilam, 2001) or coupling physical demonstrations with scientific explanations (e.g., Diakidoy & Kendeou, 2001; Vosniadou et al., 2001) translated into strong effect sizes for multiple forms of subject-matter knowledge. Finally, while texts have often been employed as tools for conceptual change in educational practice, as well as in the research literature (e.g., Murphy & Alexander, 2004), the documented effects for texts in this meta-analysis were weak to moderate for subject-matter knowledge (e.g., Mikkilä-Erdmann, 2001).

It is worth noting, however, that the nature or structure of the text employed in the intervention was often unspecified. In cases where the type of text was specified as refutational (e.g., Alsparslan, Tekkaya, & Geban, 2003), the calculated effects on knowledge were substantively stronger than in those cases where the structure of the text was unclear (e.g., Sungur, Tekkaya, & Geban, 2001). These results are similar to those reported in previous meta-analyses on conceptual change (Guzzetti, Snyder, Glass, & Gamas, 1993). In addition, the practical effects of dual position texts, such as that employed by Mason and Boscolo (2004), varied dramatically due to students' epistemic sophistication (i.e., low = 0.045 to high = 1.181).

It would be misleading to leave the reader with the impression that the instructional catalysts we catalogued in this review had disappointing effects. Although some interventions did not translate into statistically significant shifts in K–12 students' beliefs or their subject-matter knowledge, others were associated with quite strong effects such as a cognitive apprenticeship approach employed by Chiu et al. (2002) or the combination of explanations and demonstrations instituted by Vosniadou et al. (2001). Moreover, one might argue that securing even moderately sized changes in students' beliefs or knowledge from what were often relatively short treatment intervals stands as evidence of the possibilities for facilitating conceptual change in this K–12 population.

What was perhaps most interesting was that the strongest effects on knowledge or beliefs resulted from interventions that directly addressed, in some way, students' initial understandings (e.g., Nieswandt, 2001; She, 2002; Wiser & Amin, 2001). By comparison, approaches that focused more on the presentation of accurate scientific information with less attention to students' current understandings produced more modest effects (e.g., Eryilmaz, 2002; Mikkilä-Erdmann, 2001). This finding supports a number of prominent conceptual change models including Vosniadou's (1994) framework theory and the Conceptual Change Model (Posner et al., 1982).

Beyond the question of whether or not these catalysts worked at all or to what degree, there are remaining issues that must be considered for those seeking to intervene in the formation or reformation of conceptual understanding. One of those issues relates to the durability of effects and the other to their replicability. Specifically, there is no way to ascertain from this meta-analysis of the literature whether or not the influences documented herein have staying power or not. Do we expect that the newly modified beliefs or concepts that students hold about forward movement, heat transfer, or chemical equilibrium are now solidly planted in students' minds? Or, do these more accurately signal fragile transformations in what students know or believe that will wane or regress under the pressure of everyday experiences or misleading instruction?

We were also struck by the fact that many catalysts we charted in Table 22.4, even the more promising ones, have been subjected to little, if any, replication. That is to say, it is not evident if the general treatment methods (e.g., texts or demonstrations) or particular interventions (e.g., EAC) reported here would produce similar effects if the treatments were repeated under similar conditions. For instance, how are we to know whether the very strong effects for the cognitive apprenticeship approach instituted by Chiu et al. (2002) would produce similar results if executed with an alternative sample or by other researchers? If researchers other than Chinn and Malhotra (2002) attempt classroom explanations would changes in students' beliefs or understandings be as impressive?

As has begun with the work of Vosniadou and colleagues (Vosniadou et al., 2001), the conceptual change literature would clearly benefit from more interventions that have substantial track records when it comes to interpreting their overall effects. Regrettably, much of what we found within this body of work involved singular occurrences or particular treatments that have not had the benefit of repeated trials or multiple instantiations. We are hopeful that such replication is underway, especially for those programs of research with promising initial showings.

CONCLUDING THOUGHTS

In this chapter, we sought to interrogate the recent literature on conceptual change through analysis and synthesis. First, we coupled a statistical exploration with a more traditional synthesis of the 47 studies we located. The results proved enlightening. For one, we were able to view this empirical panorama and to sketch the landscape of the conceptual change literature. For another, we came to appreciate how difficult it can be for conceptual change researchers to conceptualize and operationalize the factors or forces that matter to them in this complex and dynamic process. We also came to the realization that the distance between the theoretical depictions of this complex and dynamic process and the portraits that arise from the synthesis of the empirical literature seems daunting.

Second, we delved into a meta-analytic examination of the literature reported in between 2001 and 2006 to understand the power of particular experimental interventions or instructional catalysts to spark changes in the knowledge, beliefs, or interests of K–12 students. The resulting analysis proved revealing with regard to the relative effects of an array of methods — from discussion to apprenticing — on students' subject-specific knowledge and beliefs.

We would hope that our future exploration of the domain of conceptual change theory and research will confirm that theory and research — to say nothing of educational practice — are moving into greater alignment. We believe that such an alignment will not only foster greater understanding of the very nature of concept formation and reformation but also allow us to orchestrate educational contexts that optimize learner development.

REFERENCES

Alexander, P. A. (1997). Mapping the multidimensional nature of domain learning: The interplan of cognitive, motivational, and strategic forces. In M. L. Maehr & P. R. Pintrich (Eds.), *Andvances in motivation and achievement* (Vol. 10, pp. 213–250). Greenwich, CT: JAI Press.

Alexander, P. A. (1998). The nature of disciplinary and domain learning: The knowledge, interest, and strategic dimensions of learning from subject-matter text. In C. Hynd (Ed.), *Learning from text across conceptual domains* (pp. 263–287). Mahwah, NJ: Erlbaum.

Alexander, P. A. (2006). *Psychology in learning and instruction.* Upper Saddle River, NJ: Pearson.

Alexander, P. A., Jetton, T. L., & Kulikowich, J. M. (1995). Interrelationship of knowledge, interest, and recall: Assessing a model of domain learning. *Journal of Educational Psychology, 87,* 559–575.

Alexander, P. A., Murphy, P. K., Woods, B. S., Duhon, K. E., & Parker, D. (1997). College instruction and concomitant changes in students' knowledge, interest, and strategy use: A study of domain learning. *Contemporary Educational Psychology, 22,* 125–146.

Alexander, P. A., Schallert, D. L., & Hare, V. C. (1991). Coming to terms: How researchers in learning and literacy talk about knowledge. *Review of Educational Research, 61,* 315–343.

Alexander, P. A., Sperl, C. T., Buehl, M. M., Fives, H., & Chiu, S. (2004). Modeling domain learning: Profiles from the field of special education. *Journal of Educational Psychology, 96,* 545–557.

Alsparslan, C., Tekkaya, C., & Geban, O. (2003). Using the conceptual change instruction to improve learning. *Journal of Biological Education, 37,* 133–137.

Bandura, A. (1977).Self-efficacy: Toward a unifying theory of behavioral change. *Psychological Review, 84,* 191–215.

Biemas, H. J. A., Deel, O. R., & Simons, P. R. J. (2001). Differences between successful and less successful students while working with the CONTACT-2 strategy. *Learning and Instruction, 11,* 265–282.

Bigozzi, L., Biggeri, A., Boschi, F., Conti, P., & Fiorentini, C. (2002). Children "scientists" know the reasons why and they are "poets" too. Non-randomized controlled trial to evaluate the effectiveness of a strategy aimed at improving the learning of scientific concepts. *European Journal of Psychology of Education, 17,* 343–362.

Boo, H. K., & Watson, J. R. (2001). Progression in high school students' (aged 16–18) conceptualizations about chemical reactions in solution. *Science Education, 85,* 568–585.

Carey, S. (1985). *Conceptual change in childhood.* Cambridge, MA: MIT Press.

Chan, C. K. K. (2001). Peer collaboration and discourse patterns in learning from incompatible information. *Instructional Science, 29,* 443–479.

Cheng, P. C. H., & Shipstone, D. M. (2003). Supporting learning and promoting conceptual change with box and AVOW diagrams. Part 2: Their impact on student learning at A-level. *International Journal of Science Education, 25,* 291–305.

Chi, M. H. T. (1992). Conceptual change within and across ontological categories: Examples from learning and discovery in science. In R. N. Giene (Ed.), *Cognitive models of science: Minnesota studies in the philosophy of science* (pp. 1129–1187). Minneapolis: University of Minnesota Press.

Chinn, C. A., & Brewer, W. F. (2001). Models of data: A theory of how people evaluate data. *Cognition and Instruction, 19,* 323–393.

Chinn, C. A., & Malhotra, B. A. (2002). Children's responses to anomalous scientific data: How is conceptual change impeded? *Journal of Educational Psychology, 94*, 327–343.

Chiu, M. M., Chou, C., & Liu, C. (2002). Dynamic processes of conceptual change: Analysis of constructing mental models of chemical equilibrium. *Journal of Research in Science Teaching, 39*, 688–712.

Chiu, M. M., Kessel, C., Moschkovich, J., & Muñoz-Nuñez, A. (2001). Learning to graph linear functions: A case study of conceptual change. *Cognition and Instruction, 19*, 215–252.

Diakidoy, I. A., & Kendeou, P. (2001). Facilitating conceptual change in astronomy: A comparison of the effectiveness off two instructional approaches. *Learning and Instruction, 11*, 1–20.

Diakidoy, I. A. N., Kendeou, P., & Ioannides, C. (2003). Reading about energy: The effects of text structure in science learning and conceptual change. *Contemporary Educational Psychology, 28*, 335–356.

Dole, J. A., & Sinatra, G. M. (1998). Reconceptualizing change in the cognitive construction of knowledge. *Educational Psychologist, 33*, 109–128.

Duit, R., Roth, W. M., Komorek, M., & Wilbers, J. (2001). Fostering conceptual change by analogies—between Scylla and Chrybdis. *Learning and Instruction, 11*, 283–303.

Edens, K. M., & Potter, E. (2003). Using descriptive drawings as a conceptual change strategy in elementary science. *School Science and Mathematics, 103*, 135–144.

Eryilmaz, A. (2002). Effects of conceptual assignments and conceptual change discussions on students misconceptions and achievement regarding force and motion. *Journal of Research in Science Teaching, 39*, 1001–1015.

Guzzetti, B. J., Snyder, T. E., Glass, G. V., & Gamas, W. S. (1993). Promoting conceptual change in science: A comparative meta-analysis of instructional interventions from reading education and science education. *Reading Research Quarterly, 28,* 117–159.

Harrison, A. G., & Treagust, D. F. (2001). Conceptual change using multiple interpretive perspectives: Two case studies in secondary school chemistry. *Instructional Science, 29*, 45–85.

Hayes, B. K., Goodhew, A., Heit, E., & Gillan, J. (2003). The role of diverse instruction in conceptual change. *Journal of Experimental Child Psychology, 86*, 253–276.

Kulikowich, J. M., & Hancock, G. (Eds.). (in press). Theory and method in research using latent variable models. [Special Issue] *Contemporary Educational Psychology.*

Lee, Y., & Law, N. (2001). Explorations in promoting conceptual change in electrical concepts via ontological category shift. *International Journal of Science Education, 23*, 111–149.

Mason, L. (2001a). Introducing talk and writing for conceptual change: A classroom study. *Learning and Instruction, 11*, 305–329.

Mason, L. (2001b). Responses to anomalous data on controversial topics and theory change. *Learning and Instruction, 11*, 453–483.

Mason, L., & Boscolo, P. (2004). Role of epistemological understanding and interest in interpreting a controversy and in topic-specific belief change. *Contemporary Educational Psychology, 29*, 103–128.

Mazens, K.,, & Lautrey, J. (2003). Conceptual change in physics: Children's naïve representations of sound. *Cognitive Development, 18*, 159–176.

Mikkilä-Erdmann, M. (2001). Improving conceptual change concerning photosynthesis through text design. *Learning and Instruction, 11*, 241–257.

Murphy, P. K., & Alexander, P. A. (2000). A motivated exploration of motivation terminology. *Contemporary Educational Psychology, 25*, 3–53.

Murphy, P. K., & Alexander, P. A. (2004). Persuasion as a dynamic, multidimensional process: An investigation of individual and intraindividual differences. *American Educational Research Journal, 41*, 337–364.

Murphy, P. K., & Mason, L. (2006). Changing knowledge and changing beliefs. In P. A. Alexander & P. Winne (Eds.), *Handbook of Educational Psychology* (2nd ed.). New York Erlbaum.

Murphy, P. K., Alexander, P. A., Greene, J. A., & Edwards, M. N. (in press). Epistemological threads in the fabric of conceptual change. In S. Vosniadou, A. Baltas, & X. Vamvakoussi (Eds.), *Re-framing the conceptual change approach in learning and instruction.* Dordrecht, Netherlands: Elsevier.

Nieswandt, M. (2001). Problems and possibilities for learning in an introductory chemistry course from a conceptual change perspective. *Science Education, 85*, 158–179.

Oliva, J. M. (2003). The structural coherence of students' conceptions in mechanics and conceptual change. *International Journal of Science Education, 25*, 539–561.

Osborne, R. J., & Wittrock, M. C. (1983). Learning science: A generative process. *Science Education, 67*, 489–508.

Pajares, F. (1997). Current directions in self-efficacy research. In M. Maehr & P. R. Pintrich (Eds.), *Advances in motivation and achievement* (Vol. 10, pp. 1–49). Greenwich, CT: JAI Press.

Palmer, D. H. (2001). Investigating the relationship between refutational text and conceptual change. *Research in Science and Technological Education, 19*, 193–204.

Park, J., & Han, S. (2002). Using deductive reasoning to promote the change of students' conceptions about force and motion. *International Journal of Science Education, 24*, 593–609.

Petty, R. E., & Cacioppo, J. T. (1986). The elaboration likelihood model of persuasion. In L. Berkowitz (Ed.), *Advances in experimental social psychology* (Vol. 19, pp. 123–205). New York: Academic Press.

Pnevmatikos, D. (2002). Conceptual changes in religious concepts of elementary schoolchildren: The case of the house where God lives. *Educational Psychology, 22*, 93–122.

Posner, G. J., Strike, K. A., Hewson, P. W., & Gertzog, W. A. (1982). Accommodation of a scientific conception: Toward a theory of conceptual change. *Science Education, 66*, 211–227.

Pozo, J. I., & Gómez Crespo, M. A. (1998). *Aprender y enseñar ciencia. Del conocimiento cotidiano al conocimiento científico* [Teaching and learning science: From everyday knowledge to scientific knowledge]. Madrid, Spain: Morata.

Pozo, J. I., & Gómez Crespo, M. A. (2005). The embodied nature of implicit theories: The consistency of ideas about the nature of matter. *Cognition & Instruction, 23*(3), 351–387.

Reiner, M., & Eilam, B. (2001). Conceptual classroom environment-a system view of learning. *International Journal of Science Education, 23*, 551–568.

Renninger, K. A., Hidi, S., & Krapp, A. (1992). *The role of interest in learning and development.* Hillsdale, NJ: Erlbaum.

Ross, N., Medin, D., Coley, J. D., & Atran, S. (2003). Cultural and experimental differences in the development of folkbiological induction. *Cognitive Development, 18*, 25–47.

Schur, Y., Skuy, M., Zietsman, A., & Fridjhon, P. (2002). A thinking journey based on constructivism and mediated learning experience as a vehicle for teaching science to low functioning students and enhancing their cognitive skills. *School Psychology International, 23*, 36–67.

She, H. C. (2002). Concepts of a higher hierarchical level require more dual situated learning events for conceptual change: A study of air pressure and buoyancy. *International Journal of Science Education, 24*, 981–996.

She, H. C. (2004). Fostering radical conceptual change through dual-situated learning model. *Journal of Research in Science Teaching, 41*, 142–164.

Smith, J. P. III, diSessa, A., & Roschelle, J. (1993). Misconception reconceived: A constructivist analysis of knowledge in transition. *Journal of the Learning Sciences, 3*, 115–164.

Smith, C. L., Solomon, G. E. A., & Carey, S. (2005). Never getting to zero: Elementary school students' understanding of the infinite divisibility of number and matter. *Cognitive psychology, 51*, 101–140.

Southerland, S. A., Sinatra, G. M., & Matthews, M. R. (2001). Belief, knowledge, and science education. *Educational Psychology Review, 13*, 325–351.

Stanovich, K. (1984). Intelligence, cognitive skills, and early reading progress. *Reading Research Quarterly, 29*, 278–303.

Sungur, S., Tekkaya, C., & Geban, O. (2001). The contribution of conceptual change texts accompanied by concept mapping to students' understanding of the human circulatory system. *School Science and Mathematics, 101*, 91–101.

Thagard, P. (1992). *Conceptual revolutions.* Princeton, NJ: Princeton University Press.

Tsai, C. C. (2003). Using a conflict map as an instructional tool to change student conceptions in simple series electric-circuits. *International Journal of Science Education, 25*, 307–327.

von Aufschnaiter, C., & von Aufschnaiter, S. (2003). Theoretical framework and empirical evidence of students' cognitive processes in three dimensions of content, complexity, and time. *Journal of Research in Science Teaching, 40*, 616–648.

Vosniadou, S. (1994). Capturing and modeling the process of conceptual change. *Learning and Instruction,* *4*, 45–69.

Vosniadou, S., & Brewer, W. F. (1992). Mental models of the earth: A study of conceptual change in childhood. *Cognitive Psychology, 24*, 535–585.

Vosniadou, S., Ioannides, C., Dimitrakopoulou, A., & Papademetriou, E. (2001). Designing learning environments to promote conceptual change in science. *Learning and Instruction, 11*, 381–419.

Wellman, H. M., & Gelman, S. A. (1998). Knowledge acquisition in foundational domains. In W. Damon (Ed.), *Handbook of child psychology* (5th ed., Vol. 2, pp. 523–573). New York: Wiley.

Windschitl, M. (2001). Using simulations in the middle school: Does assertiveness of dyad partners influence conceptual change? *International Journal of Science Education, 23*, 17–32.

Wiser, M., & Amin, T. (2001). "Is heat hot?" Inducing conceptual change by integrating everyday and scientific perspectives on thermal phenomena. *Learning and Instruction, 11*, 331–355.

VI

INSTRUCTIONAL APPROACHES TO PROMOTE CONCEPTUAL CHANGE

23

The Conceptual Change Approach and the Teaching of Science

Richard T. White and Richard F. Gunstone
Monash University

INTRODUCTION

In the 1970s, something remarkable happened in research in science education. For decades the dominant form of research had been the experiment, in which different forms of instruction were compared in effect on performance on a test. Quite suddenly, however, apparently independently in a wide spread of countries, instead of doing comparative experiments, researchers began to probe children's understanding of natural phenomena such as the shape of the Earth, drying of clothes, floating and sinking, and so on. They reported surprising results, with children and even older students offering explanations that differed from scientists', even after they had been taught the scientists' depiction in school. It was not only remarkable that researchers began to do this new type of study, but also that major journals accepted reports of them and that other scholars and, eventually, teachers took notice of them. Through the 1980s, uncovering alternative conceptions became the most prominent line in research. This led to considerations of how conceptions form, how amenable they are to change, and what this means for teaching.

Understanding of how all this came about is interesting for its own sake, but also important for understanding why research on conceptual change became so prominent in the latter part of the 20th century, and perhaps for guiding the course of research in the future. The focus of this chapter is on the ways research on alternative conceptions in science shaped the early years of conceptual change research. We explore this focus by addressing five key questions:

- Why did research into alternative conceptions spread rapidly in the 1970s, when a beginning 30 years earlier withered?
- What factors stimulated the widespread international involvement?
- What phases can be identified in the early years of research into alternative conceptions and conceptual change research, and what changes in research style were associated with them?
- Why, when research on alternative conceptions and conceptual change was prominent in science education, did it have little presence in research into learning of other subjects?
- What effect did this early research have on teaching?

WHY DID RESEARCH INTO ALTERNATIVE CONCEPTIONS
FLOURISH IN THE 1970S?

In 1945 Mervin Oakes published in *Science Education* a study of adults' understandings of falling objects and of Bernoulli's principle. His work does not seem to have attracted attention. Two years later, Oakes' doctoral dissertation was published as a book by Teachers College (Oakes, 1947). This dissertation was a wide ranging study of young children's explanations of a range of natural phenomena and simple experiments (e.g., motions of waves, clouds, nightfall, functions of plant roots, displacement of water, falling balls, melting snow). Oakes is clear in this study that he was not in any way interested in classifying children's explanations, and directly contrasts this with the approach of Piaget. A decade later, Oakes tried again with a paper that both revisited these earlier two studies and reported examples of his own college students' explanations given in response to his conventional examination questions about a wide range of biology and physics topics (Oakes, 1957). Again, no related studies followed. Yet, suddenly, in the 1970s a raft of studies of alternative conceptions appeared (see Pfundt & Duit, 1994, and http://www.ipn. uni-kiel.de/aktuell/stcse/stcse.html for a bibliography). None of the authors of these very large numbers of later studies cited Oakes, presumably because they were not aware of his work. Research does not occur in a social vacuum, of course, and reasons for the difference between the fate of Oakes and that of the later scholars must lie in the circumstances of the two periods and of the intervening 20–30 years.

In the United States in Oakes's time, behaviourism was the dominant theory of learning. Attention concentrated on stimulus-response connections. What learners already knew about a topic was of no concern, nor were subtleties of understanding. Oakes was outside the main stream. By the 1970s, in contrast, psychology had recovered its interest in the mind. Paivio (1971) brought back the notion of mental imagery; and the theory of information processing, with concepts of short- and long-term memory, became popular. In science education, Piaget's visit to the United States in 1964 and his subsequent article (Piaget, 1964) in the *Journal of Research in Science Teaching* brought the idea of individual construction of meaning into prominence.

At the same time as the major shift in the psychology of learning, broad social changes occurred. As populations grew around the world with better health facilities and improved economies, school enrolments rose, especially at secondary level. Universities entered a golden age, as individuals' aspirations coincided with governments' appreciation that education served the national interest. Science, especially, was seen to open the way to a bright future for both individuals and nations. To meet demands for more and better-qualified teachers, universities established and supported faculties of education. Within those faculties, in order to gain the respect of colleagues in other disciplines, scholars gave increasing attention to research.

As well as being a time of expansion in education and in science, the 1970s were years of individualism. Mao Zedong's slogan, "Let a thousand flowers bloom", may have had more impact in the West, where it was matched less poetically by "Do your own thing", than in his own country, but it represented the spirit of the time. Hippie movements, student revolts, and opposition to the Vietnam War were outcomes. A less obvious outcome was researchers' appreciation that individuals differ in their response to any situation, including the meaning that they place on what they see or hear. The time was ripe, then, for investigations of alternative conceptions.

WHAT FACTORS WERE RESPONSIBLE FOR THE WIDESPREAD
INTERNATIONAL INVOLVEMENT?

Following the Second World War, reconstruction and economic growth promoted a rise in the number of universities, many with departments of education. Australia had six universities in

1959 and 20 in 1975. In Great Britain, the number rose from 16 in 1945 to 43 in 1975; in Canada from 28 to 53, Belgium four to ten, Argentina six to 37. There were, then, potentially many scholars in many countries who could be interested in alternative conceptions and conceptual change. New journals became available to them as outlets for their research. *Science Education*, which had been the sole journal dedicated to research in science education, which began in 1917, was joined by the *Journal of Research in Science Teaching* in 1963, *Research in Science Education* in 1970, *Studies in Science Education* in 1974, and the *European Journal of Science Education* in 1979. Air travel made it possible for scholars from different countries to meet at conferences, and even though email had not yet arrived it was much easier for scholars to correspond and share ideas than it had been in the days of surface travel and surface mail. As late as 1970, Australians travelling to Europe mostly went by ship, a 6-week journey.

Although it was easier for people to meet or correspond, that did not guarantee the sharing of ideas that was necessary for a widespread research effort to arise and be maintained. There were two further requirements. What was being done had to be interesting, and there had to be openness, a readiness to share. Both requirements were met. People found the results of probes of understanding surprising and intriguing. Those who discovered them were excited, and keen to tell what they had found. Perhaps this was because, as a result of the recent expansion of universities, most were in the early years of their research careers, energetic and wanting to build up connections with other scholars. In most countries, other than the United States, these early career researchers were recruited from the ranks of experienced school science teachers, and so were engaged by this research because it informed their own professional understanding and experiences.

Readiness to meet and share ideas culminated in the formation in 1983 of a Special Interest Group of the American Educational Research Association, Cognitive Structure and Conceptual Change, which for several years supported and stimulated the research in a wide range of countries.

WHAT PHASES AND RESEARCH STYLES WERE APPARENT IN THE EARLY YEARS OF RESEARCH INTO ALTERNATIVE CONCEPTIONS AND CONCEPTUAL CHANGE?

There was an initial period of discovery, in which studies reported beliefs, mainly for secondary school students, about natural phenomena. There was at first no attempt to alter these beliefs. This was similar to Piaget's studies in the 1920s and 1930s. Like Piaget, the researchers interviewed their subjects, employing diverse stimuli to evoke responses. Nussbaum and Novak (1976) used a globe and small model human figures to probe understanding of the shape of the Earth; Osborne and his co-workers (Osborne, 1980; Osborne & Freyberg, 1985) based their interviews on drawings of stick figures; Tiberghien and Delacôte (1976) gave children the task of connecting a simple electric circuit; Champagne, Klopfer, and Anderson (1980) asked respondents to predict what was going to happen in a dynamical situation. Where the researchers differed from Piaget, at least in this initial phase, was that they did not theorise about the existence of stages that beliefs might go through.

A feature of research in this phase was how much it differed from the standard form of research that had been current. Nearly all the studies of learning published in *Science Education* and the *Journal of Research in Science Teaching* in the 1950s and 1960s were of experiments that compared the effects of different interventions. Often complex, with elegant designs, the experiments mostly employed simple pencil and paper tests. Interviews were not used. Inferential statistics determined whether groups' scores on the tests differed sufficiently for the researcher to conclude that the interventions differed in their effects. In the hunt for differences, a wide spread of scores within a group made it less likely that a difference between groups' mean scores was real and not a chance variation. Individual differences were therefore a nuisance, rather than a matter of absorbing interest.

Where these experimental studies used complex designs but simple tests, the probes of students' ideas and beliefs that emerged in the 1970s used a simple design and subtle tests. Instead of inferential statistics, there were either no statistics or merely simple counts of numbers who expressed a particular idea or belief. It is to the credit of reviewers and editors of journals that work so different from the pervading style was accepted for publication. The number of descriptive studies in *Science Education* went from two in 1975 to 14 in 1985, in *Journal of Research in Science Teaching* from six to 13, and in *Research in Science Education* from one to nine (White, 2001).

One of the consequences of the simple design of probes was that the studies were easily repeated. A problem with experiments was that, unlike experiments in science itself, they were difficult to repeat, either by the original researcher or an independent scholar. Replication of results was rare. With probes of beliefs, however, replications were common, to the extent that journal editors were flooded with them.

A problem created by the initial work was finding a satisfactory term for the knowledge that lay behind the explanations that learners proffered. One early term for the source of explanations was *misconceptions*. This term implies an error in understanding, suggesting that teaching should show why the belief was in error and then present the correct, or scientists', truth. Another term, *children's science* (Osborne & Freyberg, 1985), implies that children think like scientists by holding coherent, even though inaccurate or incomplete, theories to explain events. The term *alternative beliefs* could be taken to imply some equality of value, opening the constructivist model of learning to extremist criticisms. *Alternative frameworks* (Driver & Easley, 1978) suggests a permanent structure of knowledge. All of these terms imply a consistency and constancy of knowledge, whereas explanations might be ephemeral, produced at the moment to satisfy the social demands of the context. Knowledge might better be represented as fluid and dynamic than as stable.

That no one term was free of objections is related to difficulty in defining the key word conception. Obviously this was related to *concept*, for which theorists held two meanings. One is the ability to recognise objects or actions as members or not-members of a named class. An example of this meaning from alternative conceptions literature is Bell's (1981) study of young children's ability to class things such as cows, whales, spiders, and fish as animals or not. The second meaning of concept is the set of knowledge that a person associates with the name. This knowledge will include propositions, mental images, and recollections of personal experiences. The second meaning is more closely connected than the first with the notion of conception, but is not identical with that term. Conception seems to mean more than the sum of knowledge that comprises concept. It is not difficult to change a person's concept of anything. All you have to do is tell them something new about it, and provided they pay attention some change or some new relation between concepts will occur. Carey (1985) termed this form of learning weak restructuring. But by conceptual, or perhaps a better term would be conceptional, change theorists mean a more substantial revision of belief or understanding. Carey postulated that the distinction that matters in this *strong restructuring* is that concepts themselves alter, and not just the relations between them. She gave three criteria for such 'strong restructuring': "changes in the domain of phenomena to be accounted for by the theory, changes in explanatory mechanisms, and (most importantly) changes in individual concepts" (1985, p.187). A student who has, for example, mastered Newtonian dynamics will have a radically different notion of force from one who holds an impetus notion, such as the force of a hit remains in a moving ball, gradually dying away and so causing the ball to slow. Such a student will also see a different range of phenomena as being explained by Newtonian theory. This distinction between weak and strong restructuring is not, however, altogether clear-cut, because concepts at any degree of sophistication are determined by their relations. Even in weak restructuring concepts change. Just when there is sufficient change for this to be judged to constitute strong restructuring remains obscure.

Difficulties with terminology, about concepts and conceptions and weak and strong restructuring, were connected with practical problems raised by informed teachers of science. They made it hard to answer questions such as how could alternative beliefs persist in the face of (presumably) clear teaching. In a theoretical statement that is still cited frequently, Posner, Strike, Hewson, and Gertzog (1982) postulated that learners would not abandon an existing belief and accept a new one unless they were dissatisfied with the old and found the new one intelligible, plausible, and fruitful. The difficulty remained that although current teaching was well able to present new information clearly and plausibly, it was less obvious how to create dissatisfaction with an existing belief, which after all must have served its holder well up to this point, or how to show that the new view was rewarding (except for the purpose of passing an examination).

In the second phase of work, researchers returned to experiments in which they tested the effectiveness of methods in overcoming non-scientific beliefs. Methods included asking students to predict what would happen in a particular situation, showing them what did happen, then explaining to them why their prediction had gone wrong (Hewson & Hamlyn, 1984; Stavy, 1991). This approach was intended to bring about the conditions specified by Posner et al. (1982).

While at first it seemed likely that carefully-designed interventions would be effective, it soon became clear that the issue was more complex than had been thought. Some remarkable results exemplify that complexity. The idea was that learners would see from a demonstration that their belief had led them to an incorrect prediction. What had not been appreciated was that seeing is not a simple, objective act. Gunstone and White (1981) asked first-year university students, enrolled in a physics course, to predict the relative rates of fall of a heavy and a light ball. The balls were dropped from shoulder height, and the students were asked what they saw. Many who predicted that the heavy ball would fall faster said that they saw it hit the ground before the light one — though nobody else said that. People see what they expect to see. In this case, a clear demonstration was insufficient to shake an incorrect belief.

Gauld (1986) found a similar plasticity, this time with memory rather than observation. He had asked 14-year-olds to choose between four possibilities for electric current in a simple circuit of a battery and light globe: that current comes from one end of the battery and is all consumed in globe; that current comes from both ends and reacts in the globe; that it comes from one end, some is used up in the globe and the rest goes on back to the battery; and that it comes from one end and all returns to the battery. Many predicted that it would be less in the wire connected to the negative terminal of the battery. After the students had made their choice, they were shown with ammeters that the currents were equal in the wires on each side of the globe. Three months later they were interviewed again. In making their choice this time, several justified it by stating that the ammeters had shown less current on one side of the globe from the other. Instead of the demonstration convincing them that their model was incorrect, they had altered their memories of the demonstration to accord with their beliefs.

Champagne, Gunstone, and Klopfer (1985) provide another instance of persistence of beliefs and the emotional dimension of this persistence. An extended teaching sequence focussed on developing physics concepts was conducted with two groups: a group of middle school gifted students, in Pittsburgh, and a group of graduate trainee science teachers in Melbourne. Data collected through the sequence in Pittsburgh suggested that most students were undertaking conceptual change. A final interview at the end of the sequence however showed that all students had reverted to their pre-teaching concepts and modes of analysis of situations. Although they had learned scientists' explanations, their original beliefs remained as well. In Melbourne, with the trainee science teachers, at the end of each session in the sequence each participant wrote comments about their reactions to the experiences in that session. In one session, the students made predictions and observations of the relative times of fall of two balls of different mass dropped from the same height, and then spent considerable time with the teacher discussing predictions and observations. In reacting, one of the students wrote, "I don't know if I am going to be able to last the distance. I'm mentally exhausted after each session and the effort to hold out when I am wrong is very draining" (p.176). It was clear from a number of student comments that there can be an emotional charge to be met in conceptual change.

A conclusion from studies such as that of Champagne et al. (1985) is that conceptual change is not a simple matter of abandoning one belief and accepting another. Rather, both can be held, even when the holder is aware that they contradict. Which belief is activated at any time will depend on the context.

The persistence of alternative beliefs in the face of instruction led researchers to consider, and probe, how such beliefs form. If late instruction was ineffective, perhaps early experiences could be provided to encourage initial development of notions consistent with scientists' depictions.

In the title of Driver's (1983) book, *The Pupil as Scientist?*, the question mark prefigured a debate about how coherent a learner's beliefs might be. Did young children form consistent, even if primitive, theories about the causes and natures of phenomena? Initial beliefs must surely be context-bound: "If I push this block it moves," and then "When I push it harder it moves more." DiSessa (1988) termed these context-specific beliefs *phenomenological primitives*. Gradually, the child must see commonalities across situations, and will build *presuppositions* that constitute a naïve theory of a broader field of events, such as dynamics (Vosniadou, 1994, p. 61): for example, "There are physical objects, which have properties such as force. Inanimate objects do not move by themselves; their motion requires a force." Stavy and Tirosh (2000) propose a similar notion, that children generalise *intuitive beliefs*. An intuitive belief is employed in making comparisons, such as in the Piagetian task where children are asked about the relative volumes of liquid in a tall narrow container and a short wide one, or when asked about the relative speeds of fall of a heavy and a light object. In these comparisons there is an obvious quantity (height or weight) and a less obvious one (volume or speed). Stavy and Tirosh suggest that incorrect responses stem from an intuitive belief that more of quantity A naturally goes with more of quantity B. Presumably such a generalised belief forms from experiences across a range of contexts.

While early theories of conceptual change differed in the relative emphases they placed on the coherence and stability of children's conceptions, on the awareness children have of their beliefs, on the rate or age at which knowledge develops, and on the balance between experience and social transmission of beliefs, essentially they presented the same message: knowledge and the associated explanations for phenomena were seen to build up gradually, piece by piece, mainly from experience at first and later through an increasing degree of social transmission (adults' conversations and explanations, teaching, books, television); from time to time evidence or authoritative information would shock a revision of the conception into greater coherence and extent of application, and even bring it into line with the current scientific depiction.

LINES OF RESEARCH

Di Sessa, Vosniadou, Stavy and Tirosh, Carey, and other theorists developed their postulates from subtle probes of children's beliefs. Although Vosniadou (2002) and Stavy (1994), for example, produced valuable insights from their studies of pre-school children, in the main most studies have been of single groups of children of elementary school age or older. To put theories on a sounder base requires two lines of research, both of considerable difficulty. One is to discover the beliefs of very young children, the other to conduct longitudinal studies. Both lines could, of course, be combined in the one study.

There are at least two difficulties in finding the beliefs of very young children. One is communication. The child might not understand what the researcher is getting at, or might not be interested in it. An instance occurred, not with very young children but with 6-year-olds, in Tytler's (2000) investigation of their understanding of change of state. Tytler had the children watch a puddle evaporate, then asked them to draw what they saw happen. In all the drawings the puddle was a minor feature: the children put their effort into drawing themselves and their classmates looking at the puddle. Even if children do comprehend the researcher's purpose, they might not be able to articulate their beliefs. The second difficulty is that the act of probing might cause children to create beliefs in order to respond, when up till that moment they had none. This possibility exists with older respondents also, but is a greater risk with the very young, who are less likely to have formed settled beliefs.

Longitudinal studies also have their difficulties. White and Arzi (2005) define a longitudinal study as one in which two or more measures of a comparable form are made of the same individuals over a period of at least one year. Taking repeated measures over a long period brings the problem of access. The researcher has to have the cooperation of those tested and also the permission of parents and authorities who have to be convinced of the benefit of the study, not just to the world of scholarship but also to the children for whom they are responsible. While co-operation and permission are necessary in all forms of investigation, they have to be maintained and are particularly salient in longitudinal research. A second problem is that a measure taken at one time may influence the response given at another. Any test or interview will produce change in knowledge and will also alert the respondent to what matters are of interest to the researcher. Thus a later measure is not of what the child would have believed, but of what the child believed through being sensitised to the topic by the earlier probing. This effect becomes greater as the number of measures increases.

Despite these problems, longitudinal studies such as that by Tytler (1998), for instance, should reveal much about the formation and development of conceptions. Tytler's study supports the theoretical postulate of diSessa (1983, 1988) that children acquire knowledge piecemeal and only gradually synthesise the pieces into comprehensive principles.

WHY WAS THE EARLY RESEARCH ON CONCEPTUAL CHANGE CONFINED LARGELY TO LEARNING OF SCIENCE?

For at least the first decade of the popularity of investigations of alternative conceptions and the beginnings of research on conceptual change, there were few studies in subjects other than science. This is well illustrated by the cases of the three international seminars organised for research presentations in this field by Novak at Cornell University in the 1980s. These seminars were titled "Misconceptions and educational strategies in science *and mathematics*" (emphasis added). Yet even though the seminars were clearly attempting to attract studies of mathematics learning, there were far fewer of these than science learning studies. For example, the three published volumes of papers from the second of these seminars contain a total of 162 separate reports. Of these, 22 focus on mathematics learning, 18 were in computing education or were cross discipline in their focus, and the rest (122) were about science learning.

Even within science, there is uneven spread across topics. Pfundt and Duit (1994) noted that, of the several thousand studies listed in their bibliography at that time, 66% were about physics. Within physics, force and motion, heat and temperature, floating and sinking, change of state, light propagation and vision, and electric current have received attention. Presumably researchers were concentrating on topics where experience before formal schooling would have occurred and caused children to create their own explanations. The explanations, obviously developed from experience, are in the form of the "phenomenological primitives" of diSessa or the intuitive rules of Stavy and Tirosh (2000). Researchers might have included electric current, even though it is not open to early experience, because of its importance in the syllabus for introductory physics, or because alternative beliefs may arise in it from inappropriate analogies (either generated by pupils themselves or communicated to them by a teacher), such as fuel being consumed or water flow. Few studies were published on beliefs about atomic structure, electric and magnetic fields, and sound, either because researchers did not do them or because they did not find any interesting alternative beliefs. Since sound is experienced from birth and children might well create early beliefs about its nature as they do for light, it is strange that few studies have probed beliefs about it.

Disciplines such as history, economics, music, and mathematics may encompass divergent beliefs, but do not require children to create explanations for events, or at least not as much as some physics topics do. They might, however, have their specific issues with conceptual change. In mathematics, for instance, it might be a major shift to perceive that mathematics is not just a set of operations involving numbers but a system of logic built on axioms and rules. Conceptual change could, then, differ in nature from discipline to discipline. Each discipline would then have its own theory of conceptual change (Limón, 2002). Accordingly, Mason (2002) suggests that teaching children about the ways in which knowledge is established in a discipline could facilitate conceptual change.

WHAT EFFECT DID THE EARLY RESEARCH ON ALTERNATIVE CONCEPTIONS AND CONCEPTUAL CHANGE HAVE ON TEACHING?

Educational research frequently receives criticism for lack of relevance to the classroom (e.g., Finn, 1988; Hargreaves, 1996). A counter charge is that teachers, isolated in their classrooms, make little effort to keep informed about relevant research. Whatever the general validity of these charges, they would appear to apply much less to research on alternative conceptions and conceptual change.

Before the first phase of research, the discovering of alternative beliefs, teachers were not aware of their extent. There was no mention of them in texts about pedagogy, in subject matter texts and their associated teachers' guides, and in teachers' professional journals. The accounts of alternative beliefs were a revelation to science teachers. They were also highly relevant. Where teachers might have disputed a claim from a contrived laboratory study that one method of teaching was superior to another, on grounds that it would not transfer to the complex world of the real classroom, they had less reason to doubt the results of a probe of understanding that was not open to the charge of artificiality. Teachers could replicate the probes easily with their own students. Many did, and some also took the significant step of writing about this researching of their own practice for other teachers (e.g., Hart, 1987; Lovejoy, 1995; Stanbridge, 1990; Vance & Miller, 1995).

A professional teacher, once alerted to the existence of alternative conceptions, would want to do something about it. The difficulties that researchers had encountered in the second phase of their studies showed, however, that this was unlikely to be a simple task.

The research in the second and third phases implies that it is inevitable that for many phenomena people will acquire a primitive model, which is not totally discarded on later learning of the scientific explanation. Even though a physicist understands well Newton's laws of motion, he or she still carries Aristotelian notions such as a force is needed to keep things moving. This is not a problem as long as the physicist recognises the contradiction. So one approach to alternative conceptions and conceptual change would be to get learners to be reflective, open to new beliefs, and able to recognise contradictions between beliefs and resolve them.

Two large-scale examples of training in reflective learning are Cognitive Acceleration through Science Education (Adey & Shayer, 1994) and the Project for Enhancing Effective Learning (Baird & Mitchell, 1986; Baird & Northfield, 1992). CASE is based in science classes, PEEL is more general although it originated from concern about science teaching and learning. Although different in methods and organization, CASE and PEEL recognise that there is no quick answer, no easy way to produce reflective learners overnight.

In sum, the brief, simply-designed studies that began in the 1970s to probe understanding alerted researchers and teachers to a previously unknown or overlooked problem in teaching and learning, and although much progress has occurred in research and theory, it remains a problem of great complexity as well as importance. It warrants attention still.

REFERENCES

Adey, P., & Shayer, M. (1994). *Really raising standards: Cognitive intervention and academic achievement.* London: Routledge

Baird, J. R., & Mitchell, I. J. (Eds.). (1986). *Improving the quality of teaching and learning: An Australian case study – the PEEL project.* Melbourne: Monash University Faculty of Education.

Baird, J. R., & Northfield, J. R. (Eds.). (1992). *Learning from the PEEL experience.* Melbourne: Monash University Faculty of Education.

Bell, B. F. (1981). When is an animal, not an animal. *Journal of Biological Education, 15*, 213–218.

Carey, S. (1985). *Conceptual change in childhood.* Cambridge, MA: MIT Press.

Champagne, A. B., Klopfer, L. E., & Anderson, J. H. (1980). Factors influencing the learning of classical mechanics. *American Journal of Physics, 48*, 1074–1079.

Champagne, A. B., Gunstone, R. F., & Klopfer, L. E. (1985). Effecting changes in cognitive structures among physics students. In L. H. T. West & A. L. Pines (Eds.), *Cognitive structure and conceptual change* (pp. 163–187). New York: Academic Press.

Di Sessa, A. A. (1983). Phenomenology and the evolution of intuition. In D. Gentner & A. L. Stevens (Eds.), *Mental models* (pp. 15–33). Hillsdale, N J: Erlbaum.

DiSessa, A. A. (1988). Knowledge in pieces. In G. Forman & A. Pufall (Eds.), *Constructivism in the computer age* (pp. 49–70). Hillsdale, NJ: Erlbaum.

Driver, R. (1983). *The pupil as scientist?* Milton Keynes: Open University Press.

Driver, R., & Easley, J. (1978). Pupils and paradigms: A review of literature related to development in adolescent science students. *Studies in Science Education, 5*, 61–84.

Finn, C. E. (1988). What ails education research? *Educational Researcher, 17*(1), 5–8.

Gauld, C. (1986). Models, meters, and memory. *Research in Science Education, 16*, 49–54.

Gunstone, R.F., & White, R.T. (1981). Understanding of gravity. *Science Education, 65*, 291–299.

Hargreaves, D. H. (1996). *Teaching as a research-based profession: Possibilities and prospects.* Teacher Training Agency Annual Lecture (Teacher Training Agency, London).

Hart, C. (1987). A teaching sequence for introducing forces to year 11 physics students. *Australian Science Teachers Journal, 33*(1), 25–28.

Hewson, M. G., & Hamlyn, D. (1984). The influence of intellectual environment on conceptions of heat. *European Journal of Science Education, 6*, 254–262

Limón, M. (2002). Conceptual change in history. In M. Limón & L. Mason (Eds.), *Reconsidering conceptual change: Issues in theory and practice* (pp. 259–289). Dordrecht, The Netherlands: Kluwer.

Lovejoy, C. (1995). Using students' conceptual knowledge to teach a junior secondary topic of circulation and respiration. In B. Hand & V. Prain (Eds.), *Teaching and learning in science: The constructivist classroom* (pp. 106–121). Sydney: Harcourt Brace.

Mason, L. (2002). Developing epistemological thinking to foster conceptual change in different domains. In M. Limón & L. Mason (Eds.), *Reconsidering conceptual change: Issues in theory and practice* (pp. 301–335). Dordrecht, The Netherlands: Kluwer.

Nussbaum, J., & Novak, J. D. (1976). An assessment of children's concepts of the Earth utilizing structured interviews. *Science Education, 60*, 535–550.

Oakes, M. E. (1945). Explanations of natural phenomena by adults. *Science Education, 29*, 137–142, 190–201.

Oakes, M. E. (1947). *Children's explanations of natural phenomena*. New York: Teachers College, Colombia University.

Oakes, M. E. (1957). Explanations by college students. *Science Education, 41*, 425–428.

Osborne, R. J. (1980*). Force* (Paper no. 16). Hamilton, New Zealand: University of Waikato, Learning in Science project.

Osborne, R. J., & Freyberg, P. (1985). *Learning in science: The implications of children's science*. Auckland: Heinemann.

Paivio, A. (1971). *Imagery and verbal processes*. New York: Holt, Rinehart, & Winston.

Pfundt, H., & Duit, R. (1994). *Bibliography: Students' alternative frameworks and science education* (4th ed.). Kiel: Institute for Science Education, University of Kiel.

Piaget, J. (1964). Development and learning. *Journal of Research in Science Teaching, 2*, 176–186.

Posner, G. J., Strike, K. A., Hewson, P. W., & Gertzog, W. A. (1982). Accommodation of a scientific conception: Toward a theory of conceptual change. *Science Education, 66*, 211–227.

Stanbridge, B. (1990). A constructivist model of learning used in the teaching of junior science. *Australian Science Teachers' Journal, 36*(4), 20–28.

Stavy, R. (1991). Using analogy to overcome misconceptions about conservation of matter. *Journal of Research in Science Teaching, 28,* 305–313.

Stavy, R. (1994). States of matter — Pedagogical sequence and teaching strategies based on cognitive research. In P. Fensham, R. Gunstone, & R. White (Eds.), *The content of science: A constructivist approach to its teaching and learning* (pp. 221–236). London: Falmer Press.

Stavy, R., & Tirosh, D. (2000). *How students (mis-)understand science and mathematics: Intuitive rules.* New York: Teachers' College Press.

Tiberghien, A., & Delacôte, G. (1976). Manipulation et représentations des circuits électriques simple par des enfants de 7 à 12 ans. *Revue Française de Pedagogie, 34*, 32–44.

Tytler, R. (1998). Children's conceptions of air pressure: Exploring the nature of conceptual change. *International Journal of Science Education, 20*, 929–958.

Tytler, R. (2000). A comparison of year 1 and year 6 students' conceptions of evaporation and condensation: Dimensions of conceptual progression. *International Journal of Science Education, 22,* 447–467.

Vance, K., & Miller, K. (1995). Setting up as a constructivist teacher: Examples from a middle secondary ecology unit. In B. Hand & V. Prain (Eds.), *Teaching and learning in science: The constructivist classroom* (pp. 85–105). Sydney: Harcourt Brace.

Vosniadou, S. (1994). Capturing and modelling the process of conceptual change. *Learning and Instruction, 4*, 45–69.

Vosniadou, S. (2002). On the nature of naïve physics. In M. Limón & L. Mason (Eds.), *Reconsidering conceptual change: Issues in theory and practice* (pp. 61–76). Dordrecht: Kluwer.

White, R. T. (2001). The revolution in research on science teaching. In V. Richardson (Ed.), *Handbook of research on teaching* (4th ed.) (pp. 457–471). New York: Macmillan.

White, R. T., & Arzi, H. J. (2005). Longitudinal studies: Designs, validity, practicality, and value. *Research in Science Education, 35*, 137–149.

24

Teaching Science for Conceptual Change: Theory and Practice

Reinders Duit
IPN – Leibniz Institute for Science Education at the University of Kiel

David F. Treagust
Science and Mathematics Education Centre, Curtin University

Ari Widodo
Indonesian University of Education

INTRODUCTION

This chapter contains two parts. In the first part, we discuss a range of theoretical perspectives giving rise to different notions of conceptual change and illustrate how researchers have conceptualized teaching and learning science from these different perspectives. In the second part, we report on studies about the awareness and implementation of these perspectives in regular science classes and document that there is still a large gap between what is known about effective teaching and learning science from conceptual change perspectives and the reality of instructional practice. Finally, we argue that more research is necessary on how teachers in regular classrooms can become more familiar with the key ideas of conceptual change.

THEORETICAL DEVELOPMENTS IN THE AREA OF CONCEPTUAL CHANGE

Over the past three decades, research has shown that students come to science classes with pre-instructional conceptions and ideas about the phenomena and concepts to be learned that are not in harmony with science views. Furthermore, these conceptions and ideas are firmly held and are resistant to change (Duit, 2006; Duit & Treagust, 1998, 2003). While studies on students' learning in science that primarily investigate conceptions on the content level continue to be produced, investigations of students' conceptions at meta-levels, namely conceptions of the nature of science and views of learning, also have been given considerable attention since the 1980s.

The 1980s saw the growth of studies investigating the development of students' pre-instructional conceptions towards the intended science concepts in conceptual change approaches.

Over the past three decades, research on students' conceptions and conceptual change has been embedded in various theoretical frames with epistemological, ontological and affective orientations (Duit & Treagust, 2003; Taber, 2006; Zembylas, 2005).

Research on the role of students' pre-instructional ("alternative") conceptions in learning science developed in the 1970s drawing primarily on two theoretical perspectives (Driver & Easley, 1978). The first was Ausubel's (1968) dictum that the most important single factor influencing learning is what the learner already knows and hence to teach the learner accordingly. The second theoretical perspective was Piaget's idea of the interplay of assimilation and accommodation. His clinical interview method deeply influenced research on investigating students' conceptions (White & Gunstone, 1992). By the end of the 1970s and the beginning of the 1980s, preliminary conceptual change ideas addressing students' conceptions were revealed in the various studies that developed.

Conceptual change viewed as epistemology, namely when the research looks at students' learning of concepts, initially involved only an understanding of how students' conceptions evolved. Later, constructivist ideas developed by merging various cognitive approaches with a focus on viewing knowledge as being constructed. These approaches were influenced by the already mentioned Piagetian interplay of assimilation and accommodation, Kuhnian ideas of theory change in the history of science and radical constructivism (Duit & Treagust, 1998).

As is discussed more later in this chapter, conceptual change viewed as ontology, namely how students view the nature of the conception being investigated, sought to examine the way that students viewed scientific conceptions in terms of reality. Conceptual change from an epistemological and an ontological perspective refers to students' personal views, on the nature of coming to know — what we refer to as epistemological in this chapter — and on the nature or reality — what we refer to as ontological.

Other researchers were concerned that conceptual change had initially taken on an over rational approach (Pintrich, Marx, & Boyle, 1993). Certain limitations of the constructivist ideas of the 1980s and early 1990s led to their merger with social constructivist and social cultural orientations that more recently resulted in recommendations to employ multi-perspective epistemological frameworks in order to adequately address the complex process of learning (Duit & Treagust, 2003; Tyson, Venville, Harrison, & Treagust, 1997; Zembylas, 2005).

An Epistemological Perspective of Conceptual Change

The "classical" conceptual change approach as introduced by Posner, Strike, Hewson, and Gertzog (1982) involved the teacher making students' alternative frameworks explicit prior to designing a teaching approach consisting of ideas that do not fit students' existing conceptions and thereby promoting dissatisfaction. A new framework is then introduced based on formal science that may explain the anomaly. However, it became obvious that students' conceptual progress towards understanding and learning science concepts and principles after instruction frequently turned out to be still limited. There appears to be no study which found that a particular student's conception could be completely extinguished and then replaced by the science view (Duit & Treagust, 1998). Indeed, most studies show that the old ideas stay alive in particular contexts. Usually, the best that can be achieved is a "peripheral conceptual change" (Chinn & Brewer, 1993) in that parts of the initial idea merge with parts of the new idea to form some sort of hybrid concept (Jung, 1993) or synthetic model (Vosniadou & Brewer, 1992).

In the classical conceptual change model that emphasised students' epistemologies (Posner et al., 1982), student dissatisfaction with a prior conception was believed to initiate dramatic or revolutionary conceptual change and was embedded in radical constructivist epistemological views with an emphasis on the individual's conceptions and his/her conceptual development. If the learner was dissatisfied with his/her prior conception *and* an available replacement conception was intelligible, plausible and/or fruitful, accommodation of the new conception may follow. An intelligible conception is sensible if it is non-contradictory and its meaning is understood by the student; plausible means that in addition to the student knowing what the conception means, he/she finds the conception believable; and, the conception is fruitful if it helps the learner solve other problems or suggests new research directions. Posner et al. insist that a plausible conception must first be intelligible and a fruitful conception must be intelligible and plausible. Resultant conceptual changes may be permanent, temporary or too tenuous to detect.

In this learning model, resolution of conceptual competition is explained in terms of the comparative intelligibility, plausibility and fruitfulness of rival conceptions. Posner et al. (1982) claimed that a collection of epistemological commitments called the student's conceptual ecology (Toulmin, 1972) mediated conceptual intelligibility, plausibility, and fruitfulness. Strike and Posner (1985, pp. 216–217) expanded the conceptual ecology metaphor to include anomalies, analogies and metaphors, exemplars and images, past experiences, epistemological commitments, metaphysical beliefs and knowledge in other fields.

Different ways that researchers have measured students' conceptual change from an epistemological position are conceptual status and epistemological profiles.

Students' Conceptual Status

Conceptual status classifies a conception's status as intelligible, plausible or fruitful (Hewson, 1982; Hewson & Lemberger, 2000; Hewson & Thorley, 1989) and is particularly useful for assessing changes in students' conceptions during learning. When a competing conception does not generate dissatisfaction, the new conception may be assimilated alongside the old. When dissatisfaction between competing conceptions reveals their incompatibility, two conceptual events may happen. If the new conception achieves higher status than the prior conception, accommodation, which Hewson (1982) terms *conceptual exchange*, may occur. If the old conception retains higher status, conceptual exchange will not proceed for the time being. It should be remembered that a replaced conception is not forgotten and the learner may wholly or partly reinstate it at a later date. Both Posner et al. (1982) and Hewson (1982) stress that it is the student, not the teacher, who makes the decisions about conceptual status and conceptual changes. This position is in harmony with constructivist learning theory and the highly personal nature of mental models (Norman, 1983).

Studies utilising the notion of conceptual status include that by Treagust, Harrison, Venville and Dagher (1996) which set out to assess the efficacy of using analogies to engender conceptual change in students' science learning about the refraction of light. Following instruction by the same teacher, two classes of students, one of which was taught analogically and one that was not, were interviewed three months after instruction using an interview-about-instances protocol. Factors related to status were identified from the interview transcripts to help in the process of classifying each student's conception of refraction as being intelligible, plausible or fruitful. Hewson and Hennessey (1992, p. 177) developed descriptors to guide this process, and these were used in the research. For example, descriptors for intelligible included "I must know what the concept means — the words must be understandable, the words must make sense"; descriptors for plausible included "'it first must be intelligible — it must fit in with other ideas or concepts I know about or believe"; descriptors for fruitful included "it first must be intelligible it should be plausible and I can see it is something as useful — it will help me solve problems."

Most of the evidence from this study indicated that conceptual change which meets the criteria of dissatisfaction, intelligibility, plausibility and fruitfulness is not necessarily an exchange of conceptions for another, but rather an increased use of the kind of conception that makes better sense to the student. The two groups of students performed similarly on the teacher's classroom test. However, when students were interviewed and their conceptions were analysed graphically with elements of status — no status, intelligibility, plausibility and fruitfulness — on the ordinate and test scores on the abscissa, those student in the class introduced to the analogy held conceptions of higher status than those students in the class who were not introduced to the analogy. Consequently, the application of the idea of status of a conception showed the degree to which students understood, believed and were able to apply their scientific knowledge to otherwise unsolved problems. Nevertheless, the research showed that an increased status of a conception made possible by analogical teaching does not necessarily lead to different learning outcomes as measured on traditional tests.

Epistemological and Conceptual Profiles

A different but useful way to understand student reactions to multiple conceptions or models is Bachelard's (1968) epistemological profile. People often possess more than one way for describing objects and processes, and this is especially so in science. For example, mass can be described in everyday terms of "bigness," measured instrumentally using a spring balance, expressed in dynamic terms like F = ma or relativistically. Scientists use different methods depending on context so why should not students use the same differences as they learn? What may appear to be a change in conception by a scientist or a student could simply be a contextually-based preference for one conception or model over another. For instance, many secondary teachers and textbooks simultaneously use the electron shell or Bohr model when discussing atomic structure, use balls or space-filling models to explain kinetic theory and Lewis electron-dot diagrams for bonding.

The ability to select intelligible, plausible and fruitful representations or conceptions for a specific context is itself a measure of expertise; however, researchers need to be aware that apparent conceptual changes may in fact be context-driven choices rather than conceptual status changes. In learning settings, Mortimer (1995) proposed the use of conceptual profiles to help differentiate conceptual changes from contextual choices.

An Ontological Perspective of Conceptual Change

Researchers who use epistemology to explain conceptual changes do not overtly emphasize changes in the way students view reality. Other researchers, however, use specific ontological terms to explain changes in the way students develop their science conceptions (Chi, Slotta, & de Leeuw, 1994; Thagard, 1992; Vosniadou, 1994). Chinn and Brewer (1993, p. 17) described ontological beliefs as being about "the fundamental categories and properties of the world." In showing that "some of the child's concepts are incommensurable with the adults'," Carey (1985, p. 269) argued for strong knowledge restructuring during childhood, and Vosniadou called similar changes radical restructuring and explained that revisions to central "framework theories" (pp. 46–49) involve both ontological and epistemological changes. Chi et al. (1994) called their strongest ontological changes "Tree swapping" and Thagard (1992) also has a strongest change which he calls "tree switching." Two candidates for these types of change are heat which needs to change from a flowing fluid to kinetic energy in transit and a gene which needs to change from an inherited object to a biochemical process. There are many other concepts where scientists' *process* views are incommensurable with students' *material* conceptions, and the desired changes to students' ontologies are not often achieved in school science. Chiu, Chou, and Liu (2002) adopted Chi's ontological categories of scientific concepts to investigate how students perceived the concept of chemical equilibrium, arguing that "although Posner's theory is widely accepted by science educators and easy to comprehend and apply to learning activities, … it does not delineate what the nature of a scientific concept is, which causes difficulty in learning the concept" (p. 689).

An Affective Position of Conceptual Change

The third focus of conceptual change is the affective domain, particularly involving emotions, motivation and social aspects such as group work which has had limited attention in the epistemological position and no attention in the ontological position. Pintrich et al. (1993) proposed that a hot irrational explanation for conceptual change is as tenable as cold cognition and argued that students' self-efficacy and control beliefs, the classroom social context, and the individual's goals, intentions, purposes, expectations and needs are as important as cognitive strategies in concept learning. Similarly, Solomon (1987) and Dykstra, Boyle, and Monarch (1992) claim that group factors can advantage concept learning, and Vygotsky's theories (van der Veer & Valsiner, 1991) highlight the importance of social and motivational influences. Pintrich et al.'s review of the social and motivational literature highlights the importance of interest, personal and situational beliefs to students' engagement in learning activities. Indeed, they claim that teachers who ignore the social and affective aspects of personal and group learning may limit conceptual change. In a recent review of linking the cognitive and the emotional in teaching and learning science, Zembylas (2005) goes a step further arguing that it is necessary to develop a unity between the cognitive and emotional dimensions that views emotions not only as a moderating variable of cognitive outcomes but as a variable of equal status.

Intentional Conceptual Change

Recent studies in an edited volume, *Intentional Conceptual Change,* by Sinatra and Pintrich (2003) emphasized the importance of the learner, suggesting that the learner should play an active intentional role in the process of knowledge restructuring. While acknowledging the important contributions to the study of conceptual change from the perspectives of science education and cognitive developmental psychology, Sinatra and Pintrich note that the psychological and educational literature of the 1980s and 1990s placed greater emphasis on the role of the learner in the learning process. It is this emphasis on the impetus for change being within the learner's control that forms the basis of the chapters in the text. The notion of intentional conceptual change is in some ways analogous to that of mindfulness (Salomon & Globerson, 1987, p. 623), a "construct which reflects a voluntary state of mind, and connects among motivation, cognition and learning."

Multidimensional Perspectives of Conceptual Change

Conceptual change approaches as developed in the 1980s and early 1990s contributed substantially to improving our understanding of science learning and teaching. Most studies on learning science so far have been oriented towards views of learning that are monistic to a certain extent. Only recently have there been powerful developments towards admitting that the complex phenomenon of learning needs pluralistic epistemological frameworks (Greeno, Collins, & Resnick, 1997) in order to adequately address the many facets emphasised by different views of learning. In science education, there are a growing number of multi-perspectives of conceptual change which appear to be promising to improve science teaching and learning (Duit, 1998; Duit & Treagust, 1998, 2003; Zembylas, 2005). Briefly summarized, multi-perspectives of conceptual change that consider epistemological, ontological and affective domains have to be employed in order to adequately address the complexity of the teaching and learning processes. Only such frameworks can sufficiently model teaching and learning processes and address the ambitious levels of scientific literacy that are presented in the following paragraphs.

Much of the research on conceptual change has taken a particular perspective, namely an epistemological perspective, an ontological perspective or an affective perspective. There is ample of evidence in research on learning and instruction that cognitive and affective issues are closely linked. However, the number of studies on the interaction of cognitive and affective factors in the learning process is limited. There are, for instance, many studies on the relations between interest in science and acquisition of science concepts. However, these studies are usually restricted to correlations between interest in science and cognitive results of learning. The interplay of changes of interest in science and conceptual change has been investigated only in a small number of studies. The multi-dimensional perspectives for interpreting conceptual change by Tyson, Venville, Harrison, and Treagust (1997) includes, for instance, an epistemological, an ontological and an affective domain, though the affective domain has not been fully elaborated. A fruitful outcome for future studies is to merge ideas of conceptual change and theories on the significance of affective factors. It also seems to be most valuable to view the issue of interest in science and science teaching from the perspective of conceptual change. Clearly, an important aim of science instruction is to develop interest in much the same way as to develop students' pre-instructional conceptions towards the intended science concepts.

In contrast to the approach of being committed to one theoretical perspective of conceptual change as a framework for their data analysis and interpretation, Venville and Treagust (1998) utilized four different perspectives of conceptual change to analyse different classroom teaching situations in which analogies were used to teach genetics (also see Venville, Gribble, & Donovan, 2005). The authors used Posner et al.'s (1982) conceptual change model, Vosniadou's (1994) framework theory and mental model perspective, Chi et al.'s (1994) ontological categories, and Pintrich et al.'s (1993) motivation perspective. Venville and Treagust (1998) found that each of the perspectives of conceptual change had explanatory value and contributed a different theoretical perspective on interpreting the role that analogies played in each of the classroom situations. For example, the epistemological perspective in terms of students' conceptions of genes indicated the degree of acceptance of the conception by the students. In this study, there was likely concordance with the status of the conception and different ontological models that students used to think about genes. From a social affective perspective, almost all these grade 10 students demonstrated in interviews that they were not interested in the microscopic explanatory nature of genetics, preferring to use simple Mendelian genetics to answer questions about themselves.

THE ROLE OF COGNITIVE CONFLICT IN CONCEPTUAL CHANGE

Cognitive conflict has played a major role in various conceptual change approaches since the advent of classical conceptual change approaches in the early 1980s. As mentioned earlier, Piagetian ideas of the interplay of assimilation and accommodation have provided a powerful framework for conceptual change. Cognitive conflict plays a key role in Piagetian approaches such as the "learning cycle" (Karplus, 1977; Lawson, Abraham, & Renner, 1989) and hence also in conceptual change approaches like "constructivist teaching sequences" (Driver, 1989; Scott, Asoko, & Driver, 1992). In these constructivist approaches, however, not only Piagetian ideas but also Festingers' theory of cognitive dissonance is referred to (Driver & Erickson, 1983). Hashweh (1986) provided a critical view of the role of cognitive conflict in learning science, arguing that various forms of cognitive conflicts have to be distinguished and that it is essential that students actually experience the conflict.

Studies on the use of cognitive conflict reveal conflicting results. Guzetti, Snyder, Glass, and Gamas (1993) carried out a meta-analysis of conceptual change approaches. Those approaches employing cognitive conflict strategies were found to be more efficient than studies in which this was not the case. Some studies (e.g., Limon & Carretero, 1999; Mason, 2001) report that cognitive conflict may be linked with positive learning results such that these can facilitate conceptual change while other studies (e.g., Chan, Burtis, & Bereiter, 1997) showed that cognitive conflict may also be inefficient because even when students are confronted with contradictory information, they do not necessarily change their conceptions. In a review on the effectiveness of strategies for facilitating conceptual change within constructivist frameworks, Harlen (1999) suggested that there is no convincing evidence about the effectiveness of one strategy over the other. Vosniadou and Ioannides (1998) argued (see also Limon, 2001) that the conceptual change approaches as developed in the 1980s and early 1990s put too much emphasis on sudden insights facilitated by cognitive conflict. They claimed that learning science should be viewed as a "gradual process during which initial conceptual structures based on children's interpretations of everyday experience are continuously enriched and restructured" (p. 1213). Briefly summarized, research has shown that much care is needed if cognitive conflict strategies are used for facilitating conceptual change. It is not only necessary to carefully ensure that students experience the conflict but also to consider the role of specific, usually small scale, sudden insights within the long-lasting gradual process of conceptual change.

Impact of Research on Conceptual Change in School Practice

As outlined in the previous part, conceptual change has became a powerful domain of research on teaching and learning that developed in the early 1970s. Since this time, cognitive psychologists and science educators have worked closely together with both domains of educational research substantially profiting from this cooperation. However, what also became evident in reviewing the literature is a certain polarisation of researchers in the two domains such that one can read exellent research in one domain that has little reference to research in the other domain. The text by Sinatra and Pintrich (2003), for instance, brings many of these researchers together in one volume. But this is not always the case, as for example in the very informative text by Limon and Mason (2003) based on a symposium as part of the activities of a Special Interest Group of the European Association for Research on Learning and Instruction (EARLI), where there are virtually no references to science education and science education researchers who have worked in this area. Our intention is that the present review can help to overcome this issue of polarization of the two research domains.

In the research domain of conceptual change as outlined, multidimensional theoretical perspectives allow researchers to investigate teaching and learning processes at a fine-grained level. The perspectives also provide support for the design of teaching and learning environments that usually are superior to more traditional instructional designs. In principle, there is a large potential for improving practice. However, so far the research evidence concerning the impact of teaching informed by conceptual change instructional practices in normal classes is still rather limited. We address this issue in the following paragraphs.

Are Conceptual Change Approaches More Efficient than More Traditional Ones?

Usually, researchers who use a conceptual change approach in their classroom-based studies report that their approach is more efficient than traditional ones. Predominantly, efficiency concerns exclusively or predominantly cognitive outcomes of instruction. The development of affective variables during instruction is often not viewed as the outcome per se. This appears to be only the case in more recent multi-dimensional conceptual change perspectives that consider both cognitive and affective outcomes of learning as conceptual change as discussed by Tyson et al. (1997) and Zembylas (2005).

Quite frequently, individual research studies do provide convincing empirical evidence for this claim (e.g., more recently Bryce & MacMillan, 2005; Piquette & Heikkinen, 2005) though an actual summarizing meta-analysis is not available. Previously, Guzetti et al. (1993) provided a meta-analysis that included studies that only employed a treatment-control group design, and Wandersee, Mintzes, and Novak (1994) reviewed conceptual change approaches with a cautious remark that their analysis gave the impression that conceptual change approaches usually are more successful than traditional approaches in guiding students to the science concepts. However, a problem with research on conceptual change is that it is difficult to compare the success of conceptual change approaches and other approaches. Usually different approaches to teaching and learning address different aims, and hence it is only possible to evaluate whether the particular aims have been adequately met. An additional problem is that quite frequently the focus of conceptual change approaches is on particular pedagogical means like analogies (Bryce & Mac-Millan, 2005). Research on instructional quality, however, has shown that usually a single intervention (like addressing students' preinstructional conceptions) does not lead to better outcomes per se (Weinert, Schrader, & Helmke, 1989; Baumert & Köller, 2000). Quality of instruction is always due to a certain orchestration (Oser & Baeriswyl, 2001) of various instructional methods and strategies. Hence, conceptual change strategies may only be efficient if they are embedded in a conceptual change supporting learning environment that includes many additional features.

In summarizing the state of research on the efficiency of conceptual change approaches, there appears to be ample evidence in various studies that these approaches are more efficient than traditional approaches dominated by transmissive views of teaching and learning. This seems to be the case in particular if more inclusive conceptual change approaches based on multi-dimensional perspectives as outlined above are employed. Recent large scale programs to improve the quality of science instruction (as well as instruction in other domains) include instructional methods that are clearly oriented toward constructivist conceptual change approaches, i.e., attempts to set constructivist principles of teaching and learning into practice (Beeth, Duit, Prenzel, Ostermeier, Tytler, & Wickman, 2003). The other characteristics of quality development approaches by Beeth et al. (2003) refer to: (1) Supporting schools and teachers to rethink the representation of science in the curriculum; (2) Enlarging the repertoire of tasks, experiments, and teaching and learning strategies and resources; and (3) Promoting strategies and resources that attempt to increase students' engagement and interests. Clearly, this set of characteristics requires the teachers to be reflective practitioners (Schoen, 1983) with a non-transmissive view of teaching and learning. The students need to be seen as active, self-responsible, co-operative and self-reflective learners. Indeed, these features are at the heart of inclusive constructivist conceptual change approaches.

Scientific Literacy and Conceptual Change Approaches

The 1990s saw another intensive debate on the aims of science instruction, in many countries, namely preparing students for the demands of the 21st century (de Boer, 2000; Millar & Osborne, 1998). A widely accepted view of scientific literacy is the conception developed for the international monitoring study PISA 2000 (Programme for International Student Assesment; OECD, 1999). In PISA, scientific literacy is seen as the capacity to identify questions and to draw evidence-based conclusions in order to understand and help to make decisions about the natural world and the changes made to it through human activity. This is a rather ambitious definition which includes student competencies not only at the level of understanding science concepts and principles but also comprises understanding of science inquiry as well as views about the nature of science. Further, the focus is not only on understanding but also on using knowledge and views in everyday situations (including issues of relevance of science for modern societies). It appears that such an ambitious definition of scientific literacy may only be set into practice if the multi-dimensional conceptual change perspectives as outlined above provide the framework for instructional design. Such frameworks are at the heart of recent quality development programmes mentioned by Beeth et al. (2003).

Teachers' Views of Teaching and Learning Science

In discussing opportunities to implement science standards in the United States, Anderson and Helms (2001) highlighted the major obstacles to success — teachers usually are not well informed about the recent state of research on teaching and learning science and hold views of teaching and learning that are predominantly transmissive and not constructivist. In many studies investigating teachers' views about teaching and learning carried out since the 1990s (Duit, 2006), it becomes apparent that science teachers usually hold rather limited views of teaching and learning science. Research shows that this limited view not only holds for science but for other instructional domains as well (Borko, 2004). In their teacher professional development approach of content-focused coaching, West and Staub (2003) claimed that it is essential to encourage teachers to become familiar with the recent state of educational research and to help develop their views about efficient teaching and learning.

A video-study on the practice of German and Swiss lower secondary physics instruction supports the above findings. In the first phase of this study, 13 German teachers participated; in the second phase, 50 German and 40 Swiss teachers were involved from a variety of randomly selected schools (Prenzel, Seidel, Lehrke, Rimmele, Duit, Euler, Geiser, Hoffmann, Müller, & Widodo, 2002; Seidel, Rimmele, & Prenzel, 2005). In these two phases, lessons of each teacher were videotaped, and additional data on teachers' thinking were provided by questionnaires and interviews. Findings from the first phase concerning the practice of physics instruction and teachers' views of teaching and learning science were summarized by Duit, Widodo, and Wodzinski (2007). Additional data from the second phase are available from Duit, Fischer, Labudde, Brückmann, Gerber, Kauertz, Knierim, and Tesch (2005) and Seidel, Rimmele, and Prenzel (2005).

Analysis of these data showed that most teachers are not well informed about key ideas of conceptual change research. Their views of their students' learning usually are not consistent with the state of recent theories of teaching and learning. Indeed, many teachers appear to lack an explicit view of learning. Several teachers hold implicit theories that contain some intuitive constructivist issues; for instance, they want to be learning counselors, and they are aware of the importance of students' cognitive activity and the interpreting nature of students' observations and understanding. However, teachers were identified who characterized themselves as mediators of facts and information and who were not aware of students' interpretational frameworks and the role of students' pre-instructional conceptions. These teachers mostly think that what they consider to be good instruction is a guarantee for successful learning.

The teachers' views and beliefs about good physics teaching and learning as revealed by the teacher interviews also showed a rich repertoire of thinking patterns about instruction on the one hand and a certain narrowness on the other (Müller, 2004). Many teachers hold elaborated ideas about their way of teaching. However, considerations about the content in question predominate teacher planning. Reflections about students' perspectives and their role in the learning process play a comparably minor role.

Briefly summarized, two general orientations of instruction may be distinguished from the video-study: (1) *Transmissive* — Oriented towards physics with a focus on physics concepts and learning viewed as knowledge transmission; (2) *Constructivist* — Focus on student learning, in particular which conditions are necessary to support learning, with learning viewed as student construction.

The transmissive orientation predominates teaching behaviour and teachers' beliefs. There is a large gap between the kind of thinking about efficient teaching and learning physics as discussed in the research-based literature and the thinking of the teachers in this study. The above characteristics of teacher thinking about teaching and learning physics are valid for the above small sample of 13 teachers, but the subsequent video-study carried out in some 90 classes in Germany and Switzerland led to similar findings. However, more formal analyses are only in progress. Similar findings concerning teachers' limited familiarity of constructivist conceptual change ideas and rather limited views of teaching and learning also are reported from another video-study conducted in German classrooms (Reyer, 2004).

The Practice of Teaching Science in Normal Classes

The literature on the actual practice of science instruction in normal classes is not extensive. But there are several studies showing that normal instructional practice is somewhat far from what multi-perspective conceptual change approaches outlined in this chapter. This may be expected taking into account the findings on teachers' limited views of teaching and learning science presented in the previous section. A number of studies on teachers' views also provide information on their teaching practice (cf. Anderson & Helms, 2001) with findings from studies that deliberately address the issue of investigating practice discussed below.

In summarizing findings of student narratives from interpretive studies on students' experiences of school science in Sweden, England, and Australia, Lyons (2006, p. 595) pointed out that "students in the three studies frequently described school science pedagogy as the transmission of content expert sources — teachers and texts — to relative passive recipients." It is interesting to note that students were overwhelmingly critical of this kind of teaching practice, leaving them with an impression of science as being a body of knowledge to be memorized.

The seminal TIMSS Video Study on Mathematics Teaching (Stigler, Gonzales, Kawanaka, Knoll, & Serrano, 1999; Stigler, Gallimore, & Hiebert, 2000) compared the practice of instruction in the United States, Japan, and Germany. Instruction was observed to be primarily teacher-oriented and instructional scripts based at transmissive views of teaching and learning predominated. However, it also became apparent that there are significant differences between the participating countries according to the degree of constructivist-oriented teaching and learning. In Japan, for instance, students had many more opportunities for self-guided problem solving than in the other two countries. Although instruction in Japan was also teacher controlled, students spent much of the class time solving problems using a variety of strategies. This was not the case in the German and the United States mathematics classrooms.

The TIMSS Video Study on science teaching (Roth, Druker, Garnier, Chen, Kawanaka, Rasmussen, Trubacova, Warvi, Okamoto, Gonzales, Stigler, & Gallimore, 2006) investigated the instructional scripts of science teaching in five countries: Australia, Czech Republic, Japan, The Netherlands, and the United States. Again, the predominating impression was instructional scripts informed by traditional transmissive views of teaching and learning. However, instructional features oriented towards constructivist conceptual change perspectives, though not frequent, did occur to different degrees in the participating countries.

The video-study discussed previously in German and Swiss schools on the practice of physics instruction resulted in similar findings. Specifically, there was a strong teacher dominance in German physics instruction though students worked in groups or individually for 15% of the lesson time (Duit et al., 2005). Nevertheless, in this somewhat narrow kind of classroom discourse, experiments played a significant role in instruction but students had few opportunities for self-organized inquiry. In Switzerland, instruction was less teacher-dominated and there were also significantly more opportunities for student inquiry. But still, the percentage of instruction oriented toward constructivist conceptual change views was small.

For the first phase of the above physics video-study, more detailed analyses from constructivist conceptual change perspectives are available (Duit, Widodo, & Wodzinski, 2007). In his investigation of the practice of instruction from constructivist perspectives, including deliberate analyses from the point of view of conceptual change strategies, Widodo (2004) observed that the teaching behaviour of several teachers comprised various features that were characteristic of constructivist-oriented science classrooms. In these classrooms, teachers provided, for instance, cognitive activity by addressing thought-provoking questions as well as incorporating certain features of conceptual change supporting conditions such as dealing with everyday phenomena. Further, a key phase of constructivist-oriented teaching sequences (Driver, 1989), namely, elicitation of students' pre-instructional knowledge frequently occurred as did teachers dealing with students' conceptions, another key phase of conceptual change approaches. However, cognitive conflict was infrequent; usually, the teachers attempted to guide students step-by-step from their own ideas to the science views. Such attempts to elicitate students' ideas and to address them were not deliberately linked. For example, after extended elicitation of what students already knew about electricity or forces, the findings usually did not play any significant role in subsequent instruction. Seldom were students' initial ideas explicitly taken into account when elaborating their conceptions. Finally, there were limited examples where students followed their own ideas in the video data, indicating that students had little voice in instruction.

Briefly summarized, the normal practice of science instruction described in the above studies was not significantly informed by constructivist conceptual change perspectives. Of course, there was a large variance within the educational culture of certain countries and also between the educational cultures of the countries. But still there is a large gap between instructional design based on recent research findings on conceptual change and what is normal practice in most of the classes observed.

Conceptual Change and Teacher Professional Development

Investigating teachers' views of teaching and learning science and the means to improve teachers' views and their instructional behaviour through teacher professional development has developed into a research domain that has been given much attention since the late 1990s (Borko, 2004). Two major issues are addressed in teacher professional development projects. First, teachers are made familiar with research knowledge on teaching and learning by being introduced to recent constructivist and conceptual change views and are made familiar with instructional design that is oriented toward these views. Second, attempts to link their own content knowledge and their pedagogical knowledge play a major role. The most prominent theoretical perspective applied is Shulman's (1987) idea of content specific pedagogical knowledge — briefly referred to as PCK — Pedagogical Content Knowledge (Gess-Newsome, & Lederman, 1999; van Driel, Verloop, & de Vos, 1998; West & Staub, 2003).

The process of teacher professional development can be viewed as a set of substantial conceptual changes that teachers have to undergo. As briefly outlined in a previous section of the present chapter, teachers' views of teaching and learning are limited when seen from the perspective of the implemented constructivist conceptual change ideas about teaching and learning. Instead, deep changes are necessary. Learning to teach for conceptual change means "that teachers must undergo a process of pedagogical conceptual changes themselves" (Stofflett, 1994, p. 787).

Hence, the conceptual change perspectives developed to analyze student learning should also be valuable frameworks for teacher learning. In fact, there are several attempts to apply these frameworks in teacher education. Stofflett (1994) primarily draws on the classical conceptual change model by Posner et al. (1982) using the conceptual change quadriga of intelligibility-plausibility-dissatisfaction-fruitfulness to analyse the change processes in a teacher development project. A similar approach to teacher development using the theoretical base of classical conceptual change was proposed by Feldman (2000) who argued that because teacher practical reasoning is similar to scientific reasoning, "a model of practical conceptual change can be developed that is analogous to the conceptual change model" (Feldman, 2000, p. 606).

This classical conceptual change model by Posner et al. also provided the major orientation of a large study on professional development of biology teachers (Hewson, Tabachnick, Zeichner, Blomker, Meyer, Lemberger, Marion, Park, & Toolin, 1999a; Hewson, Tabachnick, Zeichner, & Lemberger, 1999b). Constructivist perspectives with a particular emphasis on the classical conceptual change model were observed to provide a powerful framework to design the change processes that teachers had to undergo and to analyse the characteristics of these processes. Interestingly, the changes that were initiated not only comprised teachers' views about teaching and learning but also their views of science and the nature of knowledge (Hewson et al., 1999a, p. 254): "… we use the term conception of teaching science as an inclusive one that encompasses science (the nature of science, scientific knowledge, etc.), learning, and instruction, and the relationships between these three conceptions." The various analyses that were provided clearly showed that conceptual change perspectives may not only provide powerful frameworks for designing and analysing student learning but also for teacher learning.

It is important to note, however, that attempts to explicitly employ the more recent multidimensional and inclusive conceptual change perspectives as outlined in the first part of the present chapter, currently appear to be missing. Clearly, Hewson et al. (1999a, b) take into account teacher change processes of various kinds, but the conceptual change perspectives applied appear to be largely concerned with teachers' epistemologies.

CONCLUSIONS

The present chapter discusses two distinct but closely connected issues concerning teaching science for conceptual change. In the first part, we provide on overview of theoretical conceptual change perspectives that have developed since the 1970s and that have been employed to design approaches that allow for teaching science more effectively than with instructional designs drawing on transmissive views of teaching and learning. In the second part, we discuss situations where conceptual change perspectives have been put into practice in normal schools.

Concerning the first part, it becomes obvious that conceptual change has developed to one of the leading paradigms in research on teaching and learning. It is interesting to see a continuous progress over the three decades since early conceptual change research occurred. As science educators, we note that science education research contributed greatly to the development of the broader research domain of conceptual change.

Very briefly summarized, we witness a development from early conceptual change perspectives based on Piagetian, Ausubelian, Kuhnian, and further epistemological views. In general, the conceptual change ideas of the early 1980s were based on individualistic and somewhat radical constructivist views. Only later, in parallel with the development of constructivist ideas towards including variants of social constructivism, more inclusive views of conceptual change have developed.

It is noteworthy that also the definition of what changes in conceptual change has changed substantially over the past three decades. Initially, the term change was frequently used in a somewhat naïve way — if seen from the inclusive perspectives that have since developed. The term *conceptual change* was even frequently misunderstood as exchange of the students' prein-structional (or alternative) views for the science view. However, it became clear very soon that such an exchange is not possible. Major meanings given to the term *conceptual change* (such as status change proposed by Hewson and Hennessey, 1992) are discussed in the first part of the present chapter. Conceptual change now denotes that learning science includes various changes of perspectives. Most of these changes of epistemological and ontological perspectives are not simple but rather difficult as the "everyday" perspectives and the science perspectives often are not in accordance but are at best complementary.

The role given to affective issues in the process of conceptual change is also worth noting. Already the classical conceptual change approach (Posner et al., 1982) included affective issues, but only implicitly. Pintrich et al. (1993) initiated attempts to investigate the role of emotions, interests, and motivation more fully. Affective issues were, however, mainly viewed as variables moderating conceptual change. Only more recently, cognitive and affective perspectives are viewed as equally important with both having to undergo substantial conceptual changes during instruction (Zembylas, 2005). This more recent view also provides cognitive and affective outcomes of instruction with the same importance.

Instructional design oriented at conceptual change perspectives has proven more efficient than traditional design oriented toward transmissive views of teaching and learning. However, a cautious remark is needed here: A formal meta-analysis supporting this claim is so far not available.

The significance of instructional design oriented at recent inclusive conceptual change perspectives for improving practices is twofold. First, recent, rather ambitious and multi-faceted conceptions of scientific literacy may be set into practice only if instructional design is informed by inclusive conceptual change perspectives. Second, as mentioned, usually such design leads to improved learning outcomes. For this reason, it appears that recent quality development approaches in science education are based on these designs.

In a nutshell, research on conceptual change has developed to a rich and significant domain of educational research since the 1970s. The theoretical frameworks and research methods developed allow fine-grained analyses of teaching and learning processes. The findings of research provide powerful guidance for the development of instructional design for science education that societies need.

However, there is a large gap between what is known in the research domain of conceptual change about more efficient teaching and learning and what may be set into practice in normal classes. In the second part of the present chapter, we argue that teachers usually are not well informed about actual views of efficient teaching and learning available in the research community. Most teachers hold views that are limited if seen from the recent inclusive conceptual change perspectives. At best, some isolated features of these perspectives are embedded within predominantly transmissive views. Further, instructional practice is also usually far from a practice that is informed by conceptual change perspectives. Taking into account teachers' deeply rooted views of what they perceive to be good instruction, it becomes apparent that various closely linked conceptual changes on the teachers' beliefs about teaching and learning are necessary to commence and set recent conceptual change views into practice.

Although much research is now carried out on teacher professional development, the research community involved in conceptual change appears to contribute only marginally to investigating opportunities to implement their results and ideas into practice. It may be argued that many conceptual change strategies have been developed and evaluated in actual classrooms and often in close cooperation with teachers (e.g., Driver, 1989; Biemanns, Deel, & Simons, 2001; Vosniadou, Dimitrakopoulou, & Papademetriou, 2001) but what works in special arrangements does not necessarily work in everyday practice.

The state of theory-building on conceptual change has become more and more sophisticated and the teaching and learning strategies developed have become more and more complex over the past 30 years. Of course, these developments are necessary in order to address the complex phenomena of teaching and learning science more and more adequately. But it appears that the gap between what is necessary from the researchers' perspective and what may be set into practice by normal teachers has increased. Maybe we have to address the paradox that in order to adequately model teaching and learning processes, research alienates the teachers and hence widens the theory-practice gap.

The message of the present chapter is that we should deal with this paradox. Taking into account the state of research on conceptual change as presented in the present handbook, the focus is on further developing theoretical frameworks, research methods, and more efficient conceptual change instructional strategies. However, in which way all this may become part of actual practice has been given little attention. Interestingly, the frameworks of student conceptual change — being predominantly researched so far — may also provide powerful frameworks for teacher change towards employing conceptual change ideas. There are attempts to use this potential as discussed above. However, more research in this field based on the recent inclusive conceptual change perspectives is most desirable.

REFERENCES

Anderson, R. D., & Helms, J. V. (2001). The ideal of standards and the reality of schools: needed research. *Journal of Research in Science Teaching, 38*, 3–16.

Ausubel, D. P. (1968). *Educational psychology: A cognitive view.* New York: Holt, Rinehart and Winston.

Bachelard, G. (1968). *The philosophy of No. A philosophy of the new scientific mind.* New York: The Orion Press.

Baumert, J., & Köller, O. (2000). Unterrichtsgestaltung, verständnisvolles Lernen und multiple Zielerreichung im Mathematik- und Physikunterricht der gymnasialen Oberstufe [Instructional design, learning and achievement of multiple goals in mathematics and science upper secondary instruction]. In J. Baumert, W. Bos, & R. Lehmann (Eds.), *TIMSS/III. Dritte Internationale Mathematik- und Naturwissenschaftsstudie. Vol. 2.* (pp. 271–315). Opladen, Germany: Leske + Budrich.

Beeth, M., Duit, R., Prenzel, M., Ostermeier, C., Tytler, R., & Wickman, P.O. (2003). Quality development projects in science education. In D. Psillos, P. Kariotoglou, V. Tselfes, G. Fassoulopoulos, E. Hatzikraniotis, & M. Kallery (Eds.), *Science education research in the knowledge based society* (pp. 447–457). Dordrecht, The Netherlands: Kluwer Academic Publishers.

Biemanns, H. J. A., Deel, O. R., & Simons, P. R.-J. (2001). Differences between successful and less successful students while working with the CONTACT-2 strategy. *Learning and Instruction, 11*, 265–282.

Borko, H. (2004). Professional development and teacher learning: Mapping the terrain. *Educational Researcher, 33*, 3–15.

Bryce, T., & MacMillan, K. (2005). Encouraging conceptual change: the use of bridging analogies in the teaching of action-reaction forces and the 'at rest' condition in physics. *International Journal of Science Education, 27*, 737–763.

Carey, S. (1985). *Conceptual change in childhood.* Cambridge, MA: The MIT Press.

Chan, C., Burtis, J., & Bereiter, C. (1997). Knowledge building as a mediator of conflict in conceptual change. *Cognition and Instruction, 15*(1), 1–40.

Chi, M. T. H., Slotta, J. D., & de Leeuw, N. (1994). From things to processes: A theory of conceptual change for learning science concepts. *Learning and Instruction, 4*, 27–43.

Chinn, C. A., & Brewer, W. F. (1993). The role of anomalous data in knowledge acquisition: A theoretical framework and implications for science education. *Review of Educational Research, 63*, 1–49.

Chiu, M-H, Chou, C-C, & Liu, C-J (2002). Dynamic processes of conceptual change: Analysis of constructing mental models of chemical equilibrium. *Journal of Research in Science Teaching, 39*, 713–737.

De Boer, G. E. (2000). Scientific literacy: another look at its historical and contemporary meanings and its relationship to science education reform. *Journal of Research in Science Teaching, 37*, 582–601.

Driver, R. (1989). Changing conceptions. In P. Adey, J. Bliss, J. Head, & M. Shayer (Eds.), *Adolescent development and school science* (pp. 79–104). London: The Falmer Press.

Driver, R., & Easley, J. A. (1978). Pupils and paradigms: A review of literature related to concept development in adolescent science students. *Studies in Science Education, 5*, 61–84.

Driver, R., & Erickson, G. L. (1983). Theories-in-action: Some theoretical and empirical issues in the study of students' conceptual frameworks in science. *Studies in Science Education, 10,* 37–60.

Duit, R. (1998, April). *Towards multi-perspective views of science learning and instruction.* Paper presented at the annual meeting of the American Educational Research Association in San Diego.

Duit, R. (2006). *STCSE — Bibliography: Students' and teachers' conceptions and science education.* Kiel, Germany: IPN — Leibniz Institute for Science Education (http://www.ipn.uni-kiel.de/aktuell/stcse/stcse.html).

Duit, R., & Treagust, D. F. (1998). Learning in science - From behaviourism towards social constructivism and beyond. In B. J. Fraser & K. Tobin (Eds.), *International handbook of science education, Part 1* (pp. 3–25). Dordrecht, The Netherlands: Kluwer Academic Publishers.

Duit, R., & Treagust, D. (2003). Conceptual change: a powerful framework for improving science teaching and learning. *International Journal of Science Education, 25*, 671–688.

Duit, R., Widodo, A., & Wodzinski, C. T. (2007). Conceptual change ideas — Teachers' views and their instructional practice. In S. Vosniadou, A. Baltas, & X. Vamvokoussi (Eds.), *Re-framing the problem of conceptual change in learning and instruction* (pp. 197–217). Amsterdam, The Netherlands: Elsevier.

Duit, R., Fischer, H., Labudde, P., Brückmann, M., Gerber, B., Kauertz, A., Knierim, B., & Tesch, M. (2005). Potential of video studies in research on teaching and learning science. In R. Pintó & D. Couso (Eds.), *Proceedings of the Fifth International ESERA Conference on Contributions of Research to Enhancing Students' Interests in Learning Science* (pp. 829–842). Barcelona, Spain: Universitat Autonoma de Barcelona.

Dykstra, D. I., Boyle, C. F., & Monarch, I. A. (1992). Studying conceptual change in learning physics. *Science Education, 76*, 615–652.

Feldman, A. (2000). Decision making in the practical domain: A model of practical conceptual change. *Science Education, 84*, 606–623.

Gess-Newsome, & Lederman, N. G. (1999). *Examining pedagogical content knowledge.* Dordrecht, The Netherlands: Kluwer Academic Publishers.

Greeno, J. G., Collins, A. M., & Resnick, L. B. (1997). Cognition and learning. In D. C. Berliner & R. C. Calfee (Eds.), *Handbook of educational psychology* (pp. 15–46). New York: Simon & Schuster Macmillan.

Guzetti, B. J., Snyder, T. E., Glass, G. V., & Gamas, W. S. (1993). Promoting conceptual change in science: A comparative meta-analysis of instructional interventions from reading education and science education. *Reading Research Quarterly, 28*, 116–159.

Harlen, W. (1999). *Effective teaching of science: A review of research.* Edinburgh: The Scottish Council for Research in Education.

Hashweh, M. Z. (1986). Toward an explanation of conceptual change. *European Journal of Science Education, 8*, 229–249.

Hewson, P. W. (1982). A case study of conceptual change in special relativity: The influence of prior knowledge in learning. *European Journal of Science Education, 4,* 61–78.

Hewson, P. W., & Thorley, N. R. (1989). The conditions of conceptual change in the classroom. *International Journal of Science Education, 11,* 541–553.

Hewson, P. W., Tabachnick, B. R., Zeichner, K. M., Blomker, K. B., Meyer, H., Lemberger, J., Marion, R., Park, H.-J., & Toolin, R. (1999a). Educating prospective teachers of biology: Introduction and research methods. *Science Education, 83*, 247–273.

Hewson, P. W., Tabachnick, B. R., Zeichner, K. M., & Lemberger, J. (1999b). Educating prospective teachers of biology: Findings, limitations, and recommendations. *Science Education, 83*, 373–384.

Hewson, P. W., & Lemberger (2000). Status as the hallmark of conceptual change. In R. Millar, J. Leach, & J. Osborne (Eds.), *Improving science education* (pp. 110–125). Buckingham, UK: Open University Press.

Hewson, P., & Hennessey, M. G. (1992). Making status explicit: A case study of conceptual change. In R. Duit, F. Goldberg, & H. Niedderer (Eds.), *Research in physics learning: Theoretical issues and empirical studies* (pp. 176–187). Proceedings of an international workshop. Kiel, Germany: IBN-Leibniz Institute for Science Education.

Jung, W. (1993). Hilft die Entwicklungspsychologie dem Physikdidaktiker [Does developmental psychology help the physics educator?]. In R. Duit, & W. Gräber (Eds.), *Kognitive Entwicklung und naturwissenschaftlicher Unterricht* (pp. 86–107). Kiel, Germany: IPN – Leibniz Institute for Science Education.

Karplus, R. (1977). Science teaching and the development of reasoning. *Journal of Research in Science Teaching, 14*, 33–46.

Lawson, A. E., Abraham, M., & Renner, J. (1989). *A theory of instruction: Using the Learning Cycle to teach science concepts and thinking skills* (NARST Monograph Number One). University of Cincinnati, Cincinnati, OH: National Association for Research in Science Teaching.

Limon, M. (2001). On the cognitive conflict as an instructional strategy for conceptual change: a critical appraisal. *Learning and Instruction, 11*, 357–380.

Limon, M., & Carretero, M. (1999). Conflicting data and conceptual change in history experts. In W. Schnotz, S. Vosniadou, & M. Carretero (Eds.), *New Perspective on conceptual change* (pp. 137–160). Oxford: Pergamon.

Limon, M., & Mason, L. (Eds.). (2003). *Reconsidering conceptual change. Issues in theory and practice.* Dordrecht, The Netherlands: Kluwer Academic Publishers.

Lyons, T. (2006). Different countries, same science classes: Students' experiences of school science in their own words. *International Journal of Science Education, 28*, 591–613.

Mason, L. (2001). Responses to anomalous data on controversial topics and theory change. *Learning and Instruction, 11*, 453–484.

Millar, R., & Osborne, J. (1998). *Beyond 2000: Science education for the future. The report of a seminar series funded by the Nuffield Foundation.* London: King's College London, School of Education (http://www.kcl.ac.uk/education).

Mortimer, E. F. (1995). Conceptual change or conceptual profile change? *Science & Education, 4*, 267–285.

Müller, C. T. (2004). *Subjektive Theorien und handlungsleitende Kognitionen von Lehrern als Determinanten schulischer Lehr-Lern-Prozesse im Physikunterricht* [Teachers' subjective theories and cognitions and teaching and learning processes in physics instruction]. Studien zum Physikunterricht, Band 33. Berlin: Logos.

Norman, D. A. (1983). Some observations on mental models. In D. Gentner & A. L. Stevens (Eds.), *Mental models* (pp. 7–14). Hillsdale, NJ: Erlbaum.

OECD-PISA. (1999). *Measuring student knowledge and skills: A new framework for assessment.* Paris: OECD.

Oser, F. K., & Baeriswyl, F. J. (2001). Choreographies of teaching: Bridging instruction to learning. In V. Richardson (Ed.), *AERA's handbook of research on teaching – 4th edition* (pp. 1031–1065). Washington DC: American Educational Research Association.

Piquette, J. S., & Heikkinen, H. W. (2005). Strategies reported used by instructors to address student alternate conceptions in chemical equilibrium. *Journal of Research in Science Teaching, 42*, 1112–1134.

Pintrich, P. R., Marx, R. W., & Boyle, R. A. (1993). Beyond cold conceptual change: The role of motivational beliefs and classroom contextual factors in the process of conceptual change. *Review of Educational Research, 6*, 167–199.

Posner, G. J., Strike, K. A., Hewson, P. W., & Gertzog, W. A. (1982). Accommodation of a scientific conception: Toward a theory of conceptual change. *Science Education, 66*, 211–227.

25

Teaching for Conceptual Understanding: An Approach Drawing on Individual and Sociocultural Perspectives

John T. Leach and Philip H. Scott
The University of Leeds

INTRODUCTION: A PREVIEW OF THE ISSUES

There is a rich academic literature theorizing learning, including perspectives based on the conceptual change approach. This body of literature offers a potentially useful starting point for developing approaches to teaching. However, learning theories do not in themselves provide a template for the design of teaching, and the relationships between the two can be complex with no single perspective on learning leading directly to a unique approach to teaching. The purpose of this chapter is to consider how contemporary perspectives on conceptual learning might be, and have been, drawn upon to inform the design of teaching for conceptual understanding.

We have used conceptual understanding in science as our focus, as that is the area we know most about. We appreciate that there are ontological and epistemological differences between disciplines, and that an account of teaching science for conceptual understanding cannot therefore be transferred straightforwardly to another discipline. Nevertheless, we imagine that there is common ground with disciplines such as mathematics, history, and geography and that this account may therefore be of use in exploring teaching for conceptual understanding in those fields and others.

The chapter opens with a presentation of the major perspectives on learning scientific concepts, and a review of the ways in which these perspectives have been drawn upon in the design of science teaching. We then move on to consider some key accounts of the design and evaluation of science teaching, where multiple perspectives on learning are drawn upon. Next, we present an example of the design of science teaching for conceptual understanding, from our own work. The chapter concludes with a discussion of the relationship between theoretical perspectives on conceptual learning, and the practice of designing teaching for conceptual understanding.

A key issue shaping the chapter is the way in which perspectives on learning are used to address different aspects or *foci* of the process of designing teaching, at different levels of specificity or *grain size*. We note that learning theory has been used to focus on two principle aspects of the design of teaching. The first focus is the *conceptual goals* of teaching. For example, the

Focus of the use of learning theory on the design process

Grain size		Aims of teaching	Pedagogical approach
	Large	e.g., use of alternative conceptions literature to identify the age-placement of topics	e.g., use of sociocultural theory to promote inquiry as a general pedagogic strategy
	Fine	e.g., use of alternative conceptions literature to identify detailed, content-specific aims for teaching	e.g., use of sociocultural theory to inform a specific pattern of teacher-student interaction to address a specific learning aim

FIGURE 25.1   A framework for considering how learning theory is used to inform the design of teaching for conceptual learning — focus and grain size.

alternative conceptions literature has been drawn upon to develop aims for science teaching at both a large and fine grain size. Thus, at a large grain size, a topic such as mechanics might be identified as demanding to learn, and not therefore included amongst the aims of teaching until the later stages of secondary education. At a fine grain size, the aims of teaching a particular topic (such as the normal force) might be specified in relation to what the alternative conceptions literature can tell us about learning in this area. The second focus is the *pedagogical approach taken* in the design of teaching. Once again, this aspect of teaching design can be addressed at a large or small grain size. Thus, at a large grain size, sociocultural theory might be used to justify a pedagogical approach based on learning through *inquiry*. At a fine grain size, a specific pattern of teacher-student talk, such as scaffolding, might be specified to address a particular learning aim. In practice, of course, learning theory is often used to focus upon both aims and the pedagogical approach, though the emphasis may be stronger on one than the other.

Our use of the terms *focus* and *grain size* is illustrated in Figure 25.1.

We shall draw upon these ideas of *focus* and *grain size* throughout this chapter to discuss examples of teaching that have been informed by learning theory. Our own position is that different bodies of learning theory can usefully be used to inform various aspects of the design of teaching for conceptual learning. Furthermore, we believe that many of the key decisions in designing teaching need to be taken at both a large and fine grain size, and we present an example from our own work to illustrate one approach to achieving this later in the chapter.

CHARACTERIZING PERSPECTIVES ON CONCEPTUAL LEARNING

In this section, we begin by setting out key perspectives on conceptual learning in science that have been used to inform the design of teaching for conceptual understanding. We consider the *acquisition* and *participation* metaphors for learning and relate these to individual and sociocultural perspectives.

Two Metaphors for Learning: Acquisition and Participation

Given the range of approaches taken to conceptualizing science learning, we have found it helpful to identify two key features which we use as organizing dimensions in this chapter. The first dimension is taken from the influential paper by Anna Sfard (1998) in which she proposed two metaphors for learning: the *acquisition* metaphor and the *participation* metaphor.

According to Sfard (1998), human learning has been conceived of as an *acquisition* of something "since the dawn of civilization" and, in recent decades, "the idea of learning as gaining possession over some commodity has persisted in a wide spectrum of frameworks, from moderate to radical constructivism and then to interactionism and sociocultural theories" (p. 6). Gaining possession implies that something is stored or held somewhere. Sfard makes clear that it is *concepts* which are learned and then stored in the learner's head: "Since the time of Piaget and Vygotsky, the growth of knowledge in the process of learning has been analyzed in terms of concept development. Concepts are to be understood as basic units of knowledge that can be accumulated, gradually refined, and combined to form ever richer cognitive structures" (Sfard, 1998, p. 5). In developing this chapter, we begin with perspectives on conceptual learning which belong to the *acquisition* perspective, as there are many examples in the literature where these have been drawn upon to inform the design of science teaching for conceptual understanding. Many acquisition perspectives draw fundamentally upon the Piagetian account of learning. Piaget described an interactive learning process whereby an individual makes sense of the world through cognitive schemes, which are themselves modified as a result of the individual's actions on objects in the world. This model is summarized in the phrase *"L'intelligence organise le monde en s'organisant elle-même"*[1] (Piaget, 1937, p. 311). Piaget emphasized the significance of the child's social environment on knowledge development, claiming that:

> Society is the supreme unit, and the individual can only achieve his inventions and intellectual constructions insofar as he is the seat of collective interactions that are naturally dependent, in level and value, on society as a whole. (Piaget, 1971, p. 368)

Nonetheless, in most of Piaget's writing, knowledge is portrayed as schemata in the individual's head, with little prominence being placed upon wider social aspects of learning.

Several problems have been identified with this fundamental account of learning. The first relates to the ontological status of knowledge in Piagetian accounts of learning. Michael Matthews (1992), for example, has argued that Piagetian accounts of learning do not recognize publicly warranted knowledge claims, viewing all knowledge claims as personal to an individual. Science teaching for conceptual understanding is therefore viewed as a process of supporting learners in *personal construction* of knowledge based on experience of natural phenomena, rather than a *guided introduction* to ideas that already exist within a community.

The second problem relates to the relationship between knowledge and action in Piagetian accounts of learning. Brown, Collins, and Duguid (1989), for example, suggest that the typical Piagetian view is that an individual knows something, and that this knowledge is then applied to inform action. This view, they argue, does not provide adequate explanation for empirical findings from studies of conceptual learning in action (such as studies of students learning how to perform simple arithmetic processes). Rather, learning should be portrayed as a process of learning to participate in actions that are characteristic of communities: knowing and acting are seen as inseparable.

Sfard (1998) identifies this *participation* metaphor as offering a fundamentally different perspective on learning, in which "the learner should be viewed as a person interested in participation in certain kinds of activities rather than in accumulating private possessions" (ibid., p. 6). According to this perspective, "learning a subject is now conceived of as a process of becoming a member of a certain community" (ibid., p. 6). There is now a growing body of literature which draws upon a participation metaphor for learning to inform the design and interpretation of teaching for conceptual understanding.

From the outset, it is important to recognize that the acquisition-participation dimension is not a continuum. The two metaphors offer fundamentally different perspectives on learning, or as Sfard (1998, p. 7) stated, "the acquisition/participation division is ontological in nature and draws on two radically different approaches to the fundamental question, 'What is this thing called learning?'"

Individual and Social Perspectives on Learning

Our second organizing dimension in the chapter involves the distinction between individual and social perspectives on learning. This takes us from a starting point where the main focus is on the *individual* learner, moving towards approaches where increased account is taken of various *social* aspects of the learning process and of knowledge itself. In examining different accounts of conceptual learning, it is often apparent that different aspects of the learning process are being focused upon, and the emphasis may be more upon the cognizing individual, or the group. We therefore view the individual-social dimension as a continuum. It is worth underlining that the individual-social dimension does not map directly onto the acquisition-participation dimension. In the quotation above Sfard (1998, p. 6), for example, states that both Piaget and Vygotsky use an *acquisition* metaphor for learning, though we will see later in this chapter that Piaget's and Vygotsky's perspectives on learning tend to be drawn upon by researchers working at different ends of the individual-social dimension.

PERSPECTIVES ON LEARNING AND LINKS TO TEACHING

There is a significant body of literature developing perspectives on conceptual learning and drawing out the implications of these perspectives for the practice of teaching, and we focus upon this literature in this section. Our review is organized around the acquisition/participation and individual/social dimensions, and for each combination (acquisition/individual, acquisition/social, participation/social) we discuss one or more examples where the perspective on learning has been used explicitly to inform the design of teaching.

Science Concept Learning as Acquisition: Individual Perspectives

Piagetian stage theory has been drawn upon to inform science curriculum design and sequencing (see, for example, Science Curriculum Improvement Study, USA, see Andersson, 1976; Cognitive Acceleration through Science Education, Adey and Shayer, 1993). Stage theory suggests that there are characteristic, age-related stages in the development of cognitive functioning. Cognitive ability is portrayed in terms of processes such as logico-mathematical reasoning, which promote or constrain reasoning across domains of knowledge. Various criticisms of the use of Piagetian theory in science education have been advanced. Driver (1978), Donaldson (1978) and Carey (1985) have questioned the empirical basis on which claims for characteristic stages in logico-mathematical thinking are founded. Specific criticisms include the following:

- Tasks requiring identical logico-mathematical reasoning are made easier or more difficult by the degree of familiarity with the task's context (Donaldson, 1978).
- Tasks characteristic of a given stage can be performed by much younger children (Driver, 1978).
- The analysis used in Piagetian research is designed to validate existing theory rather than account for children's reasoning (Driver, 1978; Carey, 1985).

Although there has been a decline in the influence of Piagetian approaches since the 1970s, there remains a significant line of research on domain-general reasoning skills in science learning (e.g., Kuhn, Amsel, & O'Loughlin, 1988; Kuhn, 1991; Koslowski, 1996; Metz, 1997), as well as accounts of science learning drawing on Piaget's work (e.g., Adey & Shayer, 1993; Lawson, 1985; Shayer, 2003).

Perhaps the most significant break from the Piagetian account of conceptual learning in science can be traced back to the developmental psychology of David Ausubel (1968). Ausubel argued that the most significant influence on the learner's conceptual development is their existing conceptual knowledge in the target domain. During the early 1970s, a small number of empirical studies were conducted which accounted for students' science learning in terms of domain-specific factors, rather than explaining learning in terms of global logico-mathematical reasoning skills (e.g., Driver, 1973; Viennot, 1979; McClosky, 1983).

An empirical research program subsequently developed (Novak, 1978), focusing upon the content of students' domain-specific reasoning (or students' alternative conceptions; Driver & Easley, 1978) about natural phenomena and involving researchers from around the world. Two particularly influential books in the development of research on students' alternative conceptions were *The Pupil as Scientist?* by Rosalind Driver (1983) and *Learning in Science: The Implications of Children's Science* edited by Roger Osborne and Peter Freyberg (1985). Helga Pfundt and Reinders Duit of the IPN in Kiel, Germany, developed a comprehensive bibliography, *Students' Alternative Frameworks and Science Education*, which is now in its fifth edition (Duit, 2006).

In 1982, Posner, Strike, Hewson, and Gertzog published their seminal paper *Accommodation of a scientific conception: Toward a theory of conceptual change*. This paper draws upon Ausubel's developmental psychology, and the early empirical work of Driver and others on physics learning, to present an account of conceptual change in science learning. In addition, the paper uses Kuhn's ideas about theory change in science as an analogy for conceptual change in science learning, suggesting that *assimilation* in conceptual learning is akin to Kuhnian normal science in that new information is assimilated into a well developed structure of ideas. By contrast, *accommodation* in conceptual learning is seen as more analogous to paradigm change. Although Piagetian language is used in the paper, the account of conceptual change that is presented is based upon changes in domain-specific reasoning, rather than changes in more fundamental logico-mathematical reasoning skills. Drawing upon a term introduced by Toulmin, Posner et al. refer to the concepts "which govern a conceptual change as a 'conceptual ecology'" (p. 213), recognizing that even in radical conceptual change, some concepts remain essentially unaltered.

Posner et al.'s (1982) account of conceptual change in science learning has been highly influential, being regularly cited as an account of a *constructivist* view of learning in studies of teaching and learning science concepts during the 1980s and 1990s. During the 1980s, Ernst von Glasersfeld set out a radical constructivist view of learning which was influential in shaping science and mathematics educators' approaches to designing teaching for conceptual understanding (von Glasersfeld, 1998, p. 24). This view of learning drew upon Thomas Kuhn's work in the philosophy of science as well as Piaget's perspective on learning. von Glasersfeld describes radical constructivism as introducing

a new, more tangible relationship between knowledge and reality, which I have called a relationship of "viability". Simply put, the notion of viability means that an action, operation, conceptual structure, or even a theory, is considered "viable" as long as it is useful in accomplishing a task or in achieving a goal that one has set for oneself. Thus, instead of claiming that knowledge is capable of representing a world outside of our experience, we would say, as did the pragmatists, that knowledge is a tool within the realm of experience. (p. 24)

Learning as Acquisition/Individual: Links to Teaching

We now turn our attention to the ways in which perspectives on learning based on an acquisition/individual approach have been drawn upon to inform the design and interpretation of science teaching for conceptual understanding. Some of the earliest studies in the "alternative conceptions movement" combined detailed studies of science students' conceptual understanding, based upon

Piagetian clinical interviews with students about phenomena and events in the natural world, with observational studies of students in teaching situations. Rosalind Driver's doctoral study, which led to her often-cited book *The Pupil as Scientist?* (1983), is a good example of such a study. The book presents several examples of adolescent physics students' accounts of phenomena typical to the physics curriculum. Driver shows that the "incorrect" ideas put forward by students are internally coherent, and furthermore that there are commonalities in the concepts that appear to underpin students' explanations. Although the early part of the book outlines Ausubel's perspective on conceptual learning, the examples are presented without theorization. At the beginning of the book, Driver states, "Inevitably, the book raises questions about classroom practice. Here I recognize the danger of being prescriptive and recommending simplistic solutions to complex problems" (*Preface,* unnumbered page). However, implications for secondary science courses are raised and general suggestions for classroom practice are made in the last chapter. Driver's suggestions include:

- Recognizing the difficulty experienced by learners in meeting new phenomena, and their scientific explanations, at the same time;
- Recognizing that phenomena can be conceptualized at different levels, and that simpler levels are functional in many everyday settings;
- Recognizing that meaningful learning of scientific concepts may take considerable time.

During the 1980s, a small number of papers began to be published which presented a rationale for the design of science teaching, which cited a constructivist view of learning as a key source (including Posner and colleagues' model of conceptual change, as well as Piaget's and von Glasersfeld's accounts of learning). For example, Rosalind Driver established a group of teachers and researchers in Leeds with the aim of developing "revised teaching approaches which would be informed by research on children's thinking in science and current theoretical developments in cognition" (Driver & Oldham, 1985, p. 105). Driver and Oldham (1985) cite empirical studies of children's ideas in science, a constructivist view of learning and learning as conceptual change as influences on the project to develop revised teaching approaches. A "constructivist teaching sequence" (p. 119) is then presented, which involves the following steps:

1. Orientation of students to the phenomena being studied;
2. Elicitation of the students' pre-instructional ideas, by asking them to explain various phenomena and events in their own terms;
3. Restructuring the students' ideas through clarification and exchanges between students about their pre-instructional explanations, the exposure of students to conflicting situations, and having students work in groups to construct and evaluate new ideas;
4. The application of newly-constructed ideas to the original phenomena in the elicitation phase;
5. A review of the changes in students' ideas, followed by a second phase of restructuring etc. if necessary.

Researchers working from the conceptual change model (Posner et al., 1982) have developed teaching approaches where cognitive conflict based on the careful selection of anomalous data is portrayed as a key teaching strategy. Drawing upon Thorley (1990), Hewson and Lemberger (2000) demonstrate how the status of a concept changes through group discussion between students working on problems of Mendelian inheritance in genetics. This approach acknowledges the influence of group discussion upon individual learning, though there is no particular theorizing of the role of authority sources, such as teachers, in promoting conceptual learning. Indeed,

Millar (1989) has argued that a wide variety of teaching approaches can be consistent with a constructivist view of learning and questions the wisdom of making direct links between theories of learning and approaches to teaching.

Driver and Oldham's constructivist teaching sequence addresses the design of *pedagogical approaches* at a *large grain size*. It does not articulate tight links between the account of learning that they present and the teaching sequence that they advocate, in common with much of the literature of the period. The teaching described by Thorley, and Hewson and Lemberger, focuses on the design of *pedagogical approaches* through the use of cognitive conflict. Descriptions of the use of cognitive conflict are presented at both a *large and fine grain size*, in the sense that teaching is analyzed in terms of its overall shape, and also in terms of the minute-by-minute interactions between students. However, no explicit rationale for designing teaching is presented.

More recently, Fritz Oser and Franz Baeriswyl (2001) have addressed specifically the need to develop a theory of instructional design. Oser and Baeriswyl (2001) argue that all too often teaching is not planned to address and to support specific aspects of learning. In such situations, they suggest that "a creative ordering of visible (teaching) structures without guaranteeing the possibility of basis-model sequences is like didactic theatre. Learning and learning sequences are not the focus, instruction is" (p. 1048). Their approach is far more ambitious than others presented so far in this section, in that it aims to present a generalized theory of instructional design, rather than providing guidance about teaching for specific conceptual learning. In common with the approaches set out above, it portrays learning as a process of acquisition by individuals. Two aspects of the teaching-learning situation in lessons are described, namely the visible or sight structure of the lesson and the basis-model of the lesson. The sight structure of the lesson involves the concrete activities of the students, whereas the basis-model refers to "creating conditions for inner non-visible constructive activities, namely, the learning process itself or the mental operations that refer to the deep structure of learning" (p. 1032). The "choreography of teaching" (p. 1032) involves the planning and processing of both the sight structure and base-model in the classroom. Oser and Baeriswyl (2001) claim that the number of possible base-models of learning is restricted to 12.

So, what guidance on designing teaching do Oser and Baeriswyl offer? This can be illustrated in relation to "concept building" (base-model 4). They suggest five learning steps in the trajectory of a complex concept building process (p. 1054): 1. Direct or indirect stimulation of the awareness of what the learner already knows regarding the new concept; 2. Introduction of and working through of a prototype as a valid example of the new concept; 3. Analysis of essential categories and principles that define the new concept (positive and negative distinctions); 4. Active dealing with the new concept (application, synthesis and analysis); 5. Application of the new concept in different contexts (incorporation of different but similar concepts into a more complex knowledge system). There are clear similarities between these five learning steps and the five steps of the constructivist teaching sequence offered by Driver and Oldham (1985), and both are set out at the same large grain size. For example, no guidance is offered about what might be involved in introducing and working through a prototype in relation to a particular scientific concept (such as the normal force). The reader gains an impression of what an overall sequence of learning steps might involve but little insight about what each step might entail.

Science Concept Learning as Acquisition: Social Perspectives

Posner et al.'s (1982) model of conceptual change has been criticized on various grounds. Chinn and Brewer (1993), for example, questioned the assumption that conceptual change comes about as a result of students being exposed to anomalous data. In a study of professional scientists', and science students', responses to anomalous data they present a typology of seven possible responses, only one of which involves accepting the data and changing beliefs. Other critiques of Posner et al.'s model of conceptual change have focused upon the inadequate portrayal of social aspects of learning. O'Loughlin (1992), for example, noted the absence of any theorizing about motivational aspects of learning in Posner et al.'s model. Driver, Asoko, Leach, Mortimer, and Scott (1994) argued that "knowledge and understandings, including scientific understandings, are constructed when individuals engage socially in talk and activity about shared problems or tasks. Making meaning is thus a dialogic process involving persons-in-conversation, and learning is seen as the process by which individuals are introduced to a culture by more skilled members" (p. 7).

In this section, we will consider social perspectives on science concept learning as acquisition, which attempt to address some of these critiques. We will first summarize key aspects of a Vygotskian (and neo-Vygotskian) sociocultural perspective on learning. We shall then outline a social constructivist perspective which is developed from both sociocultural and constructivist views and which we draw upon in our own work on the design of science teaching for conceptual understanding.

Sociocultural Perspective on Learning

We start with the fundamental assumption of Vygotsky's sociocultural view of learning that higher mental functioning (such as science conceptual understanding) in the individual derives from social life (Vygotsky, 1978, p. 128). In the first instance, language and other semiotic mechanisms provide the means for concepts to be talked through between people on the social (or intermental) plane. The process of *internalization* (Vygotsky, 1987) is where individuals appropriate and become able to use for themselves (on the intramental plane) conceptual tools first encountered on the social plane. Central to this view is the continuity between language and thought. It is not the case that language offers some neutral means for communicating personally and internally generated thoughts: language provides the very tools through which those thoughts are first rehearsed on the social plane and then processed and used on the intramental plane. In the sense that learning is portrayed as involving internalization to an intermental plane, sociocultural perspectives on learning that draw upon Vygotsky involve *acquisition*. Wertsch (1991, p. 46) has made the point that the Vygotskian view is limited in that there is no recognition of the *different* forms of intermental functioning which occur on the social plane. He has turned to the work of M. M. Bakhtin for the additional tools needed to develop the Vygotskian account. In his approach to discourse analysis, Bakhtin draws attention to the fact that different modes of discourse are used in different parts of society and he refers to these as *social languages*. For Bakhtin, a social language is "a discourse peculiar to a specific stratum of society (professional, age group etc.) within a given system at a given time" (Holquist & Emerson, 1981, p. 430). Thus, a social language would include a dialect used in a particular geographical area, or a particular form of professional jargon, or indeed the way of talking about the natural world which is termed *science*. In Bakhtin's view, a speaker necessarily invokes a social language in producing an utterance, and this social language shapes what the speaker's individual voice can say. All of these social languages "are specific points of view on the world, forms for conceptualizing the world in words, specific world views, each characterized by its own objects, meanings and values. As such they all may be juxtaposed to one another, mutually supplement one another and co-exist in the consciousness of real people..." (Bakhtin, 1934/1981, p. 292).

Thus the *scientific* social language, the scientific way of talking and thinking, is that which has been developed within the scientific community. It is based on the use of specific concepts such as energy, mass and entropy, it involves the development of models which provide a simpli-

fied account of phenomena in the natural world, and it is characterized by certain key epistemological features such as the development of theories which can be generally applied to different
phenomena and situations. However, it is not the case that "anything goes" in the generation of
scientific knowledge, as this knowledge should, in principle, be consistent with empirical evidence about the material world. Scientists are not in a position to create their social language in
isolation from empirical data.

In the classroom, science is often presented, either explicitly or implicitly, as the only acceptable way of talking about the natural world. However, there are other acceptable modes
of expression. In day-to-day living we are immersed in everyday ways of talking and thinking
about the world. These everyday ways of talking are usually spontaneous (Vygotsky, 1987), in
the sense that they are developed without conscious reflection and thought. Learning science
involves coming to understand and being able to use a new set of tools for talking and thinking
about the world, which can be drawn upon when circumstances and context are appropriate.
Furthermore, we would suggest that a mature understanding of science can be demonstrated in
terms of the ability to move between ways of talking and thinking about phenomena according to
context, recognizing the appropriateness, power and limitations of each.

When learning science is conceptualized as learning to talk in new ways or learning to talk
science (Lemke 1990), then the act of learning might appear deceptively straightforward: isn't it
the case that the student simply learns how to talk about familiar phenomena in new ways? This
sounds unproblematic, but as all teachers are very well aware, learning science often creates difficulties. The learning outcomes which follow from instruction are often disappointing in terms
of how much students are able to remember, how much they are able to understand, how much
they are able to apply. Why should this be the case? What are the obstacles or barriers to learning
science? We now turn to the Vygotskian notion of internalization to address these questions.

A first obvious point here is that the process of internalization, as envisaged by Vygotsky,
does not simply involve direct transfer of "ways of talking" from the social to the personal plane.
There must be a step of personal interpretation, where the individual comes to a personal understanding of the ideas encountered on the social plane. The same point is made by one of
Vygotsky's contemporaries, Leontiev, who states that "the process of internalization is not the
transferal of an external activity to a pre-existing, 'internal plane of consciousness': it is the
process in which this plane is formed" (Leontiev, 1981, p. 57). That is, individual learners must
make sense of the talk that surrounds them, relating that talk to their existing ideas and ways of
thinking. Learners must reorganize and reconstruct the talk and activities of the social plane.

This point, of course, is central to research in the individual tradition:

> ...such a psychogenetic model, it seems to me, could help the socially oriented researchers to
> ground their findings far more solidly than by assuming that the knowledge and the language of a
> social group could be instilled into its members through the simple occurrence of language games
> and other forms of social interaction. (von Glasersfeld, 1999, p. 11)

Social Constructivist Perspective on Learning

There is a clear overlap here between sociocultural and individual views which we see as providing the basis of a *social constructivist* perspective on learning (Leach & Scott, 2002). This
social constructivist view brings together the social-interactive and personal-sense-making parts
of the learning process and identifies language as the central form of mediational means on both
social and personal planes. It draws upon sociocultural approaches in conceptualizing learning
in terms of developing a new social language, and in identifying epistemological differences
between social languages. It draws upon individual views in clarifying the nature of the learning

steps, or learning demands, which learners must address as they make personal interpretations of the social language of science. Sociocultural views of learning draw attention to how scientific knowledge is talked into existence (Ogborn, Kress, Martins, & McGillicuddy, 1996) on the social plane of the classroom, for showing how teachers control discourse on the social plane, and for considering student learning in response to teaching. We shall return later to this social constructivist perspective on learning to show how it can be used as a basis for designing teaching.

Social Perspectives on Learning: Links to Teaching

How have the social perspectives on learning, outlined above, been used to inform the design of teaching?

Hodson and Hodson (1998), working from a Vygotskian sociocultural perspective on teaching and learning science, come to the conclusion that "the Vygotskian perspectives outlined here suggest that the most effective form of learning is likely to be inquiry-oriented, personalized and collaborative, and conducted in accordance with the norms and values of the community of scientists, under the guidance of a skilled practitioner" (pp. 38–39). A similar, inquiry based approach, is proposed by Wells (1999) working from sociocultural principles. Hodson and Hodson state (p. 39) that inquiries can be regarded as "either literature/media-based or as field experience/laboratory-based" and they outline five phases of the inquiry process (inititiation, design and planning, performance, interpretation, reporting and communicating) which are played out over an extended period of time. In both of these cases the focus is upon developing a *pedagogical approach* at a *large grain size*; the emphasis is not upon enhancing students' understanding of specific conceptual content.

We find this link from sociocultural theory to inquiry-based approaches to teaching surprising, given the prominent role reserved for the teacher, as the "vicar of the new culture" (Bruner, 1985) in sociocultural theory. In other words, it is the job of the teacher to introduce the ways of talking and thinking of particular cultures (such as science) to the students. We are not convinced that the most effective way of teaching scientific conceptual knowledge (which is of interest to us here) is through inquiry activities played out over extended periods of time. We shall return to this same point in the next section in discussing inquiry approaches in the context of learning as participation.

Science Concept Teaching as Participation: Situated (Social) Perspectives

The metaphor of learning as participation has largely arisen through the *situated cognition* perspective (see, for example, Brown, Collins, & Duguid, 1989; Lave & Wenger, 1991; Rogoff, 1990). The pioneering work in this field focused on the use of mathematics in the workplace and in day-to-day life. For example, Scribner (1984) analyzed the arithmetical practices of people as they worked in a dairy factory, whilst Lave (1988) focused on the use of arithmetic in everyday shopping. These studies, and others (see Hennessy, 1993, for a review), have identified forms of mathematics which are radically different from those taught in school. The skilled users of these everyday forms of arithmetic vary their problem solving approaches depending on the specific situation and problems, which appear to be structurally identical, but are solved using different strategies. In this sense, the strategies are seen to be directly linked to context and thereby *situated* in nature.

According to the situated cognition perspective, learning is seen as a process of enculturation, or participation in socially organized practices, through which specialized skills are developed by the learner as they engage in an apprenticeship in thinking (Rogoff, 1990), or in legitimate peripheral participation (Lave & Wenger, 1991). For this reason, we view situated cognition as a *social* perspective. According to Collins, Brown, and Newman (1989), the key components of the apprenticeship process include modeling, coaching, scaffolding, fading, and encouraging learners to reflect on their own problem-solving strategies. This apprenticeship leads to the learner becoming involved in the *authentic* practices of a "community of practice" (Lave & Wenger, 1991). Brown et al. (1989) argued that "Unfortunately, students are too often asked to use the tools of a discipline without being able to adopt its culture. To learn to use tools as practitioners use them, a student, like an apprentice, must enter that community and its culture." Roth (1995, p. 29) suggested that authentic practices involve activities "which have a large degree of resemblance with the activities in which core members of a community actually engage."

Jay Lemke offered a different perspective on learning science through participation in his book, *Talking Science: Language, Learning and Values* (1990). This "social semiotic" approach has been highly influential in drawing attention to the fundamental importance of language in science learning. The basic thesis which Lemke proposed is that learning science involves learning to talk science: "it means learning to communicate in the language of science and act as a member of the community of people who do so" (Lemke, 1990, p. 1). In common with other work based on the participation metaphor for learning, Vygotsky's writing about the workings of the social plane are used as a theoretical foundation. However, Lemke (1990, p. 122) questioned the value of cognitive theories of concept use based on mental processes "which we know nothing about" and suggests that "we may as well cut out the 'middleman' of *mental* concepts, and simply analyze conceptual systems in terms of the thematic patterns of language use and other forms of meaningful human action." The Vygotskian notion of the individual plane is not drawn upon. This use of Vygotskian theory clearly follows the participation metaphor rather than the acquisition metaphor.

In his more recent work, Lemke has developed the social semiotics perspective introduced in *Talking Science*, along multimodal lines to investigate "how we make meaning using the cultural resources of systems of words, images, symbols and actions" (Lemke, 2003). As part of this analysis, Lemke made the important point that it is not only the communicative activities of teacher and students in the classroom which are multimodal in character, but that science itself also involves the use of multiple semiotic systems: "science does not speak of the world in the language of words alone, and in many cases it simply cannot do so. The natural language of science is a synergistic integration of words, diagrams, pictures, graphs, maps, equations, tables, charts, and other forms of visual and mathematical expression" (Lemke, 2003, p. 3). Science thus consists of "the languages of visual representation, the languages of mathematical symbolism, and the languages of experimental operations" (p. 3). Following this perspective, Lemke argued that learning science must involve developing the ability "to use all of these languages in meaningful and appropriate ways, and, above all, to be able to functionally integrate them in the conduct of scientific activity" (p. 3).

Learning as Participation: Links to Teaching

To what extent have situated perspectives on learning been drawn upon to inform the design of science teaching for conceptual understanding? Situated perspectives on learning have been drawn upon as part of a theoretical justification for inquiry-based approaches to science teaching and learning (see, for example, Metz, 1998; Roth, 1995). These are the same kinds of approaches as those espoused by Hodson and Hodson (1998) working from an acquisition (social) perspective. Roth (1995, p. 29) suggested that "situated learning emphasizes learning through the engagement in authentic activities." He explained his use of the term *authentic* by suggesting that in classrooms focusing on scientific activities, the students would, "(1) learn in contexts constituted in part by ill-defined problems; (2) experience uncertainties, ambiguities, and the social nature of scientific work and knowledge; (3) engage in learning (curriculum) which is predicated on, and driven by, their current knowledge state; (4) experience themselves as part of communities of inquiry in which knowledge, practices, resources, and discourse are shared; and (5) participate in classroom communities, in which they can draw on the expertise of more knowledgeable others" (Roth, 1995, p. 29; see also Wells, 1999).

Drawing explicitly upon these ideas, science instruction has been planned and implemented as the enculturation of students into practices such as field ecology (e.g., Roth & Bowen, 1995), environmental activism (e.g., Roth & Désautels, 2002) and basic scientific research (e.g., Ryder, Leach & Driver, 1999). In each case, the teaching focuses more upon students' learning about various *practices* that involve science (e.g., the use of instrumentation and specific technical procedures, the construction of arguments, the social relationships of various communities) than upon the development of conceptual understanding by students.

Elsewhere, Roth (1995) has reported classroom studies in which students are faced with conceptual learning aims such as developing an understanding of chaotic systems by working with a pendulum device, or developing an understanding of aspects of Newtonian mechanics through working with a computer-based microworld. In both of these cases, the students, working in small groups, spend a considerable amount of time in carrying out inquiry based activities. A key question which emerges here concerns the balance to be set between teacher intervention and allowing the students to fumble in the dark, developing new ways of observing and explaining from the muddle of talk and experience. On the one hand, Roth acknowledges the difficulties inherent in mapping between microworlds and the real world (p. 166), and yet the students were placed in a situation where they were required to come to recognize the nature of the force and velocity vectors by themselves. Our own view on this matter is that if the aim of a sequence of teaching is to introduce aspects of scientific conceptual knowledge, then some form of clear and direct guidance by the teacher is essential. The scientific knowledge itself is authoritative in nature and some form of authoritative intervention by the teacher is therefore needed to introduce it to the social plane of the classroom. At the same time, of course, the students should be given every opportunity to apply that knowledge as they talk and use it for themselves. From this point of view we believe that there are real limitations to using inquiry-based, participation driven, approaches in teaching scientific conceptual knowledge.

EXAMPLES OF DESIGNING SCIENCE TEACHING INFORMED BY MULTIPLE PERSPECTIVES ON LEARNING

So far in this chapter, we have presented examples where a specific aspect of learning theory is drawn upon explicitly to inform the design of teaching. However, as previously noted, the relationship between perspectives on learning and instructional design is not a simple one, and it is possible to justify a broad range of teaching approaches in terms of a single perspective on learning. In this section, we turn our focus to examples of the design of teaching to promote conceptual understanding which draw upon multiple perspectives on learning, or where the process of designing teaching appears to precede the use of learning theory. Key differences between the examples that we consider here relate to the issues of *focus* and *grain size*. In practice, as previously noted, it is often the case that the focus of the design process includes both the aims of teaching and the pedagogical approach, though the emphasis may be much more on one than the other. For this reason, we have organized the examples into those which focus on the aims of instruction or pedagogical approach at a large grain size and those at a smaller grain size.

Approaches to Designing Science Teaching: Focus at a Large Grain Size

In 2000, the National Research Council (USA) published a report from its Committee on Developments in the Science of Learning, entitled *How People Learn: Brain, Mind, Experience and School* (Branford, Brown, & Cocking, 2000). The report was designed to provide a bridge, for practitioners, between research findings about learning and the practice of teaching. The book sets out a good deal of learning theory, in a way that is intended to be accessible for practitioners. In 2005, a second book was published which takes the principles and framework developed in the first and works them through in the context of three school subject areas (science, mathematics, and history) (*How Students Learn*; Donovan & Branford, 2005). Both books present *Principles* and a *Framework* which are intended to influence the design of teaching.

The *Principles* and *Framework* presented in *How People Learn* contain no surprises:

Principles:
- Engaging prior understandings;
- The essential role of factual knowledge and conceptual frameworks in understanding;
- The importance of self-monitoring (i.e., metacognition).

Framework for thinking about teaching, learning, and the design of classroom and school environments (NRC 2005, p. 13):

- The *learner-centered lens* encourages attention to preconceptions and begins instruction with what students think and know.
- The *knowledge-centered lens* focuses on what is to be taught, why it is taught, and what mastery looks like.
- The *assessment-centered lens* emphasizes the need to provide frequent opportunities to make students' thinking and learning visible as a guide for both the teacher and the student in learning and instruction.
- The *community-centered lens* encourages a culture of questioning, respect and risk taking.

Three examples of science teaching are introduced as illustrations of approaches to teaching that are consistent with the *Principles* and *Framework*. The examples are not presented as unique or best solutions to a given teaching problem, but rather illustrations of possible solutions that are consistent with how students learn science. The *Principles* and *Framework* offer guidance on pedagogical approaches at a *large grain size*, though inevitably the three examples of science teaching include design decisions at a very small grain size. The teaching design decisions presented in case studies appear to have been made without much explicit reference to particular theoretical insights. Rather, theoretical insights were used *a posteriori* to justify the approach used.

Engle and Conant (2002) draw upon both participation and acquisition metaphors to justify four principles for designing teaching that fosters *productive disciplinary engagement*. Productive disciplinary engagement is broadly defined as combining "moment-by-moment, intentional aspects of student engagement with ideas of what constitutes productive discourse in a content domain" (p. 400). The four principles are:

1. *Problematising*: Students are encouraged to take on intellectual problems
2. *Authority*: Students are given authority in addressing such problems
3. *Accountability*: Students' intellectual work is made accountable to others and to disciplinary norms
4. *Resources*: Students are provided with sufficient resources to do all of the above (pp. 400–401)

These principles offer guidance on pedagogical approaches and are framed at a *large grain size.* Unlike the *Principles* and *Framework* presented in *How People Learn,* they were developed as a result of a post-hoc analysis of teaching rather than emerging from learning theory *per se,* and both acquisition and participation metaphors for learning were drawn upon to justify them. Although several references to work in the situated cognition tradition are presented in the article, it is largely left to the reader to judge how these have been drawn upon to inform the formulation of the four principles.

The case of one sequence of teaching is presented by Engle and Conant (2002) to illustrate how the four principles were used to foster productive disciplinary engagement. The example involves an episode from an elementary school science classroom, in which the students debated whether the orca (killer whale) should actually be classified as a whale or a dolphin. Evidence is presented to show how the students took on this intellectual problem, how they were given authority to address it, how they were held accountable to others and to disciplinary norms, and how resources were made available to them to undertake the work. However, although the example focuses upon a biological taxonomy, it appears that the primary aim of the teaching is to engender learning about the norms of scientific argumentation and warranting of claims, rather than the conceptual content *per se.* It was necessary to make decisions about the progress of the teaching at a *fine grain size* that could not be informed by the design principles. In the next section, we present some examples of instructional design where the design principles focus at a finer grain size, and consider how these draw upon perspectives on learning for conceptual understanding.

Approaches to Designing Science Teaching: Focus at a Fine Grain Size

The theoretical resources that have been discussed so far in this chapter have been developed mainly by researchers working in various fields of psychology. However, there is also a well-established tradition of theorizing about learning and teaching processes in the field of education. Much of this work is carried out at a *fine grain size* focusing upon teaching and learning processes in relation to specific content, and it is to this work that we now turn our attention.

In a recent Special Issue of *Educational Researcher* (2003), focusing upon the role of design in educational research, the editor defines design-based research as attempting:

> ...to support arguments constructed around the results of active innovation and intervention in classrooms. The operative grammar, which draws upon models from design and engineering, is generative and transformative. It is directed primarily at understanding learning and teaching processes when the researcher is active as an educator. (Kelly, 2003, p. 3)

Although taken up by educationalists, the seminal work in this program was conducted by psychologists with a close interest in classroom learning (e.g., Brown, 1992). Cobb, Confrey, diSessa, Lehrer, and Schauble (2003) describe the purpose of design research as developing "theories, not merely to empirically tune 'what works'" (p. 9). These theories are portrayed as targeting domain-specific learning processes, and as such are at a *fine grain size.* It is claimed that the value of design-based research lies in its ability to improve educational practice (Design-Based Research Collective, 2003, p. 8). In a report of a design experiment addressing teaching statistics to lower secondary students, Cobb and McClain (2004) characterize the design principles as:

"five aspects of the classroom environment that proved critical in supporting the students' statistical learning:

1. The focus on central statistical ideas
2. The instructional activities
3. The classroom activity structure

4. The computer-based tools the students used
5. The classroom discourse" (p. 376).

Each design principle is then specified, with reference to evidence in the academic literature and short accounts of what happened during the design experiment.

Krajcik, McNeill, and Reiser (2006) are educational researchers who describe the goal of their research program as "narrow(ing) the gap between assessment, materials, and learning goals through the process of learning-goals-driven design" (p. 2). Drawing upon the *Principles* and *Framework* of *How People Learn*, they describe six major ideas that influence their approach to designing curriculum materials:

1. Active construction of knowledge by students
2. Situated learning
3. Social interactions
4. Cognitive tools
5. The structure of expert knowledge
6. Science as a way of knowing. (Krajcik, Blumenfeld, Marx, & Soloway, 2000)

These ideas are framed at a *large grain size*. However, Krajcik et al. (2006) develop the notion of "Learning Performances" as a tool for informing decisions about the detail of planning teaching at a smaller grain size. Learning performances are defined in terms of the content standards specified in relevant mandatory science curricula, and evidence about the nature of knowledge and practice in scientific disciplines, and are phrased as learning outcomes which students should attain following teaching. Instructional sequences are developed which draw upon evidence (from individual perspectives on learning as acquisition) about students' likely domain-specific knowledge before instruction, as well as insights (from sociocultural perspectives on learning) about social interactions during learning. The instructional sequences are then tested and iteratively improved.

There are well-established research traditions of theorizing the relationship between subject matter content, learning and teaching processes, and students' conceptual understanding in several non-Anglophone European countries. Such research is generally referred to as *didactics* (Sjøberg, 1996; Tochon, 1999). The aims of didactical research appear to be broadly similar to the aims of design-based research in that the primary focus is upon improving learners' understanding of specific content in a given domain. The early training of didactics researchers tends to be in the relevant content domain (mathematics, physics, chemistry, biology) rather than in psychology or cognitive science, and many are institutionally located in University departments of mathematics, physics, chemistry, and biology rather than in psychology or education. Different theoretical literatures tend to be cited by didactics researchers in countries with different linguistic backgrounds, with only minimal cross-referencing. In France, for example, many researchers working on the didactics of mathematics and the various scientific disciplines draw upon well-developed theoretical accounts of the process of designing teaching such as Chevellard's notion of *transposition didactique* (didactical transposition; Chevellard, 1991) and Brousseau's *théorie des situations didactiques* (theory of didactical situations; Brousseau, 1998). Didactical transposition addresses the process whereby the knowledge to be taught in particular teaching situations is developed within the institutional constraints of schooling, and in the context of disciplinary knowledge as used by practitioners of a given discipline. Tiberghien (2000), for example, draws upon Chevellard's notion of didactical transposition, Bachelard's perspective on modeling activity in physics (Bachelard, 1968), and Brousseau's notion of devolution (Brousseau, 1998) to illustrate detailed decisions in the design of physics teaching sequences. She then illustrates how these broad notions were used to specify the knowledge to be taught in the case of sound and electrical energy. By contrast, Dutch researchers in the didactics of physics and mathematics draw upon a different body of theory to justify their developmental research (e.g., Gravemeijer, 1994; Lijnse, 2000). These research programs use theory to focus upon the *aims of science teaching* at a *fine grain size*.

In other cases, didactics research draws mainly upon detailed examination of the content and structure of disciplinary knowledge, including its historical development, and a detailed account of students' domain-specific knowledge prior to instruction, to develop the aims of teaching at a fine grain size. Viennot and Rainson's (1999) work is a good example in this tradition. They recognize explicitly the need to move to a fine grain size in designing domain-specific teaching sequences:

> There is a wide choice, therefore a need for a decision, which will be by no means innocuous, in order to define the conceptual targets of a given teaching sequence. In other words, whereas a simplistic view would distinguish the 'what' of a teaching sequence from the 'how', we claim that both are interrelated and that the 'what' is to be specified in great detail after reasoned reflection. (Viennot & Rainson, 1999, p. 1)

They go on to present a careful analysis of the content and structure of a specific area of physics (i.e., the superposition of electric fields), as well as the mistakes that students commonly make when encountering teaching in this area, justifying in detail decisions about the design of a teaching sequence to address students' difficulties.

In articulating the case for didactics research, Piet Lijnse (2000) argues for the development of content-specific didactical knowledge, based on developing and justifying exemplary science teaching practices. He also bemoans the absence of this focus in "mainstream (Anglo-American) science educational research" (p. 312). However, in reviewing this small selection of papers where the implications for instructional design are at a small grain size, we are struck by the *absence* of clear presentations of content-specific theories for particular content domains in literature emanating from both North America and Europe. Lijnse (1995) perhaps goes some way towards explaining why this might be, when he states that didactical theory is:

> (a) detailed description of possible didactical structures for a certain topic, (which) may be given in what we call a scenario. A scenario describes and justifies in considerable detail the learning tasks and their interrelations, and what actions the students and teacher are supposed and expect to perform: it can be seen as the description and theoretical justification of a hypothetical interrelated learning and teaching process. (p. 196)

In other words, knowledge about how students develop conceptual understanding as a result of teaching in a specific domain is discussed through the content of a scenario (e.g., an artifact such as a teaching sequence with notes for the teacher). This kind of research is often described as similar to research and development in science and engineering, where the principal aim is to develop or improve a product. However, R+D scientists have a shared language to discuss the theory that informs their design decisions; at present, there does not appear to be such a language through which content-specific theories can be expressed and communicated between researchers. In a recent paper, Björn Andersson and Anita Wallin (2006) take up this issue explicitly. They present what they term a *content-oriented theory of teaching and learning biological evolution* as an example and specify detail around the following aspects:

1. Content-specific aspects (evolutionary time, the role of randomness, variation in hereditary characteristics, survival, reproduction and adaptation, levels of organization)

2. Aspects concerning the nature of science (evolution and religious belief, theoretical integration)
3. General aspects (the teacher as a bearer of culture) (p. 677).

Compared to other examples, this paper is more explicit about the content-specific knowledge about teaching and learning evolution that has been developed through research. However, the norms of school organization vary considerably between countries, and different teachers, schools and students have very different expectations about what counts as "good science teaching." How should this content-oriented knowledge about teaching and learning evolution be used by teachers, or other curriculum designers? Is the claim that some aspects of teaching and learning evolution are sufficiently well understood that they should always be treated as a fundamental aspect of the design of teaching? Or are there aspects that are amenable to local development and modification? Andersson and Wallin's (2006) account does not provide this level of specification.

We do not believe that there is yet an approach to designing teaching for conceptual understanding which maximizes the use of theoretical insights about learning and makes explicit how these are drawn upon, which makes explicit the content-specific theory that is developed through the research process, and is widely accepted and used by instructional designers. In the next section we present our own recent work on the design of teaching for conceptual understanding. We show how perspectives on learning are used to inform design decisions focusing upon both aims and pedagogical approaches at large and fine grain sizes.

DESIGNING TEACHING FOR CONCEPTUAL UNDERSTANDING: AN APPROACH BASED UPON A SOCIAL CONSTRUCTIVIST PERSPECTIVE

The Context for this Work

We have been involved in designing science teaching for conceptual understanding for around 20 years, both as science teachers and as professional researchers. Our experience of participation in the enterprise has left us extremely confident that, by drawing upon academic perspectives on teaching and learning, the effectiveness of science teaching to improve students' conceptual understanding of science can be positively enhanced. However, we are also aware of a significant gap between the *potential* for improving teaching by drawing upon academic perspectives on teaching and learning, and the *actual* improvements achieved. In particular, as we have indicated in this chapter there is very little work available that explains how design decisions about science teaching *at a fine grain size* can be informed by academic perspectives on teaching and learning. Furthermore, very few studies have been conducted that provide convincing evidence about improvements in students' conceptual understanding following teaching.

We decided, therefore, to conduct a study with the aim of developing an explicit account of the design of some short science teaching sequences, showing how theoretical and other insights were used with different foci and at different grain sizes, and evaluating the implementation of the teaching sequences. We worked collaboratively with a group of teachers to design three short teaching sequences, aimed at lower secondary school students. The teaching sequences addressed introductory ideas about simple electric circuits, particles and change, and plant nutrition.

From a Social Constructivist Perspective on Learning to Designing Science Teaching

We outlined the key features of our social constructivist theoretical framing perspective (Leach & Scott, 2002) earlier in the chapter. According to this perspective, we see teaching and learning science as involving an introduction to the social language of school science against a backdrop of everyday reasoning. This introduction to the social language of school science is carried out on the social plane of the classroom. Social constructivist theory thereby draws attention to the ways in which scientific knowledge might be systematically made available to students. The social constructivist perspective also draws attention to the individual sense-making step of internalization. It is important to draw upon evidence about students' likely pre-instructional knowledge in particular domains in the design of the teaching and providing teaching support for the students as they try to make sense of the science view. In the case of simple electric circuits, for example, there are well-established characterizations of students' likely pre-instructional reasoning, which we will present later in this chapter.

The Concept of Learning Demand

Such insights into learners' everyday reasoning provide a starting point for thinking about the design of teaching sequences. Building on this starting point, we have developed the notion of *learning demand* (Leach & Scott, 2002) to characterize more precisely the intellectual task faced by learners in coming to understand the scientific account of a given topic. The learning demand characterizes the ways in which the school science view of a particular natural phenomenon differs from everyday views of that phenomenon. Thus, learning science is conceptualized as coming to terms with the conceptual tools, and associated epistemology and ontology, of school science. If the differences between school science and everyday ways of reasoning are great, because there is little overlap between the concepts and associated epistemology and ontology of school science and everyday views, then the topic in question appears difficult to learn and to teach. Conversely, if there is considerable overlap between school science and everyday views, the learning demand is small and students may think that the school science account is easy or obvious.

The concept of learning demand itself follows from the social constructivist perspective on learning in setting up the comparison between everyday and school science social languages. Actually identifying learning demands involves drawing on research evidence about students' domain specific reasoning about natural phenomena. This evidence is empirical, based on students' written or oral responses to research questions (from the alternative conceptions literature), and much of it has been replicated through multiple studies around the world. The concept of learning demand therefore provides a bridge between findings of empirical research on students' reasoning, school science social language, and the design of teaching approaches.

Having identified the learning demands for each of the three teaching sequences, we then considered how these demands might be addressed through teaching. We started by identifying a set of *Teaching Goals* for each sequence. The teaching goals make explicit the ways in which the students' ideas and understandings are to be worked on through the intervention and guidance of the teacher, in order to address the identified learning demand. Once the teaching goals have been clarified, attention can be given to considering what teaching activities might be used to address these goals.

The overall approach to designing teaching, as set out above, is cast at a *large grain size*. In putting this generalized scheme into operation, it is necessary to become more specific and to work through the steps at a much finer grain size. We will illustrate this process by taking the case of the teaching sequence focusing on introductory ideas about electric circuits.

Designing a Teaching Sequence: The Case of Simple Electric Circuits

In the context of the National Curriculum for Science in England and Wales (DfEE, 1999), the school science knowledge to be taught involves developing a model of energy transfer via an electric current where:

- the current in a series circuit depends on the number of batteries and the number and nature of other components;
- current is not used up by components;
- energy is transferred from batteries and other sources to other components in electrical circuits.

This model is further developed in subsequent phases of the National Curriculum by introducing the concept of voltage. A review of the literature on teaching and learning about simple electric circuits was conducted, and the following characteristic patterns in students' reasoning were identified (see, for example, Psillos, 1998; Shipstone, 1988).

- The circuit is not viewed as a *whole system*, with changes occurring virtually simultaneously in all parts (for example, when a switch is closed charges are set into motion in all parts of the circuit together). Instead, students often explain effects in terms of *sequential* models, where any disturbance travels in one direction, affecting circuit components in succession. Thus, when an extra resistive component (such as a bulb) is added in series to a circuit, students often predict that the first component after the battery gets most, or all, of the energy.
- Students often think about electric circuits in terms of a *source* (the battery) and a *consumer* (for example, a bulb). This can lead to problems:
  — the charge which constitutes an electric current is considered to originate in the battery (the *source*).
  — the battery is considered to provide a fixed electric current.
  — when an extra battery is added to a circuit the extra current is thought to come from the additional battery (the *source*).
  — electric current and energy are not differentiated, with students suggesting that the current is used up in a bulb (the *consumer*).
- The size of the electric current is estimated to be less in high resistance parts of a circuit (such as a bulb filament) than in other parts (such as the connecting leads).

In relation to broader epistemological issues, it is likely that the students will have little experience of using a scientific model which involves moving between the theoretical world of the model (based on the abstract concepts of charge, current and energy) and the real world of observations and measurements (Tiberghien, 1996). They are also likely to have little appreciation of the fact that scientific models are intended to be applied generally to a wide range of contexts (Driver, Leach Millar, & Scott, 1996).

Identification of Learning Demands

By comparing the school science and everyday views identified above, the following *learning demands* were developed. Learning in this area involves the students in coming to:

- develop abstract scientific concepts of charge, current, resistance and energy in the context of explaining the behavior of simple electric circuits.
- understand that the battery is the source of energy for the circuit.
- understand that energy is transferred in the circuit and not the current.
- understand that the charges originate in the circuit and not in the battery.

- understand that an electric circuit behaves as a whole system such that a change in one part of the circuit affects all other parts of the circuit simultaneously.
- understand that the electric circuit model based on concepts of charge, current, resistance, energy can be used to predict and explain the behavior of a wide range of simple circuits.

The first five elements of the learning demand involve conceptual issues whilst the final element relates to more general epistemological matters. It is clear that all of these elements involve a high level of specificity in relation to learning demands: they are cast at a small grain size.

The first step in designing the teaching sequence itself involved formulating a set of teaching goals, which were based on the learning demands and specified more directly the nature of the pedagogical interventions to be taken by the teacher. The first set of teaching goals is conceptual (for example, drawing attention to ideas such as charges originating in the whole circuit rather than just the battery). The second set of teaching goals is epistemological (for example, being explicit that the concepts of charge, current, resistance and energy can be used to predict and explain the behavior of a wide range of circuits).

Designing Activities and Sequencing Them into Lessons

The teaching sequence was developed to address the teaching goals, with individual teaching activities being designed to enable teacher and students to focus upon key features of the content. In Lesson 1, for example, the teacher introduces a whole class activity involving a "BIG Circuit." This is a simple circuit including a battery and bulb, which stretches all of the way around the laboratory. The students are asked to predict what will happen when the BIG Circuit is completed. This activity was designed to challenge student thinking about the battery as source (as identified through the learning demand analysis) and debates typically ensue in class on whether the bulb will light straight away or after a short time. Completing the circuit shows that the bulb lights immediately and attention is then turned to developing a model to account for this finding: What is going on inside the circuit to allow this to happen? This activity is superficially similar to others used in science classrooms: it is a teacher demonstration with question-and-answer work. However, its design is focused specifically upon a learning demand which only becomes apparent through a comparison of students' pre-instructional knowledge and curriculum content goals.

Communicative Approach

The teaching sequences also contained guidance for teachers about different approaches to classroom communication at different points in the teaching. This guidance follows from the social constructivist framing perspective (see Leach & Scott, 2002) in acknowledging the fundamental importance of the interactions between teacher and students on the social plane, and is based on a framework developed by Mortimer and Scott (2003). Central to the analytical framework is the concept of *communicative approach*. The idea of communicative approach was introduced by Mortimer and Scott (2003) and provides a perspective on *how* the teacher works with pupils to develop ideas in the classroom. It focuses on questions such as whether or not the teacher interacts with pupils (teacher and pupils taking turns in the classroom talk), and also on whether the teacher takes account of pupils' ideas as the lessons proceed. The communicative approach is defined by characterizing the talk between teacher and pupils along each of two dimensions: *interactive-non interactive* and *dialogic-authoritative*.

Interactive teaching allows for the verbal participation of both teacher and students, and *non-interactive* teaching involves only the teacher. Thus in interactive teaching the teacher typically engages students in a series of questions and answers, whilst in non-interactive teaching the teacher presents ideas in a lecturing style. In a *dialogic* teaching approach, the teacher asks students for their points of view and explicitly takes account of them by, for example: asking for further details (for example, "Oh, that's interesting, what do you mean by..."); or writing them down for further consideration (for example, "Let's just put that down on the board, so that we don't forget it..."); or asking other students whether they agree with the ideas or not (for example, "Do you go along with what Julia has just said...?"). In short, the teacher makes room in the classroom talk for a whole range of ideas. In dialogic talk there is always the attempt to acknowledge the views of others, and through dialogic talk the teacher attends to the students' points of view as well as to the school science view. In an *authoritative* teaching approach, the teacher is likely to focus on the science point of view and if ideas or questions, which do not contribute to the development of the school science story, are raised by students they are likely to be re-shaped or ignored by the teacher.

In developing the teaching sequences, guidance was included about the communicative approach to be taken with each teaching activity. Thus, for example, with the BIG Circuit activity, the teaching purpose was to promote discussion about the how the circuit works, with the students making their points of view clear. For this particular activity, an interactive/dialogic communicative approach was therefore planned. In this way, the nature of the interactions between teacher and students on the social plane of the classroom was planned on an activity-by-activity basis. In other words the social interactions were planned at a *fine grain size*.

Reflections on the Design Process

The approach to identifying learning demands and developing teaching goals at a fine grain size, as exemplified in the previous section, is strongly informed by research evidence on students' everyday thinking. However, it is important to recognize that the process of developing teaching activities inevitably involves judgments about selecting one activity along with the associated communicative approach, rather than another, and that this step is less well informed by research evidence to evaluate different approaches. In developing teaching activities, it is also clear that effective lessons must motivate both students and teachers and conform to their expectations of what "good" science lessons look like. If a lesson is perceived as being dull, it is unlikely to prompt engagement of students and meaningful learning.

In order to move from teaching goals to sequences of lessons ready for the classroom, we drew upon the professional expertise of a group of nine teachers. These teachers attended planning meetings at the university where they contributed their professional knowledge to discussions about teaching activities to address specific teaching goals. In some cases the teachers suggested possible activities and at other times offered feedback on ideas proposed by the research team. The contribution of the teachers involved creative insight and professional knowledge about what would work rather than knowledge of research and scholarship on teaching and learning science, which came chiefly from the researchers. The researchers involved also had extensive experience in the past as classroom teachers, which they brought to bear on the design.

Looking back over this account, it is instructive to return to the question of what different insights, including research evidence, were employed in designing the teaching sequences, and what was the source of each kind of insight. The range of insights used are summarized in Figure 25.2.

We do not see the three teaching sequences as offering unique solutions in addressing the learning demands identified for the three content areas. We see them as *worked examples,* which present one way in which research evidence-informed design principles for teaching can be met.

Insight	Source of insight
1. Theoretical framing perspective: a social constructivist perspective on teaching and learning science	Scholarly writing in the academic literature on teaching and learning
2. Planning tools	
Learning demand	Developed from a social constructivist perspective on learning and teaching, and knowledge of the existence of research evidence about students' reasoning
Communicative approach	Scholarly writing in the academic literature - empirically validated as an *analytical* tool (but not as a *planning* tool leading to enhanced learning)
3. Students' reasoning	- multiple (and frequently replicated) empirical studies
4. Design of teaching sequences	
General pedagogical perspectives	- reflective articles, position papers, analytical accounts in science education and psychological research
Teaching and learning specific topics	- classroom-based empirical studies, but with limited comparative evaluation of learning data
Teachers' professional knowledge	

FIGURE 25.2   Insights informing the design of the teaching sequences.

This allows for the possibility of improving and adapting the worked examples for use in different settings, while remaining faithful to the underlying design principles.

Evaluation of the Teaching Sequences

The teaching sequences were evaluated in three ways. First, we were interested to know whether students attained conceptual understanding consistent with the aims of the teaching. The teaching sequences were taught to at least one group of students by each of the nine teachers who helped to develop them (the Development Phase teachers). We used a number of short diagnostic questions focusing upon key conceptual content to assess the students' understanding. The majority of these questions were administered both before and after teaching, although in some cases we did not judge it appropriate to ask students certain questions prior to teaching. For example, it did not seem sensible to ask questions about the readings on ammeters prior to teaching students what an ammeter is. Some of the questions were set in contexts that were covered in the teaching sequences, whilst others were designed to test students' ability in applying concepts in novel situations. The questions followed a structure whereby students were asked to make a prediction about behavior (such as whether a lamp would light in an electric circuit), followed by an explanation of that behavior based upon a taught model.

Second, we were interested to know something about the effectiveness of the teaching sequences compared to other teaching approaches. We therefore compared the conceptual understanding of the students who followed the designed sequences (as measured with the diagnostic questions) with the performance of similar students *in the same school,* who had followed the school's usual teaching program. This evidence was used to inform a judgment about the effectiveness of the designed teaching approach in promoting students' understanding, compared with the teaching approaches normally used in their schools. We have discussed the methodological difficulties in making such comparisons elsewhere (Leach & Scott, 2002).

Third, we were interested to know whether teachers who were not involved in the design of the teaching sequences could use them with similar results as the Development Phase teachers. In addition to the nine Development Phase teachers, we therefore worked with nine Transfer Phase teachers, who were not involved in developing the teaching sequences. The Transfer Phase teachers taught in schools of similar profile to those of the Development teachers (ranging from affluent outer suburban areas to the inner city), and implemented the written teaching sequences with at least one class of students. Pre- and post-test data were collected from students in Transfer Phase classes, and similar data were collected from students following the school's usual teaching approach. The chemistry teaching sequence was significantly different in structure from the two other sequences. It aimed to revise and extend students' understanding of the use of a simple particulate model of matter to account for physical and chemical change processes, rather than introduce ideas about physical and chemical change for the first time. It was not possible, however, to identify baseline classes covering similar content to the designed teaching sequence, and we did not therefore use the chemistry teaching sequence in the Transfer Phase of the study.

Data from the diagnostic questions completed by students who followed the biology and physics teaching sequences in the Development and Transfer Phases were analyzed as follows. First, students' predictions were coded as correct or not. Their explanations were then categorized into three groups:

- Responses broadly consistent with the scientific model introduced in the teaching (Consistent);
- Responses that are consistent with the taught model but incomplete in some respect (Incomplete);
- Other responses (Other).

These coded responses were averaged across all of the diagnostic questions used.

Using data from both the Development and Transfer phases (physics and biology), there are 15 pairs of experimental and baseline classes, in the same school, who had pre-test scores that are not significantly different[2] and where we therefore concluded that it is valid to make comparisons between the effectiveness of the designed teaching and the school's usual approach.

To what extent did students who followed the biology and physics teaching sequences develop conceptual understanding consistent with the teaching goals of the sequences? Ideally all students, after teaching, would be able to make correct predictions for the diagnostic questions. Looking across both sets of data, in 14 of the 15 experimental classes, at least 79.9% of student predictions were correct after following the designed teaching sequences. In addition, all students' explanations, after teaching, would ideally be consistent with the conceptual models taught. Realistically, however, it would be surprising if all students wrote explanations for *all* questions that drew upon *all* features of the taught conceptual models, particularly given that the diagnostic questions have an open format which provides minimal cueing about the level of detail required. Our more realistic aim, therefore, is that all students' explanations would be coded as either consistent or incomplete, with as many as possible being consistent. Students' actual results fall some considerable way short of this ideal. Nevertheless, looking across our evaluations of the biology and physics teaching sequences, students who followed the designed teaching sequences in all 15 cases were significantly more likely to draw upon the conceptual models introduced in teaching, when compared with students in associated baseline groups. Although mean scores for students in the Development Phase are higher than those for students in the Transfer Phase, this difference is not statistically significant.

CONCLUDING STATEMENTS

This chapter has focused upon the relationship between perspectives on conceptual learning, and the process of designing teaching. We have observed that many design decisions are at a fine grain size, and that it is not always clear how these might be informed by academic perspectives on learning and teaching. Rather, suggestions about the practice of teaching that are put forward from insights about learning are often made at a large grain size. We presented an example of our own work, to illustrate one possible approach to using perspectives on learning to inform design decisions about the aims, and pedagogical approach of teaching, starting off with a general approach cast at a large grain size and going down to a small grain size. Our approach draws upon insights about students' domain-specific reasoning to focus on design decisions about learning aims, and insights about classroom communication to propose different communicative approaches for particular purposes in the teaching, at a relatively small grain size. There are, of course, other insights about learning that we did not use explicitly in our work on the design of teaching. For example, we did not draw upon the literature on skilled performance cited by Branford et al. (2000) to build opportunities for practice into the teaching sequences (though opportunities for practice can be found in the sequences of lessons). These were informed by professional knowledge about the practice of teaching, rather than insights about learning per se.

In a recent book, Millar, Leach, Osborne, and Ratcliffe (2006) have explored the relationship between evidence from educational research and the design of subject teaching. They introduce the term *research evidence-informed (REI) practice* (pp. 9–10) to describe an educational practice (such as *teaching*) which draws explicitly upon insights from research and scholarship on learning in its design. This is contrasted with *research evidence-based (REB) practice*, which describes an educational practice which is carried out because there is empirical evidence that it achieves certain aims better than other approaches. The examples of teaching for conceptual understanding reviewed in this chapter are all, in Millar et al.'s terms, examples of REI practice in that scholarly perspectives on learning, and in some cases examples of empirical evaluations of teaching, have been drawn upon (more or less explicitly) to inform design decisions about the teaching.

Although many of the examples of teaching discussed in this chapter were developed through an iterative process of design and evaluation, none of them are presented by the authors as examples of research evidence-based practice, that is, examples which have been shown empirically to be better than other approaches at meeting a named set of goals. In spite of the prominent calls for education to become more "evidence based" (such as the No Child Left Behind Act in the USA), and in common with many educational researchers attempting to improve students' conceptual understanding through the design of teaching interventions, we believe that it is naïve to assume that any educational practice can be shown to be straightforwardly "better" than other practices. This is because decisions at a very fine grain size can make a very significant difference to students' conceptual learning following teaching, and collecting robust evidence about the implications of such decisions on students' learning is, methodologically, extremely difficult. These arguments are addressed in more detail by Leach, Ametller, Hind, Lewis, and Scott (2006).

As we stated previously, we view research evidence-informed teaching sequences as *worked examples* of how a set of design principles can be put into practice in a particular educational situation, with all of its constraints. This includes teachers' preferred ways of working in the classroom, and students' and other stakeholders' expectations about the norms of schooling. We agree with Pawson and Tilley (1997) that:

…choice is the very condition of social and individual change and not some kind of practical hindrance to understanding that change… *it is not programmes [or interventions] which work, as such, but people cooperating and choosing to make them work.* (p. 46, emphasis in original)

However, acknowledging the importance of choice in successful teaching for conceptual understanding is not the same as saying that all choices are equally effective. Many worked examples could be developed to address a set of design principles, and it is not straightforward to generate evidence about which is better or best. Nonetheless, some design principles are likely to be central to the overall teaching strategy. In the case of our teaching about electric circuits, for example, a central design principle is that the use of an analogy is the most effective way of enabling students to see how the behavior of a circuit is conceptualized as a *system*, rather than as a sequence of distinct events, operating over a temporal sequence. There is a significant body of evidence to suggest that many students are likely to have difficulties in understanding this aspect of a scientific explanation of the behavior of electric circuits without specific teaching to address the problem. An analogy is first introduced to students in its own terms, to explain the behavior of a circuit, and then students are shown how the analogy maps onto a school science explanation of the behavior of electric circuits. Eventually, students are supported in using the school science explanation without recourse to the analogy.

Teachers using the worked example will inevitably be involved in making literally thousands of choices about how to proceed in each lesson. Teachers will no doubt develop their own repertoire of anecdotes and stories to support students' understanding, and we view this as an essential aspect of the practice of teaching. Our point is that if teachers significantly modify the analogy itself, or the strategy for its introduction on the social plane of the classroom, a key design principle of the teaching has been broken, and this is likely to have a detrimental effect on students' conceptual understanding.

We believe that those involved in designing teaching to promote conceptual understanding, including ourselves, have some way to go in making explicit the design principles that underpin their worked examples, and the rationale behind these design principles (including perspectives on the nature of conceptual learning). Specifically, we believe that there is some way to go in explaining how, and whether, learning theory has been used to inform the aims of teaching for conceptual understanding, and the pedagogical approach, at a fine grain size. Achieving this would inevitably involve developing a terminology through which domain-specific theories of learning and teaching could be articulated. *Learning demand*, *focus,* and *grain size* might be included in the terminology. We believe that developing such a terminology would facilitate curriculum development, and teacher professional development, with a central focus upon teaching and learning for conceptual understanding.

ACKNOWLEDGMENTS

The authors contributed equally to this chapter. We have drawn heavily on previously published work in preparing this chapter, particularly Leach and Scott (2002), Leach and Scott (2003), Leach, Ametller, Hind, Lewis, and Scott (2006) and Scott, Asoko and Leach (2007). The work on designing and evaluating science teaching sequences was conducted as part of the Economic and Social Research Council Teaching and Learning Research Programme Research Network *Towards Evidence-based Practice in Sscience Education* (Award L139251003).

NOTES

1. Intelligence organises the world by organising itself
2. In fact, two of the experimental groups were significantly better at making predictions about the behaviour of phenomena, though their explanations were not significantly different from students in the baseline groups. On that basis, we did not exclude them from the sample.

REFERENCES

Adey, P., & Shayer, M. (1993). *Really raising standards*. London: Routledge.

Andersson, B. (1976). *Science teaching and the development of thinking*. Gothenburg: Acta Universitatis Gothoburgensis.

Andersson, B., & Wallin, A. (2006). On developing content-oriented theories taking biological evolution as an example. *International Journal of Science Education, 28*(6), 673–695.

Ausubel, D. P. (1968). *Educational psychology: A cognitive view*. New York: Holt, Rinehart and Winston.

Bachelard, G. (1968). *The philosophy of no*. G. C. Waterston (Trans.). New York: The Orion Press.

Bakhtin, M. M. (1934/1981). Discourse in the Novel. In M. M. Bakhtin (Ed.), *The dialogic imagination*, C. Emerson & M. Holquist (Trans.), (rev. ed., pp. 259–422). Austin: University of Texas Press.

Branford, J. D., Brown, A. L., & Cocking, R. R. (Eds.). (2000). *How people learn: Brain, mind, experience, and school* (expanded ed.). Washington, DC: National Research Council.

Brousseau, G. (1998). *Théorie des situations didactiques*. Grenoble: La Pensée Sauvage Éditions.

Brown, A. (1992). Design experiments: theoretical and methodological challenges in creating complex interventions. *Journal of the Learning Sciences, 2*(2), 141–178.

Brown, J. S., Collins, A., & Duguid, P. (1989). Situated cognition and the culture of learning. *Educational Researcher, 18*(1), 32–42.

Bruner, J. (1985). Vygotsky: An historical and conceptual perspective. In J.Wertsch (Ed.), *Culture, communication and cognition: Vygotskian perspectives* (pp. 21–34). Cambridge: Cambridge University Press.

Carey, S. (1985). Conceptual change in childhood. Cambridge, MA: MIT Press.

Chevellard, Y. (1991). *La transposition didactique*. Grenoble: La Pensée Sauvage Éditions.

Chinn, C., & Brewer, W. (1993). The role of anomalous data in knowledge acquisition: a theoretical framework and implications for science instruction. *Review of Educational Research, 63*(1), 1–49.

Cobb, P., Confrey, J., diSessa, A., Lehrer, R., & Schauble, L. (2003). Design experiments in educational research. *Educational Researcher, 32*(1), 9–13.

Cobb, P., & McClain, K. (2004). Proposed design principles for the teaching and learning of elementary statistics. In D. Ben-Zvi & J. Garfield (Eds.), *The challenge of developing statistical literacy, reasoning, and thinking* (pp. 375–396). Dordrecht, Netherlands: Kluwer.

Collins, A., Brown, J. S., & Newman, S. (1989). Cognitive apprenticeship: Teaching the craft of reading, writing and mathematics. In L. Resnick (Ed.), *Cognition and instruction: Issues and agendas* (pp. 453–494). Hillsdale, NJ: Erlbaum.

Design-Based Research Collective (2003). Design-based research: An emerging paradigm for educational inquiry. *Educational Researcher, 32*(1), 5–8.

DfEE (1999). *Science in the national curriculum*. London: HMSO.

Donaldson, M. (1978). *Children's minds*. London: Croom Helm.

Donovan, M. S., & Branford, J. D. (Eds.). (2005). *How students learn: science in the classroom*. Washington, DC: The National Academic Press.

Driver, R. (1973). Representation of conceptual frameworks in young adolescent science students. Unpublished PhD thesis, the University of Illinois at Urbana-Champaign.

Driver, R. (1978). When is a stage not a stage? A critique of Piaget's theory of cognitive development and its application to science education. *Educational Research, 21*(1), 54–61.

Driver, R. (1983). *The pupil as scientist?* Milton Keynes, UK: Open University Press.

Driver, R., & Easley, J. (1978). Pupils and paradigms: A review of literature related to concept development in adolescent science students. *Studies in Science Education, 5,* 3–12.

Driver, R., Asoko, H., Leach, J., Mortimer, E., & Scott, P. (1994). Constructing scientific knowledge in the classroom. *Educational Researcher, 23*(7), 5–12.

Driver, R., Leach, J., Millar, R., & Scott, P. (1996). *Young people's images of science.* Buckingham, UK: Open University Press.

Driver, R., & Oldham, V. (1985). A constructivist approach to curriculum development in science. *Studies in Science Education, 13,* 105–122.

Duit, R. (2006). Students' and Teachers' Conceptions in Science Educaton. Keil, Germany: IPN. Available at http://www.ipn.uni-kiel.de/aktuell/stcse/stcse.html (accessed 7 February 2007).

Engle, R. A., & Conant, F. R. (2002). Guiding principles for fostering productive disciplinary engagement: explaining emergent argument in a community of learners classroom. *Cognition and Instruction, 20*(4), 399–483.

Gravemeijer, K. E. P. (1994). *Developing realistic mathematics education.* Utrecht, The Netherlands: CD-B Press.

Hennessy, S. (1993). Situated cognition and cognitive apprenticeship: Implications for classroom learning. *Studies in Science Education, 22,* 1–41.

Hewson, P., & Lemberger, J. (2000). Status as the hallmark of conceptual learning. In R. Millar, J. Leach, & J. Osborne (Eds.), *Improving science education: The contribution of research* (pp. 110–125). Open University Press.

Hodson, D., & Hodson, J. (1998). From constructivism to social constructivism: A Vygotskian perspective on teaching and learning science. *School Science Review, 79*(289), 33–41.

Holquist, M., & Emerson, C. (1981). Glossary for the dialogic imagination. In M. M. Bakhtin (Ed.), *Four essays.* (pp. 423–434). University of Texas Press, Austin.

Kelly, A. E. (2003). Research as design. *Educational Researcher, 32*(1), 3–4.

Koslowski, B. (1996). *Theory and evidence: The development of scientific reasoning.* Cambridge: MIT Press.

Krajcik, J., McNeill, K., & Reiser, B. (2006). A learning goals driven design model for developing science curricula. Paper presented at the Annual Meeting of the American Educational Research Association, San Francisco, CA.

Krajcik, J., Blumenfeld, P., Marx, R., & Solway, E. (2000). Instructional, curricular and technological supports for inquiry learning in science classrooms. In J. Minstrell & E. van Zee (Eds.), *Inquiring into inquiry learning and teaching in ccience* (pp. 283–315). Washington, DC: AAAS.

Kuhn, D. (1991). *The skills of argument.* Cambridge: Cambridge University Press.

Kuhn, D., Amsel, E., & O'Loughlin, M. (1988). *The development of scientific thinking skills.* London: Academic Press.

Lave, J. (1988). *Cognition in practice: Mind, mathematics and culture in everyday life.* Cambridge: Cambridge University Press.

Lave, J., & Wenger, E. (1991). *Situated learning: legitimate peripheral participation.* New York: Cambridge University Press.

Lawson, A. (1985). A review of research on formal reasoning and science teaching. *Journal of Research in Science Teaching, 22,* 569–618.

Leach, J., Ametller, J., Hind, A., Lewis, J., & Scott, P. (2006). Implementing and evaluating teaching interventions: towards evidence-based practice? In R. Millar, J. Leach, J. Osborne, & M. Ratcliffe (Eds.), *Improving subject teaching: lessons from research in science education* (pp. 479–492). London: RoutledgeFalmer.

Leach, J., & Scott, P. (2002). Designing and evaluating science teaching sequences: an approach drawing upon the concept of learning demand and a social constructivist perspective on learning. *Studies in Science Education, 38,* 115–142.

Leach, J., & Scott, P. (2003). Learning science in the classroom: Drawing on individual and social perspectives. *Science and Education, 12*(1), 91–113.

Lemke, J. L. (1990). *Talking science. Language, learning and values.* Norwood, NJ: Ablex Publishing.

Lemke, J. L. (2003). Teaching all the languages of science: Words, symbols, images and actions. Retrieved February 1, 2008, from http://academic.brooklyn.cuny.edu/education/jlemke/papers/barcelon.htm

Leontiev, A. N. (1981). The problem of activity in psychology. In J. V. Wertsch (Ed.), *The concept of activity in Soviet psychology* (pp. 37–71). Armonk, NY: Sharpe.

Lijnse, P. (1995). 'Developmental research' as a way to an empirically based 'didactical structure' of science. *Science Education, 79*(2), 189–199.

Lijnse, P. L. (2000). Didactics of science: The forgotten dimension in science education research? In R. Millar, J. Leach, & J. Osborne (Eds.), *Improving science education: The contribution of research* (pp 308–326). Buckingham, UK: Open University Press.

Matthews, M. (1992). Constructivism and empiricism: an incomplete divorce. *Research in Science Education, 22,* 299–307.

McClosky, M. (1983). Intuitive physics. *Scientific American, 248,* 122–130.

Metz, K. (1997). Reassessment of developmental constraints on children's science instruction. *Review of Educational Research, 65,* 93–127.

Metz, K. E. (1998). Scientific inquiry within reach of young children. In B. J. Fraser & K.G. Tobin (Eds.), *International handbook of science education* (pp. 81–96). Dordrecht, The Netherlands: Kluwer Academic.

Millar, R. (1989). Constructive criticisms. *International Journal of Science Education, 11*(5), 587–596.

Millar, R., Leach, J., Osborne, J., & Ratcliffe, M. (2006). *Improving subject teaching: Lessons from science education research.* London: RoutledgeFalmer.

Mortimer, E., & Scott, P. (2003). *Meaning making in secondary science classrooms.* Milton Keynes, UK: Open University Press.

Novak, J. (1978). An alternative to Piagetian psychology for science and mathematics education. *Studies in Science Education, 5,* 1–30.

Ogborn, J., Kress, G., Martins, I., & McGillicuddy, K. (1996). Explaining science in the classroom. Buckingham, UK: Open University Press.

O'Loughlin, M. (1992). Rethinking science education: Beyond Piagetian constructivism toward a sociocultural model of teaching and learning. *Journal of Research in Science Teaching, 29*(8), 791–820.

Osborne, R., & Freyberg, P. (1985). *Learning in science: the implications of children's science.* Aukland: Henemann.

Oser, F, K., & Baeriswyl, F. J. (2001). Choreographies of teaching: bridging instruction to learning. In V. Richardson (Ed.), *Handbook of research on teaching* (4th ed.; pp. 1031–1065). Washington, DC.: AERA.

Pawson, R., & Tilley, N. (1997). *Realistic evaluation.* London: Sage.

Piaget, J. (1937). *La construction du réel chez l'enfant.* Neuchâtel: Felachaux et Niestlé.

Piaget, J. (1971). *Biology and knowledge.* Edinburgh: Edinburgh University Press.

Posner, G. J., Strike, K. A., Hewson, P. W., & Gerzog, W.A. (1982). Accommodation of a scientific conception: toward a theory of conceptual change. *Science Education, 66*(2), 211–227.

Psillos, D. (1998). Teaching introductory electricity. In A. Tiberghien, E. L. Jossem, & J. Barojas (Eds.), Connecting research in physics education with teacher education: An ICPE Book', International Commission on Physics Education. Available at http://www.physics.ohio-state.edu/~jossem/ICPE/TOC.html (accessed 4 January 2005).

Rogoff, B. (1990). *Apprenticeship in thinking: Cognitive development in social context.* Oxford: Oxford University Press.

Roth, W.-M. (1995). *Authentic school science. Knowing and learning in open-inquiry science laboratories.* Dordrecht, The Netherlands: Kluwer Academic.

Roth, W-M. (2005). *Talking science: Language and learning in science classrooms.* Lanham, MD: Rowman and Littlefield.

Roth, W-M., & Bowen, G. M. (1995). Knowing and interacting: a study of culture, practices and resources in a Grade 8 open-inquiry science classroom guided by a cognitive apprenticeship metaphor. *Cognition and Instruction, 13,* 73–128.

Roth, W-M. & Désautels, J. (2002). *Science education as/for sociopolitical action.* New York: Counterpoints.

Ryder, J., Leach, J., & Driver, R. (1999). Undergraduate science students' images of the nature of science. *Journal of Research in Science Teaching, 36*(2), 201–220.

Scott, P., Asoko, H., & Leach, J. (2007). Student conceptuions and conceptual learning in science. In S. K. Abell & N. G. Lederman (Eds.), *Handbook of research on science education.* Mahwah, NJ: Erlbaum.

Scribner, S. (1984). Studying working intelligence. In B. Rogoff & J. Lave (Eds.), *Everyday cognition: Its development in social context* (pp. 9–40). Cambridge, MA: Harvard University Press.

Sfard, A. (1998). On two metaphors for learning and the dangers of choosing just one. *Educational Researcher, 27*(2), 4–13.

Shayer, M. (2003). Not just Piaget; not just Vygotsky, and certainly not Vygotsky as alternative to Piaget. *Learning and Instruction, 13,* 465–485.

Shipstone, D. M. (1988). Students' understanding of simple electrical circuits. *Physics Education, 23*(2), 92–96.

Sjøberg, S. (1996). Science education research in Europe: some reflections for the future association. In A. G. Welford, J. Osborne, & P. Scott (Eds.), *Science education research in Europe: Current issues and themes* (pp. 399–403). London: Falmer Press.

Thorley, N. R. (1990). The role of the conceptual change model in the interpretation of classroom interactions. Unpublished doctoral dissertation, University of Wisconsin-Madison.

Tiberghien, A. (1996). Construction of prototypical situations in teaching the concept of energy. In A. G. Welford, J. Osborne, & P. Scott (Eds.), *Science education research in Europe: Current issues and themes* (pp. 100–114). London: Falmer.

Tiberghien, A. (2000). Designing teaching situations in the secondary school. In R. Millar, J. Leach, & J. Osborne (Eds.), *Improving science education: The contribution of research* (pp. 27–47). Buckingham, UK: Open University Press.

Tochon, F. V. (1999). Semiotic foundations for building the new didactics: an introduction to the prototype features of the discipline. *Instructional Science, 27*(1-2), 9–32.

von Glasersfeld, E. (1998). Why constructivism must be radical. In M. Larochelle, N. Bednarz, & J. Garrison (Eds.), *Constructivism and education* (pp. 23–28). London: Cambridge University Press.

von Glasersfeld, E. (1999). How do we mean? A constructivist sketch of semantics. *Cybernetics & Human Learning, 6*(1), 9–16.

Viennot, L. (1979). Spontaneous reasoning in elementary dynamics. *European Journal of Science Education, 1*(2), 205–221.

Viennot, L., & Rainson, S. (1999). Design and evaluation of a research based teaching sequence: the superposition of electric fields. *International Journal of Science Education, 21*(1), 1–16.

Vygotsky, L. S. (1978). *Mind in society: The development of higher psychological processes.* Cambridge, MA: Harvard University Press.

Vygotsky, L. S. (1987). *The collected works of L. S. Vygotsky, Volume 1.* R. W. Rieber & A .S. Carton (Eds.), N. Minick (Trans.). New York: Plenum.

Wells, G. (1999). *Dialogic inquiry. Toward a sociocultural practice and theory of education.* Cambridge: Cambridge University Press.

Wertsch, J.V. (1991). *Voices of the mind: A sociocultural approach to mediated action.* Cambridge, MA: Harvard University Press.

26

Model Building for Conceptual Change

David Jonassen
University of Missouri

PREMISE: MODELING FOR CONCEPTUAL CHANGE

Conceptual change is most meaningful when it is intentional (Dole & Sinatra, 1998). In order for intentional conceptual change to occur, according to Luque (2003), learners must be aware of a need to change and be able to know what to change; learners must want to change, making change as a personal goal; and learners must be able to self-regulate the process of change, that is, be able to plan, monitor, and evaluate the process (self-regulation prerequisite). The question that pervades much of the work described in the book is, "how do we engage and encourage intentional conceptual change?"

Vosniadou (1992, 1994), like many researchers, believes that conceptual change arises from interaction between experience and current conceptions during problem solving. Nersessian (1999) agrees that conceptual change results most consistently from extended problem solving or some higher-order cognitive activity. However, an unanswered question is what kind of problem solving is necessary for engaging conceptual change. Jonassen (2000) described several dimensions of problem solving (structuredness, complexity, abstractness, and dynamicity). Based largely on a continuum of problems from well structured to ill structured, he also identified several different kinds of problems (algorithms, story (word) problems, rule-using problems, troubleshooting, diagnosis-solution, strategic performance, policy problems, design problems, and dilemmas). What we need to know is which kinds of problems best engage conceptual change processes? How complex and dynamic should those problems be? Does conceptual change result more consistently from embedding problems in rich contexts?

The answers to these questions can be found, not in empirical evidence, but in principles of conceptual change. Conceptual change requires conceptual engagement (Dole & Sinatra, 1998). Learners tend to interact with information that is comprehensible, coherent, and plausible in light of their existing theories. The degree to which learners interact with new information lies on a continuum from low cognitive engagement to high metacognitive engagement. When learners are not cognitively engaged, they are processing information shallowly. *Conceptual change requires high cognitive engagement*. In order to restructure what they know, learners must become self-regulated and effortful, analyzing and synthesizing new information. At the highest level of engagement, according to Dole and Sinatra (1998), learners think deeply about arguments and counterarguments related to the message, resulting in the strongest likelihood of conceptual change. These are skills that are more consistently required of ill-structured problems rather than well-structured problems (Hong, Jonassen, & McGee, 2003); however, a great deal of empirical research is needed to isolate the problem-solving factors that more readily encourage intentional conceptual change.

The premise of this chapter is that using computer technologies to construct qualitative and quantitative models of phenomena being studied is among the most conceptually engaging tasks that students can undertake in schools, and it has significant potential for engaging and assessing conceptual change as well as supporting different kinds of problems solving. After discussing different roles for models and explicating a rationale for building models to engage conceptual change, I describe how computer formalisms can be used as cognitive tools (AKA Mindtools; Jonassen, 1996, 2000, 2006) for representing different kinds of knowledge. I conclude by describing some limitations of modeling for conceptual change.

What Are Models?

There are numerous kinds of models that can be used to represent phenomena in the world or the mental models that learners construct to represent them. Mathematicians and scientists most often refer to computational models using mathematical formalisms (e.g., calculus, differential equations, Bayesian probabilities). Data models are only one kind of model. Harris (1999) describes three kinds of models: data models, theoretical models, and experimental models. Theoretical models are abstract representations of systemic elements or factors, while experimental models are designed to test the theoretical models. They are more specific than theoretical, including directives for action; specifications of the size of sample populations; definitions of experimental variables and test statistics; and measures for comparing hypotheses and observed values. Their purpose is to predict or specify the kind of data that we are looking for and to specify analytical techniques for linking data to questions. Lehrer and Schauble (2003) describe a continuum of model types including physical models, representational systems (grounded in resemblance between the model and the world), syntactic models (summarizing essential functioning of system), and hypothetical-deductive models (formal abstractions). Whatever they are, models qualitatively, functionally, or formally resemble the real objects under study (Yu, 2002).

How Are Models Used?

Historically, much of the modeling research has focused on mathematization as the primary modeling formalism. Representing phenomena in formulas is the most succinct and exact form of modeling. However, most contemporary researchers argue that qualitative models are just as important as quantitative. Qualitative representation is a missing link in novice problem solving (Chi, Feltovich, & Glaser, 1981; Larkin, 1983). When students try to understand a problem in only one way, especially when that way conveys no conceptual information about the problem, students do not understand the underlying systems they are working in. So, it is necessary to help learners to construct a qualitative model of the problem as well as a quantitative. Qualitative models both constrain and facilitate the construction of quantitative representations (Ploetzner & Spada, 1998).

Modeling is fundamental to human cognition and scientific inquiry. Modeling helps learners to express and externalize their thinking; visualize and test components of their theories; and make materials more interesting. Models function as epistemic resources (Morrison & Morgan, 1999). We must first understand what we can demonstrate in the model before we can ask questions about the real system.

External and Internal Models

Models are conceptual systems consisting of elements, relations, operations, and rules governing interactions that are expressed using external notation systems and that are used to construct, describe, or explain the behavior of other systems (Lesh & Doerr, 2003). The models that are constructed by learners using equations, diagrams, and computer programs represent the models that exist in the minds of learners. That is, there are models in the mind (mental models) and there are models in the world that are constructed by learners. Both of these kinds of models reflect phenomena in the world. The relationship between internal and external models is not well understood, but there is good reason to believe that there is a dynamic and reciprocal relationship between internal mental models and the external models that students construct. The mental models provide the basis for external models. The external models in turn constrain and regulate internal models, providing the means for conceptual change. In this chapter, I argue for the construction of external, syntactic models using different technology-based modeling tools, because each tool imposes a different set of structural or rhetorical constraints (syntaxes) that enable student to tune their internal models.

The ability to form mental models is a basic characteristic of human cognitive system, and these mental models are essential for conceptual development and conceptual change (Vosniadou, 2002a). When solving problems, learners may construct models and apply those models to solving problems rather than by applying logical rules (Vandierendonck & deVooght, 1996). As soon as problems are presented, learners construct an initial model and integrate new information into the model in order to make the model look and function like the problem. The mental models that learners construct are generally believed to retain the structure of the world that they are representing. Mental models, according to Norman (1983), are the internal representations that humans develop of themselves and the objects they interact with in the world. Mental models are developed inductively as we interact with objects for the purpose of reasoning about causality in physical systems. These models often result in analogical, incomplete, or even fragmentary representations of how those objects and the system they are in work (Farooq & Dominick, 1988). Humans comprehend the world by constructing mental models of it (Johnson-Laird, 1983). Those models that are structural analogs of real world or imaginary situations, events, or processes. The spatial and temporal models embody representations of the relations and causal structures connecting the events and entities represented in the model.

Stronger or more radical forms of conceptual change require significant restructuring of mental models. Model building is critical to this kind of conceptual change. Conceptual change is task-dependent. The task most engages and supports the construction and reorganization of mental models uses a variety of tools for constructing physical, visual, logical, or computation models of phenomena. Building representational and interpretive models using technologies provides learners the opportunities to externalize and restructure their mental models. When students discover conceptual anomalies or inconsistencies in their own conceptual structures by modeling them, they are more likely to revise and restructure them. In order to recognize and resolve perturbations or anomalies, learners must use experimentation or some other high engagement process such as modeling to compare rival conceptions (Dole & Sinatra, 1998).

Model-Using vs. Model-Building

We learn from models by using them and by building them (Morgan, 1999). What we can learn from using models, however, depends on the extent to which we can transfer the things we learn from manipulating the model to our theory of the real world. Learning from building models involves finding out what elements fit together in order to represent the theory of the world. Modeling requires making certain choices, and it is in these choices that the learning process lays. "We do not learn much from looking at a model — we learn a lot more from building the model and from manipulating it" (Morrison & Morgan, 1999, pp. 11–12).

Despite the cognitive benefits of building models, technology-based learning environments more often exemplify model using. Models are commonly used as the cognitive engine in software. Most intelligent tutoring systems possess learner models, expert or domain models, and tutoring models. Models also provide the cognitive engine in microworlds, such as Geometric Supposer, SimCalc, and others. In microworlds, the model is implicit in the exploratory options provided by the software, but the model is not explicitly demonstrated. Learners interact with these black-box systems in order to infer the propositions embedded in the model in order to test hypotheses. Research shows that interacting with model-based environments can result in development and change of mental models (Frederiksen & White, 1998; Mellar, Bliss, Boohan, Ogborn, & Tompsett, 1994). Model using has certain cognitive limitations. For example, the model is immutable. Not only do learners have no access to the model, but also they cannot change it in order to change the assumptions of the system being modeled.

The major premise of this chapter is that building models using different qualitative and quantitative formalisms embedded in different classes of modeling software is among the most conceptually engaging classroom activities possible that has the greatest potential for engaging and encouraging conceptual change processes. Modeling is an important method for engaging conceptual change (Nersessian, 1999). Building explicit models externalizes or reifies mental models or personal theories, thereby fostering conceptual change. The multiple formalisms afforded by different modeling tools enable learners to construct syntactically different models. Comparing and contrasting those models is an essential process in comprehension. Other essential characteristics of models include the separation of model and its referent, assessment of the fit of the model to its referent, the conventionalization of the external representations used in the model, and the incorporation of models into disciplinary practice (Lehrer & Schauble, 2003). Perhaps the most important characteristic that Lehrer and Schauble cite is the evaluation of competing alternative models, that is, the comparison of two or more models for their relative fit to the world. Comparing and evaluating models requires understanding that alternative models are possible and that the activity of modeling can be used for testing rival models. That process is at the heart of conceptual change. "Inquiry takes on new meaning when one moves from identifying simple relationships and principles in existing expert models to producing a model of one's own that describes and predict the behavior of a system" (Windschitl, 2000, pp. 89–90). Interacting with model-based environments certainly can result in conceptual change. However, the models that learners build mediate between personal theories and related objects or phenomena in the world. When discrepancies between the models learners build and scientifically valid understandings occur, learners must revise their models, which reflects concomitant changes on learners' mental models. Therefore, building models is among the most conceptually embedded and engaging tasks that students can undertake, and building models of problems being solved enhances problem solving which in turn enhances conceptual change. Although building models of all kinds (physical, computational, or virtual) can engage and support conceptual change, this chapter will focus on the use of computer-based modeling tools.

RATIONALES FOR MODELING

Constructing technology-mediated models of phenomena is among the most conceptually engaging tasks that students can undertake. Modeling engages and supports conceptual change and also provides measurable evidence of conceptual change. The conceptual reasons for constructing models to support meaningful learning and mental model construction include:

- Model building is a natural cognitive phenomenon. When encountering unknown phenomena, humans naturally begin to construct personal theories about those phenomena that are represented as models.
- Modeling is essentially constructivist — constructing personal representations of experienced phenomena.
- Modeling supports hypothesis testing, conjecturing, inferring, and a host of other important cognitive skills.
- Modeling requires learners to articulate causal reasoning, the cognitive basis for most scientific reasoning.
- Modeling is important because it is among the most conceptually engaging cognitive processes that can be performed, which is a strong predictor of conceptual change.
- Modeling results in the construction of cognitive artifacts (externalized mental models).
- When students construct models, they own the knowledge. Student ownership is important to meaning making and knowledge construction.
- Modeling supports the development of epistemic beliefs. Epistemologically, what motivates our efforts to make sense of the world? According to Wittgenstein (1953), what we know is predicated on the possibility of doubt. We know many things, but we can never be certain that we know it. As already described, comparing and evaluating models requires understanding that alternative models are possible and that the activity of modeling can be used for testing rival models (Lehrer & Schauble, 2003).

Modeling Different Kinds of Knowledge Using Computer-Based Modeling Tools

If model building externalizes mental models, then learners should learn to use a variety of tools to model a variety of phenomena in a variety of ways. Each tool provides a different formalism for representing mental models in different ways (Jonassen, 2000). In this section, I briefly describe the how different kinds of knowledge can be represented using different modeling tools. Most of these models are what Lehrer and Schauble (2000) refer to as syntactic models. These are formal models, each of which imposes a different syntax on the learner that conveys a relational correspondence between the model and the phenomena it is representing. The purpose of syntactic models is to summarize the essential function of the system being represented.

Semantic Models

The primary use of modeling has been in the math and science domains. Middle school and high school students use computer-based modeling tools, such as databases or concept mapping tools, to construct their models of domain knowledge. Modeling the underlying semantics or structural knowledge (Jonassen, Beissner, & Yacci, 1993) in any domain is necessary but not sufficient for comprehending any domain. More complete comprehension also requires causal and experiential understanding (described later). For example, Figure 26.1 illustrates a semantic model of stoichiometry, the molar conversion process in chemistry, that was produced using the concept-mapping tool, Inspiration (many other concept mapping tools exist). That model illustrates the semantic relationships between all of the important stoichiometric concepts such as mole and atomic mass and the semantic relationships between them (measures/measured by). As students study domain content in a course, concept-mapping tools provides them a seman-

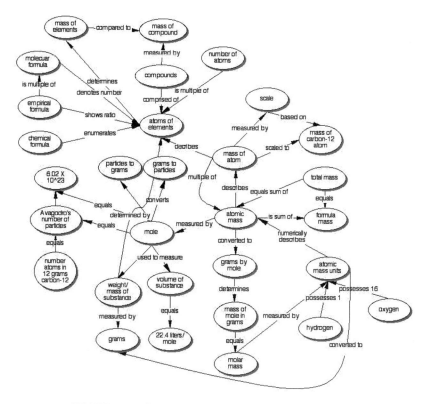

FIGURE 26.1   Semantic model of molar conversion process.

tic structure for representing their domain knowledge. In a meta-analysis of concept-mapping studies, Horton, McConney, Gallo, & Woods (1993) showed that concept mapping supports knowledge acquisition. Comparing your semantic network with others often results in conceptual change as students see how other models represent and structure the same ideas (Chularut & DeBacker, 2004), a formidable strategy for engaging conceptual change. Therefore, concept mapping is predictive of different forms of higher order thinking. Concept mapping has been significantly related to formal reasoning in chemistry (Schreiber & Abegg, 1991) and in biology (Briscoe & LeMaster, 1991; Mikulecky, 1988). Concept maps help in organizing such knowledge by integrating information into a progressively more complex conceptual framework.

In addition to concept maps, semantic models can also be constructed by students using database management systems and hypermedia construction tools (Jonassen, 2006). Databases are organized by data structures that are defined by fields and records. Those data structures constrain the ways that students interconnect ideas. Hypermedia (hypertext), on the other hand, generally has a more open associative structure that can be defined by students in various ways.

Causal Models

The reason why linking is so important to concept mapping is that linked pairs of concepts define propositions. The most important propositions to conceptual change and to scientific reasoning are causal propositions. Causal reasoning is second only to concept categorization as the most pervasive cognitive process in everyday life, as humans and other animals rely primarily on observable empirical cues to understand and predict causal sequences (Rehder, 2003). Causal reasoning is required for making predictions, drawing implications and inferences, and explaining phenomena. The cognitive process that underlies all thinking is causal reasoning (Carey, 1995; Keil, 1989).

Another impediment to comprehending causal domains is the oversimplification of causal relationships in those domains. Students tend to focus on quantitative and molar-level depictions of causality. However, causal relations are usually more complex than learners understand. They need to be able to articulate covariational attributes of causal relationships, including direction, valency, probability, duration, responsiveness, as well as mechanistic attributes, including process, conjunctions/disjunctions, and necessity/sufficiency (Jonassen & Ionas, in press).

Learners can use a variety of tools, such as spreadsheets, expert system shells, and systems modeling tools to construct dynamic, testable models of phenomena (Jonassen, 2000, 2006). These tools enable learners to represent both qualitative and quantitative representations of dynamic phenomena. Conceptual change in science domains is too frequently impeded by an exclusive use of quantitative representations of problems and the absence of conceptual representations. Qualitative and quantitative representations are complementary. Ploetzner, Fehse, Kneser, and Spada (1999) showed that when solving physics problems, qualitative problem representations are necessary prerequisites to learning quantitative representations. Qualitative representation is a missing link in novice problem solving (Chi, Feltovich, & Glaser, 1981; Larkin, 1983). When students try to understand a problem in only one way, especially when that way conveys no conceptual information about the problem, students do not understand the underlying systems they are working in. So, it is necessary to support conceptual understanding in students before solving problems by helping them to construct a qualitative representation of the problem as well as a quantitative one. Qualitative problem representations both constrain and facilitate the construction of quantitative representations (Ploetzner & Spada, 1998).

Building expert systems is a knowledge modeling process that enables experts and knowledge engineers to construct conceptual models (Adams-Webber, 1995). The expert system rule base in Figure 26.2 simulates the process of calculating molar conversions in chemistry. This is a purely qualitative representation of the process that focuses on the reasoning processes entailed. Constructing expert system rule bases is an effective method for engaging students in this simulation process. Jonassen and Wang (2003) experimented with having a seminar class develop an expert system to simulate different metacognitive reasoning processes. The design and development process was highly iterative, involving extensive discussions and very intense self-reflections about our own preferred methods. The students who participated in constructing the cognitive simulation made significantly more contributions to the seminar discussion and had stronger opinions about the material.

Causal relationships aggregate into functional systems. That is, rather than focusing on discrete causal relationships, learners must understand how those relationships cohere into systems. For example, while a sneeze may be a key causal agent in catching a cold, the system of viral transmission is much more complex than that. Students' mental models must explicate the casual factors that mediate that relationship. Germs are dispersed through the air by the sneeze, some of which attach to host cells. The virus injects its genetic material into the host cell. That genetic code is copied into the host cell, breaking out of it and invading other cells, all of which sets off complex immunological reactions, including the distribution or mast cells to the site of the infection, the release of histamines causing inflammation of the tissue causing more immune cells to be delivered to fight off the infection. If learners cannot adequately articulate and model these systems of complex causal processes, their understanding is overly simplified. Building models of systems that convey causal relationships supports the construction of internal conceptual frameworks necessary for transferable problem solving.

Context: This knowledge base is intended to simulate the processes of calculating molar conversions.

D1: You know the mass of one mole of sample.
D2: You need to determine molar (formula) mass.
D3: Divide sample mass by molar mass.
D4: Multiply number of moles by molar mass.
D5: You know atomic mass units.
D6: You know molar mass.
D7: Divide mass of sample by molar mass and multiply by Avogadro's number.
D8: Divide number of particles by Avogadro's number.
D9: Convert number of particles to moles, then convert moles to mass.
D10: Convert mass to moles using molar mass, and then convert moles to molecules using Avogadro's number.
D11: Convert from volume to moles (divide volume by volume/mole), and then convert moles to moles by multiplying by Avogadro's number.

Q1:	Do you know the number of molecules?	A	1 yes	2	no
Q2:	Do you know the mass of the sample in grams?	A	1 yes	2	no
Q3:	Do you know the molar mass of the element or compound?	A	1 yes	2	no
Q4:	Do you know the number of moles of the sample?	A	1 yes	2	no
Q5:	Do you want to know the number of molecules?	A	1 yes	2	no
Q6:	Do you want to know the mass of the sample in grams?	A	1 yes	2	no
Q7:	Do you want to know the molar mass of the compound?	A	1 yes	2	no
Q8:	Do you want to know the number of moles of the sample?	A	1 yes	2	no
Q9:	Do you know atomic mass units?	A	1 yes	2	no
Q10:	Do you know the volume of a gas?	A	1 yes	2	no

Rule1: IF q2a1 AND q8a1 THEN D2
Rule2: IF (d1 OR q3a1) AND q2a1 AND q8a1 THEN D3
Rule3: IF q4a1 AND q3a1 AND q6a1 THEN D4
Rule4: IF q3a1 THEN D1
Rule5: IF q3a1 THEN D5
Rule6: IF q9a1 THEN D6
Rule7: IF qq3a1 AND q2a1 AND q5a1 THEN D7
Rule8: IF q1a1 AND q8a1 THEN D8
Rule9: IF q1a1 AND q6a1 THEN D9
Rule10: IF q2a1 AND q5a1 THEN d10
Rule11: IF q10a1 AND q1a1 THEN d11

FIGURE 26.2   Excerpt from expert system rule base on stoichiometry.

There are a variety of computer-based tools for modeling systems. Based on systems dynamics, tools like Stella, PowerSim, and VenSim are sophisticated tools for modeling systems. These tools enable learners to construct systems models of phenomena using a graphic interface. Systems modeling tools enable students to construct models of actual problems. For example, Figure 26.6 illustrates how systems modeling tools, such as Stella, can be used to model actual stoichiometry problems (described semantically in Figure 26.2 and procedurally in Figure 26.3). After constructing the model of a molar conversion process in Figure 26.3, the students were able to run the model in order to test the accuracy of the model. The graph resulting from the test is illustrated in the lower part of Figure 26.3. Students must then interpret the results. If the results are not consistent with predictions, then the student may revise the model. This iterative testing and revising of the model to insure that it predicts theoretically viable outcomes is one of the most conceptually engaging processes possible. When expected values do not result from the model, learners are faced with a cognitive conflict that they must resolve.

Very little research has directly addressed the effects of systems modeling on conceptual change. In a recent study, fifth-grade students in Singapore who modeled problems associated with the water cycle using Model-It performed better on a knowledge test that also significantly predicted problem-solving performance (Lee, 2006). Model-It is a systems modeling tool that

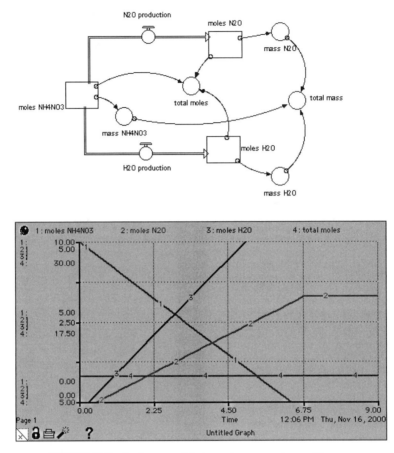

FIGURE 26.3   Systems model of a molar conversion problem.

is similar to but simpler than Stella. It was designed for use by middle school students. Rather than entering formulae into the model, students use a relationship editor to select the most accurate relationship among variables. Figure 26.4 shows one of the models that students constructed. Students' mental models were induced from the justification portion of the knowledge test. Students who constructed models of the process using Model-It generated fewer nonsensical conceptual models after modeling, more textbook repetition models and more syntactic models where students attempted to synthesize disparate pieces of information (Vosniadou & Brewer, 1992). The students who produced syntactic and scientifically viable models were also better problem solvers. This study confirmed the interrelationships among modeling, problem solving, and conceptual change.

Experiential Models

The most meaningful forms of knowledge are based on our experiences. The most common means for representing and conveying those experiences are stories, which are the oldest and most natural form of sense making. Stories are the "means [by] which human beings give meaning to their experience of temporality and personal actions" (Polkinghorne, 1988, p. 11). Stories can function as a substitute for direct experience. Some researchers believe that hearing stories is tantamount to experiencing the phenomenon oneself (Ferguson, Bareiss, Birnbaum, & Osgood,

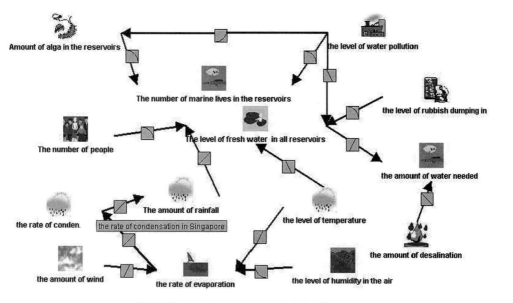

FIGURE 26.4   Systems model built by fifth grader.

1991). Therefore, we have experimented extensively with collecting stories about experiences.

The cognitive theory describing how stories are recalled and reused is case-based reasoning (CBR). An encountered problem (the new case) prompts the reasoner to retrieve cases from memory, to reuse the old case (i.e. interpret the new in terms of the old), which suggests a solution (Aamodt & Plaza, 1994). If the suggested solution will not work, then the old and or new cases are revised. When their effectiveness is confirmed, then the learned case is retained for later use. Cases or stories are reminded and retrieved by indexing them to previous cases, that is, what does the current situation have in common with previously stored cases.

Students can support their conceptual change by modeling people's experiences, that is, collecting stories about their experiences. Probably the easiest tool for capturing stories in order to model experiences is the database. Learners collect stories via interviews surveys, magazines, or news reports. The database in Figure 26.5 recounts one of many stories that were collected by students studying the conflict in Northern Ireland. The database contains many stories that have been indexed by topic, theme, context, goal, reasoning, religion, etc. When students analyze stories in order to understand the issues, they better understand the underlying complexity of a phenomenon in terms of the diverse social, cultural, political, and personal perspectives reflected in the stories. Because those stories often contain elements that result in cognitive conflict, conceptual change is often inevitable. Encountering this diversity of beliefs provides anomalous data that entails the need to change one's conceptual models of the world. Having collected stories, learners must decide what the stories teach them, so the stories must be indexed. Indexes are used to retrieve stories when needed and to compare and contrast experiences and their conceptual frameworks. Indexing requires the learners to identify relevant dimensions of the stories, such as context, goals, or lessons learned. Databases facilitate this learning process by allowing students to search or sort on any field to locate similar cases or results.

Reflective Models (Cognitive Simulations)

In virtually every course that I teach in learning psychology, I require learners to build models of the conceptual theories that they are studying. That is, they build models of thinking

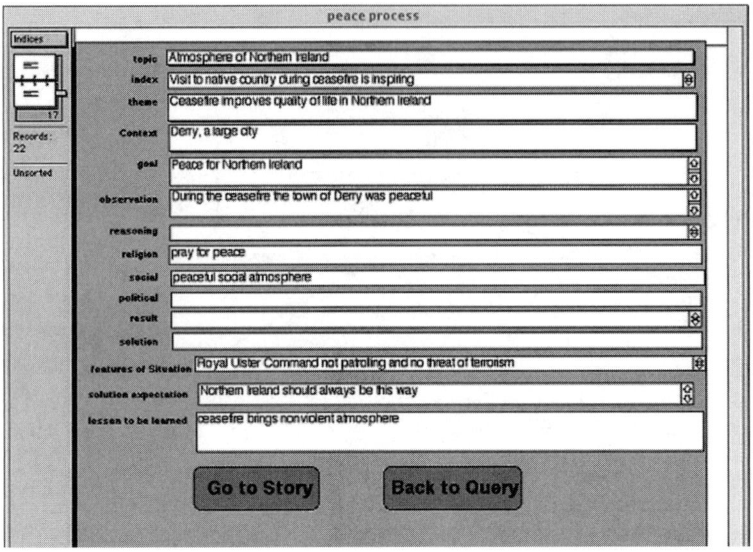

FIGURE 26.5   Record from database of stories about Northern Ireland.

processes by reflecting on the thinking processes and representing them using different modeling tools. Rather than modeling content or systems, learners model the kind of thinking that they need to perform in order to solve a problem, make a decision, or complete some other task. That is, learners use computer-based modeling tools to construct cognitive simulations.

"Cognitive simulations are runnable computer programs that represent models of human cognitive activities" (Roth, Woods, & People, 1992, p. 1163). They attempt to model mental structures and human cognitive processes. "The computer program contains explicit representations of proposed mental processes and knowledge structures" (Kieras, 1990, pp. 51–52). Building cognitive simulations attempts to reify mental constructs for analysis and theory building and testing, that is, to manifest theories and models of human mental functioning. So, rather than studying about cognitive phenomena, students construct simulation models of those phenomena. Theories of cognition all rely on constructs that may or may not exist. Cognitive simulations provide a medium for testing those theories in a computational model.

In a seminar on conceptual change that I recently taught, I required students to build models of the different theories of conceptual change that we were comparing. We collaboratively built systems models of different theories, including cognitive structures, synthetic meaning, cognitive conflict, revisionist theory, paradigm shifts, and ontology shifts. By constructing models of the different theories of conceptual change, we were able to manifest and assess our own understanding of the theories. While building models of each theory, we reconciled our naïve personal theories with the different theoretical accounts.

For example, we collaborated to construct a systems dynamics model of the cognitive conflict theory of conceptual change (see Figure 26.6). When there is a discrepancy between experienced events and the learner's intellectual expectations, a more radical form of conceptual change is necessary. When learners' current conceptions are unable to interpret their personal experiences or cannot solve problems, cognitive conflict occurs (Strike & Posner, 1985). Conceptual change results from cognitive conflicts when discrepant, dissonant, or anomalous data or events call into question their current understanding (Ferrari, & Elik, 2003).

In our model of the cognitive conflict conception of conceptual change in Figure 26.6, experiences (the level of which are under the control of the model user) flow into the model at the top.

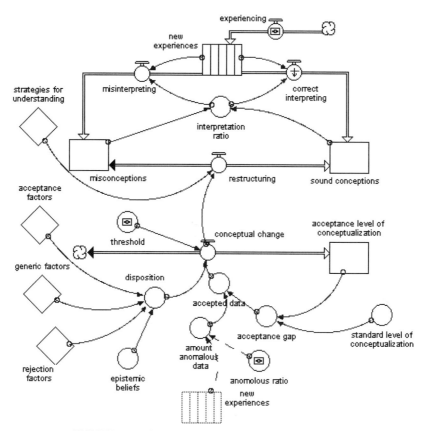

FIGURE 26.6   Cognitive conflict model of conceptual change.

The values mathematically define the flow of experiences into a stock that collects those experiences, which may be misinterpreted or correctly interpreted. Those conceptions are restructured based on the learner's conceptual change process (bottom structure in Figure 26.6). Restructuring and conceptual change are represented by a co-flow, indicating mutual interdependence between the processes. We can run this model in order to test the validity of the assumptions that are programmed into the model by examining the output of the model.

Conceptual change occurs when the learner's disposition to change and his or her acceptance of anomalous data increase. Disposition to change is a function of acceptance factors (hidden in the decision diamond of that name in Figure 26.6), including ability to interpret experiences and problem-solving ability (because conceptual change results most consistently from extended problem solving (Nersessian, 1999). Disposition also relies on necessity to change; generic factors, such as domain knowledge and experience; rejection factors, including ignoring, excluding, or reinterpreting (Chinn & Brewer, 1993); and epistemic beliefs. The acceptance, generic, and rejection factors, along with epistemic beliefs (which convey the learner's openness to alternative views) regulate the learner's disposition to change. Along with disposition to change, conceptual change also depends on the learner's acceptance of anomalous data, which depends on the amount of anomalous data (also under control of the model user), which is determined by the gap between the learner's conceptions and standard conceptions. Restructuring can be facilitated by strategies for understanding (hidden in the decision diamond of the same name in Figure 26.6), including exemplifying, analogizing, and imaging.

When we ran the model, we had to adjust the delay for new experiences and the time frame in order to manifest a rational restructuring performance. If the rate of new experiences is too high, they cannot be accommodated, let alone restructured. The importance of the rate of new anomalous experiences was a discovery that resulted from our modeling experiences. Realizing that such a model is always incomplete, the process of constructing it required intensive negotiation about which factors in the change process are most important and how the process of conceptual change looks in an operationalized form. Reifying different theories of conceptual change supported comparison-contrast thinking, an essential skill in conceptual development. We also realize that viewers of the model and its runtime performance will take issue with some of the factors and assumptions that we made. The opportunity to negotiate those differences of opinion would likely result in conceptual changes for all engaged in the negotiations.

WHICH KIND OF MODELING?

In this chapter, I have demonstrated a variety of computer-based tools (e.g., spreadsheets, expert systems, systems modeling tools, concept maps, databases) that may be used by students to model the phenomena they are studying. Each tool fosters the representation of different kinds of knowledge, and each tool imposes its own syntax, so the quality of representation within that tool depends on the affordances of that tool. Throughout this chapter, I have also cited a few studies that have demonstrated the effects of different modeling activities on conceptual change, although none of that research is systematic enough to provide advice on which tools are most effective in fostering difference kinds of conceptual change. In a study taking place over an entire semester, Jonassen (1993) showed that students who constructed concept maps in one class and expert systems in another class both improved the organization and coherence of their knowledge structures, as measured by Pathfinder Networks, an accepted method for assessing mental models. The concept-mapping group produced more hierarchically structured nets than did the expert system group, indicating that the formalism embedded in the tool has an effect on knowledge structures that learners constructed.

Advice about which tools are most effective for engaging different kinds of conceptual change is based on largely theoretical arguments. Thagard (1992) provides perhaps the best rubrics for assessing conceptual change in models in the form of explanatory coherence. Different kinds of explanatory coherence can be used to analyze models, including deductive coherence (logical consistency and entailment among members of set of propositions), probabilistic coherence (probability assignments), and semantic (similar meanings among propositions). Within models, assessors would look for symmetry, explanatory value, appropriate analogies, contradictions, competition among propositions, and acceptability of propositions. Extensive work is needed to operationalize these or any other criteria for assessing conceptual change as a result of different modeling activities. Numerous studies are easy to conceive. A major question (how can models be used to assess conceptual change?) is addressed next.

USING MODELS TO ASSESS CONCEPTUAL CHANGE

Although the theoretical accounts of conceptual change are replete (Limon & Mason, 2002; Schnotz, Vosniadou, & Carretero, 1999; Sinatra & Pintrich, 2003), there is very little literature that addresses how to effectively assess conceptual change. The dominant methods that are used include analyzing student protocols while engaged in problem solving activities (Hogan

& Fisherkeller, 2000), structured interviews (Southerland, Smith, & Cummins, 2000), and the use of concept maps (Edmundson, 2000). The analysis of interview and conversation protocols is very difficult and time-consuming and is plagued with reliability problems. Throughout this chapter, I have argued that the models that students construct while representing domain knowledge, systems, problems, experiences, and thought processes can be used to assess their conceptual change.

Limitations of Model Building

Although I have made a strong case for using technology-mediated model building for fostering conceptual change, I must acknowledge any limitations of the process.

Cognitive Load as Limitation to Modeling

A disadvantage of model building is that it places enormous demands on working memory. Construction of models places heavy cognitive load on learners. Sweller and his colleagues (Mwangi & Sweller, 1998; Tarmizi & Sweller, 1988; Ward & Sweller, 1990) found that integrating textual and diagrammatic information describing the same problems placed heavier demands on working memory, known as the split-attention effect. Requiring students to integrate multiple sources of information, a fundamental requirement of most modeling tools, is more difficult and will likely impede many learners from constructing models. Mitigating this effect will require better-developed mental models for the tools along with extensive practice.

Contradictions as Limitation to Modeling

Any activity system has potential contradictions that may impede work flow and learning (Engeström, 1987). That is, elements of any activity system (subject, goal, object, division of labor, and so on) using modeling tools may contradict each other. Because of the difficulty in producing models and integrating them in classroom activity systems, the outcomes of such activities may be compromised. As an empirical example of this notion, Barab, Barnett, Yamagata-Lynch, Squire, and Keating (2002) used activity theory as an analytical lens for understanding the transactions and pervasive tensions that characterized course activities. They discovered substantive contradictions between the use of a simulation tool, which the students enjoyed and were engaged by, and learning of the astronomy content, which was the goal of the teacher. Not only does modeling require cognitive commitment, but it must also be carefully integrated into other lesson activities.

Fidelity as Limitation to Modeling

Many tacit misconceptions prevail about models. One is the identity hypothesis. Although one goal in building models is to reify ideas and phenomena, the models themselves are not, as many people tacitly believe, identical to the phenomena themselves. Models are representations of interpretations of phenomena in the world, not the objects themselves. All models are at best inexact replicas of the real phenomenon.

Another misconception of models relates to their stability. Models are usually synchronic representations of dynamic processes. Phenomena change over time, context, and purpose. Models often do not. Assuming that models are literal and immutable representations of phenomena will surely lead to misconceptions.

Phenomena in the world are typically far more complex than anything that can be represented by any model. Modeling always involves certain simplifications and approximations that have to be decided independently of the theoretical requirements or data conditions (Morrison & Morgan, 1999).

As long as we recognize these limitations of models that we build, then we should avoid overstating the meaning of them.

CONCLUSIONS ABOUT MODELING FOR CONCEPTUAL CHANGE

In this chapter, I have argued that model building is a powerful and engaging method for fostering and assessing conceptual change. Conceptual change requires the reorganization of personal conceptual knowledge that may transpire over long periods of time or more radically while trying to accommodate anomalous information. Building models of knowledge, problems, systems, experiences, or thought processes reifies the conceptual entities requiring reorganization. Because running models often provides anomalous data, the reconciliation of the model in order to achieve expectations of theoretical standards forces learners into conceptual change. As a relatively under-researched activity, many issues regarding model building remain. Research is needed to determine which kinds of models (domain knowledge, problems, systems, experiences, or cognitive simulations) or which kinds of modeling tools are more likely to result in more complete or meaningful conceptual change. Which tools learners can more readily adopt is largely a function of individual differences in cognition. Also, because mental modes are dynamic and multi-modal, consisting of structural knowledge, procedural knowledge, executive or strategic knowledge, spatial representations, personal reflection, and even metaphorical knowledge (Jonassen & Henning, 1999, which kinds of tools afford the best representation of conceptual understanding is not known. Modeling provides rich research opportunities in the effects of knowledge representation on conceptual change.

REFERENCES

Aamodt, A., & Plaza, E. (1994). Case-based reasoning: Foundational issues, methodological variations, and system approaches. *Artificial Intelligence Communications, 7*(1), 39–59.

Adams-Webber, J. (1995). Constructivist psychology and knowledge elicitation. *Journal of Constructivist Psychology, 8*(3), 237–249.

Barab, S. A., Barnett, M., Yamagata-Lynch, L., Squire, K., & Keating, T. (2002). Using activity theory to understand the contradictions characterizing a technology-rich introductory astronomy course. *Mind, Culture, and Activity, 9*(2), 76–107.

Briscoe, C., & LeMaster, S. U. (1991). Meaningful learning in college biology through concept mapping. *American Biology Teacher, 53*(4), 214–219.

Carey, S. (1995). On the origin of causal understanding. In D. Sperber, D. Premack, & A. J. Premack (Eds.), *Causal cognition: A multidisciplinary debate* (pp. 268–302). Oxford: Clarendon Press.

Chi, M. T. H., Feltovich, P. J., & Glaser, R. (1981). Categorization and representation of physics problems by experts and novices. *Cognitive Science, 5*, 121–152.

Chinn, C. A., & Brewer, W. F. (1993). The role of anomalous data in knowledge acquisition: A theoretical framework and implications for science education. *Review of Educational Research, 63*, 1–49.

Chularut,, P., & DeBacker, T. K. (2004). The influence of concept mapping on achievement, self-regulation, and self efficacy in students of English as a second language. *Contemporary Educational Psychology, 29*, 248–263.

Dole, J. A., & Sinatra, G. M. (1998). Reconceptualizing change in the cognitive construction of knowledge. *Educational Psychologist, 33*, 109–128.

Edmundson, K. M. (2000). Assessing science understanding through concept maps. In J. J. Mintzes, J. H.

Wandersee, & J. D. Novak (Eds.), *Assessing science understanding: A human constructivist view* (pp. 19–40). San Diego: Academic Press.

Engeström, Y. (1987). *Learning by expanding: An activity-theoretical approach to developmental research.* Helsinki, Finland: Orienta-Konultit.

Farooq, M. U., & Dominick, W. D. (1988). A survey of formal tools and models for developing user interfaces. *International Journal of Man-Machine Studies, 29*, 479–496.

Ferguson, W., Bareiss, R., Birnbaum, L., & Osgood, R. (1991). ASK Systems: An approach to the realization of story-based teachers. *The Journal of the Learning Sciences, 2(1)*, 95–134.

Ferrari, M., & Elik, N. (2003). Influences on intentional conceptual change. In G. M. Sinatra & P. R. Pintrich (Eds.), *Intentional conceptual change* (pp. 21–54). Mahwah, NJ: Erlbaum

Frederiksen, J. R., & White, B. Y. (1998). Teaching and learning generic modeling and reasoning skills. *Journal of Interactive Learning Environments, 55,* 33–51.

Harris, T (1999). A hierarchy of model and electron microscopy. In L. Magnani, N. J. Nersessian, & P. Thagard (Eds.), *Models are used to represent reality.* New York: Kluwer.

Hogan, K., & Fisherkeller, J. (2000). Dialogue as data: Assessing students' scientific reasoning with interactive protocols. In J. J. Mintzes, J. H. Wandersee, & J. D. Novak (Eds.), *Assessing science understanding: A human constructivist view* (pp. 96–129). San Diego: Academic Press.

Hong, N .S., Jonassen, D. H., & McGee, S. (2003). Predictors of well-structured and ill-structured problem solving in an astronomy simulation. *Journal of Research in Science Teaching, 40(1)*, 6–33.

Horton, P. B., McConney, A. A., Gallo, M., & Woods, A.L. (1993). An investigation of the effectiveness of concept mapping as an instructional tool. *Science Education, 77*, 95–111.

Johnson-Laird, P. N. (1983). *Mental models: Towards a cognitive science of language, inference, and consciousness.* Cambridge, MA: Harvard University Press.

Jonassen, D. H. (1993). Changes in knowledge structures from building semantic net versus production rule representations of subject content. *Journal of Computer Based Instruction, 20* (4), 99–106.

Jonassen, D. H. (1996). *Computers in the classroom: Mindtools for critical thinking.* Columbus, OH: Merrill/Prentice-Hall.

Jonassen, D. H. (2000). *Computers as Mindtools for schools: Engaging critical thinking.* Columbus, OH: Merrill/Prentice-Hall.

Jonassen, D. H. (2006). *Modeling with technology: Mindtools for conceptual change.* Columbus, OH: Merrill/Prentice-Hall.

Jonassen, D. H., Beissner, K., & Yacci, M. (1993). *Structural knowledge: Techniques for assessing, conveying, and acquiring structural knowledge.* Hillsdale, NJ: Erlbaum.

Jonassen, D. H., & Henning, P. (1999). Mental models: Knowledge in the head and knowledge in the world. *Educational Technology*, (May–June), 37–42.

Jonassen, D. H., & Ionas, I. G. (in press). Learning to reason causally. *Educational Technology: Research & Development, 54* (4).

Jonassen, D. H., & Wang, S. (2003). Using expert systems to build cognitive simulations. *Journal of Educational Computing Research, 28(1)*, 1–13

Keil, F. C. (1989). *Concepts, kinds, and cognitive development.* Cambridge, MA: MIT Press.

Kieras, D. (1990). The role of cognitive simulation models in the development of advanced training and testing systems. In N. Frederickson, R. Glaser, A. Lesgold, & M. G. Shafto (Eds.), *Diagnostic monitoring of skill and knowledge acquisition* (pp. 51–74). Hillsdale, NJ: Erlbaum.

Larkin, J.H. (1983). The role of problem representation in physics. In D. Gentner & A. L. Stevens (Eds.). *Mental models* (pp. 75–98). Hillsdale, NJ: Erlbaum.

Lee, C. B. (2006). *Capturing and assessing conceptual change in problem solving.* Doctoral Dissertation, University of Missouri.

Lehrer, R., & Schauble, L. (2000). Modeling in mathematics and science. In R. Glaser (Ed.), *Advances in instructional psychology: Volume 5. Educational design and cognitive science* (pp. 101–159). Hillsdale, NJ: Erlbaum.

Lehrer, R., & Schauble, L. (2003). Origins and evolution of model-based reasoning in mathematics and science. In R. Lesh & H. M. Doerr (Eds.), *Beyond constructivism: Models and modeling perspectives on mathematics problem solving, teaching, and learning* (pp. 59– 70). Mahwah, NJ: Erlbaum.

Lesh, R., & Doerr, H. M. (2003). Foundations of a models and modeling perspective on mathematics teaching, learning, and problem solving. In R. Lesh & H. M. Doerr (Eds.), *Beyond constructivism: Models and modeling perspectives on mathematics problem solving, teaching, and learning* (pp. 3–33). Mahwah, NJ: Erlbaum.

Limon, M., & Mason, L. (2002). *Reconsidering conceptual change: Issues in theory and practice.* Amsterdam: Kluwer.

Luque, M. L. (2003). The role of domain-specific knowledge in intentional conceptual change. In G. M. Sinatra, & P. R. Pintrich (Eds.), *Intentional conceptual change.* Mahwah, NJ: Erlbaum.

Mellar, H., Bliss, J., Boohan, R., Ogborn, J., & Tompsett, C. (1994). *Learning with artificial worlds: Computer-based modeling in the curriculum.* London: Falmer Press.

Mikulecky, L. (1988). Development of interactive programs to help students transfer basic skills to college level science and behavioral sciences courses. Bloomington: Indiana University (ERIC Document No. ED 318469).

Morgan, M.S. (1999). Learning from models. In M.S. Morgan & M. Morrison (Eds.), *Models as mediators: Perspectives on natural and social science* (pp. 347–388). Cambridge: Cambridge University Press.

Morrison, M., & Morgan, M. S. (1999). Models as mediating instruments. In M. S. Morgan & M. Morrison (Eds.), *Models as mediators: Perspectives on natural and social science* (pp. 10–37). Cambridge: Cambridge University Press.

Mwangi, W., & Sweller, J. (1998). Learning to solve compare word problems: The effect of example format and generating explanations. *Cognition & Instruction, 16*, 173–199.

Nersessian, N. J. (1999). Model-based reasoning in conceptual change. In L. Magnani, N. J. Nersessian, & P. Thagard (Eds.), *Model-based reasoning in scientific discovery* (pp. 5–23). New York: Kluwer.

Norman, D. A. (1983). Some observations on mental models. In D. Gentner & A. Stevens (Eds.), *Mental models* (pp. 15–34). Hillsdale, NJ: Erlbaum.

Ploetzner, R., & Spada, H. (1998). Constructing quantitative problem representations on the basis of qualitative reasoning. *Interactive Learning Environments, 5*, 95–107.

Ploetzner, R., Fehse, E., Kneser, C., & Spada, H. (1999). Learning to relate qualitative and quantitative problem representations in a model-based setting for collaborative problem solving. *Journal of the Learning Sciences, 8*(2), 177–214.

Polkinghorne, D. (1988). *Narrative Knowing and the Human Sciences.* Albany: State University of New York Press.

Rehder, B. (2003). Categorization as causal reasoning. *Cognitive Science, 27*(5), 709–748.

Roth, E. M., Woods, D. D., & People, H. E. (1992). Cognitive simulation as a tool for cognitive task analysis. *Ergonomics, 35*(10), 1163–1198.

Schnotz, W., Vosniadou, S., & Carretero, T. (1999). *New perspectives in conceptual change.* Amsterdam: Pergamom.

Schreiber, D. A., & Abegg, G. L. (1991, April). *Scoring student-generated concept maps in introductory college chemistry.* Paper presented at the Annual Meeting of the National Association for Research in Science Teaching, Lake Geneva, WI (ERIC Document No. 347055).

Sinatra, G.M, & Pintrich, P. R. (2003). The role of intentions in conceptual change learning. In G. M. Sinatra, & P. R. Pintrich (Eds.), *Intentional conceptual change.* Mahwah, NJ: Erlbaum.

Southerland, S. A., Smith, M. U., & Cummins, C. L. (2000). "What do you mean by that?": Using structured interviews to assess science understanding. In J. J. Mintzes, J. H. Wandersee, & J. D. Novak (Eds.), *Assessing science understanding: A human constructivist view* (pp. 72–95). San Diego: Academic Press.

Strike, K. A., & Posner, G. J. (1985). A conceptual change view of learning and understanding. In L. H. T. West & A. L. Pines (Eds.), *Cognitive structure and conceptual change* (pp. 211–231). New York: Academic.

Strike, K. A., & Posner, G. J. (1992). A revisionist theory of conceptual change. In R. A. Duschl, & R. J. Hamilton (Eds.), *Philosophy of science, cognitive psychology, and educational theory and practi e* (pp.147–176). New York: State University of New York Press.

Tarmizi, R. A., & Sweller, J. (1988). Guidance during mathematical problem solving. *Journal of Educational Psychology, 80*, 424–436.

Thagard, P. (1992). *Conceptual revolutions*. Princeton, NJ: Princeton University Press.

Vandierendonck, A., & deVooght, G. (1996). Evidence for mental-model-based reasoning: A comparison of reasoning with time and space concepts. *Thinking and Reasoning, 2*(4), 249–272.

Vosniadou, S. (1992). Knowledge acquisition and conceptual change. *Applied Psychology: An International Review, 41*(4), 347–357.

Vosniadou, S. (1994). Capturing and modeling the process of conceptual change. *Learning and Instruction, 4*(1), 45–70.

Vosniadou, S. (2002a). On the nature of naïve physics. In M. Limon & L. Mason (Eds.), *Reconsidering conceptual change: Issues in theory and practice* (pp. 61–76). Dordrecht: Kluwer.

Vosniadou, S. (2002b). Mental models in conceptual development. In L. Magnani & N. J. Nersessian (Eds.), *Model-based reasoning: Science, technology, and values*. New York: Kluwer.

Vosniadou, S., & Brewer, W. F. (1992). Mental models of the earth: A study of conceptual change in childhood. *Cognitive Psychology, 24*, 535–585.

Ward, M., & Sweller, J. (1990). Structuring effective worked examples. *Cognition & Instruction, 7*, 1–39.

Windschitl, M. (2000). Supporting the development of science inquiry skills with special classes of software. *Educational Technology: Research & Development, 48*(2), 81–95.

Wittgensetein, L. (1953). *Philosophical investigations* (G. E. M. Anscombe, Trans.). Oxford: Blackwell.

Yu, Q. (2002). Model-based reasoning and similarity in the world. In L. Magnani & N. J. Nersessian (Eds.), *Model-based reasoning: Science, technology, and values* (pp. 275–285). New York: Kluwer.

27

Teaching for Conceptual Change: Distinguish or Extinguish Ideas

Marcia C. Linn
University of California, Berkeley

INTRODUCTION

Conceptual change has perplexed and intrigued researchers at least since Rousseau (1892) and Locke (1824). When Piaget published his account of child development (Piaget, 1953, 1970), he brought extensive evidence of student thinking into the conversation, drawing attention to the ideas students develop spontaneously and arguing for biological constraints on reasoning. Subsequent researchers have explored various constraints in logic or processing capacity and have also analyzed the nature of the ideas that students devise to explain the scientific phenomena they encounter both in and out of school (diSessa, 1988; Linn, 1995; Siegler, 1996).

These research directions raise the dilemma posed in the title of this chapter: Should we encourage learners to extinguish the ideas that experts dispute, or should we help students distinguish among normative and personally-constructed views? To answer the question, this chapter identifies issues that a comprehensive perspective on conceptual change needs to address and introduces the knowledge integration framework as a promising way to respond.

For the purposes of this chapter, conceptual change is identified as the individuals' lifelong trajectory of understanding of a given topic or discipline. This chapter distinguishes between individual and group or field changes in scientific views. This chapter is selective, not exhaustive; perspectives on conceptual change are used to illustrate the diversity of views of conceptual change. The focus here is instruction in science. All the examples come from research on scientific topics, and the implications also focus on science, although they may have value for other disciplines.

Conceptual change theorists disagree about the importance of extinguishing or distinguishing ideas. Some theorists, consistent with Locke, view conceptual change as the accumulation of knowledge, where new ideas replace less powerful notions. These researchers focus on acquisition, forgetting, and retrieval (Anderson, 1976; Skinner, 1956).

Others, inspired by Piagetian research, see the non-normative ideas that students articulate as obstacles that might prevent acceptance of normative views. They argue for age-related changes in reasoning that become possible as constraints on reasoning, based on biological or intellectual development, are overcome (Inhelder & Piaget, 1958/1972). These researchers identify dramatic shifts in student understanding and point to clearly contradicting accounts of scientific phenomena such as *the earth is round like a pancake* or *the earth is round like a sphere* (Carey, 1985; Chi, 2005; Gopnik & Wellman, 1994; Schnotz, Vosniadou, & Carretero, 1999; Wiser, 1988). Among those viewing some ideas as obstacles to student understanding, has grown up a group arguing that these conceptual revolutions require ontological shifts (Chi & Roscoe, 2002; Slotta & Chi, 2006; Slotta, Chi, & Joram, 1995). This group often implies that students need to replace one set of views with another — essentially extinguishing the first set and installing the scientifically normative views.

An emerging group of researchers advocates a "knowledge in pieces" or "knowledge integration" view. This group suggests that students build individual ideas in various ways and that these ideas may exist alongside each other in a repertoire (Clark & Linn, 2003; diSessa, 1988; Hammer & Elby, 2003; K. Howe, 1998; Lewis, 1996; Linn, 1986; Linn, 1995; Linn & Hsi, 2000; Metz, 1991, 2000; Siegler, 2000; Songer, 1996; Songer & Linn, 1992; White & Frederiksen, 1998). This group generally respects the intellectual work that produced the ideas and argues that the goal of instruction is to introduce more powerful ideas, as well as to encourage students to inspect, distinguish, and evaluate the ideas in a way that leads to some form of reconciliation and coherence.

Philosophers of science, analyzing the history of change in fields like physics, chemistry, and biology, have inspired those thinking about conceptual change among students. Kuhn (1970) described a revolutionary view of conceptual change in the field based on evidence for shifts from Newtonian to Einsteinian conceptions of physics. Strike and Posner (1985) apply this view to student learning, suggesting that students persist with a particular conception of a scientific phenomenon until they encounter the conditions that enable a new idea to take hold; they then substitute the new idea. Lakatos (1976) and Toulmin (1972) draw more on an evolutionary metaphor, suggesting that scientists and others hold multiple views of phenomena and that the fitter ideas survive. Lakatos (1976) argues that scientists hold core ideas surrounded by a protective belt and maintain the coherence of the core by modifying ideas in the protective belt (Linn & Siegel, 1984). Thagard (2000) argues for coherence as a force in shaping conceptual change among scientists and provides rich examples from a variety of disciplines.

In summary, conceptual change philosophers and researchers have generated a repertoire of ideas about student trajectories of understanding. Some argue that students develop well-formed theories almost like scientists and change them reluctantly. Others argue that students build a broad repertoire of ideas and select among them depending on the context. Still others argue that students go through developmental stages constrained by some biological phenomenon. And, some argue that students replace old ideas with new ones when those are presented by authorities. These views all shed light on the dilemma of how to teach so students can gain normative scientific ideas.

CONCEPTUAL CHANGE ISSUES

A comprehensive perspective on conceptual change processes and instructional remedies needs to simultaneously address several important issues. These include:

- *Explaining how memory and forgetting impact the trajectory of understanding*, including the opportunity to spontaneously revisit ideas.
- *Explaining how the development of the individual impacts the trajectory of lifelong learning*, including predictions concerning gradual or rapid change and evidence for the similarities of ideas at specific ages.

- *Explaining how learners grapple with multiple contexts for similar phenomena*, including explaining the origins of misconceptions, alternative conceptions, beliefs, and constructed ideas.
- *Describing how learners connect various kinds of explanations of scientific phenomena to each other*, including descriptive explanations, causal explanations, and explanations of unseen or dynamic processes.
- *Explaining how learners respond to instructional activities*, including instruction that promotes ability to monitor and analyze one's own ideas.

Memory and Forgetting: Desirable Difficulties

Researchers on memory and forgetting study why some ideas are retained and others, often those encountered in school, are forgotten. This research tradition contributes to understanding of conceptual change by explaining the trajectory of understanding. Researchers in this tradition often use simple materials and short retention intervals, but recent studies have used more realistic materials and shed light on more complex topics.

Research on the processes of memory and forgetting demonstrates the role of revisiting ideas and shows that spacing and interleaving topics improve recall, compared to teaching a topic without interruption (Pashler, 2006; Richland, Linn, & Bjork, 2007). Research also shows the benefit of variation in presentation format, which in science might include text, visualizations, tests, symbolic representations or everyday situations (Christina & Bjork, 1991; Reder & Klatzky, 1994).

Because schools in the United States and some other countries rush through the science curriculum, they often mass practice on each topic and infrequently have time to revisit ideas (National Research Council, 2006). In order to fit the curriculum into the instructional time, districts or states provide pacing guides that allocate instructional time to chapters in the science text with little time for review. California seventh-grade life-science standards, for example, include 40 disciplinary topics and five investigation and experimentation standards. The 40 disciplinary topics include mitosis, photosynthesis, genetic inheritance, natural selection, the rock cycle, plate tectonics, male and female reproduction, the physics of light, the role of levers and their application to the musculo-skeletal system, the food web, and the interactions between the heart and the circulatory system. Furthermore, each topic needs to be explored following five investigation and experimentation standards: use appropriate tools and technology, gather evidence from print and electronic resources, make logical connections between hypotheses and evidence, construct models, and communicate investigations in oral and written reports. Students address all 40 disciplinary topics using the five investigation and experimentation techniques in the seventh-grade school year. Because there are 180 days in the school year, several of which are devoted to standardized testing and other school-wide events — each of these 40 topics and accompanying inquiry activities receive 3–4 days of instruction. This limited time deters teachers from revisiting ideas or even emphasizing connections among ideas.

Bjork's (1999) research on desirable difficulties elegantly illustrates that when topics are spaced or interleaved, rather than taught without interruption, performance declines during learning but, remarkably, is strengthened on long term recall measures. Desirable difficulties are instructional activities, such as spacing lessons on a topic that initially is slow learning but ultimately strengthen outcomes. U.S. instructors may resist these practices because they interpret the declines in performance when the topic is spaced between other topics as meaning that students have learned less than when the topic is taught all at once. In fact, the opposite is true and could be detected with measures of cumulative understanding.

The value of revisiting ideas is evident in the role everyday observations play in views of science. Spontaneous everyday experiences with many concepts such as electricity, light, the circulatory system, plate tectonics, or genetic inheritance occur much more often and over longer intervals than classroom instruction on the same topic. Students may attempt to explain the trajectory of a soccer ball daily and under quite varied conditions but only study force and motion for 3 or 4 days in middle school or high school physical science.

If students applied class-taught ideas, spontaneous revisiting of complex scientific phenomena could provide spaced practice. However, a consequence of the fleeting coverage of science topics is that instruction features primarily abstract problems and computational formulas, rather than connections to everyday examples. As a result, in everyday situations students frequently generate what have been called misconceptions or intuitive beliefs about science based on what they can observe (diSessa, 2000; A. Howe, 2002; Linn, 1995). Everyday revisiting of these topics may provide spaced practice on intuitive ideas. Thus, the idea that objects like the soccer ball have a constant force "pushing" them while they are moving or that objects in motion come to rest is revisited regularly and is, therefore, reinforced.

In summary, research on memory and forgetting clarifies the learning trajectory by showing why intuitive ideas persist and why connecting school and out-of-school experiences matters. This research illustrates one reason why new, scientifically normative ideas fail to become established. From the desirable difficulties perspective, instruction should introduce new ideas, provide spaced practice, and enable their reuse. This means that normative ideas would be practiced and tested in new settings and contexts. To succeed in explaining conceptual change, researchers need to consider the interactions between instructed and spontaneous opportunities to learn and apply ideas.

Development and Rate of Change

A major factor in the trajectory of student understanding concerns developmental accomplishments. Developmental research looks at the lifelong trajectories of student understanding, paying attention to the rate of change in reasoning and the similarities in reasoning at specific ages. It seeks to explain why gradual or rapid change arises. Many argue that it takes time for students to develop capabilities of embracing new ideas.

Developmental theories also focus on similarities in ideas generated by students and often attempt to discern the single view students have of a phenomenon. If students give several answers, they look for the most frequent, representative, or strongly held idea.

Piaget (Inhelder & Piaget, 1958/1972; Piaget, 1970) characterized the similarities in the ideas students articulate to argue that students go through developmental stages that constrain reasoning. Piaget argued that the ideas at each stage have special characteristics — concrete for those age 5 to 11 and formal for those age 12 and older — determined by constraints on reasoning. Piaget suggested that certain ideas such as conservation of mass or length characterized the logical nature of a stage and resulted in an equilibrium that persisted until the next stage was established.

Recent research distinguishing expert and novice ontologies for views of electricity or heat also makes claims about the special status of certain ideas. These researchers argue that changing the ontology of an idea is more difficult than other forms of change (Slotta & Chi, 2006). Specifically, these researchers argue that students develop a substance-based view of heat and electricity and that embracing the normative, constraint-based view necessitates an ontological shift.

Neo-Piagetian theorists (Case, 1985; Pascual-Leone, Goodman, Ammon, & Subelman, 1978; Scardamalia, 1977) argue that constraints are determined by mental processing capacity.

These researchers claim that processing capacity increases with age. They explain the similarities in reasoning at a given age as reflecting limits in processing. Researchers often use evidence for the entrenched nature of some ideas to argue for developmental constraints. However, as studies of memory and forgetting suggest, ideas may persist because they benefit from spaced practice and because they resonate with everyday experience.

Researchers disagree about the coherence of the developmental process. Some pay attention to similarities among ideas to argue that students develop a cohesive theory of the world. They suggest that the process of conceptual change involves abandoning one cohesive view for another. Carey, for example, describes students as going through "revolutions" in understanding, consistent with the writings of Kuhn (1970).

Evidence for rapid change in reasoning capability or for revolutions in reasoning has been difficult to establish due to the small number of longitudinal studies and the methodological challenges. Many recent research programs cast doubt on developmental limitations as articulated by Piaget and others. These researchers have demonstrated stunning accomplishments of babies (Spelke, 1999), young students (Case, 1985; Gelman & Gallistel, 1986; Metz, 2000), and adolescents (diSessa, 2000; Lee & Songer, 2003; Linn & Hsi, 2000).

Starting with Piaget, developmental theorists have eschewed instructional issues, arguing that development needs to take its course. Efforts to speed accomplishment of ideas like conservation of matter have often met with failure, but more and more studies have succeeded as researchers place emphasis on disciplinary context (diSessa, 2000; Linn & Eylon, 2006), social context (Scardamalia & Bereiter, 1999), and sequences of activities (Case, 1985).

In summary, whether one views developmental constraints as based on stages, brain maturity, processing capacity, or experience, conceptual change theories need to account for the rate of student progress. Theories also need to address an important aspect of constraints, commonly held views of specific scientific topics. Placing emphasis on the many ideas that students formulate and utilize has led to a focus on the process of idea generation. Placing emphasis on specific ideas and on the similarities among ideas has led to a focus on constraints.

Context and the Repertoire of Ideas

An examination of the many creative and unique ideas that students formulate for specific contexts has led some researchers to argue for a constructive process of knowledge generation and change. Context refers to the situation where an idea is applied. When students are asked to explain scientific phenomena in the abstract they often respond quite differently from when asked to explain the phenomena in a specific context. Analyzing the trajectory of understanding involves explaining how students make sense of ideas when they occur in a new context. Unique contexts account for many of the diverse ideas students have in their repertoire. Students' methods for grappling with context differences strengthen the view that students engage in a creative process of trying to make sense of their world (Hatano & Inagaki, 2003).

Many researchers have focused on the diversity and character of contextualized ideas. These ideas have been referred to as "misconceptions," "alternative conceptions," "beliefs," "intuitive ideas," and "constructed ideas." Any theory of conceptual change needs to explain the emergence of these views, as well as their role in conceptual change. A cottage industry has emerged around gathering the varied ideas that students generate in a wide assortment of scientific domains (Duit, Treagust, & Mansfield, 1996; Eylon & Linn, 1988; Pfundt & Duit, 1994). This large body of evidence has led researchers to argue that students construct multiple, contradictory, and fragmented ideas that stem from interacting with the material and social world (diSessa, 1988; A. Howe, 2002; Linn & Hsi, 2000; Metz, 2000; Siegler, 1996). Many researchers have shown that the ideas students generate arise from observations, analogies with related events, cultural practices, or colloquial uses of language. diSessa (1988) refers to one class of explanations students generate (such as sound dies out or heavy objects fall faster than light objects, things bounce because they are springy, and continuing force is needed for continuing motion) as phenomenological primitives to capture their descriptive nature.

Many have shown that students distinguish science class context from ideas developed by interacting with the world (Gilbert & Boulter, 2000; Redish, 2003). These researchers argue that the ideas students articulate, such as the view that since metal feels cold at room temperature it has the property of cooling objects, illustrate student capabilities to make sense of confusing observations rather than developmental constraints. They see these ideas as evidence for powerful reasoning ability that can be guided by instruction (diSessa, Elby, & Hammer, 2002; Linn & Hsi, 2000).

In many textbook-driven courses, students learn abstract ideas and formulas but do not explore how to use the ideas in varied everyday problems. This approach contributes to students' propensity to separate school ideas from personal experience. Designers of textbooks often view the everyday contexts where ideas apply as potential transfer tasks. For example, many courses define heat and temperature in terms of units of measurement (temperature as degrees on a thermometer and heat as calories) or molecular kinetics. Students rarely study how to explain situations such as wilderness survival, predicting the temperature of metal and wood objects that feel differently at room temperature, or estimating the cooling curves for metal and pottery objects removed from a warming oven. When they are asked to apply their abstract ideas to these new situations they come up with creative alternatives (Linn & Hsi, 2000).

Abstract scientific ideas, often based on unseen processes such as molecular kinetic theory, have value for experts wishing to organize their knowledge across varied contexts (Chi, Feltovich, & Glaser, 1981; Larkin & Reif, 1979). However, for students who find the abstract ideas complex and inaccessible, alternative ways to structure knowledge have proven useful. Linn & Songer (1991) found, for example, that heat flow ideas were more generative for middle school students than molecular kinetics ideas for understanding thermal equilibrium, heating and cooling, insulation and conduction, direction of heat flow, and specific heat among middle school students.

Lifelong learning requires that learners both extend scientific ideas to new situations and deal with disciplinary boundaries. Thus, students might initially study energy in isolated areas — learning how plants get and use energy, how humans get and use energy, how energy is generated and used to power an automobile, etc. For many students, these are quite distinct domains that never get connected. Yet, sophisticated understanding of science requires combining these situations and developing a coherent or integrated view of concepts like energy, the nature of matter, or evolution.

Current instruction may inadvertently deter students from using their reasoning abilities to link ideas and bridge disciplines. Courses spend little time on connections and reflect self-monitoring. They often isolate topics using abstract definitions, rather than showing the benefit of explanations that connect topics. Theories of conceptual change need to explain how context contributes to the learning trajectory. Theories need to explain the variations in student ideas across contexts and disciplinary boundaries. By linking the depictions of science topics in science courses to the variation in student performance across different contexts, we can begin to determine how to guide students to develop coherent understanding and to grapple with sophisticated ideas.

Explanations and Schooling

Theories of conceptual change need to explain the trajectory and character of the scientific explanations that students and scientists employ. Scientists connect descriptive explanations, causal explanations, and various intermediate forms of explanations. Students typically bring descriptive explanations to science class and generally encounter more sophisticated accounts of phenomena for the first time. Many students segregate school explanations from everyday accounts of science rather than connecting these ideas.

Both students and scientists use descriptive explanations of everyday scientific phenomena — the challenge is to make informative connections to causal and mechanistic explanations. For example, scientists and students mention that metal objects feel colder than wooden objects at room temperature. When a thermometer reveals they have the same temperature, students might question the thermometer. Scientists might explain this phenomenon using heat flow — a mechanism commonly found in engineering courses. They might say, for example, that heat flows out of your hand faster when you touch a metal object than when you touch a wooden object, or that metal is a conductor while wood is an insulator. Others might use an atomic level explanation, talking about molecular kinetic theory. They might use a molecular visualization to illustrate that a warm hand has the potential of transferring the motion of molecules to objects that are cooler than the hand. Then they might represent insulators and conductors as varying in their reaction to the warm hand.

Some scientists are excellent at linking explanations and explaining how ideas work across multiple contexts. In other cases, scientists falter when attempting to link the causal explanations to either descriptive or mechanistic accounts of scientific phenomena. For example, Lewis (1996) reports that some natural scientists, when asked to choose between aluminum foil and a wool sweater for keeping a drink cold, actually neglect their understanding at the atomic level and talk about aluminum foil as a better choice, based on observations that people use foil to wrap drinks.

Ultimately, effective understanding of scientific phenomena requires that learners link and understand varied forms of explanations of scientific phenomena. White and Frederiksen (1998) report that students understand electricity better when they learn a series of explanations going from descriptive to causal. Some problems benefit from multiple explanations. Students might start with descriptive explanations or mechanistic accounts (Linn & Muilenburg, 1996) and then learn molecular theories. National and international assessments demonstrate that few citizens master causal explanations for most scientific phenomena (Schmidt, Raizen, Britton, Bianchi, & Wolfe, 1997).

Choosing an appropriate form of explanation is challenging. The molecular kinetic account of heat transfer, for example, draws on unseen processes and may be less generative than the heat flow account for students who are also struggling to understand the particulate nature of matter (Nussbaum, 1985).

Researchers have pointed out that students' descriptive views can interfere with understanding of causal or atomic explanations (Chi, 2005; Vosniadou, in press). Others argue that many causal or atomic explanations are challenging to apply to everyday events and should be added to science courses judiciously (Linn & Hsi, 2000).

A variety of research programs have identified ways to link explanations and promote coherent ideas. For example, students often argue that an object traveling in a specific direction has a force pushing it in that direction (impetus theory). Clement (1983) described the coin toss problem, where students were asked to explain the forces on a coin tossed in the air and allowed to come down and hit the ground. Many students reported that the coin, on its upward trajectory ,had a force pushing it up, and then on its downward trajectory had a force pushing it down. The normative view says the coin is given an initial upward velocity, and then the only force acting on it is that of gravity. Clement (1983) helped students sort out these ideas by creating bridging analogies that distinguished the descriptive and normative explanations of the coin toss.

In a similar vein, Linn and Hsi (2000) show that what they call pivotal cases, as elaborated below, can promote effective links. When students are asked to explain a variety of heat and temperature situations — surviving in the wilderness, predicting the temperature of a metal pan and a pizza stone in the oven, or clarifying why metals and wooden objects feel differently at room temperature — students articulate a complex repertoire of explanations (Clark & Linn, 2003; Linn & Hsi, 2000). Instruction introducing abstract explanations could be viewed by learners as offering another view of the phenomena. Students might isolate the abstract view rather than see it as a comprehensive account of all the situations they encounter — especially if their science course devotes little time to these connections. A more successful approach would help learners link their explanations.

Distinguishing forms of explanations is one way to make sense of phenomena like heat and electricity that involve ontological shifts. For example, descriptive explanations of electricity as flowing out of the wall or heat coming out of the furnace are legitimate colloquial expressions. Problems arise as these accounts are interpreted by students to mean that heat or electricity are substances, rather than properties of materials. Introducing causal explanations and distinguishing their ontological origins is one way to advance scientific understanding.

Thus, understanding and connecting varied types of explanations is an important aspect conceptual change. Students need to distinguish types of explanations and make links across them. Helping students embrace generative and durable ideas and to use these to explain phenomena in multiple contexts benefits from attention to the nature of explanations. Instructional designers need to identify sensible ways to help students link varied types of explanations. They need to establish appropriate sequences for teaching these views of scientific phenomena.

Instructional Design

Conceptual change perspectives need to explain how instructional design impacts the learning trajectory. Findings from research on instruction should inform conceptual change theories, just as views of conceptual change should inform the design of instruction. Instructional designers make decisions about the ideas they ask students to consider and about sequences of learning activities students perform.

Research is beginning to clarify why some formulations of scientific ideas are more effective than others. Clement's (1983) bridging analogies benefit many learners. Researchers on analogies have shown that some are better than others (Holyoak & Thagard, 1995). Research on atomic level visualizations demonstrates benefits over static diagrams. Pivotal cases (Linn, 2005) incorporate the benefits of bridging analogies and visualizations.

Researchers disagree about whether classroom activities should take advantage of the many ideas students generate about scientific situations, confront them, or eradicate them (Chi, 2005; diSessa, Hammer, Sherin, & Kolpakowski, 1991; Linn & Eylon, 2006; Siegler, 2000; Smith, diSessa, & Roschelle, 1993/1994; Vosniadou, 2002). diSessa et al. (1991) documented the advantage of building on student ideas in showing that a creative instructional sequence could motivate students to invent the idea of graphing.

Theories should explain why some sequences of activities work better than others. Research on promising instructional patterns shows that some patterns are more effective than others (Linn & Eylon, 2006; Linn & Songer, 1991). Promising sequences structure learning, rather than lead students to unguided exploration (diSessa et al., 1991; Klahr & Nigam, 2004; Linn & Hsi, 2000). In addition, sequences support learners in taking advantage of the well-designed views of scientific phenomena described above (Edelson, 2001; White & Frederiksen, 1998). Sequences also ensure that students encounter multiple contexts and take advantage of social interactions (Linn

& Eylon, 2006; Quintana, Reiser, Davis, Krajcik, Fretz, Golan, et al., 2004). Importantly, patterns encourage students to reflect and to monitor their own progress (Davis & Linn, 2000; Chi, deLeeuw, Chiu, & LaVancer,1994).

Several important instructional elements deserve special attention in conceptual change theories. First, conceptual change theories can and should offer a view of the role of new ideas and suggest criteria for these ideas. Second, conceptual change theories need to address the role of students' existing ideas — these alternative conceptions, misconceptions, or constructed ideas that students bring to science class. Third, conceptual change theories need to address the role of the social context and opportunities for students to extend each others' zone of proximal development (Vygotsky, 1978). Finally, any view of instruction should offer guidance about developing the ability to monitor and critique one's own performance and become a lifelong learner.

Design of both sequences of learning activities and of specific ideas to introduce to students has proved important for conceptual change. Views of conceptual change should incorporate research investigating the designs of new ideas that students encounter in instruction, the balance between directed, guided, and unguided instruction, and the design of sequences of instruction that supports lifelong learning.

In summary, these five issues are central to any theoretical account of conceptual change and deserve attention in contrasting perspectives. Their role in my research program is summarized in the next section.

THE KNOWLEDGE INTEGRATION PERSPECTIVE AND CONCEPTUAL CHANGE

The knowledge integration framework calls for capitalizing on students' ability to make sense of scientific phenomena by empowering them to distinguish among ideas, consider new ideas, and promote the most promising ones. Students generate a broad range of ideas about any scientific phenomenon. These ideas represent multiple types of explanations, vary across contexts, and may not be recognized as applying to the same topic. The knowledge integration framework takes these ideas as building blocks and uses the same processes that generated them to explain and focus the learning trajectory.

The knowledge integration view of conceptual change has emerged from a series of empirical studies. It was spurred by evidence for the impact of context on student reasoning (Linn, 1983). It celebrates the ideas students generate but views these as intellectual accomplishments rather than seeing them as resulting from intellectual constraints (Linn, 1995; Linn, Davis, & Bell, 2004; Linn & Hsi, 2000). Important evidence for this view comes from a longitudinal study carried out over five years that gives insight into student lifelong learning (Clark & Linn, 2003; Linn & Hsi, 2000). Studies of successful instruction demonstrate the importance of designing what are called *pivotal cases* to coalesce disparate ideas. These cases help students critique their own ideas and embrace normative views (Linn, 2005). Studies also reveal promising instructional patterns that promote self-monitoring and help students develop scientific criteria for arguments (Linn & Eylon, 2006). The patterns are all variations of a general pattern that has four parts: First, elicit the ideas held by the student so they can be analyzed; second, add well-designed normative ideas that form pivotal cases to stimulate comparisons among ideas and promote normative views; third, encourage development of criteria for promising ideas, such as looking for valid evidence; finally, enable refection on the repertoire of ideas in order to distinguish among views and select the most promising perspectives. This empirical basis explains the typical student trajectories.

To motivate the framework, I describe its roots. As an undergraduate, I had the opportunity to learn about memory and forgetting in Richard Atkinson's lab. As a graduate student, I had an opportunity to spend a year visiting Jean Piaget, learning about his approach to understanding reasoning firsthand. I was fortunate to work with Lee Cronbach as my graduate advisor, where I gained insight into the design of instruction and the analysis of computer data.

Repertoire of Views of Learning

As an undergraduate and graduate student at Stanford University, I was fortunate to encounter a broad range of views of learning. I worked with Richard Atkinson, Patrick Suppes, Ernest Hilgard, and Lee Cronbach. Atkinson was studying mathematical learning theory and using this theory to design computer assisted instruction in reading. Patrick Suppes was designing computer assisted instruction for introductory logical courses, by converting his successful classroom practices into online problems and advocating a problem-based approach. Hilgard introduced me to varied theories of learning and indulged my desire to discuss the connections between these theories and the design of instruction — a topic that was only briefly covered in a new directions chapter in his famous book (Hilgard, 1964). Cronbach broadened my view of statistical analysis of student learning by introducing me to the complex world of psychometrics, introduced the ideas of instruction interacting with learning characteristics, and eventually became my graduate advisor.

In Atkinson's group, I had the opportunity to participate in discussions about research on learning that primarily used word lists or isolated vocabulary items. The materials were selected so that prior learning or prior understanding would have minimal impact on performance. Members of the research group sought ways to eliminate the impact of prior knowledge in studies of memory. These discussions intrigued me because I wondered what advantages might accrue from prior knowledge. We read and discussed studies showing advantages for spaced versus massed practice and for various forms of feedback on student retention of decontextualized information. At the time, I wondered about the generalizability of these results to more complex and meaningful tasks.

Recently, I have had the opportunity to explore this question in collaboration with Bob Bjork at the University of California, Los Angeles. I have gained valuable insights from exploring his desirable difficulties perspective. Bjork initially identified desirable difficulties as instructional treatments that slow the process of learning, but ultimately increase the outcomes from instruction. Thus, when learning events are interleaved (so students study, for example, ecology interleaved with chemistry), learning ecology is slowed, presumably due to the spacing of practice and to potential confusion introduced by studying the other topic. Students in the interleaved condition, however, perform better on delayed post-tests than students who did not encounter interleaved material. In our Introducing Desirable Difficulties for Educational Applications in Science (IDDEAS) project, we extended these experimental manipulations to complex science material and were able to replicate this finding. Essentially by interleaving science topics and therefore, spacing practice, we showed that students learned more science content and also were better able to link science ideas together (Richland et al., 2007).

From a conceptual change perspective, these desirable difficulties findings show the benefit of instructional interventions that encourage students to consider the connections among ideas, help students strengthen connections among relevant information, and promote self-monitoring (Bjork & Linn, 2006). When students study a science topic, the information that they learn may be isolated or confused. When students reencounter the topic, they revisit the information and can make additional connections. The finding suggests that if students encounter scientific ideas in multiple contexts, they will initially be confused, but, if encouraged to compare the ideas, will ultimately gain a more robust and integrated set of ideas about the topic. These studies shed light on specific factors that impact conceptual change and suggest that the process of conceptual change involves the linking and connecting of ideas, as well as the process of revisiting those links and reconsidering their validity.

Piagetian Influence

I was able to spend a year in Geneva working with Piaget. The richness of Piaget's perspective on reasoning was exciting and stimulating. I benefited from interactions with Alina Szeminska, Bärbel Inhelder, Hermine Sinclair, Magali Bovet, and others while visiting Geneva. Piaget (1970) gave his famous lecture on structuralism during the time that I was visiting, and I had the opportunity to discuss these ideas with him. I should say that I had the opportunity to ask questions and then nod appreciatively when my questions were answered. My mastery of the French language did not extend to engaging in debate about these ideas, which endeared me to my hosts.

I found the effort of the groups to fit student ideas into the frameworks of concrete operations and formal operations, as well as the sub-stages within those stages, creative and intriguing. Researchers probed students to determine the reasoning behind their comments so they could be properly assigned. As an observer, I was enthralled when students came up with idiosyncratic explanations for scientific phenomena. In one experiment, I recall a marble rolled down a curved track and, depending on the design of the track, either followed it like a rollercoaster or flew off it. I listened to students explain this phenomenon using anthropomorphic metaphors as well as many non-normative ideas about force and motion. In addition, I watched while students constructed experiments to test their ideas, often assuming that a variable lacked impact on the outcome and so could be changed without impacting the experiment. I was extremely impressed with the creativity of the researchers in regard to the design of experiments and the elicitation of student ideas. I was fortunate to observe Piaget's group discussing results from these experiments and interpreting them using the stage theory. While I was taken by the unique, creative, and idiosyncratic ideas that students developed, the group focused more on the similarities across students of different ages, the concreteness of explanations, and the logic of the experiments.

Dissertation Research

Working under the direction of Lee Cronbach at Stanford University, I sought to understand how Vygotsky's Zone of Proximal Development could help in the design of valid and effective measures of student understanding. To this end, I looked at the effect of hints and social support on students' reasoning about Raven's progressive matrices. I studied the validity of the scores that students earned with hints compared to scores without hints. Inspired by my work in Geneva, I sought to create matrices with varied contextual characteristics and to elicit students' ideas about how to solve these problems. My research verified the hypothesis that tests given with hints provided a more valid measure of student potential (Linn, 1972). The hint conditions often helped students recognize similarities between matrices that varied in context and in the rules used to generate them. I noted that hints and social interactions sustained student interest in the task and resulted in more thoughtful responses, as well as promoting more careful comparisons, jointly accounting for the increased validity.

Adolescent Reasoning

After completing my degree, I had the opportunity to work at the Lawrence Hall of Science and explore adolescent reasoning about scientific phenomena in many different contexts. I studied reasoning among visually impaired and sighted students, as well as reasoning when students had the opportunity to guide their own experimentation and when their experiments were structured. These studies reinforced my emerging view that researchers should value the wealth of exciting and intriguing ideas that students brought to their scientific experiments. I became curious about two questions: First, the relationship between the scientific context and the student's ability to reason about it; and second, the role of instruction in improving students' reasoning skills (Linn, 1977, 1978).

To explore the relationship between the context of the problem and reasoning, I carried out a series of cross-sectional studies of the reasoning of adolescents across a variety of contexts. I summarized these results in a paper entitled "Is it formal if it's not physics?" (Linn, Clement, & Pulos, 1983) that contrasted performance on tasks commonly found in physics courses and used extensively in Piagetian research (such as pendulums, balance beams, bending rods and springs) with tasks using the same logical characteristics but involving problems such as identifying the most reasonably priced advertised special or determining which variables produce the most successful party. In this study, students' reasoning was inconsistent across contexts, but overall there was a slight advantage for the familiar contexts over the physics contexts. In addition, in the familiar contexts, students offered a much richer array of explanations and conjectures than for the physics contexts, which by-and-large weren't particularly familiar to the students.

Part of the advantage for familiar problems was that students could identify the variables. In general, students' ability to control variables was influenced by their understanding of the variables (Linn & Swiney Jr., 1981). Piagetian views called for ascertaining whether or not students could use strategies like controlling variables. But realistically, the issue was not whether, but when students could design controlled experiments. This view is very compatible with the situated cognition ideas that were also emerging at the time.

The findings from these studies suggested that students selected reasoning strategies and concepts depending on the context in which they were reasoning. It seemed that if students studied a broad range of contexts, they could gain robust ideas.

I also conducted a series of experimental studies looking at interactive instruction and its impact on student reasoning. Several studies of the Science Curriculum Improvement Study (Karplus & Thier, 1967) contrasted students who learned using an innovative, hands-on set of curriculum materials with comparable individuals in courses using the textbook. These studies (Bowyer & Linn, 1978; Linn & Thier, 1975) revealed a dramatic advantage for students who conducted experiments in the Science Curriculum Improvement Study classrooms. To understand the benefit of experimentation and inspired by my experiences in Geneva, I began to study how students explore their own ideas.

Following Piaget's view that students develop reasoning capabilities gradually and not particularly as the result of direct instruction, I designed a series of experiments involving student-initiated experimentation, often conducted in classrooms where students worked in pairs, selecting any of a broad array of questions. I gathered materials for experimentation and encouraged students to generate and investigate their own questions. These studies revealed the limitations of free choice experiences in helping students learn. By and large, in typical classrooms and small laboratory studies, students looked for guidance rather than immediately embarking on their own investigations. Often, guidance was simply not available because the idea of free choice experimentation was that students had many different sets of equipment to choose from and they could carry out whatever investigations they desired. This resulted in students constantly asking leaders for guidance. Many students reported considerable anxiety about whether the activities they chose would lead to successful performance on evaluation measures in the classroom. A few classroom leaders often determined the experiments conducted by the whole class. Experiments that caused explosions or had dramatic outcomes were far preferred to those that systematically investigated a scientific topic. Thus, at one point, every group in a class I was teaching sought to explore the interaction between vinegar and baking powder and tested their results by determining the proportions necessary to blow the tops off snap top vials, often staining the classroom ceiling.

These learning activities were engaging and motivating but did not necessarily promote adolescent reasoning. The students who learned the most seemed to be those that I tutored as I wandered around the classroom asking questions about the design and interpretations of experiments. Since I could not guide each group at the same time, I started designing introductory activities to set students on a path toward independent experimentation. These activities were highly successful. Instead of all students copying the investigations of the leaders, students chose a broad array of different topics of experimentation. In addition, students solved the progressively more complex challenges, felt confident about classroom success, and were prepared to write and explore their own challenges. Thus, I learned that structuring experimentation was valuable. These structured experiments were more effective than unstructured experiments in helping students to improve their understanding of effective experimentation and to reach valid conclusions about scientific phenomenon (Linn, 1980).

A series of studies refined understanding of structuring understanding (Linn, 1986; Linn & Songer, 1991). These studies demonstrated the importance of eliciting student ideas about scientific phenomena before engaging them in experimentation and asking students to make predictions before they conducted experiments. Eliciting ideas resulted in much richer experimentation than when students immediately embarked on their investigations without generating alternatives. When students got to consider their ideas, they often came up with more creative experiments. In addition, when students were asked to make predictions, it was more common for them to recognize that their experiments contradicted their expectations and to revise their ideas (Linn & Songer, 1991).

These findings reinforced the notion that student ideas are crucial to the development of scientific understanding and need to be built upon, rather than vilified. Art Linkletter made his reputation by showing that students say the darndest things. These studies showed that student ideas were valuable tools for subsequent learning.

In a series of studies on students' understanding of floating and sinking and eventually of density, the group explored the role of variation in student ideas in more detail. In the research on floating and sinking, first and second grade students were asked questions based on those used by Piaget, such as: "If you threw a rock into the pond everyday, would it always sink?" or "If all the students in your school threw a rock in the ponds, would all the rocks sink?" Students explained perplexing materials, such as pieces of plastic that looked similar but differed in their propensity to sink. They experimented with bottle caps that sunk only when filled with water. They tested rubber bands to explore surface tension. They found rubber bands could float if placed carefully on the water but would sink if pushed under the water. Students generated quite intriguing answers to all these questions. Often, they would have given only one explanation had only the traditional objects been used. They revealed multiple ideas, some of which were indicative of sophisticated understanding of floating and sinking and others that drew on anthropomorphic and descriptive explanations when the context was enriched. These studies confirmed the importance of context in understanding student reasoning.

Studies of density were also intriguing. Initially, our group sought to extend Siegler's (1996) ideas about rules to interpret students' reasoning about density, looking for consistency in reasoning. We found that, when asked to make predictions with cylinders of varied length, diameter, and mass, students were very consistent. For example, some students predicted that the volume of a solid would determine the amount of water it displaced, except when the two solids varied only in weight. In this case, many said the heavier one would displace more volume when they both sank (Linn & Pulos, 1983).

In density experiments, however, increasing the variety of contexts and asking students to imagine more complex situations, such as why boats float, led to more complicated reasoning, more diverse ideas, and some creativity. Students used less sophisticated reasoning, based on Piagetian scoring rubrics, than for the cylinders. For example, one respondent, in talking about why things float, was asked about sightseeing boats on the bay. At first, the student responded that the boats were made out of metal, based on personal experience. Then when asked to explain how they could float, the student thought about it for a while and decided, "Oh, the boats are made out of wood!" — essentially denying personal experience. In another example, a student predicted that a heavier object of the same volume would displace more liquid. When confronted with empirical evidence that the two objects displaced the same amount of liquid, the student told the experimenter, "You brought magic water."

One could interpret these responses and others like them in multiple ways. Some researchers argue that students' persistence with their intuitions, even when confronted with empirical evidence refuting them, calls for instruction that eradicates these ideas. Other researchers, including our group, concluded that these ideas and the students' attempts to defend them are important scientific events that resemble Lakatos' description of the protective belt (Linn & Siegel, 1984). Just as experimenters in many scientific laboratories doggedly pursue their conjectures even when preliminary evidence reveals problems, so do these students pursue their scientific ideas even when confronted with contradictions.

These experiments motivated me to wonder how to create instruction that respects student conjectures and adds opportunities for more experimentation. It was clear that instruction needed to encourage students to develop criteria to justify their ideas.

In summary, these instructional studies exploring the role of hands on experimentation and attempting to understand student reasoning provided further evidence for the value of paying attention to student ideas and the context of student learning. These studies also revealed that students' efforts to make sense of scientific information are often mistaken as ineffective, when in fact they are reasonable, once you appreciate the knowledge the students have. Perhaps student efforts could be made more effective with a better learning context and more emphasis on coherence.

Computer as Learning Partner

These views of student learning and the kinds of activities that led to improvements in student reasoning formed the groundwork for the Computer as Learning Partner (CLP) research program. This research program was motivated by the availability of temperature sensitive probes that could display the graphs from experiments about heat and temperature and by the desire to extend research on instruction to complex science topics and longer course sequences.

This research program had two important components: an iterative refinement study of instruction on thermodynamics and a longitudinal study of individual students. This research program yielded several useful findings from the standpoint of conceptual change (Clark & Linn, 2003; Linn et al., 2004; Linn & Hsi, 2000).

The research team designed and revised the thermodynamics curriculum a total of eight times, and each revision resulted in better student outcomes and more insight into the nature of student experimentation. Each iteration of the CLP curriculum was informed by assessments to establish the progress students were making in developing an integrated understanding of thermodynamics. The assessments asked students to analyze phenomena in a broad range of contexts including: the design of containers to keep picnics cool; the temperature of objects in a cold ski cabin, a hot car, and other enclosures; as well as the role of sweaters, blankets, aluminum foil, and other wrapping materials in keeping objects and organisms warm or cold. The students needed to use the ideas they were learning in the classroom to solve important, personally relevant problems. Students' responses to these problems guided the improvement of the instruction.

Student responses revealed that individuals came to science class with very little sense of normative ideas about thermodynamics and a vast array of intriguing, contradictory, descriptive, and idiosyncratic conjectures about the nature of heat and temperature, the direction of heat flow, thermal equilibrium, and the processes of insulation and conduction.

The CLP team summarized the findings from these interactions and for the longitudinal research in the scaffolded knowledge integration framework, a set of fourteen design principals organized under four main metaprinciples: make science accessible, make science visible, enable students to learn from each other, and promote autonomy (Linn & Hsi, 2000). As summarized in the metaprinciples, four main dimensions of the instruction proved helpful to guide students to integrate their ideas.

Make Science Accessible

First, to make science accessible and take advantage of the idiosyncratic and varied ideas held by students, the curriculum focuses on personally relevant problems, rather than the typical, abstract problems found in textbooks. For example, students were asked to design a house for the desert that would keep residents warm at night and cool during the day. This design challenge required students to think about the day/night cycle, the temperature of the Earth during day and night, the role of insulating materials, and the mechanisms that might be used to store solar energy and make it available during a cool desert night.

The projects specifically selected personally relevant problems, both to motivate students and to ensure that students would encounter the same topic outside of science class. A primary focus for the CLP curriculum in promoting conceptual change was to ensure that students would have the opportunity to revisit their ideas about heat and temperature outside of science class, thus increasing opportunities to practice scientific reasoning and ensuring distributed practice of topics learned in class.

Make Thinking Visible

Second, to make thinking visible, a major focus of the CLP curriculum was the use of computer technology to visualize science. Over and over again, the project demonstrated that computer representations for scientific phenomena could act as what came to be known as *pivotal cases* (Linn, 2005; Linn et al., 2004).

Pivotal cases are introductions of scientific ideas that enable students to sort out previously contradictory or disconnected views of scientific phenomena. The most famous example for the CLP curriculum concerned an animation called Heat Bars (Lewis, 1991). Extensive research on students' ideas through the first several versions of the curriculum revealed that students could understand that heat travels through materials, but had difficulty conceptualizing the ideas that heat might travel at different rates depending on the nature of the material. Some students envisioned materials as barriers and assumed that heat was only in the air between the object and the barrier and that the barrier prevented heat from flowing. Other students recognized that there were insulators and conductors but decided that insulators were barriers and conductors let heat through. The Heat Bars simulation allowed students to compare the relative rates of heat flow for different materials. Students could select materials like aluminum, steel, birch, pine, or

Styrofoam, and they could observe an animation showing the rate at which heat flowed through the material. This very short instructional activity had a dramatic impact on student learning. Its greatest impact was on questions concerning rate of heat flow, but it also impacted student un derstanding of insulation and conduction and thermal equilibrium (Davis, 2003; Davis & Linn, 2000). Once students realized that heat flowed at different rates depending on the material, they could use the information to explain the way objects feel at room temperature. They could begin to understand that when they put their hand on a metal surface heat traveled more rapidly out of their hand than when they put their hand on a wooden surface.

Eventually, four characteristics of pivotal cases were established. Research suggests that successful pivotal cases:

- Make a compelling, scientifically valid comparison between two situations.
- Draw on accessible, culturally relevant contexts, such as everyday experiences.
- Provide feedback that supports students' efforts to develop criteria and monitor their progress.
- Encourage students to create narrative accounts of their ideas using precise vocabulary so they can discuss them with others.

For example, to help explain why objects that feel differently can have the same temperature, teachers encourage students to distinguish the feel of wood and metal at home on a cool day with the feel of these materials at the beach on a hot day. This example fits the criteria for a pivotal case because it offers a rigorous comparison between hot and cool days, describes familiar situations, provides feedback that helps students evaluate ideas, and offers students an example they can discuss with others.

The Heat Bars pivotal case, as well as the opportunities to use temperature sensitive probes for graphing, both illustrate the advantages of the computer technology for making thermodynamics visible. The technology enabled the researchers to design new representations for complex phenomenon that shed light on issues students found difficult to conceptualize.

Learn from Others

The third aspect of the scaffolded knowledge integration framework, enabling students to learn from each other, takes advantage of the diversity of ideas that students bring to science class and of the need for students to evaluate their own ideas and develop criteria for distinguishing among ideas. The CLP curriculum engaged students in online discussions, classroom discussions and debates (Bell, 1998; Hsi, 1997). In these interactions, students argued with each other about such topics as what is the best principle to explain the temperature of objects in a room, or what is the best way to cool lasagna so it can be consumed at a party. Analysis of these social interactions revealed that students considered many more ideas than they would have when working alone, that students developed class norms concerning the kind of evidence that could be used to warrant assertions, and that students often changed their ideas about complex phenomenon because of arguments presented by their peers rather than those presented in the curriculum. Peer articulation of scientific ideas often made them more understandable because students used terms more accessible to their peers than those used in the curriculum. They helped their peers learn the scientific meaning of the terms in the curriculum (Linn & Hsi, 2000).

By enabling students to learn from each other, the CLP curriculum increased the number of ideas that students considered and supported their use of evidence to distinguish their ideas. This approach also helped students to clarify their ideas, using vocabulary supplied by their peers.

Promote Autonomous Learning

The fourth metaprinciple emerging from the CLP instruction concerns promoting autonomy. This principle involves motivating students to reflect and monitor their performance. Considerable research documents the benefits of reflection and monitoring (Chi, deLeeuw, Chiu, & La-Vancer, 1994; Scardamalia & Bereiter, 1983, 1991). Incorporating these opportunities into the Computer as Learning Partner curriculum involved scaffolding and prompting students to make predictions, analyze their observations, reflect on the relationship between their observations and predictions, explain anomalies, and construct reports. The CLP group experimented with varied prompts to encourage self-monitoring. Some prompts were better than others (Davis & Linn, 2000). Eventually, the research group identified patterns such as *predict, observe, and explain* that promoted autonomy.

Encouraging students to engage in activities that are consistent with autonomous learning resulted in more successful understanding of thermal phenomena than instruction neglecting these opportunities (Davis, 2003; Davis & Linn, 2000). The impact of these activities on spontaneous, autonomous performance when students encounter this material outside of science class was tested in the longitudinal research.

Longitudinal Research

After iteratively refining the CLP curriculum, we began studying the trajectories of students during and after they participated in the program (Lewis, 1991, 1996; Linn & Hsi, 2000). These longitudinal investigations provide direct indications of conceptual change. In these studies, students were interviewed regularly while participating in the CLP curriculum and then interviewed prior to entering the 10th grade and prior to entering the 12th grade. We were also able to compare students who participated in the curriculum with those from other feeder schools who did not participate in the curriculum during their physics classes in the 11th or 12th grade. In general, students who participated in the CLP curriculum were more sophisticated than those who did not participate. There were some variations in the trajectories students followed (Linn, 2006; Linn & Hsi, 2000). Most students who participated in the interviews followed a progressing trajectory, gaining more sophisticated understanding of thermal concepts over the course of the interviews (Linn, 2006).

Analysis of these longitudinal interviews clearly establishes the process that students go through in grappling with multiple conflicting ideas, sorting them out, reconsidering them and reorganizing them as they gain sophisticated understanding of thermal phenomenon. Clark (2000) analyzed a subset of student trajectories in depth to illustrate this phenomenon. One representation of student ideas as analyzed by Clark is shown in Figure 27.1. The figure captures student understanding of thermal equilibrium at seven different points during the longitudinal study. It also shows that the student holds multiple ideas at each point in the longitudinal study. Over time, students gain more sophisticated ideas and become more capable of giving normative responses to problems having to do with thermal equilibrium. Nevertheless, students also retain non-normative ideas and often return to them.

Although CLP did not deal with thermal phenomena at the atomic level, several interviews in the longitudinal study revealed that students were able to connect the CLP instruction to instruction in high school, where they encountered information at the atomic level. In these interviews, students were able to reach sensible conclusions, linking heat flow and atomic level ideas (Linn & Muilenburg, 1996).

Taken together, the instructional studies and longitudinal research reinforce the idea that students have a large repertoire of ideas and that the process of conceptual change involves dis-

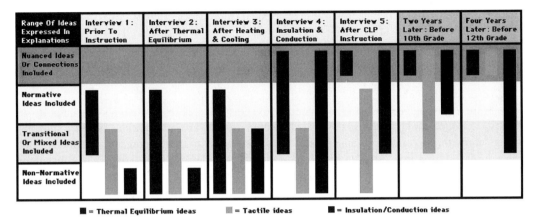

FIGURE 27.1   Types of ideas expressed by one student across seven interviews.

tinguishing and comparing these views. Well-designed instruction needs to enable students to generate, inspect, add, distinguish, and sort out a repertoire of ideas. This approach sets students on a trajectory of lifelong learning.

The CLP experience also demonstrates the benefit of an iterative refinement approach to ensure that instructional materials have the desired outcome. This is particularly difficult today when standard-setting groups frequently set curriculum expectations and instructional time allocations without attention to how long it might take someone to master a particular topic. Conceptual change takes time. When instructional programs fail to allocate sufficient time for complex topics, students may not recall any of the material they study (e.g., Linn, 1987; Linn & Hsi, 2000).

IMPLICATIONS FOR CONCEPTUAL CHANGE

The knowledge integration framework addresses the five issues identified in the introduction. This section explores the connections between knowledge integration and the other perspectives on conceptual change and suggests research directions.

Memory and Forgetting

Knowledge integration incorporates research on memory and forgetting that shows the potential impact of distributed practice of everyday explanations of scientific phenomena on development of scientific understanding. Students have many more opportunities to generate and use their everyday ideas than they do to use the scientifically normative ideas introduced in science classes. This is particularly likely if the ideas introduced in science classes are abstract, normative notions rather than pivotal cases. As a result, students may favor their everyday ideas in the repertoire of ideas they hold.

When science classes introduce abstract notions, such as differentiating heat and temperature on the basis of calories and degrees or talk solely about the motion of molecules in objects that are warming and cooling, they make it difficult for students to make connections between these ideas and everyday experience. Students have multiple opportunities to practice and link their everyday ideas, whereas normative ideas, even if they are compelling in class, may not be revisited. This situation helps explain why some intuitive student ideas are ingrained and persistent. From a knowledge integration perspective, these distributed learning opportunities call for instructional designs that enable students to refine their ideas and connect them to everyday ideas.

The knowledge integration framework responds to the potential impact of extensive practice of everyday descriptive explanations by advocating the introduction of normative ideas in the context of relevant, everyday problems. The CLP project introduced each principle in the context of an everyday problem. CLP also guided students to apply ideas from class in their lives.

From a knowledge integration perspective, the normative, abstract ideas about electricity or heat are hard to maintain because they are difficult to use in everyday situations. Science students rarely apply the abstract representations of heat and electricity they encounter in textbooks and as a result rarely have an opportunity to revisit and practice these ideas. Designers of curriculum need to think about how to ensure that scientific ideas have value outside of class.

Results on desirable difficulties resonate with the knowledge integration framework instructional practices. The knowledge integration practice of generating answers to questions rather than selecting among alternatives, for example, is supported by research showing that students who generate responses to questions perform less well during learning but have better recall later (Bjork & Linn, 2006; Pashler, 2006; Roediger & Karpicke, 2006). Research conducted in collaboration with Bjork (Richland et al., 2007) replicated and extended this finding by showing that when topics are interleaved (rather than taught in sequence) students have difficulty while learning but are more successful in making connections and succeeding on tests. These findings suggest that linking subjects, rather than segregating them, could improve outcomes.

In summary, the knowledge integration perspective on conceptual change resonates with research showing benefits of spacing and generation, first established in laboratory studies. It also helps explain why students generate and retain their descriptive ideas about scientific events, rather than embracing abstract, school-based views.

Developmental Trajectories

The knowledge integration perspective argues, consistent with the work of Case (1985) and Bereiter and Scardamalia (1986), that the main constraint on development is time. Research shows that students can use sophisticated reasoning strategies at a relatively young age when they understand the variables. Thus, students can conduct controlled experiments about floating and sinking or set up fair footraces by age 6 or 7, when the variables are understood (Case, 1985; Linn, 1990). Even natural scientists fail to control variables that they do not realize are relevant to the situation. The knowledge integration perspective stresses the importance of focusing on practicing reasoning in the context of the discipline. Appropriate methods for charting the progression of knowledge integration focus on coherence, rather than on developmental constraints, as revealed in the longitudinal research. This conjecture is consistent with recent research and analysis by Metz (2000) targeting young children.

A challenge for conceptual change concerns ideas like heat and electricity that are difficult to comprehend. For example, Chi (2005) argues that heat and electricity involve emergent phenomena and are frequently misconceived and need to be directly reflected. The knowledge integration perspective emphasizes the importance of identifying pivotal cases to help students understand these sorts of perplexing and difficult phenomena, and to appreciate their own propensity to impute concrete properties to phenomena like electricity. From the knowledge integration perspective, emergent properties are neglected and must compete with explanations that work well for everyday problems.

For example, the pivotal cases used to help students understand rate of heat flow were essential to promoting knowledge integration in CLP. A pivotal case that helped individuals understand why objects might feel differently but still have the same temperature illustrates the process. Many students believe because metal objects feel colder than wooden objects at room temperature, that metal has the property of imparting cold. Students often use this reasoning to justify the selection of aluminum foil for keeping drinks cold. To help students re-interpret and re-represent this idea, the instructor of the CLP class, Doug Kirkpatrick, experimented with different explanations. Ultimately, he hit on the idea of asking students to explain how these same objects would feel on a hot day at the beach. This turned out to be a great pivotal case. Students reported that metals would feel warmer than wooden objects on a hot day at the beach. They remembered that when they got into the car if there were metal and wooden objects, they would definitely not want to touch the metal ones. Many were able to use this idea to reconsider their ideas about why objects might feel differently. They often recognized that the feel objects had at room temperature had to do with the rate of heat flow from the object and their hand.

Thus, the knowledge integration framework recognizes that some scientific ideas require more creative instruction than others. It embraces the idea that instructional designers need to take these situations into consideration in designing effective pivotal cases and other instructional interventions to help students make sense of complex notions.

The knowledge integration approach to conceptual change suggests that learning is gradual, in part because students need to grapple with their many conflicting and confusing ideas. Students need to find evidence, to sort out those ideas, and to encounter opportunities to engage in reflection and reconsideration of their views. Knowledge integration's emphasis on pivotal cases also suggests that some science topics are more difficult because students need better representations to motivate analysis of their existing ideas or more powerful criteria to distinguish ideas. Before researchers conclude that learners go through qualitatively distinct developmental stages, they need to rule out the possibility that students make progress when motivated to revisit their ideas or when spurred by powerful new representations.

Context

Results for the context of reasoning resonate with the knowledge integration framework's emphasis on the repertoire of ideas. When students explore scientific concepts in multiple contexts, they generate a broader range of ideas. These ideas initially interfere with understanding because of their idiosyncratic and often contradictory nature, but ultimately, when integrated, have the benefit of helping students develop more robust ideas that apply in a wide range of situations.

When instruction features a broad range of contexts and applications of ideas, students can gain more robust and useful views. Multiple contexts can help students eliminate idiosyncratic aspects of concepts by contrasting situations. In addition, by considering abstract ideas in multiple practical contexts, students have the opportunity to refine those ideas and connect them to everyday situations.

Interviews with expert scientists (Lewis, 1996) reveal that even well-trained science faculty are sometimes stumped by insulation and conduction problems that have everyday entailments. If students learn insulation and conduction solely from mathematical formulas and the r-values for various materials, they are unlikely to be able to apply this information to everyday situations. As mentioned above, one expert interviewed in our studies, when asked whether aluminum foil or a wool sweater was better for keeping a drink cold, actually thought the aluminum foil would be more successful because that is what he had seen drinks being wrapped in, rather than drawing on information about insulation, conduction, and r-values to recognize that the wool sweater would be a better choice (Lewis, 1991). These examples illustrate the importance of cultivating skepticism while offering multiple contexts. Students complain that science lacks relevance to their lives, suggesting the need for multiple contexts, but at the same time, these contexts can reinforce non-normative views.

Forms of Explanation

Research on forms of explanation helps clarify the knowledge integration challenge students face. This research shows that students need both to distinguish the type of explanation of the scientific ideas they encounter and to learn how to make links across these explanations.

The CLP curriculum addressed this goal by having students explore everyday situations and then synthesize their findings in pragmatic principles. For example, in the topic of thermal equilibrium, one principle is *if all the objects are in the same surround and none of them produce their own heat, then they will all come to the same temperature.* These principles offer students an abstract, accessible explanation. They allow students to connect class experiments, everyday situations, and more abstract ideas about scientific phenomena.

Linking explanations of various types has unprecedented power for developing scientific understanding. Students who take seriously the task of linking explanations can make substantial progress in understanding. Often, however, students encounter obstacles and cannot make links. Sometimes, there are no effective criteria because students are comparing different types of explanations. For example, in the area of electricity, a descriptive view that electricity flows out of the wall has sensible implications for many problems that individuals face. Recognizing that electricity is governed by a set of constraints requires considerably more complicated reasoning. An atomic level explanation has value for interpreting complex electrical dilemmas and to clarify phenomena such as the way microchips work. Students need atomic level explanations to accompany mechanisms like heat flow. The challenge is to help students connect explanations of varied types.

Instruction

The knowledge integration perspective offers principles for instructional design that addresses conceptual change. To help students continuously engage in the process of knowledge integration throughout their lives, the framework emphasizes multiple contexts, features pivotal cases, and advocates patterns that sequence activities to encourage self-monitoring. Lifelong learning, of science especially, involves merging ideas that initially might appear to come from very different contexts and developing criteria for evaluating explanations. New disciplines, such as molecular biology or bioengineering, involve merging across previous disciplinary boundaries. Similarly, lifelong learning involves constantly dealing with new situations. Effective instruction can prepare students to engage in this process, by emphasizing reflection and critiquing of ideas.

Instruction for topics like heat and electricity that feature ontological shifts require careful instructional design. Often, students need to appreciate both the descriptive implications of the new idea and the causal explanation. To make this even more challenging, the causal explanation often requires taking on faith a dynamic process (like molecular movement) that is unseen. Rather than according special status to ideas like heat, electricity, or even the view that the earth is round, researchers need to explore the origin of student views and design pivotal cases to help distinguish scientifically normative student ideas.

The knowledge integration perspective on conceptual change stresses the importance of designing instruction to promote knowledge integration and set students on a course towards lifelong learning. The principles emerging from the Computer as Learning Partner research have been tested in the design of subsequent learning experiences. Recently, these principles have been compiled by Kali (2006) in a Design Principles Database. Researchers are continuously identifying more powerful and sophisticated principles to guide the design of instruction and to speed up the process of creating effective instructional materials.

Thus, the knowledge integration perspective connects conceptual change and effective instruction. It suggests that research on conceptual change will be most informative when combined with instructional investigations.

CONCLUSIONS

Exploring conceptual change through a knowledge integration lens raises five issues that concern all researchers investigating conceptual change: memory and forgetting, developmental accomplishments, context variation, forms of explanation, and instruction. These issues emerged in my own research program and have also been studied by numerous other investigators. This chapter focuses on the role of these issues in conceptual change in science education.

Science education researchers have promoted varied aspects of conceptual change. One group of researchers has postulated that students learning science behave like scientists, as described by philosophers like Kuhn (1970). These folks argue that developing a strong perspective on a phenomenon and defending it is valuable. Other researchers have focused on specific problematic ideas that appear to be obstacles for learners, interfering with their ability to embrace more sophisticated perspectives. Obstacle ideas include substance-like views of heat and electricity, anthropomorphic views of inanimate processes like fire or water flow, as well as perceptual views of the earth, such as that the earth is flat or round like a pancake. A large number of researchers in science education have described the intuitive, descriptive, and idiosyncratic ideas that students develop (Eylon & Linn, 1988; Duit, 1999). These ideas have been viewed as obstacles, as well as embraced as examples of effective scientific reasoning. This chapter calls for merging these research directions to reach unified conclusions.

This chapter makes the case for the knowledge integration perspective, arguing that variability in student ideas is fundamentally a valuable feature and that instruction designed to capitalize on the variability and the creativity of student ideas has potential for facilitating conceptual change. The knowledge integration framework does not advocate unguided discovery or radical constructivism, but rather argues that understanding that students generate new ideas to make sense of science leads to important and essential design decisions. Two areas where design decisions are particularly important are, first, the design of new ideas to add to the mix that students have, and second, the design of sequences of instructional activities that help students consolidate their ideas and develop more coherent understanding. Both of these instructional approaches are facilitated by an emerging group of design principles intended to help those creating materials capitalize on successful practices from instructional investigations (Kali, 2006).

Research Directions

Contrasting the knowledge integration perspective with other views of conceptual change raises some important issues for research design that permeate the field and could help researchers integrate their ideas about conceptual change. Certainly, researchers, much like students, hold a repertoire of ideas about conceptual change, and many researchers hold more than one view depending on the context in which conceptual change is sought. Thus, researchers may advocate distinguishing ideas when students are exploring some topics but believe that, for certain very difficult or entrenched views, a process of extinguishing the scientifically non-normative ideas would be preferable.

Research appropriate for resolving some of the discussions in the field evolve around the design of assessments of student understanding and the design of instruction intended to promote conceptual change. Many now call for new methods to advance the field (e.g., Vosniadou et al., 2004).

Assessments

Assessments of students' understanding of complex science concepts may reveal only part of the students' repertoire of ideas (Vosniadou, Skopeliti, & Ikospentaki, 2004). This can occur when questions asked of students come from a narrow context. For example, if all the questions are very abstract, puzzle-type questions (Linn & Pulos, 1983), students often attempt to use only their abstract ideas to explain the phenomenon under investigation and may actually sound more or less sophisticated than if they looked at the problem in a richer context. Alternatively, students may interpret a question intended to be abstract as applying only to a single context and provide a narrow, concrete answer that could have also been misinterpreted if one knew the full repertoire of ideas held by the student.

My early work on the zone of proximal development as a technique for increasing the validity of measurement of student understanding is relevant to this methodological dilemma. The zone of proximal development, as advocated by Vygotsky, had an important implication for assessment. Vygotsky argued that when students' reasoning was measured in a rich context where there were some social supports for reasoning, that a more valid outcome could be achieved. This hypothesis deserves serious investigation in conceptual change research. Researchers are encouraged to measure student ideas using a variety of contexts and to include prompts or social supports to determine how students will interpret information across these contexts. Too often, abstract assessment items yield incomplete understanding of student reasoning.

Coding Ideas

An important methodological issue concerns reporting all the ideas that students have. Some researchers minimize this issue by attempting to identify one most salient idea (e.g., Inhelder & Piaget, 1958/1972). This approach neglects important views that students may use effectively in different contexts or could use to improve their interpretation of complex settings.

The knowledge integration emphasis on the repertoire of ideas held by students empowers researchers and instructional designers to think about how to interpret the repertoire students have. Researchers have coded facets (Clark & Linn, 2003) or p-prims (diSessa, 1988), as well as characterizing specific views (Chi, 2005). Characterizing the repertoire also focuses design of new ideas. The knowledge integration framework emphasizes pivotal cases. Other research programs have identified benchmark lessons (diSessa & Minstrell, 1998), bridging analogies (Clement, 1993), didactic objects (Thompson, 2002), animations (Holyoak & Thagard, 1995) and other approaches. Characterizing the repertoire and adding the right ideas to the mix held by students has the potential of dramatically increasing the efficiency and effectiveness of instruction.

An important methodological issue concerns the design and refinement of instruction. Both experiments intended to characterize student conceptual change and instruction intended to promote conceptual change often fail to succeed because students interpret instructions or activities differently from the intentions of the designers. The CLP examples of eight versions of instruction that resulted in a 50% increase in student understanding of heat and temperature is one example. In this case, drawing on detailed analysis of student responses to instruction, the researchers were able to dramatically improve student outcomes while maintaining an equal amount of instructional time (Linn & Hsi, 2000).

Research contrasting theoretical views of conceptual change could enhance our understanding and engage the community in a collaborative process of improving research practices. Many call for either addressing non-normative views directly or creating ways for students to become better critics. We need research comparing these views.

Researchers have begun to investigate the sequence of instructional activities that promote conceptual change. Current research approaches this challenge in quite different ways. Researchers on memory distinguish distributed practice from massed practice on items. The desirable difficulties work shows that some forms of instruction will increase frustration and misunderstanding during learning, requiring considerable skill on the part of the teachers, but ultimately will have greater benefit for long-term retention (Richland et al., 2007).

Other research groups have specified the conditions under which conceptual change occurs, emphasizing readiness of students for conceptual change (Strike & Posner, 1985). The evolutionary view of the learner highlights gradually contrasting varied ideas and embracing ideas that have the most power in terms of explanatory value, durability, or generativity (Lakatos, 1976; Toulmin, 1972). These researchers also raised issues about what constitutes the criteria students hold for their own ideas and, in particular, how students evaluate the coherence of their ideas (Thagard, 2000).

These efforts to think about the sequence of instructional activities also raise issues about the forms of explanation called for in instructional programs and their relevance to the ideas students already hold. Scientists take advantage of multiple forms of explanation and often are very astute in linking across these forms, combining descriptive, mechanistic, and causal explanations for phenomena. For experts, explanations involving unseen dynamic processes, such as atomic level explanations or vector breakdowns of motion, often have the greatest generativity. However, these unseen processes and phenomena are often difficult for students to apply to everyday phenomena and may be taught in ways that make those applications particularly problematic. Research that contrasts ways to prevent unseen processes seems very promising.

In this chapter, I have argued for selecting intermediate models, such as heat flow, to stimulate reasoning. This approach is consistent with research inspired by Piagetian studies of student limitations in reasoning. Introducing explanations that are easily comprehended by students has the benefit of spurring the process of conceptual change along and making subsequent learning potentially more accessible. At the same time, researchers dispute this possibility, some arguing that it might be preferable to focus on normative ideas, rather than potentially introducing explanations such as heat flow that could reinforce substance-based models of heat.

The field of conceptual change remains contested, intriguing, and ultimately extremely important for understanding both learning and instruction. Researchers have the opportunity to let their ideas bump up against each others' ideas and to identify ways to integrate their ideas and advance the field.

ACKNOWLEDGMENT

This material is based upon work supported by the National Science Foundation under grants No. REC-0311835, ESI-0334199, and ESI-0455877, and the Introducing Desirable Difficulties for Educational Applications in Science (IDDEAS) grant from the Office of Educational Research and Improvement (OERI) Cognition and Student Learning (CASL) program. Any opinions, findings, and conclusions or recommendations expressed in this material are those of the author and do not necessarily reflect the views of the National Science Foundation.

The author benefited from helpful insights and conversations with Bat-Sheva Eylon in framing the issues in this chapter and with Hee-Sun Lee in discussing early drafts. Comments from the Technology-Enhanced Learning in Science group were valuable and informative. The author appreciates help in production of this manuscript from Jonathan Breitbart.

REFERENCES

Anderson, J. R. (1976). *Language, memory, and thought*. Hillsdale, NJ: Erlbaum.

Bell, P. (1998). Designing for students' conceptual change in science using argumentation and classroom debate. Unpublished doctoral dissertation, University of California, Berkeley, CA.

Bereiter, C., & Scardamalia, M. (1986). *The psychology of written composition*. Hillsdale, NJ: Erlbaum.

Bjork, R. A. (1999). Assessing our own competence: Heuristics and illusions. In D. Gopher & A. Koriat (Eds.), *Attention and performance XVII. Cognitive regulation of performance: Interaction of theory and application* (pp. 435–459). Cambridge, MA: MIT Press.

Bjork, R. A., & Linn, M. C. (2006). The science of learning and the learning of science: Introducing desirable difficulties. *The APS Observer, 19*(3). Retrieved February 6, 2008 from: http://www.psychologicalscience.org/observer/getArticle.cfm?id=1952.

Bowyer, J. B., & Linn, M. C. (1978). Effectiveness of the science curriculum improvement study in teaching scientific literacy. *Journal of Research in Science Teaching, 15*, 209–219.

Carey, S. (1985). *Conceptual change in childhood*. Cambridge, MA: MIT Press.

Case, R. (1985). *Intellectual development: Birth to adulthood*. Orlando, FL: Academic Press.

Chi, M. T. H. (2005). Common sense conceptions of emergent processes: Why some misconceptions are robust. *Journal of the Learning Sciences, 14*, 161–199.

Chi, M. T. H., & Roscoe, R. D. (2002). The process and challenges of conceptual change. In M. Limon & L. Mason (Eds.), *Reconsidering conceptual change: Issues in theory and practice* (pp. 3–27). Netherlands: Kluwer Academic.

Chi, M. T. H., deLeeuw, N., Chiu, M. H., & LaVancer, C. (1994). Eliciting self-explanations improves understanding. *Cognitive Science, 18*, 439–477.

Chi, M. T. H., Feltovich, P. J., & Glaser, R. (1981). Categorization and representation of physics problems by experts and novices. *Cognitive Science, 5*, 121–152.

Christina, R. W., & Bjork, R. A. (1991). Optimizing long-term retention and transfer. In D. Druckman & R. A. Bjork (Eds.), *In the mind's eye: Enhancing human performance* (pp. 23–56). Washington, DC: National Academy Press.

Clark, D. B. (2000). Scaffolding knowledge integration through curricular depth. Unpublished doctoral dissertation, University of California, Berkeley, CA.

Clark, D. B., & Linn, M. C. (2003). Scaffolding knowledge integration through curricular depth. *Journal of Learning Sciences, 12*(4), 451–494.

Clement, J. (1983). A conceptual model discussed by Galileo and used intuitively by physics students. In D. Gentner & A. L. Stevens (Eds.), *Mental models* (pp. 325–339). Hillsdale, NJ: Erlbaum.

Clement, J. (1993). Using bridging analogies and anchoring intuitions to deal with students' preconceptions in physics. *Journal of Research in Science Teaching, 30*(10), 1241–1257.

Davis, E. A. (2003). Prompting middle school science students for productive reflection: Generic and directed prompts. *The Journal of the Learning Sciences, 12*(1), 91–142.

Davis, E. A., & Linn, M. C. (2000). Scaffolding students' knowledge integration: Prompts for reflection in KIE. *International Journal of Science Education, 22*(8), 819–837.

diSessa, A. A. (1988). Knowledge in pieces. In G. Forman & P. Pufall (Eds.), *Constructivism in the computer age* (pp. 49–70). Hillsdale, NJ: Erlbaum.

diSessa, A. A. (2000). *Changing minds: Computers, learning and literacy*. Cambridge, MA: MIT Press.

diSessa, A. A., & Minstrell, J. (1998). Cultivating conceptual change with benchmark lessons. In J. G. Greeno & S. Goldman (Eds.), *Thinking practices* (pp. 155–187). Mahwah, NJ: Erlbaum.

diSessa, A. A., Elby, A., & Hammer, D. (2002). J's epistemological stance and strategies. In G. M. Sinatra & P. R. Pintrich (Eds.), *Intentional conceptual change* (pp. 237–290). Mahwah, NJ: Erlbaum.

diSessa, A. A., Hammer, D., Sherin, B., & Kolpakowski, T. (1991). Inventing graphing: Metarepresentational expertise in children. *Journal of Mathematical Behavior, 10*, 117–160.

Duit, R. (1999). Conceptual change approaches in science education. In W. Schnotz, S. Vosniadou & M. Carretero (Eds.), *New perspectives on conceptual change* (pp. 263–282). Oxford: Pergamon.

Duit, R., Treagust, D. F., & Mansfield, H. (1996). Investigating student understanding as a pre-requisite to improving teaching and learning in science and mathematics. In D. F. Treagust, R. Duit, & B. Fraser (Eds.), *Improving teaching and learning in science and mathematics* (pp. 17–31). New York: Teachers College Press.

Edelson, D. C. (2001). Learning-for-Use: A Framework for the Design of Technology-Supported inquiry Activities. *Journal of Research in Science Teaching, 38*(3), 355–385.

Eylon, B.-S., & Linn, M. C. (1988). Learning and instruction: An examination of four research perspectives in science education. *Review of Educational Research, 58*(3), 251–301.

Gelman, R., & Gallistel, C. R. (1986). *The child's understanding of number.* Cambridge, MA: Harvard University Press.

Gilbert, J. K., & Boulter, C. J. (2000). *Developing models in science education.* Dordrecht: Kluwer.

Gopnik, A., & Wellman, H. M. (1994). The theory theory. In L. A. Hirschfeld & S. A. Gelman (Eds.), *Mapping the mind: Domain specifity in cognition and culture* (pp. 257–293). New York: Cambridge University Press.

Hammer, D., & Elby, A. (2003). Tapping students' epistemological resources. *Journal of the Learning Sciences, 12*(1), 53–91.

Hatano, G., & Inagaki, K. (2003). When is conceptual change intended?: A cognitive-sociocultural view. In G. M. Sinatra & P. R. Pintrich (Eds.), *Intentional conceptual change* (pp. 407–427). Mahwah, NJ: Erlbaum.

Hilgard, E. R. (1964). *Theories of learning and instruction: The sixty-sixth yearbook of the National Society for the Study of Education.* Chicago: University of Chicago Press.

Holyoak, K. J., & Thagard, P. (1995). *Mental leaps: Analogy in creative thought.* Cambridge, MA: MIT Press.

Howe, A. (2002). *Engaging children in science.* Upper Saddle River, NJ: Merrill Prentice-Hall.

Howe, K. (1998). The interpretive turn and the new debate in education. *Educational Researcher, 27*(8), 13–21.

Hsi, S. (1997). Facilitating knowledge integration in science through electronic discussion: The Multimedia Forum Kiosk. Unpublished doctoral dissertation, University of California, Berkeley, CA.

Inhelder, B., & Piaget, J. (1958/1972). *The growth of logical thinking from childhood to adolescence; An essay on the construction of formal operational structures.* New York: Basic Books.

Kali, Y. (2006). Collaborative knowledge building using the Design Principles Database. *International Journal of Computer Support for Collaborative Learning, 1*(2), 187–201.

Karplus, R., & Thier, H. D. (1967). *A new look at elementary school science: Science curriculum improvement study.* Chicago: Rand McNally.

Klahr, D., & Nigam, M. (2004). The equivalence of learning paths in early science instruction. *Psychological Science, 15*(10), 661–667.

Kuhn, T. S. (1970). *The structure of scientific revolutions* (2nd ed.). Chicago: University of Chicago Press.

Lakatos, I. (1976). *Proofs and refutations: The logic of mathematical discovery.* Cambridge: Cambridge University Press.

Larkin, J. H., & Reif, F. (1979). Understanding and teaching problem solving in physics. *European Journal of Science Education, 1*, 191–203.

Lee, H. S., & Songer, N. (2003). Making authentic science accessible to students. *International Journal of Science Education, 25*(8), 923–948.

Lewis, E. L. (1991). The process of scientific knowledge acquisition among middle school students learning thermodynamics. Unpublished doctoral dissertation, University of California, Berkeley.

Lewis, E. L. (1996). Conceptual change among middle school students studying elementary thermodynamics. *Journal of Science Education and Technology, 5*(1), 3–31.

Linn, M. C. (1972). An experiential science curriculum for the visually impaired. *Exceptional Children, 39*, 37–43.

Linn, M. C. (1977). Scientific reasoning: Influences on task performance and response categorization. *Science Education, 61,* 357–363.

Linn, M. C. (1978). Influence of cognitive style and training on tasks requiring the separation of variables schema. *Child Development, 49,* 874–877.

Linn, M. C. (1980). Teaching children to control variables: Some investigations using free choice experiences. In S. Modgil & C. Modgil (Eds.), *Toward a theory of psychological development within the Piagetian framework* (pp. 673–697). Windsor, Berkshire, UK: National Foundation for Educational Research Publishing Company.

Linn, M. C. (1983). Content, context, and process in adolescent reasoning. *Journal of Early Adolescence, 3,* 63–82.

Linn, M. C. (1986). Science. In R. Dillon & R. J. Sternberg (Eds.), *Cognition and Instruction* (pp. 155–204). New York: Academic Press.

Linn, M. C. (1987). Cognitive consequences of technology in science education. *Journal of Research in Science Teaching, 24*(4/5 Special Issue), 285–506.

Linn, M. C. (1990). Content, context, and process in reasoning during adolescence. In R. E. Muuss (Ed.), *Adolescent behavior and society* (4th ed., pp. 67–80). New York: McGraw-Hill.

Linn, M. C. (1995). Designing computer learning environments for engineering and computer science: The Scaffolded Knowledge Integration framework. *Journal of Science Education and Technology, 4*(2), 103–126.

Linn, M. C. (2005). WISE design for lifelong learning-Pivotal Cases. In P. Gärdenfors & P. Johansson (Eds.), *Cognition, education and communication technology* (pp. 223–256). Mahwah, NJ: Erlbaum.

Linn, M. C. (2006). The Knowledge Integration Perspective on Learning and Instruction. In R. K. Sawyer (Ed.), *The Cambridge handbook of the learning sciences* (pp. 243–264). New York: Cambridge University Press.

Linn, M. C., & Eylon, B.-S. (2006). Science education: Integrating views of learning and instruction. In P. A. Alexander & P. H. Winne (Eds.), *Handbook of educational psychology* (2nd ed., pp. 511–544). Mahwah, NJ: Erlbaum.

Linn, M. C., & Hsi, S. (2000). *Computers, teachers, peers: Science learning partners.* Mahwah, NJ: Erlbaum.

Linn, M. C., & Muilenburg, L. (1996). Creating lifelong science learners: What models form a firm foundation? *Educational Researcher, 25*(5), 18–24.

Linn, M. C., & Pulos, S. (1983). Male-female differences in predicting displaced volume: Strategy usage, aptitude relationships and experience influences. *Journal of Educational Psychology, 75,* 86–96.

Linn, M. C., & Siegel, H. (1984). Post-formal reasoning: A philosophical model. In M. Commons, F. A. Richards, & C. Armon (Eds.), *Beyond formal operations: Late adolescent and adult cognitive development* (pp. 239–257). New York: Praeger.

Linn, M. C., & Songer, N. B. (1991). Teaching thermodynamics to middle school students: What are appropriate cognitive demands? *Journal of Research in Science Teaching, 28*(10), 885–918.

Linn, M. C., & Swiney Jr., J. (1981). Individual differences in formal thought: Role of expectations and aptitudes. *Journal of Educational Psychology, 73*(2), 274–286.

Linn, M. C., & Thier, H. D. (1975). The effect of experiential science on the development of logical thinking in children. *Journal of Research in Science Teaching, 12,* 49–62.

Linn, M. C., Clement, C., & Pulos, S. (1983). Is it formal if it's not physics? *Journal of Research in Science Teaching, 20*(8), 755–770.

Linn, M. C., Davis, E. A., & Bell, P. (Eds.). (2004). *Internet environments for science education.* Mahwah, NJ: Erlbaum.

Locke, J. (1824). *The works of John Locke in nine volumes* (12th ed.). London: Rivington.

Metz, K. E. (1991). Development of explanation: Incremental and fundamental change in children's phsysics knowledge. *Journal of Research in Science Teaching* (Special Issue: Students' models and epistemologies), *28*(9), 785–797.

Metz, K. E. (2000). Young children's inquiry in biology. Building the knowledge bases to empower independent inquiry. In J. Minstrell & E. Van Zee (Eds.), *Inquiring into inquiry learning and teaching in science* (pp. 3–13). Washington, DC: American Association for the Advancement of Science.

National Research Council. (2006). *Learning to think spatially*. Washington, DC: The National Academies Press.

Nussbaum, J. (1985). The particulate nature of matter in the gaseous phase. In R. Driver, E. Guesne, & A. Tiberghien (Eds.), *Children's ideas in science* (pp. 124–144). Milton Keynes, UK: Open University Press.

Pascual-Leone, J., Goodman, D., Ammon, P., & Subelman, I. (1978). Piagetian theory and neo-Piagetian analysis as psychological guides in education. In J. M. Gallagher & J. A. Easley (Eds.), *Knowledge and development* (Vol. 2, pp. 243–289). New York: Plenum Publishing Corporation.

Pashler, H. (2006). How we learn. *The APS Observer, 19*(3). Retrieved February 6, 2008 from http://www.psychologicalscience.org/observer/getArticle.cfm?id=1949.

Pfundt, H., & Duit, R. (1994). *Bibliography: Students' alternative frameworks and science education* (4th ed.). Kiel, Germany: Institute for Science Education.

Piaget, J. (1953). *The origin of intelligence in the child*. London: Routledge & Paul.

Piaget, J. (1970). *Structuralism*. New York: Basic Books.

Quintana, C., Reiser, B. J., Davis, E. A., Krajcik, J., Fretz, E., Golan, R. D., et al. (2004). A scaffolding design framework for software to support science inquiry. *Journal of the Learning Sciences, 13*(3), 337–386.

Reder, L. M., & Klatzky, R. L. (1994). Transfer: Training for performance. In D. Druckman & R. A. Bjork (Eds.), *Learning, remembering, believing: Enhancing human performance* (pp. 25–56). Washington, DC: National Academy Press.

Redish, E. F. (2003). *Teaching physics with the physics suite*. New York: Wiley.

Richland, L. E., Linn, M. C., & Bjork, R. A. (2007). Instruction. In F. T. Durso (Ed.), *Handbook of applied cognition* (2nd ed., pp. 555–583). West Sussex, UK: Wiley.

Roediger, H. L., & Karpicke, J. D. (2006). Test-enhanced learning. *Psychological Science, 17*(3), 249–255.

Rousseau, J. J. (1892). *Treatise on education* (T. W. H. Payne, Trans.). New York: Appleton and Company.

Scardamalia, M. (1977). Information processing capacity and the problem of horizontal decalage: A demonstration using combinatorial reasoning tasks. *Child Development, 48*, 23–37.

Scardamalia, M., & Bereiter, C. (1983). Child as co-investigator: Helping children gain insight into their own mental processes. In S. Paris, G. Olson, & H. Stevenson (Eds.), *Learning and motivation in the classroom* (pp. 61–82). Hillsdale, NJ: Erlbaum.

Scardamalia, M., & Bereiter, C. (1991). Higher levels of agency for children in knowledge-building: A challenge for the design of new knowledge media. *Journal of the Learning Sciences, 1*, 37–68.

Scardamalia, M., & Bereiter, C. (1999). Schools as knowledge-building organizations. In D. Keating & C. Hertzman (Eds.), *Today's children tomorrow's society: The developmental health and wealth of nations* (pp. 274–289). New York: Guildford.

Schmidt, W. H., Raizen, S. A., Britton, E. D., Bianchi, L. J., & Wolfe, R. G. (1997). *Many visions, many aims: A cross-national investigation of curricular intentions in school science*. Dordrech, The Netherlands: Kluwer Academic Publishers.

Schnotz, W., Vosniadou, S., & Carretero, M. (Eds.). (1999). *New perspectives on conceptual change*. Oxford: Killington.

Siegler, R. S. (1996). *Emerging minds: The process of change in children's thinking*. New York: Oxford University Press.

Siegler, R. S. (2000). The rebirth of children's learning. *Child Development, 71*, 26–35.

Skinner, B. F. (1956). A case history in scientific method. *American Psychologist, 11*, 221–233.

Slotta, J. D., & Chi, M. T. H. (2006). Helping students understand challenging topics in science through ontology training. *Cognition and Instruction, 24*(2), 261–289.

Slotta, J. D., Chi, M. T. H., & Joram, E. (1995). Assessing the ontological nature of conceptual physics: A contrast of experts and novices. *Cognition and Instruction, 13*, 373–400.

Smith, J. P., diSessa, A. A., & Roschelle, J. (1993/1994). Misconceptions reconceived: A constructivist analysis of knowlege in transition. *The Journal of the Learning Sciences, 3*(2), 115–163.

Songer, N. B. (1996). Exploring learning opportunities in coordinated network-enhanced classrooms — A case of kids as global scientists. *Journal of the Learning Sciences, 5*(4), 297–327.

Songer, N. B., & Linn, M. C. (1992). How do students' views of science influence knowledge integration? In M. K. Pearsall (Ed.), *Scope, sequence and coordination of secondary school science, Volume I: Relevant research* (pp. 197–219). Washington, DC: The National Science Teachers Association.

Spelke, E. S. (1999). Infant cognition. In R. A. Wilson & F. Keil (Eds.), *The MIT encyclopedia of the cognitive sciences* (pp. 402–404) Cambridge, MA: MIT Press.

Strike, K. A., & Posner, G. J. (1985). A conceptual change view of learning and understanding. In L. H. West & A. L. Pines (Eds.), *Cognitive structure and conceptual change* (pp. 211–231). Orlando, FL: Academic Press.

Thagard, P. (2000). *Coherence in thought and action*. Cambridge, MA: The MIT Press.

Thompson, P. W. (2002). Didactic objects and didactic models in radical constructivism. In K. Gravemeijer, R. Lehrer, B. v. Oers, & L. Verschaffel (Eds.), *Symbolizing and modeling in mathematics education* (pp. 191–212). Dordrecht, The Netherlands: Kluwer.

Toulmin, S. (1972). *Human understanding: An inquiry into the aims of science*. Princeton, NJ: Princeton University Press.

Vosniadou, S. (2002). On the nature of naïve physics. In M. Limón & L. Mason (Eds.), *Reconsidering conceptual change: Issues in theory and practice* (pp. 61–76). Dordrecht, The Netherlands: Kluwer Academic Publishers.

Vosniadou, S. (in press). The conceptual change approach and it re-framing. In S. Vosniadou, A. Baltas, & X. Vamvakoussi (Eds.), *Re-framing the conceptual change change approach in learning and instruction*. Oxford: Elsevier.

Vosniadou, S., Skopeliti, I., & Ikospentaki, K. (2004). Modes of knowing and ways of reasoning in elementary astronomy. *Cognitive Development, 19*, 203–222.

Vygotsky, L. S. (1978). *Mind in society: The development of higher psychological processes*. Cambridge, MA: Harvard University Press.

White, B. Y., & Frederiksen, J. R. (1998). Inquiry, modeling, and metacognition: Making science accessible to all students. *Cognition and Instruction, 16*(1), 3–118.

Wiser, M. (1988). The differentiation of heat and temperature: History of science and novice-expert shift. In S. Strauss (Ed.), *Ontogeny, phylogeny, and historical development* (pp. 28–48). Norwood, NJ: Ablex.

Index

Page numbers in italics refer to Figures or Tables.